NBA REGISTER

1988-89 EDITION

Editors/NBA Register
ALEX SACHARE
DAVE SLOAN

Contributing Editors/NBA Register
MIKE DOUCHANT
JOHN DUXBURY
TERRY LYONS
CLARE MARTIN

President-Chief Executive Officer
RICHARD WATERS

Editor
TOM BARNIDGE

Director of Books and Periodicals
RON SMITH

NBA Statistics by Elias Sports Bureau

Published by

The Sporting News

1212 North Lindbergh Boulevard
P.O. Box 56 — St. Louis, MO 63166

Copyright © 1988
The Sporting News Publishing Company

◥◤ A Times Mirror
◣ Company

ISBN 0-89204-289-3   ISSN 0739-3067

Table

of

Contents

* * *

* * *

On the cover: Most Valuable Player James Worthy averaged 22 points per game in the 1988 NBA Finals against Detroit as the Los Angeles Lakers became the first team in 19 years to successfully defend an NBA crown.
                                        Photo by Andrew Bernstein

Career Records of NBA Players

The following records are of players who appeared in at least one game during the 1987-88 NBA season. Also included are records of players with previous NBA experience who were invited to training camp this year or were on the injured list for the entire 1987-88 season.

†Indicates college freshman or junior varsity participant.

KAREEM ABDUL-JABBAR

(Formerly known as Lew Alcindor.)
Born April 16, 1947 at New York, N. Y.   Height 7:02.   Weight 267.
High School—New York, N. Y., Power Memorial.
College—University of California at Los Angeles, Los Angeles, Calif.
Drafted by Milwaukee on first round, 1969 (1st pick).

Traded by Milwaukee with Walt Wesley to Los Angeles for Elmore Smith, Brian Winters, Dave Meyers and Junior Bridgeman, June 16, 1975.

—COLLEGIATE RECORD—

Year	G.	Min.	FGA	FGM	Pct.	FTA	FTM	Pct.	Reb.	Pts.	Avg.
65-66†	21	....	432	295	.683	179	106	.592	452	696	33.1
66-67	30	....	519	346	.667	274	178	.650	466	870	29.0
67-68	28	....	480	294	.613	237	146	.616	461	734	26.2
68-69	30	....	477	303	.635	188	115	.612	440	721	24.0
Varsity Totals	88	....	1476	943	.639	699	439	.628	1367	2325	26.4

NBA REGULAR SEASON RECORD

Sea.—Team	G.	Min.	FGA	FGM	Pct.	FTA	FTM	Pct.	Reb.	Ast.	PF	Disq.	Pts.	Avg.
69-70—Milwaukee	82	3534	1810	938	.518	743	485	.653	1190	337	283	8	2361	28.8
70-71—Milwaukee	82	3288	1843	1063	.577	681	470	.690	1311	272	264	4	2596	31.7
71-72—Milwaukee	81	3583	2019	1159	.574	732	504	.689	1346	370	235	1	2822	34.8
72-73—Milwaukee	76	3254	1772	982	.554	460	328	.713	1224	379	208	0	2292	30.2

Sea.—Team	G.	Min.	FGA	FGM	Pct.	FTA	FTM	Pct.	Off.	Def.	Tot.	Ast.	PF	Dq.	Stl.	Blk.	Pts.	Avg.
73-74—Milwaukee	81	3548	1759	948	.539	420	295	.702	287	891	1178	386	238	2	112	283	2191	27.0
74-75—Milwaukee	65	2747	1584	812	.513	426	325	.763	194	718	912	264	205	2	65	212	1949	30.0
75-76—Los Angeles	82	3379	1728	914	.529	636	447	.703	272	1111	1383	413	292	6	119	338	2275	27.7
76-77—Los Angeles	82	3016	1533	888	.579	536	376	.701	266	824	1090	319	262	4	101	261	2152	26.2
77-78—Los Angeles	62	2265	1205	663	.550	350	274	.783	186	615	801	269	182	1	103	185	1600	25.8
78-79—Los Angeles	80	3157	1347	777	.577	474	349	.736	207	818	1025	431	230	3	76	316	1903	23.8
79-80—Los Angeles	82	3143	1383	835	.604	476	364	.765	190	696	886	371	216	2	81	280	2034	24.8
80-81—Los Angeles	80	2976	1457	836	.574	552	423	.766	197	624	821	272	244	4	59	228	2095	26.2
81-82—Los Angeles	76	2677	1301	753	.579	442	312	.706	172	487	659	225	224	0	63	207	1818	23.9
82-83—Los Angeles	79	2554	1228	722	.588	371	278	.749	167	425	592	200	220	1	61	170	1722	21.8
83-84—Los Angeles	80	2622	1238	716	.578	394	285	.723	169	418	587	211	211	1	55	143	1717	21.5
84-85—L.A. Lakers	79	2630	1207	723	.599	395	289	.732	162	460	622	249	238	3	63	162	1735	22.0
85-86—L.A. Lakers	79	2629	1338	755	.564	439	336	.765	133	345	478	280	248	2	67	130	1846	23.4
86-87—L.A. Lakers	78	2441	993	560	.564	343	245	.714	152	371	523	203	245	2	49	97	1366	17.5
87-88—L.A. Lakers	80	2308	903	480	.532	269	205	.762	118	360	478	135	216	1	48	92	1165	14.6
Totals	1486	55751	27648	15524	.561	9139	6590	.721			17106	5586	4461	47	1122	3104	37639	25.3

Three-Point Field Goals: 1979-80, 0-for-1. 1980-81, 0-for-1. 1981-82, 0-for-3. 1982-83, 0-for-2. 1983-84, 0-for-1. 1984-85, 0-for-1. 1985-86, 0-for-2. 1986-87, 1-for-3 (.333). 1987-88, 0-for-1. Totals, 1-for-15 (.067).

NBA PLAYOFF RECORD

Sea.—Team	G.	Min.	FGA	FGM	Pct.	FTA	FTM	Pct.	Reb.	Ast.	PF	Disq.	Pts.	Avg.
69-70—Milwaukee	10	435	245	139	.567	101	74	.733	168	41	25	1	352	35.2
70-71—Milwaukee	14	577	295	152	.515	101	68	.673	238	35	45	0	372	26.6
71-72—Milwaukee	11	510	318	139	.437	54	38	.704	200	56	35	0	316	28.7
72-73—Milwaukee	6	276	138	59	.428	35	19	.543	97	17	26	0	137	22.8

Sea.—Team	G.	Min.	FGA	FGM	Pct.	FTA	FTM	Pct.	Off.	Def.	Tot.	Ast.	PF	Dq.	Stl.	Blk.	Pts.	Avg.
73-74—Milwaukee	16	758	402	224	.557	91	67	.736	67	186	253	78	41	0	20	39	515	32.2
76-77—Los Angeles	11	467	242	147	.607	120	87	.725	51	144	195	45	42	0	19	38	381	34.6
77-78—Los Angeles	3	134	73	38	.521	9	5	.556	14	27	41	11	14	1	2	12	81	27.0
78-79—Los Angeles	8	367	152	88	.579	62	52	.839	18	83	101	38	26	0	8	33	228	28.5
79-80—Los Angeles	15	618	346	198	.572	105	83	.790	51	130	181	46	51	0	17	58	479	31.9
80-81—Los Angeles	3	134	65	30	.462	28	20	.714	13	37	50	12	14	0	3	8	80	26.7
81-82—Los Angeles	14	493	221	115	.520	87	55	.632	33	86	119	51	45	0	14	45	285	20.4
82-83—Los Angeles	15	588	287	163	.568	106	80	.755	25	90	115	42	61	1	17	55	406	27.1
83-84—Los Angeles	21	767	371	206	.555	120	90	.750	56	117	173	79	71	2	23	45	502	23.9
84-85—L.A. Lakers	19	610	300	168	.560	103	80	.777	50	104	154	76	67	1	23	36	416	21.9
85-86—L.A. Lakers	14	489	282	157	.557	61	48	.787	26	57	83	49	54	0	15	24	362	25.9

Sea.—Team	G.	Min.	FGA	FGM	Pct.	FTA	FTM	Pct.	Off.	Def.	Tot.	Ast.	PF	Dq.	Stl.	Blk.	Pts.	Avg.
									—Rebounds—									
86-87—L.A. Lakers	18	559	234	124	.530	122	97	.795	39	84	123	36	56	0	8	35	345	19.2
87-88—L.A. Lakers	24	718	304	141	.464	71	56	.789	49	82	131	36	81	1	15	37	338	14.1
Totals	222	8500	4275	2288	.535	1376	1019	.741			2422	748	754	7	184	465	5595	25.2

Three-Point Field Goals: 1982-83, 0-for-1. 1986-87, 0-for-1. 1987-88, 0-for-2. Totals, 0-for-4.

NBA ALL-STAR GAME RECORD

Season—Team	Min.	FGA	FGM	Pct.	FTA	FTM	Pct.	Reb.	Ast.	PF	Disq.	Pts.
1970—Milwaukee	18	8	4	.500	2	2	1.000	11	4	6	1	10
1971—Milwaukee	30	16	8	.500	4	3	.750	14	1	2	0	19
1972—Milwaukee	19	10	5	.500	2	2	1.000	7	2	0	0	12
1973—Milwaukee					Selected, Did Not Play.							

Season—Team	Min.	FGA	FGM	Pct.	FTA	FTM	Pct.	Off.	Def.	Tot.	Ast.	PF	Dq.	Stl.	Blk.	Pts.
								—Rebounds—								
1974—Milwaukee	23	11	7	.636	0	0	.000	1	7	8	6	2	0	1	1	14
1975—Milwaukee	19	10	3	.300	2	1	.500	5	5	10	3	2	0	0	1	7
1976—Los Angeles..	36	16	9	.563	4	4	1.000	2	13	15	3	3	0	0	3	22
1977—Los Angeles .	23	14	8	.571	6	5	.833	3	1	4	2	1	0	0	1	21
1979—Los Angeles .	28	12	5	.417	2	1	.500	1	7	8	3	4	0	1	1	11
1980—Los Angeles .	30	17	6	.353	6	5	.833	5	11	16	9	5	0	0	6	17
1981—Los Angeles .	23	9	6	.667	3	3	1.000	2	4	6	4	3	0	0	4	15
1982—Los Angeles .	22	10	1	.100	0	0	.000	1	2	3	1	3	0	0	2	2
1983—Los Angeles .	32	12	9	.750	3	2	.667	2	4	6	5	1	0	1	4	20
1984—Los Angeles .	37	19	11	.579	4	3	.750	5	8	13	2	5	0	0	1	25
1985—L.A. Lakers ..	23	10	5	.500	2	1	.500	0	6	6	1	5	0	1	1	11
1986—L.A. Lakers ..	32	15	9	.600	4	3	.750	2	5	7	2	4	0	2	2	21
1987—L.A. Lakers ..	27	9	4	.444	2	2	1.000	2	6	8	3	5	0	0	2	10
1988—L.A. Lakers ..	14	9	4	.444	2	2	1.000	2	2	4	0	3	0	0	0	10
Totals	436	207	104	.502	48	39	.813			146	51	54	1	6	29	247

Named to NBA 35th Anniversary All-Time Team, 1980. . . . NBA Most Valuable Player, 1971, 1972, 1974, 1976, 1977, 1980. . . . All-NBA First Team, 1971, 1972, 1973, 1974, 1976, 1977, 1980, 1981, 1984, 1986. . . . All-NBA Second Team, 1970, 1978, 1979, 1983, 1985. . . . NBA All-Defensive First Team, 1974, 1975, 1979, 1980, 1981. . . . NBA All-Defensive Second Team, 1970, 1971, 1976, 1977, 1978, 1984. . . . NBA Rookie of the Year, 1970. . . . NBA All-Rookie Team, 1970. . . . NBA Playoff MVP, 1971 and 1985. . . . Member of NBA championship teams, 1971, 1980, 1982, 1985, 1987, 1988. . . . Led NBA in scoring, 1971 and 1972. . . . Led NBA in rebounding, 1976. . . . Led NBA in field-goal percentage, 1977. . . . Led NBA in blocked shots, 1975, 1976, 1979, 1980. . . . Holds NBA records for most seasons played, most games played and most minutes played. . . . Holds NBA records for most points, field goals made, field goals attempted, blocked shots and personal fouls. . . . Holds NBA playoff records for most seasons, games played, field goals attempted, field goals made, points and personal fouls. . . . Holds NBA All-Star Game records for most points, games played, most minutes played, field goals attempted, field goals made and personal fouls. . . . THE SPORTING NEWS College Player of the Year, 1967 and 1969. . . . THE SPORTING NEWS All-America First Team, 1967, 1968, 1969. . . . NCAA Tournament Most Outstanding Player, 1967, 1968, 1969. . . . Member of NCAA championship teams, 1967, 1968, 1969. . . . Led NCAA in field-goal percentage, 1967 and 1969.

MARK RICHARD ACRES

Born November 15, 1962 at Inglewood, Calif.   Height 6:11.   Weight 220.

High School—Palos Verdes Estates, Calif., Palos Verdes.

College—Oral Roberts University, Tulsa, Okla.

Drafted by Dallas on second round, 1985 (40th pick).

Draft rights relinquished by Dallas, July 31, 1986; signed by Boston as a free agent, May 7, 1987. Played in Italy during 1985-86 season and in Belgium, 1986-87.

—COLLEGIATE RECORD—

Year	G.	Min.	FGA	FGM	Pct.	FTA	FTM	Pct.	Reb.	Pts.	Avg.
81-82	22	702	186	109	.586	143	104	.727	178	322	14.6
82-83	28	976	368	203	.552	167	120	.719	269	526	18.8
83-84	31	...	482	266	.552	159	114	.717	324	646	20.8
84-85	29	959	380	221	.582	163	102	.626	280	544	18.8
Totals	110	...	1416	799	.564	632	440	.696	1051	2038	18.5

ITALIAN LEAGUE RECORD

Year	G.	Min.	FGA	FGM	Pct.	FTA	FTM	Pct.	Reb.	Pts.	Avg.
85-86—Pall. Varese	5	135	41	17	.415	20	17	.850	41	51	10.2

NBA REGULAR SEASON RECORD

Sea.—Team	G.	Min.	FGA	FGM	Pct.	FTA	FTM	Pct.	Off.	Def.	Tot.	Ast.	PF	Dq.	Stl.	Blk.	Pts.	Avg.
									—Rebounds—									
87-88—Boston	79	1151	203	108	.532	111	71	.640	105	165	270	42	198	2	29	27	287	3.6

NBA PLAYOFF RECORD

Sea.—Team	G.	Min.	FGA	FGM	Pct.	FTA	FTM	Pct.	Off.	Def.	Tot.	Ast.	PF	Dq.	Stl.	Blk.	Pts.	Avg.
									—Rebounds—									
87-88—Boston	17	158	26	14	.538	18	9	.500	14	22	36	2	33	0	1	1	37	2.2

Three-Point Field Goals: 1987-88, 0-for-1.

ALVAN LEIGH ADAMS

Born July 19, 1954 at Lawrence, Kan.   Height 6:09.   Weight 220.
High School—Putnam City, Okla.
College—University of Oklahoma, Norman, Okla.
Drafted by Phoenix on first round as hardship case, 1975 (4th pick).

—COLLEGIATE RECORD—

Year	G.	Min.	FGA	FGM	Pct.	FTA	FTM	Pct.	Reb.	Pts.	Avg.
72-73	21	....	356	195	.548	110	74	.673	277	464	22.1
73-74	26	....	437	236	.540	116	80	.690	315	552	21.2
74-75	26	....	524	279	.532	183	133	.727	346	691	26.6
Totals	73	....	1317	710	.539	409	287	.702	938	1707	23.4

NBA REGULAR SEASON RECORD

Sea.—Team	G.	Min.	FGA	FGM	Pct.	FTA	FTM	Pct.	Off.	Def.	Tot.	Ast.	PF	Dq.	Stl.	Blk.	Pts.	Avg.
75-76—Phoenix	80	2656	1341	629	.469	355	261	.735	215	512	727	450	274	6	121	116	1519	19.0
76-77—Phoenix	72	2278	1102	522	.474	334	252	.754	180	472	652	322	260	4	95	87	1296	18.0
77-78—Phoenix	70	1914	895	434	.485	293	214	.730	158	407	565	225	242	8	86	63	1082	15.5
78-79—Phoenix	77	2364	1073	569	.530	289	231	.799	220	485	705	360	246	4	110	63	1369	17.8
79-80—Phoenix	75	2168	875	465	.531	236	188	.797	158	451	609	322	237	4	108	55	1118	14.9
80-81—Phoenix	75	2054	870	458	.526	259	199	.768	157	389	546	344	226	2	106	69	1115	14.9
81-82—Phoenix	79	2393	1027	507	.494	233	182	.781	138	448	586	356	269	7	114	78	1196	15.1
82-83—Phoenix	80	2447	981	477	.486	217	180	.829	161	387	548	376	287	7	114	74	1135	14.2
83-84—Phoenix	70	1452	582	269	.462	160	132	.825	118	201	319	219	195	1	73	31	670	9.6
84-85—Phoenix	82	2136	915	476	.520	283	250	.883	153	347	500	308	254	2	115	48	1202	14.7
85-86—Phoenix	78	2005	679	341	.502	203	159	.783	148	329	477	324	272	7	103	46	841	10.8
86-87—Phoenix	68	1690	618	311	.503	170	134	.788	91	247	338	223	207	3	62	37	756	11.1
87-88—Phoenix	82	1646	506	251	.496	128	108	.844	118	247	365	183	245	3	82	41	611	7.5
Totals	988	27203	11464	5709	.498	3160	2490	.788	2015	4922	6937	4012	3214	58	1289	808	13910	14.1

Three-Point Field Goals: 1979-80, 0-for-2. 1981-82, 0-for-1. 1982-83, 1-for-3 (.333). 1983-84, 0-for-4. 1985-86, 0-for-2. 1986-87, 0-for-1. 1987-88, 1-for-2 (.500). Totals, 2-for-15 (.133).

NBA PLAYOFF RECORD

Sea.—Team	G.	Min.	FGA	FGM	Pct.	FTA	FTM	Pct.	Off.	Def.	Tot.	Ast.	PF	Dq.	Stl.	Blk.	Pts.	Avg.
75-76—Phoenix	19	668	303	137	.452	82	67	.817	54	137	191	98	60	1	24	20	341	17.9
77-78—Phoenix	2	71	33	15	.455	2	2	1.000	8	8	16	4	8	0	2	1	32	16.0
78-79—Phoenix	12	372	139	66	.475	31	22	.710	25	65	90	53	41	1	11	12	154	12.8
79-80—Phoenix	8	251	99	56	.566	19	17	.895	18	59	77	46	24	1	7	10	129	16.1
80-81—Phoenix	7	218	60	27	.450	28	20	.714	11	30	41	26	20	0	4	1	74	10.6
81-82—Phoenix	7	233	92	48	.522	28	22	.786	19	32	51	26	22	0	14	10	118	16.9
82-83—Phoenix	3	84	32	15	.469	7	5	.714	3	15	18	14	15	0	2	5	35	11.7
83-84—Phoenix	17	312	126	53	.421	53	36	.679	27	60	87	42	53	0	17	11	142	8.4
84-85—Phoenix	3	79	46	23	.500	6	5	.833	4	13	17	11	8	0	7	1	51	17.0
Totals	78	2288	930	440	.473	256	196	.766	169	419	588	320	251	3	88	71	1076	13.8

NBA ALL-STAR GAME RECORD

Season—Team	Min.	FGA	FGM	Pct.	FTA	FTM	Pct.	Off.	Def.	Tot.	Ast.	PF	Dq.	Stl.	Blk.	Pts.
1976—Phoenix	11	4	2	.500	0	0	.000	2	1	3	0	1	0	0	0	4

Named NBA Rookie of the Year, 1976. . . . NBA All-Rookie Team, 1976.

MICHAEL ADAMS

Born January 19, 1963 at Hartford, Conn.   Height 5:11.   Weight 165.
High School—Hartford, Conn., Public.
College—Boston College, Chestnut Hill, Mass.
Drafted by Sacramento on third round, 1985 (66th pick).

Waived by Sacramento, December 17, 1985; signed by Washington as a free agent, May 13, 1986.
Waived by Washington, September 25, 1986; re-signed by Washington as a free agent, September 29, 1986.
Waived by Washington, October 28, 1986; re-signed by Washington as a free agent, November 21, 1986.
Traded by Washington with Jay Vincent to Denver for Mark Alarie and Darrell Walker, November 2, 1987.
Played in Continental Basketball Association with Bay State Bombardiers, 1985-86.

—COLLEGIATE RECORD—

Year	G.	Min.	FGA	FGM	Pct.	FTA	FTM	Pct.	Reb.	Pts.	Avg.
81-82	26	379	103	51	.495	61	36	.590	30	138	5.3
82-83	32	1075	405	195	.482	157	127	.809	86	517	16.2
83-84	30	1026	429	195	.455	172	130	.756	102	520	17.3
84-85	31	1044	413	193	.467	119	89	.748	102	475	15.3
Totals	119	3524	1350	634	.469	509	382	.750	320	1750	14.7

CBA REGULAR SEASON RECORD

Sea.—Team	G.	Min.	2-Point FGM	FGA	Pct.	3-Point FGM	FGA	Pct.	FTM	FTA	Pct.	Reb.	Ast.	Pts.	Avg.
85-86—Bay State	38	1526	241	487	.494	21	71	.296	125	164	.762	149	320	670	17.6

NBA REGULAR SEASON RECORD

Sea.—Team	G.	Min.	FGA	FGM	Pct.	FTA	FTM	Pct.	Rebounds Off.	Def.	Tot.	Ast.	PF	Dq.	Stl.	Blk.	Pts.	Avg.
85-86—Sacramento	18	139	44	16	.364	12	8	.667	2	4	6	22	9	0	9	1	40	2.2
86-87—Washington	63	1303	393	160	.407	124	105	.847	38	85	123	244	88	0	85	6	453	7.2
87-88—Denver	82	2778	927	416	.449	199	166	.834	40	183	223	503	138	0	168	16	1137	13.9
Totals	163	4220	1364	592	.434	335	279	.833	80	272	352	769	235	0	262	23	1630	10.0

Three-Point Field Goals: 1985-86, 0-for-3. 1986-87, 28-for-102 (.275). 1987-88, 139-for-379 (.367). Totals, 167-for-484 (.345).

NBA PLAYOFF RECORD

Sea.—Team	G.	Min.	FGA	FGM	Pct.	FTA	FTM	Pct.	Rebounds Off.	Def.	Tot.	Ast.	PF	Dq.	Stl.	Blk.	Pts.	Avg.
86-87—Washington	3	82	25	8	.320	3	1	.333	0	7	7	10	6	0	7	0	19	6.3
87-88—Denver	11	406	130	47	.362	41	36	.878	9	27	36	64	19	0	18	2	147	13.4
Totals	14	488	155	55	.355	44	37	.841	9	34	43	74	25	0	25	2	166	11.9

Three-Point Field Goals: 1986-87, 2-for-9 (.222). 1987-88, 17-for-54 (.315). Totals, 19-for-63 (.302).

Named CBA Rookie of the Year, 1986 ... CBA All-Star Second Team, 1986 ... CBA All-Defensive Second Team, 1986.

MARK ANTHONY AGUIRRE

Born December 10, 1959 at Chicago, Ill. Height 6:06. Weight 235.

High Schools—Chicago, Ill., Austin (Sophomore)
and Chicago, Ill., Westinghouse (Junior and Senior).

College—DePaul University, Chicago, Ill.

Drafted by Dallas on first round as an undergraduate, 1981 (1st pick).

—COLLEGIATE RECORD—

Year	G.	Min.	FGA	FGM	Pct.	FTA	FTM	Pct.	Reb.	Pts.	Avg.
78-79	32	....	581	302	.520	213	163	.765	244	767	24.0
79-80	28	....	520	281	.540	244	187	.766	213	749	26.8
80-81	29	1069	481	280	.582	137	106	.774	249	666	23.0
Totals	89	....	1582	863	.546	594	456	.768	706	2182	24.5

NBA REGULAR SEASON RECORD

Sea.—Team	G.	Min.	FGA	FGM	Pct.	FTA	FTM	Pct.	Rebounds Off.	Def.	Tot.	Ast.	PF	Dq.	Stl.	Blk.	Pts.	Avg.
81-82—Dallas	51	1468	820	381	.465	247	168	.680	89	160	249	164	152	0	37	22	955	18.7
82-83—Dallas	81	2784	1589	767	.483	589	429	.728	191	317	508	332	247	5	80	26	1979	24.4
83-84—Dallas	79	2900	1765	925	.524	621	465	.749	161	308	469	358	246	5	80	22	2330	29.5
84-85—Dallas	80	2699	1569	794	.506	580	440	.759	188	289	477	249	250	3	60	24	2055	25.7
85-86—Dallas	74	2501	1327	668	.503	451	318	.705	177	268	445	339	229	6	62	14	1670	22.6
86-87—Dallas	80	2663	1590	787	.495	557	429	.770	181	246	427	254	243	4	84	30	2056	25.7
87-88—Dallas	77	2610	1571	746	.475	504	388	.770	182	252	434	278	223	1	70	57	1932	25.1
Totals	522	17625	10231	5068	.495	3549	2637	.743	1169	1840	3009	1974	1590	24	473	195	12977	24.9

Three-Point Field Goals: 1981-82, 25-for-71 (.352). 1982-83, 16-for-76 (.211). 1983-84, 15-for-56 (.268). 1984-85, 27-for-85 (.318). 1985-86, 16-for-56 (.285). 1986-87, 53-for-150 (.353). 1987-88, 52-for-172 (.302). Totals, 204-for-666 (.306).

NBA PLAYOFF RECORD

Sea.—Team	G.	Min.	FGA	FGM	Pct.	FTA	FTM	Pct.	Rebounds Off.	Def.	Tot.	Ast.	PF	Dq.	Stl.	Blk.	Pts.	Avg.
83-84—Dallas	10	350	184	88	.478	57	44	.772	21	55	76	32	34	2	5	5	220	22.0
84-85—Dallas	4	164	89	44	.494	32	27	.844	16	14	30	16	16	1	3	0	116	29.0
85-86—Dallas	10	345	214	105	.491	55	35	.636	21	50	71	54	28	1	9	0	247	24.7
86-87—Dallas	4	130	62	31	.500	30	23	.767	11	13	24	8	15	1	8	0	85	21.3
87-88—Dallas	17	558	294	147	.500	86	60	.698	34	66	100	56	49	0	14	9	367	21.6
Totals	45	1547	843	415	.492	260	189	.727	103	198	301	166	142	5	39	14	1035	23.0

Three-Point Field Goals: 1983-84, 0-for-5. 1984-85, 1-for-2 (.500). 1985-86, 2-for-6 (.333). 1986-87, 0-for-4. 1987-88, 13-for-34 (.382). Totals, 16-for-51 (.314).

NBA ALL-STAR GAME RECORD

Season—Team	Min.	FGA	FGM	Pct.	FTA	FTM	Pct.	Rebounds Off.	Def.	Tot.	Ast.	PF	Dq.	Stl.	Blk.	Pts.
1984—Dallas	13	8	5	.625	4	3	.750	1	0	1	2	1	0	1	1	13
1987—Dallas	17	6	3	.500	3	2	.667	1	1	2	1	1	0	0	0	9
1988—Dallas	12	10	5	.500	3	3	1.000	0	1	1	1	3	0	1	0	14
Totals	42	24	13	.542	10	8	.800	2	2	4	4	5	0	2	1	36

Three-Point Field Goals: 1987, 1-for-2 (.500). 1988, 1-for-3 (.333). Totals, 2-for-5 (.400).

Named THE SPORTING NEWS College Player of the Year, 1981.... THE SPORTING NEWS All-America First Team, 1980 and 1981.... Member of U.S. Olympic Team, 1980.

DANNY AINGE

DANIEL RAY AINGE
(Danny)

Born March 17, 1959 at Eugene, Ore. Height 6:05. Weight 185.
High School—Eugene, Ore., North.
College—Brigham Young University, Provo, Utah.
Drafted by Boston on second round, 1981 (31st pick).

—COLLEGIATE RECORD—

Year	G.	Min.	FGA	FGM	Pct.	FTA	FTM	Pct.	Reb.	Pts.	Avg.
77-78	30	....	473	243	.514	169	146	.864	173	632	21.1
78-79	27	922	376	206	.548	112	86	.768	102	498	18.4
79-80	29	984	430	229	.533	124	97	.782	114	555	19.1
80-81	32	1212	596	309	.518	199	164	.824	152	782	24.4
Totals	118	....	1875	987	.526	604	493	.816	541	2467	20.9

NBA REGULAR SEASON RECORD

Sea.—Team	G.	Min.	FGA	FGM	Pct.	FTA	FTM	Pct.	—Rebounds— Off.	Def.	Tot.	Ast.	PF	Dq.	Stl.	Blk.	Pts.	Avg.
81-82—Boston	53	564	221	79	.357	65	56	.862	25	31	56	87	86	1	37	3	219	4.1
82-83—Boston	80	2048	720	357	.496	97	72	.742	83	131	214	251	259	2	109	6	791	9.9
83-84—Boston	71	1154	361	166	.460	56	46	.821	29	87	116	162	143	2	41	4	384	5.4
84-85—Boston	75	2564	792	419	.529	136	118	.868	76	192	268	399	228	4	122	6	971	12.9
85-86—Boston	80	2407	701	353	.504	136	123	.904	47	188	235	405	204	4	94	7	855	10.7
86-87—Boston	71	2499	844	410	.486	165	148	.897	49	193	242	400	189	3	101	14	1053	14.8
87-88—Boston	81	3018	982	482	.491	180	158	.878	59	190	249	503	203	1	115	17	1270	15.7
Totals	511	14254	4621	2266	.490	835	721	.863	368	1012	1380	2207	1312	17	619	57	5543	10.8

Three-Point Field Goals: 1981-82, 5-for-17 (.294). 1982-83, 5-for-29 (.172). 1983-84, 6-for-22 (.273). 1984-85, 15-for-56 (.268). 1985-86, 26-for-73 (.356). 1986-87, 85-for-192 (.443). 1987-88, 148-for-357 (.415). Totals, 290-for-746 (.389).

NBA PLAYOFF RECORD

Sea.—Team	G.	Min.	FGA	FGM	Pct.	FTA	FTM	Pct.	—Rebounds— Off.	Def.	Tot.	Ast.	PF	Dq.	Stl.	Blk.	Pts.	Avg.
81-82—Boston	10	129	45	19	.422	13	10	.769	6	7	13	11	21	0	2	1	50	5.0
82-83—Boston	7	201	72	28	.389	11	8	.727	2	12	14	25	24	0	5	1	66	9.4
83-84—Boston	19	253	90	41	.456	10	7	.700	4	12	16	38	36	0	9	2	91	4.8
84-85—Boston	21	687	208	97	.466	39	30	.769	20	38	58	121	76	1	32	1	231	11.0
85-86—Boston	18	652	193	107	.554	60	52	.867	22	54	76	93	57	0	41	1	280	15.6
86-87—Boston	20	762	238	116	.487	36	31	.861	13	39	52	92	62	0	24	4	295	14.8
87-88—Boston	17	670	184	71	.386	42	37	.881	15	38	53	109	64	2	9	1	198	11.6
Totals	112	3354	1030	479	.465	211	175	.829	82	200	282	489	340	3	122	11	1211	10.8

Three-Point Field Goals: 1981-82, 2-for-4 (.500). 1982-83, 2-for-5 (.400). 1983-84, 2-for-9 (.222). 1984-85, 7-for-16 (.438). 1985-86, 14-for-34 (.412). 1986-87, 32-for-73 (.438). 1987-88, 19-for-57 (.333). Totals, 78-for-198 (.394).

NBA ALL-STAR GAME RECORD

Season—Team	Min.	FGA	FGM	Pct.	FTA	FTM	Pct.	—Rebounds— Off.	Def.	Tot.	Ast.	PF	Dq.	Stl.	Blk.	Pts.
1988—Boston	19	11	4	.364	2	1	.500	1	2	3	2	1	0	1	0	12

Three-Point Field Goals: 1988, 3-for-4 (.750).

RECORD AS BASEBALL PLAYER

Year	Club	League	Pos.	G.	AB.	R.	H.	2B.	3B.	HR.	RBI.	B.A.	PO.	A.	E.	F.A.
1978	Syracuse	Int.	SS-2B	119	389	33	89	10	1	4	30	.229	206	328	29	.948
1979	Syracuse	Int.	2B	27	101	10	25	4	2	0	8	.248	56	77	4	.971
1979	Toronto	Amer.	2B	87	308	26	73	7	1	2	19	.237	198	261	11	.977
1980	Syracuse	Int.	3-O-SS	80	295	37	72	9	1	2	17	.244	111	140	3	.988
1980	Toronto	Amer.	OF-3-2	38	111	11	27	6	1	0	4	.243	69	12	1	.988
1981	Toronto	Amer.	3-SS-O-2	86	246	20	46	6	2	0	14	.187	88	146	12	.951
Major League Totals				211	665	57	146	19	4	2	37	.220	355	419	24	.970

Holds NBA record for most three-point field goals in a season, 1988.... Member of NBA championship teams, 1984 and 1986.... Named to THE SPORTING NEWS All-America First Team, 1981.... Drafted by Toronto Blue Jays in 15th round of free-agent draft, June 7, 1977.

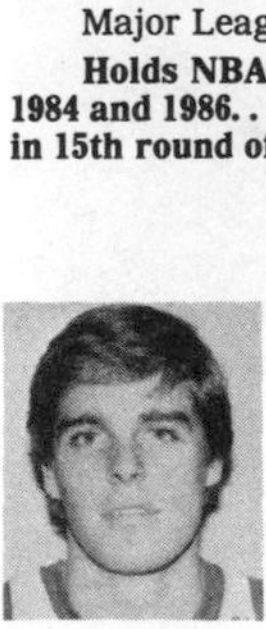

MARK STEVEN ALARIE

Born December 11, 1963 at Phoenix, Ariz. Height 6:08. Weight 217.
High School—Phoenix, Ariz., Brophy Prep.
College—Duke University, Durham, N.C.
Drafted by Denver on first round, 1986 (18th pick).

Traded by Denver with Darrell Walker to Washington for Michael Adams and Jay Vincent, November 2, 1987.

NBA REGULAR SEASON RECORD

Sea.—Team	G.	Min.	FGA	FGM	Pct.	FTA	FTM	Pct.	—Rebounds— Off.	Def.	Tot.	Ast.	PF	Dq.	Stl.	Blk.	Pts.	Avg.
87-88—San Antonio	82	1984	756	379	.501	328	198	.604	161	352	513	79	228	1	54	122	957	11.7

Three-Point Field Goals: 1987-88, 1-for-5 (.200).

NBA PLAYOFF RECORD

Sea.—Team	G.	Min.	FGA	FGM	Pct.	FTA	FTM	Pct.	—Rebounds— Off.	Def.	Tot.	Ast.	PF	Dq.	Stl.	Blk.	Pts.	Avg.
87-88—San Antonio	3	95	36	17	.472	9	4	.444	6	15	21	3	10	1	2	4	38	12.7

Named to NBA All-Rookie Team, 1988.

RICHARD ANDREW ANDERSON

Born November 19, 1960 at San Pedro, Calif.   Height 6:10.   Weight 240.

High School—Garden Grove, Calif., Rancho Alamitos.

College—University of California at Santa Barbara, Santa Barbara, Calif.

Drafted by San Diego on second round, 1982 (32nd pick).

Traded by San Diego to Denver for Billy McKinney, October 4, 1983.

Signed by Houston as a Veteran Free Agent, October 11, 1986; Denver agreed not to exercise its right of first refusal in exchange for a 1988 3rd round draft choice.

Waived by Houston, December 7, 1987; claimed off waivers by Portland, December 9, 1987.

—COLLEGIATE RECORD—

Year	G.	Min.	FGA	FGM	Pct.	FTA	FTM	Pct.	Reb.	Pts.	Avg.
78-79	20	208	84	36	.429	16	7	.438	59	79	4.0
79-80	27	906	316	141	.446	77	58	.753	164	340	12.6
80-81	27	770	367	166	.452	98	72	.735	257	404	15.0
81-82	26	926	351	165	.470	121	87	.719	289	417	16.0
Totals	100	2810	1118	508	.454	312	224	.718	769	1240	12.4

NBA REGULAR SEASON RECORD

Sea.—Team	G.	Min.	FGA	FGM	Pct.	FTA	FTM	Pct.	—Rebounds— Off.	Def.	Tot.	Ast.	PF	Dq.	Stl.	Blk.	Pts.	Avg.
82-83—San Diego	78	1274	431	174	.404	69	48	.696	111	161	272	120	170	2	57	26	403	5.2
83-84—Denver	78	1380	638	272	.426	150	116	.773	136	270	406	193	183	0	46	28	663	8.5
86-87—Houston	51	312	139	59	.424	29	22	.759	24	55	79	33	37	0	7	3	144	2.8
87-88—Hou.-Port.	74	1350	439	171	.390	77	58	.753	91	212	303	112	137	1	51	16	448	6.1
Totals	281	4316	1647	676	.410	325	244	.751	362	698	1060	458	527	3	161	73	1658	5.9

Three-Point Field Goals: 1982-83, 7-for-19 (.269). 1983-84, 3-for-19 (.158). 1986-87, 4-for-16 (.250). 1987-88, 48-for-150 (.320). Totals, 62-for-204 (.304).

NBA PLAYOFF RECORD

Sea.—Team	G.	Min.	FGA	FGM	Pct.	FTA	FTM	Pct.	—Rebounds— Off.	Def.	Tot.	Ast.	PF	Dq.	Stl.	Blk.	Pts.	Avg.
83-84—Denver	4	37	15	6	.400	6	4	.667	1	8	9	5	6	0	1	0	16	4.0
86-87—Houston	5	5	3	1	.333	2	2	1.000	1	0	1	0	1	0	0	0	5	1.0
87-88—Portland	3	63	24	11	.458	4	4	1.000	5	8	13	1	11	0	2	1	32	10.7
Totals	12	105	42	18	.429	12	10	.833	7	16	23	6	18	0	2	2	53	4.4

Three-Point Field Goals: 1983-84, 0-for-1. 1986-87, 1-for-2 (.500). 1987-88, 6-for-14 (.429). Totals, 7-for-17 (.412).

RONALD GENE ANDERSON
(Ron)

Born October 15, 1958 at Chicago, Ill.   Height 6:07.   Weight 215.

High School—Chicago, Ill., Bowen (Did not play basketball)

Colleges—Santa Barbara City College, Santa Barbara, Calif.,
and Fresno State University, Fresno, Calif.

Drafted by Cleveland on second round, 1984 (27th pick).

Traded by Cleveland to Indiana for a 1987 4th round draft choice, December 10, 1985.

—COLLEGIATE RECORD—
Santa Barbara

Year	G.	Min.	FGA	FGM	Pct.	FTA	FTM	Pct.	Reb.	Pts.	Avg.
80-81	33	....	333	167	.502	75	56	.747	328	390	11.8
81-82	32	....	448	292	.652	84	66	.786	340	650	20.3
JC Totals	65	....	781	459	.588	159	122	.767	668	1040	16.0

GREG ANDERSON

Fresno State

Year	G.	Min.	FGA	FGM	Pct.	FTA	FTM	Pct.	Reb.	Pts.	Avg.
82-83	35	1303	426	234	.549	128	104	.813	204	572	16.3
83-84	33	1197	437	249	.570	104	82	.788	200	580	17.6
Totals	68	2500	863	483	.560	232	186	.802	404	1152	16.9

NBA REGULAR SEASON RECORD

Sea.—Team	G.	Min.	FGA	FGM	Pct.	FTA	FTM	Pct.	Off.	Def.	Tot.	Ast.	PF	Dq.	Stl.	Blk.	Pts.	Avg.
84-85—Cleveland	36	520	195	84	.431	50	41	.820	39	49	88	34	40	0	9	7	210	5.8
85-86—Clev.-Ind.	77	1676	628	310	.494	127	85	.669	130	144	274	144	125	0	56	6	707	9.2
86-87—Indiana	63	721	294	139	.473	108	85	.787	73	78	151	54	65	0	31	3	363	5.8
87-88—Indiana	74	1097	436	217	.498	141	108	.766	89	127	216	78	98	0	41	6	542	7.3
Totals	250	4014	1553	750	.483	426	319	.749	331	398	729	310	328	0	137	22	1822	7.3

Three-Point Field Goals: 1984-85, 1-for-2 (.500). 1985-86, 2-for-9 (.222). 1986-87, 0-for-5. 1987-88, 0-for-2. Totals, 3-for-18 (.167).

NBA PLAYOFF RECORD

Sea.—Team	G.	Min.	FGA	FGM	Pct.	FTA	FTM	Pct.	Off.	Def.	Tot.	Ast.	PF	Dq.	Stl.	Blk.	Pts.	Avg.
84-85—Cleveland	2	9	3	0	.000	0	0	.000	1	2	3	0	0	0	0	0	0	0.0
86-87—Indiana	4	24	4	2	.500	0	0	.000	2	1	3	0	2	0	0	0	4	1.0
Totals	6	33	7	2	.286	0	0	.000	3	3	6	0	2	0	0	0	4	0.7

JOSEPH ARLAUCKAS
(Joe)

Born July 20, 1965 at Rochester, N.Y.   Height 6:09.   Weight 230.
High School—Rochester, N.Y., Jefferson.
College—Niagara University, Niagara University, N.Y.
Drafted by Sacramento on fourth round, 1987 (74th pick).

Waived by Sacramento, December 14, 1987.

—COLLEGIATE RECORD—

Year	G.	Min.	FGA	FGM	Pct.	FTA	FTM	Pct.	Reb.	Pts.	Avg.
83-84	28	423	145	66	.455	60	42	.700	131	174	6.2
84-85	27	969	405	197	.486	121	77	.636	230	471	17.4
85-86	29	965	398	209	.525	92	53	.576	244	471	16.2
86-87	29	855	410	216	.527	87	60	.690	210	494	17.0
Totals	113	3212	1358	688	.507	360	232	.644	815	1610	14.2

Three-Point Field Goals: 1986-87, 2-for-8 (.250).

NBA REGULAR SEASON RECORD

Sea.—Team	G.	Min.	FGA	FGM	Pct.	FTA	FTM	Pct.	Off.	Def.	Tot.	Ast.	PF	Dq.	Stl.	Blk.	Pts.	Avg.
87-88—Sacramento	9	85	43	14	.326	8	6	.750	6	7	13	8	16	0	3	4	34	3.8

VINCENT ASKEW

Born February 28, 1966 at Memphis, Tenn.   Height 6:06.   Weight 210.
High School—Memphis, Tenn., Frayser.
College—Memphis State University, Memphis, Tenn.
Drafted by Philadelphia on second round as an undergraduate, 1987 (39th pick).

Waived by Philadelphia, December 22, 1987.

—COLLEGIATE RECORD—

Year	G.	Min.	FGA	FGM	Pct.	FTA	FTM	Pct.	Reb.	Pts.	Avg.
84-85	35	1177	225	115	.511	93	59	.634	117	289	8.3
85-86	34	1094	306	150	.490	86	70	.814	228	370	10.9
86-87	34	1164	387	187	.483	155	122	.787	170	512	15.1
Totals	103	3435	918	452	.492	334	251	.751	515	1171	11.4

Three-Point Field Goals: 1986-87, 16-for-42 (.381).

NBA REGULAR SEASON RECORD

Sea.—Team	G.	Min.	FGA	FGM	Pct.	FTA	FTM	Pct.	Off.	Def.	Tot.	Ast.	PF	Dq.	Stl.	Blk.	Pts.	Avg.
87-88—Philadelphia	14	234	74	22	.297	11	8	.727	6	16	22	33	12	0	10	6	52	3.7

JOHN EDWARD BAGLEY

Born April 23, 1960 at Bridgeport, Conn.   Height 6:00.   Weight 192.

High School—Bridgeport, Conn., Warren Harding.

College—Boston College, Chestnut Hill, Mass.

Drafted by Cleveland on first round as an undergraduate, 1982 (12th pick).

Traded by Cleveland with Keith Lee to New Jersey for Darryl Dawkins and James Bailey, October 8, 1987.

—COLLEGIATE RECORD—

Year	G.	Min.	FGA	FGM	Pct.	FTA	FTM	Pct.	Reb.	Pts.	Avg.
79-80	29	....	270	130	.481	115	83	.722	91	343	11.8
80-81	30	965	418	209	.500	245	193	.788	115	611	20.4
81-82	32	1065	513	257	.501	202	161	.797	122	675	21.1
Totals	91	....	1201	596	.496	562	437	.778	328	1629	17.9

NBA REGULAR SEASON RECORD

Sea.—Team	G.	Min.	FGA	FGM	Pct.	FTA	FTM	Pct.	Off.	Def.	Tot.	Ast.	PF	Dq.	Stl.	Blk.	Pts.	Avg.
82-83—Cleveland	68	990	373	161	.432	84	64	.762	17	79	96	167	74	0	54	5	386	5.7
83-84—Cleveland	76	1712	607	257	.423	198	157	.793	49	107	156	333	113	1	78	4	673	8.9
84-85—Cleveland	81	2401	693	338	.488	167	125	.749	54	237	291	697	132	0	129	5	804	9.9
85-86—Cleveland	78	2472	865	366	.423	215	170	.791	76	199	275	735	165	1	122	10	911	11.7
86-87—Cleveland	72	2182	732	312	.426	136	113	.831	55	197	252	379	114	0	91	7	768	10.7
87-88—New Jersey	82	2774	896	393	.439	180	148	.822	61	196	257	479	162	0	110	10	981	12.0
Totals	457	12531	4166	1827	.439	980	777	.793	312	1015	1327	2790	760	2	584	41	4523	9.9

Three-Point Field Goals: 1982-83, 0-for-14. 1983-84, 2-for-17 (.118). 1984-85, 3-for-26 (.115). 1985-86, 9-for-37 (.243). 1986-87, 31-for-103 (.301). 1987-88, 47-for-161 (.292). Totals, 92-for-358 (.257).

NBA PLAYOFF RECORD

Sea.—Team	G.	Min.	FGA	FGM	Pct.	FTA	FTM	Pct.	Off.	Def.	Tot.	Ast.	PF	Dq.	Stl.	Blk.	Pts.	Avg.
84-85—Cleveland	4	168	56	22	.393	10	7	.700	1	15	16	40	7	0	10	0	51	12.8

Three-Point Field Goals: 1984-85, 0-for-3.

JAMES L. BAILEY

Born May 21, 1957 at Dublin, Ga.   Height 6:09.   Weight 220.

High School—Westwood, Mass., Xaverian.

College—Rutgers University, New Brunswick, N. J.

Drafted by Seattle on first round, 1979 (6th pick).

Traded by Seattle to New Jersey for Ray Tolbert and a 1984 2nd round draft choice, November 25, 1981.
Traded by New Jersey to Houston for 1983 and 1985 2nd round draft choices, November 10, 1982.
Traded by Houston with a 1985 2nd round draft choice and cash to San Antonio for John Lucas and a 1985 3rd round draft choice, October 4, 1984.
Traded by San Antonio to New York for a 1986 3rd round draft choice and cash, October 24, 1984.
Signed by New Jersey as a Veteran Free Agent, August 14, 1986; New York waived its right of first refusal.
Traded by New Jersey with Darryl Dawkins to Cleveland for Keith Lee and John Bagley, October 8, 1987.
Traded by Cleveland to Phoenix for a 1989 2nd round draft choice, October 29, 1987.

—COLLEGIATE RECORD—

Year	G.	Min.	FGA	FGM	Pct.	FTA	FTM	Pct.	Reb.	Pts.	Avg.
75-76	33	790	240	121	.504	68	40	.588	233	282	8.5
76-77	28	927	342	185	.541	141	98	.695	304	468	16.7
77-78	31	1061	533	312	.585	164	106	.646	290	730	23.5
78-79	30	1028	443	231	.521	140	92	.657	247	554	18.5
Totals	122	3806	1558	849	.545	513	336	.655	1074	2034	16.7

NBA REGULAR SEASON RECORD

Sea.—Team	G.	Min.	FGA	FGM	Pct.	FTA	FTM	Pct.	Off.	Def.	Tot.	Ast.	PF	Dq.	Stl.	Blk.	Pts.	Avg.
79-80—Seattle	67	726	271	122	.450	101	68	.673	71	126	197	28	116	1	21	54	312	4.7
80-81—Seattle	82	2539	889	444	.499	361	256	.709	192	415	607	98	332	11	74	143	1145	14.0
81-82—Sea-N.J.	77	1468	505	261	.517	224	137	.612	127	264	391	65	270	5	42	83	659	8.6
82-83—N.J.-Hou.	75	1765	774	385	.497	322	226	.702	171	303	474	67	271	7	43	60	996	13.3
83-84—Houston	73	1174	517	254	.491	192	138	.719	104	190	294	79	197	8	33	40	646	8.8
84-85—New York	74	1297	349	156	.447	108	73	.676	122	222	344	39	286	10	30	50	385	5.2
85-86—New York	48	1245	443	202	.456	167	129	.772	102	232	334	50	207	12	33	40	533	11.1
86-87—New Jersey	34	542	239	112	.469	80	58	.725	48	89	137	20	119	5	12	23	282	8.3
87-88—Phoenix	65	869	241	109	.452	89	70	.787	73	137	210	42	180	1	17	28	288	4
Totals	595	11625	4228	2045	.484	1644	1155	.703	1010	1978	2988	488	1978	60	305	521	5246	

Three-Point Field Goals: 1980-81, 1-for-2 (.500). 1982-83, 0-for-1. 1983-84, 0-for-1. 1984-85, 0-for-1. 1985-86, 0-for-4, 88, 0-for-4. Totals, 1-for-13 (.077).

THURL BAILEY

NBA PLAYOFF RECORD

Sea.—Team	G.	Min.	FGA	FGM	Pct.	FTA	FTM	Pct.	Off.	Def.	Tot.	Ast.	PF	Dq.	Stl.	Blk.	Pts.	Avg.
										—Rebounds—								
79-80—Seattle	12	138	44	21	.477	20	13	.650	8	17	25	5	22	0	9	9	55	4.6
81-82—New Jersey	2	26	3	1	.333	2	2	1.000	2	4	6	1	5	0	2	1	4	2.0
Totals	14	164	47	22	.468	22	15	.682	10	21	31	6	27	0	11	10	59	4.2

Named to THE SPORTING NEWS All-America First Team, 1979. . . . THE SPORTING NEWS All-America Second Team, 1978.

THURL LEE BAILEY

Born April 7, 1961 at Washington, D. C.   Height 6:11.   Weight 222.

High School—Bladensburg, Md.

College—North Carolina State University, Raleigh, N. C.

Drafted by Utah on first round, 1983 (7th pick).

—COLLEGIATE RECORD—

Year	G.	Min.	FGA	FGM	Pct.	FTA	FTM	Pct.	Reb.	Pts.	Avg.
79-80	28	....	101	44	.436	55	37	.673	102	125	4.5
80-81	27	....	278	146	.525	53	39	.736	165	331	12.3
81-82	32	....	312	171	.548	118	96	.814	216	438	13.7
82-83	36	....	499	250	.501	127	91	.717	276	601	16.7
Totals	123	....	1190	611	.513	353	263	.745	759	1495	12.2

Three-Point Field Goals: 1982-83, 10-for-15 (.667).

NBA REGULAR SEASON RECORD

Sea.—Team	G.	Min.	FGA	FGM	Pct.	FTA	FTM	Pct.	Off.	Def.	Tot.	Ast.	PF	Dq.	Stl.	Blk.	Pts.	Avg.
										—Rebounds—								
83-84—Utah	81	2009	590	302	.512	117	88	.752	113	349	464	129	193	1	38	122	692	8.5
84-85—Utah	80	2481	1034	507	.490	234	197	.842	153	372	525	138	215	2	51	105	1212	15.2
85-86—Utah	82	2358	1077	483	.448	277	230	.830	148	345	493	153	160	0	42	114	1196	14.6
86-87—Utah	81	2155	1036	463	.447	236	190	.805	145	287	432	102	150	0	38	88	1116	13.8
87-88—Utah	82	2804	1286	633	.492	408	337	.826	134	397	531	158	186	1	49	125	1604	19.6
Totals	406	11807	5023	2388	.475	1272	1042	.819	695	1750	2445	680	904	4	218	554	5820	14.3

Three-Point Field Goals: 1984-85, 1-for-1 (1.000). 1985-86, 0-for-7. 1986-87, 0-for-2. 1987-88, 1-for-3 (.333). Totals, 2-for-13 (.154).

NBA PLAYOFF RECORD

Sea.—Team	G.	Min.	FGA	FGM	Pct.	FTA	FTM	Pct.	Off.	Def.	Tot.	Ast.	PF	Dq.	Stl.	Blk.	Pts.	Avg.
										—Rebounds—								
83-84—Utah	11	340	97	50	.515	21	17	.810	15	46	61	10	33	0	2	11	117	10.6
84-85—Utah	10	375	152	62	.408	55	45	.818	21	71	92	27	30	0	5	18	169	16.9
85-86—Utah	4	147	77	28	.364	11	8	.727	11	21	32	13	13	0	2	2	64	16.0
86-87—Utah	5	151	63	30	.476	18	18	1.000	14	16	30	9	12	1	3	6	78	15.6
87-88—Utah	11	449	203	99	.488	68	57	.838	21	42	63	18	32	0	6	23	255	23.2
Totals	41	1462	592	269	.454	173	145	.838	82	196	278	77	120	1	18	60	683	16.7

Three-Point Field Goals: 1983-84, 0-for-2. 1985-86, 0-for-1. 1987-88, 0-for-1. Totals, 0-for-4.

Named to NBA All-Rookie Team, 1984. . . . Member of NCAA Division I championship team, 1983.

EUGENE LAVON BANKS
(Gene)

Born May 15, 1959 at Philadelphia, Pa.   Height 6:07.   Weight 215.

High School—Philadelphia, Pa., West.

College—Duke University, Durham, N. C.

Drafted by San Antonio on second round, 1981 (28th pick).

Traded by San Antonio to Chicago for Steve Johnson and a 1985 2nd round draft choice, June 18, 1985.
Missed entire 1987-88 season due to injury.

—COLLEGIATE RECORD—

Year	G.	Min.	FGA	FGM	Pct.	FTA	FTM	Pct.	Reb.	Pts.	Avg.
77-78	34	....	451	238	.528	146	105	.719	292	581	17.1
78-79	30	....	353	175	.496	126	79	.627	255	429	14.3
79-80	33	1165	404	212	.525	183	146	.798	254	570	17.3
80-81	27	933	350	202	.577	134	95	.709	184	499	18.5
Totals	124	....	1558	827	.531	589	425	.722	985	2079	16.8

NBA REGULAR SEASON RECORD

Sea.—Team	G.	Min.	FGA	FGM	Pct.	FTA	FTM	Pct.	Off.	Def.	Tot.	Ast.	PF	Dq.	Stl.	Blk.	Pts.	Avg.
										—Rebounds—								
81-82—San Antonio	80	1700	652	311	.477	212	145	.684	157	254	411	147	199	2	55	17	767	9.6

Sea.—Team	G.	Min.	FGA	FGM	Pct.	FTA	FTM	Pct.	Off.	Def.	Tot.	Ast.	PF	Dq.	Stl.	Blk.	Pts.	Avg.
82-83—San Antonio	81	2722	919	505	.550	278	196	.705	222	390	612	279	229	3	78	21	1206	14.9
83-84—San Antonio	80	2600	747	424	.568	270	200	.741	204	378	582	254	256	5	105	23	1049	13.1
84-85—San Antonio	82	2091	493	289	.586	257	199	.774	133	312	445	234	220	3	65	13	778	9.5
85-86—Chicago	82	2139	688	356	.517	255	183	.718	178	182	360	251	212	4	81	10	895	10.9
86-87—Chicago	63	1822	462	249	.539	146	112	.767	115	193	308	170	173	3	52	17	610	9.7
Totals	468	13074	3961	2134	.539	1418	1035	.730	1009	1709	2718	1335	1289	20	436	101	5305	11.3

Three-Point Field Goals: 1981-82, 0-for-8. 1982-83, 0-for-5. 1983-84, 1-for-6 (.167). 1984-85, 1-for-3 (.333). 1985-86, 0-for-19. 1986-87, 0-for-5. Totals, 2-for-46 (.043).

NBA PLAYOFF RECORD

Sea.—Team	G.	Min.	FGA	FGM	Pct.	FTA	FTM	Pct.	Off.	Def.	Tot.	Ast.	PF	Dq.	Stl.	Blk.	Pts.	Avg.
81-82—San Antonio	9	146	65	30	.462	10	4	.400	21	22	43	9	12	0	4	3	64	7.1
82-83—San Antonio	11	398	150	76	.507	35	23	.657	27	49	76	50	25	1	11	1	175	15.9
84-85—San Antonio	1	10	1	0	.000	0	0	.000	0	0	0	1	3	0	0	0	0	0.0
85-86—Chicago	3	69	18	10	.556	4	2	.500	4	6	10	5	10	0	1	0	22	7.3
86-87—Chicago	3	79	22	13	.591	8	5	.625	3	5	8	2	13	1	0	0	31	10.3
Totals	27	702	256	129	.504	57	34	.596	55	82	137	67	63	2	16	4	292	10.8

Three-Point Field Goals: 1981-82, 0-for-1. 1985-86, 0-for-2. Totals, 0-for-3.

CHARLES WADE BARKLEY

Born February 20, 1963 at Leeds, Ala.   Height 6:06.   Weight 263.

High School—Leeds, Ala.

College—Auburn University, Auburn, Ala.

Drafted by Philadelphia on first round as an undergraduate, 1984 (5th pick).

—COLLEGIATE RECORD—

Year	G.	Min.	FGA	FGM	Pct.	FTA	FTM	Pct.	Reb.	Pts.	Avg.
81-82..................	28	746	242	144	.595	107	68	.636	275	356	12.7
82-83..................	28	782	250	161	.644	130	82	.631	266	404	14.4
83-84..................	28	794	254	162	.638	145	99	.683	265	423	15.1
Totals	84	2322	746	467	.636	382	249	.652	806	1183	14.1

NBA REGULAR SEASON RECORD

Sea.—Team	G.	Min.	FGA	FGM	Pct.	FTA	FTM	Pct.	Off.	Def.	Tot.	Ast.	PF	Dq.	Stl.	Blk.	Pts.	Avg.
84-85—Philadelphia	82	2347	783	427	.545	400	293	.733	266	437	703	155	301	5	95	80	1148	14.0
85-86—Philadelphia	80	2952	1041	595	.572	578	396	.685	354	672	1026	312	333	8	173	125	1603	20.0
86-87—Philadelphia	68	2740	937	557	.594	564	429	.761	390	604	994	331	252	5	119	104	1564	23.0
87-88—Philadelphia	80	3170	1283	753	.587	951	714	.751	385	566	951	254	278	6	100	103	2264	28.3
Totals	310	11209	4044	2332	.577	2493	1832	.735	1395	2279	3674	1052	1164	24	487	412	6579	21.2

Three-Point Field Goals: 1984-85, 1-for-6 (.167). 1985-86, 17-for-75 (.227). 1986-87, 21-for-104 (.202). 1987-88, 44-for-157 (.280). Totals, 83-for-342 (.243).

NBA PLAYOFF RECORD

Sea.—Team	G.	Min.	FGA	FGM	Pct.	FTA	FTM	Pct.	Off.	Def.	Tot.	Ast.	PF	Dq.	Stl.	Blk.	Pts.	Avg.
84-85—Philadelphia	13	408	139	75	.540	63	40	.635	52	92	144	26	49	0	23	15	194	14.9
85-86—Philadelphia	12	497	180	104	.578	131	91	.695	60	129	189	67	52	2	27	15	300	25.0
86-87—Philadelphia	5	210	75	43	.573	45	36	.800	27	36	63	12	21	0	4	8	123	24.6
Totals	30	1115	394	222	.563	239	167	.699	139	257	396	105	122	2	54	38	617	20.6

Three-Point Field Goals: 1984-85, 4-for-6 (.667). 1985-86, 1-for-15 (.067). 1986-87, 1-for-8 (.125). Totals, 6-for-29 (.207).

NBA ALL-STAR GAME RECORD

Season—Team	Min.	FGA	FGM	Pct.	FTA	FTM	Pct.	Off.	Def.	Tot.	Ast.	PF	Dq.	Stl.	Blk.	Pts.
1987—Philadelphia	16	6	2	.333	6	3	.500	1	3	4	1	2	0	1	0	7
1988—Philadelphia	15	4	1	.250	2	2	1.000	1	2	3	0	2	0	1	1	4
Totals	31	10	3	.300	8	5	.625	2	5	7	1	4	0	2	1	11

Three-Point Field Goals: 1987, 0-for-2. 1988, 0-for-1. Totals, 0-for-3.

Named to All-NBA First Team, 1988. . . . All-NBA Second Team, 1986 and 1987. . . . NBA All-Rookie Team, 1985. . . . Led NBA in rebounding, 1987. . . . Recipient of Schick Pivotal Player Award, 1986, 1987, 1988.

JOHN SIDNEY BATTLE

Born November 9, 1962 at Washington, D.C.   Height 6:02.   Weight 175.

High School—Washington, D.C., McKinley.

College—Rutgers University, New Brunswick, N.J.

Drafted by Atlanta on fourth round, 1985 (84th pick).

—COLLEGIATE RECORD—

Year	G.	Min.	FGA	FGM	Pct.	FTA	FTM	Pct.	Reb.	Pts.	Avg.
81-82	29	373	67	29	.433	28	12	.429	29	70	2.4
82-83	31	443	139	68	.489	51	37	.725	48	182	5.9
83-84	25	814	420	207	.493	153	111	.725	78	525	21.0
84-85	29	1017	470	231	.491	177	129	.729	115	608	21.0
Totals	114	2647	1096	535	.488	409	289	.707	270	1385	12.1

Three-Point Field Goals: 1982-83, 9-for-18 (.500). 1984-85, 17-for-58 (.293).

NBA REGULAR SEASON RECORD

Sea.—Team	G.	Min.	FGA	FGM	Pct.	FTA	FTM	Pct.	Off.	Def.	Tot.	Ast.	PF	Dq.	Stl.	Blk.	Pts.	Avg.
85-86—Atlanta	64	639	222	101	.455	103	75	.728	12	50	62	74	80	0	23	3	277	4.3
86-87—Atlanta	64	804	315	144	.457	126	93	.738	16	44	60	124	76	0	29	5	381	6.0
87-88—Atlanta	67	1227	613	278	.454	188	141	.750	26	87	113	158	84	0	31	5	713	10.6
Totals	195	2670	1150	523	.455	417	309	.741	54	181	235	356	240	0	83	13	1371	7.0

Three-Point Field Goals: 1985-86, 0-for-7. 1986-87, 0-for-10. 1987-88, 16-for-41 (.390). Totals, 16-for-58 (.276).

NBA PLAYOFF RECORD

Sea.—Team	G.	Min.	FGA	FGM	Pct.	FTA	FTM	Pct.	Off.	Def.	Tot.	Ast.	PF	Dq.	Stl.	Blk.	Pts.	Avg.
85-86—Atlanta	6	27	11	4	.364	4	3	.750	0	4	4	2	5	0	2	0	11	1.8
86-87—Atlanta	8	78	34	15	.441	23	21	.913	2	8	10	8	13	0	1	0	53	6.6
87-88—Atlanta	12	166	67	32	.478	25	17	.680	2	18	20	26	14	0	2	0	81	6.8
Totals	26	271	112	51	.455	52	41	.788	4	30	34	36	32	0	5	0	145	5.8

Three-Point Field Goals: 1985-86, 0-for-1. 1986-87, 2-for-5 (.400). 1987-88, 0-for-2. Totals, 2-for-8 (.250).

WILLIAM BEDFORD

Born December 14, 1963 at Memphis, Tenn. Height 7:01. Weight 235.

High School—Memphis, Tenn., Melrose.

College—Memphis State University, Memphis, Tenn.

Drafted by Phoenix on first round as an undergraduate, 1986 (6th pick).

Traded by Phoenix to Detroit for a 1989 1st round draft choice, June 21, 1987.

—COLLEGIATE RECORD—

Year	G.	Min.	FGA	FGM	Pct.	FTA	FTM	Pct.	Reb.	Pts.	Avg.
83-84	26	684	187	108	.578	56	30	.536	137	246	9.5
84-85	35	1099	330	179	.542	101	68	.673	265	426	12.2
85-86	32	1038	389	227	.584	156	98	.628	273	552	17.3
Totals	93	2821	906	514	.567	313	196	.626	675	1224	13.2

NBA REGULAR SEASON RECORD

Sea.—Team	G.	Min.	FGA	FGM	Pct.	FTA	FTM	Pct.	Off.	Def.	Tot.	Ast.	PF	Dq.	Stl.	Blk.	Pts.	Avg.
86-87—Phoenix	50	979	358	142	.397	86	50	.581	79	167	246	57	125	1	18	37	334	6.7
87-88—Detroit	38	298	101	44	.436	23	13	.565	27	38	65	4	47	0	8	17	101	2.7
Totals	88	1277	459	186	.405	109	63	.578	106	205	311	61	172	1	26	54	435	4.9

Three-Point Field Goals: 1986-87, 0-for-1.

LENARD BENOIT BENJAMIN

(Known by middle name.)

Born November 22, 1964 at Monroe, La. Height 7:00. Weight 250.

High School—Monroe, La., Carroll.

College—Creighton University, Omaha, Neb.

Drafted by Los Angeles Clippers on first round as an undergraduate, 1985 (3rd pick).

—COLLEGIATE RECORD—

Year	G.	Min.	FGA	FGM	Pct.	FTA	FTM	Pct.	Reb.	Pts.	Avg.
82-83	27	871	292	162	.555	116	76	.655	259	400	14.8
83-84	30	1112	350	190	.543	144	107	.743	295	487	16.2
84-85	32	1193	443	258	.582	233	172	.738	451	688	21.5
Totals	89	3176	1085	610	.562	493	355	.720	1005	1575	

NBA REGULAR SEASON RECORD

Sea.—Team	G.	Min.	FGA	FGM	Pct.	FTA	FTM	Pct.	Off.	Def.	Tot.	Ast.	PF	Dq.	Stl.	Blk.
85-86—L.A. Clippers	79	2088	661	324	.490	307	229	.746	161	439	600	79	286	5	64	20

Sea.—Team	G.	Min.	FGA	FGM	Pct.	FTA	FTM	Pct.	Off.	Def.	Tot.	Ast.	PF	Dq.	Stl.	Blk.	Pts.	Avg.
86-87—L.A. Clippers	72	2230	713	320	.449	263	188	.715	134	452	586	135	251	7	60	187	828	11.5
87-88—L.A. Clippers	66	2171	693	340	.491	255	180	.706	112	418	530	172	203	2	50	225	860	13.0
Totals	217	6489	2067	984	.476	825	597	.724	407	1309	1716	386	740	14	174	618	2566	11.8

Three-Point Field Goals: 1985-86, 1-for-3 (.333). 1986-87, 0-for-2. 1987-88, 0-for-8. Totals, 1-for-13 (.077).

MICHAEL KENT BENSON

(Known by middle name.)

Born December 27, 1954 at New Castle, Ind. Height 6:10. Weight 240.

High School—New Castle, Ind., Chrysler.

College—Indiana University, Bloomington, Ind.

Drafted by Milwaukee on first round, 1977 (1st pick).

Traded by Milwaukee with a 1980 1st round draft choice to Detroit for Bob Lanier, February 4, 1980.

Traded by Detroit with Kelly Tripucka to Utah for Adrian Dantley and 1987 and 1990 2nd round draft choices, August 21, 1986.

Traded by Utah with Dell Curry and future 2nd round draft considerations to Cleveland for Darryl Dawkins, Mel Turpin and future 2nd round draft considerations, October 8, 1987.

—COLLEGIATE RECORD—

Year	G.	Min.	FGA	FGM	Pct.	FTA	FTM	Pct.	Reb.	Pts.	Avg.
73-74	27	....	224	113	.504	40	24	.600	222	250	9.3
74-75	32	....	366	198	.541	113	84	.743	286	480	15.0
75-76	32	....	410	237	.578	117	80	.684	282	554	17.3
76-77	23	....	346	174	.503	144	108	.750	241	456	19.8
Totals	114	....	1346	722	.536	414	296	.715	1031	1740	15.3

NBA REGULAR SEASON RECORD

Sea.—Team	G.	Min.	FGA	FGM	Pct.	FTA	FTM	Pct.	Off.	Def.	Tot.	Ast.	PF	Dq.	Stl.	Blk.	Pts.	Avg.
77-78—Milwaukee	69	1288	473	220	.465	141	92	.652	89	206	295	99	177	1	69	54	532	7.7
78-79—Milwaukee	82	2132	798	413	.518	245	180	.735	187	397	584	204	280	4	89	81	1006	12.3
79-80—Mil.-Det.	73	1891	618	299	.484	141	99	.702	126	327	453	178	246	4	73	92	698	9.6
80-81—Detroit	59	1956	770	364	.473	254	196	.772	124	276	400	172	184	1	72	67	924	15.7
81-82—Detroit	75	2467	802	405	.505	158	127	.804	219	434	653	159	214	2	66	98	940	12.5
82-83—Detroit	21	599	182	85	.467	50	38	.760	53	102	155	49	61	0	14	17	208	9.9
83-84—Detroit	82	1734	451	248	.550	101	83	.822	117	292	409	130	230	4	71	53	579	7.1
84-85—Detroit	72	1401	397	201	.506	94	76	.809	103	221	324	93	207	4	53	44	478	6.6
85-86—Detroit	72	1344	415	201	.484	83	66	.795	118	258	376	80	196	3	58	51	469	6.5
86-87—Utah	73	895	316	140	.443	58	47	.810	80	151	231	39	138	0	39	28	329	4.5
87-88—Cleveland	2	12	2	2	1.000	2	1	.500	0	1	1	0	2	0	1	1	5	2.5
Totals	680	15719	5224	2578	.493	1327	1005	.757	1216	2665	3881	1203	1935	23	605	586	6168	9.1

Three-Point Field Goals: 1979-80, 1-for-5 (.200). 1980-81, 0-for-4. 1981-82, 3-for-11 (.273). 1982-83, 0-for-1. 1983-84, 0-for-1. 1984-85, 0-for-3. 1985-86, 1-for-2 (.500). 1986-87, 2-for-7 (.286). Totals, 7-for-34 (.206).

NBA PLAYOFF RECORD

Sea.—Team	G.	Min.	FGA	FGM	Pct.	FTA	FTM	Pct.	Off.	Def.	Tot.	Ast.	PF	Dq.	Stl.	Blk.	Pts.	Avg.
77-78—Milwaukee	9	103	23	11	.478	11	6	.545	5	10	15	3	20	0	5	3	28	3.1
83-84—Detroit	5	129	37	16	.432	10	6	.600	9	21	30	7	14	0	5	7	38	7.6
84-85—Detroit	9	142	46	25	.543	15	13	.867	9	27	36	4	27	0	8	2	63	7.0
85-86—Detroit	4	55	10	4	.400	0	0	.000	3	10	13	0	11	0	0	2	8	2.0
86-87—Utah	2	3	0	0	.000	0	0	.000	0	0	0	0	0	0	0	0	0	0.0
Totals	29	432	116	56	.483	36	25	.694	26	68	94	14	72	0	18	14	137	4.7

Named to THE SPORTING NEWS All-America First Team, 1977. . . . NCAA Division I Tournament Most Outstanding Player, 1976. . . . Member of NCAA Division I championship team, 1976.

WALTER BERRY

Born May 14, 1964 at Harlem, N.Y. Height 6:08. Weight 215.

High Schools—Bronx, N.Y., Morris; Bronx, N.Y., DeWitt Clinton and New York, N.Y., Benjamin Franklin.

Colleges—San Jacinto College (Central), Pasadena, Tex., and St. John's University, Jamaica, N.Y.

Drafted by Portland on first round as an undergraduate, 1986 (14th pick).

Traded by Portland to San Antonio for Kevin Duckworth, December 18, 1986.

—COLLEGIATE RECORD—

St. John's

Year	G.	Min.	FGA	FGM	Pct.	FTA	FTM	Pct.	Reb.	Pts.	Avg.
82-83					Did Not Play—Ineligible						

San Jacinto

Year	G.	Min.	FGA	FGM	Pct.	FTA	FTM	Pct.	Reb.	Pts.	Avg.
83-84	35	....	625	419	.670	270	174	.644	489	1012	28.9

St. John's

Year	G.	Min.	FGA	FGM	Pct.	FTA	FTM	Pct.	Reb.	Pts.	Avg.
84-85	35	1200	414	231	.558	187	134	.717	304	596	17.0
85-86	36	1318	547	327	.598	248	174	.702	399	828	23.0
St. John's Totals...	71	2518	961	558	.581	435	308	.708	703	1424	20.1

NBA REGULAR SEASON RECORD

Sea.—Team	G.	Min.	FGA	FGM	Pct.	FTA	FTM	Pct.	Off.	Def.	Tot.	Ast.	PF	Dq.	Stl.	Blk.	Pts.	Avg.
86-87—Port.-S.A.	63	1586	766	407	.531	288	187	.649	136	173	309	105	196	2	38	40	1001	15.9
87-88—San Antonio	73	1922	960	540	.563	320	192	.600	176	219	395	110	207	2	55	63	1272	17.4
Totals	136	3508	1726	947	.549	608	379	.623	312	392	704	215	403	4	93	103	2273	16.7

Three-Point Field Goals: 1986-87, 0-for-3.

NBA PLAYOFF RECORD

Sea.—Team	G.	Min.	FGA	FGM	Pct.	FTA	FTM	Pct.	Off.	Def.	Tot.	Ast.	PF	Dq.	Stl.	Blk.	Pts.	Avg.
87-88—San Antonio	3	94	50	27	.540	15	12	.800	13	8	21	6	10	0	5	2	66	22.0

Three-Point Field Goals: 1987-88, 0-for-1.

Named THE SPORTING NEWS College Player of the Year, 1986. . . . THE SPORTING NEWS All-America First Team, 1986.

LARRY JOE BIRD

Born December 7, 1956 at West Baden, Ind. Height 6:09. Weight 220.

High School—French Lick, Ind., Springs Valley.

Colleges—Indiana University, Bloomington, Ind.; Northwood Institute, West Baden, Ind., and Indiana State University, Terre Haute, Ind.

Drafted by Boston on first round as junior eligible, 1978 (6th pick).

—COLLEGIATE RECORD—

Indiana

Year	G.	Min.	FGA	FGM	Pct.	FTA	FTM	Pct.	Reb.	Pts.	Avg.
74-75					Did Not Play						

Indiana State

Year	G.	Min.	FGA	FGM	Pct.	FTA	FTM	Pct.	Reb.	Pts.	Avg.
75-76					Did Not Play—Transfer Student						
76-77	28	1033	689	375	.544	200	168	.840	373	918	32.8
77-78	32	....	769	403	.524	193	153	.793	369	959	30.0
78-79	34	....	707	376	.532	266	221	.831	505	973	28.6
Totals	94	....	2165	1154	.533	659	542	.822	1247	2850	30.3

NBA REGULAR SEASON RECORD

Sea.—Team	G.	Min.	FGA	FGM	Pct.	FTA	FTM	Pct.	Off.	Def.	Tot.	Ast.	PF	Dq.	Stl.	Blk.	Pts.	Avg.
79-80—Boston	82	2955	1463	693	.474	360	301	.836	216	636	852	370	279	4	143	53	1745	21.3
80-81—Boston	82	3239	1503	719	.478	328	283	.863	191	704	895	451	239	2	161	63	1741	21.2
81-82—Boston	77	2923	1414	711	.503	380	328	.863	200	637	837	447	244	0	143	66	1761	22.9
82-83—Boston	79	2982	1481	747	.504	418	351	.840	193	677	870	458	197	0	148	71	1867	23.6
83-84—Boston	79	3028	1542	758	.492	421	374	.888	181	615	796	520	197	0	144	69	1908	24.2
84-85—Boston	80	3161	1760	918	.522	457	403	.882	164	678	842	531	208	0	129	98	2295	28.7
85-86—Boston	82	3113	1606	796	.496	492	441	.896	190	615	805	557	182	0	166	51	2115	25.8
86-87—Boston	74	3005	1497	786	.525	455	414	.910	124	558	682	566	185	3	135	70	2076	28.1
87-88—Boston	76	2965	1672	881	.527	453	415	.916	108	595	703	467	157	0	125	57	2275	29.9
Totals	711	27371	13938	7009	.503	3764	3310	.879	1567	5715	7282	4367	1888	9	1294	598	17783	25.0

Three-Point Field Goals: 1979-80, 58-for-143 (.406). 1980-81, 20-for-74 (.270). 1981-82, 11-for-52 (.212). 1982-83, 22-for-77 (.286). 1983-84, 18-for-73 (.247). 1984-85, 56-for-131 (.427). 1985-86, 82-for-194 (.423). 1986-87, 90-for-225 (.400). 1987-88, 98-for-237 (.414). Totals, 455-for-1206 (.377).

NBA PLAYOFF RECORD

Sea.—Team	G.	Min.	FGA	FGM	Pct.	FTA	FTM	Pct.	Off.	Def.	Tot.	Ast.	PF	Dq.	Stl.	Blk.	Pts.	Avg.
79-80—Boston	9	372	177	83	.469	25	22	.880	22	79	101	42	30	0	14	8	192	21.3
80-81—Boston	17	750	313	147	.470	85	76	.894	49	189	238	103	53	0	39	17	373	21.9
81-82—Boston	12	490	206	88	.427	45	37	.822	33	117	150	67	43	0	23	17	214	17.8
82-83—Boston	6	240	116	49	.422	29	24	.828	20	55	75	41	15	0	13	3	123	20.5
83-84—Boston	23	961	437	229	.524	190	167	.879	62	190	252	136	71	0	54	27	632	27.5

LARRY BIRD

Sea.—Team	G.	Min.	FGA	FGM	Pct.	FTA	FTM	Pct.	—Rebounds— Off.	Def.	Tot.	Ast.	PF	Dq.	Stl.	Blk.	Pts.	Avg.
84-85—Boston	20	815	425	196	.461	136	121	.890	53	129	182	115	54	0	34	19	520	26.0
85-86—Boston	18	770	331	171	.517	109	101	.927	34	134	168	148	55	0	37	11	466	25.9
86-87—Boston	23	1015	454	216	.476	193	176	.912	41	190	231	165	55	1	27	19	622	27.0
87-88—Boston	17	763	338	152	.450	113	101	.894	29	121	150	115	45	0	36	14	417	24.5
Totals	145	6176	2797	1331	.476	925	825	.892	343	1204	1547	932	418	1	277	135	3559	24.5

Three-Point Field Goals: 1979-80, 4-for-15 (.267). 1980-81, 3-for-8 (.375). 1981-82, 1-for-6 (.167). 1982-83, 1-for-4 (.250). 1983-84, 7-for-17 (.412). 1984-85, 7-for-25 (.280). 1985-86, 23-for-56 (.411). 1986-87, 14-for-41 (.341). 1987-88, 12-for-32 (.375). Totals, 72-for-204 (.353).

NBA ALL-STAR GAME RECORD

Season—Team	Min.	FGA	FGM	Pct.	FTA	FTM	Pct.	—Rebounds— Off.	Def.	Tot.	Ast.	PF	Dq.	Stl.	Blk.	Pts.
1980—Boston............	23	6	3	.500	0	0	.000	3	3	6	7	1	0	1	0	7
1981—Boston............	18	5	1	.200	0	0	.000	1	3	4	3	1	0	1	0	2
1982—Boston............	28	12	7	.583	8	5	.625	0	12	12	5	3	0	1	1	19
1983—Boston............	29	14	7	.500	0	0	.000	3	10	13	7	4	0	2	0	14
1984—Boston............	33	18	6	.333	4	4	1.000	1	6	7	3	1	0	2	0	16
1985—Boston............	31	16	8	.500	6	5	.833	5	3	8	2	3	0	0	1	21
1986—Boston............	35	18	8	.444	6	5	.833	2	6	8	5	5	0	7	0	23
1987—Boston............	35	18	7	.389	4	4	1.000	2	4	6	5	5	0	2	0	18
1988—Boston............	32	8	2	.250	2	2	1.000	0	7	7	1	4	0	4	1	6
Totals	264	115	49	.426	30	25	.833	17	54	71	38	27	0	20	3	126

Three-Point Field Goals: 1980, 1-for-2 (.500). 1983, 0-for-1. 1985, 0-for-1. 1986, 2-for-4 (.500). 1987, 0-for-3. 1988, 0-for-1. Totals, 3-for-12 (.250).

NBA Most Valuable Player, 1984, 1985, 1986. . . . Named to All-NBA First Team, 1980, 1981, 1982, 1983, 1984, 1985, 1986, 1987, 1988. . . . NBA All-Defensive Second Team, 1982, 1983, 1984. . . . NBA Rookie of the Year, 1980. . . . NBA All-Rookie Team, 1980. . . . Member of NBA championship teams, 1981, 1984, 1986. . . . NBA Playoff MVP, 1984 and 1986. . . . Holds NBA playoff record for most points in one year, 1984. . . . NBA's all-time three-point field goal leader. . . . Led NBA in free-throw percentage, 1984, 1986 and 1987. . . . NBA All-Star Game MVP, 1982. . . . THE SPORTING NEWS College Player of the Year, 1979. . . . THE SPORTING NEWS All-America First Team, 1978 and 1979.

OTIS LEE BIRDSONG

Born December 9, 1955 at Winter Haven, Fla.   Height 6:08.   Weight 195.

High School—Winter Haven, Fla.

College—University of Houston, Houston, Tex.

Drafted by Kansas City on first round, 1977 (2nd pick).

Traded by Kansas City with a 1981 2nd round draft choice to New Jersey for Cliff Robinson, June 8, 1981.

Year	G.	Min.	FGA	FGM	Pct.	FTA	FTM	Pct.	Reb.	Pts.	Avg.
73-74	26	673	312	154	.494	92	64	.696	110	372	14.3
74-75	26	965	460	268	.583	143	104	.727	122	640	24.6
75-76	28	1082	582	302	.519	191	126	.660	176	730	26.1
76-77	36	1342	794	452	.569	249	186	.747	159	1090	30.3
Totals	116	4062	2148	1176	.547	675	480	.711	567	2832	24.4

Title above table: —COLLEGIATE RECORD—

NBA REGULAR SEASON RECORD

Sea.—Team	G.	Min.	FGA	FGM	Pct.	FTA	FTM	Pct.	—Rebounds— Off.	Def.	Tot.	Ast.	PF	Dq.	Stl.	Blk.	Pts.	Avg.
77-78—Kansas City	73	1878	955	470	.492	310	216	.697	70	105	175	174	179	1	74	12	1156	15.8
78-79—Kansas City	82	2839	1456	741	.509	408	296	.725	176	178	354	281	255	2	125	17	1778	21.7
79-80—Kansas City	82	2885	1546	781	.505	412	286	.694	170	161	331	202	226	2	136	22	1858	22.7
80-81—Kansas City	71	2593	1306	710	.544	455	317	.697	119	139	258	233	172	2	93	18	1747	24.6
81-82—New Jersey	37	1025	480	225	.469	127	74	.583	30	67	97	124	74	0	30	5	524	14.2
82-83—New Jersey	62	1885	834	426	.511	145	82	.566	53	97	150	239	155	0	85	16	936	15.1
83-84—New Jersey	69	2168	1147	583	.508	319	194	.608	74	96	170	266	180	2	86	17	1365	19.8
84-85—New Jersey	56	1842	968	495	.511	259	161	.622	60	88	148	232	145	1	84	7	1155	20.6
85-86—New Jersey	77	2395	1056	542	.513	210	122	.581	88	114	202	261	228	8	85	17	1214	15.8
86-87—New Jersey	7	127	42	19	.452	9	6	.667	3	4	7	17	16	0	3	0	44	6.3
87-88—New Jersey	67	1882	736	337	.458	92	47	.511	73	94	167	222	143	2	54	11	730	10.9
Totals	683	21519	10526	5329	.506	2746	1801	.656	916	1143	2059	2251	1773	20	855	142	12507	18.3

Three-Point Field Goals: 1979-80, 10-for-36 (.278). 1980-81, 10-for-35 (.286). 1981-82, 0-for-10. 1982-83, 2-for-6 (.333). 1983-84, 5-for-20 (.250). 1984-85, 4-for-21 (.190). 1985-86, 8-for-22 (.364). 1986-87, 0-for-1. 1987-88, 9-for-25 (.360). Totals, 48-for-176 (.273).

NBA PLAYOFF RECORD

Sea.—Team	G.	Min.	FGA	FGM	Pct.	FTA	FTM	Pct.	—Rebounds— Off.	Def.	Tot.	Ast.	PF	Dq.	Stl.	Blk.	Pts.	Avg.
78-79—Kansas City	5	168	76	39	.513	38	27	.711	8	10	18	9	13	0	10	0	105	21.0
79-80—Kansas City	3	112	62	30	.484	14	6	.429	11	12	23	7	5	0	4	0	66	22
0-81—Kansas City	8	234	98	56	.571	18	11	.611	8	13	21	27	13	1	12	0	124	1

Sea.—Team	G.	Min.	FGA	FGM	Pct.	FTA	FTM	Pct.	—Rebounds— Off.	Def.	Tot.	Ast.	PF	Dq.	Stl.	Blk.	Pts.	Avg.
3—New Jersey	2	37	16	6	.375	2	1	.500	1	1	2	9	3	0	3	0	13	6.5
4—New Jersey	11	387	171	71	.415	48	25	.521	7	19	26	41	38	0	20	1	167	15.2
6—New Jersey	3	132	55	29	.527	19	11	.579	5	7	12	10	14	0	6	3	69	23.0
Totals	32	1070	478	231	.483	139	81	.583	40	62	102	103	86	1	55	4	544	17.0

Three-Point Field Goals: 1979-80, 0-for-3. 1980-81, 1-for-1. 1982-83, 0-for-1. 1983-84, 0-for-1. 1985-86, 0-for-3. Totals, or-9 (.111).

NBA ALL-STAR GAME RECORD

Season—Team	Min.	FGA	FGM	Pct.	FTA	FTM	Pct.	—Rebounds— Off.	Def.	Tot.	Ast.	PF	Dq.	Stl.	Blk.	Pts.
1979—Kansas City..	14	6	4	.667	2	1	.500	1	1	2	0	1	0	2	0	9
1980—Kansas City..	14	2	1	.500	0	0	.000	0	0	0	0	1	0	1	0	2
1981—Kansas City..	12	3	0	.000	2	1	.500	1	0	1	1	0	0	0	0	1
1984—New Jersey..	12	5	1	.200	0	0	.000	2	1	3	1	1	0	0	0	2
Totals	52	16	6	.375	4	2	.500	4	2	6	2	3	0	3	0	14

Named to All-NBA Second Team, 1981.... THE SPORTING NEWS All-America First Team, 1977.

UWE KONSTANTINE BLAB

Born March 26, 1962 at Munich, West Germany. Height 7:01. Weight 255.

High School—Effingham, Ill.

College—Indiana University, Bloomington, Ind.

Drafted by Dallas on first round, 1985 (17th pick).

—COLLEGIATE RECORD—

Year	G.	Min.	FGA	FGM	Pct.	FTA	FTM	Pct.	Reb.	Pts.	Avg.
81-82	24	....	124	69	.556	70	41	.586	89	179	7.5
82-83	30	....	220	114	.518	97	55	.567	148	283	9.4
83-84	31	....	284	150	.528	104	66	.635	190	366	11.8
84-85	33	....	375	212	.565	147	105	.714	207	529	16.0
Totals	118	....	1003	545	.543	418	267	.639	634	1357	11.5

NBA REGULAR SEASON RECORD

Sea.—Team	G.	Min.	FGA	FGM	Pct.	FTA	FTM	Pct.	—Rebounds— Off.	Def.	Tot.	Ast.	PF	Dq.	Stl.	Blk.	Pts.	Avg.
85-86—Dallas	48	409	94	44	.468	67	36	.537	25	66	91	17	65	0	3	12	124	2.6
86-87—Dallas	30	160	51	20	.392	28	13	.464	11	25	36	13	33	0	4	9	53	1.8
87-88—Dallas	73	658	132	58	.439	65	46	.708	52	82	134	35	108	1	8	29	162	2.2
Totals	151	1227	277	122	.440	160	95	.594	88	173	261	65	206	1	15	50	339	2.2

NBA PLAYOFF RECORD

Sea.—Team	G.	Min.	FGA	FGM	Pct.	FTA	FTM	Pct.	—Rebounds— Off.	Def.	Tot.	Ast.	PF	Dq.	Stl.	Blk.	Pts.	Avg.
85-86—Dallas	1	6	3	2	.667	0	0	.000	0	1	1	0	1	0	0	0	4	4.0
86-87—Dallas	1	10	1	1	1.000	4	1	.250	1	2	3	0	4	0	1	1	3	3.0
87-88—Dallas	3	8	2	0	.000	2	2	1.000	1	0	1	1	1	0	0	0	2	0.7
Totals	5	24	6	3	.500	6	3	.500	2	3	5	1	6	0	1	1	9	1.8

Member of West German Olympic team, 1984.

ROLANDO ANTONIO BLACKMAN

Born February 26, 1959 at Panama City, Panama. Height 6:06. Weight 194.

High School—Brooklyn, N. Y., William Grady.

College—Kansas State University, Manhattan, Kan.

Drafted by Dallas on first round, 1981 (9th pick).

—COLLEGIATE RECORD—

Year	G.	Min.	FGA	FGM	Pct.	FTA	FTM	Pct.	Reb.	Pts.	Avg.
77-78	29	....	269	127	.472	93	61	.656	187	315	10.9
78-79	28	....	392	200	.510	113	83	.735	110	483	17.3
79-80	31	....	419	226	.539	145	100	.690	145	552	17.8
80-81	33	....	380	202	.532	115	90	.783	165	494	15.0
Totals	121	....	1460	755	.517	466	334	.717	607	1844	15.2

NBA REGULAR SEASON RECORD

Sea.—Team	G.	Min.	FGA	FGM	Pct.	FTA	FTM	Pct.	—Rebounds— Off.	Def.	Tot.	Ast.	PF	Dq.	Stl.	Blk.	Pts.	Avg.
81-82—Dallas	82	1979	855	439	.513	276	212	.768	97	157	254	105	122	0	46	30	1091	13.3
82-83—Dallas	75	2349	1042	513	.492	381	297	.780	108	185	293	185	116	0	37	29	1326	17.
83-84—Dallas	81	3025	1320	721	.546	458	372	.812	124	249	373	288	127	0	56	37	1815	22
84-85—Dallas	81	2834	1230	625	.508	413	342	.828	107	193	300	289	96	0	61	16	1598	1

Sea.—Team	G.	Min.	FGA	FGM	Pct.	FTA	FTM	Pct.	—Rebounds— Off.	Def.	Tot.	Ast.	PF	Dq.	Stl.	Blk.	Pts.	Avg.
85-86—Dallas	82	2787	1318	677	.514	483	404	.836	88	203	291	271	138	0	79	25	1762	21.5
86-87—Dallas	80	2758	1264	626	.495	474	419	.884	96	182	278	266	142	0	64	21	1676	21.0
87-88—Dallas	71	2580	1050	497	.473	379	331	.873	82	164	246	262	112	0	64	18	1325	18.7
Totals	552	18312	8079	4098	.507	2864	2377	.830	702	1333	2035	1666	853	0	407	176	10593	19.2

Three-Point Field Goals: 1981-82, 1-for-4 (.250). 1982-83, 3-for-15 (.200). 1983-84, 1-for-11 (.091). 1984-85, 6-for-20 (.300). 1985-86, 4-for-29 (.138). 1986-87, 5-for-15 (.333). 1987-88, 0-for-5. Totals, 20-for-99 (.202).

NBA PLAYOFF RECORD

Sea.—Team	G.	Min.	FGA	FGM	Pct.	FTA	FTM	Pct.	—Rebounds— Off.	Def.	Tot.	Ast.	PF	Dq.	Stl.	Blk.	Pts.	Avg.
83-84—Dallas	10	397	175	93	.531	63	53	.841	15	26	41	40	15	0	6	4	239	23.9
84-85—Dallas	4	169	92	47	.511	38	36	.947	11	15	26	19	8	0	2	2	131	32.8
85-86—Dallas	10	371	167	83	.497	53	42	.792	15	20	35	32	26	1	8	1	208	20.8
86-87—Dallas	4	153	73	36	.493	24	22	.917	4	10	14	17	7	0	2	0	94	23.5
87-88—Dallas	17	672	261	126	.483	62	55	.887	26	29	55	77	28	0	15	3	307	18.1
Totals	45	1762	768	385	.501	240	208	.867	71	100	171	185	84	1	33	10	979	21.8

Three-Point Field Goals: 1984-85, 1-for-2 (.500). 1985-86, 0-for-1. 1986-87, 0-for-1. 1987-88, 0-for-3. Totals, 1-for-7 (.143).

NBA ALL-STAR GAME RECORD

Season—Team	Min.	FGA	FGM	Pct.	FTA	FTM	Pct.	—Rebounds— Off.	Def.	Tot.	Ast.	PF	Dq.	Stl.	Blk.	Pts.
1985—Dallas	23	14	7	.500	2	1	.500	1	2	3	2	1	0	1	1	15
1986—Dallas	22	11	6	.545	0	0	.000	1	3	4	8	1	0	2	1	12
1987—Dallas	22	15	9	.600	13	11	.846	1	3	4	1	2	0	0	0	29
Totals	67	40	22	.550	15	12	.800	3	8	11	11	4	0	3	2	56

Named to THE SPORTING NEWS All-America First Team, 1981. . . . Member of U.S. Olympic team, 1980.

NATHANIEL BLACKWELL
(Nate)

Born February 15, 1965 at Philadelphia, Pa. Height 6:04. Weight 170.

High School—Philadelphia, Pa., South Philadelphia.

College—Temple University, Philadelphia, Pa.

Drafted by San Antonio on second round, 1987 (27th pick).

Waived by San Antonio, December 1, 1987; signed by Golden State as a free agent, December 20, 1987.
Waived by Golden State, December 29, 1987.

—COLLEGIATE RECORD—

Year	G.	Min.	FGA	FGM	Pct.	FTA	FTM	Pct.	Reb.	Pts.	Avg.
83-84	31	735	209	82	.392	79	60	.759	55	224	7.2
84-85	31	1179	309	127	.411	105	86	.819	99	365	11.8
85-86	31	1227	363	161	.444	105	83	.790	121	405	13.1
86-87	36	1422	564	255	.452	136	123	.904	162	714	19.8
Totals	129	4563	1445	625	.433	425	352	.828	437	1708	13.2

Three-Point Field Goals: 1984-85, 25-for-69 (.362). 1986-87, 81-for-193 (.420). Totals, 106-for-262 (.405).

NBA REGULAR SEASON RECORD

Sea.—Team	G.	Min.	FGA	FGM	Pct.	FTA	FTM	Pct.	—Rebounds— Off.	Def.	Tot.	Ast.	PF	Dq.	Stl.	Blk.	Pts.	Avg.
87-88—San Antonio	10	112	41	15	.366	6	5	.833	2	4	6	18	16	0	3	0	37	3.7

Three-Point Field Goals: 1987-88, 2-for-11 (.182).

TYRONE BOGUES
(Muggsy)

Born January 9, 1965 at Baltimore, Md. Height 5:03. Weight 140.

High School—Baltimore, Md., Dunbar.

College—Wake Forest University, Winston-Salem, N.C.

Drafted by Washington on first round, 1987 (12th pick).

Selected from Washington by Charlotte in NBA expansion draft, June 23, 1988.

—COLLEGIATE RECORD—

Year	G.	Min.	FGA	FGM	Pct.	FTA	FTM	Pct.	Reb.	Pts.	Avg.
83-84	32	312	46	14	.304	13	9	.692	21	37	1.2
84-85	29	1025	162	81	.500	44	30	.682	69	192	6.6
85-86	29	....	290	132	.455	89	65	.730	90	329	11.3
86-87	29	....	318	159	.500	93	75	.806	110	428	14.8
Totals	119	....	816	386	.473	239	179	.749	290	986	8.3

Three-Point Field Goals: 1986-87, 35-for-79 (.443).

NBA REGULAR SEASON RECORD

Sea.—Team	G.	Min.	FGA	FGM	Pct.	FTA	FTM	Pct.	Off.	Def.	Tot.	Ast.	PF	Dq.	Stl.	Blk.	Pts.	Avg.
87-88—Washington	79	1628	426	166	.390	74	58	.784	35	101	136	404	138	1	127	3	393	5.0

Three-Point Field Goals: 1987-88, 3-for-16 (.188).

NBA PLAYOFF RECORD

Sea.—Team	G.	Min.	FGA	FGM	Pct.	FTA	FTM	Pct.	Off.	Def.	Tot.	Ast.	PF	Dq.	Stl.	Blk.	Pts.	Avg.
87-88—Washington	1	2	0	0	.000	0	0	.000	0	0	0	2	0	0	0	0	0	0.0

MANUTE BOL

Born October 16, 1962 at Gogrial, Sudan.   Height 7:06.   Weight 225.

High School—Attended Case Western Reserve English Language School, Cleveland, O.

College—University of Bridgeport, Bridgeport, Conn.

Drafted by San Diego on fifth round, 1983 (97th pick).

Declared ineligible for 1983 NBA draft.

Drafted by Washington on second round as an undergraduate, 1985 (31st pick).

Traded by Washington to Golden State for Dave Feitl and a 1989 2nd round draft choice, June 8, 1988.

—COLLEGIATE RECORD—

Year	G.	Min.	FGA	FGM	Pct.	FTA	FTM	Pct.	Reb.	Pts.	Avg.
84-85	31	....	496	303	.611	153	91	.595	419	697	22.5

NBA REGULAR SEASON RECORD

Sea.—Team	G.	Min.	FGA	FGM	Pct.	FTA	FTM	Pct.	Off.	Def.	Tot.	Ast.	PF	Dq.	Stl.	Blk.	Pts.	Avg.
85-86—Washington	80	2090	278	128	.460	86	42	.488	123	354	477	23	255	5	28	397	298	3.7
86-87—Washington	82	1552	231	103	.446	67	45	.672	84	278	362	11	189	1	20	302	251	3.1
87-88—Washington	77	1136	165	75	.455	49	26	.531	72	203	275	13	160	0	11	208	176	2.3
Totals	239	4778	674	306	.454	202	113	.559	279	835	1114	47	604	6	59	907	725	3.0

Three-Point Field Goals: 1985-86, 0-for-1. 1986-87, 0-for-1. 1987-88, 0-for-1. Totals, 0-for-3.

NBA PLAYOFF RECORD

Sea.—Team	G.	Min.	FGA	FGM	Pct.	FTA	FTM	Pct.	Off.	Def.	Tot.	Ast.	PF	Dq.	Stl.	Blk.	Pts.	Avg.
85-86—Washington	5	152	17	10	.588	8	3	.375	16	22	38	1	15	0	3	29	23	4.6
86-87—Washington	3	43	10	4	.400	2	0	.000	5	4	9	0	6	0	0	5	8	2.7
87-88—Washington	5	44	7	4	.571	1	1	1.000	7	5	12	0	5	0	0	2	9	1.8
Totals	13	239	34	18	.529	11	4	.364	28	31	59	1	26	0	3	36	40	3.1

Three-Point Field Goals: 1986-87, 0-for-1.

Named to NBA All-Defensive Second Team, 1986. . . . Led NBA in blocked shots, 1986.

SAMUEL PAUL BOWIE
(Sam)

Born March 17, 1961 at Lebanon, Pa.   Height 7:01.   Weight 240.

High School—Lebanon, Pa.

College—University of Kentucky, Lexington, Ky.

Drafted by Portland on first round, 1984 (2nd pick).

Missed entire 1987-88 season due to injury.

—COLLEGIATE RECORD—

Year	G.	Min.	FGA	FGM	Pct.	FTA	FTM	Pct.	Reb.	Pts.	Avg.
79-80	34	886	311	165	.531	144	110	.764	276	440	12.9
80-81	28	895	356	185	.520	164	118	.720	254	488	17.4
81-82					Did Not Play—Injured						
82-83					Did Not Play—Injured						
83-84	34	980	258	133	.516	126	91	.722	313	357	10.5
Totals	96	2761	925	483	.522	434	319	.735	843	1285	13.4

NBA REGULAR SEASON RECORD

Sea.—Team	G.	Min.	FGA	FGM	Pct.	FTA	FTM	Pct.	Off.	Def.	Tot.	Ast.	PF	Dq.	Stl.	Blk.	Pts.	Avg.
84-85—Portland	76	2216	557	299	.537	225	160	.711	207	449	656	215	278	9	55	203	758	10.0
85-86—Portland	38	1132	345	167	.484	161	114	.708	93	234	327	99	142	4	21	96	448	11.8
86-87—Portland	5	163	66	30	.455	30	20	.667	14	19	33	9	19	0	1	10	80	16.0
Totals	119	3511	968	496	.512	416	294	.707	314	702	1016	323	439	13	77	309	1286	10.8

—Rebounds—

Sea.—Team	G.	Min.	FGA	FGM	Pct.	FTA	FTM	Pct.	Off.	Def.	Tot.	Ast.	PF	Dq.	Stl.	Blk.	Pts.	Avg.
84-85—Portland	9	259	59	26	.441	25	14	.560	16	60	76	21	36	2	4	21	66	7.3

Named to NBA All-Rookie Team, 1985. . . . Member of 1980 U.S. Olympic team. . . . THE SPORTING NEWS All-America Second Team, 1984.

DUDLEY LEROY BRADLEY

Born March 19, 1957 at Baltimore, Md.   Height 6:06.   Weight 195.

High School—Edgewood, Md.

College—University of North Carolina, Chapel Hill, N. C.

Drafted by Indiana on first round, 1979 (13th pick).

Traded by Indiana to Phoenix for 1981 and 1982 2nd round draft choices, June 8, 1981.
Signed by Chicago as a Veteran Free Agent, October 1, 1982; Phoenix agreed not to exercise its right of first refusal in exchange for a 1983 3rd round draft choice, October 2, 1983.
Waived by Chicago, October 25, 1983; signed by Detroit as a free agent, July 6, 1984.
Waived by Detroit, September 4, 1984; signed by Washington as a free agent, September 27, 1984.
Signed by Milwaukee as a Veteran Free Agent, October 23, 1986; Washington waived its right of first refusal.
Waived by Milwaukee, December 10, 1987; signed by New Jersey as a free agent, December 15, 1987.
Played in Continental Basketball Association with Toronto Tornados and Detroit Spirits, 1983-84.

—COLLEGIATE RECORD—

Year	G.	Min.	FGA	FGM	Pct.	FTA	FTM	Pct.	Reb.	Pts.	Avg.
75-76	27	....	65	19	.292	16	8	.500	33	46	1.7
76-77	33	....	48	17	.354	9	2	.222	39	36	1.1
77-78	31	....	159	76	.478	41	22	.537	108	174	5.6
78-79	29	....	213	109	.512	79	48	.608	105	266	9.2
Totals	120	....	485	221	.456	145	80	.552	285	522	4.4

CBA REGULAR SEASON RECORD

			——2-Point——			——3-Point——									
Sea.—Team	G.	Min.	FGM	FGA	Pct.	FGM	FGA	Pct.	FTM	FTA	Pct.	Reb.	Ast.	Pts.	Avg.
83-84—Toronto-Detroit	38	1282	211	451	.467	8	28	.286	125	179	.698	172	154	571	15.0

NBA REGULAR SEASON RECORD

—Rebounds—

Sea.—Team	G.	Min.	FGA	FGM	Pct.	FTA	FTM	Pct.	Off.	Def.	Tot.	Ast.	PF	Dq.	Stl.	Blk.	Pts.	Avg.
79-80—Indiana	82	2027	609	275	.452	174	136	.782	69	154	223	252	194	1	211	48	688	8.4
80-81—Indiana	82	1867	559	265	.474	178	125	.702	70	123	193	188	236	2	186	37	657	8.0
81-82—Phoenix	64	937	281	125	.445	100	74	.740	30	57	87	80	115	0	78	10	325	5.1
82-83—Chicago	58	683	159	82	.516	45	36	.800	27	78	105	106	91	0	49	10	201	3.5
84-85—Washington	73	1232	299	142	.475	79	54	.684	34	100	134	173	152	0	96	21	358	4.9
85-86—Washington	70	842	209	73	.349	56	32	.571	24	71	95	107	101	0	85	3	195	2.8
86-87—Milwaukee	68	900	213	76	.357	58	47	.810	31	71	102	66	118	2	105	8	212	3.1
87-88—Mil.-N.J.	65	1437	365	156	.427	97	74	.763	25	102	127	151	172	1	114	43	423	6.5
Totals	562	9925	2694	1194	.443	787	578	.734	310	756	1066	1123	1179	6	924	180	3059	5.4

Three-Point Field Goals: 1979-80, 2-for-5 (.400). 1980-81, 2-for-16 (.125). 1981-82, 1-for-4 (.250). 1982-83, 1-for-5 (.200). 1984-85, 20-for-65 (.308). 1985-86, 17-for-68 (.250). 1986-87, 13-for-50 (.260). 1987-88, 37-for-102 (.363). Totals, 93-for-315 (.295).

NBA PLAYOFF RECORD

—Rebounds—

Sea.—Team	G.	Min.	FGA	FGM	Pct.	FTA	FTM	Pct.	Off.	Def.	Tot.	Ast.	PF	Dq.	Stl.	Blk.	Pts.	Avg.
80-81—Indiana	2	19	9	3	.333	2	2	1.000	1	1	2	4	0	2	0	0	9	4.5
81-82—Phoenix	7	24	8	2	.250	1	1	1.000	0	1	1	5	3	0	1	1	5	0.7
84-85—Washington	4	41	9	5	.556	4	3	.750	2	4	6	6	5	0	2	0	14	3.5
85-86—Washington	5	82	29	12	.414	9	6	.667	2	3	5	7	14	0	5	0	33	6.6
86-87—Milwaukee	12	46	11	4	.364	2	1	.500	0	0	0	2	9	0	3	0	9	0.8
Totals	30	212	66	26	.394	18	13	.722	5	9	14	22	35	0	13	1	70	2.3

Three-Point Field Goals: 1980-81, 1-for-1. 1984-85, 1-for-5 (.200). 1985-86, 3-for-10 (.300). 1986-87, 0-for-6. Totals, 5-for-22 (.227).

Named to NBA All-Defensive Second Team, 1981. . . . Named to CBA All-Defensive First Team, 1984.

ADRIAN FRANCIS BRANCH

Born November 17, 1963 at Washington, D.C.   Height 6:08.   Weight 185.

High School—Hyattsville, Md., DeMatha.

College—University of Maryland, College Park, Md.

Drafted by Chicago on second round, 1985 (46th pick).

Waived by Chicago, October 7, 1985; signed by Cleveland as a free agent, June 16, 1986.

Waived by Cleveland, August 22, 1986; signed by Los Angeles Lakers as a free agent, September 18, 1986.
Traded by Los Angeles Lakers to New Jersey for cash, November 5, 1987.
Waived by New Jersey, December 22, 1987.
Played in Continental Basketball Association with Baltimore Lightning, 1985-86.

—COLLEGIATE RECORD—

Year	G.	Min.	FGA	FGM	Pct.	FTA	FTM	Pct.	Reb.	Pts.	Avg.
81-82	29	976	346	164	.474	149	114	.765	125	442	15.2
82-83	29	1043	420	197	.469	165	118	.715	150	541	18.7
83-84	28	862	284	136	.479	121	91	.752	89	363	13.0
84-85	37	1298	529	270	.510	172	131	.762	182	671	18.1
Totals	123	4179	1579	767	.486	607	454	.748	546	2017	16.4

Three-Point Field Goals: 1982-83, 29-for-81 (.358).

CBA REGULAR SEASON RECORD

			——2-Point——			——3-Point——								
Sea.—Team	G.	Min.	FGM	FGA	Pct.	FGM	FGA	Pct.	FTM	FTA	Pct.	Reb.	Ast.	Pts.	Avg.
85-86—Baltimore	46	1630	430	842	.511	5	25	.200	295	388	.760	332	145	1170	25.4

NBA REGULAR SEASON RECORD

									—Rebounds—								
Sea.—Team	G.	Min.	FGA	FGM	Pct.	FTA	FTM	Pct.	Off.	Def.	Tot.	Ast.	PF	Dq.	Stl.	Blk.	Pts.	Avg.
86-87—L.A. Lakers	32	219	96	48	.500	54	42	.778	23	30	53	16	39	0	16	3	138	4.3
87-88—New Jersey	20	308	134	56	.418	23	20	.870	20	28	48	16	41	1	16	11	133	6.7
Totals	52	527	230	104	.452	77	62	.805	43	58	101	32	80	1	32	14	271	5.2

Three-Point Field Goals: 1986-87, 0-for-2. 1987-88, 1-for-5 (.200). Totals, 1-for-7 (.143).

NBA PLAYOFF RECORD

									—Rebounds—								
Sea.—Team	G.	Min.	FGA	FGM	Pct.	FTA	FTM	Pct.	Off.	Def.	Tot.	Ast.	PF	Dq.	Stl.	Blk.	Pts.	Avg.
86-87—L.A. Lakers	11	42	21	4	.190	12	6	.500	3	7	10	5	10	0	2	0	14	1.3

Three-Point Field Goals: 1986-87, 0-for-1.
Member of NBA championship team, 1987.

RANDALL W. BREUER
(Randy)

Born October 11, 1960 at Lake City, Minn.   Height 7:03.   Weight 263.

High School—Lake City, Minn.

College—University of Minnesota, Minneapolis, Minn.

Drafted by Milwaukee on first round, 1983 (18th pick).

—COLLEGIATE RECORD—

Year	G.	Min.	FGA	FGM	Pct.	FTA	FTM	Pct.	Reb.	Pts.	Avg.
79-80	31	....	172	96	.558	74	48	.648	98	240	7.7
80-81	30	....	313	180	.575	141	97	.688	166	457	15.2
81-82	29	....	325	180	.554	168	127	.756	209	487	16.8
82-83	29	....	384	225	.586	186	143	.769	257	593	20.4
Totals	119	....	1194	681	.570	569	415	.729	730	1777	14.9

NBA REGULAR SEASON RECORD

									—Rebounds—								
Sea.—Team	G.	Min.	FGA	FGM	Pct.	FTA	FTM	Pct.	Off.	Def.	Tot.	Ast.	PF	Dq.	Stl.	Blk.	Pts.	Avg.
83-84—Milwaukee	57	472	177	68	.384	46	32	.696	48	61	109	17	98	1	11	38	168	2.9
84-85—Milwaukee	78	1083	317	162	.511	127	89	.701	92	164	256	40	179	4	21	82	413	5.3
85-86—Milwaukee	82	1792	570	272	.477	198	141	.712	159	299	458	114	214	2	50	116	685	8.4
86-87—Milwaukee	76	1467	497	241	.485	202	118	.584	129	221	350	47	229	9	56	61	600	7.9
87-88—Milwaukee	81	2258	788	390	.495	286	188	.657	191	360	551	103	198	3	46	107	968	12.0
Totals	374	7072	2349	1133	.482	859	568	.661	619	1105	1724	321	918	19	184	404	2834	7.6

Three-Point Field Goals: 1985-86, 0-for-1.

NBA PLAYOFF RECORD

									—Rebounds—								
Sea.—Team	G.	Min.	FGA	FGM	Pct.	FTA	FTM	Pct.	Off.	Def.	Tot.	Ast.	PF	Dq.	Stl.	Blk.	Pts.	Avg.
83-84—Milwaukee	12	66	26	11	.423	5	3	.600	6	11	17	4	18	0	0	6	25	2.1
84-85—Milwaukee	8	104	26	15	.577	21	14	.667	9	15	24	0	15	0	2	2	44	5.5
85-86—Milwaukee	14	318	86	46	.535	38	26	.684	20	40	60	11	38	1	11	18	118	8.4
86-87—Milwaukee	12	156	33	16	.485	12	8	.667	9	22	31	4	32	1	7	9	40	3.3
87-88—Milwaukee	4	47	16	9	.563	6	1	.167	2	10	12	1	7	0	1	2	19	4.8
Totals	50	691	187	97	.519	82	52	.634	46	98	144	20	110	2	21	37	246	4.9

—DID YOU KNOW—

That no team in NBA history has ever come back from a 3-0 deficit to win a playoff series? A total of 10 teams have come back from 2-0 deficits.

FRANK BRICKOWSKI

Born August 14, 1959 at Bayville, N. Y.   Height 6:10.   Weight 240.

High School—Locust Valley, N. Y.

College—Penn State University, University Park, Pa.

Drafted by New York on third round, 1981 (57th pick).

Draft rights relinquished by New York, June 30, 1983; signed by Seattle as a free agent, September 23, 1984.

Signed by Los Angeles Lakers as a Veteran Free Agent, October 8, 1986; Seattle agreed not to exercise its right of first refusal in exchange for a 1988 3rd round draft choice and cash.

Traded by Los Angeles Lakers with Petur Gudmundsson, a 1987 1st round draft choice, a 1990 2nd round draft choice and cash to San Antonio for Mychal Thompson, February 13, 1987.

Played in Italy during 1981-82 season.

Played in France during 1982-83 season.

Played in Israel during 1983-84 season.

—COLLEGIATE RECORD—

Year	G.	Min.	FGA	FGM	Pct.	FTA	FTM	Pct.	Reb.	Pts.	Avg.
77-78	25	266	81	37	.457	25	21	.840	64	95	3.8
78-79	24	349	99	49	.495	48	38	.792	109	136	5.7
79-80	27	692	213	111	.521	105	82	.781	202	304	11.3
80-81	24	615	218	131	.601	63	49	.778	150	311	13.0
Totals	100	1922	611	328	.537	241	190	.788	525	846	8.5

NBA REGULAR SEASON RECORD

Sea.—Team	G.	Min.	FGA	FGM	Pct.	FTA	FTM	Pct.	Off.	Def.	Tot.	Ast.	PF	Dq.	Stl.	Blk.	Pts.	Avg.
									—Rebounds—									
84-85—Seattle	78	1115	305	150	.492	127	85	.669	76	184	260	100	171	1	34	15	385	4.9
85-86—Seattle	40	311	58	30	.517	27	18	.667	16	38	54	21	74	2	11	7	78	2.0
86-87—L.A.L.-S.A.	44	487	124	63	.508	70	50	.714	48	68	116	17	118	4	20	6	176	4.0
87-88—San Antonio	70	2227	805	425	.528	349	268	.768	167	316	483	266	275	11	74	36	1119	16.0
Totals	232	4140	1292	668	.517	573	421	.735	307	606	913	404	638	18	139	64	1758	7.6

Three-Point Field Goals: 1984-85, 0-for-4. 1986-87, 0-for-4. 1987-88, 1-for-5 (.200). Totals, 1-for-13 (.077).

NBA PLAYOFF RECORD

Sea.—Team	G.	Min.	FGA	FGM	Pct.	FTA	FTM	Pct.	Off.	Def.	Tot.	Ast.	PF	Dq.	Stl.	Blk.	Pts.	Avg.
									—Rebounds—									
87-88—San Antonio	3	113	44	22	.500	19	13	.684	7	15	22	14	12	0	6	2	58	19.3

Three-Point Field Goals: 1987-88, 1-for-1 (1.000).

MICHAEL ANTHONY BROOKS

Born August 17, 1958 at Philadelphia, Pa.   Height 6:07.   Weight 220.

High School—Philadelphia, Pa., West Catholic.

College—La Salle College, Philadelphia, Pa.

Drafted by San Diego on first round, 1980 (9th pick).

Missed entire 1984-85 and 1985-86 seasons due to injury.

Signed by Indiana, January 1, 1987, to the first of consecutive 10-day contracts that expired, January 21, 1987. (Los Angeles Clippers retained right of first refusal.)

Signed by Denver as a Veteran Free Agent, March 4, 1988; Los Angeles Clippers waived their right of first refusal in exchange for a 1988 3rd round draft choice.

Played in Continental Basketball Association with Tampa Bay Thrillers and Charleston Gunners, 1986-87, and Albany Patroons, 1987-88.

Selected from Denver by Charlotte in NBA expansion draft, June 23, 1988.

—COLLEGIATE RECORD—

Year	G.	Min.	FGA	FGM	Pct.	FTA	FTM	Pct.	Reb.	Pts.	Avg.
76-77	29	....	490	241	.492	152	97	.638	311	579	20.0
77-78	28	967	490	288	.588	164	120	.732	358	696	24.9
78-79	26	....	443	245	.553	161	116	.720	347	606	23.3
79-80	31	....	553	290	.524	237	167	.705	356	747	24.1
Totals	114	....	1976	1064	.538	714	500	.700	1372	2628	23.1

CBA REGULAR SEASON RECORD

Sea.—Team	G.	Min.	2-Point			3-Point			FTM	FTA	Pct.	Reb.	Ast.	Pts.	Avg.
			FGM	FGA	Pct.	FGM	FGA	Pct.							
86-87—Tampa-Char.	20	727	156	314	.497	1	1	1.000	81	113	.717	195	35	396	19.8
87-88—Albany	51	1944	314	558	.563	0	4	.000	134	172	.779	609	94	762	14.9
Totals	71	2671	470	872	.539	1	5	.200	215	285	.754	804	129	1158	16.3

NBA REGULAR SEASON RECORD

Sea.—Team	G.	Min.	FGA	FGM	Pct.	FTA	FTM	Pct.	Off.	Def.	Tot.	Ast.	PF	Dq.	Stl.	Blk.	Pts.	Avg.
									—Rebounds—									
80-81—San Diego	82	2479	1018	488	.479	320	226	.706	210	232	442	208	234	2	99	31	1202	14.7

Sea.—Team	G.	Min.	FGA	FGM	Pct.	FTA	FTM	Pct.	Off.	Def.	Tot.	Ast.	PF	Dq.	Stl.	Blk.	Pts.	Avg.
81-82—San Diego	82	2750	1066	537	.504	267	202	.757	207	417	624	236	285	7	113	39	1276	15.6
82-83—San Diego	82	2457	830	402	.484	277	193	.697	239	282	521	262	297	6	112	39	1002	12.2
83-84—San Diego	47	1405	445	213	.479	151	104	.689	142	200	342	88	125	1	50	14	530	11.3
86-87—Indiana	10	148	37	13	.351	10	7	.700	9	19	28	11	19	0	9	0	33	3.3
87-88—Denver	16	133	49	20	.408	4	3	.750	19	25	44	13	21	1	4	1	43	2.7
Totals	319	9372	3445	1673	.486	1029	735	.714	826	1175	2001	818	981	17	387	124	4086	12.8

Three-Point Field Goals: 1980-81, 0-for-6. 1981-82, 0-for-7. 1982-83, 5-for-15 (.333). 1983-84, 0-for-5. Totals, 5-for-33 (.152).

NBA PLAYOFF RECORD

Sea.—Team	G.	Min.	FGA	FGM	Pct.	FTA	FTM	Pct.	Off.	Def.	Tot.	Ast.	PF	Dq.	Stl.	Blk.	Pts.	Avg.
87-88—Denver	4	11	3	1	.333	0	0	.000	1	3	4	2	1	0	0	0	3	0.8

Three-Point Field Goals: 1987-88, 1-for-2 (.500).

Named to THE SPORTING NEWS All-America Second Team, 1980. . . . Member of U.S. Olympic team, 1980. . . . Named CBA Most Valuable Player, 1988. . . . CBA All-Star First Team, 1988. . . . CBA All-Defensive Team, 1988.

ANTHONY WILLIAM BROWN
(Tony)

Born July 29, 1960 at Chicago, Ill.   Height 6:06.   Weight 195.

High School—Chicago, Ill., Farragut.

College—University of Arkansas, Fayetteville, Ark.

Drafted by New Jersey on fourth round, 1982 (82nd pick).

Waived by New Jersey, October 25, 1982; signed by Detroit as a free agent, May 7, 1983.
Waived by Detroit, August 19, 1983; signed by Indiana as a free agent, September 28, 1984.
Waived by Indiana, October 22, 1985; signed by Chicago, February 22, 1986, to the first of consecutive 10-day contracts that expired, March 13, 1986.
Signed by New Jersey as a free agent, September 3, 1986.
Missed entire 1987-88 season due to injury.
Played in Continental Basketball Association with Ohio Mixers, 1982-83, and Kansas City Sizzlers, 1985-86.

—COLLEGIATE RECORD—

Year	G.	Min.	FGA	FGM	Pct.	FTA	FTM	Pct.	Reb.	Pts.	Avg.
78-79	23	354	66	38	.576	14	11	.786	29	87	3.8
79-80	28	299	68	37	.544	23	13	.565	39	87	3.1
80-81	32	654	113	63	.558	46	29	.630	88	155	4.8
81-82	27	826	185	109	.589	68	52	.765	87	270	10.0
Totals	110	2133	432	247	.572	151	105	.695	243	599	5.4

CBA REGULAR SEASON RECORD

Sea.—Team	G.	Min.	FGM	FGA	Pct.	FGM	FGA	Pct.	FTM	FTA	Pct.	Reb.	Ast.	Pts.	Avg.
			2-Point			3-Point									
82-83—Ohio	44	1584	371	745	.497	0	5	.000	223	321	.694	304	115	965	21.9
85-86—Kansas City	23	767	181	370	.489	3	15	.200	130	178	.730	135	144	501	21.8
Totals	67	2351	552	1115	.495	3	20	.150	353	499	.707	439	259	1466	21.9

NBA REGULAR SEASON RECORD

Sea.—Team	G.	Min.	FGA	FGM	Pct.	FTA	FTM	Pct.	Off.	Def.	Tot.	Ast.	PF	Dq.	Stl.	Blk.	Pts.	Avg.
84-85—Indiana	82	1586	465	214	.460	171	116	.678	146	142	288	159	212	3	59	12	544	6.6
85-86—Chicago	10	132	41	18	.439	13	9	.692	5	11	16	14	16	0	5	1	45	4.5
86-87—New Jersey	77	2339	810	358	.442	206	152	.738	84	135	219	259	273	12	89	14	873	11.3
Totals	169	4057	1316	590	.448	390	277	.710	235	288	523	432	501	15	153	27	1462	8.7

Three-Point Field Goals: 1984-85, 0-for-6. 1985-86, 0-for-2. 1986-87, 5-for-20 (.250). Totals, 5-for-28 (.179).

Named to CBA All-Defensive Second Team, 1983.

—DID YOU KNOW—

That Reggie Lewis is the only Boston first-round draft choice since 1981 who is still on the Celtics' roster? Charles Bradley (1981), was waived in 1983; Darren Tillis ('82) was traded in 1983; Greg Kite ('83) was waived last season; Michael Young ('84) was waived before playing a game; Sam Vincent ('85) was traded last season; Len Bias ('86) died shortly after being drafted, while Lewis ('87) played in 49 games as a rookie last year.

MICHAEL BROWN
(Mike)

Born July 19, 1963 at Newark, N.J. Height 6:10. Weight 260.
High School—East Orange, N.J., Clifford Scott.
College—George Washington University, Washington, D.C.
Drafted by Chicago on third round, 1985 (69th pick).

Selected from Chicago by Charlotte in NBA expansion draft, June 23, 1988.
Traded by Charlotte to Utah for Kelly Tripucka, June 23, 1988.
Played in Italy during 1985-86 season.

—COLLEGIATE RECORD—

Year	G.	Min.	FGA	FGM	Pct.	FTA	FTM	Pct.	Reb.	Pts.	Avg.
81-82	27	926	350	174	.497	141	73	.518	230	421	15.6
82-83	29	1058	369	192	.520	171	112	.655	298	496	17.1
83-84	29	1049	355	190	.535	256	187	.730	351	567	19.6
84-85	26	937	321	154	.480	191	124	.649	287	432	16.6
Totals	111	3970	1395	710	.509	759	496	.653	1166	1916	17.3

NBA REGULAR SEASON RECORD

Sea.—Team	G.	Min.	FGA	FGM	Pct.	FTA	FTM	Pct.	Off.	Def.	Tot.	Ast.	PF	Dq.	Stl.	Blk.	Pts.	Avg.
86-87—Chicago	62	818	201	106	.527	72	46	.639	71	143	214	24	129	2	20	7	258	4.2
87-88—Chicago	46	591	174	78	.448	71	41	.577	66	93	159	28	85	0	11	4	197	4.3
Totals	108	1409	375	184	.491	143	87	.608	137	236	373	52	214	2	31	11	455	4.2

Three-Point Field Goals: 1987-88, 0-for-1.

NBA PLAYOFF RECORD

Sea.—Team	G.	Min.	FGA	FGM	Pct.	FTA	FTM	Pct.	Off.	Def.	Tot.	Ast.	PF	Dq.	Stl.	Blk.	Pts.	Avg.
86-87—Chicago	1	3	1	0	.000	0	0	.000	0	0	0	0	1	0	1	0	0	0.0
87-88—Chicago	1	4	0	0	.000	2	1	.500	0	0	0	1	0	0	1	0	1	1.0
Totals	2	7	1	0	.000	2	1	.500	0	0	0	1	1	0	2	0	1	0.5

STEVEN DWAYNE BURTT
(Steve)

Born November 5, 1962 at New York, N. Y. Height 6:02. Weight 185.
High School—New York, N. Y., Charles Evans Hughes.
College—Iona College, New Rochelle, N. Y.
Drafted by Golden State on second round, 1984 (30th pick).

Right of first refusal relinquished by Golden State, September 26, 1985; signed by Los Angeles Clippers, March 18, 1988, to the first of consecutive 10-day contracts that expired, April 6, 1988.
Re-signed by Los Angeles Clippers, April 7, 1988, for remainder of season.
Played in Continental Basketball Association with Albany Patroons, 1984-85, and Savannah Spirits, 1987-88.

—COLLEGIATE RECORD—

Year	G.	Min.	FGA	FGM	Pct.	FTA	FTM	Pct.	Reb.	Pts.	Avg.
80-81	28	800	309	149	.482	126	83	.659	73	381	13.6
81-82	31	1148	496	251	.506	251	182	.725	108	684	22.1
82-83	31	1139	544	294	.540	171	132	.772	129	720	23.2
83-84	31	1065	574	309	.538	179	131	.732	109	749	24.2
Totals	121	4152	1923	1003	.522	727	528	.726	419	2534	20.9

—DID YOU KNOW—

That more than half of the NBA's head coaches have a higher winning percentage in the NBA playoffs than San Antonio's Larry Brown? Brown registered a modest 8-13 (.381) record in three NBA playoff years (1977-78-82). Posting better marks are the Lakers' Pat Riley (.696), Detroit's Chuck Daly (.571), Cleveland's Lenny Wilkens (.527), Dallas' John MacLeod (.480), Golden State's Don Nelson (.477), Seattle's Bernie Bickerstaff (.474), Milwaukee's Del Harris (.472), Orlando's Matt Guokas (.471), Atlanta's Mike Fratello (.457), Utah's Frank Layden (.439), Indiana's Jack Ramsay (.431), Denver's Doug Moe (.429), Washington's Wes Unseld (.400) and the Clippers' Gene Shue (.390).

Sea.—Team	G.	Min.	FGM	FGA	Pct.	FGM	FGA	Pct.	FTM	FTA	Pct.	Reb.	Ast.	Pts.	Avg.

CBA REGULAR SEASON RECORD

Sea.—Team	G.	Min.	2-Point FGM	FGA	Pct.	3-Point FGM	FGA	Pct.	FTM	FTA	Pct.	Reb.	Ast.	Pts.	Avg.
85-86—Albany	6	86	21	53	.396	0	0	.000	11	16	.687	6	4	53	8.8
87-88—Savannah	45	1449	368	717	.513	4	19	.211	299	399	.749	117	138	1047	23.3
Totals	51	1535	389	770	.505	4	19	.211	310	415	.747	123	142	1100	21.6

NBA REGULAR SEASON RECORD

Sea.—Team	G.	Min.	FGA	FGM	Pct.	FTA	FTM	Pct.	Off.	Def.	Tot.	Ast.	PF	Dq.	Stl.	Blk.	Pts.	Avg.
84-85—Golden State	47	418	188	72	.383	77	53	.688	10	18	28	20	76	0	21	4	197	4.2
87-88—L.A. Clippers	19	312	138	62	.449	69	47	.681	6	21	27	38	56	0	10	5	171	9.0
Totals	66	730	326	134	.411	146	100	.685	16	39	55	58	132	0	31	9	368	5.6

Three-Point Field Goals: 1984-85, 0-for-1. 1987-88, 0-for-4. Totals, 0-for-5.

MICHAEL JEROME CAGE

Born January 28, 1962 at West Memphis, Ark. Height 6:09. Weight 235.

High School—West Memphis, Ark.

College—San Diego State University, San Diego, Calif.

Drafted by Los Angeles Clippers on first round, 1984 (14th pick).

Traded by Los Angeles Clippers to Seattle for draft rights to Gary Grant and a 1989 1st round draft choice, June 28, 1988.

—COLLEGIATE RECORD—

Year	G.	Min.	FGA	FGM	Pct.	FTA	FTM	Pct.	Reb.	Pts.	Avg.
80-81	27	1031	206	115	.558	86	65	.756	355	295	10.9
81-82	29	1076	252	123	.488	109	72	.661	256	318	11.0
82-83	28	1070	335	191	.570	221	165	.747	354	547	19.5
83-84	28	1085	445	250	.562	251	186	.741	352	686	24.5
Totals	112	4262	1238	679	.548	667	488	.732	1317	1846	16.5

NBA REGULAR SEASON RECORD

Sea.—Team	G.	Min.	FGA	FGM	Pct.	FTA	FTM	Pct.	Off.	Def.	Tot.	Ast.	PF	Dq.	Stl.	Blk.	Pts.	Avg.
84-85—L.A. Clippers	75	1610	398	216	.543	137	101	.737	126	266	392	51	164	1	41	32	533	7.1
85-86—L.A. Clippers	78	1566	426	204	.479	174	113	.649	168	249	417	81	176	1	62	34	521	6.7
86-87—L.A. Clippers	80	2922	878	457	.521	467	341	.730	354	568	922	131	221	1	99	67	1255	15.7
87-88—L.A. Clippers	72	2660	766	360	.470	474	326	.688	371	567	938	110	194	1	91	58	1046	14.5
Totals	305	8758	2468	1237	.501	1252	881	.704	1019	1650	2669	373	755	4	293	191	3355	11.0

Three-Point Field Goals: 1985-86, 0-for-3. 1986-87, 0-for-3. 1987-88, 0-for-1. Totals, 0-for-7.

Led NBA in rebounding, 1988.

ANTHONY CAMPBELL
(Tony)

Born May 7, 1962 at Teaneck, N. J. Height 6:07. Weight 215.

High School—Teaneck, N. J.

College—Ohio State University, Columbus, Ohio.

Drafted by Detroit on first round, 1984 (20th pick).

Signed by Washington as a Veteran Free Agent, October 8, 1987; Detroit agreed not to exercise its right of first refusal in exchange for a 1989 2nd round draft choice.

Waived by Washington, November 3, 1987; signed by Los Angeles Lakers as a free agent, March 30, 1988.

Played in Continental Basketball Association with Albany Patroons, 1987-88.

—COLLEGIATE RECORD—

Year	G.	Min.	FGA	FGM	Pct.	FTA	FTM	Pct.	Reb.	Pts.	Avg.
80-81	14	55	24	10	.417	6	3	.500	9	23	1.6
81-82	31	986	356	151	.424	119	95	.798	154	397	12.8
82-83	30	1122	451	227	.503	144	115	.799	250	569	19.0
83-84	29	1095	392	201	.513	171	138	.807	215	540	18.6
Totals	104	3258	1223	589	.482	440	351	.798	628	1529	14.7

CBA REGULAR SEASON RECORD

Sea.—Team	G.	Min.	2-Point FGM	FGA	Pct.	3-Point FGM	FGA	Pct.	FTM	FTA	Pct.	Reb.	Ast.	Pts.	Avg.
87-88—Albany	38	1133	332	513	.647	3	8	.375	229	266	.861	251	51	902	23

NBA REGULAR SEASON RECORD

								—Rebounds—								
Sea.—Team	G.	Min.	FGA	FGM	Pct.	FTA	FTM	Pct.	Off.	Def.	Tot.	Ast.	PF	Dq.	Stl.	Blk.	Pts.	Avg.
84-85—Detroit	56	625	262	130	.496	70	56	.800	41	48	89	24	107	1	28	3	316	5.6
85-86—Detroit	82	1292	608	294	.484	73	58	.795	83	153	236	45	164	0	62	7	648	7.9
86-87—Detroit	40	332	145	57	.393	39	24	.615	21	37	58	19	40	0	12	1	138	3.5
87-88—L.A. Lakers	13	242	101	57	.564	39	28	.718	8	19	27	15	41	0	11	2	143	11.0
Totals	191	2491	1116	538	.482	221	166	.751	153	257	410	103	352	1	113	13	1245	6.5

Three-Point Field Goals: 1984-85, 0-for-1. 1985-86, 2-for-9 (.222). 1986-87, 0-for-3. 1987-88, 1-for-3 (.333). Totals, 3-for-16 (.188).

NBA PLAYOFF RECORD

								—Rebounds—								
Sea.—Team	G.	Min.	FGA	FGM	Pct.	FTA	FTM	Pct.	Off.	Def.	Tot.	Ast.	PF	Dq.	Stl.	Blk.	Pts.	Avg.
84-85—Detroit	2	9	3	1	.333	0	0	.000	0	2	2	1	1	0	0	0	2	1.0
85-86—Detroit	2	16	10	4	.400	2	1	.500	0	2	2	0	5	0	0	0	9	4.5
86-87—Detroit	4	13	6	3	.500	2	2	1.000	0	5	5	0	1	0	0	0	9	2.3
87-88—L.A. Lakers	15	94	42	18	.429	16	11	.688	4	6	10	5	16	0	3	0	47	3.1
Totals	23	132	61	26	.426	20	14	.700	4	15	19	6	23	0	3	0	67	2.9

Three-Point Field Goals: 1986-87, 1-for-1 (1.000). 1987-88, 0-for-1. Totals, 1-for-2 (.500).
Member of NBA championship team, 1988. . . . Named to CBA All-Star First Team, 1988. . . . CBA Newcomer of the Year, 1988.

RICHARD PRESTON CARLISLE
(Rick)

Born October 27, 1959 at Ogdensburg, N. Y. Height 6:05. Weight 210.

High School—Lisbon, N. Y., Central.

Prep School—Worcester Academy, Worcester, Mass.

Colleges—University of Maine, Orono, Me., and University of Virginia, Charlottesville, Va.

Drafted by Boston on third round, 1984 (69th pick).

Waived by Boston, November 3, 1987; signed by New York as a free agent, November 30, 1987. Played in Continental Basketball Association with Albany Patroons, 1987-88.

—COLLEGIATE RECORD—
Maine

Year	G.	Min.	FGA	FGM	Pct.	FTA	FTM	Pct.	Reb.	Pts.	Avg.
79-80	28	....	236	131	.555	97	83	.856	96	345	12.3
80-81	28	....	322	176	.547	126	102	.810	118	454	16.2
Maine Totals	56	....	558	307	.550	223	185	.830	214	799	14.3

Virginia

Year	G.	Min.	FGA	FGM	Pct.	FTA	FTM	Pct.	Reb.	Pts.	Avg.
81-82			Did Not Play—Transfer Student								
82-83	34	965	277	142	.513	104	87	.837	100	379	11.1
83-84	33	959	289	149	.516	96	67	.698	93	365	11.1
Va. Totals	67	1924	566	291	.514	200	154	.770	193	744	11.1
College Totals	123	....	1124	598	.532	443	339	.765	407	1543	12.5

Three-Point Field Goals: 1982-83, 8-for-12 (.750).

CBA REGULAR SEASON RECORD

			——2-Point——			——3-Point——								
Sea.—Team	G.	Min.	FGM	FGA	Pct.	FGM	FGA	Pct.	FTM	FTA	Pct.	Reb.	Ast.	Pts.	Avg.
87-88—Albany	6	172	38	74	.514	4	8	.500	16	19	.842	11	14	104	17.3

NBA REGULAR SEASON RECORD

								—Rebounds—								
Sea.—Team	G.	Min.	FGA	FGM	Pct.	FTA	FTM	Pct.	Off.	Def.	Tot.	Ast.	PF	Dq.	Stl.	Blk.	Pts.	Avg.
84-85—Boston	38	179	67	26	.388	17	15	.882	8	13	21	25	21	0	3	0	67	1.8
85-86—Boston	77	760	189	92	.487	23	15	.652	22	55	77	104	92	1	19	4	199	2.6
86-87—Boston	42	297	92	30	.326	20	15	.750	8	22	30	35	28	0	8	0	80	1.9
87-88—New York	26	204	67	29	.433	11	10	.909	6	7	13	32	39	1	11	4	74	2.8
Totals	183	1440	415	177	.427	71	55	.775	44	97	141	196	180	2	41	8	420	2.3

Three-Point Field Goals: 1984-85, 0-for-2. 1985-86, 0-for-10. 1986-87, 5-for-16 (.313). 1987-88, 6-for-17 (.353). Totals, 11-for-45 (.244).

NBA PLAYOFF RECORD

								—Rebounds—								
Sea.—Team	G.	Min.	FGA	FGM	Pct.	FTA	FTM	Pct.	Off.	Def.	Tot.	Ast.	PF	Dq.	Stl.	Blk.	Pts.	Avg.
85-86—Boston	10	54	15	8	.533	4	3	.750	3	2	5	8	9	0	2	0	19	1.9
87-88—New York	2	8	4	1	.250	0	0	.000	1	1	2	0	1	0	1	0	2	1.0
Totals	12	62	19	9	.474	4	3	.750	4	3	7	8	10	0	3	0	21	1.8

Three-Point Field Goals: 1987-88, 0-for-2.
Member of NBA championship team, 1986.

ANTOINE LABOTTE CARR

Born July 23, 1961 at Oklahoma City, Okla.   Height 6:09.   Weight 235.

High School—Wichita, Kan., Wichita Heights.

College—Wichita State University, Wichita, Kan.

Drafted by Detroit on first round, 1983 (8th pick).

Draft rights traded by Detroit with Cliff Levington and 1986 and 1987 2nd round draft choices to Atlanta for Dan Roundfield, June 18, 1984.

Played in Italy during 1983-84 season.

—COLLEGIATE RECORD—

Year	G.	Min.	FGA	FGM	Pct.	FTA	FTM	Pct.	Reb.	Pts.	Avg.
79-80	29	818	355	178	.501	129	86	.667	171	442	15.2
80-81	33	1030	360	211	.586	132	101	.765	241	523	15.8
81-82	28	785	316	179	.566	115	91	.791	196	449	16.0
82-83	22	727	339	195	.575	136	104	.765	168	497	22.6
Totals	112	3360	1370	763	.557	512	382	.746	776	1911	17.1

Three-Point Field Goals: 1982-83, 3-for-5 (.600).

ITALIAN LEAGUE RECORD

Year	G.	Min.	FGA	FGM	Pct.	FTA	FTM	Pct.	Reb.	Pts.	Avg.
83-84—Milan Olym.	20	701	329	183	.556	101	61	.604	174	427	21.4

NBA REGULAR SEASON RECORD

Sea.—Team	G.	Min.	FGA	FGM	Pct.	FTA	FTM	Pct.	Off.	Def.	Tot.	Ast.	PF	Dq.	Stl.	Blk.	Pts.	Avg.
84-85—Atlanta	62	1195	375	198	.528	128	101	.789	79	153	232	80	219	4	29	78	499	8.0
85-86—Atlanta	17	258	93	49	.527	27	18	.667	16	36	52	14	51	1	7	15	116	6.8
86-87—Atlanta	65	695	265	134	.506	103	73	.709	60	96	156	34	146	1	14	48	342	5.3
87-88—Atlanta	80	1483	517	281	.544	182	142	.780	94	195	289	103	272	7	38	83	705	8.8
Totals	224	3631	1250	662	.530	440	334	.759	249	480	729	231	688	13	88	224	1662	7.4

Three-Point Field Goals: 1984-85, 2-for-6 (.333). 1986-87, 1-for-3 (.333). 1987-88, 1-for-4 (.250). Totals, 4-for-13 (.308).

NBA PLAYOFF RECORD

Sea.—Team	G.	Min.	FGA	FGM	Pct.	FTA	FTM	Pct.	Off.	Def.	Tot.	Ast.	PF	Dq.	Stl.	Blk.	Pts.	Avg.
86-87—Atlanta	9	162	56	39	.696	32	26	.813	11	16	27	13	36	1	3	8	104	11.6
87-88—Atlanta	12	210	68	36	.529	14	9	.643	12	29	41	15	47	2	4	17	81	6.8
Totals	21	372	124	75	.605	46	35	.761	23	45	68	28	83	3	7	25	185	8.8

Three-Point Field Goals: 1987-88, 0-for-1.

Named to THE SPORTING NEWS All-America First Team, 1983.

JOSEPH BARRY CARROLL
(Joe Barry)

Born July 24, 1958 at Pine Bluff, Ark.   Height 7:01.   Weight 255.

High School—Denver, Colo., East.

College—Purdue University, West Lafayette, Ind.

Drafted by Golden State on first round, 1980 (1st pick).

Traded by Golden State with Eric Floyd to Houston for Ralph Sampson and Steve Harris, December 12, 1987.
Played in Italy during 1984-85 season, averaging 24.9 points in 25 games.

—COLLEGIATE RECORD—

Year	G.	Min.	FGA	FGM	Pct.	FTA	FTM	Pct.	Reb.	Pts.	Avg.
76-77	28	573	187	93	.497	54	34	.630	206	220	7.9
77-78	27	855	312	163	.522	143	95	.664	288	421	15.6
78-79	35	1235	545	318	.583	253	162	.640	352	798	22.8
79-80	33	1168	558	301	.539	203	134	.660	302	736	22.3
Totals	123	3831	1602	875	.546	653	425	.651	1148	2175	17.7

NBA REGULAR SEASON RECORD

Sea.—Team	G.	Min.	FGA	FGM	Pct.	FTA	FTM	Pct.	Off.	Def.	Tot.	Ast.	PF	Dq.	Stl.	Blk.	Pts.	Avg.
80-81—Golden State	82	2919	1254	616	.491	440	315	.716	274	485	759	117	313	10	50	121	1547	18.9
81-82—Golden State	76	2627	1016	527	.519	323	235	.728	210	423	633	64	265	8	64	127	1289	17.0
82-83—Golden State	79	2988	1529	785	.513	469	337	.719	220	468	688	169	260	7	108	155	1907	24.1
83-84—Golden State	80	2962	1390	663	.477	433	313	.723	235	401	636	193	244	9	103	142	1639	20.5

Sea.—Team	G.	Min.	FGA	FGM	Pct.	FTA	FTM	Pct.	Off.	Def.	Tot.	Ast.	PF	Dq.	Stl.	Blk.	Pts.	Avg.
85-86—Golden State	79	2801	1404	650	.463	501	377	.752	193	477	670	176	277	13	101	144	1677	21.2
86-87—Golden State	81	2724	1461	690	.472	432	340	.787	173	416	589	214	255	2	92	123	1720	21.2
87-88—G.S.-Hou.	77	2004	924	402	.435	225	172	.764	131	358	489	113	195	1	50	106	976	12.7
Totals	554	19025	8978	4333	.483	2823	2089	.740	1436	3028	4464	1051	1809	50	568	918	10755	19.4

Three-Point Field Goals: 1980-81, 0-for-2. 1981-82, 0-for-1. 1982-83, 0-for-3. 1983-84, 0-for-1. 1985-86, 0-for-2. 1987-88, 0-for-2. Totals, 0-for-11.

NBA PLAYOFF RECORD

Sea.—Team	G.	Min.	FGA	FGM	Pct.	FTA	FTM	Pct.	Off.	Def.	Tot.	Ast.	PF	Dq.	Stl.	Blk.	Pts.	Avg.
86-87--Golden State	10	334	163	74	.454	51	41	.804	16	49	65	19	42	2	14	25	189	18.9
87-88—Houston	4	116	47	18	.383	10	8	.800	8	11	19	2	12	0	3	1	44	11.0
Totals	14	450	210	92	.438	61	49	.803	24	60	84	21	54	2	17	26	233	16.6

Three-Point Field Goals: 1986-87, 0-for-1.

NBA ALL-STAR GAME RECORD

Season—Team	Min.	FGA	FGM	Pct.	FTA	FTM	Pct.	Off.	Def.	Tot.	Ast.	PF	Dq.	Stl.	Blk.	Pts.
1987—Golden State	18	7	1	.143	2	2	1.000	4	2	6	0	4	0	0	1	4

Named to NBA All-Rookie Team, 1981. . . . THE SPORTING NEWS All-America First Team, 1980.

JAMES WILLIAM CARTWRIGHT
(Bill)

Born July 30, 1957 at Lodi, Calif.   Height 7:01.   Weight 245.
High School—Elk Grove, Calif.
College—University of San Francisco, San Francisco, Calif.
Drafted by New York on first round, 1979 (3rd pick).

Traded by New York with 1988 1st and 3rd round draft choices to Chicago for Charles Oakley and 1988 1st and 3rd round draft choices, June 27, 1988.
Missed entire 1984-85 season due to injury.

—COLLEGIATE RECORD—

Year	G.	Min.	FGA	FGM	Pct.	FTA	FTM	Pct.	Reb.	Pts.	Avg.
75-76	30	845	285	151	.530	98	72	.735	207	374	12.5
76-77	31	969	426	241	.566	161	118	.733	262	600	19.4
77-78	21	712	252	168	.667	131	96	.733	213	432	20.6
78-79	29	1020	443	268	.605	237	174	.734	455	710	24.5
Totals	111	3546	1406	828	.589	627	460	.734	1137	2116	19.1

NBA REGULAR SEASON RECORD

Sea.—Team	G.	Min.	FGA	FGM	Pct.	FTA	FTM	Pct.	Off.	Def.	Tot.	Ast.	PF	Dq.	Stl.	Blk.	Pts.	Avg.
79-80—New York	82	3150	1215	665	.547	566	451	.797	194	532	726	165	279	2	48	101	1781	21.7
80-81—New York	82	2925	1118	619	.554	518	408	.788	161	452	613	111	259	2	48	83	1646	20.1
81-82—New York	72	2060	694	390	.562	337	257	.763	116	305	421	87	208	2	48	65	1037	14.4
82-83—New York	82	2468	804	455	.566	511	380	.744	185	405	590	136	315	7	41	127	1290	15.7
83-84—New York	77	2487	808	453	.561	502	404	.805	195	454	649	107	262	4	44	97	1310	17.0
85-86—New York	2	36	7	3	.429	10	6	.600	2	8	10	5	6	0	1	1	12	6.0
86-87—New York	58	1989	631	335	.531	438	346	.790	132	313	445	96	188	2	40	26	1016	17.5
87-88—New York	82	1676	528	287	.544	426	340	.798	127	257	384	85	234	4	43	43	914	11.1
Totals	537	16791	5805	3207	.552	3308	2592	.784	1112	2726	3838	792	1751	23	313	543	9006	16.8

Three-Point Field Goals: 1980-81, 0-for-1. 1983-84, 0-for-1. Totals, 0-for-2.

NBA PLAYOFF RECORD

Sea.—Team	G.	Min.	FGA	FGM	Pct.	FTA	FTM	Pct.	Off.	Def.	Tot.	Ast.	PF	Dq.	Stl.	Blk.	Pts.	Avg.
80-81—New York	2	49	17	6	.353	12	8	.667	4	9	13	1	7	0	1	1	20	10.0
82-83—New York	6	172	43	25	.581	22	17	.773	9	25	34	4	25	0	3	7	67	11.2
83-84—New York	12	398	126	70	.556	80	69	.863	27	72	99	5	44	0	2	14	209	17.4
87-88—New York	4	76	18	9	.500	15	11	.733	8	11	19	6	12	0	0	3	29	7.3
Totals	24	695	204	110	.539	129	105	.814	48	117	165	16	88	0	6	25	325	13.5

NBA ALL-STAR GAME RECORD

Season—Team	Min.	FGA	FGM	Pct.	FTA	FTM	Pct.	Off.	Def.	Tot.	Ast.	PF	Dq.	Stl.	Blk.
1980—New York.....	14	8	4	.500	0	0	.000	1	2	3	1	1	0	0	0

Named to NBA All-Rookie Team, 1980. . . . THE SPORTING NEWS All-America First Team, 1979.

TERRY DEWAYNE CATLEDGE

Born August 22, 1963 at Houston, Miss. Height 6:08. Weight 230.

High School—Houston, Miss.

Colleges—Itawamba Junior College, Fulton, Miss., and
University of South Alabama, Mobile, Ala.

Drafted by Philadelphia on first round, 1985 (21st pick).

Traded by Philadelphia with Moses Malone and 1986 and 1988 1st round draft choices to Washington for Jeff Ruland and Cliff Robinson, June 16, 1986.

—COLLEGIATE RECORD—

Itawamba

Year	G.	Min.	FGA	FGM	Pct.	FTA	FTM	Pct.	Reb.	Pts.	Avg.
81-82			Transferred before basketball season.								

South Alabama

Year	G.	Min.	FGA	FGM	Pct.	FTA	FTM	Pct.	Reb.	Pts.	Avg.
81-82			Did Not Play—Transfer Student								
82-83	28	911	387	216	.558	171	119	.696	278	551	19.7
83-84	30	1032	373	220	.590	219	157	.717	332	597	19.9
84-85	28	1038	536	285	.532	250	148	.592	322	718	25.6
Totals	86	2981	1296	721	.556	640	424	.663	932	1866	21.7

NBA REGULAR SEASON RECORD

Sea.—Team	G.	Min.	FGA	FGM	Pct.	FTA	FTM	Pct.	Off.	Def.	Tot.	Ast.	PF	Dq.	Stl.	Blk.	Pts.	Avg.
											—Rebounds—							
85-86—Philadelphia	64	1092	431	202	.469	139	90	.647	107	165	272	21	127	0	31	8	494	7.7
86-87—Washington	78	2149	835	413	.495	335	199	.594	248	312	560	56	195	1	43	14	1025	13.1
87-88—Washington	70	1610	585	296	.506	235	154	.655	180	217	397	63	172	0	33	9	746	10.7
Totals	212	4851	1851	911	.492	709	443	.625	535	694	1229	140	494	1	107	31	2265	10.7

Three-Point Field Goals: 1985-86, 0-for-4. 1986-87, 0-for-4. 1987-88, 0-for-2. Totals, 0-for-10.

NBA PLAYOFF RECORD

Sea.—Team	G.	Min.	FGA	FGM	Pct.	FTA	FTM	Pct.	Off.	Def.	Tot.	Ast.	PF	Dq.	Stl.	Blk.	Pts.	Avg.
											—Rebounds—							
85-86—Philadelphia	11	293	117	46	.393	38	22	.579	37	38	75	5	34	0	6	8	114	10.4
86-87—Washington	3	98	41	23	.561	17	9	.529	7	18	25	0	5	0	3	1	55	18.3
87-88—Washington	5	45	11	4	.364	4	3	.750	2	4	6	2	9	0	0	0	11	2.2
Totals	19	436	169	73	.432	59	34	.576	46	60	106	7	48	0	9	9	180	9.5

Three-Point Field Goals: 1987-88, 0-for-1.

THOMAS DOANE CHAMBERS
(Tom)

Born June 21, 1959 at Ogden, Utah. Height 6:10. Weight 230.

High School—Boulder, Colo., Fairview.

College—University of Utah, Salt Lake City, Utah.

Drafted by San Diego on first round, 1981 (8th pick).

Traded by San Diego with Al Wood, a 1987 2nd round draft choice and a future 3rd round draft choice to Seattle for James Donaldson, Greg Kelser, Mark Radford, a 1984 1st round draft choice and a 1985 2nd round draft choice, August 18, 1983.

Signed by Phoenix as an unrestricted free agent, July 5, 1988.

—COLLEGIATE RECORD—

Year	G.	Min.	FGA	FGM	Pct.	FTA	FTM	Pct.	Reb.	Pts.	Avg.
77-78	28	355	139	69	.496	64	40	.625	104	178	6.4
78-79	30	853	379	206	.544	127	69	.543	266	481	16.0
79-80	28	792	359	195	.543	129	92	.713	244	482	17.2
80-81	30	959	372	221	.594	155	115	.742	262	557	18.6
Totals	116	2959	1249	691	.553	475	316	.665	876	1698	14.6

NBA REGULAR SEASON RECORD

Sea.—Team	G.	Min.	FGA	FGM	Pct.	FTA	FTM	Pct.	Off.	Def.	Tot.	Ast.	PF	Dq.	Stl.	Blk.	Pts.	Avg.
											—Rebounds—							
81-82—San Diego	81	2682	1056	554	.525	458	284	.620	211	350	561	146	341	17	58	46	1392	17.2
82-83—San Diego	79	2665	1099	519	.472	488	353	.723	218	301	519	192	333	15	79	57	1391	17.6
83-84—Seattle	82	2570	1110	554	.499	469	375	.800	219	313	532	133	309	8	47	51	1483	18.1
84-85—Seattle	81	2923	1302	629	.483	571	475	.832	164	415	579	209	312	4	70	57	1739	21.5

TOM CHAMBERS

Sea.—Team	G.	Min.	FGA	FGM	Pct.	FTA	FTM	Pct.	Off.	Def.	Tot.	Ast.	PF	Dq.	Stl.	Blk.	Pts.	Avg.
									—Rebounds—									
85-86—Seattle	66	2019	928	432	.466	414	346	.836	126	305	431	132	248	6	55	37	1223	18.5
86-87—Seattle	82	3018	1446	660	.456	630	535	.849	163	382	545	245	307	9	81	50	1909	23.3
87-88—Seattle	82	2680	1364	611	.448	519	419	.807	135	355	490	212	297	4	87	53	1674	20.4
Totals	553	18557	8305	3959	.477	3549	2787	.785	1236	2421	3657	1269	2147	63	477	351	10811	19.5

Three-Point Field Goals: 1981-82, 0-for-2. 1982-83, 0-for-8. 1983-84, 0-for-12. 1984-85, 6-for-22 (.273). 1985-86, 13-for-48 (.271). 1986-87, 54-for-145 (.372). 1987-88, 33-for-109 (.303). Totals, 106-for-346 (.306).

NBA PLAYOFF RECORD

Sea.—Team	G.	Min.	FGA	FGM	Pct.	FTA	FTM	Pct.	Off.	Def.	Tot.	Ast.	PF	Dq.	Stl.	Blk.	Pts.	Avg.
									—Rebounds—									
83-84—Seattle	5	191	59	28	.475	18	12	.667	4	29	33	8	23	0	5	3	68	13.6
86-87—Seattle	14	498	263	118	.449	99	80	.808	32	58	90	32	51	0	12	13	322	23.0
87-88—Seattle	5	168	91	50	.549	35	29	.829	8	23	31	11	24	1	3	1	129	25.8
Totals	24	857	413	196	.475	152	121	.796	44	110	154	51	98	1	20	17	519	21.6

Three-Point Field Goals: 1983-84, 0-for-1. 1986-87, 6-for-17 (.353). 1987-88, 0-for-2. Totals, 6-for-21 (.286).

NBA ALL-STAR GAME RECORD

Season—Team	Min.	FGA	FGM	Pct.	FTA	FTM	Pct.	Off.	Def.	Tot.	Ast.	PF	Dq.	Stl.	Blk.	Pts.
								—Rebounds—								
1987—Seattle............	29	25	13	.520	9	6	.667	3	1	4	2	5	0	4	0	34

Three-Point Field Goals: 1987, 2-for-3 (.667).

NBA All-Star Game MVP, 1987.

MAURICE EDWARD CHEEKS

Born September 8, 1956 at Chicago, Ill.   Height 6:01.   Weight 180.

High School—Chicago, Ill., DuSable.

College—West Texas State University, Canyon, Tex.

Drafted by Philadelphia on second round, 1978 (36th pick).

—COLLEGIATE RECORD—

Year	G.	Min.	FGA	FGM	Pct.	FTA	FTM	Pct.	Reb.	Pts.	Avg.
74-75	26	....	75	35	.467	53	31	.585	56	101	3.9
75-76	23	767	170	102	.600	84	52	.619	91	256	11.1
76-77	30	1095	246	149	.606	169	119	.704	119	417	13.9
77-78	27	941	319	174	.545	147	105	.714	152	453	16.8
Totals	106	....	810	460	.568	453	307	.678	418	1227	11.6

NBA REGULAR SEASON RECORD

Sea.—Team	G.	Min.	FGA	FGM	Pct.	FTA	FTM	Pct.	Off.	Def.	Tot.	Ast.	PF	Dq.	Stl.	Blk.	Pts.	Avg.
									—Rebounds—									
78-79—Philadelphia	82	2409	572	292	.510	140	101	.721	63	191	254	431	198	2	174	12	685	8.4
79-80—Philadelphia	79	2623	661	357	.540	231	180	.779	75	199	274	556	197	1	183	32	898	11.4
80-81—Philadelphia	81	2415	581	310	.534	178	140	.787	67	178	245	560	231	1	193	39	763	9.4
81-82—Philadelphia	79	2498	676	352	.521	220	171	.777	51	197	248	667	247	0	209	33	881	11.2
82-83—Philadelphia	79	2465	745	404	.542	240	181	.754	53	156	209	543	182	0	184	31	990	12.5
83-84—Philadelphia	75	2494	702	386	.550	232	170	.733	44	161	205	478	196	1	171	20	950	12.7
84-85—Philadelphia	78	2616	741	422	.570	199	175	.879	54	163	217	497	184	0	169	24	1025	13.1
85-86—Philadelphia	82	3270	913	490	.537	335	282	.842	55	180	235	753	160	0	207	27	1266	15.4
86-87—Philadelphia	68	2624	788	415	.527	292	227	.777	47	168	215	538	109	0	180	15	1061	15.6
87-88—Philadelphia	79	2871	865	428	.495	275	227	.825	59	194	253	635	116	0	167	22	1086	13.7
Totals	782	26285	7244	3856	.532	2342	1854	.792	568	1787	2355	5658	1820	5	1837	255	9605	12.3

Three-Point Field Goals: 1979-80, 4-for-9 (.444). 1980-81, 3-for-8 (.375). 1981-82, 6-for-22 (.273). 1982-83, 1-for-6 (.167). 1983-84, 8-for-20 (.400). 1984-85, 6-for-26 (.231). 1985-86, 4-for-17 (.235). 1986-87, 4-for-17 (.235). 1987-88, 3-for-22 (.136). Totals, 39-for-147 (.265).

NBA PLAYOFF RECORD

Sea.—Team	G.	Min.	FGA	FGM	Pct.	FTA	FTM	Pct.	Off.	Def.	Tot.	Ast.	PF	Dq.	Stl.	Blk.	Pts.	Avg.
									—Rebounds—									
78-79—Philadelphia	9	330	121	66	.545	56	37	.661	13	22	35	63	29	0	37	4	169	18.8
79-80—Philadelphia	18	675	174	89	.511	41	29	.707	22	52	74	111	43	0	45	4	208	11.6
80-81—Philadelphia	16	513	125	68	.544	42	32	.762	4	47	51	116	55	1	40	12	168	10.5
81-82—Philadelphia	21	765	265	125	.472	65	50	.769	15	47	62	172	58	0	48	6	301	14.3
82-83—Philadelphia	13	483	165	83	.503	64	45	.703	11	28	39	91	23	0	26	2	212	16.3
83-84—Philadelphia	5	171	67	35	.522	15	13	.867	2	10	12	19	18	0	13	0	83	16.6
84-85—Philadelphia	13	483	153	81	.529	42	36	.857	12	34	46	67	29	0	31	5	198	15.2
85-86—Philadelphia	12	519	182	94	.516	73	62	.849	13	43	56	85	18	0	13	3	250	20.8
86-87—Philadelphia	5	210	66	35	.530	21	18	.857	1	12	13	44	14	0	9	4	88	17.6
Totals	112	4149	1318	676	.513	419	322	.768	93	295	388	768	287	1	262	40	1677	15.0

Three-Point Field Goals: 1979-80, 1-for-5 (.200). 1980-81, 0-for-3. 1981-82, 1-for-9 (.111). 1982-83, 1-for-2 (.500). 1983-84, 0-for-1. 1984-85, 0-for-5. 1985-86, 0-for-7. 1986-87, 0-for-1. Totals, 3-for-33 (.091).

Season—Team	Min.	FGA	FGM	Pct.	FTA	FTM	Pct.	Off.	Def.	Tot.	Ast.	PF	Dq.	Stl.	Blk.	Pts.
									—Rebounds—							
1983—Philadelphia	18	8	3	.375	0	0	.000	0	1	1	1	0	0	0	0	6
1986—Philadelphia	14	6	3	.500	0	0	.000	0	0	0	2	0	0	2	0	6
1987—Philadelphia	8	2	1	.500	2	2	1.000	0	0	0	0	1	0	1	0	4
1988—Philadelphia	4	0	0	.000	0	0	.000	0	2	2	1	1	0	0	0	0
Totals	44	16	7	.438	2	2	1.000	0	3	3	4	2	0	3	0	16

Named to NBA All-Defensive First Team, 1983, 1984, 1985, 1986. . . . All-Defensive Second Team, 1987. . . . Member of NBA championship team, 1983. . . . NBA all-time steals leader.

BEN COLEMAN

Born November 14, 1961 at Minneapolis, Minn. Height 6:09. Weight 235.

High School—Minneapolis, Minn., North.

Colleges—University of Minnesota, Minneapolis, Minn., and
University of Maryland, College Park, Md.

Drafted by Chicago on second round, 1984 (37th pick).

Draft rights traded by Chicago with draft rights to Ken Johnson to Portland for draft rights to Mike Smrek, June 18, 1985.
Waived by Portland, November 12, 1985; signed by New Jersey as a free agent, September 22, 1986.
Traded by New Jersey with Mike Gminski to Philadelphia for Roy Hinson, Tim McCormick and a 1989 2nd round draft choice, January 16, 1988.
Played in Italy during 1984-85 season, averaging 25.7 points in 30 games.

—COLLEGIATE RECORD—
Minnesota

Year	G.	Min.	FGA	FGM	Pct.	FTA	FTM	Pct.	Reb.	Pts.	Avg.
79-80	17	....	38	14	.369	8	3	.375	21	31	1.8
80-81	23	....	190	85	.447	35	23	.657	118	193	8.4
Minn. Totals	40	....	228	99	.434	43	26	.605	139	224	5.6

Maryland

Year	G.	Min.	FGA	FGM	Pct.	FTA	FTM	Pct.	Reb.	Pts.	Avg.
81-82			Did Not Play—Transfer Student								
82-83	30	995	319	192	.571	138	90	.652	242	454	15.1
83-84	32	1094	319	194	.608	144	103	.715	209	491	15.3
Md. Totals	62	2089	638	376	.589	282	193	.684	511	945	15.2
Col. Totals	102	....	866	475	.548	325	219	.674	650	1169	11.5

NBA REGULAR SEASON RECORD

Sea.—Team	G.	Min.	FGA	FGM	Pct.	FTA	FTM	Pct.	Off.	Def.	Tot.	Ast.	PF	Dq.	Stl.	Blk.	Pts.	Avg.
										—Rebounds—								
86-87—New Jersey	68	1029	313	182	.581	121	88	.727	99	189	288	37	200	7	32	31	452	6.6
87-88—N.J.-Phil.	70	1498	453	226	.499	185	141	.762	116	234	350	62	230	5	43	41	593	8.5
Totals	138	2527	766	408	.533	306	229	.748	215	423	638	99	430	12	75	72	1045	7.6

Three-Point Field Goals: 1986-87, 0-for-1. 1987-88, 0-for-3. Totals, 0-for-4.

NORRIS J. COLEMAN

Born September 27, 1961 at Jacksonville, Fla. Height 6:08. Weight 210.

High School—Jacksonville, Fla., Paxon.

College—Kansas State University, Manhattan, Kan.

Drafted by Los Angeles Clippers on second round as an undergraduate, 1987 (38th pick).

Played in Continental Basketball Association with Pensacola Tornados, 1987-88.
Waived by Los Angeles Clippers, February 3, 1988.
In United States Army during 1979-80 through 1984-85 seasons.

—COLLEGIATE RECORD—

Year	G.	Min.	FGA	FGM	Pct.	FTA	FTM	Pct.	Reb.	Pts.	Avg.
85-86	28	992	490	254	.518	136	101	.743	225	609	21.8
86-87	19	613	303	154	.508	113	85	.752	160	394	20.7
Totals	47	1605	793	408	.515	249	186	.747	385	1003	21.3

Three-Point Field Goals: 1986-87, 1-for-13 (.077).

CBA REGULAR SEASON RECORD

Sea.—Team	G.	Min.	FGM	FGA	Pct.	FGM	FGA	Pct.	FTM	FTA	Pct.	Reb.	Ast.	Pts.	Avg.
			—2-Point—			—3-Point—									
87-88—Pensacola	16	296	70	128	.547	0	2	.000	18	27	.667	74	11	158	9.9

Sea.—Team	G.	Min.	FGA	FGM	Pct.	FTA	FTM	Pct.	Off.	Def.	Tot.	Ast.	PF	Dq.	Stl.	Blk.	Pts.	Avg.
									—Rebounds—									
87-88—L.A. Clippers	29	431	191	66	.346	36	20	.556	36	45	81	13	51	1	11	6	153	5.3

Three-Point Field Goals: 1987-88, 1-for-2 (.500).

STEVE COLTER

Born July 24, 1962 at Phoenix, Ariz.   Height 6:03.   Weight 175.

High School—Phoenix, Ariz., Union.

College—New Mexico State University, Las Cruces, N. M.

Drafted by Portland on second round, 1984 (33rd pick).

Traded by Portland to Chicago for draft rights to Larry Krystkowiak and 1987 and 1992 2nd round draft choices, June 17, 1986.

Traded by Chicago with a future 2nd round draft choice to Philadelphia for Sedale Threatt, December 31, 1986.

Waived by Philadelphia, December 3, 1987; signed by Washington as a free agent, December 22, 1987.

Waived by Washington, December 29, 1987; re-signed by Washington, January 1, 1988, to the first of consecutive 10-day contracts that expired, January 20, 1988.

Re-signed by Washington, January 21, 1988, for remainder of season.

—COLLEGIATE RECORD—

Year	G.	Min.	FGA	FGM	Pct.	FTA	FTM	Pct.	Reb.	Pts.	Avg.
80-81	22	233	47	18	.383	41	28	.683	37	64	2.9
81-82	28	822	194	94	.485	87	66	.759	100	254	9.1
82-83	29	1079	329	166	.505	179	135	.754	137	469	16.2
83-84	28	1120	438	219	.500	138	108	.783	137	546	19.5
Totals	107	3254	1008	497	.493	445	337	.757	411	1333	12.5

Three-Point Field Goals: 1982-83, 2-for-6 (.333).

NBA REGULAR SEASON RECORD

Sea.—Team	G.	Min.	FGA	FGM	Pct.	FTA	FTM	Pct.	Off.	Def.	Tot.	Ast.	PF	Dq.	Stl.	Blk.	Pts.	Avg.
									—Rebounds—									
84-85—Portland	78	1462	477	216	.453	130	98	.754	40	110	150	243	142	0	75	9	556	7.1
85-86—Portland	81	1868	597	272	.456	164	135	.823	41	136	177	257	188	0	113	10	706	8.7
86-87—Chi.-Phil.	70	1322	397	169	.426	107	82	.766	23	85	108	210	99	0	56	12	424	6.1
87-88—Phil.-Wash.	68	1513	441	203	.460	95	75	.789	58	115	173	261	132	0	62	14	484	7.1
Totals	297	6165	1912	860	.450	496	390	.786	162	446	608	971	561	0	306	45	2170	7.3

Three-Point Field Goals: 1984-85, 26-for-74 (.351). 1985-86, 27-for-83 (.325). 1986-87, 4-for-17 (.235). 1987-88, 3-for-10 (.300). Totals, 60-for-184 (.326).

NBA PLAYOFF RECORD

Sea.—Team	G.	Min.	FGA	FGM	Pct.	FTA	FTM	Pct.	Off.	Def.	Tot.	Ast.	PF	Dq.	Stl.	Blk.	Pts.	Avg.
									—Rebounds—									
84-85—Portland	9	166	75	36	.480	8	5	.625	4	12	16	37	24	1	5	0	80	8.9
85-86—Portland	4	104	26	12	.462	2	2	1.000	3	12	15	23	13	0	5	1	26	6.5
86-87—Philadelphia	2	8	2	1	.500	0	0	.000	0	0	0	2	1	0	0	0	2	1.0
87-88—Washington	5	86	31	14	.452	7	4	.571	5	10	15	13	9	0	3	3	32	6.4
Totals	20	364	134	63	.470	17	11	.647	12	34	46	75	47	1	13	4	140	7.0

Three-Point Field Goals: 1984-85, 3-for-11 (.273). 1985-86, 0-for-1. Totals, 3-for-12 (.250).

DALLAS A. COMEGYS

Born August 17, 1964 at Philadelphia, Pa.   Height 6:09.   Weight 205.

High School—Philadelphia, Pa., Roman Catholic.

College—DePaul University, Chicago, Ill.

Drafted by Atlanta on first round, 1987 (21st pick).

Traded by Atlanta to New Jersey for a 1990 2nd round draft choice, November 4, 1987.

—COLLEGIATE RECORD—

Year	G.	Min.	FGA	FGM	Pct.	FTA	FTM	Pct.	Reb.	Pts.	Avg.
83-84	28	716	241	119	.494	116	77	.664	181	315	11.3
84-85	29	730	254	129	.508	128	84	.656	132	342	11.8
85-86	30	924	307	158	.515	154	98	.636	169	414	13.8
86-87	31	1053	378	201	.532	190	140	.737	232	542	17.5
Totals	118	3423	1180	607	.514	588	399	.679	714	1613	13.7

Three-Point Field Goals: 1986-87, 0-for-1.

NBA REGULAR SEASON RECORD

Sea.—Team	G.	Min.	FGA	FGM	Pct.	FTA	FTM	Pct.	Off.	Def.	Tot.	Ast.	PF	Dq.	Stl.	Blk.	Pts.	Avg.
									—Rebounds—									
87-88—New Jersey	75	1122	363	156	.430	150	106	.707	54	164	218	65	175	3	36	70	418	5.6

Three-Point Field Goals: 1987-88, 0-for-1.

LESTER ALLEN CONNER

Born September 17, 1959 at Memphis, Tenn.   Height 6:04.   Weight 185.
High School—Oakland, Calif., Fremont.
Colleges—Los Medanos College, Antioch, Calif.; Chabot College,
Hayward, Calif., and Oregon State University, Corvallis, Ore.
Drafted by Golden State on first round, 1982 (14th pick).

Signed by Houston as a Veteran Free Agent, October 9, 1987; Golden State agreed not to exercise its right of first refusal in exchange for a 1988 2nd round draft choice.

—COLLEGIATE RECORD—
Los Medanos

Year	G.	Min.	FGA	FGM	Pct.	FTA	FTM	Pct.	Reb.	Pts.	Avg.
78-79	31	....	...	...	....	...	...	....	....	781	25.2

Chabot

Year	G.	Min.	FGA	FGM	Pct.	FTA	FTM	Pct.	Reb.	Pts.	Avg.
79-80	35	1179	549	319	.581	217	158	.728	215	796	22.7
JC Totals	66	....	...	...	....	...	...	....	....	1577	23.9

Oregon State

Year	G.	Min.	FGA	FGM	Pct.	FTA	FTM	Pct.	Reb.	Pts.	Avg.
80-81	28	790	141	68	.482	91	61	.670	119	197	7.0
81-82	30	1106	292	151	.517	196	146	.745	163	448	14.9
Totals	58	1896	433	219	.506	287	207	.721	282	645	11.1

NBA REGULAR SEASON RECORD

Sea.—Team	G.	Min.	FGA	FGM	Pct.	FTA	FTM	Pct.	Off.	Def.	Tot.	Ast.	PF	Dq.	Stl.	Blk.	Pts.	Avg.
82-83—Golden State	75	1416	303	145	.479	113	79	.699	69	152	221	253	141	1	116	7	369	4.9
83-84—Golden State	82	2573	730	360	.493	259	186	.718	132	173	305	401	176	1	162	12	907	11.1
84-85—Golden State	79	2258	546	246	.451	192	144	.750	87	159	246	369	136	1	161	13	640	8.1
85-86—Golden State	36	413	136	51	.375	54	40	.741	25	37	62	43	23	0	24	1	144	4.0
87-88—Houston	52	399	108	50	.463	41	32	.780	20	18	38	59	31	0	38	1	132	2.5
Totals	324	7059	1823	852	.467	659	481	.730	333	539	872	1125	507	3	501	34	2192	6.8

Three-Point Field Goals: 1982-83, 0-for-4. 1983-84, 1-for-6 (.167). 1984-85, 4-for-20 (.200). 1985-86, 2-for-7 (.286). 1987-88, 0-for-7. Totals, 7-for-44 (.159).

NBA PLAYOFF RECORD

Sea.—Team	G.	Min.	FGA	FGM	Pct.	FTA	FTM	Pct.	Off.	Def.	Tot.	Ast.	PF	Dq.	Stl.	Blk.	Pts.	Avg.
87-88—Houston	1	1	0	0	.000	2	2	1.000	0	1	1	1	0	0	1	0	2	2.0

DARWIN LOUIS COOK

Born August 6, 1958 at Los Angeles, Calif. Height 6:03. Weight 195.
High School—Los Angeles, Calif., Crenshaw.
College—University of Portland, Portland, Ore.
Drafted by Detroit on fourth round, 1980 (70th pick).

Waived by Detroit, July 3, 1980; signed by New Jersey as a free agent, July 17, 1980.
Traded by New Jersey to Washington for cash, August 8, 1986.
Played in Continental Basketball Association with LaCrosse Catbirds, 1987-88.
Played in Italy, 1987-88.

—COLLEGIATE RECORD—

Year	G.	Min.	FGA	FGM	Pct.	FTA	FTM	Pct.	Reb.	Pts.	Avg.
76-77	26	790	303	146	.482	78	50	.641	71	342	13.2
77-78	27	....	300	146	.487	85	66	.776	81	358	13.3
78-79	28	985	429	201	.469	127	91	.717	121	493	17.6
79-80	28	1001	394	204	.518	99	77	.778	113	485	17.3
Totals	109	....	1426	697	.489	389	284	.730	386	1678	15.4

CBA REGULAR SEASON RECORD

Sea.—Team	G.	Min.	2-Point			3-Point			FTM	FTA	Pct.	Reb.	Ast.	Pts.	Avg.
			FGM	FGA	Pct.	FGM	FGA	Pct.							
87-88—LaCrosse	19	703	98	218	.450	18	50	.360	37	44	.841	67	120	287	15.1

NBA REGULAR SEASON RECORD

Sea.—Team	G.	Min.	FGA	FGM	Pct.	FTA	FTM	Pct.	Off.	Def.	Tot.	Ast.	PF	Dq.	Stl.	Blk.	Pts.	Avg.
80-81—New Jersey	81	1980	819	383	.468	180	132	.733	96	140	236	297	197	4	141	36	904	11.2

Sea.—Team	G.	Min.	FGA	FGM	Pct.	FTA	FTM	Pct.	Off.	Def.	Tot.	Ast.	PF	Dq.	Stl.	Blk.	Pts.	Avg.
81-82—New Jersey	82	2090	803	387	.482	162	118	.728	52	103	155	319	196	2	146	24	899	11.0
82-83—New Jersey	82	2625	986	446	.449	242	186	.769	73	167	240	448	213	2	194	48	1080	13.2
83-84—New Jersey	82	1870	687	304	.443	126	95	.754	51	105	156	356	184	3	164	36	714	8.7
84-85—New Jersey	58	1063	453	212	.468	54	47	.870	21	71	92	160	96	0	74	10	473	8.2
85-86—New Jersey	79	1965	627	267	.426	111	84	.757	51	126	177	390	172	0	156	22	629	8.0
86-87—Washington	82	1420	622	265	.426	103	82	.796	46	99	145	151	136	0	98	17	614	7.5
Totals	546	13013	4997	2264	.453	978	744	.761	390	811	1201	2121	1194	11	973	193	5313	9.7

Three-Point Field Goals: 1980-81, 6-for-25 (.240). 1981-82, 7-for-31 (.226). 1982-83, 8-for-38 (.211). 1983-84, 11-for-46 (.239). 1984-85, 2-for-23 (.087). 1985-86, 11-for-53 (.208). 1986-87, 2-for-23 (.087). Totals, 47-for-239 (.197).

NBA PLAYOFF RECORD

Sea.—Team	G.	Min.	FGA	FGM	Pct.	FTA	FTM	Pct.	Off.	Def.	Tot.	Ast.	PF	Dq.	Stl.	Blk.	Pts.	Avg.
81-82—New Jersey	2	86	33	13	.394	6	2	.333	0	3	3	9	7	0	2	2	28	14.0
82-83—New Jersey	2	63	27	9	.333	2	2	1.000	3	3	6	10	8	0	1	0	20	10.0
83-84—New Jersey	11	185	82	30	.366	24	17	.708	8	10	18	31	26	0	15	0	81	7.4
84-85—New Jersey	1	7	4	3	.750	0	0	.000	0	0	0	1	2	0	0	0	6	6.0
85-86—New Jersey	3	77	29	13	.448	6	2	.333	3	4	7	17	11	1	5	2	28	9.3
86-87—Washington	3	41	24	6	.250	2	1	.500	4	3	7	3	4	0	4	0	14	4.7
Totals	22	459	199	74	.372	40	24	.600	18	23	41	71	58	1	27	4	177	8.0

Three-Point Field Goals: 1981-82, 0-for-3. 1982-83, 0-for-1. 1983-84, 4-for-13 (.308). 1985-86, 0-for-4. 1986-87, 1-for-2 (.500). Totals, 5-for-23 (.217).

JEFF JAMES COOK

Born October 21, 1956 at West Covina, Calif.   Height 6:10.   Weight 215.

High School—West Covina, Calif., Edgewood.

College—Idaho State University, Pocatello, Idaho.

Drafted by Kansas City on third round, 1978 (49th pick).

Waived by Kansas City, October 2, 1978; signed by Phoenix as a free agent, May 22, 1979.
Traded by Phoenix with a 1983 3rd round draft choice and cash to Cleveland for James Edwards, February 7, 1983.
Traded by Cleveland to San Antonio for Edgar Jones and cash, December 14, 1984.
Traded by San Antonio with Marc Iavaroni to Utah for Jeff Wilkins, February 15, 1986.
Waived by Utah, October 28, 1986; signed by Phoenix as a free agent, October 2, 1987.
Played in Western Basketball Association with Washington Lumberjacks, 1978-79.

—COLLEGIATE RECORD—

Year	G.	Min.	FGA	FGM	Pct.	FTA	FTM	Pct.	Reb.	Pts.	Avg.
74-75	20	....	45	19	.422	12	6	.500	51	44	2.2
75-76	24	....	95	42	.442	44	26	.591	108	110	4.6
76-77	30	....	267	143	.536	60	37	.617	259	323	10.8
77-78	26	....	274	134	.489	139	104	.748	302	372	14.3
Totals	100	....	681	338	.496	255	173	.678	720	849	8.5

WBA REGULAR SEASON RECORD

Sea.—Team	G.	Min.	FGM	FGA	Pct.	FGM	FGA	Pct.	FTM	FTA	Pct.	Reb.	Ast.	Pts.	Avg.
78-79—Washington	48	1822	301	634	.475	0	1	.000	163	226	.721	612	195	765	15.9

NBA REGULAR SEASON RECORD

Sea.—Team	G.	Min.	FGA	FGM	Pct.	FTA	FTM	Pct.	Off.	Def.	Tot.	Ast.	PF	Dq.	Stl.	Blk.	Pts.	Avg.
79-80—Phoenix	66	904	275	129	.469	129	104	.806	90	151	241	84	102	0	28	18	362	5.5
80-81—Phoenix	79	2192	616	286	.464	155	100	.645	170	297	467	201	236	3	82	54	672	8.5
81-82—Phoenix	76	1298	358	151	.422	134	89	.664	112	189	301	100	174	1	37	23	391	5.1
82-83—Phoe.-Clev.	75	1333	304	148	.487	104	79	.760	119	216	335	102	181	3	39	31	375	5.0
83-84—Cleveland	81	1950	387	188	.486	130	94	.723	174	310	484	123	282	7	68	47	471	5.8
84-85—Cle.-S.A.	72	1288	279	138	.495	64	47	.734	122	192	314	62	203	2	30	23	323	4.5
85-86—S.A.-Utah	36	373	73	31	.425	42	27	.643	33	53	86	21	65	0	13	11	89	2.5
87-88—Phoenix	33	359	59	14	.237	28	23	.821	37	69	106	14	64	1	9	8	51	1.5
Totals	518	9697	2351	1085	.462	786	563	.716	857	1477	2334	707	1307	17	306	215	2734	5.3

Three-Point Field Goals: 1979-80, 0-for-3. 1980-81, 0-for-5. 1981-82, 0-for-2. 1982-83, 0-for-3. 1983-84, 1-for-2 (.500). 1984-85, 0-for-1. 1985-86, 0-for-1. 1987-88, 0-for-1. Totals, 1-for-18 (.056).

NBA PLAYOFF RECORD

Sea.—Team	G.	Min.	FGA	FGM	Pct.	FTA	FTM	Pct.	Off.	Def.	Tot.	Ast.	PF	Dq.	Stl.	Blk.	Pts.	Avg.
79-80—Phoenix	7	98	24	16	.667	26	22	.846	5	16	21	7	10	0	4	2	54	7.7
80-81—Phoenix	7	206	54	25	.463	19	14	.737	17	30	47	11	29	1	1	0	65	9.3
81-82—Phoenix	7	45	8	4	.500	0	0	.000	6	3	9	7	5	0	2	2	8	1.1
84-85—San Antonio	5	98	18	9	.500	25	17	.680	6	23	29	4	23	0	5	6	35	7.0
85-86—Utah	4	21	4	1	.250	4	3	.750	1	4	5	2	4	0	0	0	5	1.3
Totals	30	468	108	55	.509	74	56	.757	35	76	111	31	71	1	12	10	167	5.6

Three-Point Field Goals: 1980-81, 1-for-1 (1.000). 1984-85, 0-for-1. Totals, 1-for-2 (.500).

ARTIS WAYNE COOPER
(Known by middle name.)

Born November 16, 1956 at Milan, Ga.   Height 6:10.   Weight 220.

High School—McRae, Ga., Telfair County.

College—University of New Orleans, New Orleans, La.

Drafted by Golden State on second round, 1978 (40th pick).

Traded by Golden State with a 1981 2nd round draft choice to Utah for Bernard King, September 11, 1980.
Traded by Utah with Allan Bristow to Dallas for Bill Robinzine, August 20, 1981.
Traded by Dallas with a 1985 1st round draft choice to Portland for Kelvin Ransey, June 28, 1982.
Traded by Portland with Lafayette Lever, Calvin Natt, a 1984 2nd round draft choice and a 1985 1st round draft choice to Denver for Kiki Vandeweghe, June 7, 1984.

—COLLEGIATE RECORD—

Year	G.	Min.	FGA	FGM	Pct.	FTA	FTM	Pct.	Reb.	Pts.	Avg.
74-75	17	....	33	16	.485	4	3	.750	52	35	2.1
75-76	26	....	278	140	.504	47	34	.723	244	314	12.1
76-77	28	....	368	166	.451	55	38	.691	284	370	13.2
77-78	27	....	377	202	.536	111	86	.775	343	490	18.1
Totals	98	....	1056	524	.496	217	161	.742	923	1209	12.3

NBA REGULAR SEASON RECORD

Sea.—Team	G.	Min.	FGA	FGM	Pct.	FTA	FTM	Pct.	Off.	Def.	Tot.	Ast.	PF	Dq.	Stl.	Blk.	Pts.	Avg.
78-79—Golden State	65	795	293	128	.437	61	41	.672	90	190	280	21	118	0	7	44	297	4.6
79-80—Golden State	79	1781	750	367	.489	181	136	.751	202	305	507	42	246	5	20	79	871	11.0
80-81—Utah	71	1420	471	213	.452	90	62	.689	166	274	440	52	219	8	18	51	489	6.9
81-82—Dallas	76	1818	669	281	.420	160	119	.744	200	350	550	115	285	10	37	106	682	9.0
82-83—Portland	80	2099	723	320	.443	197	135	.685	214	397	611	116	318	5	27	136	775	9.7
83-84—Portland	81	1662	663	304	.459	230	185	.804	176	300	476	76	247	2	26	106	793	9.8
84-85—Denver	80	2031	856	404	.472	235	161	.685	229	402	631	86	304	2	28	197	969	12.1
85-86—Denver	78	2112	906	422	.466	219	174	.795	190	420	610	81	315	6	42	227	1021	13.1
86-87—Denver	69	1561	524	235	.448	109	79	.725	162	311	473	68	257	5	13	101	549	8.0
87-88—Denver	45	865	270	118	.437	67	50	.746	98	172	270	30	145	3	12	94	286	6.4
Totals	724	16144	6125	2792	.456	1549	1142	.737	1727	3121	4848	687	2454	46	230	1141	6732	9.3

Three-Point Field Goals: 1979-80, 1-for-4 (.250). 1980-81, 1-for-3 (.333). 1981-82, 1-for-8 (.125). 1982-83, 0-for-5. 1983-84, 0-for-7. 1984-85, 0-for-2. 1985-86, 3-for-7 (.429). 1986-87, 0-for-3. 1987-88, 0-for-1. Totals, 6-for-40 (.150).

NBA PLAYOFF RECORD

Sea.—Team	G.	Min.	FGA	FGM	Pct.	FTA	FTM	Pct.	Off.	Def.	Tot.	Ast.	PF	Dq.	Stl.	Blk.	Pts.	Avg.
82-83—Portland	7	228	74	36	.486	17	15	.882	24	32	56	9	33	3	2	8	87	12.4
83-84—Portland	5	104	27	10	.370	8	4	.500	11	9	20	4	14	0	1	4	24	4.8
84-85—Denver	15	321	143	67	.469	40	30	.750	34	59	93	20	52	0	8	36	164	10.9
85-86—Denver	8	154	56	24	.429	22	15	.682	11	29	40	7	31	2	2	5	63	7.9
86-87—Denver	3	41	12	5	.417	2	2	1.000	6	11	17	2	9	0	0	1	12	4.0
87-88—Denver	9	96	23	8	.348	2	2	1.000	16	17	33	6	19	0	3	8	18	2.0
Totals	47	944	335	150	.448	91	68	.747	102	157	259	48	158	5	16	62	368	7.8

Three-Point Field Goals: 1985-86, 0-for-1.

MICHAEL JEROME COOPER

Born April 15, 1956 at Los Angeles, Calif.   Height 6:07.   Weight 176.

High School—Pasadena, Calif.

Colleges—Pasadena City College, Pasadena, Calif., and
University of New Mexico, Albuquerque, N. M.

Drafted by Los Angeles on third round, 1978 (60th pick).

—COLLEGIATE RECORD—

Pasadena City

Year	G.	Min.	FGA	FGM	Pct.	FTA	FTM	Pct.	Reb.	Pts.	Avg.
74-75	23	....	336	177	.527	65	38	.585	91	392	17.0
75-76	28	....	473	261	.552	129	102	.791	230	624	22.3
JC Totals	51	....	809	438	.541	194	140	.722	321	1016	19.9

New Mexico

Year	G.	Min.	FGA	FGM	Pct.	FTA	FTM	Pct.	Reb.	Pts.	Av.
76-77	30	957	333	171	.514	140	112	.800	150	454	
77-78	28	830	387	189	.488	111	73	.658	158	451	
Totals	58	1787	720	360	.500	251	185	.737	308	905	

NBA REGULAR SEASON RECORD

Sea.—Team	G.	Min.	FGA	FGM	Pct.	FTA	FTM	Pct.	—Rebounds— Off.	Def.	Tot.	Ast.	PF	Dq.	Stl.	Blk.	Pts.	Avg.
78-79—Los Angeles	3	7	6	3	.500	0	0	.000	0	0	0	0	1	0	1	0	6	2.0
79-80—Los Angeles	82	1973	578	303	.524	143	111	.776	101	128	229	221	215	3	86	38	722	8.8
80-81—Los Angeles	81	2625	654	321	.491	149	117	.785	121	215	336	332	249	4	133	78	763	9.4
81-82—Los Angeles	76	2197	741	383	.517	171	139	.813	84	185	269	230	216	1	120	61	907	11.9
82-83—Los Angeles	82	2148	497	266	.535	130	102	.785	82	192	274	315	208	0	115	50	639	7.8
83-84—Los Angeles	82	2387	549	273	.497	185	155	.838	53	209	262	482	267	3	113	67	739	9.0
84-85—L.A. Lakers	82	2189	593	276	.465	133	115	.865	56	199	255	429	208	0	93	49	702	8.6
85-86—L.A. Lakers	82	2269	606	274	.452	170	147	.865	44	200	244	466	238	2	89	43	758	9.2
86-87—L.A. Lakers	82	2253	736	322	.438	148	126	.851	58	196	254	373	199	1	78	43	859	10.5
87-88—L.A. Lakers	61	1793	482	189	.392	113	97	.858	50	178	228	289	136	1	66	26	532	8.7
Totals	713	19841	5442	2610	.480	1342	1109	.826	649	1702	2351	3137	1937	15	894	455	6627	9.3

Three-Point Field Goals: 1979-80, 5-for-20 (.250). 1980-81, 4-for-19 (.211). 1981-82, 2-for-17 (.118). 1982-83, 5-for-21 (.238). 1983-84, 38-for-121 (.314). 1984-85, 35-for-123 (.285). 1985-86, 63-for-163 (.387). 1986-87, 89-for-231 (.385). 1987-88, 57-for-178 (.320). Totals, 298-for-893 (.334).

NBA PLAYOFF RECORD

Sea.—Team	G.	Min.	FGA	FGM	Pct.	FTA	FTM	Pct.	—Rebounds— Off.	Def.	Tot.	Ast.	PF	Dq.	Stl.	Blk.	Pts.	Avg.
79-80—Los Angeles	16	464	140	57	.407	36	31	.861	28	31	59	58	54	0	24	11	145	9.1
80-81—Los Angeles	3	102	20	11	.550	14	10	.714	2	8	10	7	7	0	6	0	32	10.7
81-82—Los Angeles	14	383	124	70	.565	34	25	.735	19	42	61	62	47	0	24	11	166	11.9
82-83—Los Angeles	15	453	114	53	.465	41	34	.829	12	47	59	44	54	1	26	6	141	9.4
83-84—Los Angeles	21	723	191	88	.461	62	50	.806	20	62	82	119	80	1	24	20	238	11.3
84-85—L.A. Lakers	19	501	126	71	.563	52	48	.923	12	64	76	93	46	0	21	9	198	10.4
85-86—L.A. Lakers	14	421	115	54	.470	11	9	.818	16	30	46	68	24	0	18	4	136	9.7
86-87—L.A. Lakers	18	522	159	77	.484	54	46	.852	8	51	59	90	46	0	25	14	234	13.0
87-88—L.A. Lakers	24	588	131	54	.412	27	20	.741	15	43	58	66	57	0	19	9	153	6.4
Totals	144	4157	1120	535	.478	331	273	.825	132	378	510	607	415	2	187	84	1443	10.0

Three-Point Field Goals: 1979-80, 0-for-2. 1980-81, 0-for-3. 1981-82, 1-for-2 (.500). 1982-83, 1-for-7 (.143). 1983-84, 12-for-36 (.333). 1984-85, 8-for-26 (.308). 1985-86, 19-for-41 (.463). 1986-87, 34-for-70 (.486). 1987-88, 25-for-62 (.403). Totals, 100-for-249 (.402).

Named NBA Defensive Player of the Year, 1987. . . . NBA All-Defensive First Team, 1982, 1984, 1985, 1987, 1988 . . . . NBA All-Defensive Second Team, 1981, 1983, 1986. . . . Member of NBA championship teams, 1980, 1982, 1985, 1987, 1988. . . . Holds championship series game record for most three-point field goals made, 6, vs. Boston, June 4, 1987.

TYRONE KENNEDY CORBIN

Born December 31, 1962 at Columbia, S. C.   Height 6:06.   Weight 222.

High School—Columbia, S. C., A. C. Flora.

College—DePaul University, Chicago, Ill.

Drafted by San Antonio on second round, 1985 (35th pick).

Waived by San Antonio, January 21, 1987; signed by Cleveland as a free agent, January 24, 1987.
Traded by Cleveland with Kevin Johnson, Mark West, 1988 1st and 2nd round draft choices and a 1989 2nd round draft choice to Phoenix for Larry Nance, Mike Sanders and a 1988 1st round draft choice, February 25, 1988.

—COLLEGIATE RECORD—

Year	G.	Min.	FGA	FGM	Pct.	FTA	FTM	Pct.	Reb.	Pts.	Avg.
81-82	28	602	103	43	.417	78	56	.718	172	142	5.1
82-83	33	1060	263	124	.471	132	102	.773	262	350	10.6
83-84	30	1070	316	166	.525	125	93	.744	223	425	14.2
84-85	29	1004	354	189	.534	102	83	.814	236	461	15.8
Totals	120	3736	1036	522	.504	437	334	.764	893	1378	11.5

NBA REGULAR SEASON RECORD

Sea.—Team	G.	Min.	FGA	FGM	Pct.	FTA	FTM	Pct.	—Rebounds— Off.	Def.	Tot.	Ast.	PF	Dq.	Stl.	Blk.	Pts.	Avg.
85-86—San Antonio	16	174	64	27	.422	14	10	.714	11	14	25	11	21	0	11	2	64	4.0
86-87—S.A.-Clev.	63	1170	381	156	.409	124	91	.734	88	127	215	97	129	0	55	5	404	6.4
87-88—Clev.-Phoe.	84	1739	525	257	.490	138	110	.797	127	223	350	115	181	2	72	18	625	7.4
Totals	163	3083	970	440	.453	276	211	.764	226	364	590	223	331	2	138	25	1093	6.7

Three-Point Field Goals: 1985-86, 0-for-1. 1986-87, 1-for-4 (.250). 1987-88, 1-for-6 (.167). Totals, 2-for-11 (.182).

NBA PLAYOFF RECORD

Sea.—Team	G.	Min.	FGA	FGM	Pct.	FTA	FTM	Pct.	—Rebounds— Off.	Def.	Tot.	Ast.	PF	Dq.	Stl.	Blk.	Pts.	Avg.
85-86—San Antonio	1	14	4	0	.000	0	0	.000	0	1	1	1	0	0	0	0	0	0.0

MICHAEL COOPER

DAVID JOHN CORZINE
(Dave)

Born April 25, 1956 at Arlington Heights, Ill. Height 6:11. Weight 260.
High School—Arlington Heights, Ill., Hersey.
College—DePaul University, Chicago, Ill.
Drafted by Washington on first round, 1978 (18th pick).

Traded by Washington to San Antonio for 1981 and 1982 2nd round draft choices, September 26, 1980.
Traded by San Antonio with Mark Olberding and cash to Chicago for Artis Gilmore, July 22, 1982.

—COLLEGIATE RECORD—

Year	G.	Min.	FGA	FGM	Pct.	FTA	FTM	Pct.	Reb.	Pts.	Avg.
74-75	25	....	309	134	.434	56	36	.643	216	304	12.2
75-76	29	....	386	181	.469	124	88	.710	256	450	15.5
76-77	27	....	448	219	.489	97	74	.763	339	512	19.0
77-78	30	....	462	255	.552	152	120	.789	340	630	21.0
Totals	111	....	1605	789	.492	429	318	.741	1151	1896	17.1

NBA REGULAR SEASON RECORD

Sea.—Team	G.	Min.	FGA	FGM	Pct.	FTA	FTM	Pct.	Off.	Def.	Tot.	Ast.	PF	Dq.	Stl.	Blk.	Pts.	Avg.
78-79—Washington	59	532	118	63	.534	63	49	.778	52	95	147	49	67	0	10	14	175	3.0
79-80—Washington	78	826	216	90	.417	68	45	.662	104	166	270	63	120	1	9	31	225	2.9
80-81—San Antonio	82	1960	747	366	.490	175	125	.714	228	408	636	117	212	0	42	99	857	10.5
81-82—San Antonio	82	2189	648	336	.519	213	159	.746	211	418	629	130	235	3	33	126	832	10.1
82-83—Chicago	82	2496	920	457	.497	322	232	.720	243	474	717	154	242	4	47	109	1146	14.0
83-84—Chicago	82	2674	824	385	.467	275	231	.840	169	406	575	202	227	3	58	120	1004	12.2
84-85—Chicago	82	2062	568	276	.486	200	149	.745	130	292	422	140	189	2	32	64	701	8.5
85-86—Chicago	67	1709	519	255	.491	171	127	.743	132	301	433	150	133	0	28	53	640	9.6
86-87—Chicago	82	2287	619	294	.475	129	95	.736	199	341	540	209	202	1	38	87	683	8.3
87-88—Chicago	80	2328	715	344	.481	153	115	.752	170	357	527	154	149	1	36	95	804	10.1
Totals	776	19063	5894	2866	.486	1769	1327	.750	1638	3258	4896	1368	1776	15	333	798	7067	9.1

Three-Point Field Goals: 1980-81, 0-for-3. 1981-82, 1-for-4 (.250). 1982-83, 0-for-2. 1983-84, 3-for-9 (.333). 1984-85, 0-for-1. 1985-86, 3-for-12 (.250). 1986-87, 0-for-5. 1987-88, 1-for-9 (.111). Totals, 8-for-45 (.178).

NBA PLAYOFF RECORD

Sea.—Team	G.	Min.	FGA	FGM	Pct.	FTA	FTM	Pct.	Off.	Def.	Tot.	Ast.	PF	Dq.	Stl.	Blk.	Pts.	Avg.
78-79—Washington	12	63	15	4	.267	0	0	.000	12	13	25	5	9	0	2	0	8	0.7
79-80—Washington	2	9	5	4	.800	2	2	1.000	2	1	3	0	2	0	0	0	10	5.0
80-81—San Antonio	7	161	55	27	.491	13	9	.692	12	36	48	16	15	0	4	8	63	9.0
81-82—San Antonio	9	258	106	49	.462	34	24	.706	38	47	85	17	30	0	6	9	122	13.6
84-85—Chicago	4	77	21	14	.667	6	5	.833	9	13	22	3	14	0	2	1	33	8.3
85-86—Chicago	3	103	29	16	.552	4	4	1.000	6	21	27	6	12	0	1	2	36	12.0
86-87—Chicago	3	122	22	10	.455	9	7	.778	7	14	21	7	6	0	1	3	27	9.0
87-88—Chicago	10	308	76	27	.355	13	7	.538	15	42	57	8	21	0	3	8	61	6.1
Totals	50	1101	329	151	.459	81	58	.716	101	187	288	62	109	0	19	31	360	7.2

WINSTON ARNEL CRITE

Born June 20, 1965 at Bakersfield, Calif. Height 6:07. Weight 233.
High School—Bakersfield, Calif., South.
College—Texas A&M University, College Station, Tex.
Drafted by Phoenix on third round, 1987 (53rd pick).

—COLLEGIATE RECORD—

Year	G.	Min.	FGA	FGM	Pct.	FTA	FTM	Pct.	Reb.	Pts.	Avg.
83-84	30	884	198	105	.530	83	56	.675	184	266	8.9
84-85	30	1004	247	140	.567	128	83	.648	245	363	12.1
85-86	32	1046	286	166	.580	134	94	.701	256	426	13.3
86-87	31	1115	362	203	.561	173	115	.665	228	521	16.8
Totals	123	4049	1093	614	.562	518	348	.672	913	1576	12.8

Three-Point Field Goals: 1986-87, 0-for-1.

NBA REGULAR SEASON RECORD

Sea.—Team	G.	Min.	FGA	FGM	Pct.	FTA	FTM	Pct.	Off.	Def.	Tot.	Ast.	PF	Dq.	Stl.	Blk.	Pts.	Avg.
87-88—Phoenix	29	258	68	34	.500	25	19	.760	27	37	64	15	42	0	5	8	87	3.0

PATRICK MICHAEL CUMMINGS
(Pat)

Born July 11, 1956 at Johnstown, Pa. Height 6:09. Weight 235.

High School—Johnstown, Pa.

College—University of Cincinnati, Cincinnati, O.

Drafted by Milwaukee on third round as junior eligible, 1978 (59th pick).

Traded by Milwaukee to Dallas for a 1982 2nd round draft choice, June 28, 1982.
Signed by New York as a Veteran Free Agent, June 27, 1984; Dallas agreed not to exercise its right of first refusal in exchange for a 1985 3rd round draft choice and a 1986 2nd round draft choice.

—COLLEGIATE RECORD—

Year	G.	Min.	FGA	FGM	Pct.	FTA	FTM	Pct.	Reb.	Pts.	Avg.
74-75	18	458	190	111	.584	39	29	.744	131	251	13.9
75-76	31	810	291	163	.560	57	37	.649	210	363	11.7
76-77					Did Not Play—Broken Foot						
77-78	27	854	330	212	.642	87	63	.724	206	487	18.0
78-79	27	1013	490	270	.551	147	121	.823	304	661	24.5
Totals	103	3135	1301	756	.581	330	250	.758	851	1762	17.1

NBA REGULAR SEASON RECORD

Sea.—Team	G.	Min.	FGA	FGM	Pct.	FTA	FTM	Pct.	Off.	Def.	Tot.	Ast.	PF	Dq.	Stl.	Blk.	Pts.	Avg.
79-80—Milwaukee	71	900	370	187	.505	123	94	.764	81	157	238	53	141	0	22	17	468	6.6
80-81—Milwaukee	74	1084	460	248	.539	140	99	.707	97	195	292	62	192	4	31	19	595	8.0
81-82—Milwaukee	78	1132	430	219	.509	91	67	.736	61	184	245	99	227	6	22	8	505	6.5
82-83—Dallas	81	2317	878	433	.493	196	148	.755	225	443	668	144	296	9	57	35	1014	12.5
83-84—Dallas	80	2492	915	452	.494	190	141	.742	151	507	658	158	282	2	64	23	1045	13.1
84-85—New York	63	2069	797	410	.514	227	177	.780	139	379	518	109	247	6	50	17	997	15.8
85-86—New York	31	1007	408	195	.478	139	97	.698	92	188	280	47	136	7	27	12	487	15.7
86-87—New York	49	1056	382	172	.450	110	79	.718	123	189	312	38	145	2	26	7	423	8.6
87-88—New York	62	946	307	140	.456	80	59	.738	82	153	235	37	143	0	20	10	339	5.5
Totals	589	13003	4947	2456	.496	1296	961	.742	1051	2395	3446	747	1809	36	319	148	5873	10.0

Three-Point Field Goals: 1980-81, 0-for-2. 1981-82, 0-for-2. 1982-83, 0-for-1. 1983-84, 0-for-2. 1984-85, 0-for-4 1985-86, 0-for-2. 1987-88, 0-for-1. Totals, 0-for-14.

NBA PLAYOFF RECORD

Sea.—Team	G.	Min.	FGA	FGM	Pct.	FTA	FTM	Pct.	Off.	Def.	Tot.	Ast.	PF	Dq.	Stl.	Blk.	Pts.	Avg.
79-80—Milwaukee	6	57	17	11	.647	6	5	.833	4	12	16	2	9	0	1	0	27	4.5
80-81—Milwaukee	5	25	11	3	.273	4	3	.750	3	3	6	0	2	0	1	0	9	1.8
81-82—Milwaukee	6	44	11	4	.364	2	1	.500	3	8	11	2	7	0	0	2	9	1.5
83-84—Dallas	10	300	115	47	.409	15	14	.933	26	46	72	15	30	0	4	2	108	10.8
87-88—New York	3	28	5	2	.400	4	3	.750	2	5	7	3	11	0	0	0	7	2.3
Totals	30	454	159	67	.421	31	26	.839	38	74	112	22	59	0	6	4	160	5.3

ROBERT TERRELL CUMMINGS
(Terry)

Born March 15, 1961 at Chicago, Ill. Height 6:09. Weight 235.

High School—Chicago, Ill., Carver.

College—DePaul University, Chicago, Ill.

Drafted by San Diego on first round as an undergraduate, 1982 (2nd pick).

Traded by Los Angeles Clippers with Craig Hodges and Ricky Pierce to Milwaukee for Marques Johnson, Harvey Catchings, Junior Bridgeman and cash, September 29, 1984.

—COLLEGIATE RECORD—

Year	G.	Min.	FGA	FGM	Pct.	FTA	FTM	Pct.	Reb.	Pts.	Avg.
79-80	28	....	303	154	.508	107	89	.832	263	397	14.2
80-81	29	994	303	151	.498	100	75	.750	260	377	13.0
81-82	28	1031	430	244	.567	180	136	.756	334	624	22.3
Totals	85	2025	1036	549	.530	387	300	.775	857	1398	16.4

NBA REGULAR SEASON RECORD

Sea.—Team	G.	Min.	FGA	FGM	Pct.	FTA	FTM	Pct.	Off.	Def.	Tot.	Ast.	PF	Dq.	Stl.	Blk.	Pts.	Avg.
82-83—San Diego	70	2531	1309	684	.523	412	292	.709	303	441	744	177	294	10	129	62	1660	23.7
83-84—San Diego	81	2907	1491	737	.494	528	380	.720	323	454	777	139	298	6	92	57	1854	22.9
84-85—Milwaukee	79	2722	1532	759	.495	463	343	.741	244	472	716	228	264	4	117	67	1861	23.6

Sea.—Team	G.	Min.	FGA	FGM	Pct.	FTA	FTM	Pct.	Off.	Def.	Tot.	Ast.	PF	Dq.	Stl.	Blk.	Pts.	Avg.
85-86—Milwaukee	82	2669	1438	681	.474	404	265	.656	222	472	694	193	283	4	121	51	1627	19.8
86-87—Milwaukee	82	2770	1426	729	.511	376	249	.662	214	486	700	229	296	3	129	81	1707	20.8
87-88—Milwaukee	76	2629	1392	675	.485	406	270	.665	184	369	553	181	274	6	78	46	1621	21.3
Totals	470	16228	8588	4265	.497	2589	1799	.695	1490	2694	4184	1147	1709	33	666	364	10330	22.0

Three-Point Field Goals: 1982-83, 0-for-1. 1983-84, 0-for-3. 1984-85, 0-for-1. 1985-86, 0-for-2. 1986-87, 0-for-3. 1987-88, 1-for-3 (.333). Totals, 1-for-13 (.077).

NBA PLAYOFF RECORD

Sea.—Team	G.	Min.	FGA	FGM	Pct.	FTA	FTM	Pct.	Off.	Def.	Tot.	Ast.	PF	Dq.	Stl.	Blk.	Pts.	Avg.
84-85—Milwaukee	8	311	149	86	.577	58	48	.828	21	49	70	20	33	1	12	7	220	27.5
85-86—Milwaukee	14	510	253	130	.514	62	43	.694	33	105	138	42	52	0	20	16	303	21.6
86-87—Milwaukee	12	443	215	105	.488	83	57	.687	29	66	95	28	51	1	12	13	267	22.3
87-88—Milwaukee	5	193	89	50	.562	44	29	.659	12	27	39	13	16	0	9	3	129	25.8
Totals	39	1457	706	371	.525	247	177	.717	95	247	342	103	152	2	53	39	919	23.6

Three-Point Field Goals: 1984-85, 0-for-1.

NBA ALL-STAR GAME RECORD

Season—Team	Min.	FGA	FGM	Pct.	FTA	FTM	Pct.	Off.	Def.	Tot.	Ast.	PF	Dq.	Stl.	Blk.	Pts.
1985—Milwaukee....	16	17	7	.412	4	3	.750	4	3	7	0	1	0	0	1	17

Named to All-NBA Second Team, 1985. . . . NBA Rookie of the Year, 1983. . . . NBA All-Rookie Team, 1983. . . . THE SPORTING NEWS All-America First Team, 1982.

EARL CURETON

Born September 3, 1957 at Detroit, Mich.   Height 6:09.   Weight 215.

High School—Detroit, Mich., Finney.

Colleges—Robert Morris College, Coraopolis, Pa., and
University of Detroit, Detroit, Mich.
(Robert Morris, a junior college, became a four-year college between
the 1975-76 and 1976-77 school years.)

Drafted by Philadelphia on third round as junior eligible, 1979 (58th pick).

Signed by Detroit as a Veteran Free Agent, November 12, 1983; Philadelphia agreed not to exercise its right of first refusal in exchange for 1989 and 1990 2nd round draft choices.
Traded by Detroit with a 1987 2nd round draft choice to Chicago for Sidney Green, August 21, 1986.
Traded by Chicago to Los Angeles Clippers for a 1989 2nd or 3rd round draft choice, February 11, 1987.

—COLLEGIATE RECORD—
Robert Morris JC

Year	G.	Min.	FGA	FGM	Pct.	FTA	FTM	Pct.	Reb.	Pts.	Avg.
75-76	28	....	...	...	....	...	...	....	227	405	14.5

Robert Morris (Four-year college)

Year	G.	Min.	FGA	FGM	Pct.	FTA	FTM	Pct.	Reb.	Pts.	Avg.
76-77	26	....	418	196	.469	101	54	.535	274	446	17.2

Detroit

Year	G.	Min.	FGA	FGM	Pct.	FTA	FTM	Pct.	Reb.	Pts.	Avg.
77-78					Did Not Play—Transfer Student						
78-79	28	744	270	138	.511	75	51	.680	251	327	11.7
79-80	27	893	448	236	.527	109	66	.606	246	538	19.9
Totals	55	1637	718	374	.521	184	117	.636	497	865	15.7
College Totals	81	....	1136	570	.502	285	171	.600	771	1311	16.2

NBA REGULAR SEASON RECORD

Sea.—Team	G.	Min.	FGA	FGM	Pct.	FTA	FTM	Pct.	Off.	Def.	Tot.	Ast.	PF	Dq.	Stl.	Blk.	Pts.	Avg.
80-81—Philadelphia	52	528	205	93	.454	64	33	.516	51	104	155	25	68	0	20	23	219	4.2
81-82—Philadelphia	66	956	306	149	.487	94	51	.543	90	180	270	32	142	0	31	27	349	5.3
82-83—Philadelphia	73	987	258	108	.419	67	33	.493	84	185	269	43	144	1	37	24	249	3.4
83-84—Detroit	73	907	177	81	.458	59	31	.525	86	201	287	36	143	3	24	31	193	2.6
84-85—Detroit	81	1642	428	207	.484	144	82	.569	169	250	419	83	216	1	56	42	496	6.1
85-86—Detroit	80	2017	564	285	.505	211	117	.555	198	306	504	137	239	3	58	58	687	8.6
86-87—Chi.-L.A.C.	78	1973	510	243	.476	152	82	.539	212	240	452	122	188	2	33	56	568	7.3
87-88—L.A. Clippers	69	1128	310	133	.429	63	33	.524	97	174	271	63	135	1	32	36	299	4.3
Totals	572	10138	2758	1299	.471	854	462	.541	987	1640	2627	541	1275	11	291	297	3060	5.3

Three-Point Field Goals: 1980-81, 0-for-1. 1981-82, 0-for-2. 1983-84, 0-for-1. 1984-85, 0-for-3. 1985-86, 0-for-2. 1986-87, 0-for-2. 1987-88, 0-for-3. Totals, 0-for-14.

TERRY CUMMINGS

Sea.—Team	G.	Min.	FGA	FGM	Pct.	FTA	FTM	Pct.	Off.	Def.	Tot.	Ast.	PF	Dq.	Stl.	Blk.	Pts.	Avg.
80-81—Philadelphia	9	36	18	6	.333	2	0	.000	1	8	9	2	3	0	1	2	12	1.3
81-82—Philadelphia	12	75	41	13	.317	9	6	.667	12	14	26	2	12	0	1	1	32	2.7
82-83—Philadelphia	5	25	4	1	.250	0	0	.000	0	5	5	1	5	0	2	0	2	0.4
83-84—Detroit	5	93	31	15	.484	6	2	.333	14	19	33	2	9	0	2	1	32	6.4
84-85—Detroit	9	133	34	16	.471	9	5	.556	10	31	41	4	20	0	9	2	37	4.1
85-86—Detroit	4	126	31	17	.548	8	2	.250	12	18	30	9	14	0	3	0	36	9.0
Totals	44	488	159	68	.428	34	15	.441	49	95	144	20	63	0	18	6	151	3.4

Three-Point Field Goals: 1981-82, 0-for-1. 1984-85, 0-for-1. 1985-86, 0-for-1. Totals, 0-for-3.

Member of NBA championship team, 1983.

WARDELL STEPHEN CURRY
(Dell)

Born June 25, 1964 at Harrisonburg, Va.   Height 6:05.   Weight 195.

High School—Fort Defiance, Va.

College—Virginia Polytechnic Institute and State University, Blacksburg, Va.

Drafted by Utah on first round, 1986 (15th pick).

Traded by Utah with Kent Benson and future 2nd round draft considerations to Cleveland for Darryl Dawkins, Mel Turpin and future 2nd round draft considerations, October 8, 1987.

Selected from Cleveland by Charlotte in NBA expansion draft, June 23, 1988.

—COLLEGIATE RECORD—

Year	G.	Min.	FGA	FGM	Pct.	FTA	FTM	Pct.	Reb.	Pts.	Avg.
82-83	32	1024	417	198	.475	80	68	.850	95	464	14.5
83-84	35	1166	561	293	.522	116	88	.759	143	674	19.3
84-85	29	968	467	225	.482	99	75	.758	169	529	18.2
85-86	30	1117	577	305	.529	142	112	.789	203	722	24.1
Totals	126	4275	2022	1021	.505	437	343	.785	610	2389	19.0

Three-Point Field Goals: 1984-85, 4-for-7 (.571).

NBA REGULAR SEASON RECORD

Sea.—Team	G.	Min.	FGA	FGM	Pct.	FTA	FTM	Pct.	Off.	Def.	Tot.	Ast.	PF	Dq.	Stl.	Blk.	Pts.	Avg.
86-87—Utah	67	636	326	139	.426	38	30	.789	30	48	78	58	86	0	27	4	325	4.9
87-88—Cleveland	79	1499	742	340	.458	101	79	.782	43	123	166	149	128	0	94	22	787	10.0
Totals	146	2135	1068	479	.449	139	109	.784	73	171	244	207	214	0	121	26	1112	7.6

Three-Point Field Goals: 1986-87, 17-for-60 (.283). 1987-88, 28-for-81 (.346). Totals, 45-for-141 (.319).

NBA PLAYOFF RECORD

Sea.—Team	G.	Min.	FGA	FGM	Pct.	FTA	FTM	Pct.	Off.	Def.	Tot.	Ast.	PF	Dq.	Stl.	Blk.	Pts.	Avg.
86-87—Utah	2	4	3	0	.000	1	0	.000	0	0	0	0	1	0	0	0	0	0.0
87-88—Cleveland	2	17	4	1	.250	0	0	.000	1	0	1	2	1	0	0	1	2	1.0
Totals	4	21	7	1	.143	1	0	.000	1	0	1	2	2	0	0	1	2	0.5

Three-Point Field Goals: 1986-87, 0-for-1. 1987-88, 0-for-1. Totals, 0-for-2.

Named to THE SPORTING NEWS All-America Second Team, 1986.

QUINTIN DAILEY

Born January 22, 1961 at Baltimore, Md.   Height 6:03.   Weight 180.

High School—Baltimore, Md., Cardinal Gibbons.

College—University of San Francisco, San Francisco, Calif.

Drafted by Chicago on first round as an undergraduate, 1982 (7th pick).

Signed by Los Angeles Clippers as a free agent, December 29, 1986; Chicago waived its right of first refusal. Played in Continental Basketball Association with Mississippi Jets, 1986-87.

—COLLEGIATE RECORD—

Year	G.	Min.	FGA	FGM	Pct.	FTA	FTM	Pct.	Reb.	Pts.	Avg.
79-80	29	....	292	154	.527	134	85	.634	107	393	13.6
80-81	31	....	467	267	.572	206	159	.772	170	693	22.4
81-82	30	1138	524	286	.546	232	183	.789	156	755	25.2
Totals	90	....	1283	707	.551	572	427	.747	433	1841	20.5

CBA REGULAR SEASON RECORD

Sea.—Team			—2-Point—			—3-Point—								
	G.	Min.	FGM	FGA	Pct.	FGM	FGA	Pct.	FTM	FTA	Pct.	Reb.	Ast.	Pts.	Avg.
86-87—Mississippi	8	220	54	99	.545	0	2	.000	35	47	.745	17	11	143	17.9

NBA REGULAR SEASON RECORD

Sea.—Team	G.	Min.	FGA	FGM	Pct.	FTA	FTM	Pct.	Off.	Def.	Tot.	Ast.	PF	Dq.	Stl.	Blk.	Pts.	Avg.
82-83—Chicago	76	2081	1008	470	.466	282	206	.730	87	173	260	280	248	7	72	10	1151	15.1
83-84—Chicago	82	2449	1229	583	.474	396	321	.811	61	174	235	254	218	4	109	11	1491	18.2
84-85—Chicago	79	2101	1111	525	.473	251	205	.817	57	151	208	191	192	0	71	5	1262	16.0
85-86—Chicago	35	723	470	203	.432	198	163	.823	20	48	68	67	86	0	22	5	569	16.3
86-87—L.A. Clippers	49	924	491	200	.407	155	119	.768	34	49	83	79	113	4	43	8	520	10.6
87-88—L.A. Clippers	67	1282	755	328	.434	313	243	.776	62	92	154	109	128	1	69	4	901	13.4
Totals	388	9560	5064	2309	.456	1595	1257	.788	321	687	1008	980	985	16	386	43	5894	15.2

Three-Point Field Goals: 1982-83, 5-for-25 (.200). 1983-84, 4-for-32 (.125). 1984-85, 7-for-30 (.233). 1985-86, 0-for-8. 1986-87, 1-for-10 (.100). 1987-88, 2-for-12 (.167). Totals, 19-for-117 (.162).

NBA PLAYOFF RECORD

Sea.—Team	G.	Min.	FGA	FGM	Pct.	FTA	FTM	Pct.	Off.	Def.	Tot.	Ast.	PF	Dq.	Stl.	Blk.	Pts.	Avg.
84-85—Chicago	4	129	62	26	.419	11	8	.727	5	8	13	11	9	0	4	0	61	15.3

Three-Point Field Goals: 1984-85, 1-for-7 (.143).

Named to NBA All-Rookie Team, 1983. . . . THE SPORTING NEWS All-America First Team, 1982.

ADRIAN DELANO DANTLEY

Born February 28, 1956 at Washington, D. C. Height 6:05. Weight 210.

High School—Hyattsville, Md., DeMatha.

College—University of Notre Dame, Ind.

Drafted by Buffalo on first round as hardship case, 1976 (6th pick).

Traded by Buffalo with Mike Bantom to Indiana for Billy Knight, September 1, 1977.

Traded by Indiana with Dave Robisch to Los Angeles for James Edwards, Earl Tatum and cash, December 13, 1977.

Traded by Los Angeles to Utah for Spencer Haywood, September 13, 1979.

Traded by Utah with 1987 and 1990 2nd round draft choices to Detroit for Kelly Tripucka and Kent Benson, August 21, 1986.

—COLLEGIATE RECORD—

Year	G.	Min.	FGA	FGM	Pct.	FTA	FTM	Pct.	Reb.	Pts.	Avg.
73-74	28	795	339	189	.558	161	133	.826	255	511	18.3
74-75	29	1091	581	315	.542	314	253	.806	296	883	30.4
75-76	29	1056	510	300	.588	294	229	.779	292	829	28.6
Totals	86	2942	1430	804	.562	769	615	.800	843	2223	25.8

NBA REGULAR SEASON RECORD

Sea.—Team	G.	Min.	FGA	FGM	Pct.	FTA	FTM	Pct.	Off.	Def.	Tot.	Ast.	PF	Dq.	Stl.	Blk.	Pts.	Avg.
76-77—Buffalo	77	2816	1046	544	.520	582	476	.818	251	336	587	144	215	2	91	15	1564	20.3
77-78—Ind.-L. A.	79	2933	1128	578	.512	680	541	.796	265	355	620	253	233	2	118	24	1697	21.5
78-79—Los Angeles	60	1775	733	374	.510	342	292	.854	131	211	342	138	162	0	63	12	1040	17.3
79-80—Utah	68	2674	1267	730	.576	526	443	.842	183	333	516	191	211	2	96	14	1903	28.0
80-81—Utah	80	3417	1627	909	.559	784	632	.806	192	317	509	322	245	1	109	18	2452	30.7
81-82—Utah	81	3222	1586	904	.570	818	648	.792	231	283	514	324	252	1	95	14	2457	30.3
82-83—Utah	22	887	402	233	.580	248	210	.847	58	82	140	105	62	2	20	0	676	30.7
83-84—Utah	79	2984	1438	802	.558	946	813	.859	179	269	448	310	201	0	61	4	2418	30.6
84-85—Utah	55	1971	964	512	.531	545	438	.804	148	175	323	186	133	0	57	8	1462	26.6
85-86—Utah	76	2744	1453	818	.563	796	630	.791	178	217	395	264	206	2	64	4	2267	29.8
86-87—Detroit	81	2736	1126	601	.534	664	539	.812	104	228	332	162	193	1	63	7	1742	21.5
87-88—Detroit	69	2144	863	444	.514	572	492	.860	84	143	227	171	144	0	39	10	1380	20.0
Totals	827	30303	13633	7449	.546	7503	6154	.820	2004	2949	4953	2570	2257	13	876	130	21058	25.5

Three-Point Field Goals: 1979-80, 0-for-2. 1980-81, 2-for-7 (.286). 1981-82, 1-for-3 (.333). 1983-84, 1-for-4 (.250). 1985-86, 1-for-11 (.091). 1986-87, 1-for-6 (.167). 1987-88, 0-for-2. Totals, 6-for-35 (.171).

NBA PLAYOFF RECORD

Sea.—Team	G.	Min.	FGA	FGM	Pct.	FTA	FTM	Pct.	Off.	Def.	Tot.	Ast.	PF	Dq.	Stl.	Blk.	Pts.	Avg.
77-78—Los Angeles	3	104	35	20	.571	17	11	.647	9	16	25	11	9	0	5	3	51	17.0
78-79—Los Angeles	8	236	89	50	.562	52	41	.788	10	23	33	11	24	0	6	1	141	17.5
83-84—Utah	11	454	232	117	.504	139	120	.863	37	46	83	46	30	0	10	1	354	32.2
84-85—Utah	10	398	151	79	.523	122	95	.779	25	50	75	20	39	1	16	0	253	25.3
86-87—Detroit	15	500	206	111	.539	111	86	.775	29	39	68	35	36	0	13	0	308	20.5
87-88—Detroit	23	804	292	153	.524	178	140	.787	37	70	107	46	50	0	19	1	446	19.4
Totals	70	2496	1005	530	.527	619	493	.796	147	244	391	169	188	1	69	6	1553	22.?

Three-Point Field Goals: 1984-85, 0-for-1. 1987-88, 0-for-2. Totals, 0-for-3.

NBA ALL-STAR GAME RECORD

Season—Team	Min.	FGA	FGM	Pct.	FTA	FTM	Pct.	Off.	Def.	Tot.	Ast.	PF	Dq.	Stl.	
1980—Utah	30	15	8	.533	8	7	.875	4	1	5	2	1	0	2	

Season—Team	Min.	FGA	FGM	Pct.	FTA	FTM	Pct.	—Rebounds— Off.	Def.	Tot.	Ast.	PF	Dq.	Stl.	Blk.	Pts.
1981—Utah	21	9	3	.333	2	2	1.000	2	3	5	0	1	0	1	0	8
1982—Utah	21	8	6	.750	1	0	.000	1	1	2	0	2	0	0	0	12
1984—Utah	18	8	1	.125	0	0	.000	0	2	2	1	4	0	1	0	2
1985—Utah	23	6	2	.333	6	6	1.000	0	2	2	1	4	0	1	0	10
1986—Utah	17	8	3	.375	2	2	1.000	1	6	7	3	1	0	1	0	8
Totals	130	54	23	.426	19	17	.895	8	15	23	7	13	0	6	0	63

Named to All-NBA Second Team, 1981 and 1984. . . . NBA Rookie of the Year, 1977. . . . NBA All-Rookie Team, 1977. . . . Led NBA in scoring, 1981 and 1984. . . . NBA Comeback Player of the Year, 1984. . . . Shares NBA record for most free throws made in one game, 28, vs. Houston, January 4, 1984. . . . THE SPORTING NEWS All-America First Team, 1975 and 1976. . . . Member of U.S. Olympic team, 1976.

BRADLEY LEE DAUGHERTY
(Brad)

Born October 19, 1965 at Black Mountain, N.C.   Height 7:00.   Weight 245.

High School—Swannanoa, N.C., Charles D. Owen.

College—University of North Carolina, Chapel Hill, N.C.

Drafted by Cleveland on first round, 1986 (1st pick).

—COLLEGIATE RECORD—

Year	G.	Min.	FGA	FGM	Pct.	FTA	FTM	Pct.	Reb.	Pts.	Avg.
82-83	35	....	197	110	.558	101	67	.663	181	287	8.2
83-84	30	....	210	128	.610	87	59	.678	167	315	10.5
84-85	36	....	381	238	.625	198	147	.742	349	623	17.3
85-86	34	....	438	284	.648	174	119	.684	306	687	20.2
Totals	135	....	1226	760	.620	560	392	.700	1003	1912	14.2

Three-Point Field Goals: 1982-83, 0-for-1.

NBA REGULAR SEASON RECORD

Sea.—Team	G.	Min.	FGA	FGM	Pct.	FTA	FTM	Pct.	—Rebounds— Off.	Def.	Tot.	Ast.	PF	Dq.	Stl.	Blk.	Pts.	Avg.
86-87—Cleveland	80	2695	905	487	.538	401	279	.696	152	495	647	304	248	3	49	63	1253	15.7
87-88—Cleveland	79	2957	1081	551	.510	528	378	.716	151	514	665	333	235	2	48	56	1480	18.7
Totals	159	5652	1986	1038	.523	929	657	.707	303	1009	1312	637	483	5	97	119	2733	17.2

Three-Point Field Goals: 1987-88, 0-for-2.

NBA PLAYOFF RECORD

Sea.—Team	G.	Min.	FGA	FGM	Pct.	FTA	FTM	Pct.	—Rebounds— Off.	Def.	Tot.	Ast.	PF	Dq.	Stl.	Blk.	Pts.	Avg.
87-88—Cleveland	5	204	63	29	.460	31	21	.677	10	36	46	16	11	0	2	7	79	15.8

NBA ALL-STAR GAME RECORD

Season—Team	Min.	FGA	FGM	Pct.	FTA	FTM	Pct.	—Rebounds— Off.	Def.	Tot.	Ast.	PF	Dq.	Stl.	Blk.	Pts.
1988—Cleveland	15	7	6	.857	0	0	.000	0	3	3	1	4	0	0	1	12

Named to NBA All-Rookie Team, 1987. . . . THE SPORTING NEWS All-America Second Team, 1986. . . . Led NCAA Division I in field-goal percentage, 1986.

BRADLEY ERNEST DAVIS
(Brad)

Born December 17, 1955 at Monaca, Pa.   Height 6:03.   Weight 180.

High School—Monaca, Pa.

College—University of Maryland, College Park, Md.

Drafted by Los Angeles on first round as an undergraduate, 1977 (15th pick).

Waived by Los Angeles, October 27, 1978; signed by Indiana as a free agent, February 14, 1979.
Waived by Indiana, October 22, 1979; signed by Utah to two 10-day contracts that expired March 20, 1979.
Signed by Detroit as a free agent, July 9, 1980.
Waived by Detroit, October 8, 1980; signed by Dallas as a free agent, December 2, 1980.
Played in Western Basketball Association with Montana Sky, 1978-79.
Played in Continental Basketball Association with Anchorage Northern Knights, 1979-80 and 1980-81.

—COLLEGIATE RECORD—

Year	G.	Min.	FGA	FGM	Pct.	FTA	FTM	Pct.	Reb.	Pts.	Avg.
74-75	29	....	243	141	.580	100	82	.820	95	364	12.6
75-76	28	....	228	117	.513	116	92	.793	73	326	11.6
76-77	27	....	250	128	.512	102	80	.784	94	336	12.4
Totals	84	....	721	386	.535	318	254	.799	262	1026	12.2

Sea.—Team	G.	Min.	2-Point FGM	FGA	Pct.	3-Point FGM	FGA	Pct.	FTM	FTA	Pct.	Reb.	Ast.	Pts.	Avg.
78-79—Montana WBA	34	1395	194	362	.536	3	16	.188	105	133	.789	119	224	502	14.8
79-80—Anchorage WBA	40	955	206	361	.571	0	8	.000	120	139	.863	158	291	532	13.3
80-81—Anchorage CBA	5	165	18	43	.418	0	5	.000	12	16	.750	18	41	48	9.6

NBA REGULAR SEASON RECORD

Sea.—Team	G.	Min.	FGA	FGM	Pct.	FTA	FTM	Pct.	—Rebounds— Off.	Def.	Tot.	Ast.	PF	Dq.	Stl.	Blk.	Pts.	Avg.
77-78—Los Angeles	33	334	72	30	.417	29	22	.759	4	31	35	83	39	1	15	2	82	2.5
78-79—L.A.-Ind.	27	298	55	31	.564	23	16	.696	1	16	17	52	32	0	16	2	78	2.9
79-80—Ind.-Utah	18	268	63	35	.556	16	13	.813	4	13	17	50	28	0	13	1	83	4.6
80-81—Dallas	56	1686	410	230	.561	204	163	.799	29	122	151	385	156	2	52	11	626	11.2
81-82—Dallas	82	2614	771	397	.515	230	185	.804	35	191	226	509	218	5	73	6	993	12.1
82-83—Dallas	79	2323	628	359	.572	220	186	.845	34	164	198	565	176	2	80	11	915	11.6
83-84—Dallas	81	2665	651	345	.530	238	199	.836	41	146	187	561	218	4	94	13	896	11.1
84-85—Dallas	82	2539	614	310	.505	178	158	.888	39	154	193	581	219	1	91	10	825	10.1
85-86—Dallas	82	1971	502	267	.532	228	198	.868	26	120	146	467	174	2	57	15	764	9.3
86-87—Dallas	82	1582	436	199	.456	171	147	.860	27	87	114	373	159	0	63	10	577	7.0
87-88—Dallas	75	1480	415	208	.501	108	91	.843	18	84	102	303	149	0	51	18	537	7.2
Totals	697	17760	4617	2411	.522	1645	1378	.838	258	1128	1386	2929	1568	17	605	99	6376	9.1

Three-Point Field Goals: 1979-80, 0-for-1. 1980-81, 3-for-17 (.176). 1981-82, 14-for-49 (.286). 1982-83, 11-for-43 (.256). 1983-84, 7-for-38 (.184). 1984-85, 47-for-115 (.409). 1985-86, 32-for-89 (.360). 1986-87, 32-for-106 (.302). 1987-88, 30-for-74 (.405). Totals, 176-for-532 (.331).

NBA PLAYOFF RECORD

Sea.—Team	G.	Min.	FGA	FGM	Pct.	FTA	FTM	Pct.	—Rebounds— Off.	Def.	Tot.	Ast.	PF	Dq.	Stl.	Blk.	Pts.	Avg.
83-84—Dallas	10	304	73	33	.452	19	15	.789	6	13	19	50	18	0	6	0	81	8.1
84-85—Dallas	4	113	26	13	.500	13	12	.923	1	7	8	22	11	0	4	1	41	10.3
85-86—Dallas	10	163	44	24	.545	24	19	.792	1	18	19	23	22	0	3	0	77	7.7
86-87—Dallas	4	75	23	13	.565	9	7	.778	2	7	9	17	4	0	0	0	33	8.3
87-88—Dallas	17	295	70	42	.600	26	24	.923	1	19	20	55	34	0	3	5	109	6.4
Totals	45	950	236	125	.530	91	77	.846	11	64	75	167	89	0	16	6	341	7.6

Three-Point Field Goals: 1983-84, 0-for-2. 1984-85, 3-for-8 (.375). 1985-86, 10-for-15 (.667). 1986-87, 0-for-2. 1987-88, 1-for-5 (.200). Totals, 14-for-32 (.438).

Named CBA Co-Newcomer of the Year, 1980. . . . CBA All-Star Second Team, 1980. . . . Member of CBA championship team, 1980.

CHARLES EDWARD DAVIS
(Charlie)

Born October 5, 1958 at Nashville, Tenn.   Height 6:07.   Weight 215.

High School—Nashville, Tenn., McGavock.

College—Vanderbilt University, Nashville, Tenn.

Drafted by Washington on second round, 1981 (35th pick).

Waived by Washington, November 6, 1984; signed by Milwaukee as a free agent, November 11, 1984.
Traded by Milwaukee with a 1989 2nd round draft choice to San Antonio for Larry Krystkowiak, November 18, 1987.
Waived by San Antonio, December 28, 1987.

—COLLEGIATE RECORD—

Year	G.	Min.	FGA	FGM	Pct.	FTA	FTM	Pct.	Reb.	Pts.	Avg.
76-77	26	825	368	164	.446	94	71	.755	181	399	15.3
77-78	25	889	353	178	.504	87	63	.724	178	419	16.8
78-79	27	964	352	203	.577	130	96	.738	234	502	18.6
79-80	1	15	6	3	.500	0	0	.000	3	6	6.0
80-81	26	676	249	135	.542	99	79	.798	150	349	13.4
Totals	105	3369	1328	683	.514	410	309	.754	746	1675	16.0

(Granted extra year of eligibility because he was able to play only one game in 1979-80 because of tendinitis in left ankle.)

NBA REGULAR SEASON RECORD

Sea.—Team	G.	Min.	FGA	FGM	Pct.	FTA	FTM	Pct.	—Rebounds— Off.	Def.	Tot.	Ast.	PF	Dq.	Stl.	Blk.	Pts.	Avg.
81-82—Washington	54	575	184	88	.478	37	30	.811	54	79	133	31	89	0	10	13	206	3.8
82-83—Washington	74	1161	534	251	.470	89	56	.629	83	130	213	73	122	0	32	22	560	7.6
83-84—Washington	46	467	218	103	.472	39	24	.615	34	69	103	30	58	1	14	10	231	5.0
84-85—Wash.-Mil.	61	774	356	153	.430	62	51	.823	59	94	153	51	113	1	22	5	358	5.9
85-86—Milwaukee	57	873	397	188	.474	75	61	.813	60	110	170	55	113	1	26	7	440	7.7
87-88—Mil.-S.A.	21	226	115	48	.417	10	7	.700	16	25	41	20	29	0	2	4	104	5.0
Totals	313	4076	1804	831	.461	314	229	.729	306	507	813	260	524	3	106	61	1899	6.1

Three-Point Field Goals: 1981-82, 0-for-2. 1982-83, 2-for-10 (.200). 1983-84, 1-for-9 (.111). 1984-85, 1-for-10 (.100). 1985-86, 3-for-24 (.125). 1987-88, 1-for-17 (.059). Totals, 8-for-72 (.111).

NBA PLAYOFF RECORD

Sea.—Team	G.	Min.	FGA	FGM	Pct.	FTA	FTM	Pct.	Off.	Def.	Tot.	Ast.	PF	Dq.	Stl.	Blk.	Pts.	Avg.
81-82—Washington	6	52	17	7	.412	2	2	1.000	1	4	5	3	6	0	1	1	16	2.7
83-84—Washington	3	17	12	7	.583	0	0	.000	1	2	3	0	0	0	0	0	14	4.7
84-85—Milwaukee	5	51	20	8	.400	4	3	.750	6	4	10	4	2	0	0	0	19	3.8
85-86—Milwaukee	12	145	58	21	.362	20	18	.900	9	16	25	6	28	1	4	0	60	5.0
Totals	26	265	107	43	.402	26	23	.885	17	26	43	13	36	1	5	1	109	4.2

Three-Point Field Goals: 1981-82, 0-for-1. 1984-85, 0-for-2. 1985-86, 0-for-1. Totals, 0-for-4.

WALTER PAUL DAVIS

Born September 9, 1954 at Pineville, N. C.   Height 6:06.   Weight 200.

High School—Pineville, N. C., South Mecklenberg.

Prep School—Hockessin, Del., Sanford.

College—University of North Carolina, Chapel Hill, N. C.

Drafted by Phoenix on first round, 1977 (5th pick).

Signed by Denver as an unrestricted free agent, July 6, 1988.

—COLLEGIATE RECORD—

Year	G.	Min.	FGA	FGM	Pct.	FTA	FTM	Pct.	Reb.	Pts.	Avg.
73-74	27	....	322	161	.500	82	65	.793	126	387	14.3
74-75	31	....	396	200	.505	130	98	.754	195	498	16.1
75-76	29	....	351	190	.541	130	101	.777	166	481	16.6
76-77	32	....	351	203	.578	117	91	.778	183	497	15.5
Totals	119	....	1420	754	.531	459	355	.773	670	1863	15.7

NBA REGULAR SEASON RECORD

Sea.—Team	G.	Min.	FGA	FGM	Pct.	FTA	FTM	Pct.	Off.	Def.	Tot.	Ast.	PF	Dq.	Stl.	Blk.	Pts.	Avg.
77-78—Phoenix	81	2590	1494	786	.526	466	387	.830	158	326	484	273	242	2	113	20	1959	24.2
78-79—Phoenix	79	2437	1362	764	.561	409	340	.831	111	262	373	339	250	5	147	26	1868	23.6
79-80—Phoenix	75	2309	1166	657	.563	365	299	.819	75	197	272	337	202	2	114	19	1613	21.5
80-81—Phoenix	78	2182	1101	593	.539	250	209	.836	63	137	200	302	192	3	97	12	1402	18.0
81-82—Phoenix	55	1182	669	350	.523	111	91	.820	21	82	103	162	104	1	46	3	794	14.4
82-83—Phoenix	80	2491	1289	665	.516	225	184	.818	63	134	197	397	186	2	117	12	1521	19.0
83-84—Phoenix	78	2546	1274	652	.512	270	233	.863	38	164	202	429	202	0	107	12	1557	20.0
84-85—Phoenix	23	570	309	139	.450	73	64	.877	6	29	35	98	42	0	18	0	345	15.0
85-86—Phoenix	70	2239	1287	624	.485	305	257	.843	54	149	203	361	153	1	99	3	1523	21.8
86-87—Phoenix	79	2646	1515	779	.514	334	288	.862	90	154	244	364	184	1	96	5	1867	23.6
87-88—Phoenix	68	1951	1031	488	.473	231	205	.887	32	127	159	278	131	0	86	3	1217	17.9
Totals	766	23143	12497	6497	.520	3039	2557	.841	711	1761	2472	3340	1888	17	1040	115	15666	20.5

Three-Point Field Goals: 1979-80, 0-for-4. 1980-81, 7-for-17 (.412). 1981-82, 3-for-16 (.188). 1982-83, 7-for-23 (.304). 1983-84, 20-for-87 (.230). 1984-85, 3-for-10 (.300). 1985-86, 18-for-76 (.237). 1986-87, 21-for-81 (.259). 1987-88, 36-for-96 (.375). Totals, 115-for-410 (.280).

NBA PLAYOFF RECORD

Sea.—Team	G.	Min.	FGA	FGM	Pct.	FTA	FTM	Pct.	Off.	Def.	Tot.	Ast.	PF	Dq.	Stl.	Blk.	Pts.	Avg.
77-78—Phoenix	2	66	40	19	.475	16	12	.750	4	13	17	8	8	0	3	0	50	25.0
78-79—Phoenix	15	490	244	127	.520	96	78	.813	24	45	69	79	41	0	26	5	332	22.1
79-80—Phoenix	8	245	137	69	.504	38	28	.737	9	14	23	35	20	0	4	1	166	20.8
80-81—Phoenix	7	199	106	51	.481	17	10	.588	7	12	19	22	17	0	7	1	112	16.0
81-82—Phoenix	7	173	116	52	.448	24	22	.917	5	17	22	30	19	0	5	1	127	18.1
82-83—Phoenix	3	113	69	30	.435	21	17	.810	5	10	15	13	6	0	6	5	78	26.0
83-84—Phoenix	17	623	327	175	.535	78	70	.897	15	31	46	109	55	0	29	3	423	24.9
Totals	59	1909	1039	523	.503	290	237	.817	69	142	211	296	166	0	80	16	1288	21.8

Three-Point Field Goals: 1979-80, 0-for-3. 1980-81, 0-for-1. 1981-82, 1-for-3 (.333). 1982-83, 1-for-2 (.500). 1983-84, 3-for-11 (.273). Totals, 5-for-20 (.250).

NBA ALL-STAR GAME RECORD

Season—Team	Min.	FGA	FGM	Pct.	FTA	FTM	Pct.	Off.	Def.	Tot.	Ast.	PF	Dq.	Stl.	Blk.	Pts.
1978—Phoenix.........	15	6	3	.500	4	4	1.000	0	1	1	6	1	0	1	0	10
1979—Phoenix.........	19	9	4	.444	0	0	.000	1	3	4	4	0	0	1	0	8
1980—Phoenix.........	23	10	5	.500	2	2	1.000	2	2	4	2	2	0	4	0	12
1981—Phoenix.........	22	9	5	.556	2	2	1.000	1	6	7	1	2	0	0	0	12
1984—Phoenix.........	15	9	5	.556	0	0	.000	0	2	2	1	0	0	1	0	10
1987—Phoenix.........	15	12	3	.250	0	0	.000	2	0	2	1	0	0	0	0	7
Totals	109	55	25	.455	8	8	1.000	6	14	20	15	5	0	7	0	59

Three-Point Field Goals: 1987, 1-for-1 (1.000).

Named to All-NBA Second Team, 1978 and 1979. . . . NBA Rookie of the Year, 1978. . . . NBA All-Rookie Team, 1978. . . . Member of U. S. Olympic team, 1976.

DARRYL DAWKINS

Born January 11, 1957 at Orlando, Fla.   Height 6:11.   Weight 270.

High School—Orlando, Fla., Maynard Evans.

Did not attend college.

Drafted by Philadelphia on first round as hardship case, 1975 (5th pick).

Traded by Philadelphia to New Jersey for a 1983 1st round draft choice and cash, August 27, 1982.
Traded by New Jersey with James Bailey to Cleveland for Keith Lee and John Bagley, October 8, 1987.
Traded by Cleveland with Mel Turpin and future 2nd round draft considerations to Utah for Kent Benson, Dell Curry and future 2nd round draft considerations, October 8, 1987.
Traded by Utah to Detroit for 1988 and 1990 2nd round draft choices and cash, November 26, 1987.

NBA REGULAR SEASON RECORD

								—Rebounds—								
Sea.—Team	G.	Min.	FGA	FGM	Pct.	FTA	FTM	Pct.	Off.	Def.	Tot.	Ast.	PF	Dq.	Stl.	Blk.	Pts.	Avg.
75-76—Philadelphia	37	165	82	41	.500	24	8	.333	15	34	49	3	40	1	2	9	90	2.4
76-77—Philadelphia	59	684	215	135	.628	79	40	.506	59	171	230	24	129	1	12	49	310	5.3
77-78—Philadelphia	70	1722	577	332	.575	220	156	.709	117	438	555	85	268	5	34	125	820	11.7
78-79—Philadelphia	78	2035	831	430	.517	235	158	.672	123	508	631	128	295	5	32	143	1018	13.1
79-80—Philadelphia	80	2541	946	494	.522	291	190	.653	197	496	693	149	328	8	49	142	1178	14.7
80-81—Philadelphia	76	2088	697	423	.607	304	219	.720	106	439	545	109	316	9	38	112	1065	14.0
81-82—Philadelphia	48	1124	367	207	.564	164	114	.695	68	237	305	55	193	5	19	55	528	11.0
82-83—New Jersey	81	2093	669	401	.599	257	166	.646	127	293	420	114	379	23	67	152	968	12.0
83-84—New Jersey	81	2417	855	507	.593	464	341	.735	159	382	541	123	386	22	60	136	1357	16.8
84-85—New Jersey	39	972	339	192	.566	201	143	.711	55	126	181	45	171	11	14	35	527	13.5
85-86—New Jersey	51	1207	441	284	.644	297	210	.707	85	166	251	77	227	10	16	59	778	15.3
86-87—New Jersey	6	106	32	20	.625	24	17	.708	9	10	19	2	25	0	2	3	57	9.5
87-88—Utah-Det.	6	33	9	2	.222	15	6	.400	2	3	5	2	14	0	0	2	10	1.7
Totals	712	17187	6060	3468	.572	2575	1768	.687	1122	3303	4425	916	2771	100	345	1022	8706	12.2

Three-Point Field Goals: 1979-80, 0-for-6. 1981-82, 0-for-2. 1983-84, 2-for-5 (.400). 1984-85, 0-for-1. 1985-86, 0-for-1. Totals, 2-for-15 (.133).

NBA PLAYOFF RECORD

								—Rebounds—								
Sea.—Team	G.	Min.	FGA	FGM	Pct.	FTA	FTM	Pct.	Off.	Def.	Tot.	Ast.	PF	Dq.	Stl.	Blk.	Pts.	Avg.
76-77—Philadelphia	18	331	95	50	.526	47	31	.660	9	89	98	17	46	1	8	18	131	7.3
77-78—Philadelphia	10	180	53	27	.509	17	9	.529	6	51	57	10	34	1	3	15	63	6.3
78-79—Philadelphia	9	255	106	56	.528	47	32	.681	21	61	82	12	42	1	2	16	144	16.0
79-80—Philadelphia	18	607	238	126	.529	93	60	.645	44	93	137	33	75	2	13	42	312	17.3
80-81—Philadelphia	16	421	153	86	.562	68	49	.721	28	70	98	14	71	2	3	16	221	13.8
81-82—Philadelphia	21	460	178	99	.556	50	33	.660	23	75	98	11	94	4	7	35	231	11.0
82-83—New Jersey	2	59	22	17	.773	2	2	1.000	2	8	10	2	7	0	4	5	36	18.0
83-84—New Jersey	11	340	118	66	.559	83	70	.843	22	46	68	13	52	4	5	10	202	18.4
84-85—New Jersey	3	64	23	11	.478	4	3	.750	4	10	14	4	13	1	2	6	25	8.3
85-86—New Jersey	1	17	6	4	.667	3	2	.667	1	2	3	3	4	0	0	2	10	10.0
Totals	109	2734	992	542	.546	414	291	.703	160	505	665	119	438	16	47	165	1375	12.6

Three-Point Field Goals: 1979-80, 0-for-3. 1982-83, 0-for-1. 1983-84, 0-for-3. Totals, 0-for-7.

Holds NBA record for most personal fouls in a season, 1984.

JOHNNY EARL DAWKINS JR.

Born September 28, 1963 at Washington D.C.   Height 6:02.   Weight 165.

High School—Washington, D.C., Mackin.

College—Duke University, Durham, N.C.

Drafted by San Antonio on first round, 1986 (10th pick).

—COLLEGIATE RECORD—

Year	G.	Min.	FGA	FGM	Pct.	FTA	FTM	Pct.	Reb.	Pts.	Avg.
82-83	28	1002	414	207	.500	107	73	.682	115	506	18.1
83-84	34	1306	547	263	.481	160	133	.831	138	659	19.4
84-85	31	1117	455	225	.495	166	132	.795	141	582	18.8
85-86	40	1324	603	331	.549	181	147	.812	142	809	20.2
Totals	133	4749	2019	1026	.508	614	485	.790	536	2556	19.2

Three-Point Field Goals: 1982-83, 19-for-54 (.352).

NBA REGULAR SEASON RECORD

								—Rebounds—								
Sea.—Team	G.	Min.	FGA	FGM	Pct.	FTA	FTM	Pct.	Off.	Def.	Tot.	Ast.	PF	Dq.	Stl.	Blk.	Pts.	Avg.
86-87—San Antonio	81	1682	764	334	.437	191	153	.801	56	113	169	290	118	0	67	3	835	10.3
87-88—San Antonio	65	2179	835	405	.485	221	198	.896	66	138	204	480	95	0	88	2	1027	15.8
Totals	146	3861	1599	739	.462	412	351	.852	122	251	373	770	213	0	155	5	1862	12.8

Three-Point Field Goals: 1986-87, 14-for-47 (.298). 1987-88, 19-for-61 (.311). Totals, 33-for-108 (.306).

—Rebounds—

Sea.—Team	G.	Min.	FGA	FGM	Pct.	FTA	FTM	Pct.	Off.	Def.	Tot.	Ast.	PF	Dq.	Stl.	Blk.	Pts.	Avg.
87-88—San Antonio	3	53	23	6	.261	4	3	.750	1	2	3	5	2	0	2	0	15	5.0

Three-Point Field Goals: 1987-88, 0-for-2.

Named to THE SPORTING NEWS All-America First Team, 1986. . . . THE SPORTING NEWS All-America Second Team, 1985.

DARREN KEEFE DAYE

Born November 30, 1960 at Des Moines, Iowa.   Height 6:08.   Weight 220.
High School—Granada Hills, Calif., Kennedy.
College—University of California at Los Angeles, Los Angeles, Calif.
Drafted by Washington on third round, 1983 (57th pick).

Waived by Washington, October 30, 1986; claimed by Chicago, November 3, 1986.
Waived by Chicago, December 8, 1986; signed by Boston as a free agent, December 11, 1986.
Waived by Boston, February 24, 1988.

—COLLEGIATE RECORD—

Year	G.	Min.	FGA	FGM	Pct.	FTA	FTM	Pct.	Reb.	Pts.	Avg.
79-80	32	497	103	59	.573	76	43	.566	60	161	5.0
80-81	27	717	225	131	.582	93	63	.677	117	325	12.0
81-82	26	606	140	76	.543	85	55	.647	101	207	8.0
82-83	29	979	347	186	.536	124	84	.677	174	456	15.7
Totals	114	2799	815	452	.555	378	245	.648	452	1149	10.1

NBA REGULAR SEASON RECORD

—Rebounds—

Sea.—Team	G.	Min.	FGA	FGM	Pct.	FTA	FTM	Pct.	Off.	Def.	Tot.	Ast.	PF	Dq.	Stl.	Blk.	Pts.	Avg.
83-84—Washington	75	1174	408	180	.441	133	95	.714	90	98	188	176	154	0	38	12	455	6.1
84-85—Washington	80	1573	504	258	.512	249	178	.715	93	179	272	240	164	1	53	19	695	8.7
85-86—Washington	64	1075	399	198	.496	237	159	.671	71	112	183	109	121	0	46	11	556	8.7
86-87—Chi.-Bos.	62	731	202	101	.500	65	34	.523	37	88	125	76	100	0	25	7	236	3.8
87-88—Boston	47	655	217	112	.516	87	59	.678	30	46	76	71	68	0	29	4	283	6.0
Totals	328	5208	1730	849	.491	771	525	.681	321	523	844	672	607	1	191	53	2225	6.8

Three-Point Field Goals: 1983-84, 0-for-6. 1984-85, 1-for-7 (.143). 1985-86, 1-for-3 (.333). 1987-88, 0-for-1. Totals, 2-for-17 (.118).

NBA PLAYOFF RECORD

—Rebounds—

Sea.—Team	G.	Min.	FGA	FGM	Pct.	FTA	FTM	Pct.	Off.	Def.	Tot.	Ast.	PF	Dq.	Stl.	Blk.	Pts.	Avg.
83-84—Washington	3	15	5	1	.200	2	2	1.000	0	0	0	1	2	0	0	1	4	1.3
84-85—Washington	4	85	30	17	.567	16	7	.438	6	6	12	14	8	0	3	0	41	10.3
85-86—Washington	4	32	12	4	.333	2	0	.000	3	5	8	0	3	0	0	0	8	2.0
86-87—Boston	23	240	72	42	.583	37	32	.865	11	21	32	13	33	1	9	3	116	5.0
Totals	34	372	119	64	.538	57	41	.719	20	32	52	28	46	1	12	4	169	5.0

JAMES LEE DONALDSON III

Born August 16, 1957 at Heacham, England.   Height 7:02.   Weight 278.
High School—Sacramento, Calif., Burbank.
College—Washington State University, Pullman, Wash.
Drafted by Seattle on fourth round, 1979 (73rd pick).

Traded by Seattle with Greg Kelser, Mark Radford, a 1984 1st round draft choice and a 1985 2nd round draft choice to San Diego for Tom Chambers, Al Wood, a 1987 2nd round draft choice and a 1984 3rd round draft choice, August 18, 1983.
Traded by Los Angeles Clippers to Dallas for Kurt Nimphius, November 25, 1985.
Played in Europe during 1979-80 season.

—COLLEGIATE RECORD—

Year	G.	Min.	FGA	FGM	Pct.	FTA	FTM	Pct.	Reb.	Pts.	Avg.
75-76	9	36	7	4	.571	3	2	.667	17	10	1.1
76-77	22	297	59	34	.576	19	6	.316	74	74	3.4
77-78	27	999	251	131	.522	121	79	.653	305	341	12.6
78-79	26	946	216	120	.556	98	53	.541	281	293	11.3
Totals	84	2278	533	289	.542	241	140	.581	677	718	8.5

JAMES DONALDSON

Sea.—Team	G.	Min.	FGA	FGM	Pct.	FTA	FTM	Pct.	—Rebounds— Off.	Def.	Tot.	Ast.	PF	Dq.	Stl.	Blk.	Pts.	Avg.
80-81—Seattle	68	980	238	129	.542	170	101	.594	107	202	309	42	79	0	8	74	359	5.3
81-82—Seattle	82	1710	419	255	.609	240	151	.629	138	352	490	51	186	2	27	139	661	8.1
82-83—Seattle	82	1789	496	289	.583	218	150	.688	131	370	501	97	171	1	19	101	728	8.9
83-84—San Diego	82	2525	604	360	.596	327	249	.761	165	484	649	90	214	1	40	139	969	11.8
84-85—L.A. Clippers	82	2392	551	351	.637	303	227	.749	168	500	668	48	217	1	28	130	929	11.3
85-86—L.A.C.-Dal.	83	2682	459	256	.558	254	204	.803	171	624	795	96	189	0	28	139	716	8.6
86-87—Dallas	82	3028	531	311	.586	329	267	.812	295	678	973	63	191	0	51	136	889	10.8
87-88—Dallas	81	2523	380	212	.558	189	147	.778	247	508	755	66	175	2	40	104	571	7.0
Totals	642	17629	3678	2163	.588	2030	1496	.737	1422	3718	5140	553	1422	7	241	962	5822	9.1

NBA PLAYOFF RECORD

Sea.—Team	G.	Min.	FGA	FGM	Pct.	FTA	FTM	Pct.	—Rebounds— Off.	Def.	Tot.	Ast.	PF	Dq.	Stl.	Blk.	Pts.	Avg.
81-82—Seattle	8	189	43	18	.419	24	18	.750	25	49	74	7	16	0	2	5	54	6.8
82-83—Seattle	2	47	22	11	.500	3	2	.667	5	12	17	2	4	0	0	3	24	12.0
85-86—Dallas	10	410	48	36	.750	40	37	.925	30	87	117	10	26	0	6	12	109	10.9
86-87—Dallas	3	68	5	4	.800	9	8	.889	2	15	17	2	6	0	1	3	16	5.3
87-88—Dallas	17	499	104	68	.654	37	22	.595	47	99	146	12	41	0	7	15	158	9.3
Totals	40	1213	222	137	.617	113	87	.770	109	262	371	33	93	0	16	38	361	9.0

NBA ALL-STAR GAME RECORD

Season—Team	Min.	FGA	FGM	Pct.	FTA	FTM	Pct.	—Rebounds— Off.	Def.	Tot.	Ast.	PF	Dq.	Stl.	Blk.	Pts.
1988—Dallas	8	0	0	.000	2	2	1.000	1	5	6	1	2	0	0	2	2

Led NBA in field-goal percentage, 1985.

WILLIAM DONOVAN
(Billy)

Born May 30, 1965 at Rockville Centre, N.Y.   Height 5:11.   Weight 171.

High School—Rockville Centre, N.Y., St. Agnes.

College—Providence College, Providence, R.I.

Drafted by Utah on third round, 1987 (68th pick).

Waived by Utah, November 3, 1987; signed by New York as a free agent, December 11, 1987.
Waived by New York, March 28, 1988.
Played in Continental Basketball Association with Wyoming Wildcatters, 1987-88.

—COLLEGIATE RECORD—

Year	G.	Min.	FGA	FGM	Pct.	FTA	FTM	Pct.	Reb.	Pts.	Avg.
83-84	28	446	68	25	.368	21	15	.714	23	65	2.3
84-85	29	327	87	41	.471	15	10	.667	16	92	3.2
85-86	31	964	358	183	.511	130	103	.792	49	469	15.1
86-87	34	1234	467	203	.435	236	199	.843	102	702	20.6
Totals	122	2971	980	452	.461	402	327	.813	190	1328	10.9

Three-Point Field Goals: 1986-87, 97-for-237 (.409).

CBA REGULAR SEASON RECORD

Sea.—Team	G.	Min.	—2-Point— FGM	FGA	Pct.	—3-Point— FGM	FGA	Pct.	FTM	FTA	Pct.	Reb.	Ast.	Pts.	Avg.
87-88—Wyoming	3	28	0	4	.000	1	2	.500	2	2	1.000	2	4	5	1.7

NBA REGULAR SEASON RECORD

Sea.—Team	G.	Min.	FGA	FGM	Pct.	FTA	FTM	Pct.	—Rebounds— Off.	Def.	Tot.	Ast.	PF	Dq.	Stl.	Blk.	Pts.	Avg.
87-88—New York	44	364	109	44	.404	21	17	.810	5	20	25	87	33	0	16	1	105	2.4

Three-Point Field Goals: 1987-88, 0-for-7.

GREGORY ALAN DREILING
(Greg)

Born November 7, 1963 at Wichita, Kan.   Height 7:01.   Weight 250.

High School—Wichita, Kan., Kapaun-Mt. Carmel.

Colleges—Wichita State University, Wichita, Kan., and
University of Kansas, Lawrence, Kan.

Drafted by Indiana on second round, 1986 (26th pick).

—COLLEGIATE RECORD—
Wichita State

Year	G.	Min.	FGA	FGM	Pct.	FTA	FTM	Pct.	Reb.	Pts.	Avg.
81-82	29	534	151	82	.543	93	70	.753	121	234	8.1

Kansas

Year	G.	Min.	FGA	FGM	Pct.	FTA	FTM	Pct.	Reb.	Pts.	Avg.
82-83				Did Not Play—Transfer Student							
83-84	32	742	228	121	.531	93	69	.742	153	311	9.7
84-85	34	987	300	173	.577	139	101	.727	235	447	13.1
85-86	39	1031	300	180	.600	128	91	.711	262	451	11.6
Kan. Totals	105	2760	828	474	.572	360	261	.725	650	1209	11.5
Col. Totals	134	3294	979	556	.568	453	331	.731	771	1443	10.8

NBA REGULAR SEASON RECORD

Sea.—Team	G.	Min.	FGA	FGM	Pct.	FTA	FTM	Pct.	Off.	Def.	Tot.	Ast.	PF	Dq.	Stl.	Blk.	Pts.	Avg.
86-87—Indiana	24	128	37	16	.432	12	10	.833	12	31	43	7	42	0	2	2	42	1.8
87-88—Indiana	20	74	17	8	.471	26	18	.692	3	14	17	5	19	0	2	4	34	1.7
Totals	44	202	54	24	.444	38	28	.737	15	45	60	12	61	0	4	6	76	1.7

LARRY DONNELL DREW

Born April 2, 1958 at Kansas City, Kan. Height 6:02. Weight 190.

High School—Kansas City, Kan., Wyandotte.

College—University of Missouri, Columbia, Mo.

Drafted by Detroit on first round, 1980 (17th pick).

Traded by Detroit to Kansas City for two 2nd round draft choices (1982 and 1984), August 26, 1981.

Traded by Sacramento with Mike Woodson, a 1988 1st round draft choice and a 1989 2nd round draft choice to Los Angeles Clippers for Franklin Edwards and Derek Smith, August 19, 1986.

—COLLEGIATE RECORD—

Year	G.	Min.	FGA	FGM	Pct.	FTA	FTM	Pct.	Reb.	Pts.	Avg.
76-77	28	....	175	75	.429	59	44	.746	77	194	6.9
77-78	30	1029	344	150	.436	105	80	.762	90	380	12.7
78-79	28	1037	366	181	.495	100	64	.640	73	426	15.2
79-80	31	1092	279	151	.541	121	99	.818	89	401	12.9
Totals	117	....	1164	557	.479	385	287	.745	329	1401	12.0

NBA REGULAR SEASON RECORD

Sea.—Team	G.	Min.	FGA	FGM	Pct.	FTA	FTM	Pct.	Off.	Def.	Tot.	Ast.	PF	Dq.	Stl.	Blk.	Pts.	Avg.
80-81—Detroit	76	1581	484	197	.407	133	106	.797	24	96	120	249	125	0	88	7	504	6.6
81-82—Kansas City	81	1973	757	358	.473	189	150	.794	30	119	149	419	150	0	110	1	874	10.8
82-83—Kansas City	75	2690	1218	599	.492	378	310	.820	44	163	207	610	207	1	126	10	1510	20.1
83-84—Kansas City	73	2363	1026	474	.462	313	243	.776	33	113	146	558	170	0	121	10	1194	16.4
84-85—Kansas City	72	2373	913	457	.501	194	154	.794	39	125	164	484	147	0	93	8	1075	14.9
85-86—Sacramento	75	1971	776	376	.485	161	128	.795	25	100	125	338	134	0	66	2	890	11.9
86-87—L.A. Clippers	60	1566	683	295	.432	166	139	.837	26	77	103	326	107	0	60	2	741	12.4
87-88—L.A. Clippers	74	2024	720	328	.456	108	83	.769	21	98	119	383	114	0	65	0	765	10.3
Totals	586	16541	6577	3084	.469	1642	1313	.800	242	891	1133	3367	1154	1	729	40	7553	12.9

Three-Point Field Goals: 1980-81, 4-for-17. 1981-82, 8-for-27 (.296). 1982-83, 2-for-16 (.125). 1983-84, 3-for-10 (.300). 1984-85, 7-for-28 (.250). 1985-86, 10-for-31 (.323). 1986-87, 12-for-72 (.167). 1987-88, 26-for-90 (.289). Totals, 72-for-291 (.247).

NBA PLAYOFF RECORD

Sea.—Team	G.	Min.	FGA	FGM	Pct.	FTA	FTM	Pct.	Off.	Def.	Tot.	Ast.	PF	Dq.	Stl.	Blk.	Pts.	Avg.
83-84—Kansas City	3	70	19	7	.368	3	3	1.000	0	4	4	11	5	0	3	0	17	5.7
85-86—Sacramento	3	56	25	14	.560	2	2	1.000	0	1	1	14	2	0	5	0	31	10.3
Totals	6	126	44	21	.477	5	5	1.000	0	5	5	25	7	0	8	0	48	8.0

Three-Point Field Goals: 1985-86, 1-for-3 (.333).

CLYDE DREXLER

Born June 22, 1962 at New Orleans, La. Height 6:07. Weight 215.

High School—Houston, Tex., Sterling.

College—University of Houston, Houston, Tex.

Drafted by Portland on first round as an undergraduate, 1983 (14th pick).

—COLLEGIATE RECORD—

Year	G.	Min.	FGA	FGM	Pct.	FTA	FTM	Pct.	Reb.	Pts.
80-81	30	992	303	153	.505	85	50	.588	314	356
81-82	32	1077	362	206	.569	120	73	.608	336	485
82-83	34	1186	440	236	.536	95	70	.737	298	54?
Totals	96	3255	1105	595	.538	300	193	.643	948	

NBA REGULAR SEASON RECORD

Sea.—Team	G.	Min.	FGA	FGM	Pct.	FTA	FTM	Pct.	Off.	Def.	Tot.	Ast.	PF	Dq.	Stl.	Blk.	Pts.	Avg.
										—Rebounds—								
83-84—Portland	82	1408	559	252	.451	169	123	.728	112	123	235	153	209	2	107	29	628	7.7
84-85—Portland	80	2555	1161	573	.494	294	223	.759	217	259	476	441	265	3	177	68	1377	17.2
85-86—Portland	75	2576	1142	542	.475	381	293	.769	171	250	421	600	270	8	197	46	1389	18.5
86-87—Portland	82	3114	1408	707	.502	470	357	.760	227	291	518	566	281	7	204	71	1782	21.7
87-88—Portland	81	3060	1679	849	.506	587	476	.811	261	272	533	467	250	2	203	52	2185	27.0
Totals	400	12713	5949	2923	.491	1901	1472	.774	988	1195	2183	2227	1275	22	888	266	7361	18.4

Three-Point Field Goals: 1983-84, 1-for-4 (.250). 1984-85, 8-for-37 (.216). 1985-86, 12-for-60 (.200). 1986-87, 11-for-47 (.234). 1987-88, 11-for-52 (.212). Totals, 43-for-200 (.215).

NBA PLAYOFF RECORD

Sea.—Team	G.	Min.	FGA	FGM	Pct.	FTA	FTM	Pct.	Off.	Def.	Tot.	Ast.	PF	Dq.	Stl.	Blk.	Pts.	Avg.
										—Rebounds—								
83-84—Portland	5	85	35	15	.429	7	6	.857	7	10	17	8	11	0	5	1	36	7.2
84-85—Portland	9	339	134	55	.410	45	38	.844	27	28	55	83	37	0	23	9	150	16.7
85-86—Portland	4	145	57	26	.456	23	18	.783	9	16	25	26	19	1	6	3	72	18.0
86-87—Portland	4	153	79	36	.456	29	23	.793	16	14	30	15	16	1	7	3	96	24.0
87-88—Portland	4	170	83	32	.386	29	21	.724	12	16	28	21	14	0	12	2	88	22.0
Totals	26	892	388	164	.423	133	106	.797	71	84	155	153	97	2	53	18	442	17.0

Three-Point Field Goals: 1983-84, 0-for-1. 1984-85, 2-for-7 (.286). 1985-86, 2 for-5 (.400). 1986-87, 1-for-4 (.250). 1987-88, 3-for-6 (.500). Totals, 8-for-23 (.423).

NBA ALL-STAR GAME RECORD

Season—Team	Min.	FGA	FGM	Pct.	FTA	FTM	Pct.	Off.	Def.	Tot.	Ast.	PF	Dq.	Stl.	Blk.	Pts.
									—Rebounds—							
1986—Portland	15	7	5	.714	0	0	.000	0	4	4	4	3	0	3	1	10
1988—Portland	15	5	3	.600	6	6	1.000	2	3	5	0	3	0	1	0	12
Totals	30	12	8	.667	6	6	1.000	2	7	9	4	6	0	4	1	22

Three-Point Field Goals: 1986, 0-for-1. 1988, 0-for-1. Totals, 0-for-2.

Named to All-NBA Second Team, 1988.

KEVIN JEROME DUCKWORTH

Born April 1, 1964 at Harvey, Ill.   Height 7:00.   Weight 280.

High School—Dolton, Ill., Thornridge.

College—Eastern Illinois University, Charleston, Ill.

Drafted by San Antonio on second round, 1986 (33rd pick).

Traded by San Antonio to Portland for Walter Berry, December 18, 1986.

—COLLEGIATE RECORD—

Year	G.	Min.	FGA	FGM	Pct.	FTA	FTM	Pct.	Reb.	Pts.	Avg.
82-83	30	669	212	112	.528	95	64	.674	181	288	9.6
83-84	28	642	221	132	.597	89	61	.685	191	325	11.6
84-85	28	733	258	133	.516	99	65	.657	205	331	11.8
85-86	32	1023	396	250	.631	164	125	.762	290	625	19.5
Totals	118	3067	1087	627	.577	447	315	.705	867	1569	13.3

NBA REGULAR SEASON RECORD

Sea.—Team	G.	Min.	FGA	FGM	Pct.	FTA	FTM	Pct.	Off.	Def.	Tot.	Ast.	PF	Dq.	Stl.	Blk.	Pts.	Avg.
										—Rebounds—								
86-87—S.A.-Port.	65	875	273	130	.476	134	92	.687	76	147	223	29	192	3	21	21	352	5.4
87-88—Portland	78	2223	907	450	.496	430	331	.770	224	352	576	66	280	5	31	32	1231	15.8
Totals	143	3098	1180	580	.492	564	423	.750	300	499	799	95	472	8	52	53	1583	11.1

Three-Point Field Goals: 1986-87, 0-for-1.

NBA PLAYOFF RECORD

Sea.—Team	G.	Min.	FGA	FGM	Pct.	FTA	FTM	Pct.	Off.	Def.	Tot.	Ast.	PF	Dq.	Stl.	Blk.	Pts.	Avg.
										—Rebounds—								
86-87—Portland	4	53	12	6	.500	5	2	.400	3	5	8	1	14	0	4	1	14	3.5
87-88—Portland	4	151	70	34	.486	23	18	.783	20	24	44	7	14	0	1	2	86	21.5
Totals	8	204	82	40	.488	28	20	.714	23	29	52	8	28	0	5	3	100	12.5

Three-Point Field Goals: 1987-88, 0-for-1.

Named NBA Most Improved Player, 1988.

—DID YOU KNOW—

That Nets Coach Willis Reed is the only player in NBA history to win the most valuable player award of the All-Star Game, the regular season and the playoffs in the same season? Reed achieved the feat with the New York Knicks in 1970.

KEVIN DUCKWORTH

CHRISTOPHER GUILFORD DUDLEY
(Chris)

Born February 22, 1965 at Stamford, Conn.   Height 6:11.   Weight 235.

High School—Del Mar, Calif., Torrey Pines.

College—Yale University, New Haven, Conn.

Drafted by Cleveland on fourth round, 1987 (75th pick).

—COLLEGIATE RECORD—

Year	G.	Min.	FGA	FGM	Pct.	FTA	FTM	Pct.	Reb.	Pts.	Avg.
83-84	26	498	97	45	.464	60	28	.467	132	118	4.5
84-85	26	795	294	131	.446	122	65	.533	266	327	12.6
85-86	26	756	317	171	.539	166	80	.482	256	422	16.2
86-87	24	749	290	165	.569	177	96	.542	320	426	17.8
Totals	102	2798	998	512	.513	525	269	.512	974	1293	12.7

NBA REGULAR SEASON RECORD

Sea.—Team	G.	Min.	FGA	FGM	Pct.	FTA	FTM	Pct.	Off.	Def.	Tot.	Ast.	PF	Dq.	Stl.	Blk.	Pts.	Avg.
									—Rebounds—									
87-88—Cleveland	55	513	137	65	.474	71	40	.563	74	70	144	23	87	2	13	19	170	3.1

NBA PLAYOFF RECORD

Sea.—Team	G.	Min.	FGA	FGM	Pct.	FTA	FTM	Pct.	Off.	Def.	Tot.	Ast.	PF	Dq.	Stl.	Blk.	Pts.	Avg.
									—Rebounds—									
87-88—Cleveland	4	24	4	2	.500	2	1	.500	4	2	6	2	3	0	0	0	5	1.3

JOE DUMARS III

Born May 24, 1963 at Shreveport, La.   Height 6:03.   Weight 190.

High School—Natchitoches, La., Central.

College—McNeese State University, Lake Charles, La.

Drafted by Detroit on first round, 1985 (18th pick).

—COLLEGIATE RECORD—

Year	G.	Min.	FGA	FGM	Pct.	FTA	FTM	Pct.	Reb.	Pts.	Avg.
81-82	29	....	464	206	.444	160	115	.719	64	527	18.2
82-83	29	....	487	212	.435	197	140	.711	128	569	19.6
83-84	31	....	586	276	.471	324	267	.824	164	819	26.4
84-85	27	....	501	248	.495	236	201	.852	132	697	25.8
Totals	116		2038	942	.462	917	723	.788	488	2612	22.5

Three-Point Field Goals: 1982-83, 5-for-8 (.625).

NBA REGULAR SEASON RECORD

Sea.—Team	G.	Min.	FGA	FGM	Pct.	FTA	FTM	Pct.	Off.	Def.	Tot.	Ast.	PF	Dq.	Stl.	Blk.	Pts.	Avg.
									—Rebounds—									
85-86—Detroit	82	1957	597	287	.481	238	190	.798	60	59	119	390	200	1	66	11	769	9.4
86-87—Detroit	79	2439	749	369	.493	246	184	.748	50	117	167	352	194	1	83	5	931	11.8
87-88—Detroit	82	2732	960	453	.472	308	251	.815	63	137	200	387	155	1	87	15	1161	14.2
Totals	243	7128	2306	1109	.481	792	625	.789	173	313	486	1129	549	3	236	31	2861	11.8

Three-Point Field Goals: 1985-86, 5-for-16 (.313). 1986-87, 9-for-22 (.409). 1987-88, 4-for-19 (.211). Totals, 18-for-57 (.316).

NBA PLAYOFF RECORD

Sea.—Team	G.	Min.	FGA	FGM	Pct.	FTA	FTM	Pct.	Off.	Def.	Tot.	Ast.	PF	Dq.	Stl.	Blk.	Pts.	Avg.
									—Rebounds—									
85-86—Detroit	4	147	41	25	.610	15	10	.667	6	7	13	25	16	0	4	0	60	15.0
86-87—Detroit	15	473	145	78	.538	41	32	.780	8	11	19	72	26	0	12	1	190	12.7
87-88—Detroit	23	804	247	113	.457	63	56	.889	18	32	50	112	50	1	13	2	284	12.3
Totals	42	1424	433	216	.499	119	98	.824	32	50	82	209	92	1	29	3	534	12.7

Three-Point Field Goals: 1986-87, 2-for-3 (.667). 1987-88, 2-for-6 (.333). Totals, 4-for-9 (.444).

Named to NBA All-Rookie Team, 1986. . . . THE SPORTING NEWS All-America Second Team, 1985.

THEODORE ROOSEVELT DUNN
(T. R.)

Born February 1, 1955 at Birmingham, Ala.   Height 6:04.   Weight 192.

High School—Birmingham, Ala., West End.

College—University of Alabama, University, Ala.

Drafted by Portland on second round, 1977 (41st pick).

Traded by Portland to Denver for a 1984 2nd round draft choice and other considerations, August 15, 1980.

—COLLEGIATE RECORD—

Year	G.	Min.	FGA	FGM	Pct.	FTA	FTM	Pct.	Reb.	Pts.	Avg.
73-74	25	839	232	99	.427	58	38	.655	199	236	9.4

JOE DUMARS

Year	G.	Min.	FGA	FGM	Pct.	FTA	FTM	Pct.	Reb.	Pts.	Avg.
74-75	27	948	297	140	.471	70	51	.729	176	331	12.3
75-76	28	961	303	118	.389	59	37	.627	145	273	9.8
76-77	31	1094	353	173	.490	86	61	.709	220	407	13.1
Totals	111	3842	1185	530	.447	273	187	.685	740	1247	11.2

NBA REGULAR SEASON RECORD

Sea.—Team	G.	Min.	FGA	FGM	Pct.	FTA	FTM	Pct.	Off.	Def.	Tot.	Ast.	PF	Dq.	Stl.	Blk.	Pts.	Avg.
77-78—Portland	63	768	240	100	.417	56	37	.661	63	84	147	45	74	0	46	8	237	3.8
78-79—Portland	80	1828	549	246	.448	158	122	.772	145	199	344	103	166	1	86	23	614	7.7
79-80—Portland	82	1841	551	240	.436	111	84	.757	132	192	324	147	145	1	102	31	564	6.9
80-81—Denver	82	1427	354	146	.412	121	79	.653	133	168	301	81	141	0	66	29	371	4.5
81-82—Denver	82	2519	504	258	.512	215	153	.712	211	348	559	188	210	1	135	36	669	8.2
82-83—Denver	82	2640	527	254	.482	163	119	.730	231	384	615	189	218	2	147	25	627	7.6
83-84—Denver	80	2705	370	174	.470	145	106	.731	195	379	574	228	233	5	173	32	454	5.7
84-85—Denver	81	2290	358	175	.489	116	84	.724	169	216	385	153	213	3	140	14	434	5.4
85-86—Denver	82	2401	379	172	.454	88	68	.773	143	234	377	171	228	1	155	16	412	5.0
86-87—Denver	81	1932	276	118	.428	55	36	.655	91	174	265	147	160	0	100	21	272	3.4
87-88—Denver	82	1534	156	70	.449	52	40	.769	110	130	240	87	152	0	101	11	180	2.2
Totals	877	21885	4264	1953	.458	1280	928	.725	1623	2508	4131	1539	1940	14	1251	246	4834	5.5

Three-Point Field Goals: 1979-80, 0-for-3. 1980-81, 0-for-2. 1981-82, 0-for-1. 1982-83, 0-for-1. 1983-84, 0-for-1. 1984-85, 0-for-2. 1985-86, 0-for-1. 1986-87, 0-for-2. 1987-88, 0-for-1. Totals, 0-for-14.

NBA PLAYOFF RECORD

Sea.—Team	G.	Min.	FGA	FGM	Pct.	FTA	FTM	Pct.	Off.	Def.	Tot.	Ast.	PF	Dq.	Stl.	Blk.	Pts.	Avg.
77-78—Portland	4	35	4	2	.500	0	0	.000	1	4	5	3	3	0	1	0	4	1.0
78-79—Portland	3	52	11	5	.455	0	0	.000	2	4	6	4	7	0	5	0	10	3.3
79-80—Portland	3	24	8	2	.250	2	2	1.000	1	3	4	4	3	0	1	0	6	2.0
81-82—Denver	3	81	13	6	.462	8	7	.875	10	8	18	10	11	0	8	1	19	6.3
82-83—Denver	8	300	41	18	.439	8	5	.625	27	51	78	20	21	0	12	3	41	5.1
83-84—Denver	5	178	25	14	.560	7	5	.714	20	19	39	8	19	0	10	4	33	6.6
84-85—Denver	15	371	65	27	.415	19	14	.737	27	33	60	34	45	0	24	3	68	4.5
85-86—Denver	10	276	46	20	.435	14	9	.643	22	31	53	13	34	1	16	0	49	4.9
86-87—Denver	3	22	4	1	.250	0	0	.000	1	2	3	2	3	0	1	1	2	0.7
87-88—Denver	11	185	20	11	.550	8	4	.500	11	18	29	3	20	0	8	0	26	2.4
Totals	65	1524	237	106	.447	66	46	.697	122	173	295	101	166	1	86	12	258	4.0

Named to NBA All-Defensive Second Team, 1983, 1984, 1985.

MARK E. EATON

Born January 24, 1957 at Westminister, Calif.   Height 7:04.   Weight 290.

High School—Westminster, Calif.

Colleges—Cypress College, Cypress, Calif., and University of California at Los Angeles, Los Angeles, Calif.

Drafted by Phoenix on fifth round, 1979 (107th pick). (Eligible for NBA draft because he was out of school three seasons between high school and college and his college class graduated in 1979.)

Drafted by Utah on fourth round, 1982 (72nd pick).

—COLLEGIATE RECORD—
Cypress

Year	G.	Min.	FGA	FGM	Pct.	FTA	FTM	Pct.	Reb.	Pts.	Avg.
78-79	35	....	319	202	.633	117	78	.667	381	482	13.8
79-80	25	....	289	167	.578	83	40	.482	218	374	15.0
JC Totals	60	....	608	369	.607	200	118	.590	599	856	14.3

UCLA

Year	G.	Min.	FGA	FGM	Pct.	FTA	FTM	Pct.	Reb.	Pts.	Avg.
80-81	19	155	37	17	.459	17	5	.294	49	39	2.1
81-82	11	41	12	5	.417	5	4	.800	22	14	1.3
Totals	30	196	49	22	.449	22	9	.409	71	53	1.8

NBA REGULAR SEASON RECORD

Sea.—Team	G.	Min.	FGA	FGM	Pct.	FTA	FTM	Pct.	Off.	Def.	Tot.	Ast.	PF	Dq.	Stl.	Blk.	Pts.	Avg.
82-83—Utah	81	1528	353	146	.414	90	59	.656	86	376	462	112	257	6	24	275	351	4.3
83-84—Utah	82	2139	416	194	.466	123	73	.593	148	447	595	113	303	4	25	351	461	5.6
84-85—Utah	82	2813	673	302	.449	267	190	.712	207	720	927	124	312	5	36	456	794	9.7
85-86—Utah	80	2551	589	277	.470	202	122	.604	172	503	675	101	282	5	33	369	676	8.5
86-87—Utah	79	2505	585	234	.400	213	140	.657	211	486	697	105	273	5	43	321	608	7.7
87-88—Utah	82	2731	541	226	.418	191	119	.623	230	487	717	55	320	8	41	304	571	7.0
Totals	486	14267	3157	1379	.437	1086	703	.647	1054	3019	4073	610	1747	33	202	2076	3461	7.1

Three-Point Field Goals: 1982-83, 0-for-1. 1983-84, 0-for-1. Totals, 0-for-2.

NBA PLAYOFF RECORD

Sea.—Team	G.	Min.	FGA	FGM	Pct.	FTA	FTM	Pct.	Off.	Def.	Tot.	Ast.	PF	Dq.	Stl.	Blk.	Pts.	Avg.
83-84—Utah	11	254	41	21	.512	17	8	.471	19	57	76	9	33	1	5	34	50	4.5
84-85—Utah	5	158	34	12	.353	7	5	.714	11	34	45	5	19	0	4	29	29	5.8
85-86—Utah	4	157	57	28	.491	3	2	.667	13	23	36	10	12	0	1	18	58	14.5
86-87—Utah	5	193	41	19	.463	25	16	.640	16	39	55	3	18	0	1	21	54	10.8
87-88—Utah	11	461	65	31	.477	36	23	.639	28	75	103	13	48	3	12	34	85	7.7
Totals	36	1223	238	111	.466	88	54	.614	87	228	315	40	130	4	23	136	276	7.7

Named NBA Defensive Player of the Year, 1985. . . . NBA All-Defensive First Team, 1985 and 1986. . . . NBA All-Defensive Second Team, 1987 and 1988. . . . Holds NBA record for most blocked shots in a season, 1985. . . . Holds NBA playoff game record for most blocked shots, 10, vs. Denver, April 26, 1985. . . . Led NBA in blocked shots, 1984, 1985, 1987, 1988.

FRANKLIN DELANO EDWARDS

Born February 2, 1959 at New York, N. Y.   Height 6:01.   Weight 190.

High School—New York, N. Y., Julia Richman.

College—Cleveland State University, Cleveland, O.

Drafted by Philadelphia on first round, 1981 (22nd pick).

Signed by Los Angeles Clippers as a Veteran Free Agent to two 10-day contracts that expired April 3, 1985; Philadelphia waived its right of first refusal.
Re-signed by Los Angeles Clippers, September 27, 1985.
Traded by Los Angeles Clippers with Derek Smith to Sacramento for Larry Drew, Mike Woodson, a 1988 1st round draft choice and a 1989 2nd round draft choice, August 19, 1986.
Waived by Sacramento, January 18, 1988.
Played in Continental Basketball Association with Lancaster Lightning, 1984-85.

—COLLEGIATE RECORD—

Year	G.	Min.	FGA	FGM	Pct.	FTA	FTM	Pct.	Reb.	Pts.	Avg.
77-78	25	....	416	190	.457	122	87	.713	68	467	18.7
78-79	25	....	402	198	.493	93	71	.763	90	467	18.7
79-80	25	....	486	253	.521	153	131	.856	65	637	25.5
80-81	27	....	503	265	.527	152	134	.882	86	664	24.6
Totals	102	....	1807	906	.501	520	423	.813	309	2235	21.9

CBA REGULAR SEASON RECORD

			2-Point			3-Point								
Sea.—Team	G.	Min.	FGM	FGA	Pct.	FGM	FGA	Pct.	FTM	FTA	Pct.	Reb.	Ast.	Pts.	Avg.
84-85—Lancaster	18	660	134	258	.519	1	2	.500	74	80	.925	42	173	345	19.2

NBA REGULAR SEASON RECORD

Sea.—Team	G.	Min.	FGA	FGM	Pct.	FTA	FTM	Pct.	Off.	Def.	Tot.	Ast.	PF	Dq.	Stl.	Blk.	Pts.	Avg.
81-82—Philadelphia	42	291	150	65	.433	27	20	.741	10	17	27	45	37	0	16	5	150	3.6
82-83—Philadelphia	81	1266	483	228	.472	113	86	.761	23	62	85	221	119	0	81	6	542	6.7
83-84—Philadelphia	60	654	221	84	.380	48	34	.708	12	47	59	90	78	1	31	5	202	3.4
84-85—L.A. Clippers	16	198	66	36	.545	24	19	.792	3	11	14	38	10	0	17	0	91	5.7
85-86—L.A. Clippers	73	1491	577	262	.454	151	132	.874	24	62	86	259	87	0	89	4	657	9.0
86-87—Sacramento	8	122	32	9	.281	14	10	.714	2	8	10	29	7	0	5	0	28	3.5
87-88—Sacramento	16	414	115	54	.470	32	24	.750	4	15	19	92	10	0	10	1	132	8.3
Totals	296	4456	1644	738	.449	409	325	.795	78	222	300	774	348	1	249	21	1802	6.1

Three-Point Field Goals: 1981-82, 0-for-9. 1982-83, 0-for-8. 1983-84, 0-for-1. 1985-86, 1-for-9 (.111). 1986-87, 0-for-4. 1987-88, 0-for-2. Totals, 1-for-33 (.030).

NBA PLAYOFF RECORD

Sea.—Team	G.	Min.	FGA	FGM	Pct.	FTA	FTM	Pct.	Off.	Def.	Tot.	Ast.	PF	Dq.	Stl.	Blk.	Pts.	Avg.
81-82—Philadelphia	9	32	20	12	.600	9	8	.889	2	3	5	5	0	0	3	0	33	3.7
82-83—Philadelphia	12	101	32	13	.406	17	14	.824	2	7	9	17	7	0	5	0	40	3.3
Totals	21	133	52	25	.481	26	22	.846	4	10	14	22	7	0	8	0	73	3.5

Three-Point Field Goals: 1981-82, 1-for-1 (1.000).

Member of NBA championship team, 1983.

JAMES FRANKLIN EDWARDS

Born November 22, 1955 at Seattle, Wash.   Height 7:01.   Weight 252.

High School—Seattle, Wash., Roosevelt.

College—University of Washington, Seattle, Wash.

Drafted by Los Angeles on third round, 1977 (46th pick).

Traded by Los Angeles with Earl Tatum and cash to Indiana for Adrian Dantley and Dave Robisch, December 13, 1977.

Signed by Cleveland as a Veteran Free Agent, May 25, 1981; Indiana agreed not to exercise its right of first refusal in exchange for 1981 and 1982 2nd round draft choices, June 8, 1981.

Traded by Cleveland to Phoenix for Jeff Cook, a 1983 3rd round draft choice and cash, February 7, 1983.

Traded by Phoenix to Detroit for Ron Moore and a 1991 2nd round draft choice, February 24, 1988.

—COLLEGIATE RECORD—

Year	G.	Min.	FGA	FGM	Pct.	FTA	FTM	Pct.	Reb.	Pts.	Avg.
73-74	25	....	160	68	.425	62	34	.548	115	170	6.8
74-75	26	575	264	125	.473	129	70	.543	198	320	12.3
75-76	28	811	392	205	.523	137	83	.606	200	493	17.6
76-77	27	940	404	223	.552	184	119	.647	282	565	20.9
Totals	106	....	1220	621	.509	512	306	.598	795	1548	14.6

NBA REGULAR SEASON RECORD

Sea.—Team	G.	Min.	FGA	FGM	Pct.	FTA	FTM	Pct.	Off.	Def.	Tot.	Ast.	PF	Dq.	Stl.	Blk.	Pts.	Avg.
77-78—LA-Ind.	83	2405	1093	495	.453	421	272	.646	197	418	615	85	322	12	53	78	1262	15.2
78-79—Indiana	82	2546	1065	534	.501	441	298	.676	179	514	693	92	363	16	60	109	1366	16.7
79-80—Indiana	82	2314	1032	528	.512	339	231	.681	179	399	578	127	324	12	55	104	1287	15.7
80-81—Indiana	81	2375	1004	511	.509	347	244	.703	191	380	571	212	304	7	32	128	1266	15.6
81-82—Cleveland	77	2539	1033	528	.511	339	232	.684	189	392	581	123	347	17	24	117	1288	16.7
82-83—Clev.-Phoe.	31	667	263	128	.487	108	69	.639	56	99	155	40	110	5	12	19	325	10.5
83-84—Phoenix	72	1897	817	438	.536	254	183	.720	108	240	348	184	254	3	23	30	1059	14.7
84-85—Phoenix	70	1787	766	384	.501	370	276	.746	95	292	387	153	237	5	26	52	1044	14.9
85-86—Phoenix	52	1314	587	318	.542	302	212	.702	79	222	301	74	200	5	23	29	848	16.3
86-87—Phoenix	14	304	110	57	.518	70	54	.771	20	40	60	19	42	1	6	7	168	12.0
87-88—Phoe.-Det.	69	1705	643	302	.470	321	210	.654	119	293	412	78	216	2	16	37	814	11.8
Totals	713	19853	8413	4223	.502	3312	2281	.689	1412	3289	4701	1187	2719	85	330	710	10727	15.0

Three-Point Field Goals: 1979-80, 0-for-1. 1980-81, 0-for-3. 1981-82, 0-for-4. 1983-84, 0-for-1. 1984-85, 0-for-3. 1987-88, 0-for-1. Totals, 0-for-13.

NBA PLAYOFF RECORD

Sea.—Team	G.	Min.	FGA	FGM	Pct.	FTA	FTM	Pct.	Off.	Def.	Tot.	Ast.	PF	Dq.	Stl.	Blk.	Pts.	Avg.
80-81—Indiana	2	56	24	7	.292	0	0	.000	4	10	14	5	8	0	1	1	14	7.0
82-83—Phoenix	3	54	26	11	.423	6	6	1.000	6	12	18	4	7	0	1	1	28	9.3
83-84—Phoenix	17	463	189	93	.492	68	48	.706	22	69	91	27	62	3	4	11	234	13.8
87-88—Detroit	22	308	110	56	.509	41	27	.659	23	45	68	11	55	0	2	10	139	6.3
Totals	44	881	349	167	.479	115	81	.704	55	136	191	47	132	3	8	23	415	9.4

Three-Point Field Goals: 1987-88, 0-for-1.

JOEL CRAIG EHLO

(Known by middle name.)

Born August 11, 1961 at Lubbock, Tex. Height 6:07. Weight 185.

High School—Lubbock, Tex., Monterey.

Colleges—Odessa College, Odessa, Tex., and Washington State University, Pullman, Wash.

Drafted by Houston on third round, 1983 (48th pick).

Waived by Houston, October 30, 1986; signed by Cleveland as a free agent, January 13, 1987.
Played in Continental Basketball Association with Mississippi Jets, 1986-87.

—COLLEGIATE RECORD—
Odessa

Year	G.	Min.	FGA	FGM	Pct.	FTA	FTM	Pct.	Reb.	Pts.	Avg.
79-80	28	...	300	146	.487	84	60	.714	142	352	12.6
80-81	30	...	482	241	.500	180	139	.772	204	621	20.7
JC Totals	58	...	782	387	.495	264	199	.754	346	973	16.8

Washington State

Year	G.	Min.	FGA	FGM	Pct.	FTA	FTM	Pct.	Reb.	Pts.	Avg.
81-82	30	592	119	57	.479	65	39	.600	65	153	5.1
82-83	30	911	265	145	.547	109	69	.633	97	359	12.0
Totals	60	1503	384	202	.526	174	108	.621	162	512	8.5

CBA REGULAR SEASON RECORD

Sea.—Team		G.	Min.	2-Point			3-Point			FTM	FTA	Pct.	Reb.	Ast.	Pts.	Avg.
				FGM	FGA	Pct.	FGM	FGA	Pct.							
86-87—Mississippi		6	144	20	31	.645	1	1	1.000	20	30	.667	22	20	63	10.5

NBA REGULAR SEASON RECORD

Sea.—Team	G.	Min.	FGA	FGM	Pct.	FTA	FTM	Pct.	Off.	Def.	Tot.	Ast.	PF	Dq.	Stl.	Blk.	Pts.	Avg.
83-84—Houston	7	63	27	11	.407	1	1	1.000	4	5	9	6	13	0	3	0	23	3.3
84-85—Houston	45	189	69	34	.493	30	19	.633	8	17	25	26	26	0	11	3	87	1.9
85-86—Houston	36	199	84	36	.429	29	23	.793	17	29	46	29	22	0	11	4	98	2.7
86-87—Cleveland	44	890	239	99	.414	99	70	.707	55	106	161	92	80	0	40	30	273	6.2
87-88—Cleveland	79	1709	485	226	.466	132	89	.674	86	188	274	206	182	0	82	30	563	7.1
Totals	211	3050	904	406	.449	291	202	.694	170	345	515	359	323	0	147	67	1044	4.9

Three-Point Field Goals: 1984-85, 0-for-3. 1985-86, 3-for-9 (.333). 1986-87, 5-for-29 (.172). 1987-88, 22-for-64 (.344). Totals, 30-for-105 (.286).

NBA PLAYOFF RECORD

Sea.—Team	G.	Min.	FGA	FGM	Pct.	FTA	FTM	Pct.	Off.	Def.	Tot.	Ast.	PF	Dq.	Stl.	Blk.	Pts.	Avg.
84-85—Houston	3	6	1	1	1.000	2	2	1.000	0	0	0	0	3	0	4	0	4	1.3
85-86—Houston	10	38	16	8	.500	5	4	.800	1	2	3	6	4	0	4	1	20	2.0
87-88—Cleveland	5	128	40	17	.425	16	10	.625	3	15	18	17	14	0	5	0	44	8.8
Totals	18	172	57	26	.456	23	16	.696	4	17	21	23	21	0	13	1	68	3.8

Three-Point Field Goals: 1985-86, 0-for-1. 1987-88, 0-for-8. Totals, 0-for-9.

DALE ELLIS

Born August 6, 1960 at Marietta, Ga. Height 6:07. Weight 215.

High School—Marietta, Ga.

College—University of Tennessee, Knoxville, Tenn.

Drafted by Dallas on first round, 1983 (9th pick).

Traded by Dallas to Seattle for Al Wood, July 23, 1986.

—COLLEGIATE RECORD—

Year	G.	Min.	FGA	FGM	Pct.	FTA	FTM	Pct.	Reb.	Pts.	Avg.
79-80	27	573	182	81	.445	40	31	.775	96	193	7.1
80-81	29	1057	360	215	.597	111	83	.748	185	513	17.7
81-82	30	1134	393	257	.654	152	121	.796	189	635	21.2
82-83	32	1179	464	279	.601	221	166	.751	209	724	22.6
Totals	118	4943	1399	832	.595	523	401	.767	679	2065	17.5

NBA REGULAR SEASON RECORD

Sea.—Team	G.	Min.	FGA	FGM	Pct.	FTA	FTM	Pct.	Off.	Def.	Tot.	Ast.	PF	Dq.	Stl.	Blk.	Pts.	Avg.
83-84—Dallas	67	1059	493	225	.456	121	87	.719	106	144	250	56	118	0	41	9	549	8.2
84-85—Dallas	72	1314	603	274	.454	104	77	.740	100	138	238	56	131	1	46	7	667	9.3
85-86—Dallas	72	1086	470	193	.411	82	59	.720	86	82	168	37	78	0	44	9	508	7.1
86-87—Seattle	82	3073	1520	785	.516	489	385	.787	187	260	447	238	267	2	104	32	2041	24.9
87-88—Seattle	75	2790	1519	764	.503	395	303	.767	167	173	340	197	221	1	74	11	1938	25.8
Totals	368	9322	4605	2241	.487	1191	911	.765	646	797	1443	584	815	4	305	68	5703	15.5

Three-Point Field Goals: 1983-84, 12-for-29 (.414). 1984-85, 42-for-109 (.385). 1985-86, 63-for-173 (.364). 1986-87, 86-for-240 (.358). 1987-88, 107-for-259 (.413). Totals, 310-for-810 (.383).

NBA PLAYOFF RECORD

Sea.—Team	G.	Min.	FGA	FGM	Pct.	FTA	FTM	Pct.	Off.	Def.	Tot.	Ast.	PF	Dq.	Stl.	Blk.	Pts.	Avg.
83-84—Dallas	8	178	80	26	.325	8	6	.750	19	23	42	4	17	0	10	2	59	7.4
84-85—Dallas	4	68	23	10	.435	2	1	.500	4	3	7	3	3	0	4	0	23	5.8
85-86—Dallas	7	67	22	9	.409	5	5	1.000	3	4	7	2	6	0	2	2	30	4.3
86-87—Seattle	14	530	304	148	.487	54	44	.815	37	53	90	37	54	1	10	6	353	25.2
87-88—Seattle	5	172	83	40	.482	29	21	.724	11	12	23	15	17	0	3	2	104	20.8
Totals	38	1015	512	233	.455	98	77	.786	74	95	169	61	97	1	29	12	569	15.0

Three-Point Field Goals: 1983-84, 1-for-12 (.083). 1984-85, 2-for-5 (.400). 1985-86, 7-for-12 (.583). 1986-87, 13-for-36 (.361). 1987-88, 3-for-12 (.250). Totals, 26-for-77 (.338).

Named NBA Most Improved Player, 1987.... THE SPORTING NEWS All-America First Team, 1983.

CHRISTOPHER AARON ENGLER
(Chris)

Born March 1, 1959 at Stillwater, Minn. Height 6:11. Weight 250.

High School—Stillwater, Minn.

Colleges—University of Minnesota, Minneapolis, Minn., and
University of Wyoming, Laramie, Wyo.

Drafted by Golden State on third round, 1982 (60th pick).

Waived by Golden State, October 23, 1984; signed by New Jersey, December 22, 1984, to the first of consecutive 10-day contracts that expired, January 12, 1985.
Signed by Chicago, January 14, 1985, to the first of consecutive 10-day contracts that expired, February 4, 1985.
Signed by Los Angeles Clippers to a 10-day contract that expired, February 28, 1985.
Signed by Milwaukee as a free agent, April 2, 1985.
Traded by Milwaukee to Portland for a 1987 2nd round draft choice, November 11, 1986.
Waived by Portland, December 22, 1986; signed by Milwaukee, December 26, 1986, to the first of consecutive 10-day contracts that expired, January 15, 1987.
Signed by New Jersey as a free agent, January 22, 1987.
Played in Continental Basketball Association with Wyoming Wildcatters, 1984-85.

—COLLEGIATE RECORD—
Minnesota

Year	G.	Min.	FGA	FGM	Pct.	FTA	FTM	Pct.	Reb.	Pts.	Avg.
77-78	8	....	10	4	.400	1	0	.000	10	8	1.0
78-79	8	....	4	1	.250	0	0	.000	8	2	0.3
Minn. Totals	16	....	14	5	.357	1	0	.000	18	10	0.6

Wyoming

Year	G.	Min.	FGA	FGM	Pct.	FTA	FTM	Pct.	Reb.	Pts.	Avg.
79-80					Did Not Play—Transfer Student						
80-81	30	649	190	97	.511	50	35	.700	158	229	7.6
81-82	30	877	251	144	.574	77	58	.753	192	346	11.5
Wyo. Totals	60	1526	441	241	.546	127	93	.732	350	575	9.6
College Totals	76	....	455	246	.541	128	93	.727	368	585	7.7

CBA REGULAR SEASON RECORD

Sea.—Team	G.	Min.	2-Point			3-Point			FTM	FTA	Pct.	Reb.	Ast.	Pts.	Avg.
			FGM	FGA	Pct.	FGM	FGA	Pct.							
84-85—Wyoming	25	842	135	278	.485	0	1	.000	80	104	.769	221	34	350	14.0

NBA REGULAR SEASON RECORD

Sea.—Team	G.	Min.	FGA	FGM	Pct.	FTA	FTM	Pct.	Off.	Def.	Tot.	Ast.	PF	Dq.	Stl.	Blk.	Pts.	Avg.
82-83—Golden State	54	369	94	38	.404	16	5	.313	43	61	104	11	95	1	7	17	81	1.5
83-84—Golden State	46	360	83	33	.398	23	14	.609	27	70	97	11	68	0	9	3	80	1.7
84-85—N.J.-Chi.-Mil.	11	82	20	8	.400	9	5	.556	12	18	30	0	5	0	2	5	21	1.9
86-87—Pt.-Mil.-NJ	30	195	51	23	.451	16	12	.750	23	34	57	8	33	0	5	11	58	1.9
87-88—New Jersey	54	399	88	36	.409	35	31	.886	32	66	98	15	73	1	9	6	103	1.9
Totals	195	1405	336	138	.411	99	67	.677	137	249	386	45	274	2	32	42	343	1.8

NBA PLAYOFF RECORD

Sea.—Team	G.	Min.	FGA	FGM	Pct.	FTA	FTM	Pct.	Off.	Def.	Tot.	Ast.	PF	Dq.	Stl.	Blk.	Pts.	Avg.
84-85—Milwaukee	1	6	1	1	1.000	0	0	.000	0	2	2	0	2	0	0	0	2	2.0

ALEXANDER ENGLISH
(Alex)

Born January 5, 1954 at Columbia, S. C.   Height 6:07.   Weight 190.
High School—Columbia, S. C., Dreher.
College—University of South Carolina, Columbia, S. C.
Drafted by Milwaukee on second round, 1976 (23rd pick).

Signed by Indiana as a Veteran Free Agent, June 8, 1978; Milwaukee waived its right of first refusal in exchange for a 1979 1st round draft choice, October 3, 1978.
Traded by Indiana with a 1980 1st round draft choice to Denver for George McGinnis, February 1, 1980.

—COLLEGIATE RECORD—

Year	G.	Min.	FGA	FGM	Pct.	FTA	FTM	Pct.	Reb.	Pts.	Avg.
72-73	29	1037	368	189	.514	70	44	.629	306	422	14.6
73-74	27	1007	395	209	.529	112	75	.670	237	493	18.3
74-75	28	1024	359	199	.554	77	49	.636	244	447	16.0
75-76	27	1045	468	258	.551	134	94	.701	277	610	22.6
Totals	111	4113	1590	855	.538	393	262	.667	1064	1972	17.8

NBA REGULAR SEASON RECORD

Sea.—Team	G.	Min.	FGA	FGM	Pct.	FTA	FTM	Pct.	Off.	Def.	Tot.	Ast.	PF	Dq.	Stl.	Blk.	Pts.	Avg.
76-77—Milwaukee	60	648	277	132	.477	60	46	.767	68	100	168	25	78	0	17	18	310	5.2
77-78—Milwaukee	82	1552	633	343	.542	143	104	.727	144	251	395	129	178	1	41	55	790	9.6
78-79—Indiana	81	2696	1102	563	.511	230	173	.752	253	402	655	271	214	3	70	78	1299	16.0
79-80—Ind.-Den.	78	2401	1113	553	.501	266	210	.789	269	336	605	224	206	0	73	62	1318	16.9
80-81—Denver	81	3093	1555	768	.494	459	390	.850	273	373	646	290	255	2	106	100	1929	23.8

Sea.—Team	G.	Min.	FGA	FGM	Pct.	FTA	FTM	Pct.	Off.	Def.	Tot.	Ast.	PF	Dq.	Stl.	Blk.	Pts.	Avg.
81-82—Denver	82	3015	1553	855	.551	443	372	.840	210	348	558	433	261	2	87	120	2082	25.4
82-83—Denver	82	2988	1857	959	.516	490	406	.829	263	338	601	397	235	1	116	126	2326	28.4
83-84—Denver	82	2870	1714	907	.529	427	352	.824	216	248	464	406	252	3	83	95	2167	26.4
84-85—Denver	81	2924	1812	939	.518	462	383	.829	203	255	458	344	259	1	101	46	2262	27.9
85-86—Denver	81	3024	1888	951	.504	593	511	.862	192	213	405	320	235	1	73	29	2414	29.8
86-87—Denver	82	3085	1920	965	.503	487	411	.844	146	198	344	422	216	0	73	21	2345	28.6
87-88—Denver	80	2818	1704	843	.495	379	314	.828	166	207	373	377	193	1	70	23	2000	25.0
Totals	952	31114	17128	8778	.512	4439	3672	.827	2403	3269	5672	3638	2582	15	910	773	21242	22.3

Three-Point Field Goals: 1979-80, 2-for-6 (.333). 1980-81, 3-for-5 (.600). 1981-82, 0-for-8. 1982-83, 2-for-12 (.167). 1983-84, 1-for-7 (.143). 1984-85, 1-for-5 (.200). 1985-86, 1-for-5 (.200). 1986-87, 4-for-15 (.267). 1987-88, 0-for-6. Totals, 14-for-69 (.203).

NBA PLAYOFF RECORD

Sea.—Team	G.	Min.	FGA	FGM	Pct.	FTA	FTM	Pct.	Off.	Def.	Tot.	Ast.	PF	Dq.	Stl.	Blk.	Pts.	Avg.
77-78—Milwaukee	9	208	78	48	.615	32	25	.781	16	26	42	13	20	0	6	7	121	13.4
81-82—Denver	3	118	55	26	.473	7	6	.857	8	15	23	17	6	0	3	3	58	19.3
82-83—Denver	7	270	150	67	.447	53	47	.887	20	24	44	42	21	0	4	7	181	25.9
83-84—Denver	5	203	102	60	.588	28	25	.893	16	24	40	28	17	0	3	2	145	29.0
84-85—Denver	14	536	304	163	.536	109	97	.890	36	56	92	63	40	1	17	5	423	30.2
85-86—Denver	10	394	229	106	.463	71	61	.859	18	17	35	52	29	0	4	4	273	27.3
86-87—Denver	3	76	49	25	.510	7	6	.857	10	4	14	10	9	1	0	0	56	18.7
87-88—Denver	11	438	255	116	.455	43	35	.814	31	28	59	48	34	0	7	3	267	24.3
Totals	62	2243	1222	611	.500	350	302	.863	155	194	349	273	176	2	44	31	1524	24.6

Three-Point Field Goals: 1982-83, 0-for-2. 1983-84, 0-for-1. 1984-85, 0-for-1. 1985-86, 0-for-1. 1987-88, 0-for-3. Totals, 0-for-8.

NBA ALL-STAR GAME RECORD

Season—Team	Min.	FGA	FGM	Pct.	FTA	FTM	Pct.	Off.	Def.	Tot.	Ast.	PF	Dq.	Stl.	Blk.	Pts.
1982—Denver	12	6	2	.333	0	0	.000	2	3	5	1	2	0	1	0	4
1983—Denver	23	14	7	.500	1	0	.000	2	2	4	0	2	0	1	2	14
1984—Denver	19	8	6	.750	1	1	1.000	0	0	0	2	2	0	1	1	13
1985—Denver	14	3	0	.000	0	0	.000	1	1	2	1	1	0	0	0	0
1986—Denver	16	12	8	.667	0	0	.000	1	0	1	2	0	0	0	1	16
1987—Denver	13	6	0	.000	0	0	.000	0	0	0	1	1	0	0	0	0
1988—Denver	22	10	5	.500	0	0	.000	2	1	3	4	0	0	1	0	10
Totals	119	59	28	.475	2	1	.500	8	7	15	11	8	0	4	4	57

Named to All-NBA Second Team, 1982, 1983, 1986. . . . Led NBA in scoring, 1983.

MIKE LEEROYALL EVANS

Born April 19, 1955 at Goldsboro, N. C.   Height 6:01.   Weight 170.

High School—Goldsboro, N. C.

Prep School—Laurinburg, N. C., Institute.

College—Kansas State University, Manhattan, Kan.

Drafted by Denver on first round, 1978 (21st pick).

Draft rights traded by Denver with Darnell Hillman to Kansas City for Ron Boone and a 1979 2nd round draft choice, June 26, 1978.

Waived by Kansas City, October 11, 1978; signed by San Antonio as a free agent, April 26, 1979.
Sold by San Antonio to Milwaukee, October 7, 1980.
Waived by Milwaukee, December 29, 1981; re-signed by Milwaukee, January 8, 1982.
Waived by Milwaukee, February 11, 1982; signed by Cleveland as a free agent, February 20, 1982.
Signed as Veteran Free Agent by San Diego, October 11, 1982.
Waived by San Diego, October 29, 1982; signed by Denver as a free agent, January 12, 1983.
Played in Western Basketball Association with Washington Lumberjacks, 1978-79.
Played in Continental Basketball Association with Montana Golden Nuggets, 1982-83.

—COLLEGIATE RECORD—

Year	G.	Min.	FGA	FGM	Pct.	FTA	FTM	Pct.	Reb.	Pts.	Avg.
74-75	29	....	446	213	.478	81	66	.815	103	492	17.0
75-76	28	....	425	216	.508	82	70	.854	94	502	17.9
76-77	31	....	468	227	.485	145	112	.772	110	566	18.3
77-78	29	....	471	234	.497	120	87	.725	86	555	19.1
Totals	117	....	1810	890	.492	428	335	.783	393	2115	18.1

WBA & CBA REGULAR SEASON RECORD

Sea.—Team	G.	Min.	2-Point			3-Point			FTM	FTA	Pct.	Reb.	Ast.	Pts.	Avg.
			FGM	FGA	Pct.	FGM	FGA	Pct.							
78-79—Washington WBA.....	4	94	16	36	.444	0	0	....	0	0	....	6	4	32	8.0
82-83—Montana CBA............	16	504	109	201	.542	5	14	.357	42	50	.840	35	77	275	17.2

NBA REGULAR SEASON RECORD

Sea.—Team	G.	Min.	FGA	FGM	Pct.	FTA	FTM	Pct.	Off.	Def.	Tot.	Ast.	PF	Dq.	Stl.	Blk.	Pts.	Avg.
79-80—San Antonio	79	1246	464	208	.448	85	58	.682	29	78	107	230	194	2	60	9	486	6.2
80-81—Milwaukee	71	911	291	134	.460	64	50	.781	22	65	87	167	114	0	34	4	320	4.5
81-82—Mil.-Clev.	22	270	86	35	.407	20	13	.650	5	17	22	42	36	1	13	0	83	3.8
82-83—Denver	42	695	243	115	.473	41	33	.805	4	54	58	113	94	3	23	3	263	6.3
83-84—Denver	78	1687	564	243	.431	131	111	.847	23	115	138	288	175	2	61	4	629	8.1
84-85—Denver	81	1437	661	323	.489	131	113	.863	26	93	119	231	174	2	65	12	816	10.1
85-86—Denver	81	1389	715	304	.425	149	126	.846	30	71	101	177	159	1	61	1	773	9.5
86-87—Denver	81	1567	729	334	.458	123	96	.780	36	92	128	185	149	1	79	12	817	10.1
87-88—Denver	56	656	307	139	.453	37	30	.811	9	39	48	81	78	0	34	6	344	6.1
Totals	591	9858	4060	1835	.452	781	630	.807	184	624	808	1514	1173	12	430	51	4531	7.7

Three-Point Field Goals: 1979-80, 12-for-42 (.286). 1980-81, 2-for-14 (.143). 1981-82, 0-for-6. 1982-83, 0-for-9. 1983-84, 32-for-89 (.360). 1984-85, 57-for-157 (.363). 1985-86, 39-for-176 (.222). 1986-87, 53-for-169 (.314). 1987-88, 36-for-91 (.396). Totals, 231-for-753 (.307).

NBA PLAYOFF RECORD

Sea.—Team	G.	Min.	FGA	FGM	Pct.	FTA	FTM	Pct.	Off.	Def.	Tot.	Ast.	PF	Dq.	Stl.	Blk.	Pts.	Avg.
79-80—San Antonio	2	12	8	3	.375	4	3	.750	0	2	2	2	2	0	0	0	11	5.5
80-81—Milwaukee	4	38	17	9	.529	8	7	.875	0	1	1	6	9	0	0	1	25	6.3
82-83—Denver	8	183	74	36	.486	17	11	.647	2	17	19	38	20	0	5	0	86	10.8
83-84—Denver	5	77	28	9	.321	4	4	1.000	1	2	3	12	13	0	0	0	23	4.6
84-85—Denver	15	281	143	62	.434	17	14	.824	3	29	32	46	39	0	13	3	155	10.3
85-86—Denver	10	204	82	30	.366	30	25	.833	6	14	20	25	19	0	10	3	92	9.2
86-87—Denver	3	57	19	7	.368	2	2	1.000	2	5	7	8	6	0	3	0	18	6.0
87-88—Denver	11	219	114	45	.395	15	14	.933	6	16	22	23	19	0	12	0	116	10.5
Totals	58	1071	485	201	.414	97	80	.825	20	86	106	160	127	0	43	7	526	9.1

Three-Point Field Goals: 1979-80, 2-for-4 (.500). 1980-81, 0-for-2. 1982-83, 3-for-10 (.300). 1983-84, 1-for-8 (.125). 1984-85, 17-for-51 (.333). 1985-86, 7-for-29 (.241). 1986-87, 2-for-7 (.286). 1987-88, 12-for-44 (.273). Totals, 44-for-155 (.284).

PATRICK ALOYSIUS EWING

Born August 5, 1962 at Kingston, Jamaica.   Height 7:00.   Weight 240.

High School—Cambridge, Mass., Rindge & Latin.

College—Georgetown University, Washington, D.C.

Drafted by New York on first round, 1985 (1st pick).

—COLLEGIATE RECORD—

Year	G.	Min.	FGA	FGM	Pct.	FTA	FTM	Pct.	Reb.	Pts.	Avg.
81-82	37	1064	290	183	.631	167	103	.617	279	469	12.7
82-83	32	1024	372	212	.570	224	141	.629	325	565	17.7
83-84	37	1179	368	242	.658	189	124	.656	371	608	16.4
84-85	37	1132	352	220	.625	160	102	.638	341	542	14.6
Totals	143	4399	1382	857	.620	740	470	.635	1316	2184	15.3

NBA REGULAR SEASON RECORD

Sea.—Team	G.	Min.	FGA	FGM	Pct.	FTA	FTM	Pct.	Off.	Def.	Tot.	Ast.	PF	Dq.	Stl.	Blk.	Pts.	Avg.
85-86—New York	50	1771	814	386	.474	306	226	.739	124	327	451	102	191	7	54	103	998	20.0
86-87—New York	63	2206	1053	530	.503	415	296	.713	157	398	555	104	248	5	89	147	1356	21.5
87-88—New York	82	2546	1183	656	.555	476	341	.716	245	431	676	125	332	5	104	245	1653	20.2
Totals	195	6523	3050	1572	.515	1197	863	.721	526	1156	1682	331	771	17	247	495	4007	20.5

Three-Point Field Goals: 1985-86, 0-for-5. 1986-87, 0-for-7. 1987-88, 0-for-3. Totals, 0-for-15.

NBA PLAYOFF RECORD

Sea.—Team	G.	Min.	FGA	FGM	Pct.	FTA	FTM	Pct.	Off.	Def.	Tot.	Ast.	PF	Dq.	Stl.	Blk.	Pts.	Avg.
87-88—New York	4	153	57	28	.491	22	19	.864	16	35	51	10	17	0	6	13	75	18.8

Three-Point Field Goals: 1987-88, 0-for-1.

NBA ALL-STAR GAME RECORD

Season—Team	Min.	FGA	FGM	Pct.	FTA	FTM	Pct.	Off.	Def.	Tot.	Ast.	PF	Dq.	Stl.	Blk.	Pts.
1986—New York.....							Did Not Play—Injured									
1988—New York.....	16	8	4	.500	1	1	1.000	1	5	6	0	1	0	0	1	9

Named to All-NBA Second Team, 1988. . . . NBA All-Defensive Second Team, 1988. . . . NBA Rookie of the Year, 1986. . . . NBA All-Rookie Team, 1986. . . . Member of NCAA Division I championship team, 1984. . . . Named NCAA Division I Tournament Most Outstanding Player, 1984. . . . Member of U.S. Olympic team, 1984. . . . THE SPORTING NEWS College Player of the Year, 1985. . . . THE SPORTING NEWS All-America First Team, 1985. . . . THE SPORTING NEWS All-America Second Team, 1983 and 1984.

PATRICK EWING

JAMES HUBERT FARMER III
(Jim)

Born September 23, 1964 at Dothan, Ala. Height 6:04. Weight 190.
High School—Dothan, Ala., Houston Academy.
College—University of Alabama, University, Ala.
Drafted by Dallas on first round, 1987 (20th pick).

—COLLEGIATE RECORD—

Year	G.	Min.	FGA	FGM	Pct.	FTA	FTM	Pct.	Reb.	Pts.	Avg.
82-83					Redshirted						
83-84	12	59	24	7	.292	13	7	.538	6	21	1.8
84-85	33	700	186	82	.441	65	45	.692	71	209	6.3
85-86	33	1101	326	168	.515	114	85	.746	154	421	12.8
86-87	33	1084	421	196	.466	133	118	.887	159	546	16.5
Totals	111	2944	957	453	.473	325	255	.785	390	1197	10.8

Three-Point Field Goals: 1986-87, 36-for-93 (.387).

NBA REGULAR SEASON RECORD

Sea.—Team	G.	Min.	FGA	FGM	Pct.	FTA	FTM	Pct.	Off.	Def.	Tot.	Ast.	PF	Dq.	Stl.	Blk.	Pts.	Avg.
									—Rebounds—									
87-88—Dallas	30	157	69	26	.377	10	9	.900	9	9	18	16	18	0	3	1	61	2.0

Three-Point Field Goals: 1987-88, 0-for-6.

NBA PLAYOFF RECORD

Sea.—Team	G.	Min.	FGA	FGM	Pct.	FTA	FTM	Pct.	Off.	Def.	Tot.	Ast.	PF	Dq.	Stl.	Blk.	Pts.	Avg.
									—Rebounds—									
87-88—Dallas	3	11	6	2	.333	0	0	.000	3	1	4	1	2	0	0	0	4	1.3

DAVE SCOTT FEITL

Born June 8, 1962 at Butler, Pa. Height 7:00. Weight 240.
High School—Tucson, Ariz., Santa Rita.
College—University of Texas at El Paso, El Paso, Tex.
Drafted by Houston on second round, 1986 (43rd pick).

Traded by Houston with a future 1st round draft choice to Golden State for Purvis Short, November 5, 1987.
Traded by Golden State with a 1989 2nd round draft choice to Washington for Manute Bol, June 8, 1988.

—COLLEGIATE RECORD—

Year	G.	Min.	FGA	FGM	Pct.	FTA	FTM	Pct.	Reb.	Pts.	Avg.
81-82					Did Not Play—Back Injury						
82-83	29	641	191	95	.497	89	67	.753	141	257	8.9
83-84	31	575	176	82	.466	60	40	.667	132	204	6.6
84-85	32	911	305	158	.518	156	117	.750	227	433	13.5
85-86	33	1017	412	208	.505	182	132	.725	226	548	16.6
Totals	125	3144	1084	543	.501	487	356	.731	726	1442	11.5

NBA REGULAR SEASON RECORD

Sea.—Team	G.	Min.	FGA	FGM	Pct.	FTA	FTM	Pct.	Off.	Def.	Tot.	Ast.	PF	Dq.	Stl.	Blk.	Pts.	Avg.
									—Rebounds—									
86-87—Houston	62	498	202	88	.436	71	53	.746	39	78	117	22	83	0	9	4	229	3.7
87-88—Golden State	70	1128	404	182	.450	134	94	.701	83	252	335	53	146	1	15	9	458	6.5
Totals	132	1626	606	270	.446	205	147	.717	122	330	452	75	229	1	24	13	687	5.2

Three-Point Field Goals: 1986-87, 0-for-1. 1987-88, 0-for-4. Totals, 0-for-5.

NBA PLAYOFF RECORD

Sea.—Team	G.	Min.	FGA	FGM	Pct.	FTA	FTM	Pct.	Off.	Def.	Tot.	Ast.	PF	Dq.	Stl.	Blk.	Pts.	Avg.
									—Rebounds—									
86-87—Houston	6	8	0	0	.000	2	2	1.000	0	1	1	0	0	0	0	0	2	0.3

KENNETH HENRY FIELDS
(Kenny)

Born February 9, 1962 at Iowa City, Iowa. Height 6:05. Weight 240.
High School—Los Angeles, Calif., Verbum Dei.
College—University of California at Los Angeles, Los Angeles, Calif.
Drafted by Milwaukee on first round, 1984 (21st pick).

Waived by Milwaukee, November 11, 1986; signed by Los Angeles Clippers as a free agent, November 17, 1986, for remainder of season.

Signed by Los Angeles Clippers, February 27, 1988, to the first of consecutive 10-day contracts that expired, March 16, 1988.

Played in Continental Basketball Association with Rochester Flyers, 1987-88.

—COLLEGIATE RECORD—

Year	G.	Min.	FGA	FGM	Pct.	FTA	FTM	Pct.	Reb.	Pts.	Avg.
80-81	25	588	185	110	.595	56	33	.589	122	253	10.1
81-82	27	867	286	158	.552	84	60	.714	160	376	13.9
82-83	29	998	405	224	.553	121	75	.620	192	523	18.0
83-84	28	943	384	194	.505	134	98	.731	193	486	17.4
Totals	109	3396	1260	686	.544	395	266	.673	667	1638	15.0

CBA REGULAR SEASON RECORD

Sea.—Team	G.	Min.	2-Point FGM	FGA	Pct.	3-Point FGM	FGA	Pct.	FTM	FTA	Pct.	Reb.	Ast.	Pts.	Avg.
87-88—Rochester	11	212	34	65	.523	0	0	.000	13	19	.684	43	13	81	7.4

NBA REGULAR SEASON RECORD

Sea.—Team	G.	Min.	FGA	FGM	Pct.	FTA	FTM	Pct.	Off.	Def.	Tot.	Ast.	PF	Dq.	Stl.	Blk.	Pts.	Avg.
84-85—Milwaukee	51	535	191	84	.440	36	27	.750	41	43	84	38	84	2	9	10	195	3.8
85-86—Milwaukee	78	1120	398	204	.513	132	91	.689	59	144	203	79	170	3	51	15	499	6.4
86-87—Mil.-L.A.C.	48	883	352	159	.452	94	73	.777	63	85	148	61	123	2	32	11	394	8.2
87-88—L.A. Clippers	7	154	36	16	.444	26	20	.769	13	16	29	10	17	0	5	2	52	7.4
Totals	184	2692	977	463	.474	288	211	.733	176	288	464	188	394	7	97	38	1140	6.2

Three-Point Field Goals: 1985-86, 0-for-4. 1986-87, 3-for-12 (.250). Totals, 3-for-16 (.188).

NBA PLAYOFF RECORD

Sea.—Team	G.	Min.	FGA	FGM	Pct.	FTA	FTM	Pct.	Off.	Def.	Tot.	Ast.	PF	Dq.	Stl.	Blk.	Pts.	Avg.
85-86—Milwaukee	12	158	69	38	.551	23	12	.522	7	21	28	10	23	0	8	0	89	7.4

Three-Point Field Goals: 1985-86, 1-for-3 (.333).

VERN FLEMING

Born February 4, 1961 at New York, N.Y.   Height 6:05.   Weight 195.

High School—Long Island City, N. Y., Mater Christi.

College—University of Georgia, Athens, Ga.

Drafted by Indiana on first round, 1984 (18th pick).

—COLLEGIATE RECORD—

Year	G.	Min.	FGA	FGM	Pct.	FTA	FTM	Pct.	Reb.	Pts.	Avg.
80-81	30	1082	225	108	.480	122	85	.697	80	301	10.0
81-82	31	1079	236	117	.496	114	73	.640	120	307	9.9
82-83	34	1130	424	227	.535	169	121	.716	158	575	16.9
83-84	30	1030	493	248	.503	130	98	.754	120	594	19.8
Totals	125	4321	1378	700	.508	535	377	.705	478	1777	14.2

NBA REGULAR SEASON RECORD

Sea.—Team	G.	Min.	FGA	FGM	Pct.	FTA	FTM	Pct.	Off.	Def.	Tot.	Ast.	PF	Dq.	Stl.	Blk.	Pts.	Avg.
84-85—Indiana	80	2486	922	433	.470	339	260	.767	148	175	323	247	232	4	99	8	1126	14.1
85-86—Indiana	80	2870	862	436	.506	353	263	.745	102	284	386	505	230	3	131	5	1136	14.2
86-87—Indiana	82	2549	727	370	.509	302	238	.788	109	225	334	473	222	3	109	18	980	12.0
87-88—Indiana	80	2733	845	442	.523	283	227	.802	106	258	364	568	225	0	115	11	1111	13.9
Totals	322	10638	3356	1681	.501	1277	988	.774	465	942	1407	1793	909	10	454	42	4353	13.5

Three-Point Field Goals: 1984-85, 0-for-4. 1985-86, 1-for-6 (.167). 1986-87, 2-for-10 (.200). 1987-88, 0-for-13. Totals, 3-for-33 (.091).

NBA PLAYOFF RECORD

Sea.—Team	G.	Min.	FGA	FGM	Pct.	FTA	FTM	Pct.	Off.	Def.	Tot.	Ast.	PF	Dq.	Stl.	Blk.	Pts.	Avg.
86-87—Indiana	4	141	36	13	.361	30	23	.767	9	17	26	24	15	1	4	1	49	12.3

Three-Point Field Goals: 1986-87, 0-for-1.

Member of U.S. Olympic team, 1984.

—DID YOU KNOW—

That Spurs assistant coach Ed Manning, father of Clippers rookie Danny Manning, played for Clippers Coach Gene Shue with the old Baltimore Bullets? Elgin Baylor, now the Clippers' general manager, played for the Lakers against Ed Manning.

ERIC A. FLOYD
(Sleepy)

Born March 6, 1960 at Gastonia, N.C.   Height 6:03.   Weight 175.

High School—Gastonia, N. C., Hunter Huss.

College—Georgetown University, Washington, D. C.

Drafted by New Jersey on first round, 1982 (13th pick).

Traded by New Jersey with Mickey Johnson to Golden State for Micheal Ray Richardson, February 6, 1983.

Traded by Golden State with Joe Barry Carroll to Houston for Ralph Sampson and Steve Harris, December 12, 1987.

—COLLEGIATE RECORD—

Year	G.	Min.	FGA	FGM	Pct.	FTA	FTM	Pct.	Reb.	Pts.	Avg.
78-79	29	975	388	177	.456	155	126	.813	119	480	16.6
79-80	32	1052	444	246	.554	140	106	.757	98	598	18.7
80-81	32	1115	508	237	.467	165	133	.806	133	607	19.0
81-82	37	1200	494	249	.504	168	121	.720	127	619	16.7
Totals	130	4342	1834	909	.496	628	486	.774	477	2304	17.7

NBA REGULAR SEASON RECORD

Sea.—Team	G.	Min.	FGA	FGM	Pct.	FTA	FTM	Pct.	Off.	Def.	Tot.	Ast.	PF	Dq.	Stl.	Blk.	Pts.	Avg.
82-83—N.J.-G.S.	76	1248	527	226	.429	180	150	.833	56	81	137	138	134	3	58	17	612	8.1
83-84—Golden State	77	2555	1045	484	.463	386	315	.816	87	184	271	269	216	0	103	31	1291	16.8
84-85—Golden State	82	2873	1372	610	.445	415	336	.810	62	140	202	406	226	1	134	41	1598	19.5
85-86—Golden State	82	2764	1007	510	.506	441	351	.796	76	221	297	746	199	2	157	16	1410	17.2
86-87—Golden State	82	3064	1030	503	.488	537	462	.860	56	212	268	848	199	1	146	18	1541	18.8
87-88—G.S.-Hou.	77	2514	969	420	.433	354	301	.850	77	219	296	544	190	1	95	12	1155	15.0
Totals	476	15018	5950	2753	.463	2313	1915	.828	414	1057	1471	2951	1164	8	693	135	7607	16.0

Three-Point Field Goals: 1982-83, 10-for-25 (.400). 1983-84, 8-for-45 (.178). 1984-85, 42-for-143 (.294). 1985-86, 39-for-119 (.328). 1986-87, 73-for-190 (.384). 1987-88, 14-for-72 (.194). Totals, 186-for-594 (.313).

NBA PLAYOFF RECORD

Sea.—Team	G.	Min.	FGA	FGM	Pct.	FTA	FTM	Pct.	Off.	Def.	Tot.	Ast.	PF	Dq.	Stl.	Blk.	Pts.	Avg.
86-87—Golden State	10	414	152	77	.507	51	47	.922	9	21	30	102	24	0	18	2	214	21.4
87-88—Houston	4	154	61	26	.426	22	19	.864	3	4	7	34	10	0	8	0	75	18.8
Totals	14	568	213	103	.484	73	66	.904	12	25	37	136	34	0	26	2	289	20.6

Three-Point Field Goals: 1986-87, 13-for-28 (.464). 1987-88, 4-for-8 (.500). Totals, 17-for-36 (.472).

NBA ALL-STAR GAME RECORD

Season—Team	Min.	FGA	FGM	Pct.	FTA	FTM	Pct.	Off.	Def.	Tot.	Ast.	PF	Dq.	Stl.	Blk.	Pts.
1987—Golden State	19	7	4	.571	7	5	.714	2	3	5	1	2	0	1	0	14

Three-Point Field Goals: 1987, 1-for-3 (.333).

Shares NBA record for most minutes played in one game, 64, vs. New Jersey, February 1, 1987 (4 ot). . . . Holds NBA playoff game records for most points in one half, 39, and in one quarter, 29, vs. Los Angeles Lakers, May 10, 1987. . . . Named to THE SPORTING NEWS All-America Second Team, 1982.

TELLIS JOSEPH FRANK JR.

Born April 26, 1965 at Gary, Ind.   Height 6:10.   Weight 225.

High School—Gary, Ind., Lew Wallace.

College—Western Kentucky University, Bowling Green, Ky.

Drafted by Golden State on first round, 1987 (14th pick).

—COLLEGIATE RECORD—

Year	G.	Min.	FGA	FGM	Pct.	FTA	FTM	Pct.	Reb.	Pts.	Avg.
83-84	27	....	121	42	.347	36	22	.611	92	106	3.9
84-85	27	....	213	93	.437	62	41	.661	134	227	8.4
85-86	30	....	212	109	.514	111	88	.793	157	306	10.2
86-87	38	....	542	281	.518	175	122	.697	281	684	18.0
Totals	122	....	1088	525	.483	384	273	.711	664	1323	10.8

NBA REGULAR SEASON RECORD

Sea.—Team	G.	Min.	FGA	FGM	Pct.	FTA	FTM	Pct.	Off.	Def.	Tot.	Ast.	PF	Dq.	Stl.	Blk.	Pts.	Avg.
87-88—Golden State	78	1597	565	242	.428	207	150	.725	95	235	330	111	267	5	53	23	634	8.1

Three-Point Field Goals: 1987-88, 0-for-1.

ERIC FLOYD

WORLD B. FREE
(Formerly known as Lloyd Free.)

Born December 9, 1953 at Atlanta, Ga.   Height 6:03.   Weight 190.

High School—Brooklyn, N. Y., Canarsie.

College—Guilford College, Greensboro, N. C.

Drafted by Philadelphia on second round as hardship case, 1975 (23rd pick).

Traded by Philadelphia to San Diego for a 1984 1st round draft choice, October 12, 1978.
Traded by San Diego to Golden State for Phil Smith and a 1984 1st round draft choice, August 28, 1980.
Traded by Golden State to Cleveland for Ron Brewer, December 15, 1982.
Signed by Philadelphia as a Veteran Free Agent, December 30, 1986; Cleveland agreed not to exercise its right of first refusal in exchange for a 1990 2nd round draft choice.
Waived by Philadelphia, March 4, 1987; signed by Houston as a free agent, October 1, 1987.

—COLLEGIATE RECORD—

Year	G.	Min.	FGA	FGM	Pct.	FTA	FTM	Pct.	Reb.	Pts.	Avg.
72-73	33	....	572	272	.476	217	153	.705	191	697	21.1
73-74	24	....	456	216	.474	225	165	.733	200	597	24.9
74-75	28	....	486	247	.508	291	218	.749	163	712	25.4
Totals	85	....	1514	735	.485	733	536	.731	554	2006	23.6

NBA REGULAR SEASON RECORD

Sea.—Team	G.	Min.	FGA	FGM	Pct.	FTA	FTM	Pct.	Off.	Def.	Tot.	Ast.	PF	Dq.	Stl.	Blk.	Pts.	Avg.
75-76—Philadelphia	71	1121	533	239	.448	186	112	.602	64	61	125	104	107	0	37	6	590	8.3
76-77—Philadelphia	78	2253	1022	467	.457	464	334	.720	97	140	237	266	207	2	75	25	1268	16.3
77-78—Philadelphia	76	2050	857	390	.455	562	411	.731	92	120	212	306	199	0	68	41	1191	15.7
78-79—San Diego	78	2954	1653	795	.481	865	654	.756	127	174	301	340	253	8	111	35	2244	28.8
79-80—San Diego	68	2585	1556	737	.474	760	572	.753	129	109	238	283	195	0	81	32	2055	30.2
80-81—Golden State	65	2370	1157	516	.446	649	528	.814	48	111	159	361	183	1	85	11	1565	24.1
81-82—Golden State	78	2796	1452	650	.448	647	479	.740	118	130	248	419	222	1	71	8	1789	22.9
82-83—G.S.-Clev.	73	2638	1423	649	.456	583	430	.738	92	109	201	290	241	4	97	15	1743	23.4
83-84—Cleveland	75	2375	1407	626	.445	504	395	.784	89	128	217	226	214	2	94	8	1669	22.3
84-85—Cleveland	71	2249	1328	609	.459	411	308	.749	61	150	211	320	163	0	75	16	1597	22.5
85-86—Cleveland	75	2535	1433	652	.455	486	379	.780	72	146	218	314	186	1	91	19	1754	23.4
86-87—Philadelphia	20	285	123	39	.317	47	36	.766	5	14	19	30	26	0	5	4	116	5.8
87-88—Houston	58	682	350	143	.409	100	80	.800	14	30	44	60	74	2	20	3	374	6.4
Totals	886	26893	14294	6512	.456	6264	4718	.753	1008	1422	2430	3319	2270	21	910	223	17955	20.3

Three-Point Field Goals: 1979-80, 9-for-25 (.360). 1980-81, 5-for-31 (.161). 1981-82, 10-for-56 (.179). 1982-83, 15-for-45 (.333). 1983-84, 22-for-69 (.319). 1984-85, 71-for-193 (.368). 1985-86, 71-for-169 (.420). 1986-87, 2-for-9 (.222). 1987-88, 8-for-35 (.229). Totals, 213-for-632 (.337).

NBA PLAYOFF RECORD

Sea.—Team	G.	Min.	FGA	FGM	Pct.	FTA	FTM	Pct.	Off.	Def.	Tot.	Ast.	PF	Dq.	Stl.	Blk.	Pts.	Avg.
75-76—Philadelphia	3	62	28	11	.393	13	10	.769	1	0	1	5	6	0	3	0	32	10.7
76-77—Philadelphia	15	281	170	63	.371	77	53	.688	10	22	32	29	33	0	12	8	179	11.9
77-78—Philadelphia	10	268	124	51	.411	81	59	.728	10	21	31	37	26	0	4	6	161	16.1
84-85—Cleveland	4	150	93	41	.441	25	23	.920	4	6	10	31	12	0	6	0	105	26.3
87-88—Houston	2	12	2	0	.000	0	0	.000	1	1	2	1	2	0	0	0	0	0.0
Totals	34	773	417	166	.398	196	145	.740	26	50	76	103	79	0	25	14	477	14.0

Three-Point Field Goals: 1984-85, 0-for-4. 1987-88, 0-for-1. Totals, 0-for-5.

NBA ALL-STAR GAME RECORD

Season—Team	Min.	FGA	FGM	Pct.	FTA	FTM	Pct.	Off.	Def.	Tot.	Ast.	PF	Dq.	Stl.	Blk.	Pts.
1980—San Diego	21	13	7	.538	1	0	.000	1	2	3	5	1	0	0	1	14

Named to All-NBA Second Team, 1979. . . . . **Most Valuable Player in NAIA tournament, 1973.** . . . . **Member of NAIA championship team, 1973.**

KEVIN DOUGLAS GAMBLE

Born November 13, 1965 at Springfield, Ill.   Height 6:05.   Weight 215.

High School—Springfield, Ill., Lanphier.

Colleges—Lincoln College, Lincoln, Ill., and
University of Iowa, Iowa City, Ia.

Drafted by Portland on third round, 1987 (63rd pick).

Waived by Portland, December 9, 1987.
Played in Continental Basketball Association with Quad City Thunder, 1987-88.

Lincoln

Year	G.	Min.	FGA	FGM	Pct.	FTA	FTM	Pct.	Reb.	Pts.	Avg.
83-84	30	....	469	262	.559	148	115	.777	276	639	21.3
84-85	31	....	461	267	.579	126	103	.817	301	637	20.5
J.C. Totals	61	....	930	529	.569	274	218	.796	577	1276	20.9

Iowa

Year	G.	Min.	FGA	FGM	Pct.	FTA	FTM	Pct.	Reb.	Pts.	Avg.
85-86	30	260	76	36	.474	10	7	.700	52	79	2.6
86-87	35	867	298	162	.544	99	69	.697	158	418	11.9
Iowa Totals	65	1127	374	198	.529	109	76	.697	210	497	7.6

Three-Point Field Goals: 1986-87, 35-for-76 (.329).

CBA REGULAR SEASON RECORD

Sea.—Team	G.	Min.	2-Point FGM	2-Point FGA	2-Point Pct.	3-Point FGM	3-Point FGA	3-Point Pct.	FTM	FTA	Pct.	Reb.	Ast.	Pts.	Avg.
87-88—Quad City	40	1450	299	565	.529	31	75	.413	151	184	.821	237	149	842	21.1

NBA REGULAR SEASON RECORD

Sea.—Team	G.	Min.	FGA	FGM	Pct.	FTA	FTM	Pct.	Rebounds Off.	Rebounds Def.	Rebounds Tot.	Ast.	PF	Dq.	Stl.	Blk.	Pts.	Avg.
87-88—Portland	9	19	3	0	.000	0	0	.000	2	1	3	1	2	0	2	0	0	0.0

Three-Point Field Goals: 1987-88, 0-for-1.

WINSTON KINNARD GARLAND

Born December 19, 1964 at Gary, Ind.   Height 6:02.   Weight 170.

High School—Gary, Ind., Roosevelt.

Colleges—Southeastern Community College, West Burlington, Ia.,
and Southwest Missouri State University, Springfield, Mo.

Drafted by Milwaukee on second round, 1987 (40th pick).

Waived by Milwaukee, November 4, 1987; signed by Golden State as a free agent, November 25, 1987.
Waived by Golden State, December 9, 1987; re-signed by Golden State, December 14, 1987.
Played in Continental Basketball Association with Pensacola Tornados, 1987-88.

—COLLEGIATE RECORD—
Southeastern

Year	G.	Min.	FGA	FGM	Pct.	FTA	FTM	Pct.	Reb.	Pts.	Avg.
83-84	34	1053	450	233	.518	134	112	.836	150	578	17.0
84-85	30	1006	401	207	.516	156	133	.853	107	547	18.2
J. C. Totals	64	2059	851	440	.517	290	245	.845	257	1125	17.6

Southwest Missouri State

Year	G.	Min.	FGA	FGM	Pct.	FTA	FTM	Pct.	Reb.	Pts.	Avg.
85-86	32	1006	445	205	.461	153	118	.771	116	528	16.5
86-87	34	1119	545	274	.503	153	115	.752	85	720	21.2
Totals	66	2231	990	479	.484	306	233	.761	201	1248	18.9

Three-Point Field Goals: 1986-87, 57-for-113 (.504).

CBA REGULAR SEASON RECORD

Sea.—Team	G.	Min.	2-Point FGM	2-Point FGA	2-Point Pct.	3-Point FGM	3-Point FGA	3-Point Pct.	FTM	FTA	Pct.	Reb.	Ast.	Pts.	Avg.
87-88—Pensacola	4	60	17	34	.500	0	1	.000	10	11	.909	7	5	44	11.0

NBA REGULAR SEASON RECORD

Sea.—Team	G.	Min.	FGA	FGM	Pct.	FTA	FTM	Pct.	Rebounds Off.	Rebounds Def.	Rebounds Tot.	Ast.	PF	Dq.	Stl.	Blk.	Pts.	Avg.
87-88—Golden State	67	2122	775	340	.439	157	138	.879	68	159	227	429	188	2	116	7	831	12.4

Three-Point Field Goals: 1987-88, 13-for-39 (.333).

ARMON LOUIS GILLIAM

Born May 28, 1964 at Pittsburgh, Pa.   Height 6:09.   Weight 230.

High School—Bethel Park, Pa.

Colleges—Independence Junior College, Independence, Kan., and
University of Nevada at Las Vegas, Las Vegas, Nev.

Drafted by Phoenix on first round, 1987 (2nd pick).

—COLLEGIATE RECORD—
Independence

Year	G.	Min.	FGA	FGM	Pct.	FTA	FTM	Pct.	Reb.	Pts.	Avg.
82-83	38	....	422	262	.621	185	117	.632	314	641	16.9

ARMON GILLIAM

Nevada-Las Vegas

Year	G.	Min.	FGA	FGM	Pct.	FTA	FTM	Pct.	Reb.	Pts.	Avg.
83-84				Did Not Play—Redshirted							
84-85	31	800	219	136	.621	150	98	.653	212	370	11.9
85-86	37	1243	418	221	.529	190	140	.737	315	582	15.7
86-87	39	1259	598	359	.600	254	185	.728	363	903	23.2
UNLV Totals	107	3302	1235	716	.580	594	423	.712	890	1855	17.3

NBA REGULAR SEASON RECORD

Sea.—Team	G.	Min.	FGA	FGM	Pct.	FTA	FTM	Pct.	Off.	Def.	Tot.	Ast.	PF	Dq.	Stl.	Blk.	Pts.	Avg.
									—Rebounds—									
87-88—Phoenix	55	1807	720	342	.475	193	131	.679	134	300	434	72	143	1	58	29	815	14.8

Named to NBA All-Rookie Team, 1988. . . . THE SPORTING NEWS All-America Second Team, 1987.

ARTIS GILMORE

Born September 21, 1949 at Chipley, Fla.   Height 7:02.   Weight 265.

High Schools—Chipley, Fla., Roulhac and Dothan, Ala., Carver (Senior).

Colleges—Gardner-Webb Junior College, Boiling Springs, N.C., and
Jacksonville University, Jacksonville, Fla.

Drafted by Chicago on seventh round, 1971 (117th pick).

Selected by Kentucky on first round of ABA draft, 1971.
Selected by Chicago NBA from Kentucky for $1,100,000 in ABA dispersal draft, August 5, 1976.
Traded by Chicago to San Antonio for Dave Corzine, Mark Olberding and cash, July 22, 1982.
Traded by San Antonio to Chicago for a 1988 2nd round draft choice, June 22, 1987.
Waived by Chicago, December 26, 1987; signed by Boston as a free agent, January 8, 1988.

—COLLEGIATE RECORD—
Gardner Webb JC

Year	G.	Min.	FGA	FGM	Pct.	FTA	FTM	Pct.	Reb.	Pts.	Avg.
67-68	31	....	...	296	....	...	121	....	....	713	23.0
68-69	36	....	...	326	....	...	140	....	....	792	22.0
JC Totals	67	....	....	622	....	....	261	....	....	1505	22.5

Jacksonville

Year	G.	Min.	FGA	FGM	Pct.	FTA	FTM	Pct.	Reb.	Pts.	Avg.
69-70	28	....	529	307	.580	202	128	.634	621	742	26.5
70-71	26	....	405	229	.565	188	112	.596	603	570	21.9
Totals	54		934	536	.574	390	240	.615	1224	1312	24.3

ABA REGULAR SEASON RECORD

Sea.—Team	G.	Min.	2-Point			3-Point			FTM	FTA	Pct.	Reb.	Ast.	Pts.	Avg.
			FGM	FGA	Pct.	FGM	FGA	Pct.							
71-72—Kentucky	84	3666	806	1348	.598	0	0	.000	391	605	.646	1491	230	2003	23.8
72-73—Kentucky	84	3502	686	1226	.560	1	2	.500	368	572	.643	1476	295	1743	20.9
73-74—Kentucky	84	3502	621	1257	.494	0	3	.000	326	489	.667	1538	329	1568	18.7
74-75—Kentucky	84	3493	783	1349	.580	1	2	.500	412	592	.696	1361	208	1081	23.6
75-76—Kentucky	84	3286	773	1401	.552	0	0	.000	521	764	.682	1303	211	2067	24.6
Totals	420	17449	3669	6581	.558	2	7	.286	2018	3022	.668	7169	1273	9362	22.3

ABA PLAYOFF RECORD

Sea.—Team	G.	Min.	2-Point			3-Point			FTM	FTA	Pct.	Reb.	Ast.	Pts.	Avg.
			FGM	FGA	Pct.	FGM	FGA	Pct.							
71-72—Kentucky	6	285	52	90	.577	0	0	.000	27	38	.711	106	25	131	21.8
72-73—Kentucky	19	780	142	261	.544	0	0	.000	77	123	.626	260	75	361	19.0
73-74—Kentucky	8	344	71	127	.559	0	0	.000	38	66	.576	149	28	180	22.5
74-75—Kentucky	15	679	132	245	.539	0	0	.000	98	127	.772	264	38	362	24.1
75-76—Kentucky	10	390	93	153	.608	0	0	.000	56	75	.747	152	19	242	24.2
Totals	58	2478	500	876	.571	0	0	.000	296	429	.690	931	185	1280	22.1

ABA ALL-STAR GAME RECORD

Sea.—Team	Min.	2-Point			3-Point			FTM	FTA	Pct.	Reb.	Ast.	Pts.	Avg.
		FGM	FGA	Pct.	FGM	FGA	Pct.							
1972—Kentucky	27	4	5	.800	0	0	.000	6	10	.600	10	2	14	14.0
1973—Kentucky	31	3	8	.375	0	0	.000	4	8	.500	16	0	10	10.0
1974—Kentucky	27	8	12	.667	0	0	.000	2	3	.667	13	1	18	18.0
1975—Kentucky	28	4	8	.500	0	0	.000	3	7	.429	13	2	11	11.0
1976—Kentucky	27	5	7	.714	0	0	.000	6	7	.857	7	1	14	14.0
Totals	140	24	40	.600	0	0	.000	21	35	.600	59	6	67	13.4

NBA REGULAR SEASON RECORD

Sea.—Team	G.	Min.	FGA	FGM	Pct.	FTA	FTM	Pct.	Off.	Def.	Tot.	Ast.	PF	Dq.	Stl.	Blk.	Pts.	Avg.
76-77—Chicago	82	2877	1091	570	.522	586	387	.660	313	757	1070	199	266	4	44	203	1527	18.6
77-78—Chicago	82	3067	1260	704	.559	669	471	.704	318	753	1071	263	261	4	42	181	1879	22.9
78-79—Chicago	82	3265	1310	753	.575	587	434	.739	293	750	1043	274	280	2	50	156	1940	23.7
79-80—Chicago	48	1568	513	305	.595	344	245	.712	108	324	432	133	167	5	29	59	855	17.8
80-81—Chicago	82	2832	816	547	.670	532	375	.705	220	608	828	172	295	2	47	198	1469	17.9
81-82—Chicago	82	2796	837	546	.652	552	424	.768	224	611	835	136	287	4	49	220	1517	18.5
82-83—San Antonio	82	2797	888	556	.626	496	367	.740	299	685	984	126	273	4	40	192	1479	18.0
83-84—San Antonio	64	2034	556	351	.631	390	280	.718	213	449	662	70	229	4	36	132	982	15.3
84-85—San Antonio	81	2756	854	532	.623	646	484	.749	231	615	846	131	306	4	40	173	1548	19.1
85-86—San Antonio	71	2395	684	423	.618	482	338	.701	166	434	600	102	239	3	39	108	1184	16.7
86-87—San Antonio	82	2405	580	346	.597	356	242	.680	185	394	579	150	235	2	39	95	934	11.4
87-88—Chi.-Bos.	71	893	181	99	.547	128	67	.523	69	142	211	21	148	0	15	30	265	3.7
Totals	909	29685	9570	5732	.599	5768	4114	.713	2639	6522	9161	1777	2986	38	470	1747	15579	17.1

Three-Point Field Goals: 1981-82, 1-for-1. 1982-83, 0-for-6. 1983-84, 0-for-3. 1984-85, 0-for-2. 1985-86, 0-for-1. Totals, 1-for-13 (.077).

NBA PLAYOFF RECORD

Sea.—Team	G.	Min.	FGA	FGM	Pct.	FTA	FTM	Pct.	Off.	Def.	Tot.	Ast.	PF	Dq.	Stl.	Blk.	Pts.	Avg.
76-77—Chicago	3	126	40	19	.475	23	18	.783	15	24	39	6	9	0	3	8	56	18.7
80-81—Chicago	6	247	60	35	.583	55	38	.691	24	43	67	12	15	0	6	17	108	18.0
82-83—San Antonio	11	401	132	76	.576	46	32	.696	37	105	142	18	46	1	9	34	184	16.7
84-85—San Antonio	5	185	52	29	.558	45	31	.689	10	40	50	7	18	0	2	7	89	17.8
85-86—San Antonio	3	107	24	16	.667	14	8	.571	7	11	18	3	11	0	7	1	40	13.3
87-88—Boston	14	86	8	4	.500	14	7	.500	4	16	20	1	14	0	0	4	15	1.1
Totals	42	1152	316	179	.566	197	134	.680	97	239	336	47	113	1	27	71	492	11.7

NBA ALL-STAR GAME RECORD

Season—Team	Min.	FGA	FGM	Pct.	FTA	FTM	Pct.	Off.	Def.	Tot.	Ast.	PF	Dq.	Stl.	Blk.	Pts.
1978—Chicago	13	4	2	.500	8	6	.750	0	2	2	0	1	0	1	2	10
1979—Chicago	15	4	3	.750	2	2	1.000	1	0	1	2	1	0	0	0	8
1981—Chicago	22	7	5	.714	2	1	.500	1	5	6	2	4	0	0	1	11
1982—Chicago	16	6	3	.500	1	1	1.000	1	2	3	2	4	0	0	1	7
1983—San Antonio..	16	4	2	.500	2	1	.500	1	4	5	1	4	0	1	0	5
1986—San Antonio..	13	4	3	.750	4	4	1.000	1	1	2	1	4	0	2	0	10
Totals	95	29	18	.621	19	15	.789	5	14	19	8	18	0	4	4	51

COMBINED ABA AND NBA REGULAR SEASON RECORDS

	G.	Min.	FGA	FGM	Pct.	FTA	FTM	Pct.	Off.	Def.	Tot.	Ast.	PF	Dq.	Stl.	Blk.	Pts.	Avg.
Totals	1329	47134	16158	9403	.582	8790	6132	.698	4816	11514	16330	3050	4529	na	na	3178	24941	18.8

Named to NBA All-Defensive Second Team, 1978.... NBA all-time field-goal percentage leader.... Led NBA in field-goal percentage, 1981, 1982, 1983, 1984.... ABA All-Star First Team, 1972, 1973, 1974, 1975, 1976.... ABA Most Valuable Player and Rookie of the Year, 1972.... ABA All-Rookie Team, 1972.... ABA All-Defensive Team, 1973, 1974, 1975, 1976.... ABA All-Star Game MVP, 1974.... ABA Playoff MVP, 1975.... Member of ABA championship team, 1975.... Led ABA in rebounding, 1972, 1973, 1974, 1976.... Led ABA in field-goal percentage, 1972 and 1973.... Led ABA in blocked shots, 1973.... Named to THE SPORTING NEWS All-America First Team, 1971.... THE SPORTING NEWS All-America Second Team, 1970.... NCAA career leading rebounding average, 22.7.... Led NCAA in rebounding, 1970 and 1971.... One of only seven players to average over 20 points and 20 rebounds per game during NCAA career.

MICHAEL THOMAS GMINSKI
(Mike)

Born August 3, 1959 at Monroe, Conn.   Height 6:11.   Weight 260.

High School—Monroe, Conn., Masuk.

College—Duke University, Durham, N. C.

Drafted by New Jersey on first round, 1980 (7th pick).

Traded by New Jersey with Ben Coleman to Philadelphia for Roy Hinson, Tim McCormick and a 1989 2nd round draft choice, January 16, 1988.

—COLLEGIATE RECORD—

Year	G.	Min.	FGA	FGM	Pct.	FTA	FTM	Pct.	Reb.	Pts.	Avg.
76-77	27	....	340	175	.515	91	64	.703	289	414	15.3
77-78	32	....	450	246	.547	176	148	.841	319	640	20.0
78-79	30	....	420	218	.519	177	129	.729	275	565	18.8
79-80	33	1192	487	262	.538	214	180	.841	359	704	21.3
Totals	122	....	1697	901	.531	658	521	.792	1242	2323	19.0

NBA REGULAR SEASON RECORD

Sea.—Team	G.	Min.	FGA	FGM	Pct.	FTA	FTM	Pct.	Off.	Def.	Tot.	Ast.	PF	Dq.	Stl.	Blk.	Pts.	Avg.
80-81—New Jersey	56	1579	688	291	.423	202	155	.767	137	282	419	72	127	1	54	100	737	13.2

Sea.—Team	G.	Min.	FGA	FGM	Pct.	FTA	FTM	Pct.	Off.	Def.	Tot.	Ast.	PF	Dq.	Stl.	Blk.	Pts.	Avg.
									—Rebounds—									
81-82—New Jersey	64	740	270	119	.441	118	97	.822	70	116	186	41	69	0	17	48	335	5.2
82-83—New Jersey	80	1255	426	213	.500	225	175	.778	154	228	382	61	118	0	35	116	601	7.5
83-84—New Jersey	82	1655	462	237	.513	184	147	.799	161	272	433	92	162	0	37	70	621	7.6
84-85—New Jersey	81	2418	818	380	.465	328	276	.841	229	404	633	158	135	0	38	92	1036	12.8
85-86—New Jersey	81	2525	949	491	.517	393	351	.893	206	462	668	133	163	0	56	71	1333	16.5
86-87—New Jersey	72	2272	947	433	.457	370	313	.846	192	438	630	99	159	0	52	69	1179	16.4
87-88—N.J.-Phil.	81	2961	1126	505	.448	392	355	.906	245	569	814	139	176	0	64	118	1365	16.9
Totals	597	15405	5686	2669	.469	2212	1869	.845	1394	2771	4165	795	1109	1	353	684	7207	12.1

Three-Point Field Goals: 1980-81, 0-for-1. 1982-83, 0-for-1. 1983-84, 0-for-3. 1984-85, 0-for-1. 1985-86, 0-for-1. 1987-88, 0-for-2. Totals, 0-for-9.

NBA PLAYOFF RECORD

Sea.—Team	G.	Min.	FGA	FGM	Pct.	FTA	FTM	Pct.	Off.	Def.	Tot.	Ast.	PF	Dq.	Stl.	Blk.	Pts.	Avg.
									—Rebounds—									
81-82—New Jersey	1	10	3	2	.667	2	1	.500	0	2	2	0	2	0	0	0	5	5.0
82-83—New Jersey	2	29	9	6	.667	4	3	.750	4	5	9	1	2	0	0	4	15	7.5
83-84—New Jersey	11	223	50	29	.580	52	36	.692	22	33	55	6	17	0	7	15	94	8.5
84-85—New Jersey	3	81	33	18	.545	6	6	1.000	4	15	19	4	5	0	3	5	42	14.0
85-86—New Jersey	3	109	43	16	.372	27	26	.963	11	19	30	5	11	0	4	2	58	19.3
Totals	20	452	138	71	.514	91	72	.791	41	74	115	16	37	0	14	26	214	10.7

Named to THE SPORTING NEWS All-America Second Team, 1979 and 1980.

LANCASTER GORDON

Born June 24, 1962 at Jackson, Miss. Height 6:03. Weight 195.

High School—Jackson, Miss., Jim Hill.

College—University of Louisville, Louisville, Ky.

Drafted by Los Angeles Clippers on first round, 1984 (8th pick).

Waived by Los Angeles Clippers, February 26, 1988.

—COLLEGIATE RECORD—

Year	G.	Min.	FGA	FGM	Pct.	FTA	FTM	Pct.	Reb.	Pts.	Avg.
80-81	30	630	234	109	.466	56	39	.696	74	257	8.6
81-82	33	956	301	148	.492	71	53	.746	77	349	10.6
82-83	36	1164	400	208	.520	99	76	.768	120	492	13.7
83-84	35	1177	418	217	.519	107	82	.766	122	516	14.7
Totals	143	3927	1353	682	.504	333	250	.751	393	1614	12.0

NBA REGULAR SEASON RECORD

Sea.—Team	G.	Min.	FGA	FGM	Pct.	FTA	FTM	Pct.	Off.	Def.	Tot.	Ast.	PF	Dq.	Stl.	Blk.	Pts.	Avg.
									—Rebounds—									
84-85—L.A. Clippers	63	682	287	110	.383	49	37	.755	26	35	61	88	61	0	33	6	259	4.1
85-86—L.A. Clippers	60	704	345	130	.377	56	45	.804	24	44	68	60	91	1	33	10	312	5.2
86-87—L.A. Clippers	70	1130	545	221	.406	95	70	.737	64	62	126	139	106	1	61	13	526	7.5
87-88—L.A. Clippers	8	65	31	11	.355	6	6	1.000	2	2	4	7	8	0	1	2	28	3.5
Totals	201	2581	1208	472	.391	206	158	.767	116	143	259	294	266	2	128	31	1125	5.6

Three-Point Field Goals: 1984-85, 2-for-9 (.222). 1985-86, 7-for-28 (.250). 1986-87, 14-for-48 (.292). Totals, 23-for-85 (.271).

Named to THE SPORTING NEWS All-America Second Team, 1984.

HORACE JUNIOR GRANT

Born July 4, 1965 at Augusta, Ga. Height 6:10. Weight 215.

High School—Sparta, Ga., Hancock Central.

College—Clemson University, Clemson, S.C.

Drafted by Chicago on first round, 1987 (10th pick).

—COLLEGIATE RECORD—

Year	G.	Min.	FGA	FGM	Pct.	FTA	FTM	Pct.	Reb.	Pts.	Avg.
83-84	28	551	120	64	.533	43	32	.744	129	160	5.7
84-85	29	703	238	132	.555	102	65	.637	196	329	11.3
85-86	34	1099	356	208	.584	193	140	.725	357	556	16.4
86-87	31	1010	390	256	.656	195	138	.708	299	651	21.0
Totals	122	3363	1104	660	.598	533	375	.704	981	1696	13.9

Three-Point Field Goals: 1986-87, 1-for-2 (.500).

NBA REGULAR SEASON RECORD

Sea.—Team	G.	Min.	FGA	FGM	Pct.	FTA	FTM	Pct.	Off.	Def.	Tot.	Ast.	PF	Dq.	Stl.	Blk.	Pts.	Avg.
									—Rebounds—									
87-88—Chicago	81	1827	507	254	.501	182	114	.626	155	292	447	89	221	3	51	53	622	7.7

Three-Point Field Goals: 1987-88, 0-for-2.

Sea.—Team	G.	Min.	FGA	FGM	Pct.	FTA	FTM	Pct.	—Rebounds— Off.	Def.	Tot.	Ast.	PF	Dq.	Stl.	Blk.	Pts.	Avg.
87-88—Chicago	10	299	81	46	.568	15	9	.600	25	45	70	16	35	2	14	2	101	10.1

Three-Point Field Goals: 1987-88, 0-for-1.

STUART ALLAN GRAY

Born May 27, 1963 in the Panama Canal Zone.   Height 7:00.   Weight 245.

High School—Granada Hills, Calif., Kennedy.

College—University of California at Los Angeles, Los Angeles, Calif.

Drafted by Indiana on second round as an undergraduate, 1984 (29th pick).

—COLLEGIATE RECORD—

Year	G.	Min.	FGA	FGM	Pct.	FTA	FTM	Pct.	Reb.	Pts.	Avg.
81-82	27	589	111	57	.514	44	19	.432	129	133	4.9
82-83	23	570	134	78	.582	45	20	.444	158	176	7.7
83-84	28	860	177	107	.605	90	62	.689	220	276	9.9
Totals	78	2019	422	242	.573	179	101	.564	507	585	7.5

NBA REGULAR SEASON RECORD

Sea.—Team	G.	Min.	FGA	FGM	Pct.	FTA	FTM	Pct.	—Rebounds— Off.	Def.	Tot.	Ast.	PF	Dq.	Stl.	Blk.	Pts.	Avg.
84-85—Indiana	52	391	92	35	.380	47	32	.681	29	94	123	15	82	1	9	14	102	2.0
85-86—Indiana	67	423	108	54	.500	74	47	.635	45	73	118	15	94	0	8	11	155	2.3
86-87—Indiana	55	456	101	41	.406	39	28	.718	39	90	129	26	93	0	10	28	110	2.0
87-88—Indiana	74	807	193	90	.466	73	44	.603	70	180	250	44	152	1	11	32	224	3.0
Totals	248	2077	494	220	.445	233	151	.648	183	437	620	100	421	2	38	85	591	2.4

Three-Point Field Goals: 1987-88, 0-for-1.

NBA PLAYOFF RECORD

Sea.—Team	G.	Min.	FGA	FGM	Pct.	FTA	FTM	Pct.	—Rebounds— Off.	Def.	Tot.	Ast.	PF	Dq.	Stl.	Blk.	Pts.	Avg.
86-87—Indiana	3	14	1	0	.000	4	2	.500	2	5	7	0	3	0	0	0	2	0.7

A. C. GREEN JR.

Born October 4, 1963 at Portland, Ore.   Height 6:09.   Weight 230.

High School—Portland, Ore., Benson.

College—Oregon State University, Corvallis, Ore.

Drafted by Los Angeles Lakers on first round, 1985 (23rd pick).

—COLLEGIATE RECORD—

Year	G.	Min.	FGA	FGM	Pct.	FTA	FTM	Pct.	Reb.	Pts.	Avg.
81-82	30	895	161	99	.615	100	61	.610	158	259	8.6
82-83	31	1113	290	162	.559	161	111	.689	235	435	14.0
83-84	23	853	204	134	.657	183	141	.770	201	409	17.8
84-85	31	1191	362	217	.599	231	157	.680	286	591	19.1
Totals	115	4052	1017	612	.602	675	470	.696	880	1694	14.7

NBA REGULAR SEASON RECORD

Sea.—Team	G.	Min.	FGA	FGM	Pct.	FTA	FTM	Pct.	—Rebounds— Off.	Def.	Tot.	Ast.	PF	Dq.	Stl.	Blk.	Pts.	Avg.
85-86—L.A. Lakers	82	1542	388	209	.539	167	102	.611	160	221	381	54	229	2	49	49	521	6.4
86-87—L.A. Lakers	79	2240	587	316	.538	282	220	.780	210	405	615	84	171	0	70	80	852	10.8
87-88—L.A. Lakers	82	2636	640	322	.503	379	293	.773	245	465	710	93	204	0	87	45	937	11.4
Totals	243	6418	1615	847	.524	828	615	.743	615	1091	1706	231	604	2	206	174	2310	9.5

Three-Point Field Goals: 1985-86, 1-for-6 (.167). 1986-87, 0-for-5. 1987-88, 0-for-2. Totals, 1-for-13 (.077).

NBA PLAYOFF RECORD

Sea.—Team	G.	Min.	FGA	FGM	Pct.	FTA	FTM	Pct.	—Rebounds— Off.	Def.	Tot.	Ast.	PF	Dq.	Stl.	Blk.	Pts.	Avg.
85-86—L.A. Lakers	9	106	17	9	.529	9	4	.444	3	13	16	0	13	0	1	3	22	2.4
86-87—L.A. Lakers	18	505	130	71	.546	87	65	.747	54	88	142	11	47	0	9	8	207	11.5
87-88—L.A. Lakers	24	726	169	92	.544	73	55	.753	57	118	175	20	61	0	11	12	239	10.0
Totals	51	1337	316	172	.544	169	124	.734	114	219	333	31	121	0	21	23	468	9.2

Member of NBA championship teams, 1987 and 1988.

RICKEY GREEN

Born August 18, 1954 at Chicago, Ill. Height 6:00. Weight 172.

High School—Chicago, Ill., Hirsch.

Colleges—Vincennes University, Vincennes, Ind., and
University of Michigan, Ann Arbor, Mich.

Drafted by Golden State on first round, 1977 (16th pick).

Traded by Golden State to Detroit for a 1980 2nd round draft choice, October 9, 1978.
Waived by Detroit, December 11, 1978; signed by Chicago as a free agent, August 12, 1980.
Waived by Chicago, October 8, 1980; signed by Utah as a free agent, December 2, 1980.
Selected from Utah by Charlotte in NBA expansion draft, June 23, 1988.
Played in Continental Basketball Association with Hawaii and Billings Volcanos, 1979-80 and 1980-81.

—COLLEGIATE RECORD—
Vincennes

Year	G.	Min.	FGA	FGM	Pct.	FTA	FTM	Pct.	Reb.	Pts.	Avg.
73-74	36	....	633	254	.401	163	114	.699	237	622	17.3
74-75	32	....	600	302	.503	105	69	.657	208	673	21.0
JC Totals	68	....	1233	556	.451	268	183	.683	445	1295	19.0

Michigan

Year	G.	Min.	FGA	FGM	Pct.	FTA	FTM	Pct.	Reb.	Pts.	Avg.
75-76	32	....	542	266	.491	135	106	.785	117	638	19.9
76-77	28	....	464	224	.483	128	98	.766	81	546	19.5
Totals	60	....	1006	490	.487	263	204	.776	198	1184	19.7

CBA REGULAR SEASON RECORD

| Sea.—Team | G. | Min. | 2-Point | | | 3-Point | | | FTM | FTA | Pct. | Reb. | Ast. | Pts. | Avg. |
			FGM	FGA	Pct.	FGM	FGA	Pct.							
79-80—Hawaii	44	1753	408	824	.495	3	17	.176	155	205	.756	188	345	980	22.3
80-81—Billings	5	197	47	95	.494	0	1	.000	19	24	.791	22	32	113	22.6
Totals	49	1950	455	919	.495	3	18	.167	174	229	.760	210	377	1093	22.3

NBA REGULAR SEASON RECORD

| Sea.—Team | G. | Min. | FGA | FGM | Pct. | FTA | FTM | Pct. | Off. | Def. | Tot. | Ast. | PF | Dq. | Stl. | Blk. | Pts. | Avg. |
									—Rebounds—									
77-78—Golden State	76	1098	375	143	.381	90	54	.600	49	67	116	149	95	0	58	1	340	4.5
78-79—Detroit	27	431	177	67	.379	67	45	.672	15	25	40	63	37	0	25	1	179	6.6
80-81—Utah	47	1307	366	176	.481	97	70	.722	30	86	116	235	123	2	75	1	422	9.0
81-82—Utah	81	2822	1015	500	.493	264	202	.765	85	158	243	630	183	0	185	9	1202	14.8
82-83—Utah	78	2783	942	464	.493	232	185	.797	62	161	223	697	154	0	220	4	1115	14.3
83-84—Utah	81	2768	904	439	.486	234	192	.821	56	174	230	748	155	1	215	13	1072	13.2
84-85—Utah	77	2431	798	381	.477	267	232	.869	37	152	189	597	131	0	132	3	1000	13.0
85-86—Utah	80	2012	758	357	.471	250	213	.852	32	103	135	411	130	0	106	6	932	11.7
86-87—Utah	81	2090	644	301	.467	208	172	.827	38	125	163	541	108	0	110	2	781	9.6
87-88—Utah	81	1116	370	157	.424	83	75	.904	14	66	80	300	83	0	57	1	393	4.9
Totals	709	18858	6349	2985	.470	1792	1440	.804	418	1117	1535	4371	1199	3	1183	41	7436	10.5

Three-Point Field Goals: 1980-81, 0-for-1. 1981-82, 0-for-8. 1982-83, 2-for-13 (.154). 1983-84, 2-for-17 (.118). 1984-85, 6-for-20 (.300). 1985-86, 5-for-29 (.172). 1986-87, 7-for-19 (.368). 1987-88, 4-for-19 (.211). Totals, 26-for-126 (.206).

NBA PLAYOFF RECORD

| Sea.—Team | G. | Min. | FGA | FGM | Pct. | FTA | FTM | Pct. | Off. | Def. | Tot. | Ast. | PF | Dq. | Stl. | Blk. | Pts. | Avg. |
									—Rebounds—									
83-84—Utah	11	404	151	64	.424	43	32	.744	9	25	34	104	17	0	19	4	161	14.6
84-85—Utah	10	302	106	57	.538	38	35	.921	10	20	30	75	23	0	12	0	150	15.0
85-86—Utah	4	119	43	21	.488	11	10	.909	0	9	9	38	1	0	2	0	53	13.3
86-87—Utah	4	72	23	11	.478	6	5	.833	1	7	8	25	5	0	2	0	27	6.8
87-88—Utah	7	38	8	2	.250	0	0	.000	0	1	1	9	2	0	2	0	4	0.6
Totals	36	935	331	155	.468	98	82	.837	20	62	82	251	48	0	37	4	395	11.0

Three-Point Field Goals: 1983-84, 1-for-4 (.250). 1984-85, 1-for-7 (.143). 1985-86, 1-for-2 (.500). 1986-87, 0-for-1. Totals, 3-for-14 (.214).

NBA ALL-STAR GAME RECORD

| Season—Team | Min. | FGA | FGM | Pct. | FTA | FTM | Pct. | Off. | Def. | Tot. | Ast. | PF | Dq. | Stl. | Blk. | Pts. |
								—Rebounds—								
1984—Utah	19	8	3	.375	0	0	.000	0	0	0	11	1	0	1	0	6

Led NBA in steals, 1984. . . . Named to THE SPORTING NEWS All-America First Team, 1977.

—DID YOU KNOW—

That All-NBA first-teamers Larry Bird and Akeem Olajuwon have brothers attending Indiana State, Bird's alma mater? Eddie Bird led the Sycamores with a 15.3 scoring average in 1987-88 while Taju Olajuwon was a Proposition 48 victim his freshman season.

SIDNEY GREEN

Born January 4, 1961 at Brooklyn, N. Y.   Height 6:09.   Weight 220.
High School—Brooklyn, N. Y., Jefferson.
College—University of Nevada at Las Vegas, Las Vegas, Nev.
Drafted by Chicago on first round, 1983 (5th pick).

Traded by Chicago to Detroit for Earl Cureton and a 1987 2nd round draft choice, August 21, 1986.
Traded by Detroit to New York for Ron Moore and a 1988 2nd round draft choice, October 29, 1987.

—COLLEGIATE RECORD—

Year	G.	Min.	FGA	FGM	Pct.	FTA	FTM	Pct.	Reb.	Pts.	Avg.
79-80	32	1024	388	201	.518	132	96	.727	354	498	15.6
80-81	26	817	297	153	.515	120	85	.708	284	391	15.0
81-82	30	963	374	200	.535	130	100	.769	270	500	16.7
82-83	31	1120	491	269	.548	203	142	.700	368	684	22.1
Totals	119	3924	1550	823	.531	585	423	.723	1276	2073	17.4

Three-Point Field Goals: 1982-83, 4-for-12 (.333).

NBA REGULAR SEASON RECORD

Sea.—Team	G.	Min.	FGA	FGM	Pct.	FTA	FTM	Pct.	Rebounds Off.	Rebounds Def.	Rebounds Tot.	Ast.	PF	Dq.	Stl.	Blk.	Pts.	Avg.
83-84—Chicago	49	667	228	100	.439	77	55	.714	58	116	174	25	128	1	18	17	255	5.2
84-85—Chicago	48	740	250	108	.432	98	79	.806	72	174	246	29	102	0	11	11	295	6.1
85-86—Chicago	80	2307	875	407	.465	335	262	.782	208	450	658	139	292	5	70	37	1076	13.5
86-87—Detroit	80	1792	542	256	.472	177	119	.672	196	457	653	62	197	0	41	50	631	7.9
87-88—New York	82	2049	585	258	.441	190	126	.663	221	421	642	93	318	9	65	32	642	7.8
Totals	339	7555	2480	1129	.455	877	641	.731	755	1618	2373	348	1037	15	205	147	2899	8.6

Three-Point Field Goals: 1984-85, 0-for-4. 1985-86, 0-for-8. 1986-87, 0-for-2. 1987-88, 0-for-2. Totals, 0-for-16.

NBA PLAYOFF RECORD

Sea.—Team	G.	Min.	FGA	FGM	Pct.	FTA	FTM	Pct.	Rebounds Off.	Rebounds Def.	Rebounds Tot.	Ast.	PF	Dq.	Stl.	Blk.	Pts.	Avg.
84-85—Chicago	3	54	24	12	.500	11	7	.636	10	5	15	2	8	0	0	1	31	10.3
85-86—Chicago	3	53	20	6	.300	12	6	.500	7	5	12	0	9	0	1	1	18	6.0
86-87—Detroit	9	42	10	6	.600	6	5	.833	3	6	9	1	2	0	1	2	17	1.9
87-88—New York	4	93	17	8	.471	0	0	.000	8	25	33	7	14	0	0	1	16	4.0
Totals	19	242	71	32	.451	29	18	.621	28	41	69	10	33	0	2	5	82	4.3

Named to THE SPORTING NEWS All-America Second Team, 1983.

DAVID KASIM GREENWOOD
(Dave)

Born May 27, 1957 at Lynwood, Calif.   Height 6:09.   Weight 225.
High School—Los Angeles, Calif., Verbum Dei.
College—University of California at Los Angeles, Los Angeles, Calif.
Drafted by Chicago on first round, 1979 (2nd pick).

Traded by Chicago to San Antonio for George Gervin, October 24, 1985.

—COLLEGIATE RECORD—

Year	G.	Min.	FGA	FGM	Pct.	FTA	FTM	Pct.	Reb.	Pts.	Avg.
75-76	31	403	122	62	.508	35	28	.800	114	152	4.9
76-77	29	979	395	202	.511	112	80	.714	280	484	16.7
77-78	28	978	364	196	.538	133	97	.729	319	489	17.5
78-79	30	1069	421	247	.587	126	102	.810	309	596	19.9
Totals	118	3439	1302	707	.543	406	307	.756	1022	1721	14.6

NBA REGULAR SEASON RECORD

Sea.—Team	G.	Min.	FGA	FGM	Pct.	FTA	FTM	Pct.	Rebounds Off.	Rebounds Def.	Rebounds Tot.	Ast.	PF	Dq.	Stl.	Blk.	Pts.	Avg.
79-80—Chicago	82	2791	1051	498	.474	416	337	.810	223	550	773	182	313	8	60	129	1334	16.3
80-81—Chicago	82	2710	989	481	.486	290	217	.748	243	481	724	218	282	5	77	124	1179	14.4
81-82—Chicago	82	2914	1014	480	.473	291	240	.825	192	594	786	262	292	1	70	93	1200	14.6
82-83—Chicago	79	2355	686	312	.455	233	165	.708	217	548	765	151	261	5	54	90	789	10.0
83-84—Chicago	78	2718	753	369	.490	289	213	.737	214	572	786	139	265	9	67	72	951	12.2
84-85—Chicago	61	1523	332	152	.458	94	67	.713	108	280	388	78	190	1	34	21	371	6.1
85-86—San Antonio	68	1910	388	198	.510	184	142	.772	151	380	531	90	207	3	37	52	538	7.9
86-87—San Antonio	79	2587	655	336	.513	307	241	.785	256	527	783	237	248	3	71	50	916	11.6
87-88—San Antonio	45	1236	328	151	.460	111	83	.748	92	208	300	97	134	2	33	22	385	8.6
Totals	656	20744	6196	2977	.480	2215	1705	.770	1696	4140	5836	1454	2192	37	503	653	7663	11.7

Three-Point Field Goals: 1979-80, 1-for-7 (.143). 1980-81, 0-for-2. 1981-82, 0-for-3. 1982-83, 0-for-4. 1983-84, 0-for-1. 1984-85, 0-for-1. 1985-86, 0-for-1. 1986-87, 3-for-6 (.500). 1987-88, 0-for-2. Totals, 4-for-27 (.148).

Sea.—Team	G.	Min.	FGA	FGM	Pct.	FTA	FTM	Pct.	Off.	Def.	Tot.	Ast.	PF	Dq.	Stl.	Blk.	Pts.	Avg.
										—Rebounds—								
80-81—Chicago	6	212	87	51	.586	12	5	.417	16	28	44	11	26	0	9	5	107	17.8
84-85—Chicago	4	139	28	15	.536	10	8	.800	10	21	31	5	14	0	6	4	38	9.5
85-86—San Antonio	3	101	23	12	.522	8	6	.750	1	17	18	3	12	0	3	1	30	10.0
Totals	13	452	138	78	.565	30	19	.633	27	66	93	19	52	0	18	10	175	13.5

Three-Point Field Goals: 1980-81, 0-for-2.

Named to NBA All-Rookie Team, 1980. . . . THE SPORTING NEWS All-America Second Team, 1979.

CLAUDE ANDRE GREGORY

Born December 26, 1958 at Washington, D. C.   Height 6:09.   Weight 235.

High School—Washington, D. C., Coolidge.

College—University of Wisconsin, Madison, Wis.

Drafted by Washington on second round, 1981 (41st pick).

Waived by Washington, October 13, 1981; signed by Washington, January 19, 1986, to the first of consecutive 10-day contracts that expired, February 7, 1986.
Signed by Philadelphia as a free agent, May 19, 1987.
Waived by Philadelphia, October 16, 1987; signed by Los Angeles Clippers, March 7, 1988, to the first of consecutive 10-day contracts that expired, March 26, 1988.
Re-signed by Los Angeles Clippers, March 28, 1988, for remainder of season.
Played in Continental Basketball Association with Evansville Thunder, 1984-85 and 1985-86, and LaCrosse Catbirds, 1986-87 and 1987-88.

—COLLEGIATE RECORD—

Year	G.	Min.	FGA	FGM	Pct.	FTA	FTM	Pct.	Reb.	Pts.	Avg.
77-78	27	554	245	92	.376	99	70	.707	165	254	9.4
78-79	27	866	385	168	.436	106	71	.670	236	407	15.1
79-80	29	1001	424	197	.465	189	140	.741	254	534	18.4
80-81	27	989	438	199	.454	202	152	.752	249	550	20.4
Totals	110	3410	1492	656	.440	596	433	.727	904	1745	15.9

CBA REGULAR SEASON RECORD

Sea.—Team	G.	Min.	FGM	FGA	Pct.	FGM	FGA	Pct.	FTM	FTA	Pct.	Reb.	Ast.	Pts.	Avg.
			—2-Point—			—3-Point—									
84-85—Evansville	37	1296	303	584	.518	0	3	.000	213	278	.766	401	58	819	22.1
85-86—Evansville	39	1535	339	664	.510	4	9	.444	280	378	.740	401	74	970	24.9
86-87—LaCrosse	48	1857	411	887	.463	7	23	.304	280	362	.773	505	98	1123	23.4
87-88—LaCrosse.....................	48	1774	427	848	.504	9	27	.333	230	322	.714	538	112	1111	23.1
Totals	172	6462	1480	2983	.496	20	62	.323	1003	1340	.749	1845	342	4023	23.4

NBA REGULAR SEASON RECORD

Sea.—Team	G.	Min.	FGA	FGM	Pct.	FTA	FTM	Pct.	Off.	Def.	Tot.	Ast.	PF	Dq.	Stl.	Blk.	Pts.	Avg.
										—Rebounds—								
85-86—Washington	2	2	2	1	.500	0	0	.000	2	0	2	0	1	0	1	0	2	1.0
87-88—L.A. Clippers	23	313	134	61	.455	36	12	.333	37	58	95	16	37	0	9	13	134	5.8
Totals	25	315	136	62	.456	36	12	.333	39	58	97	16	38	0	10	13	136	5.4

Three-Point Field Goals: 1987-88, 0-for-1.

Named to CBA All-Star First Team, 1988. . . . CBA All-Star Second Team, 1986.

DARRELL STEVEN GRIFFITH

Born June 16, 1958 at Louisville, Ky.   Height 6:04. Weight 190.

High School—Louisville, Ky., Male.

College—University of Louisville, Louisville, Ky.

Drafted by Utah on first round, 1980 (2nd pick).

Missed entire 1985-86 season due to injury.

—COLLEGIATE RECORD—

Year	G.	Min.	FGA	FGM	Pct.	FTA	FTM	Pct.	Reb.	Pts.	Avg.
76-77	28	652	299	150	.502	93	59	.634	109	359	12.8
77-78	30	996	460	240	.522	110	78	.709	162	558	18.6
78-79	32	1001	487	242	.497	151	107	.709	140	591	18.5
79-80	36	1246	631	349	.553	178	127	.713	174	825	22.9
Totals	126	3895	1877	981	.523	532	371	.697	585	2333	18.5

NBA REGULAR SEASON RECORD

Sea.—Team	G.	Min.	FGA	FGM	Pct.	FTA	FTM	Pct.	Off.	Def.	Tot.	Ast.	PF	Dq.	Stl.	Blk.	Pts.	Avg.
										—Rebounds—								
80-81—Utah	81	2867	1544	716	.464	320	229	.716	79	209	288	194	219	0	106	40	1671	20.6
81-82—Utah	80	2597	1429	689	.482	271	189	.697	128	177	305	187	213	0	95	34	1582	19.8

Sea.—Team	G.	Min.	FGA	FGM	Pct.	FTA	FTM	Pct.	Off.	Def.	Tot.	Ast.	PF	Dq.	Stl.	Blk.	Pts.	Avg.
82-83—Utah	77	2787	1554	752	.484	246	167	.679	100	204	304	270	184	0	138	33	1709	22.2
83-84—Utah	82	2650	1423	697	.490	217	151	.696	95	243	338	283	202	1	114	23	1636	20.0
84-85—Utah	78	2776	1593	728	.457	298	216	.725	124	220	344	243	178	1	133	30	1764	22.6
86-87—Utah	76	1843	1038	463	.446	212	149	.703	81	146	227	129	167	0	97	29	1142	15.0
87-88—Utah	52	1052	585	251	.429	92	59	.641	36	91	127	91	102	0	52	5	589	11.3
Totals	526	16572	9166	4296	.469	1656	1160	.700	643	1290	1933	1397	1265	2	735	194	10093	19.2

Three-Point Field Goals: 1980-81, 10-for-52 (.192). 1981-82, 15-for-52 (.288). 1982-83, 38-for-132 (.288). 1983-84, 91-for-252 (.361). 1984-85, 92-for-257 (.358). 1986-87, 67-for-200 (.335). 1987-88, 28-for-102 (.275). Totals, 341-for-1047 (.326).

NBA PLAYOFF RECORD

Sea.—Team	G.	Min.	FGA	FGM	Pct.	FTA	FTM	Pct.	Off.	Def.	Tot.	Ast.	PF	Dq.	Stl.	Blk.	Pts.	Avg.
83-84—Utah	11	417	183	81	.443	48	33	.688	16	49	65	41	24	0	19	2	211	19.2
84-85—Utah	10	340	158	72	.456	25	18	.720	6	23	29	25	21	0	12	5	175	17.5
86-87—Utah	5	104	65	24	.369	19	14	.737	5	7	12	8	5	0	6	2	68	13.6
Totals	26	861	406	177	.436	92	65	.707	27	79	106	74	50	0	37	9	454	17.5

Three-Point Field Goals: 1983-84, 16-for-45 (.356). 1984-85, 13-for-36 (.361). 1986-87, 6-for-15 (.400). Totals, 35-for-96 (.365).

Named NBA Rookie of the Year, 1981. . . . NBA All-Rookie Team, 1981. . . . Led NBA in three-point field goal percentage, 1984 and 1985. . . . THE SPORTING NEWS College Player of the Year, 1980. . . . THE SPORTING NEWS All-America First Team, 1979 and 1980. . . . THE SPORTING NEWS All-America Second Team, 1978. . . . NCAA Division I Tournament Most Outstanding Player, 1980. . . . Member of NCAA Division I championship team, 1980.

KARL PETUR GUDMUNDSSON
(Known by middle name.)

Born October 30, 1958 at Reykjavik, Iceland. Height 7:02. Weight 260.

High School—Mercer Island, Wash.

College—University of Washington, Seattle, Wash.

Drafted by Portland on third round, 1981 (61st pick).

Suspended by Portland, October 26, 1982.
Traded by Portland to Detroit for a 3rd round draft choice, August 18, 1983.
Waived by Detroit, October 25, 1983; signed by Los Angeles Lakers, March 19, 1986, to the first of consecutive 10-day contracts that expired, April 7, 1986.
Re-signed by Los Angeles Lakers, April 8, 1986, for remainder of season.
Re-signed by Los Angeles Lakers, June 30, 1986.
Traded by Los Angeles Lakers with Frank Brickowski, a 1987 1st round draft choice, a 1990 2nd round draft choice and cash to San Antonio for Mychal Thompson, February 13, 1987.
Missed entire 1986-87 season due to injury.
Played in Iceland during 1982-83 season.
Played in Continental Basketball Association with Tampa Bay Thrillers and Kansas City Sizzlers, 1985-86.

—COLLEGIATE RECORD—

Year	G.	Min.	FGA	FGM	Pct.	FTA	FTM	Pct.	Reb.	Pts.	Avg.
77-78	26	223	76	37	.487	30	22	.733	61	96	3.7
78-79	27	533	200	105	.525	82	63	.768	130	273	10.1
79-80	28	415	149	75	.503	44	27	.614	157	177	6.3
80-81					Dropped Out of School—Played Pro Ball in Argentina						
Totals	81	1171	425	217	.511	156	112	.718	348	546	6.7

CBA REGULAR SEASON RECORD

Sea.—Team	G.	Min.	2-Point FGM	2-Point FGA	2-Point Pct.	3-Point FGM	3-Point FGA	3-Point Pct.	FTM	FTA	Pct.	Reb.	Ast.	Pts.	Avg.
85-86—T. Bay-Kan. City	47	863	139	251	.554	0	1	.000	98	130	.754	266	62	376	8.0

NBA REGULAR SEASON RECORD

Sea.—Team	G.	Min.	FGA	FGM	Pct.	FTA	FTM	Pct.	Off.	Def.	Tot.	Ast.	PF	Dq.	Stl.	Blk.	Pts.	Avg.
81-82—Portland	68	845	166	83	.500	76	52	.684	51	135	186	59	163	2	13	30	219	3.2
85-86—L.A. Lakers	8	128	37	20	.541	27	18	.667	17	21	38	3	25	1	3	4	58	7.3
87-88—San Antonio	69	1017	280	139	.496	145	117	.807	93	230	323	86	197	5	18	61	395	5.7
Totals	145	1990	483	242	.501	248	187	.754	161	386	547	148	385	8	34	95	672	4.6

Three-Point Field Goals: 1981-82, 1-for-1 (1.000). 1987-88, 0-for-1. Totals, 1-for-2 (.500).

NBA PLAYOFF RECORD

Sea.—Team	G.	Min.	FGA	FGM	Pct.	FTA	FTM	Pct.	Off.	Def.	Tot.	Ast.	PF	Dq.	Stl.	Blk.	Pts.	Avg.
85-86—L.A. Lakers	12	111	27	16	.593	15	10	.667	8	18	26	3	23	1	3	4	42	3.5
87-88—San Antonio	2	6	2	0	.000	0	0	.000	0	0	0	1	0	0	0	0	0	0.0
Totals	14	117	29	16	.552	15	10	.667	8	18	26	4	23	1	3	4	42	3.0

Three-Point Field Goals: 1985-86, 0-for-2.

ROBERT LOUIS HANSEN II
(Bob)

Born January 18, 1961 at Des Moines, Iowa.   Height 6:06.   Weight 195.

High School—Des Moines, Iowa, Dowling.

College—University of Iowa, Iowa City, Iowa.

Drafted by Utah on third round, 1983 (54th pick).

—COLLEGIATE RECORD—

Year	G.	Min.	FGA	FGM	Pct.	FTA	FTM	Pct.	Reb.	Pts.	Avg.
79-80	33	....	167	71	.425	73	43	.589	67	185	5.6
80-81	22	....	156	70	.449	53	45	.849	75	185	8.4
81-82	25	....	237	117	.494	93	65	.699	102	299	12.0
82-83	31	....	378	184	.487	129	98	.760	166	476	15.4
Totals	111	....	938	442	.471	388	251	.647	410	1145	10.3

Three-Point Field Goals: 1982-83, 10-for-20 (.500).

NBA REGULAR SEASON RECORD

Sea.—Team	G.	Min.	FGA	FGM	Pct.	FTA	FTM	Pct.	Off.	Def.	Tot.	Ast.	PF	Dq.	Stl.	Blk.	Pts.	Avg.
83-84—Utah	55	419	145	65	.448	28	18	.643	13	35	48	44	62	0	15	4	148	2.7
84-85—Utah	54	646	225	110	.489	72	40	.556	20	50	70	75	88	0	25	1	261	4.8
85-86—Utah	82	2032	628	299	.476	132	95	.720	82	162	244	193	205	1	74	9	710	8.7
86-87—Utah	72	1453	601	272	.453	179	136	.760	84	119	203	102	146	0	44	6	696	9.7
87-88—Utah	81	1796	611	316	.517	152	113	.743	64	123	187	175	193	2	65	5	777	9.6
Totals	344	6346	2210	1062	.481	563	402	.714	263	489	752	589	694	3	223	25	2592	7.5

Three-Point Field Goals: 1983-84, 0-for-8. 1984-85, 1-for-7 (.143). 1985-86, 17-for-50 (.340). 1986-87, 16-for-45 (.356). 1987-88, 32-for-97 (.330). Totals, 66-for-207 (.319).

NBA PLAYOFF RECORD

Sea.—Team	G.	Min.	FGA	FGM	Pct.	FTA	FTM	Pct.	Off.	Def.	Tot.	Ast.	PF	Dq.	Stl.	Blk.	Pts.	Avg.
83-84—Utah	4	18	7	2	.286	2	1	.500	2	5	7	2	4	0	0	0	7	1.8
84-85—Utah	8	34	8	2	.250	8	5	.625	1	3	4	6	6	0	3	0	9	1.1
85-86—Utah	4	140	37	27	.730	9	8	.889	10	8	18	11	16	0	3	1	64	16.0
86-87—Utah	5	142	49	21	.429	20	17	.850	3	12	15	11	14	0	1	1	61	12.2
87-88—Utah	11	408	135	67	.496	22	16	.727	8	31	39	32	42	1	7	0	169	15.4
Totals	32	742	236	119	.504	61	47	.770	24	59	83	62	82	1	14	2	310	9.7

Three-Point Field Goals: 1983-84, 2-for-3 (.667). 1985-86, 2-for-3 (.667). 1986-87, 2-for-5 (.400). 1987-88, 19-for-36 (.528). Totals, 25-for-47 (.532).

WILLIAM HENRY HANZLIK
(Bill)

Born December 6, 1957 at Middletown, O.   Height 6:07.   Weight 200.

High Schools—Lake Oswego, Ore. (Junior) and

Beloit, Wis., Memorial (Senior).

College—University of Notre Dame, Notre Dame, Ind.

Drafted by Seattle on first round, 1980 (20th pick).

Traded by Seattle to Denver to complete deal for David Thompson, July 20, 1982. Seattle's earlier trade of the rights to free agent Wally Walker and a 1982 1st round draft choice for Thompson was nullified when Walker's rights were ruled non-transferable by an arbitrator.

—COLLEGIATE RECORD—

Year	G.	Min.	FGA	FGM	Pct.	FTA	FTM	Pct.	Reb.	Pts.	Avg.
76-77	28	274	91	38	.418	55	39	.709	51	115	4.1
77-78	30	307	78	40	.513	38	30	.789	57	110	3.7
78-79	29	654	164	95	.579	77	63	.818	84	253	8.7
79-80	22	603	135	61	.452	60	44	.733	74	166	7.5
Totals	109	1838	468	234	.500	230	176	.765	266	644	5.9

NBA REGULAR SEASON RECORD

Sea.—Team	G.	Min.	FGA	FGM	Pct.	FTA	FTM	Pct.	Off.	Def.	Tot.	Ast.	PF	Dq.	Stl.	Blk.	Pts.	Avg.
80-81—Seattle	74	1259	289	138	.478	150	119	.793	67	86	153	111	168	1	58	20	396	5.4
81-82—Seattle	81	1974	357	167	.468	176	138	.784	99	167	266	183	250	3	81	30	472	5.8
82-83—Denver	82	1547	437	187	.428	160	125	.781	80	156	236	268	220	0	75	15	500	6.1
83-84—Denver	80	1469	306	132	.431	207	167	.807	66	139	205	252	255	6	68	19	434	5.4
84-85—Denver	80	1673	522	220	.421	238	180	.756	88	119	207	210	291	5	84	26	621	7.8
85-86—Denver	79	1982	741	331	.447	405	318	.785	88	176	264	316	277	2	107	16	988	12.5
86-87—Denver	73	1990	746	307	.412	402	316	.786	79	177	256	280	245	3	87	28	952	13.0
87-88—Denver	77	1334	287	109	.380	163	129	.791	39	132	171	166	185	1	64	17	350	4.5
Totals	626	13228	3685	1591	.432	1901	1492	.785	606	1152	1758	1786	1891	21	624	171	4713	7.5

Three-Point Field Goals: 1980-81, 1-for-5 (.200). 1981-82, 0-for-4. 1982-83, 1-for-7 (.143). 1983-84, 3-for-12 (.250). 1984-85, 1-for-15 (.067). 1985-86, 8-for-41 (.195). 1986-87, 22-for-80 (.275). 1987-88, 3-for-16 (.188). Totals, 39-for-180 (.217).

NBA PLAYOFF RECORD

Sea.—Team	G.	Min.	FGA	FGM	Pct.	FTA	FTM	Pct.	Off.	Def.	Tot.	Ast.	PF	Dq.	Stl.	Blk.	Pts.	Avg.
81-82—Seattle	8	203	34	16	.471	22	20	.909	10	22	32	20	26	1	6	5	52	6.5
82-83—Denver	8	157	50	20	.400	17	14	.824	3	22	25	21	26	0	6	5	54	6.8
83-84—Denver	5	82	19	11	.579	6	6	1.000	3	5	8	21	16	0	3	0	28	5.6
84-85—Denver	15	310	92	45	.489	41	30	.732	24	22	46	33	57	2	14	6	120	8.0
85-86—Denver	6	102	28	15	.536	16	13	.813	2	4	6	19	12	0	1	1	44	7.3
86-87—Denver	3	76	25	8	.320	15	9	.600	0	6	6	7	6	0	4	0	25	8.3
87-88—Denver	11	212	56	20	.357	26	18	.692	11	18	29	26	40	1	5	9	58	5.3
Totals	56	1142	304	135	.444	143	110	.769	53	99	152	147	183	4	39	26	381	6.8

Three-Point Field Goals: 1981-82, 0-for-1. 1982-83, 0-for-2. 1983-84, 0-for-2. 1984-85, 0-for-1. 1985-86, 1-for-1 (1.000). 1986-87, 0-for-2. 1987-88, 0-for-8. Totals, 1-for-17 (.059).

Named to NBA All-Defensive Second Team, 1986. . . . Member of U. S. Olympic team, 1980.

DEREK RICARDO HARPER

Born October 13, 1961 at Elberton, Ga.   Height 6:04.   Weight 203.

High School—West Palm Beach, Fla., North Shore.

College—University of Illinois, Champaign, Ill.

Drafted by Dallas on first round as an undergraduate, 1983 (11th pick).

—COLLEGIATE RECORD—

Year	G.	Min.	FGA	FGM	Pct.	FTA	FTM	Pct.	Reb.	Pts.	Avg.
80-81	29	934	252	104	.413	46	33	.717	75	241	8.3
81-82	29	1059	230	105	.457	45	34	.756	133	244	8.4
82-83	32	1182	369	198	.537	123	83	.675	112	492	15.4
Totals	90	3175	851	407	.478	214	150	.701	320	977	10.9

Three-Point Field Goals: 1982-83, 13-for-24 (.542).

NBA REGULAR SEASON RECORD

Sea.—Team	G.	Min.	FGA	FGM	Pct.	FTA	FTM	Pct.	Off.	Def.	Tot.	Ast.	PF	Dq.	Stl.	Blk.	Pts.	Avg.
83-84—Dallas	82	1712	451	200	.443	98	66	.673	53	119	172	239	143	0	95	21	469	5.7
84-85—Dallas	82	2218	633	329	.520	154	111	.721	47	152	199	360	194	1	144	37	790	9.6
85-86—Dallas	79	2150	730	390	.534	229	171	.747	75	151	226	416	166	1	153	23	963	12.2
86-87—Dallas	77	2556	993	497	.501	234	160	.684	51	148	199	609	195	0	167	25	1230	16.0
87-88—Dallas	82	3032	1167	536	.459	344	261	.759	71	175	246	634	164	0	168	35	1393	17.0
Totals	402	11668	3974	1952	.491	1059	769	.726	297	745	1042	2258	862	2	727	141	4845	12.1

Three-Point Field Goals: 1983-84, 3-for-26 (.115). 1984-85, 21-for-61 (.344). 1985-86, 12-for-51 (.235). 1986-87, 76-for-212 (.358). 1987-88, 60-for-192 (.313). Totals, 172-for-542 (.317).

NBA PLAYOFF RECORD

Sea.—Team	G.	Min.	FGA	FGM	Pct.	FTA	FTM	Pct.	Off.	Def.	Tot.	Ast.	PF	Dq.	Stl.	Blk.	Pts.	Avg.
83-84—Dallas	10	226	54	21	.389	7	5	.714	8	12	20	28	16	0	11	2	50	5.0
84-85—Dallas	4	132	21	10	.476	7	5	.714	1	11	12	20	12	0	6	1	26	6.5
85-86—Dallas	10	348	107	57	.533	16	12	.750	13	6	19	76	27	0	23	0	134	13.4
86-87—Dallas	4	123	40	20	.500	30	24	.800	2	10	12	27	7	0	7	0	66	16.5
87-88—Dallas	17	602	202	89	.441	59	43	.729	11	32	43	121	44	0	32	5	230	13.5
Totals	45	1431	424	197	.465	119	89	.748	35	71	106	272	106	0	79	8	506	11.2

Three-Point Field Goals: 1983-84, 3-for-8 (.375). 1984-85, 1-for-3 (.333). 1985-86, 8-for-14 (.571). 1986-87, 2-for-9 (.222). 1987-88, 9-for-36 (.250). Totals, 23-for-70 (.329).

Named to NBA All-Defensive Second Team, 1987.

RONALD HARPER
(Ron)

Born January 20, 1964 at Dayton, O.   Height 6:06.   Weight 205.

High School—Dayton, O., Kiser.

College—Miami University, Oxford, O.

Drafted by Cleveland on first round, 1986 (8th pick).

—COLLEGIATE RECORD—

Year	G.	Min.	FGA	FGM	Pct.	FTA	FTM	Pct.	Reb.	Pts.	Avg.
82-83	28	887	298	148	.497	95	64	.674	195	360	12.9
83-84	30	989	367	197	.537	165	94	.570	229	448	16.3
84-85	31	1144	577	312	.541	224	148	.661	333	772	24.9
85-86	31	1144	572	312	.545	200	133	.665	362	757	24.4
Totals	120	4164	1814	969	.534	684	439	.642	1119	2377	19.8

DEREK HARPER

NBA REGULAR SEASON RECORD

Sea.—Team	G.	Min.	FGA	FGM	Pct.	FTA	FTM	Pct.	—Rebounds— Off.	Def.	Tot.	Ast.	PF	Dq.	Stl.	Blk.	Pts.	Avg.
86-87—Cleveland	82	3064	1614	734	.455	564	386	.684	169	223	392	394	247	3	209	84	1874	22.9
87-88—Cleveland	57	1830	732	340	.464	278	196	.705	64	159	223	281	157	3	122	52	879	15.4
Totals	139	4894	2346	1074	.458	842	582	.691	233	382	615	675	404	6	331	136	2753	19.8

Three-Point Field Goals: 1986-87, 20-for-94 (.213). 1987-88, 3-for-20 (.150). Totals, 23-for-114 (.202).

NBA PLAYOFF RECORD

Sea.—Team	G.	Min.	FGA	FGM	Pct.	FTA	FTM	Pct.	—Rebounds— Off.	Def.	Tot.	Ast.	PF	Dq.	Stl.	Blk.	Pts.	Avg.
87-88—Cleveland	4	134	63	30	.476	16	11	.688	4	16	20	15	9	0	11	4	71	17.8

Three-Point Field Goals: 1987-88, 0-for-2.

Named to NBA All-Rookie Team, 1987. . . . THE SPORTING NEWS All-America Second Team, 1986.

STEVEN DWAYNE HARRIS
(Steve)

Born October 15, 1963 at Kansas City, Mo.   Height 6:05.   Weight 195.

High School—Blue Springs, Mo.

College—University of Tulsa, Tulsa, Okla.

Drafted by Houston on first round, 1985 (19th pick).

Traded by Houston with Ralph Sampson to Golden State for Joe Barry Carroll and Eric Floyd, December 12, 1987.

—COLLEGIATE RECORD—

Year	G.	Min.	FGA	FGM	Pct.	FTA	FTM	Pct.	Reb.	Pts.	Avg.
81-82	29	587	239	137	.531	67	57	.851	60	311	10.7
82-83	31	1119	443	233	.526	119	104	.874	130	574	18.5
83-84	31	1043	468	271	.579	142	113	.796	104	655	21.1
84-85	31	1069	499	273	.547	215	186	.865	134	732	23.6
Totals	122	3818	1649	904	.548	543	460	.847	428	2272	18.6

NBA REGULAR SEASON RECORD

Sea.—Team	G.	Min.	FGA	FGM	Pct.	FTA	FTM	Pct.	—Rebounds— Off.	Def.	Tot.	Ast.	PF	Dq.	Stl.	Blk.	Pts.	Avg.
85-86—Houston	57	482	233	103	.442	54	50	.926	25	32	57	50	55	0	21	4	257	4.5
86-87—Houston	74	1174	599	251	.419	130	111	.854	71	99	170	100	111	1	37	16	613	8.3
87-88—Hou.-G.S.	58	1084	487	223	.458	113	89	.788	53	73	126	87	89	0	50	8	535	9.2
Totals	189	2740	1319	577	.437	297	250	.842	149	204	353	237	255	1	108	28	1405	7.4

Three-Point Field Goals: 1985-86, 1-for-5 (.200). 1986-87, 0-for-8. 1987-88, 0-for-7. Totals, 1-for-20 (.050).

NBA PLAYOFF RECORD

Sea.—Team	G.	Min.	FGA	FGM	Pct.	FTA	FTM	Pct.	—Rebounds— Off.	Def.	Tot.	Ast.	PF	Dq.	Stl.	Blk.	Pts.	Avg.
85-86—Houston	15	83	29	14	.483	5	2	.400	5	5	10	2	3	0	4	3	30	2.0
86-87—Houston	9	91	43	16	.372	6	5	.833	3	4	7	5	15	0	3	0	37	4.1
Totals	24	174	72	30	.417	11	7	.636	8	9	17	7	18	0	7	3	67	2.8

Three-Point Field Goals: 1986-87, 0-for-1.

SCOTT ALAN HASTINGS

Born June 3, 1960 at Independence, Kan.   Height 6:10.   Weight 235.

High School—Independence, Kan.

College—University of Arkansas, Fayetteville, Ark.

Drafted by New York on second round, 1982 (29th pick).

Traded by New York with cash to Atlanta for Rory Sparrow, February 12, 1983.
Selected from Atlanta by Miami in NBA expansion draft, June 23, 1988.

—COLLEGIATE RECORD—

Year	G.	Min.	FGA	FGM	Pct.	FTA	FTM	Pct.	Reb.	Pts.	Avg.
78-79	30	753	191	97	.508	74	54	.730	138	248	8.3
79-80	29	1033	322	172	.534	160	125	.781	194	469	16.2
80-81	32	1054	341	192	.563	189	139	.735	173	523	16.3
81-82	29	1040	369	204	.553	177	131	.740	175	539	18.6
Totals	120	3880	1223	665	.544	600	449	.748	680	1779	14.8

NBA REGULAR SEASON RECORD

Sea.—Team	G.	Min.	FGA	FGM	Pct.	FTA	FTM	Pct.	—Rebounds— Off.	Def.	Tot.	Ast.	PF	Dq.	Stl.	Blk.	Pts.	Avg.
82-83—N.Y.-Atl.	31	140	38	13	.342	20	11	.550	15	26	41	3	34	0	6	1	37	1.2

Sea.—Team	G.	Min.	FGA	FGM	Pct.	FTA	FTM	Pct.	—Rebounds— Off.	Def.	Tot.	Ast.	PF	Dq.	Stl.	Blk.	Pts.	Avg.
83-84—Atlanta	68	1135	237	111	.468	104	82	.788	96	174	270	46	220	7	40	36	305	4.5
84-85—Atlanta	64	825	188	89	.473	81	63	.778	59	100	159	46	135	1	24	23	241	3.8
85-86—Atlanta	62	650	159	65	.409	70	60	.857	44	80	124	26	118	2	14	8	193	3.1
86-87—Atlanta	40	256	68	23	.338	29	23	.793	16	54	70	13	35	0	10	7	71	1.8
87-88—Atlanta	55	403	82	40	.488	27	25	.926	27	70	97	16	67	1	8	10	110	2.0
Totals	320	3409	772	341	.442	331	264	.798	257	504	761	150	609	11	102	85	957	3.0

Three-Point Field Goals: 1982-83, 0-for-3. 1983-84, 1-for-4 (.250). 1985-86, 3-for-4 (.750). 1986-87, 2-for-12 (.167). 1987-88, 5-for-12 (.417). Totals, 11-for-35 (.314).

NBA PLAYOFF RECORD

Sea.—Team	G.	Min.	FGA	FGM	Pct.	FTA	FTM	Pct.	—Rebounds— Off.	Def.	Tot.	Ast.	PF	Dq.	Stl.	Blk.	Pts.	Avg.
83-84—Atlanta	5	32	9	2	.222	4	3	.750	2	6	8	1	4	0	1	0	7	1.4
85-86—Atlanta	9	49	14	11	.786	11	5	.455	3	7	10	2	11	0	2	0	28	3.1
86-87—Atlanta	4	21	3	2	.667	2	2	1.000	1	5	6	0	5	0	1	1	6	1.5
87-88—Atlanta	11	103	14	9	.643	8	8	1.000	7	10	17	3	21	1	3	1	26	2.4
Totals	29	205	40	24	.600	25	18	.720	13	28	41	6	41	1	7	2	67	2.3

Three-Point Field Goals: 1985-86, 1-for-4 (.250). 1987-88, 0-for-1. Totals, 1-for-5 (.200).

DAVID McKINLEY HENDERSON

Born July 21, 1964 at Henderson, N.C.   Height 6:05.   Weight 195.

High School—Warrenton, N.C., Warren County.

College—Duke University, Durham, N.C.

Drafted by Washington on third round, 1986 (58th pick).

Waived by Washington, October 30, 1986; re-signed by Washington as a free agent, October 7, 1987.
Waived by Washington, November 5, 1987; signed by Philadelphia, March 3, 1988, to the first of consecutive 10-day contracts that expired, March 22, 1988.
Re-signed by Philadelphia, March 23, 1988, for remainder of season.
Played in Continental Basketball Association with Albany Patroons, 1986-87, and Charleston Gunners and Wyoming Wildcatters, 1987-88.

—COLLEGIATE RECORD—

Year	G.	Min.	FGA	FGM	Pct.	FTA	FTM	Pct.	Reb.	Pts.	Avg.
82-83	28	697	238	100	.420	64	45	.703	120	254	9.1
83-84	33	878	318	153	.481	193	140	.725	109	446	13.5
84-85	28	660	233	116	.498	137	85	.620	98	317	11.3
85-86	39	1090	419	217	.518	160	119	.744	186	553	14.2
Totals	128	3325	1208	586	.485	554	389	.702	513	1570	12.3

Three-Point Field Goals: 1982-83, 9-for-33 (.273).

CBA REGULAR SEASON RECORD

Sea.—Team	G.	Min.	2-Point FGM	FGA	Pct.	3-Point FGM	FGA	Pct.	FTM	FTA	Pct.	Reb.	Ast.	Pts.	Avg.
86-87—Albany	25	482	96	214	.448	1	6	.167	72	100	.720	109	40	267	10.7
87-88—Char.-Wyo.	30	742	153	316	.484	2	13	.154	135	175	.771	159	57	447	14.9
Totals	55	1224	249	530	.470	3	19	.158	207	275	.753	268	97	714	13.0

NBA REGULAR SEASON RECORD

Sea.—Team	G.	Min.	FGA	FGM	Pct.	FTA	FTM	Pct.	—Rebounds— Off.	Def.	Tot.	Ast.	PF	Dq.	Stl.	Blk.	Pts.	Avg.
87-88—Philadelphia	22	351	116	47	.405	47	32	.681	11	24	35	34	41	0	12	5	126	5.7

Three-Point Field Goals: 1987-88, 0-for-1.

JEROME McKINLEY HENDERSON
(Gerald)

Born January 16, 1956 at Richmond, Va.   Height 6:02.   Weight 180.

High School—Richmond, Va., Huguenot.

College—Virginia Commonwealth University, Richmond, Va.

Drafted by San Antonio on third round, 1978 (64th pick).

Waived by San Antonio, September 20, 1978; signed by Boston as a free agent, June 25, 1979.
Traded by Boston to Seattle for a 1986 1st round draft choice, October 16, 1984.
Traded by Seattle to New York for a 1990 2nd round draft choice and the right to exchange 1987 1st round draft choices, November 12, 1986.
Waived by New York, November 14, 1987; signed by Philadelphia as a free agent, December 3, 1987.
Played in Western Basketball Association with Tucson Gunners, 1978-79.

—COLLEGIATE RECORD—

Year	G.	Min.	FGA	FGM	Pct.	FTA	FTM	Pct.	Reb.	Pts.	Avg.
74-75	25	....	182	73	.401	39	21	.538	64	167	6.7
75-76	25	....	395	196	.496	43	27	.628	71	419	16.8
76-77	25	903	465	228	.490	81	50	.617	102	506	20.2
77-78	28	939	377	185	.491	121	80	.661	94	450	16.1
Totals	103	....	1419	682	.481	284	178	.627	331	1542	15.0

WBA REGULAR SEASON RECORD

Sea.—Team	G.	Min.	2-Point FGM	FGA	Pct.	3-Point FGM	FGA	Pct.	FTM	FTA	Pct.	Reb.	Ast.	Pts.	Avg.
78-79—Tucson	48	1288	239	447	.535	1	7	.143	124	173	.717	138	140	605	12.6

NBA REGULAR SEASON RECORD

Sea.—Team	G.	Min.	FGA	FGM	Pct.	FTA	FTM	Pct.	Off.	Def.	Tot.	Ast.	PF	Dq.	Stl.	Blk.	Pts.	Avg.
79-80—Boston	76	1061	382	191	.500	129	89	.690	37	46	83	147	96	0	45	15	473	6.2
80-81—Boston	82	1608	579	261	.451	157	113	.720	43	89	132	213	177	0	79	12	636	7.8
81-82—Boston	82	1844	705	353	.501	172	125	.727	47	105	152	252	199	3	82	11	833	10.2
82-83—Boston	82	1551	618	286	.463	133	96	.722	57	67	124	195	190	6	95	3	671	8.2
83-84—Boston	78	2088	718	376	.524	177	136	.768	68	79	147	300	209	1	117	14	908	11.6
84-85—Seattle	79	2648	891	427	.479	255	199	.780	71	119	190	559	196	1	140	9	1062	13.4
85-86—Seattle	82	2568	900	434	.482	223	185	.830	89	98	187	487	230	2	138	12	1071	13.1
86-87—Sea.-N.Y.	74	2045	674	298	.442	230	190	.826	50	125	175	471	208	1	101	11	805	10.9
87-88—N.Y.-Phil.	75	1505	453	194	.428	170	138	.812	27	80	107	231	187	0	69	5	595	7.9
Totals	710	16918	5920	2820	.476	1646	1271	.772	489	808	1297	2855	1692	14	866	92	7054	9.9

Three-Point Field Goals: 1979-80, 2-for-6 (.333). 1980-81, 1-for-16 (.063). 1981-82, 2-for-12 (.167). 1982-83, 3-for-16 (.188). 1983-84, 20-for-57 (.351). 1984-85, 9-for-38 (.237). 1985-86, 18-for-52 (.346). 1986-87, 19-for-77 (.247). 1987-88, 69-for-163 (.423). Totals, 143-for-437 (.327).

NBA PLAYOFF RECORD

Sea.—Team	G.	Min.	FGA	FGM	Pct.	FTA	FTM	Pct.	Off.	Def.	Tot.	Ast.	PF	Dq.	Stl.	Blk.	Pts.	Avg.
79-80—Boston	9	101	37	15	.405	20	12	.600	4	6	10	12	8	0	4	0	42	4.7
80-81—Boston	16	228	86	41	.477	12	10	.833	10	15	25	26	24	0	10	3	92	5.8
81-82—Boston	12	310	93	38	.409	35	24	.686	12	13	25	48	30	0	14	2	100	8.3
82-83—Boston	7	187	85	35	.412	7	6	.857	8	6	14	31	25	1	11	1	76	10.9
83-84—Boston	23	616	237	115	.485	75	54	.720	23	29	52	97	78	0	34	1	287	12.5
Totals	67	1442	538	344	.639	149	106	.711	57	69	126	214	165	1	73	7	597	8.9

Three-Point Field Goals: 1979-80, 0-for-2. 1980-81, 0-for-1. 1981-82, 0-for-2. 1982-83, 0-for-3. 1983-84, 3-for-11 (.273). Totals, 3-for-19 (.158).

Member of NBA championship teams, 1981 and 1984.

KEVIN DWAYNE HENDERSON

Born March 22, 1964 at Baltimore, Md.   Height 6:04.   Weight 195.

High School—Compton, Calif., Centennial.

Colleges—Saddleback Community College, Mission Viejo, Calif., and California State University, Fullerton, Calif.

Drafted by Cleveland on third round, 1986 (50th pick).

Waived by Cleveland, October 28, 1986; signed by Golden State, February 9, 1987, to a 10-day contract that expired, February 18, 1987.
Signed by Cleveland, February 24, 1987, to a 10-day contract that expired, March 5, 1987.
Signed by Golden State as a free agent, June 14, 1987.
Waived by Golden State, December 21, 1987; signed by Cleveland as a free agent, March 29, 1988.
Played in Continental Basketball Association with Charleston Gunners, 1986-87 and 1987-88.

—COLLEGIATE RECORD—
Saddleback

Year	G.	Min.	FGA	FGM	Pct.	FTA	FTM	Pct.	Reb.	Pts.	Avg.
82-83	24	....	248	130	.524	118	79	.669	93	339	14.1

California State-Fullerton

Year	G.	Min.	FGA	FGM	Pct.	FTA	FTM	Pct.	Reb.	Pts.	Avg.
83-84	22	329	96	49	.510	29	17	.586	24	115	5.2
84-85	30	1081	387	194	.501	139	104	.748	80	518	17.3
85-86	21	575	238	125	.525	103	84	.816	40	348	16.6
CSF Totals	73	1985	721	368	.510	271	205	.756	144	981	13.4

Three-Point Field Goals: 1984-85, 26-for-53 (.491). 1985-86, 14-for-27 (.519). Totals, 40-for-80 (.500).

CBA REGULAR SEASON RECORD

Sea.—Team	G.	Min.	2-Point FGM	FGA	Pct.	3-Point FGM	FGA	Pct.	FTM	FTA	Pct.	Reb.	Ast.	Pts.	Avg.
86-87—Charleston	35	891	135	264	.511	15	41	.366	120	153	.784	120	97	435	12.4
87-88—Charleston	14	383	47	109	.431	12	21	.571	54	69	.783	29	69	184	13.1
Totals	49	1274	182	373	.488	27	62	.435	174	222	.784	149	166	619	12.6

Sea.—Team	G.	Min.	FGA	FGM	Pct.	FTA	FTM	Pct.	—Rebounds— Off.	Def.	Tot.	Ast.	PF	Dq.	Stl.	Blk.	Pts.	Avg.
86-87—Golden State	5	45	8	3	.375	2	2	1.000	1	2	3	11	9	0	1	0	8	1.6
87-88—G.S.-Clev.	17	190	53	21	.396	26	15	.577	9	12	21	23	26	0	8	0	57	3.4
Totals	22	235	61	24	.393	28	17	.607	10	14	24	34	35	0	9	0	65	3.0

Three-Point Field Goals: 1987-88, 0-for-1.

CONNER HENRY

Born July 21, 1963 at Claremont, Calif.   Height 6:07.   Weight 195.

High School—Claremont, Calif.

College—University of California at Santa Barbara, Santa Barbara, Calif.

Drafted by Houston on fourth round, 1986 (89th pick).

Waived by Houston, December 23, 1986; signed by Boston, January 1, 1987, to the first of consecutive 10-day contracts that expired, January 21, 1987.

Re-signed by Boston, January 22, 1987, for remainder of season.

Waived by Boston, November 30, 1987; signed by Milwaukee as a free agent, December 5, 1987.

Waived by Milwaukee, January 18, 1988; signed by Sacramento, March 26, 1988, to the first of consecutive 10-day contracts that expired, April 14, 1988.

Re-signed by Sacramento, April 14, 1988, for remainder of season.

Selected from Sacramento by Miami in NBA expansion draft, June 23, 1988.

—COLLEGIATE RECORD—

Year	G.	Min.	FGA	FGM	Pct.	FTA	FTM	Pct.	Reb.	Pts.	Avg.
82-83	25	524	126	42	.333	43	34	.791	52	127	5.1
83-84	27	865	275	131	.476	118	89	.754	107	351	13.0
84-85	22	789	223	93	.417	102	80	.784	116	291	13.2
85-86	27	981	369	161	.436	133	105	.789	133	468	17.3
Totals	101	3159	993	427	.430	396	308	.778	408	1237	12.2

Three-Point Field Goals: 1982-83, 9-for-28 (.321). 1984-85, 25-for-56 (.446). 1985-86, 41-for-101 (.406). Totals, 75-for-185 (.405).

NBA REGULAR SEASON RECORD

Sea.—Team	G.	Min.	FGA	FGM	Pct.	FTA	FTM	Pct.	—Rebounds— Off.	Def.	Tot.	Ast.	PF	Dq.	Stl.	Blk.	Pts.	Avg.
86-87—Hou.-Bos.	54	323	136	46	.338	27	17	.630	7	27	34	35	34	0	9	1	122	2.3
87-88—Bs-Ml-Sac	39	433	150	62	.413	47	39	.830	13	36	49	67	37	0	12	5	183	4.7
Totals	93	756	286	108	.378	74	56	.757	20	63	83	102	71	0	21	6	305	3.3

Three-Point Field Goals: 1986-87, 13-for-42 (.310). 1987-88, 20-for-45 (.444). Totals, 33-for-87 (.379).

NBA PLAYOFF RECORD

Sea.—Team	G.	Min.	FGA	FGM	Pct.	FTA	FTM	Pct.	—Rebounds— Off.	Def.	Tot.	Ast.	PF	Dq.	Stl.	Blk.	Pts.	Avg.
86-87—Boston	11	35	16	8	.500	10	5	.500	3	3	6	0	3	0	0	0	22	2.0

Three-Point Field Goals: 1986-87, 1-for-5 (.200).

RODERICK DWAYNE HIGGINS
(Rod)

Born January 31, 1960 at Monroe, La.   Height 6:07.   Weight 205.

High School—Harvey, Ill., Thornton.

College—Fresno State University, Fresno, Calif.

Drafted by Chicago on second round, 1982 (31st pick).

Waived by Chicago, October 24, 1985; signed by Seattle as a free agent, November 4, 1985.

Waived by Seattle, December 17, 1985; signed by San Antonio, January 15, 1986, to the first of consecutive 10-day contracts that expired, February 3, 1986.

Signed by New Jersey, February 21, 1986, to a 10-day contract that expired, March 2, 1986.

Signed by Chicago, March 14, 1986, to a 10-day contract that expired, March 23, 1986.

Re-signed by Chicago, March 24, 1986; released, March 27, 1986.

Signed by Golden State as a free agent, October 2, 1986.

Played in Continental Basketball Association with Tampa Bay Thrillers, 1985-86.

—COLLEGIATE RECORD—

Year	G.	Min.	FGA	FGM	Pct.	FTA	FTM	Pct.	Reb.	Pts.	Avg.
78-79	22	....	153	79	.516	66	49	.742	127	207	9.4
79-80	24	....	235	119	.506	86	72	.837	136	310	12.9
80-81	29	941	319	178	.558	108	92	.852	158	448	15.4
81-82	29	1025	335	178	.531	105	81	.771	182	437	15.1
Totals	104	....	1042	554	.532	365	294	.805	603	1402	13.5

CBA REGULAR SEASON RECORD

Sea.—Team	G.	Min.	2-Point FGM	FGA	Pct.	3-Point FGM	FGA	Pct.	FTM	FTA	Pct.	Reb.	Ast.	Pts.	Avg.
85-86—Tampa Bay	11	422	105	190	.553	4	10	.400	92	115	.800	85	30	314	28.5

NBA REGULAR SEASON RECORD

Sea.—Team	G.	Min.	FGA	FGM	Pct.	FTA	FTM	Pct.	Off.	Def.	Tot.	Ast.	PF	Dq.	Stl.	Blk.	Pts.	Avg.
82-83—Chicago	82	2196	698	313	.448	264	209	.792	159	207	366	175	248	3	66	65	848	10.3
83-84—Chicago	78	1577	432	193	.447	156	113	.724	87	119	206	116	161	0	49	29	500	6.4
84-85—Chicago	68	942	270	119	.441	90	60	.667	55	92	147	73	91	0	21	13	308	4.5
85-86—Se-SA-NJ-Ch	30	332	106	39	.368	27	19	.704	14	37	51	24	49	0	9	11	98	3.3
86-87—Golden State	73	1497	412	214	.519	240	200	.833	72	165	237	96	145	0	40	21	631	8.6
87-88—Golden State	68	2188	725	381	.526	322	273	.848	94	199	293	188	188	2	70	31	1054	15.5
Totals	399	8732	2643	1259	.476	1099	874	.795	481	819	1300	672	882	5	255	170	3439	8.6

Three-Point Field Goals: 1982-83, 13-for-41 (.317). 1983-84, 1-for-22 (.045). 1984-85, 10-for-37 (.270). 1985-86, 1-for-9 (.111). 1986-87, 3-for-17 (.176). 1987-88, 19-for-39 (.487). Totals, 47-for-165 (.285).

NBA PLAYOFF RECORD

Sea.—Team	G.	Min.	FGA	FGM	Pct.	FTA	FTM	Pct.	Off.	Def.	Tot.	Ast.	PF	Dq.	Stl.	Blk.	Pts.	Avg.
84-85—Chicago	1	1	0	0	.000	0	0	.000	0	0	0	0	0	0	0	0	0	0.0
86-87—Golden State	10	177	46	18	.391	9	6	.667	5	16	21	12	20	0	11	6	43	4.3
Totals	11	178	46	18	.391	9	6	.667	5	16	21	12	20	0	11	6	43	3.9

Three-Point Field Goals: 1986-87, 1-for-1 (1.000).

Only NBA player ever to play for four teams in one season, 1985-86. . . . CBA Playoff MVP, 1986. . . . Member of CBA championship team, 1986.

ROY MANUS HINSON

Born May 2, 1961 at Trenton, N. J.   Height 6:09.   Weight 220.

High School—Somerset, N. J., Franklin Township.

College—Rutgers University, New Brunswick, N. J.

Drafted by Cleveland on first round, 1983 (20th pick).

Traded by Cleveland with other considerations to Philadelphia for a 1986 1st round draft choice, June 16, 1986.
Traded by Philadelphia with Tim McCormick and a 1989 2nd round draft choice to New Jersey for Ben Coleman and Mike Gminski, January 16, 1988.

—COLLEGIATE RECORD—

Year	G.	Min.	FGA	FGM	Pct.	FTA	FTM	Pct.	Reb.	Pts.	Avg.
79-80	28	796	228	115	.504	76	42	.553	157	272	9.7
80-81	30	952	309	150	.485	98	59	.602	218	359	12.0
81-82	30	1015	316	153	.484	119	70	.588	215	376	12.5
82-83	31	1048	377	199	.528	184	118	.641	268	516	16.6
Totals	119	3811	1230	617	.502	477	289	.606	858	1523	12.8

NBA REGULAR SEASON RECORD

Sea.—Team	G.	Min.	FGA	FGM	Pct.	FTA	FTM	Pct.	Off.	Def.	Tot.	Ast.	PF	Dq.	Stl.	Blk.	Pts.	Avg.
83-84—Cleveland	80	1858	371	184	.496	117	69	.590	175	324	499	69	306	11	31	145	437	5.5
84-85—Cleveland	76	2344	925	465	.503	376	271	.721	186	410	596	68	311	13	51	173	1201	15.8
85-86—Cleveland	82	2834	1167	621	.532	506	364	.719	167	472	639	102	316	7	62	112	1606	19.6
86-87—Philadelphia	76	2489	823	393	.478	360	273	.758	150	338	488	60	281	4	45	161	1059	13.9
87-88—Phil.-N.J.	77	2592	930	453	.487	351	272	.775	159	358	517	99	275	6	69	140	1178	15.3
Totals	391	12117	4216	2116	.502	1710	1249	.730	837	1902	2739	398	1489	41	258	731	5481	14.0

Three-Point Field Goals: 1984-85, 0-for-3. 1985-86, 0-for-4. 1986-87, 0-for-1. 1987-88, 0-for-2. Totals, 0-for-10.

NBA PLAYOFF RECORD

Sea.—Team	G.	Min.	FGA	FGM	Pct.	FTA	FTM	Pct.	Off.	Def.	Tot.	Ast.	PF	Dq.	Stl.	Blk.	Pts.	Avg.
84-85—Cleveland	4	120	48	26	.542	23	15	652	10	20	30	3	18	1	3	9	67	16.8
86-87—Philadelphia	5	159	52	31	.596	38	24	.632	6	17	23	3	18	0	4	10	86	17.2
Totals	9	279	100	57	.570	61	39	.639	16	37	53	6	36	1	7	19	153	17.0

—DID YOU KNOW—

That the Lakers have reached the NBA Finals 22 times and the Celtics 19 times but Boston has won 16 titles compared to 11 for the Lakers? The Lakers have opposed the Celtics in the final 10 times (1959-62-63-65-66-68-69-84-85-87), with Boston winning the first eight series and the Lakers the last two. Five of the Lakers' 11 titles came in a six-year span (1949 through 1954) before the franchise moved from Minneapolis to Los Angeles.

CRAIG ANTHONY HODGES

Born June 27, 1960 at Park Forest, Ill.   Height 6:03.   Weight 195.

High School—Park Forest, Ill., Rich East.

College—California State University at Long Beach, Long Beach, Calif.

Drafted by San Diego on third round, 1982 (48th pick).

Traded by Los Angeles Clippers with Terry Cummings and Ricky Pierce to Milwaukee for Marques Johnson, Harvey Catchings, Junior Bridgeman and cash, September 29, 1984.

Traded by Milwaukee with a 1988 2nd round draft choice to Phoenix for Jay Humphries, February 25, 1988.

—COLLEGIATE RECORD—

Year	G.	Min.	FGA	FGM	Pct.	FTA	FTM	Pct.	Reb.	Pts.	Avg.
78-79	28	801	234	122	.521	49	38	.776	56	282	10.1
79-80	33	1148	361	180	.499	68	57	.838	70	417	12.6
80-81	26	755	275	127	.462	55	33	.600	67	287	11.0
81-82	28	1005	444	211	.475	92	68	.739	89	490	17.5
Totals	115	3709	1314	640	.487	264	196	.742	282	1476	12.8

NBA REGULAR SEASON RECORD

Sea.—Team	G.	Min.	FGA	FGM	Pct.	FTA	FTM	Pct.	Off.	Def.	Tot.	Ast.	PF	Dq.	Stl.	Blk.	Pts.	Avg.
82-83—San Diego	76	2022	704	318	.452	130	94	.723	53	69	122	275	192	3	82	4	750	9.9
83-84—San Diego	76	1571	573	258	.450	88	66	.750	22	64	86	116	166	2	58	1	592	7.8
84-85—Milwaukee	82	2496	733	359	.490	130	106	.815	74	112	186	349	262	8	96	1	871	10.6
85-86—Milwaukee	66	1739	568	284	.500	86	75	.872	39	78	117	229	157	3	74	2	716	10.8
86-87—Milwaukee	78	2147	682	315	.462	147	131	.891	48	92	140	240	189	3	76	7	846	10.8
87-88—Mil.-Phoe.	66	1445	523	242	.463	71	59	.831	19	59	78	153	118	1	46	2	629	9.5
Totals	444	11420	3783	1776	.469	652	531	.814	255	474	729	1362	1084	20	432	17	4404	9.9

Three-Point Field Goals: 1982-83, 20-for-90 (.222). 1983-84, 10-for-46 (.217). 1984-85, 47-for-135 (.348). 1985-86, 73-for-162 (.451). 1986-87, 85-for-228 (.373). 1987-88, 86-for-175 (.491). Totals, 321-for-836 (.384).

NBA PLAYOFF RECORD

Sea.—Team	G.	Min.	FGA	FGM	Pct.	FTA	FTM	Pct.	Off.	Def.	Tot.	Ast.	PF	Dq.	Stl.	Blk.	Pts.	Avg.
84-85—Milwaukee	8	216	77	28	.364	5	4	.800	2	11	13	26	29	2	12	1	64	8.0
85-86—Milwaukee	14	460	145	74	.510	34	27	.794	9	16	25	63	44	1	32	1	189	13.5
86-87—Milwaukee	12	226	77	40	.519	11	10	.909	11	11	22	20	16	0	9	2	95	7.9
Totals	34	902	299	142	.475	50	41	.820	22	38	60	109	89	3	53	5	348	10.2

Three-Point Field Goals: 1984-85, 4-for-23 (.174). 1985-86, 14-for-31 (.452). 1986-87, 5-for-17 (.294). Totals, 23-for-71 (.324).

Led NBA in three-point field goal percentage, 1986 and 1988.

MICHAEL DAVID HOLTON

Born August 4, 1961 at Seattle, Wash.   Height 6:04.   Weight 185.

High School—Pasadena, Calif., Pasadena.

College—University of California at Los Angeles, Los Angeles, Calif.

Drafted by Golden State on third round, 1983 (53rd pick).

Waived by Golden State, October 5, 1983; signed by Phoenix as a free agent, September 24, 1984.

Waived by Phoenix, November 4, 1985; signed by Chicago as a free agent, February 12, 1986.

Signed by Portland as a Veteran Free Agent, August 7, 1986; Chicago agreed not to exercise its right of first refusal in exchange for a 1992 2nd round draft choice.

Selected from Portland by Charlotte in NBA expansion draft, June 23, 1988.

Played in Continental Basketball Association with Puerto Rico Coquis, 1983-84, and Tampa Bay Thrillers and Florida Stingers, 1985-86.

—COLLEGIATE RECORD—

Year	G.	Min.	FGA	FGM	Pct.	FTA	FTM	Pct.	Reb.	Pts.	Avg.
79-80	32	802	105	55	.524	73	54	.740	78	164	5.1
80-81	27	734	161	79	.491	67	53	.791	75	211	7.8
81-82	27	677	154	75	.487	65	46	.708	64	196	7.3
82-83	29	721	161	88	.547	75	64	.853	78	240	8.3
Totals	115	2934	581	297	.511	280	217	.775	295	811	7.1

CBA REGULAR SEASON RECORD

Sea.—Team	G.	Min.	2-Point FGM	FGA	Pct.	3-Point FGM	FGA	Pct.	FTM	FTA	Pct.	Reb.	Ast.	Pts.	Avg.
83-84—Puerto Rico	44	1646	293	574	.510	6	23	.261	207	250	.828	149	198	811	18.4
85-86—Tampa Bay-Florida	29	1095	202	365	.553	7	30	.233	133	154	.863	85	193	558	19.2
Totals	73	2741	495	939	.527	13	53	.245	340	404	.841	234	391	1369	18.8

Sea.—Team	G.	Min.	FGA	FGM	Pct.	FTA	FTM	Pct.	Off.	Def.	Tot.	Ast.	PF	Dq.	Stl.	Blk.	Pts.	Avg.
									—Rebounds—									
84-85—Phoenix	74	1761	576	257	.446	118	96	.814	30	102	132	198	141	0	59	6	624	8.4
85-86—Phoe.-Chi.	28	512	175	77	.440	44	28	.636	11	22	33	55	47	1	25	0	183	6.5
86-87—Portland	58	479	171	70	.409	55	44	.800	9	29	38	73	51	0	16	2	191	3.3
87-88—Portland	82	1279	353	163	.462	129	107	.829	50	99	149	211	154	0	41	10	436	5.3
Totals	242	4031	1275	567	.445	346	275	.795	100	252	352	537	393	1	141	18	1434	5.9

Three-Point Field Goals: 1984-85, 14-for-45 (.311). 1985-86, 1-for-12 (.083). 1986-87, 7-for-23 (.304). 1987-88, 3-for-15 (.200). Totals, 25-for-95 (.263).

NBA PLAYOFF RECORD

Sea.—Team	G.	Min.	FGA	FGM	Pct.	FTA	FTM	Pct.	Off.	Def.	Tot.	Ast.	PF	Dq.	Stl.	Blk.	Pts.	Avg.
									—Rebounds—									
84-85—Phoenix	3	55	19	9	.474	4	4	1.000	0	2	2	9	8	0	0	0	22	7.3
86-87—Portland	2	9	2	1	.500	0	0	.000	0	1	1	0	1	0	0	0	2	1.0
87-88—Portland	4	34	13	3	.231	0	0	.000	1	4	5	6	6	0	2	0	6	1.5
Totals	9	98	34	13	.382	4	4	1.000	1	7	8	15	15	0	2	0	30	3.3

Three-Point Field Goals: 1984-85, 0-for-4. 1987-88, 0-for-1. Totals, 0-for-5.

DAVID DIRK HOPPEN
(Dave)

Born March 13, 1964 at Omaha, Neb.   Height 6:11.   Weight 235.

High School—Omaha, Neb., Benson.

College—University of Nebraska, Lincoln, Neb.

Drafted by Atlanta on third round, 1986 (65th pick).

Missed entire 1986-87 season due to injury.

Waived by Atlanta, December 29, 1987; signed by Milwaukee, January 12, 1988, to a 10-day contract that expired, January 21, 1988.

Signed by Golden State as a free agent, January 22, 1988.

Selected from Golden State by Charlotte in NBA expansion draft, June 23, 1988.

Played in Continental Basketball Association with Topeka Sizzlers, 1987-88.

—COLLEGIATE RECORD—

Year	G.	Min.	FGA	FGM	Pct.	FTA	FTM	Pct.	Reb.	Pts.	Avg.
82-83	32	829	311	163	.524	159	119	.748	161	445	13.9
83-84	30	1058	367	220	.599	208	158	.760	207	598	19.9
84-85	30	1155	418	270	.646	210	164	.781	258	704	23.5
85-86	19	669	245	151	.616	147	118	.803	147	420	22.1
Totals	111	3711	1341	804	.600	724	559	.772	773	2167	19.5

CBA REGULAR SEASON RECORD

Sea.—Team	G.	Min.	FGM	FGA	Pct.	FGM	FGA	Pct.	FTM	FTA	Pct.	Reb.	Ast.	Pts.	Avg.
			—2-Point—			—3-Point—									
87-88—Topeka	6	204	33	51	.647	0	0	.000	26	33	.788	65	11	92	15.3

NBA REGULAR SEASON RECORD

Sea.—Team	G.	Min.	FGA	FGM	Pct.	FTA	FTM	Pct.	Off.	Def.	Tot.	Ast.	PF	Dq.	Stl.	Blk.	Pts.	Avg.
									—Rebounds—									
87-88—Mil.-G.S.	39	642	183	84	.459	62	54	.871	58	116	174	32	87	1	13	6	222	5.7

Three-Point Field Goals: 1987-88, 0-for-1.

DENNIS HOPSON

Born April 22, 1965 at Toledo, O.   Height 6:05.   Weight 200.

High School—Toledo, O., Bowsher.

College—Ohio State University, Columbus, O.

Drafted by New Jersey on first round, 1987 (3rd pick).

—COLLEGIATE RECORD—

Year	G.	Min.	FGA	FGM	Pct.	FTA	FTM	Pct.	Reb.	Pts.	Avg.
83-84	29	541	133	63	.474	35	29	.829	108	155	5.3
84-85	30	764	243	120	.494	72	53	.736	142	293	9.8
85-86	33	1148	505	275	.545	180	140	.778	193	690	20.9
86-87	33	1158	653	338	.518	264	215	.814	269	958	29.0
Totals	125	3611	1534	796	.519	551	437	.793	712	2096	16.8

Three-Point Field Goals: 1986-87, 67-for-160 (.419).

NBA REGULAR SEASON RECORD

Sea.—Team	G.	Min.	FGA	FGM	Pct.	FTA	FTM	Pct.	Off.	Def.	Tot.	Ast.	PF	Dq.	Stl.	Blk.	Pts.	Avg.
									—Rebounds—									
87-88—New Jersey	61	1365	549	222	.404	177	131	.740	63	80	143	118	145	0	57	25	587	9.6

Three-Point Field Goals: 1987-88, 12-for-45 (.267).
Named to THE SPORTING NEWS All-America First Team, 1987.

JEFFREY JOHN HORNACEK
(Jeff)

Born April 3, 1963 at Elmhurst, Ill. Height 6:04. Weight 190.
High School—LaGrange, Ill., Lyons.
College—Iowa State University, Ames, Ia.
Drafted by Phoenix on second round, 1986 (46th pick).

—COLLEGIATE RECORD—

Year	G.	Min.	FGA	FGM	Pct.	FTA	FTM	Pct.	Reb.	Pts.	Avg.
81-82					Did Not Play—Redshirted						
82-83	27	583	135	57	.422	45	32	.711	62	146	5.4
83-84	29	1065	208	104	.500	105	83	.790	101	291	10.0
84-85	34	1224	330	172	.521	96	81	.844	122	425	12.5
85-86	33	1229	370	177	.478	125	97	.776	127	451	13.7
Totals	123	4101	1043	510	.489	371	293	.790	412	1313	10.7

NBA REGULAR SEASON RECORD

Sea.—Team	G.	Min.	FGA	FGM	Pct.	FTA	FTM	Pct.	Off.	Def.	Tot.	Ast.	PF	Dq.	Stl.	Blk.	Pts.	Avg.
86-87—Phoenix	80	1561	350	159	.454	121	94	.777	41	143	184	361	130	0	70	5	424	5.3
87-88—Phoenix	82	2243	605	306	.506	185	152	.822	71	191	262	540	151	0	107	10	781	9.5
Totals	162	3804	955	465	.487	306	246	.804	112	334	446	901	281	0	177	15	1205	7.4

Three-Point Field Goals: 1986-87, 12-for-43 (.279). 1987-88, 17-for-58 (.293). Totals, 29-for-101 (.287).

PHILLIP GREGORY HUBBARD
(Phil)

Born December 13, 1956 at Canton, O. Height 6:08. Weight 215.
High School—Canton, O., McKinley.
College—University of Michigan, Ann Arbor, Mich.
Drafted by Detroit on first round as junior eligible, 1979 (15th pick).

Traded by Detroit with Paul Mokeski and 1982 1st and 2nd round draft choices to Cleveland for Kenny Carr and Bill Laimbeer, February 16, 1982.

—COLLEGIATE RECORD—

Year	G.	Min.	FGA	FGM	Pct.	FTA	FTM	Pct.	Reb.	Pts.	Avg.
75-76	32	....	381	208	.546	113	66	.584	352	482	15.1
76-77	30	....	410	228	.556	195	132	.677	389	588	19.6
77-78					Did Not Play—Knee Injury						
78-79	26	....	311	154	.495	128	77	.602	238	385	14.8
Totals	88	....	1102	590	.535	436	275	.631	979	1455	16.5

NBA REGULAR SEASON RECORD

Sea.—Team	G.	Min.	FGA	FGM	Pct.	FTA	FTM	Pct.	Off.	Def.	Tot.	Ast.	PF	Dq.	Stl.	Blk.	Pts.	Avg.
79-80—Detroit	64	1189	451	210	.466	220	165	.750	114	206	320	70	202	9	48	10	585	9.1
80-81—Detroit	80	2289	880	433	.492	426	294	.690	236	350	586	150	317	14	80	20	1161	14.5
81-82—Det.-Clev.	83	1839	665	326	.490	280	191	.682	187	286	473	91	292	3	65	19	843	10.2
82-83—Cleveland	82	1953	597	288	.482	296	204	.689	222	249	471	89	271	11	87	8	780	9.5
83-84—Cleveland	80	1799	628	321	.511	299	221	.739	172	208	380	86	244	3	71	6	863	10.8
84-85—Cleveland	76	2249	822	415	.505	494	371	.751	214	265	479	114	258	8	81	9	1201	15.8
85-86—Cleveland	23	640	198	93	.470	112	76	.679	48	72	120	29	78	2	20	3	262	11.4
86-87—Cleveland	68	2083	605	321	.531	272	162	.596	178	210	388	136	224	6	66	7	804	11.8
87-88—Cleveland	78	1631	485	237	.489	243	182	.749	117	164	281	81	167	1	50	7	656	8.4
Totals	634	15672	5331	2644	.496	2642	1866	.706	1488	2010	3498	846	2053	57	568	89	7155	11.3

Three-Point Field Goals: 1979-80, 0-for-2. 1980-81, 1-for-3 (.333). 1981-82, 0-for-4. 1982-83, 0-for-2. 1983-84, 0-for-1. 1984-85, 0-for-4. 1985-86, 0-for-1. 1986-87, 0-for-4. 1987-88, 0-for-5. Totals, 1-for-26 (.038).

NBA PLAYOFF RECORD

Sea.—Team	G.	Min.	FGA	FGM	Pct.	FTA	FTM	Pct.	Off.	Def.	Tot.	Ast.	PF	Dq.	Stl.	Blk.	Pts.	Avg.
84-85—Cleveland	4	101	45	24	.533	17	13	.765	11	9	20	3	16	0	3	0	62	15.5
87-88—Cleveland	3	21	6	1	.167	1	0	.000	1	2	3	0	1	0	0	0	2	0.7
Totals	7	122	51	25	.490	18	13	.722	12	11	23	3	17	0	3	0	64	9.1

Three-Point Field Goals: 1984-85, 1-for-1 (1.000).
Member of U. S. Olympic team, 1976.

JEFF HORNACEK

EDDIE HUGHES

Born May 26, 1960 at Greenville, Miss.   Height 5:10.   Weight 165.

High School—Chicago, Ill., Austin.

College—Colorado State University, Fort Collins, Colo.

Drafted by San Diego on seventh round, 1982 (140th pick).

Waived by Utah, October 27, 1982; signed by Denver as a free agent, August 1, 1985.
Waived by Denver, October 3, 1985; signed by Utah as a free agent, October 3, 1986.
Waived by Utah, October 27, 1986; re-signed by Utah as a free agent, October 8, 1987.
Waived by Utah, November 3, 1987; signed by Utah as a free agent, March 23, 1988.
Played in Continental Basketball Association with Wyoming Wildcatters and Maine Lumberjacks, 1982-83; Bay State Bombardiers and Albuquerque Silvers, 1983-84; Albuquerque Silvers, 1984-85; LaCrosse Catbirds, 1985-86, and Pensacola Tornados, 1986-87.

—COLLEGIATE RECORD—

Year	G.	Min.	FGA	FGM	Pct.	FTA	FTM	Pct.	Reb.	Pts.	Avg.
78-79	27	....	342	175	.512	89	66	.742	77	416	15.4
79-80	27	1033	293	149	.509	77	55	.714	90	353	13.1
80-81	26	935	295	140	.475	98	66	.673	79	346	13.3
81-82	26	831	224	102	.455	62	41	.661	102	245	9.4
Totals	106	....	1154	566	.490	326	228	.699	348	1360	12.8

CBA REGULAR SEASON RECORD

Sea.—Team	G.	Min.	2-Point FGM	FGA	Pct.	3-Point FGM	FGA	Pct.	FTM	FTA	Pct.	Reb.	Ast.	Pts.	Avg.
82-83—Wyoming-Maine	42	1483	197	420	.469	38	99	.384	79	116	.681	122	304	587	14.0
83-84—Bay St.-Albu.	43	1448	185	344	.537	48	118	.407	116	154	.753	130	230	630	14.7
84-85—Albuquerque	48	1826	162	296	.547	68	153	.444	112	145	.772	135	293	640	13.3
85-86—LaCrosse	47	1620	163	354	.460	50	153	.327	151	210	.719	120	261	627	13.3
86-87—Pensacola	48	1539	143	360	.397	45	119	.378	123	154	.798	104	298	544	11.3
Totals	228	7916	850	1774	.479	249	642	.388	581	779	.745	611	1386	3028	13.3

NBA REGULAR SEASON RECORD

Sea.—Team	G.	Min.	FGA	FGM	Pct.	FTA	FTM	Pct.	Off.	Def.	Tot.	Ast.	PF	Dq.	Stl.	Blk.	Pts.	Avg.
87-88—Utah	11	42	13	5	.385	6	6	1.000	3	1	4	8	5	0	0	0	17	1.5

Three-Point Field Goals: 1987-88, 1-for-6 (.167).

NBA PLAYOFF RECORD

Sea.—Team	G.	Min.	FGA	FGM	Pct.	FTA	FTM	Pct.	Off.	Def.	Tot.	Ast.	PF	Dq.	Stl.	Blk.	Pts.	Avg.
87-88—Utah	7	16	7	2	.286	0	0	.000	0	0	0	1	1	0	1	0	5	0.7

Three-Point Field Goals: 1987-88, 1-for-3 (.333).

JOHN JAY HUMPHRIES
(Known by middle name.)

Born October 17, 1962 at Los Angeles, Calif.   Height 6:03.   Weight 185.

High School—Inglewood, Calif.

College—University of Colorado, Boulder, Colo.

Drafted by Phoenix on first round, 1984 (13th pick).

Traded by Phoenix to Milwaukee for Craig Hodges and a 1988 2nd round draft choice, February 25, 1988.

—COLLEGIATE RECORD—

Year	G.	Min.	FGA	FGM	Pct.	FTA	FTM	Pct.	Reb.	Pts.	Avg.
80-81	28	762	143	74	.517	47	31	.660	59	179	6.4
81-82	27	948	242	113	.467	83	53	.639	71	279	10.3
82-83	28	1034	339	170	.501	95	60	.632	91	400	14.3
83-84	29	1120	334	170	.509	137	108	.788	94	448	15.4
Totals	112	3864	1058	527	.498	362	252	.696	315	1306	11.7

NBA REGULAR SEASON RECORD

Sea.—Team	G.	Min.	FGA	FGM	Pct.	FTA	FTM	Pct.	Off.	Def.	Tot.	Ast.	PF	Dq.	Stl.	Blk.	Pts.	Avg.
84-85—Phoenix	80	2062	626	279	.446	170	141	.829	32	132	164	350	209	2	107	8	703	8.8
85-86—Phoenix	82	2733	735	352	.479	257	197	.767	56	204	260	526	222	1	132	9	905	11.0
86-87—Phoenix	82	2579	753	359	.477	260	200	.769	62	198	260	632	239	1	112	9	923	11.3
87-88—Phoe-Mil.	68	1809	538	284	.528	153	112	.732	49	125	174	395	177	1	81	5	683	10.0
Totals	312	9183	2652	1274	.480	840	650	.774	199	659	858	1903	847	5	432	31	3214	10.3

Three-Point Field Goals: 1984-85, 4-for-20 (.200). 1985-86, 4-for-29 (.138). 1986-87, 5-for-27 (.185). 1987-88, 3-for-18 (.167). Totals, 16-for-94 (.170).

Sea.—Team	G.	Min.	FGA	FGM	Pct.	FTA	FTM	Pct.	Off.	Def.	Tot.	Ast.	PF	Dq.	Stl.	Blk.	Pts.	Avg.
										—Rebounds—								
84-85—Phoenix	3	90	31	20	.645	12	9	.750	1	4	5	16	12	0	2	0	49	16.3
87-88—Milwaukee	2	18	5	0	.000	0	0	.000	1	2	3	1	6	0	1	0	0	0.0
Totals	5	108	36	20	.556	12	9	.750	2	6	8	17	18	0	3	0	49	9.8

MARCUS JOHN IAVARONI
(Marc)

Born September 15, 1956 at Jamaica, N. Y.   Height 6:10.   Weight 225.

High School—Plainview, N. Y., Kennedy.

College—University of Virginia, Charlottesville, Va.

Drafted by New York on third round, 1978 (55th pick).

Waived by New York, October 9, 1980; signed by Philadelphia as free agent, August, 1982.
Traded by Philadelphia to San Antonio for a 1986 3rd round draft choice, December 15, 1984.
Traded by San Antonio with Jeff Cook to Utah for Jeff Wilkins, February 15, 1986.
Played in Italy during 1978-79, 1979-80 and 1981-82 seasons.

—COLLEGIATE RECORD—

Year	G.	Min.	FGA	FGM	Pct.	FTA	FTM	Pct.	Reb.	Pts.	Avg.
74-75	25	846	213	105	.493	83	61	.735	198	271	10.8
75-76	30	830	261	138	.529	157	106	.675	168	382	12.7
76-77	28	791	272	118	.434	122	80	.656	178	316	11.3
77-78	27	800	188	97	.516	119	81	.681	174	275	10.2
Totals	110	3267	934	458	.490	481	328	.682	718	1244	11.3

ITALIAN LEAGUE RECORD

Year	G.	Min.	FGA	FGM	Pct.	FTA	FTM	Pct.	Reb.	Pts.	Avg.
78-79—P. I. Brescia	26	....	297	139	.468	87	65	.747	199	343	13.2
79-80—P. I. Brescia	27	....	291	148	.411	87	66	.758	212	362	13.4
81-82—Recoard	34	1329	592	340	.574	185	137	.741	364	817	24.0

NBA REGULAR SEASON RECORD

Sea.—Team	G.	Min.	FGA	FGM	Pct.	FTA	FTM	Pct.	Off.	Def.	Tot.	Ast.	PF	Dq.	Stl.	Blk.	Pts.	Avg.
										—Rebounds—								
82-83—Philadelphia	80	1612	353	163	.462	113	78	.690	117	212	329	83	238	0	32	44	404	5.1
83-84—Philadelphia	78	1532	322	149	.463	131	97	.740	91	219	310	95	222	1	36	55	395	5.1
84-85—Phil.-S.A.	69	1334	354	162	.458	128	87	.680	95	209	304	119	217	5	35	35	411	6.0
85-86—S.A.-Utah	68	1014	244	110	.451	115	76	.661	63	146	209	82	163	0	32	17	296	4.4
86-87—Utah	78	845	215	100	.465	116	78	.672	64	109	173	36	154	0	16	11	278	3.6
87-88—Utah	81	1238	308	143	.464	99	78	.788	94	174	268	67	162	1	23	25	364	4.5
Totals	454	7575	1796	827	.460	702	494	.704	524	1069	1593	482	1156	7	174	187	2148	4.7

Three-Point Field Goals: 1982-83, 0-for-2. 1983-84, 0-for-2. 1984-85, 0-for-4. 1985-86, 0-for-2. 1986-87, 0-for-4. 1987-88, 0-for-2. Totals, 0-for-16.

NBA PLAYOFF RECORD

Sea.—Team	G.	Min.	FGA	FGM	Pct.	FTA	FTM	Pct.	Off.	Def.	Tot.	Ast.	PF	Dq.	Stl.	Blk.	Pts.	Avg.
										—Rebounds—								
82-83—Philadelphia	13	283	52	29	.558	18	9	.500	22	35	57	19	42	1	8	7	67	5.2
83-84—Philadelphia	4	64	15	7	.467	8	7	.875	3	5	8	3	18	1	1	1	22	4.5
84-85—San Antonio	5	116	28	15	.536	20	15	.750	8	18	26	13	23	1	5	2	45	9.0
85-86—Utah	4	73	16	5	.313	4	3	.750	4	5	9	6	9	0	1	0	13	3.3
86-87—Utah	5	47	10	4	.400	3	2	.667	8	5	13	4	7	0	0	3	10	2.0
87-88—Utah	11	137	29	16	.552	14	12	.857	5	14	19	14	26	0	2	2	44	4.0
Totals	42	720	150	76	.507	67	48	.716	50	82	132	59	125	3	17	15	201	4.8

Three-Point Field Goals: 1983-84, 1-for-2 (.500). 1984-85, 0-for-1. Totals, 1-for-3 (.333).
Member of NBA championship team, 1983.

MARK A. JACKSON

Born April 1, 1965 at Brooklyn, N.Y.   Height 6:03.   Weight 205.

High School—Brooklyn, N.Y., Bishop Loughlin.

College—St. John's University, Jamaica, N.Y.

Drafted by New York on first round, 1987 (18th pick).

—COLLEGIATE RECORD—

Year	G.	Min.	FGA	FGM	Pct.	FTA	FTM	Pct.	Reb.	Pts.	Avg.
83-84	30	855	106	61	.575	77	53	.688	59	175	5.8
84-85	35	601	101	57	.564	91	66	.725	44	180	5.1
85-86	36	1340	316	151	.478	142	105	.739	125	407	11.3

MARK JACKSON

Year	G.	Min.	FGA	FGM	Pct.	FTA	FTM	Pct.	Reb.	Pts.	Avg.
86-87	30	1184	389	196	.504	155	125	.806	110	566	18.9
Totals	131	3980	912	465	.510	465	349	.751	338	1328	10.1

Three-Point Field Goals: 1986-87, 49-for-117 (.419).

NBA REGULAR SEASON RECORD

Sea.—Team	G.	Min.	FGA	FGM	Pct.	FTA	FTM	Pct.	—Rebounds— Off.	Def.	Tot.	Ast.	PF	Dq.	Stl.	Blk.	Pts.	Avg.
87-88—New York	82	3249	1013	438	.432	266	206	.774	120	276	396	868	244	2	205	6	1114	13.6

Three-Point Field Goals: 1987-88, 32-for-126 (.254).

NBA PLAYOFF RECORD

Sea.—Team	G.	Min.	FGA	FGM	Pct.	FTA	FTM	Pct.	—Rebounds— Off.	Def.	Tot.	Ast.	PF	Dq.	Stl.	Blk.	Pts.	Avg.
87-88—New York	4	171	60	22	.367	11	8	.727	6	13	19	39	13	0	10	0	57	14.3

Three-Point Field Goals: 1987-88, 5-for-12 (.417).

Named NBA Rookie of the Year, 1988. . . . NBA All-Rookie Team, 1988. . . . Led NCAA Division I in assists, 1986. . . . THE SPORTING NEWS All-America Second Team, 1987.

MICHAEL JACKSON

Born July 13, 1964 at Fairfax, Va.   Height 6:02.   Weight 185.

High School—Reston, Va., South Lakes.

College—Georgetown University, Washington, D. C.

Drafted by New York on second round, 1986 (47th pick).

Waived by New York, October 28, 1986; signed by Sacramento as a free agent, October 8, 1987.

—COLLEGIATE RECORD—

Year	G.	Min.	FGA	FGM	Pct.	FTA	FTM	Pct.	Reb.	Pts.	Avg.
82-83	32	858	278	128	.460	137	114	.832	51	370	11.6
83-84	31	833	226	115	.509	103	84	.816	52	314	10.1
84-85	36	980	234	104	.444	75	55	.733	58	263	7.3
85-86	32	947	260	130	.500	95	77	.811	64	337	10.5
Totals	131	3618	998	477	.478	410	330	.805	225	1284	9.8

NBA REGULAR SEASON RECORD

Sea.—Team	G.	Min.	FGA	FGM	Pct.	FTA	FTM	Pct.	—Rebounds— Off.	Def.	Tot.	Ast.	PF	Dq.	Stl.	Blk.	Pts.	Avg.
87-88—Sacramento	58	760	171	64	.374	32	23	.719	17	42	59	179	81	0	20	5	157	2.7

Three-Point Field Goals: 1987-88, 6-for-25 (.240).

Member of NCAA Division I championship team, 1984.

ALFONSO JOHNSON JR.
(Buck)

Born January 3, 1964 at Birmingham, Ala.   Height 6:07.   Weight 190.

High School—Birmingham, Ala., Hayes.

College—University of Alabama, University, Ala.

Drafted by Houston on first round, 1986 (20th pick).

—COLLEGIATE RECORD—

Year	G.	Min.	FGA	FGM	Pct.	FTA	FTM	Pct.	Reb.	Pts.	Avg.
82-83	32	834	217	104	.479	88	56	.636	144	264	8.3
83-84	28	1042	356	183	.514	152	111	.730	237	477	17.0
84-85	33	1172	373	209	.560	156	111	.712	310	529	16.0
85-86	29	1082	407	235	.577	155	129	.832	242	599	20.7
Totals	122	4130	1353	731	.540	551	407	.739	933	1869	15.3

NBA REGULAR SEASON RECORD

Sea.—Team	G.	Min.	FGA	FGM	Pct.	FTA	FTM	Pct.	—Rebounds— Off.	Def.	Tot.	Ast.	PF	Dq.	Stl.	Blk.	Pts.	Avg.
86-87—Houston	60	520	201	94	.468	58	40	.690	38	50	88	40	81	0	17	15	228	3.8
87-88—Houston	70	879	298	155	.520	91	67	.736	77	91	168	49	127	0	30	26	378	5.4
Totals	130	1399	499	249	.499	149	107	.718	115	141	256	89	208	0	47	41	606	4.7

Three-Point Field Goals: 1986-87, 0-for-1. 1987-88, 1-for-8 (.125). Totals, 1-for-9 (.111).

Sea.—Team	G.	Min.	FGA	FGM	Pct.	FTA	FTM	Pct.	—Rebounds— Off.	Def.	Tot.	Ast.	PF	Dq.	Stl.	Blk.	Pts.	Avg.
86-87—Houston	5	10	6	2	.333	0	0	.000	0	0	0	0	1	0	0	0	4	0.8
87-88—Houston	4	20	3	2	.667	2	1	.500	2	2	4	0	1	0	1	0	5	1.3
Totals	9	30	9	4	.444	2	1	.500	2	2	4	0	2	0	1	0	9	1.0

CLARENCE STEPHEN JOHNSON
(Steve)

Born November 3, 1957 at Akron, O.   Height 6:10.   Weight 235.

High School—San Bernardino, Calif., San Gorgonio.

College—Oregon State University, Corvallis, Ore.

Drafted by Kansas City on first round, 1981 (7th pick).

Traded by Kansas City with a 1984 2nd round draft choice and two 1985 2nd round draft choices to Chicago for Reggie Theus, February 15, 1984.

Traded by Chicago with a 1985 2nd round draft choice to San Antonio for Gene Banks, June 18, 1985.

Traded by San Antonio to Portland for Mychal Thompson and draft rights to Larry Krystkowiak, June 19, 1986.

—COLLEGIATE RECORD—

Year	G.	Min.	FGA	FGM	Pct.	FTA	FTM	Pct.	Reb.	Pts.	Avg.
76-77	28	616	267	159	.596	91	61	.670	156	379	13.5
77-78	3	62	45	26	.578	13	8	.615	29	60	20.0
78-79	27	724	298	197	.661	169	104	.615	178	498	18.4
79-80	30	711	297	211	.710	145	87	.600	207	509	17.0
80-81	28	716	315	235	.746	174	119	.684	215	589	21.0
Totals	116	2829	1222	828	.678	592	379	.640	785	2035	17.5

(Suffered broken left foot in 1977-78 season; granted extra year of eligibility).

NBA REGULAR SEASON RECORD

Sea.—Team	G.	Min.	FGA	FGM	Pct.	FTA	FTM	Pct.	—Rebounds— Off.	Def.	Tot.	Ast.	PF	Dq.	Stl.	Blk.	Pts.	Avg.
81-82—Kansas City	78	1741	644	395	.613	330	212	.642	152	307	459	91	372	25	39	89	1002	12.8
82-83—Kansas City	79	1544	595	371	.624	324	186	.574	140	258	398	95	323	9	40	83	928	11.7
83-84—K.C.-Chi.	81	1487	540	302	.559	287	165	.575	162	256	418	81	307	15	37	69	769	9.5
84-85—Chicago	74	1659	516	281	.545	252	181	.718	146	291	437	64	265	7	37	62	743	10.0
85-86—San Antonio	71	1828	573	362	.632	373	259	.694	143	319	462	95	291	13	44	66	983	13.8
86-87—Portland	79	2345	889	494	.556	490	342	.698	194	372	566	155	340	16	49	76	1330	16.8
87-88—Portland	43	1050	488	258	.529	249	146	.586	84	158	242	57	151	4	17	32	662	15.4
Totals	505	11654	4245	2463	.580	2305	1491	.647	1021	1961	2982	638	2349	89	263	477	6417	12.7

Three-Point Field Goals: 1984-85, 0-for-3. 1987-88, 0-for-1. Totals, 0-for-4.

NBA PLAYOFF RECORD

Sea.—Team	G.	Min.	FGA	FGM	Pct.	FTA	FTM	Pct.	—Rebounds— Off.	Def.	Tot.	Ast.	PF	Dq.	Stl.	Blk.	Pts.	Avg.
84-85—Chicago	3	22	7	2	.286	2	2	1.000	3	2	5	2	4	0	0	0	6	2.0
85-86—San Antonio	3	53	15	5	.333	11	5	.455	2	4	6	2	14	1	0	1	15	5.0
86-87—Portland	4	137	61	28	.459	43	27	.628	17	23	40	2	15	0	2	1	83	20.8
Totals	10	212	83	35	.422	56	34	.607	22	29	51	6	33	1	2	2	104	10.4

Led NBA in field-goal percentage, 1986.... Named to THE SPORTING NEWS All-America Second Team, 1981. ... Holds NCAA record for career field-goal percentage.... Led NCAA in field-goal percentage, 1980 and 1981.

CLEMON JOHNSON

Born September 12, 1956 at Monticello, Fla.   Height 6:10.   Weight 240.

High School—Tallahassee, Fla., Florida A&M University High.

College—Florida A&M University, Tallahassee, Fla.

Drafted by Portland on second round, 1978 (44th pick).

Traded by Portland to Indiana for a 1981 2nd round draft choice, October 9, 1979.

Traded by Indiana with a 1984 3rd round draft choice to Philadelphia for Russ Schoene, a 1983 1st round draft choice and a 1984 2nd round draft choice, February 15, 1983.

Traded by Philadelphia with a 1989 1st round draft choice to Seattle for Tim McCormick and Danny Vranes, September 29, 1986.

—COLLEGIATE RECORD—

Year	G.	Min.	FGA	FGM	Pct.	FTA	FTM	Pct.	Reb.	Pts.	Avg.
74-75	25	....	233	113	.485	45	23	.511	302	249	9.9
75-76	27	....	242	118	.488	53	30	.566	378	266	9.9
76-77	30	....	310	170	.548	89	54	.607	402	394	13.1
77-78	27	....	354	200	.565	117	72	.643	412	472	17.5
Totals	109	....	1139	601	.528	304	179	.589	1494	1381	12.7

NBA REGULAR SEASON RECORD

Sea.—Team	G.	Min.	FGA	FGM	Pct.	FTA	FTM	Pct.	Off.	Def.	Tot.	Ast.	PF	Dq.	Stl.	Blk.	Pts.	Avg.
78-79—Portland	74	794	217	102	.470	74	36	.486	83	143	226	78	121	1	23	36	240	3.2
79-80—Indiana	79	1541	396	199	.503	117	74	.632	145	249	394	115	211	2	48	121	472	6.0
80-81—Indiana	81	1643	466	235	.504	189	112	.593	173	295	468	144	185	1	44	119	582	7.2
81-82—Indiana	79	1979	641	312	.487	189	123	.651	184	387	571	127	241	3	60	112	747	9.5
82-83—Ind.-Phil.	83	1914	581	299	.515	180	111	.617	190	334	524	139	221	3	67	92	709	8.5
83-84—Philadelphia	80	1721	412	193	.468	113	69	.611	131	267	398	55	205	1	35	65	455	5.7
84-85—Philadelphia	58	875	235	117	.498	49	36	.735	92	129	221	33	112	0	15	44	270	4.7
85-86—Philadelphia	75	1069	223	105	.471	81	51	.630	106	149	255	15	129	0	23	62	261	3.5
86-87—Seattle	78	1051	178	88	.494	110	70	.636	106	171	277	21	137	0	21	42	246	3.2
87-88—Seattle	74	723	105	49	.467	32	22	.688	66	108	174	17	104	0	13	24	120	1.6
Totals	761	13310	3454	1699	.492	1134	704	.621	1276	2232	3508	744	1666	11	349	717	4102	5.4

Three-Point Field Goals: 1980-81, 0-for-1. 1982-83, 0-for-1. 1984-85, 0-for-1. 1986-87, 0-for-2. Totals, 0-for-5.

NBA PLAYOFF RECORD

Sea.—Team	G.	Min.	FGA	FGM	Pct.	FTA	FTM	Pct.	Off.	Def.	Tot.	Ast.	PF	Dq.	Stl.	Blk.	Pts.	Avg.
78-79—Portland	3	47	11	4	.364	11	6	.545	5	12	17	2	5	0	2	4	14	4.7
80-81—Indiana	2	55	12	5	.417	10	5	.500	10	10	20	3	3	0	4	2	15	7.5
82-83—Philadelphia	12	202	49	25	.510	4	0	.000	21	22	43	7	28	0	4	5	50	4.2
83-84—Philadelphia	5	45	12	4	.333	0	0	.000	3	3	6	0	8	0	1	4	8	1.6
84-85—Philadelphia	13	165	33	13	.394	21	16	.762	17	19	36	2	32	0	3	6	42	3.2
85-86—Philadelphia	12	303	53	29	.547	25	16	.640	23	37	60	8	35	0	11	15	74	6.2
86-87—Seattle	14	262	53	24	.453	19	12	.632	25	24	49	4	18	0	7	15	60	4.3
87-88—Seattle	5	39	7	3	.429	2	1	.500	0	7	7	0	10	0	1	1	7	1.4
Totals	66	1118	230	107	.465	92	56	.609	104	134	238	26	139	0	33	52	270	4.1

Three-Point Field Goals: 1984-85, 0-for-1. 1986-87, 0-for-1. Totals, 0-for-2.
Member of NBA championship team, 1983.

DENNIS WAYNE JOHNSON

Born September 18, 1954 at San Pedro, Calif. Height 6:04. Weight 200.

High School—Compton, Calif., Dominguez.

Colleges—Los Angeles Harbor Junior College, Wilmington, Calif., and
Pepperdine University, Malibu, Calif.

Drafted by Seattle on second round as hardship case, 1976 (29th pick).

Traded by Seattle to Phoenix for Paul Westphal, June 4, 1980.
Traded by Phoenix with 1983 1st and 3rd round draft choices to Boston for Rick Robey and two 1983 2nd round
draft choices, June 27, 1983.

—COLLEGIATE RECORD—
Los Angeles Harbor JC

Year	G.	Min.	FGA	FGM	Pct.	FTA	FTM	Pct.	Reb.	Pts.	Avg.
73-74	...	699	191	103	.539	82	45	.549	230	251	.....
74-75	28	967	....	....	....	....	...	....	336	511	18.3
JC Totals.................	...	1166	....	....	....	...	...	....	566	762	....

Pepperdine

Year	G.	Min.	FGA	FGM	Pct.	FTA	FTM	Pct.	Reb.	Pts.	Avg.
75-76	27	930	378	181	.479	112	63	.563	156	425	15.7

NBA REGULAR SEASON RECORD

Sea.—Team	G.	Min.	FGA	FGM	Pct.	FTA	FTM	Pct.	Off.	Def.	Tot.	Ast.	PF	Dq.	Stl.	Blk.	Pts.	Avg.
76-77—Seattle	81	1667	566	285	.504	287	179	.624	161	141	302	123	221	3	123	57	749	9.2
77-78—Seattle	81	2209	881	367	.417	406	297	.732	152	142	294	230	213	2	118	51	1031	12.7
78-79—Seattle	80	2717	1110	482	.434	392	306	.781	146	228	374	280	209	2	100	97	1270	15.9
79-80—Seattle	81	2937	1361	574	.422	487	380	.780	173	241	414	332	267	6	144	82	1540	19.0
80-81—Phoenix	79	2615	1220	532	.436	501	411	.820	160	203	363	291	244	2	136	61	1486	18.8
81-82—Phoenix	80	2937	1228	577	.470	495	399	.806	142	268	410	369	253	6	105	55	1561	19.5
82-83—Phoenix	77	2551	861	398	.462	369	292	.791	92	243	335	388	204	1	97	39	1093	14.2
83-84—Boston	80	2665	878	384	.437	330	281	.852	87	193	280	338	251	6	93	57	1053	13.2
84-85—Boston	80	2976	1066	493	.462	306	261	.853	91	226	317	543	224	2	96	39	1254	15.7
85-86—Boston	78	2732	1060	482	.455	297	243	.818	69	199	268	456	206	3	110	35	1213	15.6
86-87—Boston	79	2933	953	423	.444	251	209	.833	45	216	261	594	201	0	87	38	1062	13.4
87-88—Boston	77	2670	803	352	.438	298	255	.856	62	178	240	598	204	0	93	29	971	12.6
Totals	953	31609	11987	5349	.446	4419	3513	.795	1380	2478	3858	4542	2697	33	1302	640	14283	15.0

Three-Point Field Goals: 1979-80, 12-for-58 (.207). 1980-81, 11-for-51 (.216). 1981-82, 8-for-42 (.190). 1982-83, 5-for-31
(.161). 1983-84, 4-for-32 (.125). 1984-85, 7-for-26 (.269). 1985-86, 6-for-42 (.143). 1986-87, 7-for-62 (.113). 1987-88, 12-for-46 (.261).
Totals, 72-for-390 (.185).

Sea.—Team	G.	Min.	FGA	FGM	Pct.	FTA	FTM	Pct.	Off.	Def.	Tot.	Ast.	PF	Dq.	Stl.	Blk.	Pts.	Avg.
77-78—Seattle	22	827	294	121	.412	159	112	.704	47	54	101	72	63	0	23	23	354	16.1
78-79—Seattle	17	691	302	136	.450	109	84	.771	44	60	104	69	63	0	28	26	356	20.9
79-80—Seattle	15	582	244	100	.410	62	52	.839	25	39	64	57	48	2	27	10	257	17.1
80-81—Phoenix	7	267	110	52	.473	42	32	.762	7	26	33	20	18	0	9	9	137	19.6
81-82—Phoenix	7	271	132	63	.477	39	30	.769	13	18	31	32	28	2	15	4	156	22.3
82-83—Phoenix	3	108	48	22	.458	12	10	.833	6	17	23	17	9	0	5	2	54	18.0
83-84—Boston	22	808	319	129	.404	120	104	.867	30	49	79	97	75	1	25	7	365	16.6
84-85—Boston	21	848	319	142	.445	93	80	.860	24	60	84	154	66	0	31	9	364	17.3
85-86—Boston	18	715	245	109	.445	84	67	.798	23	53	76	107	58	2	39	5	291	16.2
86-87—Boston	23	964	361	168	.465	113	96	.850	24	67	91	205	71	0	16	8	435	18.9
87-88—Boston	17	702	210	91	.433	103	82	.796	15	62	77	139	51	0	24	8	270	15.9
Totals	172	6783	2584	1133	.438	936	749	.800	258	505	763	969	550	7	242	111	3039	17.7

Three-Point Field Goals: 1979-80, 5-for-15 (.333). 1980-81, 1-for-5 (.200). 1981-82, 0-for-3. 1982-83, 0-for-1. 1983-84, 3-for-7 (.429). 1984-85, 0-for-14. 1985-86, 6-for-16 (.375). 1986-87, 3-for-26 (.115). 1987-88, 6-for-16 (.375). Totals, 24-for-103 (.233).

NBA ALL-STAR GAME RECORD

Season—Team	Min.	FGA	FGM	Pct.	FTA	FTM	Pct.	Off.	Def.	Tot.	Ast.	PF	Dq.	Stl.	Blk.	Pts.
1979—Seattle	27	7	5	.714	2	2	1.000	1	0	1	3	3	0	0	1	12
1980—Seattle	20	13	7	.538	6	5	.833	2	2	4	1	3	0	2	1	19
1981—Phoenix	24	8	5	.625	10	9	.900	1	1	2	1	1	0	3	0	19
1982—Phoenix	15	2	0	.000	2	1	.500	2	3	5	1	1	0	0	2	1
1985—Boston	12	7	3	.429	2	2	1.000	1	5	6	3	2	0	0	0	8
Totals	98	37	20	.541	22	19	.864	7	11	18	9	10	0	5	4	59

Named to All-NBA First Team, 1981.... All-NBA Second Team, 1980.... NBA All-Defensive First Team, 1979, 1980, 1981, 1982, 1983, 1987.... NBA All-Defensive Second Team, 1984, 1985, 1986.... NBA Playoff MVP, 1979.... Member of NBA championship teams, 1979, 1984, 1986.... Shares NBA record for most free throws made in one half of championship series game, 12, vs. Los Angeles, June 12, 1984.

EARVIN JOHNSON JR.
(Magic)

Born August 14, 1959 at Lansing, Mich. Height 6:09. Weight 226.

High School—Lansing, Mich., Everett.

College—Michigan State University, East Lansing, Mich.

Drafted by Los Angeles on first round as an undergraduate, 1979 (1st pick).

—COLLEGIATE RECORD—

Year	G.	Min.	FGA	FGM	Pct.	FTA	FTM	Pct.	Reb.	Pts.	Avg.
77-78	30	....	382	175	.458	205	161	.785	237	511	17.0
78-79	32	1159	370	173	.468	240	202	.842	234	548	17.1
Totals	62	....	752	348	.463	445	363	.816	471	1059	17.1

NBA REGULAR SEASON RECORD

Sea.—Team	G.	Min.	FGA	FGM	Pct.	FTA	FTM	Pct.	Off.	Def.	Tot.	Ast.	PF	Dq.	Stl.	Blk.	Pts.	Avg.
79-80—Los Angeles	77	2795	949	503	.530	462	374	.810	166	430	596	563	218	1	187	41	1387	18.0
80-81—Los Angeles	37	1371	587	312	.532	225	171	.760	101	219	320	317	100	0	127	27	798	21.6
81-82—Los Angeles	78	2991	1036	556	.537	433	329	.760	252	499	751	743	223	1	208	34	1447	18.6
82-83—Los Angeles	79	2907	933	511	.548	380	304	.800	214	469	683	829	200	1	176	47	1326	16.8
83-84—Los Angeles	67	2567	780	441	.565	358	290	.810	99	392	491	875	169	1	150	49	1178	17.6
84-85—L.A. Lakers	77	2781	899	504	.561	464	391	.843	90	386	476	968	155	0	113	25	1406	18.3
85-86—L.A. Lakers	72	2578	918	483	.526	434	378	.871	85	341	426	907	133	0	113	16	1354	18.8
86-87—L.A. Lakers	80	2904	1308	683	.522	631	535	.848	122	382	504	977	168	0	138	36	1909	23.9
87-88—L.A. Lakers	72	2637	996	490	.492	489	417	.853	88	361	449	858	147	0	114	13	1408	19.6
Totals	639	23531	8406	4483	.533	3876	3189	.823	1217	3479	4696	7037	1513	4	1266	288	12213	19.1

Three-Point Field Goals: 1979-80, 7-for-31 (.226). 1980-81, 3-for-17 (.176). 1981-82, 6-for-29 (.207). 1982-83, 0-for-21.)983-84, 6-for-29 (.207). 1984-85, 7-for-37 (.189). 1985-86, 10-for-43 (.233). 1986-87, 8-for-39 (.205). 1987-88, 11-for-56 (.196). Totals, 58-for-302 (.192).

NBA PLAYOFF RECORD

Sea.—Team	G.	Min.	FGA	FGM	Pct.	FTA	FTM	Pct.	Off.	Def.	Tot.	Ast.	PF	Dq.	Stl.	Blk.	Pts.	Avg.
79-80—Los Angeles	16	658	199	103	.518	106	85	.802	52	116	168	151	47	1	49	6	293	18.3
80-81—Los Angeles	3	127	49	19	.388	20	13	.650	8	33	41	21	14	1	8	3	51	17.0
81-82—Los Angeles	14	562	157	83	.529	93	77	.828	54	104	158	130	50	0	40	3	243	17.4
82-83—Los Angeles	15	643	206	100	.485	81	68	.840	51	77	128	192	49	0	34	12	268	17.9
83-84—Los Angeles	21	837	274	151	.551	100	80	.800	26	113	139	284	71	0	42	20	382	18.2
84-85—L.A. Lakers	19	687	226	116	.513	118	100	.847	19	115	134	289	48	0	32	4	333	17.5
85-86—L.A. Lakers	14	541	205	110	.537	107	82	.766	21	79	100	211	43	0	27	1	302	21.6

Sea.—Team	G.	Min.	FGA	FGM	Pct.	FTA	FTM	Pct.	Off.	Def.	Tot.	Ast.	PF	Dq.	Stl.	Blk.	Pts.	Avg.
86-87—L.A. Lakers	18	666	271	146	.539	118	98	.831	28	111	139	219	37	0	31	7	392	21.8
87-88—L.A. Lakers	24	965	329	169	.514	155	132	.852	32	98	130	303	61	0	34	4	477	19.9
Totals	144	5686	1916	997	.520	898	735	.818	291	846	1137	1800	420	2	297	60	2741	19.0

Three-Point Field Goals: 1979-80, 2-for-8 (.250). 1981-82, 0-for-4. 1982-83, 0-for-11. 1983-84, 0-for-7. 1984-85, 1-for-7 (.143). 1985-86, 0-for-11. 1986-87, 2-for-10 (.200). 1987-88, 7-for-14 (.500). Totals, 12-for-72 (.167).

NBA ALL-STAR GAME RECORD

Season—Team	Min.	FGA	FGM	Pct.	FTA	FTM	Pct.	Off.	Def.	Tot.	Ast.	PF	Dq.	Stl.	Blk.	Pts.
1980—Los Angeles	24	8	5	.625	2	2	1.000	2	0	2	4	3	0	3	2	12
1982—Los Angeles	23	9	5	.556	7	6	.857	3	1	4	7	5	0	0	0	16
1983—Los Angeles	33	16	7	.438	4	3	.750	3	2	5	16	2	0	5	0	17
1984—Los Angeles .	37	13	6	.462	2	2	1.000	4	5	9	22	3	0	3	2	15
1985—L.A. Lakers ..	31	14	7	.500	8	7	.875	2	3	5	15	2	0	1	0	21
1986—L.A. Lakers ..	28	3	1	.333	4	4	1.000	0	4	4	15	4	0	1	0	6
1987—L.A. Lakers ..	34	10	4	.400	2	1	.500	1	6	7	13	2	0	4	0	9
1988—L.A. Lakers ..	39	15	4	.267	9	9	1.000	1	5	6	19	2	0	2	2	17
Totals	249	88	39	.443	38	34	.895	16	26	42	111	23	0	19	6	113

Three-Point Field Goals: 1980, 0-for-1. 1983, 0-for-2. 1984, 1-for-3 (.333). 1986, 0-for-1. 1988, 0-for-1. Totals, 1-for-7 (.143).

NBA Most Valuable Player, 1987.... Named to All-NBA First Team, 1983, 1984, 1985, 1986, 1987, 1988.... All-NBA Second Team, 1982.... NBA All-Rookie Team, 1980.... NBA Playoff MVP, 1980, 1982, 1987.... Recipient of Schick Pivotal Player Award, 1984.... Member of NBA championship teams, 1980, 1982, 1985, 1987, 1988.... Holds all-time NBA playoff record for most assists.... Holds NBA playoff game record for most assists, 24, vs. Phoenix, May 15, 1984, and most assists in one half, 15, vs. Portland, May 3, 1985.... Holds NBA championship series game records for most assists, 21, vs. Boston, June 3, 1984, most assists in one half, 14, vs. Detroit, June 19, 1988, and shares record for most assists in one quarter, 8, vs. Boston, June 3, 1984.... Holds NBA All-Star Game records for career assists and assists in one game, 22, 1984.... Led NBA in steals, 1981 and 1982.... Led NBA in assists, 1983, 1984, 1986, 1987. ... Named to THE SPORTING NEWS All-America First Team, 1979.... NCAA Division I Tournament Most Outstanding Player, 1979.... Member of NCAA championship team, 1979.

EDWARD A. JOHNSON
(Eddie)

Born May 1, 1959 at Chicago, Ill.   Height 6:09.   Weight 218.

High School—Chicago, Ill., Westinghouse.

College—University of Illinois, Champaign, Ill.

Drafted by Kansas City on second round, 1981 (29th pick).

Traded by Sacramento to Phoenix for Ed Pinckney and a 1988 2nd round draft choice, June 21, 1987.

—COLLEGIATE RECORD—

Year	G.	Min.	FGA	FGM	Pct.	FTA	FTM	Pct.	Reb.	Pts.	Avg.
77-78	27	469	234	100	.427	27	20	.741	84	220	8.1
78-79	30	786	405	168	.415	49	26	.531	170	362	12.1
79-80	35	1215	576	266	.462	119	78	.655	310	610	17.4
80-81	29	1009	443	219	.494	82	62	.756	267	500	17.2
Totals	121	3479	1658	753	.454	277	186	.671	831	1692	14.0

NBA REGULAR SEASON RECORD

Sea.—Team	G.	Min.	FGA	FGM	Pct.	FTA	FTM	Pct.	Off.	Def.	Tot.	Ast.	PF	Dq.	Stl.	Blk.	Pts.	Avg.
81-82—Kansas City	74	1517	643	295	.459	149	99	.664	128	194	322	109	210	6	50	14	690	9.3
82-83—Kansas City	82	2933	1370	677	.494	317	247	.779	191	310	501	216	259	3	70	20	1621	19.8
83-84—Kansas City	82	2920	1552	753	.485	331	268	.810	165	290	455	296	266	4	76	21	1794	21.9
84-85—Kansas City	82	3029	1565	769	.491	373	325	.871	151	256	407	273	237	2	83	22	1876	22.9
85-86—Sacramento	82	2514	1311	623	.475	343	280	.816	173	246	419	214	237	0	54	17	1530	18.7
86-87—Sacramento	81	2457	1309	606	.463	322	267	.829	146	207	353	251	218	4	42	19	1516	18.7
87-88—Phoenix	73	2177	1110	533	.480	240	204	.850	121	197	318	180	190	0	33	9	1294	17.7
Totals	556	17547	8860	4256	.480	2075	1690	.814	1075	1700	2775	1539	1617	19	408	122	10321	18.6

Three-Point Field Goals: 1981-82, 1-for-11 (.091). 1982-83, 20-for-71 (.282). 1983-84, 20-for-64 (.313). 1984-85, 13-for-54 (.241). 1985-86, 4-for-20 (.200). 1986-87, 37-for-118 (314). 1987-88, 24-for-94 (.255). Totals, 119-for-432 (.275).

NBA PLAYOFF RECORD

Sea.—Team	G.	Min.	FGA	FGM	Pct.	FTA	FTM	Pct.	Off.	Def.	Tot.	Ast.	PF	Dq.	Stl.	Blk.	Pts.	Avg.
83-84—Kansas City	3	107	48	21	.438	7	7	1.000	4	6	10	12	8	0	3	1	51	17.0
85-86—Sacramento	3	96	55	24	.436	9	8	.889	10	11	21	4	7	0	3	1	56	18.7
Totals	6	203	103	45	.437	16	15	.938	14	17	31	16	15	0	6	2	107	17.8

Three-Point Field Goals: 1983-84, 2-for-5 (.400). 1985-86, 0-for-3. Totals, 2-for-8 (.250).

MAGIC JOHNSON

FRANKLIN LENARD JOHNSON
(Frank)

Born November 23, 1958 at Weirsdale, Fla.   Height 6:03.   Weight 185.

High School—Summerfield, Fla., Lake Weir.

College—Wake Forest University, Winston-Salem, N. C.

Drafted by Washington on first round, 1981 (11th pick).

—COLLEGIATE RECORD—

Year	G.	Min.	FGA	FGM	Pct.	FTA	FTM	Pct.	Reb.	Pts.	Avg.
76-77	30	1044	328	150	.457	69	48	.696	84	348	11.6
77-78	29	999	392	193	.492	122	84	.689	91	470	16.2
78-79	27	957	354	169	.477	125	96	.768	62	434	16.1
79-80	5	109	32	9	.281	10	10	1.000	9	28	5.6
80-81	29	945	359	187	.521	116	95	.819	60	469	16.2
Totals	120	4054	1465	708	.483	442	333	.753	306	1749	14.6

(Suffered broken bone in left foot prior to 1979-80 season; granted extra year of eligibility.)

NBA REGULAR SEASON RECORD

Sea.—Team	G.	Min.	FGA	FGM	Pct.	FTA	FTM	Pct.	Off.	Def.	Tot.	Ast.	PF	Dq.	Stl.	Blk.	Pts.	Avg.
81-82—Washington	79	2027	812	336	.414	204	153	.750	34	113	147	380	196	1	76	7	842	10.7
82-83—Washington	68	2324	786	321	.408	261	196	.751	46	132	178	549	170	1	110	6	852	12.5
83-84—Washington	82	2686	840	392	.467	252	187	.742	58	126	184	567	174	1	96	6	982	12.0
84-85—Washington	46	925	358	175	.489	96	72	.750	23	40	63	143	72	0	43	3	428	9.3
85-86—Washington	14	402	154	69	.448	54	38	.704	7	21	28	76	30	0	11	1	176	12.6
86-87—Washington	18	399	128	59	.461	49	35	.714	10	20	30	58	31	0	21	0	153	8.5
87-88—Washington	75	1258	498	216	.434	149	121	.812	39	82	121	188	120	0	70	4	554	7.4
Totals	382	10021	3576	1568	.438	1065	802	.753	217	534	751	1961	793	3	427	27	3987	10.4

Three-Point Field Goals: 1981-82, 17-for-79 (.215). 1982-83, 14-for-61 (.230). 1983-84, 11-for-43 (.256). 1984-85, 6-for-17 (.353). 1985-86, 0-for-3. 1986-87, 0-for-1. 1987-88, 1-for-9 (.111). Totals, 49-for-213 (.230).

NBA PLAYOFF RECORD

Sea.—Team	G.	Min.	FGA	FGM	Pct.	FTA	FTM	Pct.	Off.	Def.	Tot.	Ast.	PF	Dq.	Stl.	Blk.	Pts.	Avg.
81-82—Washington	7	280	104	40	.385	28	24	.857	7	15	22	59	24	0	10	0	109	15.6
83-84—Washington	4	156	42	24	.571	8	8	1.000	4	9	13	25	16	0	5	0	57	14.3
84-85—Washington	2	39	14	4	.286	6	6	1.000	1	3	4	7	5	0	2	0	15	7.5
86-87—Washington	3	28	7	2	.286	4	4	1.000	2	0	2	5	3	0	1	0	8	2.7
87-88—Washington	5	44	22	7	.318	4	4	1.000	0	2	2	1	4	0	4	0	18	3.6
Totals	21	547	189	77	.407	50	46	.920	14	29	43	97	52	0	22	0	207	9.9

Three-Point Field Goals: 1981-82, 5-for-12 (.417). 1983-84, 1-for-3 (.333). 1984-85, 1-for-6 (.167). 1987-88, 0-for-2. Totals, 7-for-23 (.304).

Named to THE SPORTING NEWS All-America Second Team, 1981. . . . Brother of former NBA guard Eddie Johnson.

KANNARD JOHNSON

Born June 24, 1965 at Cincinnati, O.   Height 6:09.   Weight 220.

High School—Cincinnati, O., Taft.

College—Western Kentucky University, Bowling Green, Ky.

Drafted by Cleveland on second round, 1987 (41st pick).

Waived by Cleveland, December 29, 1987.

Played in Continental Basketball Association with Charleston Gunners, Rockford Lightning and Topeka Sizzlers, 1987-88.

—COLLEGIATE RECORD—

Year	G.	Min.	FGA	FGM	Pct.	FTA	FTM	Pct.	Reb.	Pts.	Avg.
83-84	29	....	242	147	.607	94	76	.809	178	370	12.8
84-85	28	....	326	172	.528	106	75	.708	180	419	15.0
85-86	31	....	313	150	.479	119	79	.664	172	379	12.2
86-87	38	....	413	224	.542	152	122	.803	310	570	15.0
Totals	126	....	1294	693	.536	471	352	.747	840	1738	13.8

Three-Point Field Goals: 1986-87, 0-for-1.

CBA REGULAR SEASON RECORD

Sea.—Team		2-Point			3-Point								
	G.	Min.	FGM	FGA	Pct.	FGM	FGA	Pct.	FTM	FTA	Pct.	Reb.	Ast.	Pts.	Avg.
87-88—Char-Rock-Top	34	917	177	329	.538	0	9	.000	121	160	.756	211	29	475	14.0

NBA REGULAR SEASON RECORD

Sea.—Team	G.	Min.	FGA	FGM	Pct.	FTA	FTM	Pct.	Off.	Def.	Tot.	Ast.	PF	Dq.	Stl.	Blk.	Pts.	Avg.
87-88—Cleveland	4	12	3	1	.333	0	0	.000	0	0	0	0	1	0	1	0	2	0.5

KEVIN M. JOHNSON

Born March 4, 1966 at Sacramento, Calif.   Height 6:01.   Weight 180.

High School—Sacramento, Calif., Sacramento.

College—University of California, Berkeley, Calif.

Drafted by Cleveland on first round, 1987 (7th pick).

Traded by Cleveland with Tyrone Corbin, Mark West, 1988 1st and 2nd round draft choices and a 1989 2nd round draft choice to Phoenix for Larry Nance, Mike Sanders and a 1988 2nd round draft choice, February 25, 1988.

—COLLEGIATE RECORD—

Year	G.	Min.	FGA	FGM	Pct.	FTA	FTM	Pct.	Reb.	Pts.	Avg.
83-84	28	....	192	98	.510	104	75	.721	83	271	9.7
84-85	27	....	282	127	.450	142	94	.662	104	348	12.9
85-86	29	....	335	164	.490	151	123	.815	104	451	15.6
86-87	34	....	450	212	.471	138	113	.819	132	585	17.2
Totals	118	....	1259	601	.477	535	405	.757	423	1655	14.0

Three-Point Field Goals: 1986-87, 48-for-124 (.387).

NBA REGULAR SEASON RECORD

Sea.—Team	G.	Min.	FGA	FGM	Pct.	FTA	FTM	Pct.	—Rebounds—Off.	Def.	Tot.	Ast.	PF	Dq.	Stl.	Blk.	Pts.	Avg.
87-88—Clev.-Phoe.	80	1917	596	275	.461	211	177	.839	36	155	191	437	155	1	103	24	732	9.2

Three-Point Field Goals: 1987-88, 5-for-24 (.208).

MARQUES KEVIN JOHNSON

Born February 8, 1956 at Nachitoches, La.   Height 6:07.   Weight 224.

High School—Los Angeles, Calif., Crenshaw.

College—University of California at Los Angeles, Los Angeles, Calif.

Drafted by Milwaukee on first round, 1977 (3rd pick).

Traded by Milwaukee with Harvey Catchings, Junior Bridgeman and cash to Los Angeles Clippers for Terry Cummings, Craig Hodges and Ricky Pierce, September 29, 1984.
Missed entire 1987-88 season due to injury.

—COLLEGIATE RECORD—

Year	G.	Min.	FGA	FGM	Pct.	FTA	FTM	Pct.	Reb.	Pts.	Avg.
73-74	27	....	131	83	.634	38	28	.737	90	194	7.2
74-75	29	....	254	138	.543	86	59	.686	205	335	11.6
75-76	32	1165	413	223	.540	140	106	.757	301	552	17.3
76-77	27	1004	413	244	.591	145	90	.621	301	578	21.4
Totals	115	....	1211	688	.568	409	283	.692	897	1659	14.4

NBA REGULAR SEASON RECORD

Sea.—Team	G.	Min.	FGA	FGM	Pct.	FTA	FTM	Pct.	—Rebounds—Off.	Def.	Tot.	Ast.	PF	Dq.	Stl.	Blk.	Pts.	Avg.
77-78—Milwaukee	80	2765	1204	628	.522	409	301	.736	292	555	847	190	221	3	92	103	1557	19.5
78-79—Milwaukee	77	2779	1491	820	.550	437	332	.760	212	374	586	234	186	1	116	89	1972	25.6
79-80—Milwaukee	77	2686	1267	689	.544	368	291	.791	217	349	566	273	173	0	100	70	1671	21.7
80-81—Milwaukee	76	2542	1153	636	.552	381	269	.706	225	293	518	346	196	1	115	41	1541	20.3
81-82—Milwaukee	60	1900	760	404	.532	260	182	.700	153	211	364	213	142	1	59	35	990	16.5
82-83—Milwaukee	80	2853	1420	723	.509	359	264	.735	196	366	562	363	211	0	100	56	1714	21.4
83-84—Milwaukee	74	2715	1288	646	.502	340	241	.709	173	307	480	315	194	1	115	44	1535	20.7
84-85—L.A. Clippers	72	2448	1094	494	.452	260	190	.731	184	244	428	248	193	2	72	30	1181	16.4
85-86—L.A. Clippers	75	2605	1201	613	.510	392	298	.760	156	260	416	283	214	2	107	50	1525	20.3
86-87—L.A. Clippers	10	302	155	68	.439	42	30	.714	9	24	33	28	24	0	12	5	166	16.6
Totals	681	23595	11033	5721	.519	3248	2398	.738	1817	2983	4800	2493	1754	11	888	524	13852	20.3

Three-Point Field Goals: 1979-80, 2-for-9 (.222). 1980-81, 0-for-9. 1981-82, 0-for-4. 1982-83, 4-for-20 (.200). 1983-84, 2-for-13 (.154). 1984-85, 3-for-13 (.231). 1985-86, 1-for-15 (.067). 1986-87, 0-for-6. Totals, 12-for-89 (.135).

NBA PLAYOFF RECORD

Sea.—Team	G.	Min.	FGA	FGM	Pct.	FTA	FTM	Pct.	—Rebounds—Off.	Def.	Tot.	Ast.	PF	Dq.	Stl.	Blk.	Pts.	Avg.
77-78—Milwaukee	9	321	153	84	.549	64	48	.750	35	77	112	31	25	0	10	17	216	24.0
79-80—Milwaukee	7	303	128	54	.422	40	30	.750	17	31	48	20	20	0	5	6	139	19.9
80-81—Milwaukee	7	266	135	75	.556	32	23	.719	41	25	66	34	14	0	10	7	173	24.7
81-82—Milwaukee	6	235	100	44	.440	42	24	.571	23	21	44	20	25	0	6	2	113	18.8
82-83—Milwaukee	9	382	175	85	.486	43	28	.651	28	44	72	38	22	0	8	7	198	22.0
83-84—Milwaukee	16	605	273	129	.473	90	65	.722	29	56	85	55	50	0	17	6	324	20.3
Totals	54	2112	964	471	.489	311	218	.701	173	254	427	198	156	0	56	45	1163	21.5

Three-Point Field Goals: 1979-80, 1-for-3 (.333). 1980-81, 0-for-1. 1981-82, 1-for-4 (.250). 1982-83, 0-for-1. 1983-84, 1-for-4 (.250). Totals, 3-for-13 (.231).

Season—Team	Min.	FGA	FGM	Pct.	FTA	FTM	Pct.	Rebounds Off.	Rebounds Def.	Rebounds Tot.	Ast.	PF	Dq.	Stl.	Blk.	Pts.
1979—Milwaukee....	20	11	3	.273	6	4	.667	3	3	6	2	1	0	0	0	10
1980—Milwaukee....	34	6	1	.167	2	2	1.000	1	3	4	1	2	0	1	1	4
1981—Milwaukee....	19	2	1	.500	6	5	.833	1	3	4	2	2	0	0	0	7
1983—Milwaukee....	20	10	3	.300	2	1	.500	2	0	2	2	1	0	0	1	7
1986—L.A. Clippers	13	6	3	.500	0	0	.000	2	1	3	2	3	0	0	0	6
Totals	106	35	11	.314	16	12	.750	9	10	19	9	9	0	1	2	34

Named to All-NBA First Team, 1979. . . . All-NBA Second Team, 1980 and 1981. . . . NBA All-Rookie Team, 1978. . . . NBA Comeback Player of the Year, 1986. . . . THE SPORTING NEWS College Player of the Year, 1977. . . . THE SPORTING NEWS All-America First Team, 1977. . . . Member of NCAA Division I championship team, 1975.

VINCENT JOHNSON
(Vinnie)

Born September 1, 1956 at Brooklyn, N. Y.   Height 6:02.   Weight 200.

High School—Brooklyn, N. Y., Franklin Roosevelt.

Colleges—McLennan Community College, Waco, Tex., and Baylor University, Waco, Tex.

Drafted by Seattle on first round, 1979 (7th pick).

Traded by Seattle to Detroit for Greg Kelser, November 23, 1981.

—COLLEGIATE RECORD—
McLennan CC

Year	G.	Min.	FGA	FGM	Pct.	FTA	FTM	Pct.	Reb.	Pts.	Avg.
75-76	35	....	...	398	....	...	169	....	....	965	27.6
76-77	31	....	...	382	....	...	152	....	....	916	29.5
JC Totals.................	66	....	....	780	....	...	321	....	....	1881	28.5

Baylor

Year	G.	Min.	FGA	FGM	Pct.	FTA	FTM	Pct.	Reb.	Pts.	Avg.
77-78	25	....	481	241	.501	141	93	.660	140	575	23.0
78-79	26	....	502	262	.522	170	132	.776	128	656	25.2
Totals	51	....	983	503	.512	311	225	.723	268	1231	24.1

NBA REGULAR SEASON RECORD

Sea.—Team	G.	Min.	FGA	FGM	Pct.	FTA	FTM	Pct.	Rebounds Off.	Rebounds Def.	Rebounds Tot.	Ast.	PF	Dq.	Stl.	Blk.	Pts.	Avg.
79-80—Seattle	38	325	115	45	.391	39	31	.795	19	36	55	54	40	0	19	4	121	3.2
80-81—Seattle	81	2311	785	419	.534	270	214	.793	193	173	366	341	198	0	78	20	1053	13.0
81-82—Sea.-Det.	74	1295	444	217	.489	142	107	.754	82	77	159	171	101	0	56	25	544	7.4
82-83—Detroit	82	2511	1013	520	.513	315	245	.778	167	186	353	301	263	2	93	49	1296	15.8
83-84—Detroit	82	1909	901	426	.473	275	207	.753	130	107	237	271	196	1	44	19	1063	13.0
84-85—Detroit	82	2093	942	428	.454	247	190	.769	134	118	252	325	205	2	71	20	1051	12.8
85-86—Detroit	79	1978	996	465	.467	214	165	.771	119	107	226	269	180	2	80	23	1097	13.9
86-87—Detroit	78	2166	1154	533	.462	201	158	.786	123	134	257	300	159	0	92	16	1228	15.7
87-88—Detroit	82	1935	959	425	.443	217	147	.677	90	141	231	267	164	0	58	18	1002	12.2
Totals	678	16523	7309	3478	.476	1920	1464	.763	1057	1079	2136	2299	1506	7	591	194	8455	12.5

Three-Point Field Goals: 1979-80, 0-for-1. 1980-81, 1-for-5 (.200). 1981-82, 3-for-12 (.250). 1982-83, 11-for-40 (.275). 1983-84, 4-for-19 (.211). 1984-85, 5-for-27 (.185). 1985-86, 2-for-13 (.154). 1986-87, 4-for-14 (.286). 1987-88, 5-for-24 (.208). Totals, 35-for-155 (.226).

NBA PLAYOFF RECORD

Sea.—Team	G.	Min.	FGA	FGM	Pct.	FTA	FTM	Pct.	Rebounds Off.	Rebounds Def.	Rebounds Tot.	Ast.	PF	Dq.	Stl.	Blk.	Pts.	Avg.
79-80—Seattle	5	12	3	1	.333	0	0	.000	0	2	2	2	1	0	1	0	2	0.4
83-84—Detroit	5	132	46	17	.370	19	17	.895	5	9	14	12	9	0	1	1	51	10.2
84-85—Detroit	9	235	103	53	.515	28	22	.786	15	12	27	29	24	0	6	1	128	14.2
85-86—Detroit	4	85	49	22	.449	13	7	.538	8	9	17	11	9	0	3	0	51	12.8
86-87—Detroit	15	388	207	95	.459	36	31	.861	20	24	44	62	33	0	9	4	221	14.7
87-88—Detroit	23	477	239	101	.423	50	33	.660	35	40	75	43	48	0	17	4	236	10.3
Totals	61	1329	647	289	.447	146	110	.753	83	96	179	159	124	0	37	10	689	11.3

Three-Point Field Goals: 1983-84, 0-for-1. 1984-85, 0-for-3. 1985-86, 0-for-1. 1986-87, 0-for-2. 1987-88, 1-for-7 (.143). Totals, 1-for-14 (.071).

CALDWELL JONES

Born August 4, 1950 at McGehee, Ark.   Height 6:11.   Weight 225.

High School—Rohwer, Ark., Desha Central.

College—Albany State College, Albany, Ga.

Drafted by Philadelphia on second round, 1973 (32nd pick).

Selected by Virginia on third round of ABA draft, 1973.

Signed by San Diego; Larry Miller sent by San Diego to Virginia as compensation, October 29, 1973.
Signed by Philadelphia (for future services), February 25, 1975.
Purchased by Kentucky from disbanded San Diego franchise, November 14, 1975.
Traded by Kentucky to St. Louis for Maurice Lucas, December 17, 1975.
Traded by Philadelphia with a 1983 1st round draft choice to Houston for Moses Malone, September 15, 1982.
Traded by Houston to Chicago for Mitchell Wiggins and 1985 2nd and 3rd round draft choices, August 10, 1984.
Signed by Portland as a Veteran Free Agent, October 1, 1985; Chicago agreed not to exercise its right of first refusal in exchange for a 1987 2nd round draft choice.

—COLLEGIATE RECORD—

Year	G.	Min.	FGA	FGM	Pct.	FTA	FTM	Pct.	Reb.	Pts.	Avg.
69-70†	25	....	367	185	.504	108	80	.741	440	450	18.0
70-71	27	....	437	206	.471	137	76	.555	576	488	18.1
71-72	28	....	539	288	.534	219	156	.712	567	732	26.1
72-73	29	....	470	238	.506	134	91	.679	633	567	19.6
Varsity Totals	109	....	1813	917	.506	598	403	.674	2216	2237	20.5

ABA REGULAR SEASON RECORD

Sea.—Team	G.	Min.	2-Point FGM	FGA	Pct.	3-Point FGM	FGA	Pct.	FTM	FTA	Pct.	Reb.	Ast.	Pts.	Avg.
73-74—San Diego	79	2929	505	1083	.466	2	8	.250	171	230	.743	1095	144	1187	15.0
74-75—San Diego	76	3004	603	1229	.491	3	11	.273	264	335	.788	1074	162	1479	19.5
75-76—SD-Ky-St.L.	76	2674	423	893	.474	0	7	.000	140	186	.753	853	147	986	13.0
Totals	231	8607	1531	3205	.478	5	26	.192	575	751	.766	3022	453	3652	15.8

ABA PLAYOFF RECORD

Sea.—Team	G.	Min.	2-Point FGM	FGA	Pct.	3-Point FGM	FGA	Pct.	FTM	FTA	Pct.	Reb.	Ast.	Pts.	Avg.
73-74—San Diego	6	277	36	88	.409	0	0	.000	11	16	.688	94	15	83	13.8

ABA ALL-STAR GAME RECORD

Sea.—Team	Min.	2-Point FGM	FGA	Pct.	3-Point FGM	FGA	Pct.	FTM	FTA	Pct.	Reb.	Ast.	Pts.	Avg.
1975—San Diego	15	2	4	.500	0	0	.000	1	1	1.000	4	0	5	5.0

NBA REGULAR SEASON RECORD

Sea.—Team	G	Min.	FGA	FGM	Pct.	FTA	FTM	Pct.	Rebounds Off.	Def.	Tot.	Ast.	PF	Dq.	Stl.	Blk.	Pts.	Avg.
76-77—Philadelphia	82	2023	424	215	.507	116	64	.552	190	476	666	92	301	3	43	200	494	6.0
77-78—Philadelphia	80	1636	359	169	.471	153	96	.627	165	405	570	92	281	4	26	127	434	5.4
78-79—Philadelphia	78	2171	637	302	.474	162	121	.747	177	570	747	151	303	10	39	157	725	9.3
79-80—Philadelphia	80	2771	532	232	.436	178	124	.697	219	731	950	164	298	5	43	162	588	7.4
80-81—Philadelphia	81	2639	485	218	.449	193	148	.767	200	613	813	122	271	2	53	134	584	7.2
81-82—Philadelphia	81	2446	465	231	.497	219	179	.817	164	544	708	100	301	3	38	146	641	7.9
82-83—Houston	82	2440	677	307	.453	206	162	.786	222	446	668	138	278	2	46	131	776	9.5
83-84—Houston	81	2506	633	318	.502	196	164	.837	168	414	582	156	335	7	46	80	801	9.9
84-85—Chicago	42	885	115	53	.461	47	36	.766	49	162	211	34	125	3	12	31	142	3.4
85-86—Portland	80	1437	254	126	.496	150	124	.827	105	250	355	74	244	2	38	61	376	4.7
86-87—Portland	78	1578	224	111	.496	124	97	.782	114	341	455	64	227	5	23	77	319	4.1
87-88—Portland	79	1778	263	128	.487	106	78	.736	105	303	408	81	251	0	29	99	334	4.2
Totals	924	24310	5068	2410	.476	1850	1393	.753	1878	5255	7133	1268	3215	46	436	1405	6214	6.7

Three-Point Field Goals: 1979-80, 0-for-2. 1981-82, 0-for-3. 1982-83, 0-for-2. 1983-84, 1-for-3 (.333). 1984-85, 0-for-2. 1985-86, 0-for-7. 1986-87, 0-for-2. 1987-88, 0-for-4. Totals, 1-for-25 (.040).

NBA PLAYOFF RECORD

Sea.—Team	G.	Min.	FGA	FGM	Pct.	FTA	FTM	Pct.	Rebounds Off.	Def.	Tot.	Ast.	PF	Dq.	Stl.	Blk.	Pts.	Avg.
76-77—Philadelphia	19	513	73	37	.507	30	18	.600	38	112	150	20	81	4	9	40	92	4.8
77-78—Philadelphia	10	301	56	28	.500	10	8	.800	22	84	106	14	36	2	5	30	64	6.4
78-79—Philadelphia	9	320	89	43	.483	36	28	.778	37	84	121	21	36	0	4	22	114	12.7
79-80—Philadelphia	18	639	129	58	.450	52	42	.808	50	135	185	34	75	1	13	37	158	8.8
80-81—Philadelphia	16	580	95	54	.568	42	31	.738	37	118	155	27	53	0	7	31	139	8.7
81-82—Philadelphia	21	679	160	74	.463	41	35	.854	52	137	189	19	77	1	11	40	183	8.7
84-85—Chicago	2	18	6	5	.833	0	0	.000	1	4	5	0	7	1	0	1	10	5.0
85-86—Portland	4	73	17	6	.353	4	2	.500	9	10	19	3	13	0	0	2	14	3.5
86-87—Portland	4	129	12	5	.417	6	5	.833	9	22	31	6	15	0	0	6	15	3.8
87-88—Portland	4	98	16	6	.375	2	1	.500	4	13	17	1	17	0	2	8	13	3.3
Totals	107	3350	653	316	.484	223	170	.762	259	719	978	145	410	9	51	217	802	7.5

Three-Point Field Goals: 1979-80, 0-for-3. 1984-85, 0-for-1. Totals, 0-for-4.

COMBINED ABA AND NBA REGULAR SEASON RECORDS

	G.	Min.	FGA	FGM	Pct.	FTA	FTM	Pct.	Rebounds Off.	Def.	Tot.	Ast.	PF	Dq.	Stl.	Blk.	Pts.	Avg.
Totals	1155	32917	8299	3946	.476	2601	1968	.757	2757	7398	10155	1721	4124	46	641	2185	9866	8.5

Named to NBA All-Defensive First Team, 1981 and 1982. . . . Shares ABA record for most blocked shots in one game, 12, vs. Carolina, January 6, 1974. . . . Led ABA in blocked shots, 1974 and 1975. . . . Brother of Washington Bullets forward-center Charles Jones.

CHARLES JONES

Born April 3, 1957 at McGehee, Ark.   Height 6:09.   Weight 215.
High School—McGehee, Ark., Delta.
College—Albany State College, Albany, Ga.
Drafted by Phoenix on eighth round, 1979 (165th pick).

Waived by Phoenix, October 1, 1979; signed by Portland as a free agent, April 14, 1980.
Waived by Portland, July 21, 1980; signed by New York as a free agent, September 30, 1983.
Waived by New York, October 24, 1983; signed by Philadelphia to a 10-day contract that expired March 2, 1984.
Signed by San Antonio as a free agent, May 2, 1984.
Waived by San Antonio, September 11, 1984; signed by Chicago as a free agent, September 20, 1984.
Waived by Chicago, November 16, 1984; signed by Washington as a free agent, February 14, 1985.
Played in Continental Basketball Association with Maine Lumberjacks during 1979-80 and 1982-83 seasons, with Bay State Bombardiers during 1983-84 season and with Tampa Bay Thrillers during 1984-85 season.
Played in France during 1980-81 season.
Played in Italy during 1981-82 season.

—COLLEGIATE RECORD—

Year	G.	Min.	FGA	FGM	Pct.	FTA	FTM	Pct.	Reb.	Pts.	Avg.
75-76	24	....	206	106	.515	35	16	.457	198	228	9.5
76-77	27	....	284	136	.479	84	39	.464	374	311	11.5
77-78	27	....	276	148	.536	100	68	.680	368	364	13.5
78-79	29	....	352	182	.517	97	66	.680	438	430	14.8
Totals	107	....	1118	572	.512	316	189	.598	1378	1333	12.5

CBA REGULAR SEASON RECORD

Sea.—Team	G.	Min.	2-Point FGM	FGA	Pct.	3-Point FGM	FGA	Pct.	FTM	FTA	Pct.	Reb.	Ast.	Pts.	Avg.
79-80—Maine	39	1606	222	459	.484	0	2	.000	60	94	.619	506	70	504	12.9
82-83—Maine	24	914	105	215	.488	0	1	.000	70	89	.786	223	35	280	11.7
83-84—Bay State	37	1365	149	297	.501	0	1	.000	94	139	.676	293	73	392	10.6
84-85—Tampa Bay	24	802	80	154	.519	0	1	.000	38	53	.716	227	38	198	8.3
Totals	124	4687	556	1125	.494	0	5	.000	262	760	.560	1249	216	1374	11.1

ITALIAN LEAGUE

Year	G.	Min.	FGA	FGM	Pct.	FTA	FTM	Pct.	Reb.	Pts.	Avg.
81-82—S. Benedetto	38	1458	398	215	.540	114	73	.640	429	503	13.2

NBA REGULAR SEASON RECORD

Sea.—Team	G.	Min.	FGA	FGM	Pct.	FTA	FTM	Pct.	Rebounds Off.	Def.	Tot.	Ast.	PF	Dq.	Stl.	Blk.	Pts.	Avg.
83-84—Philadelphia	1	3	1	0	.000	4	1	.250	0	0	0	0	1	0	0	0	1	1.0
84-85—Chi.-Wash.	31	667	127	67	.528	58	40	.690	71	113	184	26	107	3	22	79	174	5.6
85-86—Washington	81	1609	254	129	.508	86	54	.628	122	199	321	76	235	2	57	133	312	3.9
86-87—Washington	79	1609	249	118	.474	76	48	.632	144	212	356	80	252	2	67	165	284	3.6
87-88—Washington	69	1313	177	72	.407	75	53	.707	106	219	325	59	226	5	53	113	197	2.9
Totals	261	5201	808	386	.478	299	196	.656	443	743	1186	241	821	12	199	490	968	3.7

Three-Point Field Goals: 1985-86, 0-for-2. 1986-87, 0-for-1. 1987-88, 0-for-1. Totals, 0-for-4.

NBA PLAYOFF RECORD

Sea.—Team	G.	Min.	FGA	FGM	Pct.	FTA	FTM	Pct.	Rebounds Off.	Def.	Tot.	Ast.	PF	Dq.	Stl.	Blk.	Pts.	Avg.
84-85—Washington	4	110	19	10	.526	16	9	.563	11	15	26	3	16	0	3	10	29	7.3
85-86—Washington	5	72	11	4	.364	4	4	1.000	6	3	9	3	13	0	2	2	12	2.4
86-87—Washington	3	56	5	3	.600	0	0	.000	1	7	8	3	9	0	2	5	6	2.0
87-88—Washington	5	95	5	1	.200	2	1	.500	5	12	17	2	18	0	2	4	3	0.6
Totals	17	333	40	18	.450	22	14	.636	23	37	60	11	56	0	9	21	50	2.9

Led CBA in blocked shots, 1980, 1983 and 1984. . . . Named to CBA All-Star Second Team, 1984. . . . CBA All-Defensive First Team, 1983 and 1984. . . . CBA All-Defensive Second Team, 1985. . . . Brother of Caldwell Jones, forward-center with Portland Trail Blazers.

CHARLES ALEXANDER JONES

Born January 12, 1962 at Scooba, Miss.   Height 6:08.   Weight 215.
High School—Scooba, Miss., East Kemper.
College—University of Louisville, Louisville, Ky.
Drafted by Phoenix on second round, 1984 (36th pick).

Waived by Phoenix, October 28, 1986; signed by Portland as a free agent, April 16, 1987.

—COLLEGIATE RECORD—

Year	G.	Min.	FGA	FGM	Pct.	FTA	FTM	Pct.	Reb.	Pts.	Avg.
80-81	27	538	105	54	.514	68	38	.559	106	146	5.4
81-82	31	553	102	60	.588	92	65	.707	122	185	6.0
82-83	36	1088	243	134	.551	184	123	.668	247	391	10.9
83-84	35	1210	280	159	.568	169	84	.497	338	402	11.5
Totals	129	3389	730	407	.558	513	310	.604	813	1124	8.7

NBA REGULAR SEASON RECORD

Sea.—Team	G.	Min.	FGA	FGM	Pct.	FTA	FTM	Pct.	Off.	Def.	Tot.	Ast.	PF	Dq.	Stl.	Blk.	Pts.	Avg.
84-85—Phoenix	78	1565	454	236	.520	281	182	.648	139	255	394	128	149	0	45	61	654	8.4
85-86—Phoenix	43	742	164	75	.457	98	50	.510	65	128	193	52	87	0	32	25	200	4.7
87-88—Portland	37	186	40	16	.400	33	19	.576	11	20	31	8	28	0	3	6	51	1.4
Totals	158	2493	658	327	.497	412	251	.609	215	403	618	188	264	0	80	92	905	5.7

Three-Point Field Goals: 1984-85, 0-for-4. 1985-86, 0-for-1. 1987-88, 0-for-1. Totals, 0-for-6.

NBA PLAYOFF RECORD

Sea.—Team	G.	Min.	FGA	FGM	Pct.	FTA	FTM	Pct.	Off.	Def.	Tot.	Ast.	PF	Dq.	Stl.	Blk.	Pts.	Avg.
84-85—Phoenix	2	34	5	3	.600	6	6	1.000	1	2	3	3	4	0	0	3	12	6.0
87-88—Portland	2	2	1	0	.000	0	0	.000	0	1	1	0	0	0	0	0	0	0.0
Totals	4	36	6	3	.500	6	6	1.000	1	3	4	3	4	0	0	3	12	3.0

MICHAEL JEFFREY JORDAN

Born February 17, 1963 at Brooklyn, N. Y.   Height 6:06.   Weight 195.

High School—Wilmington, N. C., Laney.

College—University of North Carolina, Chapel Hill, N. C.

Drafted by Chicago on first round as an undergraduate, 1984 (3rd pick).

—COLLEGIATE RECORD—

Year	G.	Min.	FGA	FGM	Pct.	FTA	FTM	Pct.	Reb.	Pts.	Avg.
81-82	34	....	358	191	.534	108	78	.722	149	460	13.5
82-83	36	....	527	182	.535	167	123	.737	197	721	20.0
83-84	31	....	448	247	.551	145	113	.779	163	607	19.6
Totals	101	....	1333	720	.540	420	314	.748	509	1788	17.7

Three-Point Field Goals: 1982-83, 34-for-76 (.447).

NBA REGULAR SEASON RECORD

Sea.—Team	G.	Min.	FGA	FGM	Pct.	FTA	FTM	Pct.	Off.	Def.	Tot.	Ast.	PF	Dq.	Stl.	Blk.	Pts.	Avg.
84-85—Chicago	82	3144	1625	837	.515	746	630	.845	167	367	534	481	285	4	196	69	2313	28.2
85-86—Chicago	18	451	328	150	.457	125	105	.840	23	41	64	53	46	0	37	21	408	22.7
86-87—Chicago	82	3281	2279	1098	.482	972	833	.857	166	264	430	377	237	0	236	125	3041	37.1
87-88—Chicago	82	3311	1998	1069	.535	860	723	.841	139	310	449	485	270	2	259	131	2868	35.0
Totals	264	10187	6230	3154	.506	2703	2291	.848	495	982	1477	1396	838	6	728	346	8630	32.7

Three-Point Field Goals: 1984-85, 9-for-52 (.173). 1985-86, 3-for-18 (.167). 1986-87, 12-for-66 (.182). 1987-88, 7-for-53 (.132). Totals, 31-for-189 (.164).

NBA PLAYOFF RECORD

Sea.—Team	G.	Min.	FGA	FGM	Pct.	FTA	FTM	Pct.	Off.	Def.	Tot.	Ast.	PF	Dq.	Stl.	Blk.	Pts.	Avg.
84-85—Chicago	4	171	78	34	.436	58	48	.828	7	16	23	34	15	0	11	4	117	29.3
85-86—Chicago	3	135	95	48	.505	39	34	.872	5	14	19	17	13	1	7	4	131	43.7
86-87—Chicago	3	128	84	35	.417	39	35	.897	7	14	21	18	11	0	6	7	107	35.7
87-88—Chicago	10	427	260	138	.531	99	86	.869	23	48	71	47	38	1	24	11	363	36.3
Totals	20	861	517	255	.493	235	203	.864	42	92	134	116	77	2	48	26	718	35.9

Three-Point Field Goals: 1984-85, 1-for-8 (.125). 1985-86, 1-for-1 (1.000). 1986-87, 2-for-5 (.400). 1987-88, 1-for-3 (.333). Totals, 5-for-17 (.294).

NBA ALL-STAR GAME RECORD

Season—Team	Min.	FGA	FGM	Pct.	FTA	FTM	Pct.	Off.	Def.	Tot.	Ast.	PF	Dq.	Stl.	Blk.	Pts.
1985—Chicago	22	9	2	.222	4	3	.750	3	3	6	2	4	0	3	1	7
1987—Chicago	28	12	5	.417	2	1	.500	0	0	0	4	2	0	2	0	11
1988—Chicago	29	23	17	.739	6	6	1.000	3	5	8	3	5	0	4	4	40
Totals	79	44	24	.545	12	10	.833	6	8	14	9	11	0	9	5	58

Three-Point Field Goals: 1985, 0-for-1. 1987, 0-for-1. Totals, 0-for-2.

NBA Most Valuable Player, 1988. . . . Named to All-NBA First Team, 1987 and 1988. . . . All-NBA Second Team, 1985. . . . NBA Defensive Player of the Year, 1988. . . . NBA All-Defensive First Team, 1988. . . . NBA All-Star Game MVP, 1988. . . . NBA Rookie of the Year, 1985. . . . NBA All-Rookie Team, 1985. . . . Recipient of Schick Pivotal Player Award, 1985. . . . Led NBA in scoring, 1987 and 1988. . . . Led NBA in steals, 1988. . . . Holds NBA playoff game record for most points, 63, vs. Boston, April 20, 1986. . . . Member of NCAA Division I championship team, 1982. . . . Member of U.S. Olympic Team, 1984. . . . Named THE SPORTING NEWS College Player of the Year, 1983 and 1984. . . . THE SPORTING NEWS All-America First Team, 1983 and 1984.

MICHAEL JORDAN

JEROME KERSEY

Born June 26, 1962 at Clarksville, Va.   Height 6:07.   Weight 222.

High School—Clarksville, Va., Bluestone.

College—Longwood College, Farmville, Va.

Drafted by Portland on second round, 1984 (46th pick).

—COLLEGIATE RECORD—

Year	G.	Min.	FGA	FGM	Pct.	FTA	FTM	Pct.	Reb.	Pts.	Avg.
80-81	28	....	313	197	.629	133	78	.586	249	472	16.9
81-82	23	....	282	165	.585	98	62	.633	260	392	17.0
82-83	25	....	257	144	.560	125	76	.608	270	364	14.6
83-84	27	....	411	214	.521	165	100	.606	383	528	19.6
Totals	103	....	1263	720	.570	521	316	.607	1162	1756	17.0

NBA REGULAR SEASON RECORD

Sea.—Team	G.	Min.	FGA	FGM	Pct.	FTA	FTM	Pct.	Off.	Def.	Tot.	Ast.	PF	Dq.	Stl.	Blk.	Pts.	Avg.
84-85—Portland	77	958	372	178	.478	181	117	.646	95	111	206	63	147	1	49	29	473	6.1
85-86—Portland	79	1217	470	258	.549	229	156	.681	137	156	293	83	208	2	85	32	672	8.5
86-87—Portland	82	2088	733	373	.509	364	262	.720	201	295	496	194	328	5	122	77	1009	12.3
87-88—Portland	79	2888	1225	611	.499	396	291	.735	211	446	657	243	302	8	127	65	1516	19.2
Totals	317	7151	2800	1420	.507	1170	826	.706	644	1008	1652	583	985	16	383	203	3670	11.6

Three-Point Field Goals: 1984-85, 0-for-3. 1985-86, 0-for-6. 1986-87, 1-for-23 (.043). 1987-88, 3-for-15 (.200). Totals, 4-for-47 (.085).

NBA PLAYOFF RECORD

Sea.—Team	G.	Min.	FGA	FGM	Pct.	FTA	FTM	Pct.	Off.	Def.	Tot.	Ast.	PF	Dq.	Stl.	Blk.	Pts.	Avg.
84-85—Portland	8	60	31	16	.516	8	6	.750	5	4	9	6	11	0	7	2	38	4.8
85-86—Portland	4	56	22	9	.409	4	4	1.000	7	8	15	4	13	0	1	4	22	5.5
86-87—Portland	4	60	25	10	.400	4	4	1.000	6	13	19	3	13	0	5	1	24	6.0
87-88—Portland	4	127	65	32	.492	21	15	.714	17	13	30	9	17	1	7	4	79	19.8
Totals	20	303	143	67	.469	37	29	.784	35	38	73	22	54	1	20	11	163	8.2

Three-Point Field Goals: 1985-86, 0-for-1. 1987-88, 0-for-1. Totals, 0-for-2.

Led NCAA Division II in rebounding, 1984.

ALBERT KING

Born December 17, 1959 at Brooklyn, N. Y.   Height 6:06.   Weight 215.

High School—Brooklyn, N. Y., Fort Hamilton.

College—University of Maryland, College Park, Md.

Drafted by New Jersey on first round, 1981 (10th pick).

Signed by Philadelphia as a Veteran Free Agent, November 24, 1987; New Jersey agreed not to exercise its right of first refusal in exchange for a 1988 2nd round draft choice.

—COLLEGIATE RECORD—

Year	G.	Min.	FGA	FGM	Pct.	FTA	FTM	Pct.	Reb.	Pts.	Avg.
77-78	28	....	327	164	.502	82	53	.646	187	381	13.6
78-79	28	....	387	191	.494	81	62	.765	144	444	15.9
79-80	31	...	497	275	.553	151	124	.821	207	674	21.7
80-81	31	1075	462	232	.502	117	95	.812	177	559	18.0
Totals	118	....	1673	862	.515	531	334	.629	715	2058	17.4

NBA REGULAR SEASON RECORD

Sea.—Team	G.	Min.	FGA	FGM	Pct.	FTA	FTM	Pct.	Off.	Def.	Tot.	Ast.	PF	Dq.	Stl.	Blk.	Pts.	Avg.
81-82—New Jersey	76	1694	812	391	.482	171	133	.778	105	207	312	142	261	4	64	36	918	12.1
82-83—New Jersey	79	2447	1226	582	.475	227	176	.775	157	299	456	291	278	5	95	41	1346	17.0
83-84—New Jersey	79	2103	946	465	.492	295	232	.786	125	263	388	203	258	6	91	33	1165	14.7
84-85—New Jersey	42	860	460	226	.491	104	85	.817	70	89	159	58	110	0	41	9	537	12.8
85-86—New Jersey	73	1998	961	438	.456	203	167	.823	116	250	366	181	205	4	58	24	1047	14.3
86-87—New Jersey	61	1291	573	244	.426	100	81	.810	82	132	214	103	177	5	34	28	582	9.5
87-88—Philadelphia	72	1593	540	211	.391	103	78	.757	71	145	216	109	219	4	39	18	517	7.2
Totals	482	11986	5518	2557	.463	1203	952	.791	726	1385	2111	1087	1508	28	422	189	6112	12.7

Three-Point Field Goals: 1981-82, 3-for-13 (.231). 1982-83, 6-for-23 (.261). 1983-84, 3-for-22 (.136). 1984-85, 0-for-8. 1985-86, 4-for-23 (.174). 1986-87, 13-for-32 (.406). 1987-88, 17-for-49 (.347). Totals, 46-for-170 (.271).

NBA PLAYOFF RECORD

Sea.—Team	G.	Min.	FGA	FGM	Pct.	FTA	FTM	Pct.	Off.	Def.	Tot.	Ast.	PF	Dq.	Stl.	Blk.	Pts.	Avg.
81-82—New Jersey	2	58	33	18	.545	5	4	.800	3	5	8	6	8	0	5	1	40	20.0
82-83—New Jersey	2	68	38	18	.474	6	5	.833	4	4	8	3	12	2	2	0	42	21.0

Sea.—Team	G.	Min.	FGA	FGM	Pct.	FTA	FTM	Pct.	Off.	Def.	Tot.	Ast.	PF	Dq.	Stl.	Blk.	Pts.	Avg.
83-84—New Jersey	11	295	128	53	.414	46	32	.696	25	33	58	25	32	0	10	4	138	12.5
84-85—New Jersey	3	105	57	28	.491	13	9	.692	4	19	23	5	14	0	7	2	66	22.0
85-86—New Jersey	3	98	42	18	.429	4	4	1.000	8	5	13	10	15	1	2	1	41	13.7
Totals	21	624	298	135	.453	74	54	.730	44	66	110	49	81	3	26	8	327	15.6

Three-Point Field Goals: 1982-83, 1-for-2 (.500). 1983-84, 0-for-2. 1984-85, 1-for-1 (1.000). 1985-86, 1-for-4 (.250). Totals, 3-for-9 (.333).

Named to THE SPORTING NEWS All-America First Team, 1981. . . . Brother of Washington Bullets forward Bernard King.

BERNARD KING

Born December 4, 1956 at Brooklyn, N. Y.   Height 6:07.   Weight 205.

High School—Brooklyn, N. Y., Fort Hamilton.

College—University of Tennessee, Knoxville, Tenn.

Drafted by New Jersey on first round as an undergraduate, 1977 (7th pick).

Traded by New Jersey with John Gianelli and Jim Boylan to Utah for Rich Kelley, October 2, 1979.
Traded by Utah to Golden State for Wayne Cooper and a 1981 2nd round draft choice, September 11, 1980.
Signed by New York as a Veteran Free Agent, September 28, 1982; Golden State matched offer and traded King to New York for Micheal Ray Richardson and a 1984 5th round draft choice, October 22, 1982.
Signed by Washington as a free agent, October 16, 1987.
Missed entire 1985-86 season due to injury.

—COLLEGIATE RECORD—

Year	G.	Min.	FGA	FGM	Pct.	FTA	FTM	Pct.	Reb.	Pts.	Avg.
74-75	25	....	439	273	.622	147	115	.782	308	661	26.4
75-76	25	....	454	260	.573	163	109	.669	325	629	25.2
76-77	26	....	481	278	.578	163	116	.712	371	672	25.8
Totals	76	....	1374	811	.590	473	340	.719	1004	1962	25.8

NBA REGULAR SEASON RECORD

Sea.—Team	G.	Min.	FGA	FGM	Pct.	FTA	FTM	Pct.	Off.	Def.	Tot.	Ast.	PF	Dq.	Stl.	Blk.	Pts.	Avg.
77-78—New Jersey	79	3092	1665	798	.479	462	313	.677	265	486	751	193	302	5	122	36	1909	24.2
78-79—New Jersey	82	2859	1359	710	.522	619	349	.564	251	418	669	295	326	10	118	39	1769	21.6
79-80—Utah	19	419	137	71	.518	63	34	.540	24	64	88	52	66	3	7	4	176	9.3
80-81—Golden State	81	2914	1244	731	.588	437	307	.703	178	373	551	287	304	5	72	34	1771	21.9
81-82—Golden State	79	2861	1307	740	.566	499	352	.705	140	329	469	282	285	6	78	23	1833	23.2
82-83—New York	68	2207	1142	603	.528	388	280	.722	99	227	326	195	233	5	90	13	1486	21.9
83-84—New York	77	2667	1391	795	.572	561	437	.779	123	271	394	164	273	2	75	17	2027	26.3
84-85—New York	55	2063	1303	691	.530	552	426	.772	114	203	317	204	191	8	71	15	1809	32.9
86-87—New York	6	214	105	52	.495	43	32	.744	13	19	32	19	14	0	2	0	136	22.7
87-88—Washington	69	2044	938	470	.501	324	247	.762	86	194	280	192	202	3	49	10	1188	17.2
Totals	615	21340	10591	5661	.535	3948	2777	.703	1293	2584	3877	1883	2196	42	684	191	14104	22.9

Three-Point Field Goals: 1980-81, 2-for-6 (.333). 1981-82, 1-for-5 (.200). 1982-83, 0-for-6. 1983-84, 0-for-4. 1984-85, 1-for-10 (.100). 1987-88, 1-for-6 (.167). Totals, 5-for-37 (.135).

NBA PLAYOFF RECORD

Sea.—Team	G.	Min.	FGA	FGM	Pct.	FTA	FTM	Pct.	Off.	Def.	Tot.	Ast.	PF	Dq.	Stl.	Blk.	Pts.	Avg.
78-79—New Jersey	2	81	42	21	.500	24	10	.417	5	6	11	7	10	0	4	0	52	26.0
82-83—New York	6	184	97	56	.577	35	28	.800	8	16	24	13	16	0	2	0	141	23.5
83-84—New York	12	477	282	162	.574	123	93	.756	28	46	74	36	48	0	14	6	417	34.8
87-88—Washington	5	168	53	26	.491	21	17	.810	3	8	11	9	17	0	3	0	69	13.8
Totals	25	910	474	265	.559	203	148	.729	44	76	120	65	91	0	23	6	679	27.2

Three-Point Field Goals: 1982-83, 1-for-3 (.333). 1983-84, 0-for-1. Totals, 1-for-4 (.250).

NBA ALL-STAR GAME RECORD

Season—Team	Min.	FGA	FGM	Pct.	FTA	FTM	Pct.	Off.	Def.	Tot.	Ast.	PF	Dq.	Stl.	Blk.	Pts.
1982—Golden State	14	7	2	.286	2	2	1.000	0	4	4	1	2	0	3	1	6
1984—New York	22	13	8	.615	5	2	.400	2	1	3	4	2	0	0	0	18
1985—New York	22	10	6	.600	2	1	.500	4	3	7	1	5	0	0	0	13
Totals	58	30	16	.533	9	5	.556	6	8	14	6	9	0	3	1	37

Named to All-NBA First Team, 1984 and 1985. . . . Named to All-NBA Second Team, 1982. . . . Led NBA in scoring, 1985. . . . NBA All-Rookie Team, 1978. . . . NBA Comeback Player of the Year, 1981. . . . Named to THE SPORTING NEWS All-America Second Team, 1977. . . . Led NCAA in field-goal percentage, 1975. . . . Brother of Philadelphia 76ers forward Albert King.

GREGORY FULLER KITE
(Greg)

Born August 5, 1961 at Houston, Tex.   Height 6:11.   Weight 250.

High School—Houston, Tex., Madison.

College—Brigham Young University, Provo, Utah.

Drafted by Boston on first round, 1983 (21st pick).

Waived by Boston, February 1, 1988; claimed off waivers by Los Angeles Clippers, February 3, 1988.

—COLLEGIATE RECORD—

Year	G.	Min.	FGA	FGM	Pct.	FTA	FTM	Pct.	Reb.	Pts.	Avg.
79-80	21	192	48	14	.292	25	12	.480	86	40	1.9
80-81	32	1002	221	108	.489	101	50	.495	272	266	8.3
81-82	30	853	169	79	.467	65	29	.446	234	187	6.2
82-83	29	896	206	90	.437	77	44	.571	255	224	7.7
Totals	112	2943	644	291	.452	268	135	.504	847	717	6.4

NBA REGULAR SEASON RECORD

Sea.—Team	G.	Min.	FGA	FGM	Pct.	FTA	FTM	Pct.	—Rebounds— Off.	Def.	Tot.	Ast.	PF	Dq.	Stl.	Blk.	Pts.	Avg.
83-84—Boston	35	197	66	30	.455	16	5	.313	27	35	62	7	42	0	1	5	65	1.9
84-85—Boston	55	424	88	33	.375	32	22	.688	38	51	89	17	84	3	3	10	88	1.6
85-86—Boston	64	464	91	34	.374	39	15	.385	35	93	128	17	81	1	3	28	83	1.3
86-87—Boston	74	745	110	47	.427	76	29	.382	61	108	169	27	148	2	17	46	123	1.7
87-88—Bos.-L.A.C.	53	1063	205	92	.449	79	40	.506	85	179	264	47	153	1	19	58	224	4.2
Totals	281	2893	560	236	.421	242	111	.459	246	466	712	115	508	7	43	147	583	2.1

Three-Point Field Goals: 1985-86, 0-for-1. 1986-87, 0-for-1. 1987-88, 0-for-1. Totals, 0-for-3.

NBA PLAYOFF RECORD

Sea.—Team	G.	Min.	FGA	FGM	Pct.	FTA	FTM	Pct.	—Rebounds— Off.	Def.	Tot.	Ast.	PF	Dq.	Stl.	Blk.	Pts.	Avg.
83-84—Boston	11	38	8	1	.125	6	5	.833	5	4	9	3	9	0	0	1	7	0.6
84-85—Boston	9	63	12	5	.417	2	1	.500	5	11	16	3	13	0	1	0	11	1.2
85-86—Boston	13	78	10	7	.700	7	4	.571	5	14	19	3	20	0	2	4	18	1.4
86-87—Boston	20	172	20	7	.350	7	3	.429	15	31	46	8	43	1	2	8	17	0.9
Totals	53	351	50	20	.400	22	13	.591	30	60	90	17	85	1	5	13	53	1.0

Member of NBA championship teams, 1984 and 1986.

JOSEPH WILLIAM KLEINE
(Joe)

Born January 4, 1962 at Colorado Springs, Colo.   Height 7:00.   Weight 271.

High School—Slater, Mo.

Colleges—University of Notre Dame, Notre Dame, Ind., and
University of Arkansas, Fayetteville, Ark.

Drafted by Sacramento on first round, 1985 (6th pick).

—COLLEGIATE RECORD—
Notre Dame

Year	G.	Min.	FGA	FGM	Pct.	FTA	FTM	Pct.	Reb.	Pts.	Avg.
80-81	29	291	50	32	.640	16	12	.750	71	76	2.6

Arkansas

Year	G.	Min.	FGA	FGM	Pct.	FTA	FTM	Pct.	Reb.	Pts.	Avg.
81-82					Did Not Play—Transfer Student						
82-83	30	950	307	165	.537	109	69	.633	219	399	13.3
83-84	32	1173	351	209	.595	211	163	.773	293	581	18.2
84-85	35	1289	484	294	.607	257	185	.720	294	773	22.1
Ark. Totals	97	3412	1142	668	.585	577	417	.723	806	1753	18.1
College Totals	126	3703	1192	700	.587	593	429	.723	877	1829	14.5

NBA REGULAR SEASON RECORD

Sea.—Team	G.	Min.	FGA	FGM	Pct.	FTA	FTM	Pct.	—Rebounds— Off.	Def.	Tot.	Ast.	PF	Dq.	Stl.	Blk.	Pts.	Avg.
85-86—Sacramento	80	1180	344	160	.465	130	94	.723	113	260	373	46	224	1	24	34	414	5.2
86-87—Sacramento	79	1658	543	256	.471	140	110	.786	173	310	483	71	213	2	35	30	622	7.9
87-88—Sacramento	82	1999	686	324	.472	188	153	.814	179	400	579	93	228	1	28	59	801	9.8
Totals	241	4837	1573	740	.470	458	357	.779	465	970	1435	210	665	4	87	123	1837	7.6

Three-Point Field Goals: 1986-87, 0-for-1.

Sea.—Team	G.	Min.	FGA	FGM	Pct.	FTA	FTM	Pct.	—Rebounds— Off.	Def.	Tot.	Ast.	PF	Dq.	Stl.	Blk.	Pts.	Avg.
85-86—Sacramento	3	45	13	5	.385	6	5	.833	8	6	14	1	8	0	1	1	15	5.0

Member of U.S. Olympic team, 1984. . . . Cousin of Washington Redskins offensive lineman Wally Kleine.

BART KOFOED

Born March 24, 1964 at Omaha, Neb.   Height 6:04.   Weight 210.

High School—Omaha, Neb., Westside.

Colleges—Hastings College, Hastings, Neb., and
Kearney State College, Kearney, Neb.

Drafted by Utah on fifth round, 1987 (107th pick).

—COLLEGIATE RECORD—
Hastings

Year	G.	Min.	FGA	FGM	Pct.	FTA	FTM	Pct.	Reb.	Pts.	Avg.
82-83	28	....	116	55	.474	31	18	.581	75	128	4.6
83-84					Statistics Unavailable						

Kearney State

Year	G.	Min.	FGA	FGM	Pct.	FTA	FTM	Pct.	Reb.	Pts.	Avg.
84-85				Did Not Play—Transfer Student							
85-86	32	....	566	288	.509	146	102	.699	186	678	21.2
86-87	34	....	747	358	.479	203	148	.729	184	902	26.5
K.S. Totals	66	....	1313	646	.492	349	250	.716	370	1580	23.9

Three-Point Field Goals: 1986-87, 38-for-114 (.333).

NBA REGULAR SEASON RECORD

Sea.—Team	G.	Min.	FGA	FGM	Pct.	FTA	FTM	Pct.	—Rebounds— Off.	Def.	Tot.	Ast.	PF	Dq.	Stl.	Blk.	Pts.	Avg.
87-88—Utah	36	225	48	18	.375	13	8	.615	4	11	15	23	42	0	6	1	46	1.3

Three-Point Field Goals: 1987-88, 2-for-7 (.286).

NBA PLAYOFF RECORD

Sea.—Team	G.	Min.	FGA	FGM	Pct.	FTA	FTM	Pct.	—Rebounds— Off.	Def.	Tot.	Ast.	PF	Dq.	Stl.	Blk.	Pts.	Avg.
87-88—Utah	10	109	23	9	.391	2	2	1.000	3	11	14	11	18	0	1	0	21	2.1

Three-Point Field Goals: 1987-88, 1-for-5 (.200).

JON FRANCIS KONCAK

Born May 17, 1963 at Cedar Rapids, Ia.   Height 7:00.   Weight 260.

High School—Kansas City, Mo., Center.

College—Southern Methodist University, Dallas, Tex.

Drafted by Atlanta on first round, 1985 (5th pick).

—COLLEGIATE RECORD—

Year	G.	Min.	FGA	FGM	Pct.	FTA	FTM	Pct.	Reb.	Pts.	Avg.
81-82	27	745	232	107	.461	92	57	.620	155	271	10.0
82-83	30	980	334	176	.527	123	85	.691	282	437	14.6
83-84	33	1162	340	211	.621	145	88	.607	378	510	15.5
84-85	33	1084	370	219	.592	192	128	.667	354	566	17.2
Totals	123	3971	1276	713	.559	552	358	.649	1169	1784	14.5

NBA REGULAR SEASON RECORD

Sea.—Team	G.	Min.	FGA	FGM	Pct.	FTA	FTM	Pct.	—Rebounds— Off.	Def.	Tot.	Ast.	PF	Dq.	Stl.	Blk.	Pts.	Avg.
85-86—Atlanta	82	1695	519	263	.507	257	156	.607	171	296	467	55	296	10	37	69	682	8.3
86-87—Atlanta	82	1684	352	169	.480	191	125	.654	153	340	493	31	262	2	52	76	463	5.6
87-88—Atlanta	49	1073	203	98	.483	136	83	.610	103	230	333	19	161	1	36	56	279	5.7
Totals	213	4452	1074	530	.493	584	364	.623	427	866	1293	105	719	13	125	201	1424	6.7

Three-Point Field Goals: 1985-86, 0-for-1. 1986-87, 0-for-1. 1987-88, 0-for-2. Totals, 0-for-4.

NBA PLAYOFF RECORD

Sea.—Team	G.	Min.	FGA	FGM	Pct.	FTA	FTM	Pct.	—Rebounds— Off.	Def.	Tot.	Ast.	PF	Dq.	Stl.	Blk.	Pts.	Avg.
85-86—Atlanta	9	193	29	14	.483	46	26	.565	11	23	34	5	27	2	6	10	54	6.0
86-87—Atlanta	8	86	13	7	.538	8	6	.750	5	20	25	3	24	0	3	4	20	2.5
Totals	17	279	42	21	.500	54	32	.593	16	43	59	8	51	2	9	14	74	4.4

Member of U.S. Olympic team, 1984. . . . Named to THE SPORTING NEWS All-America Second Team, 1985.

LARRY BRETT KRYSTKOWIAK

Born September 23, 1964 at Missoula, Mont.   Height 6:09.   Weight 220.

High School—Missoula, Mont., Big Sky.

College—University of Montana, Missoula, Mont.

Drafted by Chicago on second round, 1986 (28th pick).

Draft rights traded by Chicago with 1987 and 1992 2nd round draft choices to Portland for Steve Colter, June 17, 1986.

Draft rights traded by Portland with Mychal Thompson to San Antonio for Steve Johnson, June 20, 1986.

Traded by San Antonio to Milwaukee for Charles Davis and a 1989 2nd round draft choice, November 18, 1987.

—COLLEGIATE RECORD—

Year	G.	Min.	FGA	FGM	Pct.	FTA	FTM	Pct.	Reb.	Pts.	Avg.
82-83	28	396	97	42	.433	77	53	.688	120	137	4.9
83-84	30	1068	338	185	.547	210	169	.805	315	539	18.0
84-85	30	1079	366	214	.585	243	204	.840	306	632	21.1
85-86	32	1118	446	258	.578	254	193	.760	364	709	22.2
Totals	120	3661	1247	699	.561	784	619	.790	1105	2017	16.8

NBA REGULAR SEASON RECORD

Sea.—Team	G.	Min.	FGA	FGM	Pct.	FTA	FTM	Pct.	Off.	Def.	Tot.	Ast.	PF	Dq.	Stl.	Blk.	Pts.	Avg.
86-87—San Antonio	68	1004	373	170	.456	148	110	.743	77	162	239	85	141	1	22	12	451	6.6
87-88—Milwaukee	50	1050	266	128	.481	127	103	.811	88	143	231	50	137	0	18	8	359	7.2
Totals	118	2054	639	298	.466	275	213	.775	165	305	470	135	278	1	40	20	810	6.9

Three-Point Field Goals: 1986-87, 1-for-12 (.083). 1987-88, 0-for-3. Totals, 1-for-15 (.067).

NBA PLAYOFF RECORD

Sea.—Team	G.	Min.	FGA	FGM	Pct.	FTA	FTM	Pct.	Off.	Def.	Tot.	Ast.	PF	Dq.	Stl.	Blk.	Pts.	Avg.
87-88—Milwaukee	5	163	29	13	.448	18	16	.889	13	21	34	7	17	0	4	0	42	8.4

WILLIAM LAIMBEER JR.
(Bill)

Born May 19, 1957 at Boston, Mass.   Height 6:11.   Weight 260.

High School—Palos Verdes, Calif.

Colleges—University of Notre Dame, Notre Dame, Ind.,
and Owens Technical College, Toledo, O.

Drafted by Cleveland on third round, 1979 (65th pick).

Traded by Cleveland with Kenny Carr to Detroit for Phil Hubbard, Paul Mokeski and 1982 1st and 2nd round draft choices, February 16, 1982.

Played in Italy during 1979-80 season.

—COLLEGIATE RECORD—
Notre Dame

Year	G.	Min.	FGA	FGM	Pct.	FTA	FTM	Pct.	Reb.	Pts.	Avg.
75-76	10	190	65	32	.492	23	18	.783	79	82	8.2

Owens Tech

Year	G.	Min.	FGA	FGM	Pct.	FTA	FTM	Pct.	Reb.	Pts.	Avg.
76-77					Did Not Play						

Notre Dame

Year	G.	Min.	FGA	FGM	Pct.	FTA	FTM	Pct.	Reb.	Pts.	Avg.
77-78	29	654	175	97	.554	62	42	.677	190	236	8.1
78-79	30	614	145	78	.538	50	35	.700	164	191	6.4
Totals	69	1458	385	207	.538	135	95	.704	433	509	7.4

ITALIAN LEAGUE RECORD

Year	G.	Min.	FGA	FGM	Pct.	FTA	FTM	Pct.	Reb.	Pts.	Avg.
79-80—Brescia	29	....	465	258	.555	124	97	.782	363	613	21.1

NBA REGULAR SEASON RECORD

Sea.—Team	G.	Min.	FGA	FGM	Pct.	FTA	FTM	Pct.	Off.	Def.	Tot.	Ast.	PF	Dq.	Stl.	Blk.	Pts.	Avg.
80-81—Cleveland	81	2460	670	337	.503	153	117	.765	266	427	693	216	332	14	56	78	791	9.8
81-82—Clev.-Det.	80	1829	536	265	.494	232	184	.793	234	383	617	100	296	5	39	64	718	9.0
82-83—Detroit	82	2871	877	436	.497	310	245	.790	282	711	993	263	320	9	51	118	1119	13.6
83-84—Detroit	82	2864	1044	553	.530	365	316	.866	329	674	1003	149	273	4	49	84	1422	17.3

Sea.—Team	G.	Min.	FGA	FGM	Pct.	FTA	FTM	Pct.	Off.	Def.	Tot.	Ast.	PF	Dq.	Stl.	Blk.	Pts.	Avg.
									\-Rebounds\-									
84-85—Detroit	82	2892	1177	595	.506	306	244	.797	295	718	1013	154	308	4	69	71	1438	17.5
85-86—Detroit	82	2891	1107	545	.492	319	266	.834	305	770	1075	146	291	4	59	65	1360	16.6
86-87—Detroit	82	2854	1010	506	.501	274	245	.894	243	712	955	151	283	4	72	69	1263	15.4
87-88—Detroit	82	2897	923	455	.493	214	187	.874	165	667	832	199	284	6	66	78	1110	13.5
Totals	653	21558	7344	3692	.503	2173	1804	.830	2119	5062	7181	1378	2387	50	461	627	9221	14.1

Three-Point Field Goals: 1981-82, 4-for-13 (.308). 1982-83, 2-for-13 (.154). 1983-84, 0-for-11. 1984-85, 4-for-18 (.222). 1985-86, 4-for-14 (.286). 1986-87, 6-for-21 (.286). 1987-88, 13-for-39 (.333). Totals, 33-for-129 (.256).

NBA PLAYOFF RECORD

Sea.—Team	G.	Min.	FGA	FGM	Pct.	FTA	FTM	Pct.	Off.	Def.	Tot.	Ast.	PF	Dq.	Stl.	Blk.	Pts.	Avg.
									\-Rebounds\-									
83-84—Detroit	5	165	51	29	.569	20	18	.900	14	48	62	12	23	2	4	3	76	15.2
84-85—Detroit	9	325	107	48	.449	51	36	.706	36	60	96	15	32	1	7	7	132	14.7
85-86—Detroit	4	168	68	34	.500	23	21	.913	20	36	56	1	19	1	2	3	90	22.5
86-87—Detroit	15	543	163	84	.515	24	15	.625	30	126	156	37	53	2	15	12	184	12.3
87-88—Detroit	23	779	250	114	.456	45	40	.889	43	178	221	44	77	2	18	19	273	11.9
Totals	56	1980	639	309	.484	163	130	.798	143	448	591	109	204	8	46	44	755	13.5

Three-Point Field Goals: 1984-85, 0-for-2. 1985-86, 1-for-1 (1.000). 1986-87, 1-for-5 (.200). 1987-88, 5-for-17 (.294). Totals, 7-for-25 (.280).

NBA ALL-STAR GAME RECORD

Season—Team	Min.	FGA	FGM	Pct.	FTA	FTM	Pct.	Off.	Def.	Tot.	Ast.	PF	Dq.	Stl.	Blk.	Pts.
								\-Rebounds\-								
1983—Detroit..........	6	1	1	1.000	0	0	.000	1	0	1	0	1	0	0	0	2
1984—Detroit..........	17	8	6	.750	1	1	1.000	1	4	5	0	3	0	1	2	13
1985—Detroit..........	11	4	2	.500	2	1	.500	1	2	3	1	1	0	0	0	5
1987—Detroit..........	11	7	4	.571	0	0	.000	0	2	2	1	2	0	1	0	8
Totals	45	20	13	.650	3	2	.667	3	8	11	2	7	0	2	2	28

Led NBA in rebounding, 1986.

JEFFREY ALAN LAMP
(Jeff)

Born March 9, 1959 at Minneapolis, Minn.   Height 6:06.   Weight 195.

High School—Louisville, Ky., Ballard.

College—University of Virginia, Charlottesville, Va.

Drafted by Portland on first round, 1981 (15th pick).

Waived by Portland, June 21, 1984; signed by Milwaukee as a free agent, September 26, 1985.

Waived by Milwaukee, February 3, 1986; signed by San Antonio as a free agent, February 11, 1986, for remainder of season.

Signed by Los Angeles Lakers as a Veteran Free Agent, October 7, 1987; San Antonio agreed not to exercise its right of first refusal in exchange for a 1988 3rd round draft choice.

—COLLEGIATE RECORD—

Year	G.	Min.	FGA	FGM	Pct.	FTA	FTM	Pct.	Reb.	Pts.	Avg.
77-78	28	930	382	156	.408	205	173	.844	124	485	17.3
78-79	28	967	477	230	.482	214	181	.846	121	641	22.9
79-80	34	1200	445	232	.521	151	127	.841	133	591	17.4
80-81	33	1134	406	223	.549	178	154	.865	137	600	18.2
Totals	123	4231	1710	841	.492	748	635	.849	515	2317	18.8

NBA REGULAR SEASON RECORD

Sea.—Team	G.	Min.	FGA	FGM	Pct.	FTA	FTM	Pct.	Off.	Def.	Tot.	Ast.	PF	Dq.	Stl.	Blk.	Pts.	Avg.
									\-Rebounds\-									
81-82—Portland	54	617	196	100	.510	61	50	.820	24	40	64	28	83	0	16	1	250	4.6
82-83—Portland	59	690	252	107	.425	52	42	.808	25	51	76	58	67	0	20	3	257	4.4
83-84—Portland	64	660	261	128	.490	67	60	.896	23	40	63	51	67	0	22	4	318	5.0
85-86—Mil.-S.A.	74	1321	514	245	.477	133	111	.835	53	147	200	117	155	1	39	4	608	8.2
87-88—L.A. Lakers	3	7	0	0	.000	2	2	1.000	0	0	0	0	1	0	0	0	2	0.7
Totals	254	3295	1223	580	.474	315	265	.841	125	278	403	254	373	1	97	12	1435	5.6

Three-Point Field Goals: 1981-82, 0-for-1. 1982-83, 1-for-6 (.167). 1983-84, 2-for-13 (.154). 1985-86, 7-for-30 (.233). Totals, 10-for-50 (.200).

NBA PLAYOFF RECORD

Sea.—Team	G.	Min.	FGA	FGM	Pct.	FTA	FTM	Pct.	Off.	Def.	Tot.	Ast.	PF	Dq.	Stl.	Blk.	Pts.	Avg.
									\-Rebounds\-									
82-83—Portland	1	1	2	1	.500	0	0	.000	0	0	0	0	0	0	0	0	2	2.0
83-84—Portland	3	19	6	2	.333	0	0	.000	0	0	0	0	1	0	0	0	4	1.3
85-86—San Antonio	3	45	18	7	.389	0	0	.000	1	0	1	7	6	0	1	0	15	5.0
Totals	7	65	26	10	.385	0	0	.000	1	0	1	7	7	0	1	0	21	3.0

Three-Point Field Goals: 1985-86, 1-for-3 (.333).

BILL LAIMBEER

ALLEN FRAZIER LEAVELL

Born May 27, 1957 at Muncie, Ind.   Height 6.02.   Weight 190.

High School—Muncie, Ind., Central.

College—Oklahoma City University, Oklahoma City, Okla.

Drafted by Houston on fifth round, 1979 (104th pick).

Waived by Houston, November 17, 1986; re-signed by Houston as a free agent, January 13, 1987.

—COLLEGIATE RECORD—

Year	G.	Min.	FGA	FGM	Pct.	FTA	FTM	Pct.	Reb.	Pts.	Avg.
75-76	24	....	80	34	.425	26	19	.731	40	87	3.6
76-77	18	....	125	61	.488	25	18	.720	20	140	7.8
77-78	27	....	494	248	.502	72	54	.750	107	550	20.4
78-79	21	....	404	192	.475	103	83	.806	67	467	22.2
Totals	)0	....	1103	535	.485	236	174	.737	234	1244	13.8

NBA REGULAR SEASON RECORD

Sea.—Team	G.	Min.	FGA	FGM	Pct.	FTA	FTM	Pct.	Off.	Def.	Tot.	Ast.	PF	Dq.	Stl.	Blk.	Pts.	Avg.
79-80—Houston	77	2123	656	330	.503	221	180	.814	57	127	184	417	197	1	127	28	843	10.9
80-81—Houston	79	1686	548	258	.471	149	124	.832	30	104	134	384	160	1	97	15	642	8.1
81-82—Houston	79	2150	793	370	.467	135	115	.852	49	119	168	457	182	2	150	15	864	10.9
82-83—Houston	79	2602	1059	439	.415	297	247	.832	64	131	195	530	215	0	165	14	1167	14.8
83-84—Houston	82	2009	731	349	.477	286	238	.832	31	86	117	459	199	2	107	12	947	11.5
84-85—Houston	42	536	209	88	.421	57	44	.772	8	29	37	102	61	0	23	4	228	5.4
85-86—Houston	74	1190	458	212	.463	158	135	.854	6	61	67	234	126	1	58	8	583	7.9
86-87—Houston	53	1175	358	147	.411	119	100	.840	14	47	61	224	126	1	53	10	412	7.8
87-88—Houston	80	2150	666	291	.437	251	218	.869	22	126	148	405	162	1	124	9	819	10.2
Totals	645	15621	5478	2484	.453	1673	1401	.837	281	830	1111	3212	1428	9	904	115	6505	10.1

Three-Point Field Goals: 1979-80, 3-for-19 (.158). 1980-81, 2-for-17 (.118). 1981-82, 9-for-31 (.290). 1982-83, 42-for-175 (.240). 1983-84, 11-for-71 (.155). 1984-85, 8-for-37 (.216). 1985-86, 24-for-67 (.358). 1986-87, 18-for-57 (.316). 1987-88, 19-for-88 (.216). Totals, 136-for-562 (.242).

NBA PLAYOFF RECORD

Sea.—Team	G.	Min.	FGA	FGM	Pct.	FTA	FTM	Pct.	Off.	Def.	Tot.	Ast.	PF	Dq.	Stl.	Blk.	Pts.	Avg.
79-80—Houston	7	149	38	10	.263	21	19	.905	2	10	12	24	12	0	6	0	39	5.6
80-81—Houston	17	217	77	30	.390	17	15	.882	5	12	17	44	26	0	18	4	75	4.4
81-82—Houston	3	93	47	20	.426	2	2	1.000	1	4	5	10	9	0	3	1	42	14.0
84-85—Houston	5	16	6	2	.333	2	2	1.000	1	2	3	3	2	0	0	0	6	1.2
85-86—Houston	15	170	80	24	.300	23	20	.870	3	12	15	40	12	0	9	0	75	5.0
86-87—Houston	10	384	107	44	.411	60	49	.817	6	19	25	72	42	2	19	3	141	14.1
87-88—Houston	4	38	19	7	.368	4	4	1.000	0	3	3	9	6	0	2	0	20	5.0
Totals	61	1067	374	137	.366	129	111	.860	18	62	80	202	109	2	57	8	398	6.5

Three-Point Field Goals: 1979-80, 0-for-4. 1981-82, 0-for-1. 1984-85, 0-for-2. 1985-86, 7-for-15 (.467). 1986-87, 4-for-16 (.250). 1987-88, 2-for-6 (.333). Totals, 13-for-44 (.295).

KEITH DEYWANE LEE

Born December 28, 1962 at West Memphis, Ark.   Height 6:10.   Weight 220.

High School—West Memphis, Ark.

College—Memphis State University, Memphis, Tenn.

Drafted by Chicago on first round, 1985 (11th pick).

Draft rights traded by Chicago with Ennis Whatley to Cleveland for draft rights to Charles Oakley and Calvin Duncan, June 18, 1985.

Traded by Cleveland with John Bagley to New Jersey for Darryl Dawkins and James Bailey, October 8, 1987. Missed entire 1987-88 season due to injury.

—COLLEGIATE RECORD—

Year	G.	Min.	FGA	FGM	Pct.	FTA	FTM	Pct.	Reb.	Pts.	Avg.
81-82	29	1041	370	199	.538	178	134	.753	320	532	18.3
82-83	31	1109	438	220	.502	172	141	.820	336	581	18.7
83-84	33	1139	453	245	.541	151	117	.775	357	607	18.4
84-85	35	1141	536	266	.496	200	156	.780	323	688	19.7
Totals	128	4430	1797	930	.518	701	548	.782	1336	2408	18.8

NBA REGULAR SEASON RECORD

Sea.—Team	G.	Min.	FGA	FGM	Pct.	FTA	FTM	Pct.	Off.	Def.	Tot.	Ast.	PF	Dq.	Stl.	Blk.	Pts.	Avg.
85-86—Cleveland	58	1197	380	177	.466	96	75	.781	116	235	351	67	204	9	29	37	431	7.4
86-87—Cleveland	67	870	374	170	.455	101	72	.713	93	158	251	69	147	0	25	40	412	6.1
Totals	125	2067	754	347	.460	197	147	.746	209	393	602	136	351	9	54	77	843	6.7

Three-Point Field Goals: 1985-86, 2-for-9 (.222). 1986-87, 0-for-1. Totals, 2-for-10 (.200).
Named to THE SPORTING NEWS All-America First Team, 1983 and 1985.

LAFAYETTE LEVER
(Fat)

Born August 18, 1960 at Pine Bluff, Ark.   Height 6:03.   Weight 175.

High School—Tucson, Ariz., Pueblo.

College—Arizona State University, Tempe, Ariz.

Drafted by Portland on first round, 1982 (11th pick).

Traded by Portland with Calvin Natt, Wayne Cooper, a 1984 2nd round draft choice and a 1985 1st round draft choice to Denver for Kiki Vandeweghe, June 7, 1984.

—COLLEGIATE RECORD—

Year	G	Min.	FGA	FGM	Pct.	FTA	FTM	Pct.	Reb.	Pts.	Avg.
78-79	29	377	92	38	.413	38	28	.737	44	104	3.6
79-80	29	974	220	98	.445	103	72	.699	125	268	9.2
80-81	28	1038	259	120	.463	116	84	.724	138	324	11.6
81-82	27	1032	357	162	.454	143	117	.818	146	441	16.3
Totals	113	3421	928	418	.450	400	301	.753	453	1137	10.1

NBA REGULAR SEASON RECORD

| | | | | | | | | | —Rebounds— | | | | | | | | | |
Sea.—Team	G.	Min.	FGA	FGM	Pct.	FTA	FTM	Pct.	Off.	Def.	Tot.	Ast.	PF	Dq.	Stl.	Blk.	Pts.	Avg.
82-83—Portland	81	2020	594	256	.431	116	159	.730	85	140	225	426	179	2	153	15	633	7.8
83-84—Portland	81	2010	701	313	.447	214	159	.743	96	122	218	372	178	1	135	31	788	9.7
84-85—Denver	82	2559	985	424	.430	256	197	.770	147	264	411	613	226	1	202	30	1051	12.8
85-86—Denver	78	2616	1061	468	.441	182	132	.725	136	284	420	584	204	3	178	15	1080	13.8
86-87—Denver	82	3054	1370	643	.469	312	244	.782	216	513	729	654	219	1	201	34	1552	18.9
87-88—Denver	82	3061	1360	643	.473	316	248	.785	203	462	665	639	214	0	223	21	1546	18.9
Totals	486	15320	6071	2747	.452	1439	1096	.762	883	1785	2668	3288	1220	8	1092	146	6650	13.7

Three-Point Field Goals: 1982-83, 5-for-15 (.333). 1983-84, 3-for-15 (.200). 1984-85, 6-for-24 (.250). 1985-86, 12-for-38 (.316). 1986-87, 22-for-92 (.239). 1987-88, 12-for-57 (.211). Totals, 60-for-241 (.249).

NBA PLAYOFF RECORD

| | | | | | | | | | —Rebounds— | | | | | | | | | |
Sea.—Team	G.	Min.	FGA	FGM	Pct.	FTA	FTM	Pct.	Off.	Def.	Tot.	Ast.	PF	Dq.	Stl.	Blk.	Pts.	Avg.
82-83—Portland	7	134	42	19	.452	5	4	.800	3	11	14	31	13	0	7	0	42	6.0
83-84—Portland	5	75	30	8	.267	10	8	.800	10	5	15	9	6	0	4	0	26	5.2
84-85—Denver	11	342	122	49	.402	63	48	.762	23	48	71	93	33	0	26	2	146	13.3
85-86—Denver	10	347	131	59	.450	24	17	.708	15	33	48	53	33	0	20	2	143	14.3
86-87—Denver	3	99	50	19	.380	9	6	.667	5	13	18	22	7	0	7	0	46	15.3
87-88—Denver	7	273	98	45	.459	33	26	.788	16	49	65	49	15	0	13	4	119	17.0
Totals	43	1270	473	199	.421	144	109	.757	72	159	231	257	107	0	77	8	522	12.1

Three-Point Field Goals: 1983-84, 2-for-3 (.667). 1984-85, 0-for-2. 1985-86, 8-for-14 (.571). 1986-87, 2-for-8 (.250). 1987-88, 3-for-7 (.429). Totals, 15-for-34 (.441).

NBA ALL-STAR GAME RECORD

| | | | | | | | | —Rebounds— | | | | | | | |
Season—Team	Min.	FGA	FGM	Pct.	FTA	FTM	Pct.	Off.	Def.	Tot.	Ast.	PF	Dq.	Stl.	Blk.	Pts.
1988—Denver	31	14	7	.500	4	3	.750	0	4	4	3	4	0	0	0	17

Named to All-NBA Second Team, 1987. . . . NBA All-Defensive Second Team, 1988.

CLIFFORD EUGENE LEVINGSTON
(Cliff)

Born January 4, 1961 at San Diego, Calif.   Height 6:08.   Weight 220.

High School—San Diego, Calif., Morse.

College—Wichita State University, Wichita, Kan.

Drafted by Detroit on first round as an undergraduate, 1982 (9th pick).

Traded by Detroit with the draft rights to Antoine Carr and 1986 and 1987 2nd round draft choices to Atlanta for Dan Roundfield, June 18, 1984.

—COLLEGIATE RECORD—

Year	G.	Min.	FGA	FGM	Pct.	FTA	FTM	Pct.	Reb.	Pts.	Avg.
79-80	29	914	346	189	.546	127	79	.622	294	457	15.8
80-81	33	1108	452	246	.544	194	120	.619	376	612	18.5
81-82	29	902	312	162	.519	125	78	.624	295	402	13.9
Totals	91	2924	1110	597	.538	446	277	.621	965	1471	16.2

Sea.—Team	G.	Min.	FGA	FGM	Pct.	FTA	FTM	Pct.	Off.	Def.	Tot.	Ast.	PF	Dq.	Stl.	Blk.	Pts.	Avg.
									—Rebounds—									
82-83—Detroit	62	879	270	131	.485	147	84	.571	104	128	232	52	125	2	23	36	346	5.6
83-84—Detroit	80	1746	436	229	.525	186	125	.672	234	311	545	109	281	7	44	78	583	7.3
84-85—Atlanta	74	2017	552	291	.527	222	145	.653	230	336	566	104	231	3	70	69	727	9.8
85-86—Atlanta	81	1945	551	294	.534	242	164	.678	193	341	534	72	260	5	76	39	752	9.3
86-87—Atlanta	82	1848	496	251	.506	212	155	.731	219	314	533	40	261	4	48	68	657	8.0
87-88—Atlanta	82	2135	564	314	.557	246	190	.772	228	276	504	71	287	5	52	84	819	10.0
Totals	461	10570	2869	1510	.526	1255	863	.688	1208	1706	2914	448	1445	26	313	374	3884	8.4

Three-Point Field Goals: 1982-83, 0-for-1. 1983-84, 0-for-3. 1984-85, 0-for-2. 1985-86, 0-for-1. 1986-87, 0-for-3. 1987-88, 1-for-2 (.500). Totals, 1-for-12 (.083).

NBA PLAYOFF RECORD

Sea.—Team	G.	Min.	FGA	FGM	Pct.	FTA	FTM	Pct.	Off.	Def.	Tot.	Ast.	PF	Dq.	Stl.	Blk.	Pts.	Avg.
									—Rebounds—									
83-84—Detroit	5	101	19	15	.789	16	10	.625	11	13	24	1	15	0	1	2	40	8.0
85-86—Atlanta	9	180	37	22	.595	9	7	.778	15	26	41	3	23	0	4	9	52	5.8
86-87—Atlanta	9	108	18	7	.389	18	14	.778	12	22	34	3	21	0	0	3	28	3.1
87-88—Atlanta	12	163	50	24	.480	16	12	.750	14	12	26	7	25	0	5	5	60	5.0
Totals	35	552	124	68	.548	59	43	.729	52	73	125	14	84	0	10	19	180	5.1

Three-Point Field Goals: 1985-86, 1-for-1 (1.000). 1986-87, 0-for-1. Totals, 1-for-2 (.500).

RALPH ADOLPHUS LEWIS

Born March 28, 1963 at Philadelphia, Pa. Height 6:06. Weight 200.

High School—Philadelphia, Pa., Frankford.

College—La Salle University, Philadelphia, Pa.

Drafted by Boston on sixth round, 1985 (139th pick).

Draft rights relinquished by Boston, September 30, 1986.
Signed by Detroit as a free agent, October 6, 1987.
Selected from Detroit by Charlotte in NBA expansion draft, June 23, 1988.
Played in Continental Basketball Association with Bay State Bombardiers, 1985-86, and Pensacola Tornados, 1986-87.

—COLLEGIATE RECORD—

Year	G.	Min.	FGA	FGM	Pct.	FTA	FTM	Pct.	Reb.	Pts.	Avg.
81-82	25	....	174	83	.477	100	61	.610	158	227	9.1
82-83	32	1071	339	156	.460	158	106	.671	259	418	13.1
83-84	31	....	404	237	.587	220	164	.745	281	638	20.6
84-85	28	....	360	201	.558	165	122	.739	268	524	18.7
Totals	116	....	1277	677	.530	643	453	.705	966	1807	15.6

CBA REGULAR SEASON RECORD

Sea.—Team	G.	Min.	FGM	FGA	Pct.	FGM	FGA	Pct.	FTM	FTA	Pct.	Reb.	Ast.	Pts.	Avg.
			—2-Point—			—3-Point—									
85-86—Bay State	38	444	74	151	.490	0	2	.000	41	74	.554	89	23	189	5.0
86-87—Pensacola..................	48	1742	353	684	.516	1	9	.111	296	388	.762	293	104	1005	20.9
Totals	86	2186	427	835	.511	1	11	.091	337	462	.729	382	127	1194	13.9

NBA REGULAR SEASON RECORD

Sea.—Team	G.	Min.	FGA	FGM	Pct.	FTA	FTM	Pct.	Off.	Def.	Tot.	Ast.	PF	Dq.	Stl.	Blk.	Pts.	Avg.
									—Rebounds—									
87-88—Detroit	50	310	87	27	.310	48	29	.604	17	34	51	14	36	0	13	4	83	1.7

Three-Point Field Goals: 1987-88, 0-for-1.

NBA PLAYOFF RECORD

Sea.—Team	G.	Min.	FGA	FGM	Pct.	FTA	FTM	Pct.	Off.	Def.	Tot.	Ast.	PF	Dq.	Stl.	Blk.	Pts.	Avg.
									—Rebounds—									
1987-88—Detroit	10	17	6	2	.333	0	0	.000	3	5	8	1	2	0	0	0	4	0.4

Three-Point Field Goals: 1987-88, 0-for-1.

REGGIE LEWIS

Born November 21, 1965 at Baltimore, Md. Height 6:07. Weight 195.

High School—Baltimore, Md., Dunbar.

College—Northeastern University, Boston, Mass.

Drafted by Boston on first round, 1987 (22nd pick).

—COLLEGIATE RECORD—

Year	G.	Min.	FGA	FGM	Pct.	FTA	FTM	Pct.	Reb.	Pts.	Avg.
83-84	32	1030	447	236	.528	144	99	.688	198	571	17.8

Year	G.	Min.	FGA	FGM	Pct.	FTA	FTM	Pct.	Reb.	Pts.	Avg.
84-85	31	1082	585	294	.503	213	159	.746	241	747	24.1
85-86	30	1118	559	265	.474	229	184	.803	279	714	23.8
86-87	29	957	507	248	.489	197	150	.761	246	676	23.3
Totals	122	4187	2098	1043	.497	783	592	.756	964	2708	22.2

Three-Point Field Goals: 1986-87, 30-for-91 (.330).

NBA REGULAR SEASON RECORD

Sea.—Team	G.	Min.	FGA	FGM	Pct.	FTA	FTM	Pct.	Off.	Def.	Tot.	Ast.	PF	Dq.	Stl.	Blk.	Pts.	Avg.
87-88—Boston	49	405	193	90	.466	57	40	.702	28	35	63	26	54	0	16	15	220	4.5

Three-Point Field Goals: 1987-88, 0-for-4.

NBA PLAYOFF RECORD

Sea.—Team	G.	Min.	FGA	FGM	Pct.	FTA	FTM	Pct.	Off.	Def.	Tot.	Ast.	PF	Dq.	Stl.	Blk.	Pts.	Avg.
87-88—Boston	12	70	34	13	.382	5	3	.600	9	7	16	4	13	0	3	2	29	2.4

Three-Point Field Goals: 1987-88, 0-for-1.

ALTON LAVELLE LISTER

Born October 1, 1958 at Dallas, Tex.   Height 7:00.   Weight 240.

High School—Dallas, Tex., Woodrow Wilson.

Colleges—San Jacinto College, Pasadena, Tex., and
Arizona State University, Tempe, Ariz.

Drafted by Milwaukee on first round, 1981 (21st pick).

Traded by Milwaukee with 1987 and 1989 1st round draft choices to Seattle for Jack Sikma and 1987 and 1989 2nd round draft choices, July 1, 1986.

—COLLEGIATE RECORD—
San Jacinto

Year	G.	Min.	FGA	FGM	Pct.	FTA	FTM	Pct.	Reb.	Pts.	Avg.
76-77	40	....	....	....		....	....	....	640	680	17.0
77-78					Did Not Play—Redshirted						

Arizona State

Year	G.	Min.	FGA	FGM	Pct.	FTA	FTM	Pct.	Reb.	Pts.	Avg.
78-79	29	584	209	104	.498	84	47	.560	194	255	8.8
79-80	27	793	264	133	.504	104	58	.558	231	324	12.0
80-81	26	845	282	158	.560	123	85	.691	251	401	15.4
Totals	82	2222	755	395	.523	311	190	.611	676	980	12.0

NBA REGULAR SEASON RECORD

Sea.—Team	G.	Min.	FGA	FGM	Pct.	FTA	FTM	Pct.	Off.	Def.	Tot.	Ast.	PF	Dq.	Stl.	Blk.	Pts.	Avg.
81-82—Milwaukee	80	1186	287	149	.519	123	64	.520	108	279	387	84	239	4	18	118	362	4.5
82-83—Milwaukee	80	1885	514	272	.529	242	130	.537	168	400	568	111	328	18	50	177	674	8.4
83-84—Milwaukee	82	1955	512	256	.500	182	114	.626	156	447	603	110	327	11	41	140	626	7.6
84-85—Milwaukee	81	2091	598	322	.538	262	154	.588	219	428	647	127	287	5	49	167	798	9.9
85-86—Milwaukee	81	1812	577	318	.551	266	160	.602	199	393	592	101	300	8	49	142	796	9.8
86-87—Seattle	75	2288	687	346	.504	265	179	.675	223	482	705	110	289	11	32	180	871	11.6
87-88—Seattle	82	1812	343	173	.504	188	114	.606	200	427	627	58	319	8	27	140	461	5.6
Totals	561	13029	3518	1836	.522	1528	915	.599	1273	2856	4129	701	2089	65	266	1064	4588	8.2

Three-Point Field Goals: 1984-85, 0-for-1. 1985-86, 0-for-2. 1986-87, 0-for-1. 1987-88, 1-for-2 (.500). Totals, 1-for-6 (.167).

NBA PLAYOFF RECORD

Sea.—Team	G.	Min.	FGA	FGM	Pct.	FTA	FTM	Pct.	Off.	Def.	Tot.	Ast.	PF	Dq.	Stl.	Blk.	Pts.	Avg.
81-82—Milwaukee	6	112	24	14	.583	7	5	.714	6	21	27	5	23	0	2	15	33	5.5
82-83—Milwaukee	9	206	63	27	.429	5	4	.800	21	40	61	11	30	1	9	15	58	6.4
83-84—Milwaukee	16	368	78	39	.500	48	30	.625	26	70	96	10	63	2	5	24	108	6.8
84-85—Milwaukee	8	203	60	27	.450	32	15	.469	27	35	62	15	36	1	6	15	69	8.6
85-86—Milwaukee	14	335	103	66	.641	58	35	.603	37	59	96	12	56	3	7	22	167	11.9
86-87—Seattle	9	206	50	20	.400	20	14	.700	29	27	56	7	37	3	7	13	54	6.0
87-88—Seattle	5	77	17	12	.706	5	4	.800	9	20	29	5	17	0	1	5	28	5.6
Totals	67	1507	395	205	.519	175	107	.611	155	272	427	65	262	10	37	109	517	7.7

Three-Point Field Goals: 1982-83, 0-for-1. 1985-86, 0-for-1. Totals, 0-for-2.

Member of U.S. Olympic team, 1980.

—DID YOU KNOW—

That the New Jersey Nets have had fewer victories than the previous season each of the last six years? The Milwaukee Bucks and Philadelphia 76ers have had fewer wins than the previous season each of the last four years.

BRAD ALLEN LOHAUS

Born September 29, 1964 at New Ulm, Minn.   Height 7:00.   Weight 235.

High School—Phoenix, Ariz., Greenway.

College—University of Iowa, Iowa City, Ia.

Drafted by Boston on second round, 1987 (45th pick).

—COLLEGIATE RECORD—

Year	G.	Min.	FGA	FGM	Pct.	FTA	FTM	Pct.	Reb.	Pts.	Avg.
82-83	20	....	29	9	.310	13	7	.538	11	26	1.3
83-84	28	626	193	78	.404	52	35	.673	146	191	6.8
84-85				Did Not Play—Redshirted							
85-86	32	407	102	44	.431	34	27	.794	101	115	3.6
86-87	35	943	276	149	.540	104	72	.692	268	395	11.3
Totals	115	....	600	280	.467	203	141	.695	526	727	6.3

Three-Point Field Goals: 1982-83, 1-for-1 (1.000). 1986-87, 25-for-72 (.347). Totals, 26-for-73 (.356).

NBA REGULAR SEASON RECORD

									—Rebounds—								
Sea.—Team	G.	Min.	FGA	FGM	Pct.	FTA	FTM	Pct.	Off.	Def.	Tot.	Ast.	PF	Dq.	Stl.	Blk.	Pts.	Avg.
87-88—Boston	70	718	246	122	.496	62	50	.806	46	92	138	49	123	1	20	41	297	4.2

Three-Point Field Goals: 1987-88, 3-for-13 (.231).

NBA PLAYOFF RECORD

									—Rebounds—								
Sea.—Team	G.	Min.	FGA	FGM	Pct.	FTA	FTM	Pct.	Off.	Def.	Tot.	Ast.	PF	Dq.	Stl.	Blk.	Pts.	Avg.
87-88—Boston	9	26	11	8	.727	0	0	.000	1	3	4	0	4	0	0	1	16	1.8

Three-Point Field Goals: 1987-88, 0-for-2.

JOHN EDDIE LONG

Born August 28, 1956 at Romulus, Mich.   Height 6:05.   Weight 200.

High School—Romulus, Mich.

College—University of Detroit, Detroit, Mich.

Drafted by Detroit on second round, 1978 (29th pick).

Traded by Detroit to Seattle for 1987 and 1991 2nd round draft choices, September 30, 1986.
Traded by Seattle with a future 2nd round draft choice to Indiana for Russ Schoene and Terence Stansbury, October 2, 1986.

—COLLEGIATE RECORD—

Year	G.	Min.	FGA	FGM	Pct.	FTA	FTM	Pct.	Reb.	Pts.	Avg.
74-75	26	654	419	200	.477	58	45	.776	168	445	17.1
75-76	27	872	524	230	.439	95	72	.758	240	532	19.7
76-77	28	891	508	245	.482	102	78	.765	189	568	20.3
77-78	29	798	491	265	.540	114	92	.807	218	622	21.4
Totals	110	3215	1942	940	.484	369	287	.778	815	2167	19.7

NBA REGULAR SEASON RECORD

									—Rebounds—								
Sea.—Team	G.	Min.	FGA	FGM	Pct.	FTA	FTM	Pct.	Off.	Def.	Tot.	Ast.	PF	Dq.	Stl.	Blk.	Pts.	Avg.
78-79—Detroit	82	2498	1240	581	.469	190	157	.826	127	139	266	121	224	1	102	19	1319	16.1
79-80—Detroit	69	2364	1164	588	.505	194	160	.825	152	185	337	206	221	4	129	26	1337	19.4
80-81—Detroit	59	1750	957	441	.461	184	160	.870	95	102	197	106	164	3	95	22	1044	17.7
81-82—Detroit	69	2211	1294	637	.492	275	238	.865	95	162	257	148	173	0	65	25	1514	21.9
82-83—Detroit	70	1485	692	312	.451	146	111	.760	56	124	180	105	130	1	44	12	737	10.5
83-84—Detroit	82	2514	1155	545	.472	275	243	.884	139	150	289	205	199	1	93	18	1334	16.3
84-85—Detroit	66	1820	885	431	.487	123	106	.862	81	109	190	130	139	0	71	14	973	14.7
85-86—Detroit	62	1176	548	264	.482	104	89	.856	47	51	98	82	92	0	41	13	620	10.0
86-87—Indiana	80	2265	1170	490	.419	246	219	.890	75	142	217	258	167	1	96	8	1218	15.2
87-88—Indiana	81	2022	879	417	.474	183	166	.907	72	157	229	173	164	1	84	11	1034	12.8
Totals	720	20105	9984	4706	.471	1920	1649	.859	939	1321	2260	1534	1673	12	820	168	11130	15.5

Three-Point Field Goals: 1979-80, 1-for-12 (083). 1980-81, 2-for-11 (.182). 1981-82, 2-for-15 (.133). 1982-83, 2-for-7 (.286). 1983-84, 1-for-5 (.200). 1984-85, 5-for-15 (.333). 1985-86, 3-for-16 (.188). 1986-87, 19-for-67 (.284). 1987-88, 34-for-77 (.442). Totals, 69-for-225 (.307).

NBA PLAYOFF RECORD

									—Rebounds—								
Sea.—Team	G.	Min.	FGA	FGM	Pct.	FTA	FTM	Pct.	Off.	Def.	Tot.	Ast.	PF	Dq.	Stl.	Blk.	Pts.	Avg.
83-84—Detroit	5	149	55	20	.364	15	15	1.000	7	4	11	2	15	0	7	0	55	11.0
84-85—Detroit	9	255	105	48	.457	15	15	1.000	10	7	17	13	22	0	14	2	112	12.4
85-86—Detroit	1	13	5	2	.400	3	3	1.000	0	1	1	0	1	0	1	0	7	7.0
86-87—Indiana	4	109	52	16	.308	13	11	.846	2	4	6	9	16	0	6	0	44	11.0
Totals	19	526	217	86	.396	46	44	.957	19	16	35	24	54	0	28	2	218	11.5

Three-Point Field Goals: 1983-84, 0-for-1. 1984-85, 1-for-4 (.250). 1986-87, 1-for-6 (.167). Totals, 2-for-11 (.182).
Uncle of Grant Long, rookie forward with Miami Heat.

JOHN HARDING LUCAS JR.

Born October 31, 1953 at Durham, N. C.   Height 6:03.   Weight 185.
High School—Durham, N. C., Hillside.
College—University of Maryland, College Park, Md.
Drafted by Houston on first round, 1976 (1st pick).

Awarded from Houston with cash to Golden State as compensation for earlier signing of Veteran Free Agent Rick Barry, September 5, 1978.
Traded by Golden State to Washington for 1982 and 1984 2nd round draft choices, October 19, 1981.
Waived by Washington, January 25, 1983; signed by Cleveland as a free agent, August 29, 1983.
Waived by Cleveland, September 21, 1983; signed by San Antonio as a free agent, December 4, 1983.
Traded by San Antonio with a 1985 3rd round draft choice to Houston for James Bailey, a 1985 2nd round draft choice and cash, October 4, 1984.
Waived by Houston, December 10, 1984; re-signed by Houston, February 19, 1985.
Waived by Houston, March 14, 1986; signed by Milwaukee as a free agent, January 17, 1987.
Played in Continental Basketball Association with Lancaster Lightning, 1983-84.

—COLLEGIATE RECORD—

Year	G.	Min.	FGA	FGM	Pct.	FTA	FTM	Pct.	Reb.	Pts.	Avg.
72-73	30	....	353	190	.538	64	45	.703	83	425	14.2
73-74	28	....	495	253	.511	77	58	.753	82	564	20.1
74-75	24	....	339	186	.549	116	97	.836	100	469	19.5
75-76	28	....	456	233	.511	117	91	.778	109	557	19.9
Totals	110	....	1643	862	.525	374	291	.778	374	2015	18.3

CBA REGULAR SEASON RECORD

Sea.—Team	G.	Min.	2-Point FGM	FGA	Pct.	3-Point FGM	FGA	Pct.	FTM	FTA	Pct.	Reb.	Ast.	Pts.	Avg.
83-84—Lancaster	2	48	11	17	.647	1	1	1.000	6	6	1.000	1	8	31	15.5

NBA REGULAR SEASON RECORD

Sea.—Team	G.	Min.	FGA	FGM	Pct.	FTA	FTM	Pct.	Off.	Def.	Tot.	Ast.	PF	Dq.	Stl.	Blk.	Pts.	Avg.
76-77—Houston	82	2531	814	388	.477	171	135	.789	55	164	219	463	174	0	125	19	911	11.1
77-78—Houston	82	2933	947	412	.435	250	193	.772	51	204	255	768	208	1	160	9	1017	12.4
78-79—Golden State	82	3095	1146	530	.462	321	264	.822	65	182	247	762	229	1	152	9	1324	16.1
79-80—Golden State	80	2763	830	388	.467	289	222	.768	61	159	220	602	196	2	138	3	1010	12.6
80-81—Golden State	66	1919	506	222	.439	145	107	.738	34	120	154	464	140	1	83	2	555	8.4
81-82—Washington	79	1940	618	263	.426	176	138	.784	40	126	166	551	105	0	95	6	666	8.4
82-83—Washington	35	386	131	62	.473	42	21	.500	8	21	29	102	18	0	25	1	145	4.1
83-84—San Antonio	63	1807	595	275	.462	157	120	.764	23	157	180	673	123	1	92	5	689	10.9
84-85—Houston	47	1158	446	206	.462	129	103	.798	21	64	85	318	78	0	62	2	536	11.4
85-86—Houston	65	2120	818	365	.446	298	231	.775	33	110	143	571	124	0	77	5	1006	15.5
86-87—Milwaukee	43	1358	624	285	.457	174	137	.787	29	96	125	290	82	0	71	6	753	17.5
87-88—Milwaukee	81	1766	631	281	.445	162	130	.802	29	130	159	392	102	1	88	3	743	9.2
Totals	805	23776	8106	3677	.454	2314	1801	.778	449	1533	1982	5956	1579	7	1168	70	9355	11.6

Three-Point Field Goals: 1979-80, 12-for-42 (.286). 1980-81, 4-for-24 (.167). 1981-82, 2-for-22 (.091). 1982-83, 0-for-5. 1983-84, 19-for-69 (.275). 1984-85, 21-for-66 (.318). 1985-86, 45-for-146 (.308). 1986-87, 46-for-126 (.365). 1987-88, 51-for-151 (.338). Totals, 200-for-651 (.307).

NBA PLAYOFF RECORD

Sea.—Team	G.	Min.	FGA	FGM	Pct.	FTA	FTM	Pct.	Off.	Def.	Tot.	Ast.	PF	Dq.	Stl.	Blk.	Pts.	Avg.
76-77—Houston	12	430	139	75	.540	34	26	.765	4	29	33	83	33	1	24	4	176	14.7
81-82—Washington	7	74	26	14	.538	3	2	.667	0	8	8	20	6	0	3	1	31	4.4
84-85—Houston	5	152	80	26	.325	22	14	.636	7	14	21	27	14	0	6	0	68	13.6
86-87—Milwaukee	12	362	150	68	.453	48	39	.813	4	21	25	62	17	0	14	1	187	15.6
87-88—Milwaukee	5	80	27	10	.370	9	6	.667	5	3	8	19	5	0	5	0	29	5.8
Totals	41	1098	422	193	.457	116	87	.750	20	75	95	211	75	1	52	6	491	12.0

Three-Point Field Goals: 1981-82, 1-for-3 (.333). 1984-85, 2-for-14 (.143). 1986-87, 12-for-36 (.333). 1987-88, 3-for-13 (.231). Totals, 18-for-66 (.273).

Named to NBA All-Rookie Team, 1977. . . . Holds NBA record for most assists in one quarter, 14, vs. Denver, April 15, 1984. . . . Played World Team Tennis with Golden Gaters and New Orleans Nets, 1977 and 1978. . . . Named to THE SPORTING NEWS All-America First Team, 1975 and 1976. . . . THE SPORTING NEWS All-America Second Team, 1974.

—DID YOU KNOW—

That Boston's Larry Bird has shot better than 50 percent from the floor in the playoffs only two times in his nine NBA seasons? He shot .524 from the field in 23 playoff games in 1984 and .517 in 18 playoff games in 1986. The Celtics won the NBA title both years.

MAURICE LUCAS

Born February 18, 1952 at Pittsburgh, Pa.   Height 6:09.   Weight 238.

High School—Pittsburgh, Pa., Schenley.

College—Marquette University, Milwaukee, Wis.

Drafted by Chicago on first round as hardship case, 1974 (14th pick).

Selected by Carolina on first round of ABA undergraduate draft, 1973; Carolina franchise transferred to St. Louis, 1974.

Traded by St. Louis to Kentucky for Caldwell Jones, December 17, 1975.

Selected by Portland NBA from Kentucky in ABA dispersal draft, August 5, 1976.

Traded by Portland with 1980 and 1981 1st round draft choices to New Jersey for Calvin Natt, February 8, 1980.

Traded by New Jersey to New York in exchange for the Knicks not exercising their right of first refusal on Ray Williams, October 25, 1981.

Traded by New York to Phoenix for Leonard (Truck) Robinson, July 7, 1982.

Traded by Phoenix to Los Angeles Lakers for 1988 and 1989 2nd round draft choices, August 19, 1985.

Waived by Los Angeles Lakers, September 26, 1986; claimed by Seattle, September 30, 1986.

Signed by Portland as a Veteran Free Agent, November 10, 1987; Seattle agreed not to exercise its right of first refusal in exchange for a 1990 2nd round draft choice.

—COLLEGIATE RECORD—

Year	G.	Min.	FGA	FGM	Pct.	FTA	FTM	Pct.	Reb.	Pts.	Avg.
71-72†	17	....	345	203	.588	112	81	.723	286	487	28.6
72-73	29	....	374	186	.497	97	76	.784	315	448	15.4
73-74	31	....	429	211	.492	94	69	.734	328	491	15.8
Varsity Totals	60	....	803	397	.494	191	145	.759	643	939	15.7

ABA REGULAR SEASON RECORD

Sea.—Team	G.	Min.	2-Point FGM	FGA	Pct.	3-Point FGM	FGA	Pct.	FTM	FTA	Pct.	Reb.	Ast.	Pts.	Avg.
74-75—St. Louis	80	2464	436	928	.470	2	9	.222	180	229	.786	816	287	1058	13.2
75-76—St.L.-Ky.	86	2861	617	1328	.465	3	18	.167	217	283	.767	970	224	1460	17.0
Totals	166	5325	1053	2256	.467	5	27	.185	397	512	.775	1786	511	2518	15.2

ABA PLAYOFF RECORD

Sea.—Team	G.	Min.	2-Point FGM	FGA	Pct.	3-Point FGM	FGA	Pct.	FTM	FTA	Pct.	Reb.	Ast.	Pts.	Avg.
74-75—St. Louis	10	375	68	152	.447	0	1	.000	27	41	.659	147	50	163	16.3
75-76—Kentucky	10	330	75	152	.493	0	0	.000	15	19	.789	108	22	165	16.5
Totals	20	705	143	304	.470	0	1	.000	42	60	.700	255	72	328	16.4

ABA ALL-STAR GAME RECORD

Sea.—Team	Min.	2-Point FGM	FGA	Pct.	3-Point FGM	FGA	Pct.	FTM	FTA	Pct.	Reb.	Ast.	Pts.	Avg.
1976—Kentucky	14	2	5	.400	0	0	.000	1	1	1.000	5	3	5	5.0

NBA REGULAR SEASON RECORD

Sea.—Team	G.	Min.	FGA	FGM	Pct.	FTA	FTM	Pct.	Rebounds Off.	Def.	Tot.	Ast.	PF	Dq.	Stl.	Blk.	Pts.	Avg.
76-77—Portland	79	2863	1357	632	.466	438	335	.765	271	628	899	229	294	6	83	56	1599	20.2
77-78—Portland	68	2119	989	453	.458	270	207	.767	186	435	621	173	221	3	61	56	1113	16.4
78-79—Portland	69	2462	1208	568	.470	345	270	.783	192	524	716	215	254	3	66	81	1406	20.4
79-80—Port.-N.J.	63	1884	813	371	.456	239	179	.749	143	394	537	208	223	2	42	62	923	14.7
80-81—New Jersey	68	2162	835	404	.484	254	191	.752	153	422	575	173	260	3	57	59	999	14.7
81-82—New York	80	2671	1001	505	.504	349	253	.725	274	629	903	179	309	4	68	70	1263	15.8
82-83—Phoenix	77	2586	1045	495	.474	356	278	.781	201	598	799	219	274	5	56	43	1269	16.5
83-84—Phoenix	75	2309	908	451	.497	383	293	.765	208	517	725	203	235	2	55	39	1195	15.9
84-85—Phoenix	63	1670	727	346	.476	200	150	.750	138	419	557	145	183	0	39	17	842	13.4
85-86—L.A. Lakers	77	1750	653	302	.462	230	180	.783	164	402	566	84	253	1	45	24	785	10.2
86-87—Seattle	63	1120	388	175	.451	187	150	.802	88	219	307	65	171	1	34	21	500	7.9
87-88—Portland	73	1191	373	168	.450	148	109	.736	101	214	315	94	188	0	33	10	445	6.1
Totals	855	24787	10297	4870	.473	3399	2595	.763	2119	5401	7520	1987	2865	30	639	538	12339	14.4

Three-Point Field Goals: 1979-80, 2-for-9 (.222). 1980-81, 0-for-2. 1981-82, 0-for-3, 1982-83, 1-for-3 (.333). 1983-84, 0-for-5. 1984-85, 0-for-4. 1985-86, 1-for-2 (.500). 1986-87, 0-for-5. 1987-88, 0-for-3. Totals, 4-for-36 (.111).

NBA PLAYOFF RECORD

Sea.—Team	G.	Min.	FGA	FGM	Pct.	FTA	FTM	Pct.	Rebounds Off.	Def.	Tot.	Ast.	PF	Dq.	Stl.	Blk.	Pts.	Avg.
76-77—Portland	19	731	316	164	.519	101	75	.743	43	145	188	79	79	3	28	23	403	21.2
77-78—Portland	6	233	108	46	.426	19	11	.579	19	56	75	15	28	0	4	2	103	17.2
78-79—Portland	3	104	41	14	.341	7	5	.714	2	30	32	18	12	0	3	1	33	11.0
82-83—Phoenix	2	57	21	12	.571	4	2	.500	5	7	12	8	5	0	3	0	26	13.0
83-84—Phoenix	17	570	227	116	.511	78	63	.808	42	127	169	61	66	2	12	8	295	17.4
84-85—Phoenix	3	84	47	22	.468	19	15	.789	12	21	33	10	12	0	2	2	59	19.7
85-86—L.A. Lakers	14	319	112	59	.527	19	14	.737	29	62	91	10	53	0	6	5	132	9.4
86-87—Seattle	14	265	90	35	.389	38	28	.737	19	46	65	19	43	1	12	5	98	7.0

Sea.—Team	G.	Min.	FGA	FGM	Pct.	FTA	FTM	Pct.	Off.	Def.	Tot.	Ast.	PF	Dq.	Stl.	Blk.	Pts.	Avg.
87-88—Portland	4	63	13	4	.308	4	2	.500	9	16	25	5	12	0	1	0	10	2.5
Totals	82	2426	975	472	.484	289	215	.744	180	510	690	225	310	6	71	46	1159	14.1

Three-Point Field Goals: 1986-87, 0-for-1. Totals, 0-for-1.

NBA ALL-STAR GAME RECORD

							—Rebounds—							
Season—Team	Min.	FGA	FGM	Pct.	FTA	FTM	Pct.	Off.	Def.	Tot.	Ast.	PF	Dq.	Stl.	Blk.	Pts.
1977—Portland	11	9	3	.333	0	0	.000	2	2	4	2	2	0	1	1	6
1978—Portland	33	13	6	.462	0	0	.000	6	7	13	4	2	0	1	0	12
1979—Portland	19	10	4	.400	2	2	1.000	1	6	7	1	5	0	0	0	10
1983—Phoenix	27	8	3	.375	1	0	.000	1	6	7	1	1	0	0	0	6
Totals	90	40	16	.400	3	2	.667	10	21	31	8	10	0	2	1	34

COMBINED ABA AND NBA REGULAR SEASON RECORDS

								—Rebounds—								
	G.	Min.	FGA	FGM	Pct.	FTA	FTM	Pct.	Off.	Def.	Tot.	Ast.	PF	Dq.	Stl.	Blk.	Pts.	Avg.
Totals	1021	30112	12580	5928	.471	3911	2992	.765	2698	6608	9306	2498	3498	30	803	659	14857	14.6

Named to All-NBA Second Team, 1978. . . . NBA All-Defensive First Team, 1978. . . . NBA All-Defensive Second Team, 1979. . . . Member of NBA championship team, 1977.

DERRICK ALLEN MAHORN
(Ricky)

Born September 21, 1958 at Hartford, Conn.   Height 6:10.   Weight 255.

High School—Hartford, Conn., Weaver.

College—Hampton Institute, Hampton, Va.

Drafted by Washington on second round, 1980 (35th pick).

Traded by Washington with Mike Gibson to Detroit for Dan Roundfield, June 17, 1985.

—COLLEGIATE RECORD—

Year	G.	Min.	FGA	FGM	Pct.	FTA	FTM	Pct.	Reb.	Pts.	Avg.
76-77	28	....	159	65	.409	44	29	.659	168	159	5.7
77-78	30	....	570	291	.511	202	137	.678	377	719	24.0
78-79	30	....	489	274	.560	200	137	.685	430	685	22.8
79-80	31	1123	621	352	.567	220	151	.686	490	855	27.6
Totals	119	....	1839	982	.534	666	454	.682	1465	2418	20.3

NBA REGULAR SEASON RECORD

									—Rebounds—									
Sea.—Team	G.	Min.	FGA	FGM	Pct.	FTA	FTM	Pct.	Off.	Def.	Tot.	Ast.	PF	Dq.	Stl.	Blk.	Pts.	Avg.
80-81—Washington	52	696	219	111	.507	40	27	.675	67	148	215	25	134	3	21	44	249	4.8
81-82—Washington	80	2664	816	414	.507	234	148	.632	149	555	704	150	349	12	57	138	976	12.2
82-83—Washington	82	3023	768	376	.490	254	146	.575	171	608	779	115	335	13	86	148	898	11.0
83-84—Washington	82	2701	605	307	.507	192	125	.651	169	569	738	131	358	14	62	123	739	9.0
84-85—Washington	77	2072	413	206	.499	104	71	.683	150	458	608	121	308	11	59	104	483	6.3
85-86—Detroit	80	1442	345	157	.455	119	81	.681	121	291	412	64	261	4	40	61	395	4.9
86-87—Detroit	63	1278	322	144	.447	117	96	.821	93	282	375	38	221	4	32	50	384	6.1
87-88—Detroit	67	1963	481	276	.574	217	164	.756	159	406	565	60	262	4	43	42	717	10.7
Totals	583	15839	3969	1991	.502	1277	858	.672	1079	3317	4396	704	2228	65	400	710	4841	8.3

Three-Point Field Goals: 1981-82, 0-for-3. 1982-83, 0-for-3. 1985-86, 0-for-1. 1987-88, 1-for-2 (.500). Totals, 1-for-9 (.111).

NBA PLAYOFF RECORD

									—Rebounds—									
Sea.—Team	G.	Min.	FGA	FGM	Pct.	FTA	FTM	Pct.	Off.	Def.	Tot.	Ast.	PF	Dq.	Stl.	Blk.	Pts.	Avg.
81-82—Washington	7	242	73	32	.438	14	10	.714	14	47	61	13	30	1	10	5	74	10.6
83-84—Washington	4	154	25	15	.600	10	8	.800	7	36	43	6	19	0	1	6	38	9.5
84-85—Washington	4	41	8	4	.500	4	4	1.000	2	5	7	0	9	0	0	3	12	3.0
85-86—Detroit	4	61	13	5	.385	2	2	1.000	3	9	12	0	14	0	1	0	12	3.0
86-87—Detroit	15	483	109	59	.541	35	28	.800	42	100	142	5	60	1	6	11	146	9.7
87-88—Detroit	23	409	90	31	.344	19	13	.684	19	70	89	13	64	2	5	10	75	3.3
Totals	57	1390	318	146	.459	84	65	.774	87	267	354	37	196	4	23	35	357	6.3

Three-Point Field Goals: 1983-84, 0-for-1. 1986-87, 0-for-1. Totals, 0-for-2.

Led NCAA Division II in rebounding, 1980.

JEFFREY NIGEL MALONE
(Jeff)

Born June 28, 1961 at Mobile, Ala.   Height 6:04.   Weight 205.

High School—Macon, Ga., Southwest.

College—Mississippi State University, Mississippi State, Miss.

Drafted by Washington on first round, 1983 (10th pick).

—COLLEGIATE RECORD—

Year	G.	Min.	FGA	FGM	Pct.	FTA	FTM	Pct.	Reb.	Pts.	Avg.
79-80	27	781	303	139	.459	51	42	.824	90	320	11.9
80-81	27	999	447	219	.490	128	105	.820	113	543	20.1
81-82	27	1001	410	225	.549	70	52	.743	111	502	18.6
82-83	29	1070	608	323	.531	159	131	.824	106	777	26.8
Totals	110	3851	1768	906	.512	408	330	.809	420	2142	19.5

NBA REGULAR SEASON RECORD

Sea.—Team	G.	Min.	FGA	FGM	Pct.	FTA	FTM	Pct.	Off.	Def.	Tot.	Ast.	PF	Dq.	Stl.	Blk.	Pts.	Avg.
83-84—Washington	81	1976	918	408	.444	172	142	.826	57	98	155	151	162	1	23	13	982	12.1
84-85—Washington	76	2613	1213	605	.499	250	211	.844	60	146	206	184	176	1	52	9	1436	18.9
85-86—Washington	80	2992	1522	735	.483	371	322	.868	66	222	288	191	180	2	70	12	1795	22.4
86-87—Washington	80	2763	1509	689	.457	425	376	.885	50	168	218	298	154	0	75	13	1758	22.0
87-88—Washington	80	2655	1360	648	.476	380	335	.882	44	162	206	237	198	1	51	13	1641	20.5
Totals	397	12999	6522	3085	.473	1598	1386	.867	277	796	1073	1061	870	5	271	60	7612	19.2

Three-Point Field Goals: 1983-84, 24-for-74 (.324). 1984-85, 15-for-72 (.208). 1985-86, 3-for-17 (.176). 1986-87, 4-for-26 (.154). 1987-88, 10-for-24 (.417). Totals, 56-for-213 (.263).

NBA PLAYOFF RECORD

Sea.—Team	G.	Min.	FGA	FGM	Pct.	FTA	FTM	Pct.	Off.	Def.	Tot.	Ast.	PF	Dq.	Stl.	Blk.	Pts.	Avg.
83-84—Washington	4	71	26	12	.462	0	0	.000	2	3	5	2	6	0	1	0	24	6.0
84-85—Washington	4	126	56	27	.482	13	10	.769	3	3	6	8	14	1	5	0	65	16.3
85-86—Washington	5	197	103	42	.408	29	26	.897	4	12	16	17	13	0	7	3	110	22.0
86-87—Washington	3	105	46	17	.370	11	11	1.000	1	6	7	9	8	0	1	0	45	15.0
87-88—Washington	5	199	97	50	.515	37	28	.757	3	14	17	11	16	0	5	5	128	25.6
Totals	21	698	328	148	.451	90	75	.833	13	38	51	47	57	1	19	8	372	17.7

Three-Point Field Goals: 1983-84, 0-for-1. 1984-85, 1-for-3 (.333). 1985-86, 0-for-2. 1987-88, 0-for-1. Totals, 2-for-7 (.286).

NBA ALL-STAR GAME RECORD

Season—Team	Min.	FGA	FGM	Pct.	FTA	FTM	Pct.	Off.	Def.	Tot.	Ast.	PF	Dq.	Stl.	Blk.	Pts.
1986—Washington	12	5	3	.600	0	0	.000	0	1	1	4	0	0	1	0	6
1987—Washington	13	5	3	.600	0	0	.000	1	1	2	2	1	0	0	0	6
Totals	25	10	6	.600	0	0	.000	1	2	3	6	1	0	1	0	12

Three-Point Field Goals: 1987, 0-for-1.

Named to NBA All-Rookie Team, 1984. . . . Named to THE SPORTING NEWS All-America First Team, 1983.

KARL MALONE

Born July 24, 1963 at Summerfield, La.   Height 6:09.   Weight 254.

High School—Summerfield, La.

College—Louisiana Tech University, Ruston, La.

Drafted by Utah on first round as an undergraduate, 1985 (13th pick).

—COLLEGIATE RECORD—

Year	G.	Min.	FGA	FGM	Pct.	FTA	FTM	Pct.	Reb.	Pts.	Avg.
81-82			Did Not Play—Scholastically Ineligible								
82-83	28	....	373	217	.583	244	152	.623	289	586	20.9
83-84	32	....	382	220	.576	236	161	.682	282	601	18.8
84-85	32	....	399	216	.541	170	97	.571	288	529	16.5
Totals	92	....	1154	653	.566	650	410	.631	859	1716	18.7

NBA REGULAR SEASON RECORD

Sea.—Team	G.	Min.	FGA	FGM	Pct.	FTA	FTM	Pct.	Off.	Def.	Tot.	Ast.	PF	Dq.	Stl.	Blk.	Pts.	Avg.
85-86—Utah	81	2475	1016	504	.496	405	195	.481	174	544	718	236	295	2	105	44	1203	14.9
86-87—Utah	82	2857	1422	728	.512	540	323	.598	278	577	855	158	323	6	104	60	1779	21.7
87-88—Utah	82	3198	1650	858	.520	789	552	.700	277	709	986	199	296	2	117	50	2268	27.7
Totals	245	8530	4088	2090	.511	1734	1070	.617	729	1830	2559	593	914	10	326	154	5250	21.4

Three-Point Field Goals: 1985-86, 0-for-2. 1986-87, 0-for-7. 1987-88, 0-for-5. Totals, 0-for-14.

NBA PLAYOFF RECORD

Sea.—Team	G.	Min.	FGA	FGM	Pct.	FTA	FTM	Pct.	Off.	Def.	Tot.	Ast.	PF	Dq.	Stl.	Blk.	Pts.	Avg.
85-86—Utah	4	144	72	38	.528	26	11	.423	6	24	30	4	18	1	8	0	87	21.8
86-87—Utah	5	200	88	37	.420	36	26	.722	15	33	48	6	20	1	11	4	100	20.0
87-88—Utah	11	494	255	123	.482	112	81	.723	33	97	130	17	35	0	13	7	327	29.7
Totals	20	838	415	198	.477	174	118	.678	54	154	208	27	73	2	32	11	514	25.7

Three-Point Field Goals: 1987-88, 0-for-1.

NBA ALL-STAR GAME RECORD

Season—Team	Min.	FGA	FGM	Pct.	FTA	FTM	Pct.	—Rebounds— Off.	Def.	Tot.	Ast.	PF	Dq.	Stl.	Blk.	Pts.
1988—Utah	33	19	9	.474	5	4	.800	4	6	10	2	4	0	2	0	22

Named to All-NBA Second Team, 1988. . . . NBA All-Defensive Second Team, 1988. . . . NBA All-Rookie Team, 1986.

MOSES EUGENE MALONE

Born March 23, 1955 at Petersburg, Va. Height 6:10. Weight 255.

High School—Petersburg, Va.

Did not attend college.

Selected as an undergraduate by Utah on third round of ABA draft, 1974.
Sold by Utah to St. Louis, December 2, 1975.
Selected by Portland NBA from St. Louis in ABA dispersal draft, August 5, 1976.
Traded by Portland to Buffalo for 1978 1st round draft choice, October 18, 1976.
Traded by Buffalo to Houston for 1977 and 1978 1st round draft choices, October 24, 1976.
Signed by Philadelphia as a Veteran Free Agent, September 2, 1982; Houston matched offer and traded Malone to Philadelphia for Caldwell Jones and a 1983 1st round draft choice, September 15, 1982.
Traded by Philadelphia with Terry Catledge and 1986 and 1988 1st round draft choices to Washington for Jeff Ruland and Cliff Robinson, June 16, 1986.
Signed by Atlanta as an unrestricted free agent, August 16, 1988.

ABA REGULAR SEASON RECORD

Sea.—Team	G.	Min.	—2-Point— FGM	FGA	Pct.	—3-Point— FGM	FGA	Pct.	FTM	FTA	Pct.	Reb.	Ast.	Pts.	Avg.
74-75—Utah	83	3205	591	1034	.572	0	1	.000	375	591	.635	1209	82	1557	18.8
75-76—St. Louis	43	1168	251	488	.514	0	2	.000	112	183	.612	413	58	614	14.3
Totals..................	126	4373	842	1522	.553	0	3	.000	487	774	.629	1622	140	2171	17.2

ABA PLAYOFF RECORD

Sea.—Team	G.	Min.	—2-Point— FGM	FGA	Pct.	—3-Point— FGM	FGA	Pct.	FTM	FTA	Pct.	Reb.	Ast.	Pts.	Avg.
74-75—Utah	6	235	51	80	.638	0	0	.000	34	51	.667	105	9	136	22.7

ABA ALL-STAR GAME RECORD

Sea.—Team	Min.	—2-Point— FGM	FGA	Pct.	—3-Point— FGM	FGA	Pct.	FTM	FTA	Pct.	Reb.	Ast.	Pts.	Avg.
1975—Utah....................	20	2	3	.667	0	0	.000	2	5	.400	10	0	6	6.0

NBA REGULAR SEASON RECORD

Sea.—Team	G.	Min.	FGA	FGM	Pct.	FTA	FTM	Pct.	—Rebounds— Off.	Def.	Tot.	Ast.	PF	Dq.	Stl.	Blk.	Pts.	Avg.
76-77—Buf-Hou	82	2506	810	389	.480	440	305	.693	437	635	1072	89	275	3	67	181	1083	13.2
77-78—Houston	59	2107	828	413	.499	443	318	.718	380	506	886	31	179	2	48	76	1144	19.4
78-79—Houston	82	3390	1325	716	.540	811	599	.739	587	857	1444	147	223	0	79	119	2031	24.8
79-80—Houston	82	3140	1549	778	.502	783	563	.719	573	617	1190	147	210	0	80	107	2119	25.8
80-81—Houston	80	3245	1545	806	.522	804	609	.757	474	706	1180	141	223	0	83	150	2222	27.8
81-82—Houston	81	3398	1822	945	.519	827	630	.762	558	630	1188	142	208	0	76	125	2520	31.1
82-83—Philadelphia	78	2922	1305	654	.501	788	600	.761	445	749	1194	101	206	0	89	157	1908	24.5
83-84—Philadelphia	71	2613	1101	532	.483	727	545	.750	352	598	950	96	188	0	71	110	1609	22.7
84-85—Philadelphia	79	2957	1284	602	.469	904	737	.815	385	646	1031	130	216	0	67	123	1941	24.6
85-86—Philadelphia	74	2706	1246	571	.458	784	617	.787	339	533	872	90	194	0	67	71	1759	23.8
86-87—Washington	73	2488	1311	595	.454	692	570	.824	340	484	824	120	139	0	59	92	1760	24.1
87-88—Washington	79	2692	1090	531	.487	689	543	.788	372	512	884	112	160	0	59	72	1607	20.3
Totals	920	34164	15216	7532	.495	8692	6636	.763	5242	7473	12715	1346	2421	5	845	1383	21703	23.6

Three-Point Field Goals: 1979-80, 0-for-6. 1980-81, 1-for-3 (.333). 1981-82, 0-for-6. 1982-83, 0-for-1. 1983-84, 0-for-4. 1984-85, 0-for-2. 1985-86, 0-for-1. 1986-87, 0-for-11. 1987-88, 2-for-7 (.286). Totals, 3-for-41 (.073).

NBA PLAYOFF RECORD

Sea.—Team	G.	Min.	FGA	FGM	Pct.	FTA	FTM	Pct.	—Rebounds— Off.	Def.	Tot.	Ast.	PF	Dq.	Stl.	Blk.	Pts.	Avg.
76-77—Houston	12	518	162	81	.500	91	63	.692	84	119	203	7	42	0	13	21	225	18.8
78-79—Houston	2	78	41	18	.439	18	13	.722	25	16	41	2	5	0	1	8	49	24.5
79-80—Houston	7	275	138	74	.536	43	33	.767	42	55	97	7	18	0	4	16	181	25.9
80-81—Houston	21	955	432	207	.479	208	148	.711	125	180	305	35	54	0	13	34	562	26.8
81-82—Houston	3	136	67	29	.433	15	14	.933	28	23	51	10	8	0	2	2	72	24.0
82-83—Philadelphia	13	524	235	126	.536	120	86	.717	70	136	206	20	40	0	19	25	338	26.0
83-84—Philadelphia	5	212	83	38	.458	32	31	.969	20	49	69	7	15	0	3	11	107	21.4
84-85—Philadelphia	13	505	212	90	.425	103	82	.796	36	102	138	24	39	0	17	22	262	20.2
86-87—Washington	3	114	47	21	.447	21	20	.952	15	23	38	5	5	0	3	3	62	20.7
87-88—Washington	5	198	65	30	.462	40	33	.825	22	34	56	7	9	0	3	4	93	18.6
Totals	84	3515	1482	714	.482	691	523	.757	467	737	1204	124	235	0	75	146	1951	23.2

Three-Point Field Goals: 1979-80, 0-for-1. 1980-81, 0-for-2. 1982-83, 0-for-1. 1984-85, 0-for-1. 1987-88, 0-for-1. Totals, 0-for-6.

Season—Team	Min.	FGA	FGM	Pct.	FTA	FTM	Pct.	Off.	Def.	Tot.	Ast.	PF	Dq.	Stl.	Blk.	Pts.
1978—Houston	14	1	1	1.000	4	2	.500	1	3	4	1	1	0	1	0	4
1979—Houston	17	2	2	1.000	5	4	.800	2	5	7	1	0	0	1	0	8
1980—Houston	31	12	7	.583	12	6	.500	6	6	12	2	4	0	1	2	20
1981—Houston	22	8	3	.375	4	2	.500	2	4	6	3	3	0	1	0	8
1982—Houston	20	11	5	.455	6	2	.333	5	6	11	0	2	0	1	1	12
1983—Philadelphia	24	8	3	.375	6	4	.667	2	6	8	3	1	0	0	1	10
1984—Philadelphia					Selected but did not play											
1985—Philadelphia	33	10	2	.200	6	3	.500	5	7	12	1	4	0	0	0	7
1986—Philadelphia	34	12	5	.417	9	6	.667	5	8	13	0	4	0	1	0	16
1987—Washington	35	19	11	.579	6	5	.833	7	11	18	2	4	0	2	1	27
1988—Washington	22	6	2	.333	6	3	.500	5	4	9	2	2	0	0	0	7
Totals	252	89	41	.461	64	37	.578	40	60	100	15	25	0	8	5	119

COMBINED ABA AND NBA REGULAR SEASON RECORDS

	G.	Min.	FGA	FGM	Pct.	FTA	FTM	Pct.	Off.	Def.	Tot.	Ast.	PF	Dq.	Stl.	Blk.	Pts.	Avg.
Totals	1046	38537	16741	8374	.500	9466	7123	.753	5893	8444	14337	1486	2822	5	955	1539	23874	22.8

Named NBA Most Valuable Player, 1979, 1982, 1983. . . . All-NBA First Team, 1979, 1982, 1983, 1985. . . . All-NBA Second Team, 1980, 1981, 1984, 1987. . . . NBA All-Defensive First Team, 1983. . . . NBA All-Defensive Second Team, 1979. . . . NBA Playoff MVP, 1983. . . . Member of NBA championship team, 1983. . . . Led NBA in rebounding, 1979, 1981, 1982, 1983, 1984, 1985. . . . Named to ABA All-Rookie Team, 1975.

PACE SHEWAN MANNION

Born September 22, 1960 at Salt Lake City, Utah. Height 6:07. Weight 190.

High School—Las Vegas, Nev., Chaparral.

College—University of Utah, Salt Lake City, Utah.

Drafted by Golden State on second round, 1983 (43rd pick).

Waived by Golden State, October 15, 1984; signed by Utah as a free agent, December 22, 1984.
Waived by Utah, April 10, 1986; signed by New Jersey as a free agent, September 11, 1986.
Waived by New Jersey, February 17, 1987; signed by Milwaukee as a free agent, October 8, 1987.
Waived by Milwaukee, March 14, 1988.
Played in Continental Basketball Association with Rockford Lightning, 1986-87.

—COLLEGIATE RECORD—

Year	G.	Min.	FGA	FGM	Pct.	FTA	FTM	Pct.	Reb.	Pts.	Avg.
79-80	28	457	82	31	.378	30	26	.867	53	88	3.1
80-81	28	902	163	73	.448	79	47	.595	93	193	6.9
81-82	28	1061	263	114	.433	97	64	.660	122	292	10.4
82-83	32	1195	344	166	.483	138	112	.812	147	444	13.9
Totals	116	3615	852	384	.451	344	249	.724	415	1017	8.8

CBA REGULAR SEASON RECORD

Sea.—Team	G.	Min.	2-Point FGM	FGA	Pct.	3-Point FGM	FGA	Pct.	FTM	FTA	Pct.	Reb.	Ast.	Pts.	Avg.
86-87—Rockford	1	41	3	7	.429	2	5	.400	9	14	.643	11	2	21	21.0

NBA REGULAR SEASON RECORD

Sea.—Team	G.	Min.	FGA	FGM	Pct.	FTA	FTM	Pct.	Off.	Def.	Tot.	Ast.	PF	Dq.	Stl.	Blk.	Pts.	Avg.
83-84—Golden State	57	469	126	50	.397	23	18	.783	23	36	59	47	63	0	25	2	121	2.1
84-85—Utah	34	190	63	27	.429	23	16	.696	12	11	23	27	17	0	16	3	70	2.1
85-86—Utah	57	673	214	97	.453	82	53	.646	26	56	82	55	68	0	32	5	255	4.5
86-87—New Jersey	23	284	94	31	.330	31	18	.581	10	29	39	45	32	0	18	4	83	3.6
87-88—Milwaukee	35	477	118	48	.407	37	25	.676	17	34	51	34	51	0	13	7	123	3.5
Totals	206	2093	615	253	.411	196	130	.663	88	166	254	229	233	0	104	21	652	3.2

Three-Point Field Goals: 1983-84, 3-for-13 (.231). 1984-85, 0-for-1. 1985-86, 8-for-42 (.190). 1986-87, 3-for-9 (.333). 1987-88, 2-for-12 (.167). Totals, 16-for-77 (.208).

NBA PLAYOFF RECORD

Sea.—Team	G.	Min.	FGA	FGM	Pct.	FTA	FTM	Pct.	Off.	Def.	Tot.	Ast.	PF	Dq.	Stl.	Blk.	Pts.	Avg.
84-85—Utah	8	41	12	4	.333	12	10	.833	3	4	7	4	5	0	1	2	18	2.3

Three Point Field Goals: 1984-85, 0-for-1.

MAURICE MARTIN

Born July 2, 1964 at Liberty, N.Y. Height 6:06. Weight 200.

High School—Liberty, N.Y., Central.

College—St. Joseph's University, Philadelphia, Pa.

Drafted by Denver on first round, 1986 (16th pick).

Year	G.	Min.	FGA	FGM	Pct.	FTA	FTM	Pct.	Reb.	Pts.	Avg.
82-83	28	934	203	105	.517	114	82	.719	135	292	10.4
83-84	28	928	329	190	.578	82	58	.707	140	438	15.6
84-85	28	917	351	172	.490	126	95	.754	173	462	16.5
85-86	30	997	406	198	.488	184	138	.750	174	534	17.8
Totals	114	3776	1289	665	.516	506	373	.737	622	1726	15.1

Three-Point Field Goals: 1984-85, 23-for-57 (.404).

NBA REGULAR SEASON RECORD

Sea.—Team	G.	Min.	FGA	FGM	Pct.	FTA	FTM	Pct.	Off.	Def.	Tot.	Ast.	PF	Dq.	Stl.	Blk.	Pts.	Avg.
									—Rebounds—									
86-87—Denver	43	286	135	51	.378	66	42	.636	12	29	41	35	48	0	13	6	147	3.4
87-88—Denver	26	136	61	23	.377	21	10	.476	13	11	24	14	21	0	6	3	57	2.2
Totals	69	422	196	74	.378	87	52	.598	25	40	65	49	69	0	19	9	204	3.0

Three-Point Field Goals: 1986-87, 3-for-15 (.200). 1987-88, 1-for-4 (.250). Totals, 4-for-19 (.211).

NBA PLAYOFF RECORD

Sea.—Team	G.	Min.	FGA	FGM	Pct.	FTA	FTM	Pct.	Off.	Def.	Tot.	Ast.	PF	Dq.	Stl.	Blk.	Pts.	Avg.
									—Rebounds—									
86-87—Denver	3	54	29	12	.414	12	7	.583	4	5	9	10	12	0	0	1	31	10.3
87-88—Denver	3	9	5	1	.200	6	5	.833	0	1	1	0	1	0	0	1	7	2.3
Totals	6	63	34	13	.382	18	12	.667	4	6	10	10	13	0	0	2	38	6.3

Three-Point Field Goals: 1986-87, 0-for-1. 1987-88, 0-for-1. Totals, 0-for-2.

WILLIAM MARTIN
(Bill)

Born August 16, 1962 at Washington, D.C.   Height 6:07.   Weight 205.

High School—Washington, D.C., McKinley.

College—Georgetown University, Washington, D.C.

Drafted by Indiana on second round, 1985 (26th pick).

Waived by Indiana, October 28, 1986; signed by New York, March 29, 1987, to the first of consecutive 10-day contracts that expired, April 18, 1987.
Signed by Phoenix as a free agent, June 11, 1987.
Waived by Phoenix, December 28, 1987.
Played in Continental Basketball Association with Cincinnati Slammers, 1986-87, and Topeka Sizzlers, 1987-88.

Year	G.	Min.	FGA	FGM	Pct.	FTA	FTM	Pct.	Reb.	Pts.	Avg.
81-82	35	468	126	63	.500	74	46	.622	84	172	4.9
82-83	32	917	260	131	.504	102	78	.765	203	340	10.6
83-84	37	800	232	118	.509	132	93	.705	219	329	8.9
84-85	38	1147	361	196	.543	117	76	.650	234	468	12.3
Totals	142	3332	979	508	.519	425	293	.689	740	1309	9.2

CBA REGULAR SEASON RECORD

Sea.—Team	G.	Min.	FGM	FGA	Pct.	FGM	FGA	Pct.	FTM	FTA	Pct.	Reb.	Ast.	Pts.	Avg.
			—2-Point—			—3-Point—									
86-87—Cincinnati	45	1574	365	711	.513	2	5	.400	144	194	.742	298	136	880	19.6
87-88—Topeka	33	1179	232	466	.498	1	9	.111	153	187	.818	213	99	620	18.8
Totals	78	2753	597	1177	.507	3	14	.214	297	381	.780	511	235	1500	19.2

NBA REGULAR SEASON RECORD

Sea.—Team	G.	Min.	FGA	FGM	Pct.	FTA	FTM	Pct.	Off.	Def.	Tot.	Ast.	PF	Dq.	Stl.	Blk.	Pts.	Avg.
									—Rebounds—									
85-86—Indiana	66	691	298	143	.480	54	46	.852	42	60	102	52	108	1	21	7	332	5.0
86-87—New York	8	68	25	9	.360	8	7	.875	2	5	7	0	5	0	4	2	25	3.1
87-88—Phoenix	10	101	51	16	.314	13	8	.615	9	18	27	6	16	0	5	0	40	4.0
Totals	84	860	374	168	.449	75	61	.813	53	83	136	58	129	1	30	9	397	4.7

Three-Point Field Goals: 1985-86, 0-for-8. 1987-88, 0-for-1. Totals, 0-for-9.

Named to CBA All-Star Second Team, 1987. . . . CBA All-Defensive Second Team, 1987. . . . Member of NCAA Division I championship team, 1984.

WES JOEL MATTHEWS

Born August 24, 1959 at Sarasota, Fla.   Height 6:01.   Weight 170.

High School—Bridgeport, Conn., Harding.

College—University of Wisconsin, Madison, Wis.

Drafted by Washington on first round as an undergraduate, 1980 (14th pick).

Traded by Washington to Atlanta for Don Collins, January 17, 1981.

Traded by Atlanta with Kevin Figaro to San Diego for a conditional 2nd round draft choice, October 6, 1983.
Waived by San Diego, October 17, 1983; signed by Atlanta to a 10-day contract that expired, March 5, 1984.
Signed by Philadelphia, March 22, 1984, to the first of consecutive 10-day contracts that expired, April 11, 1984.
Signed by Chicago as a free agent, October 26, 1984; Chicago relinquished its right of first refusal, July 1, 1985.
Signed by San Antonio as a free agent, October 23, 1985.
Waived by San Antonio, October 9, 1986; signed by Los Angeles Lakers as a free agent, October 13, 1986.
Played in Continental Basketball Association with Ohio Mixers, 1983-84.

—COLLEGIATE RECORD—

Year	G.	Min.	FGA	FGM	Pct.	FTA	FTM	Pct.	Reb.	Pts.	Avg.
77-78	14	408	197	83	.421	52	37	.712	47	203	14.5
78-79	27	986	417	195	.468	139	109	.784	69	499	18.5
79-80	28	955	412	211	.512	143	127	.888	73	549	19.6
Totals	69	2349	1026	489	.477	334	273	.817	189	1251	18.1

CBA REGULAR SEASON RECORD

Sea.—Team	G.	Min.	2-Point FGM	FGA	Pct.	3-Point FGM	FGA	Pct.	FTM	FTA	Pct.	Reb.	Ast.	Pts.	Avg.
83-84—Ohio	8	235	69	121	.570	1	10	.100	28	37	.756	21	66	169	21.1

NBA REGULAR SEASON RECORD

Sea.—Team	G.	Min.	FGA	FGM	Pct.	FTA	FTM	Pct.	Rebounds Off.	Def.	Tot.	Ast.	PF	Dq.	Stl.	Blk.	Pts.	Avg.
80-81—Wash.-Atl.	79	2266	779	385	.494	252	202	.802	46	93	139	411	242	2	107	17	977	12.4
81-82—Atlanta	47	837	298	131	.440	79	60	.759	19	39	58	139	129	3	53	2	324	6.9
82-83—Atlanta	64	1187	424	171	.403	112	86	.768	25	66	91	249	129	0	60	8	442	6.9
83-84—Atl.-Phil.	20	388	131	61	.466	36	27	.750	7	20	27	83	45	0	16	3	150	7.5
84-85—Chicago	78	1523	386	191	.495	85	59	.694	16	51	67	354	133	0	73	12	443	5.7
85-86—San Antonio	75	1853	603	320	.531	211	173	.820	30	101	131	476	168	1	87	32	817	10.9
86-87—L.A. Lakers	50	532	187	89	.476	36	29	.806	13	34	47	100	53	0	23	4	208	4.2
87-88—L.A. Lakers	51	706	248	114	.460	65	54	.831	16	50	66	138	65	0	25	3	289	5.7
Totals	464	9292	3056	1462	.478	876	690	.788	172	454	626	1950	964	6	444	81	3650	7.9

Three-Point Field Goals: 1980-81, 5-for-21 (.238). 1981-82, 2-for-8 (.250). 1982-83, 14-for-48 (.292). 1983-84, 1-for-8 (.125). 1984-85, 2-for-16 (.125). 1985-86, 4-for-25 (.160). 1986-87, 1-for-3 (.333). 1987-88, 7-for-30 (.233). Totals, 36-for-159 (.226).

NBA PLAYOFF RECORD

Sea.—Team	G.	Min.	FGA	FGM	Pct.	FTA	FTM	Pct.	Rebounds Off.	Def.	Tot.	Ast.	PF	Dq.	Stl.	Blk.	Pts.	Avg.
81-82—Atlanta	2	28	10	2	.200	4	4	1.000	0	0	0	4	4	0	0	1	8	4.0
82-83—Atlanta	3	38	9	3	.333	5	4	.800	0	0	0	11	5	0	0	1	10	3.3
83-84—Philadelphia	4	23	8	4	.500	2	1	.500	0	0	0	4	4	0	1	0	10	2.5
84-85—Chicago	4	91	32	11	.344	9	7	.778	2	4	6	12	10	0	5	0	29	7.3
85-86—San Antonio	3	116	54	35	.648	8	6	.750	1	6	7	24	7	0	6	0	76	25.3
86-87—L.A. Lakers	12	61	23	11	.478	7	6	.857	0	4	4	9	9	0	1	0	28	2.3
87-88—L.A. Lakers	10	27	5	2	.400	10	8	.800	0	1	1	2	4	0	1	0	12	1.2
Totals	38	384	141	68	.482	45	36	.800	3	15	18	66	43	0	14	2	173	4.6

Three-Point Field Goals: 1982-83, 0-for-1. 1983-84, 1-for-2 (.500). 1984-85, 0-for-3. 1985-86, 0-for-1. 1986-87, 0-for-1. 1987-88, 0-for-1. Totals, 1-for-9 (.111).

Member of NBA championship teams, 1987 and 1988.

CEDRIC BRYAN MAXWELL

Born November 21, 1955 at Kinston, N. C.   Height 6:08.   Weight 225.

High School—Kinston, N. C.

College—University of North Carolina at Charlotte, Charlotte, N. C.

Drafted by Boston on first round, 1977 (12th pick).

Traded by Boston with a 1986 1st round draft choice and cash to Los Angeles Clippers for Bill Walton, September 6, 1985.
Traded by Los Angeles Clippers to Houston for a 1987 1st round draft choice and a 1989 2nd or 3rd round draft choice, January 16, 1987.

—COLLEGIATE RECORD—

Year	G.	Min.	FGA	FGM	Pct.	FTA	FTM	Pct.	Reb.	Pts.	Avg.
73-74	26	....	154	98	.636	77	41	.532	161	237	9.1
74-75	26	....	237	127	.535	88	64	.727	230	318	12.2
75-76	29	....	371	201	.541	215	177	.823	350	579	20.0
76-77	31	....	381	244	.640	263	202	.768	376	690	22.3
Totals	112	....	1143	670	.586	643	484	.753	1117	1824	16.3

NBA REGULAR SEASON RECORD

Sea.—Team	G.	Min.	FGA	FGM	Pct.	FTA	FTM	Pct.	Rebounds Off.	Def.	Tot.	Ast.	PF	Dq.	Stl.	Blk.	Pts.	Avg.
77-78—Boston	72	1213	316	170	.538	250	188	.752	138	241	379	68	151	2	53	48	528	7.3
78-79—Boston	80	2969	808	472	.584	716	574	.802	272	519	791	228	266	4	98	74	1518	19.0
79-80—Boston	80	2744	750	457	.609	554	436	.787	284	420	704	199	266	6	76	61	1350	16.9
80-81—Boston	81	2730	750	441	.588	450	352	.782	222	303	525	219	256	5	79	68	1234	15.2

Sea.—Team	G.	Min.	FGA	FGM	Pct.	FTA	FTM	Pct.	Off.	Def.	Tot.	Ast.	PF	Dq.	Stl.	Blk.	Pts.	Avg.
										—Rebounds—								
81-82—Boston	78	2590	724	397	.548	478	357	.747	218	281	499	183	263	6	79	49	1151	14.8
82-83—Boston	79	2252	663	331	.499	345	280	.812	185	237	422	186	202	3	65	39	942	11.9
83-84—Boston	80	2502	596	317	.532	425	320	.753	201	260	461	205	224	4	63	24	955	11.9
84-85—Boston	57	1495	377	201	.533	278	231	.831	98	144	242	102	140	2	36	15	633	11.1
85-86—L.A. Clippers	76	2458	661	314	.475	562	447	.795	241	383	624	215	252	2	61	29	1075	14.1
86-87—L.A.C.-Hou.	81	1968	477	253	.530	391	303	.775	175	260	435	197	178	1	39	14	809	10.0
87-88—Houston	71	848	171	80	.468	143	110	.769	74	105	179	60	75	0	22	12	270	3.8
Totals	835	23769	6293	3433	.546	4592	3598	.784	2108	3153	5261	1862	2273	35	671	433	10465	12.5

Three-Point Field Goals: 1980-81, 0-for-1. 1981-82, 0-for-3. 1982-83, 0-for-1. 1983-84, 1-for-6 (.167). 1984-85, 0-for-2. 1985-86, 0-for-3. 1986-87, 0-for-1. 1987-88, 0-for-2. Totals, 1-for-19 (.053).

NBA PLAYOFF RECORD

Sea.—Team	G.	Min.	FGA	FGM	Pct.	FTA	FTM	Pct.	Off.	Def.	Tot.	Ast.	PF	Dq.	Stl.	Blk.	Pts.	Avg.
										—Rebounds—								
79-80—Boston	9	320	93	59	.634	61	46	.754	31	59	90	19	25	0	5	10	164	18.2
80-81—Boston	17	598	174	101	.580	88	72	.818	61	64	125	46	53	0	12	16	274	16.1
81-82—Boston	12	385	120	62	.517	70	50	.714	37	50	87	26	40	0	18	11	174	14.5
82-83—Boston	7	246	55	29	.527	38	32	.842	23	28	51	23	18	0	4	4	90	12.9
83-84—Boston	23	752	167	84	.503	136	106	.779	52	67	119	55	77	1	22	7	274	11.9
84-85—Boston	20	238	43	21	.488	43	34	.791	17	30	47	7	29	0	9	2	76	3.8
86-87—Houston	10	177	34	18	.529	35	26	.743	11	22	33	17	17	1	4	0	62	6.2
87-88—Houston	4	15	2	1	.500	0	0	.000	1	0	1	1	1	0	0	0	2	0.5
Totals	102	2731	688	375	.545	471	366	.777	233	320	553	194	260	2	74	50	1116	10.9

Three-Point Field Goals: 1983-84, 0-for-1. 1986-87, 0-for-1. Totals, 0-for-2.

Named NBA Playoff MVP, 1981. . . . Member of NBA championship teams, 1981 and 1984. . . . Led NBA in field-goal percentage, 1979 and 1980.

TIMOTHY DANIEL McCORMICK
(Tim)

Born March 10, 1962 at Detroit, Mich. Height 7:00. Weight 240.

High School—Clarkston, Mich.

College—University of Michigan, Ann Arbor, Mich.

Drafted by Cleveland on first round as an undergraduate, 1984 (12th pick).

Draft rights traded by Cleveland with Cliff Robinson and cash to Washington for draft rights to Melvin Turpin, June 19, 1984.

Draft rights traded by Washington with Ricky Sobers to Seattle for Gus Williams, June 19, 1984.

Traded by Seattle with Danny Vranes to Philadelphia for Clemon Johnson and a 1989 1st round draft choice, September 29, 1986.

Traded by Philadelphia with Roy Hinson and a 1989 2nd round draft choice to New Jersey for Mike Gminski and Ben Coleman, January 16, 1988.

—COLLEGIATE RECORD—

Year	G.	Min.	FGA	FGM	Pct.	FTA	FTM	Pct.	Reb.	Pts.	Avg.
80-81	30	524	106	54	.509	60	47	.783	106	155	5.2
81-82					Did Not Play—Knee Operations						
82-83	28	....	220	122	.555	134	109	.813	180	353	12.6
83-84	32	960	226	131	.580	186	124	.667	189	386	12.1
Totals	90	....	552	307	.556	380	280	.737	475	894	9.9

NBA REGULAR SEASON RECORD

Sea.—Team	G.	Min.	FGA	FGM	Pct.	FTA	FTM	Pct.	Off.	Def.	Tot.	Ast.	PF	Dq.	Stl.	Blk.	Pts.	Avg.
										—Rebounds—								
84-85—Seattle	78	1584	483	269	.557	263	188	.715	146	252	398	78	207	2	18	33	726	9.3
85-86—Seattle	77	1705	444	253	.570	244	174	.713	140	263	403	83	219	4	19	28	681	8.8
86-87—Philadelphia	81	2817	718	391	.545	349	251	.719	180	431	611	114	270	4	36	64	1033	12.8
87-88—Phil.-N.J.	70	2114	648	348	.537	215	145	.674	146	321	467	118	234	3	32	23	841	12.0
Totals	306	8220	2293	1261	.550	1071	758	.708	612	1267	1879	393	930	13	105	148	3281	10.7

Three-Point Field Goals: 1984-85, 0-for-1. 1985-86, 1-for-2 (.500). 1986-87, 0-for-4. 1987-88, 0-for-2. Totals, 1-for-9 (.111).

NBA PLAYOFF RECORD

Sea.—Team	G.	Min.	FGA	FGM	Pct.	FTA	FTM	Pct.	Off.	Def.	Tot.	Ast.	PF	Dq.	Stl.	Blk.	Pts.	Avg.
										—Rebounds—								
86-87—Philadelphia	5	121	24	12	.500	4	4	1.000	7	24	31	6	19	0	1	2	28	5.6

RODNEY EARL McCRAY

Born August 29, 1961 at Mt. Vernon, N.Y. Height 6:08. Weight 235.

High School—Mt. Vernon, N.Y.

College—University of Louisville, Louisville, Ky.

Drafted by Houston on first round, 1983 (3rd pick).

—COLLEGIATE RECORD—

Year	G.	Min.	FGA	FGM	Pct.	FTA	FTM	Pct.	Reb.	Pts.	Avg.
79-80	36	1178	197	107	.543	102	66	.647	269	280	7.8
80-81	30	917	194	114	.588	90	60	.667	222	288	9.6
81-82	33	961	196	112	.571	84	59	.702	234	283	8.6
82-83	36	1197	259	152	.587	124	92	.742	304	396	11.0
Totals	135	4253	846	485	.573	400	277	.693	1029	1247	9.2

NBA REGULAR SEASON RECORD

Sea.—Team	G.	Min.	FGA	FGM	Pct.	FTA	FTM	Pct.	Off.	Def.	Tot.	Ast.	PF	Dq.	Stl.	Blk.	Pts.	Avg.
83-84—Houston	79	2081	672	335	.499	249	182	.731	173	277	450	176	205	1	53	54	853	10.8
84-85—Houston	82	3001	890	476	.535	313	231	.738	201	338	539	355	215	2	90	75	1183	14.4
85-86—Houston	82	2610	629	338	.537	222	171	.770	159	361	520	292	197	2	50	58	847	10.3
86-87—Houston	81	3136	783	432	.552	393	306	.779	190	388	578	434	172	2	88	53	1170	14.4
87-88—Houston	81	2689	746	359	.481	367	288	.785	232	399	631	264	166	2	57	51	1006	12.4
Totals	405	13517	3720	1940	.522	1544	1178	.763	955	1763	2718	1521	955	9	338	291	5059	12.5

Three-Point Field Goals: 1983-84, 1-for-4 (.250). 1984-85, 0-for-6. 1985-86, 0-for-3. 1986-87, 0-for-9. 1987-88, 0-for-4. Totals, 1-for-26 (.038).

NBA PLAYOFF RECORD

Sea.—Team	G.	Min.	FGA	FGM	Pct.	FTA	FTM	Pct.	Off.	Def.	Tot.	Ast.	PF	Dq.	Stl.	Blk.	Pts.	Avg.
84-85—Houston	5	181	34	19	.559	23	15	.652	9	21	30	11	17	0	6	1	53	10.6
85-86—Houston	20	835	202	108	.535	58	43	.741	23	95	118	125	45	0	18	19	259	13.0
86-87—Houston	10	436	101	57	.564	54	43	.796	32	51	83	56	21	0	5	9	157	15.7
87-88—Houston	4	159	31	12	.387	12	8	.667	15	12	27	9	12	0	4	3	32	8.0
Totals	39	1611	368	196	.533	147	109	.741	79	179	258	201	95	0	33	32	501	12.8

Three-Point Field Goals: 1985-86, 0-for-3. 1986-87, 0-for-2. 1987-88, 0-for-1. Totals, 0-for-6.

Named to NBA All-Defensive First Team, 1988. . . . All-Defensive Second Team, 1987. . . . Member of U.S. Olympic team, 1980. . . . Member of NCAA Division I championship team, 1980. . . . Brother of former NBA forward Carlton (Scooter) McCray.

XAVIER MAURICE McDANIEL

Born June 4, 1963 at Columbia, S.C.   Height 6:07.   Weight 205.

High School—Columbia, S.C., A.C. Flora.

College—Wichita State University, Wichita, Kan.

Drafted by Seattle on first round, 1985 (4th pick).

—COLLEGIATE RECORD—

Year	G.	Min.	FGA	FGM	Pct.	FTA	FTM	Pct.	Reb.	Pts.	Avg.
81-82	28	378	135	68	.504	43	27	.628	103	163	5.8
82-83	28	987	376	223	.593	148	80	.541	403	526	18.8
83-84	30	1130	445	251	.564	172	117	.680	393	619	20.6
84-85	31	1143	628	351	.559	224	142	.634	460	844	27.2
Totals	117	3638	1584	893	.564	587	366	.624	1359	2152	18.4

NBA REGULAR SEASON RECORD

Sea.—Team	G.	Min.	FGA	FGM	Pct.	FTA	FTM	Pct.	Off.	Def.	Tot.	Ast.	PF	Dq.	Stl.	Blk.	Pts.	Avg.
85-86—Seattle	82	2706	1176	576	.490	364	250	.687	307	348	655	193	305	8	101	37	1404	17.1
86-87—Seattle	82	3031	1583	806	.509	395	275	.696	338	367	705	207	300	4	115	52	1890	23.0
87-88—Seattle	78	2703	1407	687	.488	393	281	.715	206	312	518	263	230	2	96	52	1669	21.4
Totals	242	8440	4166	2069	.497	1152	806	.700	851	1027	1878	663	835	14	312	141	4963	20.5

Three-Point Field Goals: 1985-86, 2-for-10 (.200). 1986-87, 3-for-14 (.214). 1987-88, 14-for-50 (.280). Totals, 19-for-74 (.257).

NBA PLAYOFF RECORD

Sea.—Team	G.	Min.	FGA	FGM	Pct.	FTA	FTM	Pct.	Off.	Def.	Tot.	Ast.	PF	Dq.	Stl.	Blk.	Pts.	Avg.
86-87—Seattle	14	528	254	124	.488	56	34	.607	52	65	117	42	63	2	21	9	284	20.3
87-88—Seattle	5	180	81	45	.556	24	12	.500	14	34	48	25	15	0	3	1	106	21.2
Totals	19	708	335	169	.504	80	46	.575	66	99	165	67	78	2	24	10	390	20.5

Three-Point Field Goals: 1986-87, 2-for-10 (.200). 1987-88, 4-for-8 (.500). Totals, 6-for-18 (.333).

NBA ALL-STAR GAME RECORD

Season—Team	Min.	FGA	FGM	Pct.	FTA	FTM	Pct.	Off.	Def.	Tot.	Ast.	PF	Dq.	Stl.	Blk.	Pts.
1988—Seattle	13	9	1	.111	0	0	.000	1	1	2	0	1	0	0	0	2

Named to NBA All-Rookie Team, 1986. . . . Only player in NCAA history to lead nation in both scoring and rebounding in same season, 1985. . . . Led NCAA Division I in scoring, 1985. . . . Led NCAA Division I in rebounding, 1983 and 1985.

XAVIER McDANIEL

BENJAMIN McDONALD
(Ben)

Born July 20, 1962 at Torrance, Calif.   Height 6:08.   Weight 225.

High School—Long Beach, Calif., Poly.

College—University of California at Irvine, Irvine, Calif.

Drafted by Cleveland on third round, 1984 (50th pick).

Signed by Cleveland, March 4, 1986, to the first of consecutive 10-day contracts that expired, March 23, 1986.
Re-signed by Cleveland, March 24, 1986, for remainder of season.
Signed by Golden State as a free agent, September 24, 1986.

—COLLEGIATE RECORD—

Year	G.	Min.	FGA	FGM	Pct.	FTA	FTM	Pct.	Reb.	Pts.	Avg.
80-81	27	899	247	128	.518	61	40	.656	140	296	11.0
81-82	30	1012	259	143	.552	74	52	.703	151	338	11.3
82-83	28	953	342	180	.526	101	66	.653	214	426	15.2
83-84	29	1001	373	188	.504	105	76	.724	166	452	15.6
Totals	114	3865	1221	639	.523	341	234	.686	671	1512	13.3

NBA REGULAR SEASON RECORD

Sea.—Team	G.	Min.	FGA	FGM	Pct.	FTA	FTM	Pct.	Off.	Def.	Tot.	Ast.	PF	Dq.	Stl.	Blk.	Pts.	Avg.
85-86—Cleveland	21	266	58	28	.483	8	5	.625	15	23	38	9	30	0	7	1	61	2.9
86-87—Golden State	63	1284	360	164	.456	38	24	.632	63	120	183	84	200	5	27	8	353	5.6
87-88—Golden State	81	2039	552	258	.467	111	87	.784	133	202	335	138	246	4	39	8	612	7.6
Totals	165	3589	970	450	.464	157	116	.739	211	345	556	231	476	9	73	17	1026	6.2

Three-Point Field Goals: 1985-86, 0-for-1. 1986-87, 1-for-8 (.125). 1987-88, 9-for-35 (.257). Totals, 10-for-44 (.227).

NBA PLAYOFF RECORD

Sea.—Team	G.	Min.	FGA	FGM	Pct.	FTA	FTM	Pct.	Off.	Def.	Tot.	Ast.	PF	Dq.	Stl.	Blk.	Pts.	Avg.
86-87—Golden State	5	45	11	1	.091	0	0	.000	2	4	6	9	7	0	2	0	2	0.4

Three-Point Field Goals: 1986-87, 0-for-2.

MICHAEL RAY McGEE
(Mike)

Born July 29, 1959 at Tyler, Tex.   Height 6:05.   Weight 207.

High School—Omaha, Neb., North.

College—University of Michigan, Ann Arbor, Mich.

Drafted by Los Angeles on first round, 1981 (19th pick).

Traded by Los Angeles Lakers with draft rights to Ken Barlow to Atlanta for draft rights to Billy Thompson and Ron Kellogg, June 17, 1986.
Traded by Atlanta to Sacramento for 1991 and 1995 2nd round draft choices, December 14, 1987.

—COLLEGIATE RECORD—

Year	G.	Min.	FGA	FGM	Pct.	FTA	FTM	Pct.	Reb.	Pts.	Avg.
77-78	27	....	439	217	.494	122	97	.795	132	531	19.7
78-79	27	....	454	207	.456	146	97	.664	150	511	18.9
79-80	30	....	584	277	.474	159	111	.698	130	665	22.2
80-81	30	1070	600	309	.515	169	114	.675	118	732	24.4
Totals	114	....	2077	1010	.486	596	419	.703	530	2439	21.4

NBA REGULAR SEASON RECORD

Sea.—Team	G.	Min.	FGA	FGM	Pct.	FTA	FTM	Pct.	Off.	Def.	Tot.	Ast.	PF	Dq.	Stl.	Blk.	Pts.	Avg.
81-82—Los Angeles	39	352	172	80	.465	53	31	.585	34	15	49	16	59	0	18	3	191	4.9
82-83—Los Angeles	39	381	163	69	.423	23	17	.739	33	20	53	26	50	1	11	5	156	4.0
83-84—Los Angeles	77	1425	584	347	.594	113	61	.540	117	76	193	81	176	0	49	6	757	9.8
84-85—L.A. Lakers	76	1170	612	329	.538	160	94	.588	97	68	165	71	147	1	39	7	774	10.2
85-86—L.A. Lakers	71	1213	544	252	.463	64	42	.656	51	89	140	83	131	0	53	7	587	8.3
86-87—Atlanta	76	1420	677	311	.459	137	80	.584	71	88	159	149	156	1	61	2	788	10.4
87-88—Atl.-Sac.	48	1003	530	223	.421	102	76	.745	55	73	128	71	81	0	52	6	575	12.0
Totals	426	6964	3282	1611	.491	652	401	.615	458	429	887	497	800	3	283	36	3828	9.0

Three-Point Field Goals: 1981-82, 0-for-4. 1982-83, 1-for-7 (.143). 1983-84, 2-for-13 (.154). 1984-85, 22-for-61 (.361). 1985-86, 41-for-114 (.360). 1986-87, 86-for-229 (.376). 1987-88, 53-for-160 (.331). Totals, 205-for-588 (.349).

NBA PLAYOFF RECORD

Sea.—Team	G.	Min.	FGA	FGM	Pct.	FTA	FTM	Pct.	Off.	Def.	Tot.	Ast.	PF	Dq.	Stl.	Blk.	Pts.	Avg.
										—Rebounds—								
81-82—Los Angeles	4	10	13	6	.462	0	0	.000	3	0	3	0	1	0	0	0	12	3.0
82-83—Los Angeles	6	25	11	4	.364	4	3	.750	5	2	7	1	5	0	0	0	12	2.0
83-84—Los Angeles	17	370	157	90	.573	39	25	.641	22	12	34	23	52	0	11	1	211	12.4
84-85—L.A. Lakers	17	260	142	76	.535	42	29	.690	20	16	36	12	26	0	7	1	190	11.2
85-86—L.A. Lakers	6	28	18	8	.444	4	0	.000	3	2	5	2	3	0	0	0	16	2.7
86-87—Atlanta	8	101	39	10	256	10	5	.500	9	11	20	15	7	0	4	0	27	3.4
Totals	58	794	380	194	.510	97	62	.626	62	43	105	53	94	0	22	2	468	8.1

Three-Point Field Goals: 1981-82, 0-for-1. 1982-83, 1-for-1 (1.000). 1983-84, 6-for-17 (.353). 1984-85, 9-for-18 (.500). 1985-86, 0-for-3. 1986-87, 2-for-14 (.143). Totals, 18-for-54 (.333).

Member of NBA championship teams, 1982 and 1985.

KEVIN EDWARD McHALE

Born December 19, 1957 at Hibbing, Minn.   Height 6:10.   Weight 225.

High School—Hibbing, Minn.

College—University of Minnesota, Minneapolis, Minn.

Drafted by Boston on first round, 1980 (3rd pick).

—COLLEGIATE RECORD—

Year	G.	Min.	FGA	FGM	Pct.	FTA	FTM	Pct.	Reb.	Pts.	Avg.
76-77	27	....	241	133	.552	77	58	.753	218	324	12.0
77-78	26	....	242	143	.591	77	54	.701	192	340	13.1
78.79	27	....	391	202	.517	96	79	.823	259	483	17.9
79-80	32	....	416	236	.567	107	85	.794	281	557	17.4
Totals	112	....	1290	714	.553	357	276	.773	950	1704	15.2

NBA REGULAR SEASON RECORD

Sea.—Team	G.	Min.	FGA	FGM	Pct.	FTA	FTM	Pct.	Off.	Def.	Tot.	Ast	PF	Dq.	Stl.	Blk.	Pts.	Avg.
										—Rebounds—								
80-81—Boston	82	1645	666	355	.533	159	108	.679	155	204	359	55	260	3	27	151	818	10.0
81-82—Boston	82	2332	875	465	.531	248	187	.754	191	365	556	91	264	1	30	185	1117	13.6
82-83—Boston	82	2345	893	483	.541	269	193	.717	215	338	553	104	241	3	34	192	1159	14.1
83-84—Boston	82	2577	1055	587	.556	439	336	.765	208	402	610	104	243	5	23	126	1511	18.4
84-85—Boston	79	2653	1062	605	.570	467	355	.760	229	483	712	141	234	3	28	120	1565	19.8
85-86—Boston	68	2397	978	561	.574	420	326	.776	171	380	551	181	192	2	29	134	1448	21.3
86-87—Boston	77	3060	1307	790	.604	512	428	.836	247	516	763	198	240	1	38	172	2008	26.1
87-88—Boston	64	2390	911	550	.604	434	346	.797	159	377	536	171	179	1	27	92	1446	22.6
Totals	616	19399	7747	4396	.567	2948	2279	.773	1575	3065	4640	1045	1853	19	236	1172	11072	18.0

Three-Point Field Goals: 1980-81, 0-for-2. 1982-83, 0-for-1. 1983-84, 1-for-3 (.333). 1984-85, 0-for-6. 1986-87, 0-for-4. Totals, 1-for-16 (.063).

NBA PLAYOFF RECORD

Sea.—Team	G.	Min.	FGA	FGM	Pct.	FTA	FTM	Pct.	Off.	Def.	Tot.	Ast.	PF	Dq.	Stl.	Blk.	Pts.	Avg.
										—Rebounds—								
80-81—Boston	17	296	113	61	.540	36	23	.639	29	30	59	14	51	1	4	25	145	8.5
81-82—Boston	12	344	134	77	.575	53	40	.755	41	44	85	11	44	0	5	27	194	16.2
82-83—Boston	7	177	62	34	.548	18	10	.556	15	27	42	5	16	0	3	7	78	11.1
83-84—Boston	23	702	244	123	.504	121	94	.777	62	81	143	27	75	1	3	35	340	14.8
84-85—Boston	21	837	303	172	.568	150	121	.807	74	134	208	32	73	3	13	46	465	22.1
85-86—Boston	18	715	290	168	.579	141	112	.794	51	104	155	48	64	0	8	43	448	24.9
86-87—Boston	21	827	298	174	.584	126	96	.762	66	128	194	39	71	2	7	30	444	21.1
87-88—Boston	17	716	262	158	.603	137	115	.839	55	81	136	40	65	1	7	30	432	25.4
Totals	136	4614	1706	967	.567	782	611	.781	393	629	1022	216	459	8	50	243	2546	18.7

Three-Point Field Goals: 1982-83, 0-for-1. 1983-84, 0-for-3. 1985-86, 0-for-1. 1987-88, 1-for-1 (1.000). Totals, 1-for-6 (.167).

NBA ALL-STAR GAME RECORD

Season—Team	Min.	FGA	FGM	Pct.	FTA	FTM	Pct.	Off.	Def.	Tot.	Ast.	PF	Dq.	Stl.	Blk.	Pts.
									—Rebounds—							
1984—Boston............	11	7	3	.429	6	4	.667	2	3	5	0	1	0	0	0	10
1986—Boston............	20	8	3	.375	2	2	1.000	3	7	10	2	4	0	0	4	8
1987—Boston............	30	11	7	.636	2	2	1.000	4	3	7	2	5	0	0	4	16
1988—Boston............	14	1	0	.000	2	2	1.000	0	1	1	1	2	0	0	2	2
Totals	75	27	13	.481	12	10	.833	9	14	23	5	12	0	0	10	36

Named to All-NBA First Team, 1987. . . . NBA All-Rookie Team, 1981. . . . Recipient of NBA Sixth Man Award, 1984 and 1985. . . . Member of NBA championship teams, 1981, 1984, 1986. . . . NBA All-Defensive First Team, 1986, 1987, 1988. . . . NBA All-Defensive Second Team, 1983. . . . Led NBA in field-goal percentage, 1987 and 1988.

—DID YOU KNOW—

That only one of the 23 players selected by the Charlotte Hornets and Miami Heat in the expansion draft last June scored in double figures in 1987-88? Guard Dell Curry, chosen by Charlotte, averaged 10 points per game for the Cleveland Cavaliers.

KEVIN ROBERT McKENNA

Born January 8, 1959 at St. Paul, Minn.   Height 6:05.   Weight 195.

High School—Palatine, Ill.

College—Creighton University, Omaha, Neb.

Drafted by Los Angeles on fourth round, 1981 (88th pick).

Waived by Los Angeles, October 8, 1982; signed by Indiana as a free agent, September 30, 1983.
Traded by Indiana to Houston for a 1985 5th round draft choice, September 17, 1984.
Waived by Houston, October 23, 1984; signed by New Jersey as a free agent, December 10, 1984.
Waived by New Jersey, December 18, 1984; re signed by New Jersey, December 20, 1984.
Waived by New Jersey, April 15, 1985; signed by Washington, January 28, 1986, to a 10-day contract that expired, February 6, 1986.
Re-signed by Washington, February 10, 1986, to a second 10-day contract that expired, February 19, 1986.
Re-signed by Washington, February 20, 1986, for remainder of season.
Waived by Washington, June 17, 1986; signed by New Jersey as a free agent, December 9, 1986.
Played in Continental Basketball Association with Las Vegas-Albuquerque Silvers, 1982-83, and Kansas City Sizzlers, 1985-86.

—COLLEGIATE RECORD—

Year	G.	Min.	FGA	FGM	Pct.	FTA	FTM	Pct.	Reb.	Pts.	Avg.
77-78	28	....	223	104	.466	51	36	.706	80	244	8.7
78-79	27	....	282	130	.461	82	59	.720	102	319	11.8
79-80	28	....	362	182	.503	124	99	.798	123	463	16.5
80-81	30	....	388	181	.466	135	112	.830	121	474	15.8
Totals	113	....	1255	597	.476	392	306	.781	426	1500	13.3

CBA REGULAR SEASON RECORD

| Sea.—Team | G. | Min. | —2-Point— | | | —3-Point— | | | FTM | FTA | Pct. | Reb. | Ast. | Pts. | Avg. |
			FGM	FGA	Pct.	FGM	FGA	Pct.							
82-83—Las Vegas-Albu.	42	1251	267	515	.518	1	21	.048	189	224	.843	154	96	726	17.3
85-86—Kansas City	20	571	115	236	.487	17	50	.340	68	83	.819	71	84	349	17.5
Totals	62	1822	382	751	.508	18	71	.254	257	307	.837	225	180	1075	17.3

NBA REGULAR SEASON RECORD

| Sea.—Team | G. | Min. | FGA | FGM | Pct. | FTA | FTM | Pct. | —Rebounds— | | | Ast. | PF | Dq. | Stl. | Blk. | Pts. | Avg. |
									Off.	Def.	Tot.							
81-82—Los Angeles	36	237	87	28	.322	17	11	.647	18	11	29	14	45	0	10	2	67	1.9
83-84—Indiana	61	923	371	152	.410	98	80	.816	30	65	95	114	133	3	46	5	387	6.3
84-85—New Jersey	29	535	134	61	.455	43	38	.884	20	29	49	58	63	0	30	7	165	5.7
85-86—Washington	30	430	166	61	.367	30	25	.833	9	27	36	23	54	1	29	2	174	5.8
86-87—New Jersey	56	942	337	153	.454	57	43	.754	21	56	77	93	141	0	54	7	401	7.2
87-88—New Jersey	31	393	109	43	.394	25	24	.960	4	27	31	40	55	1	15	2	126	4.1
Totals	243	3460	1204	498	.414	270	221	.819	102	215	317	342	491	5	184	25	1320	5.4

Three-Point Field Goals: 1981-82, 0-for-2. 1983-84, 3-for-17 (.176). 1984-85, 5-for-13 (.385). 1985-86, 27-for-77 (.351). 1986-87, 52-for-124 (.419). 1987-88, 16-for-50 (.320). Totals, 103-for-283 (.364).

NBA PLAYOFF RECORD

| Sea.—Team | G. | Min. | FGA | FGM | Pct. | FTA | FTM | Pct. | —Rebounds— | | | Ast. | PF | Dq. | Stl. | Blk. | Pts. | Avg. |
									Off.	Def.	Tot.							
85-86—Washington	1	2	0	0	.000	0	0	.000	0	0	0	0	0	0	0	0	0	0.0

DERRICK WAYNE McKEY

Born October 10, 1966 at Meridian, Miss.   Height 6:09.   Weight 205.

High School—Meridian, Miss.

College—University of Alabama, University, Ala.

Drafted by Seattle on first round as an undergraduate, 1987 (9th pick).

—COLLEGIATE RECORD—

Year	G.	Min.	FGA	FGM	Pct.	FTA	FTM	Pct.	Reb.	Pts.	Avg.
84-85	33	728	155	74	.477	33	20	.606	134	168	5.1
85-86	33	1117	280	178	.636	117	92	.786	262	448	13.6
86-87	33	1199	425	247	.581	116	100	.862	247	615	18.6
Totals	99	3044	860	499	.580	266	212	.797	643	1231	12.4

Three-Point Field Goals: 1986-87, 21-for-50 (.420).

NBA REGULAR SEASON RECORD

| Sea.—Team | G. | Min. | FGA | FGM | Pct. | FTA | FTM | Pct. | —Rebounds— | | | Ast. | PF | Dq. | Stl. | Blk. | Pts. | Avg. |
									Off.	Def.	Tot.							
87-88—Seattle	82	1706	519	255	.491	224	173	.772	115	213	328	107	237	3	70	63	694	8.5

Three-Point Field Goals: 1987-88, 11-for-30 (.367).

DERRICK McKEY

Sea.—Team	G.	Min.	FGA	FGM	Pct.	FTA	FTM	Pct.	Off.	Def.	Tot.	Ast.	PF	Dq.	Stl.	Blk.	Pts.	Avg.
									—Rebounds—									
87-88—Seattle	5	109	38	24	.632	17	10	.588	7	13	20	8	12	0	3	5	60	12.0

Three-Point Field Goals: 1987-88, 2-for-6 (.333).

Named to NBA All-Rookie Team, 1988. . . . THE SPORTING NEWS All-America Second Team, 1987.

NATHANIEL McMILLAN
(Nate)

Born August 3, 1964 at Raleigh, N.C. Height 6:05. Weight 195.

High School—Raleigh, N.C., Enloe.

Colleges—Chowan College, Murfreesboro, N.C., and North Carolina State University, Raleigh, N.C.

Drafted by Seattle on second round, 1986 (30th pick).

—COLLEGIATE RECORD—
Chowan

Year	G.	Min.	FGA	FGM	Pct.	FTA	FTM	Pct.	Reb.	Pts.	Avg.
82-83	27	....	174	101	.580	92	64	.696	134	266	9.9
83-84	35	....	331	180	.544	130	100	.769	342	460	13.1
J.C. Totals	62	....	505	281	.556	222	164	.739	476	726	11.7

North Carolina State

Year	G.	Min.	FGA	FGM	Pct.	FTA	FTM	Pct.	Reb.	Pts.	Avg.
84-85	33	973	207	94	.454	95	64	.674	189	252	7.6
85-86	34	1208	262	127	.485	90	66	.733	155	320	9.4
N.C. St. Tot.	67	2181	469	221	.471	185	130	.703	344	572	8.5

NBA REGULAR SEASON RECORD

Sea.—Team	G.	Min.	FGA	FGM	Pct.	FTA	FTM	Pct.	Off.	Def.	Tot.	Ast.	PF	Dq.	Stl.	Blk.	Pts.	Avg.
									—Rebounds—									
86-87—Seattle	71	1972	301	143	.475	141	87	.617	101	230	331	583	238	4	125	45	373	5.3
87-88—Seattle	82	2453	496	235	.474	205	145	.707	117	221	338	702	238	1	169	47	624	7.6
Totals	153	4425	797	378	.474	346	232	.671	218	451	669	1285	476	5	294	92	997	6.5

Three-Point Field Goals: 1986-87, 0-for-7. 1987-88, 9-for-24 (.375). Totals, 9-for-31 (.290).

NBA PLAYOFF RECORD

Sea.—Team	G.	Min.	FGA	FGM	Pct.	FTA	FTM	Pct.	Off.	Def.	Tot.	Ast.	PF	Dq.	Stl.	Blk.	Pts.	Avg.
									—Rebounds—									
86-87—Seattle	14	356	62	27	.435	24	17	.708	13	41	54	112	42	1	14	10	71	5.1
87-88—Seattle	5	127	35	12	.343	14	9	.643	6	15	21	33	11	0	2	3	33	6.6
Totals	19	483	97	39	.402	38	26	.684	19	56	75	145	53	1	16	13	104	5.5

Three-Point Field Goals: 1987-88, 0-for-1.

MARK ROBERT McNAMARA

Born June 8, 1959 at San Jose, Calif. Height 6:11. Weight 235.

High School—San Jose, Calif., Del Mar.

Colleges—Santa Clara University, Santa Clara, Calif., and University of California, Berkeley, Calif.

Drafted by Philadelphia on first round, 1982 (22nd pick).

Traded by Philadelphia to San Antonio for a 1986 2nd round draft choice, November 4, 1983.
Traded by San Antonio to Kansas City for Billy Knight, December 11, 1984.
Traded by Kansas City to Milwaukee for a 1986 4th round draft choice, August 9, 1985.
Waived by Milwaukee, October 22, 1985; signed by Philadelphia as a free agent, March 4, 1987.

—COLLEGIATE RECORD—
Santa Clara

Year	G.	Min.	FGA	FGM	Pct.	FTA	FTM	Pct.	Reb.	Pts.	Avg.
77-78	29	....	229	143	.624	98	46	.469	197	332	11.4
78-79	25	652	266	153	.575	123	71	.577	167	377	15.1
SC Totals	54	....	495	296	.598	221	117	.529	364	709	13.1

California

Year	G.	Min.	FGA	FGM	Pct.	FTA	FTM	Pct.	Reb.	Pts.	Avg.
79-80					Did Not Play—Transfer Student						
80-81	26	....	295	182	.617	168	84	.500	272	448	17.2
81-82	27	....	329	231	.702	242	131	.541	341	593	22.0
Cal Totals	53	....	624	413	.662	410	215	.524	613	1041	19.6
College Totals	107	....	1119	709	.634	631	332	.526	977	1750	16.4

NBA REGULAR SEASON RECORD

Sea.—Team	G.	Min.	FGA	FGM	Pct.	FTA	FTM	Pct.	Off.	Def.	Tot.	Ast.	PF	Dq.	Stl.	Blk.	Pts.	Avg.
									\-Rebounds\-									
82-83—Philadelphia	36	182	64	29	.453	45	20	.444	34	42	76	7	42	1	3	3	78	2.2
83-84—San Antonio	70	1037	253	157	.621	157	74	.471	137	180	317	31	138	2	14	12	388	5.5
84-85—S.A.-K.C.	45	273	76	40	.526	62	32	.516	31	43	74	6	27	0	7	8	112	2.5
86-87—Philadelphia	11	113	30	14	.467	19	7	.368	17	19	36	2	17	0	1	0	35	3.2
87-88—Philadelphia	42	581	133	52	.391	66	48	.727	66	91	157	18	67	0	4	12	152	3.6
Totals	204	2186	556	292	.525	349	181	.519	285	375	660	64	291	3	29	35	765	3.8

NBA PLAYOFF RECORD

Sea.—Team	G.	Min.	FGA	FGM	Pct.	FTA	FTM	Pct.	Off.	Def.	Tot.	Ast.	PF	Dq.	Stl.	Blk.	Pts.	Avg.
									\-Rebounds\-									
82-83—Philadelphia	2	2	2	2	1.000	0	0	.000	0	1	1	0	0	0	0	0	4	2.0
86-87—Philadelphia	1	2	1	1	1.000	0	0	.000	0	1	1	0	0	0	0	0	2	2.0
Totals	3	4	3	3	1.000	0	0	.000	0	2	2	0	0	0	0	0	6	2.0

Member of NBA championship team, 1983. . . . Led NCAA Division I in field-goal percentage, 1982.

CHRISTOPHER McNEALY
(Chris)

Born July 15, 1961 at Fresno, Calif.   Height 6:07.   Weight 215.

High School—Fresno, Calif., Roosevelt.

Colleges—Santa Barbara City College, Santa Barbara, Calif.,
and San Jose State University, San Jose, Calif.

Drafted by Kansas City on second round, 1983 (38th pick).

Draft rights traded by Kansas City with draft rights to Ennis Whatley and a 1984 2nd round draft choice to Chicago for Mark Olberding and draft rights to Larry Micheaux, June 28, 1983.
Played in Italy, 1983-84.
Signed by Golden State as a free agent, September 12, 1985.
Waived by Golden State, October 24, 1985; signed by New York to a 10-day contract that expired, February 22, 1986.
Re-signed by New York, February 23, 1986, for remainder of season.
Re-signed by New York as a free agent, June 17, 1986.
Waived by New York, December 15, 1987.
Played in Continental Basketball Association with Bay State Bombardiers and Albany Patroons, 1985-86, and LaCrosse Catbirds, 1987-88.

—COLLEGIATE RECORD—
Santa Barbara City College

Year	G.	Min.	FGA	FGM	Pct.	FTA	FTM	Pct.	Reb.	Pts.	Avg.
79-80	32	1170	302	180	.596	72	49	.681	331	409	12.8

San Jose State

Year	G.	Min.	FGA	FGM	Pct.	FTA	FTM	Pct.	Reb.	Pts.	Avg.
80-81	30	1100	296	149	.503	84	50	.595	193	348	11.6
81-82	23	822	250	138	.552	113	71	.628	222	347	15.1
82-83	28	1048	368	217	.589	157	105	.669	263	541	19.3
Totals	81	2970	914	504	.551	354	226	.638	678	1236	15.3

Three-Point Field Goals: 1982-83, 2-for-2.

CBA REGULAR SEASON RECORD

Sea.—Team	G.	Min.	2-Point			3-Point			FTM	FTA	Pct.	Reb.	Ast.	Pts.	Avg.
			FGM	FGA	Pct.	FGM	FGA	Pct.							
85-86—Bay State-Albany......	26	1019	200	379	.527	0	1	.000	102	142	.718	294	77	502	19.3
87-88—LaCrosse..................	14	393	65	127	.512	0	0	....	38	66	.576	107	29	168	12.0
Totals	40	1412	265	506	.524	0	1	.000	140	208	.673	401	106	670	16.8

NBA REGULAR SEASON RECORD

Sea.—Team	G.	Min.	FGA	FGM	Pct.	FTA	FTM	Pct.	Off.	Def.	Tot.	Ast.	PF	Dq.	Stl.	Blk.	Pts.	Avg.
									\-Rebounds\-									
85-86—New York	30	627	144	70	.486	47	31	.660	62	141	203	41	88	2	38	12	171	5.7
86-87—New York	59	972	179	88	.492	80	52	.650	74	153	227	46	136	1	36	16	228	3.9
87-88—New York	19	265	74	23	.311	31	21	.677	24	40	64	23	50	1	16	2	67	3.5
Totals ...	108	1864	397	181	.456	158	104	.658	160	334	494	110	274	4	90	30	466	4.3

Named to CBA All-Defensive First Team, 1986.

REGINALD WAYNE MILLER
(Reggie)

Born August 24, 1965 at Riverside, Calif.   Height 6:07.   Weight 190.

High School—Riverside, Calif., Poly.

College—University of California at Los Angeles, Los Angeles, Calif.

Drafted by Indiana on first round, 1987 (11th pick).

Year	G.	Min.	FGA	FGM	Pct.	FTA	FTM	Pct.	Reb.	Pts.	Avg.
83-84	28	384	110	56	.509	28	18	.643	42	130	4.6
84-85	33	1174	347	192	.553	148	119	.804	141	503	15.2
85-86	29	1112	493	274	.556	229	202	.882	153	750	25.9
86-87	32	1166	455	247	.543	179	149	.832	173	712	22.3
Totals	122	3836	1405	769	.547	584	488	.836	509	2095	17.2

Three-Point Field Goals: 1986-87, 69-for-157 (.439).

NBA REGULAR SEASON RECORD

Sea.—Team	G.	Min.	FGA	FGM	Pct.	FTA	FTM	Pct.	—Rebounds— Off.	Def.	Tot.	Ast.	PF	Dq.	Stl.	Blk.	Pts.	Avg.
87-88—Indiana	82	1840	627	306	.488	186	149	.801	95	95	190	132	157	0	53	19	822	10.0

Three-Point Field Goals: 1987-88, 61-for-172 (.355).

Brother of California Angels catcher Darrell Miller and basketball player Cheryl Miller.

DIRK DeWAYNE MINNIEFIELD

Born January 17, 1961 at Lexington, Ky.   Height 6:03.   Weight 180.

High School—Lexington, Ky., Lafayette.

College—University of Kentucky, Lexington, Ky.

Drafted by Dallas on second round, 1983 (33rd pick).

Draft rights traded by Dallas to New Jersey for a 1986 2nd round draft choice and the option to exchange 2nd round picks in 1987, June 30, 1983.

Waived by New Jersey, October 25, 1983; signed by Chicago as a free agent, September 27, 1984.

Waived by Chicago, October 22, 1984; signed by Cleveland as a free agent, August 26, 1985.

Traded by Cleveland to Houston for a 1989 2nd or 3rd round draft choice, December 8, 1986.

Signed by Golden State as a Veteran Free Agent, November 5, 1987; Houston agreed not to exercise its right of first refusal.

Waived by Golden State, November 25, 1987; signed by Boston as a free agent, December 17, 1987.

Played in Continental Basketball Association with Louisville Catbirds, 1983-84 and 1984-85.

—COLLEGIATE RECORD—

Year	G.	Min.	FGA	FGM	Pct.	FTA	FTM	Pct.	Reb.	Pts.	Avg.
79-80	34	691	142	68	.479	49	35	.714	70	171	5.0
80-81	28	890	213	118	.554	63	55	.873	79	291	10.4
81-82	30	1034	251	128	.510	111	84	.757	94	340	11.3
82-83	31	951	199	108	.543	68	51	.750	88	267	8.6
Totals	123	3566	805	422	.524	291	225	.773	331	1069	8.7

CBA REGULAR SEASON RECORD

Sea.—Team	G.	Min.	—2-Point— FGM	FGA	Pct.	—3-Point— FGM	FGA	Pct.	FTM	FTA	Pct.	Reb.	Ast.	Pts.	Avg.
83-84—Louisville	43	1423	234	490	.478	9	45	.200	138	165	.836	105	284	633	14.7
84-85—Louisville	48	1869	345	733	.470	23	113	.204	157	190	.826	171	287	916	19.1
Totals	91	3292	579	1223	.473	32	158	.203	295	355	.830	276	571	1549	17.0

NBA REGULAR SEASON RECORD

Sea.—Team	G.	Min.	FGA	FGM	Pct.	FTA	FTM	Pct.	—Rebounds— Off.	Def.	Tot.	Ast.	PF	Dq.	Stl.	Blk.	Pts.	Avg.
85-86—Cleveland	76	1131	347	167	.481	93	73	.785	43	88	131	269	165	1	65	1	417	5.5
86-87—Clev.-Hou.	74	1600	482	218	.452	90	62	.689	29	111	140	348	174	2	72	7	509	6.9
87-88—G.S.-Bos.	72	1070	221	108	.489	55	41	.745	30	66	96	228	133	0	59	3	261	3.6
Totals	222	3801	1050	493	.470	238	176	.739	102	265	367	845	472	3	196	11	1187	5.3

Three-Point Field Goals: 1985-86, 10-for-37 (.270). 1986-87, 11-for-39 (.282). 1987-88, 4-for-16 (.250). Totals, 25-for-92 (.271).

NBA PLAYOFF RECORD

Sea.—Team	G.	Min.	FGA	FGM	Pct.	FTA	FTM	Pct.	—Rebounds— Off.	Def.	Tot.	Ast.	PF	Dq.	Stl.	Blk.	Pts.	Avg.
86-87—Houston	8	27	8	4	.500	6	6	1.000	2	0	2	2	8	0	1	0	14	1.8
87-88—Boston	11	50	14	6	.429	2	2	1.000	1	1	2	11	13	0	2	0	16	1.5
Totals	19	77	22	10	.455	8	8	1.000	3	1	4	13	21	0	3	0	30	1.6

Three-Point Field Goals: 1986-87, 0-for-1. 1987-88, 2-for-4 (.500). Totals, 2-for-5 (.400).

Cousin of Frank Minnifield, cornerback with Cleveland Browns.

—DID YOU KNOW—

That Bill Russell, K.C. Jones and Pat Riley are the only three men who have played in the championship game of the NCAA Tournament and coached an NBA titlist? Russell and Jones were teammates for the University of San Francisco and coached the Boston Celtics to NBA crowns. Riley played for Kentucky and coaches the Los Angeles Lakers.

MICHAEL ANTHONY MITCHELL
(Mike)

Born January 1, 1956 at Atlanta, Ga.   Height 6:07.   Weight 215.

High School—Atlanta, Ga., Price.

College—Auburn University, Auburn, Ala.

Drafted by Cleveland on first round, 1978 (15th pick).

Traded by Cleveland with Roger Phegley to San Antonio for Ron Brewer, Reggie Johnson and cash, December 23, 1981.

—COLLEGIATE RECORD—

Year	G.	Min.	FGA	FGM	Pct.	FTA	FTM	Pct.	Reb.	Pts.	Avg.
74-75	25	....	426	204	.479	98	53	.541	286	461	18.4
75-76	26	....	431	210	.487	96	66	.688	249	486	18.7
76-77	26	....	429	229	.534	69	47	.681	220	505	19.4
77-78	27	....	544	283	.520	135	105	.778	241	671	24.9
Totals	104	....	1830	926	.506	398	271	.681	996	2123	20.4

NBA REGULAR SEASON RECORD

Sea.—Team	G.	Min.	FGA	FGM	Pct.	FTA	FTM	Pct.	Off.	Def.	Tot.	Ast.	PF	Dq.	Stl.	Blk.	Pts.	Avg.
78-79—Cleveland	80	1576	706	362	.513	178	131	.736	127	202	329	60	215	6	51	29	855	10.7
79-80—Cleveland	82	2802	1482	775	.523	343	270	.787	206	385	591	93	259	4	70	77	1820	22.2
80-81—Cleveland	82	3194	1791	853	.476	385	302	.784	215	287	502	139	199	0	63	52	2012	24.5
81-82—Clev.-S.A.	84	3063	1477	753	.510	302	220	.728	244	346	590	82	277	4	60	43	1726	20.5
82-83—San Antonio	80	2803	1342	686	.511	289	219	.758	188	349	537	98	248	6	57	52	1591	19.9
83-84—San Antonio	79	2853	1597	779	.488	353	275	.779	188	382	570	93	251	6	62	73	1839	23.3
84-85—San Antonio	82	2853	1558	775	.497	346	269	.777	145	272	417	151	219	1	61	27	1824	22.2
85-86—San Antonio	82	2970	1697	802	.473	392	317	.809	134	275	409	188	175	0	56	25	1921	23.4
86-87—San Antonio	40	922	478	208	.435	112	92	.821	38	65	103	38	68	0	19	9	509	12.7
87-88—San Antonio	68	1501	784	378	.482	194	160	.825	54	144	198	68	101	0	31	13	919	13.5
Totals	759	24537	12912	6371	.493	2894	2255	.779	1539	2707	4246	1010	2012	27	530	400	15016	19.8

Three-Point Field Goals: 1979-80, 0-for-6. 1980-81, 4-for-9 (.444). 1981-82, 0-for-7. 1982-83, 0-for-3. 1983-84, 6-for-14 (.429). 1984-85, 5-for-23 (.217). 1985-86, 0-for-12. 1986-87, 1-for-2 (.500). 1987-88, 3-for-12 (.250). Totals, 19-for-88 (.216).

NBA PLAYOFF RECORD

Sea.—Team	G.	Min.	FGA	FGM	Pct.	FTA	FTM	Pct.	Off.	Def.	Tot.	Ast.	PF	Dq.	Stl.	Blk.	Pts.	Avg.
81-82—San Antonio	9	365	169	90	.533	57	43	.754	28	45	73	7	22	0	5	1	223	24.8
82-83—San Antonio	11	422	200	102	.501	33	25	.758	33	72	105	12	34	0	7	19	230	20.9
84-85—San Antonio	5	180	78	44	.564	24	21	.875	5	14	19	12	19	1	3	4	109	21.8
85-86—San Antonio	3	107	52	21	.404	10	5	.500	3	6	9	10	8	1	3	3	47	15.7
87-88—San Antonio	3	74	37	13	.351	6	5	.833	6	9	15	4	5	0	1	1	31	10.3
Totals	31	1148	536	270	.504	130	99	.762	75	146	221	45	88	2	19	28	640	20.6

Three-Point Field Goals: 1982-83, 1-for-2 (.500). 1984-85, 0-for-1. Totals, 1-for-3 (.333).

NBA ALL-STAR GAME RECORD

Season—Team	Min.	FGA	FGM	Pct.	FTA	FTM	Pct.	Off.	Def.	Tot.	Ast.	PF	Dq.	Stl.	Blk.	Pts.
1981—Cleveland	15	12	6	.500	2	2	1.000	4	0	4	2	2	0	1	0	14

PAUL KEEN MOKESKI

Born January 3, 1957 at Spokane, Wash.   Height 7:00.   Weight 255.

High School—Encino, Calif., Crespi Carmelite.

College—University of Kansas, Lawrence, Kan.

Drafted by Houston on second round, 1979 (42nd pick).

Traded by Houston to Detroit for a 1982 2nd round draft choice, October 7, 1980.
Traded by Detroit with Phil Hubbard and 1982 1st and 2nd round draft choices to Cleveland for Kenny Carr and Bill Laimbeer, February 16, 1982.
Waived by Cleveland, December 20, 1982; signed by Milwaukee as a free agent, December 24, 1982.

—COLLEGIATE RECORD—

Year	G.	Min.	FGA	FGM	Pct.	FTA	FTM	Pct.	Reb.	Pts.	Avg.
75-76	18	474	170	82	.482	37	27	.730	115	191	10.6
76-77	14	250	96	38	.396	16	10	.625	86	86	6.1
77-78	28	653	220	114	.518	54	31	.574	237	259	9.3
78-79	29	974	323	161	.498	120	87	.725	242	409	14.1
Totals	89	2351	809	395	.488	227	155	.683	680	945	10.6

NBA REGULAR SEASON RECORD

Sea.—Team	G.	Min.	FGA	FGM	Pct.	FTA	FTM	Pct.	Rebounds Off.	Rebounds Def.	Rebounds Tot.	Ast.	PF	Dq.	Stl.	Blk.	Pts.	Avg.
79-80—Houston	12	113	33	11	.333	9	7	.778	14	15	29	2	24	0	1	6	29	2.4
80-81—Detroit	80	1815	458	224	.489	200	120	.600	141	277	418	135	267	7	38	73	568	7.1
81-82—Det.-Clev.	67	868	193	84	.435	63	48	.762	59	149	208	35	171	2	33	40	216	3.2
82-83—Clev.-Milw.	73	1128	260	119	.458	68	50	.735	76	184	260	49	223	9	21	44	288	3.9
83-84—Milwaukee	68	838	213	102	.479	72	50	.694	51	115	166	44	168	1	11	29	255	3.8
84-85—Milwaukee	79	1586	429	205	.478	116	81	.698	107	303	410	99	266	6	28	35	491	6.2
85-86—Milwaukee	45	521	139	59	.424	34	25	.735	36	103	139	30	92	1	6	6	143	3.2
86-87—Milwaukee	62	626	129	52	.403	64	46	.719	45	93	138	22	126	0	18	13	150	2.4
87-88—Milwaukee	60	848	210	100	.476	72	51	.708	70	151	221	22	194	5	27	29	251	4.2
Totals	546	8343	2064	956	.463	698	478	.685	599	1390	1989	438	1531	31	183	275	2391	4.4

Three-Point Field Goals: 1980-81, 0-for-1. 1981-82, 0-for-3. 1982-83, 0-for-1. 1983-84, 1-for-3 (.333). 1984-85, 0-for-2. 1986-87, 0-for-1. 1987-88, 0-for-4. Totals, 1-for-15 (.067).

NBA PLAYOFF RECORD

Sea.—Team	G.	Min.	FGA	FGM	Pct.	FTA	FTM	Pct.	Rebounds Off.	Rebounds Def.	Rebounds Tot.	Ast.	PF	Dq.	Stl.	Blk.	Pts.	Avg.
82-83—Milwaukee	4	12	4	2	.500	0	0	.000	1	1	2	1	1	0	1	0	4	1.0
83-84—Milwaukee	16	322	63	34	.540	45	30	.667	20	68	88	6	62	0	9	11	98	6.1
84-85—Milwaukee	8	154	36	16	.444	12	12	1.000	8	26	34	12	28	1	2	4	44	5.5
85-86—Milwaukee	14	101	27	14	.519	9	6	.667	5	19	24	8	27	1	6	3	34	2.4
86-87—Milwaukee	12	107	22	8	.364	15	12	.800	12	17	29	2	22	1	3	2	28	2.3
87-88—Milwaukee	4	40	14	5	.357	6	4	.667	5	4	9	0	4	0	3	2	14	3.5
Totals	58	736	166	79	.476	87	64	.736	51	135	186	29	144	3	24	22	222	3.8

Three-Point Field Goals: 1983-84, 0-for-2. 1986-87, 0-for-1. Totals, 0-for-3.

SIDNEY A. MONCRIEF

Born September 21, 1957 at Little Rock, Ark. Height 6:04. Weight 180.

High School—Little Rock, Ark., Hall.

College—University of Arkansas, Fayetteville, Ark.

Drafted by Milwaukee on first round, 1979 (5th pick).

—COLLEGIATE RECORD—

Year	G.	Min.	FGA	FGM	Pct.	FTA	FTM	Pct.	Reb.	Pts.	Avg.
75-76	28	....	224	149	.665	77	56	.727	213	354	12.6
76-77	28	997	242	157	.649	171	117	.684	235	431	15.4
77-78	36	1293	354	209	.590	256	203	.793	278	621	17.3
78-79	30	1157	400	224	.560	248	212	.855	289	660	22.0
Totals	122	....	1220	739	.606	752	588	.782	1015	2066	16.9

NBA REGULAR SEASON RECORD

Sea.—Team	G.	Min.	FGA	FGM	Pct.	FTA	FTM	Pct.	Rebounds Off.	Rebounds Def.	Rebounds Tot.	Ast.	PF	Dq.	Stl.	Blk.	Pts.	Avg.
79-80—Milwaukee	77	1557	451	211	.468	292	232	.795	154	184	338	133	106	0	72	16	654	8.5
80-81—Milwaukee	80	2417	739	400	.541	398	320	.804	186	220	406	264	156	1	90	37	1122	14.0
81-82—Milwaukee	80	2980	1063	556	.523	573	468	.817	221	313	534	382	206	3	138	22	1581	19.8
82-83—Milwaukee	76	2710	1156	606	.524	604	499	.826	192	245	437	300	180	1	113	23	1712	22.5
83-84—Milwaukee	79	3075	1125	560	.498	624	529	.848	215	313	528	358	204	2	108	27	1654	20.9
84-85—Milwaukee	73	2734	1162	561	.483	548	454	.828	149	242	391	382	197	1	117	39	1585	21.7
85-86—Milwaukee	73	2567	962	470	.489	580	498	.859	115	219	334	357	178	1	103	18	1471	20.2
86-87—Milwaukee	39	992	324	158	.488	162	136	.840	57	70	127	121	73	0	27	10	460	11.8
87-88—Milwaukee	56	1428	444	217	.489	196	164	.837	58	122	180	204	109	0	41	12	603	10.8
Totals	633	20460	7426	3739	.504	3977	3300	.830	1347	1928	3275	2501	1409	9	809	204	10842	17.1

Three-Point Field Goals: 1979-80, 0-for-1. 1980-81, 2-for-9 (.222). 1981-82, 1-for-14 (.071). 1982-83, 1-for-10 (.100). 1983-84, 5-for-18 (.278). 1984-85, 9-for-33 (.273). 1985-86, 33-for-103 (.320). 1986-87, 8-for-31 (.258). 1987-88, 5-for-31 (.161). Totals, 64-for-250 (.256).

NBA PLAYOFF RECORD

Sea.—Team	G.	Min.	FGA	FGM	Pct.	FTA	FTM	Pct.	Rebounds Off.	Rebounds Def.	Rebounds Tot.	Ast.	PF	Dq.	Stl.	Blk.	Pts.	Avg.
79-80—Milwaukee	7	182	51	30	.588	31	27	.871	17	14	31	11	14	0	5	1	87	12.4
80-81—Milwaukee	7	277	69	30	.435	51	38	.745	19	28	47	20	24	0	12	3	98	14.0
81-82—Milwaukee	6	252	74	31	.419	38	30	.789	15	15	30	24	22	1	9	2	92	15.3
82-83—Milwaukee	9	377	142	62	.437	61	46	.754	28	32	60	33	25	1	18	3	170	18.9
83-84—Milwaukee	16	618	191	99	.518	134	106	.791	44	67	111	68	54	1	28	9	305	19.1
84-85—Milwaukee	8	319	99	55	.556	75	70	.933	10	24	34	40	26	0	5	4	184	23.0
85-86—Milwaukee	9	327	122	52	.426	63	44	.698	15	26	41	44	30	0	5	5	152	16.9
86-87—Milwaukee	12	426	165	78	.473	90	73	.811	21	33	54	36	43	0	13	6	233	19.4
87-88—Milwaukee	5	173	50	24	.480	27	26	.963	6	13	19	26	14	0	3	1	75	15.0
Totals	79	2951	963	461	.479	570	460	.807	175	252	427	302	252	3	98	34	1396	17.7

Three-Point Field Goals: 1981-82, 0-for-1. 1982-83, 0-for-1. 1983-84, 1-for-4 (.250). 1984-85, 4-for-10 (.400). 1985-86, 4-for-14 (.286). 1986-87, 4-for-14 (.286). 1987-88, 1-for-1 (1.000). Totals, 14-for-45 (.311).

NBA ALL-STAR GAME RECORD

Season—Team	Min.	FGA	FGM	Pct.	FTA	FTM	Pct.	—Rebounds— Off.	Def.	Tot.	Ast.	PF	Dq.	Stl.	Blk.	Pts.
1982—Milwaukee....	22	11	3	.273	2	0	.000	3	1	4	1	2	0	1	0	6
1983—Milwaukee....	23	14	8	.571	5	4	.800	3	2	5	4	1	0	6	1	20
1984—Milwaukee....	26	6	3	.500	2	2	1.000	1	4	5	2	3	0	5	0	8
1985—Milwaukee....	22	5	1	.200	6	6	1.000	2	3	5	4	1	0	0	0	8
1986—Milwaukee....	26	11	4	.364	7	7	1.000	3	0	3	1	0	0	0	1	16
Totals	119	47	19	.404	22	19	.864	12	10	22	12	7	0	12	2	58

Three-Point Field Goals: 1986, 1-for-1 (1.000).

Named to All-NBA First Team, 1983.... All-NBA Second Team, 1982, 1984, 1985, 1986.... NBA Defensive Player of the Year, 1983 and 1984.... NBA All-Defensive First Team, 1983, 1984, 1985, 1986.... NBA All-Defensive Second Team, 1982.... Named to THE SPORTING NEWS All-America Second Team, 1979.... Led NCAA in field-goal percentage, 1976.

ANDRE M. MOORE

Born July 2, 1964 at Chicago, Ill.   Height 6:09.   Weight 215.

High School—Chicago, Ill., Carver.

Colleges—University of Illinois at Chicago, Chicago, Ill., and
Loyola University, Chicago, Ill.

Drafted by Denver on second round, 1987 (31st pick).

Waived by Denver, December 3, 1987; signed by Milwaukee as a free agent, December 11, 1987.
Waived by Milwaukee, December 28, 1987.

—COLLEGIATE RECORD—
Illinois-Chicago

Year	G.	Min.	FGA	FGM	Pct.	FTA	FTM	Pct.	Reb.	Pts.	Avg.
82-83				Did Not Play							

Loyola (Ill.)

Year	G.	Min.	FGA	FGM	Pct.	FTA	FTM	Pct.	Reb.	Pts.	Avg.
83-84				Did Not Play—Transfer Student							
84-85	29	986	260	139	.535	56	42	.750	300	320	11.0
85-86	27	1047	381	201	.528	112	80	.714	269	482	17.9
86-87	29	1134	509	257	.505	123	84	.683	360	598	20.6
Totals	85	3167	1150	597	.519	291	206	.708	929	1400	16.5

Three-Point Field Goals: 1986-87, 0-for-10.

NBA REGULAR SEASON RECORD

Sea.—Team	G.	Min.	FGA	FGM	Pct.	FTA	FTM	Pct.	—Rebounds— Off.	Def.	Tot.	Ast.	PF	Dq.	Stl.	Blk.	Pts.	Avg.
87-88—Den.-Mil.	10	50	27	9	.333	8	6	.750	6	8	14	6	6	0	2	1	24	2.4

JOHN BRIAN MOORE
(Johnny)

Born March 3, 1958 at Altoona, Pa.   Height 6:03.   Weight 185.

High School—Altoona, Pa.

College—University of Texas, Austin, Tex.

Drafted by Seattle on second round, 1979 (43rd pick).

Draft rights sold by Seattle to San Antonio, June 26, 1979.
Waived by San Antonio, October 12, 1979; re-signed by San Antonio, March 9, 1980.
Waived by San Antonio, November 19, 1987; signed by New Jersey as a free agent, December 3, 1987.
Waived by New Jersey, December 15, 1987.

—COLLEGIATE RECORD—

Year	G.	Min.	FGA	FGM	Pct.	FTA	FTM	Pct.	Reb.	Pts.	Avg.
75-76	26	....	353	154	.436	61	45	.738	61	353	13.6
76-77	26	....	387	168	.434	97	78	.804	97	414	15.9
77-78	31	....	344	168	.488	110	81	.736	159	417	13.5
78-79	29	....	254	119	.469	88	57	.648	129	295	10.2
Totals	112	....	1338	609	.455	356	261	.733	446	1479	13.2

NBA REGULAR SEASON RECORD

Sea.—Team	G.	Min.	FGA	FGM	Pct.	FTA	FTM	Pct.	—Rebounds— Off.	Def.	Tot.	Ast.	PF	Dq.	Stl.	Blk.	Pts.	Avg.
80-81—San Antonio	82	1578	520	249	.479	172	105	.610	58	138	196	373	178	0	120	22	604	7.4
81-82—San Antonio	79	2294	667	309	.463	182	122	.670	62	213	275	762	254	6	163	12	741	9.4
82-83—San Antonio	77	2552	841	394	.468	199	148	.744	65	212	277	753	247	2	194	32	941	12.2
83-84—San Antonio	59	1650	518	231	.446	139	105	.755	37	141	178	566	168	2	123	20	595	10.1
84-85—San Antonio	82	2689	910	416	.457	248	189	.762	94	284	378	816	247	3	229	18	1046	12.8

<table>
<tr><th>Sea.—Team</th><th>G.</th><th>Min.</th><th>FGA</th><th>FGM</th><th>Pct.</th><th>FTA</th><th>FTM</th><th>Pct.</th><th colspan="3">—Rebounds—</th><th></th><th></th><th></th><th></th><th></th><th></th><th></th></tr>
<tr><th></th><th></th><th></th><th></th><th></th><th></th><th></th><th></th><th></th><th>Off.</th><th>Def.</th><th>Tot.</th><th>Ast.</th><th>PF</th><th>Dq.</th><th>Stl.</th><th>Blk.</th><th>Pts.</th><th>Avg.</th></tr>
<tr><td>85-86—San Antonio</td><td>28</td><td>856</td><td>303</td><td>150</td><td>.495</td><td>86</td><td>59</td><td>.686</td><td>25</td><td>61</td><td>86</td><td>252</td><td>78</td><td>0</td><td>70</td><td>6</td><td>363</td><td>13.0</td></tr>
<tr><td>86-87—San Antonio</td><td>55</td><td>1234</td><td>448</td><td>198</td><td>.442</td><td>70</td><td>56</td><td>.800</td><td>32</td><td>68</td><td>100</td><td>250</td><td>97</td><td>0</td><td>83</td><td>3</td><td>474</td><td>8.6</td></tr>
<tr><td>87-88—S.A.-N.J.</td><td>5</td><td>61</td><td>10</td><td>4</td><td>.400</td><td>0</td><td>0</td><td>.000</td><td>2</td><td>4</td><td>6</td><td>12</td><td>1</td><td>0</td><td>3</td><td>0</td><td>8</td><td>1.6</td></tr>
<tr><td>Totals ....</td><td>467</td><td>12914</td><td>4217</td><td>1951</td><td>.463</td><td>1096</td><td>784</td><td>.715</td><td>375</td><td>1121</td><td>1496</td><td>3784</td><td>1270</td><td>13</td><td>985</td><td>113</td><td>4772</td><td>10.2</td></tr>
</table>

Three-Point Field Goals: 1980-81, 1-for-19 (.053). 1981-82, 1-for-21 (.048). 1982-83, 5-for-22 (.277). 1983-84, 28-for-87 (.322). 1984-85, 25-for-89 (.281). 1985-86, 4-for-22 (.182). 1986-87, 22-for-79 (.278). 1987-88, 0-for-1. Totals, 86-for-340 (.253).

NBA PLAYOFF RECORD

<table>
<tr><th>Sea.—Team</th><th>G.</th><th>Min.</th><th>FGA</th><th>FGM</th><th>Pct.</th><th>FTA</th><th>FTM</th><th>Pct.</th><th colspan="3">—Rebounds—</th><th></th><th></th><th></th><th></th><th></th><th></th><th></th></tr>
<tr><th></th><th></th><th></th><th></th><th></th><th></th><th></th><th></th><th></th><th>Off.</th><th>Def.</th><th>Tot.</th><th>Ast.</th><th>PF</th><th>Dq.</th><th>Stl.</th><th>Blk.</th><th>Pts.</th><th>Avg.</th></tr>
<tr><td>80-81—San Antonio</td><td>7</td><td>124</td><td>37</td><td>18</td><td>.486</td><td>8</td><td>6</td><td>.750</td><td>8</td><td>5</td><td>13</td><td>27</td><td>14</td><td>0</td><td>10</td><td>1</td><td>42</td><td>6.0</td></tr>
<tr><td>81-82—San Antonio</td><td>9</td><td>292</td><td>82</td><td>39</td><td>.476</td><td>27</td><td>16</td><td>.593</td><td>9</td><td>22</td><td>31</td><td>93</td><td>38</td><td>0</td><td>15</td><td>6</td><td>94</td><td>10.4</td></tr>
<tr><td>82-83—San Antonio</td><td>11</td><td>414</td><td>197</td><td>105</td><td>.533</td><td>35</td><td>28</td><td>.800</td><td>8</td><td>39</td><td>47</td><td>161</td><td>41</td><td>0</td><td>28</td><td>3</td><td>247</td><td>22.5</td></tr>
<tr><td>84-85—San Antonio</td><td>5</td><td>168</td><td>54</td><td>25</td><td>.463</td><td>23</td><td>15</td><td>.652</td><td>13</td><td>17</td><td>30</td><td>42</td><td>17</td><td>0</td><td>10</td><td>2</td><td>66</td><td>13.2</td></tr>
<tr><td>Totals ....</td><td>32</td><td>998</td><td>370</td><td>187</td><td>.505</td><td>93</td><td>65</td><td>.699</td><td>38</td><td>83</td><td>121</td><td>323</td><td>110</td><td>0</td><td>63</td><td>12</td><td>449</td><td>14.0</td></tr>
</table>

Three-Point Field Goals: 1980-81, 0-for-3. 1981-82, 0-for-3. 1982-83, 9-for-17 (.529). 1984-85, 1-for-3 (.333). Totals, 10-for-26 (.385).

Led NBA in assists, 1982.

RONALD KEITH MOORE
(Ron)

Born June 16, 1962 at New York, N.Y. Height 7:00. Weight 260.

High Schools—Brooklyn, N.Y., Thomas Jefferson (Freshman and Sophomore) and Clarksville, Ark. (Junior and Senior).

Colleges—Salem College, Salem, W. Va., and West Virginia State College, Institute, W. Va.

Drafted by New York on second round, 1987 (25th pick).

Traded by New York with a 1988 2nd round draft choice to Detroit for Sidney Green, October 28, 1987.
Traded by Detroit with a 1991 2nd round draft choice to Phoenix for James Edwards, February 24, 1988.

—COLLEGIATE RECORD—
Salem

<table>
<tr><th>Year</th><th>G.</th><th>Min.</th><th>FGA</th><th>FGM</th><th>Pct.</th><th>FTA</th><th>FTM</th><th>Pct.</th><th>Reb.</th><th>Pts.</th><th>Avg.</th></tr>
<tr><td>82-83 ....</td><td>31</td><td>....</td><td>347</td><td>186</td><td>.536</td><td>139</td><td>81</td><td>.583</td><td>333</td><td>453</td><td>14.6</td></tr>
<tr><td>83-84 ....</td><td>27</td><td>....</td><td>366</td><td>229</td><td>.626</td><td>146</td><td>90</td><td>.616</td><td>292</td><td>548</td><td>20.3</td></tr>
<tr><td>Totals ....</td><td>58</td><td>....</td><td>713</td><td>415</td><td>.582</td><td>285</td><td>171</td><td>.600</td><td>625</td><td>1001</td><td>17.3</td></tr>
</table>

West Virginia State

<table>
<tr><th>Year</th><th>G.</th><th>Min.</th><th>FGA</th><th>FGM</th><th>Pct.</th><th>FTA</th><th>FTM</th><th>Pct.</th><th>Reb.</th><th>Pts.</th><th>Avg.</th></tr>
<tr><td>84-85</td><td colspan="11">Did Not Play—Transfer Student</td></tr>
<tr><td>85-86 ....</td><td>30</td><td>....</td><td>549</td><td>289</td><td>.526</td><td>180</td><td>105</td><td>.583</td><td>325</td><td>683</td><td>22.8</td></tr>
<tr><td>86-87 ....</td><td>35</td><td>1122</td><td>704</td><td>407</td><td>.578</td><td>278</td><td>152</td><td>.547</td><td>383</td><td>966</td><td>27.6</td></tr>
<tr><td>Totals ....</td><td>65</td><td></td><td>1253</td><td>696</td><td>.555</td><td>458</td><td>257</td><td>.561</td><td>708</td><td>1649</td><td>25.4</td></tr>
<tr><td>College Totals ....</td><td>123</td><td>....</td><td>1966</td><td>1111</td><td>.565</td><td>743</td><td>428</td><td>.576</td><td>1333</td><td>2650</td><td>21.5</td></tr>
</table>

Three-Point Field Goals: 1986-87, 0-for-2.

NBA REGULAR SEASON RECORD

<table>
<tr><th>Sea.—Team</th><th>G.</th><th>Min.</th><th>FGA</th><th>FGM</th><th>Pct.</th><th>FTA</th><th>FTM</th><th>Pct.</th><th colspan="3">—Rebounds—</th><th></th><th></th><th></th><th></th><th></th><th></th><th></th></tr>
<tr><th></th><th></th><th></th><th></th><th></th><th></th><th></th><th></th><th></th><th>Off.</th><th>Def.</th><th>Tot.</th><th>Ast.</th><th>PF</th><th>Dq.</th><th>Stl.</th><th>Blk.</th><th>Pts.</th><th>Avg.</th></tr>
<tr><td>87-88—Det.-Phoe.</td><td>14</td><td>59</td><td>29</td><td>9</td><td>.310</td><td>8</td><td>6</td><td>.750</td><td>2</td><td>6</td><td>8</td><td>1</td><td>21</td><td>0</td><td>5</td><td>0</td><td>24</td><td>1.7</td></tr>
</table>

CHRISTOPHER PAUL MULLIN
(Chris)

Born July 30, 1963 at New York, N.Y. Height, 6:07. Weight 220.

High School—Brooklyn, N.Y., Xaverian.

College—St. John's University, Jamaica, N.Y.

Drafted by Golden State on first round, 1985 (7th pick).

—COLLEGIATE RECORD—

<table>
<tr><th>Year</th><th>G.</th><th>Min.</th><th>FGA</th><th>FGM</th><th>Pct.</th><th>FTA</th><th>FTM</th><th>Pct.</th><th>Reb.</th><th>Pts.</th><th>Avg.</th></tr>
<tr><td>81-82 ....</td><td>30</td><td>1061</td><td>328</td><td>175</td><td>.534</td><td>187</td><td>148</td><td>.791</td><td>97</td><td>498</td><td>16.6</td></tr>
<tr><td>82-83 ....</td><td>33</td><td>1210</td><td>395</td><td>228</td><td>.577</td><td>197</td><td>173</td><td>.878</td><td>123</td><td>629</td><td>19.1</td></tr>
<tr><td>83-84 ....</td><td>27</td><td>1070</td><td>394</td><td>225</td><td>.571</td><td>187</td><td>169</td><td>.904</td><td>120</td><td>619</td><td>22.9</td></tr>
<tr><td>84-85 ....</td><td>35</td><td>1327</td><td>482</td><td>251</td><td>.521</td><td>233</td><td>192</td><td>.824</td><td>169</td><td>694</td><td>19.8</td></tr>
<tr><td>Totals ....</td><td>125</td><td>4668</td><td>1599</td><td>879</td><td>.550</td><td>804</td><td>682</td><td>.848</td><td>509</td><td>2440</td><td>19.5</td></tr>
</table>

NBA REGULAR SEASON RECORD

Sea.—Team	G.	Min.	FGA	FGM	Pct.	FTA	FTM	Pct.	Off.	Def.	Tot.	Ast.	PF	Dq.	Stl.	Blk.	Pts.	Avg.
85-86—Golden State	55	1391	620	287	.463	211	189	.896	42	73	115	105	130	1	70	23	768	14.0
86-87—Golden State	82	2377	928	477	.514	326	269	.825	39	142	181	261	217	1	98	36	1242	15.1
87-88—Golden State	60	2033	926	470	.508	270	239	.885	58	147	205	290	136	3	113	32	1213	20.2
Totals	197	5801	2474	1234	.499	807	697	.864	139	362	501	656	483	5	281	91	3223	16.4

Three-Point Field Goals: 1985-86, 5-for-27 (.185). 1986-87, 19-for-63 (.302). 1987-88, 34-for-97 (.351). Totals, 58-for-187 (.310).

NBA PLAYOFF RECORD

Sea.—Team	G.	Min.	FGA	FGM	Pct.	FTA	FTM	Pct.	Off.	Def.	Tot.	Ast.	PF	Dq.	Stl.	Blk.	Pts.	Avg.
86-87—Golden State	10	262	98	49	.500	16	12	.750	2	13	15	23	31	0	9	2	113	11.3

Three-Point Field Goals: 1986-87, 3-for-4 (.750).

Member of U.S. Olympic team, 1984. . . . Named to THE SPORTING NEWS All-America First Team, 1985. . . . THE SPORTING NEWS All-America Second Team, 1984.

JAY DENNIS MURPHY

Born June 26, 1962 at Meriden, Conn.   Height 6:09.   Weight 220.

High School—Meriden, Conn., Maloney.

College—Boston College, Chestnut Hill, Mass.

Drafted by Golden State on second round, 1984 (31st pick).

Draft rights traded by Golden State to Los Angeles Clippers for Jerome Whitehead, June 19, 1984.
Waived by Los Angeles Clippers, December 17, 1985; signed by Washington as a free agent, September 3, 1986.

—COLLEGIATE RECORD—

Year	G.	Min.	FGA	FGM	Pct.	FTA	FTM	Pct.	Reb.	Pts.	Avg.
80-81	30	676	210	108	.514	93	63	.677	132	279	9.3
81-82	31	735	236	126	.534	147	105	.714	153	357	11.5
82-83	32	957	455	224	.492	158	117	.741	260	565	17.7
83-84	30	958	481	227	.472	175	140	.800	218	594	19.8
Totals	123	3326	1382	685	.496	573	425	.742	763	1795	14.6

NBA REGULAR SEASON RECORD

Sea.—Team	G.	Min.	FGA	FGM	Pct.	FTA	FTM	Pct.	Off.	Def.	Tot.	Ast.	PF	Dq.	Stl.	Blk.	Pts.	Avg.
84-85—L.A. Clippers	23	149	50	8	.160	21	12	.571	6	35	41	4	21	0	1	2	28	1.2
85-86—L.A. Clippers	14	100	45	16	.356	14	9	.643	7	8	15	3	12	0	4	3	41	2.9
86-87—Washington	21	141	72	31	.431	16	9	.563	17	22	39	5	21	0	3	2	71	3.4
87-88—Washington	9	46	23	8	.348	5	4	.800	4	12	16	1	5	0	0	0	20	2.2
Totals	67	436	190	63	.332	56	34	.607	34	77	111	13	59	0	8	7	160	2.4

Three-Point Field Goals: 1984-85, 0-for-1. 1985-86, 0-for-2. Totals, 0-for-3.

RONALD T. MURPHY
(Ronnie)

Born July 29, 1964 at Dover, Del.   Height 6:05.   Weight 225.

High School—Ovideo, Fla.

College—Jacksonville University, Jacksonville, Fla.

Drafted by Portland on first round, 1987 (17th pick).

—COLLEGIATE RECORD—

Year	G.	Min.	FGA	FGM	Pct.	FTA	FTM	Pct.	Reb.	Pts.	Avg.
83-84	26	1012	404	193	.478	104	79	.760	152	465	17.9
84-85	28	847	368	152	.413	84	58	.690	93	362	12.9
85-86	30	1004	406	182	.448	121	85	.702	129	449	15.0
86-87	30	1004	521	243	.466	134	106	.791	169	661	22.0
Totals	114	3867	1699	770	.453	443	328	.740	543	1937	17.0

Three-Point Field Goals: 1986-87, 69-for-145 (.476).

NBA REGULAR SEASON RECORD

Sea.—Team	G.	Min.	FGA	FGM	Pct.	FTA	FTM	Pct.	Off.	Def.	Tot.	Ast.	PF	Dq.	Stl.	Blk.	Pts.	Avg.
87-88—Portland	18	89	49	14	.286	11	7	.636	5	6	11	6	14	0	5	1	36	2.0

Three-Point Field Goals: 1987-88, 1-for-4 (.250).

TOD JAMES MURPHY

Born December 24, 1963 at Long Beach, Calif. Height 6:09. Weight 220.

High School—Lakewood, Calif.

College—University of California-Irvine, Irvine, Calif.

Drafted by Seattle on third round, 1986 (53rd pick).

Draft rights relinquished by Seattle, September 17, 1987; signed by Los Angeles Clippers as a free agent, October 6, 1987.

Waived by Los Angeles Clippers, November 9, 1987.

Played in Continental Basketball Association with Albany Patroons, 1987-88.

—COLLEGIATE RECORD—

Year	G.	Min.	FGA	FGM	Pct.	FTA	FTM	Pct.	Reb.	Pts.	Avg.
82-83	28	704	172	89	.517	93	66	.710	150	244	8.7
83-84	29	872	268	154	.575	135	110	.815	203	418	14.4
84-85	30	1047	340	190	.559	153	130	.850	268	511	17.0
85-86	30	1116	378	211	.558	244	182	.746	216	605	20.2
Totals	117	3739	1158	644	.556	625	488	.781	837	1778	15.2

Three-Point Field Goals: 1984-85, 1-for-3 (.333). 1985-86, 1-for-1 (1.000). Totals, 2-for-4 (.500).

CBA REGULAR SEASON RECORD

Sea.—Team	G.	Min.	2-Point FGM	FGA	Pct.	3-Point FGM	FGA	Pct.	FTM	FTA	Pct.	Reb.	Ast.	Pts.	Avg.
87-88—Albany	32	751	104	175	.594	0	2	.000	98	120	.817	214	28	306	9.6

NBA REGULAR SEASON RECORD

Sea.—Team	G.	Min.	FGA	FGM	Pct.	FTA	FTM	Pct.	Off.	Def.	Tot.	Ast.	PF	Dq.	Stl.	Blk.	Pts.	Avg.
87-88—L.A. Clippers	1	19	1	1	1.000	4	3	.750	1	1	2	2	2	0	1	0	5	5.0

CBA Playoff MVP, 1988.

PETER E. MYERS
(Pete)

Born September 15, 1963 at Mobile, Ala. Height 6:06. Weight 180.

High School—Mobile, Ala., Williamson.

Colleges—Faulkner State Junior College, Bay Minette, Ala., and University of Arkansas at Little Rock, Little Rock, Ark.

Drafted by Chicago on sixth round, 1986 (120th pick).

Waived by Chicago, November 3, 1987; signed by San Antonio as a free agent, January 29, 1988.

Played in Continental Basketball Association with Rockford Lightning, 1987-88.

—COLLEGIATE RECORD—
Faulkner State

Year	G.	Min.	FGA	FGM	Pct.	FTA	FTM	Pct.	Reb.	Pts.	Avg.
81-82	26	....	199	109	.548	140	104	.743	132	322	12.4
82-83	26	....	249	144	.578	169	106	.627	196	394	15.2
J.C. Totals	52	....	448	253	.565	309	210	.680	328	716	13.8

Arkansas-Little Rock

Year	G.	Min.	FGA	FGM	Pct.	FTA	FTM	Pct.	Reb.	Pts.	Avg.
83-84						Did Not Play					
84-85	30	....	359	162	.451	167	120	.719	213	444	14.8
85-86	34	1142	429	229	.534	261	195	.747	270	653	19.2
Ark.-LR Totals	64	....	788	391	.496	428	315	.736	483	1097	17.1

CBA REGULAR SEASON RECORD

Sea.—Team	G.	Min.	2-Point FGM	FGA	Pct.	3-Point FGM	FGA	Pct.	FTM	FTA	Pct.	Reb.	Ast.	Pts.	Avg.
87-88—Rockford	28	1134	206	380	.542	10	26	.385	146	199	.734	103	147	588	21.0

NBA REGULAR SEASON RECORD

Sea.—Team	G.	Min.	FGA	FGM	Pct.	FTA	FTM	Pct.	Off.	Def.	Tot.	Ast.	PF	Dq.	Stl.	Blk.	Pts.	Avg.
86-87—Chicago	29	155	52	19	.365	28	8	.651	8	9	17	21	25	0	14	2	66	2.3
87-88—San Antonio	22	328	95	43	.453	39	26	.667	11	26	37	48	30	0	17	6	112	5.1
Totals	51	483	147	62	.422	82	54	.659	19	35	54	69	55	0	31	8	178	3.5

Three-Point Field Goals: 1986-87, 0-for-6. 1987-88, 0-for-4. Totals, 0-for-10.

Sea.—Team	G.	Min.	FGA	FGM	Pct.	FTA	FTM	Pct.	—Rebounds— Off.	Def.	Tot.	Ast.	PF	Dq.	Stl.	Blk.	Pts.	Avg.
86-87—Chicago	1	1	1	0	.000	0	0	.000	0	0	0	0	0	0	0	0	0	0.0

Named to CBA All-Star Second Team, 1988.

LARRY DONELL NANCE

Born February 12, 1959 at Anderson, S. C.   Height 6:10.   Weight 215.

High School—Anderson, S. C., McDuffie.

College—Clemson University, Clemson, S. C.

Drafted by Phoenix on first round, 1981 (20th pick).

Traded by Phoenix with Mike Sanders and a 1988 1st round draft choice to Cleveland for Tyrone Corbin, Kevin Johnson, Mark West, 1988 1st and 2nd round draft choices and a 1989 2nd round draft choice, February 25, 1988.

—COLLEGIATE RECORD—

Year	G.	Min.	FGA	FGM	Pct.	FTA	FTM	Pct.	Reb.	Pts.	Avg.
77-78	25	273	75	35	.467	17	8	.471	78	78	3.1
78-79	29	837	264	137	.519	77	49	.636	210	323	11.1
79-80	32	961	338	174	.515	164	98	.598	259	446	13.9
80-81	31	887	360	207	.575	116	80	.690	237	494	15.9
Totals	117	2958	1037	553	.533	374	235	.628	834	1341	11.5

NBA REGULAR SEASON RECORD

Sea.—Team	G.	Min.	FGA	FGM	Pct.	FTA	FTM	Pct.	—Rebounds— Off.	Def.	Tot.	Ast.	PF	Dq.	Stl.	Blk.	Pts.	Avg.
81-82—Phoenix	80	1186	436	227	.521	117	75	.641	95	161	256	82	169	2	42	71	529	6.6
82-83—Phoenix	82	2914	1069	588	.550	287	193	.672	239	471	710	197	254	4	99	217	1370	16.7
83-84—Phoenix	82	2899	1044	601	.576	352	249	.707	227	451	678	214	274	5	86	174	1451	17.7
84-85—Phoenix	61	2202	877	515	.587	254	180	.709	195	341	536	159	185	2	88	104	1211	19.9
85-86—Phoenix	73	2484	1001	582	.581	444	310	.698	169	449	618	240	247	6	70	130	1474	20.2
86-87—Phoenix	69	2569	1062	585	.551	493	381	.773	188	411	599	233	223	4	86	148	1552	22.5
87-88—Phoe.-Clev.	67	2383	920	487	.529	390	304	.779	193	414	607	207	242	10	63	159	1280	19.1
Totals	514	16637	6409	3585	.559	2337	1692	.724	1306	2698	4004	1332	1594	33	534	1003	8867	17.3

Three-Point Field Goals: 1981-82, 0-for-1. 1982-83, 1-for-3 (.333). 1983-84, 0-for-7. 1984-85, 1-for-2 (.500). 1985-86, 0-for-8. 1986-87, 1-for-5 (.200). 1987-88, 2-for-6 (.333). Totals, 5-for-32 (.156).

NBA PLAYOFF RECORD

Sea.—Team	G.	Min.	FGA	FGM	Pct.	FTA	FTM	Pct.	—Rebounds— Off.	Def.	Tot.	Ast.	PF	Dq.	Stl.	Blk.	Pts.	Avg.
81-82—Phoenix	7	128	41	25	.610	8	4	.500	13	19	32	7	15	1	10	11	54	7.7
82-83—Phoenix	3	103	35	14	.400	10	8	.800	10	15	25	3	12	1	3	6	36	12.0
83-84—Phoenix	17	633	200	118	.590	76	51	.671	51	97	148	40	59	1	16	34	287	16.9
87-88—Cleveland	5	200	64	34	.531	18	16	.889	10	26	36	18	13	0	2	11	84	16.8
Totals	32	1064	340	191	.562	112	79	.705	84	157	241	68	99	3	31	62	461	14.4

NBA ALL-STAR GAME RECORD

Season—Team	Min.	FGA	FGM	Pct.	FTA	FTM	Pct.	—Rebounds— Off.	Def.	Tot.	Ast.	PF	Dq.	Stl.	Blk.	Pts.
1985—Phoenix	15	8	7	.875	2	2	1.000	1	4	5	0	5	0	0	2	16

CALVIN LEON NATT

Born January 8, 1957 at Monroe, La.   Height 6:06.   Weight 220.

High School—Bastrop, La.

College—Northeast Louisiana University, Monroe, La.

Drafted by New Jersey on first round, 1979 (8th pick).

Traded by New Jersey to Portland for Maurice Lucas and 1980 and 1981 1st round draft choices, February 8, 1980. Traded by Portland with Lafayette Lever, Wayne Cooper, a 1984 2nd round draft choice and a 1985 1st round draft choice to Denver for Kiki Vandeweghe, June 7, 1984.

—COLLEGIATE RECORD—

Year	G.	Min.	FGA	FGM	Pct.	FTA	FTM	Pct.	Reb.	Pts.	Avg.
75-76	25	....	371	207	.558	129	102	.791	274	516	20.6
76-77	27	....	493	307	.623	226	168	.743	340	782	29.0
77-78	27	....	401	220	.549	186	136	.731	356	576	21.3
78-79	29	....	506	283	.559	178	141	.792	315	707	24.4
Totals	108	....	1771	1017	.574	719	547	.761	1285	2581	23.9

LARRY NANCE

NBA REGULAR SEASON RECORD

Sea.—Team	G.	Min.	FGA	FGM	Pct.	FTA	FTM	Pct.	Off.	Def.	Tot.	Ast.	PF	Dq.	Stl.	Blk.	Pts.	Avg.
79-80—N.J.-Port.	78	2857	1298	622	.479	419	306	.730	239	452	691	169	205	1	102	34	1553	19.9
80-81—Portland	74	2111	794	395	.497	283	200	.707	149	282	431	159	188	2	73	18	994	13.4
81-82—Portland	75	2599	894	515	.576	392	294	.750	193	420	613	150	175	1	62	36	1326	17.7
82-83—Portland	80	2879	1187	644	.543	428	339	.792	214	385	599	171	184	2	63	29	1630	20.4
83-84—Portland	79	2638	857	500	.583	345	275	.797	166	310	476	179	218	3	69	22	1277	16.2
84-85—Denver	78	2657	1255	685	.546	564	447	.793	209	401	610	238	182	1	75	33	1817	23.3
85-86—Denver	69	2007	930	469	.504	347	278	.801	125	311	436	164	143	0	58	13	1218	17.7
86-87—Denver	1	20	10	4	.400	2	2	1.000	2	3	5	2	2	0	1	0	10	10.0
87-88—Denver	27	533	208	102	.490	73	54	.740	35	61	96	47	43	0	13	3	258	9.6
Totals	561	18301	7433	3936	.530	2853	2195	.769	1332	2625	3957	1279	1340	10	516	188	10083	18.0

Three-Point Field Goals: 1979-80, 3-for-9 (.333). 1980-81, 4-for-8 (.500). 1981-82, 2-for-8 (.250). 1982-83, 3-for-20 (.150). 1983-84, 2-for-17 (.118). 1984-85, 0-for-3. 1985-86, 2-for-6 (.333). 1987-88, 0-for-1. Totals, 16-for-72 (.222).

NBA PLAYOFF RECORD

Sea.—Team	G.	Min.	FGA	FGM	Pct.	FTA	FTM	Pct.	Off.	Def.	Tot.	Ast.	PF	Dq.	Stl.	Blk.	Pts.	Avg.
79-80—Portland	3	125	48	21	.438	10	6	.600	9	15	24	2	7	0	2	1	48	16.0
80-81—Portland	3	95	31	14	.452	8	4	.500	6	14	20	1	4	0	1	1	32	10.7
82-83—Portland	7	274	102	50	.490	48	31	.646	22	42	64	11	14	0	8	1	132	18.9
83-84—Portland	5	195	72	37	.514	36	25	.694	11	27	38	9	10	0	6	1	99	19.8
84-85—Denver	15	508	238	131	.550	89	72	.809	31	68	99	57	35	0	8	5	334	22.3
85-86—Denver	10	293	142	66	.465	59	46	.780	17	62	79	28	25	0	2	3	179	17.9
Totals	43	1490	633	319	.504	250	184	.736	96	228	324	108	95	0	27	12	824	19.2

Three-Point Field Goals: 1979-80, 0-for-2. 1982-83, 1-for-2 (.500). 1983-84, 0-for-3. 1985-86, 1-for-2 (.500). Totals, 2-for-9 (.222).

NBA ALL-STAR GAME RECORD

Season—Team	Min.	FGA	FGM	Pct.	FTA	FTM	Pct.	Off.	Def.	Tot.	Ast.	PF	Dq.	Stl.	Blk.	Pts.
1985—Denver	11	3	1	.333	2	1	.500	0	3	3	1	1	0	0	0	3

Named to NBA All-Rookie Team, 1980. . . . THE SPORTING NEWS All-America Second Team, 1979.

EDDIE CARL NEALY
(Ed)

Born February 19, 1960 at Pittsburg, Kan. Height 6:07. Weight 238.

High School—Bonner Springs, Kan.

College—Kansas State University, Manhattan, Kan.

Drafted by Kansas City on eighth round, 1982 (166th pick).

Waived by Kansas City, July 10, 1984; re-signed by Kansas City as a free agent, July 20, 1984.
Waived by Kansas City, October 24, 1984; re-signed by Kansas City as a free agent, February 27, 1985.
Waived by Kansas City, October 21, 1985; signed by San Antonio as a free agent, July 15, 1986.
Played in Continental Basketball Association with Sarasota Stingers, 1984-85, and Tampa Bay Thrillers, 1985-86.

—COLLEGIATE RECORD—

Year	G.	Min.	FGA	FGM	Pct.	FTA	FTM	Pct.	Reb.	Pts.	Avg.
78-79	28	....	266	115	.432	71	56	.789	230	286	10.2
79-80	31	....	242	114	.471	105	76	.724	272	304	9.8
80-81	33	....	289	152	.526	82	59	.720	301	363	11.0
81-82	31	....	243	138	.568	122	75	.615	268	351	11.3
Totals	123	....	1040	519	.499	380	266	.700	1071	1304	10.6

CBA REGULAR SEASON RECORD

Sea.—Team	G.	Min.	2-Point			3-Point			FTM	FTA	Pct.	Reb.	Ast.	Pts.	Avg.
			FGM	FGA	Pct.	FGM	FGA	Pct.							
84-85—Sarasota	39	1350	156	267	.584	1	2	.500	113	142	.795	371	53	428	11.0
85-86—Tampa Bay	29	926	91	169	.538	0	1	.000	59	79	.746	309	34	241	8.3
Totals	68	2276	247	436	.566	1	3	.333	172	221	.778	680	87	669	9.8

NBA REGULAR SEASON RECORD

Sea.—Team	G.	Min.	FGA	FGM	Pct.	FTA	FTM	Pct.	Off.	Def.	Tot.	Ast.	PF	Dq.	Stl.	Blk.	Pts.	Avg.
82-83—Kansas City	82	1643	247	147	.595	114	70	.614	170	315	485	62	247	4	68	12	364	4.4
83-84—Kansas City	71	960	126	63	.500	60	48	.800	73	149	222	50	138	1	41	9	174	2.5
84-85—Kansas City	22	225	44	26	.591	19	10	.526	15	29	44	18	26	0	3	1	62	2.8
86-87—San Antonio	60	980	192	84	.438	69	51	.739	96	188	284	83	144	1	40	11	223	3.7
87-88—San Antonio	68	837	109	50	.459	63	41	.651	82	140	222	49	94	0	29	5	142	2.1
Totals	303	4645	718	370	.515	325	220	.677	436	821	1257	262	649	6	181	38	965	3.2

Three-Point Field Goals: 1986-87, 4-for-31 (.129). 1987-88, 1-for-2 (.500). Totals, 5-for-33 (.152).

NBA PLAYOFF RECORD

Sea.—Team	G.	Min.	FGA	FGM	Pct.	FTA	FTM	Pct.	Rebounds Off.	Def.	Tot.	Ast.	PF	Dq.	Stl.	Blk.	Pts.	Avg.
83-84—Kansas City	2	19	2	2	1.000	2	2	1.000	2	4	6	2	1	0	0	0	6	3.0
87-88—San Antonio	2	36	4	2	.500	0	0	.000	3	4	7	4	6	0	1	0	4	2.0
Totals	4	55	6	4	.667	2	2	1.000	5	8	13	6	7	0	1	0	10	2.5

MARTIN SCOTT NESSLEY

Born February 16, 1965 at Columbus, O.   Height 7:02.   Weight 260.

High School—Whitehall, Ohio, Whitehall-Yearling.

College—Duke University, Durham, N.C.

Drafted by Los Angeles Clippers on sixth round, 1987 (116th pick).

Waived by Los Angeles Clippers, March 23, 1988; signed by Sacramento, April 1, 1988, to the first of consecutive 10-day contracts that expired, April 20, 1988.
Re-signed by Sacramento, April 21, 1988, for remainder of season.
Waived by Sacramento, April 25, 1988.

—COLLEGIATE RECORD—

Year	G.	Min.	FGA	FGM	Pct.	FTA	FTM	Pct.	Reb.	Pts.	Avg.
83-84	22	147	40	12	.300	15	7	.467	38	31	1.4
84-85	17	101	11	7	.636	2	2	1.000	18	16	0.9
85-86	20	107	36	14	.389	9	6	.667	38	34	1.7
86-87	33	375	93	53	.570	57	37	.649	97	143	4.3
Totals	92	730	180	86	.478	83	52	.627	191	224	2.4

NBA REGULAR SEASON RECORD

Sea.—Team	G.	Min.	FGA	FGM	Pct.	FTA	FTM	Pct.	Rebounds Off.	Def.	Tot.	Ast.	PF	Dq.	Stl.	Blk.	Pts.	Avg.
87-88—L.A.C.-Sac.	44	336	52	20	.385	18	8	.444	23	59	82	16	89	1	8	12	48	1.1

CHARLES GOODRICH NEVITT
(Chuck)

Born June 13, 1959 at Cortez, Colo.   Height 7:05.   Weight 237.

High School—Marietta, Ga., Sprayberry.

College—North Carolina State University, Raleigh, N. C.

Drafted by Houston on third round, 1982 (63rd pick).

Waived by Houston and claimed by Milwaukee on waivers, October 22, 1982.
Waived by Milwaukee, October 28, 1982; signed by Houston as a free agent, June 1, 1983.
Waived by Houston, November 29, 1983; signed by Los Angeles Lakers as a free agent, September 15, 1984.
Waived by Los Angeles Lakers, November 6, 1984; re-signed by Los Angeles Lakers, March 5, 1985, to the first of consecutive 10-day contracts that expired, March 24, 1985.
Re-signed by Los Angeles Lakers, March 25, 1985.
Waived by Los Angeles Lakers, November 22, 1985; signed by Detroit as a free agent, November 29, 1985.

—COLLEGIATE RECORD—

Year	G.	Min.	FGA	FGM	Pct.	FTA	FTM	Pct.	Reb.	Pts.	Avg.
77-78					Did Not Play—Injured						
78-79	19	....	20	10	.500	15	4	.267	25	24	1.3
79-80	19	....	23	14	.609	10	2	.200	34	30	1.6
80-81	21	....	26	15	.577	23	10	.435	24	40	1.9
81-82	31	....	119	70	.588	57	32	.561	137	172	5.5
Totals	90	....	188	109	.580	105	48	.457	220	266	3.0

NBA REGULAR SEASON RECORD

Sea.—Team	G.	Min.	FGA	FGM	Pct.	FTA	FTM	Pct.	Rebounds Off.	Def.	Tot.	Ast.	PF	Dq.	Stl.	Blk.	Pts.	Avg.
82-83—Houston	6	64	15	11	.733	4	1	.250	6	11	17	0	14	0	1	12	23	3.8
84-85—L.A. Lakers	11	59	17	5	.294	8	2	.250	5	15	20	3	20	0	0	15	12	1.1
85-86—L.A.L.-Det.	29	126	43	15	.349	26	19	.731	13	19	32	7	35	0	4	19	49	1.7
86-87—Detroit	41	267	63	31	.492	24	14	.583	36	47	83	4	73	0	7	30	76	1.9
87-88—Detroit	17	63	21	7	.333	6	3	.500	4	14	18	0	12	0	1	5	17	1.0
Totals	104	579	159	69	.434	68	39	.574	64	106	170	14	154	0	13	81	177	1.7

NBA PLAYOFF RECORD

Sea.—Team	G.	Min.	FGA	FGM	Pct.	FTA	FTM	Pct.	Rebounds Off.	Def.	Tot.	Ast.	PF	Dq.	Stl.	Blk.	Pts.	Avg.
84-85—L.A. Lakers	7	37	9	3	.333	8	4	.500	3	3	6	1	11	0	4	6	10	1.4
85-86—Detroit	1	1	0	0	.000	0	0	.000	0	0	0	0	0	0	0	0	0	0.0
86-87—Detroit	3	10	5	1	.200	2	2	1.000	1	5	6	0	1	0	0	3	4	1.3
87-88—Detroit	3	4	2	1	.500	0	0	.000	2	1	3	0	1	0	0	0	2	0.7
Totals	14	52	16	5	.313	10	6	.600	6	9	15	1	13	0	4	9	16	1.1

Member of NBA championship team, 1985.

JOHN SYLVESTER NEWMAN JR.

Born November 28, 1963 at Danville, Va.   Height 6:07.   Weight 190.

High School—Danville, Va., George Washington.

College—University of Richmond, Richmond, Va.

Drafted by Cleveland on second round, 1986 (29th pick).

Waived by Cleveland, November 5, 1987; signed by New York as a free agent, November 12, 1987.

—COLLEGIATE RECORD—

Year	G.	Min.	FGA	FGM	Pct.	FTA	FTM	Pct.	Reb.	Pts.	Avg.
82-83	28	763	259	137	.528	96	69	.718	87	343	12.3
83-84	32	1189	517	273	.528	197	155	.786	196	701	21.9
84-85	32	1128	490	270	.551	181	140	.773	166	680	21.3
85-86	30	1123	489	253	.517	172	153	.895	219	659	22.0
Totals	122	4203	1755	933	.532	646	517	.800	668	2383	19.5

NBA REGULAR SEASON RECORD

Sea.—Team	G.	Min.	FGA	FGM	Pct.	FTA	FTM	Pct.	Off.	Def.	Tot.	Ast.	PF	Dq.	Stl.	Blk.	Pts.	Avg.
86-87—Cleveland	59	630	275	113	.411	76	66	.868	36	34	70	27	67	0	20	7	293	5.0
87-88—New York	77	1589	620	270	.435	246	207	.841	87	72	159	62	204	5	72	11	773	10.0
Totals	136	2219	895	383	.428	322	273	.848	123	106	229	89	271	5	92	18	1066	7.8

Three-Point Field Goals: 1986-87, 1-for-22 (.045). 1987-88, 26-for-93 (.280). Totals, 27-for-115 (.235).

NBA PLAYOFF RECORD

Sea.—Team	G.	Min.	FGA	FGM	Pct.	FTA	FTM	Pct.	Off.	Def.	Tot.	Ast.	PF	Dq.	Stl.	Blk.	Pts.	Avg.
87-88—New York	4	113	68	31	.456	16	14	.875	8	3	11	7	16	0	6	1	76	19.0

Three-Point Field Goals: 1987-88, 0-for-9.

KURT ALLEN NIMPHIUS

Born March 13, 1958 at Milwaukee, Wis.   Height 6:11.   Weight 225.

High School—South Milwaukee, Wis.

College—Arizona State University, Tempe, Ariz.

Drafted by Denver on third round, 1980 (47th pick).

Waived by Denver and signed same day by Dallas as a free agent, September 2, 1981.
Traded by Dallas to Los Angeles Clippers for James Donaldson, November 25, 1985.
Traded by Los Angeles Clippers to Detroit for 1987 1st and 2nd round draft choices, January 29, 1987.
Signed by San Antonio as a Veteran Free Agent, October 27, 1987; Detroit agreed not to exercise its right of first refusal in exchange for a 1988 2nd round draft choice.
Played in Continental Basketball Association with Alberta Dusters, 1980-81.
Played in Italy during 1980-81 season.

—COLLEGIATE RECORD—

Year	G.	Min.	FGA	FGM	Pct.	FTA	FTM	Pct.	Reb.	Pts.	Avg.
76-77†	3	....	....	28	....	14	10	.714	44	66	22.0
76-77	18	76	19	10	.526	12	7	.583	28	27	1.5
77-78	27	670	176	98	.557	53	34	.642	166	230	8.5
78-79	30	576	180	105	.583	90	59	.656	150	269	9.0
79-80	29	977	304	185	.609	155	110	.710	277	480	16.6
Varsity Totals	104	2299	679	398	.586	310	210	.677	621	1006	9.7

CBA REGULAR SEASON RECORD

Sea.—Team	G.	Min.	2-Point FGM	FGA	Pct.	3-Point FGM	FGA	Pct.	FTM	FTA	Pct.	Reb.	Ast.	Pts.	Avg.
80-81—Alberta	18	498	92	181	.508	0	1	.000	53	67	.791	156	20	237	13.2

NBA REGULAR SEASON RECORD

Sea.—Team	G.	Min.	FGA	FGM	Pct.	FTA	FTM	Pct.	Off.	Def.	Tot.	Ast.	PF	Dq.	Stl.	Blk.	Pts.	Avg.
81-82—Dallas	63	1085	297	137	.461	108	63	.583	92	203	295	61	190	5	17	82	337	5.3
82-83—Dallas	81	1515	355	174	.490	140	77	.550	157	247	404	115	287	11	24	111	426	5.3
83-84—Dallas	82	2284	523	272	.520	162	101	.623	182	331	513	176	283	5	41	144	646	7.9
84-85—Dallas	82	2010	434	196	.452	140	108	.771	136	272	408	183	262	4	30	126	500	6.1
85-86—Dal.-L.A.C.	80	2226	694	351	.506	262	194	.740	152	301	453	62	267	8	33	105	896	11.2
86-87—L.A.C.-Det.	66	1088	330	155	.470	120	81	.675	80	107	187	25	156	1	20	54	391	5.9
87-88—San Antonio	72	919	257	128	.498	83	60	.723	62	91	153	53	141	2	22	56	316	4.4
Totals	526	11127	2890	1413	.489	1015	684	.674	861	1552	2413	675	1586	36	187	678	3512	6.7

Three-Point Field Goals: 1982-83, 1-for-1 (1.000). 1983-84, 1-for-4 (.250). 1984-85, 0-for-6. 1985-86, 0-for-3. 1986-87, 0-for-4. 1987-88, 0-for-1. Totals, 2-for-19 (.105).

NBA PLAYOFF RECORD

Sea.—Team	G.	Min.	FGA	FGM	Pct.	FTA	FTM	Pct.	Off.	Def.	Tot.	Ast.	PF	Dq.	Stl.	Blk.	Pts.	Avg.
83-84—Dallas	10	178	33	14	.424	17	14	.824	20	33	53	13	24	0	0	14	42	4.2
84-85—Dallas	4	50	6	3	.500	0	0	.000	3	3	6	3	10	0	1	1	6	1.5
86-87—Detroit	4	30	9	3	.333	4	2	.500	5	5	10	0	10	0	0	2	8	2.0
87-88—San Antonio	3	30	10	5	.500	2	2	1.000	3	5	8	2	7	0	0	1	12	4.0
Totals	21	288	58	25	.431	23	18	.783	31	46	77	18	51	0	1	18	68	3.2

NORMAN ELLARD NIXON
(Norm)

Born October 11, 1955 at Macon, Ga.   Height 6:02.   Weight 170.

High School—Macon, Ga., Southwest.

College—Duquesne University, Pittsburgh, Pa.

Drafted by Los Angeles on first round, 1977 (22nd pick).

Traded by Los Angeles with Eddie Jordan and 1986 and 1987 2nd round draft choices to San Diego for Swen Nater and the draft rights to Byron Scott, October 10, 1983.
Missed entire 1986-87 and 1987-88 seasons due to injury.

—COLLEGIATE RECORD—

Year	G.	Min.	FGA	FGM	Pct.	FTA	FTM	Pct.	Reb.	Pts.	Avg.
73-74	24	....	257	113	.440	45	31	.689	99	257	10.7
74-75	25	....	282	147	.521	92	69	.750	88	363	14.5
75-76	25	....	434	214	.493	127	96	.756	105	524	21.0
76-77	30	1106	539	279	.518	138	103	.746	119	661	22.0
Totals	104	....	1512	753	.498	402	299	.744	411	1805	17.4

NBA REGULAR SEASON RECORD

Sea.—Team	G.	Min.	FGA	FGM	Pct.	FTA	FTM	Pct.	Off.	Def.	Tot.	Ast.	PF	Dq.	Stl.	Blk.	Pts.	Avg.
77-78—Los Angeles	81	2779	998	496	.497	161	115	.714	41	198	239	553	259	3	138	7	1107	13.7
78-79—Los Angeles	82	3145	1149	623	.542	204	158	.775	48	183	231	737	250	6	201	17	1404	17.1
79-80—Los Angeles	82	3226	1209	624	.516	253	197	.779	52	177	229	642	241	1	147	14	1446	17.6
80-81—Los Angeles	79	2962	1210	576	.476	252	196	.778	64	168	232	696	226	2	146	11	1350	17.1
81-82—Los Angeles	82	3024	1274	628	.493	224	181	.808	38	138	176	652	264	3	132	7	1440	17.6
82-83—Los Angeles	79	2711	1123	533	.475	168	125	.744	61	144	205	566	176	1	104	4	1191	15.1
83-84—San Diego	82	3053	1270	587	.462	271	206	.760	56	147	203	914	180	1	94	4	1391	17.0
84-85—L.A. Clippers	81	2894	1281	596	.465	218	170	.780	55	163	218	711	175	2	95	4	1395	17.2
85-86—L.A. Clippers	67	2138	921	403	.438	162	131	.809	45	135	180	576	143	0	84	3	979	14.6
Totals	715	25932	10435	5066	.485	1913	1479	.773	460	1453	1913	6047	1914	19	1141	71	11703	16.4

Three-Point Field Goals: 1979-80, 1-for-8 (.125). 1980-81, 2-for-12 (.167). 1981-82, 3-for-12 (.250). 1982-83, 0-for-13. 1983-84, 11-for-46 (.239). 1984-85, 33-for-99 (.333). 1985-86, 42-for-121 (.347). Totals, 92-for-311 (.296).

NBA PLAYOFF RECORD

Sea.—Team	G.	Min.	FGA	FGM	Pct.	FTA	FTM	Pct.	Off.	Def.	Tot.	Ast.	PF	Dq.	Stl.	Blk.	Pts.	Avg.
77-78—Los Angeles	3	92	24	11	.458	3	2	.667	4	5	9	16	13	0	4	1	24	8.0
78-79—Los Angeles	8	327	119	56	.471	15	11	.733	6	22	28	94	37	1	11	0	123	15.4
79-80—Los Angeles	16	648	239	114	.477	51	41	.804	13	43	56	125	59	0	32	3	270	16.9
80-81—Los Angeles	3	133	49	25	.510	10	8	.800	1	10	11	26	9	0	1	1	58	19.3
81-82—Los Angeles	14	549	253	121	.478	57	43	.754	13	30	43	114	43	0	23	2	286	20.4
82-83—Los Angeles	14	538	237	113	.477	50	37	.740	13	35	48	89	40	0	18	1	266	19.0
Totals	58	2287	921	440	.478	186	142	.763	50	145	195	464	201	1	89	8	1027	17.7

Three-Point Field Goals: 1979-80, 1-for-5 (.200). 1981-82, 1-for-3 (.333). 1982-83, 3-for-7 (.429). Totals, 5-for-15 (.333).

NBA ALL-STAR GAME RECORD

Season—Team	Min.	FGA	FGM	Pct.	FTA	FTM	Pct.	Off.	Def.	Tot.	Ast.	PF	Dq.	Stl.	Blk.	Pts.
1982—Los Angeles	19	14	7	.500	0	0	.000	0	0	0	2	0	0	1	0	14
1985—L.A. Clippers	19	7	5	.714	2	1	.500	0	2	2	8	0	0	1	0	11
Totals	38	21	12	.571	2	1	.500	0	2	2	10	0	0	2	0	25

Named to NBA All-Rookie Team, 1978. . . . Member of NBA championship teams, 1980 and 1982. . . . Shares NBA record for most minutes played in one game, 64, vs. Cleveland, January 29, 1980 (4 ot).

—DID YOU KNOW—

That Larry Bird made the biggest impact among all rookies in NBA history? The Celtics improved by 32 games in Bird's rookie season, going from 29-53 in 1978-79 to 61-21 in 1979-80. Kareem Abdul-Jabbar is runner-up in that category as the Milwaukee Bucks improved by 29 games after selecting him.

KENNETH DARNEL NORMAN
(Snake)

(Known as Ken Colliers in high school.)

Born September 5, 1964 at Chicago, Ill.   Height 6:08.   Weight 215.

High School—Chicago, Ill., Crane.

Colleges—Wabash Valley College, Mt. Carmel, Ill., and
University of Illinois, Champaign, Ill.

Drafted by Los Angeles Clippers on first round, 1987 (19th pick).

—COLLEGIATE RECORD—
Wabash Valley

Year	G.	Min.	FGA	FGM	Pct.	FTA	FTM	Pct.	Reb.	Pts.	Avg.
82-83	35	....	499	302	.605	165	111	.673	362	715	20.4

Illinois

Year	G.	Min.	FGA	FGM	Pct.	FTA	FTM	Pct.	Reb.	Pts.	Avg.
83-84					Did Not Play—Redshirted						
84-85	29	462	136	86	.632	83	55	.663	107	227	7.8
85-86	32	1015	337	216	.641	116	93	.802	226	525	16.4
86-87	31	1112	443	256	.578	176	128	.727	303	641	20.7
Ill. Totals	92	2589	916	558	.609	375	276	.736	636	1393	15.1

Three-Point Field Goals: 1986-87, 1-for-4 (.250).

NBA REGULAR SEASON RECORD

Sea.—Team	G.	Min.	FGA	FGM	Pct.	FTA	FTM	Pct.	Off.	Def.	Tot.	Ast.	PF	Dq.	Stl.	Blk.	Pts.	Avg.
										—Rebounds—								
87-88—L.A. Clippers	66	1435	500	241	.482	170	87	.512	100	163	263	78	123	0	44	34	569	8.6

Three-Point Field Goals: 1987-88, 0-for-10.

**Named to THE SPORTING NEWS All-America Second Team, 1987. . . . Half-brother of former NFL wide
receiver Bobby Duckworth.**

CHARLES OAKLEY

Born December 18, 1963 at Cleveland, O.   Height 6:08.   Weight 225.

High School—Cleveland, O., John Hay.

College—Virginia Union University, Richmond, Va.

Drafted by Cleveland on first round, 1985 (9th pick).

Draft rights traded by Cleveland with draft rights to Calvin Duncan to Chicago for Ennis Whatley and draft rights
to Keith Lee, June 18, 1985.

Traded by Chicago with 1988 1st and 3rd round draft choices to New York for Bill Cartwright and 1988 1st and 3rd
round draft choices, June 27, 1988.

—COLLEGIATE RECORD—

Year	G.	Min.	FGA	FGM	Pct.	FTA	FTM	Pct.	Reb.	Pts.	Avg.
81-82					Statistics Unavailable						
82-83	28	....	378	220	.582	170	100	.588	365	540	19.3
83-84	30	....	418	256	.612	...	139	...	393	651	21.7
84-85	31	....	453	283	.625	266	178	.669	535	744	24.0

NBA REGULAR SEASON RECORD

Sea.—Team	G.	Min.	FGA	FGM	Pct.	FTA	FTM	Pct.	Off.	Def.	Tot.	Ast.	PF	Dq.	Stl.	Blk.	Pts.	Avg.
85-86—Chicago	77	1772	541	281	.519	269	178	.662	255	409	664	133	250	9	68	30	740	9.6
86-87—Chicago	82	2980	1052	468	.445	357	245	.686	299	775	1074	296	315	4	85	36	1192	14.5
87-88—Chicago	82	2816	776	375	.483	359	261	.727	326	740	1066	248	272	2	68	28	1014	12.4
Totals	241	7568	2369	1124	.474	985	684	.694	880	1924	2804	677	837	15	221	94	2946	12.2

Three-Point Field Goals: 1985-86, 0-for-3. 1986-87, 11-for-30 (.367). 1987-88, 3-for-12 (.250). Totals, 14-for-45 (.311).

NBA PLAYOFF RECORD

Sea.—Team	G.	Min.	FGA	FGM	Pct.	FTA	FTM	Pct.	Off.	Def.	Tot.	Ast.	PF	Dq.	Stl.	Blk.	Pts.	Avg.
85-86—Chicago	3	88	21	11	.524	13	8	.615	10	20	30	3	13	0	6	2	30	10.0
86-87—Chicago	3	129	50	19	.380	24	20	.833	17	29	46	6	13	0	4	1	60	20.0
87-88—Chicago	10	373	91	40	.440	24	21	.875	39	89	128	32	33	0	6	4	101	10.1
Totals	16	590	162	70	.432	61	49	.803	66	138	204	41	59	0	16	7	191	11.9

Three-Point Field Goals: 1986-87, 2-for-4 (.500). 1987-88, 0-for-2. Totals, 2-for-6 (.333).

Named to NBA All-Rookie Team, 1986. . . . Led NCAA Division II in rebounding, 1985.

CHARLES OAKLEY

MICHAEL F. O'KOREN
(Mike)

Born February 7, 1958 at Jersey City, N. J.   Height 6:07.   Weight 225.

High School—Jersey City, N. J., Hudson Catholic.

College—University of North Carolina, Chapel Hill, N. C.

Drafted by New Jersey on first round, 1980 (6th pick).

Traded by New Jersey to Washington for Leon Wood, October 30, 1986.
Waived by Washington, February 26, 1987; signed by Boston as a free agent, October 2, 1987.
Traded by Boston to New Jersey for cash, November 2, 1987.
Waived by New Jersey, November 5, 1987; signed by New Jersey as a free agent, December 22, 1987.

—COLLEGIATE RECORD—

Year	G.	Min.	FGA	FGM	Pct.	FTA	FTM	Pct.	Reb.	Pts.	Avg.
76-77	33	....	298	172	.577	157	114	.726	217	458	13.9
77-78	27	....	269	173	.643	163	122	.748	180	468	17.3
78-79	28	....	259	135	.521	188	144	.766	202	414	14.8
79-80	29	....	298	163	.547	152	99	.651	216	425	14.7
Totals	117	....	1124	643	.572	660	479	.726	815	1765	15.1

NBA REGULAR SEASON RECORD

Sea.—Team	G.	Min.	FGA	FGM	Pct.	FTA	FTM	Pct.	Off.	Def.	Tot.	Ast.	PF	Dq.	Stl.	Blk.	Pts.	Avg.
80-81—New Jersey	79	2473	751	365	.486	212	135	.637	179	299	478	252	243	8	86	27	870	11.0
81-82—New Jersey	80	2018	778	383	.492	189	135	.714	111	194	305	192	175	0	83	13	909	11.4
82-83—New Jersey	46	803	259	136	.525	48	34	.708	42	72	114	82	67	0	42	11	308	6.7
83-84—New Jersey	73	1191	385	186	.483	87	53	.609	71	104	175	95	148	3	34	11	430	5.9
84-85—New Jersey	43	1119	393	194	.494	67	42	.627	46	120	166	102	115	1	32	16	438	10.2
85-86—New Jersey	67	1031	336	160	.476	39	23	.590	33	102	135	118	134	3	29	9	350	5.2
86-87—Washington	15	123	42	16	.381	2	0	.000	6	8	14	13	10	0	2	0	32	2.1
87-88—New Jersey	4	52	16	9	.563	4	0	.000	1	3	4	2	2	0	3	2	18	4.5
Totals	407	8810	2960	1449	.490	648	422	.651	489	902	1391	856	894	15	311	89	3355	8.2

Three-Point Field Goals: 1980-81, 5-for-18 (.278). 1981-82, 8-for-23 (.348). 1982-83, 2-for-9 (.222). 1983-84, 5-for-28 (.179). 1984-85, 8-for-21 (.381). 1985-86, 7-for-27 (.259). 1986-87, 0-for-2. 1987-88, 0-for-1. Totals, 35-for-129 (.271).

NBA PLAYOFF RECORD

Sea.—Team	G.	Min.	FGA	FGM	Pct.	FTA	FTM	Pct.	Off.	Def.	Tot.	Ast.	PF	Dq.	Stl.	Blk.	Pts.	Avg.
81-82—New Jersey	2	44	11	3	.273	2	1	.500	0	8	8	3	8	1	1	0	7	3.5
82-83—New Jersey	2	18	8	2	.250	0	0	.000	1	5	6	3	3	0	0	4	2.0
83-84—New Jersey	11	216	59	25	.424	6	5	.833	18	17	35	21	37	1	3	4	55	5.0
84-85—New Jersey	3	34	7	3	.429	2	0	.000	1	9	10	4	6	0	0	0	6	2.0
85-86—New Jersey	2	21	6	1	.167	0	0	.000	1	1	2	2	5	0	2	1	2	1.0
Totals	20	333	91	34	.374	10	6	.600	21	40	61	33	59	2	6	5	74	3.7

Three-Point Field Goals: 1981-82, 0-for-1. 1983-84, 0-for-1. 1985-86, 0-for-1. Totals, 0-for-3.

Named to THE SPORTING NEWS All-America First Team, 1979 and 1980.

AKEEM ABDUL OLAJUWON

Born January 21, 1963 at Lagos, Nigeria.   Height 7:00.   Weight 250.

High School—Lagos, Nigeria, Moslem Teachers College.

College—University of Houston, Houston, Tex.

Drafted by Houston on first round as an undergraduate, 1984 (1st pick).

—COLLEGIATE RECORD—

Year	G.	Min.	FGA	FGM	Pct.	FTA	FTM	Pct.	Reb.	Pts.	Avg.
80-81					Did Not Play						
81-82	29	529	150	91	.607	103	58	.563	179	240	8.3
82-83	34	932	314	192	.612	148	88	.595	388	472	13.9
83-84	37	1260	369	249	.675	232	122	.526	500	620	16.8
Totals	100	2721	833	532	.639	483	168	.555	1067	1332	13.3

NBA REGULAR SEASON RECORD

Sea.—Team	G.	Min.	FGA	FGM	Pct.	FTA	FTM	Pct.	Off.	Def.	Tot.	Ast.	PF	Dq.	Stl.	Blk.	Pts.	Avg.
84-85—Houston	82	2914	1258	677	.538	551	338	.613	440	534	974	111	344	10	99	220	1692	20.6
85-86—Houston	68	2467	1188	625	.526	538	347	.645	333	448	781	137	271	9	134	231	1597	23.5
86-87—Houston	75	2760	1332	677	.508	570	400	.702	315	543	858	220	294	8	140	254	1755	23.4
87-88—Houston	79	2825	1385	712	.514	548	381	.695	302	657	959	163	324	7	162	214	1805	22.8
Totals	304	10966	5163	2691	.521	2207	1466	.664	1390	2182	3572	631	1233	34	535	919	6849	22.5

Three-Point Field Goals: 1986-87, 1-for-5 (.200). 1987-88, 0-for-4. Totals, 1-for-9 (.111).

Sea.—Team	G.	Min.	FGA	FGM	Pct.	FTA	FTM	Pct.	Off.	Def.	Tot.	Ast.	PF	Dq.	Stl.	Blk.	Pts.	Avg.
84-85—Houston	5	187	88	42	.477	46	22	.478	33	32	65	7	22	0	7	13	106	21.2
85-86—Houston	20	766	387	205	.530	199	127	.638	101	135	236	39	87	3	40	69	537	26.9
86-87—Houston	10	389	179	110	.615	97	72	.742	39	74	113	25	44	1	13	43	292	29.2
87-88—Houston	4	162	98	56	.571	43	38	.884	20	47	67	7	14	0	9	11	150	37.5
Totals	39	1504	752	413	.549	385	259	.673	193	288	481	78	167	4	69	136	1085	27.8

Three-Point Field Goals: 1985-86, 0-for-1. 1986-87, 0-for-1. 1987-88, 0-for-1. Totals, 0-for-3.

NBA ALL-STAR GAME RECORD

Season—Team	Min.	FGA	FGM	Pct.	FTA	FTM	Pct.	Off.	Def.	Tot.	Ast.	PF	Dq.	Stl.	Blk.	Pts.
1985—Houston	15	2	2	1.000	6	2	.333	2	3	5	1	1	0	0	2	6
1986—Houston	15	8	1	.125	2	1	.500	1	4	5	0	3	0	1	2	3
1987—Houston	26	6	2	.333	8	6	.750	4	9	13	2	6	1	0	3	10
1988—Houston	28	13	8	.615	7	5	.714	7	2	9	2	3	0	2	2	21
Totals	84	29	13	.448	23	14	.609	14	18	32	5	13	1	3	9	40

Named to All-NBA First Team, 1987 and 1988.... All-NBA Second Team, 1986.... NBA All-Rookie Team, 1985. ... NBA All-Defensive First Team, 1987 and 1988.... NBA All-Defensive Second Team, 1985.... NCAA Division I Tournament Most Outstanding Player, 1983. ... THE SPORTING NEWS All-America First Team, 1984. ... Led NCAA Division I in field-goal percentage, rebounding and blocked shots, 1984.

JAWANN OLDHAM

Born July 4, 1957 at Chicago, Ill.   Height 7:00.   Weight 215.

High School—Seattle, Wash., Cleveland.

College—Seattle University, Seattle, Wash.

Drafted by Denver on second round, 1980 (41st pick).

Waived by Denver, October 21, 1980; signed by Houston as a free agent, August 28, 1981.
Waived by Houston, October 26, 1982; signed by Chicago as a free agent, February 16, 1983.
Traded by Chicago to New York for a 1987 1st round draft choice and a future 2nd round draft choice, October 30, 1986.
Traded by New York to Sacramento for a 1988 2nd round draft choice, October 15, 1987.
Played in Continental Basketball Association with Montana Golden Nuggets, 1980-81.

—COLLEGIATE RECORD—

Year	G.	Min.	FGA	FGM	Pct.	FTA	FTM	Pct.	Reb.	Pts.	Avg.
76-77	27	....	300	145	.483	51	31	.608	212	321	11.9
77-78	25	....	282	140	.496	74	32	.432	205	312	12.5
78-79	24	....	367	194	.529	73	42	.575	262	430	17.9
79-80	27	....	333	188	.565	143	81	.566	282	457	16.9
Totals	103	....	1282	667	.520	341	186	.545	961	1520	14.8

CBA REGULAR SEASON RECORD

Sea.—Team	G.	Min.	2-Point			3-Point			FTM	FTA	Pct.	Reb.	Ast.	Pts.	Avg.
			FGM	FGA	Pct.	FGM	FGA	Pct.							
80-81—Montana	7	172	36	83	.433	0	0	.000	7	15	.466	57	3	79	11.3

NBA REGULAR SEASON RECORD

Sea.—Team	G.	Min.	FGA	FGM	Pct.	FTA	FTM	Pct.	Off.	Def.	Tot.	Ast.	PF	Dq.	Stl.	Blk.	Pts.	Avg.
80-81—Denver	4	21	6	2	.333	0	0	.000	3	2	5	0	3	0	0	2	4	1.0
81-82—Houston	22	124	36	13	.361	14	8	.571	7	17	24	3	8	0	2	10	34	1.5
82-83—Chicago	16	171	58	31	.534	22	12	.545	18	29	47	5	30	1	5	13	74	4.6
83-84—Chicago	64	870	218	110	.505	66	39	.591	75	158	233	33	139	2	15	76	259	4.0
84-85—Chicago	63	993	192	89	.464	50	34	.680	79	157	236	31	166	3	11	127	212	3.4
85-86—Chicago	52	1276	323	167	.517	91	53	.582	112	194	306	37	206	6	28	134	387	7.4
86-87—New York	44	776	174	71	.408	57	31	.544	51	128	179	19	95	1	22	71	173	3.9
87-88—Sacramento	54	946	250	119	.476	87	59	.678	82	222	304	33	143	2	12	110	297	5.5
Totals	319	5177	1257	602	.479	387	236	.610	427	907	1334	161	790	15	95	543	1440	4.5

Three-Point Field Goals: 1984-85, 0-for-1. 1985-86, 0-for-1. 1986-87, 0-for-1. Totals, 0-for-3.

NBA PLAYOFF RECORD

Sea.—Team	G.	Min.	FGA	FGM	Pct.	FTA	FTM	Pct.	Off.	Def.	Tot.	Ast.	PF	Dq.	Stl.	Blk.	Pts.	Avg.
84-85—Chicago	4	91	15	7	.467	0	0	.000	8	14	22	3	19	1	6	7	14	3.5
85-86—Chicago	1	4	1	0	.000	0	0	.000	1	1	2	0	0	0	0	0	0	0.0
Totals	5	95	16	7	.438	0	0	.000	9	15	24	3	19	1	6	7	14	2.8

—DID YOU KNOW—

That two of the last five NBA champions won only 30 percent of their road playoff games? The 1988 Lakers and the '84 Celtics each posted a 3-7 record in playoff games away from home.

LOUIS M. ORR

Born May 7, 1958 at Cincinnati, O. Height 6:09. Weight 200.
High School—Cincinnati, O., Withrow.
College—Syracuse University, Syracuse, N. Y.
Drafted by Indiana on second round, 1980 (29th pick).

Signed by New York as a Veteran Free Agent, October 15, 1982; Indiana matched offer and traded Orr to New York for a 1983 2nd round draft choice and cash, October 22, 1982.

—COLLEGIATE RECORD—

Year	G.	Min.	FGA	FGM	Pct.	FTA	FTM	Pct.	Reb.	Pts.	Avg.
76-77	30	....	186	105	.565	96	72	.750	194	282	9.4
77-78	28	....	302	157	.520	59	43	.729	217	357	12.8
78-79	28	....	248	142	.573	117	85	.726	215	369	13.2
79-80	30	....	332	189	.569	119	101	.849	255	479	16.0
Totals	116	....	1068	593	.555	391	301	.770	881	1487	12.8

NBA REGULAR SEASON RECORD

Sea.—Team	G.	Min.	FGA	FGM	Pct.	FTA	FTM	Pct.	Off.	Def.	Tot.	Ast.	PF	Dq.	Stl.	Blk.	Pts.	Avg.
80-81—Indiana	82	1787	709	348	.491	202	163	.807	172	189	361	132	153	0	55	25	859	10.5
81-82—Indiana	80	1951	719	357	.497	254	203	.799	127	204	331	134	182	1	56	26	918	11.5
82-83—New York	82	1666	593	274	.462	175	140	.800	94	134	228	94	134	0	64	24	688	8.4
83-84—New York	78	1640	572	262	.458	211	173	.820	101	127	228	61	142	0	66	17	697	8.9
84-85—New York	79	2452	766	372	.486	334	262	.784	171	220	391	134	195	1	100	27	1007	12.7
85-86—New York	74	2237	741	330	.445	278	218	.784	123	189	312	179	177	4	61	26	878	11.9
86-87—New York	65	1440	389	166	.427	172	125	.727	102	130	232	110	123	0	47	18	458	7.0
87-88—New York	29	180	50	16	.320	16	8	.500	13	21	34	9	27	0	6	0	40	1.4
Totals	569	13353	4539	2125	.468	1642	1292	.787	903	1214	2117	853	1133	6	455	163	5545	9.7

Three-Point Field Goals: 1980-81, 0-for-6. 1981-82, 1-for-8 (.125). 1982-83, 0-for-2. 1984-85, 1-for-10 (.100). 1985-86, 0-for-4. 1986-87, 1-for-5 (.200). 1987-88, 0-for-1. Totals, 3-for-36 (.083).

NBA PLAYOFF RECORD

Sea.—Team	G.	Min.	FGA	FGM	Pct.	FTA	FTM	Pct.	Off.	Def.	Tot.	Ast.	PF	Dq.	Stl.	Blk.	Pts.	Avg.
80-81—Indiana	2	56	25	9	.360	7	6	.857	6	4	10	4	4	0	5	1	24	12.0
82-83—New York	6	105	47	18	.383	10	10	1.000	8	13	21	3	10	0	5	4	46	7.7
83-84—New York	12	229	70	29	.414	19	15	.789	22	28	50	6	32	1	4	1	73	6.1
87-88—New York	2	3	1	0	.000	2	1	.500	1	1	2	0	0	0	0	0	1	0.5
Totals	22	393	143	56	.392	38	32	.842	37	46	83	13	46	1	14	6	144	6.5

ROBERT L. PARISH

Born August 30, 1953 at Shreveport, La. Height 7:00. Weight 230.
High School—Shreveport, La., Woodlawn.
College—Centenary College, Shreveport, La.
Drafted by Golden State on first round, 1976 (8th pick).

Traded by Golden State with a 1980 1st round draft choice to Boston for two 1980 1st round draft choices, June 9, 1980.

—COLLEGIATE RECORD—

Year	G.	Min.	FGA	FGM	Pct.	FTA	FTM	Pct.	Reb.	Pts.	Avg.
72-73	27	885	492	285	.579	82	50	.610	505	620	23.0
73-74	25	841	428	224	.523	78	49	.628	382	497	19.9
74-75	29	900	423	237	.560	112	74	.660	447	548	18.9
75-76	27	939	489	288	.589	134	93	.694	486	669	24.8
Totals	108	3565	1832	1034	.564	406	266	.655	1820	2334	21.6

NBA REGULAR SEASON RECORD

Sea.—Team	G.	Min.	FGA	FGM	Pct.	FTA	FTM	Pct.	Off.	Def.	Tot.	Ast.	PF	Dq.	Stl.	Blk.	Pts.	Avg.
76-77—Golden State	77	1384	573	288	.503	171	121	.708	201	342	543	74	224	7	55	94	697	9.1
77-78—Golden State	82	1969	911	430	.472	264	165	.625	211	469	680	95	291	10	79	123	1025	12.5
78-79—Golden State	76	2411	1110	554	.499	281	196	.698	265	651	916	115	303	10	100	217	1304	17.2
79-80—Golden State	72	2119	1006	510	.507	284	203	.715	247	536	783	122	248	6	58	115	1223	17.0
80-81—Boston	82	2298	1166	635	.545	397	282	.710	245	532	777	144	310	9	81	214	1552	18.9
81-82—Boston	80	2534	1235	669	.542	355	252	.710	288	578	866	140	267	5	68	192	1590	19.9
82-83—Boston	78	2459	1125	619	.550	388	271	.698	260	567	827	141	222	4	79	148	1509	19.3
83-84—Boston	80	2867	1140	623	.546	368	274	.745	243	614	857	139	266	7	55	116	1520	19.0
84-85—Boston	79	2850	1016	551	.542	393	292	.743	263	577	840	125	223	2	56	101	1394	17.6
85-86—Boston	81	2567	966	530	.549	335	245	.731	246	524	770	145	215	3	65	116	1305	16.1

Sea.—Team	G.	Min.	FGA	FGM	Pct.	FTA	FTM	Pct.	Off.	Def.	Tot.	Ast.	PF	Dq.	Stl.	Blk.	Pts.	Avg.
86-87—Boston	80	2995	1057	588	.556	309	227	.735	254	597	851	173	266	5	64	144	1403	17.5
87-88—Boston	74	2312	750	442	.589	241	177	.734	173	455	628	115	198	5	55	84	1061	14.3
Totals	941	28765	12055	6439	.534	3786	2705	.714	2896	6442	9338	1528	3033	73	815	1664	15583	16.6

Three-Point Field Goals: 1979-80, 0-for-1. 1980-81, 0-for-1. 1982-83, 0-for-1. 1986-87, 0-for-1. 1987-88, 0-for-1. Totals, 0-for-5.

NBA PLAYOFF RECORD

Sea.—Team	G.	Min.	FGA	FGM	Pct.	FTA	FTM	Pct.	Off.	Def.	Tot.	Ast.	PF	Dq.	Stl.	Blk.	Pts.	Avg.
76-77—Golden State	10	239	108	52	.481	26	17	.654	43	60	103	11	42	1	7	11	121	12.1
80-81—Boston	17	492	219	108	.493	58	39	.672	50	96	146	19	74	2	21	39	255	15.0
81-82—Boston	12	426	209	102	.488	75	51	.680	43	92	135	18	47	1	5	48	255	21.3
82-83—Boston	7	249	89	43	.483	20	17	.850	21	53	74	9	18	0	5	9	103	14.7
83-84—Boston	23	869	291	139	.478	99	64	.646	76	172	248	27	100	6	23	41	342	14.9
84-85—Boston	21	803	276	136	.493	111	87	.784	57	162	219	31	68	0	21	34	359	17.1
85-86—Boston	18	591	225	106	.471	89	58	.652	52	106	158	25	47	1	9	30	270	15.0
86-87—Boston	21	734	263	149	.567	103	79	.767	59	139	198	28	79	4	18	35	377	18.0
87-88—Boston	17	626	188	100	.532	61	50	.820	51	117	168	21	42	0	11	19	250	14.7
Totals	146	5029	1868	935	.501	642	462	.720	452	997	1449	189	517	15	120	266	2332	16.0

Three-Point Field Goals, 1986-87, 0-for-1.

NBA ALL-STAR GAME RECORD

Season—Team	Min.	FGA	FGM	Pct.	FTA	FTM	Pct.	Off.	Def.	Tot.	Ast.	PF	Dq.	Stl.	Blk.	Pts.
1981—Boston...........	25	18	5	.278	6	6	1.000	6	4	10	2	3	0	0	2	16
1982—Boston...........	20	12	9	.750	4	3	.750	0	7	7	1	2	0	0	2	21
1983—Boston...........	18	6	5	.833	4	3	.750	0	3	3	0	2	0	1	1	13
1984—Boston...........	28	11	5	.455	4	2	.500	4	11	15	2	1	0	3	0	12
1985—Boston...........	10	5	2	.400	0	0	.000	3	3	6	1	0	0	0	0	4
1986—Boston...........	7	0	0	.000	2	0	.000	0	1	1	0	0	0	0	1	0
1987—Boston...........	8	3	2	.667	0	0	.000	0	3	3	0	1	0	0	1	4
Totals	116	55	28	.509	20	14	.700	13	32	45	6	9	0	0	7	70

Named to All-NBA Second Team, 1982. . . . Member of NBA championship teams, 1981, 1984, 1986. . . . Named to THE SPORTING NEWS All-America First Team, 1976.

JAMES JOSEPH PAXSON JR.
(Jim)

Born July 9, 1957 at Kettering, O.   Height 6:06.   Weight 210.

High School—Kettering, O., Alter.

College—University of Dayton, Dayton, O.

Drafted by Portland on first round, 1979 (12th pick).

Traded by Portland to Boston for Jerry Sichting and future considerations, February 23, 1988.

—COLLEGIATE RECORD—

Year	G.	Min.	FGA	FGM	Pct.	FTA	FTM	Pct.	Reb.	Pts.	Avg.
75-76	27	1061	308	149	.484	73	55	.753	127	353	13.1
76-77	27	1012	401	219	.546	87	69	.793	157	507	18.8
77-78	29	1066	399	208	.521	115	89	.774	96	505	17.4
78-79	25	929	449	236	.526	134	108	.806	104	580	23.2
Totals	108	4068	1557	812	.521	409	321	.785	484	1945	18.0

NBA REGULAR SEASON RECORD

Sea.—Team	G.	Min.	FGA	FGM	Pct.	FTA	FTM	Pct.	Off.	Def.	Tot.	Ast.	PF	Dq.	Stl.	Blk.	Pts.	Avg.
79-80—Portland	72	1270	460	189	.411	90	64	.711	25	84	109	144	97	0	48	5	443	6.2
80-81—Portland	79	2701	1092	585	.536	248	182	.734	74	137	211	299	172	1	140	9	1354	17.1
81-82—Portland	82	2756	1258	662	.526	287	220	.767	75	146	221	276	159	0	129	12	1552	18.9
82-83—Portland	81	2740	1323	682	.515	478	388	.812	68	106	174	231	160	0	140	17	1756	21.7
83-84—Portland	81	2686	1322	680	.514	410	345	.841	68	105	173	251	165	0	122	10	1722	21.3
84-85—Portland	68	2253	988	508	.514	248	196	.790	69	153	222	264	115	0	101	5	1218	17.9
85-86—Portland	75	1931	792	372	.470	244	217	.889	42	106	148	278	156	3	94	5	981	13.1
86-87—Portland	72	1798	733	337	.460	216	174	.806	41	98	139	237	134	0	76	12	874	12.1
87-88—Port.-Bos.	45	801	298	137	.460	79	68	.861	15	30	45	76	73	0	30	5	347	7.7
Totals	655	18936	8266	4152	.502	2300	1854	.806	477	965	1442	2056	1231	4	880	80	10247	15.6

Three-Point Field Goals: 1979-80, 1-for-22 (.045). 1980-81, 2-for-30 (.067). 1981-82, 8-for-35 (.229). 1982-83, 4-for-25 (.160). 1983-84, 17-for-59 (.288). 1984-85, 6-for-39 (.154). 1985-86, 20-for-62 (.323). 1986-87, 26-for-98 (.265). 1987-88, 5-for-21 (.238). Totals, 89-for-391 (.228).

NBA PLAYOFF RECORD

Sea.—Team	G.	Min.	FGA	FGM	Pct.	FTA	FTM	Pct.	Off.	Def.	Tot.	Ast.	PF	Dq.	Stl.	Blk.	Pts.	Avg.
79-80—Portland	3	44	16	5	.313	6	6	1.000	0	4	4	3	2	0	2	1	16	5.3

Sea.—Team	G.	Min.	FGA	FGM	Pct.	FTA	FTM	Pct.	Off.	Def.	Tot.	Ast.	PF	Dq.	Stl.	Blk.	Pts.	Avg.
80-81—Portland	1	4	3	0	.000	0	0	.000	0	0	0	0	0	0	0	0	0	0.0
82-83—Portland	7	260	116	68	.586	33	25	.758	4	11	15	18	11	0	9	1	163	23.3
83-84—Portland	5	172	78	40	.513	40	33	.825	11	8	19	12	13	0	2	0	114	22.8
84-85—Portland	9	212	101	47	.465	24	19	.792	6	14	20	21	16	0	6	0	116	12.9
85-86—Portland	4	71	37	14	.378	15	12	.800	1	3	4	15	12	1	3	0	42	10.5
86-87—Portland	4	94	32	13	.406	9	8	.889	4	5	9	13	8	0	5	0	34	8.5
87-88—Boston	15	188	59	17	.288	20	16	.800	1	8	9	11	18	0	6	2	50	3.3
Totals	48	1045	442	204	.462	147	119	.810	27	53	80	93	80	1	33	4	535	11.1

Three-Point Field Goals: 1982-83, 2-for-4 (.500). 1983-84, 1-for-5 (.200). 1984-85, 3-for-10 (.300). 1985-86, 2-for-6 (.333). 1986-87, 0-for-2. 1987-88, 0-for-2. Totals, 8-for-29 (.276).

NBA ALL-STAR GAME RECORD

Season—Team	Min.	FGA	FGM	Pct.	FTA	FTM	Pct.	Off.	Def.	Tot.	Ast.	PF	Dq.	Stl.	Blk.	Pts.
1983—Portland........	17	7	5	.714	2	1	.500	0	0	0	1	0	0	2	0	11
1984—Portland........	14	9	5	.556	0	0	.000	1	2	3	2	0	0	0	0	10
Totals	31	16	10	.625	2	1	.500	1	2	3	3	0	0	2	0	21

Named to All-NBA Second Team, 1984. . . . Son of Jim Paxson Sr., forward with Minneapolis Lakers (1956-57) and Cincinnati Royals (1957-58) and brother of Chicago Bulls guard John Paxson.

JOHN MacBETH PAXSON

Born September 29, 1960 at Dayton, O.   Height 6:02.   Weight 185.

High School—Kettering, O., Archbishop Alter.

College—University of Notre Dame, Notre Dame, Ind.

Drafted by San Antonio on first round, 1983 (19th pick).

Signed by Chicago as a Veteran Free Agent, October 29, 1985; San Antonio relinquished its right of first refusal in exchange for cash.

—COLLEGIATE RECORD—

Year	G.	Min.	FGA	FGM	Pct.	FTA	FTM	Pct.	Reb.	Pts.	Avg.
79-80	27	459	87	42	.483	55	41	.745	34	125	4.6
80-81	29	1062	218	113	.518	89	61	.685	53	287	9.9
81-82	27	1055	346	185	.535	93	72	.774	55	442	16.4
82-83	29	1082	411	219	.533	100	74	.740	63	512	17.7
Totals	112	3658	1062	559	.526	337	248	.736	205	1366	12.2

NBA REGULAR SEASON RECORD

Sea.—Team	G.	Min.	FGA	FGM	Pct.	FTA	FTM	Pct.	Off.	Def.	Tot.	Ast.	PF	Dq.	Stl.	Blk.	Pts.	Avg.
83-84—San Antonio	49	458	137	61	.445	26	16	.615	4	29	33	149	47	0	10	2	142	2.9
84-85—San Antonio	78	1259	385	196	.509	100	84	.840	19	49	68	215	117	0	45	3	486	6.2
85-86—Chicago	75	1570	328	153	.466	92	74	.804	18	76	94	274	172	2	55	2	395	5.3
86-87—Chicago	82	2689	793	386	.487	131	106	.809	22	117	139	467	207	1	66	8	930	11.3
87-88—Chicago	81	1888	582	287	.493	45	33	.733	16	88	104	303	154	2	49	1	640	7.9
Totals	365	7864	2225	1083	.487	394	313	.794	79	359	438	1408	697	5	225	16	2593	7.1

Three-Point Field Goals: 1983-84, 4-for-22 (.182). 1984-85, 10-for-34 (.294). 1985-86, 15-for-51 (.294). 1986-87, 52-for-140 (.371). 1987-88, 33-for-95 (.347). Totals, 114-for-342 (.333).

NBA PLAYOFF RECORD

Sea.—Team	G.	Min.	FGA	FGM	Pct.	FTA	FTM	Pct.	Off.	Def.	Tot.	Ast.	PF	Dq.	Stl.	Blk.	Pts.	Avg.
84-85—San Antonio	5	114	42	21	.500	9	7	.778	0	5	5	21	9	0	5	0	51	10.2
85-86—Chicago	3	80	15	7	.467	17	13	.765	0	0	0	5	9	0	3	0	27	9.0
86-87—Chicago	3	87	22	11	.500	1	1	1.000	0	3	3	11	9	0	2	0	26	8.7
87-88—Chicago	10	165	53	20	.377	4	4	1.000	0	4	4	30	24	1	1	1	46	4.6
Totals	21	446	132	59	.447	31	25	.806	0	12	12	67	51	1	11	1	150	7.1

Three-Point Field Goals: 1984-85, 2-for-9 (.222). 1986-87, 3-for-7 (.429). 1987-88, 2-for-12 (.167). Totals, 7-for-28 (.250).

Brother of Boston Celtics guard Jim Paxson Jr.; son of Jim Paxson Sr., forward with Minneapolis Lakers (1956-57) and Cincinnati Royals (1957-58). . . . Named to THE SPORTING NEWS All-America Second Team, 1983.

SAMUEL BRUCE PERKINS
(Sam)

Born June 14, 1961 at Brooklyn, N. Y.   Height 6:09.   Weight 235.

High School—Latham, N. Y., Shaker.

College—University of North Carolina, Chapel Hill, N. C.

Drafted by Dallas on first round, 1984 (4th pick).

Year	G.	Min.	FGA	FGM	Pct.	FTA	FTM	Pct.	Reb.	Pts.	Avg.
80-81	37	....	318	199	.626	205	152	.741	289	550	14.9
81-82	32	....	301	174	.578	142	109	.768	250	457	14.3
82-83	35	....	414	218	.527	177	145	.819	330	593	16.9
83-84	31	....	331	195	.589	181	155	.856	298	545	17.6
Totals	135		1364	786	.576	705	561	.796	1167	2145	15.9

Three-Point Field Goals: 1982-83, 12-for-28 (.429).

NBA REGULAR SEASON RECORD

Sea.—Team	G.	Min.	FGA	FGM	Pct.	FTA	FTM	Pct.	Off.	Def.	Tot.	Ast.	PF	Dq.	Stl.	Blk.	Pts.	Avg.
									Rebounds									
84-85—Dallas	82	2317	736	347	.471	244	200	.820	189	416	605	135	236	1	63	63	903	11.0
85-86—Dallas	80	2626	910	458	.503	377	307	.814	195	490	685	153	212	2	75	94	1234	15.4
86-87—Dallas	80	2687	957	461	.482	296	245	.828	197	419	616	146	269	6	109	77	1186	14.8
87-88—Dallas	75	2499	876	394	.450	332	273	.822	201	400	601	118	227	2	74	54	1066	14.2
Totals	317	10129	3479	1660	.477	1249	1025	.821	782	1725	2507	552	944	11	321	288	4389	13.8

Three-Point Field Goals: 1984-85, 9-for-36 (.250). 1985-86, 11-for-33 (.333). 1986-87, 19-for-54 (.352). 1987-88, 5-for-30 (.167). Totals, 44-for-153 (.286).

NBA PLAYOFF RECORD

Sea.—Team	G.	Min.	FGA	FGM	Pct.	FTA	FTM	Pct.	Off.	Def.	Tot.	Ast.	PF	Dq.	Stl.	Blk.	Pts.	Avg.
									Rebounds									
84-85—Dallas	4	169	49	24	.490	34	26	.765	16	35	51	11	13	1	2	1	75	18.8
85-86—Dallas	10	347	133	57	.429	43	33	.767	30	53	83	24	32	0	9	14	149	14.9
86-87—Dallas	4	133	52	26	.500	23	16	.696	12	22	34	5	16	0	4	1	68	17.0
87-88—Dallas	17	572	195	88	.451	66	53	.803	39	73	112	31	51	1	25	17	230	13.5
Totals	35	1221	429	195	.455	166	128	.771	97	183	280	71	112	2	40	33	522	14.9

Three-Point Field Goals: 1984-85, 1-for-4 (.250). 1985-86, 2-for-8 (.250). 1986-87, 0-for-4. 1987-88, 1-for-7 (.143). Totals, 4-for-23 (.174).

Named to NBA All-Rookie Team, 1985.... Member of NCAA Division I championship team, 1982.... Member of U.S. Olympic team, 1984.... Named to THE SPORTING NEWS All-America First Team, 1984.... Named to THE SPORTING NEWS All-America Second Team, 1982 and 1983.

CHUCK CONNORS PERSON

Born June 27, 1964 at Brantley, Ala.   Height 6:08.   Weight 225.

High School—Brantley, Ala.

College—Auburn University, Auburn, Ala.

Drafted by Indiana on first round, 1986 (4th pick).

—COLLEGIATE RECORD—

Year	G.	Min.	FGA	FGM	Pct.	FTA	FTM	Pct.	Reb.	Pts.	Avg.
82-83	28	636	218	118	.541	33	25	.758	128	261	9.3
83-84	31	1079	470	255	.543	114	83	.728	249	593	19.1
84-85	34	1240	614	334	.544	107	79	.738	303	747	22.0
85-86	33	1178	597	310	.519	112	90	.804	260	710	21.5
Totals	126	4133	1899	1017	.536	366	277	.757	940	2311	18.3

NBA REGULAR SEASON RECORD

Sea.—Team	G.	Min.	FGA	FGM	Pct.	FTA	FTM	Pct.	Off.	Def.	Tot.	Ast.	PF	Dq.	Stl.	Blk.	Pts.	Avg.
									Rebounds									
86-87—Indiana	82	2956	1358	635	.468	297	222	.747	168	509	677	295	310	4	90	16	1541	18.8
87-88—Indiana	79	2807	1252	575	.459	197	132	.670	171	365	536	309	266	4	73	8	1341	17.0
Totals	161	5763	2610	1210	.464	494	354	.717	339	874	1213	604	576	8	163	24	2882	17.9

Three-Point Field Goals: 1986-87, 49-for-138 (.355). 1987-88, 59-for-177 (.333). Total, 108-for-315 (.343).

NBA PLAYOFF RECORD

Sea.—Team	G.	Min.	FGA	FGM	Pct.	FTA	FTM	Pct.	Off.	Def.	Tot.	Ast.	PF	Dq.	Stl.	Blk.	Pts.	Avg.
									Rebounds									
86-87—Indiana	4	159	74	38	.514	39	30	.769	6	27	33	20	14	0	5	2	108	27.0

Three-Point Field Goals: 1986-87, 2-for-8 (.250).

Named NBA Rookie of the Year, 1987.... NBA All-Rookie Team, 1987.... THE SPORTING NEWS All-America Second Team, 1985 and 1986.

JAMES RICHARD PETERSEN
(Jim)

Born February 22, 1962 at Minneapolis, Minn.   Height 6:10.   Weight 235.

High School—St. Louis Park, Minn.

College—University of Minnesota, Minneapolis, Minn.

Drafted by Houston on third round, 1984 (51st pick).

SAM PERKINS

Year	G.	Min.	FGA	FGM	Pct.	FTA	FTM	Pct.	Reb.	Pts.	Avg.
80-81	22	....	26	13	.500	4	1	.250	22	27	1.2
81-82	21	....	52	24	.462	22	14	.636	43	62	3.0
82-83	29	....	149	82	.550	28	18	.643	155	182	6.3
83-84	24	....	180	115	.639	54	39	.722	166	269	11.2
Totals	96	....	407	234	.575	108	72	.667	386	540	5.6

NBA REGULAR SEASON RECORD

Sea.—Team	G.	Min.	FGA	FGM	Pct.	FTA	FTM	Pct.	Off.	Def.	Tot.	Ast.	PF	Dq.	Stl.	Blk.	Pts.	Avg.
84-85—Houston	60	714	144	70	.486	66	50	.758	44	103	147	29	125	1	14	32	190	3.2
85-86—Houston	82	1664	411	196	.477	160	113	.706	149	247	396	85	231	2	38	54	505	6.2
86-87—Houston	82	2403	755	386	.511	209	152	.727	177	380	557	127	268	5	43	102	924	11.3
87-88—Houston	69	1793	488	249	.510	153	114	.745	145	291	436	106	203	3	36	40	613	8.9
Totals	293	6574	1798	901	.501	588	429	.730	515	1021	1536	347	827	11	131	228	2232	7.6

Three-Point Field Goals: 1985-86, 0-for-3. 1986-87, 0-for-4. 1987-88, 1-for-6 (.167). Totals, 1-for-13 (.077).

NBA PLAYOFF RECORD

Sea.—Team	G.	Min.	FGA	FGM	Pct.	FTA	FTM	Pct.	Off.	Def.	Tot.	Ast.	PF	Dq.	Stl.	Blk.	Pts.	Avg.
84-85—Houston	3	8	1	1	1.000	0	0	.000	1	1	2	1	2	0	0	0	2	0.7
85-86—Houston	20	378	108	44	.407	33	23	.697	47	64	111	21	58	1	9	9	111	5.6
86-87—Houston	10	187	51	28	.549	18	12	.667	14	32	46	6	26	1	5	2	68	6.8
87-88—Houston	4	98	23	12	.522	12	7	.583	7	14	21	6	11	1	1	2	31	7.8
Totals	37	671	183	85	.464	63	42	.667	69	111	180	34	97	3	15	13	212	5.7

MICHAEL PHELPS

Born October 3, 1961 at Vicksburg, Miss.   Height 6:04.   Weight 185.

High School—Vicksburg, Miss.

College—Alcorn State University, Lorman, Miss.

Drafted by Seattle on seventh round, 1985 (144th pick).

Waived by Seattle, October 28, 1987; signed by Los Angeles Clippers, January 20, 1988, to a 10-day contract that expired, January 29, 1988.
Played in Continental Basketball Association with Wyoming Wildcatters, 1987-88.

—COLLEGIATE RECORD—

Year	G.	Min.	FGA	FGM	Pct.	FTA	FTM	Pct.	Reb.	Pts.	Avg.
80-81					Did Not Play						
81-82	29	745	251	122	.486	85	51	.600	106	295	10.2
82-83	30	861	340	162	.476	131	93	.710	118	417	13.9
83-84	25	683	281	148	.527	160	121	.756	94	417	16.7
84-85	30	841	433	214	.494	154	107	.695	102	535	17.8
Totals	114	3130	1305	646	.495	530	372	.702	420	1664	14.6

CBA REGULAR SEASON RECORD

Sea.—Team	G.	Min.	2-Point			3-Point			FTM	FTA	Pct.	Reb.	Ast.	Pts.	Avg.
			FGM	FGA	Pct.	FGM	FGA	Pct.							
87-88—Wyoming	26	815	148	313	.473	14	45	.311	87	125	.696	128	70	425	16.3

NBA REGULAR SEASON RECORD

Sea.—Team	G.	Min.	FGA	FGM	Pct.	FTA	FTM	Pct.	Off.	Def.	Tot.	Ast.	PF	Dq.	Stl.	Blk.	Pts.	Avg.
85-86—Seattle	70	880	286	117	.409	74	44	.595	29	60	89	71	86	0	45	1	279	4.0
86-87—Seattle	60	469	176	75	.426	44	31	.705	16	34	50	64	60	0	21	2	182	3.0
87-88—L.A. Clippers	2	23	7	3	.429	4	3	.750	0	2	2	3	1	0	5	0	9	4.5
Totals	132	1372	469	195	.416	122	78	.639	45	96	141	138	147	0	71	3	470	3.6

Three-Point Field Goals: 1985-86, 1-for-12 (.083). 1986-87, 1-for-10 (.100). Totals, 2-for-22 (.091).

RICKY CHARLES PIERCE

Born August 19, 1959 at Dallas, Tex.   Height 6:04.   Weight 222.

High School—Garland Tex., South Garland.

Colleges—Walla Walla Community College, Walla Walla, Wash., and Rice University, Houston, Tex.

Drafted by Detroit on first round, 1982 (18th pick).

Traded by Detroit to San Diego for 1986 and 1987 2nd round draft choices, October 17, 1983.
Traded by Los Angeles Clippers with Terry Cummings and Craig Hodges to Milwaukee for Marques Johnson, Harvey Catchings, Junior Bridgeman and cash, September 29, 1984.

Walla Walla CC

Year	G.	Min.	FGA	FGM	Pct.	FTA	FTM	Pct.	Reb.	Pts.	Avg.
78-79	..	....	...	...	....	...	...	....	....	....	19.0

Rice

Year	G.	Min.	FGA	FGM	Pct.	FTA	FTM	Pct.	Reb.	Pts.	Avg.
79-80	26	878	421	202	.480	131	94	.718	214	498	19.2
80-81	26	901	444	230	.518	119	84	.706	181	544	20.9
81-82	30	1104	614	314	.511	223	177	.794	226	805	26.8
Totals	82	2883	1479	746	.504	473	355	.751	621	1847	22.5

NBA REGULAR SEASON RECORD

Sea.—Team	G.	Min.	FGA	FGM	Pct.	FTA	FTM	Pct.	Off.	Def.	Tot.	Ast.	PF	Dq.	Stl.	Blk.	Pts.	Avg.
82-83—Detroit	39	265	88	33	.375	32	18	.563	15	20	35	14	42	0	8	4	85	2.2
83-84—San Diego	69	1280	570	268	.470	173	149	.861	59	76	135	60	143	1	27	13	685	9.9
84-85—Milwaukee	44	882	307	165	.537	124	102	.823	49	68	117	94	117	0	34	5	433	9.8
85-86—Milwaukee	81	2147	798	429	.538	310	266	.858	94	137	231	177	252	6	83	6	1127	13.9
86-87—Milwaukee	79	2505	1077	575	.534	440	387	.880	117	149	266	144	222	0	64	24	1540	19.5
87-88—Milwaukee	37	965	486	248	.510	122	107	.877	30	53	83	73	94	0	21	7	606	16.4
Totals	349	8044	3326	1718	.517	1201	1029	.857	364	503	867	562	870	7	237	59	4476	12.8

Three-Point Field Goals: 1982-83, 1-for-7 (.143). 1983-84, 0-for-9. 1984-85, 1-for-4 (.250). 1985-86, 3-for-23 (.130). 1986-87, 3-for-28 (.107). 1987-88, 3-for-14 (.214). Totals, 10-for-85 (.118).

NBA PLAYOFF RECORD

Sea.—Team	G.	Min.	FGA	FGM	Pct.	FTA	FTM	Pct.	Off.	Def.	Tot.	Ast.	PF	Dq.	Stl.	Blk.	Pts.	Avg.
84-85—Milwaukee	8	198	73	36	.493	9	7	.778	8	10	18	15	26	0	3	1	79	9.9
85-86—Milwaukee	13	322	113	52	.460	45	40	.889	20	16	36	20	42	0	8	3	144	11.1
86-87—Milwaukee	12	317	142	68	.479	67	55	.821	12	16	28	16	39	0	10	5	191	15.9
87-88—Milwaukee	5	105	53	25	.472	9	8	.889	6	8	14	9	9	0	1	2	59	11.8
Totals	38	942	381	181	.475	130	110	.846	46	50	96	60	116	0	22	11	473	12.4

Three-Point Field Goals: 1984-85, 0-for-2. 1985-86, 0-for-2. 1987-88, 1-for-5 (.200). Totals, 1-for-9 (.111).
Recipient of NBA Sixth Man Award, 1987.

EDWARD LEWIS PINCKNEY
(Ed)

Born March 27, 1963 at Bronx, N.Y. Height 6:09. Weight 215.
High School—Bronx, N.Y., Adlai Stevenson.
College—Villanova University, Villanova, Pa.
Drafted by Phoenix on first round, 1985 (10th pick).

Traded by Phoenix with a 1988 2nd round draft choice to Sacramento for Eddie Johnson, June 21, 1987.

—COLLEGIATE RECORD—

Year	G.	Min.	FGA	FGM	Pct.	FTA	FTM	Pct.	Reb.	Pts.	Avg.
81-82	32	1083	264	169	.640	161	115	.714	249	453	14.2
82-83	31	1029	227	129	.568	171	130	.760	301	388	12.5
83-84	31	1068	268	162	.604	222	154	.694	246	478	15.4
84-85	35	1186	295	177	.600	263	192	.730	311	546	15.6
Totals	129	4366	1054	637	.604	817	591	.723	1107	1865	14.5

NBA REGULAR SEASON RECORD

Sea.—Team	G.	Min.	FGA	FGM	Pct.	FTA	FTM	Pct.	Off.	Def.	Tot.	Ast.	PF	Dq.	Stl.	Blk.	Pts.	Avg.
85-86—Phoenix	80	1602	457	255	.558	254	171	.673	95	213	308	90	190	3	71	37	681	8.5
86-87—Phoenix	80	2250	497	290	.584	348	257	.739	179	401	580	116	196	1	86	54	837	10.5
87-88—Sacramento	79	1177	343	179	.522	178	133	.747	94	136	230	66	118	0	39	32	491	6.2
Totals	239	5029	1297	724	.558	780	561	.719	368	750	1118	272	504	4	196	123	2009	8.4

Three-Point Field Goals: 1985-86, 0-for-2. 1986-87, 0-for-2. 1987-88, 0-for-2. Totals, 0-for-6.
Member of NCAA Division I championship team, 1985. . . . Named NCAA Division I Tournament Most Outstanding Player, 1985.

SCOTTIE PIPPEN

Born September 25, 1965 at Hamburg, Ark. Height 6:08. Weight 210.
High School—Hamburg, Ark.
College—University of Central Arkansas, Conway, Ark.
Drafted by Seattle on first round, 1987 (5th pick).

Draft rights traded by Seattle to Chicago for draft rights to Olden Polynice, a 1988 or 1989 2nd round draft choice and the option to exchange 1988 or 1989 1st round draft choices, June 22, 1987.

—COLLEGIATE RECORD—

Year	G.	Min.	FGA	FGM	Pct.	FTA	FTM	Pct.	Reb.	Pts.	Avg.
83-84	20	....	79	36	.456	19	13	.684	59	85	4.3
84-85	19	....	250	141	.564	102	69	.676	175	351	18.5
85-86	29	....	412	229	.556	169	116	.686	266	574	19.8
86-87	25	....	390	231	.592	146	105	.719	249	590	23.6
Totals	93	....	1131	637	.563	436	303	.695	749	1600	17.2

Three-Point Field Goals: 1986-87, 23-for-40 (.575).

NBA REGULAR SEASON RECORD

Sea.—Team	G.	Min.	FGA	FGM	Pct.	FTA	FTM	Pct.	Rebounds Off.	Def.	Tot.	Ast.	PF	Dq.	Stl.	Blk.	Pts.	Avg.
87-88—Chicago	79	1650	564	261	.463	172	99	.576	115	183	298	169	214	3	91	52	625	7.9

Three-Point Field Goals: 1987-88, 4-for-23 (.174).

NBA PLAYOFF RECORD

Sea.—Team	G.	Min.	FGA	FGM	Pct.	FTA	FTM	Pct.	Rebounds Off.	Def.	Tot.	Ast.	PF	Dq.	Stl.	Blk.	Pts.	Avg.
87-88—Chicago	10	294	99	46	.465	7	5	.714	24	28	52	24	33	1	8	8	100	10.0

Three-Point Field Goals: 1987-88, 3-for-6 (.500).

OLDEN POLYNICE

Born November 21, 1964 at Port-Au-Prince, Haiti.   Height 6:11.   Weight 220.

High School—Bronx, N.Y., All Hallows.

College—University of Virginia, Charlottesville, Va.

Drafted by Chicago on first round as an undergraduate, 1987 (8th pick).

Draft rights traded with a 1988 or 1989 2nd round draft choice and the option to exchange 1988 or 1989 1st round draft choices by Chicago to Seattle for the draft rights to Scottie Pippen, June 22, 1987.
Played in Italy during 1986-87 season.

—COLLEGIATE RECORD—

Year	G.	Min.	FGA	FGM	Pct.	FTA	FTM	Pct.	Reb.	Pts.	Avg.
83-84	33	866	178	98	.551	97	57	.588	184	253	7.7
84-85	32	1095	267	161	.603	157	94	.599	243	416	13.0
85-86	30	1074	320	183	.572	182	116	.637	240	482	16.1
Totals	95	3035	765	442	.578	436	267	.612	667	1151	12.1

NBA REGULAR SEASON RECORD

Sea.—Team	G.	Min.	FGA	FGM	Pct.	FTA	FTM	Pct.	Rebounds Off.	Def.	Tot.	Ast.	PF	Dq.	Stl.	Blk.	Pts.	Avg.
87-88—Seattle	82	1080	254	118	.465	158	101	.639	122	208	330	33	215	1	32	26	337	4.1

Three-Point Field Goals: 1987-88, 0-for-2.

NBA PLAYOFF RECORD

Sea.—Team	G.	Min.	FGA	FGM	Pct.	FTA	FTM	Pct.	Rebounds Off.	Def.	Tot.	Ast.	PF	Dq.	Stl.	Blk.	Pts.	Avg.
87-88—Seattle	5	44	11	5	.455	2	0	.000	2	6	8	0	6	0	3	0	10	2.0

TERRY PORTER

Born April 8, 1963 at Milwaukee, Wis.   Height 6:03.   Weight 195.

High School—Milwaukee, Wis., South Division.

College—University of Wisconsin at Stevens Point,
Stevens Point, Wisc.

Drafted by Portland on first round, 1985 (24th pick).

—COLLEGIATE RECORD—

Year	G.	Min.	FGA	FGM	Pct.	FTA	FTM	Pct.	Reb.	Pts.	Avg.
81-82	25	273	57	21	.368	13	9	.692	13	51	2.0
82-83	30	949	229	140	.611	89	62	.697	117	342	11.4
83-84	32	1040	392	244	.622	135	112	.830	165	600	18.8
84-85	30	1042	405	233	.575	151	126	.834	155	592	19.7
Totals	117	3304	1083	638	.589	388	309	.796	450	1585	13.5

NBA REGULAR SEASON RECORD

Sea.—Team	G.	Min.	FGA	FGM	Pct.	FTA	FTM	Pct.	Rebounds Off.	Def.	Tot.	Ast.	PF	Dq.	Stl.	Blk.	Pts.	Avg.
85-86—Portland	79	1214	447	212	.474	155	125	.806	35	82	117	198	136	0	81	1	562	7.1

Sea.—Team	G.	Min.	FGA	FGM	Pct.	FTA	FTM	Pct.	Off.	Def.	Tot.	Ast.	PF	Dq.	Stl.	Blk.	Pts.	Avg.
									—Rebounds—									
86-87—Portland	80	2714	770	376	.488	334	280	.838	70	267	337	715	192	0	159	9	1045	13.1
87-88—Portland	82	2991	890	462	.519	324	274	.846	65	313	378	831	204	1	150	16	1222	14.9
Totals	241	6919	2107	1050	.498	813	679	.835	170	662	832	1744	532	1	390	26	2829	11.7

Three-Point Field Goals: 1985-86, 13-for-42 (.310). 1986-87, 13-for-60 (.217). 1987-88, 24-for-69 (.348). Totals, 50-for-171 (.292).

NBA PLAYOFF RECORD

Sea.—Team	G.	Min.	FGA	FGM	Pct.	FTA	FTM	Pct.	Off.	Def.	Tot.	Ast.	PF	Dq.	Stl.	Blk.	Pts.	Avg.
									—Rebounds—									
85-86—Portland	4	68	27	12	.444	4	2	.500	1	4	5	12	10	0	3	2	27	6.8
86-87—Portland	4	150	50	24	.480	20	18	.900	1	18	19	40	14	0	10	2	68	17.0
87-88—Portland	4	149	52	29	.558	13	9	.692	4	10	14	28	13	0	10	0	68	17.0
Totals	12	367	129	65	.504	37	29	.784	6	32	38	80	37	0	23	4	163	13.6

Three-Point Field Goals: 1985-86, 1-for-6 (.167). 1986-87, 2-for-5 (.400). 1987-88, 1-for-3 (.333). Totals, 4-for-14 (.286).

PAUL MATTHEW PRESSEY

Born December 24, 1958 at Richmond, Va. Height 6:05. Weight 205.

High School—Richmond, Va., George Wythe.

Colleges—Western Texas College, Snyder, Tex., and University of Tulsa, Tulsa, Okla.

Drafted by Milwaukee on first round, 1982 (20th pick).

—COLLEGIATE RECORD—
Western Texas

Year	G.	Min.	FGA	FGM	Pct.	FTA	FTM	Pct.	Reb.	Pts.	Avg.
78-79	33	....	286	191	.668	103	78	.757	262	460	13.9
79-80	37	....	327	213	.651	122	93	.762	291	519	14.0
J.C. Totals	70	....	613	404	.659	225	171	.760	553	979	14.0

Tulsa

Year	G.	Min.	FGA	FGM	Pct.	FTA	FTM	Pct.	Reb.	Pts.	Avg.
80-81	33	1050	288	137	.476	114	66	.579	178	340	10.3
81-82	30	973	275	154	.560	131	87	.664	192	395	13.2
Totals	63	2023	563	291	.517	245	153	.624	370	735	11.7

NBA REGULAR SEASON RECORD

Sea.—Team	G.	Min.	FGA	FGM	Pct.	FTA	FTM	Pct.	Off.	Def.	Tot.	Ast.	PF	Dq.	Stl.	Blk.	Pts.	Avg.
									—Rebounds—									
82-83—Milwaukee	79	1528	466	213	.457	176	105	.597	83	198	281	207	174	2	99	47	532	6.7
83-84—Milwaukee	81	1730	528	276	.523	200	120	.600	102	180	282	252	241	6	86	50	674	8.3
84-85—Milwaukee	80	2876	928	480	.517	418	317	.758	149	280	429	543	258	4	129	56	1284	16.1
85-86—Milwaukee	80	2704	843	411	.488	392	316	.806	127	272	399	623	247	4	168	71	1146	14.3
86-87—Milwaukee	61	2057	616	294	.477	328	242	.738	98	198	296	441	213	4	110	47	846	13.9
87-88—Milwaukee	75	2484	702	345	.491	357	285	.798	130	245	375	523	233	6	112	34	983	13.1
Totals	456	13379	4083	2019	.494	1871	1385	.740	689	1373	2062	2589	1366	26	704	305	5465	12.0

Three-Point Field Goals: 1982-83, 1-for-9 (.111). 1983-84, 2-for-9 (.222). 1984-85, 7-for-20 (.350). 1985-86, 8-for-44 (.182). 1986-87, 16-for-55 (.291). 1987-88, 8-for-39 (.205). Totals, 42-for-176 (.239).

NBA PLAYOFF RECORD

Sea.—Team	G.	Min.	FGA	FGM	Pct.	FTA	FTM	Pct.	Off.	Def.	Tot.	Ast.	PF	Dq.	Stl.	Blk.	Pts.	Avg.
									—Rebounds—									
82-83—Milwaukee	9	150	47	19	.404	20	8	.400	14	19	33	14	23	0	9	6	46	5.1
83-84—Milwaukee	16	351	100	52	.520	56	38	.679	17	42	59	50	53	1	22	9	142	8.9
84-85—Milwaukee	8	296	88	45	.511	38	31	.816	15	33	48	61	27	1	18	5	122	15.3
85-86—Milwaukee	14	530	157	76	.484	88	67	.761	19	41	60	110	48	0	18	13	225	16.1
86-87—Milwaukee	12	465	146	68	.466	46	34	.739	28	34	62	103	51	3	28	8	171	14.3
87-88—Milwaukee	5	178	50	23	.460	30	23	.767	6	13	19	33	21	0	4	3	70	14.0
Totals	64	1970	588	283	.481	278	201	.723	99	182	281	371	223	5	99	44	776	12.1

Three-Point Field Goals: 1982-83, 0-for-1. 1983-84, 0-for-3. 1984-85, 1-for-3 (.333). 1985-86, 6-for-18 (.333). 1986-87, 1-for-8 (.125). 1987-88, 1-for-3 (.333). Totals, 9-for-36 (.250).

Named to NBA All-Defensive First Team, 1985 and 1986. . . . NBA All-Defensive Second Team, 1987.

HAROLD PRESSLEY

Born July 14, 1963 at Bronx, N.Y. Height 6:08. Weight 210.

High School—Uncasville, Conn., St. Bernard.

College—Villanova University, Villanova, Pa.

Drafted by Sacramento on first round, 1986 (17th pick).

Year	G.	Min.	FGA	FGM	Pct.	FTA	FTM	Pct.	Reb.	Pts.	Avg.
82-83	32	681	170	66	.388	24	11	.458	143	143	4.5
83-84	31	1126	303	156	.515	118	78	.661	221	390	12.6
84-85	35	1191	340	166	.488	135	87	.644	278	419	12.0
85-86	37	1288	442	224	.507	224	172	.768	374	620	16.8
Totals	135	4286	1255	612	.488	501	348	.695	1016	1572	11.6

NBA REGULAR SEASON RECORD

Sea.—Team	G.	Min.	FGA	FGM	Pct.	FTA	FTM	Pct.	Off.	Def.	Tot.	Ast.	PF	Dq.	Stl.	Blk.	Pts.	Avg.
										—Rebounds—								
86-87—Sacramento	67	913	317	134	.423	48	35	.729	68	108	176	120	96	1	40	21	310	4.6
87-88—Sacramento	80	2029	702	318	.453	130	103	.792	139	230	369	185	211	4	84	55	775	9.7
Totals	147	2942	1019	452	.445	178	138	.775	207	338	545	305	307	5	124	76	1085	7.4

Three-Point Field Goals: 1986-87, 7-for-28 (.250). 1987-88, 36-for-110 (.327). Totals, 43-for-138 (.312).
Member of NCAA Division I championship team, 1985.

WILLIAM MARK PRICE
(Known by middle name.)

Born February 16, 1964 at Bartlesville, Okla.   Height 6:01.   Weight 175.

High School—Enid, Okla.

College—Georgia Institute of Technology, Atlanta, Ga.

Drafted by Dallas on second round, 1986 (25th pick).

Draft rights traded by Dallas to Cleveland for a 1989 2nd round draft choice and cash, June 17, 1986.

—COLLEGIATE RECORD—

Year	G.	Min.	FGA	FGM	Pct.	FTA	FTM	Pct.	Reb.	Pts.	Avg.
82-83	28	1020	462	201	.435	106	93	.877	105	568	20.3
83-84	29	1078	375	191	.509	85	70	.824	61	452	15.6
84-85	35	1302	462	223	.483	163	137	.840	71	583	16.7
85-86	34	1204	441	233	.528	145	124	.855	94	590	17.4
Totals	126	4604	1740	848	.487	499	424	.850	331	2193	17.4

Three-Point Field Goals: 1982-83, 73-for-166 (.440).

NBA REGULAR SEASON RECORD

Sea.—Team	G.	Min.	FGA	FGM	Pct.	FTA	FTM	Pct.	Off.	Def.	Tot.	Ast.	PF	Dq.	Stl.	Blk.	Pts.	Avg.
										—Rebounds—								
86-87—Cleveland	67	1217	424	173	.408	114	95	.833	33	84	117	202	75	1	43	4	464	6.9
87-88—Cleveland	80	2626	974	493	.506	252	221	.877	54	126	180	480	119	1	99	12	1279	16.0
Totals	147	3843	1398	666	.476	366	316	.863	87	210	297	682	194	2	142	16	1743	11.9

Three-Point Field Goals: 1986-87, 23-for-70 (.329). 1987-88, 72-for-148 (.486). Totals, 95-for-218 (.436).

NBA PLAYOFF RECORD

Sea.—Team	G.	Min.	FGA	FGM	Pct.	FTA	FTM	Pct.	Off.	Def.	Tot.	Ast.	PF	Dq.	Stl.	Blk.	Pts.	Avg.
										—Rebounds—								
87-88—Cleveland	5	205	67	38	.567	25	24	.960	3	15	18	38	11	1	3	0	105	21.0

Three-Point Field Goals: 1987-88, 5-for-12 (.417).

DARRELL KURT RAMBIS
(Known by middle name.)

Born February 25, 1958 at Cupertino, Calif.   Height 6:08.   Weight 213.

High School—Cupertino, Calif.

College—University of Santa Clara, Santa Clara, Calif.

Drafted by New York on third round, 1980 (58th pick).

Waived by New York, September 18, 1980; re-signed by New York to 10-day contract that expired January 30, 1981.
Signed by Los Angeles as a free agent, September 13, 1981.
Signed by Charlotte as an unrestricted free agent, July 28, 1988.
Played in Greece during 1980-81 season.

—COLLEGIATE RECORD—

Year	G.	Min.	FGA	FGM	Pct.	FTA	FTM	Pct.	Reb.	Pts.	Avg.
76-77	27	....	317	167	.527	125	70	.560	313	404	15.0
77-78	27	....	268	136	.507	143	99	.692	231	371	13.7
78-79	27	763	336	172	.512	109	78	.716	226	422	15.6
79-80	27	860	395	211	.534	168	107	.637	267	529	19.6
Totals	108	....	1316	686	.521	545	354	.650	1037	1726	16.0

MARK PRICE

NBA REGULAR SEASON RECORD

Sea.—Team	G.	Min.	FGA	FGM	Pct.	FTA	FTM	Pct.	Off.	Def.	Tot.	Ast.	PF	Dq.	Stl.	Blk.	Pts.	Avg.
81-82—Los Angeles	64	1131	228	118	.518	117	59	.504	116	232	348	56	167	2	60	76	295	4.6
82-83—Los Angeles	78	1806	413	235	.569	166	114	.687	164	367	531	90	233	2	105	63	584	7.5
83-84—Los Angeles	47	743	113	63	.558	66	42	.636	82	184	266	34	108	0	30	14	168	3.6
84-85—L.A. Lakers	82	1617	327	181	.554	103	68	.660	164	364	528	69	211	0	82	47	430	5.2
85-86—L.A. Lakers	74	1573	269	160	.595	122	88	.721	156	361	517	69	198	0	66	33	408	5.5
86-87—L.A. Lakers	78	1514	313	163	.521	157	120	.764	159	294	453	63	201	1	74	41	446	5.7
87-88—L.A. Lakers	70	845	186	102	.548	93	73	.785	103	165	268	54	103	0	39	13	277	4.0
Totals	493	9229	1849	1022	.553	824	564	.684	944	1967	2911	435	1221	5	456	287	2608	5.3

Three-Point Field Goals: 1981-82, 0-for-1. 1982-83, 0-for-2. Totals, 0-for-3.

NBA PLAYOFF RECORD

Sea.—Team	G.	Min.	FGA	FGM	Pct.	FTA	FTM	Pct.	Off.	Def.	Tot.	Ast.	PF	Dq.	Stl.	Blk.	Pts.	Avg.
81-82—Los Angeles	14	279	64	33	.516	26	16	.615	32	54	86	11	47	0	8	12	82	5.9
82-83—Los Angeles	15	377	79	45	.570	35	23	.657	27	63	90	19	51	0	13	16	113	7.5
83-84—Los Angeles	21	428	92	60	.652	33	21	.636	33	88	121	14	57	0	10	10	141	6.7
84-85—L.A. Lakers	19	375	81	48	.593	28	19	.679	42	87	129	17	52	0	18	9	115	6.1
85-86—L.A. Lakers	14	267	45	27	.600	18	13	.722	26	57	83	14	39	0	10	7	67	4.8
86-87—L.A. Lakers	17	215	41	24	.585	34	31	.912	16	51	67	9	42	0	8	3	79	4.6
87-88—L.A. Lakers	19	186	34	21	.618	13	9	.692	13	38	51	9	28	0	5	2	51	2.7
Totals	119	2127	436	258	.592	187	132	.706	189	438	627	93	316	0	72	59	648	5.4

Member of NBA championship teams, 1982, 1985, 1987 and 1988.

BLAIR ALLEN RASMUSSEN

Born November 13, 1962 at Auburn, Wash.   Height 7:00.   Weight 250.

High School—Auburn, Wash.

College—University of Oregon, Eugene, Ore.

Drafted by Denver on first round, 1985 (15th pick).

—COLLEGIATE RECORD—

Year	G.	Min.	FGA	FGM	Pct.	FTA	FTM	Pct.	Reb.	Pts.	Avg.
81-82	27	521	141	67	.475	53	39	.736	129	173	6.4
82-83	27	819	296	160	.540	116	80	.690	146	400	14.8
83-84	29	1017	377	196	.520	112	90	.804	176	482	16.6
84-85	31	1081	381	195	.512	151	109	.722	222	499	16.1
Totals	114	3438	1195	618	.517	432	318	.736	673	1554	13.6

NBA REGULAR SEASON RECORD

Sea.—Team	G.	Min.	FGA	FGM	Pct.	FTA	FTM	Pct.	Off.	Def.	Tot.	Ast.	PF	Dq.	Stl.	Blk.	Pts.	Avg.
85-86—Denver	48	330	150	61	.407	39	31	.795	37	60	97	16	63	0	3	10	153	3.2
86-87—Denver	74	1421	570	268	.470	231	169	.732	183	282	465	60	224	6	24	58	705	9.5
87-88—Denver	79	1779	884	435	.492	170	132	.776	130	307	437	78	241	2	22	81	1002	12.7
Totals	201	3530	1604	764	.476	440	332	.755	350	649	999	154	528	8	49	149	1860	9.3

NBA PLAYOFF RECORD

Sea.—Team	G.	Min.	FGA	FGM	Pct.	FTA	FTM	Pct.	Off.	Def.	Tot.	Ast.	PF	Dq.	Stl.	Blk.	Pts.	Avg.
85-86—Denver	10	175	96	39	.406	41	33	.805	27	33	60	10	28	1	5	9	111	11.1
86-87—Denver	3	92	45	22	.489	10	5	.500	8	15	23	7	12	0	2	2	49	16.3
87-88—Denver	11	277	127	60	.472	20	18	.900	25	46	71	7	33	0	1	12	138	12.5
Totals	24	544	268	121	.451	71	56	.789	60	94	154	24	73	1	8	23	298	12.4

ROBERT KEITH REID

Born August 30, 1955 at Atlanta, Ga.   Height 6:08.   Weight 215.

High School—Schertz, Tex., Samuel Clemens.

College—St. Mary's University, San Antonio, Tex.

Drafted by Houston on second round, 1977 (40th pick).

Traded by Houston to Charlotte for Bernard Thompson and a 1990 2nd round draft choice, July 18, 1988. Sat out 1982-83 season for religious reasons.

—COLLEGIATE RECORD—

Year	G.	Min.	FGA	FGM	Pct.	FTA	FTM	Pct.	Reb.	Pts.	Avg.
73-74	19	....	30	14	.467	21	11	.524	14	39	2.1
74-75	33	....	368	197	.535	73	53	.726	286	447	13.5
75-76	28	....	458	237	.517	85	74	.871	288	548	19.6
76-77	29	....	405	196	.484	115	83	.722	244	475	16.4
Totals	109	...	1261	644	.511	294	221	.752	832	1509	13.8

Sea.—Team	G.	Min.	FGA	FGM	Pct.	FTA	FTM	Pct.	Off.	Def.	Tot.	Ast.	PF	Dq.	Stl.	Blk.	Pts.	Avg.
77-78—Houston	80	1849	574	261	.455	96	63	.656	111	248	359	121	277	8	67	51	585	7.3
78-79—Houston	82	2259	777	382	.492	186	131	.704	129	354	483	230	302	7	75	48	895	10.9
79-80—Houston	76	2304	861	419	.487	208	153	.736	140	301	441	244	281	2	132	57	991	13.0
80-81—Houston	82	2963	1113	536	.482	303	229	.756	164	419	583	344	325	4	163	66	1301	15.9
81-82—Houston	77	2913	958	437	.456	214	160	.748	175	336	511	314	297	2	115	48	1035	13.4
83-84—Houston	64	1936	857	406	.474	123	81	.659	97	244	341	217	243	5	88	30	895	14.0
84-85—Houston	82	1763	648	312	.481	126	88	.698	81	192	273	171	196	1	48	22	713	8.7
85-86—Houston	82	2157	881	409	.464	214	162	.757	67	234	301	222	231	3	91	16	986	12.0
86-87—Houston	75	2594	1006	420	.417	177	136	.768	47	242	289	323	232	2	75	21	1029	13.7
87-88—Houston	62	980	356	165	.463	63	50	.794	38	87	125	67	118	0	27	5	393	6.3
Totals	762	21718	8031	3747	.467	1710	1253	.733	1049	2657	3706	2253	2502	34	881	364	8823	11.6

Three-Point Field Goals: 1979-80, 0-for-3. 1980-81, 0-for-4. 1981-82, 1-for-10 (.100). 1983-84, 2-for-8 (.250). 1984-85, 1-for-16 (.063). 1985-86, 6-for-33 (.182). 1986-87, 53-for-162 (.327). 1987-88, 13-for-34 (.382). Totals, 76-for-270 (.281).

NBA PLAYOFF RECORD

Sea.—Team	G.	Min.	FGA	FGM	Pct.	FTA	FTM	Pct.	Off.	Def.	Tot.	Ast.	PF	Dq.	Stl.	Blk.	Pts.	Avg.
78-79—Houston	2	45	17	7	.412	9	6	.667	5	4	9	2	7	0	1	2	20	10.0
79-80—Houston	7	266	102	52	.510	26	22	.846	14	41	55	26	28	0	6	7	126	18.0
80-81—Houston	21	868	303	139	.459	92	61	.663	56	86	142	98	80	2	50	24	339	16.1
81-82—Houston	3	115	31	15	.484	5	4	.800	9	17	26	9	10	0	5	2	34	11.3
84-85—Houston	5	87	45	19	.422	0	0	.000	3	14	17	5	22	0	4	2	38	7.6
85-86—Houston	20	773	288	124	.431	59	47	.797	13	70	83	137	74	1	27	1	298	14.9
86-87—Houston	10	431	155	56	.361	23	15	.652	6	30	36	48	36	0	10	3	129	12.9
87-88—Houston	4	114	33	15	.455	3	2	.667	3	12	15	8	13	0	2	0	35	8.8
Totals	72	2699	974	427	.438	217	157	.724	109	274	383	333	270	3	105	41	1019	14.2

Three-Point Field Goals: 1979-80, 0-for-1. 1980-81, 0-for-2. 1984-85, 0-for-4. 1985-86, 3-for-21 (.143). 1986-87, 2-for-17 (.118). 1987-88, 3-for-7 (.429). Totals, 8-for-52 (.154).

RICHARD ALLEN RELLFORD

Born February 16, 1964 at Riviera Beach, Fla.   Height 6:06.   Weight 230.

High School—Riviera Beach, Fla., Suncoast.

College—University of Michigan, Ann Arbor, Mich.

Drafted by Indiana on fifth round, 1986 (95th pick).

Draft rights relinquished by Indiana, July 22, 1987; signed by San Antonio as a free agent, October 1, 1987.
Waived by San Antonio, October 28, 1987; re-signed by San Antonio, April 8, 1988, to a 10-day contract that expired, April 17, 1988.
Re-signed by San Antonio, April 18, 1988, for remainder of season.
Played in Continental Basketball Association with Rapid City Thrillers and Rockford Lightning, 1986-87, and Rockford Lightning and Wyoming Wildcatters, 1987-88.

COLLEGIATE RECORD

Year	G.	Min.	FGA	FGM	Pct.	FTA	FTM	Pct.	Reb.	Pts.	Avg.
82-83	28	....	181	85	.471	67	53	.791	98	223	8.0
83-84	33	698	185	105	.568	63	49	.778	107	259	7.8
84-85	30	732	230	133	.578	94	75	.798	126	341	11.4
85-86	33	782	249	149	.598	113	90	.796	156	388	11.8
Totals	124	....	845	472	.559	337	267	.792	487	1211	9.8

CBA REGULAR SEASON RECORD

Sea.—Team	G.	Min.	2-Point FGM	FGA	Pct.	3-Point FGM	FGA	Pct.	FTM	FTA	Pct.	Reb.	Ast.	Pts.	Avg.
86-87—Rapid City-Rock.	47	1147	284	521	.545	1	9	.111	205	276	.742	184	25	776	16.5
87-88—Rock.-Wyo.	52	1515	327	607	.539	0	2	.000	285	373	.764	277	60	939	18.1
Totals	99	2662	611	1128	.542	1	11	.091	490	649	.755	461	85	1715	17.3

NBA REGULAR SEASON RECORD

Sea.—Team	G.	Min.	FGA	FGM	Pct.	FTA	FTM	Pct.	Off.	Def.	Tot.	Ast.	PF	Dq.	Stl.	Blk.	Pts.	Avg.
87-88—San Antonio	4	42	8	5	.625	8	6	.750	2	5	7	1	3	0	0	3	16	4.0

JERRY REYNOLDS

Born December 23, 1962 at Brooklyn, N.Y.   Height 6:08.   Weight 206.

High School—Brooklyn, N.Y., Alexander Hamilton.

Colleges—Madison Area Technical College, Madison, Wisc., and
Louisiana State University, Baton Rouge, La.

Drafted by Milwaukee on first round as an undergraduate, 1985 (22nd pick).

—COLLEGIATE RECORD—
Madison Tech

Year	G.	Min.	FGA	FGM	Pct.	FTA	FTM	Pct.	Reb.	Pts.	Avg.
81-82				Did Not Play							

Louisiana State

Year	G.	Min.	FGA	FGM	Pct.	FTA	FTM	Pct.	Reb.	Pts.	Avg.
82-83	32	888	236	126	.534	142	88	.620	198	340	10.6
83-84	29	899	307	162	.528	158	85	.538	239	409	14.1
84-85	29	803	255	128	.502	107	64	.598	176	320	11.0
Totals	90	2590	798	416	.521	407	237	.582	613	1069	11.9

NBA REGULAR SEASON RECORD

Sea.—Team	G.	Min.	FGA	FGM	Pct.	FTA	FTM	Pct.	Off.	Def.	Tot.	Ast.	PF	Dq.	Stl.	Blk.	Pts.	Avg.
85-86—Milwaukee	55	508	162	72	.444	104	58	.558	37	43	80	86	57	0	43	19	203	3.7
86-87—Milwaukee	58	963	356	140	.393	184	118	.641	72	101	173	106	91	0	50	30	404	7.0
87-88—Milwaukee	62	1161	419	188	.449	154	119	.773	70	90	160	104	97	0	74	32	498	8.0
Totals	175	2632	937	400	.427	442	295	.667	179	234	413	296	245	0	167	81	1105	6.3

Three-Point Field Goals: 1985-86, 1-for-2 (.500). 1986-87, 6-for-18 (.333). 1987-88, 3-for-7 (.429). Totals, 10-for-27 (.370).

NBA PLAYOFF RECORD

Sea.—Team	G.	Min.	FGA	FGM	Pct.	FTA	FTM	Pct.	Off.	Def.	Tot.	Ast.	PF	Dq.	Stl.	Blk.	Pts.	Avg.
85-86—Milwaukee	7	40	17	7	.412	11	6	.545	3	6	9	4	5	0	4	3	20	2.9
86-87—Milwaukee	4	5	3	1	.333	2	1	.500	1	0	1	2	0	0	3	0	3	0.8
87-88—Milwaukee	3	12	6	4	.667	0	0	.000	0	1	1	1	1	0	0	0	8	2.7
Totals	14	57	26	12	.462	13	7	.538	4	7	11	7	6	0	7	3	31	2.2

Three-Point Field Goals: 1985-86, 0-for-1. 1986-87, 0-for-1. Totals, 0-for-2.

MICHEAL RAY RICHARDSON
(Sugar Ray)

Born April 11, 1955 at Lubbock, Tex.   Height 6:05.   Weight 195.

High School—Denver, Colo., Manual.

College—University of Montana, Missoula, Mont.

Drafted by New York on first round, 1978 (4th pick).

Traded by New York with a 1984 5th round draft choice to Golden State for Bernard King, October 22, 1982.
Traded by Golden State to New Jersey for Eric Floyd and Mickey Johnson, February 6, 1983.
Waived by New Jersey, October 11, 1983; reinstated by New Jersey, December 21, 1983.
Disqualified from the NBA under rules of the league's Anti-Drug Program, February 25, 1986.
Reinstated by NBA, July 21, 1988.
Played in Continental Basketball Association with Albany Patroons, 1987-88.

—COLLEGIATE RECORD—

Year	G.	Min.	FGA	FGM	Pct.	FTA	FTM	Pct.	Reb.	Pts.	Avg.
74-75†	11	....	139	73	.525	50	38	.760	182	184	16.7
74-75	29	....	188	92	.489	58	34	.586	104	218	7.5
75-76	25	....	356	187	.525	113	82	.726	157	456	18.2
76-77	26	....	466	221	.474	96	58	.604	224	500	19.2
77-78	27	....	567	272	.480	159	109	.686	185	653	24.2
Varsity Totals	107	....	1577	772	.490	426	283	.664	670	1827	17.1

CBA REGULAR SEASON RECORD

Sea.—Team	G.	Min.	2-Point FGM	FGA	Pct.	3-Point FGM	FGA	Pct.	FTM	FTA	Pct.	Reb.	Ast.	Pts.	Avg.
87-88—Albany	54	1411	306	647	.473	9	48	.188	115	158	.728	260	170	754	14.0

NBA REGULAR SEASON RECORD

Sea.—Team	G.	Min.	FGA	FGM	Pct.	FTA	FTM	Pct.	Off.	Def.	Tot.	Ast.	PF	Dq.	Stl.	Blk.	Pts.	Avg.
78-79—New York	72	1218	483	200	.414	128	69	.539	78	155	233	213	188	2	100	18	469	6.5
79-80—New York	82	3060	1063	502	.472	338	223	.660	151	388	539	832	260	3	265	35	1254	15.3
80-81—New York	79	3175	1116	523	.469	338	224	.663	173	372	545	627	258	2	232	35	1293	16.4
81-82—New York	82	3044	1343	619	.461	303	212	.700	177	388	565	572	317	3	213	41	1469	17.9
82-83—G.S.-N.J.	64	2076	815	346	.425	163	106	.650	113	182	295	432	240	4	182	24	806	12.6
83-84—New Jersey	48	1285	528	243	.460	108	76	.704	56	116	172	214	156	4	103	20	576	12.0
84-85—New Jersey	82	3127	1470	690	.469	313	240	.767	156	301	457	669	277	3	243	22	1649	20.1
85-86—New Jersey	47	1604	661	296	.448	179	141	.788	77	173	250	340	163	2	125	11	737	15.7
Totals	556	18589	7479	3419	.457	1870	1291	.690	981	2075	3056	3899	1859	23	1463	206	8253	14.8

Three-Point Field Goals: 1979-80, 27-for-110 (.245). 1980-81, 23-for-102 (.225). 1981-82, 19-for-101 (.188). 1982-83, 8-for-51 (.157). 1983-84, 14-for-48 (.241). 1984-85, 29-for-115 (.252). 1985-86, 4-for-27 (.148). Totals, 124-for-564 (.220).

NBA PLAYOFF RECORD

Sea.—Team	G.	Min.	FGA	FGM	Pct.	FTA	FTM	Pct.	Off.	Def.	Tot.	Ast.	PF	Dq.	Stl.	Blk.	Pts.	Avg.
										—Rebounds—								
80-81—New York	2	86	33	8	.242	12	7	.583	6	13	19	11	8	0	7	0	23	11.5
82-83—New Jersey	2	58	21	8	.381	5	3	.600	2	6	8	5	3	0	5	0	19	9.5
83-84—New Jersey	11	443	169	69	.408	56	41	.732	20	34	54	79	40	1	34	4	185	16.8
84-85—New Jersey	3	125	57	23	.404	14	9	.643	4	14	18	34	12	0	4	0	55	18.3
Totals	18	712	280	108	.386	87	60	.690	32	67	99	129	63	1	50	4	282	15.7

Three-Point Field Goals: 1980-81, 0-for-4. 1982-83, 0-for-1. 1983-84, 6-for-22 (.273). 1984-85, 0-for-2. Totals, 6-for-29 (.207).

NBA ALL-STAR GAME RECORD

Season—Team	Min.	FGA	FGM	Pct.	FTA	FTM	Pct.	Off.	Def.	Tot.	Ast.	PF	Dq.	Stl.	Blk.	Pts.
									—Rebounds—							
1980—New York.....	13	7	3	.429	0	0	.000	1	0	1	2	2	0	1	0	6
1981—New York.....	24	7	5	.714	2	1	.500	2	3	5	3	3	0	4	0	11
1982—New York.....	20	10	5	.500	0	0	.000	0	2	2	4	1	0	2	0	10
1985—New Jersey..	13	8	2	.250	2	1	.500	2	0	2	1	3	0	2	0	5
Totals	70	32	15	.563	4	2	.500	5	5	10	10	9	0	9	0	32

Three-Point Field Goals: 1981, 0-for-1. 1985, 0-for-2. Totals, 0-for-3.

Named to NBA All-Defensive First Team, 1980 and 1981. . . . NBA Comeback Player of the Year, 1985. . . . Led NBA in steals, 1980, 1983, 1985. . . . Led NBA in assists, 1980.

GLENN ANTON RIVERS
(Doc)

Born October 13, 1961 at Maywood, Ill.   Height 6:04.   Weight 185.

High School—Maywood, Ill., Proviso East.

College—Marquette University, Milwaukee, Wis.

Drafted by Atlanta on second round as an undergraduate, 1983 (31st pick).

—COLLEGIATE RECORD—

Year	G.	Min.	FGA	FGM	Pct.	FTA	FTM	Pct.	Reb.	Pts.	Avg.
80-81	31	....	329	182	.553	119	70	.588	99	434	14.0
81-82	29	....	382	173	.453	108	70	.648	99	416	14.3
82-83	29	....	373	163	.437	95	58	.611	94	384	13.2
Totals	80	....	1084	518	.478	322	198	.615	292	1234	13.9

NBA REGULAR SEASON RECORD

Sea.—Team	G.	Min.	FGA	FGM	Pct.	FTA	FTM	Pct.	Off.	Def.	Tot.	Ast.	PF	Dq.	Stl.	Blk.	Pts.	Avg.
										—Rebounds—								
83-84—Atlanta	81	1938	541	250	.462	325	255	.785	72	148	220	314	286	8	127	30	757	9.3
84-85—Atlanta	69	2126	701	334	.476	378	291	.770	66	148	214	410	250	7	163	53	974	14.1
85-86—Atlanta	53	1571	464	220	.474	283	172	.608	49	113	162	443	185	2	120	13	612	11.5
86-87—Atlanta	82	2590	758	342	.451	441	365	.828	83	216	299	823	287	5	171	30	1053	12.8
87-88—Atlanta	80	2502	890	403	.453	421	319	.758	83	283	366	747	272	3	140	41	1134	14.2
Totals	365	10727	3354	1549	.462	1848	1402	.759	353	908	1261	2737	1280	25	721	167	4530	12.4

Three-Point Field Goals: 1983-84, 2-for-12 (.167). 1984-85, 15-for-36 (.417). 1985-86, 0-for-16. 1986-87, 4-for-21 (.190). 1987-88, 9-for-33 (.273). Totals, 30-for-118 (.254).

NBA PLAYOFF RECORD

Sea.—Team	G.	Min.	FGA	FGM	Pct.	FTA	FTM	Pct.	Off.	Def.	Tot.	Ast.	PF	Dq.	Stl.	Blk.	Pts.	Avg.
										—Rebounds—								
83-84—Atlanta	5	130	32	16	.500	41	36	.878	7	3	10	16	16	0	12	4	68	13.6
85-86—Atlanta	9	262	92	40	.435	42	31	.738	10	32	42	78	38	2	18	0	114	12.7
86-87—Atlanta	8	245	47	18	.383	52	26	.500	6	21	27	90	32	0	9	3	62	7.8
87-88—Atlanta	12	409	139	71	.511	43	39	.907	8	51	59	115	40	1	25	2	188	15.7
Totals	34	1046	310	145	.468	178	132	.742	31	107	138	299	126	3	64	9	432	12.7

Three-Point Field Goals: 1983-84, 0-for-3. 1985-86, 3-for-6 (.500). 1987-88, 7-for-22 (.318). Totals, 10-for-31 (.323).

NBA ALL-STAR GAME RECORD

Season—Team	Min.	FGA	FGM	Pct.	FTA	FTM	Pct.	Off.	Def.	Tot.	Ast.	PF	Dq.	Stl.	Blk.	Pts.
									—Rebounds—							
1988—Atlanta	16	4	2	.500	11	5	.455	0	3	3	6	3	0	0	0	9

Nephew of former NBA forward Jim Brewer. . . . Cousin of former major league outfielder Ken Singleton.

FREDERICK CLARK ROBERTS
(Fred)

Born August 14, 1960 at Provo, Utah.   Height 6:10.   Weight 220.

High School—Riverton, Utah, Bingham.

College—Brigham Young University, Provo, Utah.

Drafted by Milwaukee on second round, 1982 (27th pick).

Draft rights traded by Milwaukee with Mickey Johnson to New Jersey for Phil Ford and a 1983 2nd round draft choice, November 10, 1982.
Draft rights traded by New Jersey with a 1983 2nd round draft choice and cash to San Antonio in exchange for the Spurs' relinquishing their rights to Coach Stan Albeck, June 7, 1983.
Traded by San Antonio to Utah for 1986 and 1988 2nd round draft choices, December 18, 1984.
Traded by Utah to Boston for a 1987 3rd round draft choice, September 25, 1986.
Selected from Boston by Miami in NBA expansion draft, June 23, 1988.
Traded by Miami to Milwaukee for a 1988 2nd round draft choice, June 23, 1988.
Played in Italian League during 1982-83 season.

—COLLEGIATE RECORD—

Year	G.	Min.	FGA	FGM	Pct.	FTA	FTM	Pct.	Reb.	Pts.	Avg.
78-79	28	861	291	158	.543	106	83	.783	191	399	14.3
79-80	29	891	257	151	.588	98	71	.724	177	373	12.9
80-81	32	1188	373	216	.579	220	171	.777	255	603	18.8
81-82	30	1118	338	162	.479	178	142	.798	215	466	15.5
Totals	119	4058	1259	687	.546	602	467	.776	838	1841	15.5

ITALIAN LEAGUE RECORD

Year	G.	Min.	FGA	FGM	Pct.	FTA	FTM	Pct.	Reb.	Pts.	Avg.
82-83—Fort. Bologna.	30	1114	462	233	.504	148	106	.716	258	572	19.1

NBA REGULAR SEASON RECORD

Sea.—Team	G.	Min.	FGA	FGM	Pct.	FTA	FTM	Pct.	Off.	Def.	Tot.	Ast.	PF	Dq.	Stl.	Blk.	Pts.	Avg.
83-84—San Antonio	79	1531	399	214	.536	172	144	.837	102	202	304	98	219	4	52	38	573	7.3
84-85—S.A.-Utah	74	1178	418	208	.498	182	150	.824	78	108	186	87	141	0	28	22	567	7.7
85-86—Utah	58	469	167	74	.443	87	67	.770	31	49	80	27	72	0	8	6	216	3.7
86-87—Boston	73	1079	270	139	.515	153	124	.810	54	136	190	62	129	1	22	20	402	5.5
87-88—Boston	74	1032	330	161	.488	165	128	.776	60	102	162	81	118	0	16	15	450	6.1
Totals	358	5289	1584	796	.503	759	613	.808	325	597	922	355	679	5	126	101	2208	6.2

Three-Point Field Goals: 1983-84, 1-for-4 (.250). 1984-85, 1-for-1. 1985-86, 1-for-2 (.500). 1986-87, 0-for-3. 1987-88, 0-for-6. Totals, 3-for-16 (.188).

NBA PLAYOFF RECORD

Sea.—Team	G.	Min.	FGA	FGM	Pct.	FTA	FTM	Pct.	Off.	Def.	Tot.	Ast.	PF	Dq.	Stl.	Blk.	Pts.	Avg.
84-85—Utah	10	130	43	19	.442	20	16	.800	6	11	17	9	16	0	7	3	54	5.4
85-86—Utah	4	31	15	7	.467	9	8	.889	4	3	7	3	5	0	0	0	22	5.5
86-87—Boston	20	265	59	30	.508	44	31	.705	15	18	33	12	47	0	6	3	91	4.6
87-88—Boston	15	100	21	11	.524	11	7	.636	8	8	16	3	20	1	3	0	29	1.9
Totals	49	526	138	67	.486	84	62	.738	33	40	73	27	88	1	16	6	196	4.0

ALVIN CYRRALE ROBERTSON

Born July 22, 1962 at Barberton, O.   Height 6:04.   Weight 190.

High School—Barberton, O.

Colleges—Crowder Junior College, Neosho, Mo., and
University of Arkansas, Fayetteville, Ark.

Drafted by San Antonio on first round, 1984 (7th pick).

—COLLEGIATE RECORD—
Crowder JC

Year	G.	Min.	FGA	FGM	Pct.	FTA	FTM	Pct.	Reb.	Pts.	Avg.
80-81	34	....	470	269	.572	112	73	.652	284	611	18.0

Arkansas

Year	G.	Min.	FGA	FGM	Pct.	FTA	FTM	Pct.	Reb.	Pts.	Avg.
81-82	28	495	159	84	.528	58	35	.603	62	203	7.3
82-83	28	915	294	161	.548	115	76	.661	137	398	14.2
83-84	32	1109	375	187	.499	182	122	.670	175	496	15.5
Ark. Totals	88	2519	828	432	.522	355	233	.656	374	1097	12.5

NBA REGULAR SEASON RECORD

Sea.—Team	G.	Min.	FGA	FGM	Pct.	FTA	FTM	Pct.	Off.	Def.	Tot.	Ast.	PF	Dq.	Stl.	Blk.	Pts.	Avg.
84-85—San Antonio	79	1685	600	299	.498	169	124	.734	116	149	265	275	217	1	127	24	726	9.2
85-86—San Antonio	82	2878	1093	562	.514	327	260	.795	184	332	516	448	296	4	301	40	1392	17.0
86-87—San Antonio	81	2697	1264	589	.466	324	244	.753	186	238	424	421	264	2	260	35	1435	17.7
87-88—San Antonio	82	2978	1408	655	.465	365	273	.748	165	333	498	557	300	4	243	69	1610	19.6
Totals	324	10238	4365	2105	.482	1185	901	.760	651	1052	1703	1701	1077	11	931	168	5163	15.9

Three-Point Field Goals: 1984-85, 4-for-11 (.364). 1985-86, 8-for-29 (.276). 1986-87, 13-for-48 (.271). 1987-88, 27-for-95 (.284). Totals, 52-for-183 (.284).

ALVIN ROBERTSON

NBA PLAYOFF RECORD

Sea.—Team	G.	Min.	FGA	FGM	Pct.	FTA	FTM	Pct.	Off.	Def.	Tot.	Ast.	PF	Dq.	Stl.	Blk.	Pts.	Avg.
										—Rebounds—								
85-86—San Antonio	3	98	29	8	.276	13	11	.846	5	9	14	19	10	0	7	1	27	9.0
87-88—San Antonio	3	119	53	30	.566	9	7	.778	5	9	14	28	15	1	12	1	70	23.3
Totals	6	217	82	38	.463	22	18	.818	10	18	28	47	25	1	19	2	97	16.2

Three-Point Field Goals: 1987-88, 3-for-7 (.429).

NBA ALL-STAR GAME RECORD

Season—Team	Min.	FGA	FGM	Pct.	FTA	FTM	Pct.	Off.	Def.	Tot.	Ast.	PF	Dq.	Stl.	Blk.	Pts.
									—Rebounds—							
1986—San Antonio..	20	6	2	.333	0	0	.000	1	8	9	5	1	0	0	0	4
1987—San Antonio..	16	5	2	.400	2	2	1.000	2	0	2	1	1	0	0	0	6
1988—San Antonio..	12	3	1	.333	0	0	.000	0	0	0	1	1	0	2	0	2
Totals	48	14	5	.357	2	2	1.000	3	8	11	7	3	0	2	0	12

Named to All-NBA Second Team, 1986. . . . NBA All-Defensive First Team, 1987. . . . NBA All-Defensive Second Team, 1986 and 1988. . . . NBA Defensive Player of the Year, 1986. . . . NBA Most Improved Player, 1986. . . . Holds NBA record for most steals in a season, 1986. . . . Led NBA in steals, 1986 and 1987. . . . Member of U.S. Olympic team, 1984.

CLIFFORD TRENT ROBINSON
(Cliff)

Born March 13, 1960 at Oakland, Calif.   Height 6:09.   Weight 240.

High School—Oakland, Calif., Castlemont.

College—University of Southern California, Los Angeles, Calif.

Drafted by New Jersey on first round as an undergraduate, 1979 (11th pick).

Traded by New Jersey to Kansas City for Otis Birdsong and a 1981 2nd round draft choice, June 8, 1981.
Traded by Kansas City to Cleveland for Reggie Johnson, February 16, 1982.
Traded by Cleveland with the draft rights to Tim McCormick and cash to Washington for the draft rights to Melvin Turpin, June 19, 1984.
Traded by Washington with Jeff Ruland to Philadelphia for Moses Malone, Terry Catledge, a 1986 1st round draft choice and a 1988 1st round draft choice, June 16, 1986.

—COLLEGIATE RECORD—

Year	G.	Min.	FGA	FGM	Pct.	FTA	FTM	Pct.	Reb.	Pts.	Avg.
77-78	24	724	367	191	.520	100	60	.600	231	442	18.4
78-79	21	670	338	159	.470	107	76	.710	243	394	18.8
Totals	45	1394	705	350	.496	207	136	.657	474	836	18.6

NBA REGULAR SEASON RECORD

Sea.—Team	G.	Min.	FGA	FGM	Pct.	FTA	FTM	Pct.	Off.	Def.	Tot.	Ast.	PF	Dq.	Stl.	Blk.	Pts.	Avg.
										—Rebounds—								
79-80—New Jersey	70	1661	833	391	.469	242	168	.694	174	332	506	98	178	1	61	34	951	13.6
80-81—New Jersey	63	1822	1070	525	.491	248	178	.718	120	361	481	105	216	6	58	52	1229	19.5
81-82—K.C.-Clev.	68	2175	1143	518	.453	313	222	.709	174	435	609	120	222	4	88	103	1258	18.5
82-83—Cleveland	77	2601	1230	587	.477	301	213	.708	190	666	856	145	272	7	61	58	1387	18.0
83-84—Cleveland	73	2402	1185	533	.450	334	234	.701	156	597	753	185	195	2	51	32	1301	17.8
84-85—Washington	60	1870	896	422	.471	213	158	.742	141	405	546	149	187	4	51	47	1003	16.7
85-86—Washington	78	2563	1255	595	.474	353	269	.762	180	500	680	186	217	2	98	44	1460	18.7
86-87—Philadelphia	55	1586	729	338	.464	184	139	.755	86	221	307	89	150	1	86	30	815	14.8
87-88—Philadelphia	62	2110	1041	483	.464	293	210	.717	116	289	405	131	192	4	79	39	1178	19.0
Totals	606	18790	9382	4392	.468	2481	1791	.722	1337	3806	5143	1208	1829	31	633	439	10582	17.5

Three-Point Field Goals: 1979-80, 1-for-4 (.250). 1980-81, 1-for-1. 1981-82, 0-for-4. 1982-83, 0-for-5. 1983-84, 1-for-2 (.500). 1984-85, 1-for-2 (.500). 1985-86, 1-for-3 (.333). 1986-87, 0-for-4. 1987-88, 2-for-9 (.222). Totals, 7-for-34 (.206).

NBA PLAYOFF RECORD

Sea.—Team	G.	Min.	FGA	FGM	Pct.	FTA	FTM	Pct.	Off.	Def.	Tot.	Ast.	PF	Dq.	Stl.	Blk.	Pts.	Avg.
										—Rebounds—								
84-85—Washington	4	123	56	25	.446	12	9	.750	12	18	30	4	14	0	4	2	59	14.8
85-86—Washington	5	177	93	46	.495	31	15	.484	17	26	43	17	19	1	10	3	107	21.4
86-87—Philadelphia	5	138	61	30	.492	15	13	.867	10	33	43	6	15	0	3	7	73	14.6
Totals	14	438	210	101	.481	58	37	.638	39	77	116	27	48	1	17	12	239	17.1

DENNIS KEITH RODMAN
(Worm)

Born May 13, 1961 at Trenton, N.J.   Height 6:08.   Weight 210.

High School—Dallas, Tex., South Oak Cliff.

(Did not play high school basketball.)

Colleges—Cooke County Junior College, Gainesville, Tex., and Southeastern Oklahoma State University, Durant, Okla.

Drafted by Detroit on second round, 1986 (27th pick).

—COLLEGIATE RECORD—
Cooke County

Year	G.	Min.	FGA	FGM	Pct.	FTA	FTM	Pct.	Reb.	Pts.	Avg.
82-83	16	....	185	114	.616	91	53	.582	212	281	17.6

Southeastern Oklahoma

Year	G.	Min.	FGA	FGM	Pct.	FTA	FTM	Pct.	Reb.	Pts.	Avg.
83-84	30	....	490	303	.618	264	173	.655	392	779	26.0
84-85	32	....	545	353	.648	267	151	.566	510	857	26.8
85-86	34	....	515	332	.645	252	165	.655	605	829	24.4
Totals	96	....	1550	988	.637	783	489	.625	1507	2465	25.7

NBA REGULAR SEASON RECORD

Sea.—Team	G.	Min.	FGA	FGM	Pct.	FTA	FTM	Pct.	Off.	Def.	Tot.	Ast.	PF	Dq.	Stl.	Blk.	Pts.	Avg.
86-87—Detroit	77	1155	391	213	.545	126	74	.587	163	169	332	56	166	1	38	48	500	6.5
87-88—Detroit	82	2147	709	398	.561	284	152	.535	318	397	715	110	273	5	75	45	953	11.6
Totals	159	3302	1100	611	.555	410	226	.551	481	566	1047	166	439	6	113	93	1453	9.1

Three-Point Field Goals: 1986-87, 0-for-1. 1987-88, 5-for-17 (.294). Totals, 5-for-18 (.278).

NBA PLAYOFF RECORD

Sea.—Team	G.	Min.	FGA	FGM	Pct.	FTA	FTM	Pct.	Off.	Def.	Tot.	Ast.	PF	Dq.	Stl.	Blk.	Pts.	Avg.
86-87—Detroit	15	245	74	40	.541	22	18	.563	32	39	71	3	48	0	6	17	98	6.5
87-88—Detroit	23	474	136	71	.522	54	22	.407	51	85	136	21	87	1	14	14	164	7.1
Totals	38	719	210	111	.529	86	40	.465	83	124	207	24	135	1	20	31	262	6.9

Three-Point Field Goals: 1987-88, 0-for-2.

Led NAIA in scoring, 1985 and 1986. . . . Led NAIA in rebounding, 1986.

JOHN BERNARD ROGERS
(Johnny)

Born December 30, 1963 at Fullerton, Calif. Height 6:11. Weight 231.

High School—Westminster, Calif., LaQuinta.

Colleges—Stanford University, Stanford, Calif., and
University of California-Irvine, Irvine, Calif.

Drafted by Sacramento on second round, 1986 (34th pick).

Waived by Sacramento, November 3, 1987; signed by Cleveland as a free agent, November 10, 1987.

—COLLEGIATE RECORD—
Stanford

Year	G.	Min.	FGA	FGM	Pct.	FTA	FTM	Pct.	Reb.	Pts.	Avg.
81-82	27	766	237	131	.553	93	76	.817	128	338	12.5
82-83	28	671	204	120	.588	62	51	.823	112	291	10.4
Stanford Totals	55	1437	441	251	.569	155	127	.819	240	629	11.4

California-Irvine

Year	G.	Min.	FGA	FGM	Pct.	FTA	FTM	Pct.	Reb.	Pts.	Avg.
83-84					Did Not Play—Transfer Student						
84-85	30	1045	471	246	.522	178	152	.854	221	650	21.7
85-86	29	1030	438	229	.523	148	122	.824	250	599	20.7
UCI Totals	59	2075	909	475	.523	326	274	.840	471	1249	21.2
Totals	114	3512	1350	726	.538	481	401	.834	711	1878	16.5

Three-Point Field Goals: 1984-85, 6-for-13 (.462). 1985-86, 19-for-35 (.543). Totals, 25-for-48 (.521).

NBA REGULAR SEASON RECORD

Sea.—Team	G.	Min.	FGA	FGM	Pct.	FTA	FTM	Pct.	Off.	Def.	Tot.	Ast.	PF	Dq.	Stl.	Blk.	Pts.	Avg.
86-87—Sacramento	45	468	185	90	.486	15	9	.600	30	47	77	26	66	0	9	8	189	4.2
87-88—Cleveland	24	168	61	26	.426	13	10	.769	8	19	27	3	23	0	4	3	62	2.6
Totals	69	636	246	116	.472	28	19	.679	38	66	104	29	89	0	13	11	251	3.6

Three-Point Field Goals: 1986-87, 0-for-5. 1987-88, 0-for-2. Totals, 0-for-7.

WAYNE MONTE ROLLINS
(Tree)

Born June 16, 1955 at Winter Haven, Fla. Height 7:01. Weight 240.

High School—Cordele, Ga., Crisp County.

College—Clemson University, Clemson, S. C.

Drafted by Atlanta on first round, 1977 (14th pick).

Signed by Cleveland as an unrestricted free agent, August 2, 1988.

Year	G.	Min.	FGA	FGM	Pct.	FTA	FTM	Pct.	Reb.	Pts.	Avg.
73-74	26	....	265	144	.543	54	34	.630	316	322	12.4
74-75	28	....	326	162	.497	67	40	.597	328	364	13.0
75-76	28	....	313	170	.543	76	43	.566	308	383	13.7
76-77	28	....	288	167	.580	95	60	.632	359	394	14.1
Totals	110	....	1192	643	.539	292	177	.606	1311	1463	13.3

NBA REGULAR SEASON RECORD

Sea —Team	G.	Min.	FGA	FGM	Pct.	FTA	FTM	Pct.	Off.	Def.	Tot.	Ast.	PF	Dq.	Stl.	Blk.	Pts.	Avg.
77-78—Atlanta	80	1795	520	253	.487	148	104	.703	179	373	552	79	326	16	57	218	610	7.6
78-79—Atlanta	81	1900	555	297	.535	141	89	.631	219	369	588	49	328	19	46	254	683	8.4
79-80—Atlanta	82	2123	514	287	.558	220	157	.714	283	491	774	76	322	12	54	244	731	8.9
80-81—Atlanta	40	1044	210	116	.552	57	46	.807	102	184	286	35	151	7	29	117	278	7.0
81-82—Atlanta	79	2018	346	202	.584	129	79	.612	168	443	611	59	285	4	35	224	483	6.1
82-83—Atlanta	80	2472	512	261	.510	135	98	.726	210	533	743	75	294	7	49	343	620	7.8
83-84—Atlanta	77	2351	529	274	.518	190	118	.621	200	393	593	62	297	9	35	277	666	8.6
84-85—Atlanta	70	1750	339	186	.549	93	67	.720	113	329	442	52	213	6	35	167	439	6.3
85-86—Atlanta	74	1781	347	173	.499	90	69	.767	131	327	458	41	239	5	38	167	415	5.6
86-87—Atlanta	78	1764	313	171	.546	87	63	.724	155	333	488	22	240	1	43	140	405	5.4
87-88—Atlanta	76	1765	260	133	.512	80	70	.875	142	317	459	20	229	2	31	132	336	4.4
Totals	817	20763	4445	2353	.529	1370	960	.701	1902	4092	5994	570	2924	88	452	2283	5666	6.9

Three-Point Field Goals: 1980-81, 0-for-1. 1982-83, 0-for-1. 1985-86, 0-for-1. Totals, 0-for-3.

NBA PLAYOFF RECORD

Sea.—Team	G.	Min.	FGA	FGM	Pct.	FTA	FTM	Pct.	Off.	Def.	Tot.	Ast.	PF	Dq.	Stl.	Blk.	Pts.	Avg.
77-78—Atlanta	2	51	12	7	.583	8	2	.250	3	6	9	1	8	1	1	4	16	8.0
78-79—Atlanta	9	212	51	21	.412	13	9	.692	19	52	71	5	29	1	3	24	51	5.7
79-80—Atlanta	5	134	31	18	.581	10	6	.600	18	20	38	3	25	3	2	14	42	8.4
81-82—Atlanta	2	65	6	2	.333	4	3	.750	5	3	8	2	8	1	0	6	7	3.5
82-83—Atlanta	3	118	27	13	.481	9	3	.333	10	20	30	3	12	1	1	10	29	9.7
83-84—Atlanta	5	152	25	10	.400	8	5	.625	10	24	34	1	23	1	2	10	25	5.0
85-86—Atlanta	9	248	47	26	.553	11	7	.636	18	60	78	3	32	2	2	15	59	6.6
86-87—Atlanta	9	221	28	15	.536	14	10	.714	19	34	53	3	33	0	3	16	40	4.4
87-88—Atlanta	12	333	36	20	.556	15	13	.867	23	48	71	6	46	0	10	19	53	4.4
Totals	56	1534	263	132	.502	92	58	.630	125	267	392	27	216	10	24	118	322	5.8

Named to NBA All-Defensive First Team, 1984. . . . NBA All-Defensive Second Team, 1983. . . . Led NBA in blocked shots, 1983.

SCOTT EDWARD ROTH

Born June 3, 1963 at Cleveland, O.   Height 6:08.   Weight 212.

High School—Brecksville, O.

College—University of Wisconsin, Madison, Wis.

Drafted by San Antonio on fourth round, 1985 (82nd pick).

Draft rights relinquished by San Antonio, June 2, 1987; signed by Utah as a free agent, February 25, 1988.
Played with EFES Pilsen Beer Co. in Istanbul, Turkey, 1985-86 and 1986-87.
Played in Continental Basketball Association with Albany Patroons, 1987-88.

—COLLEGIATE RECORD—

Year	G.	Min.	FGA	FGM	Pct.	FTA	FTM	Pct.	Reb.	Pts.	Avg.
81-82	25	330	102	47	.461	18	10	.556	47	104	4.2
82-83	28	710	156	59	.378	60	43	.717	94	162	5.8
83-84	28	973	304	151	.497	96	76	.792	83	378	13.5
84-85	28	927	365	198	.542	156	117	.750	86	513	18.3
Totals	109	2940	927	455	.491	330	246	.745	310	1157	10.6

Three-Point Field Goals: 1982-83, 1-for-5 (.200).

CBA REGULAR SEASON RECORD

Sea.—Team	G.	Min.	2-Point			3-Point			FTM	FTA	Pct.	Reb.	Ast.	Pts.	Avg.
			FGM	FGA	Pct.	FGM	FGA	Pct.							
87-88—Albany	47	1571	318	601	.529	13	26	.500	243	320	.759	220	107	918	19.5

NBA REGULAR SEASON RECORD

Sea.—Team	G.	Min.	FGA	FGM	Pct.	FTA	FTM	Pct.	Off.	Def.	Tot.	Ast.	PF	Dq.	Stl.	Blk.	Pts.	Avg.
87-88—Utah	26	201	74	30	.405	30	22	.733	7	21	28	16	37	0	12	0	84	3.2

Three-Point Field Goals: 1987-88, 2-for-11 (.182).

NBA PLAYOFF RECORD

Sea.—Team	G.	Min.	FGA	FGM	Pct.	FTA	FTM	Pct.	Off.	Def.	Tot.	Ast.	PF	Dq.	Stl.	Blk.	Pts.	Avg.
87-88—Utah	6	10	3	1	.333	0	0	.000	0	0	0	0	0	0	2	0	2	0.3

BRIAN MAURICE ROWSOM

Born October 23, 1965 at Newark, N.J.   Height 6:09.   Weight 220.
High School—Columbia, N.C.
College—University of North Carolina at Wilmington, Wilmington, N.C.
Drafted by Indiana on second round, 1987 (34th pick).

—COLLEGIATE RECORD—

Year	G.	Min.	FGA	FGM	Pct.	FTA	FTM	Pct.	Reb.	Pts.	Avg.
83-84	28	....	150	85	.567	69	47	.681	135	217	7.8
84-85	28	939	381	212	.556	126	90	.714	260	514	18.4
85-86	29	1056	418	224	.536	181	142	.785	275	590	20.3
86-87	30	1077	492	254	.516	194	144	.742	345	653	21.8
Totals	115		1441	775	.538	570	423	.742	1015	1974	17.2

Three-Point Field Goals: 1986-87, 1-for-4 (.250).

NBA REGULAR SEASON RECORD

Sea.—Team	G.	Min.	FGA	FGM	Pct.	FTA	FTM	Pct.	Off.	Def.	Tot.	Ast.	PF	Dq.	Stl.	Blk.	Pts.	Avg.
									—	Rebounds	—							
87-88—Indiana	4	16	6	0	.000	6	6	1.000	1	4	5	1	3	0	1	0	6	1.5

WALKER D. RUSSELL

Born October 26, 1960 at Pontiac, Mich.   Height 6:05.   Weight 195.
High School—Pontiac, Mich., Central.
Colleges—Oakland Community College, Union Lake, Mich.; University of Houston, Houston, Tex., and Western Michigan University, Kalamazoo, Mich.
Drafted by Detroit on fourth round, 1982 (78th pick).

Waived by Detroit, December 20, 1983; signed by Atlanta as a free agent, July 11, 1984.
Waived by Atlanta, December 18, 1984; signed by Detroit as a free agent, November 4, 1985.
Waived by Detroit, November 18, 1985; signed by Indiana as a free agent, October 2, 1986.
Signed by Detroit as a Veteran Free Agent, April 24, 1988; Indiana agreed not to exercise its right of first refusal.
Played in Continental Basketball Association with Detroit Spirits, 1983-84, Detroit Spirits and Kansas City Sizzlers, 1985-86, and Savannah Spirits, 1987-88.

—COLLEGIATE RECORD—
Oakland CC

Year	G.	Min.	FGA	FGM	Pct.	FTA	FTM	Pct.	Reb.	Pts.	Avg.
78-79	..	....	...	...	....	...	...	....	....	....	20.4

Houston

Year	G.	Min.	FGA	FGM	Pct.	FTA	FTM	Pct.	Reb.	Pts.	Avg.
79-80	8	186	73	34	.466	20	10	.500	19	78	9.8

Western Michigan

Year	G.	Min.	FGA	FGM	Pct.	FTA	FTM	Pct.	Reb.	Pts.	Avg.
80-81	17	....	243	110	.453	69	52	.754	82	272	16.0
81-82	29	....	471	230	.488	139	116	.835	102	576	19.9
WMU Totals	46	....	714	340	.476	208	168	.808	184	848	18.4
College Totals	54	...	787	374	.475	228	178	.781	203	926	17.1

CBA REGULAR SEASON RECORD

Sea.—Team	G.	Min.	FGM	FGA	Pct.	FGM	FGA	Pct.	FTM	FTA	Pct.	Reb.	Ast.	Pts.	Avg.
			—2-Point—			—3-Point—									
83-84—Detroit	30	951	182	349	.521	2	17	.117	83	96	.864	116	270	453	15
85-86—Kansas City-Detroit	26	723	140	274	.510	0	4	.000	56	67	.835	87	130	336	12.9
87-88—Savannah	49	1742	280	566	.495	13	58	.224	216	261	.828	208	336	815	16.6
Totals	105	3416	602	1189	.506	15	79	.190	355	424	.837	411	736	1604	15.3

NBA REGULAR SEASON RECORD

Sea.—Team	G.	Min.	FGA	FGM	Pct.	FTA	FTM	Pct.	Off.	Def.	Tot.	Ast.	PF	Dq.	Stl.	Blk.	Pts.	Avg.
									—	Rebounds	—							
82-83—Detroit	68	757	184	67	.364	58	47	.810	19	54	73	131	71	0	16	1	183	2.7
83-84—Detroit	16	119	42	14	.333	13	12	.923	6	13	19	22	25	0	4	0	41	2.6
84-85—Atlanta	21	377	63	34	.540	17	14	.824	8	32	40	66	37	1	17	4	83	4.0
85-86—Detroit	1	2	1	0	.000	0	0	.000	0	0	0	1	0	0	0	0	0	0.0
86-87—Indiana	48	511	165	64	.388	37	27	.730	18	37	55	129	62	0	20	5	157	3.3
87-88—Detroit	1	1	1	0	.000	0	0	.000	0	0	0	1	0	0	0	0	0	0.0
Totals	155	1767	456	179	.393	125	100	.800	51	136	187	350	195	1	57	10	464	3.0

Three-Point Field Goals: 1982-83, 2-for-18 (.111). 1983-84, 1-for-2 (.500). 1984-85, 1-for-1. (1.000). 1986-87, 2-for-16 (.125). 1987-88, 0-for-1. Totals, 6-for-38 (.158).

Sea.—Team	G.	Min.	FGA	FGM	Pct.	FTA	FTM	Pct.	—Rebounds— Off.	Def.	Tot.	Ast.	PF	Dq.	Stl.	Blk.	Pts.	Avg.
87-88—Detroit	7	10	5	2	.400	2	2	1.000	0	0	0	1	1	0	1	0	6	0.9

Led CBA in assists, 1984. . . . Brother of former NBA forward Campy Russell and guard Frank Russell.

JOHN THOMAS SALLEY

Born May 16, 1964 at Brooklyn, N.Y. Height 7:00. Weight 230.

High School—Brooklyn, N.Y., Canarsie.

College—Georgia Institute of Technology, Atlanta, Ga.

Drafted by Detroit on first round, 1986 (11th pick).

—COLLEGIATE RECORD—

Year	G.	Min.	FGA	FGM	Pct.	FTA	FTM	Pct.	Reb.	Pts.	Avg.
82-83	27	829	207	104	.502	160	102	.638	153	310	11.5
83-84	29	992	214	126	.589	132	89	.674	167	341	11.8
84-85	35	1231	308	193	.627	165	105	.636	250	491	14.0
85-86	34	1145	284	172	.606	170	101	.594	228	445	13.1
Totals	125	4197	1013	595	.587	627	397	.633	798	1587	12.7

NBA REGULAR SEASON RECORD

Sea.—Team	G.	Min.	FGA	FGM	Pct.	FTA	FTM	Pct.	—Rebounds— Off.	Def.	Tot.	Ast.	PF	Dq.	Stl.	Blk.	Pts.	Avg.
86-87—Detroit	82	1463	290	163	.562	171	105	.614	108	188	296	54	256	5	44	125	431	5.3
87-88—Detroit	82	2003	456	258	.566	261	185	.709	166	236	402	113	294	4	53	137	701	8.5
Totals	164	3466	746	421	.564	432	290	.671	274	424	698	167	550	9	97	262	1132	6.9

Three-Point Field Goals: 1986-87, 0-for-1.

NBA PLAYOFF RECORD

Sea.—Team	G.	Min.	FGA	FGM	Pct.	FTA	FTM	Pct.	—Rebounds— Off.	Def.	Tot.	Ast.	PF	Dq.	Stl.	Blk.	Pts.	Avg.
86-87—Detroit	15	311	66	33	.500	42	27	.643	30	42	72	11	60	1	3	17	93	6.2
87-88—Detroit	23	623	104	56	.538	69	49	.710	64	91	155	21	88	2	15	37	161	7.0
Totals	38	934	170	89	.524	111	76	.685	94	133	227	32	148	3	18	54	254	6.7

Three-Point Field Goals: 1987-88, 0-for-1.

RALPH LEE SAMPSON

Born July 7, 1960 at Harrisonburg, Va. Height 7:04. Weight 230.

High School—Harrisonburg, Va.

College—University of Virginia, Charlottesville, Va.

Drafted by Houston on first round, 1983 (1st pick).

Traded by Houston with Steve Harris to Golden State for Joe Barry Carroll and Eric Floyd, December 12, 1987.

—COLLEGIATE RECORD—

Year	G.	Min.	FGA	FGM	Pct.	FTA	FTM	Pct.	Reb.	Pts.	Avg.
79-80	34	1017	404	221	.547	94	66	.702	381	508	14.9
80-81	33	1056	413	230	.557	198	125	.631	378	585	17.7
81-82	32	1002	353	198	.561	179	110	.615	366	506	15.8
82-83	33	995	414	250	.604	179	126	.704	386	629	19.1
Totals	132	4070	1584	899	.568	650	427	.457	1511	2228	16.9

NBA REGULAR SEASON RECORD

Sea.—Team	G.	Min.	FGA	FGM	Pct.	FTA	FTM	Pct.	—Rebounds— Off.	Def.	Tot.	Ast.	PF	Dq.	Stl.	Blk.	Pts.	Avg.
83-84—Houston	82	2693	1369	716	.523	434	287	.661	293	620	913	163	339	16	70	197	1720	21.0
84-85—Houston	82	3086	1499	753	.502	448	303	.676	227	626	853	224	306	10	81	168	1809	22.1
85-86—Houston	79	2864	1280	624	.488	376	241	.641	258	621	879	283	308	12	99	129	1491	18.9
86-87—Houston	43	1326	566	277	.489	189	118	.624	88	284	372	120	169	6	40	58	672	15.6
87-88—Hou.-G.S.	48	1663	682	299	.438	196	149	.760	140	322	462	122	164	3	41	88	749	15.6
Totals	334	11632	5396	2669	.495	1643	1098	.668	1006	2473	3479	912	1286	47	331	640	6441	19.3

Three-Point Field Goals: 1983-84, 1-for-4 (.250). 1984-85, 0-for-6. 1985-86, 2-for-15 (.133). 1986-87, 0-for-3. 1987-88, 2-for-11 (.182). Totals, 5-for-39 (.128).

NBA PLAYOFF RECORD

Sea.—Team	G.	Min.	FGA	FGM	Pct.	FTA	FTM	Pct.	—Rebounds— Off.	Def.	Tot.	Ast.	PF	Dq.	Stl.	Blk.	Pts.	Avg.
84-85—Houston	5	193	100	43	.430	37	19	.514	25	58	83	7	23	2	2	8	106	21.2
85-86—Houston	20	741	301	156	.518	118	86	.729	66	149	215	80	79	1	30	35	399	20.0
86-87—Houston	10	330	146	75	.514	43	35	.814	27	61	88	21	47	1	2	12	186	18.6
Totals	35	1264	547	274	.501	198	140	.707	118	268	386	108	149	4	34	55	691	19.7

Three-Point Field Goals: 1984-85, 1-for-1 (1.000). 1985-86, 1-for-1 (1.000). 1986-87, 1-for-2 (.500). Totals, 3-for-4 (.750).

NBA ALL-STAR GAME RECORD

Season—Team	Min.	FGA	FGM	Pct.	FTA	FTM	Pct.	Rebounds— Off.	Def.	Tot.	Ast.	PF	Dq.	Stl.	Blk.	Pts.
1984—Houston	16	7	4	.571	2	1	.500	1	4	5	0	4	0	0	0	9
1985—Houston	29	15	10	.667	6	4	.667	3	7	10	1	5	0	0	1	24
1986—Houston	21	11	7	.636	2	2	1.000	1	3	4	1	4	0	0	0	16
Totals	66	33	21	.636	10	7	.700	5	14	19	2	13	0	0	1	49

Named to All-NBA Second Team, 1985. . . . NBA All-Star Game MVP, 1985. . . . NBA Rookie of the Year, 1984. . . . NBA All-Rookie Team, 1984. . . . THE SPORTING NEWS College Player of the Year, 1982. . . . THE SPORTING NEWS All-America First Team, 1981, 1982, 1983.

MICHAEL ANTHONY SANDERS
(Mike)

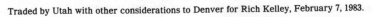

Born May 7, 1960 at Vidalia, La.   Height 6:06.   Weight 210.

High School—DeRidder, La.

College—University of California at Los Angeles, Los Angeles, Calif.

Drafted by Kansas City on fourth round, 1982 (74th pick).

Waived by Kansas City, October 4, 1982; signed by San Antonio as a free agent, February 9, 1983.
Waived by San Antonio, October 17, 1983; signed by Phoenix as a free agent, December 19, 1983.
Traded by Phoenix with Larry Nance and a 1988 1st round draft choice to Cleveland for Tyrone Corbin, Kevin Johnson, Mark West, 1988 1st and 2nd round draft choices and a 1989 2nd round draft choice, February 25, 1988.
Played in Continental Basketball Association with Montana Golden Nuggets, 1982-83, and Sarasota Stingers, 1983-84.

—COLLEGIATE RECORD—

Year	G.	Min.	FGA	FGM	Pct.	FTA	FTM	Pct.	Reb.	Pts.	Avg.
78-79	23	138	38	16	.421	16	11	.688	35	43	1.9
79-80	32	805	248	142	.573	96	76	.792	190	360	11.3
80-81	27	814	287	161	.561	124	95	.766	179	417	15.4
81-82	27	943	299	150	.502	116	90	.776	173	390	14.4
Totals	109	2700	872	469	.538	352	272	.773	577	1210	11.1

CBA REGULAR SEASON RECORD

Sea.—Team	G.	Min.	2-Point FGM	FGA	Pct.	3-Point FGM	FGA	Pct.	FTM	FTA	Pct.	Reb.	Ast.	Pts.	Avg.
82-83—Montana	30	1036	273	473	.577	0	0	....	123	149	.825	247	42	669	22.3
83-84—Sarasota	7	295	69	126	.547	0	1	.000	56	65	.861	52	8	194	27.7
Totals	37	1331	342	599	.571	0	1	.000	179	214	.836	299	50	863	23.3

NBA REGULAR SEASON RECORD

Sea.—Team	G.	Min.	FGA	FGM	Pct.	FTA	FTM	Pct.	Rebounds— Off.	Def.	Tot.	Ast.	PF	Dq.	Stl.	Blk.	Pts.	Avg.
82-83—San Antonio	26	393	157	76	.484	43	31	.721	31	63	94	19	57	0	18	6	183	7.0
83-84—Phoenix	50	586	203	97	.478	42	29	.690	40	63	103	44	101	0	23	12	223	4.5
84-85—Phoenix	21	418	175	85	.486	59	45	.763	38	51	89	29	59	0	23	4	215	10.2
85-86—Phoenix	82	1644	676	347	.513	257	208	.809	104	169	273	150	236	3	76	31	905	11.0
86-87—Phoenix	82	1655	722	357	.494	183	143	.781	101	170	271	126	210	1	61	23	859	10.5
87-88—Phoe.-Clev.	59	883	303	153	.505	76	59	.776	38	71	109	56	131	1	31	9	365	6.2
Totals	320	5579	2236	1115	.499	670	515	.769	352	587	939	424	794	5	232	85	2750	8.6

Three-Point Field Goals: 1982-83, 0-for-2. 1985-86, 3-for-15 (.200). 1986-87, 2-for-17 (.118). 1987-88, 0-for-1. Totals, 5-for-35 (.143).

NBA PLAYOFF RECORD

Sea.—Team	G.	Min.	FGA	FGM	Pct.	FTA	FTM	Pct.	Rebounds— Off.	Def.	Tot.	Ast.	PF	Dq.	Stl.	Blk.	Pts.	Avg.
82-83—San Antonio	6	25	13	7	.538	0	0	.000	2	7	9	4	3	0	0	0	14	2.3
83-84—Phoenix	15	152	46	22	.478	17	16	.941	10	10	20	7	31	0	6	4	60	4.0
84-85—Phoenix	3	91	37	22	.595	10	8	.800	8	7	15	10	8	0	5	0	52	17.3
87-88—Cleveland	5	134	52	28	.538	10	8	.800	11	14	25	7	21	0	3	2	64	12.8
Totals	29	402	148	79	.534	37	32	.865	31	38	69	28	63	0	14	6	190	6.6

Three-Point Field Goals: 1987-88, 0-for-1.

Named to CBA All-Star First Team, 1983. . . . CBA All-Defensive Second Team, 1983. . . . CBA Rookie of the Year, 1983.

DANIEL LESLIE SCHAYES
(Dan)

Born May 10, 1959 at Syracuse, N. Y.   Height 6:11.   Weight 245.

High School—DeWitt, N. Y., Jamesville-DeWitt.

College—Syracuse University, Syracuse, N. Y.

Drafted by Utah on first round, 1981 (13th pick).

Traded by Utah with other considerations to Denver for Rich Kelley, February 7, 1983.

—COLLEGIATE RECORD—

Year	G.	Min.	FGA	FGM	Pct.	FTA	FTM	Pct.	Reb.	Pts.	Avg.
77-78	24	....	69	39	.565	45	34	.756	96	112	4.7
78-79	29	....	117	62	.530	66	55	.833	121	179	6.2
79-80	30	....	116	59	.509	78	60	.769	134	178	5.9
80-81	34	....	285	165	.579	202	166	.822	284	496	14.6
Totals	117	....	587	325	.554	391	315	.806	635	965	8.2

NBA REGULAR SEASON RECORD

Sea.—Team	G.	Min.	FGA	FGM	Pct.	FTA	FTM	Pct.	Off.	Def.	Tot.	Ast.	PF	Dq.	Stl.	Blk.	Pts.	Avg.
81-82—Utah	82	1623	524	252	.481	185	140	.757	131	296	427	146	292	4	46	72	644	7.9
82-83—Utah-Den.	82	2284	749	342	.457	295	228	.773	200	435	635	205	325	8	54	98	912	11.1
83-84—Denver	82	1420	371	183	.493	272	215	.790	145	288	433	91	308	5	32	60	581	7.1
84-85—Denver	56	542	129	60	.465	97	79	.814	48	96	144	38	98	2	20	25	199	3.6
85-86—Denver	80	1654	440	221	.502	278	216	.777	154	285	439	79	298	7	42	63	658	8.2
86-87—Denver	76	1556	405	210	.519	294	229	.779	120	260	380	85	266	5	20	74	649	8.5
87-88—Denver	81	2166	668	361	.540	487	407	.836	200	462	662	106	323	9	62	92	1129	13.9
Totals	539	11245	3286	1629	.496	1908	1514	.794	998	2122	3120	750	1910	40	276	484	4772	8.9

Three-Point Field Goals: 1981-82, 0-for-1. 1982-83, 0-for-1. 1983-84, 0-for-2. 1985-86, 0-for-1. 1987-88, 0-for-2. Totals, 0-for-7.

NBA PLAYOFF RECORD

Sea.—Team	G.	Min.	FGA	FGM	Pct.	FTA	FTM	Pct.	Off.	Def.	Tot.	Ast.	PF	Dq.	Stl.	Blk.	Pts.	Avg.
82-83—Denver	8	163	43	21	.488	15	15	1.000	11	29	40	14	25	0	2	5	57	7.1
83-84—Denver	5	81	18	11	.611	8	6	.750	3	21	24	4	20	0	4	3	28	5.6
84-85—Denver	9	118	26	11	.423	20	14	.700	8	22	30	12	22	0	3	4	36	4.0
85-86—Denver	10	295	86	46	.535	30	24	.800	34	48	82	9	37	1	4	17	116	11.6
86-87—Denver	3	75	17	12	.706	9	6	.667	6	11	17	2	10	0	1	2	30	10.0
87-88—Denver	11	314	88	55	.625	83	70	.843	30	49	79	18	46	1	3	10	180	16.4
Totals	46	1046	278	156	.561	165	135	.818	92	180	272	59	160	2	17	41	447	9.7

Son of Dolph Schayes, former NBA forward, former NBA Supervisor of Referees and a member of the Naismith Memorial Basketball Hall of Fame.

RUSS SCHOENE

Born April 16, 1960 at Trenton, Ill. Height 6:10. Weight 210.

High School—Trenton, Ill., Wesclin.

Colleges—Mineral Area College, Flat River, Mo., and University of Tennessee-Chattanooga, Chattanooga, Tenn.

Drafted by Philadelphia on second round, 1982 (45th pick).

Traded by Philadelphia with a 1983 1st round draft choice and 1984 2nd round draft choice to Indiana for Clemon Johnson and a 1984 3rd round draft choice, February 15, 1983.

Traded by Indiana with Terence Stansbury to Seattle for John Long and a future 2nd round draft choice, October 2, 1986.

—COLLEGIATE RECORD—

Mineral Area

Year	G.	Min.	FGA	FGM	Pct.	FTA	FTM	Pct.	Reb.	Pts.	Avg.
78-79	31	....	206	96	.466	54	34	.630	141	226	7.3
79-80	32	....	428	220	.514	124	86	.694	268	526	16.4
J.C. Totals	63	....	634	316	.498	178	120	.674	409	752	11.9

Tennessee-Chattanooga

Year	G.	Min.	FGA	FGM	Pct.	FTA	FTM	Pct.	Reb.	Pts.	Avg.
80-81	28	....	154	80	.519	57	42	.737	113	202	7.2
81-82	31	....	350	193	.551	55	36	.655	217	422	13.6
UTC Totals	59	....	504	273	.542	112	78	.696	330	624	10.6

NBA REGULAR SEASON RECORD

Sea.—Team	G.	Min.	FGA	FGM	Pct.	FTA	FTM	Pct.	Off.	Def.	Tot.	Ast.	PF	Dq.	Stl.	Blk.	Pts.	Avg.
82-83—Phil.-Ind.	77	1222	435	207	.476	83	61	.735	96	159	255	59	192	3	25	23	476	6.2
86-87—Seattle	63	579	190	71	.374	46	29	.630	52	65	117	27	94	1	20	11	173	2.7
87-88—Seattle	81	973	454	208	.458	63	51	.810	78	120	198	53	151	0	39	13	484	6.0
Totals	221	2774	1079	486	.450	192	141	.734	226	344	570	139	437	4	84	47	1133	5.1

Three-Point Field Goals: 1982-83, 1-for-4 (.250). 1986-87, 2-for-13 (.154). 1987-88, 17-for-58 (.293). Totals, 20-for-75 (.267).

NBA PLAYOFF RECORD

Sea.—Team	G.	Min.	FGA	FGM	Pct.	FTA	FTM	Pct.	Off.	Def.	Tot.	Ast.	PF	Dq.	Stl.	Blk.	Pts.	Avg.
86-87—Seattle	14	123	28	10	.357	12	9	.750	6	20	26	3	16	1	1	4	31	2.2
87-88—Seattle	5	39	12	7	.583	0	0	.000	1	6	7	2	8	0	1	0	16	3.2
Totals	19	162	40	17	.425	12	9	.750	7	26	33	5	24	1	2	4	47	2.5

Three-Point Field Goals: 1986-87, 2-for-6 (.333). 1987-88, 2-for-4 (.500). Totals, 4-for-10 (.400).

DETLEF SCHREMPF

Born January 21, 1963 at Leverkusen, West Germany. Height 6:10. Weight 214.

High School—Centralia, Wash.

College—University of Washington, Seattle, Wash.

Drafted by Dallas on first round, 1985 (8th pick).

—COLLEGIATE RECORD—

Year	G.	Min.	FGA	FGM	Pct.	FTA	FTM	Pct.	Reb.	Pts.	Avg.
81-82	28	314	73	33	.452	47	26	.553	56	92	3.3
82-83	31	958	266	124	.466	113	81	.717	211	329	10.6
83-84	31	1186	362	195	.539	178	131	.736	230	521	16.8
84-85	32	1180	342	191	.558	175	125	.714	255	507	15.8
Totals	122	3638	1043	543	.521	513	363	.708	752	1449	11.9

NBA REGULAR SEASON RECORD

Sea.—Team	G.	Min.	FGA	FGM	Pct.	FTA	FTM	Pct.	Off.	Def.	Tot.	Ast.	PF	Dq.	Stl.	Blk.	Pts.	Avg.
85-86—Dallas	64	969	315	142	.451	152	110	.724	70	128	198	88	166	1	23	10	397	6.2
86-87—Dallas	81	1711	561	265	.472	260	193	.742	87	216	303	161	224	2	50	16	756	9.3
87-88—Dallas	82	1587	539	246	.456	266	201	.756	102	177	279	159	189	0	42	32	698	8.5
Totals	227	4267	1415	653	.461	678	504	.743	259	521	780	408	579	3	115	58	1851	8.2

Three-Point Field Goals: 1985-86, 3-for-7 (.429). 1986-87, 33-for-69 (.478). 1987-88, 5-for-32 (.156). Totals, 41-for-108 (.380).

NBA PLAYOFF RECORD

Sea.—Team	G.	Min.	FGA	FGM	Pct.	FTA	FTM	Pct.	Off.	Def.	Tot.	Ast.	PF	Dq.	Stl.	Blk.	Pts.	Avg.
85-86—Dallas	10	120	28	13	.464	17	11	.647	7	16	23	14	24	0	2	1	37	3.7
86-87—Dallas	4	97	35	13	.371	11	5	.455	4	8	12	6	13	0	3	2	31	7.8
87-88—Dallas	15	274	86	40	.465	51	36	.706	25	30	55	24	29	0	8	7	117	7.8
Totals	29	491	149	66	.443	79	52	.658	36	54	90	44	66	0	13	10	185	6.4

Three-Point Field Goals: 1985-86, 0-for-1. 1986-87, 0-for-3. 1987-88, 1-for-3 (.333). Totals, 1-for-7 (.143).

Member of West German Olympic team, 1984. . . . Named to THE SPORTING NEWS All-America Second Team, 1985.

BYRON ANTOM SCOTT

Born March 28, 1961 at Ogden, Utah. Height 6:04. Weight 195.

High School—Inglewood, Calif., Morningside.

College—Arizona State University, Tempe, Ariz.

Drafted by San Diego on first round as an undergraduate, 1983 (4th pick).

Draft rights traded by San Diego with Swen Nater to Los Angeles for Norm Nixon and Eddie Jordan and 1986 and 1987 2nd round draft choices, October 10, 1983.

—COLLEGIATE RECORD—

Year	G.	Min.	FGA	FGM	Pct.	FTA	FTM	Pct.	Reb.	Pts.	Avg.
79-80	29	936	332	166	.500	86	63	.733	79	395	13.6
80-81	28	1003	390	197	.505	101	70	.693	106	464	16.6
81-82				Did Not Play—Academic and Personal Reasons							
82-83	33	1206	552	283	.513	188	147	.782	177	713	21.6
Totals	90	3145	1274	646	.507	375	280	.747	362	1572	17.5

NBA REGULAR SEASON RECORD

Sea.—Team	G.	Min.	FGA	FGM	Pct.	FTA	FTM	Pct.	Off.	Def.	Tot.	Ast.	PF	Dq.	Stl.	Blk.	Pts.	Avg.
83-84—Los Angeles	74	1637	690	334	.484	139	112	.806	50	114	164	177	174	0	81	19	788	10.6
84-85—L.A. Lakers	81	2305	1003	541	.539	228	187	.820	57	153	210	244	197	1	100	17	1295	16.0
85-86—L.A. Lakers	76	2190	989	507	.513	176	138	.784	55	134	189	164	167	0	85	15	1174	15.4
86-87—L.A. Lakers	82	2729	1134	554	.489	251	224	.892	63	223	286	281	163	0	125	18	1397	17.0
87-88—L.A. Lakers	81	3048	1348	710	.527	317	272	.858	76	257	333	335	204	2	155	27	1754	21.7
Totals	394	11909	5164	2646	.512	1111	933	.840	301	881	1182	1201	905	3	546	96	6408	16.3

Three-Point Field Goals: 1983-84, 8-for-34 (.235). 1984-85, 26-for-60 (.433). 1985-86, 22-for-61 (.361). 1986-87, 65-for-149 (.436). 1987-88, 62-for-179 (.346). Totals, 183-for-483 (.379).

NBA PLAYOFF RECORD

Sea.—Team	G.	Min.	FGA	FGM	Pct.	FTA	FTM	Pct.	Off.	Def.	Tot.	Ast.	PF	Dq.	Stl.	Blk.	Pts.	Avg.
83-84—Los Angeles	20	404	161	74	.460	35	21	.600	11	26	37	34	39	1	18	2	171	8.6
84-85—L.A. Lakers	19	585	267	138	.517	44	35	.795	16	36	52	50	47	0	41	4	321	16.9
85-86—L.A. Lakers	14	470	181	90	.497	42	38	.905	15	40	55	42	38	0	19	2	224	16.0
86-87—L.A. Lakers	18	608	210	103	.490	67	53	.791	20	42	62	57	52	0	19	4	266	14.8
87-88—L.A. Lakers	24	897	357	178	.499	104	90	.865	26	74	100	60	65	0	34	5	470	19.6
Totals	95	2964	1176	583	.496	292	237	.812	88	218	306	243	241	1	131	17	1452	15.3

Three-Point Field Goals: 1983-84, 2-for-10 (.200). 1984-85, 10-for-21 (.476). 1985-86, 6-for-17 (.353). 1986-87, 7-for-34 (.206). 1987-88, 24-for-55 (.436). Totals, 49-for-137 (.358).

Named to NBA All-Rookie Team, 1984.... Member of NBA championship teams, 1985, 1987, 1988.... Led NBA in three-point field goal percentage, 1985.

CAREY SCURRY

Born December 4, 1962 at Brooklyn, N.Y.   Height 6:07.   Weight 190.

High School—Brooklyn, N.Y., Alexander Hamilton.

Colleges—Northeastern Oklahoma A&M College, Miami, Okla.,
and Long Island University, Brooklyn, N.Y.

Drafted by Utah on second round, 1985 (37th pick).

Waived by Utah, January 20, 1988; signed by New York, March 2, 1988, to the first of consecutive 10-day contracts that expired, March 21, 1988.

—COLLEGIATE RECORD—
Northeastern Oklahoma A&M

Year	G.	Min.	FGA	FGM	Pct.	FTA	FTM	Pct.	Reb.	Pts.	Avg.
81-82	12	....	127	69	.543	23	13	.565	79	151	12.6

Long Island

Year	G.	Min.	FGA	FGM	Pct.	FTA	FTM	Pct.	Reb.	Pts.	Avg.
82-83	20	....	191	99	.518	69	47	.681	201	245	12.3
83-84	31	....	417	226	.542	175	126	.720	418	578	18.6
84-85	28	....	413	224	.542	200	142	.710	394	590	21.1
LIU Totals	79	....	1021	549	.538	444	315	.709	1013	1413	17.9

NBA REGULAR SEASON RECORD

Sea.—Team	G.	Min.	FGA	FGM	Pct.	FTA	FTM	Pct.	Off.	Def.	Tot.	Ast.	PF	Dq.	Stl.	Blk.	Pts.	Avg.
85-86—Utah	78	1168	301	142	.472	126	78	.619	97	145	242	85	171	2	78	66	363	4.7
86-87—Utah	69	753	247	123	.498	134	94	.701	97	101	198	57	124	1	55	54	344	5.0
87-88—Utah-N.Y.	33	455	118	55	.466	39	27	.692	30	54	84	50	81	0	49	23	140	4.2
Totals	180	2376	666	320	.480	299	199	.666	224	300	524	192	376	3	182	143	847	4.7

Three-Point Field Goals: 1985-86, 1-for-11 (.091). 1986-87, 4-for-14 (.286). 1987-88, 3-for-8 (.375). Totals, 8-for-33 (.242).

NBA PLAYOFF RECORD

Sea.—Team	G.	Min.	FGA	FGM	Pct.	FTA	FTM	Pct.	Off.	Def.	Tot.	Ast.	PF	Dq.	Stl.	Blk.	Pts.	Avg.
85-86—Utah	4	54	20	8	.400	2	1	.500	10	6	16	3	12	0	1	4	17	4.3
86-87—Utah	4	57	22	10	.455	7	3	.429	7	7	14	0	10	0	4	5	24	6.0
Totals	8	111	42	18	.429	9	4	.444	17	13	30	3	22	0	5	9	41	5.1

Three-Point Field Goals: 1985-86, 0-for-2. 1986-87, 1-for-2 (.500). Totals, 1-for-4 (.250).

BRADLEY DONN SELLERS
(Brad)

Born December 17, 1962 at Warrensville Heights, O.   Height 7:00.   Weight 210.

High School—Warrensville Heights, O.

Colleges—University of Wisconsin, Madison, Wisc., and
Ohio State University, Columbus, O.

Drafted by Chicago on first round, 1986 (9th pick).

—COLLEGIATE RECORD—
Wisconsin

Year	G.	Min.	FGA	FGM	Pct.	FTA	FTM	Pct.	Reb.	Pts.	Avg.
81-82	27	964	351	167	.476	67	44	.657	254	378	14.0
82-83	28	1009	372	189	.508	99	82	.828	219	460	16.4
Wisc. Totals	55	1973	723	356	.492	166	126	.759	473	838	15.2

Ohio State

Year	G.	Min.	FGA	FGM	Pct.	FTA	FTM	Pct.	Reb.	Pts.	Avg.
83-84					Did Not Play—Transfer Student						
84-85	30	979	354	186	.525	125	97	.776	264	469	15.6
85-86	33	1234	492	234	.476	226	185	.819	416	653	19.8
Ohio St. Totals	63	2213	846	420	.496	351	282	.803	680	1122	17.8
Totals	118	4186	1569	776	.495	517	408	.789	1153	1960	16.6

Three-Point Field Goals: 1982-83, 0-for-1.

NBA REGULAR SEASON RECORD

Sea.—Team	G.	Min.	FGA	FGM	Pct.	FTA	FTM	Pct.	—Rebounds— Off.	Def.	Tot.	Ast.	PF	Dq.	Stl.	Blk.	Pts.	Avg.
86-87—Chicago	80	1751	606	276	.455	173	126	.728	155	218	373	102	194	1	44	68	680	8.5
87-88—Chicago	82	2212	714	326	.457	157	124	.790	107	143	250	141	174	0	34	66	777	9.5
Totals	162	3963	1320	602	.456	330	250	.758	262	361	623	243	368	1	78	134	1457	9.0

Three-Point Field Goals: 1986-87, 2-for-10 (.200). 1987-88, 1-for-7 (.143). Totals, 3-for-17 (.176).

NBA PLAYOFF RECORD

Sea.—Team	G.	Min.	FGA	FGM	Pct.	FTA	FTM	Pct.	—Rebounds— Off.	Def.	Tot.	Ast.	PF	Dq.	Stl.	Blk.	Pts.	Avg.
86-87—Chicago	3	68	19	6	.316	3	3	1.000	2	5	7	3	8	0	0	1	15	5.0
87-88—Chicago	10	144	43	15	.349	17	15	.882	10	11	21	8	18	0	2	5	45	4.5
Totals	13	212	62	21	.339	20	18	.900	12	16	28	11	26	0	2	6	60	4.6

PURVIS SHORT

Born July 2, 1957 at Hattiesburg, Miss. Height 6:07. Weight 220.

High School—Hattiesburg, Miss., Blair.

College—Jackson State University, Jackson, Miss.

Drafted by Golden State on first round, 1978 (5th pick).

Traded by Golden State to Houston for Dave Feitl and a future 1st round draft choice, November 5, 1987.

—COLLEGIATE RECORD—

Year	G.	Min.	FGA	FGM	Pct.	FTA	FTM	Pct.	Reb.	Pts.	Avg.
74-75	28	....	325	190	.585	66	44	.667	218	424	15.1
75-76	28	....	635	324	.510	91	66	.725	283	714	25.5
76-77	26	....	541	288	.532	92	70	.761	218	646	24.8
77-78	22	....	535	285	.532	111	80	.721	250	650	29.5
Totals	104	....	2036	1087	.534	360	260	.722	969	2434	23.4

NBA REGULAR SEASON RECORD

Sea.—Team	G.	Min.	FGA	FGM	Pct.	FTA	FTM	Pct.	—Rebounds— Off.	Def.	Tot.	Ast.	PF	Dq.	Stl.	Blk.	Pts.	Avg.
78-79—Golden State	75	1703	771	369	.479	85	57	.671	127	220	347	97	233	6	54	12	795	10.6
79-80—Golden State	62	1636	916	461	.503	165	134	.812	119	197	316	123	186	4	63	9	1056	17.0
80-81—Golden State	79	2309	1157	549	.475	205	168	.820	151	240	391	249	244	3	78	19	1269	16.1
81-82—Golden State	76	1782	935	456	.488	221	177	.801	123	143	266	209	220	3	65	10	1095	14.4
82-83—Golden State	67	2397	1209	589	.487	308	255	.828	145	209	354	228	242	3	94	14	1437	21.4
83-84—Golden State	79	2945	1509	714	.473	445	353	.793	184	254	438	246	252	2	103	11	1803	22.8
84-85—Golden State	78	3081	1780	819	.460	613	501	.817	157	241	398	234	255	4	116	27	2186	28.0
85-86—Golden State	64	2427	1313	633	.482	406	351	.865	126	203	329	237	229	5	92	22	1632	25.5
86-87—Golden State	34	950	501	240	.479	160	137	.856	55	82	137	86	103	1	45	7	621	18.3
87-88—Houston	81	1949	986	474	.481	240	206	.858	71	151	222	162	197	0	58	14	1159	14.3
Totals	695	21179	11077	5304	.479	2848	2339	.821	1258	1940	3198	1871	2161	31	768	145	13053	18.8

Three-Point Field Goals: 1979-80, 0-for-6. 1980-81, 3-for-17 (.176). 1981-82, 6-for-28 (.214). 1982-83, 4-for-15 (.267). 1983-84, 22-for-72 (.306). 1984-85, 47-for-150 (.313). 1985-86, 15-for-49 (.306). 1986-87, 4-for-17 (.253). 1987-88, 5-for-21 (.238). Totals, 106-for-375 (.283).

NBA PLAYOFF RECORD

Sea.—Team	G.	Min.	FGA	FGM	Pct.	FTA	FTM	Pct.	—Rebounds— Off.	Def.	Tot.	Ast.	PF	Dq.	Stl.	Blk.	Pts.	Avg.
86-87—Golden State	10	253	123	57	.463	36	32	.889	12	21	33	27	34	0	12	2	146	14.6
87-88—Houston	4	71	26	7	.269	8	8	1.000	4	5	9	1	8	0	1	0	22	5.5
Totals	14	324	149	64	.430	44	40	.909	16	26	42	28	42	0	13	2	168	12.0

Three-Point Field Goals: 1986-87, 0-for-2. 1987-88, 0-for-1. Totals, 0-for-3.

JERRY LEE SICHTING

Born November 29, 1956 at Martinsville, Ind. Height 6:01. Weight 180.

High School—Martinsville, Ind.

College—Purdue University, West Lafayette, Ind.

Drafted by Golden State on fourth round, 1979 (82nd pick).

Waived by Golden State, October 4, 1979; signed by Indiana as a free agent, October 9, 1980.
Traded by Indiana to Boston for a 1990 2nd round draft choice, October 3, 1985.
Traded by Boston with future considerations to Portland for Jim Paxson, February 23, 1988.

—COLLEGIATE RECORD—

Year	G.	Min.	FGA	FGM	Pct.	FTA	FTM	Pct.	Reb.	Pts.	Avg.
75-76	27	436	123	67	.545	38	31	.816	42	165	6.1

Year	G.	Min.	FGA	FGM	Pct.	FTA	FTM	Pct.	Reb.	Pts.	Avg.
76-77	28	536	131	71	.542	69	61	.884	36	203	7.3
77-78	27	975	233	120	.515	90	78	.867	67	318	11.8
78-79	35	1202	367	186	.507	118	103	.873	97	475	13.6
Totals	117	3149	854	444	.520	315	273	.867	242	1161	9.9

NBA REGULAR SEASON RECORD

Sea.—Team	G.	Min.	FGA	FGM	Pct.	FTA	FTM	Pct.	Off.	Def.	Tot.	Ast.	PF	Dq.	Stl.	Blk.	Pts.	Avg.
									—Rebounds—									
80-81—Indiana	47	450	95	34	.358	32	25	.781	11	32	43	70	38	0	23	1	93	2.0
81-82—Indiana	51	800	194	91	.469	38	29	.763	14	41	55	117	63	0	33	1	212	4.2
82-83—Indiana	78	2435	661	316	.478	107	92	.860	33	122	155	433	185	0	104	2	727	9.3
83-84—Indiana	80	2497	746	397	.532	135	117	.867	44	127	171	457	179	0	90	8	917	11.5
84-85—Indiana	70	1808	624	325	.521	128	112	.875	24	90	114	264	116	0	47	4	771	11.0
85-86—Boston	82	1596	412	235	.570	66	61	.924	27	77	104	188	118	0	50	0	537	6.5
86-87—Boston	78	1566	398	202	.508	42	37	.881	22	69	91	187	124	0	40	1	448	5.7
87-88—Bos.-Port.	52	694	172	93	.541	23	17	.739	9	27	36	93	60	0	21	0	213	4.1
Totals	538	11846	3302	1693	.513	571	490	.858	184	585	769	1809	883	0	408	17	3918	7.3

Three-Point Field Goals: 1980-81, 0-for-5. 1981-82, 1-for-9 (.111). 1982-83, 3-for-18 (.167). 1983-84, 6-for-20 (.300). 1984-85, 9-for-37 (.243). 1985-86, 6-for-16 (.375). 1986-87, 7-for-26 (.269). 1987-88, 10-for-22 (.455). Totals, 42-for-153 (.275).

NBA PLAYOFF RECORD

Sea.—Team	G.	Min.	FGA	FGM	Pct.	FTA	FTM	Pct.	Off.	Def.	Tot.	Ast.	PF	Dq.	Stl.	Blk.	Pts.	Avg.
									—Rebounds—									
80-81—Indiana	1	1	0	0	.000	0	0	.000	0	0	0	0	0	0	1	0	0	0.0
85-86—Boston	18	274	61	27	.443	7	3	.429	5	11	16	40	18	0	5	0	57	3.2
86-87—Boston	23	338	82	35	.427	10	8	.800	5	15	20	33	36	0	9	0	79	3.4
87-88—Portland	4	31	7	2	.286	0	0	.000	1	1	2	5	4	0	1	0	4	1.0
Totals	46	644	150	64	.427	17	11	.647	11	27	38	78	58	0	16	0	140	3.0

Three-Point Field Goals: 1985-86, 0-for-1. 1986-87, 1-for-6 (.167). Totals, 1-for-7 (.143).
Member of NBA championship team, 1986.

JACK WAYNE SIKMA

Born November 14, 1955 at Kankakee, Ill.   Height 7:00.   Weight 260.

High School—St. Anne, Ill.

College—Illinois Wesleyan University, Bloomington, Ill.

Drafted by Seattle on first round, 1977 (8th pick).

Traded by Seattle with 1987 and 1989 2nd round draft choices to Milwaukee for Alton Lister and 1987 and 1989 1st round draft choices, July 1, 1986.

—COLLEGIATE RECORD—

Year	G.	Min.	FGA	FGM	Pct.	FTA	FTM	Pct.	Reb.	Pts.	Avg.
73-74	21	....	306	148	.484	37	28	.757	223	324	15.4
74-75	30	....	537	265	.493	112	80	.714	415	610	20.3
75-76	25	....	385	204	.530	126	93	.738	290	501	20.0
76-77	31	....	302	324	.528	235	189	.804	477	837	27.0
Totals	107	....	1530	941	.514	510	390	.765	1405	2272	21.2

NBA REGULAR SEASON RECORD

Sea.—Team	G.	Min.	FGA	FGM	Pct.	FTA	FTM	Pct.	Off.	Def.	Tot.	Ast.	PF	Dq.	Stl.	Blk.	Pts.	Avg.
									—Rebounds—									
77-78—Seattle	82	2238	752	342	.455	247	192	.777	196	482	678	134	300	6	68	40	876	10.7
78-79—Seattle	82	2958	1034	476	.460	404	329	.814	232	781	1013	261	295	4	82	67	1281	15.6
79-80—Seattle	82	2793	989	470	.475	292	235	.805	198	710	908	279	232	5	68	77	1175	14.3
80-81—Seattle	82	2920	1311	595	.454	413	340	.823	184	668	852	248	282	5	78	93	1530	18.7
81-82—Seattle	82	3049	1212	581	.479	523	447	.855	223	815	1038	277	268	5	102	107	1611	19.6
82-83—Seattle	75	2564	1043	484	.464	478	400	.837	213	645	858	233	263	4	87	65	1368	18.2
83-84—Seattle	82	2993	1155	576	.499	480	411	.856	225	686	911	327	301	6	95	92	1563	19.1
84-85—Seattle	68	2402	943	461	.489	393	335	.852	164	559	723	285	239	1	83	91	1259	18.5
85-86—Seattle	80	2790	1100	508	.462	411	355	.864	146	602	748	301	293	4	92	73	1371	17.1
86-87—Milwaukee	82	2536	842	390	.463	313	265	.847	208	614	822	203	328	14	88	90	1045	12.7
87-88—Milwaukee	82	2923	1058	514	.486	348	321	.922	195	514	709	279	316	11	93	80	1352	16.5
Totals	879	30166	11439	5397	.472	4302	3630	.844	2184	7076	9260	2827	3117	65	936	875	14431	16.4

Three-Point Field Goals: 1979-80, 0-for-1. 1980-81, 0-for-5. 1981-82, 2-for-13 (.154). 1982-83, 0-for-8. 1983-84, 0-for-2. 1984-85, 2-for-10 (.200). 1985-86, 0-for-13. 1986-87, 0-for-2. 1987-88, 3-for-14 (.214). Totals, 7-for-68 (.103).

NBA PLAYOFF RECORD

Sea.—Team	G.	Min.	FGA	FGM	Pct.	FTA	FTM	Pct.	Off.	Def.	Tot.	Ast.	PF	Dq.	Stl.	Blk.	Pts.	Avg.
									—Rebounds—									
77-78—Seattle	22	701	247	115	.466	91	71	.780	50	128	178	27	101	7	18	11	301	13.7
78-79—Seattle	17	655	224	103	.460	61	48	.787	39	160	199	43	70	2	16	24	254	14.9
79-80—Seattle	15	534	163	65	.399	54	46	.852	30	96	126	55	55	1	17	5	176	11.7
81-82—Seattle	8	315	128	57	.445	58	50	.862	21	76	97	24	34	1	9	8	164	20.5
82-83—Seattle	2	75	31	11	.355	12	8	.667	6	20	26	11	7	0	2	2	30	15.0

Sea.—Team	G.	Min.	FGA	FGM	Pct.	FTA	FTM	Pct.	—Rebounds— Off.	Def.	Tot.	Ast.	PF	Dq.	Stl.	Blk.	Pts.	Avg.
83-84—Seattle	5	193	98	49	.500	14	12	.857	11	40	51	5	22	1	3	7	110	22.0
86-87—Milwaukee	12	426	150	73	.487	49	48	.980	33	97	130	23	56	3	15	10	194	16.2
87-88—Milwaukee	5	190	76	35	.461	30	25	.833	24	38	62	13	23	0	2	4	95	19.0
Totals	86	3089	1117	508	.455	369	308	.835	214	655	869	201	368	15	82	71	1324	15.4

Three-Point Field Goals: 1979-80, 0-for-2. 1982-83, 0-for-1. 1983-84, 0-for-1. 1986-87, 0-for-1. 1987-88, 0-for-3. Totals, 0-for-8.

NBA ALL-STAR GAME RECORD

Season—Team	Min.	FGA	FGM	Pct.	FTA	FTM	Pct.	—Rebounds— Off.	Def.	Tot.	Ast.	PF	Dq.	Stl.	Blk.	Pts.
1979—Seattle	18	5	4	.800	0	0	.000	1	3	4	0	1	0	0	0	8
1980—Seattle	28	10	4	.400	0	0	.000	2	6	8	4	5	0	2	3	8
1981—Seattle	21	5	2	.400	2	2	1.000	1	3	4	4	5	0	1	1	6
1982—Seattle	21	11	5	.455	0	0	.000	2	7	9	1	2	0	2	1	10
1983—Seattle	17	6	4	.667	0	0	.000	1	2	3	1	2	0	1	1	5
1984—Seattle	30	12	5	.417	6	5	.833	5	7	12	1	4	0	3	0	15
1985—Seattle	12	2	0	.000	0	0	.000	0	2	2	0	1	0	0	1	0
Totals	147	51	24	.471	8	7	.875	12	30	42	11	20	0	9	7	52

Three-Point Field Goals: 1980, 0-for-1. 1981, 0-for-1. 1983, 0-for-1. Totals, 0-for-3.

Named to NBA All-Defensive Second Team, 1982. . . . NBA All-Rookie Team, 1978. . . . Member of NBA championship team, 1979. . . . Led NBA in free-throw percentage, 1988.

SCOTT ALLEN SKILES

Born March 5, 1964 at LaPorte, Ind. Height 6:01. Weight 200.

High School—Plymouth, Ind.

College—Michigan State University, East Lansing, Mich.

Drafted by Milwaukee on first round, 1986 (22nd pick).

Traded by Milwaukee to Indiana for a future 2nd round draft choice, June 21, 1987.

—COLLEGIATE RECORD—

Year	G.	Min.	FGA	FGM	Pct.	FTA	FTM	Pct.	Reb.	Pts.	Avg.
82-83	30	1023	286	141	.493	83	69	.831	63	376	12.5
83-84	28	983	319	153	.480	119	99	.832	62	405	14.5
84-85	29	1107	420	212	.505	114	90	.790	93	514	17.7
85-86	31	1172	598	331	.554	209	188	.900	135	850	27.4
Totals	118	4285	1623	837	.516	525	446	.850	353	2145	18.2

Three-Point Field Goals: 1982-83, 25-for-50 (.500).

NBA REGULAR SEASON RECORD

Sea.—Team	G.	Min.	FGA	FGM	Pct.	FTA	FTM	Pct.	—Rebounds— Off.	Def.	Tot.	Ast.	PF	Dq.	Stl.	Blk.	Pts.	Avg.
86-87—Milwaukee	13	205	62	18	.290	12	10	.833	6	20	26	45	18	0	5	1	49	3.8
87-88—Indiana	51	760	209	86	.411	54	45	.833	11	55	66	180	97	0	22	3	223	4.4
Totals	64	965	271	104	.384	66	55	.833	17	75	92	225	115	0	27	4	272	4.3

Three-Point Field Goals: 1986-87, 3-for-14 (.214). 1987-88, 6-for-20 (.300). Totals, 9-for-34 (.265).
Named to THE SPORTING NEWS All-America First Team, 1986.

DEREK ERVIN SMITH

Born November 1, 1961 at Hogansville, Ga. Height 6:06. Weight 218.

High School—Hogansville, Ga.

College—University of Louisville, Louisville, Ky.

Drafted by Golden State on second round, 1982 (35th pick).

Waived by Golden State, September 8, 1983; signed by San Diego as a free agent, September 13, 1983.
Traded by Los Angeles Clippers with Junior Bridgeman and Franklin Edwards to Sacramento for Larry Drew, Mike Woodson, a 1988 1st round draft choice and a 1989 2nd round draft choice, August 19, 1986.

—COLLEGIATE RECORD—

Year	G.	Min.	FGA	FGM	Pct.	FTA	FTM	Pct.	Reb.	Pts.	Avg.
78-79	32	622	185	117	.632	123	79	.642	153	313	9.8
79-80	36	1222	372	213	.573	150	105	.700	299	531	14.8
80-81	30	964	348	188	.540	135	89	.659	233	465	15.5
81-82	33	950	346	204	.590	162	109	.673	199	517	15.7
Totals	131	3758	1251	722	.577	570	382	.670	884	1826	13.9

Sea.—Team	G.	Min.	FGA	FGM	Pct.	FTA	FTM	Pct.	Off.	Def.	Tot.	Ast.	PF	Dq.	Stl.	Blk.	Pts.	Avg.
									—Rebounds—									
82-83—Golden State	27	154	51	21	.412	25	17	.680	10	28	38	2	40	0	0	4	59	2.2
83-84—San Diego	61	1297	436	238	.546	163	123	.755	54	116	170	82	165	2	33	22	600	9.8
84-85—L.A. Clippers	80	2762	1271	682	.537	504	400	.794	174	253	427	216	317	8	77	52	1767	22.1
85-86—L.A. Clippers	11	339	181	100	.552	84	58	.690	20	21	41	31	35	2	9	13	259	23.5
86-87—Sacramento	52	1658	757	338	.447	228	178	.781	60	122	182	204	184	3	46	23	863	16.6
87-88—Sacramento	35	899	364	174	.478	113	87	.770	35	68	103	89	108	2	21	17	443	12.7
Totals	266	7109	3060	1553	.508	1117	863	.773	353	608	961	624	849	17	186	131	3991	15.0

Three-Point Field Goals: 1982-83, 0-for-2. 1983-84, 1-for-6 (.167). 1984-85, 3-for-19 (.158). 1985-86, 1-for-2 (.500). 1986-87, 9-for-33 (.273). 1987-88, 8-for-23 (.348). Totals, 22-for-85 (.259).

Member of NCAA Division I championship team, 1980.

KEITH LeWAYNE SMITH

Born March 9, 1964 at Flint, Mich.   Height 6:03.   Weight 193.

High School—West Covina, Calif.

College—Loyola Marymount University, Los Angeles, Calif.

Drafted by Milwaukee on second round, 1986 (45th pick).

Waived by Milwaukee, November 4, 1987.
Played in Continental Basketball Association with LaCrosse Catbirds, 1987-88.

—COLLEGIATE RECORD—

Year	G.	Min.	FGA	FGM	Pct.	FTA	FTM	Pct.	Reb.	Pts.	Avg.
82-86	27	651	189	91	.481	49	30	.612	52	213	7.9
83-84	27	1022	415	202	.487	105	77	.733	57	481	17.8
84-85	27	1028	599	283	.472	160	112	.700	78	678	25.1
85-86	29	1005	476	238	.500	172	132	.767	53	608	21.0
Totals	110	3706	1679	814	.485	486	351	.722	240	1980	18.0

Three-Point Field Goals: 1982-83, 1-for-4 (.250).

CBA REGULAR SEASON RECORD

				—2-Point—			—3-Point—								
Sea.—Team	G.	Min.	FGM	FGA	Pct.	FGM	FGA	Pct.	FTM	FTA	Pct.	Reb.	Ast.	Pts.	Avg.
87-88—LaCrosse.....................	7	80	9	25	.360	1	2	.500	8	13	.615	5	11	29	4.1

NBA REGULAR SEASON RECORD

									—Rebounds—									
Sea.—Team	G.	Min.	FGA	FGM	Pct.	FTA	FTM	Pct.	Off.	Def.	Tot.	Ast.	PF	Dq.	Stl.	Blk.	Pts.	Avg.
86-87—Milwaukee	42	461	150	57	.380	28	21	.750	13	19	32	43	74	0	25	3	138	3.3

Three-Point Field Goals: 1986-87, 3-for-9 (.333).

KENNY SMITH

Born March 8, 1965 at Queens, N.Y.   Height 6:03.   Weight 170.

High School—Jamaica, N.Y., Archbishop Molloy.

College—University of North Carolina, Chapel Hill, N.C.

Drafted by Sacramento on first round, 1987 (6th pick).

—COLLEGIATE RECORD—

Year	G.	Min.	FGA	FGM	Pct.	FTA	FTM	Pct.	Reb.	Pts.	Avg.
83-84	23	....	160	83	.519	55	44	.800	40	210	9.1
84-85	36	....	334	173	.518	114	98	.860	92	444	12.3
85-86	34	....	318	164	.516	99	80	.808	75	408	12.0
86-87	34	....	414	208	.502	88	71	.807	76	574	16.9
Totals	127	....	1226	628	.512	356	293	.823	283	1636	12.9

NBA REGULAR SEASON RECORD

									—Rebounds—									
Sea.—Team	G.	Min.	FGA	FGM	Pct.	FTA	FTM	Pct.	Off.	Def.	Tot.	Ast.	PF	Dq.	Stl.	Blk.	Pts.	Avg.
87-88—Sacramento	61	2170	694	331	.477	204	167	.819	40	98	138	434	140	1	92	8	841	13.8

Three-Point Field Goals: 1986-87, 87-for-213 (.408). 1987-88, 12-for-39 (.308).

Named to NBA All-Rookie Team, 1988. . . . THE SPORTING NEWS All-America First Team, 1987.

—DID YOU KNOW—

That 1987 first-round draft choices Reggie Williams (L.A. Clippers), Tyrone Bogues (Washington) and Reggie Lewis (Boston) were prep teammates at Baltimore's Dunbar High, marking the first time three players from the same high school were selected in the opening round in the same year?

KENNY SMITH

LARRY SMITH

Born January 18, 1958 at Rolling Fork, Miss.   Height 6:08.   Weight 235.

High School—Hollandale, Miss., Simmons.

College—Alcorn State University, Lorman, Miss.

Drafted by Golden State on second round, 1980 (24th pick).

—COLLEGIATE RECORD—

Year	G.	Min.	FGA	FGM	Pct.	FTA	FTM	Pct.	Reb.	Pts.	Avg.
76-77	34	....	402	212	.526	124	74	.596	222	498	14.6
77-78	22	....	231	137	.593	74	45	.608	222	319	14.5
78-79	29	....	360	216	.600	142	81	.570	398	513	17.7
79-80	26	849	342	198	.579	182	126	.692	392	522	20.1
Totals	111	....	1335	763	.572	522	326	.625	1234	1852	16.7

NBA REGULAR SEASON RECORD

Sea.—Team	G.	Min.	FGA	FGM	Pct.	FTA	FTM	Pct.	Off.	Def.	Tot.	Ast.	PF	Dq.	Stl.	Blk.	Pts.	Avg.
80-81—Golden State	82	2578	594	304	.512	301	177	.588	433	561	994	93	316	10	70	63	785	9.6
81-82—Golden State	74	2213	412	220	.534	159	88	.553	279	534	813	83	291	7	65	54	528	7.1
82-83—Golden State	49	1433	306	180	.588	99	53	.535	209	276	485	46	186	5	36	20	413	8.4
83-84—Golden State	75	2091	436	244	.560	168	94	.560	282	390	672	72	274	6	61	22	582	7.8
84-85—Golden State	80	2497	690	366	.530	256	155	.605	405	464	869	96	285	5	78	54	887	11.1
85-86—Golden State	77	2441	586	314	.536	227	112	.493	384	472	856	95	286	7	62	50	740	9.6
86-87—Golden State	80	2374	544	297	.546	197	113	.574	366	551	917	95	295	7	71	56	707	8.8
87-88—Golden State	20	499	123	58	.472	27	11	.407	79	103	182	25	63	1	12	11	127	6.4
Totals	537	16126	3691	1983	.537	1434	803	.560	2437	3351	5788	605	1996	48	455	330	4769	8.9

Three-Point Field Goals: 1981-82, 0-for-1. 1985-86, 0-for-1. 1986-87, 0-for-1. 1987-88, 0-for-1. Totals, 0-for-4.

NBA PLAYOFF RECORD

Sea.—Team	G.	Min.	FGA	FGM	Pct.	FTA	FTM	Pct.	Off.	Def.	Tot.	Ast.	PF	Dq.	Stl.	Blk.	Pts.	Avg.
86-87—Golden State	10	329	81	43	.531	24	17	.708	61	76	137	17	39	0	12	6	103	10.3

Named to NBA All-Rookie Team, 1981. . . . Led NCAA Division I in rebounding, 1980.

OTIS FITZGERALD SMITH

Born January 30, 1964 at Jacksonville, Fla.   Height 6:05.   Weight 210.

High School—Jacksonville, Fla., Forrest.

College—Jacksonville University, Jacksonville, Fla.

Drafted by Denver on second round, 1986 (41st pick).

Traded by Denver to Golden State for cash, December 22, 1987.

—COLLEGIATE RECORD—

Year	G.	Min.	FGA	FGM	Pct.	FTA	FTM	Pct.	Reb.	Pts.	Avg.
82-83	29	979	362	171	.472	102	70	.686	251	414	14.3
83-84	28	1095	375	183	.488	120	87	.725	215	453	16.2
84-85	29	1025	313	151	.482	99	73	.737	197	375	12.9
85-86	31	1164	387	180	.465	149	113	.758	248	473	15.3
Totals	117	4263	1437	685	.477	470	343	.730	911	1715	14.7

Three-Point Field Goals: 1982-83, 2-for-7 (.286).

NBA REGULAR SEASON RECORD

Sea.—Team	G.	Min.	FGA	FGM	Pct.	FTA	FTM	Pct.	Off.	Def.	Tot.	Ast.	PF	Dq.	Stl.	Blk.	Pts.	Avg.
86-87—Denver	28	168	79	33	.418	21	12	.571	17	17	34	22	30	0	1	1	78	2.8
87-88—Den.-G.S.	72	1549	662	325	.491	229	178	.777	126	121	247	155	160	0	91	42	841	11.7
Totals	100	1717	741	358	.483	250	190	.760	143	138	281	177	190	0	92	43	919	9.2

Three-Point Field Goals: 1986-87, 0-for-2. 1987-88, 13-for-41 (.317). Totals, 13-for-43 (.302).

NBA PLAYOFF RECORD

Sea.—Team	G.	Min.	FGA	FGM	Pct.	FTA	FTM	Pct.	Off.	Def.	Tot.	Ast.	PF	Dq.	Stl.	Blk.	Pts.	Avg.
86-87—Denver	3	19	6	2	.333	9	6	.667	1	4	5	4	1	0	0	2	10	3.3

—DID YOU KNOW—

That Hall of Famers Paul Arizin, Rick Barry and Walt Frazier have sons currently playing NCAA Division I basketball? The "sons of guns" include Drexel's Chris Arizin, Kansas' Richard (Scooter) Barry and Jon Barry and Penn's Walt Frazier Jr.

MICHAEL FRANK SMREK
(Mike)

Born August 31, 1962 at Welland, Ontario. Height 7:00. Weight 260.
High School—Port Robinson, Ontario, Eastdale.
College—Canisius College, Buffalo, N.Y.
Drafted by Portland on second round, 1985 (25th pick).

Draft rights traded by Portland to Chicago for draft rights to Ben Coleman and Ken Johnson, June 18, 1985.
Waived by Chicago, October 30, 1986; signed by Los Angeles Lakers as a free agent, November 7, 1986.

—COLLEGIATE RECORD—

Year	G.	Min.	FGA	FGM	Pct.	FTA	FTM	Pct.	Reb.	Pts.	Avg.
81-82	22	311	54	24	.444	14	7	.500	68	55	2.5
82-83	28	560	106	49	.462	52	27	.519	131	125	4.5
83-84	30	829	242	153	.632	96	56	.583	175	362	12.1
84-85	28	812	286	172	.601	148	97	.655	192	441	15.8
Totals	108	2512	688	398	.578	310	187	.603	566	983	9.1

NBA REGULAR SEASON RECORD

Sea.—Team	G.	Min.	FGA	FGM	Pct.	FTA	FTM	Pct.	Off.	Def.	Tot.	Ast.	PF	Dq.	Stl.	Blk.	Pts.	Avg.
85-86—Chicago	38	408	122	46	.377	29	16	.552	46	64	110	19	95	0	6	23	108	2.8
86-87—L.A. Lakers	35	233	60	30	.500	25	16	.640	13	24	37	5	70	1	4	13	76	2.2
87-88—L.A. Lakers	48	421	103	44	.427	66	44	.667	27	58	85	8	105	3	7	42	132	2.8
Totals	121	1062	285	120	.421	120	76	.633	86	146	232	32	270	4	17	78	316	2.6

Three-Point Field Goals: 1985-86, 0-for-2.

NBA PLAYOFF RECORD

Sea.—Team	G.	Min.	FGA	FGM	Pct.	FTA	FTM	Pct.	Off.	Def.	Tot.	Ast.	PF	Dq.	Stl.	Blk.	Pts.	Avg.
85-86—Chicago	3	5	1	0	.000	0	0	.000	0	0	0	0	2	0	0	1	0	0.0
86-87—L.A. Lakers	10	33	10	2	.200	6	4	.667	3	4	7	0	15	0	0	6	8	0.8
87-88—L.A. Lakers	8	34	5	1	.200	3	1	.333	1	5	6	0	4	0	1	3	3	0.4
Totals	21	72	16	3	.188	9	5	.556	4	9	13	0	21	0	1	10	11	0.5

Member of NBA championship teams, 1987 and 1988.

RORY DARNELL SPARROW

Born June 12, 1958 at Suffolk, Va. Height 6:02. Weight 175.
High School—Paterson, N. J., Eastside.
College—Villanova University, Villanova, Pa.
Drafted by New Jersey on fourth round, 1980 (75th pick).

Waived by New Jersey, October 7, 1980; re-signed by New Jersey to a 10-day contract that expired, December 29, 1980.
Re-signed by New Jersey, February 18, 1981.
Traded by New Jersey to Atlanta for a 1982 4th round draft choice, August 12, 1981.
Traded by Atlanta to New York for Scott Hastings and cash, February 12, 1983.
Traded by New York to Chicago for a 1988 2nd round draft choice, November 12, 1987.
Played in Continental Basketball Association with Scranton Aces, 1980-81.

—COLLEGIATE RECORD—

Year	G.	Min.	FGA	FGM	Pct.	FTA	FTM	Pct.	Reb.	Pts.	Avg.
76-77	33	....	193	99	.513	42	34	.810	69	232	7.0
77-78	32	1036	213	109	.512	79	57	.722	74	275	8.6
78-79	28	877	282	145	.514	61	50	.820	60	340	12.1
79-80	31	937	243	136	.560	77	64	.831	75	336	10.8
Totals	124	....	931	489	.525	259	205	.792	278	1183	9.5

CBA REGULAR SEASON RECORD

			—2-Point—			—3-Point—								
Sea.—Team	G.	Min.	FGM	FGA	Pct.	FGM	FGA	Pct.	FTM	FTA	Pct.	Reb.	Ast.	Pts.	Avg.
80-81—Scranton	20	827	196	388	.505	2	8	.250	83	107	.775	82	180	481	24.1

NBA REGULAR SEASON RECORD

Sea.—Team	G.	Min.	FGA	FGM	Pct.	FTA	FTM	Pct.	Off.	Def.	Tot.	Ast.	PF	Dq.	Stl.	Blk.	Pts.	Avg.
80-81—New Jersey	15	212	63	22	.349	16	12	.750	7	11	18	32	15	0	13	3	56	3.7
81-82—Atlanta	82	2610	730	366	.501	148	124	.838	53	171	224	424	240	2	87	13	857	10.5
82-83—Atl.-N.Y.	81	2428	810	392	.484	199	147	.739	61	169	230	397	255	4	107	5	936	11.6
83-84—New York	79	2436	738	350	.474	131	108	.824	48	141	189	539	230	4	100	8	818	10.4

Sea.—Team	G.	Min.	FGA	FGM	Pct.	FTA	FTM	Pct.	Off.	Def.	Tot.	Ast.	PF	Dq.	Stl.	Blk.	Pts.	Avg.
84-85—New York	79	2292	662	326	.492	141	122	.865	38	131	169	557	200	2	81	9	781	9.9
85-86—New York	74	2344	723	345	.477	127	101	.795	50	120	170	472	182	1	85	14	796	10.8
86-87—New York	80	1951	590	263	.446	89	71	.798	29	86	115	432	160	0	67	6	608	7.6
87-88—N.Y.-Chi.	58	1044	293	117	.399	33	24	.727	15	57	72	167	79	1	41	3	260	4.5
Totals	548	15317	4609	2181	.473	884	709	.802	301	886	1187	3020	1361	14	581	61	5112	9.3

Three-Point Field Goals: 1981-82, 1-for-15 (.067). 1982-83, 5-for-22 (.227). 1983-84, 10-for-39 (.256). 1984-85, 7-for-31 (.226). 1985-86, 5-for-20 (.250). 1986-87, 11-for-42 (.262). 1987-88, 2-for-13 (.154). Totals, 41-for-182 (.225).

NBA PLAYOFF RECORD

—Rebounds—

Sea.—Team	G.	Min.	FGA	FGM	Pct.	FTA	FTM	Pct.	Off.	Def.	Tot.	Ast.	PF	Dq.	Stl.	Blk.	Pts.	Avg.
81-82—Atlanta	2	69	12	5	.417	4	4	1.000	2	6	8	11	7	0	2	0	14	7.0
82-83—New York	6	202	71	30	.423	21	17	.810	3	10	13	42	18	1	7	0	78	13.0
83-84—New York	12	389	121	54	.446	30	24	.800	10	16	26	86	41	2	12	1	134	11.2
87-88—Chicago	7	106	32	10	.313	6	4	.667	0	3	3	18	11	0	4	0	26	3.7
Totals	27	766	236	99	.419	61	49	.803	15	35	50	157	77	3	25	1	252	9.3

Three-Point Field Goals: 1981-82, 0-for-1. 1982-83, 1-for-5 (.200). 1983-84, 2-for-6 (.333). 1987-88, 2-for-4 (.500). Totals, 5-for-16 (.313).

STEPHEN SAMUEL STIPANOVICH
(Steve)

Born November 17, 1960 at St. Louis, Mo.   Height 7:00.   Weight 250.

High School—Creve Coeur, Mo., DeSmet.

College—University of Missouri, Columbia, Mo.

Drafted by Indiana on first round, 1983 (2nd pick).

—COLLEGIATE RECORD—

Year	G.	Min.	FGA	FGM	Pct.	FTA	FTM	Pct.	Reb.	Pts.	Avg.
79-80	31	1034	301	180	.598	127	85	.669	199	445	14.4
80-81	32	970	286	143	.500	162	120	.741	237	406	12.7
81-82	31	956	278	140	.504	104	79	.760	248	359	11.6
82-83	34	1264	454	246	.542	187	134	.717	300	626	18.4
Totals	128	4224	1319	709	.538	580	418	.721	984	1836	14.3

NBA REGULAR SEASON RECORD

—Rebounds—

Sea.—Team	G.	Min.	FGA	FGM	Pct.	FTA	FTM	Pct.	Off.	Def.	Tot.	Ast.	PF	Dq.	Stl.	Blk.	Pts.	Avg.
83-84—Indiana	81	2426	816	392	.480	243	183	.753	116	446	562	170	303	4	73	67	970	12.0
84-85—Indiana	82	2315	871	414	.475	372	297	.798	141	473	614	199	265	4	71	78	1126	13.7
85-86—Indiana	79	2397	885	416	.470	315	242	.768	173	450	623	206	261	1	75	69	1076	13.6
86-87—Indiana	81	2761	760	382	.503	367	307	.837	184	486	670	180	304	9	106	97	1072	13.2
87-88—Indiana	80	2692	828	411	.496	314	254	.809	157	505	662	183	302	8	90	69	1079	13.5
Totals	403	12591	4160	2015	.484	1611	1283	.796	771	2360	3131	938	1435	26	415	380	5323	13.2

Three-Point Field Goals: 1983-84, 3-for-16 (.188). 1984-85, 1-for-11 (.091). 1985-86, 2-for-10 (.200). 1986-87, 1-for-4 (.250). 1987-88, 3-for-15 (.200). Totals, 10-for-56 (.179).

NBA PLAYOFF RECORD

—Rebounds—

Sea.—Team	G.	Min.	FGA	FGM	Pct.	FTA	FTM	Pct.	Off.	Def.	Tot.	Ast.	PF	Dq.	Stl.	Blk.	Pts.	Avg.
86-87—Indiana	4	149	38	21	.553	19	13	.684	7	23	30	3	14	0	3	2	55	13.8

Three-Point Field Goal: 1986-87, 0-for-1.

Named to NBA All-Rookie Team, 1984. . . . Named to THE SPORTING NEWS All-America Second Team, 1983.

JOHN HOUSTON STOCKTON

Born March 26, 1962 at Spokane, Wash.   Height 6:01.   Weight 175.

High School—Spokane, Wash., Gonzaga Prep.

College—Gonzaga University, Spokane, Wash.

Drafted by Utah on first round, 1984 (16th pick).

—COLLEGIATE RECORD—

Year	G.	Min.	FGA	FGM	Pct.	FTA	FTM	Pct.	Reb.	Pts.	Avg.
80-81	25	235	45	26	.578	35	26	.743	11	78	3.1
81-82	27	1054	203	117	.576	102	69	.676	67	303	11.2
82-83	27	1036	274	142	.518	115	91	.791	87	375	13.9
83-84	28	1053	397	229	.577	182	126	.692	66	584	20.9
Totals	107	3378	919	514	.559	434	312	.719	231	1340	12.5

JOHN STOCKTON

NBA REGULAR SEASON RECORD

Sea.—Team	G.	Min.	FGA	FGM	Pct.	FTA	FTM	Pct.	Off.	Def.	Tot.	Ast.	PF	Dq.	Stl.	Blk.	Pts.	Avg.
										—Rebounds—								
84-85—Utah	82	1490	333	157	.471	193	142	.736	26	79	105	415	203	3	109	11	458	5.6
85-86—Utah	82	1935	466	228	.489	205	172	.839	33	146	179	610	227	2	157	10	630	7.7
86-87—Utah	82	1858	463	231	.499	229	179	.782	32	119	151	670	224	1	177	14	648	7.9
87-88—Utah	82	2842	791	454	.574	324	272	.840	54	183	237	1128	247	5	242	16	1204	14.7
Totals	328	8125	2053	1070	.521	951	765	.804	145	527	672	2823	901	11	685	51	2940	9.0

Three-Point Field Goals: 1984-85, 2-for-11 (.182). 1985-86, 2-for-15 (.133). 1986-87, 7-for-38 (.184). 1987-88, 24-for-67 (.358). Totals, 35-for-131 (.267).

NBA PLAYOFF RECORD

Sea.—Team	G.	Min.	FGA	FGM	Pct.	FTA	FTM	Pct.	Off.	Def.	Tot.	Ast.	PF	Dq.	Stl.	Blk.	Pts.	Avg.
										—Rebounds—								
84-85—Utah	10	186	45	21	.467	35	26	.743	7	21	28	43	30	0	11	2	68	6.8
85-86—Utah	4	73	17	9	.529	9	8	.889	3	3	6	14	10	0	5	0	27	6.8
86-87—Utah	5	157	29	18	.621	13	10	.769	2	9	11	40	18	0	15	1	50	10.0
87-88—Utah	11	478	134	68	.507	91	75	.824	14	31	45	163	36	0	37	3	215	19.5
Totals	30	894	225	116	.516	148	119	.804	26	64	90	260	94	0	68	6	360	12.0

Three-Point Field Goals: 1984-85, 0-for-2. 1985-86, 1-for-1 (1.000). 1986-87, 4-for-5 (.800). 1987-88, 4-for-14 (.286). Totals, 9-for-22 (.409).

Named to All-NBA Second Team, 1988.... Holds NBA record for most assists in one season, 1988.... Led NBA in assists, 1988.

JOHN STROEDER

Born July 24, 1958 at Bremerton, Wash.   Height 6:10.   Weight 260.

High School—Port Townsend, Wash.

College—University of Montana, Missoula, Mont.

Drafted by Portland on eighth round, 1980 (168th pick).

Draft rights relinquished by Portland, July 27, 1981.
Signed by Milwaukee as a free agent, October 8, 1987.
Selected from Milwaukee by Miami in NBA expansion draft, June 23, 1988.
Played in Continental Basketball Association with Montana Golden Nuggets, 1982-83, and Rapid City Thrillers, 1986-87.
Played with Fiat in England, 1980-81 and 1981-82.
Played with Lorient Cep in France, 1983-84, 1984-85 and 1985-86.

—COLLEGIATE RECORD—

Year	G.	Min.	FGA	FGM	Pct.	FTA	FTM	Pct.	Reb.	Pts.	Avg.
76-77	19	....	22	10	.455	18	10	.556	17	30	1.6
77-78	28	....	216	116	.537	71	49	.690	191	281	10.0
78-79	27	....	283	143	.505	123	84	.683	211	370	13.7
79-80	24	653	211	102	.483	86	62	.721	162	266	11.1
Totals	98	....	732	371	.507	298	205	.688	581	947	9.7

CBA REGULAR SEASON RECORD

Sea.—Team	G.	Min.	FGM 2-Point	FGA	Pct.	FGM 3-Point	FGA	Pct.	FTM	FTA	Pct.	Reb.	Ast.	Pts.	Avg.
82-83—Montana.....................	43	936	89	219	.406	2	3	.667	55	73	.753	226	25	239	5.6
86-87—Rapid City	17	408	70	146	.479	0	0	.—	29	38	.763	109	28	169	9.9
Totals	60	1344	159	365	.435	2	3	.667	84	111	.756	335	53	408	6.8

NBA REGULAR SEASON RECORD

Sea.—Team	G.	Min.	FGA	FGM	Pct.	FTA	FTM	Pct.	Off.	Def.	Tot.	Ast.	PF	Dq.	Stl.	Blk.	Pts.	Avg.
										—Rebounds—								
87-88—Milwaukee	41	271	79	29	.367	30	20	.667	24	47	71	20	48	0	3	12	78	1.9

Three-Point Field Goals: 1987-88, 0-for-2.

NBA PLAYOFF RECORD

Sea.—Team	G.	Min.	FGA	FGM	Pct.	FTA	FTM	Pct.	Off.	Def.	Tot.	Ast.	PF	Dq.	Stl.	Blk.	Pts.	Avg.
										—Rebounds—								
87-88—Milwaukee	1	1	1	1	1.000	0	0	.000	0	0	0	0	0	0	0	0	3	3.0

Three-Point Field Goals: 1987-88, 1-for-1 (1.000).

JON THOMAS SUNDVOLD

Born July 2, 1961 at Sioux Falls, S. D.   Height 6:02.   Weight 170.

High School—Blue Springs, Mo.

College—University of Missouri, Columbia, Mo.

Drafted by Seattle on first round, 1983 (16th pick).

Traded by Seattle to San Antonio for a 1986 2nd round draft choice, October 23, 1985.
Selected from San Antonio by Miami in NBA expansion draft, June 23, 1988.

—COLLEGIATE RECORD—

Year	G.	Min.	FGA	FGM	Pct.	FTA	FTM	Pct.	Reb.	Pts.	Avg.
79-80	31	790	169	76	.450	59	44	.746	52	196	6.3
80-81	32	1134	350	178	.509	99	85	.859	54	441	13.8
81-82	31	1062	307	149	.485	93	81	.871	66	379	12.2
82-83	34	1303	447	225	.503	151	131	.868	82	581	17.1
Totals	128	4289	1273	628	.493	402	341	.848	254	1597	12.5

NBA REGULAR SEASON RECORD

Sea.—Team	G.	Min.	FGA	FGM	Pct.	FTA	FTM	Pct.	—Rebounds— Off.	Def.	Tot.	Ast.	PF	Dq.	Stl.	Blk.	Pts.	Avg.
83-84—Seattle	73	1284	488	217	.445	72	64	.889	23	68	91	239	81	0	29	1	507	6.9
84-85—Seattle	73	1150	400	170	.425	59	48	.814	17	53	70	206	87	0	36	1	400	5.5
85-86—San Antonio	70	1150	476	220	.462	48	39	.813	22	58	80	261	110	0	34	0	500	7.1
86-87—San Antonio	76	1765	751	365	.486	84	70	.833	20	78	98	315	109	1	35	0	850	11.2
87-88—San Antonio	52	1024	379	176	.464	48	43	.896	14	34	48	183	54	0	27	2	421	8.1
Totals	344	6373	2494	1148	.460	311	264	.849	96	291	387	1204	441	1	161	4	2678	7.8

Three-Point Field Goals: 1983-84, 9-for-37 (.243). 1984-85, 12-for-38 (.316). 1985-86, 21-for-60 (.350). 1986-87, 50-for-149 (.336). 1987-88, 26-for-64 (.406). Totals, 118-for-348 (.339).

NBA PLAYOFF RECORD

Sea.—Team	G.	Min.	FGA	FGM	Pct.	FTA	FTM	Pct.	—Rebounds— Off.	Def.	Tot.	Ast.	PF	Dq.	Stl.	Blk.	Pts.	Avg.
83-84—Seattle	3	22	8	3	.375	2	2	1.000	1	1	2	5	1	0	0	0	8	2.7
85-86—San Antonio	3	43	18	7	.389	1	1	1.000	0	1	1	5	1	0	0	0	16	5.3
87-88—San Antonio	3	90	30	15	.500	3	2	.667	1	3	4	15	3	0	4	0	35	11.7
Totals	9	155	56	25	.446	6	5	.833	2	5	7	25	5	0	4	0	59	6.6

Three-Point Field Goals: 1983-84, 0-for-3. 1985-86, 1-for-6 (.167). 1987-88, 3-for-9 (.333). Totals, 4-for-18 (.222).

ROY JAMES TARPLEY JR.

Born November 28, 1964 at New York, N.Y. Height 6:11. Weight 240.

High School—Detroit, Mich , Cooley.

College—University of Michigan, Ann Arbor, Mich.

Drafted by Dallas on first round, 1986 (7th pick).

—COLLEGIATE RECORD—

Year	G.	Min.	FGA	FGM	Pct.	FTA	FTM	Pct.	Reb.	Pts.	Avg.
82-83	26	....	86	35	.407	38	22	.579	83	92	3.5
83-84	33	932	315	166	.527	102	81	.794	266	413	12.5
84-85	30	1018	425	223	.525	160	124	.775	313	570	19.0
85-86	33	1045	379	205	.541	143	116	.811	291	526	15.9
Totals	122	....	1205	629	.522	443	343	.774	953	1601	13.1

NBA REGULAR SEASON RECORD

Sea.—Team	G.	Min.	FGA	FGM	Pct.	FTA	FTM	Pct.	—Rebounds— Off.	Def.	Tot.	Ast.	PF	Dq.	Stl.	Blk.	Pts.	Avg.
86-87—Dallas	75	1405	499	233	.467	139	94	.676	180	353	533	52	232	3	56	79	561	7.5
87-88—Dallas	81	2307	888	444	.500	277	205	.740	360	599	959	86	313	8	103	86	1093	13.5
Totals	156	3712	1387	677	.488	416	299	.719	540	952	1492	138	545	11	159	165	1654	10.6

Three-Point Field Goals: 1986-87, 1-for-3 (.333). 1987-88, 0-for-5. Totals, 1-for-8 (.125).

NBA PLAYOFF RECORD

Sea.—Team	G.	Min.	FGA	FGM	Pct.	FTA	FTM	Pct.	—Rebounds— Off.	Def.	Tot.	Ast.	PF	Dq.	Stl.	Blk.	Pts.	Avg.
86-87—Dallas	4	114	48	24	.500	7	5	.714	18	24	42	1	18	1	1	7	53	13.3
87-88—Dallas	17	563	241	125	.519	73	54	.740	88	131	219	30	69	3	21	26	304	17.9
Totals	21	677	289	149	.516	80	59	.738	106	155	261	31	87	4	22	33	357	17.0

Three-Point Field Goals: 1987-88, 0-for-3.

Recipient of NBA Sixth Man Award, 1988. . . . Named to NBA All-Rookie Team, 1987.

TERRY MICHAEL TEAGLE

Born April 10, 1960 at Broaddus, Tex. Height 6:05. Weight 195.

High School—Broaddus, Tex.

College—Baylor University, Waco, Tex.

Drafted by Houston on first round, 1982 (16th pick).

Waived by Houston, October 23, 1984; signed by Detroit as a free agent, November 7, 1984.

Waived by Detroit, November 20, 1984; signed by Golden State as a free agent, March 11, 1985.
Played in Continental Basketball Association with Detroit Spirits, 1984-85.

—COLLEGIATE RECORD—

Year	G.	Min.	FGA	FGM	Pct.	FTA	FTM	Pct.	Reb.	Pts.	Avg.
78-79	28	....	310	164	.529	113	80	.708	183	408	14.6
79-80	27	....	440	239	.543	171	142	.830	222	620	23.0
80-81	27	....	399	214	.536	151	111	.735	190	539	20.0
81-82	28	....	479	259	.541	144	104	.722	210	622	22.2
Totals	110	....	1628	876	.538	579	437	.755	805	2189	19.9

CBA REGULAR SEASON RECORD

| | | | ——2-Point—— | | | ——3-Point—— | | | | | | | | |
Sea.—Team	G.	Min.	FGM	FGA	Pct.	FGM	FGA	Pct.	FTM	FTA	Pct.	Reb.	Ast.	Pts.	Avg.
84-85—Detroit	40	1146	294	532	.552	2	14	.143	187	222	.842	171	67	781	19.5

NBA REGULAR SEASON RECORD

| | | | | | | | | | —Rebounds— | | | | | | | | | |
Sea.—Team	G.	Min.	FGA	FGM	Pct.	FTA	FTM	Pct.	Off.	Def.	Tot.	Ast.	PF	Dq.	Stl.	Blk.	Pts.	Avg.
82-83—Houston	73	1708	776	332	.428	125	87	.696	74	120	194	150	171	0	53	18	761	10.4
83-84—Houston	68	616	315	148	.470	44	37	.841	28	50	78	63	81	1	13	4	340	5.0
84-85—Det.-G.S.	21	349	137	74	.540	35	25	.714	22	21	43	14	36	0	13	5	175	8.3
85-86—Golden State	82	2158	958	475	.496	265	211	.796	96	139	235	115	241	2	71	34	1165	14.2
86-87—Golden State	82	1650	808	370	.458	234	182	.778	68	107	175	105	190	0	68	13	922	11.2
87-88—Golden State	47	958	546	248	.454	121	97	.802	41	40	81	61	95	0	32	4	594	12.6
Totals	373	7439	3540	1647	.465	824	639	.775	329	477	806	508	814	3	250	78	3957	10.6

Three-Point Field Goals: 1982-83, 10-for-29 (.345). 1983-84, 7-for-27 (.259). 1984-85, 2-for-4 (.500). 1985-86, 4-for-25 (.160). 1986-87, 0-for-10. 1987-88, 1-for-9 (.111). Totals, 24-for-104 (.231).

NBA PLAYOFF RECORD

| | | | | | | | | | —Rebounds— | | | | | | | | | |
Sea.—Team	G.	Min.	FGA	FGM	Pct.	FTA	FTM	Pct.	Off.	Def.	Tot.	Ast.	PF	Dq.	Stl.	Blk.	Pts.	Avg.
86-87—Golden State	10	233	124	57	.460	38	30	.789	13	7	20	13	27	0	8	1	144	14.4

Three-Point Field Goals: 1986-87, 0-for-2.

REGGIE WAYNE THEUS

Born October 13, 1957 at Inglewood, Calif. Height 6:07. Weight 213.

High School.—Inglewood, Calif.

College—University of Nevada at Las Vegas, Las Vegas, Nev.

Drafted by Chicago on first round as an undergraduate, 1978 (9th pick).

Traded by Chicago to Kansas City for Steve Johnson, a 1984 2nd round draft choice and two 1985 2nd round draft choices, February 15, 1984.
Traded by Sacramento with a 1988 3rd round draft choice and future considerations to Atlanta for Randy Wittman and a 1988 1st round draft choice, June 27, 1988.

—COLLEGIATE RECORD—

Year	G.	Min.	FGA	FGM	Pct.	FTA	FTM	Pct.	Reb.	Pts.	Avg.
75-76	31	....	163	68	.417	60	48	.800	53	184	5.9
76-77	32	....	358	178	.497	132	108	.818	145	464	14.5
77-78	28	....	389	181	.465	207	167	.807	191	529	18.9
Totals	91	....	910	427	.469	399	323	.810	389	1177	12.9

NBA REGULAR SEASON RECORD

| | | | | | | | | | —Rebounds— | | | | | | | | | |
Sea.—Team	G.	Min.	FGA	FGM	Pct.	FTA	FTM	Pct.	Off.	Def.	Tot.	Ast.	PF	Dq.	Stl.	Blk.	Pts.	Avg.
78-79—Chicago	82	2753	1119	537	.480	347	264	.761	92	136	228	429	270	2	93	18	1338	16.3
79-80—Chicago	82	3029	1172	566	.483	597	500	.838	143	186	329	515	262	4	114	20	1660	20.2
80-81—Chicago	82	2820	1097	543	.495	550	445	.809	124	163	287	426	258	1	122	20	1549	18.9
81-82—Chicago	82	2838	1194	560	.469	449	363	.808	115	197	312	476	243	1	87	16	1508	18.4
82-83—Chicago	82	2856	1567	749	.478	542	434	.801	91	209	300	484	281	6	143	17	1953	23.8
83-84—Chi.-K.C.	61	1498	625	262	.419	281	214	.762	50	79	129	352	171	3	50	12	745	12.2
84-85—Kansas City	82	2543	1029	501	.487	387	334	.863	106	164	270	656	250	0	95	18	1341	16.4
85-86—Sacramento	82	2919	1137	546	.480	490	405	.827	73	231	304	788	231	3	112	20	1503	18.3
86-87—Sacramento	79	2872	1223	577	.472	495	429	.867	86	180	266	692	208	3	78	16	1600	20.3
87-88—Sacramento	73	2653	1318	619	.470	385	320	.831	72	160	232	463	173	0	59	16	1574	21.6
Totals	787	26781	11481	5460	.476	4523	3708	.820	952	1705	2657	5281	2347	23	953	173	14771	18.8

Three-Point Field Goals: 1979-80, 28-for-105 (.267). 1980-81, 18-for-90 (.200). 1981-82, 25-for-100 (.250). 1982-83, 21-for-91 (.231). 1983-84, 7-for-42 (.167). 1984-85, 5-for-38 (.132). 1985-86, 6-for-35 (.171). 1986-87, 17-for-78 (.218). 1987-88, 16-for-59 (.271). Totals, 143-for-638 (.224).

NBA PLAYOFF RECORD

| | | | | | | | | | —Rebounds— | | | | | | | | | |
Sea.—Team	G.	Min.	FGA	FGM	Pct.	FTA	FTM	Pct.	Off.	Def.	Tot.	Ast.	PF	Dq.	Stl.	Blk.	Pts.	Avg.
80-81—Chicago	6	232	90	40	.444	43	37	.860	7	14	21	38	22	0	9	0	119	19.8

Sea.—Team	G.	Min.	FGA	FGM	Pct.	FTA	FTM	Pct.	Off.	Def.	Tot.	Ast.	PF	Dq.	Stl.	Blk.	Pts.	Avg.
83-84—Kansas City	3	81	43	17	.395	10	9	.900	4	7	11	16	9	0	5	0	43	14.3
85-86—Sacramento	3	102	46	18	.391	12	9	.750	3	5	8	19	9	0	3	2	45	15.0
Totals	12	415	179	75	.419	65	55	.846	14	26	40	73	40	0	17	2	207	17.3

Three-Point Field Goals: 1980-81, 2-for-9 (.222). 1983-84, 0-for-3. 1985-86, 0-for-1. Totals, 2-for-13 (.154).

NBA ALL-STAR GAME RECORD

Season—Team	Min.	FGA	FGM	Pct.	FTA	FTM	Pct.	Off.	Def.	Tot.	Ast.	PF	Dq.	Stl.	Blk.	Pts.
1981—Chicago	19	7	4	.571	0	0	.000	0	1	1	3	0	0	2	0	8
1983—Chicago	8	5	0	.000	0	0	.000	1	0	1	1	1	0	0	0	0
Totals	27	12	4	.333	0	0	.000	1	1	2	4	1	0	2	0	8

Named to NBA All-Rookie Team, 1979.

ISIAH LORD THOMAS III

Born April 30, 1961 at Chicago, Ill.   Height 6:01.   Weight 185.

High School—Westchester, Ill., St. Joseph's.

College—Indiana University, Bloomington, Ind.

Drafted by Detroit on first round as an undergraduate, 1981 (2nd pick).

—COLLEGIATE RECORD—

Year	G.	Min.	FGA	FGM	Pct.	FTA	FTM	Pct.	Reb.	Pts.	Avg
79-80	29	....	302	154	.510	149	115	.772	116	423	14.6
80-81	34	....	383	212	.554	163	121	.742	105	545	16.0
Totals	63	....	685	366	.534	312	236	.756	221	968	15.4

NBA REGULAR SEASON RECORD

Sea.—Team	G.	Min.	FGA	FGM	Pct.	FTA	FTM	Pct.	Off.	Def.	Tot.	Ast.	PF	Dq.	Stl.	Blk.	Pts.	Avg.
81-82—Detroit	72	2433	1068	453	.424	429	302	.704	57	152	209	565	253	2	150	17	1225	17.0
82-83—Detroit	81	3093	1537	725	.472	518	368	.710	105	223	328	634	318	8	199	29	1854	22.9
83-84—Detroit	82	3007	1448	669	.462	529	388	.733	103	224	327	914	324	8	204	33	1748	21.3
84-85—Detroit	81	3089	1410	646	.458	493	399	.809	114	247	361	1123	288	8	187	25	1720	21.2
85-86—Detroit	77	2790	1248	609	.488	462	365	.790	83	194	277	830	245	9	171	20	1609	20.9
86-87—Detroit	81	3013	1353	626	.463	521	400	.768	82	237	319	813	251	5	153	20	1671	20.6
87-88—Detroit	81	2927	1341	621	.463	394	305	.774	64	214	278	678	217	0	141	17	1577	19.5
Totals	555	20352	9405	4349	.462	3346	2527	.755	608	1491	2099	5557	1896	40	1205	161	11404	20.5

Three-Point Field Goals: 1981-82, 17-for-59 (.288). 1982-83, 36-for-125 (.288). 1983-84, 22-for-65 (.338). 1984-85, 29-for-113 (.257). 1985-86, 26-for-84 (.310). 1986-87, 19-for-98 (.194). 1987-88, 30-for-97 (.309). Totals, 179-for-641 (.279).

NBA PLAYOFF RECORD

Sea.—Team	G.	Min.	FGA	FGM	Pct.	FTA	FTM	Pct.	Off.	Def.	Tot.	Ast.	PF	Dq.	Stl.	Blk.	Pts.	Avg.
83-84—Detroit	5	198	83	39	.470	35	27	.771	7	12	19	55	22	1	13	6	107	21.4
84-85—Detroit	9	355	166	83	.500	62	47	.758	11	36	47	101	39	2	19	4	219	24.3
85-86—Detroit	4	163	91	41	.451	36	24	.667	8	14	22	48	17	0	9	3	106	26.5
86-87—Detroit	15	562	297	134	.451	110	83	.755	21	46	67	130	51	1	39	4	361	24.1
87-88—Detroit	23	911	419	183	.437	151	125	.828	26	81	107	201	71	2	66	8	504	21.9
Totals	56	2189	1056	480	.455	394	306	.777	73	189	262	535	200	6	146	25	1297	23.2

Three-Point Field Goals: 1983-84, 2-for-6 (.333). 1984-85, 6-for-15 (.400). 1985-86, 0-for-5. 1986-87, 10-for-33 (.303). 1987-88, 13-for-44 (.295). Totals, 31-for-103 (.301).

NBA ALL-STAR GAME RECORD

Season—Team	Min.	FGA	FGM	Pct.	FTA	FTM	Pct.	Off.	Def.	Tot.	Ast.	PF	Dq.	Stl.	Blk.	Pts.
1982—Detroit	17	7	5	.714	4	2	.500	1	0	1	4	1	0	3	0	12
1983—Detroit	29	14	9	.643	1	1	1.000	3	1	4	7	0	0	4	0	19
1984—Detroit	39	17	9	.529	3	3	1.000	3	2	5	15	4	0	4	0	21
1985—Detroit	25	14	9	.643	1	1	1.000	1	1	2	5	2	0	2	0	22
1986—Detroit	36	19	11	.579	9	8	.889	0	1	1	10	2	0	5	0	30
1987—Detroit	24	6	4	.667	9	8	.889	2	1	3	9	3	0	0	0	16
1988—Detroit	28	10	4	.400	0	0	.000	1	1	2	15	1	0	1	0	8
Totals	198	87	51	.586	27	23	.852	11	7	18	65	13	0	19	0	128

Three-Point Field Goals: 1984, 0-for-2. 1985, 3-for-4 (.750). 1986, 0-for-1. Totals, 3-for-7 (.429).

Named to All-NBA First Team, 1984, 1985, 1986. . . . All-NBA Second Team, 1983 and 1987. . . . NBA All-Rookie Team, 1982. . . . NBA All-Star Game MVP, 1984 and 1986. . . . Holds NBA championship series record for most points in one quarter, 25, vs. L.A. Lakers, June 19, 1988. . . . Led NBA in assists, 1985. . . . Named to THE SPORTING NEWS All-America First Team, 1981. . . . NCAA Division I Tournament Most Outstanding Player, 1981. . . . Member of NCAA Division I championship team, 1981. . . . Member of U.S. Olympic team, 1980.

BERNARD THOMPSON

Born August 30, 1962 at Phoenix, Ariz.   Height 6:06.   Weight 210.

High School—Phoenix, Ariz., South Mountain.

College—Fresno State University, Fresno, Calif.

Drafted by Portland on first round, 1984 (19th pick).

Traded by Portland to Phoenix for a 1987 2nd round draft choice, June 14, 1985.
Selected from Phoenix by Charlotte in NBA expansion draft, June 23, 1988.
Traded by Charlotte with a 1990 2nd round draft choice to Houston for Robert Reid, July 18, 1988.

—COLLEGIATE RECORD—

Year	G.	Min.	FGA	FGM	Pct.	FTA	FTM	Pct.	Reb.	Pts.	Avg.
80-81	23	259	53	28	.528	48	34	.708	45	90	3.9
81-82	30	837	177	103	.582	92	71	.772	115	277	9.2
82-83	35	1211	363	214	.590	187	138	.738	207	566	16.2
83-84	33	1151	338	192	.568	174	135	.776	193	519	15.7
Totals	121	3458	931	537	.577	501	378	.754	560	1452	12.0

NBA REGULAR SEASON RECORD

Sea.—Team	G.	Min.	FGA	FGM	Pct.	FTA	FTM	Pct.	Off.	Def.	Tot.	Ast.	PF	Dq.	Stl.	Blk.	Pts.	Avg.
84-85—Portland	59	535	212	79	.373	51	39	.765	37	39	76	52	79	0	31	10	197	3.3
85-86—Phoenix	61	1281	399	195	.489	157	127	.809	58	83	141	132	151	0	51	10	517	8.5
86-87—Phoenix	24	331	105	42	.400	33	27	.818	20	11	31	18	53	0	11	5	111	4.6
87-88—Phoenix	37	566	159	74	.465	60	43	.717	40	36	76	51	75	1	21	1	191	5.2
Totals	181	2713	875	390	.446	301	236	.784	155	169	324	253	358	1	114	26	1016	5.6

Three-Point Field Goals: 1984-85, 0-for-8. 1985-86, 0-for-2. 1986-87, 0-for-3. 1987-88, 0-for-2. Totals, 0-for-15.

NBA PLAYOFF RECORD

Sea.—Team	G.	Min.	FGA	FGM	Pct.	FTA	FTM	Pct.	Off.	Def.	Tot.	Ast.	PF	Dq.	Stl.	Blk.	Pts.	Avg.
84-85—Portland	2	10	5	0	.000	2	2	1.000	1	2	3	2	1	0	0	1	2	1.0

LaSALLE THOMPSON III

Born June 23, 1961 at Cincinnati, O.   Height 6:10.   Weight 253.

High School—Cincinnati, O., Withrow.

College—University of Texas, Austin, Tex.

Drafted by Kansas City on first round as an undergraduate, 1982 (5th pick).

—COLLEGIATE RECORD—

Year	G.	Min.	FGA	FGM	Pct.	FTA	FTM	Pct.	Reb.	Pts.	Avg.
79-80	30	971	274	153	.558	103	77	.748	292	383	12.8
80-81	30	1106	411	235	.572	147	107	.728	370	577	19.2
81-82	27	1042	371	196	.528	164	111	.677	365	503	18.6
Totals	87	3119	1056	584	.553	414	295	.713	1027	1463	16.8

NBA REGULAR SEASON RECORD

Sea.—Team	G.	Min.	FGA	FGM	Pct.	FTA	FTM	Pct.	Off.	Def.	Tot.	Ast.	PF	Dq.	Stl.	Blk.	Pts.	Avg.
82-83—Kansas City	71	987	287	147	.512	137	89	.650	133	242	375	33	186	1	40	61	383	5.4
83-84—Kansas City	80	1915	637	333	.523	223	160	.717	260	449	709	86	327	8	71	145	826	10.3
84-85—Kansas City	82	2458	695	369	.531	315	227	.721	274	580	854	130	328	4	98	128	965	11.8
85-86—Sacramento	80	2377	794	411	.518	276	202	.732	252	518	770	168	295	8	71	109	1024	12.8
86-87—Sacramento	82	2166	752	362	.481	255	188	.737	237	450	687	122	290	6	69	126	912	11.1
87-88—Sacramento	69	1257	456	215	.471	164	118	.720	138	289	427	68	217	1	54	73	550	8.0
Totals	464	11160	3621	1837	.507	1370	984	.718	1294	2528	3822	607	1643	28	403	642	4660	10.0

Three-Point Field Goals: 1982-83, 0-for-1. 1985-86, 0-for-1. 1986-87, 0-for-5. 1987-88, 2-for-5 (.400). Totals, 2-for-12 (.167).

NBA PLAYOFF RECORD

Sea.—Team	G.	Min.	FGA	FGM	Pct.	FTA	FTM	Pct.	Off.	Def.	Tot.	Ast.	PF	Dq.	Stl.	Blk.	Pts.	Avg.
83-84—Kansas City	3	93	40	18	.450	11	9	.818	11	19	30	4	14	0	3	4	45	15.0
85-86—Sacramento	3	99	32	11	.344	12	7	.583	14	21	35	2	8	0	2	6	29	9.7
Totals	6	192	72	29	.403	23	16	.696	25	40	65	6	22	0	5	10	74	12.3

Led NCAA Division I in rebounding, 1982.

—DID YOU KNOW—

That Kareem Abdul-Jabbar was born on the same day (April 16, 1947) that the first NBA championship series game was played? The Philadelphia Warriors defeated the Chicago Stags, 84-71, in Game 1 of the 1947 NBA Finals.

MYCHAL GEORGE THOMPSON

Born January 30, 1955 at Nassau, Bahamas.   Height 6:10.   Weight 235.

High School—Miami, Fla., Jackson.

College—University of Minnesota, Minneapolis, Minn.

Drafted by Portland on first round, 1978 (1st pick).

Missed entire 1979-80 season due to injury.
Traded by Portland with draft rights to Larry Krystkowiak to San Antonio for Steve Johnson, June 19, 1986.
Traded by San Antonio to Los Angeles Lakers for Frank Brickowski, Petur Gudmundsson, a 1987 1st round draft choice, a 1990 2nd round draft choice and cash, February 13, 1987.

—COLLEGIATE RECORD—

Year	G.	Min.	FGA	FGM	Pct.	FTA	FTM	Pct.	Reb.	Pts.	Avg.
74-75	23	....	215	114	.530	78	59	.756	176	287	12.5
75-76	25	....	461	264	.573	171	119	.696	312	647	25.9
76-77	27	....	414	251	.606	132	93	.705	240	595	22.0
77-78	21	....	362	194	.536	119	75	.630	228	463	22.0
Totals	96	....	1452	823	.567	500	346	.692	956	1992	20.8

NBA REGULAR SEASON RECORD

Sea.—Team	G.	Min.	FGA	FGM	Pct.	FTA	FTM	Pct.	Off.	Def.	Tot.	Ast.	PF	Dq.	Stl.	Blk.	Pts.	Avg.
78-79—Portland	73	2144	938	460	.490	269	154	.572	198	406	604	176	270	10	67	134	1074	14.7
80-81—Portland	79	2790	1151	569	.494	323	207	.641	223	463	686	284	260	5	62	170	1345	17.0
81-82—Portland	79	3129	1303	681	.523	446	280	.628	258	663	921	329	233	2	69	107	1642	20.8
82-83—Portland	80	3017	1033	505	.489	401	249	.621	183	570	753	380	213	1	68	110	1259	15.7
83-84—Portland	79	2648	929	487	.524	399	266	.667	235	453	688	308	237	2	84	108	1240	15.7
84-85—Portland	79	2616	1111	572	.515	449	307	.684	211	407	618	205	216	0	78	104	1451	18.4
85-86—Portland	82	2569	1011	503	.498	309	198	.641	181	427	608	176	267	5	76	35	1204	14.7
86-87—S.A.-L.A.L.	82	1890	797	359	.450	297	219	.737	138	274	412	115	202	1	45	71	938	11.4
87-88—L.A. Lakers	80	2007	722	370	.512	292	185	.634	198	291	489	66	251	1	38	79	925	11.6
Totals	713	22810	8995	4506	.501	3185	2065	.648	1825	3954	5779	2029	2149	27	587	918	11078	15.5

Three-Point Field Goals: 1980-81, 0-for-1. 1982-83, 0-for-1. 1983-84, 0-for-2. 1986-87, 1-for-2 (.500). 1987-88, 0-for-3. Totals, 1-for-9 (.111).

NBA PLAYOFF RECORD

Sea.—Team	G.	Min.	FGA	FGM	Pct.	FTA	FTM	Pct.	Off.	Def.	Tot.	Ast.	PF	Dq.	Stl.	Blk.	Pts.	Avg.
78-79—Portland	3	121	54	27	.500	10	5	.500	9	22	31	6	11	0	2	5	59	19.7
80-81—Portland	3	132	51	31	.608	18	13	.722	5	18	23	4	10	0	3	9	75	25.0
82-83—Portland	7	284	85	40	.471	38	25	.658	16	40	56	39	24	0	6	8	105	15.0
83-84—Portland	4	121	44	22	.500	22	17	.773	9	20	29	15	11	0	5	3	61	15.3
84-85—Portland	9	250	102	50	.490	49	33	.673	25	47	72	14	32	2	7	12	133	14.8
85-86—Portland	4	140	54	31	.574	26	14	.538	11	22	33	14	13	0	1	3	76	19.0
86-87—L.A. Lakers	18	401	137	62	.453	50	34	.680	29	59	88	9	50	0	7	17	158	8.8
87-88—L.A. Lakers	24	615	191	98	.513	62	36	.581	63	107	170	12	70	1	17	21	232	9.7
Totals	72	2064	718	361	.503	275	177	.644	167	335	502	113	221	3	48	78	899	12.5

Named to NBA All-Rookie Team, 1979. . . . Member of NBA championship teams, 1987 and 1988. . . . THE SPORTING NEWS All-America First Team, 1978. . . . THE SPORTING NEWS All-America Second Team, 1977.

WILLIAM STANSBURY THOMPSON
(Billy)

Born December 1, 1963 at Camden, N.J.   Height 6:07.   Weight 220.

High School—Camden, N.J.

College—University of Louisville, Louisville, Ky.

Drafted by Atlanta on first round, 1986 (19th pick).

Draft rights traded by Atlanta with draft rights to Ron Kellogg to Los Angeles Lakers for **Mike McGee and draft** rights to Ken Barlow, June 17, 1986.
Selected from Los Angeles Lakers by Miami in NBA expansion draft, June 23, 1988.

—COLLEGIATE RECORD—

Year	G.	Min.	FGA	FGM	Pct.	FTA	FTM	Pct.	Reb.	Pts.	Avg.
82-83	36	710	213	104	.488	81	53	.654	140	261	7.3
83-84	31	877	209	106	.507	98	72	.735	173	284	9.2
84-85	37	1262	427	220	.515	158	118	.747	311	558	15.1
85-86	39	1216	384	221	.576	196	140	.714	304	582	14.9
Totals	143	4065	1233	651	.528	533	383	.719	928	1685	11.8

NBA REGULAR SEASON RECORD

Sea.—Team	G.	Min.	FGA	FGM	Pct.	FTA	FTM	Pct.	Off.	Def.	Tot.	Ast.	PF	Dq.	Stl.	Blk.	Pts.	Avg.
86-87—L.A. Lakers	59	762	261	142	.544	74	48	.649	69	102	171	60	148	1	15	30	332	5.6

Sea.—Team	G.	Min.	FGA	FGM	Pct.	FTA	FTM	Pct.	—Rebounds— Off.	Def.	Tot.	Ast.	PF	Dq.	Stl.	Blk.	Pts.	Avg.
87-88—L.A. Lakers	9	38	13	3	.231	10	8	.800	2	7	9	1	11	0	1	0	14	1.6
Totals	68	800	274	145	.529	84	56	.667	71	109	180	61	159	1	16	30	346	5.1

Three-Point Field Goals: 1986-87, 0-for-1.

NBA PLAYOFF RECORD

Sea.—Team	G.	Min.	FGA	FGM	Pct.	FTA	FTM	Pct.	—Rebounds— Off.	Def.	Tot.	Ast.	PF	Dq.	Stl.	Blk.	Pts.	Avg.
86-87—L.A. Lakers	3	27	11	6	.545	2	2	1.000	3	3	6	2	2	0	4	0	14	4.7

Member of NBA championship teams, 1987 and 1988. . . . Member of NCAA Division I championship team, 1986.

ROBERT GEORGE THORNTON
(Bob)

Born July 10, 1962 at Los Angeles, Calif.   Height 6:10.   Weight 225.

High School—Mission Viejo, Calif.

Colleges—Saddleback Community College, Mission Viejo,
Calif., and University of California at Irvine, Irvine, Calif.

Drafted by New York on fourth round, 1984 (87th pick).

Waived by New York, December 16, 1987; signed by Philadelphia as a free agent, December 19, 1987.
Played in Spanish National League with Madrid Caja, 1984-85.

—COLLEGIATE RECORD—
Saddleback

Year	G.	Min.	FGA	FGM	Pct.	FTA	FTM	Pct.	Reb.	Pts.	Avg.
80-81	28	....	136	70	.515	50	31	.620	149	171	6.1

California-Irvine

Year	G.	Min.	FGA	FGM	Pct.	FTA	FTM	Pct.	Reb.	Pts.	Avg.
81-82	29	452	88	44	.500	45	33	.733	93	121	4.2
82-83	27	639	216	125	.579	117	75	.641	161	325	12.0
83-84	29	817	236	151	.640	118	65	.551	236	367	12.7
Totals	85	1908	540	320	.593	280	173	.618	490	813	9.6

NBA REGULAR SEASON RECORD

Sea.—Team	G.	Min.	FGA	FGM	Pct.	FTA	FTM	Pct.	—Rebounds— Off.	Def.	Tot.	Ast.	PF	Dq.	Stl.	Blk.	Pts.	Avg.
85-86—New York	71	1323	274	125	.456	162	86	.531	113	177	290	43	209	5	30	7	336	4.7
86-87—New York	33	282	67	29	.433	20	13	.650	18	38	56	8	48	0	4	3	71	2.2
87-88—N.Y.-Phil.	48	593	130	65	.500	55	34	.618	46	66	112	15	103	1	11	3	164	3.4
Totals	152	2198	471	219	.465	237	133	.561	177	281	458	66	360	6	45	13	571	3.8

Three-Point Field Goals: 1986-87, 0-for-1. 1987-88, 0-for-2. Totals, 0-for-3.

OTIS THORPE

Born August 5, 1962 at Boynton Beach, Fla.   Height 6:11.   Weight 236.

High School—Lake Worth, Fla.

College—Providence College, Providence, R.I.

Drafted by Kansas City on first round, 1984 (9th pick).

—COLLEGIATE RECORD—

Year	G.	Min.	FGA	FGM	Pct.	FTA	FTM	Pct.	Reb.	Pts.	Avg.
80-81	26	668	194	100	.515	76	50	.658	137	250	9.6
81-82	27	942	283	153	.541	115	74	.643	216	380	14.1
82-83	31	1041	321	204	.636	138	91	.659	249	499	16.1
83-84	29	1051	288	167	.580	248	162	.653	300	496	17.1
Totals	113	3702	1086	624	.575	577	377	.653	902	1625	14.4

NBA REGULAR SEASON RECORD

Sea.—Team	G.	Min.	FGA	FGM	Pct.	FTA	FTM	Pct.	—Rebounds— Off.	Def.	Tot.	Ast.	PF	Dq.	Stl.	Blk.	Pts.	Avg.
84-85—Kansas City	82	1918	685	411	.600	371	230	.620	187	369	556	111	256	2	34	37	1052	12.8
85-86—Sacramento	75	1675	492	289	.587	248	164	.661	137	283	420	84	233	3	35	34	742	9.9
86-87—Sacramento	82	2956	1050	567	.540	543	413	.761	259	560	819	201	292	11	46	60	1547	18.9
87-88—Sacramento	82	3072	1226	622	.507	609	460	.755	279	558	837	266	264	3	62	56	1704	20.8
Totals	321	9621	3453	1889	.547	1771	1267	.715	862	1770	2632	662	1045	19	177	187	5045	15.7

Three-Point Field Goals: 1984-85, 0-for-2. 1986-87, 0-for-3. 1987-88, 0-for-6. Totals, 0-for-11.

NBA PLAYOFF RECORD

Sea.—Team	G.	Min.	FGA	FGM	Pct.	FTA	FTM	Pct.	—Rebounds— Off.	Def.	Tot.	Ast.	PF	Dq.	Stl.	Blk.	Pts.	Avg.
85-86—Sacramento	3	35	13	3	.231	13	6	.462	8	4	12	0	4	0	0	1	12	4.0

SEDALE EUGENE THREATT

Born September 10, 1961, at Atlanta, Ga.   Height 6:02.   Weight 177.
High School—Atlanta, Ga., Therrell.
College—West Virginia Institute of Technology, Montgomery, W. Va.
Drafted by Philadelphia on sixth round, 1983 (139th pick).

Traded by Philadelphia to Chicago for Steve Colter and a future 2nd round draft choice, December 31, 1986.
Traded by Chicago to Seattle for Sam Vincent, February 25, 1988.

—COLLEGIATE RECORD—

Year	G.	Min.	FGA	FGM	Pct.	FTA	FTM	Pct.	Reb.	Pts.	Avg.
79-80	28	....	424	204	.481	126	90	.714	97	498	17.8
80-81	31	....	524	237	.452	104	74	.712	122	548	17.7
81-82	34	....	598	299	.500	214	156	.729	118	754	22.2
82-83	27	951	510	284	.557	164	120	.732	104	688	25.5
Totals	120	....	2056	1024	.498	608	440	.724	441	2488	20.7

NBA REGULAR SEASON RECORD

Sea.—Team	G.	Min.	FGA	FGM	Pct.	FTA	FTM	Pct.	Off.	Def.	Tot.	Ast.	PF	Dq.	Stl.	Blk.	Pts.	Avg.
										—Rebounds—								
83-84—Philadelphia	45	464	148	62	.419	28	23	.821	17	23	40	41	65	1	13	2	148	3.3
84-85—Philadelphia	82	1304	416	188	.452	90	66	.733	21	78	99	175	171	2	80	16	446	5.4
85-86—Philadelphia	70	1754	684	310	.453	90	75	.833	21	100	121	193	157	1	93	5	696	9.9
86-87—Phil.-Chi.	68	1446	534	239	.448	119	95	.798	26	82	108	259	164	0	74	13	580	8.5
87-88—Chi.-Sea.	71	1055	425	216	.508	71	57	.803	23	65	88	160	100	0	60	8	492	6.9
Totals	336	6023	2207	1015	.460	398	316	.794	108	348	456	828	657	4	320	44	2362	7.1

Three-Point Field Goals: 1983-84, 1-for-8 (.125). 1984-85, 4-for-22 (.182). 1985-86, 1-for-24 (.042). 1986-87, 7-for-32 (.219). 1987-88, 3-for-27 (.111). Totals, 16-for-113 (.142).

NBA PLAYOFF RECORD

Sea.—Team	G.	Min.	FGA	FGM	Pct.	FTA	FTM	Pct.	Off.	Def.	Tot.	Ast.	PF	Dq.	Stl.	Blk.	Pts.	Avg.
										—Rebounds—								
83-84—Philadelphia	3	6	3	1	.333	0	0	.000	1	1	2	1	0	0	1	0	2	0.7
84-85—Philadelphia	4	28	7	2	.286	0	0	.000	1	0	1	5	2	0	1	0	4	1.0
85-86—Philadelphia	12	312	143	67	.469	33	26	.788	6	19	25	42	35	0	23	2	160	13.3
86-87—Chicago	3	70	17	8	.471	4	4	1.000	2	3	5	16	11	0	1	0	20	6.7
87-88—Seattle	5	80	34	14	.412	4	4	1.000	2	9	11	11	7	0	1	0	32	6.4
Totals	27	496	204	92	.451	41	34	.829	12	32	44	75	55	0	27	2	218	8.1

Three-Point Field Goals: 1983-84, 0-for-2. 1985-86, 0-for-2. 1987-88, 0-for-1. Totals, 0-for-5.

WAYMAN LAWRENCE TISDALE

Born June 9, 1964 at Tulsa, Okla.   Height 6:09.   Weight 240.
High School—Tulsa, Okla., Washington.
College—University of Oklahoma, Norman, Okla.
Drafted by Indiana on first round as an undergraduate, 1985 (2nd pick).

—COLLEGIATE RECORD—

Year	G.	Min.	FGA	FGM	Pct.	FTA	FTM	Pct.	Reb.	Pts.	Avg.
82-83	33	1138	583	338	.580	211	134	.635	341	810	24.5
83-84	34	1232	639	369	.577	283	181	.640	329	919	27.0
84-85	37	1283	640	370	.578	273	192	.703	378	932	25.2
Totals	104	3653	1862	1077	.578	767	507	.661	1048	2661	25.6

NBA REGULAR SEASON RECORD

Sea.—Team	G.	Min.	FGA	FGM	Pct.	FTA	FTM	Pct.	Off.	Def.	Tot.	Ast.	PF	Dq.	Stl.	Blk.	Pts.	Avg.
										—Rebounds—								
85-86—Indiana	81	2277	1002	516	.515	234	160	.684	191	393	584	79	290	3	32	44	1192	14.7
86-87—Indiana	81	2159	892	458	.513	364	258	.709	217	258	475	117	293	9	50	26	1174	14.5
87-88—Indiana	79	2378	998	511	.512	314	246	.783	168	323	491	103	274	5	54	34	1268	16.1
Totals	241	6814	2892	1485	.513	912	664	.728	576	974	1550	299	857	17	136	104	3634	15.1

Three-Point Field Goals: 1985-86, 0-for-2. 1986-87, 0-for-2. 1987-88, 0-for-2. Totals 0-for-6.

NBA PLAYOFF RECORD

Sea.—Team	G.	Min.	FGA	FGM	Pct.	FTA	FTM	Pct.	Off.	Def.	Tot.	Ast.	PF	Dq.	Stl.	Blk.	Pts.	Avg.
										—Rebounds—								
86-87—Indiana	4	108	31	19	.613	23	13	.565	5	11	16	9	17	1	1	0	51	12.8

Member of U.S. Olympic team, 1984. . . . Named to THE SPORTING NEWS All-America First Team, 1984 and 1985. . . . THE SPORTING NEWS All-America Second Team, 1983.

WAYMAN TISDALE

RAYMOND L. TOLBERT
(Ray)

Born September 10, 1958 at Anderson, Ind.   Height 6:09.   Weight 225.

High School—Anderson, Ind., Madison Heights.

College—Indiana University, Bloomington, Ind.

Drafted by New Jersey on first round, 1981 (18th pick).

Traded by New Jersey to Seattle for James Bailey, November 25, 1981.
Traded by Seattle in a three-way deal to Detroit, February 13, 1983. Atlanta traded Steve Hawes to Seattle and Detroit traded two second-round draft choices (1984 and 1985) to Atlanta.
Waived by Detroit, October 23, 1984; signed by New York as a free agent, October 9, 1987.
Waived by New York, December 9, 1987; signed by Los Angeles Lakers as a free agent, December 12, 1987.
Waived by Los Angeles Lakers, March 14, 1988.
Played in Continental Basketball Association with Tampa Bay Thrillers and Bay State Bombardiers, 1985-86, and Pensacola Tornados and LaCrosse Catbirds, 1986-87.

—COLLEGIATE RECORD—

Year	G.	Min.	FGA	FGM	Pct.	FTA	FTM	Pct.	Reb.	Pts.	Avg.
77-78	29	....	269	121	.450	77	50	.649	201	292	10.1
78-79	34	....	309	168	.544	102	71	.696	241	407	12.0
79-80	29	....	241	127	.527	75	46	.613	208	300	10.3
80-81	35	....	301	177	.588	100	74	.740	224	428	12.2
Totals	127	....	1120	593	.529	354	241	.681	874	1427	11.2

CBA REGULAR SEASON RECORD

Sea.—Team	G.	Min.	2-Point			3-Point			FTM	FTA	Pct.	Reb.	Ast.	Pts.	Avg.
			FGM	FGA	Pct.	FGM	FGA	Pct.							
85-86—Tampa Bay-Bay St...	49	1291	228	383	.595	0	2	.000	95	144	.659	359	63	551	11.2
86-87—Pensacola-LaCrosse	33	1073	212	397	.534	0	0	.....	114	156	.730	228	75	538	16.3
Totals	82	2364	440	780	.564	0	2	.000	209	300	.696	587	138	1089	13.3

NBA REGULAR SEASON RECORD

Sea.—Team	G.	Min.	FGA	FGM	Pct.	FTA	FTM	Pct.	Off.	Def.	Tot.	Ast.	PF	Dq.	Stl.	Blk.	Pts.	Avg.
									—Rebounds—									
81-82—N.J.-Sea.	64	607	202	100	.495	35	19	.543	50	76	126	33	83	0	12	16	219	3.4
82-83—Sea.-Det.	73	1107	314	157	.500	103	52	.505	72	170	242	50	153	1	26	47	366	5.0
83-84—Detroit	49	475	121	64	.529	45	23	.511	45	53	98	26	88	1	12	20	151	3.1
87-88—N.Y.-L.A.L.	25	259	69	35	.507	30	19	.633	23	32	55	10	39	0	8	5	89	3.6
Totals	211	2448	706	356	.504	213	113	.531	190	331	521	110	363	2	58	88	825	3.9

Three-Point Field Goals: 1981-82, 0-for-2. 1982-83, 0-for-3. 1983-84, 0-for-1. Totals, 0-for-6.

NBA PLAYOFF RECORD

Sea.—Team	G.	Min.	FGA	FGM	Pct.	FTA	FTM	Pct.	Off.	Def.	Tot.	Ast.	PF	Dq.	Stl.	Blk.	Pts.	Avg.
									—Rebounds—									
81-82—Seattle	4	31	5	3	.600	8	4	.500	1	4	5	1	7	0	4	0	10	2.5

Named to CBA All-Defensive Second Team, 1986. . . . Member of NCAA Division I championship team, 1981.

ANDREW TONEY

Born November 23, 1957 at Birmingham, Ala.   Height 6:03.   Weight 190.

High School—Birmingham, Ala., Glenn.

College—University of Southwestern Louisiana, Lafayette, La.

Drafted by Philadelphia on first round, 1980 (8th pick).

—COLLEGIATE RECORD—

Year	G.	Min.	FGA	FGM	Pct.	FTA	FTM	Pct.	Reb.	Pts.	Avg.
76-77	29	933	489	253	.517	133	102	.767	89	608	21.0
77-78	27	885	468	262	.560	179	137	.765	71	661	24.5
78-79	27	900	500	242	.484	193	146	.756	90	630	23.3
79-80	24	809	425	239	.562	185	149	.805	90	627	26.1
Totals	107	3527	1882	996	.529	690	534	.774	340	2526	23.6

NBA REGULAR SEASON RECORD

Sea.—Team	G.	Min.	FGA	FGM	Pct.	FTA	FTM	Pct.	Off.	Def.	Tot.	Ast.	PF	Dq.	Stl.	Blk.	Pts.	Avg.
									—Rebounds—									
80-81—Philadelphia	75	1768	806	399	.495	226	161	.712	32	111	143	273	234	5	59	10	968	12.9
81-82—Philadelphia	77	1909	979	511	.522	306	227	.742	43	91	134	283	269	5	64	17	1274	16.5
82-83—Philadelphia	81	2474	1250	626	.501	411	324	.788	42	183	225	365	255	0	80	17	1598	19.7
83-84—Philadelphia	78	2556	1125	593	.527	465	390	.839	57	136	193	373	251	1	70	23	1588	20.4
84-85—Philadelphia	70	2237	914	450	.492	355	306	.862	35	142	177	363	211	1	65	24	1245	17.8
85-86—Philadelphia	6	84	36	11	.306	8	3	.375	2	3	5	12	8	0	2	0	25	4.2
86-87—Philadelphia	52	1058	437	197	.451	167	133	.796	16	69	85	188	78	0	18	8	549	10.6
87-88—Philadelphia	29	522	171	72	.421	72	58	.806	8	39	47	108	35	0	11	6	211	7.3
Totals	468	12608	5718	2859	.500	2010	1602	.797	235	774	1009	1965	1341	12	369	105	7458	15.9

Three-Point Field Goals: 1980-81, 9-for-29 (.310). 1981-82, 25-for-59 (.424). 1982-83, 22-for-76 (.289). 1983-84, 12-for-38 (.316). 1984-85, 39-for-105 (.371). 1985-86, 0-for-2. 1986-87, 22-for-67 (.328). 1987-88, 9-for-27 (.333). Totals, 138-for-403 (.342).

NBA PLAYOFF RECORD

Sea.—Team	G.	Min.	FGA	FGM	Pct.	FTA	FTM	Pct.	Off.	Def.	Tot.	Ast.	PF	Dq.	Stl.	Blk.	Pts.	Avg.
									—Rebounds—									
80-81—Philadelphia	16	356	180	77	.428	81	66	.815	10	27	37	54	50	0	11	7	221	13.8
81-82—Philadelphia	21	707	365	185	.507	103	82	.796	20	31	51	102	86	1	18	2	457	21.8
82-83—Philadelphia	12	357	185	87	.470	69	52	.754	11	17	28	55	43	1	11	1	226	18.8
83-84—Philadelphia	5	180	77	40	.519	30	23	.767	5	6	11	19	24	0	4	1	103	20.6
84-85—Philadelphia	13	442	174	83	.477	61	47	.770	8	24	32	66	46	0	12	5	219	16.8
86-87—Philadelphia	5	104	34	13	.382	2	2	1.000	2	7	9	27	16	1	2	2	28	5.6
Totals	72	2146	1015	485	.478	346	272	.786	56	112	168	323	265	3	58	18	1254	17.4

Three-Point Field Goals: 1980-81, 1-for-9 (.111). 1981-82, 5-for-15 (.333). 1982-83, 0-for-5. 1983-84, 0-for-5. 1984-85, 6-for-14 (.429). 1986-87, 0-for-3. Totals, 12-for-51 (.235).

NBA ALL-STAR GAME RECORD

Season—Team	Min.	FGA	FGM	Pct.	FTA	FTM	Pct.	Off.	Def.	Tot.	Ast.	PF	Dq.	Stl.	Blk.	Pts.
								—Rebounds—								
1983—Philadelphia	18	5	4	.800	0	0	.000	0	1	1	7	3	0	2	0	8
1984—Philadelphia	22	11	6	.545	1	1	1.000	0	0	0	3	0	0	2	0	13
Totals	40	16	10	.625	1	1	1.000	0	1	1	10	3	0	4	0	21

Three-Point Field Goals: 1982-83, 0-for-1.

Member of NBA championship team, 1983.

SEDRIC ANDRE TONEY

Born April 13, 1962 at Columbus, Miss.   Height 6:02.   Weight 178.

High School—Dayton, O., Wilbur Wright.

Colleges—Nebraska Western Junior College, Scottsbluff, Neb. and University of Dayton, Dayton, O.

Drafted by Atlanta on third round, 1985 (59th pick).

Waived by Atlanta, November 4, 1985; signed by Phoenix as a free agent, March 29, 1986.
Waived by Phoenix, October 23, 1986; signed by Denver as a free agent, October 7, 1987.
Waived by Denver, October 29, 1987; signed by New York, March 13, 1988, to a 10-day contract that expired, March 22, 1988.
Re-signed by New York, March 23, 1988, for remainder of season.
Selected from New York by Charlotte in NBA expansion draft, June 23, 1988.
Played in Continental Basketball Association with Cincinnati Slammers, 1985-86, and LaCrosse Catbirds and Cincinnati Slammers, 1986-87.

—COLLEGIATE RECORD—

Year	G.	Min.	FGA	FGM	Pct.	FTA	FTM	Pct.	Reb.	Pts.	Avg.
83-84	32	963	295	150	.508	108	72	.667	79	372	11.6
84-85	27	834	274	130	.474	115	90	.783	78	350	13.0
Totals	59	1797	569	280	.492	223	162	.726	157	722	12.3

CBA REGULAR SEASON RECORD

Sea.—Team	G.	Min.	2-Point			3-Point			FTM	FTA	Pct.	Reb.	Ast.	Pts.	Avg.
			FGM	FGA	Pct.	FGM	FGA	Pct.							
85-86—Cincinnati	48	989	169	337	.501	1	4	.250	146	186	.784	63	138	487	10.1
86-87—LaCrosse-Cincinnati	32	605	78	181	.430	7	27	.259	64	89	.719	39	96	241	7.5
Totals	80	1594	247	518	.476	8	31	.258	210	275	.763	102	234	728	9.1

NBA REGULAR SEASON RECORD

Sea.—Team	G.	Min.	FGA	FGM	Pct.	FTA	FTM	Pct.	Off.	Def.	Tot.	Ast.	PF	Dq.	Stl.	Blk.	Pts.	Avg.
									—Rebounds—									
85-86—Atl.-Phoe.	13	230	66	28	.424	31	21	.677	3	22	25	26	24	0	6	0	80	6.2
87-88—New York	21	139	48	21	.438	11	10	.909	3	5	8	24	20	0	9	1	57	2.7
Totals	34	369	114	49	.430	42	31	.738	6	27	33	50	44	0	15	1	137	4.0

Three-Point Field Goals: 1985-86, 3-for-10 (.300). 1987-88, 5-for-14 (.357). Totals, 8-for-24 (.333).

NBA PLAYOFF RECORD

Sea.—Team	G.	Min.	FGA	FGM	Pct.	FTA	FTM	Pct.	Off.	Def.	Tot.	Ast.	PF	Dq.	Stl.	Blk.	Pts.	Avg.
									—Rebounds—									
87-88—New York	3	15	6	3	.500	2	2	1.000	0	0	0	2	4	0	1	0	11	3.7

Three-Point Field Goals: 1987-88, 3-for-6 (.500).

—DID YOU KNOW—

That veteran NBA standouts Larry Nance (3.1 points per game for Clemson), Kiki Vandeweghe (3.6 ppg for UCLA), Maurice Cheeks (3.9 ppg for West Texas State) and Orlando Woolridge (4.1 ppg for Notre Dame) each averaged less than five points per game as college freshmen?

PETER KELLY TRIPUCKA
(Known by middle name.)

Born February 16, 1959 at Glen Ridge, N. J.   Height 6:06.   Weight 225.

High School—Bloomfield, N. J.

College—University of Notre Dame, Notre Dame, Ind.

Drafted by Detroit on first round, 1981 (12th pick).

Traded by Detroit with Kent Benson to Utah for Adrian Dantley and 1987 and 1990 2nd round draft choices, August 21, 1986.

Traded by Utah to Charlotte for Mike Brown, June 23, 1988.

—COLLEGIATE RECORD—

Year	G.	Min.	FGA	FGM	Pct.	FTA	FTM	Pct.	Reb.	Pts.	Avg.
77-78	31	643	247	141	.571	108	80	.741	161	362	11.7
78-79	29	807	277	143	.516	151	129	.854	125	415	14.3
79-80	23	691	270	150	.556	151	115	.762	151	415	18.0
80-81	29	919	354	195	.551	168	137	.815	169	527	18.2
Totals	112	3060	1148	629	.548	578	461	.798	606	1719	15.3

NBA REGULAR SEASON RECORD

Sea.—Team	G.	Min.	FGA	FGM	Pct.	FTA	FTM	Pct.	Off.	Def.	Tot.	Ast.	PF	Dq.	Stl.	Blk.	Pts.	Avg.
81-82—Detroit	82	3077	1281	636	.496	621	495	.797	219	224	443	270	241	0	89	16	1772	21.6
82-83—Detroit	58	2252	1156	565	.489	464	392	.845	126	138	264	237	157	0	67	20	1536	26.5
83-84—Detroit	76	2493	1296	595	.459	523	426	.815	119	187	306	228	190	0	65	17	1618	21.3
84-85—Detroit	55	1675	831	396	.477	288	255	.885	66	152	218	135	118	1	49	14	1049	19.1
85-86—Detroit	81	2626	1236	615	.498	444	380	.856	116	232	348	265	167	0	93	10	1622	20.0
86-87—Utah	79	1865	621	291	.469	226	197	.872	54	188	242	243	147	0	85	11	798	10.1
87-88—Utah	49	976	303	139	.459	68	59	.868	30	87	117	105*	68	1	34	4	368	7.5
Totals	480	14964	6724	3237	.481	2634	2204	.837	730	1208	1938	1483	1088	2	482	92	8763	18.3

Three-Point Field Goals: 1981-82, 5-for-22 (.227). 1982-83, 14-for-37 (.378). 1983-84, 2-for-17 (.118). 1984-85, 2-for-5 (.400). 1985-86, 12-for-25 (.480). 1986-87, 19-for-52 (.365). 1987-88, 31-for-74 (.419). Totals, 85-for-232 (.366).

NBA PLAYOFF RECORD

Sea.—Team	G.	Min.	FGA	FGM	Pct.	FTA	FTM	Pct.	Off.	Def.	Tot.	Ast.	PF	Dq.	Stl.	Blk.	Pts.	Avg.
83-84—Detroit	5	208	102	48	.471	51	41	.804	10	13	23	15	22	1	11	0	137	27.4
84-85—Detroit	9	288	118	49	.415	40	35	.875	19	20	39	29	22	0	4	3	133	14.8
85-86—Detroit	4	175	71	33	.465	23	21	.913	10	13	23	9	14	1	3	2	87	21.8
86-87—Utah	5	70	20	14	.700	4	4	1.000	1	6	7	3	6	0	4	0	32	6.4
87-88—Utah	2	9	3	1	.333	0	0	.000	1	0	1	1	1	0	0	0	2	1.0
Totals	25	750	314	145	.462	118	101	.856	41	52	93	57	65	2	22	5	391	15.6

Three-Point Field Goals: 1983-84, 0-for-1. 1984-85, 0-for-1. 1986-87, 0-for-3. Totals, 0-for-5.

NBA ALL-STAR GAME RECORD

Season—Team	Min.	FGA	FGM	Pct.	FTA	FTM	Pct.	Off.	Def.	Tot.	Ast.	PF	Dq.	Stl.	Blk.	Pts.
1982—Detroit	15	7	3	.429	0	0	.000	0	1	1	2	0	0	0	0	6
1984—Detroit	6	0	0	.000	2	1	.500	0	0	0	2	1	0	1	0	1
Totals	21	7	3	.429	2	1	.500	0	1	1	4	1	0	1	0	7

Named to NBA All-Rookie Team, 1982.

KELVIN TRENT TUCKER
(Known by middle name.)

Born December 20, 1959 at Tarboro, N. C.   Height 6:05.   Weight 193.

High School—Flint, Mich., Northwestern.

College—University of Minnesota, Minneapolis, Minn.

Drafted by New York on first round, 1982 (6th pick).

—COLLEGIATE RECORD—

Year	G.	Min.	FGA	FGM	Pct.	FTA	FTM	Pct.	Reb.	Pts.	Avg.
78-79	25	....	239	114	.477	32	19	.594	85	247	9.9
79-80	32	....	310	152	.490	46	34	.739	103	338	10.6
80-81	29	....	362	187	.517	69	56	.812	102	430	14.8
81-82	29	....	353	178	.504	90	74	.822	103	430	14.8
Totals	115	....	1264	631	.499	237	183	.772	393	1445	12.6

NBA REGULAR SEASON RECORD

Sea.—Team	G.	Min.	FGA	FGM	Pct.	FTA	FTM	Pct.	Off.	Def.	Tot.	Ast.	PF	Dq.	Stl.	Blk.	Pts.	Avg.
82-83—New York	78	1830	647	299	.462	64	43	.672	75	141	216	195	235	1	56	6	655	8.4
83-84—New York	63	1228	450	225	.500	33	25	.758	43	87	130	138	124	0	63	8	481	7.6

Sea.—Team	G.	Min.	FGA	FGM	Pct.	FTA	FTM	Pct.	—Rebounds— Off.	Def.	Tot.	Ast.	PF	Dq.	Stl.	Blk.	Pts.	Avg.
84-85—New York	77	1819	606	293	.483	48	38	.792	74	114	188	199	195	0	75	15	653	8.5
85-86—New York	77	1788	740	349	.472	100	79	.790	70	99	169	192	167	0	65	8	818	10.6
86-87—New York	70	1691	691	325	.470	101	77	.762	49	86	135	166	169	1	116	13	795	11.4
87-88—New York	71	1248	455	193	.424	71	51	.718	32	87	119	117	158	3	53	6	506	7.1
Totals	436	9604	3589	1684	.469	417	313	.751	343	614	957	1007	1048	5	428	56	3908	9.0

Three-Point Field Goals: 1982-83, 14-for-30 (.467). 1983-84, 6-for-16 (.375). 1984-85, 29-for-72 (.403). 1985-86, 41-for-91 (.451). 1986-87, 68-for-161 (.422). 1987-88, 69-for-167 (.413). Totals, 227-for-537 (.423).

NBA PLAYOFF RECORD

Sea.—Team	G.	Min.	FGA	FGM	Pct.	FTA	FTM	Pct.	—Rebounds— Off.	Def.	Tot.	Ast.	PF	Dq.	Stl.	Blk.	Pts.	Avg.
82-83—New York	6	85	15	9	.600	10	7	.700	2	7	9	5	7	0	2	0	26	4.3
83-84—New York	12	254	84	42	.500	10	6	.600	6	12	18	27	32	0	11	3	91	7.6
87-88—New York	4	71	19	8	.421	4	3	.750	0	2	2	4	4	0	3	0	25	6.3
Totals	22	410	118	59	.500	24	16	.667	8	21	29	36	43	0	16	3	142	6.5

Three-Point Field Goals: 1982-83, 1-for-2 (.500). 1983-84, 1-for-5 (.200). 1987-88, 6-for-13 (.462). Totals, 8-for-20 (.400).

Named to THE SPORTING NEWS All-America First Team, 1982.

ANDRE TURNER

Born December 13, 1964 at Memphis, Tenn.   Height 5:11.   Weight 160.

High School—Memphis, Tenn., Mitchell.

College—Memphis State University, Memphis, Tenn.

Drafted by Los Angeles Lakers on third round, 1986 (69th pick).

Waived by Los Angeles Lakers, October 28, 1986; signed by Boston as a free agent, November 6, 1986.
Waived by Boston, November 25, 1986; signed by Houston as a free agent, October 9, 1987.
Selected from Houston by Miami in NBA expansion draft, June 23, 1988.
Played in Continental Basketball Association with Rockford Lightning and LaCrosse Catbirds, 1986-87.

—COLLEGIATE RECORD—

Year	G.	Min.	FGA	FGM	Pct.	FTA	FTM	Pct.	Reb.	Pts.	Avg.
82-83	31	1006	245	127	.518	67	54	.806	35	308	9.9
83-84	33	1052	234	107	.457	87	58	.667	45	272	8.2
84-85	34	1157	309	154	.498	112	80	.714	79	388	11.4
85-86	34	1137	410	196	.478	96	82	.854	67	474	13.9
Totals	132	4352	1198	584	.487	362	274	.757	226	1442	10.9

CBA REGULAR SEASON RECORD

Sea.—Team	G.	Min.	—2-Point— FGM	FGA	Pct.	—3-Point— FGM	FGA	Pct.	FTM	FTA	Pct.	Reb.	Ast.	Pts.	Avg.
86-87—Rock.-LaCrosse	47	1329	228	475	.480	5	35	.143	117	142	.824	110	240	588	12.5

NBA REGULAR SEASON RECORD

Sea.—Team	G.	Min.	FGA	FGM	Pct.	FTA	FTM	Pct.	—Rebounds— Off.	Def.	Tot.	Ast.	PF	Dq.	Stl.	Blk.	Pts.	Avg.
86-87—Boston	3	18	5	2	.400	0	0	.000	1	1	2	1	1	0	0	0	4	1.3
87-88—Houston	12	99	34	12	.353	14	10	.714	4	4	8	23	13	0	7	1	35	2.9
Totals	15	117	39	14	.359	14	10	.714	5	5	10	24	14	0	7	1	39	2.6

Three-Point Field Goals: 1986-87, 0-for-1. 1987-88, 1-for-7 (.143). Totals, 1-for-8 (.125).

ELSTON HOWARD TURNER

Born June 10, 1959 at Knoxville, Tenn.   Height 6:05.   Weight 200.

High School—Knoxville, Tenn., Austin-East.

College—University of Mississippi, University, Miss.

Drafted by Dallas on second round, 1981 (43rd pick).

Signed by Denver as a Veteran Free Agent, August 3, 1984; Dallas agreed not to exercise its right of first refusal in exchange for Howard Carter.
Signed by Chicago as a Veteran Free Agent, October 4, 1986; Denver agreed not to exercise its right of first refusal in exchange for a 1988 2nd round draft choice.
Played in Continental Basketball Association with Rockford Lightning, 1987-88.

—COLLEGIATE RECORD—

Year	G.	Min.	FGA	FGM	Pct.	FTA	FTM	Pct.	Reb.	Pts.	Avg.
77-78	27	936	268	113	.422	65	43	.662	210	269	10.0
78-79	27	1035	366	183	.500	83	64	.771	173	430	15.9
79-80	30	1070	388	212	.546	110	84	.764	209	508	16.9
80-81	29	1068	473	246	.520	161	106	.658	236	598	20.6
Totals	113	4109	1495	754	.504	419	297	.709	828	1805	16.0

CBA REGULAR SEASON RECORD

Sea.—Team	G.	Min.	2-Point FGM	FGA	Pct.	3-Point FGM	FGA	Pct.	FTM	FTA	Pct.	Reb.	Ast.	Pts.	Avg.
87-88—Rockford	24	782	117	258	.453	8	25	.320	46	68	.676	124	78	304	12.7

NBA REGULAR SEASON RECORD

Sea.—Team	G.	Min.	FGA	FGM	Pct.	FTA	FTM	Pct.	Off.	Def.	Tot.	Ast.	PF	Dq.	Stl.	Blk.	Pts.	Avg.
81-82—Dallas	80	1996	639	282	.441	138	97	.703	143	158	301	189	182	1	75	2	661	8.3
82-83—Dallas	59	879	238	96	.403	30	20	.667	68	84	152	88	75	0	47	0	214	3.6
83-84—Dallas	47	536	150	54	.360	34	28	.824	42	51	93	59	40	0	26	0	137	2.9
84-85—Denver	81	1491	388	181	.466	65	51	.785	88	128	216	158	152	0	96	7	414	5.1
85-86—Denver	73	1324	379	165	.435	53	39	.736	64	137	201	165	150	1	70	6	369	5.1
86-87—Chicago	70	936	252	112	.444	31	23	.742	34	81	115	102	97	1	30	4	248	3.5
87-88—Chicago	17	98	30	8	.267	2	1	.500	8	2	10	9	5	0	8	0	17	1.0
Totals	427	7260	2076	898	.433	353	259	.734	447	641	1088	770	701	3	352	19	2060	4.8

Three-Point Field Goals: 1981-82, 0-for-4. 1982-83, 2-for-3 (.667). 1983-84, 1-for-9 (.111). 1984-85, 1-for-6 (.167). 1985-86, 0-for-9. 1986-87, 1-for-8 (.125). Totals, 5-for-39 (.128).

NBA PLAYOFF RECORD

Sea.—Team	G.	Min.	FGA	FGM	Pct.	FTA	FTM	Pct.	Off.	Def.	Tot.	Ast.	PF	Dq.	Stl.	Blk.	Pts.	Avg.
83-84—Dallas	8	53	20	7	.350	0	0	.000	5	5	10	8	4	0	6	1	14	1.8
84-85—Denver	15	358	102	50	.490	19	12	.632	30	43	73	46	42	0	17	1	114	7.6
85-86—Denver	10	196	54	29	.537	8	7	.875	12	17	29	22	19	1	7	0	66	6.6
86-87—Chicago	3	25	5	4	.800	0	0	.000	1	1	2	1	3	0	2	0	8	2.7
87-88—Chicago	4	29	6	1	.167	0	0	.000	1	4	5	6	2	0	0	0	2	0.5
Totals	40	661	187	91	.487	27	19	.704	49	70	119	83	70	1	32	2	204	5.1

Three-Point Field Goals: 1984-85, 2-for-2 (1.000). 1985-86, 1-for-1 (1.000). Totals, 3-for-3 (1.000).

MELVIN HARRISON TURPIN

Born December 28, 1960 at Lexington, Ky.   Height 6:11.   Weight 240.

High School—Lexington, Ky., Bryan Station.

Prep School—Fork Union Military Academy, Fork Union, Va.

College—University of Kentucky, Lexington, Ky.

Drafted by Washington on first round, 1984 (6th pick).

Draft rights traded by Washington to Cleveland for Cliff Robinson, the draft rights to Tim McCormick and cash, June 19, 1984.

Traded by Cleveland with Darryl Dawkins and future 2nd round draft considerations to Utah for Kent Benson, Dell Curry and future 2nd round draft considerations, October 8, 1987.

—COLLEGIATE RECORD—

Year	G.	Min.	FGA	FGM	Pct.	FTA	FTM	Pct.	Reb.	Pts.	Avg.
80-81	28	380	95	50	.526	44	31	.705	106	131	4.7
81-82	30	912	275	160	.582	106	72	.679	212	392	13.1
82-83	31	962	311	192	.617	125	84	.672	195	468	15.1
83-84	34	1071	378	224	.593	94	70	.745	217	518	15.2
Totals	123	3325	1059	626	.591	369	257	.696	730	1509	12.3

NBA REGULAR SEASON RECORD

Sea.—Team	G.	Min.	FGA	FGM	Pct.	FTA	FTM	Pct.	Off.	Def.	Tot.	Ast.	PF	Dq.	Stl.	Blk.	Pts.	Avg.
84-85—Cleveland	79	1949	711	363	.511	139	109	.784	155	297	452	36	211	3	38	87	835	10.6
85-86—Cleveland	80	2292	838	456	.544	228	185	.811	182	374	556	55	260	6	65	106	1097	13.7
86-87—Cleveland	64	801	366	169	.462	77	55	.714	62	128	190	33	90	1	11	40	393	6.1
87-88—Utah	79	1011	389	199	.512	98	71	.724	88	148	236	32	157	2	26	68	470	5.9
Totals	302	6053	2304	1187	.515	542	420	.775	487	947	1434	156	718	12	140	301	2795	9.3

Three-Point Field Goals: 1985-86, 0-for-4. 1987-88, 1-for-3 (.333). Totals, 1-for-7 (.143).

NBA PLAYOFF RECORD

Sea.—Team	G.	Min.	FGA	FGM	Pct.	FTA	FTM	Pct.	Off.	Def.	Tot.	Ast.	PF	Dq.	Stl.	Blk.	Pts.	Avg.
84-85—Cleveland	4	45	19	12	.632	2	1	.500	3	5	8	0	3	0	4	1	25	6.3
87-88—Utah	7	31	9	3	.333	2	2	1.000	3	3	6	2	5	0	1	4	8	1.1
Totals	11	76	28	15	.536	4	3	.750	6	8	14	2	8	0	5	5	33	3.0

TERRY CHRISTOPHER TYLER

Born October 30, 1956 at Detroit, Mich.   Height 6:07.   Weight 228.

High School—Detroit, Mich., Northwestern.

College—University of Detroit, Detroit, Mich.

Drafted by Detroit on second round, 1978 (23rd pick).

Signed by Sacramento as a Veteran Free Agent, November 18, 1985; Detroit agreed not to exercise its right of first refusal in exchange for a 1987 2nd round draft choice, the right to switch 1986 1st round draft positions and cash.

—COLLEGIATE RECORD—

Year	G.	Min.	FGA	FGM	Pct.	FTA	FTM	Pct.	Reb.	Pts.	Avg.
74-75	26	629	184	98	.533	47	24	.511	182	220	8.5
75-76	27	804	358	197	.550	108	70	.648	298	464	17.2
76-77	29	901	360	212	.589	109	81	.743	319	505	17.4
77-78	28	912	336	195	.580	98	70	.714	352	460	16.4
Totals	110	3246	1238	702	.567	362	245	.677	1151	1649	15.0

NBA REGULAR SEASON RECORD

Sea.—Team	G.	Min.	FGA	FGM	Pct.	FTA	FTM	Pct.	Off.	Def.	Tot.	Ast.	PF	Dq.	Stl.	Blk.	Pts.	Avg.
78-79—Detroit	82	2560	946	456	.482	219	144	.658	211	437	648	89	254	3	104	201	1056	12.9
79-80—Detroit	82	2672	925	430	.465	187	143	.765	228	399	627	129	237	3	107	220	1005	12.3
80-81—Detroit	82	2549	895	476	.532	250	148	.592	198	369	567	136	215	2	112	180	1100	13.4
81-82—Detroit	82	1989	643	336	.523	192	142	.740	154	339	493	126	182	1	77	160	815	9.9
82-83—Detroit	82	2543	880	421	.478	196	146	.745	180	360	540	157	221	3	103	160	990	12.1
83-84—Detroit	82	1602	691	313	.453	132	94	.712	104	181	285	76	151	1	63	59	722	8.8
84-85—Detroit	82	2004	855	422	.494	148	106	.716	148	275	423	63	192	0	49	90	950	11.6
85-86—Sacramento	71	1651	649	295	.455	112	84	.750	109	204	313	94	159	0	64	108	674	9.5
86-87—Sacramento	82	1930	664	329	.495	140	101	.721	116	212	328	73	151	1	55	78	760	9.3
87-88—Sacramento	74	1185	407	184	.452	64	41	.641	87	155	242	56	85	0	43	47	410	5.5
Totals	801	20685	7555	3662	.485	1640	1149	.701	1535	2931	4466	999	1847	14	777	1303	8482	10.6

Three-Point Field Goals: 1979-80, 2-for-12 (.167). 1980-81, 0-for-8. 1981-82, 1-for-4 (.250). 1982-83, 2-for-15 (.133). 1983-84, 2-for-13 (.154). 1984-85, 0-for-8. 1985-86, 0-for-3. 1986-87, 1-for-7 (.333). 1987-88, 1-for-7 (.143). Totals, 9-for-73 (.123).

NBA PLAYOFF RECORD

Sea.—Team	G.	Min.	FGA	FGM	Pct.	FTA	FTM	Pct.	Off.	Def.	Tot.	Ast.	PF	Dq.	Stl.	Blk.	Pts.	Avg.
83-84—Detroit	5	42	24	10	.417	9	5	.556	5	2	7	1	4	0	0	3	25	5.0
84-85—Detroit	9	179	100	49	.490	27	22	.815	15	25	40	3	17	0	6	4	120	13.3
85-86—Sacramento	3	51	10	2	.200	4	4	1.000	3	5	8	4	5	0	2	3	8	2.7
Totals	17	272	134	61	.455	40	31	.775	23	32	55	8	26	0	8	10	153	9.0

Three-Point Field Goals: 1984-85, 0-for-1.
Named to NBA All-Rookie Team, 1979.

DARNELL TERRELL VALENTINE

Born February 3, 1959 at Chicago, Ill.   Height 6:01.   Weight 183.

High School—Wichita, Kan., Wichita Heights.

College—University of Kansas, Lawrence, Kan.

Drafted by Portland on first round, 1981 (16th pick).

Traded by Portland to Los Angeles Clippers for a 1986 1st round draft choice and future considerations, January 14, 1986.
Selected from Los Angeles Clippers by Miami in NBA expansion draft, June 23, 1988.
Traded by Miami to Cleveland for a future 2nd round draft choice, June 23, 1988.

—COLLEGIATE RECORD—

Year	G.	Min.	FGA	FGM	Pct.	FTA	FTM	Pct.	Reb.	Pts.	Avg.
77-78	29	761	297	143	.413	143	106	.741	82	392	13.5
78-79	29	1008	375	166	.443	200	136	.680	133	468	16.1
79-80	28	951	322	155	.481	197	153	.777	89	463	16.5
80-81	32	1186	350	176	.503	214	146	.682	118	498	15.6
Totals	118	3906	1344	640	.476	754	541	.718	408	1821	15.4

NBA REGULAR SEASON RECORD

Sea.—Team	G.	Min.	FGA	FGM	Pct.	FTA	FTM	Pct.	Off.	Def.	Tot.	Ast.	PF	Dq.	Stl.	Blk.	Pts.	Avg.
81-82—Portland	82	1387	453	187	.413	200	152	.760	48	101	149	270	187	1	94	3	526	6.4
82-83—Portland	47	1298	460	209	.454	213	169	.793	34	83	117	293	139	1	101	5	587	12.5
83-84—Portland	68	1893	561	251	.447	246	194	.789	49	78	127	395	179	1	107	6	696	10.2
84-85—Portland	75	2278	679	321	.473	290	230	.793	54	165	219	522	189	1	143	5	872	11.6
85-86—Port.-L.A.C.	62	1217	388	161	.415	175	130	.743	32	93	125	246	123	0	72	2	456	7.4
86-87—L.A. Clippers	65	1759	671	275	.410	200	163	.815	38	112	150	447	148	3	116	10	726	11.2
87-88—L.A. Clippers	79	1636	533	223	.418	136	101	.743	37	119	156	382	135	0	122	8	562	7.1
Totals	478	11468	3745	1627	.434	1460	1139	.780	292	751	1043	2555	1100	7	755	39	4425	9.3

Three-Point Field Goals: 1981-82, 0-for-9. 1982-83, 0-for-1. 1983-84, 0-for-3. 1984-85, 0-for-2. 1985-86, 4-for-14 (.286). 1986-87, 13-for-56 (.232). 1987-88, 15-for-33 (.455). Totals, 32-for-118 (.271).

NBA PLAYOFF RECORD

Sea.—Team	G.	Min.	FGA	FGM	Pct.	FTA	FTM	Pct.	Off.	Def.	Tot.	Ast.	PF	Dq.	Stl.	Blk.	Pts.	Avg.
82-83—Portland	7	205	80	34	.425	21	16	.762	5	10	15	61	21	0	10	3	85	12.1

Sea.—Team	G.	Min.	FGA	FGM	Pct.	FTA	FTM	Pct.	—Rebounds— Off.	Def.	Tot.	Ast.	PF	Dq.	Stl.	Blk.	Pts.	Avg.
83-84—Portland	5	178	60	30	.500	35	32	.914	3	8	11	42	23	2	9	1	92	18.4
84-85—Portland	9	244	88	43	.489	31	29	.935	6	11	17	58	28	1	16	0	115	12.8
Totals	21	627	228	107	.469	87	77	.885	14	29	43	161	72	3	35	4	292	13.9

Three-Point Field Goals: 1982-83, 1-for-2 (.500).

Named to THE SPORTING NEWS All-America Second Team, 1979 and 1981. . . . Member of U. S. Olympic team, 1980.

ERNEST MAURICE VANDEWEGHE
(Kiki)

Born August 1, 1958 at Weisbaden, Germany.   Height 6:08.   Weight 220.

High School—Pacific Palisades, Calif., Palisades.

College—University of California at Los Angeles, Los Angeles, Calif.

Drafted by Dallas on first round, 1980 (11th pick).

Traded by Dallas with a 1986 1st round draft choice to Denver for 1981 and 1985 1st round draft choices, December 3, 1980.

Traded by Denver to Portland for Lafayette Lever, Calvin Natt, Wayne Cooper, a 1985 1st round draft choice and a 1984 2nd round draft choice, June 7, 1984.

—COLLEGIATE RECORD—

Year	G.	Min.	FGA	FGM	Pct.	FTA	FTM	Pct.	Reb.	Pts.	Avg.
76-77	23	230	70	35	.500	17	12	.706	41	82	3.6
77-78	28	592	184	101	.549	67	46	.687	123	248	8.9
78-79	30	916	267	166	.622	117	95	.812	189	427	14.2
79-80	32	1081	420	234	.557	196	155	.791	216	623	19.5
Totals	113	2819	941	536	.570	397	308	.776	569	1380	12.2

NBA REGULAR SEASON RECORD

Sea.—Team	G.	Min.	FGA	FGM	Pct.	FTA	FTM	Pct.	—Rebounds— Off.	Def.	Tot.	Ast.	PF	Dq.	Stl.	Blk.	Pts.	Avg.
80-81—Denver	51	1376	537	229	.426	159	130	.818	86	184	270	94	116	0	29	24	588	11.5
81-82—Denver	82	2775	1260	706	.560	405	347	.857	149	312	461	247	217	1	52	29	1760	21.5
82-83—Denver	82	2909	1537	841	.547	559	489	.875	124	313	437	203	198	0	66	38	2186	26.7
83-84—Denver	78	2734	1603	895	.558	580	494	.852	84	289	373	238	187	1	53	50	2295	29.4
84-85—Portland	72	2502	1158	618	.534	412	369	.896	74	154	228	106	116	0	37	22	1616	22.4
85-86—Portland	79	2791	1332	719	.540	602	523	.869	92	124	216	187	161	0	54	17	1962	24.8
86-87—Portland	79	3029	1545	808	.523	527	467	.886	86	165	251	220	137	0	52	17	2122	26.9
87-88—Portland	37	1038	557	283	.508	181	159	.878	36	73	109	71	68	0	21	7	747	20.2
Totals	560	19154	9529	5099	.535	3425	2978	.869	731	1614	2345	1366	1200	2	364	204	13276	23.7

Three-Point Field Goals: 1980-81, 0-for-7. 1981-82, 1-for-13 (.077). 1982-83, 15-for-51 (.294). 1983-84, 11-for-30 (.367). 1984-85, 11-for-33 (.333). 1985-86, 1-for-8 (.125). 1986-87, 39-for-81 (.481). 1987-88, 22-for-58 (.379). Totals, 100-for-281 (.356).

NBA PLAYOFF RECORD

Sea.—Team	G.	Min.	FGA	FGM	Pct.	FTA	FTM	Pct.	—Rebounds— Off.	Def.	Tot.	Ast.	PF	Dq.	Stl.	Blk.	Pts.	Avg.
81-82—Denver	3	109	43	25	.581	18	18	1.000	4	14	18	9	7	0	2	4	68	22.7
82-83—Denver	8	317	160	87	.544	50	40	.800	6	46	52	32	16	0	4	7	214	26.8
83-84—Denver	5	180	96	49	.510	28	27	.964	6	17	23	20	14	1	9	5	127	25.4
84-85—Portland	9	311	158	85	.538	33	31	.939	14	13	27	17	23	0	8	3	202	22.4
85-86—Portland	4	149	69	40	.580	32	32	1.000	2	3	5	8	12	0	2	2	112	28.0
86-87—Portland	4	174	71	38	.535	26	22	.846	5	8	13	11	10	0	1	1	99	24.8
87-88—Portland	4	72	40	11	.275	9	9	1.000	3	10	13	7	8	0	1	0	31	7.8
Totals	37	1312	637	335	.526	196	179	.913	40	111	151	104	90	1	27	22	853	23.1

Three-Point Field Goals: 1982-83, 0-for-4. 1983-84, 2-for-5 (.400). 1984-85, 1-for-7 (.143). 1985-86, 0-for-2. 1986-87, 1-for-4 (.250). 1987-88, 0-for-5. Totals, 4-for-27 (.148).

NBA ALL-STAR GAME RECORD

Season—Team	Min.	FGA	FGM	Pct.	FTA	FTM	Pct.	—Rebounds— Off.	Def.	Tot.	Ast.	PF	Dq.	Stl.	Blk.	Pts.
1983—Denver	14	4	3	.750	2	1	.500	0	3	3	1	0	0	1	0	7
1984—Denver	26	13	7	.538	0	0	.000	1	2	3	1	2	0	0	0	14
Totals	40	17	10	.588	2	1	.500	1	5	6	2	2	0	1	0	21

Led NBA in three-point field goal percentage, 1987. . . . Son of former NBA forward-guard Ernie Vandeweghe and nephew of former NBA forward-center Mel Hutchins.

—DID YOU KNOW—

That eight teams in NBA history have made the playoffs despite not winning at least 40 percent of their regular-season games? The worst of the eight were the 1952-53 Washington Bullets, who won just 16 of 70 games (.229) before losing their only two playoff games.

JAMES SAMUEL VINCENT
(Sam)

Born May 18, 1963 at Lansing, Mich.   Height 6:02.   Weight 185.

High School—Lansing, Mich., Eastern.

College—Michigan State University, Lansing, Mich.

Drafted by Boston on first round, 1985 (20th pick).

Traded by Boston with Scott Wedman to Seattle for a 1989 2nd round draft choice, October 16, 1987.
Traded by Seattle to Chicago for Sedale Threatt, February 25, 1988.

—COLLEGIATE RECORD—

Year	G.	Min.	FGA	FGM	Pct.	FTA	FTM	Pct.	Reb.	Pts.	Avg.
81-82	28	965	282	130	.461	91	68	.747	78	328	11.7
82-83	30	1066	401	180	.449	172	133	.773	79	498	16.6
83-84	23	740	261	130	.498	122	99	.811	62	359	15.6
84-85	29	1093	450	245	.544	208	176	.846	112	666	23.0
Totals	110	3864	1394	685	.491	593	476	.803	331	1851	16.8

Three-Point Field Goals: 1982-83, 5-for-11 (.455).

NBA REGULAR SEASON RECORD

Sea.—Team	G.	Min.	FGA	FGM	Pct.	FTA	FTM	Pct.	Off.	Def.	Tot.	Ast.	PF	Dq.	Stl.	Blk.	Pts.	Avg.
85-86—Boston	57	432	162	59	.364	70	65	.929	11	37	48	69	59	0	17	4	184	3.2
86-87—Boston	46	374	136	60	.441	55	51	.927	5	22	27	59	33	0	13	1	171	3.7
87-88—Sea.-Chi.	72	1501	461	210	.456	167	145	.868	35	117	152	381	145	0	55	16	573	8.0
Totals	175	2307	759	329	.433	292	261	.894	51	176	227	509	237	0	85	21	928	5.3

Three-Point Field Goals: 1985-86, 1-for-4 (.250). 1987-88, 8-for-21 (.381). Totals, 9-for-25 (.360).

NBA PLAYOFF RECORD

Sea.—Team	G.	Min.	FGA	FGM	Pct.	FTA	FTM	Pct.	Off.	Def.	Tot.	Ast.	PF	Dq.	Stl.	Blk.	Pts.	Avg.
85-86—Boston	9	41	28	8	.286	6	6	1.000	1	6	7	5	9	0	2	0	22	2.4
86-87—Boston	17	141	56	23	.411	35	27	.771	3	9	12	19	13	0	3	2	74	4.4
87-88—Chicago	10	251	110	41	.373	25	20	.800	6	13	19	44	23	0	8	1	102	10.2
Totals	36	433	194	72	.371	66	53	.803	10	28	38	68	45	0	13	3	198	5.5

Three-Point Field Goals: 1985-86, 0-for-1. 1986-87, 1-for-2 (.500). 1987-88, 0-for-3. Totals, 1-for-6 (.167).

Member of NBA championship team, 1986. . . . Named to THE SPORTING NEWS All-America First Team, 1985. . . . Brother of Denver Nuggets forward Jay Vincent.

JAY FLETCHER VINCENT

Born June 10, 1959 at Kalamazoo, Mich.   Height 6:07.   Weight 220.

High School—Lansing, Mich., Eastern.

College—Michigan State University, East Lansing, Mich.

Drafted by Dallas on second round, 1981 (24th pick).

Traded by Dallas to Washington for a 1990 1st round draft choice, September 3, 1986.
Traded by Washington with Michael Adams to Denver for Mark Alarie and Darrell Walker, November 2, 1987.

—COLLEGIATE RECORD—

Year	G.	Min.	FGA	FGM	Pct.	FTA	FTM	Pct.	Reb.	Pts.	Avg.
77-78	29	....	239	137	.573	86	55	.640	110	329	11.3
78-79	31	939	343	170	.496	93	54	.581	161	394	12.7
79-80	27	965	451	233	.517	161	116	.720	209	582	21.6
80-81	27	1001	522	259	.496	141	91	.645	229	609	22.6
Totals	114	....	1555	799	.514	481	316	.657	709	1914	16.8

NBA REGULAR SEASON RECORD

Sea.—Team	G.	Min.	FGA	FGM	Pct.	FTA	FTM	Pct.	Off.	Def.	Tot.	Ast.	PF	Dq.	Stl.	Blk.	Pts.	Avg.
81-82—Dallas	81	2626	1448	719	.497	409	293	.716	182	383	565	176	308	8	89	22	1732	21.4
82-83—Dallas	81	2726	1272	622	.489	343	269	.784	217	375	592	212	295	4	70	45	1513	18.7
83-84—Dallas	61	1421	579	252	.435	215	168	.781	81	166	247	114	159	1	30	10	672	11.0
84-85—Dallas	79	2543	1138	545	.479	420	351	.836	185	519	704	169	226	0	48	22	1441	18.2
85-86—Dallas	80	1994	919	442	.481	274	222	.810	107	261	368	180	193	2	66	21	1106	13.8
86-87—Washington	51	1386	613	274	.447	169	130	.769	69	141	210	85	127	0	40	17	678	13.3
87-88—Denver	73	1755	958	446	.466	287	231	.805	80	229	309	143	198	1	46	26	1124	15.4
Totals	506	14451	6927	3300	.476	2117	1664	.786	921	2074	2995	1079	1506	16	389	163	8266	16.3

Three-Point Field Goals: 1981-82, 1-for-4 (.250). 1982-83, 0-for-3. 1983-84, 0-for-1. 1984-85, 0-for-4. 1985-86, 0-for-3. 1986-87, 0-for-3. 1987-88, 1-for-4 (.250). Totals, 2-for-22 (.091).

NBA PLAYOFF RECORD

								—Rebounds—								
Sea.—Team	G.	Min.	FGA	FGM	Pct.	FTA	FTM	Pct.	Off.	Def.	Tot.	Ast.	PF	Dq.	Stl.	Blk.	Pts.	Avg.
83-84—Dallas	10	353	124	48	.387	62	56	.903	29	41	70	19	36	1	7	1	152	15.2
84-85—Dallas	4	134	56	20	.357	29	22	.759	9	13	22	3	16	0	6	3	62	15.5
85-86—Dallas	10	204	99	38	.384	34	30	.882	15	24	39	15	19	0	4	1	106	10.6
86-87—Washington	3	72	30	11	.367	9	8	.889	2	7	9	3	10	0	2	0	30	10.0
87-88—Denver	8	200	104	53	.510	40	34	.850	10	27	37	6	25	0	5	4	140	17.5
Totals	35	963	413	170	.412	174	150	.862	65	112	177	46	106	1	24	9	490	14.0

Three-Point Field Goals: 1983-84, 0-for-1. 1987-88, 0-for-1. Totals, 0-for-2.

Named to NBA All-Rookie Team, 1982. . . . Member of NCAA championship team, 1979. . . . Brother of Chicago Bulls guard Sam Vincent.

DANIEL LaDREW VRANES
(Danny)

Born October 29, 1958 at Salt Lake City, Utah. Height 6:08. Weight 220.

High School—Salt Lake City, Utah, Skyline.

College—University of Utah, Salt Lake City, Utah.

Drafted by Seattle on first round, 1981 (5th pick).

Traded by Seattle with Tim McCormick to Philadelphia for Clemon Johnson and a 1989 1st round draft choice, September 29, 1986.

—COLLEGIATE RECORD—

Year	G.	Min.	FGA	FGM	Pct.	FTA	FTM	Pct.	Reb.	Pts.	Avg.
77-78	29	851	265	145	.547	113	65	.575	210	355	12.2
78-79	28	867	292	180	.616	148	101	.682	283	455	16.3
79-80	24	760	242	138	.570	141	105	.745	228	380	15.8
80-81	30	977	304	181	.595	206	164	.796	230	526	17.5
Totals	111	3455	1103	644	.584	608	435	.715	951	1716	15.5

NBA REGULAR SEASON RECORD

								—Rebounds—								
Sea.—Team	G.	Min.	FGA	FGM	Pct.	FTA	FTM	Pct.	Off.	Def.	Tot.	Ast.	PF	Dq.	Stl.	Blk.	Pts.	Avg.
81-82—Seattle	77	1075	262	143	.546	148	89	.601	71	127	108	56	150	0	28	21	375	4.9
82-83—Seattle	82	2054	429	226	.527	209	115	.550	177	248	425	120	254	2	53	49	567	6.9
83-84—Seattle	80	2174	495	258	.521	236	153	.648	150	245	395	132	263	4	51	54	669	8.4
84-85—Seattle	76	2163	402	186	.463	127	67	.528	154	282	436	152	256	4	76	57	440	5.8
85-86—Seattle	80	1569	284	131	.461	75	39	.520	115	166	281	68	218	3	63	31	301	3.8
86-87—Philadelphia	58	817	138	59	.428	45	21	.467	51	95	146	30	127	0	35	25	140	2.4
87-88—Philadelphia	57	772	121	53	.438	35	15	.429	45	72	117	36	100	0	27	33	121	2.1
Totals	510	10624	2131	1056	.496	875	499	.570	763	1235	1998	594	1368	13	333	270	2613	5.1

Three-Point Field Goals: 1981-82, 0-for-1. 1982-83, 0-for-1. 1983-84, 0-for-1. 1984-85, 1-for-4 (.250). 1985-86, 0-for-4. 1986-87, 1-for-5 (.200). 1987-88, 0-for-3. Totals, 2-for-19 (.105).

NBA PLAYOFF RECORD

								—Rebounds—								
Sea.—Team	G.	Min.	FGA	FGM	Pct.	FTA	FTM	Pct.	Off.	Def.	Tot.	Ast.	PF	Dq.	Stl.	Blk.	Pts.	Avg.
81-82—Seattle	6	29	5	1	.200	2	1	.500	1	1	2	0	2	0	1	0	3	0.5
82-83—Seattle	2	56	17	6	.353	0	0	.000	9	10	19	1	7	0	0	1	12	6.0
83-84—Seattle	5	147	39	16	.410	7	4	.571	16	22	38	11	24	1	3	6	36	7.2
86-87—Philadelphia	2	3	0	0	.000	0	0	.000	0	3	3	0	1	0	0	0	0	0.0
Totals	15	235	61	23	.377	9	5	.556	26	36	62	12	34	1	4	7	51	3.4

Three-Point Field Goals: 1983-84, 0-for-1.

Named to NBA All-Defensive Second Team, 1985. . . . Named to THE SPORTING NEWS All-America Second Team, 1981. . . . Member of U. S. Olympic team, 1980.

MARK A. WADE

Born October 15, 1965 at Torrance, Calif. Height 5:11. Weight 160.

High School—Los Angeles, Calif., Banning.

Colleges—University of Oklahoma, Norman, Okla.; El Camino College, Torrance, Calif., and University of Nevada at Las Vegas, Las Vegas, Nev.

Never drafted by an NBA franchise.

Signed by Golden State, March 30, 1988, to the first of consecutive 10-day contracts that expired, April 18, 1988.
Re-signed by Golden State, April 20, 1988, for remainder of season.
Played in Continental Basketball Association with Quad City Thunder and Pensacola Tornados, 1987-88.

—COLLEGIATE RECORD—

Oklahoma

Year	G.	Min.	FGA	FGM	Pct.	FTA	FTM	Pct.	Reb.	Pts.	Avg.
83-84	6	45	8	3	.875	7	6	.857	5	12	2.0

El Camino

Year	G.	Min.	FGA	FGM	Pct.	FTA	FTM	Pct.	Reb.	Pts.	Avg.
84-85	35	....	154	85	.552	78	56	.718	82	226	6.5

Nevada-Las Vegas

Year	G.	Min.	FGA	FGM	Pct.	FTA	FTM	Pct.	Reb.	Pts.	Avg.
85-86	38	1054	65	28	.431	73	50	.685	81	106	2.8
86-87	38	1169	142	60	.423	49	38	.776	103	180	4.7
UNLV Totals........	76	2223	207	88	.425	122	88	.721	184	286	3.8
College Totals.......	82	2268	215	91	.423	129	94	.729	189	298	3.6

Three-Point Field Goals: 1985-86, 0-for-5. 1986-87, 22-for-60 (.367). Totals, 22-for-65 (.338).

CBA REGULAR SEASON RECORD

			—2-Point—			—3-Point—								
Sea.—Team	G.	Min.	FGM	FGA	Pct.	FGM	FGA	Pct.	FTM	FTA	Pct.	Reb.	Ast.	Pts.	Avg.
87-88—Quad City-Pen.	37	1459	62	168	.369	33	80	.413	54	73	.740	127	417	277	7.5

NBA REGULAR SEASON RECORD

								—Rebounds—									
Sea.—Team	G.	Min.	FGA	FGM	Pct.	FTA	FTM	Pct.	Off.	Def.	Tot.	Ast.	PF	Dq.	Stl.	Blk.	Pts.	Avg.
87-88—Golden State	11	123	20	3	.150	4	2	.500	3	12	15	34	13	0	7	1	8	0.7

Three-Point Field Goals: 1987-88, 0-for-2.

MILTON WAGNER JR.
(Milt)

Born February 20, 1963 at Camden, N.J.   Height 6:05.   Weight 185.

High School—Camden, N.J.

College—University of Louisville, Louisville, Ky.

Drafted by Dallas on second round, 1986 (35th pick).

Waived by Dallas, October 17, 1986; signed by Los Angeles Lakers as a free agent, October 7, 1987.
Played in Continental Basketball Association with LaCrosse Catbirds and Rockford Lightning, 1986-87.

—COLLEGIATE RECORD—

Year	G.	Min.	FGA	FGM	Pct.	FTA	FTM	Pct.	Reb.	Pts.	Avg.
81-82	32	444	131	63	.481	19	11	.579	33	137	4.3
82-83	36	1111	437	227	.519	86	61	.709	92	517	14.4
83-84	35	1157	458	228	.498	146	124	.849	103	580	16.6
84-85	2	59	27	11	.407	3	3	1.000	5	25	12.5
85-86	39	1312	444	220	.495	159	137	.862	122	577	14.8
Totals	144	4083	1497	749	.500	413	336	.814	355	1836	12.8

(Suffered broken foot in 1984-85 season; granted extra year of eligibility.)
Three-Point Field Goals: 1982-83, 2-for-4 (.500).

CBA REGULAR SEASON RECORD

			—2-Point—			—3-Point—								
Sea.—Team	G.	Min.	FGM	FGA	Pct.	FGM	FGA	Pct.	FTM	FTA	Pct.	Reb.	Ast.	Pts.	Avg.
86-87—LaCrosse-Rock.	47	1387	265	540	.490	16	51	.314	114	139	.820	114	153	692	14.7

NBA REGULAR SEASON RECORD

								—Rebounds—									
Sea.—Team	G.	Min.	FGA	FGM	Pct.	FTA	FTM	Pct.	Off.	Def.	Tot.	Ast.	PF	Dq.	Stl.	Blk.	Pts.	Avg.
87-88—L.A. Lakers	40	380	147	62	.422	29	26	.897	4	24	28	61	42	0	6	4	152	3.8

Three-Point Field Goals: 1987-88, 2-for-10 (.200).

NBA PLAYOFF RECORD

								—Rebounds—									
Sea.—Team	G.	Min.	FGA	FGM	Pct.	FTA	FTM	Pct.	Off.	Def.	Tot.	Ast.	PF	Dq.	Stl.	Blk.	Pts.	Avg.
87-88—L.A. Lakers	5	14	5	2	.400	2	2	1.000	0	2	2	3	3	0	0	1	6	1.2

Three-Point Field Goals: 1987-88, 0-for-1.

Member of NBA championship team, 1988. . . . Member of NCAA Division I championship team, 1986.

GRANVILLE S. WAITERS

Born January 8, 1961 at Columbus, O.   Height 6:11.   Weight 225.

High School—Columbus, O., East.

College—Ohio State University, Columbus, O.

Drafted by Portland on second round, 1983 (39th pick).

Draft rights traded by Portland to Indiana for a 1984 2nd round draft choice, August 18, 1983.
Traded by Indiana to Houston for a 1987 3rd round draft choice, August 1, 1985.
Waived by Houston, December 17, 1985; re-signed by Houston as a free agent, December 21, 1985.

Traded by Houston to Chicago for a 1989 3rd or 4th round draft choice, October 23, 1986.

—COLLEGIATE RECORD—

Year	G.	Min.	FGA	FGM	Pct.	FTA	FTM	Pct.	Reb.	Pts.	Avg.
79-80	17	49	11	6	.545	0	0	.000	14	12	0.7
80-81	26	232	50	27	.540	10	3	.300	39	57	2.2
81-82	31	941	166	93	.560	53	35	.660	156	221	7.1
82-83	30	993	246	131	.533	68	49	.721	225	311	10.4
Totals	104	2215	473	257	.543	131	87	.664	434	601	5.8

NBA REGULAR SEASON RECORD

Sea.—Team	G.	Min.	FGA	FGM	Pct.	FTA	FTM	Pct.	Off.	Def.	Tot.	Ast.	PF	Dq.	Stl.	Blk.	Pts.	Avg.
83-84—Indiana	78	1040	238	123	.517	51	31	.608	64	163	227	60	164	2	24	85	277	3.6
84-85—Indiana	62	703	190	85	.447	50	29	.580	57	113	170	30	107	2	16	44	199	3.2
85-86—Houston	43	156	39	13	.333	6	1	.167	15	13	28	8	30	0	4	10	27	0.6
86-87—Chicago	44	534	93	40	.430	9	5	.556	38	49	87	22	83	1	10	31	85	1.9
87-88—Chicago	22	114	29	9	.310	2	0	.000	9	19	28	1	26	0	2	15	18	0.8
Totals	249	2547	589	270	.458	118	66	.559	183	357	540	121	410	5	56	185	606	2.4

Three-Point Field Goals: 1983-84, 0-for-1. 1984-85, 0-for-1. 1985-86, 0-for-1. 1986-87, 0-for-1. 1987-88, 0-for-1. Totals, 0-for-5.

NBA PLAYOFF RECORD

Sea.—Team	G.	Min.	FGA	FGM	Pct.	FTA	FTM	Pct.	Off.	Def.	Tot.	Ast.	PF	Dq.	Stl.	Blk.	Pts.	Avg.
85-86—Houston	11	26	7	4	.571	0	0	.000	2	3	5	0	3	0	1	3	8	0.7
86-87—Chicago	2	8	0	0	.000	0	0	.000	0	1	1	0	1	0	0	1	0	0.0
Totals	13	34	7	4	.571	0	0	.000	2	4	6	0	4	0	1	4	8	0.6

DARRELL WALKER

Born March 9, 1961 at Chicago, Ill. Height 6:04. Weight 180.

High School—Chicago, Ill., Corliss.

Colleges—Westark Community College, Fort Smith, Ark., and University of Arkansas, Fayetteville, Ark.

Drafted by New York on first round, 1983 (12th pick).

Traded by New York to Denver for a 1987 1st round draft choice, October 2, 1986.
Traded by Denver with Mark Alarie to Washington for Michael Adams and Jay Vincent, November 2, 1987.

—COLLEGIATE RECORD—

Westark CC

Year	G.	Min.	FGA	FGM	Pct.	FTA	FTM	Pct.	Reb.	Pts.	Avg.
79-80	37	1332	472	255	.540	178	117	.657	259	627	16.9

Arkansas

Year	G.	Min.	FGA	FGM	Pct.	FTA	FTM	Pct.	Reb.	Pts.	Avg.
80-81	31	926	269	137	.509	125	75	.600	139	349	11.3
81-82	29	1039	316	162	.513	161	106	.658	152	430	14.8
82-83	30	1105	374	197	.527	238	152	.639	172	546	18.2
Totals	90	3070	959	496	.517	524	333	.635	463	1325	14.7

NBA REGULAR SEASON RECORD

Sea.—Team	G.	Min.	FGA	FGM	Pct.	FTA	FTM	Pct.	Off.	Def.	Tot.	Ast.	PF	Dq.	Stl.	Blk.	Pts.	Avg.
83-84—New York	82	1324	518	216	.417	263	208	.791	74	93	167	284	202	1	127	15	644	7.9
84-85—New York	82	2489	989	430	.435	347	243	.700	128	150	278	408	244	2	167	21	1103	13.5
85-86—New York	81	2023	753	324	.430	277	190	.686	100	120	220	337	216	1	146	36	838	10.3
86-87—Denver	81	2020	742	358	.482	365	272	.745	157	170	327	282	229	0	120	37	988	12.2
87-88—Washington	52	940	291	114	.392	105	82	.781	43	84	127	100	105	2	62	10	310	6.0
Totals	378	8796	3293	1442	.438	1357	995	.733	502	617	1119	1411	996	6	622	119	3883	10.3

Three-Point Field Goals: 1983-84, 4-for-15 (.267). 1984-85, 0-for-17. 1985-86, 0-for-10. 1986-87, 0-for-4. 1987-88, 0-for-6. Totals, 4-for-52 (.077).

NBA PLAYOFF RECORD

Sea.—Team	G.	Min.	FGA	FGM	Pct.	FTA	FTM	Pct.	Off.	Def.	Tot.	Ast.	PF	Dq.	Stl.	Blk.	Pts.	Avg.
83-84—New York	12	195	73	27	.370	46	28	.609	20	15	35	20	29	0	24	2	82	6.8
86-87—Denver	3	68	34	11	.324	7	4	.571	3	7	10	5	4	0	2	0	26	8.7
87-88—Washington	5	155	54	22	.407	16	11	.688	9	15	24	14	18	0	7	4	55	11.0
Totals	20	418	161	60	.373	69	43	.623	32	37	69	39	51	0	33	6	163	8.2

Three-Point Field Goals: 1987-88, 0-for-1.

Named to NBA All-Rookie Team, 1984.

KENNETH WALKER
(Kenny)

Born August 18, 1964 at Roberta, Ga.   Height 6:08.   Weight 210.

High School—Roberta, Ga., Crawford County.

College—University of Kentucky, Lexington, Ky.

Drafted by New York on first round, 1986 (5th pick).

—COLLEGIATE RECORD—

Year	G.	Min.	FGA	FGM	Pct.	FTA	FTM	Pct.	Reb.	Pts.	Avg.
82-83	31	599	144	88	.611	77	51	.662	151	227	7.3
83-84	34	1087	308	171	.555	109	80	.734	200	422	12.4
84-85	31	1139	440	246	.559	284	218	.768	315	710	22.9
85-86	36	1254	447	260	.582	263	201	.764	276	721	20.0
Totals	132	4079	1339	765	.571	733	550	.750	942	2080	15.8

NBA REGULAR SEASON RECORD

Sea.—Team	G.	Min.	FGA	FGM	Pct.	FTA	FTM	Pct.	—Rebounds— Off.	Def.	Tot.	Ast.	PF	Dq.	Stl.	Blk.	Pts.	Avg.
86-87—New York	68	1719	581	285	.491	185	140	.757	118	220	338	75	236	7	49	49	710	10.4
87-88—New York	82	2139	728	344	.473	178	138	.775	192	197	389	86	290	5	63	59	826	10.1
Totals	150	3858	1309	629	.481	363	278	.766	310	417	727	161	526	12	112	108	1536	10.2

Three-Point Field Goals: 1986-87, 0-for-4. 1987-88, 0-for-1. Totals, 0-for-5.

NBA PLAYOFF RECORD

Sea.—Team	G.	Min.	FGA	FGM	Pct.	FTA	FTM	Pct.	—Rebounds— Off.	Def.	Tot.	Ast.	PF	Dq.	Stl.	Blk.	Pts.	Avg.
87-88—New York	4	80	24	8	.333	2	2	1.000	3	6	9	5	11	0	2	3	18	4.5

Named to THE SPORTING NEWS All-America Second Team, 1986.

JAMIE ANTONIO WALLER

Born November 20, 1964 at South Boston, Va.   Height 6:04.   Weight 215.

High School—South Boston, Va., Halifax County.

College—Virginia Union University, Richmond, Va.

Drafted by New Jersey on third round, 1987 (48th pick).

Waived by New Jersey, December 3, 1987.
Played in Continental Basketball Association with Quad City Thunder and Charleston Gunners, 1987-88.

—COLLEGIATE RECORD—

Year	G.	Min.	FGA	FGM	Pct.	FTA	FTM	Pct.	Reb.	Pts.	Avg.
83-84	32	....	209	108	.517	71	43	.606	116	259	8.1
84-85	32	....	450	275	.611	184	115	.625	226	665	20.8
85-86	32	....	528	244	.462	214	139	.650	299	630	19.6
86-87	32	....	553	303	.548	198	126	.636	302	744	23.3
Totals	128	....	1740	930	.534	667	423	.634	943	2298	18.0

CBA REGULAR SEASON RECORD

Sea.—Team	G.	Min.	—2-Point— FGM	FGA	Pct.	—3-Point— FGM	FGA	Pct.	FTM	FTA	Pct.	Reb.	Ast.	Pts.	Avg.
87-88—Quad City-Char.	32	1064	281	548	.513	13	36	.361	139	199	.698	189	87	740	23.1

NBA REGULAR SEASON RECORD

Sea.—Team	G.	Min.	FGA	FGM	Pct.	FTA	FTM	Pct.	—Rebounds— Off.	Def.	Tot.	Ast.	PF	Dq.	Stl.	Blk.	Pts.	Avg.
87-88—New Jersey	9	91	40	16	.400	18	10	.556	9	4	13	3	13	0	4	1	42	4.7

Three-Point Field Goals: 1987-88, 0-for-2.

Named CBA Rookie of the Year, 1988. . . . CBA All-Rookie Team, 1988.

WILLIAM THEODORE WALTON
(Bill)

Born November 5, 1952 at La Mesa, Calif.   Height 6:11.   Weight 235.

High School—La Mesa, Calif., Helix.

College—University of California at Los Angeles, Los Angeles, Calif.

Drafted by Portland on first round, 1974 (1st pick).

Missed entire 1978-79, 1980-81, 1981-82 and 1987-88 seasons due to injury.
Signed by San Diego as a Veteran Free Agent, May 13, 1979; Portland received Kevin Kunnert, Kermit Washington, a 1980 1st round draft choice and cash as compensation, September 18, 1979.

Traded by Los Angeles Clippers to Boston for Cedric Maxwell, a 1986 1st round draft choice and cash, September 6, 1985.

—COLLEGIATE RECORD—

Year	G.	Min.	FGA	FGM	Pct.	FTA	FTM	Pct.	Reb.	Pts.	Avg.
70-71†	20	....	266	155	.686	82	52	.634	321	362	18.1
71-72	30	....	372	238	.640	223	157	.704	466	633	21.1
72-73	30	....	426	277	.650	102	59	.569	506	612	20.4
73-74	27	....	349	232	.665	100	58	.580	398	522	19.3
Varsity Totals	87	....	1147	747	.651	425	273	.642	1370	1767	20.3

NBA REGULAR SEASON RECORD

Sea.—Team	G.	Min.	FGA	FGM	Pct.	FTA	FTM	Pct.	Off.	Def.	Tot.	Ast.	PF	Dq.	Stl.	Blk.	Pts.	Avg.
74-75—Portland	35	1153	345	177	.513	137	94	.686	92	349	441	167	115	4	29	94	448	12.8
75-76—Portland	51	1687	732	345	.471	228	133	.583	132	549	681	220	144	3	49	82	823	16.1
76-77—Portland	65	2264	930	491	.528	327	228	.697	211	723	934	245	174	5	66	211	1210	18.6
77-78—Portland	58	1929	882	460	.522	246	177	.720	118	648	766	291	145	3	60	146	1097	18.9
79-80—San Diego	14	337	161	81	.503	54	32	.593	28	98	126	34	37	0	8	38	194	13.9
82-83—San Diego	33	1099	379	200	.528	117	65	.556	75	248	323	120	113	0	34	119	465	14.1
83-84—San Diego	55	1476	518	288	.556	154	92	.597	132	345	477	183	153	1	45	88	668	12.1
84-85—L.A. Clippers	67	1647	516	269	.521	203	138	.680	168	432	600	156	184	0	50	140	676	10.1
85-86—Boston	80	1546	411	231	.562	202	144	.713	136	408	544	165	210	1	38	106	606	7.6
86-87—Boston	10	112	26	10	.385	15	8	.533	11	20	31	9	23	0	1	10	28	2.8
Totals	468	13250	4900	2552	.521	1683	1111	.660	1103	3820	4923	1590	1298	17	380	1034	6215	13.3

Three-Point Field Goals: 1983-84, 0-for-2. 1984-85, 0-for-2. Totals, 0-for-4.

NBA PLAYOFF RECORD

Sea.—Team	G.	Min.	FGA	FGM	Pct.	FTA	FTM	Pct.	Off.	Def.	Tot.	Ast.	PF	Dq.	Stl.	Blk.	Pts.	Avg.
76-77—Portland	19	755	302	153	.507	57	39	.684	56	232	288	104	80	3	20	64	345	18.2
77-78—Portland	2	49	18	11	.611	7	5	.714	5	17	22	4	1	0	3	3	27	13.5
85-86—Boston	16	291	93	54	.581	23	19	.826	25	78	103	27	45	1	6	12	127	7.9
86-87—Boston	12	102	25	12	.480	14	5	.357	9	22	31	10	23	0	3	4	29	2.4
Totals	49	1197	438	230	.525	101	68	.673	95	349	444	145	149	4	32	83	528	10.8

Three-Point Field Goals: 1985-86, 0-for-1.

NBA ALL-STAR GAME RECORD

Season—Team	Min.	FGA	FGM	Pct.	FTA	FTM	Pct.	Off.	Def.	Tot.	Ast.	PF	Dq.	Stl.	Blk.	Pts.
1977—Portland					Selected—Injured, Did Not Play											
1978—Portland	31	14	6	.429	3	3	1.000	2	8	10	2	3	0	3	2	15

Named NBA Most Valuable Player, 1978.... All-NBA First Team, 1978.... All-NBA Second Team, 1977.... NBA All-Defensive First Team, 1977 and 1978.... NBA Playoff MVP, 1977.... Member of NBA championship teams, 1977 and 1986.... Recipient of NBA Sixth Man Award, 1986.... Shares NBA championship series game record for most blocked shots, 8, vs. Philadelphia, June 5, 1977.... Led NBA in blocked shots, 1977.... Led NBA in rebounding, 1977. ... THE SPORTING NEWS College Player of the Year, 1972, 1973, 1974. ... Named to THE SPORTING NEWS All-America First Team, 1972, 1973, 1974.... NCAA Division I Tournament Most Outstanding Player, 1972 and 1973. ... Member of NCAA Division I championship teams, 1972 and 1973.... Holds NCAA tournament record for highest field-goal percentage in one year (minimum of 40 made), 76.3 percent (45-of-59), 1973.... Holds NCAA tournament record for highest field-goal percentage in career (minimum of 60 made), 68.6 percent (109-of-159), 1972 through 1974.... Brother of former National Football League tackle Bruce Walton.

BRYAN ANTHONY WARRICK

Born July 22, 1959 at Moses Lake, Wash. Height 6:05. Weight 195.

High School—Burlington, N. J., Township.

College—St. Joseph's University, Philadelphia, Pa.

Drafted by Washington on second round, 1982 (25th pick).

Waived by Washington, October 26, 1983; re-signed by Washington as a free agent, November 17, 1983.
Traded by Washington to Los Angeles Clippers for a 1985 3rd round draft choice, September 25, 1984.
Waived by Los Angeles Clippers, March 8, 1985; signed by Milwaukee as a free agent, September 30, 1985.
Waived by Milwaukee, November 11, 1985; signed by Indiana, February 13, 1986, to the first of consecutive 10-day contracts that expired, March 4, 1986.
Re-signed by Indiana, March 5, 1986, for remainder of season.
Signed by Golden State as a Veteran Free Agent, October 2, 1986; Indiana relinquished its right of first refusal.
Waived by Golden State, October 20, 1986; signed by New Jersey as a free agent, July 19, 1988.
Played in Continental Basketball Association with Wisconsin Flyers, 1985-86, and Rockford Lightning, 1986-87.
Played in West Germany, 1987-88.

—COLLEGIATE RECORD—

Year	G.	Min.	FGA	FGM	Pct.	FTA	FTM	Pct.	Reb.	Pts.	Avg.
78-79	24	217	77	31	.403	24	16	.667	23	78	3.3
79-80	30	1031	298	141	.473	102	75	.735	81	357	11.9
80-81	29	967	355	160	.451	104	71	.683	79	391	13.5

Year	G.	Min.	FGA	FGM	Pct.	FTA	FTM	Pct.	Reb.	Pts.	Avg.
81-82	30	1057	345	175	.507	125	97	.776	97	447	14.9
Totals	113	3272	1075	507	.472	355	259	.730	280	1273	11.3

CBA REGULAR SEASON RECORD

Sea.—Team	G.	Min.	2-Point			3-Point			FTM	FTA	Pct.	Reb.	Ast.	Pts.	Avg.
			FGM	FGA	Pct.	FGM	FGA	Pct.							
85-86—Wisconsin	29	961	162	328	.494	5	13	.385	123	152	.809	86	287	462	15.9
86-87—Rockford	48	1782	288	531	.542	4	18	.222	175	219	.799	164	306	763	15.9
Totals	77	2743	450	859	.524	9	31	.290	298	371	.803	250	593	1225	15.9

NBA REGULAR SEASON RECORD

Sea.—Team	G.	Min.	FGA	FGM	Pct.	FTA	FTM	Pct.	—Rebounds—			Ast.	PF	Dq.	Stl.	Blk.	Pts.	Avg.
									Off.	Def.	Tot.							
82-83—Washington	43	727	171	65	.380	57	42	.737	15	54	69	126	103	5	21	8	172	4.0
83-84—Washington	32	254	66	27	.409	16	8	.500	5	17	22	43	37	0	9	3	63	2.0
84-85—L.A. Clippers	58	713	173	85	.491	57	44	.772	10	48	58	153	85	0	23	6	215	3.7
85-86—Mil.-Ind.	36	685	182	85	.467	68	54	.794	10	59	69	115	79	0	27	2	227	6.3
Totals	169	2379	592	262	.443	198	148	.747	40	178	218	437	.304	5	80	19	677	4.0

Three-Point Field Goals: 1982-83, 0-for-5. 1983-84, 1-for-3 (.333). 1984-85, 1-for-4 (.250). 1985-86, 3-for-12 (.250). Totals, 5-for-24 (.208).

Led CBA in assists, 1984.

CHRISTOPHER SCOTT WASHBURN
(Chris)

Born May 13, 1965 at Hickory, N.C.   Height 6:11.   Weight 255.

High School—Hickory, N.C.

Prep Schools—Fork Union Military Academy, Fork Union, Va.,
and Laurinburg Institute, Laurinburg, N.C.

College—North Carolina State University, Raleigh, N.C.

Drafted by Golden State on first round as an undergraduate, 1986 (3rd pick).

Traded by Golden State to Atlanta for the draft rights to Ken Barlow, December 15, 1987.

—COLLEGIATE RECORD—

Year	G.	Min.	FGA	FGM	Pct.	FTA	FTM	Pct.	Reb.	Pts.	Avg.
84-85	7	181	67	32	.478	26	11	.423	41	75	10.7
85-86	34	1185	429	241	.562	176	117	.665	229	599	17.6
Totals	41	1366	496	273	.550	202	128	.634	270	674	16.4

NBA REGULAR SEASON RECORD

Sea.—Team	G.	Min.	FGA	FGM	Pct.	FTA	FTM	Pct.	—Rebounds—			Ast.	PF	Dq.	Stl.	Blk.	Pts.	Avg.
									Off.	Def.	Tot.							
86-87—Golden State	35	385	145	57	.393	51	18	.353	36	65	101	16	51	0	6	8	132	3.8
87-88—G.S.-Atl.	37	260	81	36	.444	31	18	.581	28	47	75	6	29	0	5	8	90	2.4
Totals	72	645	226	93	.412	82	36	.439	64	112	176	22	80	0	11	16	222	3.1

Three-Point Field Goals: 1986-87, 0-for-1.

NBA PLAYOFF RECORD

Sea.—Team	G.	Min.	FGA	FGM	Pct.	FTA	FTM	Pct.	—Rebounds—			Ast.	PF	Dq.	Stl.	Blk.	Pts.	Avg.
									Off.	Def.	Tot.							
86-87—Golden State	5	29	7	3	.429	6	5	.833	0	1	1	2	2	0	0	0	11	2.2
87-88—Atlanta	1	2	0	0	.000	0	0	.000	0	0	0	0	0	0	0	0	0	0.0
Totals	6	31	7	3	.429	6	5	.833	0	1	1	2	2	0	0	0	11	1.8

DUANE E. WASHINGTON

Born August 31, 1964 at Little Rock, Ark.   Height 6:04.   Weight 195.

High School—Little Rock, Ark., Parkview.

Colleges—Laredo Junior College, Laredo, Tex., and
Middle Tennessee State University, Murfreesboro, Tenn.

Drafted by Washington on second round, 1987 (36th pick).

Waived by Washington, October 21, 1987; signed by New Jersey, March 19, 1988, to the first of consecutive 10-day contracts that expired, April 7, 1988.
Re-signed by New Jersey, April 8, 1988, for remainder of season.
Played in Continental Basketball Association with Rapid City Thrillers, 1987-88.

—COLLEGIATE RECORD—

Laredo

Year	G.	Min.	FGA	FGM	Pct.	FTA	FTM	Pct.	Reb.	Pts.	Avg.
83-84					Statistics unavailable						
84-85					Statistics unavailable						

Middle Tennessee State

Year	G.	Min.	FGA	FGM	Pct.	FTA	FTM	Pct.	Reb.	Pts.	Avg.
85-86	34	....	161	61	.379	59	45	.763	101	167	4.9
86-87	29	....	222	108	.486	91	75	.824	115	294	10.1
Totals	63	....	383	169	.441	150	120	.800	216	461	7.3

Three-Point Field Goals: 1986-87, 3-for-12 (.250).

CBA REGULAR SEASON RECORD

			—2-Point—			—3-Point—								
Sea.—Team	G.	Min.	FGM	FGA	Pct.	FGM	FGA	Pct.	FTM	FTA	Pct.	Reb.	Ast.	Pts.	Avg.
87-88—Rapid City	41	1181	112	241	.465	68	178	.382	76	105	.724	134	172	504	12.3

NBA REGULAR SEASON RECORD

									—Rebounds—								
Sea.—Team	G.	Min.	FGA	FGM	Pct.	FTA	FTM	Pct.	Off.	Def.	Tot.	Ast.	PF	Dq.	Stl.	Blk.	Pts.	Avg.
87-88—New Jersey	15	156	42	18	.429	20	16	.800	5	17	22	34	23	0	12	0	54	3.6

Three-Point Field Goals: 1987-88, 2-for-4 (.500).

DWAYNE ALONZO WASHINGTON
(Pearl)

Born January 6, 1964 at Brooklyn, N.Y.   Height 6:02.   Weight 195.

High School—Brooklyn, N.Y., Boys and Girls.

College—Syracuse University, Syracuse, N.Y.

Drafted by New Jersey on first round as an undergraduate, 1986 (13th pick).

Selected from New Jersey by Miami in NBA expansion draft, June 23, 1988.

—COLLEGIATE RECORD—

Year	G.	Min.	FGA	FGM	Pct.	FTA	FTM	Pct.	Reb.	Pts.	Avg.
83-84	32	1107	340	185	.544	136	90	.662	83	460	14.4
84-85	31	1057	339	169	.499	176	138	.784	91	476	15.4
85-86	32	1034	404	216	.535	168	122	.726	79	554	17.3
Totals	95	3198	1083	570	.526	480	350	.729	253	1490	15.7

NBA REGULAR SEASON RECORD

									—Rebounds—								
Sea.—Team	G.	Min.	FGA	FGM	Pct.	FTA	FTM	Pct.	Off.	Def.	Tot.	Ast.	PF	Dq.	Stl.	Blk.	Pts.	Avg.
86-87—New Jersey	72	1600	538	257	.478	125	98	.784	37	92	129	301	184	5	92	7	616	8.6
87-88—New Jersey	68	1379	547	245	.448	189	132	.698	54	64	118	206	163	2	91	4	633	9.3
Totals	140	2979	1085	502	.463	314	230	.732	91	156	247	507	347	7	183	11	1249	8.9

Three-Point Field Goals: 1986-87, 4-for-24 (.167). 1987-88, 11-for-49 (.224). Totals, 15-for-73 (.205).

KERMIT A. WASHINGTON

Born September 17, 1951 at Washington, D. C.   Height 6:08.   Weight 230.

High School—Washington, D. C., Coolidge.

College—American University, Washington, D. C.

Drafted by Los Angeles on first round, 1973 (5th pick).

Traded by Los Angeles with Don Chaney and a 1978 1st round draft choice to Boston for Charlie Scott, December 27, 1977.
Traded by Boston with Sidney Wicks, Kevin Kunnert and the draft rights to Freeman Williams to San Diego for Nate Archibald, Marvin Barnes, Billy Knight and 1981 and 1983 2nd round draft choices, August 4, 1978.
Awarded from San Diego with Kevin Kunnert, cash and a 1980 1st round draft choice to Portland as compensation for earlier signing of Veteran Free Agent Bill Walton, September 18, 1979.
Traded by Portland to Golden State for a 1988 3rd round draft choice, October 13, 1987.
Waived by Golden State, November 25, 1987.

—COLLEGIATE RECORD—

Year	G.	Min.	FGA	FGM	Pct.	FTA	FTM	Pct.	Reb.	Pts.	Avg.
69-70†	17	....	287	129	.449	116	72	.621	379	330	19.4
70-71	25	....	370	173	.468	183	119	.650	512	465	18.6
71-72	23	....	355	193	.544	144	96	.667	455	482	21.0
72-73	25	899	426	211	.495	132	98	.742	511	520	20.8
Varsity Totals	73	....	1151	577	.501	459	313	.682	1478	1467	20.1

Sea.—Team	G.	Min.	FGA	FGM	Pct.	FTA	FTM	Pct.	Off.	Def.	Tot.	Ast.	PF	Dq.	Stl.	Blk.	Pts.	Avg.
										—Rebounds—								
73-74—Los Angeles	45	400	151	73	.483	49	26	.531	62	85	147	19	77	0	21	18	172	3.8
74-75—Los Angeles	55	949	207	87	.420	122	72	.500	106	244	350	66	155	2	25	32	246	4.5
75-76—Los Angeles	36	492	90	39	.433	66	45	.682	51	114	165	20	76	0	11	26	123	3.4
76-77—Los Angeles	53	1342	380	191	.503	187	132	.706	182	310	492	48	183	1	43	52	514	9.7
77-78—L.A.-Bos.	57	1617	507	247	.487	246	170	.691	215	399	614	72	188	3	47	64	664	11.6
78-79—San Diego	82	2764	623	350	.562	330	227	.688	296	504	800	125	317	11	85	121	927	11.3
79-80—Portland	80	2657	761	421	.553	360	231	.642	325	517	842	167	307	8	73	131	1073	13.4
80-81—Portland	73	2120	571	325	.569	288	181	.628	236	450	686	149	258	5	85	86	831	11.4
81-82—Portland	20	418	78	38	.487	41	24	.585	40	77	117	29	56	0	9	16	100	5.0
87-88—Golden State	6	56	14	7	.500	2	2	1.000	9	10	19	0	13	0	4	4	16	2.7
Totals	507	12815	3382	1778	.526	1691	1110	.656	1522	2710	4232	695	1630	30	403	550	4666	9.2

Three-Point Field Goals: 1979-80, 0-for-3. 1980-81, 0-for-1. Totals, 0-for-4.

NBA PLAYOFF RECORD

Sea.—Team	G.	Min.	FGA	FGM	Pct.	FTA	FTM	Pct.	Off.	Def.	Tot.	Ast.	PF	Dq.	Stl.	Blk.	Pts.	Avg.
										—Rebounds—								
73-74—Los Angeles	3	14	11	5	.455	7	5	.714	9	1	10	1	0	0	1	0	15	5.0
79-80—Portland	3	121	26	13	.500	8	5	.625	12	19	31	6	9	0	1	4	31	10.3
80-81—Portland	3	128	23	12	.522	2	2	1.000	14	38	52	7	9	0	8	2	26	8.7
Totals	9	263	60	30	.500	17	12	.706	35	58	93	14	18	0	10	6	72	8.0

Three-Point Field Goals: 1979-80, 0-for-1. 1980-81, 0-for-1. Totals, 0-for-2.

NBA ALL-STAR GAME RECORD

Season—Team	Min.	FGA	FGM	Pct.	FTA	FTM	Pct.	Off.	Def.	Tot.	Ast.	PF	Dq.	Stl.	Blk.	Pts.
									—Rebounds—							
1980—Portland........	14	6	1	.167	4	2	.500	4	4	8	1	4	0	0	1	4

Named to NBA All-Defensive Second Team, 1980 and 1981.... Led NCAA in rebounding, 1972 and 1973.... One of only seven players to average over 20 points and 20 rebounds per game during NCAA career.

ANTHONY JEROME WEBB
(Spud)

Born July 13, 1963 at Dallas, Tex.   Height 5:07.   Weight 135.

High School—Dallas, Tex., Wilmer-Hutchins.

Colleges—Midland College, Midland, Tex., and North Carolina State University, Raleigh, N.C.

Drafted by Detroit on fourth round, 1985 (87th pick).

Draft rights relinquished by Detroit, September 24, 1985; signed by Atlanta as a free agent, September 26, 1985.

—COLLEGIATE RECORD—

Midland

Year	G.	Min.	FGA	FGM	Pct.	FTA	FTM	Pct.	Reb.	Pts.	Avg.
81-82	38	....	538	277	.515	301	235	.781	77	789	20.8
82-83	35	....	440	196	.445	155	120	.774	106	512	14.6
J.C. Totals...............	73	....	978	473	.484	456	355	.779	183	1301	17.8

North Carolina State

Year	G.	Min.	FGA	FGM	Pct.	FTA	FTM	Pct.	Reb.	Pts.	Avg.
83-84	33	980	279	128	.459	88	67	.761	59	323	9.8
84-85	33	919	291	140	.481	113	86	.761	66	366	11.1
N.C. St. Totals........	66	1899	570	268	.470	201	153	.761	125	689	10.4

NBA REGULAR SEASON RECORD

Sea.—Team	G.	Min.	FGA	FGM	Pct.	FTA	FTM	Pct.	Off.	Def.	Tot.	Ast.	PF	Dq.	Stl.	Blk.	Pts.	Avg.
										—Rebounds—								
85-86—Atlanta	79	1229	412	199	.483	275	216	.785	27	96	123	337	164	1	82	5	616	7.8
86-87—Atlanta	33	532	162	71	.438	105	80	.762	6	54	60	167	65	1	34	2	223	6.8
87-88—Atlanta	82	1347	402	191	.475	131	107	.817	16	130	146	337	125	0	63	11	490	6.0
Totals	194	3108	976	461	.472	511	403	.789	49	280	329	841	354	2	179	18	1329	6.9

Three-Point Field Goals: 1985-86, 2-for-11 (.182). 1986-87, 1-for-6 (.167). 1987-88, 1-for-19 (.053). Totals, 4-for-36 (.111).

NBA PLAYOFF RECORD

Sea.—Team	G.	Min.	FGA	FGM	Pct.	FTA	FTM	Pct.	Off.	Def.	Tot.	Ast.	PF	Dq.	Stl.	Blk.	Pts.	Avg.
										—Rebounds—								
85-86—Atlanta	9	183	81	42	.519	33	26	.788	6	25	31	65	13	0	4	1	110	12.2
86-87—Atlanta	8	122	19	9	.474	17	13	.765	1	7	8	38	10	0	6	0	31	3.9
87-88—Atlanta	12	211	81	35	.432	37	34	.919	4	16	20	56	22	0	9	0	106	8.8
Totals	29	516	181	86	.475	87	73	.839	11	48	59	159	45	0	19	1	247	8.5

Three-Point Field Goals: 1985-86, 0-for-2. 1986-87, 0-for-1. 1987-88, 2-for-8 (.250). Totals, 2-for-11 (.182).

SCOTT DEAN WEDMAN

Born July 29, 1952 at Harper, Kan. Height 6:07. Weight 220.
High School—Denver, Colo., Mullen.
College—University of Colorado, Boulder, Colo.
Drafted by Kansas City-Omaha on first round, 1974 (6th pick).

Signed by Cleveland as a Veteran Free Agent, June 2, 1981; Kansas City agreed not to exercise its right of first refusal and traded a 1981 2nd round draft choice to Cleveland for a 1981 1st round draft choice, June 8, 1981.
Traded by Cleveland to Boston for Darren Tillis, a 1983 1st round draft choice and cash, January 14, 1983.
Traded by Boston with Sam Vincent to Seattle for a 1989 2nd round draft choice, October 16, 1987.

—COLLEGIATE RECORD—

Year	G.	Min.	FGA	FGM	Pct.	FTA	FTM	Pct.	Reb.	Pts.	Avg.
70-71†	10	....	...	66	....	53	46	.768	....	175	17.5
71-72	26	....	291	132	.454	103	68	.660	228	332	12.8
72-73	26	....	383	185	.483	111	90	.811	242	460	17.7
73-74	23	....	372	199	.535	97	61	.629	214	459	20.0
Varsity Totals	75	....	1046	516	.493	311	219	.704	684	1251	16.7

NBA REGULAR SEASON RECORD

Sea.—Team	G.	Min.	FGA	FGM	Pct.	FTA	FTM	Pct.	Off.	Def.	Tot.	Ast.	PF	Dq.	Stl.	Blk.	Pts.	Avg.
74-75—K.C.-Omaha	80	2554	806	375	.465	170	139	.818	202	288	490	129	270	2	81	27	889	11.1
75-76—Kansas City	82	2968	1181	538	.456	245	191	.780	199	407	606	199	280	8	103	36	1267	15.5
76-77—Kansas City	81	2743	1133	521	.460	241	206	.855	187	319	506	227	226	3	100	23	1248	15.4
77-78—Kansas City	81	2961	1192	607	.509	254	221	.870	144	319	463	201	242	2	99	22	1435	17.7
78-79—Kansas City	73	2498	1050	561	.534	271	216	.797	135	251	386	144	239	4	76	30	1338	18.3
79-80—Kansas City	68	2347	1112	569	.512	181	145	.801	114	272	386	145	230	1	84	45	1290	19.0
80-81—Kansas City	81	2902	1437	685	.477	204	140	.686	128	305	433	226	294	4	97	46	1535	19.0
81-82—Cleveland	54	1638	589	260	.441	90	66	.733	128	176	304	133	189	4	73	14	591	10.9
82-83—Clev.-Bos.	75	1793	788	374	.475	107	85	.794	98	184	282	117	228	6	43	17	843	11.2
83-84—Boston	68	916	333	148	.444	35	29	.829	41	98	139	67	107	0	27	7	327	4.8
84-85—Boston	78	1127	460	220	.478	55	42	.764	57	102	159	94	111	0	23	10	499	6.4
85-86—Boston	79	1402	605	286	.473	68	45	.662	66	126	192	83	127	0	38	22	634	8.0
86-87—Boston	6	78	27	9	.333	2	1	.500	3	6	9	0	6	0	2	2	20	3.3
Totals	906	25927	10713	5153	.481	1923	1526	.794	1502	2853	4355	1771	2549	34	846	301	11916	13.2

Three-Point Field Goals: 1979-80, 7-for-22 (.318). 1980-81, 25-for-77 (.325). 1981-82, 5-for-23 (.217). 1982-83, 10-for-32 (.313). 1983-84, 2-for-13 (.154). 1984-85, 17-for-34 (.500). 1985-86, 17-for-48 (.354). 1986-87, 1-for-2 (.500). Totals, 84-for-251 (.335).

NBA PLAYOFF RECORD

Sea.—Team	G.	Min.	FGA	FGM	Pct.	FTA	FTM	Pct.	Off.	Def.	Tot.	Ast.	PF	Dq.	Stl.	Blk.	Pts.	Avg.
74-75—K.C.-Omaha	6	230	68	27	.397	18	12	.667	10	25	35	16	17	0	6	3	66	11.0
78-79—Kansas City	5	174	78	36	.462	32	24	.750	13	24	37	9	18	0	9	3	96	19.2
79-80—Kansas City	3	116	64	29	.453	11	8	.727	6	15	21	9	9	0	1	3	68	22.7
80-81—Kansas City	15	657	297	129	.434	56	40	.714	16	71	87	58	51	0	18	8	307	20.5
82-83—Boston	6	66	24	14	.583	2	1	.500	3	11	14	0	11	0	1	0	29	4.8
83-84—Boston	17	226	96	40	.417	10	5	.500	24	23	47	17	19	0	6	0	89	5.2
84-85—Boston	21	350	134	73	.545	38	26	.684	22	37	59	33	50	1	13	0	182	8.7
85-86—Boston	12	142	51	20	.392	4	3	.750	11	11	22	8	14	0	9	3	45	3.8
Totals	85	1961	812	368	.453	171	119	.696	105	217	322	150	189	1	63	20	882	10.4

Three-Point Field Goals: 1979-80, 2-for-3 (.667). 1980-81, 9-for-32 (.281). 1982-83, 0-for-2. 1983-84, 4-for-7 (.571). 1984-85, 10-for-22 (.455). 1985-86, 2-for-4 (.500). Totals, 27-for-70 (.386).

NBA ALL-STAR GAME RECORD

Season—Team	Min.	FGA	FGM	Pct.	FTA	FTM	Pct.	Off.	Def.	Tot.	Ast.	PF	Dq.	Stl.	Blk.	Pts.
1976—Kansas City	20	5	4	.800	0	0	.000	0	6	6	2	2	0	1	0	8

Named to NBA All-Defensive Second Team, 1980. . . . NBA All-Rookie Team, 1975. . . . Member of NBA championship teams, 1984 and 1986. . . . Holds NBA championship series game record for highest field-goal percentage, 1.000 (11-for-11), vs. Los Angeles Lakers, May 27, 1985.

CHRISTIAN ANSGAR WELP
(Chris)

Born January 2, 1964 at Delmenhorst, West Germany. Height 7:00. Weight 245.
High School—Silverdale, Wash., Olympia.
College—University of Washington, Seattle, Wash.
Drafted by Philadelphia on first round, 1987 (16th pick).

—COLLEGIATE RECORD—

Year	G.	Min.	FGA	FGM	Pct.	FTA	FTM	Pct.	Reb.	Pts.	Avg.
83-84	31	947	237	135	.570	89	58	.652	192	328	10.6
84-85	32	971	294	170	.578	108	75	.694	225	415	13.0
85-86	31	1053	436	234	.537	177	133	.751	263	601	19.4
86-87	35	1143	473	281	.594	226	167	.739	315	729	20.8
Totals	129	4114	1440	820	.569	600	433	.722	995	2073	16.1

NBA REGULAR SEASON RECORD

Sea.—Team	G.	Min.	FGA	FGM	Pct.	FTA	FTM	Pct.	Off.	Def.	Tot.	Ast.	PF	Dq.	Stl.	Blk.	Pts.	Avg.
87-88—Philadelphia	10	132	31	18	.581	18	12	.667	11	13	24	5	25	0	5	5	48	4.8

Member of West German Olympic team, 1984.

WILLIAM PERCEY WENNINGTON
(Bill)

Born December 26, 1964 at Montreal, Can.   Height 7:00.   Weight 245.

High School—Brookville, N.Y., Long Island Lutheran.

College—St. John's University, Jamaica, N.Y.

Drafted by Dallas on first round, 1985 (16th pick).

—COLLEGIATE RECORD—

Year	G.	Min.	FGA	FGM	Pct.	FTA	FTM	Pct.	Reb.	Pts.	Avg.
81-82	30	505	85	37	.435	34	23	.676	126	97	3.2
82-83	33	656	114	69	.605	63	44	.698	146	182	5.5
83-84	26	735	209	124	.593	83	56	.675	148	304	11.7
84-85	35	1099	279	168	.602	125	102	.816	224	438	12.5
Totals	124	2995	687	398	.579	305	225	.738	644	1021	8.2

NBA REGULAR SEASON RECORD

Sea.—Team	G.	Min.	FGA	FGM	Pct.	FTA	FTM	Pct.	Off.	Def.	Tot.	Ast.	PF	Dq.	Stl.	Blk.	Pts.	Avg.
85-86—Dallas	56	562	153	72	.471	62	45	.726	32	100	132	21	83	0	11	22	189	3.4
86-87—Dallas	58	560	132	56	.424	60	45	.750	53	76	129	24	95	0	13	10	157	2.7
87-88—Dallas	30	125	49	25	.510	19	12	.632	14	25	39	4	33	0	5	9	63	2.1
Totals	144	1247	334	153	.458	141	102	.723	99	201	300	49	211	0	29	41	409	2.8

Three-Point Field Goals: 1985-86, 0-for-4. 1986-87, 0-for-2. 1987-88, 1-for-2 (.500). Totals, 1-for-8 (.125).

NBA PLAYOFF RECORD

Sea.—Team	G.	Min.	FGA	FGM	Pct.	FTA	FTM	Pct.	Off.	Def.	Tot.	Ast.	PF	Dq.	Stl.	Blk.	Pts.	Avg.
85-86—Dallas	6	18	6	2	.333	2	2	1.000	4	1	5	0	4	0	0	0	7	1.2
86-87—Dallas	4	47	12	6	.500	5	3	.600	4	6	10	4	9	0	0	3	15	3.8
87-88—Dallas	6	14	4	0	.000	0	0	.000	3	1	4	1	5	0	1	0	0	0.0
Totals	16	79	22	8	.364	7	5	.714	11	8	19	5	18	0	1	3	22	1.4

Three-Point Field Goals: 1986-87, 1-for-1 (1.000).

Member of Canadian Olympic team, 1984.

MARK ANDRE WEST

Born November 5, 1960 at Petersburg, Va.   Height 6:10.   Weight 230.

High School—Petersburg, Va.

College—Old Dominion University, Norfolk, Va.

Drafted by Dallas on second round, 1983 (30th pick).

Waived by Dallas, October 23, 1984; signed by Milwaukee as a free agent, November 6, 1984.

Waived by Milwaukee, November 12, 1984; signed by Cleveland as a free agent, November 23, 1984.

Traded by Cleveland with Tyrone Corbin, Kevin Johnson, 1988 1st and 2nd round draft choices and a 1989 2nd round draft choice to Phoenix for Larry Nance, Mike Sanders and a 1988 1st round draft choice, February 25, 1988.

—COLLEGIATE RECORD—

Year	G.	Min.	FGA	FGM	Pct.	FTA	FTM	Pct.	Reb.	Pts.	Avg.
79-80	30	679	141	67	.475	27	10	.370	212	144	4.8
80-81	28	845	243	128	.527	83	48	.578	287	304	10.9
81-82	30	1007	323	197	.610	147	78	.531	300	472	15.7
82-83	29	1005	297	169	.569	163	80	.491	314	418	14.4
Totals	117	3536	1004	561	.559	420	216	.514	1113	1338	11.4

NBA REGULAR SEASON RECORD

Sea.—Team	G.	Min.	FGA	FGM	Pct.	FTA	FTM	Pct.	Off.	Def.	Tot.	Ast.	PF	Dq.	Stl.	Blk.	Pts.	Avg.
83-84—Dallas	34	202	42	15	.357	22	7	.318	19	27	46	13	55	0	1	15	37	1.1

Sea.—Team	G.	Min.	FGA	FGM	Pct.	FTA	FTM	Pct.	Off.	Def.	Tot.	Ast.	PF	Dq.	Stl.	Blk.	Pts.	Avg.
84-85—Mil.-Clev.	66	888	194	106	.546	87	43	.494	90	161	251	15	197	7	13	49	255	3.9
85-86—Cleveland	67	1172	209	113	.541	103	54	.524	97	225	322	20	235	6	27	62	280	4.2
86-87—Cleveland	78	1333	385	209	.543	173	89	.514	126	213	339	41	229	5	22	81	507	6.5
87-88—Clev.-Phoe.	83	2098	573	316	.551	285	170	.596	165	358	523	74	265	4	47	147	802	9.7
Totals	328	5693	1403	759	.541	670	363	.542	497	984	1481	163	981	22	110	354	1881	5.7

Three-Point Field Goals: 1984-85, 0-for-1. 1986-87, 0-for-2. 1987-88, 0-for-1. Totals, 0-for-4.

NBA PLAYOFF RECORD

Sea.—Team	G.	Min.	FGA	FGM	Pct.	FTA	FTM	Pct.	Off.	Def.	Tot.	Ast.	PF	Dq.	Stl.	Blk.	Pts.	Avg.
83-84—Dallas	4	32	9	5	.556	3	2	.667	0	7	7	3	11	1	0	3	12	3.0
84-85—Cleveland	4	68	5	3	.600	5	2	.400	5	13	18	4	19	0	2	0	8	2.0
Totals	8	100	14	8	.571	8	4	.500	5	20	25	7	30	1	2	3	20	2.5

Led NCAA Division I in blocked shots, 1981 and 1982.

ENNIS WHATLEY

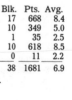

Born August 11, 1962 at Birmingham, Ala. Height 6:03. Weight 177.

High School—Birmingham, Ala., Phillips.

College—University of Alabama, University, Ala.

Drafted by Kansas City on first round as an undergraduate, 1983 (13th pick).

Draft rights traded by Kansas City with draft rights to Chris McNealy and a 1984 2nd round draft choice to Chicago for Mark Olberding and draft rights to Larry Micheaux, June 28, 1983.
Traded by Chicago with draft rights to Keith Lee to Cleveland for draft rights to Charles Oakley and Calvin Duncan, June 18, 1985.
Waived by Cleveland, December 16, 1985; signed by Washington, January 2, 1986, to a 10-day contract that expired, January 11, 1986.
Signed by San Antonio, February 1, 1986, to a 10-day contract that expired, February 10, 1986.
Signed by Washington as a free agent, September 4, 1986.
Waived by Washington, November 3, 1987; signed by Atlanta, February 11, 1988, to the first of consecutive 10-day contracts that expired, March 1, 1988.
Played in Continental Basketball Association with Mississippi Jets, 1987-88.

—COLLEGIATE RECORD—

Year	G.	Min.	FGA	FGM	Pct.	FTA	FTM	Pct.	Reb.	Pts.	Avg.
81-82	31	996	285	141	.495	129	93	.721	76	375	12.1
82-83	32	1109	366	183	.500	157	121	.771	128	487	15.2
Totals	63	2105	651	324	.498	286	214	.748	204	862	13.7

CBA REGULAR SEASON RECORD

			—2-Point—			—3-Point—								
Sea.—Team	G.	Min.	FGM	FGA	Pct.	FGM	FGA	Pct.	FTM	FTA	Pct.	Reb.	Ast.	Pts.	Avg.
87-88—Mississippi.................	29	1070	207	365	.567	2	16	.125	150	189	.794	116	218	570	19.7

NBA REGULAR SEASON RECORD

Sea.—Team	G.	Min.	FGA	FGM	Pct.	FTA	FTM	Pct.	Off.	Def.	Tot.	Ast.	PF	Dq.	Stl.	Blk.	Pts.	Avg.
83-84—Chicago	80	2159	556	261	.469	200	146	.730	63	134	197	662	223	4	119	17	668	8.4
84-85—Chicago	70	1385	313	140	.447	86	68	.791	34	67	101	381	141	1	66	10	349	5.0
85-86—Cl.-Wsh.-SA	14	107	35	15	.429	10	5	.500	4	10	14	23	10	0	5	1	35	2.5
86-87—Washington	73	1816	515	246	.478	165	126	.764	58	136	194	392	172	0	92	10	618	8.5
87-88—Atlanta	5	24	9	4	.444	4	3	.750	0	4	4	2	3	0	2	0	11	2.2
Totals	242	5491	1428	666	.466	465	348	.748	159	351	510	1460	549	5	284	38	1681	6.9

Three-Point Field Goals: 1983-84, 0-for-2. 1984-85, 1-for-9 (.111). 1986-87, 0-for-2. Totals, 1-for-13 (.077).

NBA PLAYOFF RECORD

Sea.—Team	G.	Min.	FGA	FGM	Pct.	FTA	FTM	Pct.	Off.	Def.	Tot.	Ast.	PF	Dq.	Stl.	Blk.	Pts.	Avg.
86-87—Washington	2	32	12	3	.250	0	0	.000	1	2	3	6	2	0	2	0	6	3.0

Named to THE SPORTING NEWS All-America Second Team, 1983.

CLINTON WHEELER

Born October 27, 1959 at Neptune, N.J. Height 6:01. Weight 185.

High School—Long Branch, N.J.

College—William Paterson College, Wayne, N.J.

Drafted by Kansas City on seventh round, 1981 (150th pick).

Waived by Kansas City, September 25, 1981; signed by New York as a free agent, August 1, 1984.
Waived by New York, October 24, 1984; re-signed by New York as a free agent, September 27, 1985.
Waived by New York, October 22, 1985; signed by Indiana as a free agent, October 5, 1987.
Selected from Indiana by Charlotte in NBA expansion draft, June 23, 1988.

Played in West Germany, 1981-82 and 1982-83, and in the Philippines, 1983-84.
Played in Continental Basketball Association with Albany Patroons, 1984-85 and 1985-86, and Rapid City Thrillers, 1986-87.

—COLLEGIATE RECORD—

Year	G.	Min.	FGA	FGM	Pct.	FTA	FTM	Pct.	Reb.	Pts.	Avg.
77-78				Statistics Unavailable							
78-79				Statistics Unavailable							
79-80	27	....	450	283	.629	185	139	.751	...	705	26.1
80-81	25	....	....	217	....	...	125	....	....	559	22.4
Totals	..	....	...	...	....	...	....	....	......	1624	....

CBA REGULAR SEASON RECORD

| Sea.—Team | G. | Min. | 2-Point | | | 3-Point | | | FTM | FTA | Pct. | Reb. | Ast. | Pts. | Avg. |
			FGM	FGA	Pct.	FGM	FGA	Pct.							
84-85—Albany	47	1108	285	562	.507	6	21	.286	193	237	.814	83	187	781	16.6
85-86—Albany	47	1863	435	918	.473	7	31	.226	271	337	.804	163	416	1162	24.7
86-87—Rapid City	48	1996	327	641	.510	3	8	.375	198	233	.849	156	381	861	17.9
Totals	142	4967	1047	2121	.494	16	60	.267	662	807	.820	402	984	2804	19.7

NBA REGULAR SEASON RECORD

| Sea.—Team | G. | Min. | FGA | FGM | Pct. | FTA | FTM | Pct. | Rebounds | | | Ast. | PF | Dq. | Stl. | Blk. | Pts. | Avg. |
									Off.	Def.	Tot.							
87-88—Indiana	59	513	132	62	.470	34	25	.735	19	21	40	103	37	0	36	2	149	2.5

Named CBA Playoff MVP, 1987.... CBA All-Defensive First Team, 1985, 1986, 1987.... CBA All-Star First Team, 1986.

ERIC L. WHITE

Born December 30, 1965 at San Francisco, Calif.   Height 6:08.   Weight 200.

High School—San Francisco, Calif., Sacred Heart.

College—Pepperdine University, Malibu, Calif.

Drafted by Detroit on third round, 1987 (65th pick).

Waived by Detroit, October 12, 1987; signed by Los Angeles Clippers, March 23, 1988, to the first of consecutive 10-day contracts that expired, April 11, 1988.
Re-signed by Los Angeles Clippers, April 12, 1988, for remainder of season.
Played in Continental Basketball Association with Mississippi Jets, 1987-88.

—COLLEGIATE RECORD—

Year	G.	Min.	FGA	FGM	Pct.	FTA	FTM	Pct.	Reb.	Pts.	Avg.
83-84	28	559	131	73	.557	46	28	.609	119	174	6.2
84-85	29	971	359	196	.546	97	69	.711	266	461	15.9
85-86	30	985	350	198	.566	83	64	.771	196	460	15.3
86-87	30	1067	492	232	.472	159	115	.723	230	579	19.3
Totals	117	3582	1332	699	.525	385	276	.717	811	1674	14.3

Three-Point Field Goals: 1986-87, 0-for-1.

CBA REGULAR SEASON RECORD

| Sea.—Team | G. | Min. | 2-Point | | | 3-Point | | | FTM | FTA | Pct. | Reb. | Ast. | Pts. | Avg. |
			FGM	FGA	Pct.	FGM	FGA	Pct.							
87-88—Mississippi	54	2157	423	767	.551	1	4	.250	295	363	.813	489	68	1144	21.2

NBA REGULAR SEASON RECORD

| Sea.—Team | G. | Min. | FGA | FGM | Pct. | FTA | FTM | Pct. | Rebounds | | | Ast. | PF | Dq. | Stl. | Blk. | Pts. | Avg. |
									Off.	Def.	Tot.							
87-88—L.A. Clippers	17	352	124	66	.532	57	45	.789	31	31	62	9	32	0	7	3	178	10.5

Three-Point Field Goals: 1987-88, 1-for-1 (1.000).

Named to CBA All-Rookie Team, 1988.

TONY F. WHITE

Born February 15, 1965 at Charlotte, N.C.   Height 6:02.   Weight 170.

High School—Charlotte, N.C., Independence.

College—University of Tennessee, Knoxville, Tenn.

Drafted by Chicago on second round, 1987 (33rd pick).

Waived by Chicago, November 12, 1987; claimed off waivers by New York, November 16, 1987.
Waived by New York, December 11, 1987; claimed off waivers by Golden State, December 15, 1987.

—COLLEGIATE RECORD—

Year	G.	Min.	FGA	FGM	Pct.	FTA	FTM	Pct.	Reb.	Pts.	Avg.
83-84	34	796	249	117	.470	107	79	.738	43	313	9.2
84-85	36	1117	432	221	.512	162	131	.809	88	573	15.9
85-86	28	1031	493	249	.505	142	124	.873	59	622	22.2
86-87	29	1090	530	259	.489	183	165	.902	95	711	24.5
Totals	127	4034	1704	846	.496	594	499	.840	285	2219	17.5

Three-Point Field Goals: 1986-87, 28-for-68 (.412).

NBA REGULAR SEASON RECORD

Sea.—Team	G.	Min.	FGA	FGM	Pct.	FTA	FTM	Pct.	Off.	Def.	Tot.	Ast.	PF	Dq.	Stl.	Blk.	Pts.	Avg.
87-88—Chi-NY-GS	49	581	249	111	.446	54	39	.722	12	19	31	59	57	0	20	2	261	5.3

Three-Point Field Goals: 1987-88, 0-for-6.

JEROME CLAY WHITEHEAD

Born September 30, 1956 at Waukegan, Ill. Height 6:10. Weight 225.

High School—Waukegan, Ill.

Colleges—Riverside City College, Riverside, Calif., and
Marquette University, Milwaukee, Wis.

Drafted by Buffalo on second round, 1978 (41st pick).

Waived by San Diego, December 4, 1979; signed by Utah as a free agent, January 18, 1980.
Selected from Utah by Dallas in expansion draft, May 28, 1980.
Traded by Dallas with Richard Washington to Cleveland for Bill Robinzine and 1983 and 1986 1st round draft choices, October 30, 1980.
Waived by Cleveland, November 17, 1980; signed by San Diego as a free agent, January 9, 1981.
Traded by Los Angeles Clippers to Golden State for the draft rights to Jay Murphy, June 19, 1984.

—COLLEGIATE RECORD—
Riverside City

Year	G.	Min.	FGA	FGM	Pct.	FTA	FTM	Pct.	Reb.	Pts.	Avg.
74-75	..	....	...	...	....	...	...	....	....	....	21.0

Marquette

Year	G.	Min.	FGA	FGM	Pct.	FTA	FTM	Pct.	Reb.	Pts.	Avg.
75-76	29	766	211	111	.526	56	37	.661	186	259	8.9
76-77	32	1022	290	150	.517	62	36	.581	266	336	10.5
77-78	28	884	276	165	.598	97	62	.639	232	392	14.0
Totals	89	2672	777	426	.548	215	135	.628	684	987	11.1

NBA REGULAR SEASON RECORD

Sea.—Team	G.	Min.	FGA	FGM	Pct.	FTA	FTM	Pct.	Off.	Def.	Tot.	Ast.	PF	Dq.	Stl.	Blk.	Pts.	Avg.
78-79—San Diego	31	152	34	15	.441	18	8	.444	16	34	50	7	29	0	3	4	38	1.2
79-80—SD-Utah	50	553	114	58	.509	35	10	.286	56	111	167	24	97	3	8	17	126	2.5
80-81—Dal-Cle-SD	48	688	180	83	.461	56	28	.500	58	156	214	26	122	2	20	9	194	4.0
81-82—San Diego	72	2214	726	406	.559	241	184	.763	231	433	664	102	290	16	48	44	996	13.8
82-83—San Diego	46	905	306	164	.536	87	72	.828	105	156	261	42	139	2	21	15	400	8.7
83-84—San Diego	70	921	294	144	.490	107	88	.822	94	151	245	19	159	2	17	12	376	5.4
84-85—Golden State	79	2536	825	421	.510	235	184	.783	219	403	622	53	322	8	45	43	1026	13.0
85-86—Golden State	81	1079	294	126	.429	97	60	.619	94	234	328	19	176	2	18	19	312	3.9
86-87—Golden State	73	937	327	147	.450	113	79	.699	110	152	262	24	175	1	16	12	373	5.1
87-88—Golden State	72	1221	360	174	.483	82	59	.720	109	212	321	39	209	3	32	21	407	5.7
Totals	622	11206	3460	1738	.502	1071	772	.721	1092	2042	3134	355	1718	39	228	196	4248	6.8

Three-Point Field Goals: 1980-81, 0-for-1. 1986-87, 0-for-1. Totals, 0-for-2.

NBA PLAYOFF RECORD

Sea.—Team	G.	Min.	FGA	FGM	Pct.	FTA	FTM	Pct.	Off.	Def.	Tot.	Ast.	PF	Dq.	Stl.	Blk.	Pts.	Avg.
86-87—Golden State	10	100	27	9	.333	10	4	.400	5	9	14	3	22	1	2	2	22	2.2

Member of NCAA Division I championship team, 1977.

EDDIE LEE WILKINS

Born May 7, 1962 at Cartersville, Ga. Height 6:10. Weight 220.

High School—Cartersville, Ga., Cass.

College—Gardner-Webb College, Boiling Springs, N. C.

Drafted by New York on sixth round, 1984 (133rd pick).

Missed entire 1985-86 season due to injury.
Played in Continental Basketball Association with Rockford Lightning, 1986-87, and Savannah Spirits and Quad City Thunder, 1987-88.

Year	G.	Min.	FGA	FGM	Pct.	FTA	FTM	Pct.	Reb.	Pts.	Avg.
80-81	36	....	296	166	.561	163	104	.638	242	436	12.1
81-82	29	....	350	217	.620	211	142	.673	257	576	19.9
82-83	32	....	463	295	.637	284	203	.715	340	793	24.8
83-84	29	....	376	214	.569	209	128	.612	264	556	19.2
Totals	126	....	1485	892	.601	867	577	.666	1103	2361	18.7

CBA REGULAR SEASON RECORD

Sea.—Team	G.	Min.	2-Point FGM	2-Point FGA	2-Point Pct.	3-Point FGM	3-Point FGA	3-Point Pct.	FTM	FTA	Pct.	Reb.	Ast.	Pts.	Avg.
86-87—Rockford	4	126	31	48	.646	0	1	.000	7	18	.389	32	3	69	17.3
87-88—Sav.-Quad City	54	1880	484	838	.578	0	4	.000	262	392	.668	498	31	1230	22.8
Totals	58	2006	515	886	.581	0	5	.000	269	410	.656	530	34	1299	22.4

NBA REGULAR SEASON RECORD

Sea.—Team	G.	Min.	FGA	FGM	Pct.	FTA	FTM	Pct.	Off.	Def.	Tot.	Ast.	PF	Dq.	Stl.	Blk.	Pts.	Avg.
84-85—New York	54	917	233	116	.498	122	66	.541	86	176	262	16	155	3	21	16	298	5.5
86-87—New York	24	454	127	56	.441	58	27	.466	45	62	107	6	67	1	9	2	139	5.8
Totals	78	1371	360	172	.478	180	93	.517	131	238	369	22	222	4	30	18	437	5.6

Three-Point Field Goals: 1984-85, 0-for-2. 1986-87, 0-for-1. Totals, 0-for-3.

GERALD BERNARD WILKINS

Born September 11, 1963 at Atlanta, Ga.   Height 6:06.   Weight 190.

High School—Atlanta, Ga., Mays Academy.

Colleges—Moberly Area Junior College, Moberly, Mo., and University of Tennessee-Chattanooga, Chattanooga, Tenn.

Drafted by New York on second round, 1985 (47th pick).

—COLLEGIATE RECORD—
Moberly

Year	G.	Min.	FGA	FGM	Pct.	FTA	FTM	Pct.	Reb.	Pts.	Avg.
81-82	39	1340	566	312	.551	126	97	.770	229	721	18.5

Tennessee-Chattanooga

Year	G.	Min.	FGA	FGM	Pct.	FTA	FTM	Pct.	Reb.	Pts.	Avg.
82-83	30	....	350	169	.483	62	41	.661	113	379	12.6
83-84	23	737	297	161	.542	105	73	.695	92	398	17.3
84-85	32	1188	532	276	.519	190	120	.632	147	672	21.0
UTC Totals	85	....	1179	606	.514	357	234	.655	352	1449	17.0

NBA REGULAR SEASON RECORD

Sea.—Team	G.	Min.	FGA	FGM	Pct.	FTA	FTM	Pct.	Off.	Def.	Tot.	Ast.	PF	Dq.	Stl.	Blk.	Pts.	Avg.
85-86—New York	81	2025	934	437	.468	237	132	.557	92	116	208	161	155	0	68	9	1013	12.5
86-87—New York	80	2758	1302	633	.486	335	235	.701	120	174	294	354	165	0	88	18	1527	19.1
87-88—New York	81	2703	1324	591	.446	243	191	.786	106	164	270	326	183	1	90	22	1412	17.4
Totals	242	7486	3560	1661	.467	815	558	.685	318	454	772	841	503	1	246	49	3952	16.3

Three-Point Field Goals: 1985-86, 7-for-25 (.280). 1986-87, 26-for-74 (.351). 1987-88, 39-for-129 (.302). Totals, 72-for-228 (.316).

NBA PLAYOFF RECORD

Sea.—Team	G.	Min.	FGA	FGM	Pct.	FTA	FTM	Pct.	Off.	Def.	Tot.	Ast.	PF	Dq.	Stl.	Blk.	Pts.	Avg.
87-88—New York	4	149	69	33	.478	14	12	.857	1	7	8	19	12	0	4	0	80	20.0

Three-Point Field Goals: 1987-88, 2-for-4 (.500).

Brother of Atlanta Hawks forward Dominique Wilkins.

JACQUES DOMINIQUE WILKINS
(Known by middle name.)

Born January 12, 1960 at Paris, France.   Height 6:08.   Weight 200.

High School—Washington, N. C.

College—University of Georgia, Athens, Ga.

Drafted by Utah on first round as an undergraduate, 1982 (3rd pick).

Draft rights traded by Utah to Atlanta for John Drew, Freeman Williams and cash, September 2, 1982.

GERALD WILKINS

—COLLEGIATE RECORD—

Year	G.	Min.	FGA	FGM	Pct.	FTA	FTM	Pct.	Reb.	Pts.	Avg.
79-80	16	508	257	135	.525	37	27	.730	104	297	18.6
80-81	31	1157	582	310	.533	149	112	.752	234	732	23.6
81-82	31	1083	526	278	.529	160	103	.644	250	659	21.3
Totals	78	2748	1365	723	.530	346	242	.699	588	1688	21.6

NBA REGULAR SEASON RECORD

Sea.—Team	G.	Min.	FGA	FGM	Pct.	FTA	FTM	Pct.	Off.	Def.	Tot.	Ast.	PF	Dq.	Stl.	Blk.	Pts.	Avg.
82-83—Atlanta	82	2697	1220	601	.493	337	230	.682	226	252	478	129	210	1	84	63	1434	17.5
83-84—Atlanta	81	2961	1429	684	.479	496	382	.770	254	328	582	126	197	1	117	87	1750	21.6
84-85—Atlanta	81	3023	1891	853	.451	603	486	.806	226	331	557	200	170	0	135	54	2217	27.4
85-86—Atlanta	78	3049	1897	888	.468	705	577	.818	261	357	618	206	170	0	138	49	2366	30.3
86-87—Atlanta	79	2969	1787	828	.463	742	607	.818	210	284	494	261	149	0	117	51	2294	29.0
87-88—Atlanta	78	2948	1957	909	.464	655	541	.826	211	291	502	224	162	0	103	47	2397	30.7
Totals	479	17647	10181	4763	.468	3538	2823	.798	1388	1843	3231	1146	1058	2	694	351	12458	26.0

Three-Point Field Goals: 1982-83, 2-for-11 (.182). 1983-84, 0-for-11. 1984-85, 25-for-81 (.309). 1985-86, 13-for-70 (.186). 1986-87, 31-for-106 (.292). 1987-88, 38-for-129 (.295). Totals, 109-for-408 (.267).

NBA PLAYOFF RECORD

Sea.—Team	G.	Min.	FGA	FGM	Pct.	FTA	FTM	Pct.	Off.	Def.	Tot.	Ast.	PF	Dq.	Stl.	Blk.	Pts.	Avg.
82-83—Atlanta	3	109	42	17	.405	14	12	.887	8	7	15	1	9	0	2	1	47	15.7
83-84—Atlanta	5	197	84	35	.417	31	26	.839	21	20	41	11	13	0	12	1	96	19.2
85-86—Atlanta	9	360	217	94	.433	79	68	.861	20	34	54	25	24	0	9	2	257	28.6
86-87—Atlanta	9	360	210	86	.410	74	66	.892	27	43	70	25	25	0	16	6	241	26.8
87-88—Atlanta	12	473	300	137	.457	125	96	.768	37	40	77	34	24	0	16	6	374	31.2
Totals	38	1499	853	369	.433	323	268	.830	113	144	257	96	95	0	55	18	1015	26.7

Three-Point Field Goals: 1982-83, 1-for-1 (1.000). 1983-84, 0-for-1. 1985-86, 1-for-5 (.200). 1986-87, 3-for-10 (.300). 1987-88, 4-for-18 (.222). Totals, 9-for-35 (.257).

NBA ALL-STAR GAME RECORD

Season—Team	Min.	FGA	FGM	Pct.	FTA	FTM	Pct.	Off.	Def.	Tot.	Ast.	PF	Dq.	Stl.	Blk.	Pts.
1986—Atlanta	17	15	6	.400	2	1	.500	2	1	3	2	2	0	0	1	13
1987—Atlanta	24	9	3	.333	7	4	.571	3	2	5	1	2	0	0	1	10
1988—Atlanta	30	22	12	.545	6	5	.833	1	4	5	0	3	0	0	1	29
Totals	71	46	21	.457	15	10	.667	6	7	13	3	7	0	0	3	52

Named to All-NBA First Team, 1986.... All-NBA Second Team, 1987 and 1988.... NBA All-Rookie Team, 1983... . Led NBA in scoring, 1986.... THE SPORTING NEWS All-America Second Team, 1981 and 1982.... Brother of New York Knicks forward Gerald Wilkins.

CHARLES LINWOOD WILLIAMS
(Buck)

Born March 8, 1960 at Rocky Mount, N. C.   Height 6:08.   Weight 225.

High School—Rocky Mount, N. C.

College—University of Maryland, College Park, Md.

Drafted by New Jersey on first round as an undergraduate, 1981 (3rd pick).

—COLLEGIATE RECORD—

Year	G.	Min.	FGA	FGM	Pct.	FTA	FTM	Pct.	Reb.	Pts.	Avg.
78-79	30	....	206	120	.583	109	60	.550	323	300	10.0
79-80	24	....	236	143	.606	128	85	.664	242	371	15.5
80-81	31	1080	283	183	.647	182	116	.637	363	482	15.5
Totals	85	....	725	446	.615	419	261	.623	928	1153	13.6

NBA REGULAR SEASON RECORD

Sea.—Team	G.	Min.	FGA	FGM	Pct.	FTA	FTM	Pct.	Off.	Def.	Tot.	Ast.	PF	Dq.	Stl.	Blk.	Pts.	Avg.
81-82—New Jersey	82	2825	881	513	.582	388	242	.624	347	658	1005	107	285	5	84	84	1268	15.5
82-83—New Jersey	82	2961	912	536	.588	523	324	.620	365	662	1027	125	270	4	91	110	1396	17.0
83-84—New Jersey	81	3003	926	495	.535	498	284	.570	355	645	1000	130	298	3	81	125	1274	15.7
84-85—New Jersey	82	3182	1089	577	.530	538	336	.625	323	682	1005	167	293	7	63	110	1491	18.2
85-86—New Jersey	82	3070	956	500	.523	445	301	.676	329	657	986	131	294	9	73	96	1301	15.9
86-87—New Jersey	82	2976	936	521	.557	588	430	.731	322	701	1023	129	315	8	78	91	1472	18.0
87-88—New Jersey	70	2637	832	466	.560	518	346	.668	298	536	834	109	266	5	68	44	1279	18.3
Totals	561	20654	6532	3608	.552	3498	2263	.647	2339	4541	6880	898	2021	41	538	660	9481	16.9

Three-Point Field Goals: 1981-82, 0-for-1. 1982-83, 0-for-4. 1983-84, 0-for-4. 1984-85, 1-for-4 (.250). 1985-86, 0-for-2. 1986-87, 0-for-1. 1987-88, 1-for-1 (1.000). Totals, 2-for-17 (.118).

Sea.—Team	G.	Min.	FGA	FGM	Pct.	FTA	FTM	Pct.	Rebounds—Off.	Def.	Tot.	Ast.	PF	Dq.	Stl.	Blk.	Pts.	Avg.
81-82—New Jersey	2	79	26	14	.538	15	7	.467	11	10	21	3	7	0	1	2	35	17.5
82-83—New Jersey	2	85	22	11	.500	20	16	.800	9	14	23	4	12	2	2	2	38	19.0
83-84—New Jersey	11	473	130	63	.485	81	45	.556	57	98	155	16	44	2	15	17	171	15.5
84-85—New Jersey	3	123	40	26	.650	30	22	.733	14	18	32	1	12	0	3	5	74	24.7
85-86—New Jersey	3	126	29	21	.724	26	20	.769	12	19	31	2	15	1	6	1	62	20.7
Totals	21	886	247	135	.547	172	110	.640	103	159	262	26	90	5	27	27	380	18.1

NBA ALL-STAR GAME RECORD

Season—Team	Min.	FGA	FGM	Pct.	FTA	FTM	Pct.	Rebounds—Off.	Def.	Tot.	Ast.	PF	Dq.	Stl.	Blk.	Pts.
1982—New Jersey ..	22	7	2	.286	2	0	.000	1	9	10	1	3	0	0	2	4
1983—New Jersey ..	19	4	3	.750	4	2	.500	3	4	7	1	0	0	1	0	8
1986—New Jersey ..	20	8	5	.625	5	3	.600	3	4	7	4	0	0	0	0	13
Totals	61	19	10	.526	11	5	.455	7	17	24	6	3	0	1	2	25

Named to All-NBA Second Team, 1983. . . . NBA All-Defensive Second Team, 1988. . . . NBA Rookie of the Year, 1982. . . . NBA All-Rookie Team, 1982. . . . Member of U.S. Olympic team, 1980.

HERBERT L. WILLIAMS
(Herb)

Born February 16, 1958 at Columbus, O.   Height 6:11.   Weight 242.
High School—Columbus, O., Marion Franklin.
College—Ohio State University, Columbus, O.
Drafted by Indiana on first round, 1981 (14th pick).

—COLLEGIATE RECORD—

Year	G.	Min.	FGA	FGM	Pct.	FTA	FTM	Pct.	Reb.	Pts.	Avg.
77-78	27	992	407	196	.482	91	60	.659	308	452	16.7
78-79	31	1212	483	253	.524	166	111	.669	325	617	19.9
79-80	29	1069	415	206	.496	147	97	.660	263	509	17.6
80-81	27	1020	368	179	.486	109	75	.688	215	433	16.0
Totals	114	4293	1673	834	.499	513	343	.669	1111	2011	17.6

NBA REGULAR SEASON RECORD

Sea.—Team	G.	Min.	FGA	FGM	Pct.	FTA	FTM	Pct.	Rebounds—Off.	Def.	Tot.	Ast.	PF	Dq.	Stl.	Blk.	Pts.	Avg.
81-82—Indiana	82	2277	854	407	.477	188	126	.670	175	430	605	139	200	0	53	178	942	11.5
82-83—Indiana	78	2513	1163	580	.499	220	155	.705	151	432	583	262	230	4	54	171	1315	16.9
83-84—Indiana	69	2279	860	411	.478	295	207	.702	154	400	554	215	193	4	60	108	1029	14.9
84-85—Indiana	75	2557	1211	575	.475	341	224	.657	154	480	634	252	218	1	54	134	1375	18.3
85-86—Indiana	78	2770	1275	627	.492	403	294	.730	172	538	710	174	244	2	50	184	1549	19.9
86-87—Indiana	74	2526	939	451	.480	269	199	.740	143	400	543	174	255	9	59	93	1101	14.9
87-88—Indiana	75	1966	732	311	.425	171	126	.737	116	353	469	98	244	1	37	146	748	10.0
Totals	531	16888	7034	3362	.478	1887	1331	.705	1065	3033	4098	1314	1584	21	367	1014	8059	15.2

Three-Point Field Goals: 1981-82, 2-for-7 (.286). 1982-83, 0-for-7. 1983-84, 0-for-4. 1984-85, 1-for-9 (.111). 1985-86, 1-for-12 (.083). 1986-87, 0-for-9. 1987-88, 0-for-6. Totals, 4-for-54 (.074).

NBA PLAYOFF RECORD

Sea.—Team	G.	Min.	FGA	FGM	Pct.	FTA	FTM	Pct.	Rebounds—Off.	Def.	Tot.	Ast.	PF	Dq.	Stl.	Blk.	Pts.	Avg.
86-87—Indiana	4	134	34	20	.588	13	7	.538	3	17	20	7	12	0	0	1	47	11.8

JOHN WILLIAMS

Born August 9, 1961 at Sorrento, La.   Height 6:11.   Weight 230.
High School—Sorrento, La., St. Amant.
College—Tulane University, New Orleans, La.
Drafted by Cleveland on second round, 1985 (45th pick).

—COLLEGIATE RECORD—

Year	G.	Min.	FGA	FGM	Pct.	FTA	FTM	Pct.	Reb.	Pts.	Avg.
81-82	28	932	279	163	.584	133	88	.662	202	414	14.8
82-83	31	996	317	151	.476	118	83	.703	166	385	12.4
83-84	28	1038	355	202	.569	184	140	.761	222	544	19.4
84-85	28	1006	334	189	.566	155	120	.774	219	498	17.8
Totals	115	3972	1285	705	.549	590	431	.731	809	1841	16.0

NBA REGULAR SEASON RECORD

Sea.—Team	G.	Min.	FGA	FGM	Pct.	FTA	FTM	Pct.	Off.	Def.	Tot.	Ast.	PF	Dq.	Stl.	Blk.	Pts.	Avg.
									—Rebounds—									
86-87—Cleveland	80	2714	897	435	.485	400	298	.745	222	407	629	154	197	0	58	167	1168	14.6
87-88—Cleveland	77	2106	663	316	.477	279	211	.756	159	347	506	103	203	2	61	145	843	10.9
Totals	157	4820	1560	751	.481	679	509	.750	381	754	1135	257	400	2	119	312	2011	12.8

Three-Point Field Goals: 1986-87, 0-for-1. 1987-88, 0-for-1. Totals, 0-for-2.

NBA PLAYOFF RECORD

Sea.—Team	G.	Min.	FGA	FGM	Pct.	FTA	FTM	Pct.	Off.	Def.	Tot.	Ast.	PF	Dq.	Stl.	Blk.	Pts.	Avg.
									—Rebounds—									
87-88—Cleveland	5	133	40	20	.500	13	6	.462	13	16	29	4	13	0	3	7	46	9.2

Named to NBA All-Rookie Team, 1987.

JOHN SAM WILLIAMS

Born October 26, 1966 at Los Angeles, Calif.   Height 6:09.   Weight 235.

High School—Los Angeles, Calif., Crenshaw.

College—Louisiana State University, Baton Rouge, La.

Drafted by Washington on first round as an undergraduate, 1986 (12th pick).

—COLLEGIATE RECORD—

Year	G.	Min.	FGA	FGM	Pct.	FTA	FTM	Pct.	Reb.	Pts.	Avg.
84-85	29	935	305	163	.534	81	62	.765	190	388	13.4
85-86	37	1277	540	269	.498	155	120	.774	313	658	17.8
Totals	66	2212	845	432	.511	236	182	.771	503	1046	15.8

NBA REGULAR SEASON RECORD

Sea.—Team	G.	Min.	FGA	FGM	Pct.	FTA	FTM	Pct.	Off.	Def.	Tot.	Ast.	PF	Dq.	Stl.	Blk.	Pts.	Avg.
									—Rebounds—									
86-87—Washington	78	1773	624	283	.454	223	144	.646	130	236	366	191	173	1	129	30	718	9.2
87-88—Washington	82	2428	910	427	.469	256	188	.734	127	317	444	232	217	3	117	34	1047	12.8
Totals	160	4201	1534	710	.463	479	332	.693	257	553	810	423	390	4	246	64	1765	11.0

Three-Point Field Goals: 1986-87, 8-for-36 (.222). 1987-88, 5-for-38 (.132). Totals, 13-for-74 (.176).

NBA PLAYOFF RECORD

Sea.—Team	G.	Min.	FGA	FGM	Pct.	FTA	FTM	Pct.	Off.	Def.	Tot.	Ast.	PF	Dq.	Stl.	Blk.	Pts.	Avg.
									—Rebounds—									
86-87—Washington	3	49	14	8	.571	7	4	.571	4	7	11	2	3	0	2	0	20	6.7
87-88—Washington	5	185	48	23	.479	32	19	.594	11	18	29	21	18	1	8	4	65	13.0
Totals	8	234	62	31	.500	39	23	.590	15	25	40	23	21	1	10	4	85	10.6

Three-Point Field Goals: 1986-87, 0-for-1. 1987-88, 0-for-1. Totals, 0-for-2.

KEVIN EUGENE WILLIAMS

Born September 11, 1961 at New York, N. Y.   Height 6:02.   Weight 180.

High School—New York, N. Y., Charles E. Hughes.

College—St. John's University, Jamaica, N. Y.

Drafted by San Antonio on second round, 1983 (46th pick).

Waived by San Antonio, December 12, 1983; signed by Cleveland as a free agent, December 20, 1984.
Waived by Cleveland, September 17, 1985; signed by Seattle as a free agent, July 11, 1986.
Selected from Seattle by Miami in NBA expansion draft, June 23, 1988.
Played in Continental Basketball Association with Ohio Mixers, 1983-84, Bay State Bombardiers, 1984-85, and Bay State Bombardiers and Tampa Bay Thrillers, 1985-86.

—COLLEGIATE RECORD—

Year	G.	Min.	FGA	FGM	Pct.	FTA	FTM	Pct.	Reb.	Pts.	Avg.
79-80	12	65	29	13	.448	26	21	.808	18	47	3.9
80-81	27	348	104	54	.519	52	35	.673	31	143	5.3
81-82	30	431	136	69	.507	78	64	.821	41	202	6.7
82-83	33	727	217	123	.567	92	71	.772	64	317	9.6
Totals	102	1571	486	259	.533	248	191	.770	154	709	7.0

CBA REGULAR SEASON RECORD

Sea.—Team	G.	Min.	2-Point			3-Point			FTM	FTA	Pct.	Reb.	Ast.	Pts.	Avg.
			FGM	FGA	Pct.	FGM	FGA	Pct.							
83-84—Ohio..............................	32	895	210	410	.512	1	4	.250	187	229	.816	134	136	610	19.1
84-85—Bay State	8	322	93	187	.497	1	4	.250	65	77	.844	40	46	254	31.8
85-86—Bay St.-Tampa Bay..	35	1349	406	830	.489	2	7	.286	259	316	.820	149	146	1077	30.8
Totals	75	2566	709	1427	.497	4	15	.267	511	622	.822	323	328	1941	25.9

NBA REGULAR SEASON RECORD

Sea.—Team	G.	Min.	FGA	FGM	Pct.	FTA	FTM	Pct.	Off.	Def.	Tot.	Ast.	PF	Dq.	Stl.	Blk.	Pts.	Avg.
										—Rebounds—								
83-84—San Antonio	19	200	58	25	.431	32	25	.781	4	9	13	43	42	1	8	4	75	3.9
84-85—Cleveland	46	413	134	58	.433	64	47	.734	19	44	63	61	86	1	22	4	163	3.5
86-87—Seattle	65	703	296	132	.446	66	55	.833	47	36	83	66	154	1	45	8	319	4.9
87-88—Seattle	80	1084	450	199	.442	122	103	.844	61	66	127	96	207	1	62	7	502	6.3
Totals	210	2400	938	414	.441	284	230	.810	131	155	286	266	489	4	137	23	1059	5.0

Three-Point Field Goals: 1983-84, 0-for-1. 1984-85, 0-for-5. 1986-87, 0-for-7. 1987-88, 1-for-7 (.143). Totals, 1-for-20 (.050).

NBA PLAYOFF RECORD

Sea.—Team	G.	Min.	FGA	FGM	Pct.	FTA	FTM	Pct.	Off.	Def.	Tot.	Ast.	PF	Dq.	Stl.	Blk.	Pts.	Avg.
										—Rebounds—								
84-85—Cleveland	2	7	2	1	.500	0	0	.000	0	0	0	1	1	0	0	0	2	1.0
86-87—Seattle	14	255	94	45	.479	40	30	.750	19	15	34	30	44	0	16	1	120	8.6
87-88—Seattle	5	70	16	7	.438	0	0	.000	6	2	8	9	15	0	3	0	14	2.8
Totals	21	332	112	53	.473	40	30	.750	25	17	42	40	60	0	19	1	136	6.5

Three-Point Field Goals: 1986-87, 0-for-2. 1987-88, 0-for-2. Totals, 0-for-4.

REGGIE WILLIAMS

Born March 5, 1964 at Baltimore, Md.   Height 6:07.   Weight 190.

High School—Baltimore, Md., Dunbar.

College—Georgetown University, Washington, D.C.

Drafted by Los Angeles Clippers on first round, 1987 (4th pick).

—COLLEGIATE RECORD—

Year	G.	Min.	FGA	FGM	Pct.	FTA	FTM	Pct.	Reb.	Pts.	Avg.
83-84	37	764	300	130	.433	99	76	.768	131	336	9.1
84-85	35	1043	332	168	.506	106	80	.755	200	416	11.9
85-86	32	1013	430	227	.528	149	109	.732	261	563	17.6
86-87	34	1205	589	284	.482	194	156	.804	294	802	23.6
Totals	138	4025	1651	809	.490	548	421	.768	886	2117	15.3

Three-Point Field Goals: 1986-87, 78-for-202 (.386).

NBA REGULAR SEASON RECORD

Sea.—Team	G.	Min.	FGA	FGM	Pct.	FTA	FTM	Pct.	Off.	Def.	Tot.	Ast.	PF	Dq.	Stl.	Blk.	Pts.	Avg.
										—Rebounds—								
87-88—L.A. Clippers	35	857	427	152	.356	66	48	.727	55	63	118	58	108	1	29	21	365	10.4

Three-Point Field Goals: 1987-88, 13-for-58 (.224).

Member of NCAA Division I championship team, 1984. . . . Named to THE SPORTING NEWS All-America First Team, 1987.

KEVIN ANDRE WILLIS

Born September 6, 1962 at Los Angeles, Calif.   Height 7:00.   Weight 235.

High School—Detroit, Mich., Pershing.

Colleges—Jackson Community College, Jackson, Mich., and Michigan State University, East Lansing, Mich.

Drafted by Atlanta on first round, 1984 (11th pick).

—COLLEGIATE RECORD—
Jackson CC

Year	G.	Min.	FGA	FGM	Pct.	FTA	FTM	Pct.	Reb.	Pts.	Avg.
80-81	....	....	....	....	....	....	....	....	....	....	19.0

Michigan State

Year	G.	Min.	FGA	FGM	Pct.	FTA	FTM	Pct.	Reb.	Pts.	Avg.
81-82	27	518	154	73	.474	30	17	.567	113	163	6.0
82-83	27	865	272	162	.596	70	36	.514	258	360	13.3
83-84	25	738	240	118	.492	59	39	.661	192	275	11.0
MSU Totals	79	2121	666	353	.530	159	92	.579	563	798	10.1

Three-Point Field Goals: 1982-83, 0-for-1.

NBA REGULAR SEASON RECORD

Sea.—Team	G.	Min.	FGA	FGM	Pct.	FTA	FTM	Pct.	Off.	Def.	Tot.	Ast.	PF	Dq.	Stl.	Blk.	Pts.	Avg.
										—Rebounds—								
84-85—Atlanta	82	1785	690	322	.467	181	119	.657	177	345	522	36	226	4	31	49	765	9.3
85-86—Atlanta	82	2300	511	419	.517	263	172	.654	243	461	704	45	294	6	66	44	1010	12.3
86-87—Atlanta	81	2626	1003	538	.536	320	227	.709	321	528	849	62	313	4	65	61	1304	16.1
87-88—Atlanta	75	2091	687	356	.518	245	159	.649	235	312	547	28	240	2	68	42	871	11.6
Totals	320	8802	3091	1635	.529	1009	677	.671	976	1646	2622	171	1073	16	230	196	3950	12.3

Three-Point Field Goals: 1984-85, 2-for-9 (.222). 1985-86, 0-for-6. 1986-87, 1-for-4 (.250). 1987-88, 0-for-2. Totals, 3-for-21 (.143).

KEVIN WILLIS

Sea.—Team	G.	Min.	FGA	FGM	Pct.	FTA	FTM	Pct.	—Rebounds— Off.	Def.	Tot.	Ast.	PF	Dq.	Stl.	Blk.	Pts.	Avg.
85-86—Atlanta	9	280	98	55	.561	23	15	.652	31	34	65	5	38	2	7	8	125	13.9
86-87—Atlanta	9	356	115	60	.522	31	21	.677	33	50	83	6	33	0	9	7	141	15.7
87-88—Atlanta	12	462	138	80	.580	50	34	.680	36	72	108	11	51	1	10	10	194	16.2
Totals	30	1098	351	195	.556	104	70	.673	100	156	256	22	122	3	26	25	460	15.3

Three-Point Field Goals: 1987-88, 0-for-1.

NIKITA FRANCISCUS WILSON

Born February 25, 1964 at Pineville, La. Height 6:08. Weight 200.

High School—Leesville, La.

College—Louisiana State University, Baton Rouge, La.

Drafted by Portland on second round, 1987 (30th pick).

—COLLEGIATE RECORD—

Year	G.	Min.	FGA	FGM	Pct.	FTA	FTM	Pct.	Reb.	Pts.	Avg.
83-84	28	520	130	70	.538	48	27	.563	146	167	6.0
84-85	29	933	313	183	.585	90	70	.778	201	436	15.0
85-86	18	520	165	90	.545	71	56	.789	108	236	13.1
86-87	35	1219	429	220	.513	156	105	.673	244	545	15.6
Totals	110	3192	1037	563	.543	365	258	.707	699	1384	12.6

NBA REGULAR SEASON RECORD

Sea.—Team	G.	Min.	FGA	FGM	Pct.	FTA	FTM	Pct.	—Rebounds— Off.	Def.	Tot.	Ast.	PF	Dq.	Stl.	Blk.	Pts.	Avg.
87-88—Portland	15	54	23	7	.304	6	5	.833	2	9	11	3	7	0	0	0	19	1.3

RICKY WILSON

Born July 16, 1964 at Hampton, Va. Height 6:03. Weight 195.

High School—Hampton, Va., Phoebus.

College—George Mason University, Fairfax, Va.

Drafted by Chicago on third round, 1986 (52nd pick).

Waived by Chicago, October 27, 1986; signed by Seattle as a free agent, October 7, 1987.

Waived by Seattle, October 20, 1987; signed by New Jersey, February 27, 1988, to the first of consecutive 10-day contracts that expired, March 17, 1988.

Signed by San Antonio, March 22, 1988, to the first of consecutive 10-day contracts that expired, April 10, 1988.

Re-signed by San Antonio, April 11, 1988, for remainder of season.

Played in Continental Basketball Association with Mississippi Jets, 1986-87 and 1987-88.

—COLLEGIATE RECORD—

Year	G.	Min.	FGA	FGM	Pct.	FTA	FTM	Pct.	Reb.	Pts.	Avg.
82-83	27	644	187	90	.481	53	37	.698	52	217	8.0
83-84	28	966	377	178	.472	124	80	.645	119	436	15.6
84-85	29	1000	300	139	.463	126	91	.722	90	369	12.7
85-86	32	1050	371	179	.482	182	125	.687	100	483	15.1
Totals	116	3660	1235	586	.474	485	333	.687	361	1505	13.0

CBA REGULAR SEASON RECORD

Sea.—Team	G.	Min.	—2-Point— FGM	FGA	Pct.	—3-Point— FGM	FGA	Pct.	FTM	FTA	Pct.	Reb.	Ast.	Pts.	Avg.
86-87—Mississippi................	48	1534	299	565	.529	1	10	.100	180	246	.731	164	161	781	16.3
87-88—Mississippi................	45	1862	397	791	.502	6	42	.143	246	333	.739	182	281	1058	23.5
Totals	93	3396	696	1356	.513	7	52	.135	426	579	.736	346	442	1839	19.8

NBA REGULAR SEASON RECORD

Sea.—Team	G.	Min.	FGA	FGM	Pct.	FTA	FTM	Pct.	—Rebounds— Off.	Def.	Tot.	Ast.	PF	Dq.	Stl.	Blk.	Pts.	Avg.
87-88—N.J.-S.A.	24	420	110	43	.391	40	29	.725	2	25	27	69	40	0	23	3	125	5.2

Three-Point Field Goals: 1987-88, 10-for-26 (.385).

NBA PLAYOFF RECORD

Sea.—Team	G.	Min.	FGA	FGM	Pct.	FTA	FTM	Pct.	—Rebounds— Off.	Def.	Tot.	Ast.	PF	Dq.	Stl.	Blk.	Pts.	Avg.
87-88—San Antonio	2	9	2	0	.000	0	0	.000	0	0	0	1	2	0	0	0	0	0.0

Named to CBA All-Star First Team, 1988. . . . CBA All-Defensive Team, 1988.

DAVID WINGATE

Born December 15, 1963 at Baltimore, Md.   Height 6:05.   Weight 185.
High School—Baltimore, Md., Dunbar.
College—Georgetown University, Washington, D.C.
Drafted by Philadelphia on second round, 1986 (44th pick).

—COLLEGIATE RECORD—

Year	G.	Min.	FGA	FGM	Pct.	FTA	FTM	Pct.	Reb.	Pts.	Avg.
82-83	32	855	335	149	.445	124	87	.702	95	385	12.0
83-84	37	1005	370	161	.435	129	93	.721	135	415	11.2
84-85	38	1128	395	191	.484	132	91	.689	135	473	12.4
85-86	32	956	394	196	.497	155	117	.755	129	509	15.9
Totals	139	3944	1494	697	.467	540	388	.719	494	1782	12.8

NBA REGULAR SEASON RECORD

Sea.—Team	G.	Min.	FGA	FGM	Pct.	FTA	FTM	Pct.	Off.	Def.	Tot.	Ast.	PF	Dq.	Stl.	Blk.	Pts.	Avg.
86-87—Philadelphia	77	1612	602	259	.430	201	149	.741	70	86	156	155	169	1	93	19	680	8.8
87-88—Philadelphia	61	1419	545	218	.400	132	99	.750	44	57	101	119	125	0	47	22	545	8.9
Totals	138	3031	1147	477	.416	333	248	.745	114	143	257	274	294	1	140	41	1225	8.9

Three-Point Field Goals: 1986-87, 13-for-52 (.250). 1987-88, 10-for-40 (.250). Totals, 23-for-92 (.250).

NBA PLAYOFF RECORD

Sea.—Team	G.	Min.	FGA	FGM	Pct.	FTA	FTM	Pct.	Off.	Def.	Tot.	Ast.	PF	Dq.	Stl.	Blk.	Pts.	Avg.
86-87—Philadelphia	5	90	37	15	.405	14	9	.643	5	7	12	9	11	1	5	1	41	8.2

Three-Point Field Goals: 1986-87, 2-for-2 (1.000).

Member of NCAA Division I championship team, 1984.

RICKIE O'NEAL WINSLOW

Born July 26, 1964 at Houston, Tex.   Height 6:08.   Weight 225.
High School—Houston, Tex., Yates.
College—University of Houston, Houston, Tex.
Drafted by Chicago on second round, 1987 (28th pick).

Waived by Chicago, November 9, 1987; signed by Milwaukee as a free agent, November 13, 1987.
Waived by Milwaukee, December 22, 1987.

—COLLEGIATE RECORD—

Year	G.	Min.	FGA	FGM	Pct.	FTA	FTM	Pct.	Reb.	Pts.	Avg.
83-84	37	1030	233	133	.571	82	50	.610	203	316	8.5
84-85	30	1037	315	180	.571	109	67	.615	263	427	14.2
85-86	27	985	299	159	.532	149	103	.691	281	421	15.6
86-87	30	1035	307	159	.518	109	63	.578	222	384	12.8
Totals	124	4087	1154	631	.547	449	283	.630	969	1548	12.5

Three-Point Field Goals: 1986-87, 3-for-8 (.375).

NBA REGULAR SEASON RECORD

Sea.—Team	G.	Min.	FGA	FGM	Pct.	FTA	FTM	Pct.	Off.	Def.	Tot.	Ast.	PF	Dq.	Stl.	Blk.	Pts.	Avg.
87-88—Milwaukee	7	45	13	3	.231	2	1	.500	3	4	7	2	9	0	1	0	7	1.0

Three-Point Field Goals: 1987-88, 0-for-1.

RANDY SCOTT WITTMAN

Born October 28, 1959 at Indianapolis, Ind.   Height 6:06.   Weight 210.
High School—Indianapolis, Ind., Ben Davis.
College—Indiana University, Bloomington, Ind.
Drafted by Washington on first round, 1983 (22nd pick).

Draft rights traded by Washington to Atlanta for Tom McMillen and a 1984 2nd round draft choice, July 5, 1983.
Traded by Atlanta with a 1988 1st round draft choice to Sacramento for Reggie Theus, a 1988 3rd round draft choice and future considerations, June 27, 1988.

—COLLEGIATE RECORD—

Year	G.	Min.	FGA	FGM	Pct.	FTA	FTM	Pct.	Reb.	Pts.	Avg.
78-79	34	....	190	101	.532	53	39	.736	90	241	7.1
79-80	5	....	28	13	.464	4	3	.750	7	29	5.8
80-81	35	....	286	155	.542	69	53	.768	79	363	10.4

Year	G.	Min.	FGA	FGM	Pct.	FTA	FTM	Pct.	Reb.	Pts.	Avg.
81-82	29	....	299	144	.482	78	59	.756	94	347	12.0
82-83	30	....	435	236	.543	108	89	.824	135	569	19.0
Totals	133	....	1238	649	.524	312	243	.779	405	1549	11.6

Three-Point Field Goals: 1982-83, 8-for-18 (.444).
(Suffered stress fracture of right ankle in 1979-80 season; granted extra year of eligibility.)

NBA REGULAR SEASON RECORD

Sea.—Team	G.	Min.	FGA	FGM	Pct.	FTA	FTM	Pct.	Off.	Def.	Tot.	Ast.	PF	Dq.	Stl.	Blk.	Pts.	Avg.
										—Rebounds—								
83-84—Atlanta	78	1071	318	160	.503	46	28	.609	14	57	71	71	82	0	17	0	350	4.5
84-85—Atlanta	41	1168	352	187	.531	41	30	.732	16	57	73	125	58	0	28	7	406	9.9
85-86—Atlanta	81	2760	881	467	.530	135	104	.770	51	119	170	306	118	0	81	14	1043	12.9
86-87—Atlanta	71	2049	792	398	.503	127	100	.787	30	94	124	211	107	0	39	16	900	12.7
87-88—Atlanta	82	2412	787	376	.478	89	71	.798	39	131	170	302	117	0	50	18	823	10.0
Totals	353	9460	3130	1588	.507	438	333	.760	150	458	608	1015	482	0	215	55	3522	10.0

Three-Point Field Goals: 1983-84, 2-for-5 (.400). 1984-85, 2-for-7 (.286). 1985-86, 5-for-16 (.313). 1986-87, 4-for-12 (.333). Totals, 13-for-40 (.325).

NBA PLAYOFF RECORD

Sea.—Team	G.	Min.	FGA	FGM	Pct.	FTA	FTM	Pct.	Off.	Def.	Tot.	Ast.	PF	Dq.	Stl.	Blk.	Pts.	Avg.
										—Rebounds—								
83-84—Atlanta	5	96	37	20	.541	0	0	.000	5	4	9	11	5	0	1	0	40	8.0
85-86—Atlanta	9	348	135	71	.526	26	18	.692	4	20	24	30	16	0	10	1	160	17.8
86-87—Atlanta	9	300	121	67	.554	17	14	.824	3	15	18	30	22	0	4	4	148	16.4
87-88—Atlanta	12	344	122	66	.541	7	5	.714	9	17	26	43	24	0	7	1	137	11.4
Totals	35	1088	415	224	.540	50	37	.740	21	56	77	114	67	0	22	6	485	13.9

Three-Point Field Goals: 1985-86, 0-for-2.
Member of NCAA Division I championship team, 1981.

JOSEPH JAMES WOLF
(Joe)

Born December 17, 1964 at Kohler, Wis. Height 6:11. Weight 230.
High School—Kohler, Wis.
College—University of North Carolina, Chapel Hill, N.C.
Drafted by Los Angeles Clippers on first round, 1987 (13th pick).

—COLLEGIATE RECORD—

Year	G.	Min.	FGA	FGM	Pct.	FTA	FTM	Pct.	Reb.	Pts.	Avg.
83-84	30	....	79	38	.481	33	25	.758	85	101	3.4
84-85	30	....	198	112	.566	64	50	.781	158	274	9.1
85-86	34	....	280	149	.532	59	42	.712	224	340	10.0
86-87	34	....	371	212	.571	87	69	.793	240	516	15.2
Totals	128	....	928	511	.551	243	186	.765	707	1231	9.6

Three-Point Field Goals: 1986-87, 23-for-40 (.575).

NBA REGULAR SEASON RECORD

Sea.—Team	G.	Min.	FGA	FGM	Pct.	FTA	FTM	Pct.	Off.	Def.	Tot.	Ast.	PF	Dq.	Stl.	Blk.	Pts.	Avg.
										—Rebounds—								
87-88—L.A. Clippers	42	1137	334	136	.407	54	45	.833	51	136	187	98	139	8	38	16	320	7.6

Three-Point Field Goals: 1987-88, 3-for-15 (.200).

OSIE LEON WOOD III
(Known by middle name.)

Born March 25, 1962 at Columbia S. C. Height 6:03. Weight 185.
High School—Santa Monica, Calif., St. Monica.
Colleges—University of Arizona, Tucson, Ariz., and
California State University at Fullerton, Fullerton, Calif.
Drafted by Philadelphia on first round, 1984 (10th pick).

Traded by Philadelphia to Washington for Kenny Green, January 10, 1986.
Traded by Washington to New Jersey for Mike O'Koren, October 30, 1986.
Waived by New Jersey, November 5, 1987; signed by San Antonio as a free agent, November 12, 1987.
Waived by San Antonio, February 17, 1988; signed by Atlanta, March 4, 1988, to the first of consecutive 10-day contracts that expired, March 24, 1988.
Re-signed by Atlanta, March 25, 1988, for remainder of season.

—COLLEGIATE RECORD—
Arizona

Year	G.	Min.	FGA	FGM	Pct.	FTA	FTM	Pct.	Reb.	Pts.	Avg.
79-80	25	221	111	43	.387	26	19	.731	6	105	4.2

Cal State-Fullerton

Year	G.	Min.	FGA	FGM	Pct.	FTA	FTM	Pct.	Reb.	Pts.	Avg.
80-81				Did Not Play—Transfer Student							
81-82	32	1263	448	222	.496	229	187	.817	57	631	19.7
82-83	29	1076	378	178	.471	180	142	.789	72	526	18.1
83-84	30	1170	540	254	.470	257	211	.821	78	719	24.0
CSF Totals.............	91	3509	1366	654	.479	666	540	.811	207	1876	20.6
College Totals.......	116	3730	1477	697	.472	692	559	.808	213	1981	17.1

Three-Point Field Goals: 1982-83, 28-for-63 (.444).

NBA REGULAR SEASON RECORD

Sea.—Team	G.	Min.	FGA	FGM	Pct.	FTA	FTM	Pct.	—Rebounds— Off.	Def.	Tot.	Ast.	PF	Dq.	Stl.	Blk.	Pts.	Avg.
84-85—Philadelphia	38	269	134	50	.373	26	18	.692	3	15	18	45	17	0	8	0	122	3.2
85-86—Phil.-Wash.	68	1198	466	184	.395	155	123	.794	25	65	90	182	70	0	34	0	532	7.8
86-87—New Jersey	76	1733	501	187	.373	154	123	.799	23	97	120	370	126	0	48	3	557	7.3
87-88—S.A.-Atl.	52	909	312	136	.436	99	76	.768	17	40	57	174	50	0	26	1	400	7.7
Totals	234	4109	1413	557	.394	434	340	.783	68	217	285	771	263	0	116	4	1611	6.9

Three-Point Field Goals: 1984-85, 4-for-30 (.133). 1985-86, 41-for-114 (.360). 1986-87, 60-for-200 (.300). 1987-88, 52-for-127 (.409). Totals, 157-for-471 (.333).

NBA PLAYOFF RECORD

Sea.—Team	G.	Min.	FGA	FGM	Pct.	FTA	FTM	Pct.	—Rebounds— Off.	Def.	Tot.	Ast.	PF	Dq.	Stl.	Blk.	Pts.	Avg.
84-85—Philadelphia	5	15	9	4	.444	8	6	.750	0	1	1	2	0	0	0	0	14	2.8
85-86—Washington	1	2	5	1	.200	2	2	1.000	0	0	0	0	0	0	0	0	5	5.0
87-88—Atlanta	4	4	1	1	1.000	0	0	.000	0	0	0	1	0	0	0	0	3	0.8
Totals	10	21	15	6	.400	10	8	.800	0	1	1	3	0	0	0	0	22	2.2

Three-Point Field Goals: 1984-85, 0-for-1. 1985-86, 1-for-1 (1.000). 1987-88, 1-for-1 (1.000). Totals, 2-for-3 (.667).

Member of U.S. Olympic team, 1984. . . . Named to THE SPORTING NEWS All-America First Team, 1984.

MICHAEL WOODSON
(Mike)

Born March 24, 1958 at Indianapolis, Ind. Height 6:05. Weight 198.

High School—Indianapolis, Ind., Broad Ripple.

College—Indiana University, Bloomington, Ind.

Drafted by New York on first round, 1980 (12th pick).

Traded by New York to New Jersey for Mike Newlin, June 10, 1981.
Traded by New Jersey with a 1982 1st round draft choice to Kansas City for Sam Lacey, November 12, 1981.
Traded by Sacramento with Larry Drew, a 1988 1st round draft choice and a 1989 2nd round draft choice to Los Angeles Clippers for Junior Bridgeman, Franklin Edwards and Derek Smith, August 19, 1986.
Signed by Houston as an unrestricted free agent, July 19, 1988.

—COLLEGIATE RECORD—

Year	G.	Min.	FGA	FGM	Pct.	FTA	FTM	Pct.	Reb.	Pts.	Avg.
76-77	27	....	407	212	.521	96	76	.792	182	500	18.5
77-78	29	....	462	242	.524	121	93	.769	157	577	19.9
78-79	34	....	532	265	.498	241	184	.763	193	714	21.0
79-80	14	....	225	102	.453	79	66	.835	49	270	19.3
Totals	104	....	1626	821	.505	537	419	.780	581	2061	19.8

NBA REGULAR SEASON RECORD

Sea.—Team	G.	Min.	FGA	FGM	Pct.	FTA	FTM	Pct.	—Rebounds— Off.	Def.	Tot.	Ast.	PF	Dq.	Stl.	Blk.	Pts.	Avg.
80-81—New York	81	949	373	165	.442	64	49	.766	33	64	97	75	95	0	36	12	380	4.7
81-82—N.J.-K.C.	83	2331	1069	538	.503	286	221	.773	102	145	247	222	220	3	142	35	1304	15.7
82-83—Kansas City	81	2426	1154	584	.506	377	298	.790	84	164	248	254	203	0	137	59	1473	18.2
83-84—Kansas City	71	1838	816	389	.477	302	247	.818	62	113	175	175	174	2	83	28	1027	14.5
84-85—Kansas City	78	1998	1068	530	.496	330	264	.800	69	129	198	143	216	1	117	28	1329	17.0
85-86—Sacramento	81	2417	1073	510	.475	289	242	.837	94	132	226	197	215	1	92	37	1264	15.6
86-87—L.A. Clippers	74	2126	1130	494	.437	290	240	.828	68	94	162	196	201	1	100	16	1262	17.1
87-88—L.A. Clippers	80	2534	1263	562	.445	341	296	.868	64	126	190	273	210	1	109	26	1438	18.0
Totals	629	16619	7946	3772	.475	2279	1857	.815	576	967	1543	1535	1534	9	816	241	9477	15.1

Three-Point Field Goals: 1980-81, 1-for-5 (.200). 1981-82, 7-for-25 (.280). 1982-83, 7-for-33 (.212). 1983-84, 2-for-8 (.250). 1984-85, 5-for-21 (.238). 1985-86, 2-for-13 (.154). 1986-87, 34-for-123 (.276). 1987-88, 18-for-78 (.231). Totals, 76-for-306 (.248).

NBA PLAYOFF RECORD

Sea.—Team	G.	Min.	FGA	FGM	Pct.	FTA	FTM	Pct.	—Rebounds— Off.	Def.	Tot.	Ast.	PF	Dq.	Stl.	Blk.	Pts.	Avg.
80-81—New York	2	8	3	1	.333	2	2	1.000	2	0	2	0	3	0	0	0	4	2.0
83-84—Kansas City	3	87	44	18	.409	15	13	.867	4	4	8	9	11	0	2	0	49	16.3
85-86—Sacramento	3	110	49	22	.449	12	12	1.000	7	4	11	5	13	0	4	2	56	18.7
Totals	8	205	96	41	.427	29	27	.931	13	8	21	14	27	0	6	2	109	13.6

Three-Point Field Goals: 1983-84, 0-for-1. 1985-86, 0-for-2. Totals, 0-for-3.

ORLANDO VERNADA WOOLRIDGE

Born December 16, 1959 at Bernice, La.   Height 6:09.   Weight 215.

High Schools—Pelican, La., All Saints (Freshman, Sophomore and Junior) and Mansfield, La. (Senior).

College—University of Notre Dame, Notre Dame, Ind.

Drafted by Chicago on first round, 1981 (6th pick).

Signed by New Jersey as a Veteran Free Agent, October 2, 1986; Chicago agreed not to exercise its right of first refusal in exchange for a 1987 1st round draft choice and 1988 and 1990 2nd round draft choices.
Signed by Los Angeles Lakers as an unrestricted free agent, August 10, 1988.

—COLLEGIATE RECORD—

Year	G.	Min.	FGA	FGM	Pct.	FTA	FTM	Pct.	Reb.	Pts.	Avg.
77-78	24	230	78	41	.526	33	16	.485	51	98	4.1
78-79	30	752	253	145	.573	56	41	.732	145	331	11.0
79-80	27	835	212	124	.585	117	81	.692	186	329	12.2
80-81	28	924	240	156	.650	135	90	.667	168	402	14.4
Totals	109	2741	783	466	.595	341	228	.669	550	1160	10.6

NBA REGULAR SEASON RECORD

Sea.—Team	G.	Min.	FGA	FGM	Pct.	FTA	FTM	Pct.	Off.	Def.	Tot.	Ast.	PF	Dq.	Stl.	Blk.	Pts.	Avg.
81-82—Chicago	75	1188	394	202	.513	206	144	.699	82	145	227	81	152	1	23	24	548	7.3
82-83—Chicago	57	1627	622	361	.580	340	217	.638	122	176	298	97	177	1	38	44	939	16.5
83-84—Chicago	75	2544	1086	570	.525	424	303	.715	130	239	369	136	253	6	71	60	1444	19.3
84-85—Chicago	77	2816	1225	679	.554	521	409	.785	158	277	435	135	185	0	58	38	1767	22.9
85-86—Chicago	70	2248	1090	540	.495	462	364	.788	150	200	350	213	186	2	49	47	1448	20.7
86-87—New Jersey	75	2638	1067	556	.521	564	438	.777	118	249	367	261	243	4	54	86	1551	20.7
87-88—New Jersey	19	622	247	110	.445	130	92	.708	31	60	91	71	73	2	13	20	312	16.4
Totals	448	13683	5731	3018	.527	2647	1967	.743	791	1346	2137	994	1269	16	306	319	8009	17.9

Three-Point Field Goals: 1981-82, 0-for-3. 1982-83, 0-for-3. 1983-84, 1-for-2 (.500). 1984-85, 0-for-5. 1985-86, 4-for-23 (.174). 1986-87, 1-for-8 (.125). 1987-88, 0-for-2. Totals, 6-for-46 (.130).

NBA PLAYOFF RECORD

Sea.—Team	G.	Min.	FGA	FGM	Pct.	FTA	FTM	Pct.	Off.	Def.	Tot.	Ast.	PF	Dq.	Stl.	Blk.	Pts.	Avg.
84-85—Chicago	4	167	68	34	.500	18	14	.778	6	7	13	8	19	1	6	1	82	20.5
85-86—Chicago	3	135	62	25	.403	15	13	.867	6	8	14	4	12	0	3	1	63	21.0
Totals	7	302	130	59	.454	33	27	.818	12	15	27	12	31	1	9	2	145	20.7

Three-Point Field Goals: 1985-86, 0-for-1.

Named to THE SPORTING NEWS All-America Second Team, 1981.

JAMES AGER WORTHY

Born February 27, 1961 at Gastonia, N. C.   Height 6:09.   Weight 235.

High School—Gastonia, N. C., Ashbrook.

College—University of North Carolina, Chapel Hill, N. C.

Drafted by Los Angeles on first round as an undergraduate, 1982 (1st pick).

—COLLEGIATE RECORD—

Year	G.	Min.	FGA	FGM	Pct.	FTA	FTM	Pct.	Reb.	Pts.	Avg.
79-80	14	....	126	74	.587	45	27	.600	104	175	12.5
80-81	36	....	416	208	.500	150	96	.640	301	512	14.2
81-82	34	....	354	203	.573	187	126	.674	215	532	15.6
Totals	84	....	896	485	.541	382	249	.652	620	1219	14.5

NBA REGULAR SEASON RECORD

Sea.—Team	G.	Min.	FGA	FGM	Pct.	FTA	FTM	Pct.	Off.	Def.	Tot.	Ast.	PF	Dq.	Stl.	Blk.	Pts.	Avg.
82-83—Los Angeles	77	1970	772	447	.579	221	138	.624	157	242	399	132	221	2	91	64	1033	13.4
83-84—Los Angeles	82	2415	890	495	.556	257	195	.759	157	358	515	207	244	5	77	70	1185	14.5
84-85—L.A. Lakers	80	2696	1066	610	.572	245	190	.776	169	342	511	201	196	0	87	67	1410	17.6
85-86—L.A. Lakers	75	2454	1086	629	.579	314	242	.771	136	251	387	201	195	0	82	77	1500	20.0
86-87—L.A. Lakers	82	2819	1207	651	.539	389	292	.751	158	308	466	226	206	0	108	83	1594	19.4
87-88—L.A. Lakers	75	2655	1161	617	.531	304	242	.796	129	245	374	289	175	1	72	55	1478	19.7
Totals	471	15009	6182	3449	.558	1730	1299	.751	906	1746	2652	1256	1237	8	517	416	8200	17.4

Three-Point Field Goals: 1982-83, 1-for-4 (.250). 1983-84, 0-for-6. 1984-85, 0-for-7. 1985-86, 0-for-13. 1986-87, 0-for-13. 1987-88, 2-for-16 (.125). Totals, 3-for-59 (.051).

NBA PLAYOFF RECORD

Sea.—Team	G.	Min.	FGA	FGM	Pct.	FTA	FTM	Pct.	Off.	Def.	Tot.	Ast.	PF	Dq.	Stl.	Blk.	Pts.	Avg.
83-84—Los Angeles	21	708	274	164	.599	69	42	.609	36	69	105	56	57	0	27	11	371	17.7
84-85—L.A. Lakers	19	626	267	166	.622	111	75	.676	35	61	96	41	53	1	17	13	408	21.5

Sea.—Team	G.	Min.	FGA	FGM	Pct.	FTA	FTM	Pct.	Off.	Def.	Tot.	Ast.	PF	Dq.	Stl.	Blk.	Pts.	Avg.
										—Rebounds—								
85-86—L.A. Lakers	14	539	217	121	.558	47	32	.681	22	43	65	45	43	0	16	10	274	19.6
86-87—L.A. Lakers	18	681	298	176	.591	97	73	.753	31	70	101	63	42	1	28	22	425	23.6
87-88—L.A. Lakers	24	896	390	204	.523	128	97	.758	53	86	139	106	58	0	33	19	506	21.1
Totals	96	3450	1446	831	.575	452	319	.706	177	329	506	311	253	2	121	75	1984	20.7

Three-Point Field Goals: 1983-84, 1-for-2 (.500). 1984-85, 1-for-2 (.500). 1985-86, 0-for-4. 1986-87, 0-for-2. 1987-88, 1-for-9 (.111). Totals, 3-for-19 (.158).

NBA ALL-STAR GAME RECORD

Season—Team	Min.	FGA	FGM	Pct.	FTA	FTM	Pct.	Off.	Def.	Tot.	Ast.	PF	Dq.	Stl.	Blk.	Pts.
									—Rebounds—							
1986—L.A. Lakers ..	28	19	10	.526	0	0	.000	2	1	3	2	3	0	0	2	20
1987—L.A. Lakers ..	29	14	10	.714	2	2	1.000	6	2	8	3	3	0	1	0	22
1988—L.A. Lakers ..	13	8	2	.250	1	0	.000	1	2	3	1	1	0	0	1	4
Totals	70	41	22	.537	3	2	.667	9	5	14	6	7	0	1	3	46

Three-Point Field Goals: 1986, 0-for-2.

Named to NBA All-Rookie Team, 1983. . . . Member of NBA championship teams, 1985, 1987, 1988. . . . NBA Playoff MVP, 1988. . . . THE SPORTING NEWS All-America First Team, 1982. . . . NCAA Division I Tournament Most Outstanding Player, 1982. . . . Member of NCAA Division I championship team, 1982.

BRADFORD WILLIAM WRIGHT
(Brad)

Born March 27, 1962 at Hollywood, Calif. Height 6:11. Weight 225.

High School—Los Angeles, Calif., Murphy.

College—University of California at Los Angeles, Los Angeles, Calif.

Drafted by Golden State on third round, 1985 (49th pick).

Draft rights relinquished by Golden State, September 17, 1986; signed by New York as a free agent, March 21, 1987. Waived by New York, October 12, 1987; signed by Denver, February 21, 1988, to a 10-day contract that expired, March 1, 1988.

Played in Continental Basketball Association with Cincinnati Slammers, 1985-86, Wyoming Wildcatters, 1986-87, and Wyoming Wildcatters and Rockford Lightning, 1987-88.

—COLLEGIATE RECORD—

Year	G.	Min.	FGA	FGM	Pct.	FTA	FTM	Pct.	Reb.	Pts.	Avg.
81-82	10	33	15	8	.533	5	3	.600	20	19	1.9
82-83	28	318	74	40	.541	27	14	.519	88	94	3.4
83-84	28	257	59	30	.508	64	40	.625	66	100	3.6
84-85	33	1069	251	131	.522	131	83	.634	287	345	10.5
Totals	99	1677	399	209	.524	227	140	.617	461	558	5.6

CBA REGULAR SEASON RECORD

Sea.—Team	G.	Min.	FGM	FGA	Pct.	FGM	FGA	Pct.	FTM	FTA	Pct.	Reb.	Ast.	Pts.	Avg.
			—2-Point—			—3-Point—									
85-86—Cincinnati	44	584	105	166	.632	0	0	....	58	85	.682	200	12	268	6.1
86-87—Wyoming	46	1479	241	457	.527	0	3	.000	163	249	.655	465	63	645	14.0
87-88—Wyo.-Rock.	37	1058	219	382	.573	1	1	1.000	147	234	.628	357	58	588	15.9
Totals	127	3121	565	1005	.562	1	4	.250	368	568	.648	1022	133	1501	11.8

NBA REGULAR SEASON RECORD

Sea.—Team	G.	Min.	FGA	FGM	Pct.	FTA	FTM	Pct.	Off.	Def.	Tot.	Ast.	PF	Dq.	Stl.	Blk.	Pts.	Avg.
										—Rebounds—								
86-87—New York	14	138	46	20	.435	28	12	.429	25	28	53	1	20	0	3	6	52	3.7
87-88—Denver	2	7	5	1	.200	0	0	.000	0	1	1	0	3	0	0	0	2	1.0
Totals	16	145	51	21	.412	28	12	.429	25	29	54	1	23	0	3	6	54	3.4

Three-Point Field Goals: 1986-87, 0-for-1.

Named to CBA All-Star Second Team, 1987 and 1988.

DANNY YOUNG

Born July 26, 1962 at Raleigh, N.C. Height 6:04. Weight 175.

High School—Raleigh, N. C., Enloe.

College—Wake Forest University, Winston-Salem, N. C.

Drafted by Seattle on second round, 1984 (39th pick).

Waived by Seattle, November 13, 1984; re-signed by Seattle as a free agent, August 9, 1985.
Played in Continental Basketball Association with Wyoming Wildcatters, 1984-85.

Year	G.	Min.	FGA	FGM	Pct.	FTA	FTM	Pct.	Reb.	Pts.	Avg.
80-81	29	491	117	58	.496	48	33	.688	38	149	5.1
81-82	30	946	254	129	.508	84	60	.714	74	318	10.6
82-83	31	999	315	144	.457	115	82	.713	66	397	12.8
83-84	32	1043	272	124	.456	82	58	.707	59	306	9.6
Totals	122	3479	958	455	.475	329	233	.708	237	1170	9.6

Three-Point Field Goals: 1982-83, 27-for-73 (.370).

CBA REGULAR SEASON RECORD

Sea.—Team	G.	Min.	FGM	FGA	Pct.	FGM	FGA	Pct.	FTM	FTA	Pct.	Reb.	Ast.	Pts.	Avg.
			—2-Point—			—3-Point—									
84-85—Wyoming	26	489	77	156	.493	4	12	.333	59	61	.967	34	95	225	8.7

NBA REGULAR SEASON RECORD

Sea.—Team	G.	Min.	FGA	FGM	Pct.	FTA	FTM	Pct.	Off.	Def.	Tot.	Ast.	PF	Dq.	Stl.	Blk.	Pts.	Avg.
									—Rebounds—									
84-85—Seattle	3	26	10	2	.200	0	0	.000	0	3	3	2	2	0	3	0	4	1.3
85-86—Seattle	82	1901	449	227	.506	106	90	.849	29	91	120	303	113	0	110	9	568	6.9
86-87—Seattle	73	1482	288	132	.458	71	59	.831	23	90	113	353	72	0	74	3	352	4.8
87-88—Seattle	77	949	218	89	.408	53	43	.811	18	57	75	218	69	0	52	2	243	3.2
Totals	235	4358	965	450	.466	230	192	.835	70	241	311	876	256	0	239	14	1167	5.0

Three-Point Field Goals: 1984-85, 0-for-1. 1985-86, 24-for-74 (.324). 1986-87, 29-for-79 (.367). 1987-88, 22-for-77 (.286). Totals, 75-for-231 (.325).

NBA PLAYOFF RECORD

Sea.—Team	G.	Min.	FGA	FGM	Pct.	FTA	FTM	Pct.	Off.	Def.	Tot.	Ast.	PF	Dq.	Stl.	Blk.	Pts.	Avg.
									—Rebounds—									
86-87—Seattle	14	208	52	21	.404	10	10	1.000	4	12	16	48	21	1	15	0	57	4.1
87-88—Seattle	5	95	21	11	.524	10	10	1.000	3	7	10	19	7	0	2	2	32	6.4
Totals	19	303	73	32	.438	20	20	1.000	7	19	26	67	28	1	17	2	89	4.7

Three-Point Field Goals: 1986-87, 5-for-16 (.313). 1987-88, 0-for-3. Totals, 5-for-19 (.263).

PHIL ZEVENBERGEN

Born April 13, 1964 at Seattle, Wash. Height 6:10. Weight 230.

High School—Edmonds, Wash., Woodway.

Colleges—Seattle Pacific University, Seattle, Wash.; Edmonds Community College, Lynwood, Wash., and University of Washington, Seattle, Wash.

Drafted by San Antonio on third round, 1987 (50th pick).

Played in Italy and Spain, 1987-88.

Seattle Pacific

Year	G.	Min.	FGA	FGM	Pct.	FTA	FTM	Pct.	Reb.	Pts.	Avg.
82-83	1	....	2	1	.500	0	0	.000	2	2	2.0

Edmonds C.C.

Year	G.	Min.	FGA	FGM	Pct.	FTA	FTM	Pct.	Reb.	Pts.	Avg.
83-84					Statistics Unavailable						
84-85					Statistics Unavailable						

Washington

Year	G.	Min.	FGA	FGM	Pct.	FTA	FTM	Pct.	Reb.	Pts.	Avg.
85-86	31	450	93	41	.441	48	27	.563	98	109	3.5
86-87	35	1173	408	210	.515	181	138	.762	311	558	15.9
Wash. Totals	66	1623	501	251	.501	229	165	.721	409	667	10.1
College Totals	67	....	503	252	.501	229	165	.721	411	669	10.0

NBA REGULAR SEASON RECORD

Sea.—Team	G.	Min.	FGA	FGM	Pct.	FTA	FTM	Pct.	Off.	Def.	Tot.	Ast.	PF	Dq.	Stl.	Blk.	Pts.	Avg.
									—Rebounds—									
87-88—San Antonio	8	58	27	15	.556	2	0	.000	4	9	13	3	12	0	3	1	30	3.8

NBA PLAYOFF RECORD

Sea.—Team	G.	Min.	FGA	FGM	Pct.	FTA	FTM	Pct.	Off.	Def.	Tot.	Ast.	PF	Dq.	Stl.	Blk.	Pts.	Avg.
									—Rebounds—									
87-88—San Antonio	1	1	0	0	.000	0	0	.000	0	0	0	0	0	0	0	0	0	0.0

INDIVIDUAL CAREER HIGHS
REGULAR SEASON

Player	FGM	FGA	FTM	FTA	Reb.	Ast.	Pts.
Kareem Abdul-Jabbar	24	39	20	25	34	14	55
Mark Acres	7	9	6	10	12	4	19
Alvan Adams	18	31	14	17	19	13	47
Michael Adams	12	22	10	10	7	14	32
Mark Aguirre	21	40	14	20	15	16	49
Danny Ainge	14	24	11	12	11	15	35
Mark Alarie	9	16	6	6	11	4	21
Steve Alford	4	6	4	4	4	5	10
Greg Anderson	13	19	11	15	21	6	31
Richard Anderson	11	20	8	10	14	8	23
Ron Anderson	13	23	8	12	13	7	28
Joe Arlauckas	6	14	5	6	5	3	17
Vincent Askew	4	11	2	2	5	6	9
John Bagley	16	21	10	12	11	19	35
James Bailey	14	22	13	14	21	6	35
Thurl Bailey	17	27	13	16	17	9	41
Gene Banks	19	24	11	16	17	11	44
Charles Barkley	18	30	21	26	25	14	47
John Battle	12	22	10	12	7	14	27
William Bedford	8	18	6	8	13	4	17
Benoit Benjamin	12	23	12	13	18	9	30
Kent Benson	12	23	10	13	22	9	28
Walter Berry	14	24	15	21	14	8	31
Larry Bird	22	36	16	17	21	17	60
Otis Birdsong	20	31	12	17	11	11	49
Uwe Blab	5	11	6	8	10	3	14
Rolando Blackman	19	32	22	23	11	10	46
Nate Blackwell	5	9	2	2	1	5	10
Tyrone Bogues	7	14	4	5	5	14	16
Manute Bol	7	14	8	14	19	3	18
Sam Bowie	11	20	12	16	20	7	31
Dudley Bradley	11	16	10	13	8	10	22
Adrian Branch	9	22	6	7	6	4	20
Randy Breuer	14	21	10	11	17	6	33
Frank Brickowski	12	28	13	19	15	10	34
Michael Brooks	16	27	11	13	17	12	37
Mike Brown	7	11	4	7	12	4	17
Steve Burtt	6	14	9	10	4	5	17
Michael Cage	12	19	15	19	30	5	29
Tony Campbell	10	20	8	13	8	4	28
Rick Carlisle	9	12	3	4	5	7	21
Antoine Carr	10	16	9	9	11	8	24
Joe Barry Carroll	22	37	14	18	24	7	52
Bill Cartwright	16	26	16	18	18	8	38
Terry Catledge	13	22	8	11	20	4	32
Tom Chambers	15	29	18	20	18	8	46
Maurice Cheeks	15	23	11	14	10	21	32
Ben Coleman	10	17	8	11	18	3	23
Norris Coleman	6	18	4	4	12	2	16
Steve Colter	14	21	12	14	10	12	35
Dallas Comegys	8	15	9	14	13	4	21
Lester Conner	10	17	11	13	9	12	24
Darwin Cook	14	21	9	11	13	15	35
Jeff Cook	8	15	9	10	16	6	18
Michael Cooper	13	22	10	11	13	17	31
Wayne Cooper	13	22	12	14	19	7	32
Tyrone Corbin	11	20	7	9	12	7	23
Dave Corzine	15	29	17	19	22	9	35
Winston Crite	5	10	5	6	8	3	13
Pat Cummings	14	25	10	13	20	6	34
Terry Cummings	17	32	13	20	24	10	39
Earl Cureton	11	17	7	12	18	6	25
Dell Curry	11	22	6	6	8	7	27
Quintin Dailey	17	26	15	18	10	9	44
Adrian Dantley	24	36	28	31	19	11	57
Brad Daugherty	15	22	14	18	17	13	44
Brad Davis	14	17	11	14	8	17	32

Player	FGM	FGA	FTM	FTA	Reb.	Ast.	Pts.
Charles Davis	15	22	5	7	13	5	33
Walter Davis	19	33	19	21	13	12	45
Darryl Dawkins	14	25	12	19	19	7	36
Johnny Dawkins	13	25	13	14	8	14	30
Darren Daye	11	17	11	12	9	10	27
James Donaldson	12	17	13	17	22	7	29
Billy Donovan	7	10	9	10	3	7	14
Greg Dreiling	3	5	5	6	5	2	8
Larry Drew	13	27	15	18	8	17	33
Clyde Drexler	18	33	15	17	15	16	42
Kevin Duckworth	12	24	10	15	17	4	32
Chris Dudley	5	10	4	4	10	3	14
Joe Dumars	11	24	10	12	8	14	25
T.R. Dunn	10	18	11	14	17	8	23
Mark Eaton	8	18	10	12	25	7	20
Franklin Edwards	13	20	11	13	6	16	28
James Edwards	16	29	18	19	18	7	39
Craig Ehlo	8	17	8	11	14	9	26
Dale Ellis	19	34	14	17	12	9	47
Chris Engler	6	9	5	6	9	2	14
Alex English	22	37	17	19	20	16	54
Mike Evans	15	23	12	12	6	10	38
Patrick Ewing	18	30	14	20	21	7	43
Jim Farmer	4	7	2	2	4	3	8
Dave Feitl	8	16	10	10	16	4	20
Kenny Fields	10	18	8	12	12	6	23
Vern Fleming	12	20	14	18	12	17	30
Eric Floyd	13	26	14	17	13	18	41
Tellis Frank	11	18	8	11	15	6	23
World B. Free	21	33	22	29	11	13	49
Kevin Gamble	0	1	0	0	1	1	0
Winston Garland	12	21	7	10	11	13	27
Armon Gilliam	12	20	8	11	14	5	25
Artis Gilmore	16	26	20	25	28	9	42
Mike Gminski	15	23	15	16	22	9	41
Lancaster Gordon	13	28	7	8	7	7	33
Horace Grant	10	13	7	9	13	4	20
Stuart Gray	6	8	7	8	12	3	15
A.C. Green	10	16	12	15	18	5	28
Rickey Green	16	25	13	17	9	20	45
Sidney Green	13	27	13	14	23	8	31
David Greenwood	14	26	12	14	23	10	35
Claude Gregory	10	15	3	7	12	3	21
Darrell Griffith	19	32	10	12	12	10	41
Petur Gudmundsson	10	15	10	12	15	5	21
Bob Hansen	12	20	9	11	11	9	28
Bill Hanzlik	11	25	17	18	11	11	33
Derek Harper	13	22	10	14	9	16	35
Ron Harper	15	29	15	19	16	12	40
Steve Harris	10	18	16	17	8	6	24
Scott Hastings	8	16	9	10	17	6	16
David Henderson	6	13	4	6	5	5	15
Gerald Henderson	12	20	9	12	9	17	31
Kevin Henderson	6	13	5	12	7	5	14
Conner Henry	8	13	7	8	6	6	21
Rod Higgins	15	20	14	14	12	9	41
Roy Hinson	14	26	17	20	18	5	39
Craig Hodges	13	23	8	8	9	12	29
Mike Holton	10	17	8	8	9	10	25
Dave Hoppen	6	11	5	6	14	4	17
Dennis Hopson	10	22	8	10	6	6	25
Jeff Hornacek	10	15	7	8	9	18	21
Phil Hubbard	15	22	14	19	21	7	37
Eddie Hughes	2	5	2	2	1	3	6
Jay Humphries	13	21	12	15	9	16	30
Marc Iavaroni	8	14	7	9	19	7	19
Mark Jackson	10	27	12	12	10	18	33
Michael Jackson	5	13	5	5	4	13	11
Buck Johnson	9	12	5	6	9	4	19
Clemon Johnson	11	22	9	10	18	7	22
Dennis Johnson	14	29	16	18	12	17	39

Player	FGM	FGA	FTM	FTA	Reb.	Ast.	Pts.
Eddie A. Johnson	18	31	11	14	15	10	43
Frank Johnson	12	23	18	19	8	15	36
Kannard Johnson	1	2	0	0	0	0	2
Kevin Johnson	11	24	8	11	13	16	31
Magic Johnson	18	36	17	21	18	23	46
Marques Johnson	18	32	14	18	18	11	40
Steve Johnson	14	23	17	19	18	9	40
Vinnie Johnson	15	25	11	12	11	15	35
Caldwell Jones	12	22	13	14	27	7	29
Charles Jones	7	13	5	7	14	7	17
Charles A. Jones	9	15	13	15	14	8	27
Michael Jordan	22	43	26	27	15	16	61
Jerome Kersey	15	26	11	15	20	10	36
Albert King	17	29	12	12	14	11	34
Bernard King	20	34	22	26	18	13	60
Greg Kite	7	13	6	8	13	5	16
Joe Kleine	10	17	8	10	18	8	23
Bart Kofoed	2	5	3	4	3	3	8
Jon Koncak	9	19	9	16	20	3	25
Larry Krystkowiak	9	18	10	13	13	7	24
Bill Laimbeer	16	27	12	13	24	11	35
Jeff Lamp	10	16	7	9	8	6	25
Allen Leavell	15	26	15	17	8	22	42
Keith Lee	8	15	9	9	17	7	25
Lafayette Lever	16	26	11	14	21	18	36
Cliff Levingston	11	18	11	14	17	7	29
Ralph Lewis	4	11	5	7	6	2	10
Reggie Lewis	7	15	5	9	7	3	14
Alton Lister	13	16	8	12	21	6	30
Brad Lohaus	8	13	5	7	9	4	20
John Long	18	31	13	15	13	12	44
John Lucas	15	26	11	15	11	24	35
Maurice Lucas	19	32	15	19	26	10	46
Rick Mahorn	12	23	14	15	20	7	34
Jeff Malone	18	30	14	15	11	10	48
Karl Malone	17	33	16	20	21	8	41
Moses Malone	20	35	21	26	37	7	53
Pace Mannion	9	15	6	8	7	6	25
Bill Martin	8	17	4	5	8	5	20
Mo Martin	6	11	8	10	6	5	12
Wes Matthews	13	20	12	13	7	18	29
Cedric Maxwell	13	20	19	22	19	10	35
Tim McCormick	13	19	11	15	16	8	29
Rodney McCray	12	21	12	14	18	14	28
Xavier McDaniel	17	28	12	16	19	8	41
Ben McDonald	10	16	6	6	14	7	22
Mike McGee	18	30	9	12	10	12	41
Kevin McHale	22	28	15	19	18	10	56
Kevin McKenna	8	15	8	8	8	7	25
Derrick McKey	8	14	7	8	12	6	20
Nate McMillan	7	13	10	13	13	25	21
Mark McNamara	9	15	5	8	22	2	22
Chris McNealy	7	14	6	6	15	6	17
Reggie Miller	10	16	9	12	7	5	31
Dirk Minniefield	8	15	6	8	6	16	20
Mike Mitchell	20	36	14	15	19	10	47
Paul Mokeski	9	16	9	10	13	6	21
Sidney Moncrief	16	26	18	21	15	12	43
Andre Moore	4	10	4	4	7	4	10
Johnny Moore	12	22	10	12	11	20	30
Ron Moore	3	5	2	4	3	1	6
Chris Mullin	15	24	12	12	11	11	38
Jay Murphy	3	10	4	4	9	2	8
Ronnie Murphy	4	9	2	3	2	1	11
Tod Murphy	1	1	3	4	2	2	5
Pete Myers	6	10	5	9	5	7	13
Larry Nance	19	29	13	18	21	11	45
Calvin Natt	16	29	16	22	19	8	39
Ed Nealy	9	15	8	10	16	5	23
Martin Nessley	3	5	2	4	7	2	6
Chuck Nevitt	5	6	4	4	10	2	12

Player	FGM	FGA	FTM	FTA	Reb.	Ast.	Pts.
Johnny Newman	12	20	13	13	7	4	29
Kurt Nimphius	11	20	9	10	15	10	26
Norm Nixon	18	28	13	13	9	21	39
Ken Norman	14	22	6	13	14	5	31
Charles Oakley	14	27	13	15	35	15	35
Mike O'Koren	12	19	11	14	16	10	28
Akeem Olajuwon	19	33	14	19	25	7	44
Jawann Oldham	8	14	5	8	15	4	19
Louis Orr	12	24	14	17	12	7	28
Robert Parish	16	31	13	18	32	10	40
Jim Paxson	18	33	13	15	8	11	41
John Paxson	12	20	9	10	6	14	25
Sam Perkins	12	29	11	12	20	7	32
Chuck Person	18	28	10	12	18	10	42
Jim Petersen	11	19	9	13	16	6	28
Mike Phelps	8	15	4	6	8	7	18
Ricky Pierce	14	21	14	15	12	6	32
Ed Pinckney	10	16	10	12	17	6	27
Scottie Pippen	8	18	8	10	9	6	24
Olden Polynice	6	11	8	10	12	4	15
Terry Porter	14	20	12	13	11	19	40
Paul Pressey	13	23	17	19	15	16	30
Harold Pressley	12	25	14	14	12	7	31
Mark Price	11	20	9	10	7	14	32
Kurt Rambis	10	14	8	9	18	5	21
Blair Rasmussen	16	28	10	11	15	5	35
Robert Reid	15	26	12	13	16	12	32
Richard Rellford	2	4	4	6	4	1	8
Jerry Reynolds	11	20	9	12	12	10	26
Micheal Ray Richardson	16	31	16	17	16	19	38
Glenn Rivers	14	22	17	17	14	21	37
Fred Roberts	10	17	9	12	15	7	25
Alvin Robertson	17	29	14	15	15	14	41
Cliff Robinson	19	29	15	20	23	10	45
Dennis Rodman	13	17	8	11	19	5	30
Johnny Rogers	7	11	2	3	6	5	14
Wayne Rollins	11	20	8	9	23	6	26
Scott Roth	5	9	4	4	3	3	12
Brian Rowsom	0	3	4	4	3	1	4
Walker Russell	8	12	6	6	10	10	16
John Salley	10	15	8	11	11	4	28
Ralph Sampson	19	33	15	17	25	9	43
Mike Sanders	14	19	11	14	13	7	29
Danny Schayes	11	21	18	18	24	11	32
Russ Schoene	12	17	5	7	12	5	25
Detlef Schrempf	9	17	10	13	14	10	23
Byron Scott	15	27	13	14	9	10	38
Carey Scurry	8	17	11	13	11	6	21
Brad Sellers	12	20	9	12	13	8	27
Purvis Short	24	38	18	20	15	14	59
Jerry Sichting	12	18	10	11	7	16	29
Jack Sikma	15	28	21	23	25	10	39
Scott Skiles	7	15	5	6	9	13	16
Derek Smith	14	26	13	17	11	10	41
Keith Smith	7	13	4	4	3	9	15
Kenny Smith	11	21	9	10	8	15	30
Larry Smith	11	19	9	14	31	6	25
Otis Smith	12	21	10	12	9	7	29
Mike Smrek	6	11	5	7	11	4	15
Rory Sparrow	13	23	10	12	10	17	30
Steve Stipanovich	14	23	12	14	16	10	34
John Stockton	10	17	11	11	8	26	27
John Stroeder	3	9	4	6	7	3	10
Jon Sundvold	11	19	8	9	7	14	25
Roy Tarpley	13	21	11	12	24	5	29
Terry Teagle	16	25	11	13	12	7	34
Reggie Theus	18	33	16	18	17	18	46
Isiah Thomas	19	34	16	20	12	25	47
Bernard Thompson	8	14	10	11	9	8	23
Billy Thompson	6	11	5	6	13	5	13
LaSalle Thompson	13	20	12	13	21	8	28

Player	FGM	FGA	FTM	FTA	Reb.	Ast.	Pts.
Mychal Thompson	17	28	12	20	22	11	38
Bob Thornton	7	13	6	8	14	3	17
Otis Thorpe	14	27	14	19	19	9	35
Sedale Threatt	13	22	7	8	7	15	31
Wayman Tisdale	15	25	11	14	15	6	35
Ray Tolbert	9	18	6	10	13	5	20
Andrew Toney	21	29	15	18	11	13	46
Sedric Toney	7	11	7	10	5	6	22
Kelly Tripucka	19	30	20	22	14	11	56
Trent Tucker	13	21	8	10	9	11	34
Andre Turner	4	7	3	4	2	8	8
Elston Turner	9	16	7	8	11	8	19
Mel Turpin	13	23	14	15	17	4	32
Terry Tyler	14	25	10	12	18	8	32
Darnell Valentine	14	19	13	15	8	15	30
Kiki Vandeweghe	21	31	18	22	13	10	51
Jay Vincent	17	33	17	20	17	8	42
Sam Vincent	9	20	12	13	8	17	23
Danny Vranes	10	15	9	12	15	8	24
Mark Wade	1	4	2	4	4	10	4
Milt Wagner	6	14	4	6	4	6	14
Granville Waiters	6	11	5	8	10	3	14
Darrell Walker	14	25	13	16	12	15	39
Kenny Walker	11	19	11	14	13	5	26
Jamie Waller	5	9	4	4	4	1	10
Bill Walton	17	31	12	17	26	14	36
Bryan Warrick	8	12	6	8	6	14	18
Chris Washburn	8	13	2	6	12	2	17
Duane Washington	6	9	8	9	5	10	18
Dwayne Washington	12	29	8	13	8	12	29
Kermit Washington	13	20	11	15	21	7	29
Spud Webb	9	14	13	14	8	15	23
Scott Wedman	19	31	11	16	18	11	45
Chris Welp	5	6	8	10	6	1	18
Bill Wennington	7	11	8	8	11	3	15
Mark West	11	17	7	11	18	5	27
Ennis Whatley	9	16	9	11	8	22	21
Clint Wheeler	8	9	4	4	4	7	18
Eric White	10	18	7	9	9	3	20
Tony White	12	17	4	6	3	5	24
Jerome Whitehead	13	20	13	14	23	6	31
Dominique Wilkins	21	42	20	22	17	10	57
Eddie Lee Wilkins	9	15	6	11	15	3	24
Gerald Wilkins	18	30	13	14	9	13	43
Buck Williams	14	22	18	19	27	7	35
Herb Williams	17	32	17	20	17	8	40
John Williams	11	21	13	15	18	7	27
John S. Williams	12	22	8	10	14	8	28
Kevin Williams	8	15	9	10	9	9	21
Reggie Williams	15	27	9	9	9	6	34
Kevin Willis	16	23	8	12	21	4	39
Nikita Wilson	1	4	2	2	3	1	3
Ricky Wilson	6	12	5	6	5	11	14
David Wingate	11	24	11	13	6	13	28
Rickie Winslow	2	5	1	2	2	1	5
Randy Wittman	14	22	9	9	7	12	30
Joe Wolf	9	16	5	6	12	7	23
Leon Wood	10	20	10	12	7	13	30
Mike Woodson	22	28	12	15	11	9	48
Orlando Woolridge	18	28	14	19	16	10	44
James Worthy	17	27	11	15	17	10	38
Brad Wright	5	9	5	8	13	1	13
Danny Young	9	13	5	6	6	13	20
Phil Zevenbergen	4	7	0	1	5	1	8

PLAYOFFS

Player	FGM	FGA	FTM	FTA	Reb.	Ast.	Pts.
Kareem Abdul-Jabbar	20	37	13	18	31	11	46
Mark Acres	3	5	4	4	7	1	6
Alvan Adams	14	27	8	10	20	12	33
Michael Adams	8	19	7	8	6	9	22
Mark Aguirre	19	30	11	12	17	10	39
Danny Ainge	12	22	7	9	10	14	30
Mark Alarie	4	7	2	2	3	1	8
Steve Alford	1	3	0	0	1	1	2
Greg Anderson	8	14	2	4	8	2	18
Richard Anderson	6	13	4	4	5	3	14
Ron Anderson	2	2	0	0	2	0	4
John Bagley	11	19	4	6	7	15	22
James Bailey	6	11	5	7	7	1	13
Thurl Bailey	15	25	12	15	14	6	39
Gene Banks	11	20	6	8	11	7	24
Charles Barkley	13	21	15	19	22	12	39
John Battle	7	13	5	8	6	5	19
Kent Benson	8	12	5	5	14	3	18
Walter Berry	12	18	9	10	8	2	27
Larry Bird	17	33	14	15	21	13	43
Otis Birdsong	14	24	7	12	9	7	30
Uwe Blab	2	3	2	4	3	1	4
Rolando Blackman	19	33	13	14	10	11	43
Tyrone Bogues	0	0	0	0	0	2	0
Manute Bol	3	5	2	4	12	1	8
Sam Bowie	5	11	6	12	20	5	12
Dudley Bradley	4	8	3	4	4	6	10
Adrian Branch	1	5	3	4	2	1	3
Randy Breuer	9	14	7	8	9	2	21
Frank Brickowski	8	16	5	10	12	5	22
Michael Brooks	1	2	0	0	3	1	3
Mike Brown	0	1	1	2	0	1	1
Tony Campbell	6	12	4	4	3	2	14
Rick Carlisle	3	6	3	4	3	2	6
Antoine Carr	7	10	6	7	6	2	20
Joe Barry Carroll	10	19	8	10	11	4	24
Bill Cartwright	10	19	11	13	14	3	29
Terry Catledge	13	22	6	9	12	2	27
Tom Chambers	14	29	14	16	9	5	38
Maurice Cheeks	12	20	11	14	10	14	33
Steve Colter	11	15	3	5	6	8	26
Lester Conner	0	0	2	2	1	1	2
Darwin Cook	7	18	7	10	5	7	15
Jeff Cook	7	12	5	7	12	4	17
Michael Cooper	9	16	10	12	8	12	23
Wayne Cooper	10	18	4	8	14	7	23
Tyrone Corbin	0	4	0	0	1	1	0
Dave Corzine	9	17	5	7	15	7	23
Pat Cummings	8	16	4	4	14	3	16
Terry Cummings	15	25	13	16	18	6	41
Earl Cureton	7	15	3	6	10	4	14
Dell Curry	1	3	0	0	1	2	2
Quintin Dailey	12	20	4	4	5	5	25
Adrian Dantley	16	27	15	20	14	7	46
Brad Daugherty	9	17	6	10	13	5	21
Brad Davis	8	10	6	7	6	10	26
Charles Davis	4	12	5	6	7	3	13
Walter Davis	14	28	11	13	10	13	34
Darryl Dawkins	14	25	16	18	16	6	32
Johnny Dawkins	5	11	2	2	2	3	11
Darren Daye	8	13	5	10	7	9	19
James Donaldson	8	12	9	10	20	3	18
Larry Drew	9	13	3	3	3	7	20
Clyde Drexler	12	24	12	12	13	14	32
Kevin Duckworth	14	20	5	7	16	2	33
Chris Dudley	1	1	1	2	4	2	2
Joe Dumars	15	21	7	7	7	11	35
T.R. Dunn	10	16	4	4	12	6	21
Mark Eaton	10	17	8	10	15	5	20

Player	FGM	FGA	FTM	FTA	Reb.	Ast.	Pts.
Franklin Edwards	5	10	8	8	3	3	11
James Edwards	10	18	9	10	9	4	23
Craig Ehlo	9	18	3	5	6	6	21
Dale Ellis	18	30	8	10	14	6	43
Chris Engler	1	1	0	0	2	0	2
Alex English	17	31	13	14	11	12	42
Mike Evans	9	24	7	8	8	11	23
Patrick Ewing	10	16	11	12	20	5	31
Jim Farmer	1	3	0	0	2	1	2
Dave Feitl	0	0	2	2	1	0	2
Kenny Fields	8	11	3	5	6	3	18
Vern Fleming	4	14	9	11	11	8	17
Eric Floyd	18	26	13	14	6	14	51
World B. Free	13	27	11	13	6	9	32
Artis Gilmore	11	19	9	13	20	3	27
Mike Gminski	8	17	12	12	13	3	28
Horace Grant	10	14	3	4	14	4	20
Stuart Gray	0	1	2	2	4	0	2
A.C. Green	9	13	10	13	14	3	21
Rickey Green	12	24	8	10	10	16	32
Sidney Green	7	14	3	6	12	3	17
David Greenwood	11	18	5	6	13	3	24
Darrell Griffith	11	21	7	10	10	8	28
Petur Gudmundsson	4	7	5	7	4	1	10
Bob Hansen	10	19	5	6	7	7	25
Bill Hanzlik	7	12	7	9	8	7	21
Derek Harper	12	21	9	12	6	16	35
Ron Harper	12	23	6	6	8	5	30
Steve Harris	6	12	4	5	3	2	12
Scott Hastings	4	5	4	5	4	2	10
Gerald Henderson	10	17	5	7	6	9	22
Conner Henry	3	4	2	2	2	0	8
Rod Higgins	5	12	3	4	5	3	11
Roy Hinson	10	17	8	13	11	3	28
Craig Hodges	10	16	5	5	5	9	25
Mike Holton	5	7	4	4	3	5	10
Phil Hubbard	10	15	7	8	7	1	23
Eddie Hughes	1	2	0	0	0	1	3
Jay Humphries	7	11	7	7	3	8	21
Marc Iavaroni	5	8	8	10	11	4	15
Mark Jackson	11	24	4	5	7	14	28
Buck Johnson	2	4	1	2	2	0	4
Clemon Johnson	9	13	4	7	13	2	20
Dennis Johnson	13	27	13	17	12	17	33
Eddie A. Johnson	13	25	7	8	8	6	33
Frank Johnson	9	22	7	9	7	11	26
Magic Johnson	14	25	16	17	18	24	42
Marques Johnson	16	26	11	16	17	9	36
Steve Johnson	9	18	11	16	12	2	29
Vinnie Johnson	16	21	8	9	12	13	34
Caldwell Jones	8	15	8	11	26	5	24
Charles Jones	5	9	4	6	9	2	11
Charles A. Jones	3	3	6	6	3	2	12
Michael Jordan	24	45	19	21	11	12	63
Jerome Kersey	13	18	9	11	10	3	26
Albert King	12	22	5	8	9	4	28
Bernard King	19	35	12	15	12	5	46
Greg Kite	4	5	2	3	9	2	8
Joe Kleine	2	5	3	4	5	1	7
Bart Kofoed	3	6	2	2	3	4	7
Jon Koncak	4	6	11	11	8	2	19
Larry Krystkowiak	5	10	8	8	10	3	13
Bill Laimbeer	10	23	13	13	17	6	31
Jeff Lamp	3	7	0	0	1	3	7
Allen Leavell	9	20	11	12	5	13	28
Lafayette Lever	12	22	12	12	16	18	30
Cliff Levingston	6	9	6	8	9	2	17
Ralph Lewis	1	2	0	0	2	1	2
Reggie Lewis	4	6	1	2	6	1	8
Alton Lister	9	14	9	13	17	3	22
Brad Lohaus	3	5	0	0	2	0	6

Player	FGM	FGA	FTM	FTA	Reb.	Ast.	Pts.
John Long	9	17	7	7	5	3	20
John Lucas	12	20	10	12	10	14	30
Maurice Lucas	14	24	12	14	17	9	29
Rick Mahorn	8	14	8	8	18	4	17
Jeff Malone	15	24	9	11	8	6	35
Karl Malone	17	29	17	22	16	4	38
Moses Malone	16	34	18	20	26	6	42
Pace Mannion	3	5	3	4	2	2	9
Mo Martin	6	18	6	11	4	5	18
Wes Matthews	14	21	4	6	5	10	30
Cedric Maxwell	10	16	14	17	15	8	28
Tim McCormick	5	7	2	2	9	3	12
Rodney McCray	10	19	10	10	12	11	24
Xavier McDaniel	20	29	8	12	17	8	42
Ben McDonald	1	4	0	0	3	4	2
Mike McGee	12	19	6	8	7	4	27
Kevin McHale	15	25	14	16	17	7	34
Kevin McKenna	0	0	0	0	0	0	0
Derrick McKey	8	11	4	6	7	2	19
Nate McMillan	5	9	7	8	8	16	15
Mark McNamara	2	2	0	0	1	0	4
Dirk Minniefield	3	5	4	4	2	4	10
Mike Mitchell	17	30	11	12	16	4	37
Paul Mokeski	7	10	6	8	12	6	17
Sidney Moncrief	13	24	14	16	13	8	34
Johnny Moore	16	24	8	10	10	20	39
Chris Mullin	8	17	3	4	4	4	20
Pete Myers	0	1	0	0	0	0	0
Larry Nance	12	22	9	13	15	8	29
Calvin Natt	15	24	12	17	12	10	40
Ed Nealy	2	4	2	2	6	3	6
Chuck Nevitt	2	5	2	2	5	1	6
Johnny Newman	14	25	6	7	6	3	34
Kurt Nimphius	4	7	4	4	10	3	10
Norm Nixon	17	25	8	9	7	19	36
Charles Oakley	8	20	10	12	20	7	25
Mike O'Koren	5	9	2	2	6	3	10
Akeem Olajuwon	19	33	13	20	26	6	49
Jawann Oldham	3	5	0	0	9	2	6
Louis Orr	7	17	4	4	8	3	16
Robert Parish	14	25	11	15	19	6	33
Jim Paxson	13	21	8	12	6	5	32
John Paxson	6	13	11	15	2	8	23
Sam Perkins	13	22	11	13	19	5	29
Chuck Person	14	27	12	15	17	7	40
Jim Petersen	7	12	9	11	13	4	15
Ricky Pierce	10	16	14	17	7	3	29
Scottie Pippen	10	20	4	4	12	5	24
Olden Polynice	3	7	0	2	4	0	6
Terry Porter	9	15	6	8	8	15	23
Paul Pressey	12	20	15	17	10	16	28
Mark Price	11	15	9	9	6	12	31
Kurt Rambis	8	11	5	7	15	4	19
Blair Rasmussen	13	23	6	8	13	4	28
Robert Reid	12	25	11	14	14	17	33
Jerry Reynolds	4	7	4	6	4	2	8
Micheal Ray Richardson	12	26	9	10	13	14	32
Glenn Rivers	10	17	15	16	13	22	32
Fred Roberts	6	12	7	9	5	5	16
Alvin Robertson	15	23	7	8	6	12	34
Cliff Robinson	15	27	6	9	11	6	31
Dennis Rodman	10	16	5	10	12	3	23
Wayne Rollins	8	14	6	10	17	3	18
Scott Roth	1	1	0	0	0	0	2
Walker Russell	1	3	2	2	0	1	2
John Salley	6	9	9	12	13	3	17
Ralph Sampson	13	25	10	14	24	10	33
Mike Sanders	8	17	6	6	8	4	20
Danny Schayes	11	16	13	15	14	5	33
Russ Schoene	4	7	4	4	7	2	11
Detlef Schrempf	6	12	6	8	8	4	14

Player	FGM	FGA	FTM	FTA	Reb.	Ast.	Pts.
Byron Scott	14	24	9	12	7	7	31
Carey Scurry	5	10	2	4	8	2	10
Brad Sellers	8	14	6	6	6	2	22
Purvis Short	13	20	7	7	7	4	32
Jerry Sichting	5	11	2	2	4	8	12
Jack Sikma	12	24	14	15	21	8	33
Larry Smith	8	15	4	5	23	4	18
Otis Smith	1	4	4	5	3	2	6
Mike Smrek	1	4	4	6	2	0	4
Rory Sparrow	8	16	8	8	8	11	22
Steve Stipanovich	11	18	7	10	13	2	22
John Stockton	10	16	16	19	9	24	29
John Stroeder	1	1	0	0	0	0	3
Jon Sundvold	6	11	2	2	2	7	14
Roy Tarpley	12	24	9	15	20	6	27
Terry Teagle	13	20	7	8	4	4	30
Reggie Theus	10	20	17	18	8	11	37
Isiah Thomas	18	33	13	17	12	16	43
Bernard Thompson	0	3	2	2	2	2	2
Billy Thompson	4	7	2	2	4	2	8
LaSalle Thompson	9	19	5	6	17	2	23
Mychal Thompson	15	23	10	12	17	8	40
Otis Thorpe	2	8	3	6	8	0	6
Sedale Threatt	12	16	6	9	7	7	28
Wayman Tisdale	8	13	5	8	5	3	20
Ray Tolbert	3	4	4	8	4	1	10
Andrew Toney	14	25	13	14	7	11	39
Sedric Toney	3	5	2	2	0	1	9
Kelly Tripucka	15	27	11	14	11	6	40
Trent Tucker	9	13	3	4	6	6	18
Elston Turner	9	12	4	6	11	10	18
Mel Turpin	5	9	2	2	3	1	10
Terry Tyler	9	19	11	12	11	3	23
Darnell Valentine	9	16	15	16	5	15	29
Kiki Vandeweghe	17	24	12	12	14	7	37
Jay Vincent	10	20	10	14	11	5	28
Sam Vincent	11	17	9	11	4	14	31
Danny Vranes	6	16	2	3	18	4	12
Milt Wagner	1	2	2	2	1	2	4
Granville Waiters	2	2	0	0	2	0	4
Darrell Walker	8	17	7	10	9	7	20
Kenny Walker	4	12	2	2	6	2	8
Bill Walton	12	22	6	7	24	10	28
Chris Washburn	1	3	2	2	1	1	4
Kermit Washington	7	13	3	4	17	6	15
Spud Webb	10	19	13	16	7	18	21
Scott Wedman	14	25	7	9	11	9	32
Bill Wennington	4	7	2	3	5	2	10
Mark West	2	6	2	3	6	2	5
Ennis Whatley	3	8	0	0	2	4	6
Jerome Whitehead	3	5	1	4	3	1	6
Dominique Wilkins	19	37	15	17	14	6	50
Gerald Wilkins	10	21	4	5	3	7	24
Buck Williams	12	17	11	16	18	5	28
Herb Williams	9	12	2	5	8	4	19
John Williams	8	13	4	8	8	2	20
John S. Williams	7	14	6	10	7	9	19
Kevin Williams	7	14	11	12	7	5	19
Kevin Willis	12	19	8	10	14	3	27
Ricky Wilson	0	2	0	0	0	1	0
David Wingate	5	14	5	6	5	5	16
Randy Wittman	16	25	9	12	7	8	35
Leon Wood	2	5	6	7	1	1	10
Mike Woodson	9	21	7	7	8	5	25
Orlando Woolridge	11	27	8	8	9	4	28
James Worthy	16	25	9	11	16	10	39
Danny Young	3	7	6	6	4	8	12
Phil Zevenbergen	0	0	0	0	0	0	0

Promising Newcomers

WILLIE LLOYD ANDERSON

Born January 8, 1967 at Greenville, S.C.   Height 6:07.   Weight 190.
High School—Atlanta, Ga., East Atlanta.
College—University of Georgia, Athens, Ga.
Drafted by San Antonio on first round, 1988 (10th pick).

—COLLEGIATE RECORD—

Year	G.	Min.	FGA	FGM	Pct.	FTA	FTM	Pct.	Reb.	Pts.	Avg.
84-85	13	80	39	19	.487	8	5	.625	19	43	3.3
85-86	29	493	197	99	.503	61	48	.787	98	246	8.5
86-87	30	1047	374	187	.500	97	77	.794	123	476	15.9
87-88	35	1161	482	241	.500	116	91	.784	177	583	16.7
Totals	107	2781	1092	546	.500	282	221	.784	417	1348	12.6

Three-Point Field Goals: 1986-87, 25-for-64 (.391). 1987-88, 10-for-44 (.227). Totals, 35-for-108 (.324).

KENNETH BARLOW
(Ken)

Born October 20, 1964 at Indianapolis, Ind.   Height 6:10.   Weight 220.
High School—Indianapolis, Ind., Cathedral.
College—University of Notre Dame, Notre Dame, Ind.
Drafted by Los Angeles Lakers on first round, 1986 (23rd pick).

Draft rights traded by Los Angeles Lakers with Mike McGee to Atlanta for draft rights to Billy Thompson and Ron Kellogg, June 17, 1986.
Draft rights traded by Atlanta to Golden State for Chris Washburn, December 15, 1987.
Played in Italy, 1986-87, and in Israel, 1987-88.

—COLLEGIATE RECORD—

Year	G.	Min.	FGA	FGM	Pct.	FTA	FTM	Pct.	Reb.	Pts.	Avg.
82-83	29	689	148	85	.574	35	22	.629	120	192	6.6
83-84	33	951	221	121	.548	71	54	.761	183	296	9.0
84-85	30	1026	363	179	.493	105	80	.762	194	438	14.6
85-86	28	775	312	165	.529	97	86	.887	152	416	14.9
Totals	120	3441	1044	550	.527	308	242	.786	649	1342	11.2

RICKY ALAN BERRY

Born October 6, 1964 at Lansing, Mich.   Height 6:08.   Weight 207.
High School—Morgan Hill, Calif., Live Oak.
Colleges—Oregon State University, Corvallis, Ore.,
and San Jose State University, San Jose, Calif.
Drafted by Sacramento on first round, 1988 (18th pick).

—COLLEGIATE RECORD—

Oregon State

Year	G.	Min.	FGA	FGM	Pct.	FTA	FTM	Pct.	Reb.	Pts.	Avg.
83-84	21	387	81	32	.395	22	15	.682	27	79	3.8

San Jose State

Year	G.	Min.	FGA	FGM	Pct.	FTA	FTM	Pct.	Reb.	Pts.	Avg.
84-85				Did Not Play—Transfer Student							
85-86	28	892	369	179	.485	164	137	.835	138	519	18.5
86-87	27	876	412	190	.461	165	134	.812	121	546	20.2
87-88	29	1058	520	250	.481	178	145	.815	210	702	24.2
S.J. St. Totals	84	2826	1301	619	.476	507	416	.821	469	1767	21.0
College Totals	105	3213	1382	651	.471	529	431	.815	496	1846	17.6

Three-Point Field Goals: 1985-86, 24-for-40 (.600). 1986-87, 32-for-78 (.410). 1987-88, 57-for-128 (.445). Totals, 113-for-246 (.459).

MARK BRYANT

Born April 25, 1965 at Glen Ridge, N.J.   Height 6:09.   Weight 245.
High School—South Orange, N.J., Columbia.
College—Seton Hall University, South Orange, N.J.
Drafted by Portland on first round, 1988 (21st pick).

—COLLEGIATE RECORD—

Year	G.	Min.	FGA	FGM	Pct.	FTA	FTM	Pct.	Reb.	Pts.	Avg.
84-85	26	774	257	122	.475	114	74	.649	177	318	12.2
85-86	30	901	323	169	.523	121	82	.678	226	420	14.0
86-87	28	891	345	171	.496	180	127	.706	198	470	16.8
87-88	34	1105	473	267	.564	218	163	.748	311	698	20.5
Totals	118	3671	1398	729	.521	633	446	.705	912	1906	16.2

Three-Point Field Goals: 1986-87, 1-for-1 (1.000). 1987-88, 1-for-2 (.500). Totals, 2-for-3 (.667).

GREG EDWARD BUTLER

Born March 11, 1966 at Inglewood, Calif.   Height 6:11.   Weight 240.
High School—Rolling Hills Estates, Calif., Rolling Hills.
College—Stanford University, Stanford, Calif.
Drafted by New York on second round, 1988 (37th pick).

—COLLEGIATE RECORD—

Year	G.	Min.	FGA	FGM	Pct.	FTA	FTM	Pct.	Reb.	Pts.	Avg.
84-85	27	395	158	70	.443	40	24	.600	68	164	6.1
85-86	30	635	244	122	.500	61	45	.738	118	289	9.6
86-87	27	566	140	62	.443	56	38	.679	107	163	6.0
87-88	33	967	299	169	.565	114	83	.728	193	422	12.8
Totals	117	2563	841	423	.503	271	190	.701	486	1038	8.9

Three-Point Field Goals: 1986-87, 1-for-3 (.333). 1987-88, 1-for-1 (1.000). Totals, 2-for-4 (.500).

REX EVERETT CHAPMAN

Born October 5, 1967 at Bowling Green, Ky.   Height 6:04.   Weight 185.
High School—Owensboro, Ky., Apollo.
College—University of Kentucky, Lexington, Ky.
Drafted by Charlotte on first round as an undergraduate, 1988 (8th pick).

—COLLEGIATE RECORD—

Year	G.	Min.	FGA	FGM	Pct.	FTA	FTM	Pct.	Reb.	Pts.	Avg.
86-87	29	962	390	173	.444	68	50	.735	66	464	16.0
87-88	32	1108	461	231	.501	102	81	.794	93	609	19.0
Totals	61	2070	851	404	.475	170	131	.771	159	1073	17.6

Three-Point Field Goals: 1986-87, 68-for-176 (.386). 1987-88, 66-for-159 (.415). Totals, 134-for-335 (.400).
Son of Wayne Chapman, who played for Kentucky, Denver and Indiana in the ABA, 1968-69 through 1971-72.

DERRICK JOSEPH CHIEVOUS

Born July 3, 1967 at New York, N.Y.   Height 6:07.   Weight 195.
High School—Flushing, N.Y., Holy Cross.
College—University of Missouri, Columbia, Mo.
Drafted by Houston on first round, 1988 (16th pick).

—COLLEGIATE RECORD—

Year	G.	Min.	FGA	FGM	Pct.	FTA	FTM	Pct.	Reb.	Pts.	Avg.
84-85	32	1019	278	142	.511	168	134	.798	170	418	13.1
85-86	34	1091	433	227	.524	232	186	.802	262	640	18.8
86-87	34	1215	522	282	.540	302	244	.808	291	821	24.1
87-88	30	943	477	242	.507	261	200	.766	256	701	23.4
Totals	130	4268	1710	893	.522	963	764	.793	979	2580	19.8

Three-Point Field Goals: 1986-87, 13-for-33 (.394). 1987-88, 17-for-33 (.515). Totals, 30-for-66 (.455).

—DID YOU KNOW—

That Gene Shue has twice been coach of the same franchise in two different cities? He coached the Baltimore and Washington (Landover, Md.) Bullets, and the San Diego and Los Angeles Clippers.

VINCENT JOSEPH DEL NEGRO
(Vinny)

Born August 9, 1966 at Springfield, Mass. Height 6:05. Weight 185.
High School—Suffield, Conn., Suffield Academy.
College—North Carolina State University, Raleigh, N.C.
Drafted by Sacramento on second round, 1988 (29th pick).

—COLLEGIATE RECORD—

Year	G.	Min.	FGA	FGM	Pct.	FTA	FTM	Pct.	Reb.	Pts.	Avg.
84-85	19	125	21	12	.571	23	15	.652	14	39	2.1
85-86	17	139	30	11	.367	11	7	.636	14	29	1.7
86-87	35	918	269	133	.494	71	63	.887	115	265	10.4
87-88	32	1093	363	187	.515	124	104	.839	158	509	15.9
Totals	103	2275	683	343	.502	229	189	.825	301	942	9.1

Three-Point Field Goals: 1986-87, 36-for-72 (.500). 1987-88, 31-for-78 (.397). Totals, 67-for-150 (.447).

FENNIS MARX DEMBO

Born January 24, 1966 at Mobile, Ala. Height 6:05. Weight 215.
High School—San Antonio, Tex., Fox Tech.
College—University of Wyoming, Laramie, Wyo.
Drafted by Detroit on second round, 1988 (30th pick).

—COLLEGIATE RECORD—

Year	G.	Min.	FGA	FGM	Pct.	FTA	FTM	Pct.	Reb.	Pts.	Avg.
84-85	29	1064	309	151	.489	130	90	.692	212	392	13.5
85-86	34	1169	420	227	.540	161	123	.764	229	577	17.0
86-87	34	1236	469	240	.512	171	131	.766	282	689	20.3
87-88	32	1076	430	205	.477	216	178	.824	231	653	20.4
Totals	129	4545	1628	823	.506	678	522	.770	954	2311	17.9

Three-Point Field Goals: 1986-87, 78-for-184 (.424). 1987-88, 65-for-177 (.367). Totals, 143-for-361 (.396).

LEDELL EACKLES

Born November 24, 1966 at Baton Rouge, La. Height 6:05. Weight 220.
High School—Baton Rouge, La., Broadmoor.
Colleges—San Jacinto College, Pasadena, Tex.,
and University of New Orleans, New Orleans, La.
Drafted by Washington on second round, 1988 (36th pick).

—COLLEGIATE RECORD—
San Jacinto

Year	G.	Min.	FGA	FGM	Pct.	FTA	FTM	Pct.	Reb.	Pts.	Avg.
84-85					Statistics Unavailable						
85-86	37	....	715	417	.583	229	173	.755	238	1007	27.2

New Orleans

Year	G.	Min.	FGA	FGM	Pct.	FTA	FTM	Pct.	Reb.	Pts.	Avg.
86-87	28	902	554	239	.456	116	84	.724	114	632	22.6
87-88	31	982	512	260	.508	232	186	.802	153	726	23.4
Totals	59	1884	1036	499	.482	348	270	.776	267	1358	23.0

Three-Point Field Goals: 1986-87, 70-for-172 (.407). 1987-88, 20-for-84 (.238). Totals, 90-for-256 (.352).

KEVIN EDWARDS

Born October 30, 1965 at Cleveland Heights, O. Height 6:03. Weight 200.
High School—Cleveland, O., St. Joseph.
Colleges—Lakeland Community College, Mentor, O.,
and DePaul University, Chicago, Ill.
Drafted by Miami on first round, 1988 (20th pick).

—COLLEGIATE RECORD—
Lakeland

Year	G.	Min.	FGA	FGM	Pct.	FTA	FTM	Pct.	Reb.	Pts.	Avg.
84-85	33	....	435	256	.589	144	103	.715	178	615	18.6
85-86	32	....	519	325	.626	159	121	.761	239	771	24.1
J.C. Totals	65	....	954	581	.609	303	224	.739	417	1386	21.3

Year	G.	Min.	FGA	FGM	Pct.	FTA	FTM	Pct.	Reb.	Pts.	Avg.
86-87	31	1060	343	184	.536	78	63	.808	156	447	14.4
87-88	30	999	413	220	.533	106	83	.783	158	548	18.3
DePaul Totals	61	2059	756	404	.534	184	146	.793	314	995	16.3

Three-Point Field Goals: 1986-87, 16-for-36 (.444). 1987-88, 25-for-56 (.446). Totals, 41-for-92 (.446).

ROLANDO FERREIRA JR.

Born May 24, 1964 at Curitiba, Brazil.   Height 7:01.   Weight 240.

High School—Sao Paulo, Brazil, Colegro Objectivo.

College—University of Houston, Houston, Tex.

Drafted by Portland on second round, 1988 (26th pick).

—COLLEGIATE RECORD—

Year	G.	Min.	FGA	FGM	Pct.	FTA	FTM	Pct.	Reb.	Pts.	Avg.
86-87	30	892	277	127	.458	49	36	.735	169	293	9.8
87-88	31	992	353	193	.547	116	81	.698	212	467	15.1
Totals	61	1884	630	320	.508	165	117	.709	381	760	12.5

Three-Point Field Goals: 1986-87, 3-for-17 (.176). 1987-88, 0-for-2. Totals, 3-for-19 (.158).

(Limited to two years of college eligibility in United States because of NCAA rule deducting one year of eligibility for each year of age a foreign athlete is over 20 years of age.)

Member of Brazil National Team, 1982-83 through 1985-86.

LESTER FONVILLE

Born February 15, 1963 at Mound Bayou, Miss.   Height 7:02.   Weight 245.

High School—Mound Bayou, Miss.

Colleges—Lake City Community College, Lake City, Fla.,
and Jackson State University, Jackson, Miss.

Drafted by Portland on second round, 1987 (29th pick).

Waived by Portland, February 29, 1988; re-signed by Portland as a free agent, April 20, 1988.
Played in Continental Basketball Association with Mississippi Jets, 1987-88.

—COLLEGIATE RECORD—

Year	G.	Min.	FGA	FGM	Pct.	FTA	FTM	Pct.	Reb.	Pts.	Avg.
82-83				Statistics Unavailable							

Jackson State

Year	G.	Min.	FGA	FGM	Pct.	FTA	FTM	Pct.	Reb.	Pts.	Avg.
83-84				Did Not Play—Redshirted							
84-85	25	434	167	78	.467	45	22	.489	142	178	7.1
85-86	29	695	206	92	.447	51	27	.529	225	211	7.3
86-87	29	880	335	152	.454	141	93	.660	300	397	13.7
Totals	83	2009	708	322	.455	237	142	.599	667	786	9.5

CBA REGULAR SEASON RECORD

Sea.—Team	G.	Min.	2-Point			3-Point			FTM	FTA	Pct.	Reb.	Ast.	Pts.	Avg.
			FGM	FGA	Pct.	FGM	FGA	Pct.							
87-88—Mississippi	28	496	48	103	.466	0	0	.....	16	37	.432	160	9	112	4.0

DEAN HEATH GARRETT

Born November 27, 1966 at Los Angeles, Calif.   Height 6:10.   Weight 225.

High School—San Clemente, Calif.

Colleges—City College of San Francisco, San Francisco, Calif.,
and Indiana University, Bloomington, Ind.

Drafted by Phoenix on second round, 1988 (38th pick).

—COLLEGIATE RECORD—

City College of San Francisco

Year	G.	Min.	FGA	FGM	Pct.	FTA	FTM	Pct.	Reb.	Pts.	Avg.
84-85				Statistics Unavailable							
85-86				Statistics Unavailable							

Indiana

Year	G.	Min.	FGA	FGM	Pct.	FTA	FTM	Pct.	Reb.	Pts.	Avg.
86-87	34	....	301	163	.542	96	61	.635	288	387	11.4
87-88	29	....	344	184	.535	142	99	.697	246	467	16.1
Totals	63	....	645	347	.538	238	160	.672	534	854	13.6

Member of NCAA Division I championship team, 1987.

THOMAS S. GARRICK
(Tom)

Born July 7, 1966 at West Warwick, R.I.   Height 6:02.   Weight 185.
High School—West Warwick, R.I.
College—University of Rhode Island, Kingston, R.I.
Drafted by Los Angeles Clippers on second round, 1988 (45th pick).

—COLLEGIATE RECORD—

Year	G.	Min.	FGA	FGM	Pct.	FTA	FTM	Pct.	Reb.	Pts.	Avg.
84-85	28	739	114	54	.474	78	58	.744	102	166	5.9
85-86	27	623	135	65	.481	66	49	.742	76	179	6.6
86-87	30	1037	421	192	.456	132	108	.818	129	510	17.0
87-88	35	1241	561	273	.487	174	138	.793	143	718	20.5
Totals	120	3640	1231	584	.474	450	353	.784	450	1573	13.1

Three-Point Field Goals: 1986-87, 18-for-55 (.327). 1987-88, 34-for-62 (.548). Totals, 52-for-117 (.444).

HANS-JURGEN GNAD
(Hansi)

Born June 4, 1963 at Darmstadt, West Germany.   Height 6:10.   Weight 200.
High School—Darmstadt, West Germany.
College—University of Alaska at Anchorage, Anchorage, Alaska.
Drafted by Philadelphia on third round, 1987 (57th pick).

Selected from Philadelphia by Miami in NBA expansion draft, June 23, 1988.

—COLLEGIATE RECORD—

Year	G.	Min.	FGA	FGM	Pct.	FTA	FTM	Pct.	Reb.	Pts.	Avg.
83-84	28	565	187	90	.481	64	38	.594	174	218	7.8
84-85	28	862	361	165	.457	157	104	.662	244	434	15.5
85-86	32	977	385	191	.496	163	106	.650	339	488	15.3
86-87	30	526	409	207	.506	167	107	.641	367	526	17.5
Totals	118	2930	1342	653	.487	551	355	.644	1124	1666	14.1

Three-Point Field Goals: 1986-87, 5-for-13 (.385).

ORLANDO GRAHAM

Born May 5, 1965 at Montgomery, Ala.   Height 6:08.   Weight 220.
High School—Montgomery, Ala., Lanier.
Colleges—West Texas State University, Canyon, Tex.,
and Auburn University at Montgomery, Auburn, Ala.
Drafted by Miami on second round, 1988 (40th pick).

—COLLEGIATE RECORD—
West Texas State

Year	G.	Min.	FGA	FGM	Pct.	FTA	FTM	Pct.	Reb.	Pts.	Avg.
83-84				Did Not Play—Red Shirted							
84-85	28	787	234	125	.534	101	69	.683	179	319	11.4
85-86	23	776	247	115	.466	165	85	.515	209	315	13.7
W. Texas Totals	51	1563	481	240	.499	266	154	.579	388	634	12.4

Auburn-Montgomery

Year	G.	Min.	FGA	FGM	Pct.	FTA	FTM	Pct.	Reb.	Pts.	Avg.
86-87	20	471	187	103	.551	94	50	.532	165	256	12.8
87-88	35	1001	423	261	.617	207	123	.594	401	645	18.4
Aub.-Mon. Totals	55	1472	610	364	.597	301	173	.575	566	901	16.4
College Totals	106	3035	1091	604	.554	567	327	.577	954	1535	14.5

GARY GRANT

Born April 21, 1965 at Parson, Kan.   Height 6:03.   Weight 195.
High School—Canton, O., McKinley.
College—University of Michigan, Ann Arbor, Mich.
Drafted by Seattle on first round, 1988 (15th pick).

Draft rights traded by Seattle with a 1989 1st round draft choice to Los Angeles Clippers for Michael Cage, June 28, 1988.

—COLLEGIATE RECORD—

Year	G.	Min.	FGA	FGM	Pct.	FTA	FTM	Pct.	Reb.	Pts.	Avg.
84-85	30	950	307	169	.550	60	49	.817	76	387	12.9
85-86	33	1010	348	172	.494	78	58	.744	104	402	12.2
86-87	32	....	533	286	.537	142	111	.782	159	716	22.4
87-88	34	....	508	269	.530	167	135	.808	116	717	21.1
Totals	129	....	1696	896	.528	447	353	.790	455	2222	17.2

Three-Point Field Goals: 1986-87, 33-for-68 (.485). 1987-88, 44-for-99 (.444). Totals, 77-for-167. (.461).
Named to THE SPORTING NEWS All-America Second Team, 1988.

HARVEY GRANT

Born July 4, 1965 at Augusta, Ga.   Height 6:08.   Weight 200.
High School—Sparta, Ga., Hancock Central.
Colleges—Clemson University, Clemson, S.C.; Independence Junior College, Independence, Kan., and University of Oklahoma, Norman, Okla.
Drafted by Washington on first round, 1988 (12th pick).

—COLLEGIATE RECORD—
Clemson

Year	G.	Min.	FGA	FGM	Pct.	FTA	FTM	Pct.	Reb.	Pts.	Avg.
83-84					Did Not Play—Red Shirted						
84-85	28	418	121	60	.496	41	24	.585	126	144	5.1

Independence

Year	G.	Min.	FGA	FGM	Pct.	FTA	FTM	Pct.	Reb.	Pts.	Avg.
85-86	33	....	580	340	.586	82	58	.707	388	738	22.4

Oklahoma

Year	G.	Min.	FGA	FGM	Pct.	FTA	FTM	Pct.	Reb.	Pts.	Avg.
86-87	34	1165	427	228	.534	163	119	.730	338	575	16.9
87-88	39	1339	640	350	.547	155	113	.729	365	816	20.9
Okla. Totals	73	2504	1067	578	.542	318	232	.730	703	1391	19.1
College Totals	101	2922	1188	638	.537	359	256	.713	829	1535	15.2

Three-Point Field Goals: 1986-87, 0-for-1. 1987-88, 3-for-14 (.214). Totals, 3-for-15 (.200).
Twin brother of Chicago Bulls forward Horace Grant.

SYLVESTER GRAY

Born July 8, 1967 at Millington, Tenn.   Height 6:06.   Weight 230.
High School—Arlington, Tenn., Bolton.
College—Memphis State University, Memphis, Tenn.
Drafted by Miami on second round as an undergraduate, 1988 (35th pick).

—COLLEGIATE RECORD—

Year	G.	Min.	FGA	FGM	Pct.	FTA	FTM	Pct.	Reb.	Pts.	Avg.
86-87	34	979	334	180	.539	106	54	.509	257	414	12.2
87-88	5	146	62	35	.565	10	6	.600	41	76	15.2
Totals	39	1125	396	215	.543	116	60	.517	298	490	12.6

Three-Point Field Goals: 1986-87, 0-for-1.

JEFFREY GRAYER
(Jeff)

Born December 17, 1965 at Flint, Mich.   Height 6:05.   Weight 200.
High School—Flint, Mich., Northwestern.
College—Iowa State University, Ames, Iowa.
Drafted by Milwaukee on first round, 1988 (13th pick).

—COLLEGIATE RECORD—

Year	G.	Min.	FGA	FGM	Pct.	FTA	FTM	Pct.	Reb.	Pts.	Avg.
84-85	33	1119	289	153	.529	147	96	.653	213	402	12.2
85-86	33	1159	514	281	.547	194	122	.629	208	684	20.7
86-87	27	995	452	228	.504	192	142	.740	189	605	22.4
87-88	32	1165	597	312	.523	235	167	.711	300	811	25.3
Totals	125	4438	1852	974	.526	768	527	.686	910	2502	20.0

Three-Point Field Goals: 1986-87, 7-for-21 (.333). 1987-88, 20-for-61 (.328). Totals, 27-for-82 (.329).

HERSEY R. HAWKINS JR.

Born September 29, 1965 at Chicago, Ill.   Height 6:03.   Weight 190.

High School—Chicago, Ill., Westinghouse.

College—Bradley University, Peoria, Ill.

Drafted by Los Angeles Clippers on first round, 1988 (6th pick).

Draft rights traded with a 1989 1st round draft choice by Los Angeles Clippers to Philadelphia for draft rights to Charles Smith, June 28, 1988.

—COLLEGIATE RECORD—

Year	G.	Min.	FGA	FGM	Pct.	FTA	FTM	Pct.	Reb.	Pts.	Avg.
84-85	30	1121	308	179	.581	105	81	.771	182	439	14.6
85-86	35	1291	461	250	.542	203	156	.768	200	656	18.7
86-87	29	1102	552	294	.533	213	169	.793	195	788	27.2
87-88	31	1202	720	377	.524	335	284	.848	241	1125	36.3
Totals	125	4716	2041	1100	.539	856	690	.806	818	3008	24.1

Three-Point Field Goals: 1986-87, 31-for-108 (.287). 1987-88, 87-for-221 (.394). Totals, 118-for-329 (.359).

Led NCAA Division I in scoring, 1988. . . . Named THE SPORTING NEWS College Player of the Year, 1988. . . . THE SPORTING NEWS All-America First Team, 1988.

ALFREDO WILLIAM HORFORD
(Tito)

Born January 19, 1966 at LaRomana, Dominican Republic.   Height 7:01.   Weight 245.

High School—Houston, Tex., Marian Christian.

Colleges—Louisiana State University, Baton Rouge, La.,
and University of Miami, Coral Gables, Fla.

Drafted by Milwaukee on second round as an undergraduate, 1988 (39th pick).

—COLLEGIATE RECORD—
Louisiana State

Year	G.	Min.	FGA	FGM	Pct.	FTA	FTM	Pct.	Reb.	Pts.	Avg.
85-86				Did Not Play—Left School Before Basketball Season							

Miami (Fla.)

Year	G.	Min.	FGA	FGM	Pct.	FTA	FTM	Pct.	Reb.	Pts.	Avg.
85-86				Did Not Play—Transfer Student							
86-87	25	803	287	137	.477	152	84	.533	241	358	14.3
87-88	30	963	326	176	.540	126	73	.579	271	425	14.2
Totals	55	1766	613	313	.511	278	157	.565	512	783	14.2

SHELTON JONES

Born April 6, 1966 at Copiague, N.Y.   Height 6:09.   Weight 210.

High School—Amityville, N.Y., Memorial.

College—St. John's University, Jamaica, N.Y.

Drafted by San Antonio on second round, 1988 (27th pick).

—COLLEGIATE RECORD—

Year	G.	Min.	FGA	FGM	Pct.	FTA	FTM	Pct.	Reb.	Pts.	Avg.
84-85	32	317	59	32	.542	42	26	.619	52	90	2.8
85-86	36	1022	217	114	.525	97	79	.814	205	307	8.5
86-87	30	1078	354	165	.466	149	108	.725	234	438	14.6
87-88	29	1108	399	202	.506	177	134	.757	256	539	18.6
Totals	127	3525	1029	513	.499	465	347	.746	747	1374	10.8

Three-Point Field Goals: 1986-87, 0-for-2. 1987-88, 1-for-6 (.167). Totals, 1-for-8 (.125).

STEPHEN DOUGLAS KERR
(Steve)

Born September 27, 1965 at Beirut, Lebanon.   Height 6:03.   Weight 175.

High School—Pacific Palisades, Calif.

College—University of Arizona, Tucson, Ariz.

Drafted by Phoenix on second round, 1988 (50th pick).

—COLLEGIATE RECORD—

Year	G.	Min.	FGA	FGM	Pct.	FTA	FTM	Pct.	Reb.	Pts.	Avg.
83-84	28	633	157	81	.516	52	36	.692	33	198	7.1

Year	G.	Min.	FGA	FGM	Pct.	FTA	FTM	Pct.	Reb.	Pts.	Avg.
84-85	31	1036	222	126	.568	71	57	.803	73	309	10.0
85-86	32	1228	361	195	.540	79	71	.899	101	461	14.4
86-87				Did Not Play—Knee Injury							
87-88	38	1239	270	151	.559	74	61	.824	76	477	12.6
Totals	129	4136	1010	553	.548	276	225	.815	283	1445	11.2

Three-Point Field Goals: 1987-88, 114-for-199 (.573).

RANDOLPH KEYS

Born April 19, 1966 at Collins, Miss.   Height 6:09.   Weight 195.

High School—Collins, Miss.

College—University of Southern Mississippi, Hattiesburg, Miss.

Drafted by Cleveland on first round, 1988 (22nd pick).

—COLLEGIATE RECORD—

Year	G.	Min.	FGA	FGM	Pct.	FTA	FTM	Pct.	Reb.	Pts.	Avg.
84-85	28	396	112	51	.455	36	26	.722	70	128	4.6
85-86	29	923	366	184	.503	72	42	.583	164	410	14.1
86-87	34	1142	525	243	.463	85	60	.706	268	558	16.4
87-88	30	978	455	216	.475	102	78	.765	221	530	17.7
Totals	121	3439	1458	694	.476	295	206	.698	723	1626	13.4

Three-Point Field Goals: 1986-87, 12-for-51 (.235). 1987-88, 20-for-58 (.345). Totals, 32-for-109 (.294).

JEROME LANE

Born December 4, 1966 at Akron, O.   Height 6:06.   Weight 230.

High School—Akron, O., St. Vincent-St. Mary.

College—University of Pittsburgh, Pittsburgh, Pa.

Drafted by Denver on first round as an undergraduate, 1988 (23rd pick).

—COLLEGIATE RECORD—

Year	G.	Min.	FGA	FGM	Pct.	FTA	FTM	Pct.	Reb.	Pts.	Avg.
85-86	29	711	202	95	.470	113	74	.655	148	264	9.1
86-87	33	1169	329	187	.568	230	114	.626	444	522	15.8
87-88	31	1090	300	154	.513	200	123	.615	378	431	13.9
Totals	93	2970	831	436	.525	543	341	.628	970	1217	13.1

Three-Point Field Goals: 1986-87, 4-for-8 (.500). 1987-88, 0-for-7. Totals, 4-for-15 (.267).

Led NCAA Division I in rebounding, 1987.

ANDREW CHARLES LANG

Born June 28, 1966 at Pine Bluff, Ark.   Height 6:11.   Weight 250.

High School—Pine Bluff, Ark., Dollarway.

College—University of Arkansas, Fayetteville, Ark.

Drafted by Phoenix on second round, 1988 (28th pick).

—COLLEGIATE RECORD—

Year	G.	Min.	FGA	FGM	Pct.	FTA	FTM	Pct.	Reb.	Pts.	Avg.
84-85	33	467	84	34	.405	32	18	.563	67	86	2.6
85-86	26	694	189	88	.466	61	37	.607	168	213	8.2
86-87	32	722	204	102	.500	87	56	.644	240	260	8.1
87-88	30	743	239	126	.527	60	27	.450	218	279	9.3
Totals	121	2626	716	350	.489	230	138	.600	693	838	6.9

ERIC C. LECKNER

Born May 27, 1966 at Inglewood, Calif.   Height 6.11.   Weight 265.

High School—Manhattan Beach, Calif., Mira Costa.

College—University of Wyoming, Laramie, Wyo.

Drafted by Utah on first round, 1988 (17th pick).

—COLLEGIATE RECORD—

Year	G.	Min.	FGA	FGM	Pct.	FTA	FTM	Pct.	Reb.	Pts.	Avg.
84-85	29	600	168	98	.583	78	48	.615	112	244	8.4
85-86	36	1113	392	228	.582	183	112	.612	207	568	15.8
86-87	34	1123	390	246	.631	201	142	.706	245	634	18.6
87-88	32	972	281	181	.644	172	130	.756	210	492	15.4
Totals	131	3808	1231	753	.612	634	432	.681	774	1938	14.8

GRANT ANDREW LONG

Born March 12, 1966 at Wayne, Mich. Height 6:08. Weight 225.
High School—Romulus, Mich.
College—Eastern Michigan University, Ypsilanti, Mich.
Drafted by Miami on second round, 1988 (33rd pick).

—COLLEGIATE RECORD—

Year	G.	Min.	FGA	FGM	Pct.	FTA	FTM	Pct.	Reb.	Pts.	Avg.
84-85	28	551	78	44	.564	46	28	.609	112	116	4.1
85-86	27	803	175	92	.526	73	47	.644	178	231	8.6
86-87	29	879	308	169	.549	131	95	.725	260	433	14.9
87-88	30	1026	427	237	.555	281	215	.765	313	689	23.0
Totals	114	3259	988	542	.549	531	385	.725	863	1469	12.9

Nephew of Indiana Pacers guard John Long.

DANIEL LEWIS MAJERLE

Name pronounced MAR-lee.

(Dan)

Born September 9, 1965 at Traverse City, Mich. Height 6:06. Weight 215.
High School—Traverse City, Mich.
College—Central Michigan University, Mt. Pleasant, Mich.
Drafted by Phoenix on first round, 1988 (14th pick).

—COLLEGIATE RECORD—

Year	G.	Min.	FGA	FGM	Pct.	FTA	FTM	Pct.	Reb.	Pts.	Avg.
83-84					Did Not Play—Back Injury						
84-85	12	360	162	92	.568	67	39	.582	80	223	18.6
85-86	27	1002	433	228	.527	170	122	.718	212	578	21.4
86-87	23	824	344	191	.555	183	101	.552	196	485	21.1
87-88	32	1197	535	279	.521	242	156	.645	346	759	23.7
Totals	94	3383	1474	790	.536	662	418	.631	834	2045	21.8

Three-Point Field Goals: 1986-87, 2-for-8 (.250). 1987-88, 45-for-101 (.446). Totals, 47-for-109 (.431).

DANIEL RICARDO MANNING
(Danny)

Born May 17, 1966 at Hattiesburg, Miss. Height 6:10. Weight 230.
High Schools—Greensboro, N.C., Page (Soph. and Jr.) and Lawrence, Kan.
College—University of Kansas, Lawrence, Kan.
Drafted by Los Angeles Clippers on first round, 1988 (1st pick).

—COLLEGIATE RECORD—

Year	G.	Min.	FGA	FGM	Pct.	FTA	FTM	Pct.	Reb.	Pts.	Avg.
84-85	34	1120	369	209	.566	102	78	.765	258	496	14.6
85-86	39	1256	465	279	.600	127	95	.748	245	653	16.7
86-87	36	1249	562	347	.617	226	165	.730	342	860	23.9
87-88	38	1336	653	381	.583	233	171	.734	342	942	24.8
Totals	147	4961	2049	1216	.593	688	509	.740	1187	2951	20.1

Three-Point Field Goals: 1986-87, 1-for-3 (.333). 1987-88, 9-for-26 (.346). Totals, 10-for-29 (.345).

Member of NCAA Division I championship team, 1988. . . . Named to THE SPORTING NEWS All-America First Team, 1987 and 1988. . . . Named Outstanding Player in NCAA Division I tournament, 1988. . . . Son of Ed Manning, currently an assistant coach with San Antonio Spurs and forward with Baltimore, Chicago and Portland of the NBA and Carolina, New York and Indiana of the ABA, 1967-68 through 1975-76.

—DID YOU KNOW—

That only four times in the 182 seven-game playoff series in NBA history has a team rebounded to win from an 0-2 deficit? Los Angeles beat San Francisco, 4-2, in the 1969 Western Conference semifinals; Boston edged Los Angeles, 4-3, in the 1969 NBA Finals; Baltimore defeated New York, 4-3, in the 1971 Eastern Conference finals and Portland beat Philadelphia, 4-3, in the 1977 NBA Finals.

DANNY MANNING

VERNON MAXWELL

Born September 12, 1965 at Gainesville, Fla.   Height 6:04.   Weight 180.

High School—Gainesville, Fla., Buchholz.

College—University of Florida, Gainesville, Fla.

Drafted by Denver on second round, 1988 (47th pick).

Draft rights traded by Denver to San Antonio for a 1989 2nd round draft choice, June 28, 1988.

—COLLEGIATE RECORD—

Year	G.	Min.	FGA	FGM	Pct.	FTA	FTM	Pct.	Reb.	Pts.	Avg.
84-85	30	752	366	163	.445	105	72	.686	72	398	13.3
85-86	33	1142	566	262	.463	177	124	.701	147	648	19.6
86-87	34	1086	548	266	.485	217	161	.742	125	738	21.7
87-88	33	1214	515	230	.447	207	148	.715	138	666	20.2
Totals	130	4194	1995	921	.462	706	505	.715	482	2450	18.8

Three-Point Field Goals: 1986-87, 45-for-128 (.352). 1987-88, 58-for-147 (.395). Totals, 103-for-255 (.404).

ROBERT McCANN
(Bob)

Born April 22, 1964 at Morristown, N.J.   Height 6:06.   Weight 245.

High School—Morristown, N.J.

Colleges—Upsala College, East Orange, N.J., and
Morehead State University, Morehead, Ky.

Drafted by Milwaukee on second round, 1987 (32nd pick).

Waived by Milwaukee, November 4, 1987.

—COLLEGIATE RECORD—
Upsala

Year	G.	Min.	FGA	FGM	Pct.	FTA	FTM	Pct.	Reb.	Pts.	Avg.
82-83	26	....	236	112	.475	64	34	.531	208	258	9.9

Morehead State

Year	G.	Min.	FGA	FGM	Pct.	FTA	FTM	Pct.	Reb.	Pts.	Avg.
83-84					Did Not Play—Transfer Student						
84-85	27	911	383	188	.491	152	85	.559	263	461	17.1
85-86	27	803	320	171	.534	173	113	.653	282	455	16.9
86-87	28	872	376	206	.548	170	107	.629	317	520	18.6
M.S. Totals	82	2586	1079	565	.524	495	305	.616	862	1436	17.5
Col. Totals	108	....	1315	677	.515	559	339	.606	1070	1694	15.7

Three-Point Field Goals: 1986-87, 1-for-3 (.333).

TODD ERNEST MITCHELL

Born July 26, 1966 at Toledo, O.   Height 6:07.   Weight 205.

High School—Toledo, O., St. Francis.

College—Purdue University, West Lafayette, Ind.

Drafted by Denver on second round, 1988 (43rd pick).

—COLLEGIATE RECORD—

Year	G.	Min.	FGA	FGM	Pct.	FTA	FTM	Pct.	Reb.	Pts.	Avg.
84-85	29	531	144	70	.486	87	59	.678	125	199	6.9
85-86	32	1049	307	173	.564	211	169	.801	230	515	16.1
86-87	30	900	323	174	.539	157	118	.752	195	467	15.6
87-88	33	982	345	188	.545	198	140	.707	190	518	15.7
Totals	124	3462	1119	605	.541	653	486	.744	740	1699	13.7

Three-Point Field Goals: 1986-87, 1-for-4 (.250). 1987-88, 2-for-5 (.400). Totals, 3-for-9 (.333).

JEFFREY J. MOE

Born May 19, 1966 at Indianapolis, Ind.   Height 6:03.   Weight 195.

High School—Indianapolis, Ind., Brebeuf.

College—University of Iowa, Iowa City, Iowa.

Drafted by Utah on second round, 1988 (42nd pick).

Year	G.	Min.	FGA	FGM	Pct.	FTA	FTM	Pct.	Reb.	Pts.	Avg.
84-85	30	669	205	91	.444	63	49	.778	43	231	7.7
85-86	32	482	158	84	.532	29	23	.793	11	191	6.0
86-87	35	652	289	135	.467	77	59	.766	75	389	11.1
87-88	34	792	275	135	.491	122	96	.787	72	437	12.9
Totals	131	2595	927	445	.480	291	227	.780	201	1248	9.5

Three-Point Field Goals: 1986-87, 60-for-136 (.441). 1987-88, 71-for-178 (.399). Totals, 131-for-314 (.417).

CHRISTOPHER VERNARD MORRIS
(Chris)

Born January 20, 1966 at Atlanta, Ga.   Height 6:08.   Weight 210.

High School—Atlanta, Ga., Douglass.

College—Auburn University, Auburn University, Ala.

Drafted by New Jersey on first round, 1988 (4th pick).

—COLLEGIATE RECORD—

Year	G.	Min.	FGA	FGM	Pct.	FTA	FTM	Pct.	Reb.	Pts.	Avg.
84-85	34	1032	325	155	.477	71	44	.620	169	354	10.4
85-86	33	1023	256	128	.500	103	69	.670	171	325	9.8
86-87	31	985	304	170	.559	97	69	.711	225	418	13.5
87-88	30	1018	501	241	.481	132	105	.795	295	620	20.7
Totals	128	4058	1386	694	.501	403	287	.712	860	1717	13.4

Three-Point Field Goals: 1986-87, 9-for-27 (.333). 1987-88, 33-for-97 (.340). Totals, 42-for-124 (.339).

JOSE RAFAEL ORTIZ

Born October 25, 1963 at Albonito, Puerto Rico.   Height 6:10.   Weight 225.

High School—Cayey, Puerto Rico, Benjamin Harrison.

College—Oregon State University, Corvallis, Ore.

Graduated from high school in 1981; played with San German in Puerto Rico
Superior League prior to enrolling at Oregon State in January, 1985.

Drafted by Utah on first round, 1987 (15th pick).

Played in Spain, 1987-88.

—COLLEGIATE RECORD—

Year	G.	Min.	FGA	FGM	Pct.	FTA	FTM	Pct.	Reb.	Pts.	Avg.
84-85					Did Not Play						
85-86	22	765	266	137	.515	131	87	.664	188	361	16.4
86-87	30	1100	425	248	.584	236	171	.725	262	668	22.3
Totals	52	1865	681	385	.557	367	258	.703	450	1029	19.8

Three-Point Field Goals: 1986-87, 1-for-2 (.500).

WILLIAM EDWARD PERDUE
(Will)

Born August 29, 1965 at Melbourne, Fla.   Height 7:00.   Weight 240.

High School—Merritt Island, Fla.

College—Vanderbilt University, Nashville, Tenn.

Drafted by Chicago on first round, 1988 (11th pick).

—COLLEGIATE RECORD—

Year	G.	Min.	FGA	FGM	Pct.	FTA	FTM	Pct.	Reb.	Pts.	Avg.
83-84	17	111	45	21	.467	9	4	.444	38	46	2.7
84-85				Did Not Play—Red Shirted							
85-86	22	181	53	31	.585	32	14	.438	61	76	3.5
86-87	34	1033	389	233	.599	204	126	.618	295	592	17.4
87-88	31	1013	369	234	.624	147	99	.673	314	567	18.3
Totals	104	2338	856	519	.606	392	243	.620	708	1281	12.3

TIMOTHY D. PERRY
(Tim)

Born June 4, 1965 at Freehold, N.J.   Height 6:09.   Weight 200.

High School—Freehold, N.J.

College—Temple University, Philadelphia, Pa.

Drafted by Phoenix on first round, 1988 (7th pick).

Year	G.	Min.	FGA	FGM	Pct.	FTA	FTM	Pct.	Reb.	Pts.	Avg.
84-85	30	621	70	29	.414	20	10	.500	118	68	2.3
85-86	31	1101	249	141	.566	134	77	.575	293	359	11.6
86-87	36	1271	350	180	.514	166	103	.620	310	463	12.9
87-88	33	1103	347	203	.585	113	72	.637	264	478	14.5
Totals	130	4096	1016	553	.544	433	262	.605	985	1368	10.5

MITCHELL JAMES RICHMOND
(Mitch)

Born June 30, 1965 at Fort Lauderdale, Fla. Height 6:05. Weight 225.

High School—Fort Lauderdale, Fla., Boyd Anderson.

Colleges—Moberly Area Junior College, Moberly, Mo.,
and Kansas State University, Manhattan, Kan.

Drafted by Golden State on first round, 1988 (5th pick).

—COLLEGIATE RECORD—

Moberly

Year	G.	Min.	FGA	FGM	Pct.	FTA	FTM	Pct.	Reb.	Pts.	Avg.
84-85	40	....	375	180	.480	85	55	.647	185	415	10.4
85-86	38	....	506	242	.478	180	124	.689	251	608	16.0
J.C. Totals	78	....	881	422	.479	265	179	.675	436	1023	13.1

Kansas State

Year	G.	Min.	FGA	FGM	Pct.	FTA	FTM	Pct.	Reb.	Pts.	Avg.
86-87	30	964	450	201	.447	155	118	.761	170	559	18.6
87-88	34	1200	521	268	.514	240	186	.775	213	768	22.6
K.S. Totals	64	2164	971	469	.483	395	304	.770	383	1327	20.7

Three-Point Field Goals: 1986-87, 39-for-108 (.361). 1987-88, 46-for-98 (.469). Totals, 85-for-206 (.412).
Named to THE SPORTING NEWS All-America Second Team, 1988.

DAVID LEE RIVERS

Born January 20, 1965 at Jersey City, N.J. Height 6:00. Weight 170.

High School—Jersey City, N.J., St. Anthony's.

College—University of Notre Dame, Notre Dame, Ind.

Drafted by Los Angeles Lakers on first round, 1988 (25th pick).

—COLLEGIATE RECORD—

Year	G.	Min.	FGA	FGM	Pct.	FTA	FTM	Pct.	Reb.	Pts.	Avg.
84-85	30	1068	398	168	.422	173	138	.798	78	474	15.8
85-86	28	930	353	159	.450	186	149	.801	84	467	16.7
86-87	32	1179	380	172	.453	159	134	.843	116	501	15.7
87-88	28	1027	462	205	.444	199	162	.814	115	616	22.0
Totals	118	4204	1593	704	.442	717	583	.813	393	2058	17.4

Three-Point Field Goals: 1986-87, 23-for-60 (.383). 1987-88, 44-for-105 (.419). Totals, 67-for-165 (.406).

RONY F. SEIKALY

Born May 10, 1965 at Athens, Greece. Height 6:11. Weight 230.

High School—Athens, Greece, American School.

College—Syracuse University, Syracuse, N.Y.

Drafted by Miami on first round, 1988 (9th pick).

—COLLEGIATE RECORD—

Year	G.	Min.	FGA	FGM	Pct.	FTA	FTM	Pct.	Reb.	Pts.	Avg.
84-85	31	775	177	96	.542	104	58	.558	198	250	8.1
85-86	32	875	223	122	.547	142	80	.563	250	324	10.1
86-87	38	*1032	380	216	.568	235	141	.600	311	573	15.1
87-88	35	1084	385	218	.566	234	133	.568	335	569	16.3
Totals	136	*3766	1165	652	.560	715	412	.576	1094	1716	12.6

*Missing one game.
Three-Point Field Goals: 1986-87, 0-for-1.

—DID YOU KNOW—
That Pacers rookie center Rik Smits' father was a 6-10 European judo champion?

CHARLES EDWARD SHACKLEFORD

Born April 22, 1966 at Kinston, N.C.   Height 6:10.   Weight 225.

High School—Kinston, N.C.

College—North Carolina State University, Raleigh, N.C.

Drafted by New Jersey on second round as an undergraduate, 1988 (32nd pick).

—COLLEGIATE RECORD—

Year	G.	Min.	FGA	FGM	Pct.	FTA	FTM	Pct.	Reb.	Pts.	Avg.
85-86	29	876	244	128	.525	68	42	.618	178	298	10.3
86-87	34	1079	429	204	.476	127	66	.520	260	474	13.9
87-88	31	942	416	224	.538	115	68	.591	297	516	16.6
Totals	94	2897	1089	556	.511	310	176	.568	735	1288	13.7

Three-Point Field Goals: 1986-87, 0-for-1.

BRIAN K. SHAW

Born March 22, 1966 at Oakland, Calif.   Height 6:06.   Weight 190.

High School—Oakland, Calif., Bishop O'Dowd.

Colleges—St. Mary's College, Moraga, Calif., and University of California at Santa Barbara, Santa Barbara, Calif.

Drafted by Boston on first round, 1988 (24th pick).

—COLLEGIATE RECORD—

St. Mary's

Year	G.	Min.	FGA	FGM	Pct.	FTA	FTM	Pct.	Reb.	Pts.	Avg.
83-84	14	129	36	13	.361	19	14	.737	12	40	2.9
84-85	27	976	246	99	.402	76	55	.724	144	253	9.4
St. M. Tot.	41	1105	282	112	.397	95	69	.726	156	293	7.1

California-Santa Barbara

Year	G.	Min.	FGA	FGM	Pct.	FTA	FTM	Pct.	Reb.	Pts.	Avg.
85-86				Did Not Play—Transfer Student							
86-87	29	1013	288	125	.434	66	47	.712	224	315	10.9
87-88	30	1073	324	151	.466	96	71	.740	260	399	13.3
UCSB Totals	59	2086	612	276	.451	162	118	.728	484	714	12.1
College Totals	100	3191	894	388	.434	257	187	.728	640	1007	10.1

Three-Point Field Goals: 1986-87, 18-for-42 (.429). 1987-88, 26-for-74 (.351). Totals, 44-for-116 (.379).

JONATHAN KEITH SMART

(Known by middle name.)

Born September 21, 1964 at Baton Rouge, La.   Height 6:01.   Weight 175.

High School—Baton Rouge, La., McKinley.

Colleges—Garden City Community College, Garden City, Kan., and Indiana University, Bloomington, Ind.

Drafted by Golden State on second round, 1988 (41st pick).

—COLLEGIATE RECORD—

Garden City

Year	G.	Min.	FGA	FGM	Pct.	FTA	FTM	Pct.	Reb.	Pts.	Avg.
84-85				Statistics Unavailable							
85-86	28	....	455	221	.486	150	121	.807	149	563	20.1

Indiana

Year	G.	Min.	FGA	FGM	Pct.	FTA	FTM	Pct.	Reb.	Pts.	Avg.
86-87	34	....	286	148	.517	88	74	.841	100	382	11.2
87-88	29	....	284	147	.518	92	80	.870	86	383	13.2
Ind. Totals	63	....	570	295	.518	180	154	.856	186	765	12.1

Three-Point Field Goals: 1986-87, 12-for-33 (.364). 1987-88, 9-for-28 (.321). Totals, 21-for-61 (.344).

Member of NCAA Division I championship team, 1987. . . . Named Outstanding Player in NCAA Division I tournament, 1987.

—DID YOU KNOW—

That Clippers Coach Gene Shue was the guard who had the highest scoring average for an NBA season before Oscar Robertson and Jerry West broke into the league? With the Pistons in 1959-60, Shue averaged 22.8 points per game.

CHARLES DANIEL SMITH

Born July 16, 1965 at Bridgeport, Conn.   Height 6:10.   Weight 230.
High School—Bridgeport, Conn., Harding.
College—University of Pittsburgh, Pittsburgh, Pa.
Drafted by Philadelphia on first round, 1988 (3rd pick).

Draft rights traded by Philadelphia to Los Angeles Clippers for draft rights to Hersey Hawkins and a 1989 1st round draft choice, June 28, 1988.

—COLLEGIATE RECORD—

Year	G.	Min.	FGA	FGM	Pct.	FTA	FTM	Pct.	Reb.	Pts.	Avg.
84-85	29	956	301	151	.502	175	133	.760	231	435	15.0
85-86	29	1077	408	165	.404	172	131	.762	235	461	15.9
86-87	33	1050	327	180	.550	275	202	.735	282	562	17.0
87-88	31	1020	378	211	.558	212	162	.764	239	587	18.9
Totals	122	4103	1414	707	.500	834	628	.753	987	2045	16.8

Three-Point Field Goals: 1987-88, 3-for-11 (.273).

RIK SMITS

Born August 23, 1966 at Eindhoven, Holland.   Height 7:04.   Weight 250.
High School—Eindhoven, Holland, Almonta.
College—Marist College, Poughkeepsie, N.Y.
Drafted by Indiana on first round, 1988 (2nd pick).

—COLLEGIATE RECORD—

Year	G.	Min.	FGA	FGM	Pct.	FTA	FTM	Pct.	Reb.	Pts.	Avg.
84-85	29	776	233	132	.567	104	60	.577	162	324	11.2
85-86	30	870	347	216	.622	144	98	.681	242	530	17.7
86-87	21	634	258	157	.609	151	109	.722	171	423	20.1
87-88	27	861	403	251	.623	226	166	.735	236	668	24.7
Totals	107	3141	1241	756	.609	625	433	.693	811	1945	18.2

Three-Point Field Goals: 1987-88, 0-for-2.

EVERETTE LOUIS STEPHENS

Born October 21, 1966 at Evanston, Ill.   Height 6:02.   Weight 175.
High School—Evanston, Ill.
College—Purdue University, West Lafayette, Ind.
Drafted by Philadelphia on second round, 1988 (31st pick).

—COLLEGIATE RECORD—

Year	G.	Min.	FGA	FGM	Pct.	FTA	FTM	Pct.	Reb.	Pts.	Avg.
84-85	25	166	63	25	.397	17	7	.412	17	57	2.3
85-86	31	574	159	77	.484	68	50	.735	46	204	6.6
86-87	30	909	244	130	.533	83	60	.723	79	361	12.0
87-88	33	1040	292	146	.500	109	83	.761	98	422	12.8
Totals	119	2689	758	378	.499	277	200	.722	240	1044	8.8

Three-Point Field Goals: 1986-87, 41-for-90 (.456). 1987-88, 47-for-107 (.439). Totals, 88-for-197 (.447).

RODNEY STRICKLAND
(Rod)

Born July 11, 1966 at Bronx, N.Y.   Height 6:03.   Weight 180.
High Schools—Bronx, N.Y., Harry S Truman (Jr.) and
Mouth of Wilson, Va., Oak Hill (Sr.).
College—DePaul University, Chicago, Ill.
Drafted by New York on first round as an undergraduate, 1988 (19th pick).

—COLLEGIATE RECORD—

Year	G.	Min.	FGA	FGM	Pct.	FTA	FTM	Pct.	Reb.	Pts.	Avg.
85-86	31	1063	354	176	.497	126	85	.675	84	437	14.1
86-87	30	980	323	188	.582	175	106	.606	113	490	16.3
87-88	26	837	392	207	.528	137	83	.606	98	521	20.0
Totals	87	2880	1069	571	.534	438	274	.626	295	1448	16.6

Three-Point Field Goals: 1986-87, 8-for-15 (.533). 1987-88, 24-for-54 (.444). Totals, 32-for-69 (.464).
Named to THE SPORTING NEWS All-America First Team, 1988.

RIK SMITS

ANTHONY PAUL TAYLOR

Born November 30, 1965 at Los Angeles, Calif.   Height 6:04.   Weight 175.
High School—Beaverton, Ore.
College—University of Oregon, Eugene, Ore.
Drafted by Atlanta on second round, 1988 (44th pick).

—COLLEGIATE RECORD—

Year	G.	Min.	FGA	FGM	Pct.	FTA	FTM	Pct.	Reb.	Pts.	Avg.
84-85	31	1060	253	127	.502	94	64	.681	109	318	10.3
85-86	28	1004	374	172	.460	164	133	.811	109	477	17.0
86-87	30	1112	476	224	.471	155	125	.806	132	589	19.6
87-88	26	966	417	191	.458	157	131	.834	112	555	21.3
Totals	115	4142	1520	714	.470	570	453	.795	462	1939	16.9

Three-Point Field Goals: 1986-87, 16-for-49 (.327). 1987-88, 42-for-95 (.442). Totals, 58-for-144 (.403).

BYRON THOMAS TOLBERT
(Tom)

Born October 16, 1965 at Long Beach, Calif.   Height 6:07.   Weight 240.
High School—Lakewood, Calif.
Colleges—University of California at Irvine, Irvine, Calif.; Cerritos College, Norwalk, Calif., and University of Arizona, Tucson, Ariz.
Drafted by Charlotte on second round, 1988 (34th pick).

—COLLEGIATE RECORD—
California-Irvine

Year	G.	Min.	FGA	FGM	Pct.	FTA	FTM	Pct.	Reb.	Pts.	Avg.
83-84	4	15	4	3	.750	0	0	.000	1	6	1.5
84-85	6	53	19	6	.316	5	4	.800	12	16	2.7
UCI Totals	10	68	23	9	.391	5	4	.800	13	22	2.2

Cerritos

Year	G.	Min.	FGA	FGM	Pct.	FTA	FTM	Pct.	Reb.	Pts.	Avg.
85-86	32	....	354	217	.613	125	85	.680	251	519	16.2

Arizona

Year	G.	Min.	FGA	FGM	Pct.	FTA	FTM	Pct.	Reb.	Pts.	Avg.
86-87	30	803	305	156	.511	139	98	.705	186	418	13.9
87-88	38	1034	351	192	.547	186	151	.812	220	536	14.1
Ariz. Totals	68	1837	656	348	.530	325	249	.766	406	954	14.0
College Totals	78	1905	679	357	.526	330	253	.767	419	976	12.5

(Suffered shoulder injury in 1983-84 season; granted extra year of eligibility.)
Three-Point Field Goals: 1986-87, 8-for-18 (.444). 1987-88, 1-for-2 (.500). Totals, 9-for-20 (.450).

JOSE VARGAS

Born June 23, 1963 at LaRomana, Dominican Republic.   Height 6:10.   Weight 225.
High School—LaRomana, Dominican Republic, Evangelico Central.
College—Louisiana State University, Baton Rouge, La.
Drafted by Dallas on second round, 1988 (49th pick).

—COLLEGIATE RECORD—

Year	G.	Min.	FGA	FGM	Pct.	FTA	FTM	Pct.	Reb.	Pts.	Avg.
84-85	25	256	72	34	.472	23	13	.565	51	81	3.2
85-86	37	478	101	47	.465	33	17	.515	94	111	3.0
86-87	38	764	231	120	.519	118	63	.534	184	303	8.0
87-88	30	922	334	171	.512	148	94	.635	247	436	14.5
Totals	130	2420	738	372	.504	322	187	.581	576	931	7.2

—DID YOU KNOW—

That when Dale Ellis increased his scoring average from 7.1 points per game with Dallas in 1985-86 to 24.9 ppg with Seattle in 1986-87, he became one of only four players ever to have increased their scoring averages by more than 15 points per game in one year? Other players who posted 15-point increases were Philadelphia's Neil Johnston (16.3-point increase from 1951-52 to 1952-53), Buffalo's Bob Kauffman (16.1 from 1969-70 to 1970-71) and Chicago's Bob Love (15.1 from 1968-69 to 1969-70).

MORLON DAVID WILEY

Born September 24, 1966 at New Orleans, La.   Height 6:04.   Weight 185.

High School—Long Beach, Calif., Poly.

College—California State University at Long Beach, Long Beach, Calif.

Drafted by Dallas on second round, 1988 (46th pick).

—COLLEGIATE RECORD—

Year	G.	Min.	FGA	FGM	Pct.	FTA	FTM	Pct.	Reb.	Pts.	Avg.
84-85	27	641	152	58	.382	32	24	.750	50	157	5.8
85-86	29	802	299	137	.458	68	54	.794	76	338	11.7
86-87	28	783	324	125	.386	80	64	.800	80	357	12.8
87-88	29	977	425	218	.513	111	85	.766	116	578	19.9
Totals	113	3203	1200	538	.448	291	227	.780	322	1430	12.7

Three-Point Field Goals: 1984-85, 17-for-41 (.415). 1985-86, 10-for-39 (.256). 1986-87, 43-for-109 (.394). 1987-88, 57-for-137 (.416). Totals, 127-for-326 (.390).

Brother of Michael Wiley, forward with San Antonio Spurs and San Diego Clippers of the NBA, 1980-81 and 1981-82.

MICHAEL DOUGLAS WILLIAMS

Born July 23, 1966 at Dallas, Tex.   Height 6:02.   Weight 175.

High School—Dallas, Tex., David Carter.

College—Baylor University, Waco, Tex.

Drafted by Detroit on second round, 1988 (48th pick).

—COLLEGIATE RECORD—

Year	G.	Min.	FGA	FGM	Pct.	FTA	FTM	Pct.	Reb.	Pts.	Avg.
84-85	28	787	306	149	.487	140	111	.793	66	409	14.6
85-86	22	....	225	104	.462	98	79	.806	63	287	13.0
86-87	31	1112	396	188	.475	192	137	.714	94	534	17.2
87-88	34	1262	428	216	.505	231	161	.697	108	625	18.4
Totals	115	....	1355	657	.485	661	488	.738	331	1855	16.1

Three-Point Field Goals: 1986-87, 21-for-67 (.313). 1987-88, 32-for-85 (.376). Totals, 53-for-152 (.349).

NBA Head Coaches

BERNARD TYRONE BICKERSTAFF
(Bernie)
Seattle SuperSonics

Born February 11, 1944 at Benham, Ky.   Height 6:03.   Weight 185.

High School—East Benham, Ky.

Colleges—Rio Grande College, Rio Grande, O., and
University of San Diego, San Diego, Calif.

—COLLEGIATE PLAYING RECORD—

Played with 1964-65 and 1965-66 University of San Diego teams; statistics unavailable.

—COLLEGIATE COACHING RECORD—

		Regular Season			
Sea.	Club	W.	L.	Pct.	Pos.
1969-70—San Diego U.......		14	12	.538	..
1970-71—San Diego U.......		10	14	.417	..
1971-72—San Diego U.......		12	14	.462	..
1972-73—San Diego U.......		19	9	.679	..
Totals (4 seasons)		55	49	.529	

Assistant coach, San Diego University, 1967-68 and 1968-69.
Also served as coach of National Puerto Rican team, winning Caribbean Tournament championship in 1975-76 and finishing second in 1976-77.

NBA COACHING RECORD

		Regular Season				Playoffs	
Sea.	Club	W.	L.	Pct.	Pos.	W.	L.
1985-86—Seattle		31	51	.378	5†	..	..
1986-87—Seattle		39	43	.476	4†	7	7
1987-88—Seattle		44	38	.537	3†	2	3
Totals (3 seasons)		114	132	.463		9	10

†Pacific Division.

Assistant coach, Capital Bullets, 1973-74, and Washington Bullets, 1974-85.

LAWRENCE HARVEY BROWN
(Larry)
San Antonio Spurs

Born September 14, 1940 at Brooklyn, N. Y.   Height 5:09.   Weight 160.

High School—Long Beach, N. Y.

Prep School—Hargrave Military Academy, Chatham, Va.

College—University of North Carolina, Chapel Hill, N. C.

Signed by New Orleans ABA, 1967.
Traded by New Orleans with Doug Moe to Oakland for Steve Jones, Ron Franz and Barry Leibowitz, June 18, 1968.
Oakland franchise transferred to Washington, 1969.
Washington franchise transferred to Virginia, 1970.
Sold by Virginia to Denver, January 23, 1971.

—COLLEGIATE PLAYING RECORD—

Year	G.	Min.	FGA	FGM	Pct.	FTA	FTM	Pct.	Reb.	Pts.	Avg.
59-60†	15	....	....	88	....	143	100	.699	....	276	18.4
60-61	18	....	54	28	.519	34	25	.735	28	81	4.5
61-62	17	....	204	90	.441	127	101	.795	52	281	16.5
62-63	21	....	231	102	.442	122	95	.779	50	299	14.2
Varsity Totals	56	....	489	220	.450	283	221	.781	130	661	11.8

AMATEUR PLAYING RECORD
Akron (Ohio) Goodyears

Year	G.	Min.	FGA	FGM	Pct.	FTA	FTM	Pct.	Reb.	Pts.	Avg.
63-64	..	....	....	....	....	....	....	....	....	398	....
64-65	32	....	297	144	.485	167	139	.832	90	427	13.3

ABA REGULAR SEASON RECORD

Sea.—Team	G.	Min.	2-Point FGM	FGA	Pct.	3-Point FGM	FGA	Pct.	FTM	FTA	Pct.	Reb.	Ast.	Pts.	Avg.
67-68—New Orleans	78	2807	311	812	.383	19	89	.213	366	450	.813	249	506	1045	13.4
68-69—Oakland	77	2381	300	671	.447	8	35	.229	301	379	.794	235	544	925	12.0
69-70—Washington	82	2766	366	815	.449	10	39	.256	362	439	.825	246	580	1124	13.7
70-71—Virginia-Denver	63	1343	121	319	.379	6	21	.286	186	225	.827	109	330	446	7.1
71-72—Denver	76	2012	238	531	.448	5	25	.200	198	244	.811	166	549	689	9.1
Totals	376	11309	1336	3148	.424	48	209	.230	1413	1737	.813	1005	2509	4229	11.3

ABA PLAYOFF RECORD

Sea.—Team	G.	Min.	2-Point FGM	FGA	Pct.	3-Point FGM	FGA	Pct.	FTM	FTA	Pct.	Reb.	Ast.	Pts.	Avg.
67-68—New Orleans	17	696	86	194	.443	4	18	.222	100	122	.820	59	129	284	16.7
68-69—Oakland	16	534	74	170	.435	0	3	.000	76	90	.844	52	87	224	14.0
69-70—Washington	7	269	32	68	.471	1	5	.200	30	34	.882	35	68	97	13.9
71-72—Denver	7	211	21	47	.447	0	3	.000	23	24	.958	10	36	65	9.3
Totals	47	1710	213	479	.445	5	29	.172	229	270	.848	156	285	670	14.3

ABA ALL-STAR GAME RECORD

Sea.—Team	Min.	2-Point FGM	FGA	Pct.	3-Point FGM	FGA	Pct.	FTM	FTA	Pct.	Reb.	Ast.	Pts.	Avg.
1968—New Orleans	22	5	7	.714	2	2	1.000	1	1	1.000	3	5	17	17.0
1969—Oakland	25	1	6	.167	0	1	.000	3	5	.600	0	7	5	5.0
1970—Washington	15	0	2	.000	0	0	.000	3	3	1.000	3	3	3	3.0
Totals	62	6	15	.400	2	3	.667	7	9	.778	6	15	25	8.3

COLLEGIATE COACHING RECORD

Sea.	Club	Regular Season W.	L.	Pct.	Pos.
1979-80—UCLA		22	10	.688	4
1980-81—UCLA		20	7	.741	3
1983-84—Kansas		22	10	.688	
1984-85—Kansas		26	8	.765	
1985-86—Kansas		35	4	.897	
1986-87—Kansas		25	11	.694	
1987-88—Kansas		21	11	.656	
Totals (7 seasons)		171	61	.737	

Assistant coach at University of North Carolina, 1965-67.

ABA COACHING RECORD

Sea.	Club	Regular Season W.	L.	Pct.	Pos.	Playoffs W.	L.
1972-73—Carolina		57	27	.679	1†	7	5
1973-74—Carolina		47	37	.560	3†	0	4
1974-75—Denver		65	19	.774	1‡	7	6
1975-76—Denver		60	24	.714	1	6	7
Totals (4 seasons)		229	107	.682		20	22

NBA COACHING RECORD

Sea.	Club	Regular Season W.	L.	Pct.	Pos.	Playoffs W.	L.
1976-77—Denver		50	32	.610	1§	2	4
1977-78—Denver		48	34	.585	1§	6	7
1978-79—Denver		28	25	.528	2§	..	..
1981-82—New Jersey		44	38	.537	3x	0	2
1982-83—New Jersey		47	29	.618	..x	..	..
Totals (5 seasons)		217	158	.579		8	13

†Eastern Division. ‡Western Division. §Midwest Division. xAtlantic Division.

Named to ABA All-Star Second Team, 1968.... Led ABA in assists, 1968, 1969, 1970.... ABA All-Star Game MVP, 1968.... Member of ABA championship team, 1969.... Member of U.S. Olympic team, 1964.... ABA Coach of the Year, 1973, 1975, 1976.... Coach of NCAA Division I championship team, 1988.

DONALD CHANEY
(Don)
Houston Rockets

Born March 22, 1946 at Baton Rouge, La.   Height 6:05.   Weight 210.

High School—Baton Rouge, La., McKinley.

College—University of Houston, Houston, Tex.

Drafted by Boston on first round, 1968 (12th pick).

Signed by St. Louis ABA, September 27, 1974, for 1975-76 season.
Played out option with Boston, September 1, 1975; signed by Los Angeles as a free agent, September 22, 1976.
Traded by Los Angeles with Kermit Washington and a 1978 1st round draft choice to Boston for Charlie Scott, December 27, 1977.

—COLLEGIATE RECORD—

Year	G.	Min.	FGA	FGM	Pct.	FTA	FTM	Pct.	Reb.	Pts.	Avg.
64-65†	21	....	421	186	.442	123	84	.683	183	456	21.7
65-66	26	627	243	105	.432	38	21	.553	124	231	8.9
66-67	31	1038	448	197	.440	116	80	.690	160	474	15.3
67-68	33	1010	431	189	.439	84	50	.595	191	428	13.0
Varsity Totals	90	2675	1122	491	.438	238	151	.634	475	1133	12.6

ABA REGULAR SEASON RECORD

			——2-Point——			——3-Point——							
Sea.—Team	G.	Min.	FGM	FGA	Pct.	FGM	FGA	Pct.	FTM	FTA	Pct.	Reb.	Ast.	Pts.	Avg.
75-76—St. Louis	48	1475	190	453	.419	1	4	.250	64	82	.780	234	169	447	9.3

NBA REGULAR SEASON RECORD

									—Rebounds—									
Sea.—Team	G.	Min.	FGA	FGM	Pct.	FTA	FTM	Pct.	Off.	Def.	Tot.	Ast.	PF	Dq.	Stl.	Blk.	Pts.	Avg.
68-69—Boston	20	209	113	36	.319	20	8	.400			46	19	32	0			80	4.0
69-70—Boston	63	839	320	115	.359	109	82	.752			152	72	118	0			312	5.0
70-71—Boston	81	2289	766	348	.454	313	234	.748			463	235	288	11			930	11.5
71-72—Boston	79	2275	786	373	.475	255	197	.773			395	202	295	7			943	11.9
72-73—Boston	79	2488	859	414	.482	267	210	.787			449	221	276	6			1038	13.1
73-74—Boston	81	2258	750	348	.464	180	149	.828	210	168	378	176	247	7	83	62	845	10.4
74-75—Boston	82	2208	750	321	.428	165	133	.806	171	199	370	181	244	5	122	66	775	9.5
76-77—Los Angeles	81	2408	522	213	.408	94	70	.745	120	210	330	308	224	4	140	33	496	6.1
77-78—L.A.-Boston	51	835	269	104	.387	45	38	.844	40	76	116	66	107	0	44	13	246	4.8
78-79—Boston	65	1074	414	174	.420	42	36	.857	63	78	141	75	167	3	72	11	384	5.9
79-80—Boston	60	523	189	67	.354	42	32	.762	31	42	73	38	80	1	31	11	167	2.8
Totals	742	17406	5738	2513	.438	1532	1189	.776			2913	1593	2078	44	492	196	6216	8.4

Three-Point Field Goals: 1979-80, 1-for-6 (.167).

NBA PLAYOFF RECORD

									—Rebounds—									
Sea.—Team	G.	Min.	FGA	FGM	Pct.	FTA	FTM	Pct.	Off.	Def.	Tot.	Ast.	PF	Dq.	Stl.	Blk.	Pts.	Avg.
68-69—Boston	7	25	6	1	.167	4	3	.750			4	0	7	0			5	0.7
71-72—Boston	11	271	81	41	.506	20	15	.750			39	22	39	0			97	8.8
72-73—Boston	12	288	82	39	.476	17	12	.706			40	25	41	1			90	7.5
73-74—Boston	18	545	141	65	.461	50	41	.820	37	40	77	40	64	0	24	9	171	9.5
74-75—Boston	11	294	105	48	.457	29	23	.793	24	14	38	21	46	2	21	5	119	10.8
76-77—Los Angeles	11	412	96	36	.375	22	16	.727	24	28	52	48	32	0	21	3	88	8.0
Totals	70	1835	511	230	.450	142	110	.775			250	156	229	3	66	17	570	8.1

NBA COACHING RECORD

		Regular Season			
Sea.	Club	W.	L.	Pct.	Pos.
1984-85—L.A. Clippers		9	12	.429	..
1985-86—L.A. Clippers		32	50	.390	3T†
1986-87—L.A. Clippers		12	70	.146	6†
Totals (3 seasons)		53	132	.286	

†Pacific Division.

Assistant coach, Detroit Pistons, 1980-83, Los Angeles Clippers, 1983-85, and Atlanta Hawks, 1987-88.
Member of NBA championship teams, 1969 and 1974.... Named to NBA All-Defensive Second Team, 1972, 1973, 1974, 1975, 1977.

PAUL DOUGLAS COLLINS
(Doug)
Chicago Bulls

Born July 28, 1951 at Christopher, Ill.   Height 6:06.   Weight 180.
High School—Benton, Ill.
College—Illinois State University, Normal, Ill.
Drafted by Philadelphia on first round, 1973 (1st pick).

—COLLEGIATE RECORD—

Year	G.	Min.	FGA	FGM	Pct.	FTA	FTM	Pct.	Reb.	Pts.	Avg.
69-70†	21	....	376	173	.460	113	95	.841	196	441	21.0
70-71	26	....	609	273	.448	235	197	.838	166	743	28.6
71-72	26	....	704	352	.500	177	143	.808	133	847	32.6
72-73	25	....	565	269	.476	137	112	.818	126	650	26.0
Varsity Totals	77	....	1878	894	.476	549	452	.823	425	2240	29.1

NBA REGULAR SEASON RECORD

									—Rebounds—									
Sea.—Team	G.	Min.	FGA	FGM	Pct.	FTA	FTM	Pct.	Off.	Def.	Tot.	Ast.	PF	Dq.	Stl.	Blk.	Pts.	Avg.
73-74—Philadelphia	25	436	194	72	.371	72	55	.764	7	39	46	40	65	1	13	2	199	8.0

Sea.—Team	G.	Min.	FGA	FGM	Pct.	FTA	FTM	Pct.	Off.	Def.	Tot.	Ast.	PF	Dq.	Stl.	Blk.	Pts.	Avg.
										—Rebounds—								
74-75—Philadelphia	81	2820	1150	561	.488	392	331	.844	104	211	315	213	291	6	108	17	1453	17.9
75-76—Philadelphia	77	2995	1196	614	.513	445	372	.836	126	181	307	191	249	2	110	24	1600	20.8
76-77—Philadelphia	58	2037	823	426	.518	250	210	.840	64	131	195	271	174	2	70	15	1062	18.3
77-78—Philadelphia	79	2770	1223	643	.526	329	267	.812	87	143	230	320	228	2	129	25	1553	19.7
78-79—Philadelphia	47	1595	717	358	.499	247	201	.814	36	87	123	191	139	1	52	20	917	19.5
79-80—Philadelphia	36	963	410	191	.466	124	113	.911	29	65	94	100	76	0	30	7	495	13.8
80-81—Philadelphia	12	329	126	62	.492	29	24	.828	6	23	29	42	23	0	7	4	148	12.3
Totals	415	13945	5839	2927	.501	1888	1573	.833	459	880	1339	1368	1245	14	518	114	7427	17.9

Three-Point Field Goals: 1979-80, 0-for-1.

NBA PLAYOFF RECORD

Sea.—Team	G.	Min.	FGA	FGM	Pct.	FTA	FTM	Pct.	Off.	Def.	Tot.	Ast.	PF	Dq.	Stl.	Blk.	Pts.	Avg.
										—Rebounds—								
75-76—Philadelphia	3	117	53	23	.434	14	12	.857	13	8	21	10	9	0	3	1	58	19.3
76-77—Philadelphia	19	759	318	177	.557	96	71	.740	30	49	79	74	57	0	28	3	425	22.4
77-78—Philadelphia	10	342	165	82	.497	49	40	.816	8	23	31	27	29	0	3	0	204	20.4
Totals	32	1218	536	282	.526	159	123	.774	51	80	131	111	95	0	34	4	687	21.5

NBA ALL-STAR GAME RECORD

Season—Team	Min.	FGA	FGM	Pct.	FTA	FTM	Pct.	Off.	Def.	Tot.	Ast.	PF	Dq.	Stl.	Blk.	Pts.
									—Rebounds—							
1976—Philadelphia	20	10	5	.500	2	2	1.000	2	4	6	3	3	0	3	0	12
1977—Philadelphia	21	6	3	.500	2	2	1.000	1	1	2	6	2	0	1	0	8
1978—Philadelphia	27	8	3	.375	11	8	.727	4	1	5	8	3	0	2	0	14
1979—Philadelphia							Did Not Play—Injured									
Totals	68	24	11	.458	15	12	.800	7	6	13	17	8	0	6	0	34

NBA COACHING RECORD

Sea.	Club	Regular Season				Playoffs	
		W.	L.	Pct.	Pos.	W.	L.
1986-87—Chicago		40	42	.488	5†	0	3
1987-88—Chicago		50	32	.610	2T†	4	6
Totals (2 seasons)		90	74	.549		4	9

†Central Division.

Member of U.S. Olympic team, 1972. . . . Named to THE SPORTING NEWS All-America First Team, 1973.

CHARLES JOSEPH DALY
(Chuck)
Detroit Pistons

Born July 20, 1930 at St. Mary's, Pa.   Height 6:02.   Weight 180.

High School—Kane, Pa.

Colleges—St. Bonaventure University, Olean, N. Y.;
Bloomsburg State College, Bloomsburg, Pa., and graduate work at
Penn State University, University Park, Pa.

COLLEGIATE PLAYING RECORD
St. Bonaventure

Year	G.	Min.	FGA	FGM	Pct.	FTA	FTM	Pct.	Reb.	Pts.	Avg.
48-49†				Statistics Unavailable							

Bloomsburg State

Year	G.	Min.	FGA	FGM	Pct.	FTA	FTM	Pct.	Reb.	Pts.	Avg.
49-50				Did Not Play—Transfer Student							
50-51	16	....	...	...	...	...	...	...	....	215	13.4
51-52	16	....	...	...	...	...	...	...	....	203	12.7
Totals	32	....	...	...	...	...	...	...	....	418	13.1

COLLEGIATE COACHING RECORD

Sea.	Club	Regular Season				Sea.	Club	Regular Season			
		W.	L.	Pct.	Pos.			W.	L.	Pct.	Pos.
1969-70—Boston College ..		11	13	.458	..	1975-76—Penn		17	9	.654	2
1970-71—Boston College ..		15	11	.577	..	1976-77—Penn		18	8	.692	2
1971-72—Penn		25	3	.893	1	Totals B. C. (2 sea.)		26	24	.520	
1972-73—Penn		21	7	.750	1	Totals Penn (6 sea.)		125	38	.767	
1973-74—Penn		21	6	.778	1	Totals (8 seasons)		151	62	.709	
1974-75—Penn		23	5	.821	1						

Assistant coach, Duke University, 1963 to 1969.

NOTE: Penn advanced to the NCAA championship tournament in 1972, 1973, 1974 and 1975.

NBA COACHING RECORD

Sea.	Club	Regular Season W.	L.	Pct.	Pos.	Playoffs W.	L.
1981-82	Cleveland............	9	32	.220	..	..	..
1983-84	Detroit.................	49	33	.598	2†	2	3
1984-85	Detroit.................	46	36	.561	2†	5	4
1985-86	Detroit.................	46	36	.561	3†	1	3
1986-87	Detroit.................	52	30	.634	2†	10	5
1987-88	Detroit.................	54	28	.659	1†	14	9
	Totals (6 seasons)	256	195	.568		32	24

†Central Division.
Assistant coach, Philadelphia 76ers, 1978-82.

LOWELL FITZSIMMONS
(Cotton)
Phoenix Suns

Born October 7, 1931 at Hannibal, Mo.

High School—Bowling Green, Mo.

Colleges—Hannibal-LaGrange College, Hannibal, Mo.,
and Midwestern State University, Wichita Falls, Tex.

—COLLEGIATE PLAYING RECORD—
Hannibal-LaGrange

Year	G.	Min.	FGA	FGM	Pct.	FTA	FTM	Pct.	Reb.	Pts.	Avg.
52-53	33	....	...	...	....	...	...	....	....	838	25.4

Midwestern State

Year	G.	Min.	FGA	FGM	Pct.	FTA	FTM	Pct.	Reb.	Pts.	Avg.
53-54	27	....	161	53	.329	173	128	.740	....	234	8.7
54-55	27	....	258	118	.457	210	162	.771	....	398	14.7
55-56	28	....	319	148	.464	223	164	.735	....	460	16.4
Totals	82	....	738	319	.432	606	454	.749	....	1092	13.3

COLLEGIATE COACHING RECORD

Sea.	Club	Regular Season W.	L.	Pct.	Pos.	Sea.	Club	Regular Season W.	L.	Pct.	Pos.
1958-59	Moberly J.C.......	16	15	.516	..	1965-66	Moberly J.C.......	29	5	.853	..
1959-60	Moberly J.C.......	19	8	.704	..	1966-67	Moberly J.C.......	31	2	.939	..
1960-61	Moberly J.C.......	26	5	.839	..	1968-69	Kansas State......	14	12	.538	2T*
1961-62	Moberly J.C.......	26	9	.743	..	1969-70	Kansas State......	20	8	.714	1*
1962-63	Moberly J.C.......	26	6	.813	..		Totals (JC)	222	60	.787	
1963-64	Moberly J.C.......	24	5	.828	..		Totals (College)	34	20	.630	
1964-65	Moberly J.C.......	25	5	.833	..						

Assistant coach at Kansas State, 1967-68. *Big Eight Conference.

NBA COACHING RECORD

Sea.	Club	Regular Season W.	L.	Pct.	Pos.	Playoffs W.	L.	Sea.	Club	Regular Season W.	L.	Pct.	Pos.	Playoffs W.	L.
1970-71	Phoenix.............	48	34	.585	3†	..	..	1979-80	Kansas City........	47	35	.573	2†	1	2
1971-72	Phoenix.............	49	33	.598	3†	..	..	1980-81	Kansas City........	40	42	.488	2T†	7	8
1972-73	Atlanta	46	36	.561	2‡	2	4	1981-82	Kansas City........	30	52	.366	4†	..	..
1973-74	Atlanta	35	47	.427	2‡	..	..	1982-83	Kansas City........	45	37	.549	2T†	..	..
1974-75	Atlanta	31	51	.378	4‡	..	..	1983-84	Kansas City........	38	44	.463	3T†	0	3
1975-76	Atlanta	28	46	.378	5‡	..	..	1984-85	San Antonio.......	41	41	.500	4T†	2	3
1977-78	Buffalo...............	27	55	.329	4§	..	..	1985-86	San Antonio.......	35	47	.427	6†	0	3
1978-79	Kansas City........	48	34	.585	1†	1	4		Totals (15 seasons)	588	634	.481		13	27

†Midwest Division. ‡Central Division. §Atlantic Division.

NBA Coach of the Year, 1979. . . . Father of Gary Fitzsimmons, Director of Player Personnel for Cleveland Cavaliers.

—DID YOU KNOW—

That only three of the coaches for the NBA's previous 11 expansion teams—Larry Costello of Milwaukee, Bill Fitch of Cleveland and Dick Motta of Dallas—were still coaching those clubs when those franchises posted their first winning records? If the latest group of NBA expansion teams (Charlotte, Miami, Minnesota and Orlando) follow the norm, they can expect to win 21 or 22 games in their first season and take five years before they post a winning record.

MICHAEL ROBERT FRATELLO
(Mike)
Atlanta Hawks

Born February 24, 1947 at Hackensack, N. J. Height 5:07. Weight 150.

High School—Hackensack, N. J.

Colleges—Montclair State College, Montclair, N. J., and
graduate work at University of Rhode Island, Kingston, R. I.

—COLLEGIATE PLAYING RECORD—

Played with 1965-66 Montclair State team; statistics unavailable.

COLLEGIATE COACHING RECORD

Assistant, Rhode Island (1971), James Madison (1972 through 1975), and Villanova (1976 through 1978).

NBA COACHING RECORD

Sea. Club	Regular Season				Playoffs	
	W.	L.	Pct.	Pos.	W.	L.
1983-84—Atlanta	40	42	.488	3†	2	3
1984-85—Atlanta	33	49	.402	5†	..	..
1985-86—Atlanta	50	32	.610	2†	4	5
1986-87—Atlanta	57	25	.695	1†	4	5
1987-88—Atlanta	50	32	.610	2T†	6	6
Totals (5 seasons)	230	180	.561		16	19

†Central Division.

Assistant coach, Atlanta Hawks (1978-82) and New York Knicks (1982-83).
Named NBA Coach of the Year, 1986.

DELMER HARRIS
(Del)
Milwaukee Bucks

Born June 18, 1937 at Orleans, Ind.

High School—Plainfield, Ind.

College—Milligan College, Milligan, Tenn.

—COLLEGIATE PLAYING RECORD—

Year	G.	Min.	FGA	FGM	Pct.	FTA	FTM	Pct.	Reb.	Pts.	Avg.
55-56	24	....	232	101	.435	126	89	.706	122	291	12.1
56-57	24	....	197	162	....	197	141	.716	165	465	19.4
57-58	22	....	272	167	.614	149	119	.799	144	453	20.6
58-59	21	....	346	136	.393	202	158	.782	338	430	20.5
Totals	91		1047	566	....	674	507	.752	769	1639	18.0

Note: Field-goal attempts for five games and rebounds for 13 games are unavailable.

COLLEGIATE COACHING RECORD

Sea. Club	Regular Season			
	W.	L.	Pct.	Pos.
1965-66—Earlham Col.	14	8	.636	....
1966-67—Earlham Col.	15	9	.625	4
1967-68—Earlham Col.	25	3	.893	1
1968-69—Earlham Col.	18	8	.692	2
1969-70—Earlham Col.	22	8	.733	1
1970-71—Earlham Col.	24	5	.828	1
1971-72—Earlham Col.	21	9	.700	1
1972-73—Earlham Col.	17	11	.607	3
1973-74—Earlham Col.	19	9	.679	3
Totals (9 seasons)	175	70	.714	

Assistant coach at Utah, 1975-76.

NBA COACHING RECORD

Sea. Club	Regular Season				Playoffs	
	W.	L.	Pct.	Pos.	W.	L.
1979-80—Houston	41	41	.500	2T†	2	5
1980-81—Houston	40	42	.488	2T‡	12	9
1981-82—Houston	46	36	.561	2T‡	1	2
1982-83—Houston	14	68	.171	6‡	..	..
1987-88—Milwaukee	42	40	.512	4T†	2	3
Totals (5 seasons)	183	227	.446		17	19

†Central Division.   ‡Midwest Division.

Assistant coach, Milwaukee Bucks, 1986-87.

RICHARD HARTER
(Dick)
Charlotte Hornets

Born October 19, 1930 at Philadelphia, Pa. Height 6:01. Weight 180.

High School—Pottstown, Pa., Hill.

College—University of Pennsylvania, Philadelphia, Pa.

—COLLEGIATE RECORD—

Year	G.	Min.	FGA	FGM	Pct.	FTA	FTM	Pct.	Reb.	Pts.	Avg.
49-50†				Statistics Unavailable							
50-51	18	....	...	10	....	...	10	....	42	40	2.2
51-52	27	....	116	48	.414	37	22	.595	69	118	4.4
52-53	23	....	...	13	....	...	18	....	...	44	1.9
Varsity Totals	68	....	...	76	...	...	50	....	...	202	3.0

COLLEGIATE COACHING RECORD

Sea. Club	Regular Season W.	L.	Pct.	Pos.	Sea. Club	Regular Season W.	L.	Pct.	Pos.
1965-66—Rider	16	9	.640	..	1975-76—Oregon	19	10	.655	..
1966-67—Penn	11	14	.440	..	1976-77—Oregon	18	9	.667	..
1967-68—Penn	9	17	.346	..	1977-78—Oregon	16	11	.593	..
1968-69—Penn	15	10	.600	..	1978-79—Penn State	12	18	.400	..
1969-70—Penn	25	2	.926	..	1979-80—Penn State	18	10	.643	..
1970-71—Penn	28	1	.966	..	1980-81—Penn State	17	10	.630	..
1971-72—Oregon	6	20	.231	..	1981-82—Penn State	15	12	.556	..
1972-73—Oregon	16	10	.615	..	1982-83—Penn State	17	11	.607	..
1973-74—Oregon	15	11	.577	..	Totals (18 seasons)	291	193	.601	
1974-75—Oregon	18	8	.692	..					

NBA COACHING RECORD

Assistant coach, Detroit Pistons, 1983-86, and Indiana Pacers, 1986-88.

FRANCIS PATRICK LAYDEN
(Frank)
Utah Jazz

Born January 5, 1932 at Brooklyn, N. Y. Height 6:01. Weight 212.

High School—Brooklyn, N. Y., Fort Hamilton.

College—Niagara University, Niagara Falls, N. Y.

COLLEGIATE PLAYING RECORD

Year	G.	Min.	FGA	FGM	Pct.	FTA	FTM	Pct.	Reb.	Pts.	Avg.
51-52	5	....	...	0	....	6	3	.500	....	3	0.6
52-53	13	....	...	14	...	...	5	....	....	33	2.5
53-54					Did Not Play—Freshman Coach						
54-55					Did Not Play—Freshman Coach						
Totals	18	....	...	14	....	...	8	....	....	36	2.0

COLLEGIATE COACHING RECORD

Sea. Club	Regular Season W.	L.	Pct.	Pos.	Sea. Club	Regular Season W.	L.	Pct.	Pos.
1968-69—Niagara	11	13	.458	..	1973-74—Niagara	12	14	.462	..
1969-70—Niagara	22	7	.759	..	1974-75—Niagara	13	14	.481	..
1970-71—Niagara	14	12	.538	..	1975-76—Niagara	17	12	.586	..
1971-72—Niagara	21	9	.700	..	Totals	119	97	.551	
1972-73—Niagara	9	16	.360	..					

NOTE: Niagara posted a 1-2 record in 1970 NCAA tournament and was runner-up in 1972 NIT.

NBA COACHING RECORD

Sea. Club	Regular Season W.	L.	Pct.	Pos.	Playoffs W.	L.
1981-82—Utah	17	45	.274	6†	..	..
1982-83—Utah	30	52	.366	5†	..	..
1983-84—Utah	45	37	.549	1†	5	6
1984-85—Utah	41	41	.500	T4†	4	6
1985-86—Utah	42	40	.512	4†	1	3
1986-87—Utah	44	38	.537	2†	2	3
1987-88—Utah	47	35	.573	3†	6	5
Totals (7 seasons)	266	288	.480		18	23

†Midwest Division.

Assistant coach, Atlanta Hawks, 1976-79.

Named NBA Coach of the Year, 1984. . . . NBA Executive of the Year, 1984. . . . Father of Scott Layden, an assistant coach with Utah Jazz.

JAMES F. LYNAM
(Jim)
Philadelphia 76ers

Born September 15, 1941 at Philadelphia, Pa.   Height 5:08.   Weight 160.
High School—Philadelphia, Pa., West Catholic.
College—St. Joseph's University, Philadelphia, Pa.

—COLLEGIATE PLAYING RECORD—

Year	G.	Min.	FGA	FGM	Pct.	FTA	FTM	Pct.	Reb.	Pts.	Avg.
59-60†	14	....	...	88	....	...	94	....	43	270	19.3
60-61	30	....	260	110	.423	143	118	.825	71	338	11.3
61-62	27	....	228	98	.430	140	111	.793	49	307	11.4
62-63	26	....	281	139	.495	131	89	.679	95	367	14.1
Varsity Totals	83	....	769	347	.451	414	318	.768	215	1012	12.2

COLLEGIATE COACHING RECORD

		Regular Season			
Sea.	Club	W.	L.	Pct.	Pos.
1968-69—Fairfield		10	16	.385	..
1969-70—Fairfield		13	13	.500	..
1973-74—American U.		16	10	.615	..
1974-75—American U.		16	10	.615	..
1975-76—American U.		9	16	.360	..
1976-77—American U.		13	13	.500	..
1977-78—American U.		16	12	.571	..
1978-79—St. Joseph's		19	11	.633	..
1979-80—St. Joseph's		21	9	.700	..
1980-81—St. Joseph's		25	8	.758	..
Totals (10 seasons)		158	118	.572	

Assistant coach, St. Joseph's (Pa.), 1970 through 1973.
NOTE: St. Joseph's played in the NIT in 1979 and 1980 and the NCAA tournament in 1981.

NBA COACHING RECORD

		Regular Season			
Sea.	Club	W.	L.	Pct.	Pos.
1983-84—San Diego		30	52	.366	6†
1984-85—L.A. Clippers		22	39	.361	..†
1987-88—Philadelphia		16	23	.410	..‡
Totals (3 seasons)		68	114	.374	

†Pacific Division. ‡Atlantic Division.
Assistant coach, Portland Trail Blazers, 1981-82, and Philadelphia 76ers, 1985-88.

JOHN MATTHEW MacLEOD
Dallas Mavericks

Born October 3, 1937 at New Albany, Ind.   Height 6:00.   Weight 170.
High School—Clarksville, Ind., New Providence.
College—Bellarmine College, Louisville, Ky.

—COLLEGIATE PLAYING RECORD—

Year	G.	Min.	FGA	FGM	Pct.	FTA	FTM	Pct.	Reb.	Pts.	Avg.
55-56					Statistics Unavailable						
56-57	10	....	...	0	....	...	1	....	....	1	0.1
57-58	8	....	...	2	....	10	3	.300	....	7	0.8
58-59	5	....	...	2	....	...	4	....	....	8	1.6

COLLEGIATE COACHING RECORD

		Regular Season			
Sea.	Club	W.	L.	Pct.	Pos.
1967-68—Oklahoma		13	13	.500	3T§
1968-69—Oklahoma		7	19	.269	8§
1969-70—Oklahoma		9	19	.321	3§
1970-71—Oklahoma		19	8	.704	2§
1971-72—Oklahoma		14	12	.538	3§
1972-73—Oklahoma		18	8	.692	4§
Totals (6 seasons)		80	79	.503	

Assistant coach at Oklahoma, 1966-67. §Big Eight Conference.

Sea. Club	W.	L.	Pct.	Pos.	Playoffs W.	L.	Sea. Club	W.	L.	Pct.	Pos.	Playoffs W.	L.
1973-74—Phoenix	30	52	.366	4†	..	..	1981-82—Phoenix	46	36	.561	3†	2	5
1974-75—Phoenix	32	50	.390	4†	..	..	1982-83—Phoenix	53	29	.646	2†	1	2
1975-76—Phoenix	42	40	.512	3†	10	9	1983-84—Phoenix	41	41	.500	4†	9	8
1976-77—Phoenix	34	48	.415	5†	..	..	1984-85—Phoenix	36	46	.439	3†	0	3
1977-78—Phoenix	49	33	.598	2†	0	2	1985-86—Phoenix	32	50	.390	3T†	..	..
1978-79—Phoenix	50	32	.610	2†	9	6	1986-87—Phoenix	22	34	.393	...†	..	..
1979-80—Phoenix	55	27	.671	3†	3	5	1987-88—Dallas	53	29	.646	2‡	10	7
1980-81—Phoenix	57	25	.695	1†	3	4	Totals (15 seasons)	632	572	.525		47	51

†Pacific Division. ‡Midwest Division.

DOUGLAS EDWIN MOE
(Doug)
Denver Nuggets

Born September 21, 1938 at Brooklyn, N. Y.   Height 6:05.   Weight 220.

High School—Brooklyn, N. Y., Erasmus Hall.

Prep School—Silver Springs, Md., Bullis.

Colleges—University of North Carolina, Chapel Hill, N. C.

and Elon College, Elon College, N. C.

Signed by New Orleans ABA, 1967.

Traded by New Orleans with Larry Brown to Oakland for Steve Jones, Ron Franz and Barry Leibowitz, June 18, 1968.

Traded by Oakland to Carolina in three-team deal that sent Stew Johnson from Carolina to Pittsburgh and Frank Card from Pittsburgh to Oakland, June 12, 1969.

Traded by Carolina to Washington for Gary Bradds and Ira Harge, July 24, 1970.

Washington franchise transferred to Virginia, 1970.

Played with Padua, Italy, during 1965-66 and 1966-67 seasons.

—COLLEGIATE PLAYING RECORD—
North Carolina

Year	G.	Min.	FGA	FGM	Pct.	FTA	FTM	Pct.	Reb.	Pts.	Avg.
57-58†					Statistics Unavailable						
58-59	25	....	265	106	.400	164	104	.634	179	316	12.6
59-60	12	....	144	60	.417	113	82	.726	135	202	16.8
60-61	23	....	401	163	.406	207	143	.691	321	469	20.4
Varsity Totals	60	....	810	329	.406	484	329	.680	635	987	16.5

ABA REGULAR SEASON RECORD

Sea.—Team	G.	Min.	2-Point FGM	FGA	Pct.	3-Point FGM	FGA	Pct.	FTM	FTA	Pct.	Reb.	Ast.	Pts.	Avg.
67-68—New Orleans	78	3113	662	1588	.417	3	22	.136	551	693	.795	795	202	1884	24.2
68-69—Oakland	75	2528	524	1213	.432	5	14	.357	360	444	.811	614	151	1423	19.0
69-70—Carolina	80	2671	527	1220	.432	8	34	.235	304	399	.762	437	425	1382	17.2
70-71—Virginia	78	2297	395	861	.459	2	10	.200	221	259	.853	473	270	1017	13.0
71-72—Virginia	67	1472	174	406	.429	1	9	.111	104	129	.806	241	149	455	6.8
Totals	378	12081	2282	5288	.432	19	89	.213	1540	1924	.800	2560	1197	6161	16.3

ABA PLAYOFF RECORD

Sea.—Team	G.	Min.	2-Point FGM	FGA	Pct.	3-Point FGM	FGA	Pct.	FTM	FTA	Pct.	Reb.	Ast.	Pts.	Avg.
67-68—New Orleans	17	715	140	335	.418	4	11	.364	107	149	.718	169	40	399	23.5
68-69—Oakland	16	593	115	280	.411	0	4	.000	87	111	.784	124	31	317	19.8
69-70—Carolina	4	168	25	72	.347	0	4	.000	12	16	.750	26	25	62	15.5
70-71—Virginia	12	421	89	174	.511	1	3	.333	31	41	.756	57	37	212	17.7
71-72—Virginia	11	245	37	84	.440	0	1	.000	22	25	.880	43	27	96	8.7
Totals	60	2142	406	945	.430	5	23	.217	259	342	.757	419	160	1086	18.1

ABA ALL-STAR GAME RECORD

Sea.—Team	Min.	2-Point FGM	FGA	Pct.	3-Point FGM	FGA	Pct.	FTM	FTA	Pct.	Reb.	Ast.	Pts.	Avg.
1968—New Orleans	29	7	12	.583	0	1	.000	3	5	.600	7	5	17	17.0
1969—Oakland	26	6	13	.462	0	0	.000	5	8	.625	6	6	17	17.0
1970—Carolina	36	0	5	.000	0	0	.000	2	3	.667	8	6	2	2.0
Totals	91	13	30	.433	0	1	.000	10	16	.625	21	17	36	12.0

NBA COACHING RECORD

Sea. Club	W.	L.	Pct.	Pos.	Playoffs W.	L.	Sea. Club	W.	L.	Pct.	Pos.	Playoffs W.	L.
1976-77—San Antonio	44	38	.537	3†	0	2	1979-80—San Antonio	33	33	.500	2T†	..	..
1977-78—San Antonio	52	30	.634	1†	2	4	1980-81—Denver	26	25	.510	4‡	..	..
1978-79—San Antonio	48	34	.585	1†	7	7	1981-82—Denver	46	36	.561	2T†	1	2

Sea. Club	Regular Season W.	L.	Pct.	Pos.	Playoffs W.	L.
1982-83—Denver	45	37	.549	2T‡	3	5
1983-84—Denver	38	44	.463	3T‡	2	3
1984-85—Denver	52	30	.634	1‡	8	7
1985-86—Denver	47	35	.573	2‡	5	5

Sea. Club	Regular Season W.	L.	Pct.	Pos.	Playoffs W.	L.
1986-87—Denver	37	45	.451	4‡	0	3
1987-88—Denver	54	28	.659	1‡	5	6
Totals (12 seasons)	522	415	.557		33	44

†Central Division. ‡Midwest Division.

Named NBA Coach of the Year, 1988.... ABA All-Star First Team, 1968.... ABA All-Star Second Team, 1969.... Member of ABA championship team, 1969.... Named to THE SPORTING NEWS All-America Second Team, 1959 and 1961.

DONALD ARVID NELSON
(Don)
Golden State Warriors

Born May 15, 1940 at Muskegon, Mich. Height 6:06. Weight 210.

High School—Rock Island, Ill.

College—University of Iowa, Iowa City, Iowa.

Drafted by Chicago on third round, 1962 (19th pick).

Sold by Chicago (Baltimore) to Los Angeles, September 6, 1963.
Waived by Los Angeles, October 21, 1965; signed by Boston as a free agent, October 28, 1965.

—COLLEGIATE PLAYING RECORD—

Year	G.	Min.	FGA	FGM	Pct.	FTA	FTM	Pct.	Reb.	Pts.	Avg.
58-59†				(Freshman team did not play intercollegiate schedule.)							
59-60	24	....	320	140	.438	155	100	.645	241	380	15.8
60-61	24	....	377	197	.523	268	176	.657	258	570	23.8
61-62	24	....	348	193	.555	264	186	.705	285	572	23.8
Varsity Totals	72	....	1045	530	.507	687	462	.672	784	1522	21.1

NBA REGULAR SEASON RECORD

Sea.—Team	G.	Min.	FGA	FGM	Pct.	FTA	FTM	Pct.	Reb.	Ast.	PF	Disq.	Pts.	Avg.
62-63—Chicago	62	1071	293	129	.440	221	161	.729	279	72	136	3	419	6.8
63-64—Los Angeles	80	1406	323	135	.418	201	149	.741	323	76	181	1	419	5.2
64-65—Los Angeles	39	238	85	36	.424	26	20	.769	73	24	40	1	92	2.4
65-66—Boston	75	1765	618	271	.439	326	223	.684	403	79	187	1	765	10.2
66-67—Boston	79	1202	509	227	.446	190	141	.742	295	65	143	0	595	7.5
67-68—Boston	82	1498	632	312	.494	268	195	.728	431	103	178	1	819	10.0
68-69—Boston	82	1773	771	374	.485	259	201	.776	458	92	198	2	949	11.6
69-70—Boston	82	2224	920	461	.501	435	337	.775	601	148	238	3	1259	15.4
70-71—Boston	82	2254	881	412	.468	426	317	.744	565	153	232	2	1141	13.9
71-72—Boston	82	2086	811	389	.480	452	356	.788	453	192	220	3	1134	13.8
72-73—Boston	72	1425	649	309	.476	188	159	.846	315	102	155	1	777	10.8

Sea.—Team	G.	Min.	FGA	FGM	Pct.	FTA	FTM	Pct.	—Rebounds— Off.	Def.	Tot.	Ast.	PF	Dq.	Stl.	Blk.	Pts.	Avg.
73-74—Boston	82	1748	717	364	.508	273	215	.788	90	255	345	162	189	1	19	13	943	11.5
74-75—Boston	79	2052	785	423	.539	318	263	.827	127	342	469	181	239	2	32	15	1109	14.0
75-76—Boston	75	943	379	175	.462	161	127	.789	56	126	182	77	115	0	14	7	477	6.4
Totals	1053	21685	8373	4017	.480	3744	2864	.765			5192	1526	2451	21	65	35	10898	10.3

NBA PLAYOFF RECORD

Sea.—Team	G.	Min.	FGA	FGM	Pct.	FTA	FTM	Pct.	Reb.	Ast.	PF	Disq.	Pts.	Avg.
63-64—Los Angeles	5	56	13	7	.538	3	3	1.000	13	2	11	1	17	3.4
64-65—Los Angeles	11	212	53	24	.453	25	19	.760	59	19	31	0	67	6.1
65-66—Boston	17	316	118	50	.424	52	42	.808	85	13	50	0	142	8.4
66-67—Boston	9	142	59	27	.458	17	10	.588	42	9	12	0	64	7.1
67-68—Boston	19	468	175	91	.520	74	55	.743	143	32	49	0	237	12.5
68-69—Boston	18	348	168	87	.518	60	50	.833	83	21	51	0	224	12.4
71-72—Boston	11	308	99	52	.525	48	41	.854	61	21	30	0	145	13.2
72-73—Boston	13	303	101	47	.465	56	49	.875	38	15	29	0	143	11.0

Sea.—Team	G.	Min.	FGA	FGM	Pct.	FTA	FTM	Pct.	—Rebounds— Off.	Def.	Tot.	Ast.	PF	Dq.	Stl.	Blk.	Pts.	Avg.
73-74—Boston	18	467	164	82	.500	53	41	.774	25	72	97	35	54	2	8	3	205	11.4
74-75—Boston	11	274	117	66	.564	41	37	.902	18	27	45	26	36	1	2	2	169	15.4
75-76—Boston	18	315	108	52	.481	69	60	.870	17	36	53	17	46	1	3	2	164	9.1
Totals	150	3209	1175	585	.498	498	407	.817			719	210	399	5	13	7	1577	10.5

NBA COACHING RECORD

Sea. Club	Regular Season W.	L.	Pct.	Pos.	Playoffs W.	L.
1976-77—Milwaukee	27	37	.422	6†	...	...
1977-78—Milwaukee	44	38	.537	2†	5	4
1978-79—Milwaukee	38	44	.463	4†	...	...

Sea. Club	Regular Season W.	L.	Pct.	Pos.	Playoffs W.	L.
1979-80—Milwaukee	49	33	.598	1†	3	4
1980-81—Milwaukee	60	22	.732	1‡	3	4
1981-82—Milwaukee	55	27	.671	1‡	2	4

Sea. Club	Regular Season W. L. Pct. Pos.	Playoffs W. L.	Sea. Club	Regular Season W. L. Pct. Pos.	Playoffs W. L.
1982-83—Milwaukee	51 31 .622 1‡	5 4	1985-86—Milwaukee	57 25 .695 1‡	7 7
1983-84—Milwaukee	50 32 .610 1‡	8 8	1986-87—Milwaukee	50 32 .610 3‡	6 6
1984-85—Milwaukee	59 23 .720 1‡	3 5	Totals (11 seasons)	540 344 .610	42 46

†Midwest Division. ‡Central Division.

Led NBA in field-goal percentage, 1975. . . . Member of NBA championship teams, 1966, 1968, 1969, 1974, 1976. . . . Named NBA Coach of the Year, 1983 and 1985.

RICHARD PITINO
(Rick)
New York Knicks

Born September 18, 1952 at New York, N.Y. Height 6:00. Weight 165.

High School—Oyster Bay, N.Y., St. Dominic's.

College—University of Massachusetts, Amherst, Mass.

—COLLEGIATE RECORD—

Year	G.	Min.	FGA	FGM	Pct.	FTA	FTM	Pct.	Reb.	Pts.	Avg.
70-71†	19	....	274	123	.449	87	60	.690	64	306	16.1
71-72					Statistics Unavailable						
72-73	27	....	....	37	....	...	41	....	...	115	4.3
73-74	26	867	127	63	.496	15	10	.667	51	136	5.2

COLLEGIATE COACHING RECORD

Sea. Club	Regular Season W. L. Pct. Pos.
1978-79—Boston Univ.	17 9 .654 ..
1979-80—Boston Univ.	21 9 .700 ..
1980-81—Boston Univ.	13 14 .481 ..
1981-82—Boston Univ.	19 9 .679 ..
1982-83—Boston Univ.	21 10 .677 ..
1985-86—Providence	17 14 .548 ..
1986-87—Providence	25 8 .758 ..
Totals (7 seasons)	133 73 .646

NBA COACHING RECORD

Sea. Club	Regular Season W. L. Pct. Pos.	Playoffs W. L.
1987-88—New York	38 44 .463 2T†	1 3

Assistant coach, University of Hawaii, 1975-76, and Syracuse University, 1976-78.
Assistant coach, New York Knicks, 1983-85.
Named THE SPORTING NEWS College Coach of the Year, 1987.

JOHN T. RAMSAY
(Jack)
Indiana Pacers

Born February 21, 1925 at Philadelphia, Pa. Height 6:01. Weight 180.

High School—Upper Darby, Pa.

Colleges—St. Joseph's University, Philadelphia, Pa.,
and Villanova University, Villanova, Pa.

Played with San Diego Dons, an Amateur Athletic Union team, during 1945-46 season.
Played in Eastern Basketball League with Harrisburg and Sunbury, 1949 through 1955.

—COLLEGIATE PLAYING RECORD—
St. Joseph's

Year	G.	Min.	FGA	FGM	Pct.	FTA	FTM	Pct.	Reb.	Pts.	Avg.
42-43						Statistics Unavailable					
46-47	21	....	214	72	.336	32	20	.625	....	164	7.8
47-48	14	....	....	60	....	...	38	....	....	158	11.3
48-49	23	....	...	75	....	...	52	....	....	202	8.8

NOTE: In military service (Navy) during 1943-44, 1944-45 and 1945-46 seasons.

COLLEGIATE COACHING RECORD

Sea. Club	Regular Season W. L. Pct. Pos.	Sea. Club	Regular Season W. L. Pct. Pos.
1955-56—St. Joseph's	23 6 .793 ..	1961-62—St. Joseph's	18 10 .643 1
1956-57—St. Joseph's	17 7 .708 ..	1962-63—St. Joseph's	23 5 .821 2
1957-58—St. Joseph's	18 9 .667 ..	1963-64—St. Joseph's	18 10 .643 2
1958-59—St. Joseph's	22 5 .815 ..	1964-65—St. Joseph's	26 3 .897 1
1959-60—St. Joseph's	20 7 .741 1	1965-66—St. Joseph's	24 5 .828 1
1960-61—St. Joseph's	25 5 .833 1	Totals (11 seasons)	234 72 .765

NBA COACHING RECORD

Sea.	Club	W.	L.	Pct.	Pos.	Playoffs W.	L.
1968-69	Philadelphia	55	27	.671	2†	1	4
1969-70	Philadelphia	42	40	.512	4†	1	4
1970-71	Philadelphia	47	35	.573	2‡	3	4
1971-72	Philadelphia	30	52	.366	3‡	..	..
1972-73	Buffalo	21	61	.256	3‡	..	..
1973-74	Buffalo	42	40	.512	3‡	2	4
1974-75	Buffalo	49	33	.598	2‡	3	4
1975-76	Buffalo	46	36	.561	2T‡	4	5
1976-77	Portland*	49	33	.598	2§	14	5
1977-78	Portland	58	24	.707	1§	2	4
1978-79	Portland	45	37	.549	4§	1	2

Sea.	Club	W.	L.	Pct.	Pos.	Playoffs W.	L.
1979-80	Portland	38	44	.463	4§	1	2
1980-81	Portland	45	37	.549	3§	1	2
1981-82	Portland	42	40	.512	5§	..	..
1982-83	Portland	46	36	.561	4§	3	4
1983-84	Portland	48	34	.585	2§	2	3
1984-85	Portland	42	40	.512	2§	4	5
1985-86	Portland	40	42	.488	2§	1	3
1986-87	Indiana	41	41	.500	4x	1	3
1987-88	Indiana	38	44	.463	6x	..	..
	Totals (20 seasons)	864	776	.527		44	58

*Won NBA championship. †Eastern Division. ‡Atlantic Division. §Pacific Division. xCentral Division.
Coach of NBA championship team, 1977.

WILLIS REED JR.
New Jersey Nets

Born June 25, 1942 at Hico, La.   Height 6:10.   Weight 240.
High School—Lillie, La., West Side.
College—Grambling College, Grambling, La.
Drafted by New York on second round, 1964 (10th pick).

—COLLEGIATE RECORD—

Year	G.	Min.	FGA	FGM	Pct.	FTA	FTM	Pct.	Reb.	Pts.	Avg.
60-61	35	....	239	146	.611	122	86	.705	312	378	10.8
61-62	26	....	323	189	.585	102	80	.784	380	458	17.6
62-63	33	....	489	282	.565	177	135	.763	563	699	21.2
63-64	28	....	486	301	.619	199	143	.719	596	745	26.6
Totals	122	....	1537	918	.597	600	444	.740	1851	2280	18.7

NBA REGULAR SEASON RECORD

Sea.—Team	G.	Min.	FGA	FGM	Pct.	FTA	FTM	Pct.	Reb.	Ast.	PF	Disq.	Pts.	Avg.
64-65—New York	80	3042	1457	629	.432	407	302	.742	1175	133	339	14	1560	19.5
65-66—New York	76	2537	1009	438	.434	399	302	.757	883	91	323	13	1178	15.5
66-67—New York	78	2824	1298	635	.489	487	358	.735	1136	126	293	9	1628	20.9
67-68—New York	81	2879	1346	659	.490	509	367	.721	1073	159	343	12	1685	20.8
68-69—New York	82	3108	1351	704	.521	435	325	.747	1191	190	314	7	1733	21.1
69-70—New York	81	3089	1385	702	.507	464	351	.756	1126	161	287	2	1755	21.7
70-71—New York	73	2855	1330	614	.462	381	299	.785	1003	148	228	1	1527	20.9
71-72—New York	11	363	137	60	.438	39	27	.692	96	22	30	0	147	13.4
72-73—New York	69	1876	705	334	.474	124	92	.742	590	126	205	0	760	11.0

Sea.—Team	G.	Min.	FGA	FGM	Pct.	FTA	FTM	Pct.	Off.	Def.	Tot.	Ast.	PF	Dq.	Stl.	Blk.	Pts.	Avg.
73-74—N. Y.	19	500	184	84	.457	53	42	.792	47	94	141	30	49	0	12	21	210	11.1
Totals	650	23073	10202	4859	.476	3298	2465	.747			8414	1186	2411	58			12183	18.7

NBA PLAYOFF RECORD

Sea.—Team	G.	Min.	FGA	FGM	Pct.	FTA	FTM	Pct.	Reb.	Ast.	PF	Disq.	Pts.	Avg.
66-67—New York	4	148	80	43	.538	25	24	.960	55	7	19	1	110	27.5
67-68—New York	6	210	98	53	.541	30	22	.733	62	11	24	1	128	21.3
68-69—New York	10	429	198	101	.510	70	55	.786	141	19	40	1	257	25.7
69-70—New York	18	732	378	178	.471	95	70	.737	248	51	60	0	426	23.7
70-71—New York	12	504	196	81	.413	39	26	.667	144	27	41	0	188	15.7
72-73—New York	17	486	208	97	.466	21	18	.857	129	30	65	1	212	12.5

Sea.—Team	G.	Min.	FGA	FGM	Pct.	FTA	FTM	Pct.	Off.	Def.	Tot.	Ast.	PF	Dq.	Stl.	Blk.	Pts.	Avg.
73-74—N.Y.	11	132	45	17	.378	5	3	.600	4	18	22	4	26	0	2	0	37	3.4
Totals	78	2641	1203	570	.474	285	218	.765			801	149	275	4			1358	17.4

NBA ALL-STAR GAME RECORD

Season—Team	Min.	FGA	FGM	Pct.	FTA	FTM	Pct.	Reb.	Ast.	PF	Disq.	Pts.
1965—New York	25	11	3	.273	2	1	.500	5	1	2	0	7
1966—New York	23	11	7	.636	2	2	1.000	8	1	3	0	16
1967—New York	17	6	2	.333	0	0	.000	9	1	0	0	4
1968—New York	25	14	7	.500	3	2	.667	8	1	4	0	16
1969—New York	14	8	5	.625	0	0	.000	4	2	2	0	10
1970—New York	30	18	9	.500	3	3	1.000	11	0	6	1	21
1971—New York	27	16	5	.313	6	4	.667	13	1	3	0	14
Totals	161	84	38	.452	16	12	.750	58	7	20	1	88

COLLEGIATE COACHING RECORD

Sea.	Club	Regular Season W.	L.	Pct.	Pos.
1981-82	Creighton	7	20	.259	‡8
1982-83	Creighton	8	19	.296	‡10
1983-84	Creighton	17	14	.548	‡4
1984-85	Creighton	20	11	.645	‡4
	Totals (4 seasons)	52	64	.448	

†Atlantic Division.
‡Missouri Valley Conference.

NBA COACHING RECORD

Sea.	Club	Regular Season W.	L.	Pct.	Pos.	Playoffs W.	L.
1977-78	New York	43	39	.524	2†	2	4
1978-79	New York	6	8	.429	..†	..	..
1987-88	New Jersey	7	21	.250	..†	..	..
	Totals (3 seasons)	56	68	.452		2	4

Assistant, Atlanta Hawks, 1985-87, and Sacramento Kings, 1987-88.

Elected to Naismith Memorial Basketball Hall of Fame, 1981.... NBA Most Valuable Player, 1970.... Named to NBA All-Star First Team, 1970.... NBA All-Star Second Team, 1967, 1968, 1969, 1971.... NBA All-Defensive First Team, 1970.... NBA Rookie of the Year, 1965.... NBA All-Rookie Team, 1965.... NBA Playoff MVP, 1970 and 1973. ... NBA All-Star Game MVP, 1970.... Member of NBA championship teams, 1970 and 1973.... Member of NAIA championship team, 1961.... Elected to NAIA Basketball Hall of Fame, 1970.

JERRY OWEN REYNOLDS
Sacramento Kings

Born January 29, 1944 at French Lick, Ind.   Height 5:09.   Weight 175.

High School—French Lick, Ind., Springs Valley.

Colleges—Vincennes University, Vincennes, Ind.; Oakland City College, Oakland City, Ind.; graduate work at Indiana State University, Terre Haute, Ind.

—COLLEGIATE RECORD—

Played at Vincennes (a junior college), 1962-63 and 1963-64, and at Oakland City, 1964-65 and 1965-66. Statistics unavailable.

COLLEGIATE COACHING RECORD

Sea.	Club	Regular Season W.	L.	Pct.	Pos.
1975-76	Rockhurst	15	13	.536	..
1976-77	Rockhurst	17	12	.586	..
1977-78	Rockhurst	21	7	.750	..
1978-79	Rockhurst	21	8	.724	..
1979-80	Rockhurst	24	5	.828	..
1980-81	Rockhurst	25	4	.862	..
1981-82	Rockhurst	20	8	.714	..
1982-83	Rockhurst	25	5	.833	..
1983-84	Rockhurst	14	12	.539	..
1984-85	Pittsburg State	16	15	.516	..
	Totals (10 seasons)	198	89	.690	

NBA COACHING RECORD

Sea.	Club	Regular Season W.	L.	Pct.	Pos.
1986-87	Sacramento	15	21	.417	5†
1987-88	Sacramento	7	17	.292	..†
	Totals (2 seasons)	22	38	.367	

†Midwest Division.
Assistant coach, Sacramento Kings, 1985-86, most of 1986-87 and 1987-88.

PATRICK JAMES RILEY
(Pat)
Los Angeles Lakers

Born March 20, 1945 at Rome, N. Y.   Height 6:04.   Weight 205.

High School—Schenectady, N. Y., Linton.

College—University of Kentucky, Lexington, Ky.

Drafted by San Diego on first round, 1967 (7th pick).

Selected from San Diego by Portland in expansion draft, May 11, 1970.

Sold by Portland to Los Angeles, October 9, 1970.
Traded by Los Angeles to Phoenix for draft rights to John Roche and a 1976 2nd round draft choice, November 3, 1975.

—COLLEGIATE RECORD—

Year	G.	Min.	FGA	FGM	Pct.	FTA	FTM	Pct.	Reb.	Pts.	Avg.
63-64†	16	....	259	120	.463	146	93	.637	235	333	20.8
64-65	25	825	370	160	.432	89	55	.618	212	375	15.0
65-66	29	1078	514	265	.516	153	107	.699	259	637	22.0
66-67	26	953	373	165	.442	156	122	.782	201	452	17.4
Varsity Totals	80	2856	1257	590	.469	398	284	.714	672	1464	18.3

NBA REGULAR SEASON RECORD

Sea.—Team	G.	Min.	FGA	FGM	Pct.	FTA	FTM	Pct.	Reb.	Ast.	PF	Disq.	Pts.	Avg.
67-68—San Diego	80	1263	660	250	.379	202	128	.634	177	138	205	1	628	7.9
68-69—San Diego	56	1027	498	202	.406	134	90	.672	112	136	146	1	494	8.8
69-70—San Diego	36	474	180	75	.417	55	40	.727	57	85	68	0	190	5.3
70-71—Los Angeles	54	506	254	105	.413	87	56	.644	54	72	84	0	266	4.9
71-72—Los Angeles	67	926	441	197	.447	74	55	.743	127	75	110	0	449	6.7
72-73—Los Angeles	55	801	390	167	.428	82	65	.793	65	81	126	0	399	7.3

Sea.—Team	G.	Min.	FGA	FGM	Pct.	FTA	FTM	Pct.	Off.	Def.	Tot.	Ast.	PF	Dq.	Stl.	Blk.	Pts.	Avg.
									—Rebounds—									
73-74—Los Angeles	72	1361	667	287	.430	144	110	.764	38	90	128	148	173	1	54	3	684	9.5
74-75—Los Angeles	46	1016	523	219	.419	93	69	.742	25	60	85	121	128	0	36	4	507	11.0
75-76—LA-Phoe.	62	813	301	117	.389	77	55	.714	16	34	50	57	112	0	22	6	289	4.7
Totals	528	8187	3914	1619	.414	948	668	.705			855	913	1152	3	112	13	3906	7.4

NBA PLAYOFF RECORD

Sea.—Team	G.	Min.	FGA	FGM	Pct.	FTA	FTM	Pct.	Reb.	Ast.	PF	Disq.	Pts.	Avg.
68-69—San Diego	5	76	37	16	.432	6	5	.833	11	2	13	0	37	7.4
70-71—Los Angeles	7	135	69	29	.420	11	8	.727	15	14	12	0	66	9.4
71-72—Los Angeles	15	244	99	33	.333	16	12	.750	29	14	37	0	78	5.2
72-73—Los Angeles	7	53	27	9	.333	0	0	.000	5	7	10	0	18	2.6

Sea.—Team	G.	Min.	FGA	FGM	Pct.	FTA	FTM	Pct.	Off.	Def.	Tot.	Ast.	PF	Dq.	Stl.	Blk.	Pts.	Avg.
									—Rebounds—									
73-74—Los Angeles	5	106	50	18	.360	4	3	.750	3	3	6	10	11	0	4	0	39	7.8
75-76—Phoenix	5	27	15	6	.400	1	1	1.000	0	0	0	5	3	0	0	0	13	2.6
Totals	44	641	297	111	.374	38	29	.763			66	52	86	0	4	0	251	5.7

NBA COACHING RECORD

Sea. Club	Regular Season W.	L.	Pct.	Pos.	Playoffs W.	L.	Sea. Club	Regular Season W.	L.	Pct.	Pos.	Playoffs W.	L.
1981-82—Los Angeles*	50	21	.704	1†	12	2	1985-86—L.A. Lakers	62	20	.756	1†	8	6
1982-83—Los Angeles	58	24	.707	1†	8	7	1986-87—L.A. Lakers*	65	17	.793	1†	15	3
1983-84—Los Angeles	54	28	.659	1†	14	7	1987-88—L.A. Lakers*	62	20	.756	1†	15	9
1984-85—L.A. Lakers*	62	20	.756	1†	15	4	Totals (7 seasons)	413	150	.734		87	38

*Won NBA championship.   †Pacific Division.

Member of NBA championship team, 1972. . . . Coach of NBA championship teams, 1982, 1985, 1987, 1988. . . . Son of former major league catcher and minor league manager Leon Riley. . . . Brother of former National Football League defensive back Lee Riley. . . . Drafted by Dallas Cowboys in 11th round of 1967 NFL draft.

JAMES DONALD RODGERS
(Jimmy)
Boston Celtics

Born March 12, 1943 at Oak Park, Ill.   Height 6:03.   Weight 190.
High School—Franklin Park, Ill., East Leyden.
College—University of Iowa, Iowa City, Ia.

—COLLEGIATE RECORD—

Year	G.	Min.	FGA	FGM	Pct.	FTA	FTM	Pct.	Reb.	Pts.	Avg.
61-62†		Freshman Team Did Not Play An Intercollegiate Schedule									
62-63	24	....	265	89	.336	115	92	.800	120	270	11.3
63-64	23	....	271	105	.387	105	87	.829	103	297	12.9
64-65	24	....	234	102	.436	110	93	.845	68	297	12.4
Varsity Totals	71	....	770	296	.384	330	272	.824	291	864	12.2

COLLEGIATE COACHING RECORD

Sea. Club	Regular Season W.	L.	Pct.	Pos.	Sea. Club	Regular Season W.	L.	Pct.	Pos.
1967-68—North Dakota	15	9	.625		1969-70—North Dakota	13	12	.520	
1968-69—North Dakota	11	14	.440		Totals (3 seasons)	39	35	.527	

Assistant coach, North Dakota, 1965-67.
Assistant coach, Arkansas, 1970-71.

NBA COACHING RECORD
Assistant coach, Cleveland Cavaliers, 1971-79, and Boston Celtics, 1979-88.

RONALD ROTHSTEIN
(Ron)
Miami Heat

Born December 27, 1942 at Bronxville, N.Y. Height 5:08. Weight 165.

High School—Yonkers, N.Y., Roosevelt.

College—University of Rhode Island, Kingston, R.I.

—COLLEGIATE RECORD—

Year	G.	Min.	FGA	FGM	Pct.	FTA	FTM	Pct.	Reb.	Pts.	Avg.
60-61†					Statistics Unavailable						
61-62	25	....	85	37	.435	40	34	.850	35	108	4.3
62-63	26	....	138	45	.326	68	52	.765	68	142	5.5
63-64	24	....	107	48	.449	48	32	.667	75	128	5.3
Varsity Totals	75	....	330	130	.394	156	118	.756	178	378	5.0

NBA COACHING RECORD

Assistant coach, Atlanta Hawks, 1983-86, and Detroit Pistons, 1986-88.

MICHAEL HAROLD SCHULER
(Mike)
Portland Trail Blazers

Born September 22, 1940 at Portsmouth, O. Height 5:11. Weight 165.

High School—Portsmouth, O.

College—Ohio University, Athens, O.

—COLLEGIATE RECORD—

Year	G.	Min.	FGA	FGM	Pct.	FTA	FTM	Pct.	Reb.	Pts.	Avg.
58-59†	11	....		9		4	3	.750	....	21	1.9
59-60	12	....	12	5	.417	2	0	.000	0	10	0.8
60-61	18	....	36	6	.167	3	3	1.000	12	15	0.8
61-62	8	....	13	3	.231	2	1	.500	5	7	0.9
Varsity Totals	38	....	61	14	.230	7	4	.571	17	32	0.8

COLLEGIATE COACHING RECORD

Sea. Club	Regular Season W.	L.	Pct.	Pos.	Sea. Club	Regular Season W.	L.	Pct.	Pos.
1969-70—VMI	6	19	.240		1980-81—Rice	12	15	.444	
1970-71—VMI	1	25	.038		Totals VMI (3 seasons)	13	63	.171	
1971-72—VMI	6	19	.240		Totals Rice (4 seasons)	30	76	.283	
1977-78—Rice	4	22	.154		Totals (7 seasons)	43	139	.236	
1978-79—Rice	7	20	.259						
1979-80—Rice	7	19	.269						

Assistant coach, Army, 1965-66.

Assistant coach, Ohio University, 1966 through 1969.

Assistant coach, University of Virginia, 1972 through 1977.

NBA COACHING RECORD

Sea. Club	Regular Season W.	L.	Pct.	Pos.	Playoffs W.	L.
1986-87—Portland	49	33	.598	2†	1	3
1987-88—Portland	53	29	.646	2†	1	3
Totals (2 seasons)	102	62	.622		2	6

†Pacific Division.

Assistant coach, New Jersey Nets, 1981-83.

Assistant coach, Milwaukee Bucks, 1983-86.

Named NBA Coach of the Year, 1987.

EUGENE WILLIAM SHUE
(Gene)
Los Angeles Clippers

Born December 18, 1931 at Baltimore, Md. Height 6:02. Weight 175.

High School—Towson, Md., Catholic.

College—University of Maryland, College Park, Md.

Drafted by Philadelphia on first round, 1954 (3rd pick).

Sold by Philadelphia to New York, November 29, 1954.

Traded by New York to Fort Wayne for rights to Ron Sobieszczyk, April 30, 1956.

Fort Wayne franchise transferred to Detroit, 1957.
Traded by Detroit to New York for Darrell Imhoff and cash, August 29, 1962.
Traded by New York with Paul Hogue to Baltimore for Bill McGill, October 30, 1963.

—COLLEGIATE PLAYING RECORD—

Year	G.	Min.	FGA	FGM	Pct.	FTA	FTM	Pct.	Reb.	Pts.	Avg.
50-51†	14	....	....	....	....	....	....	....	....	181	12.9
51-52	22	....	243	91	.374	75	53	.707	....	235	10.7
52-53	23	....	375	176	.469	223	156	.700	....	508	22.1
53-54	30	....	469	237	.505	228	180	.789	....	654	21.8
Varsity Totals	75	....	1087	504	.464	526	389	.740	....	1397	18.6

NBA REGULAR SEASON RECORD

Sea.—Team	G.	Min.	FGA	FGM	Pct.	FTA	FTM	Pct.	Reb.	Ast.	PF	Disq.	Pts.	Avg.
54-55—Phila.-N. Y.	62	947	289	100	.346	78	59	.756	154	89	64	0	259	4.2
55-56—New York	72	1750	625	240	.384	237	181	.764	212	179	111	0	661	9.2
56-57—Fort Wayne	72	2470	710	273	.385	316	241	.763	421	238	137	0	787	10.9
57-58—Detroit	63	2333	919	353	.384	327	276	.844	333	172	150	1	982	15.6
58-59—Detroit	72	2745	1197	464	.388	421	338	.803	335	231	129	1	1266	17.6
59-60—Detroit	75	3338	1501	620	.413	541	472	.872	409	295	146	2	1712	22.8
60-61—Detroit	78	3361	1545	650	.421	543	465	.856	334	530	207	1	1765	22.6
61-62—Detroit	80	3143	1422	580	.408	447	362	.810	372	465	192	1	1522	19.0
62-63—New York	78	2288	894	354	.396	302	208	.689	191	259	171	0	916	11.7
63-64—Baltimore	47	963	276	81	.293	61	36	.590	94	150	98	2	198	4.2
Totals	699	23338	9378	3715	.396	3273	2638	.806	2855	2608	1405	8	10068	14.4

NBA PLAYOFF RECORD

Sea.—Team	G.	Min.	FGA	FGM	Pct.	FTA	FTM	Pct.	Reb.	Ast.	PF	Disq.	Pts.	Avg.
54-55—New York	3	49	17	8	.471	7	6	.857	12	4	5	0	22	7.3
56-57—Fort Wayne	2	79	27	14	.519	4	4	1.000	7	8	3	0	32	16.0
57-58—Detroit	7	281	123	45	.366	43	40	.930	46	33	15	0	130	18.6
58-59—Detroit	3	118	60	28	.467	33	27	.818	14	10	7	0	83	27.7
59-60—Detroit	2	89	38	15	.395	20	18	.900	12	6	5	0	48	24.0
60-61—Detroit	5	186	72	35	.486	29	23	.793	12	22	11	0	93	18.6
61-62—Detroit	10	369	151	62	.410	48	37	.771	30	49	29	0	161	16.1
Totals	32	1171	488	207	.424	184	155	.842	133	132	75	0	569	17.8

NBA ALL-STAR GAME RECORD

Season—Team	Min.	FGA	FGM	Pct.	FTA	FTM	Pct.	Reb.	Ast.	PF	Disq.	Pts.
1958—Detroit	25	11	8	.727	3	2	.667	2	0	3	0	18
1959—Detroit	31	12	6	.500	2	1	.500	4	3	4	0	13
1960—Detroit	34	13	6	.462	2	1	.500	6	6	0	0	13
1961—Detroit	23	10	6	.600	4	3	.750	3	6	1	0	15
1962—Detroit	17	6	3	.500	1	1	1.000	5	4	3	0	7
Totals	130	52	29	.558	12	8	.667	20	19	11	0	66

NBA COACHING RECORD

	Regular Season				Playoffs				Regular Season				Playoffs	
Sea. Club	W.	L.	Pct.	Pos.	W.	L.	Sea. Club	W.	L.	Pct.	Pos.	W.	L.
1966-67—Baltimore	16	40	.286	5†	...	...	1977-78—Philadelphia	2	4	.333	...§	...	...
1967-68—Baltimore	36	46	.439	6†	...	...	1978-79—San Diego	43	39	.524	5x	...	...
1968-69—Baltimore	57	25	.695	1†	0	4	1979-80—San Diego	35	47	.427	5x	...	...
1969-70—Baltimore	50	32	.610	3†	3	4	1980-81—Washington	39	43	.476	4§	...	...
1970-71—Baltimore	42	40	.512	1‡	8	10	1981-82—Washington	43	39	.524	4§	3	4
1971-72—Baltimore	38	44	.463	1‡	2	4	1982-83—Washington	42	40	.512	5§	...	...
1972-73—Baltimore	52	30	.634	1‡	1	4	1983-84—Washington	35	47	.427	5§	1	3
1973-74—Philadelphia	25	57	.305	4§	...	...	1984-85—Washington	40	42	.488	4§	1	3
1974-75—Philadelphia	34	48	.415	4§	...	...	1985-86—Washington	32	37	.464	...§	...	...
1975-76—Philadelphia	46	36	.561	2T§	1	2	1987-88—L.A. Clippers......	17	65	.207	6x	..	..
1976-77—Philadelphia	50	32	.610	1§	10	9	Totals (21 seasons)	774	833	.482		30	47

†Eastern Division. ‡Central Division. §Atlantic Division. xPacific Division.
Named to All-NBA First Team, 1960. . . . All-NBA Second Team, 1961. . . . NBA Coach of the Year, 1969 and 1982.

WESTLEY SISSEL UNSELD
(Wes)
Washington Bullets

Born March 14, 1946 at Louisville, Ky.   Height 6:07.   Weight 245.
High School—Louisville, Ky., Seneca.
College—University of Louisville, Louisville, Ky.
Drafted by Baltimore on first round, 1968 (2nd pick).

—COLLEGIATE RECORD—

Year	G.	Min.	FGA	FGM	Pct.	FTA	FTM	Pct.	Reb.	Pts.	Avg.
64-65†	14	....	312	214	.686	124	73	.589	331	501	35.8

Year	G.	Min.	FGA	FGM	Pct.	FTA	FTM	Pct.	Reb.	Pts.	Avg.
65-66	26	....	374	195	.521	202	128	.634	505	518	19.9
66-67	28	....	374	201	.537	177	121	.684	533	523	18.7
67-68	28	....	382	234	.613	275	177	.644	513	645	23.0
Varsity Totals	82	....	1130	630	.558	654	426	.651	1551	1686	20.6

NBA REGULAR SEASON RECORD

Sea.—Team	G.	Min.	FGA	FGM	Pct.	FTA	FTM	Pct.	Reb.	Ast.	PF	Disq.	Pts.	Avg.
68-69—Baltimore	82	2970	897	427	.476	458	277	.605	1491	213	276	4	1131	13.8
69-70—Baltimore	82	3234	1015	526	.518	428	273	.638	1370	291	250	2	1325	16.2
70-71—Baltimore	74	2904	846	424	.501	303	199	.657	1253	293	235	2	1047	14.1
71-72—Baltimore	76	3171	822	409	.498	272	171	.629	1336	278	218	1	989	13.0
72-73—Baltimore	79	3085	854	421	.493	212	149	.703	1260	347	168	0	991	12.5

Sea.—Team	G.	Min.	FGA	FGM	Pct.	FTA	FTM	Pct.	—Rebounds— Off.	Def.	Tot.	Ast.	PF	Dq.	Stl.	Blk.	Pts.	Avg.
73-74—Capital	56	1727	333	146	.438	55	36	.655	152	365	517	159	121	1	56	16	328	5.9
74-75—Washington	73	2904	544	273	.502	184	126	.685	318	759	1077	297	180	1	115	68	672	9.2
75-76—Washington	78	2922	567	318	.561	195	114	.585	271	765	1036	404	203	3	84	59	750	9.6
76-77—Washington	82	2860	551	270	.490	166	100	.602	243	634	877	363	253	5	87	45	640	7.8
77-78—Washington	80	2644	491	257	.523	173	93	.538	286	669	955	326	234	2	98	45	607	7.6
78-79—Washington	77	2406	600	346	.577	235	151	.643	274	556	830	315	204	2	71	37	843	10.9
79-80—Washington	82	2973	637	327	.513	209	139	.665	334	760	1094	366	249	5	65	61	794	9.7
80-81—Washington	63	2032	429	225	.524	86	55	.640	207	466	673	170	171	1	52	36	507	8.0
Totals	984	35832	8586	4369	.509	2976	1883	.633			13769	3822	2762	29	628	367	10624	10.8

Three-Point Field Goals: 1979-80, 1-for-2 (.500). 1980-81, 2-for-4 (.500). Totals, 3-for-6 (.500).

NBA PLAYOFF RECORD

Sea.—Team	G.	Min.	FGA	FGM	Pct.	FTA	FTM	Pct.	Reb.	Ast.	PF	Disq.	Pts.	Avg.
68-69—Baltimore	4	165	57	30	.526	19	15	.789	74	5	14	0	75	18.8
69-70—Baltimore	7	289	70	29	.414	19	15	.789	165	24	25	1	73	10.4
70-71—Baltimore	18	759	208	96	.462	81	46	.568	339	69	60	0	238	13.2
71-72—Baltimore	6	266	65	32	.492	19	10	.526	75	25	22	0	74	12.3
72-73—Baltimore	5	201	48	20	.417	19	9	.474	76	17	12	0	49	9.8

Sea.—Team	G.	Min.	FGA	FGM	Pct.	FTA	FTM	Pct.	—Rebounds— Off.	Def.	Tot.	Ast.	PF	Dq.	Stl.	Blk.	Pts.	Avg.
73-74—Capital	7	297	63	31	.492	15	9	.600	22	63	85	27	15	0	4	1	71	10.1
74-75—Washington	17	734	130	71	.546	61	40	.656	65	211	276	64	39	0	15	20	182	10.7
75-76—Washington	7	310	39	18	.462	24	13	.542	26	59	85	28	19	0	6	4	49	7.0
76-77—Washington	9	368	54	30	.556	12	7	.583	24	81	105	44	32	0	8	6	67	7.4
77-78—Washington	18	677	134	71	.530	46	27	.587	72	144	216	79	62	2	17	7	169	9.4
78-79—Washington	19	736	158	78	.494	64	39	.609	90	163	253	64	66	2	17	14	195	10.3
79-80—Washington	2	87	14	7	.500	6	4	.667	7	21	28	7	5	0	0	3	18	9.0
Totals	119	4889	1040	513	.493	385	234	.608			1777	453	371	5	67	55	1260	10.6

Three-Point Field Goals: 1979-80, 0-for-1.

NBA ALL-STAR GAME RECORD

Season—Team	Min.	FGA	FGM	Pct.	FTA	FTM	Pct.	Reb.	Ast.	PF	Disq.	Pts.
1969—Baltimore	14	7	5	.714	3	1	.333	8	1	3	0	11
1971—Baltimore	21	9	4	.444	0	0	.000	10	2	2	0	8
1972—Baltimore	16	5	1	.200	0	0	.000	7	1	3	0	2
1973—Baltimore	11	4	2	.500	0	0	.000	5	1	0	0	4

Season—Team	Min.	FGA	FGM	Pct.	FTA	FTM	Pct.	—Rebounds— Off.	Def.	Tot.	Ast.	PF	Dq.	Stl.	Blk.	Pts.
1975—Washington	15	3	2	.667	2	2	1.000	2	4	6	1	2	0	2	0	6
Totals	77	28	14	.500	5	3	.600			36	6	10	0			31

NBA COACHING RECORD

		Regular Season				Playoffs	
Sea.	Club	W.	L.	Pct.	Pos.	W.	L.
1987-88—Washington		30	25	.545	T2†	2	3

†Atlantic Division.

Elected to Naismith Memorial Basketball Hall of Fame, 1987.... NBA Most Valuable Player, 1969.... NBA Rookie of the Year, 1969.... Named to NBA All-Star First Team, 1969.... NBA All-Rookie Team, 1969.... NBA Playoff MVP, 1978.... Member of NBA championship team, 1978.... Led NBA in rebounding, 1975.... Led NBA in field-goal percentage, 1976.... Named to THE SPORTING NEWS All-America Second Team, 1967 and 1968.

LEONARD RANDOLPH WILKENS
(Lenny)
Cleveland Cavaliers

Born October 28, 1937 at Brooklyn, N. Y. Height 6:01. Weight 180.

High School—Brooklyn, N. Y., Boys.

College—Providence College, Providence, R. I.

Drafted by St. Louis on first round, 1960.

St. Louis franchise transferred to Atlanta, 1968.
Traded by Atlanta to Seattle for Walt Hazzard, October 12, 1968.
Traded by Seattle with Barry Clemens to Cleveland for Butch Beard, August 23, 1972.
Playing rights transferred from Cleveland to Portland, October 7, 1974.

—COLLEGIATE PLAYING RECORD—

Year	G.	Min.	FGA	FGM	Pct.	FTA	FTM	Pct.	Reb.	Pts.	Avg.
56-57†	23	....	....	....	....	....	....	....	....	488	21.2
57-58	24	....	....	137	.431	....	84	.651	190	358	14.9
58-59	27	....	....	167	.428	....	89	.618	188	423	15.7
59-60	29	....	362	157	.434	140	98	.700	205	412	14.2
Varsity Totals	80	....	....	461	....	....	271	....	583	1193	14.9

NBA REGULAR SEASON RECORD

Sea.—Team	G.	Min.	FGA	FGM	Pct.	FTA	FTM	Pct.	Reb.	Ast.	PF	Disq.	Pts.	Avg.
60-61—St. Louis	75	1898	783	333	.425	300	214	.713	335	212	215	5	880	11.7
61-62—St. Louis	20	870	364	140	.385	110	84	.764	131	116	63	0	364	18.2
62-63—St. Louis	75	2569	834	333	.399	319	222	.696	403	381	256	6	888	11.8
63-64—St. Louis	78	2526	808	334	.413	365	270	.740	335	359	287	7	938	12.0
64-65—St. Louis	78	2854	1048	434	.414	558	416	.746	365	431	283	7	1284	16.5
65-66—St. Louis	69	2692	954	411	.431	532	422	.793	322	429	248	4	1244	18.0
66-67—St. Louis	78	2974	1036	448	.432	583	459	.787	412	442	280	6	1355	17.4
67-68—St. Louis	82	3169	1246	546	.438	711	546	.768	438	679	255	3	1638	20.0
68-69—Seattle	82	3463	1462	644	.440	710	547	.770	511	674	294	8	1835	22.4
69-70—Seattle	75	2802	1066	448	.420	556	438	.788	378	683	212	5	1334	17.8
70-71—Seattle	71	2641	1125	471	.419	574	461	.803	319	654	201	3	1403	19.8
71-72—Seattle	80	2989	1027	479	.466	620	480	.774	338	766	209	4	1438	18.0
72-73—Cleveland	75	2973	1275	572	.449	476	394	.828	346	628	221	2	1538	20.5

Sea.—Team	G.	Min.	FGA	FGM	Pct.	FTA	FTM	Pct.	Off.	Def.	Tot.	Ast.	PF	Dq.	Stl.	Blk.	Pts.	Avg.
									Rebounds									
73-74—Cleveland	74	2483	994	462	.465	361	289	.801	80	197	277	522	165	2	97	17	1213	16.4
74-75—Portland	65	1161	305	134	.439	198	152	.768	38	82	120	235	96	1	77	9	420	6.5
Totals	1077	38064	14327	6189	.432	6973	5394	.774			5030	7211	3285	63	174	26	17772	16.5

NBA PLAYOFF RECORD

Sea.—Team	G.	Min.	FGA	FGM	Pct.	FTA	FTM	Pct.	Reb.	Ast.	PF	Disq.	Pts.	Avg.
60-61—St. Louis	12	437	166	63	.380	58	44	.759	72	42	51	4	170	14.2
62-63—St. Louis	11	400	154	57	.370	49	37	.755	69	69	51	2	151	13.7
63-64—St. Louis	12	413	143	64	.448	58	44	.759	60	64	42	0	172	14.3
64-65—St. Louis	4	147	57	20	.351	29	24	.828	12	15	14	0	64	16.0
65-66—St. Louis	10	391	143	57	.399	83	57	.687	54	70	43	0	171	17.1
66-67—St. Louis	9	378	145	58	.400	90	77	.856	68	65	34	0	193	21.4
67-68—St. Louis	6	237	91	40	.440	40	30	.750	38	47	23	1	110	18.3
Totals	64	2403	899	359	.399	407	313	.769	373	372	258	7	1031	16.1

NBA ALL-STAR GAME RECORD

Season—Team	Min.	FGA	FGM	Pct.	FTA	FTM	Pct.	Reb.	Ast.	PF	Disq.	Pts.
1963—St. Louis	25	7	2	.286	1	0	.000	2	3	0	0	4
1964—St. Louis	14	5	1	.200	1	1	1.000	0	0	3	0	3
1965—St. Louis	20	6	2	.333	4	4	1.000	3	3	3	0	8
1967—St. Louis	16	6	2	.333	3	2	.667	2	6	2	0	6
1968—St. Louis	22	10	4	.400	8	6	.750	3	3	1	0	14
1969—Seattle	24	15	3	.200	5	4	.800	7	5	3	0	10
1970—Seattle	17	7	5	.714	3	2	.667	2	4	1	0	12
1971—Seattle	20	11	8	.727	5	5	1.000	1	1	1	0	21
1973—Cleveland	24	8	3	.375	2	1	.500	2	1	1	0	7
Totals (9 games)	182	75	30	.400	32	25	.781	22	26	15	0	85

NBA COACHING RECORD

Sea. Club	Regular Season				Playoffs	
	W.	L.	Pct.	Pos.	W.	L.
1969-70—Seattle	36	46	.439	5†	...	...
1970-71—Seattle	38	44	.463	4‡	...	...
1971-72—Seattle	47	35	.573	3‡	...	...
1974-75—Portland	38	44	.463	3‡	...	...
1975-76—Portland	37	45	.451	5‡	...	...
1977-78—Seattle	42	18	.700	3‡	13	9
1978-79—Seattle*	52	30	.634	1‡	12	5
1979-80—Seattle	56	26	.683	2‡	7	8
1980-81—Seattle	34	48	.415	6‡	...	...
1981-82—Seattle	52	30	.634	2‡	3	5
1982-83—Seattle	48	34	.585	3‡	0	2
1983-84—Seattle	42	40	.512	3‡	2	3
1984-85—Seattle	31	51	.378	4‡	..	..
1986-87—Cleveland	31	51	.378	6§	..	..
1987-88—Cleveland	42	40	.512	4T§	2	3
Totals (15 seasons)	626	582	.518		39	35

*Won NBA Championship.   †Western Division.   ‡Pacific Division.   §Central Division.

NBA All-Star Game MVP, 1971. . . . Led NBA in assists, 1970. . . . Coach of NBA championship team, 1979. . . . Named to THE SPORTING NEWS All-America Second Team, 1960.

ALL-TIME GREATS

Included are coaches and non-active players who reached one or more of the following plateaus: 17,000 points; 10,000 rebounds; 5,000 assists and 10,000 points; named to either the 25th or 35th NBA Anniversary All-Time Teams; NBA Most Valuable Player; four-time First or Second Team NBA All-Star; six NBA All-Star Games; career scoring average of 23 points per game; 400 regular-season coaching victories in NBA with winning percentage of better than .500.

PLAYERS

NATHANIEL ARCHIBALD
(Tiny or Nate)

Born September 2, 1948 at New York, N. Y.   Height 6:01.   Weight 160.
High School—Bronx, N. Y., DeWitt Clinton.
Colleges—Arizona Western College, Yuma, Ariz., and
University of Texas-El Paso, El Paso, Tex.
Drafted by Cincinnati on second round, 1970 (19th pick).

Traded by Kansas City to New York Nets for Brian Taylor, Jim Eakins and two 1st round draft choices (1977 and 1978), September 10, 1976.
Traded by New Jersey to Buffalo for George Johnson and a 1979 1st round draft choice, September 1, 1977.
Traded by San Diego with Marvin Barnes, Billy Knight and two 2nd round draft choices (1981 and 1983) to Boston for Kermit Washington, Kevin Kunnert, Sidney Wicks and the draft rights to Freeman Williams, August 4, 1978.
Waived by Boston, July 22, 1983; signed by Milwaukee as a free agent, August 1, 1983.

—COLLEGIATE RECORD—
Arizona Western

Year	G.	Min.	FGA	FGM	Pct.	FTA	FTM	Pct.	Reb.	Pts.	Avg.
66-67	27	....	....	303	....	....	190	....	....	796	29.5

Texas-El Paso

Year	G.	Min.	FGA	FGM	Pct.	FTA	FTM	Pct.	Reb.	Pts.	Avg.
67-68	23	....	281	131	.466	140	102	.729	81	364	15.8
68-69	25	....	374	199	.532	194	161	.830	69	559	22.4
69-70	25	....	351	180	.512	225	176	.782	66	536	21.4
Totals	73	....	1006	510	.507	559	439	.785	216	1459	20.0

NBA REGULAR SEASON RECORD

Sea.—Team	G.	Min.	FGA	FGM	Pct.	FTA	FTM	Pct.	Reb.	Ast.	PF	Disq.	Pts.	Avg.
70-71—Cincinnati	82	2867	1095	486	.444	444	336	.757	242	450	218	2	1308	16.0
71-72—Cincinnati	76	3272	1511	734	.486	824	677	.822	222	701	198	3	2145	28.2
72-73—K.C.-Omaha	80	3681	2106	1028	.488	783	663	.847	223	910	207	2	2719	34.0

| | | | | | | | | | —Rebounds— | | | | | | | |
Sea.—Team	G.	Min.	FGA	FGM	Pct.	FTA	FTM	Pct.	Off.	Def.	Tot.	Ast.	PF	Dq.	Stl.	Blk.	Pts.	Avg.
73-74—KC-Omaha	35	1272	492	222	.451	211	173	.820	21	64	85	266	76	0	56	7	617	17.6
74-75—KC-Omaha	82	3244	1664	759	.456	748	652	.872	48	174	222	557	187	0	119	7	2170	26.5
75-76—Kan. City	78	3184	1583	717	.453	625	501	.802	67	146	213	615	169	0	126	15	1935	24.8
76-77—NY Nets	34	1277	560	250	.446	251	197	.785	22	58	80	254	77	1	59	11	697	20.5
77-78—Buffalo								Injured—Torn Achilles Tendon										
78-79—Boston	69	1662	573	259	.452	307	242	.788	25	78	103	324	132	2	55	6	760	11.0
79-80—Boston	80	2864	794	383	.482	435	361	.830	59	138	197	671	218	2	106	10	1131	14.1
80-81—Boston	80	2820	766	382	.499	419	342	.816	36	140	176	618	201	1	75	18	1106	13.8
81-82—Boston	68	2167	652	308	.472	316	236	.747	25	91	116	541	131	1	52	3	858	12.6
82-83—Boston	66	1811	553	235	.425	296	220	.743	25	66	91	409	110	1	38	4	695	10.5
83-84—Milwaukee	46	1038	279	136	.487	101	64	.634	16	60	76	160	78	0	33	0	340	7.4
Totals	876	31159	12628	5899	.467	5760	4664	.810			2046	6476	2002	15	719	81	16481	18.8

Three-Point Field Goals: 1979-80, 4-for-18 (.222). 1980-81, 0-for-9. 1981-82, 6-for-16 (.375). 1982-83, 5-for-24 (.208). 1983-84, 4-for-18 (.222). Totals, 19-for-85 (.224).

NBA PLAYOFF RECORD

| | | | | | | | | | —Rebounds— | | | | | | | |
Sea.—Team	G.	Min.	FGA	FGM	Pct.	FTA	FTM	Pct.	Off.	Def.	Tot.	Ast.	PF	Dq.	Stl.	Blk.	Pts.	Avg.
74-75—KC-Omaha	6	242	118	43	.364	43	35	.814	2	9	11	32	18	0	4	0	121	20.2
79-80—Boston	9	332	89	45	.506	42	37	.881	3	8	11	71	28	1	10	0	128	14.2
80-81—Boston	17	630	211	95	.450	94	76	.809	6	22	28	107	39	0	13	0	266	15.6
81-82—Boston	8	277	70	30	.429	28	25	.893	1	16	17	52	21	0	5	2	85	10.6
82-83—Boston	7	161	68	22	.324	29	22	.759	3	7	10	44	12	0	2	0	67	9.6
Totals	47	1642	556	235	.423	236	195	.826	15	62	77	306	118	1	34	2	667	14.2

Three-Point Field Goals: 1979-80, 1-for-2 (.500). 1980-81, 0-for-5. 1981-82, 0-for-4. 1982-83, 1-for-6. (.167). Totals, 2-for-17 (.118).

Season—Team	Min.	FGA	FGM	Pct.	FTA	FTM	Pct.	Off.	Def.	Tot.	Ast.	PF	Dq.	Stl.	Blk.	Pts.
									—Rebounds—							
1973—K.C.-Omaha ..	27	12	6	.500	5	5	1.000			1	5	1	0			17
1975—K.C.-Omaha ..	36	15	10	.667	8	7	.875	1	1	2	6	2	0	3	1	27
1976—Kansas City ..	30	13	5	.385	3	3	1.000	2	3	5	7	0	0	2	0	13
1980—Boston............	21	8	0	.000	3	2	.667	1	2	3	6	1	0	2	0	2
1981—Boston............	25	7	4	.571	3	1	.333	0	5	5	9	3	0	3	0	9
1982—Boston............	23	5	2	.400	2	2	1.000	1	1	2	7	3	0	1	0	6
Totals	162	60	27	.450	24	20	.833	5	13	18	40	10	0	11	1	74

Named to All-NBA First Team, 1973, 1975, 1976.... All-NBA Second Team, 1972 and 1981.... Member of NBA championship team, 1981.... Led NBA in scoring, 1973.... Led NBA in assists, 1973.... NBA All-Star Game MVP, 1981.

PAUL JOSEPH ARIZIN

Born April 9, 1928 at Philadelphia, Pa.   Height 6:04.   Weight 200.

High School—Philadelphia, Pa., La Salle (Did not play varsity basketball).

College—Villanova University, Villanova, Pa.

Drafted by Philadelphia on first round, 1950.

Played in Eastern Basketball League with Camden Bullets, 1962-63 through 1964-65.

—COLLEGIATE RECORD—

Year	G.	Min.	FGA	FGM	Pct.	FTA	FTM	Pct.	Reb.	Pts.	Avg.
46-47					Did Not Play						
47-48	24	....	...	101	....	...	65	....	...	267	11.1
48-49	27	....	...	210		233	174	.747	...	594	22.0
49-50	29	....	527	260	.493	277	215	.776	...	735	25.3
Totals	80	....	...	571	....	...	454	....	...	1596	20.0

NBA REGULAR SEASON RECORD

Sea.—Team	G.	Min.	FGA	FGM	Pct.	FTA	FTM	Pct.	Reb.	Ast.	PF	Disq.	Pts.	Avg.
50-51—Philadelphia	65	....	864	352	.407	526	417	.793	640	138	284	18	1121	17.2
51-52—Philadelphia	66	2939	1222	548	.448	707	578	.818	745	170	250	5	1674	25.4
52-53—Philadelphia					Did Not Play—Military Service									
53-54—Philadelphia					Did Not Play—Military Service									
54-55—Philadelphia	72	2953	1325	529	.399	585	454	.776	675	210	270	5	1512	21.0
55-56—Philadelphia	72	2724	1378	617	.448	626	507	.810	539	189	282	11	1741	24.2
56-57—Philadelphia	71	2767	1451	613	.422	713	591	.829	561	150	274	13	1817	25.6
57-58—Philadelphia	68	2377	1229	483	.393	544	440	.809	503	135	235	7	1406	20.7
58-59—Philadelphia	70	2799	1466	632	.431	722	587	.813	637	119	264	7	1851	26.4
59-60—Philadelphia	72	2618	1400	593	.423	526	420	.798	621	165	263	6	1606	22.3
60-61—Philadelphia	79	2905	1529	650	.425	639	532	.832	681	188	335	11	1832	23.2
61-62—Philadelphia	78	2785	1490	611	.410	601	484	.805	527	201	307	18	1706	21.9
Totals	713	....	13354	5628	.421	6189	5010	.810	6129	1665	2764	101	16266	22.8

NBA PLAYOFF RECORD

Sea.—Team	G.	Min.	FGA	FGM	Pct.	FTA	FTM	Pct.	Reb.	Ast.	PF	Disq.	Pts.	Avg.
50-51—Philadelphia	2	....	27	14	.519	16	13	.813	20	3	10	1	41	20.5
51-52—Philadelphia	3	120	53	24	.453	33	29	.879	38	8	17	2	77	25.7
55-56—Philadelphia	10	409	229	103	.450	99	83	.838	84	29	31	1	289	28.9
56-57—Philadelphia	2	22	8	3	.375	5	3	.600	8	1	3	0	9	4.5
57-58—Philadelphia	8	309	169	66	.391	72	56	.778	62	16	26	1	188	23.5
59-60—Philadelphia	9	371	195	84	.431	79	69	.873	86	33	29	0	237	26.3
60-61—Philadelphia	3	125	67	22	.328	33	23	.697	26	12	17	2	67	22.3
61-62—Philadelphia	12	459	253	95	.375	102	88	.863	80	26	44	1	278	23.2
Totals	49	....	1001	411	.411	439	364	.829	404	128	177	8	1186	24.2

NBA ALL-STAR GAME RECORD

Season—Team	Min.	FGA	FGM	Pct.	FTA	FTM	Pct.	Reb.	Ast.	PF	Disq.	Pts.
1951—Philadelphia	..	12	7	.583	2	1	.500	7	0	2	0	15
1952—Philadelphia	32	13	9	.692	8	8	1.000	6	0	1	0	26
1955—Philadelphia	23	9	4	.444	2	1	.500	2	2	5	0	9
1956—Philadelphia	28	13	5	.385	5	3	.600	7	1	6	1	13
1957—Philadelphia	26	13	6	.462	2	1	.500	5	0	2	0	13
1958—Philadelphia	29	17	11	.647	2	2	1.000	8	2	3	0	24
1959—Philadelphia	30	15	4	.267	9	8	.889	8	0	2	0	16
1960—Philadelphia					Selected—Injured, Did Not Play							
1961—Philadelphia	17	12	6	.500	5	5	1.000	2	1	4	0	17
1962—Philadelphia	21	12	2	.167	0	0	.000	2	0	4	1	4
Totals (9 games)	...	116	54	.466	35	29	.829	47	6	29	1	137

EBL REGULAR SEASON RECORD

Sea.—Team	G.	Min.	2-Point FGM	FGA	Pct.	3-Point FGM	FGA	Pct.	FTM	FTA	Pct.	Reb.	Ast.	Pts.	Avg.
62-63—Camden	28	....	264	...	...	...	...	...	196	249	.787	203	42	724	27.4
63-64—Camden	27	....	261	...	...	...	...	...	174	218	.798	226	52	696	25.8
64-65—Camden	28	....	226	...	...	3	...	...	196	244	.803	164	50	657	23.5

Named to NBA 25th Anniversary All-Time Team, 1970. . . . Elected to Naismith Memorial Basketball Hall of Fame, 1977. . . . Named to NBA All-Star First Team, 1952, 1956, 1957. . . . NBA All-Star Second Team, 1959. . . . NBA All-Star Game MVP, 1952. . . . Member of NBA championship team, 1956. . . . Led NBA in field-goal percentage, 1952. . . . Led NBA in scoring, 1952 and 1957. . . . Eastern Basketball League MVP, 1963. . . . Named to EBL All-Star First Team, 1963, 1964. . . . EBL All-Star Second Team, 1965. . . . Led NCAA Division I in scoring, 1950. . . . THE SPORTING NEWS College Player of the Year, 1950. . . . Named to THE SPORTING NEWS All-America First Team, 1950.

RICHARD FRANCIS DENNIS BARRY, III
(Rick)

Born March 28, 1944 at Elizabeth, N. J. Height 6:07. Weight 220.

High School—Roselle Park, N. J.

College—University of Miami, Coral Gables, Fla.

Drafted by San Francisco on first round, 1965.

Signed as free agent by Oakland ABA for 1968-69 season (sat out option season with San Francisco NBA, 1967-68). Oakland franchise transferred to Washington, 1969.
Washington franchise transferred to Virginia, 1970.
Traded by Virginia to New York for a 1st round draft choice and cash, August, 1970.
Returned to NBA with Golden State, 1972.
Signed by Houston as a Veteran Free Agent, June 17, 1978; Golden State waived its right of first refusal in exchange for John Lucas and cash.

—COLLEGIATE RECORD—

Year	G.	Min.	FGA	FGM	Pct.	FTA	FTM	Pct.	Reb.	Pts.	Avg.
61-62†	17	....		208			73			489	28.8
62-63	24	....	341	162	.475	158	131	.829	351	455	19.0
63-64	27	....	572	314	.549	287	242	.843	448	870	32.2
64-65	26	....	651	340	.522	341	293	.859	475	973	37.4
Varsity Totals	77	....	1564	816	.522	786	666	.847	1274	2298	29.8

ABA REGULAR SEASON RECORD

Sea.—Team	G.	Min.	2-Point FGM	FGA	Pct.	3-Point FGM	FGA	Pct.	FTM	FTA	Pct.	Reb.	Ast.	Pts.	Avg.
67-68						Did Not Play—Sat Out Option Year									
68-69—Oakland	35	1361	389	757	.514	3	10	.300	403	454	.888	329	136	1190	34.0
69-70—Washington	52	1849	509	907	.511	8	39	.205	400	463	.864	363	178	1442	27.7
70-71—New York	59	2502	613	1262	.486	19	86	.221	451	507	.890	401	294	1734	29.4
71-72—New York	80	3616	829	1732	.479	73	237	.308	641	730	.878	602	327	2518	31.5
Totals	226	9328	2340	4748	.493	103	374	.275	1895	2154	.880	1695	935	6884	30.5

ABA PLAYOFF RECORD

Sea.—Team	G.	Min.	2-Point FGM	FGA	Pct.	3-Point FGM	FGA	Pct.	FTM	FTA	Pct.	Reb.	Ast.	Pts.	Avg.
69-70—Washington	7	302	105	194	.541	3	9	.333	62	68	.912	70	23	281	40.1
70-71—New York	6	287	46	108	.426	14	27	.519	48	59	.814	66	17	202	33.7
71-72—New York	18	749	180	368	.489	23	66	.348	125	146	.856	117	69	554	30.7
Totals	31	1338	331	670	.494	40	102	.392	235	273	.861	253	109	1037	33.5

ABA ALL-STAR GAME RECORD

Sea.—Team	Min.	2-Point FGM	FGA	Pct.	3-Point FGM	FGA	Pct.	FTM	FTA	Pct.	Reb.	Ast.	Pts.	Avg.
68-69—Oakland	12	3	9	.333	0	0	.000	4	5	.800	3	1	10	10.0
69-70—Washington	27	7	12	.583	0	0	.000	2	2	1.000	7	7	16	16.0
70-71—New York	17	4	6	.667	0	0	.000	6	6	1.000	2	2	14	14.0
71-72—New York	26	2	10	.200	0	0	.000	0	1	.000	12	8	4	4.0
Totals	82	16	37	.432	0	0	.000	12	14	.857	24	18	44	11.0

NBA REGULAR SEASON RECORD

Sea.—Team	G.	Min.	FGA	FGM	Pct.	FTA	FTM	Pct.	Reb.	Ast.	PF	Disq.	Pts.	Avg.
65-66—San Fran.	80	2990	1698	745	.439	660	569	.862	850	173	297	2	2059	25.7
66-67—San Fran.	78	3175	2240	1011	.451	852	753	.884	714	282	258	1	2775	35.6
72-73—Golden St.	82	3075	1630	737	.452	397	358	.902	728	399	245	2	1832	22.3

Sea.—Team	G.	Min.	FGA	FGM	Pct.	FTA	FTM	Pct.	Rebounds— Off.	Def.	Tot.	Ast.	PF	Dq.	Stl.	Blk.	Pts.	Avg.
73-74—Golden St.	80	2918	1746	796	.456	464	417	.899	103	437	540	484	265	4	169	40	2009	25.1
74-75—Golden St.	80	3235	2217	1028	.464	436	394	.904	92	364	456	492	225	0	228	33	2450	30.6
75-76—Golden St.	81	3122	1624	707	.435	311	287	.923	74	422	496	496	215	1	202	27	1701	21.0
76-77—Golden St.	79	2904	1551	682	.440	392	359	.916	73	349	422	475	194	2	172	58	1723	21.8

RICK BARRY

Sea.—Team	G.	Min.	FGA	FGM	Pct.	FTA	FTM	Pct.	Off.	Def.	Tot.	Ast.	PF	Dq.	Stl.	Blk.	Pts.	Avg.
									—Rebounds—									
77-78—Golden St.	82	3024	1686	760	.451	409	378	.924	75	374	449	446	188	1	158	45	1898	23.1
78-79—Houston	80	2566	1000	461	.461	169	160	.947	40	237	277	502	195	0	95	38	1082	13.5
79-80—Houston	72	1816	771	325	.422	153	143	.935	53	183	236	268	182	0	80	28	866	12.0
Totals	794	28825	16163	7252	.449	4243	3818	.900			5168	4017	2264	13	1104	269	18395	23.2

Three-Point Field Goals: 1979-80, 73-for-221 (.330).

NBA PLAYOFF RECORD

Sea.—Team	G.	Min.	FGA	FGM	Pct.	FTA	FTM	Pct.	Reb.	Ast.	PF	Disq.	Pts.	Avg.
66-67—San Fran.	15	614	489	197	.403	157	127	.809	113	58	49	0	521	34.7
72-73—Golden St.	11	292	164	65	.396	55	50	.909	54	24	41	1	180	16.4

Sea.—Team	G.	Min.	FGA	FGM	Pct.	FTA	FTM	Pct.	Off.	Def.	Tot.	Ast.	PF	Dq.	Stl.	Blk.	Pts.	Avg.
									—Rebounds—									
74-75—Golden St.	17	726	426	189	.444	110	101	.918	22	72	94	103	51	1	50	15	479	28.2
75-76—Golden St.	13	532	289	126	.436	68	60	.882	20	64	84	84	40	1	38	14	312	24.0
76-77—Golden St.	10	415	262	122	.466	44	40	.909	25	34	59	47	32	0	17	7	284	28.4
78-79—Houston	2	65	25	8	.320	8	8	1.000	2	6	8	9	8	0	0	2	24	12.0
79-80—Houston	6	79	33	12	.364	6	6	1.000	0	6	6	15	11	0	1	1	33	5.5
Totals	74	2723	1688	719	.426	448	392	.875			418	340	232	3	106	39	1833	24.8

Three-Point Field Goals: 1979-80, 3-for-12 (.250).

NBA ALL-STAR GAME RECORD

Season—Team	Min.	FGA	FGM	Pct.	FTA	FTM	Pct.	Reb.	Ast.	PF	Disq.	Pts.
1966—San Francisco	17	10	4	.400	4	2	.500	2	2	6	1	10
1967—San Francisco	34	27	16	.593	8	6	.750	6	3	5	0	38
1973—Golden State				Selected—Injured, Did Not Play								

Season—Team	Min.	FGA	FGM	Pct.	FTA	FTM	Pct.	Off.	Def.	Tot.	Ast.	PF	Dq.	Stl.	Blk.	Pts.
								—Rebounds—								
1974—Golden St......	19	6	3	.500	2	2	1.000	1	3	4	3	3	0	1	0	8
1975—Golden St......	38	20	11	.550	0	0	.000	1	4	5	8	4	0	8	1	22
1976—Golden St......	28	15	6	.400	5	5	1.000	2	2	4	2	5	0	2	0	17
1977—Golden St......	29	16	7	.438	4	4	1.000	1	3	4	8	1	0	2	0	18
1978—Golden St......	30	17	7	.412	1	1	1.000	2	2	4	5	6	1	3	0	15
Totals...............	195	111	54	.486	24	20	.833			29	31	30	2	16	1	128

Elected to Naismith Memorial Basketball Hall of Fame, 1986. . . . Named to NBA All-Star First Team, 1966, 1967, 1974, 1975, 1976. . . . NBA All-Star Second Team, 1973. . . . NBA Rookie of the Year, 1966. . . . NBA All-Rookie Team, 1966. . . . NBA Playoff MVP, 1975. . . . Shares NBA record for most free throws made in one quarter, 14, vs. New York, December 6, 1966. . . . NBA all-time leader in free-throw percentage. . . . NBA All-Star Game MVP, 1967. . . . Holds NBA All-Star Game record for most field goals attempted in one game, 27, in 1967. . . . Shares NBA All-Star Game record for most free throws made in one half, 10, in 1967. . . . Holds NBA record for most field-goal attempts in championship series game, 48, and shares record for most field goals, 22, vs. Philadelphia, April 18, 1967. . . . Shares NBA record for most free throws made in one half of championship series game, 12, vs. Philadelphia, April 24, 1967. . . . Holds NBA record for most field-goal attempts in one quarter of championship series game, 17, vs. Philadelphia, April 14, 1967. . . . Shares NBA record for most three-point field goals, 8, vs. Utah, February 9, 1980. . . . Member of NBA championship team, 1975. . . . Led NBA in scoring, 1967. . . . Led NBA in steals, 1975. . . . Led NBA in free-throw percentage, 1973, 1975, 1976, 1978, 1979, 1980. . . . ABA All-Star First Team, 1969, 1970, 1971, 1972. . . . Led ABA in scoring, 1969. . . . Led ABA in free-throw percentage, 1969, 1971, 1972. . . . Named to THE SPORTING NEWS All-America Second Team, 1965.

ELGIN GAY BAYLOR

Born September 16, 1934 at Washington, D. C.   Height 6:05.   Weight 225.

High Schools—Washington, D. C., Phelps Vocational (Fr.-Jr.) and Spingarn (Sr.).

Colleges—The College of Idaho, Caldwell, Idaho, and
Seattle University, Seattle, Wash.

Drafted by Minneapolis on first round as junior eligible, 1958.

—COLLEGIATE RECORD—
College of Idaho

Year	G.	Min.	FGA	FGM	Pct.	FTA	FTM	Pct.	Reb.	Pts.	Avg.
54-55	26	....	651	332	.510	232	150	.647	492	814	31.3

Seattle

Year	G.	Min.	FGA	FGM	Pct.	FTA	FTM	Pct.	Reb.	Pts.	Avg.
55-56				Did Not Play—Transfer Student							
56-57	25	....	555	271	.488	251	201	.801	508	743	29.7
57-58	29	....	697	353	.506	308	237	.769	559	943	32.5
Totals	54	....	1252	624	.498	559	438	.784	1067	1686	31.2
College Totals	80	....	1903	956	.502	791	588	.743	1559	2500	31.3

NOTE: 1954-55 rebound figures are for 24 games. Baylor played for Westside Ford, an AAU team in Seattle, during 1955-56 season (averaged 34 points per game).

ELGIN BAYLOR

NBA REGULAR SEASON RECORD

Sea.—Team	G.	Min.	FGA	FGM	Pct.	FTA	FTM	Pct.	Reb.	Ast.	PF	Disq.	Pts.	Avg.
58-59—Minneapolis	70	2855	1482	605	.408	685	532	.777	1050	287	270	4	1742	24.9
59-60—Minneapolis	70	2873	1781	755	.424	770	564	.732	1150	243	234	2	2074	29.6
60-61—Los Angeles	73	3133	2166	931	.430	863	676	.783	1447	371	279	3	2538	34.8
61-62—Los Angeles	48	2129	1588	680	.428	631	476	.754	892	222	155	1	1836	38.3
62-63—Los Angeles	80	3370	2273	1029	.453	790	661	.837	1146	386	226	1	2719	34.0
63-64—Los Angeles	78	3164	1778	756	.425	586	471	.804	936	347	235	1	1983	25.4
64-65—Los Angeles	74	3056	1903	763	.401	610	483	.792	950	280	235	0	2009	27.1
65-66—Los Angeles	65	1975	1034	415	.401	337	249	.739	621	224	157	0	1079	16.6
66-67—Los Angeles	70	2706	1658	711	.429	541	440	.813	898	215	211	1	1862	26.6
67-68—Los Angeles	77	3029	1709	757	.443	621	488	.786	941	355	232	0	2002	26.0
68-69—Los Angeles	76	3064	1632	730	.447	567	421	.743	805	408	204	0	1881	24.8
69-70—Los Angeles	54	2213	1051	511	.486	357	276	.773	559	292	132	1	1298	24.0
70-71—Los Angeles	2	57	19	8	.421	6	4	.667	11	2	6	0	20	10.0
71-72—Los Angeles	9	239	97	42	.433	27	22	.815	57	18	20	0	106	11.8
Totals	846	33863	20171	8693	.431	7391	5763	.780	11463	3650	2596	14	23149	27.4

NBA PLAYOFF RECORD

Sea.—Team	G.	Min.	FGA	FGM	Pct.	FTA	FTM	Pct.	Reb.	Ast.	PF	Disq.	Pts.	Avg.
58-59—Minneapolis	13	556	303	122	.403	113	87	.770	156	43	52	0	331	25.5
59-60—Minneapolis	9	408	234	111	.474	94	79	.840	128	31	38	0	301	33.4
60-61—Los Angeles	12	540	362	170	.470	142	117	.824	183	55	44	1	457	38.1
61-62—Los Angeles	13	571	425	186	.428	168	130	.774	230	47	45	1	502	38.6
62-63—Los Angeles	13	562	362	160	.442	126	104	.825	177	58	58	0	424	32.6
63-64—Los Angeles	5	221	119	45	.378	40	31	.775	58	28	17	0	121	24.2
64-65—Los Angeles	1	5	2	0	.000	0	0	.000	0	1	0	0	0	0.0
65-66—Los Angeles	14	586	328	145	.442	105	85	.810	197	52	38	0	375	26.8
66-67—Los Angeles	3	121	76	28	.368	20	15	.750	39	9	6	0	71	23.7
67-68—Los Angeles	15	633	376	176	.468	112	76	.679	218	60	41	0	428	28.5
68-69—Los Angeles	18	640	278	107	.385	100	63	.630	166	74	56	0	277	15.4
69-70—Los Angeles	18	667	296	138	.466	81	60	.741	173	83	50	1	336	18.7
Totals	134	5510	3161	1388	.439	1101	847	.769	1725	541	445	3	3623	27.0

NBA ALL-STAR GAME RECORD

Season—Team	Min.	FGA	FGM	Pct.	FTA	FTM	Pct.	Reb.	Ast.	PF	Disq.	Pts.
1959—Minneapolis	32	20	10	.500	5	4	.800	11	1	3	0	24
1960—Minneapolis	28	18	10	.556	7	5	.714	13	3	4	0	25
1961—Los Angeles	27	11	3	.273	10	9	.900	10	4	5	0	15
1962—Los Angeles	37	23	10	.435	14	12	.857	9	4	2	0	32
1963—Los Angeles	36	15	4	.267	13	9	.692	14	7	0	0	17
1964—Los Angeles	29	15	5	.333	11	5	.455	8	5	1	0	15
1965—Los Angeles	27	13	5	.385	8	8	1.000	7	0	4	0	18
1967—Los Angeles	20	14	8	.571	4	4	1.000	5	5	2	0	20
1968—Los Angeles	27	13	8	.615	7	6	.857	6	1	5	0	22
1969—Los Angeles	32	13	5	.385	12	11	.917	9	5	2	0	21
1970—Los Angeles	26	9	2	.222	7	5	.714	7	3	3	0	9
Totals	321	164	70	.427	98	78	.796	99	38	31	0	218

NBA COACHING RECORD

		Regular Season				Playoffs	
Sea.	Club	W.	L.	Pct.	Pos.	W.	L.
1974-75—New Orleans		0	1	.000	...†	..	..
1976-77—New Orleans		21	35	.375	5†	..	..
1977-78—New Orleans		39	43	.476	5†	..	..
1978-79—New Orleans		26	56	.317	6†	..	..
Totals (4 seasons)		86	135	.389		..	..

†Central Division.

Named to NBA 35th Anniversary All-Time Team, 1980. . . . . Elected to Naismith Memorial Basketball Hall of Fame, 1976. . . . . Named to NBA All-Star First Team, 1959, 1960, 1961, 1962, 1963, 1964, 1965, 1967, 1968, 1969. . . . . NBA Rookie of the Year, 1959. . . . . Shares NBA record for most field goals in championship series game, 22, vs. Boston, April 14, 1962. . . . . Holds NBA records for most points, 33, and most field-goal attempts, 25, in one half of championship series game, vs. Boston, April 14, 1962. . . . . NBA All-Star Game co-MVP, 1959. . . . . Holds NBA All-Star Game records for most career free throws made and most field goals attempted in one half, 15, in 1959. . . . . Shares NBA All-Star Game records for most career free throws attempted and most free throws made in one game, 12, in 1962. . . . . Led NCAA Division I in rebounding, 1957. . . . . NCAA University Division tournament MVP, 1958. . . . . Named to THE SPORTING NEWS All-America First Team, 1958.

WALTER JONES BELLAMY
(Walt)

Born July 24, 1939 at New Bern, N. C.   Height 6:11.   Weight 245.

High School—New Bern, N. C., J. T. Barber.

College—Indiana University, Bloomington, Ind.

Drafted by Chicago on first round, 1961.

Chicago franchise moved to Baltimore, 1963.

Traded by Baltimore to New York for John Green, John Egan, Jim Barnes and cash, November 2, 1965.
Traded by New York with Howard Komives to Detroit for Dave DeBusschere, December 19, 1968.
Traded by Detroit to Atlanta for a player to be designated, February 1, 1970. Detroit received John Arthurs from Milwaukee as part of deal.
Selected from Atlanta by New Orleans in expansion draft, May 20, 1974.
Waived by New Orleans, October 18, 1974.

—COLLEGIATE RECORD—

Year	G.	Min.	FGA	FGM	Pct.	FTA	FTM	Pct.	Reb.	Pts.	Avg.
57-58†			(Freshman team did not play intercollegiate schedule.)								
58-59	22	....	289	148	.512	141	86	.610	335	382	17.4
59-60	24	....	396	212	.535	161	113	.702	324	537	22.4
60-61	24	....	389	195	.501	204	132	.647	428	522	21.8
Varsity Totals	70	....	1074	555	.517	506	331	.654	1087	1441	20.6

NBA REGULAR SEASON RECORD

Sea.—Team	G.	Min.	FGA	FGM	Pct.	FTA	FTM	Pct.	Reb.	Ast.	PF	Disq.	Pts.	Avg.
61-62—Chicago	79	3344	1875	973	.519	853	549	.644	1500	210	281	6	2495	31.6
62-63—Chicago	80	3306	1595	840	.527	821	553	.674	1309	233	283	7	2233	27.9
63-64—Baltimore	80	3394	1582	811	.513	825	537	.651	1361	126	300	7	2159	27.0
64-65—Baltimore	80	3301	1441	733	.509	752	515	.685	1166	191	260	2	1981	24.8
65-66—Balt.-N.Y.	80	3352	1373	695	.506	689	430	.624	1254	235	294	9	1820	22.8
66-67—New York	79	3010	1084	565	.521	580	369	.637	1064	206	275	5	1499	19.0
67-68—New York	82	2695	944	511	.541	529	350	.662	961	164	259	3	1372	16.7
68-69—N.Y.-Det.	88	3159	1103	563	.510	618	401	.649	1101	176	320	5	1527	17.4
69-70—Det.-Atl.	79	2028	671	351	.523	373	215	.576	707	143	260	5	917	11.6
70-71—Atlanta	82	2908	879	433	.493	556	336	.604	1060	230	271	4	1202	14.7
71-72—Atlanta	82	3187	1089	593	.544	581	340	.585	1049	262	255	2	1526	18.6
72-73—Atlanta	74	2802	901	455	.505	526	283	.538	964	179	244	1	1193	16.1

Sea.—Team	G.	Min.	FGA	FGM	Pct.	FTA	FTM	Pct.	Off.	Def.	Tot.	Ast.	PF	Dq.	Stl.	Blk.	Pts.	Avg.
										—Rebounds—								
73-74—Atlanta	77	2440	801	389	.486	383	233	.608	264	476	740	189	232	2	52	48	1011	13.1
74-75—N. O.	1	14	2	2	1.000	2	2	1.000	0	5	5	0	2	0	0	0	6	6.0
Totals	1043	38940	15340	7914	.516	8088	5113	.632			14241	2544	3536	58	52	48	20941	20.1

NBA PLAYOFF RECORD

Sea.—Team	G.	Min.	FGA	FGM	Pct.	FTA	FTM	Pct.	Reb.	Ast.	PF	Disq.	Pts.	Avg.
64-65—Baltimore	10	427	158	74	.468	92	61	.663	151	34	38	0	209	20.9
66-67—New York	4	157	54	28	.519	29	17	.586	66	12	15	0	73	18.3
67-68—New York	6	277	107	45	.421	48	30	.625	96	21	22	0	120	20.0
69-70—Atlanta	9	368	126	59	.468	46	33	.717	140	35	32	0	151	16.8
70-71—Atlanta	5	216	69	41	.594	29	22	.759	72	10	16	0	104	20.8
71-72—Atlanta	6	247	86	42	.488	43	27	.628	82	11	20	0	111	18.5
72-73—Atlanta	6	247	86	34	.395	31	14	.452	73	13	17	0	82	13.7
Totals	46	1939	686	323	.471	318	204	.642	680	136	160	0	850	18.5

NBA ALL-STAR GAME RECORD

Season—Team	Min.	FGA	FGM	Pct.	FTA	FTM	Pct.	Reb.	Ast.	PF	Disq.	Pts.
1962—Chicago	29	18	10	.556	8	3	.375	17	1	6	1	23
1963—Chicago	14	4	1	.250	2	0	.000	1	2	3	0	2
1964—Baltimore	23	11	4	.364	5	3	.600	7	0	3	0	11
1965—Baltimore	17	5	4	.800	4	4	1.000	5	1	3	0	12
Totals	83	38	19	.500	19	10	.526	30	4	15	1	48

NBA Rookie of the Year, 1962. . . . Led NBA in field-goal percentage, 1962. . . . Holds NBA record for most games played in one season, 1969. . . . Member of U.S. Olympic Team, 1960. . . . Named to THE SPORTING NEWS All-America Second Team, 1961.

DAVID BING
(Dave)

Born November 24, 1943 at Washington, D. C.   Height 6:03.   Weight 185.

High School—Washington, D. C., Spingarn.

College—Syracuse University, Syracuse, N. Y.

Drafted by Detroit on first round, 1966 (1st pick).

Traded by Detroit with a 1977 1st round draft choice to Washington for Kevin Porter, August 28, 1975.
Waived by Washington, September 20, 1977; signed by Boston as a free agent, September 28, 1977.

—COLLEGIATE RECORD—

Year	G.	Min.	FGA	FGM	Pct.	FTA	FTM	Pct.	Reb.	Pts.	Avg.
62-63†	17	....	341	170	.499	131	97	.740	192	437	25.7
63-64	25	....	460	215	.467	172	126	.733	206	556	22.2
64-65	23	....	444	206	.464	162	121	.747	277	533	23.2
65-66	28	....	569	308	.541	222	178	.802	303	794	28.4
Varsity Totals	76	....	1473	729	.495	556	425	.764	786	1883	24.8

NBA REGULAR SEASON RECORD

Sea.—Team	G.	Min.	FGA	FGM	Pct.	FTA	FTM	Pct.	Reb.	Ast.	PF	Disq.	Pts.	Avg.
66-67—Detroit	80	2762	1522	664	.436	370	273	.738	359	330	217	2	1601	20.6
67-68—Detroit	79	3209	1893	835	.441	668	472	.707	373	509	254	2	2142	27.1
68-69—Detroit	77	3039	1594	678	.425	623	444	.713	382	546	256	3	1800	23.4
69-70—Detroit	70	2334	1295	575	.444	580	454	.783	299	418	196	0	1604	22.9
70-71—Detroit	82	3065	1710	799	.467	772	615	.797	364	408	228	4	2213	27.0
71-72—Detroit	45	1936	891	369	.414	354	278	.785	186	317	138	3	1016	22.6
72-73—Detroit	82	3361	1545	692	.448	560	456	.814	298	637	229	1	1840	22.4

Sea.—Team	G.	Min.	FGA	FGM	Pct.	FTA	FTM	Pct.	—Rebounds— Off.	Def.	Tot.	Ast.	PF	Dq.	Stl.	Blk.	Pts.	Avg.
73-74—Detroit	81	3124	1336	582	.436	438	356	.813	108	173	281	555	216	1	109	17	1520	18.0
74-75—Detroit	79	3222	1333	578	.434	424	343	.809	86	200	286	610	222	3	116	26	1499	19.0
75-76—Wash.	82	2945	1113	497	.447	422	332	.787	94	143	237	492	262	0	118	23	1326	16.2
76-77—Wash.	64	1516	597	271	.454	176	136	.773	54	89	143	275	150	1	61	5	678	10.6
77-78—Boston	80	2256	940	422	.449	296	244	.824	76	136	212	300	247	2	79	18	1088	13.6
Totals	901	32769	15769	6962	.441	5683	4403	.775			3420	5397	2615	22	483	89	18327	20.3

NBA PLAYOFF RECORD

Sea.—Team	G.	Min.	FGA	FGM	Pct.	FTA	FTM	Pct.	—Rebounds— Off.	Def.	Tot.	Ast.	PF	Dq.	Stl.	Blk.	Pts.	Avg.
67-68—Detroit	6	254	166	68	.410	45	33	.763			24	29	21	0			169	28.2
73-74—Detroit	7	312	131	55	.420	30	22	.733	6	20	26	42	20	0	3	1	132	18.9
74-75—Detroit	3	134	47	20	.426	13	8	.615	3	8	11	29	12	0	5	0	48	16.0
75-76—Wash.	7	209	76	34	.447	35	28	.800	6	12	18	28	18	0	7	2	96	13.7
76-77—Wash.	8	55	32	14	.438	4	4	1.000	3	3	6	5	5	0	1		32	4.0
Totals	31	964	452	191	.423	127	95	.748			85	133	76	0	15	4	477	15.4

NBA ALL-STAR GAME RECORD

Season—Team	Min.	FGA	FGM	Pct.	FTA	FTM	Pct.	Reb.	Ast.	PF	Disq.	Pts.
1968—Detroit	20	7	4	.571	1	1	1.000	2	4	3	0	9
1969—Detroit	13	3	1	.333	1	1	1.000	0	3	0	0	3
1971—Detroit	19	7	2	.286	0	0	.000	2	2	1	0	4
1973—Detroit	19	4	0	.000	2	2	1.000	3	0	1	0	2

Season—Team	Min.	FGA	FGM	Pct.	FTA	FTM	Pct.	—Rebounds— Off.	Def.	Tot.	Ast.	PF	Dq.	Stl.	Blk.	Pts.
1974—Detroit	16	9	2	.222	1	1	1.000	1	5	6	2	1	0	0	0	5
1975—Detroit	12	2	0	.000	2	2	1.000	0	0	0	1	0	0	0	0	2
1976—Washington	26	11	7	.636	2	2	1.000	1	2	3	4	1	0	0	0	16
Totals	125	43	16	.372	9	9	1.000			16	16	7	0	0	0	41

Named to NBA All-Star First Team, 1968 and 1971.... NBA All-Star Second Team, 1974.... NBA Rookie of the Year, 1967.... NBA All-Rookie Team, 1967.... Led NBA in scoring, 1968.... NBA All-Star Game MVP, 1976.... Named to THE SPORTING NEWS All-America First Team, 1965.

RONALD BRUCE BOONE

Born September 6, 1946 at Oklahoma City, Okla.   Height 6:02.   Weight 200.

High School—Omaha, Neb., Tech.

Colleges—Iowa Western Community College, Clarinda, Iowa, and Idaho State University, Pocatello, Idaho.

Drafted by Phoenix on eleventh round, 1968 (147th pick).

Selected by Dallas on eighth round of ABA draft, 1968.
Traded by Dallas with Glen Combs to Utah for Donnie Freeman and Wayne Hightower, January 8, 1971.
Sold by Utah to St. Louis, December 2, 1975.
Selected by Kansas City NBA from St. Louis for $250,000 in ABA dispersal draft, August 5, 1976.
Traded by Kansas City with a 1979 2nd round draft choice to Denver for Darnell Hillman and the draft rights to Mike Evans, June 26, 1978.
Traded by Denver with two 1979 2nd round draft choices to Los Angeles for Charlie Scott, June 26, 1978.
Traded by Los Angeles to Utah for a 1981 3rd round draft choice, October 25, 1979.
Waived by Utah, January 26, 1981.

Iowa Western CC

Year	G.	Min.	FGA	FGM	Pct.	FTA	FTM	Pct.	Reb.	Pts.	Avg.
64-65	9	....	....	....	....	....	....	....	....	227	25.2

Idaho State

Year	G.	Min.	FGA	FGM	Pct.	FTA	FTM	Pct.	Reb.	Pts.	Avg.
65-66	10	....	119	46	.387	26	17	.654	95	109	10.9
66-67	25	....	416	199	.478	215	160	.744	128	558	22.3
67-68	26	....	519	223	.430	159	108	.679	110	554	21.3
Totals	61	....	1054	468	.444	400	285	.713	333	1221	20.0

ABA REGULAR SEASON RECORD

Sea.—Team	G.	Min.	2-Point FGM	FGA	Pct.	3-Point FGM	FGA	Pct.	FTM	FTA	Pct.	Reb.	Ast.	Pts.	Avg.
68-69—Dallas	78	2682	518	1182	.438	2	15	.133	436	537	.812	394	279	1478	18.9
69-70—Dallas	84	2340	406	925	.439	17	55	.309	300	382	.785	366	272	1163	13.9
70-71—Dallas-Utah	86	2476	561	1257	.446	49	138	.355	278	357	.779	564	256	1547	18.0
71-72—Utah	84	2040	391	897	.436	13	65	.200	271	341	.795	393	233	1092	13.0
72-73—Utah	84	2585	556	1096	.507	10	40	.250	415	479	.866	423	353	1557	18.5
73-74—Utah	84	3098	581	1162	.500	6	26	.231	300	343	.875	435	417	1480	17.6
74-75—Utah	84	3414	862	1743	.495	10	33	.303	363	422	.860	406	372	2117	25.2
75-76—Utah-St. Louis	78	2961	697	1424	.489	16	43	.372	277	318	.871	319	387	1719	22.0
Totals	662	21586	4572	9686	.472	123	415	.296	2640	3179	.830	3302	2569	12153	18.4

ABA PLAYOFF RECORD

Sea.—Team	G.	Min.	2-Point FGM	FGA	Pct.	3-Point FGM	FGA	Pct.	FTM	FTA	Pct.	Reb.	Ast.	Pts.	Avg.
68-69—Dallas	7	196	38	81	.469	0	4	.000	21	25	.840	22	27	97	13.9
69-70—Dallas	6	193	43	89	.483	3	8	.375	15	21	.714	27	27	110	18.3
70-71—Utah	18	569	104	229	.454	9	27	.333	74	86	.860	110	94	309	17.2
71-72—Utah	11	209	49	100	.490	1	5	.200	25	29	.862	24	26	126	11.5
72-73—Utah	10	360	68	132	.515	0	3	.000	33	34	.971	43	47	169	16.9
73-74—Utah	18	747	137	282	.486	0	7	.000	34	37	.919	108	109	308	17.1
74-75—Utah	6	219	54	127	.425	0	0	.000	34	38	.895	24	41	142	23.7
Totals	76	2493	493	1040	.474	13	54	.240	236	270	.874	358	371	1261	16.6

ABA ALL-STAR GAME RECORD

Sea.—Team	Min.	2-Point FGM	FGA	Pct.	3-Point FGM	FGA	Pct.	FTM	FTA	Pct.	Reb.	Ast.	Pts.	Avg.
1971—Utah	4	2	4	.500	0	0	.000	2	3	.667	2	0	6	6.0
1974—Utah	24	6	11	.545	1	2	.500	0	0	.000	3	5	15	15.0
1975—Utah	23	4	8	.500	0	0	.000	2	2	1.000	2	2	10	10.0
1976—St. Louis	16	5	11	.455	0	0	.000	0	0	.000	3	2	10	10.0
Totals	67	17	34	.500	1	2	.500	4	5	.800	10	9	41	10.3

NBA REGULAR SEASON RECORD

Sea.—Team	G.	Min.	FGA	FGM	Pct.	FTA	FTM	Pct.	Rebounds— Off.	Def.	Tot.	Ast.	PF	Dq.	Stl.	Blk.	Pts.	Avg.
76-77—Kan. City	82	3021	1577	747	.474	384	324	.844	128	193	321	338	258	1	119	19	1818	22.2
77-78—Kan. City	82	2653	1271	563	.443	377	322	.854	112	157	269	311	233	3	105	11	1448	17.7
78-79—Los Ang.	82	1583	569	259	.455	104	90	.865	53	92	145	154	171	1	66	11	608	7.4
79-80—L.A.-Utah	81	2392	915	405	.443	196	175	.893	54	173	227	309	232	3	97	3	1004	12.4
80-81—Utah	52	1146	371	160	.431	94	75	.798	17	67	84	161	126	0	33	8	406	7.8
Totals	379	10795	4703	2134	.454	1155	986	.854	364	682	1046	1273	1020	8	420	52	5284	13.9

Three-Point Field Goals: 1979-80, 19-for-50 (.380). 1980-81, 11-for-39 (.282). Totals, 30-for-89 (.337).

NBA PLAYOFF RECORD

Sea.—Team	G.	Min.	FGA	FGM	Pct.	FTA	FTM	Pct.	Rebounds— Off.	Def.	Tot.	Ast.	PF	Dq.	Stl.	Blk.	Pts.	Avg.
78-79—Los Ang.	8	226	77	37	.481	21	20	.952	7	8	15	14	28	0	9	0	94	11.8

Set professional basketball record by playing in 1,041 consecutive games. . . . Named to ABA All-Star First Team, 1975. . . . ABA All-Star Second Team, 1974. . . . ABA All-Rookie Team, 1969. . . . Member of ABA championship team, 1971.

WILLIAM WARREN BRADLEY
(Bill)

Born July 28, 1943 at Crystal City, Mo.   Height 6:05.   Weight 210.

High School—Crystal City, Mo.

Colleges—Princeton University, Princeton, N. J., and
graduate work at Oxford University, Oxford, England.

Drafted by New York on first round (territorial choice), 1965.

Played with Milan Simmenthal of Italian Basketball League, 1965-66.
Played with Oxford University in England, 1966-67.

—COLLEGIATE RECORD—

Year	G.	Min.	FGA	FGM	Pct.	FTA	FTM	Pct.	Reb.	Pts.	Avg.
61-62†	13	....	265	142	.536	125	114	.912	232	398	30.6
62-63	25	....	445	212	.476	289	258	.893	306	682	27.3
63-64	29	....	648	338	.522	306	260	.850	360	936	32.3
64-65	29	....	574	306	.533	308	273	.886	342	885	30.5
Varsity Totals	83	....	1667	856	.513	903	791	.876	1008	2503	30.2

NBA REGULAR SEASON RECORD

Sea.—Team	G.	Min.	FGA	FGM	Pct.	FTA	FTM	Pct.	Reb.	Ast.	PF	Disq.	Pts.	Avg.
67-68—New York	45	874	341	142	.416	104	76	.731	113	137	138	2	360	8.0
68-69—New York	82	2413	948	401	.429	253	206	.814	350	302	295	4	1020	12.4
69-70—New York	67	2098	897	413	.460	176	145	.824	239	268	219	0	971	14.5
70-71—New York	78	2300	912	413	.453	175	144	.823	260	280	245	3	970	12.4
71-72—New York	78	2780	1085	504	.465	199	169	.849	250	315	254	4	1177	15.1
72-73—New York	82	2998	1252	575	.459	194	169	.871	301	367	273	5	1319	16.1

									—Rebounds—									
Sea.—Team	G.	Min.	FGA	FGM	Pct.	FTA	FTM	Pct.	Off.	Def.	Tot.	Ast.	PF	Dq.	Stl.	Blk.	Pts.	Avg.
73-74—New York	82	2813	1112	502	.451	167	146	.874	59	194	253	242	278	2	42	21	1150	14.0
74-75—New York	79	2787	1036	452	.436	165	144	.873	65	186	251	247	283	5	74	18	1048	13.3
75-76—New York	82	2709	906	392	.433	148	130	.878	47	187	234	247	256	2	68	18	914	11.1
76-77—New York	67	1027	274	127	.464	42	34	.810	27	76	103	128	122	0	25	8	288	4.3
Totals	742	22799	8763	3927	.448	1623	1363	.840			2354	2533	2363	27			9217	12.4

NBA ALL-STAR GAME RECORD

Season—Team	Min.	FGA	FGM	Pct.	FTA	FTM	Pct.	Reb.	Ast.	PF	Disq.	Pts.
1973—New York.................	12	5	2	.400	0	0	.000	1	0	2	0	4

NBA PLAYOFF RECORD

Sea.—Team	G.	Min.	FGA	FGM	Pct.	FTA	FTM	Pct.	Reb.	Ast.	PF	Disq.	Pts.	Avg.
67-68—New York	6	64	28	12	.429	13	9	.692	6	2	7	0	33	5.5
68-69—New York	10	419	141	65	.461	39	30	.769	73	40	38	1	160	16.0
69-70—New York	19	616	233	100	.429	43	35	.814	72	60	59	1	235	12.4
70-71—New York	12	368	132	56	.424	19	14	.737	41	43	40	0	126	10.5
71-72—New York	16	594	227	106	.467	56	47	.839	47	54	66	1	259	16.2
72-73—New York	17	587	221	99	.448	50	40	.800	57	45	59	1	238	14.0

									—Rebounds—									
Sea.—Team	G.	Min.	FGA	FGM	Pct.	FTA	FTM	Pct.	Off.	Def.	Tot.	Ast.	PF	Dq.	Stl.	Blk.	Pts.	Avg.
73-74—New York	12	425	159	63	.396	29	25	.862	8	20	28	13	39	1	7	3	151	12.6
74-75—New York	3	88	24	9	.375	2	2	1.000	4	5	9	6	5	0	2	0	20	6.7
Totals	95	3161	1165	510	.438	251	202	.805			333	263	313	5			1222	12.9

Elected to Naismith Memorial Basketball Hall of Fame, 1982. . . . Member of NBA championship teams, 1970 and 1973. . . . Named THE SPORTING NEWS College Player of the Year, 1964 and 1965. . . . THE SPORTING NEWS All-America First Team, 1963, 1964, 1965. . . . Outstanding player in NCAA University Division tourney, 1965. . . . Led NCAA University Division in free-throw percentage, 1965. . . . Member of U.S. Olympic Team, 1964. . . . Currently a U.S. Senator (D) from New Jersey.

BILL BRIDGES

Born April 4, 1939 at Hobbs, N. M. Height 6:06. Weight 235.

High School—Hobbs, N. M.

College—University of Kansas, Lawrence, Kan.

Drafted by Chicago on third round, 1961. (32nd pick).

Draft rights traded by Chicago (Baltimore) with Ralph Davis to St. Louis for Al Ferrari and Shellie McMillion, June 14, 1962.

Traded by Atlanta to Philadelphia for Jim Washington, November 19, 1971.

Traded by Philadelphia with Mel Counts to Los Angeles for Leroy Ellis and John Q. Trapp, November 2, 1972.

Waived by Los Angeles, December 6, 1974; signed by Golden State as a free agent, March 1, 1975.

Played in American Basketball League with Kansas City Steers, 1961-62 and 1962-63.

—COLLEGIATE RECORD—

Year	G.	Min.	FGA	FGM	Pct.	FTA	FTM	Pct.	Reb.	Pts.	Avg.
57-58†	(Freshman team did not play intercollegiate schedule)										
58-59	25	....	307	117	.381	129	74	.574	343	308	12.3
59-60	28	....	293	112	.382	142	94	.662	385	318	11.4
60-61	25	....	334	146	.437	155	110	.710	353	402	16.1
Varsity Totals	78	....	934	375	.401	426	278	.653	1081	1028	13.2

ABL REGULAR SEASON RECORD

			—2-Point—			—3-Point—									
Sea.—Team	G.	Min.	FGM	FGA	Pct.	FGM	FGA	Pct.	FTM	FTA	Pct.	Reb.	Ast.	Pts.	Avg.
61-62—Kan. City...................	79	3259	638	1400	.456	3	12	.250	412	587	.702	1059	181	1697	21.4
62-63—Kan. City...................	29	1185	312	606	.515	0	2	.000	225	289	.779	437	87	849	29.2

NBA REGULAR SEASON RECORD

Sea.—Team	G.	Min.	FGA	FGM	Pct.	FTA	FTM	Pct.	Reb.	Ast.	PF	Disq.	Pts.	Avg.
62-63—St. Louis	27	374	160	66	.413	51	32	.627	144	23	58	0	164	6.1
63-64—St. Louis	80	1949	675	268	.397	224	146	.652	680	181	269	6	682	8.5
64-65—St. Louis	79	2362	938	362	.386	275	186	.676	853	187	276	3	910	11.5
65-66—St. Louis	78	2677	927	377	.407	364	257	.706	951	208	333	11	1011	13.0
66-67—St. Louis	79	3130	1106	503	.455	523	367	.702	1190	222	325	12	1373	17.4
67-68—St. Louis	82	3197	1009	466	.462	484	347	.717	1102	253	366	12	1279	15.6

Sea.—Team	G.	Min.	FGA	FGM	Pct.	FTA	FTM	Pct.	Reb.	Ast.	PF	Disq.	Pts.	Avg.
68-69—Atlanta	80	2930	775	351	.453	353	239	.677	1132	298	290	3	941	11.8
69-70—Atlanta	82	3269	932	443	.475	451	331	.734	1181	345	292	6	1217	14.8
70-71—Atlanta	82	3140	834	382	.458	330	211	.639	1233	240	317	7	975	11.9
71-72—Atl.-Phil.	78	2756	779	379	.487	316	222	.703	1051	198	269	6	980	12.6
72-73—Phil-LA	82	2867	722	333	.461	255	179	.702	904	219	296	3	845	10.3

Sea.—Team	G.	Min.	FGA	FGM	Pct.	FTA	FTM	Pct.	Off.	Def.	Tot.	Ast.	PF	Dq.	Stl.	Blk.	Pts.	Avg.
								—Rebounds—									
73-74—L.A.	65	1812	513	216	.421	164	116	.707	193	306	499	148	219	3	58	31	548	8.4
74-75—LA-GS	32	415	93	35	.376	34	17	.500	64	70	134	31	65	1	11	5	87	2.7
Totals	926	30878	9463	4181	.442	3824	2650	.693			11054	2553	3375	73	69	36	11012	11.9

NBA PLAYOFF RECORD

Sea.—Team	G.	Min.	FGA	FGM	Pct.	FTA	FTM	Pct.	Reb.	Ast.	PF	Disq.	Pts.	Avg.
62-63—St. Louis	11	204	96	41	.427	27	20	.741	86	9	31	0	102	9.3
63-64—St. Louis	12	240	83	26	.313	19	12	.632	84	24	40	0	64	5.3
64-65—St. Louis	4	145	59	21	.356	15	10	.667	67	9	19	1	52	13.0
65-66—St. Louis	10	421	170	86	.506	43	31	.721	149	28	47	2	203	20.3
66-67—St. Louis	9	369	128	48	.375	67	45	.672	169	22	36	2	141	15.7
67-68—St. Louis	6	216	75	38	.507	25	18	.720	77	14	23	0	94	15.7
68-69—Atlanta	11	442	156	69	.442	48	34	.708	178	37	48	2	172	15.6
69-70—Atlanta	9	381	110	44	.400	27	16	.593	154	29	37	1	104	11.6
70-71—Atlanta	5	229	58	23	.397	9	3	.333	104	5	17	0	49	9.8
72-73—Los Ang.	17	582	136	57	.419	49	38	.776	158	29	68	2	152	8.9

Sea.—Team	G.	Min.	FGA	FGM	Pct.	FTA	FTM	Pct.	Off.	Def.	Tot.	Ast.	PF	Dq.	Stl.	Blk.	Pts.	Avg.
								—Rebounds—									
73-74—L.A.	5	144	41	12	.293	13	6	.462	14	16	30	6	19	0	7	0	30	6.0
74-75—G.S.	14	148	23	10	.435	7	2	.286	13	36	49	7	23	0	9	4	22	1.6
Totals	113	3521	1135	475	.419	349	235	.673			1305	219	408	10	16	4	1185	10.5

NBA ALL-STAR GAME RECORD

Season—Team	Min.	FGA	FGM	Pct.	FTA	FTM	Pct.	Reb.	Ast.	PF	Disq.	Pts.
1967—St. Louis	17	5	4	.800	2	0	.000	3	3	1	0	8
1968—St. Louis	21	9	7	.778	4	1	.250	7	1	4	0	15
1970—Atlanta	15	2	2	1.000	5	1	.200	4	2	1	0	5
Totals	53	16	13	.813	11	2	.182	14	6	6	0	28

Named to NBA All-Defensive Second Team, 1969 and 1970. . . . Member of NBA championship team, 1975. . . . Named to ABL All-Star First Team, 1962. . . . Led ABL in scoring, 1963. . . . Led ABL in rebounding, 1962 and 1963. . . . Set ABL single-game scoring record with 55 points vs. Oakland, December 9, 1962. . . . Member of ABL championship team, 1963.

WILTON NORMAN CHAMBERLAIN
(Wilt)

Born August 21, 1936 at Philadelphia, Pa.   Height 7:01.   Weight 275.

High School—Philadelphia, Pa., Overbrook.

College—University of Kansas, Lawrence, Kan.

Drafted by Philadelphia on first round (territorial choice), 1959.

Philadelphia franchise moved to San Francisco, 1962.
Traded by San Francisco to Philadelphia for Paul Neumann, Connie Dierking, Lee Shaffer and cash, January 15, 1965.
Traded by Philadelphia to Los Angeles for Jerry Chambers, Archie Clark and Darrall Imhoff, July 9, 1968.
Played with Harlem Globetrotters during 1958-59 season.

—COLLEGIATE RECORD—

Year	G.	Min.	FGA	FGM	Pct.	FTA	FTM	Pct.	Reb.	Pts.	Avg.
55-56†					(Freshmen team did not play an intercollegiate schedule)						
56-57	27	....	588	275	.468	399	250	.627	510	800	29.6
57-58	21	....	482	228	.473	291	177	.608	367	633	30.1
Varsity Totals	48	....	1070	503	.470	690	427	.619	877	1433	29.9

NBA REGULAR SEASON RECORD

Sea.—Team	G.	Min.	FGA	FGM	Pct.	FTA	FTM	Pct.	Reb.	Ast.	PF	Disq.	Pts.	Avg.
59-60—Philadelphia	72	3338	2311	1065	.461	991	577	.582	1941	168	150	0	2707	37.6
60-61—Philadelphia	79	3773	2457	1251	.509	1054	531	.504	2149	148	130	0	3033	38.4
61-62—Philadelphia	80	3882	3159	1597	.505	1363	835	.613	2052	192	123	0	4029	50.4
62-63—San Francisco	80	3806	2770	1463	.528	1113	660	.593	1946	275	136	0	3586	44.8
63-64—San Francisco	80	3689	2298	1204	.524	1016	540	.531	1787	403	182	0	2948	36.9
64-65—S.F.-Phila.	73	3301	2083	1063	.510	880	408	.464	1673	250	146	0	2534	34.7
65-66—Philadelphia	79	3737	1990	1074	.540	976	501	.513	1943	414	171	0	2649	33.5
66-67—Philadelphia	81	3682	1150	785	.683	875	386	.441	1957	630	143	0	1956	24.1
67-68—Philadelphia	82	3836	1377	819	.595	932	354	.380	1952	702	160	0	1992	24.3
68-69—Los Angeles	81	3669	1099	641	.583	857	382	.446	1712	366	142	0	1664	20.5
69-70—Los Angeles	12	505	227	129	.568	157	70	.446	221	49	31	0	328	27.3
70-71—Los Angeles	82	3630	1226	668	.545	669	360	.538	1493	352	174	0	1696	20.7
71-72—Los Angeles	82	3469	764	496	.649	524	221	.422	1572	329	196	0	1213	14.8
72-73—Los Angeles	82	3542	586	426	.727	455	232	.510	1526	365	191	0	1084	13.2
Totals	1045	47859	23497	12681	.540	11862	6057	.511	23924	4643	2075	0	31419	30.1

WILT CHAMBERLAIN

NBA PLAYOFF RECORD

Sea.—Team	G.	Min.	FGA	FGM	Pct.	FTA	FTM	Pct.	Reb.	Ast.	PF	Disq.	Pts.	Avg.
59-60—Philadelphia	9	415	252	125	.496	110	49	.445	232	19	17	0	299	33.2
60-61—Philadelphia	3	144	96	45	.469	38	21	.553	69	6	10	0	111	37.0
61-62—Philadelphia	12	576	347	162	.467	151	96	.636	319	37	27	0	420	35.0
63-64—San Francisco	12	558	322	175	.543	139	66	.475	302	39	27	0	416	34.7
64-65—Philadelphia	11	536	232	123	.530	136	76	.559	299	48	29	0	322	29.3
65-66—Philadelphia	5	240	110	56	.509	68	28	.412	151	15	10	0	140	28.0
66-67—Philadelphia	15	718	228	132	.579	160	62	.388	437	135	37	0	326	21.7
67-68—Philadelphia	13	631	232	124	.534	158	60	.380	321	85	29	0	308	23.7
68-69—Los Angeles	18	832	176	96	.545	148	58	.392	444	46	56	0	250	13.9
69-70—Los Angeles	18	851	288	158	.549	202	82	.406	399	81	42	0	398	22.1
70-71—Los Angeles	12	554	187	85	.455	97	50	.515	242	53	33	0	220	18.3
71-72—Los Angeles	15	703	142	80	.563	122	60	.492	315	49	47	0	220	14.7
72-73—Los Angeles	17	801	116	64	.552	98	49	.500	383	60	48	0	177	10.4
Totals	160	7559	2728	1425	.522	1627	757	.465	3913	673	412	0	3607	22.5

NBA ALL-STAR GAME RECORD

Season—Team	Min.	FGA	FGM	Pct.	FTA	FTM	Pct.	Reb.	Ast.	PF	Disq.	Pts.
1960—Philadelphia	30	20	9	.450	7	5	.714	25	2	1	0	23
1961—Philadelphia	38	8	2	.250	15	8	.533	18	5	1	0	12
1962—Philadelphia	37	23	17	.739	16	8	.500	24	1	4	0	42
1963—San Francisco	35	11	7	.636	7	3	.429	19	0	2	0	17
1964—San Francisco	37	14	4	.286	14	11	.786	20	1	2	0	19
1965—San Francisco	31	15	9	.600	8	2	.250	16	1	4	0	20
1966—Philadelphia	25	11	8	.727	9	5	.556	9	3	2	0	21
1967—Philadelphia	39	7	6	.857	5	2	.400	22	4	1	0	14
1968—Philadelphia	25	4	3	.750	4	1	.250	7	6	2	0	7
1969—Los Angeles	27	3	2	.667	1	0	.000	12	2	2	0	4
1971—Los Angeles	18	1	1	1.000	0	0	.000	8	5	0	0	2
1972—Los Angeles	24	3	3	1.000	8	2	.250	10	3	2	0	8
1973—Los Angeles	22	2	1	.500	0	0	.000	7	3	0	0	2
Totals	.388	122	72	.590	94	47	.500	197	36	23	0	191

ABA COACHING RECORD

		Regular Season				Playoffs	
Sea.	Club	W.	L.	Pct.	Pos.	W.	L.
1973-74—San Diego		37	47	.440	T4	2	4

Named to NBA 35th Anniversary All-Time Team, 1980. . . . Elected to Naismith Memorial Basketball Hall of Fame, 1978. . . . NBA Most Valuable Player, 1960, 1966, 1967, 1968. . . . Named to NBA All-Star First Team, 1960, 1961, 1962, 1964, 1966, 1967, 1968. . . . NBA All-Star Second Team, 1963, 1965, 1972. . . . NBA Rookie of the Year, 1960. . . . NBA All-Defensive First Team, 1972 and 1973. . . . NBA Playoff MVP, 1972. . . . Only NBA player ever to score over 4,000 points in a season. . . . Holds NBA single game records for most points, 100, most field-goals attempted, 63, most field-goals made, 36, and shares record for most free-throws made, 28, vs. New York at Hershey, Pa., March 2, 1962. . . . Holds NBA record for most consecutive field goals, 35, February 17-28, 1967. . . . Holds NBA single game record for most consecutive field goals, 18, vs. New York at Boston, November 27, 1963, and vs. Baltimore at Pittsburgh, February 24, 1967. . . . Holds NBA single game record for most free throws attempted, 34, vs. St. Louis, February 22, 1962. . . . Holds NBA single game record for most rebounds, 55, vs. Boston, November 24, 1960. . . . Holds NBA records for most points, 59, most field-goal attempts, 37, and most field-goals made, 22, in one half, vs. New York at Hershey, Pa., March 2, 1962. . . . Holds NBA record for most field-goals attempted in one quarter, 21, vs. New York at Hershey, Pa., March 2, 1962. . . . Holds NBA career records for most free-throw attempts, most rebounds and highest scoring average. . . . NBA all-time playoff leader in free-throw attempts. . . . Holds NBA playoff game record for most rebounds, 41, vs. Boston, April 5, 1967. . . . Shares NBA playoff game record for most field goals, 24, vs. Syracuse, March 14, 1960. . . . Holds NBA championship series game record for most rebounds in one half, 26, vs. San Francisco, April 16, 1967. . . . Shares NBA championship series record for most free-throw attempts in one quarter, 11, vs. San Francisco, April 16, 1967. . . . NBA All-Star Game MVP, 1960. . . . Holds NBA All-Star Game career records for most rebounds. . . . Holds NBA All-Star Game records for most points in one game, 42, in 1962; most field goals made in one game, 17, in 1962; most free throws attempted in one game, 16, in 1962; most points in one half, 23, in 1962, and most field goals made in one half, 10, in 1962. . . . Shares NBA All-Star Game record for most rebounds in one half, 16, in 1960. . . . Member of NBA championship teams, 1967 and 1972. . . . Led NBA in scoring, 1960, 1961, 1962, 1963, 1964, 1965, 1966. . . . Led NBA in rebounding, 1960, 1961, 1962, 1963, 1966, 1967, 1968, 1969, 1971, 1972, 1973. . . . Led NBA in field-goal percentage, 1961, 1963, 1965, 1966, 1967, 1968, 1969, 1972, 1973. . . . Led NBA in assists, 1968. . . . Named to THE SPORTING NEWS All-America First Team, 1958.

ROBERT JOSEPH COUSY
(Bob)

Born August 9, 1928 at New York, N. Y.   Height 6:01.   Weight 175.
High School—Queens, N. Y., Andrew Jackson.
College—Holy Cross College, Worcester, Mass.
Drafted by Tri-Cities on first round, 1950.

Traded by Tri-Cities to Chicago for Gene Vance, 1950.
NBA rights drawn out of a hat by Boston for $8,500 in dispersal of Chicago franchise, 1950.
Traded by Boston to Cincinnati for Bill Dinwiddie, November 18, 1969.

—COLLEGIATE RECORD—

Year	G.	Min.	FGA	FGM	Pct.	FTA	FTM	Pct.	Reb.	Pts.	Avg.
46-47	30	....	....	91	....	....	45	....	....	227	7.6
47-48	30	....	....	207	....	108	72	.667	....	486	16.2
48-49	27	....	....	195	....	134	90	.672	....	480	17.8
49-50	30	....	659	216	.328	199	150	.754	....	582	19.4
Totals	117	....	....	709		....	357		....	1775	15.2

NBA REGULAR SEASON RECORD

Sea.—Team	G.	Min.	FGA	FGM	Pct.	FTA	FTM	Pct.	Reb.	Ast.	PF	Disq.	Pts.	Avg.
50-51—Boston	69	....	1138	401	.352	365	276	.756	474	341	185	2	1078	15.6
51-52—Boston	66	2681	1388	512	.369	506	409	.808	421	441	190	5	1433	21.7
52-53—Boston	71	2945	1320	464	.352	587	479	.816	449	547	227	4	1407	19.8
53-54—Boston	72	2857	1262	486	.385	522	411	.787	394	518	201	3	1383	19.2
54-55—Boston	71	2747	1316	522	.397	570	460	.807	424	557	165	1	1504	21.2
55-56—Boston	72	2767	1223	440	.360	564	476	.844	492	642	206	2	1356	18.8
56-57—Boston	64	2364	1264	478	.378	442	363	.821	309	478	134	0	1319	20.6
57-58—Boston	65	2222	1262	445	.353	326	277	.850	322	463	136	1	1167	18.0
58-59—Boston	65	2403	1260	484	.384	385	329	.855	359	557	135	0	1297	20.0
59-60—Boston	75	2588	1481	568	.383	403	319	.791	352	715	146	2	1455	19.4
60-61—Boston	76	2468	1382	513	.371	452	352	.779	331	587	196	0	1378	18.1
61-62—Boston	75	2114	1181	462	.391	333	251	.754	261	584	135	0	1175	15.7
62-63—Boston	76	1975	988	392	.397	298	219	.735	193	515	175	0	1003	13.2
69-70—Cincinnati	7	34	3	1	.333	3	3	1.000	5	10	11	0	5	0.7
Totals	924	....	16468	6168	.375	5756	4624	.803	4786	6955	2242	20	16960	18.4

NBA PLAYOFF RECORD

Sea.—Team	G.	Min.	FGA	FGM	Pct.	FTA	FTM	Pct.	Reb.	Ast.	PF	Disq.	Pts.	Avg.
50-51—Boston	2	....	42	9	.214	12	10	.833	15	12	8	...	28	14.0
51-52—Boston	3	138	65	26	.400	44	41	.932	12	19	13	1	93	31.0
52-53—Boston	6	270	120	46	.383	73	61	.836	25	37	21	0	153	25.5
53-54—Boston	6	260	116	33	.284	75	60	.800	32	38	20	0	126	21.0
54-55—Boston	7	299	139	53	.381	48	46	.958	43	65	26	0	152	21.7
55-56—Boston	3	124	56	28	.500	25	23	.920	24	26	4	0	79	26.3
56-57—Boston	10	440	207	67	.324	91	68	.747	61	93	27	0	202	20.2
57-58—Boston	11	457	196	67	.342	75	64	.853	71	82	20	0	198	18.0
58-59—Boston	11	460	221	72	.326	94	70	.745	76	119	28	0	214	19.5
59-60—Boston	13	468	262	80	.305	51	39	.765	48	116	27	0	199	15.3
60-61—Boston	10	337	147	50	.340	88	67	.761	43	91	33	1	167	16.7
61-62—Boston	14	474	241	86	.357	76	52	.684	64	123	43	0	224	16.0
62-63—Boston	13	413	204	72	.353	47	39	.830	32	116	44	2	183	14.1
Totals	109	....	2016	689	.326	799	640	.801	546	937	314	4	2018	18.5

NBA ALL-STAR GAME RECORD

Season—Team	Min.	FGA	FGM	Pct.	FTA	FTM	Pct.	Reb.	Ast.	PF	Disq.	Pts.
1951—Boston	....	12	2	.167	5	4	.800	9	8	3	0	8
1952—Boston	33	14	4	.286	2	1	.500	4	13	3	0	9
1953—Boston	36	11	4	.364	7	7	1.000	5	3	1	0	15
1954—Boston	34	15	6	.400	8	8	1.000	11	4	1	0	20
1955—Boston	35	14	7	.500	7	6	.857	9	5	1	0	20
1956—Boston	24	8	2	.250	4	3	.750	7	2	6	1	7
1957—Boston	28	14	4	.286	2	2	1.000	5	7	0	0	10
1958—Boston	31	20	8	.400	6	4	.667	5	10	0	0	20
1959—Boston	32	8	4	.500	6	5	.833	5	4	0	0	13
1960—Boston	26	7	1	.143	0	0	.000	5	8	2	0	2
1961—Boston	33	11	2	.182	0	0	.000	3	8	6	1	4
1962—Boston	31	13	4	.308	4	3	.750	6	8	2	0	11
1963—Boston	25	11	4	.364	0	0	.000	4	6	2	0	8
Totals	....	158	52	.329	51	43	.843	78	86	27	2	147

COLLEGIATE COACHING RECORD

		Regular Season			
Sea.	Club	W.	L.	Pct.	Pos.
1963-64—Boston College		10	11	.455	...
1964-65—Boston College		22	7	.759	...
1965-66—Boston College		21	5	.808	...
1966-67—Boston College		23	3	.885	...
1967-68—Boston College		17	8	.680	...
1968-69—Boston College		24	4	.857	
Totals (6 seasons)		117	38	.755	

NOTE: Cousy guided Boston College to NIT in 1965, 1966 and 1969 and to NCAA Tournament in 1967 and 1968.

NBA COACHING RECORD

		Regular Season						Regular Season			
Sea.	Club	W.	L.	Pct.	Pos.	Sea.	Club	W.	L.	Pct.	Pos.
1969-70—Cincinnati		36	46	.439	5†	1972-73—K.C.-Omaha		36	46	.439	4§
1970-71—Cincinnati		33	49	.402	3‡	1973-74—K.C.-Omaha		6	16	.375	...§
1971-72—Cincinnati		30	52	.366	3‡	Totals (5 seasons)		141	209	.403	

†Eastern Division. ‡Central Division. §Midwest Division.

BOB COUSY

Elected to Naismith Memorial Basketball Hall of Fame, 1970. . . . Named to NBA 25th Anniversary All-Time Team, 1970, and 35th Anniversary All-Time Team, 1980. . . . NBA Most Valuable Player, 1957. . . . Named to NBA All-Star First Team, 1952, 1953, 1954, 1955, 1956, 1957, 1958, 1959, 1960, 1961. . . . NBA All-Star Second Team, 1962 and 1963. . . . Holds NBA record for most assists in one half, 19, vs. Minneapolis, February 27, 1959. . . . Holds NBA playoff game records for most free-throw attempts, 32, and most free throws made, 30, vs. Syracuse, March 21, 1953. . . . Holds NBA playoff game record for most points in an overtime period, 12, vs. Syracuse, March 17, 1954. . . . Shares NBA championship series record for most assists in one quarter, 8, vs. St. Louis, April 9, 1957. . . . NBA All-Star Game MVP, 1954 and 1957. . . . Member of NBA championship teams, 1957, 1959, 1960, 1961, 1962, 1963. . . . Led NBA in assists, 1953, 1954, 1955, 1956, 1957, 1958, 1959, 1960. . . . Named to THE SPORTING NEWS All-America First Team, 1950. . . . Named to THE SPORTING NEWS All-America Second Team, 1949. . . . Member of NCAA championship team, 1947. . . . Commissioner of American Soccer League, 1975 through mid-1980 season.

DAVID WILLIAM COWENS
(Dave)

Born October 25, 1948 at Newport, Ky.   Height 6:09.   Weight 230.

High School—Newport, Ky., Catholic.

College—Florida State University, Tallahassee, Fla.

Drafted by Boston on first round, 1970 (4th pick).

Traded by Boston to Milwaukee for Quinn Buckner, September 9, 1982.

—COLLEGIATE RECORD—

Year	G.	Min.	FGA	FGM	Pct.	FTA	FTM	Pct.	Reb.	Pts.	Avg.
66-67†	18	....	208	105	.505	90	49	.544	357	259	14.4
67-68	27	....	383	206	.538	131	96	.733	456	508	18.8
68-69	25	....	384	202	.526	164	104	.634	437	508	20.3
69-70	26	....	355	174	.490	169	115	.680	447	463	17.8
Varsity Totals	78	....	1122	582	.519	464	315	.679	1340	1479	19.0

NBA REGULAR SEASON RECORD

Sea.—Team	G.	Min.	FGA	FGM	Pct.	FTA	FTM	Pct.	Reb.	Ast.	PF	Disq.	Pts.	Avg.
70-71—Boston	81	3076	1302	550	.422	373	273	.732	1216	228	350	15	1373	17.0
71-72—Boston	79	3186	1357	657	.484	243	175	.720	1203	245	314	10	1489	18.8
72-73—Boston	82	3425	1637	740	.452	262	204	.779	1329	333	311	7	1684	20.5

Sea.—Team	G.	Min.	FGA	FGM	Pct.	FTA	FTM	Pct.	Off.	Def.	Tot.	Ast.	PF	Dq.	Stl.	Blk.	Pts.	Avg.
73-74—Boston	80	3352	1475	645	.437	274	228	.832	264	993	1257	354	294	7	95	101	1518	19.0
74-75—Boston	65	2632	1199	569	.475	244	191	.783	229	729	958	296	243	7	87	73	1329	20.4
75-76—Boston	78	3101	1305	611	.468	340	257	.756	335	911	1246	325	314	10	94	71	1479	19.0
76-77—Boston	50	1888	756	328	.434	198	162	.818	147	550	697	248	181	7	46	49	818	16.4
77-78—Boston	77	3215	1220	598	.490	284	239	.842	248	830	1078	351	297	5	102	67	1435	18.6
78-79—Boston	68	2517	1010	488	.483	187	151	.807	152	500	652	242	263	16	76	51	1127	16.6
79-80—Boston	66	2159	932	422	.453	122	95	.779	126	408	534	206	216	2	69	61	940	14.2
82-83—Milwaukee	40	1014	306	136	.444	63	52	.825	73	201	274	82	137	4	30	15	324	8.1
Totals	766	29565	12499	5744	.460	2590	2027	.783			10444	2910	2920	90	599	488	13516	17.6

Three-Point Field Goals: 1979-80, 1-for-12 (.083). 1982-83, 0-for-2. Totals, 1-for-14 (.071).

NBA PLAYOFF RECORD

Sea.—Team	G.	Min.	FGA	FGM	Pct.	FTA	FTM	Pct.	Reb.	Ast.	PF	Disq.	Pts.	Avg.
71-72—Boston	11	441	156	71	.455	47	28	.596	152	33	50	2	170	15.5
72-73—Boston	13	598	273	129	.473	41	27	.659	216	48	54	2	285	21.9

Sea.—Team	G.	Min.	FGA	FGM	Pct.	FTA	FTM	Pct.	Off.	Def.	Tot.	Ast.	PF	Dq.	Stl.	Blk.	Pts.	Avg.
73-74—Boston	18	772	370	161	.435	59	47	.797	60	180	240	66	85	2	21	17	369	20.5
74-75—Boston	11	479	236	101	.428	26	23	.885	49	132	181	46	50	2	18	6	225	20.5
75-76—Boston	18	798	341	156	.457	87	66	.759	87	209	296	83	85	4	22	13	378	21.0
76-77—Boston	9	379	148	66	.446	22	17	.773	29	105	134	36	37	3	8	13	149	16.6
79-80—Boston	9	301	103	49	.476	11	10	.909	18	48	66	21	37	0	9	7	108	12.0
Totals	89	3768	1627	733	.451	293	218	.744			1285	333	398	15	78	56	1684	18.9

Three-Point Field Goals: 1979-80, 0-for-2.

NBA ALL-STAR GAME RECORD

Season—Team	Min.	FGA	FGM	Pct.	FTA	FTM	Pct.	Reb.	Ast.	PF	Disq.	Pts.
1972—Boston	32	12	5	.417	5	4	.800	20	1	4	0	14
1973—Boston	30	15	7	.467	1	1	1.000	13	1	2	0	15

Season—Team	Min.	FGA	FGM	Pct.	FTA	FTM	Pct.	Off.	Def.	Tot.	Ast.	PF	Dq.	Stl.	Blk.	Pts.
1974—Boston	26	10	5	.500	3	1	.333	6	6	12	1	3	0	0	1	11
1975—Boston	15	7	3	.429	0	0	.000	0	6	6	3	4	0	1	0	6
1976—Boston	23	13	6	.462	5	4	.800	8	8	16	1	3	0	1	0	16
1977—Boston					Selected—Injured, Did Not Play											
1978—Boston	28	9	7	.778	0	0	.000	6	8	14	5	5	0	2	0	14
Totals	154	66	33	.500	14	10	.714			81	12	21	0	4	1	76

		Regular Season			
Sea.	Club	W.	L.	Pct.	Pos.
1978-79—Boston		27	41	.397	5†

†Atlantic Division.

CBA COACHING RECORD

		Regular Season			
Sea.	Club	W.	L.	Pct.	Pos.
1984-85—Bay State		20	28	.417	6

NBA Most Valuable Player, 1973. . . . Named to NBA All-Star Second Team, 1973, 1975, 1976. . . . NBA All-Defensive First Team, 1976. . . . NBA All-Defensive Second Team, 1975 and 1980. . . . NBA Co-Rookie of the Year, 1971. . . . NBA All-Rookie Team, 1971. . . . NBA All-Star Game MVP, 1973. . . . Member of NBA championship teams, 1974 and 1976. . . . Named to THE SPORTING NEWS All-America Second Team, 1970.

ROBERT EDRIS DAVIES
(Bob)

Born January 15, 1920 at Harrisburg, Pa. Height 6:01. Weight 175.

High School—Harrisburg, Pa., John Harris.

Colleges—Franklin & Marshall College, Lancaster, Pa., and

Seton Hall University, South Orange, N.J.

Signed as free agent by Rochester NBL, 1945.

In military service during 1942-43, 1943-44 and 1944-45 seasons.
Played with Great Lakes (Ill.) Naval Training Station during 1942-43 season.
Led team in scoring with 269 points (114 field goals and 41 free throws).
Played in American Basketball League with Brooklyn, 1943-44, and New York, 1944-45.

—COLLEGIATE RECORD—

Year	G.	Min.	FGA	FGM	Pct.	FTA	FTM	Pct.	Reb.	Pts.	Avg.
38-39†					Statistics Unavailable						
39-40	18	....	....	78	....	....	56	....	....	212	11.8
40-41	22	....	....	91	....	....	42	....	....	224	10.2
41-42	19	....	....	81	....	....	63	....	....	225	11.8
Varsity Totals	59	....	....	250	....	....	161	....	....	661	11.2

NBL AND NBA REGULAR SEASON RECORD

Sea.—Team	G.	Min.	FGA	FGM	Pct.	FTA	FTM	Pct.	Reb.	Ast.	PF	Disq.	Pts.	Avg.
45-46—Roch.-NBL	27	....	....	86	....	103	70	.680	....	....	85	..	242	9.0
46-47—Roch.-NBL	32	....	....	166	....	166	130	.783	....	....	90	..	462	14.4
47-48—Roch.-NBL	48	....	....	176	....	161	121	.752	....	....	111	..	473	9.9
48-49—Rochester	60	....	871	317	.364	348	270	.776	....	321	197	..	904	15.1
49-50—Rochester	64	....	887	317	.357	347	261	.752	....	294	187	..	895	14.0
50-51—Rochester	63	....	877	326	.372	381	303	.795	197	287	208	7	955	15.2
51-52—Rochester	65	2394	990	379	.383	379	294	.776	189	390	269	10	1052	16.2
52-53—Rochester	66	2216	880	339	.385	466	351	.753	195	280	261	7	1029	15.6
53-54—Rochester	72	2137	777	288	.371	433	311	.718	194	323	224	4	887	12.3
54-55—Rochester	72	1870	785	326	.415	293	220	.751	205	155	220	2	872	12.1
Totals	569	....	....	2720	....	3077	2331	.758	....	....	1852	..	7771	13.7

NBL AND NBA PLAYOFF RECORD

Sea.—Team	G.	Min.	FGA	FGM	Pct.	FTA	FTM	Pct.	Reb.	Ast.	PF	Disq.	Pts.	Avg.
45-46—Roch.-NBL	7	....	...	28	....	41	30	.732	....	....	13	..	86	12.3
46-47—Roch.-NBL	11	....	....	54	....	63	43	.683	....	....	30	..	151	13.7
47-48—Roch.-NBL	11	....	....	56	....	64	49	.766	....	....	26	..	161	14.6
48-49—Rochester	4	....	51	19	.373	13	10	.769	....	13	12	..	48	12.0
49-50—Rochester	2	....	17	4	.235	8	7	.875	....	9	11	..	15	7.5
50-51—Rochester	14	....	234	79	.338	80	64	.800	43	75	45	1	222	15.9
51-52—Rochester	6	233	92	37	.402	55	45	.818	13	28	18	0	119	19.8
52-53—Rochester	3	91	29	6	.207	20	14	.700	4	14	11	0	26	8.7
53-54—Rochester	6	172	52	17	.327	23	17	.739	12	14	16	0	51	8.5
54-55—Rochester	3	75	33	11	.333	4	3	.750	6	9	11	0	25	8.3
Totals	67	....	....	311	....	371	282	.752	....	....	193	..	904	13.5

NBA ALL-STAR GAME RECORD

Season—Team	Min.	FGA	FGM	Pct.	FTA	FTM	Pct.	Reb.	Ast.	PF	Disq.	Pts.
1951—Rochester	....	6	4	.667	5	5	1.000	5	5	3	0	13
1952—Rochester	27	11	4	.364	0	0	.000	0	5	4	0	8
1953—Rochester	17	7	3	.429	6	3	.500	3	2	2	0	9
1954—Rochester	31	16	8	.500	3	2	.667	5	5	4	0	18
Totals	....	40	19	.475	14	10	.714	13	17	13	0	48

COLLEGIATE COACHING RECORD

		Regular Season			
Sea.	Club	W.	L.	Pct.	Pos.
1946-47—Seton Hall		24	3	.888	..
1955-56—Gettysburg		..	..	..	..
1956-57—Gettysburg		..	..	..	..

Named to NBA 25th Anniversary All-Time Team, 1970. . . . Elected to Naismith Memorial Basketball Hall of Fame, 1969. . . . NBA All-Star First Team, 1949, 1950, 1951, 1952. . . . NBA All-Star Second Team, 1953. . . . Led NBA in assists, 1949. . . . Member of NBA championship team, 1951. . . . NBL All-Star First Team, 1947 and 1948. . . . NBL Most Valuable Player, 1947. . . . Member of NBL championship team, 1946. . . . BAA All-Star First Team, 1949.

DAVID ALBERT DeBUSSCHERE
(Dave)

Born October 16, 1940 at Detroit, Mich. Height 6:06. Weight 235.

High School—Detroit, Mich., Austin Catholic.

College—University of Detroit, Detroit, Mich.

Drafted by Detroit on first round (territorial choice), 1962.

Traded by Detroit to New York for Walt Bellamy and Howard Komives, December 19, 1968.

—COLLEGIATE RECORD—

Year	G.	Min.	FGA	FGM	Pct.	FTA	FTM	Pct.	Reb.	Pts.	Avg.
58-59†	15	....	306	144	.471	101	68	.673	305	356	23.7
59-60	27	....	665	288	.433	196	115	.587	540	691	25.6
60-61	27	....	636	256	.403	155	86	.555	514	598	22.1
61-62	26	....	616	267	.433	242	162	.669	498	696	26.8
Varsity Totals	80	....	1917	811	.423	593	363	.612	1552	1985	24.8

NBA REGULAR SEASON RECORD

Sea.—Team	G.	Min.	FGA	FGM	Pct.	FTA	FTM	Pct.	Reb.	Ast.	PF	Disq.	Pts.	Avg.
62-63—Detroit	80	2352	944	406	.430	287	206	.718	694	207	247	2	1018	12.7
63-64—Detroit	15	304	133	52	.391	43	25	.581	105	23	32	1	129	8.6
64-65—Detroit	79	2769	1196	508	.425	437	306	.700	874	253	242	5	1322	16.7
65-66—Detroit	79	2696	1284	524	.408	378	249	.659	916	209	252	5	1297	16.4
66-67—Detroit	78	2897	1278	531	.415	512	361	.705	924	216	297	7	1423	18.2
67-68—Detroit	80	3125	1295	573	.442	435	289	.664	1081	181	304	3	1435	17.9
68-69—Det.-N. Y.	76	2943	1140	506	.444	328	229	.698	888	191	290	6	1241	16.3
69-70—New York	79	2627	1082	488	.451	256	176	.688	790	194	244	2	1152	14.6
70-71—New York	81	2891	1243	523	.421	312	217	.696	901	220	237	2	1263	15.6
71-72—New York	80	3072	1218	520	.427	265	193	.728	901	291	219	1	1233	15.4
72-73—New York	77	2827	1224	532	.435	260	194	.746	787	259	215	1	1258	16.3

Sea.—Team	G.	Min.	FGA	FGM	Pct.	FTA	FTM	Pct.	Off.	Def.	Tot.	Ast.	PF	Dq.	Stl.	Blk.	Pts.	Avg.
									Rebounds									
73-74—New York	71	2899	1212	559	.461	217	164	.756	134	623	757	253	222	2	67	39	1282	18.1
Totals	875	31202	13249	5722	.432	3730	2609	.699			9618	2497	2801	37			14053	16.1

NBA PLAYOFF RECORD

Sea.—Team	G.	Min.	FGA	FGM	Pct.	FTA	FTM	Pct.	Reb.	Ast.	PF	Disq.	Pts.	Avg.
62-63—Detroit	4	159	59	25	.424	44	30	.682	63	6	14	1	80	20.0
67-68—Detroit	6	263	106	45	.425	45	26	.578	97	13	23	0	116	19.3
68-69—New York	10	419	174	61	.351	50	41	.820	148	33	43	0	163	16.3
69-70—New York	19	701	309	130	.421	68	45	.662	220	46	63	1	305	16.1
70-71—New York	12	488	202	84	.416	44	29	.659	156	22	40	1	197	16.4
71-72—New York	16	616	242	109	.450	64	48	.750	193	37	51	2	266	16.6
72-73—New York	17	632	265	117	.442	40	31	.775	179	58	57	0	265	15.6

Sea.—Team	G.	Min.	FGA	FGM	Pct.	FTA	FTM	Pct.	Off.	Def.	Tot.	Ast.	PF	Dq.	Stl.	Blk.	Pts.	Avg.
									Rebounds									
73-74—New York	12	404	166	63	380	29	18	.621	25	74	99	38	36	0	7	4	144	12.0
Totals	96	3682	1523	634	416	384	268	.698			1155	253	327	5			1536	16.0

NBA ALL-STAR GAME RECORD

Season—Team	Min.	FGA	FGM	Pct.	FTA	FTM	Pct.	Reb.	Ast.	PF	Disq.	Pts.
1966—Detroit	22	14	1	.071	2	2	1.000	6	1	1	0	4
1967—Detroit	25	17	11	.647	0	0	.000	6	0	1	0	22
1968—Detroit	12	3	0	.000	0	0	.000	4	0	1	0	0
1970—New York	14	10	5	.500	0	0	.000	7	2	1	0	10
1971—New York	19	7	4	.571	0	0	.000	7	3	3	0	8
1972—New York	26	8	4	.500	0	0	.000	11	0	2	0	8
1973—New York	25	8	4	.500	2	1	.500	7	2	1	0	9

Season—Team	Min.	FGA	FGM	Pct.	FTA	FTM	Pct.	Off.	Def.	Tot.	Ast.	PF	Dq.	Stl.	Blk.	Pts.
								Rebounds								
1974—New York	24	14	8	.571	0	0	.000	2	1	3	3	2	0	1	0	16
Totals	167	81	37	.457	4	3	.750			51	11	12	0			77

NBA COACHING RECORD

Sea. Club	Regular Season W.	L.	Pct.	Pos.	Sea. Club	Regular Season W.	L.	Pct.	Pos.
1964-65—Detroit	29	40	.420	4†	1966-67—Detroit	28	45	.384	5†
1965-66—Detroit	22	58	.275	5†	Totals (3 seasons)	79	143	.356	

†Western Division.

Elected to Naismith Memorial Basketball Hall of Fame, 1982. . . . Named to NBA All-Star Second Team, 1969. . . . NBA All-Defensive First Team, 1969, 1970, 1971, 1972, 1973, 1974. . . . Holds NBA All-Star Game record for most field goals made in one quarter, 8, in 1967. . . . Member of NBA championship teams, 1970 and 1973. . . . Youngest coach (24) in NBA history. . . . ABA Commissioner during 1975-76 season. . . . Played major league baseball as a pitcher with the Chicago White Sox, 1962 and 1963 (had 3-4 record in 36 games).

JULIUS WINFIELD ERVING II
(Dr. J)

Born February 22, 1950 at Roosevelt, N. Y.   Height 6:07.   Weight 210.

High School—Roosevelt, N. Y.

College—University of Massachusetts, Amherst, Mass.

Drafted by Milwaukee on first round, 1972 (12th pick).

Signed as an undergraduate free agent by Virginia ABA, April 6, 1971.
Traded by Virginia with Willie Sojourner to New York for George Carter, draft rights to Kermit Washington and cash, August 1, 1973.
Entered NBA with New York Nets, 1976.
Sold by Nets to Philadelphia, October 20, 1976.

—COLLEGIATE RECORD—

Year	G.	Min.	FGA	FGM	Pct.	FTA	FTM	Pct.	Reb.	Pts.	Avg.
68-69†	15	....	216	112	.519	81	49	.605	214	273	18.2
69-70	25	969	468	238	.509	230	167	.726	522	643	25.7
70-71	27	1029	609	286	.470	206	155	.752	527	727	26.9
Varsity Totals	52	1998	1077	524	.487	436	322	.739	1049	1370	26.3

ABA REGULAR SEASON RECORD

Sea.—Team	G.	Min.	2-Point FGM	FGA	Pct.	3-Point FGM	FGA	Pct.	FTM	FTA	Pct.	Reb.	Ast.	Pts.	Avg.
1971-72—Virginia	84	3513	907	1810	.501	3	16	.188	467	627	.745	1319	335	2290	27.3
1972-73—Virginia	71	2993	889	1780	.499	5	24	.208	475	612	.776	867	298	2268	31.9
1973-74—New York	84	3398	897	1742	.515	17	43	.395	454	593	.766	899	434	2299	27.4
1974-75—New York	84	3402	885	1719	.515	29	87	.333	486	608	.799	914	462	2343	27.9
1975-76—New York	84	3244	915	1770	.517	34	103	.330	530	662	.801	925	423	2462	29.3
Totals	407	16550	4493	8821	.509	88	273	.322	2412	3102	.778	4924	1952	11662	28.7

ABA PLAYOFF RECORD

Sea.—Team	G.	Min.	2-Point FGM	FGA	Pct.	3-Point FGM	FGA	Pct.	FTM	FTA	Pct.	Reb.	Ast.	Pts.	Avg.
71-72—Virginia	11	504	146	280	521	1	4	.250	71	85	.835	224	72	366	33.3
72-73—Virginia	5	219	59	109	.541	0	3	.000	30	40	.750	45	16	148	29.6
73-74—New York	14	579	156	294	.531	5	11	.455	63	85	.741	135	67	390	27.9
74-75—New York	5	211	55	113	.487	0	8	.000	27	32	.844	49	28	137	27.4
75-76—New York	13	551	156	286	.545	4	14	.286	127	158	.804	164	64	451	34.7
Totals	48	2064	572	1082	.529	10	40	.250	318	400	.795	617	247	1492	31.1

ABA ALL-STAR GAME RECORD

Sea.—Team	Min.	2-Point FGM	FGA	Pct.	3-Point FGM	FGA	Pct.	FTM	FTA	Pct.	Reb.	Ast.	Pts.	Avg.
1972—Virginia	25	9	15	.600	0	0	.000	2	2	1.000	6	3	20	20.0
1973—Virginia	30	8	16	.500	0	0	.000	6	8	.750	5	1	22	22.0
1974—New York	27	6	15	.400	0	0	.000	2	2	1.000	11	8	14	14.0
1975—New York	27	5	11	.455	1	1	1.000	8	10	.800	7	7	21	21.0
1976—New York	25	9	12	.750	0	1	.000	5	7	.714	7	5	23	23.0
Totals	134	37	69	.536	1	2	.500	23	29	.793	36	24	100	20.0

NBA REGULAR SEASON RECORD

Sea.—Team	G.	Min.	FGA	FGM	Pct.	FTA	FTM	Pct.	Rebounds Off.	Def.	Tot.	Ast.	PF	Dq.	Stl.	Blk.	Pts.	Avg.
76-77—Philadelphia	82	2940	1373	685	.499	515	400	.777	192	503	695	306	251	1	159	113	1770	21.6
77-78—Philadelphia	74	2429	1217	611	.502	362	306	.845	179	302	481	279	207	0	135	97	1528	20.6
78-79—Philadelphia	78	2802	1455	715	.491	501	373	.745	198	366	564	357	207	0	133	100	1803	23.1
79-80—Philadelphia	78	2812	1614	838	.519	534	420	.787	215	361	576	355	208	0	170	140	2100	26.9
80-81—Philadelphia	82	2874	1524	794	.521	536	422	.787	244	413	657	364	233	0	173	147	2014	24.6
81-82—Philadelphia	81	2789	1428	780	.546	539	411	.763	220	337	557	319	229	1	161	141	1974	24.4
82-83—Philadelphia	72	2421	1170	605	.517	435	330	.759	173	318	491	263	202	1	112	131	1542	21.4
83-84—Philadelphia	77	2683	1324	678	.512	483	364	.754	190	342	532	309	217	3	141	139	1727	22.4
84-85—Philadelphia	78	2535	1236	610	.494	442	338	.765	172	242	414	233	199	0	135	109	1561	20.0
85-86—Philadelphia	74	2474	1085	521	.480	368	289	.785	169	201	370	248	196	3	113	82	1340	18.1
86-87—Philadelphia	60	1918	850	400	.471	235	191	.813	115	149	264	191	137	0	76	94	1005	16.8
Totals	836	28677	14276	7237	.507	4950	3844	.777	2067	3534	5601	3224	2286	9	1508	1293	18364	22.0

Three-Point Field Goals: 1979-80, 4-for-20 (.200). 1980-81, 4-for-18 (.222). 1981-82, 3-for-11 (.273). 1982-83, 2-for-7 (.286). 1983-84, 7-for-21 (.333). 1984-85, 3-for-14 (.214). 1985-86, 9-for-32 (.281). 1986-87, 14-for-53 (.264). Totals, 46-for-176 (.261).

NBA PLAYOFF RECORD

Sea.—Team	G.	Min.	FGA	FGM	Pct.	FTA	FTM	Pct.	Off.	Def.	Tot.	Ast.	PF	Dq.	Stl.	Blk.	Pts.	Avg.
								—Rebounds—										
76-77—Philadelphia	19	758	390	204	.523	134	110	.821	41	81	122	85	45	0	41	23	518	27.3
77-78—Philadelphia	10	358	180	88	.489	56	42	.750	40	57	97	40	30	0	15	18	218	21.8
78-79—Philadelphia	9	372	172	89	.517	67	51	.761	29	41	70	53	22	0	18	17	229	25.4
79-80—Philadelphia	18	694	338	165	.488	136	108	.794	31	105	136	79	56	0	36	37	440	24.4
80-81—Philadelphia	16	592	301	143	.475	107	81	.757	52	62	114	54	54	0	22	41	367	22.9
81-82—Philadelphia	21	780	324	168	.519	165	124	.752	57	99	156	99	55	0	37	37	461	22.0
82-83—Philadelphia	13	493	211	95	.450	68	49	.721	32	67	99	44	42	1	15	27	239	18.4
83-84—Philadelphia	5	194	76	36	.474	22	19	.864	9	23	32	25	14	0	8	6	91	18.2
84-85—Philadelphia	13	434	187	84	.449	63	54	.857	29	44	73	48	34	0	25	11	222	17.1
85-86—Philadelphia	12	433	180	81	.450	65	48	.738	26	44	70	50	32	0	11	16	212	17.7
86-87—Philadelphia	5	180	82	34	.415	25	21	.840	14	11	25	17	19	0	7	6	91	18.2
Totals	141	5288	2441	1187	.486	908	707	.779	360	634	994	594	403	1	235	239	3088	21.9

Three-Point Field Goals: 1979-80, 2-for-9 (.222). 1980-81, 0-for-1. 1981-82, 1-for-6 (.167). 1982-83, 0-for-1. 1983-84, 0-for-1. 1984-85, 0-for-1. 1985-86, 2-for-11 (.182). Totals, 5-for-30 (.167).

NBA ALL-STAR GAME RECORD

Season—Team	Min.	FGA	FGM	Pct.	FTA	FTM	Pct.	Off.	Def.	Tot.	Ast.	PF	Dq.	Stl.	Blk.	Pts.
								—Rebounds—								
1977—Philadelphia	30	20	12	.600	6	6	1.000	5	7	12	3	2	0	4	1	30
1978—Philadelphia	27	14	3	.214	12	10	.833	2	6	8	3	1	0	0	1	16
1979—Philadelphia	39	22	10	.455	12	9	.750	6	2	8	5	4	0	2	0	29
1980—Philadelphia	20	12	4	.333	4	3	.750	2	3	5	2	5	0	2	1	11
1981—Philadelphia	29	15	6	.400	7	6	.857	3	0	3	2	2	0	2	1	18
1982—Philadelphia	32	16	7	.438	4	2	.500	3	5	8	2	4	0	1	2	16
1983—Philadelphia	28	19	11	.579	3	3	1.000	3	3	6	3	1	0	1	2	25
1984—Philadelphia	36	22	14	.636	8	6	.750	4	4	8	5	4	0	2	2	34
1985—Philadelphia	23	15	5	.333	2	2	1.000	2	2	4	3	3	0	1	0	12
1986—Philadelphia	19	10	4	.400	2	0	.000	1	3	4	2	2	0	2	0	8
1987—Philadelphia	33	13	9	.692	3	3	1.000	3	1	4	5	3	0	1	1	22
Totals	316	178	85	.478	63	50	.794	34	36	70	35	31	0	18	11	221

Three-Point Field Goals: 1987, 1-for-1 (1.000).

COMBINED ABA AND NBA REGULAR SEASON RECORDS

	G.	Min.	FGA	FGM	Pct.	FTA	FTM	Pct.	Off.	Def.	Tot.	Ast.	PF	Dq.	Stl.	Blk.	Pts.	Avg.
								—Rebounds—										
Totals.................	1243	45227	23370	11818	.506	8052	6256	.777	3689	6836	10525	5176	3494	na	2272	1941	30026	24.2

Named to NBA 35th Anniversary All-Time Team, 1980. . . . Named NBA Most Valuable Player, 1981. . . . Named to All-NBA First Team, 1978, 1980, 1981, 1982, 1983. . . . All-NBA Second Team, 1977 and 1984. . . . Member of NBA championship team, 1983. . . . NBA All-Star Game MVP, 1977 and 1983. . . . Holds NBA All-Star Game record for most free throws attempted in one quarter, 11, in 1978. . . . Shares NBA All-Star Game record for most free throws made in one quarter, 9, in 1978. . . . ABA Most Valuable Player, 1974 and 1976. . . . ABA co-MVP, 1975. . . . ABA All-Star First Team, 1973, 1974, 1975, 1976. . . . ABA All-Star Second Team, 1972. . . . ABA Playoff MVP, 1974 and 1976. . . . Member of ABA championship teams, 1974 and 1976. . . . ABA All-Defensive Team, 1976. . . . ABA All-Rookie Team, 1972. . . . Led ABA in scoring, 1973, 1974, 1976. . . . One of only seven players to average over 20 points and 20 rebounds per game during NCAA career.

LAWRENCE MICHAEL FOUST
(Larry)

Born June 24, 1928 at Painesville, O.   Height 6:09. Weight 250.

Died October 27, 1984.

High School—Philadelphia, Pa., South Catholic.

College—LaSalle College, Philadelphia, Pa.

Drafted by Chicago on first round, 1950.

Draft rights selected by Fort Wayne in dispersal of Chicago franchise, 1950.
Fort Wayne franchise transferred to Detroit, April, 1957.
Traded by Detroit with cash to Minneapolis for Walt Dukes, September 12, 1957.
Traded by Minneapolis to St. Louis for Charlie Share, cash and draft rights to Nick Mantis and Willie Merriweather, February 1, 1960.

—COLLEGIATE RECORD—

Year	G.	Min.	FGA	FGM	Pct.	FTA	FTM	Pct.	Reb.	Pts.	Avg.
46-47	26	....	...	103	....	...	49	....	....	255	9.8
47-48	24	....	...	157	....	...	87	....	....	401	16.7
48-49	28	....	...	177	....	164	99	.604	....	453	16.2
49-50	25	....	...	136	....	122	83	.680	....	355	14.2
Totals	103	....	...	573	....	...	318	....	....	1464	14.2

NBA REGULAR SEASON RECORD

Sea.—Team	G.	Min.	FGA	FGM	Pct.	FTA	FTM	Pct.	Reb.	Ast.	PF	Disq.	Pts.	Avg.
50-51—Ft. Wayne	68	....	944	327	.346	396	261	.659	681	90	247	6	915	13.5
51-52—Ft. Wayne	66	2615	989	390	.394	394	267	.678	880	200	245	10	1047	15.9
52-53—Ft. Wayne	67	2303	865	311	.360	465	336	.723	769	151	267	16	958	14.3
53-54—Ft. Wayne	72	2693	919	376	.409	475	338	.712	967	161	258	4	1090	15.1
54-55—Ft. Wayne	70	2264	818	398	.487	513	393	.766	700	118	264	9	1189	17.0

Sea.—Team	G.	Min.	FGA	FGM	Pct.	FTA	FTM	Pct.	Reb.	Ast.	PF	Disq.	Pts.	Avg.
55-56—Ft. Wayne	72	2024	821	367	.447	555	432	.778	648	127	263	7	1166	16.2
56-57—Ft. Wayne	61	1533	617	243	.394	380	273	.718	555	71	221	7	759	12.4
57-58—Minn.	72	2200	982	391	.398	566	428	.756	876	108	299	11	1210	16.8
58-59—Minn.	72	1933	771	301	.390	366	280	.765	627	91	233	5	882	12.3
59-60—Minn.-StL.	72	1964	766	312	.407	320	253	.791	621	96	241	7	877	12.2
60-61—St. Louis	68	1208	489	194	.397	208	164	.788	389	77	165	0	552	8.1
61-62—St. Louis	57	1153	433	204	.471	178	145	.815	328	78	186	2	553	9.7
Totals	817	21880	9414	3814	.405	4816	3570	.741	8041	1368	2889	84	11198	13.7

NBA PLAYOFF RECORD

Sea.—Team	G.	Min.	FGA	FGM	Pct.	FTA	FTM	Pct.	Reb.	Ast.	PF	Disq.	Pts.	Avg.
50-51—Ft. Wayne	3	....	45	14	.311	10	8	.800	37	5	5	....	36	12.0
51-52—Ft. Wayne	2	77	23	12	.522	7	6	.857	30	5	8	1	30	15.0
52-53—Ft. Wayne	8	332	121	48	.397	68	57	.838	111	6	34	2	153	19.1
53-54—Ft. Wayne	4	129	41	11	.268	25	19	.760	38	7	21	2	41	10.3
54-55—Ft. Wayne	11	331	152	60	.395	73	52	.712	107	26	43	0	172	15.6
55-56—Ft. Wayne	10	289	130	49	.377	89	70	.787	127	14	38	2	168	16.8
56-57—Ft. Wayne	2	64	23	13	.565	23	19	.826	25	6	10	0	45	22.5
58-59—Minn.	13	404	134	56	.418	50	41	.820	136	12	47	2	153	11.8
59-60—St. Louis	12	205	74	29	.391	25	20	.800	68	11	36	0	78	6.5
60-61—St. Louis	8	89	20	9	.450	14	8	.571	28	2	13	0	26	3.2
Totals	73	1920	763	301	.394	384	300	.781	707	94	255	9	902	12.4

NBA ALL-STAR GAME RECORD

Season—Team	Min.	FGA	FGM	Pct.	FTA	FTM	Pct.	Reb.	Ast.	PF	Disq.	Pts.
1951—Fort Wayne	..	6	1	.167	0	0	.000	5	2	3	0	2
1952—Fort Wayne				Selected—Injured, Did Not Play								
1953—Fort Wayne	18	7	5	.714	0	0	.000	6	0	4	0	10
1954—Fort Wayne	27	9	1	.111	1	1	1.000	15	0	1	0	3
1955—Fort Wayne	24	10	3	.300	1	1	1.000	7	1	1	0	7
1956—Fort Wayne	20	9	3	.333	4	3	.750	4	0	1	0	9
1958—Minneapolis	13	4	1	.250	8	8	1.000	3	0	3	0	10
1959—Minneapolis	16	9	3	.333	2	2	1.000	9	0	3	0	8
Totals	118	54	17	.315	16	15	.938	49	3	16	0	49

Named to NBA All-Star First Team, 1955. . . . NBA All-Star Second Team, 1952. . . . Led NBA in field-goal percentage, 1955. . . . Shared lead in NBA for rebounding, 1952. . . . Named to THE SPORTING NEWS All-America Fifth Team, 1950.

WALTER FRAZIER JR.
(Clyde)

Born March 29, 1945 at Atlanta, Ga. Height 6:04. Weight 205.

High School—Atlanta, Ga., David Howard.

College—Southern Illinois University, Carbondale, Ill.

Drafted by New York on first round, 1967 (5th pick).

Acquired from New York by Cleveland as compensation for anticipated signing of Veteran Free Agent Jim Cleamons, October 7, 1977.

Waived by Cleveland, October 19, 1979.

—COLLEGIATE RECORD—

Year	G.	Min.	FGA	FGM	Pct.	FTA	FTM	Pct.	Reb.	Pts.	Avg.
63-64†	14	....	225	133	.591	85	52	.612	129	318	22.7
64-65	24	....	353	161	.456	111	88	.793	221	410	17.1
65-66					Did Not Play—Ineligible						
66-67	26	....	397	192	.484	126	90	.714	310	474	18.2
Varsity Totals	50	....	750	353	.471	237	178	.751	531	884	17.7

NBA REGULAR SEASON RECORD

Sea.—Team	G.	Min.	FGA	FGM	Pct.	FTA	FTM	Pct.	Reb.	Ast.	PF	Disq.	Pts.	Avg.
67-68—New York	74	1588	568	256	.451	235	154	.655	313	305	199	2	666	9.0
68-69—New York	80	2949	1052	531	.505	457	341	.746	499	635	245	2	1403	17.5
69-70—New York	77	3040	1158	600	.518	547	409	.748	465	629	203	1	1609	20.9
70-71—New York	80	3455	1317	651	.494	557	434	.779	544	536	240	1	1736	21.7
71-72—New York	77	3126	1307	669	.512	557	450	.808	513	446	185	0	1788	23.2
72-73—New York	78	3181	1389	681	.490	350	286	.817	570	461	186	0	1648	21.1

									—Rebounds—								
Sea.—Team	G.	Min.	FGA	FGM	Pct.	FTA	FTM	Pct.	Off.	Def.	Tot.	Ast.	PF	Dq.	Stl.	Blk.	Pts.	Avg.
73-74—New York	80	3338	1429	674	.472	352	295	.838	120	416	536	551	212	2	161	15	1643	20.5
74-75—New York	78	3204	1391	672	.483	400	331	.828	90	375	465	474	205	2	190	14	1675	21.5
75-76—New York	59	2427	969	470	.485	226	186	.823	79	321	400	351	163	1	106	9	1126	19.1
76-77—Knicks	76	2687	1089	532	.489	336	259	.771	52	241	293	403	194	0	132	9	1323	17.4
77-78—Cleveland	51	1664	714	336	.471	180	153	.850	54	155	209	209	124	1	77	9	825	16.2
78-79—Cleveland	12	279	122	54	.443	27	21	.778	7	13	20	32	22	0	13	2	129	10.8
79-80—Cleveland	3	27	11	4	.364	2	2	1.000	1	2	3	8	2	0	2	1	10	3.3
Totals	825	30965	12516	6130	.490	4226	3321	.786			4830	5040	2180	12	681	59	15581	18.9

Three-Point Field Goals: 1979-80, 0-for-1.

Sea.—Team	G.	Min.	FGA	FGM	Pct.	FTA	FTM	Pct.	Reb.	Ast.	PF	Disq.	Pts.	Avg.
67-68—New York	4	119	33	12	.364	18	14	.778	22	25	12	0	38	9.5
68-69—New York	10	415	177	89	.503	57	34	.596	74	91	30	0	212	21.2
69-70—New York	19	834	247	118	.478	89	68	.764	149	156	53	0	304	16.0
70-71—New York	12	501	204	108	.529	75	55	.733	70	54	45	0	271	22.6
71-72—New York	16	704	276	148	.536	125	92	.736	112	98	48	0	388	24.3
72-73—New York	17	765	292	150	.514	94	73	.777	124	106	52	1	373	21.9

Sea.—Team	G.	Min.	FGA	FGM	Pct.	FTA	FTM	Pct.	—Rebounds— Off.	Def.	Tot.	Ast.	PF	Dq.	Stl.	Blk.	Pts.	Avg.
73-74—New York	12	491	225	113	.502	49	44	.898	21	74	95	48	41	1	21	4	270	22.5
74-75—New York	3	124	46	29	.630	16	13	.813	3	17	20	21	4	0	11	0	71	23.7
Totals	93	3953	1500	767	.511	523	393	.751			666	599	285	2	32	4	1927	20.7

NBA ALL-STAR GAME RECORD

Season—Team	Min.	FGA	FGM	Pct.	FTA	FTM	Pct.	Reb.	Ast.	PF	Disq.	Pts.
1970—New York	24	7	3	.429	2	1	.500	3	4	2	0	7
1971—New York	26	9	3	.333	0	0	.000	6	5	2	0	6
1972—New York	25	11	7	.636	2	1	.500	3	5	2	0	15
1973—New York	26	15	5	.333	0	0	.000	6	2	1	0	10

Season—Team	Min.	FGA	FGM	Pct.	FTA	FTM	Pct.	—Rebounds— Off.	Def.	Tot.	Ast.	PF	Dq.	Stl.	Blk.	Pts.
1974—New York	28	12	5	.417	2	2	1.000	1	1	2	5	1	0	3	0	12
1975—New York	35	17	10	.588	11	10	.909	0	5	5	2	2	0	4	0	30
1976—New York	19	7	2	.286	4	4	1.000	0	2	2	3	0	0	2	0	8
Totals	183	78	35	.449	21	18	.857			27	26	10	0	9	0	88

Elected to Naismith Memorial Basketball Hall of Fame, 1986. . . . Named to NBA All-Star First Team, 1970, 1972, 1974, 1975. . . . NBA All-Star Second Team, 1971 and 1973. . . . NBA All-Defensive First Team, 1969, 1970, 1971, 1972, 1973, 1974, 1975. . . . NBA All-Rookie Team, 1968. . . . NBA All-Star Game MVP, 1975. . . . Member of NBA championship teams, 1970 and 1973. . . . Named to THE SPORTING NEWS All-America Second Team, 1967.

JOSEPH E. FULKS
(Joe)

Born October 26, 1921 at Birmingham, Ky. Height 6:05. Weight 190.

Died March 21, 1976.

High Schools—Birmingham, Ky. (Fr.-Jr.), and Kuttawa, Ky. (Sr.).

College—Murray State College, Murray, Ky.

Signed by Philadelphia BAA, 1946.

—COLLEGIATE RECORD—

Year	G.	Min.	FGA	FGM	Pct.	FTA	FTM	Pct.	Reb.	Pts.	Avg.
41-42	22	....	...	117		76	50	.658	....	284	12.9
42-43	25	....	...	135		100	67	.670	....	337	13.5
Totals	47	....	...	252		176	117	.664	....	621	13.2

NOTE: In military service (Marines) during 1943-44, 1944-45 and 1945-46 seasons.

NBA REGULAR SEASON RECORD

Sea.—Team	G.	Min.	FGA	FGM	Pct.	FTA	FTM	Pct.	Reb.	Ast.	PF	Disq.	Pts.	Avg.
1946-47—Philadelphia	60	....	1557	475	.305	601	439	.730	....	25	199	..	1389	23.2
1947-48—Philadelphia	43	....	1258	326	.259	390	297	.762	....	26	162	..	949	22.1
1948-49—Philadelphia	60	....	1689	529	.313	638	502	.787	....	74	262	..	1560	26.0
1949-50—Philadelphia	68	....	1209	336	.278	421	293	.696	....	56	240	..	965	14.2
1950-51—Philadelphia	66	....	1358	429	.316	442	378	.855	523	117	247	8	1236	18.7
1951-52—Philadelphia	61	1904	1078	336	.312	303	250	.825	368	123	255	13	922	15.1
1952-53—Philadelphia	70	2085	960	332	.346	231	168	.727	387	138	319	20	832	11.9
1953-54—Philadelphia	61	501	229	61	.266	49	28	.571	101	28	90	0	150	2.5
Totals	489	....	9338	2824	.302	3075	2355	.766	....	587	1774	..	8003	16.4

NBA PLAYOFF RECORD

Sea.—Team	G.	Min.	FGA	FGM	Pct.	FTA	FTM	Pct.	Reb.	Ast.	PF	Disq.	Pts.	Avg.
1946-47—Philadelphia	10	....	257	74	.288	94	74	.787	....	3	32	..	222	22.2
1947-48—Philadelphia	13	....	380	92	.242	121	98	.810	....	3	55	..	282	21.7
1948-49—Philadelphia	1	....	0	0	.000	0	0	.000	....	0	1	..	0	0.0
1949-50—Philadelphia	2	....	26	5	.192	10	5	.500	....	2	10	..	15	7.5
1950-51—Philadelphia	2	....	49	16	.327	27	20	.741	16	1	9	0	52	26.0
1951-52—Philadelphia	3	70	33	5	.152	9	7	.778	12	2	13	1	17	5.7
Totals	31	....	745	192	.258	261	204	.782	....	11	120	..	588	19.0

NBA ALL-STAR GAME RECORD

Season—Team	Min.	FGA	FGM	Pct.	FTA	FTM	Pct.	Reb.	Ast.	PF	Disq.	Pts.
1951—Philadelphia	....	15	6	.400	9	7	.778	7	3	5	0	19
1952—Philadelphia	9	7	3	.429	1	0	.000	5	2	2	0	6
Totals	....	22	9	.409	10	7	.700	12	5	7	0	25

Named to NBA 25th Anniversary All-Time Team, 1970. . . . Elected to Naismith Memorial Basketball Hall of Fame, 1977. . . . Named to NBA All-Star First Team, 1947, 1948, 1949. . . . NBA All-Star Second Team, 1951. . . . Member of NBA championship team, 1947. . . . Led NBA in scoring, 1947. . . . Led NBA in free-throw percentage, 1951.

HARRY J. GALLATIN

Born April 26, 1927 at Roxana, Ill.   Height 6:06. Weight 215.

High School—Roxana, Ill.

College—Northeast Missouri State Teachers College, Kirksville, Mo.

Drafted by New York on first round of BAA draft, 1948.

Traded by New York with Dick Atha and Nat Clifton to Detroit for Mel Hutchins and a 1st round draft choice, April 3, 1957.

—COLLEGIATE RECORD—

Year	G.	Min.	FGA	FGM	Pct.	FTA	FTM	Pct.	Reb.	Pts.	Avg.
46-47	31	....	...	149	....	89	53	.596	....	351	11.3
47-48	31	....	465	178	.383	162	109	.673	....	465	15.0
Totals	62	....		327	....	251	162	.645	....	816	13.2

NOTE: Played only two years of college basketball.

NBA REGULAR SEASON RECORD

Sea.—Team	G.	Min.	FGA	FGM	Pct.	FTA	FTM	Pct.	Reb.	Ast.	PF	Disq.	Pts.	Avg.
48-49—New York	52	....	479	157	.328	169	120	.710	....	63	127	....	434	8.3
49-50—New York	68	....	664	263	.396	366	277	.757	....	56	215	....	803	11.8
50-51—New York	66	....	705	293	.416	354	259	.732	800	180	244	4	845	12.8
51-52—New York	66	1931	527	233	.442	341	275	.807	661	115	223	5	741	11.2
52-53—New York	70	2333	635	282	.444	430	301	.700	916	126	224	6	865	12.4
53-54—New York	72	2690	639	258	.404	552	433	.784	1098	153	208	2	949	13.2
54-55—New York	72	2548	859	330	.384	483	393	.814	995	176	206	5	1053	14.6
55-56—New York	72	2378	834	322	.386	455	358	.787	740	168	220	6	1002	13.9
56-57—New York	72	1943	817	332	.406	519	415	.802	725	85	202	1	1079	15.0
57-58—Detroit	72	1990	898	340	.379	498	392	.787	749	86	217	5	1072	14.9
Totals	682	....	7057	2810	.398	4167	3223	.773	....	1208	2086	....	8843	13.0

NBA PLAYOFF RECORD

Sea.—Team	G.	Min.	FGA	FGM	Pct.	FTA	FTM	Pct.	Reb.	Ast.	PF	Disq.	Pts.	Avg.
48-49—New York	6	....	56	20	.357	39	32	.821	....	10	31	....	72	12.0
49-50—New York	5	....	52	20	.385	32	25	.781	....	6	23	....	65	13.0
50-51—New York	14	....	140	49	.350	87	67	.770	163	26	57	3	165	11.8
51-52—New York	14	471	122	50	.410	66	51	.773	134	19	45	1	151	10.8
52-53—New York	11	303	86	36	.419	59	44	.746	120	15	29	0	116	10.5
53-54—New York	4	151	35	16	.457	31	22	.710	61	6	12	0	54	13.5
54-55—New York	3	108	42	19	.452	22	17	.773	44	7	11	0	55	18.3
57-58—Detroit	7	182	87	32	.368	37	26	.703	70	11	27	1	90	12.9
Totals	64	....	620	242	.390	373	284	.762	....	100	235	....	768	12.0

NBA ALL-STAR GAME RECORD

Season—Team	Min.	FGA	FGM	Pct.	FTA	FTM	Pct.	Reb.	Ast.	PF	Disq.	Pts.
1951—New York	....	4	2	.500	1	1	1.000	5	2	4	0	5
1952—New York	22	5	3	.600	4	1	.250	9	3	3	0	7
1953—New York	19	4	1	.250	2	1	.500	3	2	1	0	3
1954—New York	28	2	0	.000	6	5	.833	18	3	0	0	5
1955—New York	36	7	4	.571	5	5	1.000	14	3	2	0	13
1956—New York	30	12	5	.417	7	6	.857	5	2	4	1	16
1957—New York	24	7	4	.571	2	0	.000	11	1	3	0	8
Totals (7 games)	....	41	19	.463	27	19	.704	65	16	17	0	57

COLLEGIATE COACHING RECORD

		Regular Season			
Sea.	Club	W.	L.	Pct.	Pos.
1958-59—Southern Ill.		17	10	.630	
1959-60—Southern Ill.		20	9	.690	
1960-61—Southern Ill.		21	6	.778	
1961-62—Southern Ill.		21	10	.677	

NBA COACHING RECORD

Sea.	Club	Regular Season				Playoffs		Sea.	Club	Regular Season				Playoffs	
		W.	L.	Pct.	Pos.	W.	L.			W.	L.	Pct.	Pos.	W.	L.
1962-63—St. Louis		48	32	.600	2	6	5	1964-65—New York		19	23	.452	4	..	..
1963-64—St. Louis		46	34	.575	2	6	6	1965-66—New York		6	15	.286	...	..	..
1964-65—St. Louis		17	16	.515	...	..	..	Totals (4 years)		136	120	.531		12	11

Named to NBA All-Star First Team, 1954. . . . NBA All-Star Second Team, 1955. . . . Led NBA in rebounding, 1954. . . . NBA Coach of the Year, 1963. . . . Named to NAIA Basketball Hall of Fame, 1957.

GEORGE GERVIN

Born April 27, 1952 at Detroit, Mich.   Height 6:07.   Weight 185.

High School—Detroit, Mich., Martin Luther King.

Colleges—Long Beach State, Long Beach, Calif., and Eastern Michigan University, Ypsilanti, Mich.

Drafted by Phoenix on third round, 1974 (40th pick).

Selected as an undergraduate by Virginia on first round of ABA special circumstance draft, 1973.
Sold by Virginia to San Antonio, January 30, 1974.
Entered NBA with San Antonio, 1976.
Traded by San Antonio to Chicago for David Greenwood, October 24, 1985.
Played in Continental Basketball Association with the Pontiac Capparells during 1972-73 season (averaged 37.4 points per game).

—COLLEGIATE RECORD—
Long Beach State

Year	G.	Min.	FGA	FGM	Pct.	FTA	FTM	Pct.	Reb.	Pts.	Avg.
69-70			Dropped out of school prior to basketball season.								

Eastern Michigan

Year	G.	Min.	FGA	FGM	Pct.	FTA	FTM	Pct.	Reb.	Pts.	Avg.
70-71	9	300	123	65	.528	39	28	.718	104	158	17.6
71-72	30	1098	571	339	.594	265	208	.785	458	886	29.5
Totals	39	1398	694	404	.582	304	236	.776	562	1044	26.8

ABA REGULAR SEASON RECORD

Sea.—Team	G.	Min.	2-Point FGM	FGA	Pct.	3-Point FGM	FGA	Pct.	FTM	FTA	Pct.	Reb.	Ast.	Pts.	Avg.
72-73—Virginia	30	689	155	315	.492	6	26	.231	96	118	.814	128	34	424	14.1
73-74—Va.-S.A.	74	2511	664	1370	.485	8	56	.143	378	464	.815	624	142	1730	23.4
74-75—San Antonio	84	3113	767	1600	.479	17	55	.309	380	458	.830	697	207	1965	23.4
75-76—San Antonio	81	2748	692	1359	.509	14	55	.255	342	399	.857	546	201	1768	21.8
Totals	269	9061	2278	4644	.491	45	192	.234	1196	1439	.831	1977	584	5887	21.9

ABA PLAYOFF RECORD

Sea.—Team	G.	Min.	2-Point FGM	FGA	Pct.	3-Point FGM	FGA	Pct.	FTM	FTA	Pct.	Reb.	Ast.	Pts.	Avg.
72-73—Virginia	5	200	33	72	.458	1	5	.200	23	34	.676	38	8	93	18.6
73-74—San Antonio	7	226	56	114	.491	1	1	1.000	29	31	.935	52	19	144	20.6
74-75—San Antonio	6	276	76	159	.478	3	12	.250	43	52	.827	84	8	204	34.0
75-76—San Antonio	7	288	67	125	.536	0	3	.000	56	69	.812	64	19	190	27.1
Totals	25	990	232	470	.494	5	21	.238	151	186	.812	238	54	631	25.2

ABA ALL-STAR GAME RECORD

Sea.—Team	Min.	2-Point FGM	FGA	Pct.	3-Point FGM	FGA	Pct.	FTM	FTA	Pct.	Reb.	Ast.	Pts.	Avg.
1974—Virginia	21	3	8	.375	0	1	.000	3	4	.750	5	3	9	9.0
1975—San Antonio	30	8	14	.571	0	1	.000	7	8	.875	6	3	23	23.0
1976—San Antonio	16	3	13	.231	0	0	.000	1	2	.500	6	1	8	8.0
Totals	67	14	35	.400	0	2	.000	11	14	.786	17	7	40	13.3

NBA REGULAR SEASON RECORD

Sea.—Team	G.	Min.	FGA	FGM	Pct.	FTA	FTM	Pct.	Rebounds Off.	Def.	Tot.	Ast.	PF	Dq.	Stl.	Blk.	Pts.	Avg.
76-77—San Antonio	82	2705	1335	726	.544	532	443	.833	134	320	454	238	286	12	105	104	1895	23.1
77-78—San Antonio	82	2857	1611	864	.536	607	504	.830	118	302	420	302	255	3	136	110	2232	27.2
78-79—San Antonio	80	2888	1749	947	.541	570	471	.826	142	258	400	219	275	5	137	91	2365	29.6
79-80—San Antonio	78	2934	1940	1024	.528	593	505	.852	154	249	403	202	208	0	110	79	2585	33.1
80-81—San Antonio	82	2765	1729	850	.492	620	512	.826	126	293	419	260	212	4	94	56	2221	27.1
81-82—San Antonio	79	2817	1987	993	.500	642	555	.864	138	254	392	187	215	2	77	45	2551	32.3
82-83—San Antonio	78	2830	1553	757	.487	606	517	.853	111	246	357	264	243	5	88	67	2043	26.2
83-84—San Antonio	76	2584	1561	765	.490	507	427	.842	106	207	313	220	219	3	79	47	1967	25.9
84-85—San Antonio	72	2091	1182	600	.508	384	324	.844	79	155	234	178	208	2	66	48	1524	21.2
85-86—Chicago	82	2065	1100	519	.472	322	283	.879	78	137	215	144	210	4	49	23	1325	16.2
Totals	791	26536	15747	8045	.511	5383	4541	.844	1186	2421	3607	2214	2331	40	941	670	20708	26.2

Three-Point Field Goals: 1979-80, 32-for-102 (.314). 1980-81, 9-for-35 (.257). 1981-82, 10-for-36 (.278). 1982-83, 12-for-33 (.364). 1983-84, 10-for-24 (.417). 1984-85, 0-for-10. 1985-86, 4-for-19 (.211). Totals, 77-for-259 (.297).

NBA PLAYOFF RECORD

Sea.—Team	G.	Min.	FGA	FGM	Pct.	FTA	FTM	Pct.	Rebounds Off.	Def.	Tot.	Ast.	PF	Dq.	Stl.	Blk.	Pts.	Avg.
76-77—San Antonio	2	62	44	19	.432	15	12	.800	5	6	11	3	9	1	1	2	50	25.0
77-78—San Antonio	6	227	142	78	.549	56	43	.768	11	23	34	19	23	0	6	16	199	33.2
78-79—San Antonio	14	513	295	158	.536	104	84	.808	33	49	82	35	51	1	27	14	400	28.6
79-80—San Antonio	3	122	74	37	.500	30	26	.867	9	11	20	12	8	0	5	3	100	33.3
80-81—San Antonio	7	274	154	77	.500	45	36	.800	9	26	35	24	19	1	5	5	190	27.1
81-82—San Antonio	9	373	228	103	.452	71	59	.831	19	47	66	41	36	1	10	4	265	29.4
82-83—San Antonio	11	437	208	108	.519	69	61	.884	21	53	74	37	39	1	12	4	277	25.2
84-85—San Antonio	5	183	79	42	.532	34	27	.794	3	15	18	14	19	0	3	3	111	22.2
85-86—Chicago	2	11	1	0	.000	0	0	.000	0	1	1	1	3	0	0	0	0	0.0
Totals	59	2202	1225	622	.508	424	348	.821	110	231	341	186	207	5	69	51	1592	27.0

Three-Point Field Goals: 1979-80, 0-for-2. 1980-81, 0-for-3. 1981-82, 0-for-3. 1982-83, 0-for-2. 1984-85, 0-for-3. Totals, 0-for-13.

NBA ALL-STAR GAME RECORD

Season—Team	Min.	FGA	FGM	Pct.	FTA	FTM	Pct.	—Rebounds— Off.	Def.	Tot.	Ast.	PF	Dq.	Stl.	Blk.	Pts.
1977—San Antonio..	12	6	0	.000	0	0	.000	0	1	1	0	1	0	0	1	0
1978—San Antonio..	18	11	4	.364	3	1	.333	1	1	2	1	2	0	2	1	9
1979—San Antonio..	34	16	8	.500	11	10	.909	2	4	6	2	4	0	1	1	26
1980—San Antonio..	40	26	14	.538	9	6	.667	4	6	10	3	2	0	3	0	34
1981—San Antonio..	24	9	5	.556	2	1	.500	1	2	3	0	3	0	2	1	11
1982—San Antonio..	27	14	5	.357	2	2	1.000	1	5	6	1	3	0	3	3	12
1983—San Antonio..	14	8	3	.375	2	2	1.000	0	0	0	3	3	0	2	0	9
1984—San Antonio..	21	6	5	.833	3	3	1.000	0	2	2	1	5	0	0	1	13
1985—San Antonio..	25	12	10	.833	4	3	.750	0	3	3	1	2	0	3	1	23
Totals	215	108	54	.500	36	28	.778	9	24	33	12	25	0	16	9	137

Named to All-NBA First Team, 1978, 1979, 1980, 1981, 1982 .... All-NBA Second Team, 1977 and 1983.... NBA All-Star Game MVP, 1980.... Holds NBA record for most points in one quarter, 33, against New Orleans, April 9, 1978.... Led NBA in scoring, 1978, 1979, 1980, 1982.... One of only two players in NBA history to win four scoring titles.... Named to ABA All-Star Second Team, 1975 and 1976.

THOMAS JOSEPH GOLA
(Tom)

Born January 13, 1933 at Philadelphia, Pa.   Height 6:06.   Weight 205.

High School—Philadelphia, Pa., La Salle.

College—La Salle College, Philadelphia, Pa.

Drafted by Philadelphia on first round (territorial choice), 1955.

Philadelphia franchise transferred to San Francisco, 1962.
Traded by San Francisco to New York for Willie Naulls and Ken Sears, December 5, 1962.

—COLLEGIATE PLAYING RECORD—

Year	G.	Min.	FGA	FGM	Pct.	FTA	FTM	Pct.	Reb.	Pts.	Avg.
51-52	29	....	528	192	.364	170	121	.712	497	505	17.4
52-53	28	....	451	186	.412	186	145	.780	434	517	18.5
53-54	30	....	619	252	.407	254	186	.732	652	690	23.0
54-55	31	....	624	274	.439	267	202	.757	618	750	24.2
Totals	118	....	2222	904	.407	877	654	.746	2201	2462	20.9

NBA REGULAR SEASON RECORD

Sea.—Team	G.	Min.	FGA	FGM	Pct.	FTA	FTM	Pct.	Reb.	Ast.	PF	Disq.	Pts.	Avg.
55-56—Philadelphia	68	2346	592	244	.412	333	244	.733	616	404	272	11	732	10.8
56-57—Philadelphia				Did Not Play—In Military Service										
57-58—Philadelphia	59	2126	711	295	.415	299	223	.746	639	327	225	11	813	13.8
58-59—Philadelphia	64	2333	773	310	.401	357	281	.787	710	269	243	7	901	14.1
59-60—Philadelphia	75	2870	983	426	.433	340	270	.794	779	409	311	9	1122	15.0
60-61—Philadelphia	74	2735	940	420	.447	281	210	.747	692	292	321	13	1050	14.2
61-62—Philadelphia	60	2462	765	322	.421	230	176	.765	585	286	266	16	820	13.7
62-63—S.F.-N.Y.	73	2670	781	363	.465	219	170	.776	507	298	316	7	896	12.3
63-64—New York	74	2156	602	258	.429	212	154	.726	469	257	278	7	670	9.1
64-65—New York	77	1727	455	204	.448	180	133	.739	319	220	269	8	541	7.0
65-66—New York	74	1127	271	122	.450	105	82	.781	289	191	207	3	326	4.4
Totals	698	22552	6873	2964	.431	2556	1943	.760	5605	2953	2708	91	7871	11.3

NBA PLAYOFF RECORD

Sea.—Team	G.	Min.	FGA	FGM	Pct.	FTA	FTM	Pct.	Reb.	Ast.	PF	Disq.	Pts.	Avg.
55-56—Philadelphia	10	360	107	38	.355	60	47	.783	101	58	47	2	123	12.3
57-58—Philadelphia	8	327	109	36	.330	51	38	.745	84	32	24	0	110	13.8
59-60—Philadelphia	9	340	102	42	.412	36	29	.805	95	50	41	3	113	12.5
60-61—Philadelphia	3	127	34	7	.206	20	15	.750	37	15	14	1	29	9.7
61-62—Philadelphia	9	316	70	19	.271	25	19	.760	74	24	38	2	57	6.3
Totals	39	1470	422	142	.336	192	148	.771	391	179	164	8	432	11.1

NBA ALL-STAR GAME RECORD

Season—Team	Min.	FGA	FGM	Pct.	FTA	FTM	Pct.	Reb.	Ast.	PF	Disq.	Pts.
1960—Philadelphia	20	13	5	.385	3	2	.667	4	2	3	0	12
1961—Philadelphia	25	13	6	.462	4	2	.500	5	3	2	0	14
1962—Philadelphia				Injured—Did Not Play								
1963—New York	18	3	1	.333	0	0	.000	2	1	3	0	2
1964—New York................	7	0	0	.000	2	1	.500	0	1	2	0	1
Totals	70	29	12	.414	9	5	.556	11	7	10	0	2.9

COLLEGIATE COACHING RECORD

Sea. Club	Regular Season W.	L.	Pct.	Pos.
1968-69—LaSalle	23	1	.958	..
1969-70—LaSalle	14	12	.538	..

Elected to Naismith Memorial Basketball Hall of Fame, 1975.... Named to NBA All-Star Second Team, 1958.... Member of NBA championship team, 1956.... NCAA University Division Tournament MVP, 1954.... Member of NCAA University Division championship team, 1954.... One of only two major-college players ever to score over 2,000 points and grab over 2,000 rebounds in a career.... Served as a legislator in Pennsylvania General Assembly.

GAIL CHARLES GOODRICH

Born April 23, 1943 at Los Angeles, Calif.   Height 6:01. Weight 175.

High School—Los Angeles, Calif., Polytechnic.

College—University of California at Los Angeles, Los Angeles, Calif.

Drafted by Los Angeles on first round (territorial choice), 1965.

Selected from Los Angeles by Phoenix in expansion draft, May 6, 1968.
Traded by Phoenix to Los Angeles for Mel Counts, May 20, 1970.
Played out option with Los Angeles; signed by New Orleans as a Veteran Free Agent, July 19, 1976. Los Angeles received two 1st round draft choices (1977 and 1979) and a 1980 2nd round draft choice as compensation. New Orleans received a 1977 2nd round draft choice to complete transaction, October 6, 1976.

—COLLEGIATE RECORD—

Year	G.	Min.	FGA	FGM	Pct.	FTA	FTM	Pct.	Reb.	Pts.	Avg.
61-62†	20	....	385	189	.491	155	110	.710	122	488	24.4
62-63	29	....	280	117	.418	103	66	.641	101	300	10.3
63-64	30	....	530	243	.458	225	160	.711	156	646	21.5
64-65	30	....	528	277	.525	265	190	.717	158	744	24.8
Varsity Totals	89	....	1338	637	.476	593	416	.702	415	1690	19.0

NBA REGULAR SEASON RECORD

Sea.—Team	G.	Min.	FGA	FGM	Pct.	FTA	FTM	Pct.	Reb.	Ast.	PF	Disq.	Pts.	Avg.
65-66—Los Ang.	65	1008	503	203	.404	149	103	.891	130	103	103	1	509	7.8
66-67—Los Ang.	77	1780	776	352	.454	337	253	.751	251	210	194	3	957	12.4
67-68—Los Ang.	79	2057	812	395	.486	392	302	.770	199	205	228	2	1092	13.8
68-69—Phoenix	81	3236	1746	718	.411	663	495	.747	437	518	253	3	1931	23.8
69-70—Phoenix	81	3234	1251	508	.454	604	488	.808	340	605	251	3	1624	20.0
70-71—Los Ang.	79	2808	1174	558	.475	343	264	.770	260	380	258	3	1380	17.5
71-72—Los Ang.	82	3040	1695	826	.487	559	475	.850	295	365	210	0	2127	25.9
72-73—Los Ang.	76	2697	1615	750	.464	374	314	.840	263	332	193	1	1814	23.9

Sea.—Team	G.	Min.	FGA	FGM	Pct.	FTA	FTM	Pct.	Off.	Def.	Tot.	Ast.	PF	Dq.	Stl.	Blk.	Pts.	Avg.
									—Rebounds—									
73-74—L.A.	82	3061	1773	784	.442	588	508	.864	95	155	250	427	227	3	126	12	2076	25.3
74-75—L.A.	72	2668	1429	656	.459	378	318	.841	96	123	219	420	214	1	102	6	1630	22.6
75-76—L.A.	75	2646	1321	583	.441	346	293	.847	94	120	214	421	238	3	123	17	1459	19.5
76-77—N.O.	27	609	305	136	.446	85	68	.800	25	36	61	74	43	0	22	2	340	12.6
77-78—N.O.	81	2553	1050	520	.495	332	264	.795	75	102	177	388	186	0	82	22	1304	16.1
78-79—N.O.	74	2130	850	382	.449	204	174	.853	68	115	183	357	177	1	90	13	938	12.7
Totals	1031	33527	16300	7431	.456	5354	4319	.807			3279	4805	2775	24	545	72	19181	18.6

NBA PLAYOFF RECORD

Sea.—Team	G.	Min.	FGA	FGM	Pct.	FTA	FTM	Pct.	Reb.	Ast.	PF	Disq.	Pts.	Avg.
65-66—Los Ang.	11	290	92	43	.467	43	29	.674	42	33	35	0	115	10.5
66-67—Los Ang.	3	81	31	11	.355	18	11	.611	9	10	5	0	33	11.0
67-68—Los Ang.	10	100	47	23	.489	18	14	.778	14	14	10	0	60	6.0
69-70—Phoenix	7	265	118	56	.475	35	30	.857	32	38	21	0	142	20.3
70-71—Los Ang.	12	518	247	105	.425	113	95	.841	38	91	38	0	305	25.4
71-72—Los Ang.	15	575	292	130	.445	108	97	.898	38	50	50	0	357	23.8
72-73—Los Ang.	17	604	310	139	.448	79	62	.785	61	67	53	1	340	20.0

Sea.—Team	G.	Min.	FGA	FGM	Pct.	FTA	FTM	Pct.	Off.	Def.	Tot.	Ast.	PF	Dq.	Stl.	Blk.	Pts.	Avg.
									—Rebounds—									
73-74—L.A.	5	189	90	35	.389	33	28	.848	7	9	16	30	7	0	7	1	98	19.6
Totals	80	2622	1227	542	.442	447	366	.819			250	333	219	1			1450	18.1

NBA ALL-STAR GAME RECORD

Season—Team	Min.	FGA	FGM	Pct.	FTA	FTM	Pct.	Reb.	Ast.	PF	Disq.	Pts.
1969—Phoenix	6	4	2	.500	2	1	.500	1	1	1	0	5
1972—Los Angeles	14	7	2	.286	0	0	.000	1	2	2	0	4
1973—Los Angeles	16	7	1	.143	0	0	.000	2	1	2	0	2

Season—Team	Min.	FGA	FGM	Pct.	FTA	FTM	Pct.	Off.	Def.	Tot.	Ast.	PF	Dq.	Stl.	Blk.	Pts.
								—Rebounds—								
1974—Los Angeles	26	16	9	.563	0	0	.000	1	3	4	6	2	0	1	0	18
1975—LosAngeles	15	4	2	.500	0	0	.000	0	1	1	4	1	0	0	0	4
Totals	77	38	16	.421	2	1	.500			9	14	8	0	1		33

Named to NBA All-Star First Team, 1974.... Member of NBA championship team, 1972.... Named to THE SPORTING NEWS All-America First Team, 1964.... Member of NCAA Division I championship teams, 1964 and 1965.

HAROLD EVERETT GREER
(Hal)

Born June 26, 1936 at Huntington, W. Va.   Height 6:02.   Weight 175.
High School—Huntington, W. Va., Douglass.
College—Marshall College, Huntington, W. Va.
Drafted by Syracuse on second round, 1958.

Syracuse franchise transferred to Philadelphia, 1963.

—COLLEGIATE RECORD—

Year	G.	Min.	FGA	FGM	Pct.	FTA	FTM	Pct.	Reb.	Pts.	Avg.
54-55†	..	....	....	...	...	145	....	...	...	...	18.0
55-56	23	....	213	128	.601	145	101	.697	153	357	15.5
56-57	24	....	329	167	.508	156	119	.763	332	453	18.9
57-58	24	....	432	236	.546	114	95	.833	280	567	23.6
Varsity Totals	71	....	974	531	.545	415	315	.759	765	1377	19.4

NBA REGULAR SEASON RECORD

Sea.—Team	G.	Min.	FGA	FGM	Pct.	FTA	FTM	Pct.	Reb.	Ast.	PF	Disq.	Pts.	Avg.
58-59—Syracuse	68	1625	679	308	.454	176	137	.778	196	101	189	1	753	11.1
59-60—Syracuse	70	1979	815	388	.476	189	148	.783	303	188	208	4	924	13.2
60-61—Syracuse	79	2763	1381	623	.451	394	305	.774	455	302	242	0	1551	19.6
61-62—Syracuse	71	2705	1442	644	.446	404	331	.819	524	313	252	2	1619	22.8
62-63—Syracuse	80	2631	1293	600	.464	434	362	.834	457	275	286	4	1562	19.5
63-64—Philadelphia	80	3157	1611	715	.444	525	435	.829	484	374	291	6	1865	23.3
64-65—Philadelphia	70	2600	1245	539	.433	413	335	.811	355	313	254	7	1413	20.2
65-66—Philadelphia	80	3326	1580	703	.445	514	413	.804	473	384	315	6	1819	22.7
66-67—Philadelphia	80	3086	1524	699	.459	466	367	.788	422	303	302	5	1765	22.1
67-68—Philadelphia	82	3263	1626	777	.478	549	422	.769	444	372	289	6	1976	24.1
68-69—Philadelphia	82	3311	1595	732	.459	543	432	.796	435	414	294	8	1896	23.1
69-70—Philadelphia	80	3024	1551	705	.455	432	352	.815	376	405	300	8	1762	22.0
70-71—Philadelphia	81	3060	1371	591	.431	405	326	.805	364	369	289	4	1508	18.6
71-72—Philadelphia	81	2410	866	389	.449	234	181	.774	271	316	268	10	959	11.8
72-73—Philadelphia	38	848	232	91	.392	39	32	.821	106	111	76	1	214	5.6
Totals	1122	39788	18811	8504	.452	5717	4578	.801	5665	4540	3855	72	21586	19.2

NBA PLAYOFF RECORD

Sea.—Team	G.	Min.	FGA	FGM	Pct.	FTA	FTM	Pct.	Reb.	Ast.	PF	Disq.	Pts.	Avg.
58-59—Syracuse	9	277	93	39	.419	32	26	.813	47	20	35	2	104	11.6
59-60—Syracuse	3	84	43	22	.512	4	3	.750	14	10	5	0	47	15.7
60-61—Syracuse	8	232	106	41	.387	40	33	.825	33	19	32	1	115	14.4
61-62—Syracuse	1	5	0	0	.000	0	0	.000	0	0	1	0	0	0.0
62-63—Syracuse	5	214	87	44	.506	35	29	.829	27	21	21	1	117	23.4
63-64—Philadelphia	5	211	95	37	.389	39	33	.846	28	30	19	1	107	21.4
64-65—Philadelphia	11	505	222	101	.455	87	69	.793	81	55	45	2	271	24.6
65-66—Philadelphia	5	226	91	32	.352	23	18	.783	36	21	21	0	82	16.4
66-67—Philadelphia	15	688	375	161	.429	118	94	.797	88	79	55	1	416	27.7
67-68—Philadelphia	13	553	278	120	.432	111	95	.858	79	55	49	1	335	25.8
68-69—Philadelphia	5	204	81	26	.321	36	28	.778	30	23	23	0	80	16.0
69-70—Philadelphia	5	178	74	33	.446	13	11	.846	17	27	16	0	77	15.4
70-71—Philadelphia	7	265	112	49	.438	36	27	.750	25	33	35	4	125	17.9
Totals	92	3642	1657	705	.425	574	466	.812	505	393	357	13	1876	20.4

NBA ALL-STAR GAME RECORD

Season—Team	Min.	FGA	FGM	Pct.	FTA	FTM	Pct.	Reb.	Ast.	PF	Disq.	Pts.
1961—Syracuse	18	11	7	.636	0	0	.000	6	2	2	0	14
1962—Syracuse	24	14	3	.214	7	2	.286	10	9	3	0	8
1963—Syracuse	15	7	3	.429	0	0	.000	3	2	4	0	6
1964—Philadelphia	20	10	5	.500	4	3	.750	3	4	1	0	13
1965—Philadelphia	21	11	5	.455	4	3	.750	4	1	2	0	13
1966—Philadelphia	23	13	4	.308	1	1	1.000	5	1	4	0	9
1967—Philadelphia	31	16	5	.313	8	7	.875	4	1	5	0	17
1968—Philadelphia	17	8	8	1.000	7	5	.714	3	3	2	0	21
1969—Philadelphia	17	1	0	.000	5	4	.800	3	2	2	0	4
1970—Philadelphia	21	11	7	.636	1	1	1.000	4	3	4	0	15
Totals	207	102	47	.461	37	26	.703	45	28	29	0	120

CBA COACHING RECORD

		Regular Season				Playoffs	
Sea.	Club	W.	L.	Pct.	Pos.	W.	L.
1980-81—Phila. Kings		17	23	.425	3†	6	6

†Eastern Division.

Elected to Naismith Memorial Basketball Hall of Fame 1981. . . . Named to NBA All-Star Second Team, 1963, 1964, 1965, 1966, 1967, 1968, 1969. . . . NBA All-Star Game MVP, 1968. . . . Holds NBA All-Star Game record for most points in one quarter, 19, in 1968. . . . Member of NBA championship team, 1967.

RICHARD V. GUERIN

Born May 29, 1932 at New York, N. Y.   Height 6:04.   Weight 210.

High School—Bronx, N. Y., Mt. St. Michael.

College—Iona College, New Rochelle, N. Y.

Drafted by New York on second round, 1954.

In military service, 1954-55 and 1955-56 seasons, played with Quantico Marines and Marine All-Star teams.
Traded by New York to St. Louis for cash and a 2nd round draft choice, October 18, 1963.

—COLLEGIATE RECORD—

Year	G.	Min.	FGA	FGM	Pct.	FTA	FTM	Pct.	Reb.	Pts.	Avg.
50-51†	..	....	...	....	....	...	....	....	....	....	....
51-52	27	....	...	159	....	...	146	....	....	464	17.2
52-53	21	....	...	139	.491	...	114	.662	....	392	18.7
53-54	21	....	405	171	.422	249	177	.711	....	519	24.7
Varsity Totals	69	....	...	469	....	...	437	....	....	1375	19.9

NBA REGULAR SEASON RECORD

Sea.—Team	G.	Min.	FGA	FGM	Pct.	FTA	FTM	Pct.	Reb.	Ast.	PF	Disq.	Pts.	Avg.
56-57—New York	72	1793	699	257	.368	292	181	.620	334	182	186	3	695	9.7
57-58—New York	63	2368	973	344	.354	511	353	.691	489	317	202	3	1041	16.5
58-59—New York	71	2558	1046	443	.424	505	405	.802	518	364	255	1	1291	18.2
59-60—New York	74	2429	1379	579	.420	591	457	.773	505	468	242	3	1615	21.8
60-61—New York	79	3023	1545	612	.396	626	496	.792	628	503	310	3	1720	21.8
61-62—New York	78	3346	1897	839	.442	762	625	.820	501	539	299	3	2303	29.5
62-63—New York	79	2712	1380	596	.432	600	509	.848	331	348	228	2	1701	21.5
63-64—N.Y.-St.L.	80	2366	846	351	.415	424	347	.818	256	375	276	4	1049	13.1
64-65—St. Louis	57	1678	662	295	.446	301	231	.767	149	271	193	1	821	14.4
65-66—St. Louis	80	2363	998	414	.415	446	362	.812	314	388	256	4	1190	14.9
66-67—St. Louis	79	2275	904	394	.436	416	304	.731	192	345	247	2	1092	13.8
67-68—			Voluntarily Retired											
68-69—Atlanta	27	472	111	47	.423	74	57	.770	59	99	66	0	151	5.6
69-70—Atlanta	8	64	11	3	.273	1	1	1.000	2	12	9	0	7	0.9
Totals	847	27447	12451	5174	.416	5549	4328	.780	4278	4211	2769	29	14676	17.3

NBA PLAYOFF RECORD

Sea.—Team	G.	Min.	FGA	FGM	Pct.	FTA	FTM	Pct.	Reb.	Ast.	PF	Disq.	Pts.	Avg.
58-59—New York	2	77	35	9	.257	14	12	.857	18	15	11	1	30	15.0
63-64—St. Louis	12	428	169	75	.444	85	67	.788	50	49	54	1	217	18.1
64-65—St. Louis	4	125	65	25	.385	25	19	.760	8	21	14	0	69	17.3
65-66—St. Louis	10	399	159	72	.453	76	62	.816	37	79	41	0	206	20.6
66-67—St. Louis	9	228	86	36	.419	30	24	.800	23	39	23	0	96	10.7
68-69—Atlanta	3	32	4	1	.250	2	1	.500	5	7	8	0	3	1.0
69-70—Atlanta	2	56	21	13	.619	7	7	1.000	8	4	6	0	33	16.5
Totals	42	1345	539	231	.429	239	192	.803	149	214	157	2	654	15.6

NBA ALL-STAR GAME RECORD

Season—Team	Min.	FGA	FGM	Pct.	FTA	FTM	Pct.	Reb.	Ast.	PF	Disq.	Pts.
1958—New York	22	10	2	.200	4	3	.750	8	7	3	0	7
1959—New York	22	7	1	.143	5	3	.600	3	3	1	0	5
1960—New York	22	11	5	.455	2	2	1.000	4	4	4	0	12
1961—New York	15	8	3	.375	6	5	.833	0	2	1	0	11
1962—New York	27	17	10	.588	6	3	.500	3	1	6	0	23
1963—New York	14	3	2	.667	3	1	.333	1	1	2	0	5
Totals	122	56	23	.411	26	17	.654	19	18	17	0	63

NBA COACHING RECORD

Sea.	Club	Regular Season W.	L.	Pct.	Pos.	Playoffs W.	L.	Sea.	Club	Regular Season W.	L.	Pct.	Pos.	Playoffs W.	L.
1964-65—St. Louis		28	19	.596	2	1	3	1969-70—Atlanta		48	34	.585	1	4	5
1965-66—St. Louis		36	44	.450	3	6	4	1970-71—Atlanta		36	46	.439	2	1	4
1966-67—St. Louis		39	42	.476	2	5	4	1971-72—Atlanta		36	46	.439	2	2	4
1967-68—St. Louis		56	26	.683	1	2	4	Totals (8 years)		327	291	.529		26	34
1968-69—Atlanta		48	34	.585	2	5	6								

Named to NBA All-Star Second Team, 1959, 1960, 1962. . . . NBA Coach of the Year, 1968.

CLIFFORD OLDHAM HAGAN
(Cliff)

Born December 9, 1931 at Owensboro, Ky.   Height 6:04.   Weight 215.

High School—Owensboro, Ky.

College—University of Kentucky, Lexington, Ky.

Drafted by Boston on third round, 1953.

In military service, 1954-55 and 1955-56, played at Andrews Air Force Base.

Draft rights traded by Boston with Ed Macauley to St. Louis for 1st round draft choice, April 30, 1956.
Signed as player-coach by Dallas ABA, June, 1967.

—COLLEGIATE RECORD—

Year†	G.	Min.	FGA	FGM	Pct.	FTA	FTM	Pct.	Reb.	Pts.	Avg.
49-50†	12	....	244	114	.467	58	42	.724	...	270	22.5
50-51	20	....	188	69	.367	61	45	.738	169	183	9.2
51-52	32	....	633	264	.417	235	164	.698	528	692	21.6
52-53	Did Not Play—Kentucky had no team										
53-54	25	....	514	234	.455	191	132	.691	338	600	24.0
Varsity Totals	77	....	1335	567	.425	487	341	.700	1035	1475	19.2

NBA REGULAR SEASON RECORD

Sea.—Team	G.	Min.	FGA	FGM	Pct.	FTA	FTM	Pct.	Reb.	Ast.	PF	Disq.	Pts.	Avg.
56-57—St. Louis	67	971	371	134	.361	145	100	.690	247	86	165	3	368	5.5
57-58—St. Louis	70	2190	1135	503	.443	501	385	.768	707	175	267	9	1391	19.9
58-59—St. Louis	72	2702	1417	646	.456	536	415	.774	783	245	275	10	1707	23.7
59-60—St. Louis	75	2798	1549	719	.464	524	421	.803	803	299	270	4	1859	24.8
60-61—St. Louis	78	2701	1490	661	.441	467	383	.820	718	381	286	9	1705	21.9
61-62—St. Louis	77	2784	1490	701	.470	439	362	.825	533	370	282	8	1764	22.9
62-63—St. Louis	79	1716	1055	491	.465	305	244	.800	341	191	221	2	1226	15.5
63-64—St. Louis	77	2279	1280	572	.447	331	269	.813	377	189	272	4	1413	18.4
64-65—St. Louis	77	1739	901	393	.436	268	214	.799	276	136	182	0	1000	13.0
65-66—St. Louis	74	1851	942	419	.445	206	176	.854	234	164	177	1	1014	13.7
Totals	746	21731	11630	5239	.450	3722	2969	.798	5019	2236	2397	50	13447	18.0

NBA PLAYOFF RECORD

Sea.—Team	G.	Min.	FGA	FGM	Pct.	FTA	FTM	Pct.	Reb.	Ast.	PF	Disq.	Pts.	Avg.
56-57—St. Louis	10	419	143	62	.434	63	46	.730	112	28	47	3	170	17.0
57-58—St. Louis	11	418	221	111	.502	99	83	.838	115	37	48	3	305	27.7
58-59—St. Louis	6	259	123	63	.512	54	45	.833	72	16	21	0	171	28.5
59-60—St. Louis	14	544	296	125	.422	109	89	.816	138	54	54	1	339	24.2
60-61—St. Louis	12	455	235	104	.442	69	56	.811	118	54	45	1	264	22.0
62-63—St. Louis	11	255	179	83	.464	53	37	.698	55	34	42	4	203	18.5
63-64—St. Louis	12	392	175	75	.429	54	45	.833	74	57	34	0	195	16.2
64-65—St. Louis	4	123	75	34	.453	12	6	.500	26	7	14	0	74	18.5
65-66—St. Louis	10	200	97	44	.454	27	25	.926	34	18	15	0	113	11.3
Totals	90	3065	1544	701	.454	540	432	.800	744	305	320	12	1834	20.4

NBA ALL-STAR GAME RECORD

Season—Team	Min.	FGA	FGM	Pct.	FTA	FTM	Pct.	Reb.	Ast.	PF	Disq.	Pts.
1958—St. Louis	Chosen—Injured, Did Not Play											
1959—St. Louis	22	12	6	.500	3	3	1.000	8	3	5	0	15
1960—St. Louis	21	9	1	.111	0	0	.000	3	2	1	0	2
1961—St. Louis	13	2	9	.000	2	2	1.000	2	0	1	0	2
1962—St. Louis	9	3	1	.333	0	0	.000	2	1	1	0	2
Totals	65	26	8	.308	5	5	1.000	15	6	8	0	21

ABA REGULAR SEASON RECORD

Sea.—Team	G.	Min.	2-Point FGM	2-Point FGA	2-Point Pct.	3-Point FGM	3-Point FGA	3-Point Pct.	FTM	FTA	Pct.	Reb.	Ast.	Pts.	Avg.
67-68—Dallas	56	1737	371	756	.491	0	3	.000	277	351	.789	334	276	1019	18.2
68-69—Dallas	35	579	132	258	.512	0	1	.000	123	144	.854	102	122	387	11.1
69-70—Dallas	3	27	8	12	.667	0	1	.000	1	2	.500	....	....	17	5.7
Totals	94	2343	511	1026	.498	0	5	.000	401	497	.807	436	398	1423	15.1

ABA PLAYOFF RECORD

Sea.—Team	G.	Min.	2-Point FGM	2-Point FGA	2-Point Pct.	3-Point FGM	3-Point FGA	3-Point Pct.	FTM	FTA	Pct.	Reb.	Ast.	Pts.	Avg.
67-68—Dallas	3	70	14	37	.378	0	0	.000	9	13	.692	13	9	37	12.3
68-69—Dallas	2	45	5	14	.357	0	0	.000	8	10	.800	6	14	18	9.0
Totals	5	115	19	51	.373	0	0	.000	17	23	.739	19	23	55	11.0

ABA ALL-STAR GAME RECORD

Sea.—Team	G.	Min.	2-Point FGM	2-Point FGA	2-Point Pct.	3-Point FGM	3-Point FGA	3-Point Pct.	FTM	FTA	Pct.	Reb.	Ast.	Pts.	Avg.
67-68—Dallas	1	24	4	11	.364	0	0	.000	2	2	1.000	0	5	10	10.0

ABA COACHING RECORD

Sea.	Club	Regular Season W.	L.	Pct.	Pos.	Playoffs W.	L.
1967-68—Dallas		46	32	.590	2†	4	4
1968-69—Dallas		41	37	.526	4†	3	4
1969-70—Dallas		22	21	.512	..	..	..
Totals		109	90	.548		7	8

†Western Division.

**Elected to Naismith Memorial Basketball Hall of Fame, 1977.... Member of NBA championship team, 1958....
Named to NBA All-Star Second Team, 1958 and 1959.... Member of NCAA championship team, 1951.**

JOHN J. HAVLICEK
(Hondo)

Born April 8, 1940 at Martins Ferry, O.   Height 6:05.   Weight 205.

High School—Bridgeport, O.

College—Ohio State University, Columbus, O.

Drafted by Boston on first round, 1962.

—COLLEGIATE RECORD—

Year	G.	Min.	FGA	FGM	Pct.	FTA	FTM	Pct.	Reb.	Pts.	Avg.
58-59†					Freshman team did not play an intercollegiate schedule.						
59-60	28	....	312	144	.462	74	53	.716	205	341	12.2
60-61	28	....	321	173	.539	87	61	.701	244	407	14.5
61-62	28	....	377	196	.520	109	83	.761	271	475	17.0
Varsity Totals	84	....	1010	513	.508	270	197	.730	720	1223	14.6

NBA REGULAR SEASON RECORD

Sea.—Team	G.	Min.	FGA	FGM	Pct.	FTA	FTM	Pct.	Reb.	Ast.	PF	Disq.	Pts.	Avg.
62-63—Boston	80	2200	1085	483	.445	239	174	.728	534	179	189	2	1140	14.3
63-64—Boston	80	2587	1535	640	.417	422	315	.746	428	238	227	1	1595	19.9
64-65—Boston	75	2169	1420	570	.401	316	235	.744	371	199	200	2	1375	18.3
65-66—Boston	71	2175	1328	530	.399	349	274	.785	423	210	158	1	1334	18.8
66-67—Boston	81	2602	1540	684	.444	441	365	.828	532	278	210	0	1733	21.4
67-68—Boston	82	2921	1551	666	.429	453	368	.812	546	384	237	2	1700	20.7
68-69—Boston	82	3174	1709	692	.405	496	387	.780	570	441	247	0	1771	21.6
69-70—Boston	81	3369	1585	736	.464	578	488	.844	635	550	211	1	1960	24.2
70-71—Boston	81	3678	1982	892	.450	677	554	.818	730	607	200	0	2338	28.9
71-72—Boston	82	3698	1957	897	.458	549	458	.834	672	614	183	1	2252	27.5
72-73—Boston	80	3367	1704	766	.450	431	370	.858	567	529	195	1	1902	23.8

Sea.—Team	G.	Min.	FGA	FGM	Pct.	FTA	FTM	Pct.	Off.	Def.	Tot.	Ast.	PF	Dq.	Stl.	Blk.	Pts.	Avg.
73-74—Boston	76	3091	1502	685	.456	416	346	.832	138	349	487	447	196	1	95	32	1716	22.6
74-75—Boston	82	3132	1411	642	.455	332	289	.870	154	330	484	432	231	2	110	16	1573	19.2
75-76—Boston	76	2598	1121	504	.450	333	281	.844	116	198	314	278	204	1	97	29	1289	17.0
76-77—Boston	79	2913	1283	580	.452	288	235	.816	109	273	382	400	208	4	84	18	1395	17.7
77-78—Boston	82	2797	1217	546	.449	269	230	.855	93	239	332	328	185	2	90	22	1322	16.1
Totals	1270	46471	23930	10513	.439	6589	5309	.815			8007	6114	3281	21	476	117	26395	20.8

NBA PLAYOFF RECORD

Sea.—Team	G.	Min.	FGA	FGM	Pct.	FTA	FTM	Pct.	Reb.	Ast.	PF	Disq.	Pts.	Avg.
62-63—Boston	11	254	125	56	.448	27	18	.667	53	17	28	1	130	11.8
63-64—Boston	10	289	159	61	.384	44	35	.795	42	32	26	0	157	15.7
64-65—Boston	12	405	250	88	.352	55	46	.836	88	29	44	1	222	18.5
65-66—Boston	17	719	374	153	.409	113	95	.841	154	70	69	2	401	23.6
66-67—Boston	9	330	212	95	.448	71	57	.803	73	28	30	0	247	27.4
67-68—Boston	19	862	407	184	.452	151	125	.828	164	142	67	1	493	25.9
68-69—Boston	18	850	382	170	.445	138	118	.855	179	100	58	2	458	25.4
71-72—Boston	11	517	235	108	.460	99	85	.859	92	70	35	1	301	27.4
72-73—Boston	12	479	235	112	.477	74	61	.824	62	65	24	0	285	23.8

Sea.—Team	G.	Min.	FGA	FGM	Pct.	FTA	FTM	Pct.	Off.	Def.	Tot.	Ast.	PF	Dq.	Stl.	Blk.	Pts.	Avg.
73-74—Boston	18	811	411	199	.484	101	89	.881	28	88	116	108	43	0	24	6	487	27.1
74-75—Boston	11	464	192	83	.432	76	66	.868	18	39	57	51	51	1	16	1	232	21.1
75-76—Boston	15	505	180	80	.444	47	38	.809	18	38	56	51	22	0	12	5	198	13.2
76-77—Boston	9	375	167	62	.371	50	41	.820	15	34	49	62	33	0	8	4	165	18.3
Totals	172	6860	3329	1451	.436	1046	874	.836			1186	825	517	9	60	16	3776	22.0

NBA ALL-STAR GAME RECORD

Season—Team	Min.	FGA	FGM	Pct.	FTA	FTM	Pct.	Reb.	Ast.	PF	Disq.	Pts.
1966—Boston	25	16	6	.375	6	6	1.000	6	1	2	0	18
1967—Boston	17	14	7	.500	0	0	.000	2	1	1	0	14
1968—Boston	22	15	9	.600	11	8	.727	5	4	0	0	26
1969—Boston	31	14	6	.429	2	2	1.000	7	2	2	0	14
1970—Boston	29	15	7	.467	3	3	1.000	5	7	2	0	17
1971—Boston	24	12	6	.500	2	0	.000	3	2	3	0	12
1972—Boston	24	13	5	.385	5	5	1.000	3	2	2	0	15
1973—Boston	22	10	6	.600	5	2	.400	3	5	1	0	14

Season—Team	Min.	FGA	FGM	Pct.	FTA	FTM	Pct.	Off.	Def.	Tot.	Ast.	PF	Dq.	Stl.	Blk.	Pts.
1974—Boston	18	10	5	.500	2	0	.000	0	0	0	2	2	0	1	0	10
1975—Boston	31	12	7	.583	2	2	1.000	1	5	6	1	2	0	2	0	16
1976—Boston	21	10	3	.300	3	3	1.000	1	1	2	2	0	0	1	0	9
1977—Boston	17	5	2	.400	0	0	.000	0	1	1	1	1	0	0	0	4
1978—Boston	22	8	5	.625	0	0	.000	0	3	3	1	2	0	0	0	10
Totals	303	154	74	.481	41	31	.756			46	31	20	0	4	0	179

Elected to Naismith Memorial Basketball Hall of Fame, 1983. . . . Named to NBA 35th Anniversary All-Time Team, 1980. . . . NBA All-Star First Team, 1971, 1972, 1973, 1974. . . . NBA All-Star Second Team, 1964, 1966, 1968, 1969, 1970, 1975, 1976. . . . NBA All-Defensive First Team, 1972, 1973, 1974, 1975, 1976. . . . NBA All-Defensive Second Team,

JOHN HAVLICEK

1969, 1970, 1971. . . . NBA Playoff MVP, 1974. . . . Shares NBA playoff game record for most field goals made, 24, vs. Atlanta, April 1, 1973. . . . Holds NBA championship series record for most points in overtime period, 9, vs. Milwaukee, May 10, 1974. . . . Member of NBA championship teams, 1963, 1964, 1965, 1966, 1968, 1969, 1974, 1976. . . . Selected as wide receiver by Cleveland Browns on seventh round of 1962 National Football League draft. . . . Named to THE SPORTING NEWS All-America Second Team, 1962. . . . Member of NCAA championship team, 1960.

ELVIN ERNEST HAYES

Born November 17, 1945 at Rayville, La.   Height 6:09.   Weight 235.

High School—Rayville, La., Eula D. Britton.

College—University of Houston, Houston, Tex.

Drafted by San Diego on first round, 1968 (1st pick).

Traded by Houston to Baltimore for Jack Marin and future considerations, June 23, 1972.
Traded by Washington to Houston for 1981 and 1983 2nd round draft choices, June 8, 1981.

—COLLEGIATE RECORD—

Year	G.	Min.	FGA	FGM	Pct.	FTA	FTM	Pct.	Reb.	Pts.	Avg.
64-65†	21	......	478	217	.454	176	93	.528	500	527	25.1
65-66	29	946	570	323	.567	257	143	.556	490	789	27.2
66-67	31	1119	750	373	.497	227	135	.595	488	881	28.4
67-68	33	1270	945	519	.549	285	176	.618	624	1214	36.8
Varsity Totals	93	3335	2265	1215	.536	769	454	.590	1602	2884	31.0

NBA REGULAR SEASON RECORD

Sea.—Team	G.	Min.	FGA	FGM	Pct.	FTA	FTM	Pct.	Reb.	Ast.	PF	Disq.	Pts.	Avg.
68-69—San Diego	82	3695	2082	930	.447	746	467	.626	1406	113	266	2	2327	28.4
69-70—San Diego	82	3665	2020	914	.452	622	428	.688	1386	162	270	5	2256	27.5
70-71—San Diego	82	3633	2215	948	.428	676	454	.672	1362	186	225	1	2350	28.7
71-72—Houston	82	3461	1918	832	.434	615	399	.649	1197	270	233	1	2063	25.2
72-73—Baltimore	81	3347	1607	713	.444	434	291	.671	1177	127	232	3	1717	21.2

									—Rebounds—					
Sea.—Team	G.	Min.	FGA	FGM	Pct.	FTA	FTM	Pct.	Off.	Def.	Tot.	Ast.	PF	Dq.	Stl.	Blk.	Pts.	Avg.

Sea.—Team	G.	Min.	FGA	FGM	Pct.	FTA	FTM	Pct.	Off.	Def.	Tot.	Ast.	PF	Dq.	Stl.	Blk.	Pts.	Avg.
73-74—Capital	81	3602	1627	689	.423	495	357	.721	354	1109	1463	163	252	1	86	240	1735	21.4
74-75—Washington	82	3465	1668	739	.443	534	409	.766	221	783	1004	206	238	0	158	187	1887	23.0
75-76—Washington	80	2975	1381	649	.470	457	287	.628	210	668	878	121	293	5	104	202	1585	19.8
76-77—Washington	82	3364	1516	760	.501	614	422	.687	289	740	1029	158	312	1	87	220	1942	23.7
77-78—Washington	81	3246	1409	636	.451	514	326	.634	335	740	1075	149	313	7	96	159	1598	19.7
78-79—Washington	82	3105	1477	720	.487	534	349	.654	312	682	994	143	308	5	75	190	1789	21.8
79-80—Washington	81	3183	1677	761	.454	478	334	.699	269	627	896	129	309	9	62	189	1859	23.0
80-81—Washington	81	2931	1296	584	.451	439	271	.617	235	554	789	98	300	6	68	171	1439	17.8
81-82—Houston	82	3032	1100	519	.472	422	280	.664	267	480	747	144	287	4	62	104	1318	16.1
82-83—Houston	81	2302	890	424	.476	287	196	.683	199	417	616	158	232	2	50	81	1046	12.9
83-84—Houston	81	994	389	158	.406	132	86	.652	87	173	260	71	123	1	16	28	402	5.0
Totals	1303	50000	24272	10976	.452	7999	5356	.670			16279	2398	4193	53	864	1771	27313	21.0

Three-Point Field Goals: 1979-80, 3-for-13 (.231). 1980-81, 0-for-10. 1981-82, 0-for-5. 1982-83, 2-for-4 (.500). 1983-84, 0-for-2. Totals, 5-for-34 (.147).

NBA PLAYOFF RECORD

Sea.—Team	G.	Min.	FGA	FGM	Pct.	FTA	FTM	Pct.	Reb.	Ast.	PF	Disq.	Pts.	Avg.
68-69—San Diego	6	278	114	60	.526	53	35	.660	83	5	21	0	155	25.8
72-73—Baltimore	5	228	105	53	.505	33	23	.697	57	5	16	0	129	25.8

									—Rebounds—					

Sea.—Team	G.	Min.	FGA	FGM	Pct.	FTA	FTM	Pct.	Off.	Def.	Tot.	Ast.	PF	Dq.	Stl.	Blk.	Pts.	Avg.
73-74—Capital	7	323	143	76	.531	41	29	.707	31	80	111	21	23	0	5	15	181	25.9
74-75—Washington	17	751	372	174	.468	127	86	.677	46	140	186	37	70	3	26	39	434	25.5
75-76—Washington	7	305	122	54	.443	55	32	.582	16	72	88	10	24	0	5	28	140	20.0
76-77—Washington	9	405	173	74	.428	59	41	.695	29	93	122	17	39	0	10	22	189	21.0
77-78—Washington	21	868	385	189	.491	133	79	.594	103	176	279	43	86	2	32	52	457	21.8
78-79—Washington	19	786	396	170	.429	130	87	.669	94	172	266	38	79	3	17	52	427	22.5
79-80—Washington	2	92	41	16	.390	10	8	.800	10	12	22	6	8	0	0	4	40	20.0
81-82—Houston	3	124	50	17	.340	15	8	.533	7	23	30	3	12	0	2	10	42	14.0
Totals	96	4160	1901	883	.464	656	428	.652			1244	185	378	8	97	222	2194	22.9

NBA ALL-STAR GAME RECORD

Season—Team	Min.	FGA	FGM	Pct.	FTA	FTM	Pct.	Reb.	Ast.	PF	Disq.	Pts.
1969—San Diego	21	9	4	.444	3	3	1.000	5	0	4	0	11
1970—San Diego	35	21	9	.429	12	6	.500	15	1	1	0	24
1971—San Diego	19	13	4	.308	3	2	.667	4	2	1	0	10
1972—Houston	11	6	1	.167	2	2	1.000	2	0	2	0	4
1973—Baltimore	16	13	4	.308	2	2	1.000	12	0	0	0	10

								—Rebounds—						

Season—Team	Min.	FGA	FGM	Pct.	FTA	FTM	Pct.	Off.	Def.	Tot.	Ast.	PF	Dq.	Stl.	Blk.	Pts.
1974—Capital	35	13	5	.385	3	2	.667	4	11	15	6	4	0	0	1	12
1975—Washington	17	6	2	.333	0	0	.000	0	5	5	2	1	0	1	0	4
1976—Washington	31	14	6	.429	2	0	.000	3	7	10	1	5	0	1	0	12

Season—Team	Min.	FGA	FGM	Pct.	FTA	FTM	Pct.	Off.	Def.	Tot.	Ast.	PF	Dq.	Stl.	Blk.	Pts.
								—Rebounds—								
1977—Washington	11	6	6	1.000	0	0	.000	0	2	2	1	5	0	0	0	12
1978—Washington	11	7	1	.143	0	0	.000	3	1	4	0	4	0	1	0	2
1979—Washington..	28	11	5	.455	5	3	.600	4	9	13	0	5	0	1	1	13
1980—Washington..	29	10	5	.500	2	2	1.000	2	3	5	4	5	0	1	4	12
Totals	264	129	52	.403	34	22	.647			92	17	37	0	5	6	126

Named to All-NBA First Team, 1975, 1977, 1979. . . . All-NBA Second Team, 1973, 1974, 1976. . . . NBA All-Rookie Team, 1969. . . . NBA All-Defensive Second Team, 1974 and 1975. . . . Led NBA in scoring, 1969. . . . Led NBA in rebounding, 1970 and 1974. . . . Member of NBA championship team, 1978. . . . THE SPORTING NEWS College Player of the Year, 1968. . . . Named to THE SPORTING NEWS All-America First Team, 1967 and 1968. . . . THE SPORTING NEWS All-America Second Team, 1966.

SPENCER HAYWOOD

Born April 22, 1949 at Silver City, Miss. Height 6:09. Weight 225.

High School—Detroit, Mich., Pershing.

Colleges—Trinidad State Junior College, Trinidad, Colo., and University of Detroit, Detroit, Mich.

Drafted by Buffalo on second round, 1971 (30th pick).

Signed as undergraduate free agent by Denver ABA, August 16, 1969.
Terminated contract with Denver ABA and signed by Seattle NBA, 1971.
Traded by Seattle to New York for cash and the option of Eugene Short or a future draft choice, October 24, 1975.
Traded by New York to New Orleans for Joe C. Meriweather, January 5, 1979.
Traded by Utah to Los Angeles for Adrian Dantley, September 13, 1979.
Waived by Los Angeles, August 19, 1980; signed by Washington as a free agent, October 24, 1981.
Waived by Washington, March 9, 1983.
Played in Italy during 1980-81 and 1981-82 seasons.

—COLLEGIATE RECORD—
Trinidad State JC

Year	G.	Min.	FGA	FGM	Pct.	FTA	FTM	Pct.	Reb.	Pts.	Avg.
67-68	30	......	675	358	.530	195	129	.662	663	845	28.2

Detroit

Year	G.	Min.	FGA	FGM	Pct.	FTA	FTM	Pct.	Reb.	Pts.	Avg.
68-69	24	......	508	288	.567	254	195	.768	530	771	32.1

ITALIAN LEAGUE RECORD

Year	G.	Min.	FGA	FGM	Pct.	FTA	FTM	Pct.	Reb.	Pts.	Avg.
80-81—Venezia	34	....	601	334	.556	179	132	.737	354	800	23.5
81-82—Carrera	5	175	100	63	.630	32	24	.750	37	150	30.0

ABA REGULAR SEASON RECORD

Sea.—Team	G.	Min.	2-Point			3-Point			FTM	FTA	Pct.	Reb.	Ast.	Pts.	Avg.
			FGM	FGA	Pct.	FGM	FGA	Pct.							
69-70—Denver	84	3808	986	1987	.496	0	11	.000	547	705	.776	1637	190	2519	30.0

NBA REGULAR SEASON RECORD

Sea.—Team	G.	Min.	FGA	FGM	Pct.	FTA	FTM	Pct.	Reb.	Ast.	PF	Disq.	Pts.	Avg.
70-71—Seattle	33	1162	579	260	.449	218	160	.733	396	48	84	1	680	20.6
71-72—Seattle	73	3167	1557	717	.461	586	480	.819	926	148	208	0	1914	26.2
72-73—Seattle	77	3259	1868	889	.476	564	473	.839	995	196	213	2	2251	29.2

Sea.—Team	G.	Min.	FGA	FGM	Pct.	FTA	FTM	Pct.	Off.	Def.	Tot.	Ast.	PF	Dq.	Stl.	Blk.	Pts.	Avg.
									—Rebounds—									
73-74—Seattle	75	3039	1520	694	.457	458	373	.814	318	689	1007	240	198	2	65	106	1761	23.5
74-75—Seattle	68	2529	1325	608	.459	381	309	.811	198	432	630	137	173	1	54	108	1525	22.4
75-76—New York	78	2892	1360	605	.445	448	339	.757	234	644	878	92	255	1	53	80	1549	19.9
76-77—Knicks	31	1021	449	202	.450	131	109	.832	77	203	280	50	72	0	14	29	513	16.5
77-78—New York	67	1765	852	412	.484	135	96	.711	141	301	442	126	188	1	37	72	920	13.7
78-79—N.Y.-N.O.	68	2361	1205	595	.494	292	231	.791	172	361	533	127	236	8	40	82	1421	20.9
79-80—Los Ang.	76	1544	591	288	.487	206	159	.772	132	214	346	93	197	2	35	57	736	9.7
81-82—Washington	76	2086	829	395	.476	260	219	.842	144	278	422	64	249	6	45	68	1009	13.3
82-83—Washington	38	775	312	125	.401	87	63	.724	77	106	183	30	94	2	12	27	313	8.2
Totals	760	25600	12447	5790	.465	3766	3011	.800			7038	1351	2167	26	355	629	14592	19.2

Three-Point Field Goals: 1979-80, 1-for-4 (.250). 1981-82, 0-for-3. 1982-83, 0-for-1. Totals, 1-for-8 (.125).

NBA PLAYOFF RECORD

Sea.—Team	G.	Min.	FGA	FGM	Pct.	FTA	FTM	Pct.	Off.	Def.	Tot.	Ast.	PF	Dq.	Stl.	Blk.	Pts.	Avg.
									—Rebounds—									
74-75—Seattle	9	337	131	47	.359	61	47	.770	20	61	81	18	29	0	7	11	141	15.7
77-78—New York	6	177	85	43	.506	11	11	1.000	19	23	42	12	24	1	2	5	97	16.2
79-80—Los Ang.	11	145	53	25	.472	16	13	.813	14	12	26	4	17	0	0	6	63	5.7
81-82—Washington	7	231	115	57	.496	35	26	.743	16	23	39	7	28	0	4	14	140	20.0
Totals	33	890	384	172	.448	123	97	.789	69	119	188	41	98	1	13	36	441	13.4

Three-Point Field Goals: 1979-80, 0-for-1.

NBA ALL-STAR GAME RECORD

Season—Team	Min.	FGA	FGM	Pct.	FTA	FTM	Pct.	Reb.	Ast.	PF	Disq.	Pts.
1972—Seattle	25	10	4	.400	4	3	.750	7	1	2	0	11
1973—Seattle	22	10	5	.500	2	2	1.000	10	0	5	0	12

Season—Team	Min.	FGA	FGM	Pct.	FTA	FTM	Pct.	Off.	Def.	Tot.	Ast.	PF	Dq.	Stl.	Blk.	Pts.
								—Rebounds—								
1974—Seattle	33	17	10	.588	3	3	1.000	2	9	11	5	5	0	0	3	23
1975—Seattle	17	9	1	.111	0	0	.000	1	2	3	0	1	0	0	0	2
Totals	97	46	20	.435	9	8	.889			31	6	13	0	0	3	48

Named to NBA All-Star First Team, 1972 and 1973. . . . NBA All-Star Second Team, 1974 and 1975. . . . Member of NBA championship team, 1980. . . . Named to ABA All-Star First Team, 1970. . . . ABA Most Valuable Player and Rookie of the Year, 1970. . . . ABA All-Star Game MVP, 1970. . . . Led ABA in scoring and rebounding, 1970. . . . Led NCAA in rebounding, 1969. . . . Member of U. S. Olympic team, 1968. . . . THE SPORTING NEWS All-America First Team, 1969.

BAILEY E. HOWELL

Born January 20, 1937 at Middleton, Tenn.   Height 6:07.   Weight 220.

High School—Middleton, Tenn.

College—Mississippi State University, Mississippi State, Miss.

Drafted by Detroit on first round, 1959.

Traded by Detroit with Bob Ferry, Don Ohl, Wally Jones and Les Hunter to Baltimore for Terry Dischinger, Don Kojis and Rod Thorn, June 18, 1964.
Traded by Baltimore to Boston for Mel Counts, September 1, 1966.
Selected from Boston by Buffalo in expansion draft, May 11, 1970.
Traded by Buffalo to Philadelphia for Bob Kauffman and cash or a draft choice, May 11, 1970.

—COLLEGIATE RECORD—

Year	G.	Min.	FGA	FGM	Pct.	FTA	FTM	Pct.	Reb.	Pts.	Avg.
55-56†					(Statistics unavailable)						
56-57	25	....	382	217	.568	285	213	.747	492	647	25.9
57-58	25	....	439	226	.515	315	243	.771	406	695	27.8
58-59	25	....	464	231	.498	292	226	.774	379	688	27.5
Varsity Totals	75	....	1285	674	.525	892	682	.765	1277	2030	27.1

NBA REGULAR SEASON RECORD

Sea.—Team	G.	Min.	FGA	FGM	Pct.	FTA	FTM	Pct.	Reb.	Ast.	PF	Disq.	Pts.	Avg.
59-60—Detroit	75	2346	1119	510	.456	422	312	.739	790	63	282	13	1332	17.8
60-61—Detroit	77	2752	1293	607	.469	798	601	.753	1111	196	297	10	1815	23.6
61-62—Detroit	79	2857	1193	553	.464	612	470	.768	996	186	317	10	1576	19.9
62-63—Detroit	79	2971	1235	637	.516	650	519	.798	910	232	301	9	1793	22.7
63-64—Detroit	77	2700	1267	598	.472	581	470	.809	776	205	290	9	1666	21.6
64-65—Baltimore	80	2975	1040	515	.495	629	504	.801	869	208	345	10	1534	19.2
65-66—Baltimore	79	2328	986	481	.488	551	402	.730	773	155	306	12	1364	17.3
66-67—Boston	81	2503	1242	636	.512	471	349	.741	677	103	296	4	1621	20.0
67-68—Boston	82	2801	1336	643	.481	461	335	.727	805	133	285	4	1621	19.8
68-69—Boston	78	2527	1257	612	.487	426	313	.735	685	137	285	3	1537	19.7
69-70—Boston	82	2078	931	399	.429	308	235	.763	550	120	261	4	1033	12.6
70-71—Philadelphia	82	1589	686	324	.472	315	230	.730	441	115	234	2	878	10.7
Totals	951	30427	13585	6515	.480	6224	4740	.762	9383	1853	3499	90	17770	18.7

NBA PLAYOFF RECORD

Sea.—Team	G.	Min.	FGA	FGM	Pct.	FTA	FTM	Pct.	Reb.	Ast.	PF	Disq.	Pts.	Avg.
59-60—Detroit	2	72	41	14	.341	8	6	.750	17	3	8	0	34	17.0
60-61—Detroit	5	144	57	20	.351	23	16	.696	46	22	22	1	56	11.2
61-62—Detroit	10	378	163	69	.423	75	62	.827	96	23	48	3	200	20.0
62-63—Detroit	4	163	64	24	.375	27	23	.852	42	11	19	1	71	17.8
64-65—Baltimore	9	350	130	67	.515	70	53	.757	105	19	38	3	187	20.8
65-66—Baltimore	3	94	50	23	.460	11	8	.727	30	2	13	1	54	18.0
66-67—Boston	9	241	122	59	.484	30	20	.667	66	5	35	2	138	15.3
67-68—Boston	19	597	264	135	.511	107	74	.692	146	22	84	6	344	18.1
68-69—Boston	18	551	229	112	.489	64	46	.719	118	19	84	3	270	15.0
70-71—Philadelphia	7	122	45	19	.422	18	9	.500	31	4	25	1	47	6.7
Totals	86	2712	1165	542	.465	433	317	.732	697	130	376	21	1401	16.3

NBA ALL-STAR GAME RECORD

Season—Team	Min.	FGA	FGM	Pct.	FTA	FTM	Pct.	Reb.	Ast.	PF	Disq.	Pts.
1961—Detroit	16	10	5	.500	4	3	.750	3	3	4	0	13
1962—Detroit	8	2	1	.500	0	0	.000	0	1	1	0	2
1963—Detroit	11	3	2	.667	0	0	.000	1	1	2	0	4
1964—Detroit	6	3	1	.333	0	0	.000	2	0	0	0	2
1966—Baltimore	26	11	3	.273	2	1	.500	2	2	4	0	7
1967—Boston	14	4	1	.250	2	2	1.000	2	1	1	0	4
Totals	81	33	13	.394	8	6	.750	10	8	12	0	32

Named to NBA All-Star Second Team, 1963. . . . Member of NBA championship teams, 1968 and 1969. . . . Led NCAA major college division in field-goal percentage, 1957. . . . Named to THE SPORTING NEWS All-America First Team, 1959.

LOUIS C. HUDSON
(Lou)

Born July 11, 1944 at Greensboro, N. C.   Height 6:05.   Weight 210.
High School—Greensboro, N. C., Dudley.
College—University of Minnesota, Minneapolis, Minn.
Drafted by St. Louis on first round, 1966 (4th pick).

Traded by Atlanta to Los Angeles for Ollie Johnson, September 30, 1977.

—COLLEGIATE RECORD—

Year	G.	Min.	FGA	FGM	Pct.	FTA	FTM	Pct.	Reb.	Pts.	Avg.
62-63				(Freshman team did not play intercollegiate schedule.)							
63-64	24	....	435	191	.439	85	53	.624	191	435	18.1
64-65	24	....	463	231	.499	123	96	.780	247	558	23.3
65-66	17	....	303	143	.472	77	50	.649	138	336	19.8
Totals	65	....	1201	565	.470	285	199	.698	576	1329	20.4

NBA REGULAR SEASON RECORD

Sea.—Team	G.	Min.	FGA	FGM	Pct.	FTA	FTM	Pct.	Reb.	Ast.	PF	Disq.	Pts.	Avg.
66-67—St. Louis	80	2446	1328	620	.467	327	231	.706	435	95	277	3	1471	18.4
67-68—St. Louis	46	966	500	227	.454	164	120	.732	193	65	113	2	574	12.5
68-69—Atlanta	81	2869	1455	716	.492	435	338	.777	533	216	248	0	1770	21.9
69-70—Atlanta	80	3091	1564	830	.531	450	371	.824	373	276	225	1	2031	25.4
70-71—Atlanta	76	3113	1713	829	.484	502	381	.759	386	257	186	0	2039	26.8
71-72—Atlanta	77	3042	1540	775	.503	430	349	.812	385	309	225	0	1899	24.7
72-73—Atlanta	75	3027	1710	816	.477	481	397	.825	467	258	197	1	2029	27.1

Sea.—Team	G.	Min.	FGA	FGM	Pct.	FTA	FTM	Pct.	Off.	Def.	Tot.	Ast.	PF	Dq.	Stl.	Blk.	Pts.	Avg.
										—Rebounds—								
73-74—Atl.	65	2588	1356	678	.500	353	295	.836	126	224	350	216	205	3	160	29	1651	25.4
74-75—Atl.	11	380	225	97	.431	57	48	.842	14	33	47	40	33	1	13	2	242	22.0
75-76—Atl.	81	2558	1205	569	.472	291	237	.814	104	196	300	214	241	3	124	17	1375	17.0
76-77—Atl.	58	1745	905	413	.456	169	142	.840	48	81	129	155	160	2	67	19	968	16.7
77-78—L.A.	82	2283	992	493	.497	177	137	.774	80	108	188	193	196	0	94	14	1123	13.7
78-79—L.A.	78	1686	636	329	.517	124	110	.887	64	76	140	141	133	1	58	17	768	9.8
Totals	890	29794	15129	7392	.489	3960	3156	.797			3926	2432	2439	17	516	98	17940	20.2

NBA PLAYOFF RECORD

Sea.—Team	G.	Min.	FGA	FGM	Pct.	FTA	FTM	Pct.	Reb.	Ast.	PF	Disq.	Pts.	Avg.
66-67—St. Louis	9	317	179	77	.430	68	49	.723	48	15	35	1	203	22.6
67-68—St. Louis	6	181	99	44	.444	47	42	.894	43	14	21	0	130	21.7
68-69—Atlanta	11	424	216	101	.468	52	40	.769	59	32	43	1	242	22.0
69-70—Atlanta	9	360	187	78	.417	50	41	.820	40	33	34	2	197	21.9
70-71—Atlanta	5	213	108	49	.454	39	29	.744	35	15	19	0	127	25.4
71-72—Atlanta	6	266	139	63	.453	29	24	.828	33	21	13	0	150	25.0
72-73—Atlanta	6	255	166	76	.458	29	26	.897	47	17	16	0	178	29.7

Sea.—Team	G.	Min.	FGA	FGM	Pct.	FTA	FTM	Pct.	Off.	Def.	Tot.	Ast.	PF	Dq.	Stl.	Blk.	Pts.	Avg.
										—Rebounds—								
77-78—L.A.	3	93	38	14	.368	8	7	.875	7	2	9	9	9	0	5	0	35	11.7
78-79—L.A.	6	90	32	17	.531	4	4	1.000	1	3	4	8	6	0	1	0	38	6.3
Totals	61	2199	1164	519	.446	326	262	.804			318	164	196	4	6	0	1300	21.3

NBA ALL-STAR GAME RECORD

Season—Team	Min.	FGA	FGM	Pct.	FTA	FTM	Pct.	Reb.	Ast.	PF	Disq.	Pts.
1969—Atlanta	20	13	6	.462	1	1	1.000	1	1	0	0	13
1970—Atlanta	18	12	5	.417	5	5	1.000	1	0	1	0	15
1971—Atlanta	17	13	6	.462	3	2	.667	3	1	3	0	14
1972—Atlanta	18	7	2	.286	2	2	1.000	3	3	3	0	6
1973—Atlanta	9	8	2	.250	2	2	1.000	2	0	2	0	6

Season—Team	Min.	FGA	FGM	Pct.	FTA	FTM	Pct.	Off.	Def.	Tot.	Ast.	PF	Dq.	Stl.	Blk.	Pts.
									—Rebounds—							
1974—Atlanta	17	8	5	.625	2	2	1.000	1	2	3	1	2	0	0	1	12
Totals	99	61	26	.426	15	14	.933			13	6	11	0			66

Named to NBA All-Star Second Team, 1970. . . . NBA All-Rookie Team, 1967.

DANIEL PAUL ISSEL
(Dan)

Born October 25, 1948 at Batavia, Ill.   Height 6:09.   Weight 240.
High School—Batavia, Ill.
College—University of Kentucky, Lexington, Ky.
Drafted by Detroit on eighth round, 1970 (122nd pick).

Selected by Kentucky on first round of ABA draft, 1970.
Traded by Kentucky to Baltimore for Tom Owens and cash, September 19, 1975.

Traded by Baltimore to Denver for Dave Robisch and cash, October 8, 1975.
Entered NBA with Denver, 1976.

—COLLEGIATE RECORD—

Year	G.	Min.	FGA	FGM	Pct.	FTA	FTM	Pct.	Reb.	Pts.	Avg.
66-67†	20	....	332	168	.506	111	80	.721	355	416	20.8
67-68	27	836	390	171	.438	154	102	.662	328	444	16.4
68-69	28	1063	534	285	.534	232	176	.759	381	746	26.6
69-70	28	1044	667	369	.553	275	210	.764	369	948	33.9
Varsity Totals	83	2943	1591	825	.519	661	488	.738	1078	2138	25.8

ABA REGULAR SEASON RECORD

Sea.—Team	G.	Min.	2-Point FGM	FGA	Pct.	3-Point FGM	FGA	Pct.	FTM	FTA	Pct.	Reb.	Ast.	Pts.	Avg.
70-71—Kentucky	83	3274	938	1989	.472	0	5	.000	604	748	.807	1093	162	2480	29.9
71-72—Kentucky	83	3570	969	1990	.487	3	11	.273	591	753	.785	931	195	2538	30.6
72-73—Kentucky	84	3531	899	1742	.516	3	15	.200	485	635	.764	922	220	2292	27.3
73-74—Kentucky	83	3347	826	1709	.483	3	17	.176	457	581	.787	847	137	2118	25.5
74-75—Kentucky	83	2864	614	1298	.473	0	5	.000	237	321	.738	710	188	1465	17.7
75-76—Denver	84	2858	751	1468	.512	1	4	.250	425	521	.816	923	201	1930	23.0
Totals	500	19444	4997	10196	.490	10	57	.175	2799	3559	.787	5426	1103	12823	25.6

ABA PLAYOFF RECORD

Sea.—Team	G.	Min.	2-Point FGM	FGA	Pct.	3-Point FGM	FGA	Pct.	FTM	FTA	Pct.	Reb.	Ast.	Pts.	Avg.
70-71—Kentucky	19	670	207	408	.507	0	0	.000	123	141	.872	221	28	536	27.9
71-72—Kentucky	6	269	47	113	.416	0	1	.000	38	50	.760	54	5	132	22.0
72-73—Kentucky	19	821	197	392	.503	1	6	.167	124	156	.795	225	28	521	27.4
73-74—Kentucky	8	311	60	135	.444	0	0	.000	28	33	.848	87	14	148	18.5
74-75—Kentucky	15	578	122	261	.467	0	0	.000	60	74	.811	119	29	304	20.3
75-76—Denver	13	470	111	226	.491	0	1	.000	44	56	.786	156	32	266	20.5
Totals	80	3119	744	1535	.485	1	8	.125	417	510	.818	949	136	1907	23.8

ABA ALL-STAR GAME RECORD

Sea.—Team	Min.	2-Point FGM	FGA	Pct.	3-Point FGM	FGA	Pct.	FTM	FTA	Pct.	Reb.	Ast.	Pts.	Avg.
1971—Kentucky	34	8	15	.533	0	0	.000	5	8	.625	11	0	21	21.0
1972—Kentucky	23	9	13	.692	0	0	.000	3	4	.750	9	5	21	21.0
1973—Kentucky	29	6	14	.429	0	0	.000	2	2	1.000	7	4	14	14.0
1974—Kentucky	26	10	15	.667	0	0	.000	1	1	1.000	4	1	21	21.0
1975—Kentucky	20	3	6	.500	0	0	.000	1	2	.500	7	1	7	7.0
1976—Denver	31	6	16	.375	0	0	.000	7	9	.778	9	5	19	19.0
Totals	163	42	79	.532	0	0	.000	19	26	.731	41	16	103	17.2

NBA REGULAR SEASON RECORD

Sea.—Team	G.	Min.	FGA	FGM	Pct.	FTA	FTM	Pct.	Rebounds Off.	Def.	Tot.	Ast.	PF	Dq.	Stl.	Blk.	Pts.	Avg.
76-77—Denver	79	2507	1282	660	.515	558	445	.797	211	485	696	177	246	7	91	29	1765	22.3
77-78—Denver	82	2851	1287	659	.512	547	428	.782	253	577	830	304	279	5	100	41	1746	21.3
78-79—Denver	81	2742	1030	532	.517	419	316	.754	240	498	738	255	233	6	61	46	1380	17.0
79-80—Denver	82	2938	1416	715	.505	667	517	.775	236	483	719	198	190	1	88	54	1951	23.8
80-81—Denver	80	2641	1220	614	.503	684	519	.759	229	447	676	158	249	6	83	53	1749	21.9
81-82—Denver	81	2472	1236	651	.527	655	546	.834	174	434	608	179	245	4	67	55	1852	22.9
82-83—Denver	80	2431	1296	661	.510	479	400	.835	151	445	596	223	227	0	83	43	1726	21.6
83-84—Denver	76	2076	1153	569	.493	428	364	.850	112	401	513	173	182	2	60	44	1506	19.8
84-85—Denver	77	1684	791	363	.459	319	257	.806	80	251	331	137	171	1	65	31	984	12.8
Totals	718	22342	10711	5424	.506	4756	3792	.797	1686	4021	5707	1804	2022	32	698	396	14659	20.4

Three-Point Field Goals: 1979-80, 4-for-12 (.333). 1980-81, 2-for-12 (.167). 1981-82, 4-for-6 (.667). 1982-83, 4-for-19 (.211). 1983-84, 4-for-19 (.211). 1984-85, 1-for-7 (.143). Totals, 19-for-75 (.253).

NBA PLAYOFF RECORD

Sea.—Team	G.	Min.	FGA	FGM	Pct.	FTA	FTM	Pct.	Rebounds Off.	Def.	Tot.	Ast.	PF	Dq.	Stl.	Blk.	Pts.	Avg.
76-77—Denver	6	222	96	49	.510	45	34	.756	18	40	58	17	20	0	5	4	132	22.0
77-78—Denver	13	460	212	103	.486	65	56	.862	41	93	134	53	43	1	7	3	262	20.2
78-79—Denver	3	109	45	24	.533	31	25	.806	7	21	28	10	15	0	0	0	73	24.3
81-82—Denver	3	103	60	32	.533	12	12	1.000	8	13	21	5	10	0	3	1	76	25.3
82-83—Denver	8	227	136	69	.507	29	25	.862	13	45	58	25	18	0	9	5	163	20.4
83-84—Denver	5	153	102	52	.510	39	32	.821	10	30	40	8	15	0	6	6	137	27.4
84-85—Denver	15	325	159	73	.459	48	39	.813	14	40	54	27	36	0	12	5	186	12.4
Totals	53	1599	810	402	.496	269	223	.829	111	282	393	145	157	1	42	24	1029	19.4

Three-Point Field Goals: 1982-83, 0-for-1. 1983-84, 1-for-2 (.500). 1984-85, 1-for-1 (1.000). Totals, 2-for-4 (.500).

NBA ALL-STAR GAME RECORD

Season—Team	Min.	FGA	FGM	Pct.	FTA	FTM	Pct.	Rebounds Off.	Def.	Tot.	Ast.	PF	Dq.	Stl.	Blk.	Pts.
1977—Denver	10	3	0	.000	0	0	.000	1	0	1	0	1	0	0	0	0

Named to ABA All-Star First Team, 1972. . . . ABA All-Star Second Team, 1971, 1973, 1974, 1976. . . . ABA Rookie of the Year, 1971. . . . ABA All-Rookie Team, 1971. . . . ABA All-Star Game MVP, 1972. . . . Member of ABA championship team, 1975. . . . Led ABA in scoring, 1971. . . . Set ABA record for most points in one season, 1972. . . . Named to THE SPORTING NEWS All-America First Team, 1970. . . . THE SPORTING NEWS All-America Second Team, 1969.

GUS JOHNSON JR.

Born December 13, 1938 at Akron, O.   Height 6:06.   Weight 235.

Died April 29, 1987.

High School—Akron, O., Central.

Colleges—University of Akron, Akron, O.; Boise Junior
College, Boise, Idaho, and University of Idaho, Moscow, Ida.

Drafted by Baltimore on second round, 1963 (11th pick).

Traded by Baltimore to Phoenix for a draft choice, April 10, 1972.
Waived by Phoenix NBA, December 1, 1972; signed by Indiana ABA as a free agent, December 15, 1972.

—COLLEGIATE RECORD—
Akron

Year	G.	Min.	FGA	FGM	Pct.	FTA	FTM	Pct.	Reb.	Pts.	Avg.
59-60				(Left school before start of basketball season.)							

Idaho

Year	G.	Min.	FGA	FGM	Pct.	FTA	FTM	Pct.	Reb.	Pts.	Avg.
62-63	23	....	438	188	.429	105	62	.590	466	438	19.0

NBA REGULAR SEASON RECORD

Sea.—Team	G.	Min.	FGA	FGM	Pct.	FTA	FTM	Pct.	Reb.	Ast.	PF	Disq.	Pts.	Avg.
63-64—Baltimore	78	2847	1329	571	.430	319	210	.658	1064	169	321	11	1352	17.3
64-65—Baltimore	76	2899	1379	577	.418	386	261	.676	988	270	258	4	1415	18.6
65-66—Baltimore	42	1284	661	273	.413	178	131	.736	546	114	136	3	677	16.1
66-67—Baltimore	73	2626	1377	620	.450	383	271	.708	855	194	281	7	1511	20.7
67-68—Baltimore	60	2271	1033	482	.467	270	180	.667	782	159	223	7	1144	19.1
68-69—Baltimore	49	1671	782	359	.459	223	160	.717	568	97	176	1	878	17.9
69-70—Baltimore	78	2919	1282	578	.451	272	197	.724	1086	264	269	6	1353	17.3
70-71—Baltimore	66	2538	1090	494	.453	290	214	.738	1128	192	227	4	1202	18.2
71-72—Baltimore	39	668	269	103	.383	63	43	.683	226	51	91	0	249	6.4
72-73—Phoenix	21	417	181	69	.381	36	25	.694	136	31	55	0	163	7.8
Totals	582	20140	9383	4126	.440	2420	1692	.699	7379	1541	2037	43	9944	17.1

NBA PLAYOFF RECORD

Sea.—Team	G.	Min.	FGA	FGM	Pct.	FTA	FTM	Pct.	Reb.	Ast.	PF	Disq.	Pts.	Avg.
64-65—Baltimore	10	377	173	62	.358	46	34	.739	111	34	38	1	158	15.8
65-66—Baltimore	1	8	4	1	.250	0	0	.000	0	0	1	0	2	2.0
69-70—Baltimore	7	298	111	51	.459	34	27	.794	80	9	20	0	129	18.4
70-71—Baltimore	11	365	128	54	.422	47	35	.745	114	30	34	0	143	13.0
71-72—Baltimore	5	77	30	9	.300	2	2	1.000	25	3	17	0	20	4.0
Totals	34	1125	446	177	.397	129	98	.760	330	76	110	1	452	13.3

NBA ALL-STAR GAME RECORD

Season—Team	Min.	FGA	FGM	Pct.	FTA	FTM	Pct.	Reb.	Ast.	PF	Disq.	Pts.
1965—Baltimore	25	13	7	.538	13	11	.846	8	2	2	0	25
1968—Baltimore	16	9	3	.333	2	1	.500	6	1	2	0	7
1969—Baltimore	18	10	4	.400	8	5	.625	10	0	3	0	13
1970—Baltimore	17	12	5	.417	0	0	.000	7	1	2	0	10
1971—Baltimore	23	12	5	.417	2	2	1.000	4	2	3	0	12
Totals	99	56	24	.429	25	19	.760	35	6	12	0	67

ABA REGULAR SEASON RECORD

Sea.—Team	G.	Min.	2-Point			3-Point			FTM	FTA	Pct.	Reb.	Ast.	Pts.	Avg.
			FGM	FGA	Pct.	FGM	FGA	Pct.							
72-73—Indiana	50	753	128	278	.460	4	21	.190	31	42	.738	245	62	299	6.0

ABA PLAYOFF RECORD

Sea.—Team	G.	Min.	2-Point			3-Point			FTM	FTA	Pct.	Reb.	Ast.	Pts.	Avg.
			FGM	FGA	Pct.	FGM	FGA	Pct.							
72-73—Indiana	17	184	15	56	.268	0	3	.000	3	4	.750	69	15	42	2.5

Named to NBA All-Star Second Team, 1965, 1966, 1970, 1971. . . . NBA All-Rookie Team, 1964. . . . NBA All-Defensive First Team, 1970 and 1971. . . . Member of ABA championship team, 1973.

—DID YOU KNOW—

That Wilt Chamberlain's highest scoring quarter in his NBA-record 100-point game for Philadelphia against New York at Hershey, Pa., on March 2, 1962 was 31 points in the fourth period? Chamberlain's single-quarter output was surpassed by two different players on the final day of the 1977-78 season. George Gervin scored 33 points in the second period for San Antonio at New Orleans and David Thompson 32 in the first period for Denver at Detroit on April 9, 1978. Gervin edged Thompson for the league scoring title that season, 27.22 to 27.15.

DONALD NEIL JOHNSTON
(Known by middle name.)

Born February 4, 1929 at Chillicothe, O.   Height 6:08.   Weight 210.

Died September 27, 1978.

High School—Chillicothe, O.

College—Ohio State University, Columbus, O.

Signed by Philadelphia as a free agent, 1951.
Signed as player-coach by Pittsburgh, ABL, 1961.

—COLLEGIATE RECORD—

Year	G.	Min.	FGA	FGM	Pct.	FTA	FTM	Pct.	Reb.	Pts.	Avg.
46-47	7	....	....	5	....	8	3	.375	....	13	1.9
47-48	20	....	219	67	.306	87	46	.529	....	180	9.0
Totals	27	....	....	72	....	95	49	.516	....	193	7.1

(Signed pro baseball contract in 1948 and became ineligible for his final two years at Ohio State.)

NBA REGULAR SEASON RECORD

Sea.—Team	G.	Min.	FGA	FGM	Pct.	FTA	FTM	Pct.	Reb.	Ast.	PF	Disq.	Pts.	Avg.
51-52—Philadelphia	64	993	299	141	.472	151	100	.662	342	39	154	5	382	6.0
52-53—Philadelphia	70	3166	1114	504	.452	794	556	.700	976	197	248	6	1564	22.3
53-54—Philadelphia	72	3296	1317	591	.449	772	577	.747	797	203	259	7	1759	24.4
54-55—Philadelphia	72	2917	1184	521	.440	769	589	.766	1085	215	255	4	1631	22.7
55-56—Philadelphia	70	2594	1092	499	.457	685	549	.801	872	225	251	8	1547	22.1
56-57—Philadelphia	69	2531	1163	520	.447	648	535	.826	855	203	231	2	1575	22.8
57-58—Philadelphia	71	2408	1102	473	.429	540	442	.819	790	166	233	4	1388	19.5
58-59—Philadelphia	28	393	164	54	.329	88	69	.784	139	21	50	0	177	6.3
Totals	516	18298	7435	3303	.444	4447	3417	.768	5856	1269	1681	36	10023	19.4

NBA PLAYOFF RECORD

Sea.—Team	G.	Min.	FGA	FGM	Pct.	FTA	FTM	Pct.	Reb.	Ast.	PF	Disq.	Pts.	Avg.
51-52—Philadelphia	3	32	10	5	.500	8	6	.750	10	1	8	0	16	5.3
55-56—Philadelphia	10	397	169	69	.408	92	65	.707	143	51	41	0	203	20.3
56-57—Philadelphia	2	84	53	17	.321	6	4	.667	35	9	9	0	38	19.0
57-58—Philadelphia	8	189	78	30	.385	33	27	.818	69	14	18	0	87	10.9
Totals	23	702	310	121	.390	139	102	.734	257	75	76	0	344	15.0

NBA ALL-STAR GAME RECORD

Season—Team	Min.	FGA	FGM	Pct.	FTA	FTM	Pct.	Reb.	Ast.	PF	Disq.	Pts.
1953—Philadelphia	27	13	5	.385	2	1	.500	12	0	2	0	11
1954—Philadelphia	20	9	2	.222	4	2	.500	7	2	1	0	6
1955—Philadelphia	15	7	1	.143	1	1	1.000	6	1	0	0	3
1956—Philadelphia	25	9	5	.556	11	7	.636	10	1	3	0	17
1957—Philadelphia	23	12	8	.667	3	3	1.000	9	1	2	0	19
1958—Philadelpnia	22	13	6	.462	2	2	1.000	8	1	5	0	14
Totals	132	63	27	.429	23	16	.696	52	6	13	0	70

AMERICAN BASKETBALL LEAGUE PLAYING RECORD

			2-Point			3-Point							
Sea.—Team	G.	Min.	FGM	FGA	Pct.	FGM	FGA	Pct.	FTM	FTA	Pct.	Reb.	Ast.	Pts.	Avg.
61-62—Pittsburgh	5	106	37	15	.405	1	1	1.000	24	16	.667	18	10	49	9.8

ABL COACHING RECORD

	Regular Season				Playoffs	
Sea. Club	W.	L.	Pct.	Pos.	W.	L.
1961-62—Pittsburgh	41	40	.506	2†	0	1
1962-63—Pittsburgh	12	10	.545	3	..	..

NBA COACHING RECORD

	Regular Season				Playoffs	
Sea. Club	W.	L.	Pct.	Pos.	W.	L.
1959-60—Philadelphia	49	26	.653	2†	4	5
1960-61—Philadelphia	46	33	.582	2†	0	3
Totals (2 seasons)	95	59	.617		4	8

†Eastern Division.

EBL COACHING RECORD

	Regular Season				Playoffs	
Sea. Club	W.	L.	Pct.	Pos.	W.	L.
1964-65—Wilmington	12	16	.429	5	..	..
1965-66—Wilmington	20	8	.714	1†	4	2

†Eastern Division

Named to NBA All-Star First Team, 1953, 1954, 1955, 1956.... NBA All-Star Second Team, 1957.... Member of NBA championship team, 1956.... Led NBA in scoring, 1953, 1954, 1955.... Led NBA in rebounding, 1955.... Led NBA in field-goal percentage, 1953, 1956, 1957.... Played minor league baseball as a pitcher in the Philadelphia Phillies' organization, 1949 through 1951.

SAM JONES

Born June 24, 1933 at Wilmington, N. C.   Height 6:04.   Weight 205.
High School—Laurinburg, N. C., Institute.
College—North Carolina Central College, Durham, N. C.
Drafted by Boston on first round, 1957.

—COLLEGIATE RECORD—

Year	G.	Min.	FGA	FGM	Pct.	FTA	FTM	Pct.	Reb.	Pts.	Avg.
51-52	22	....	263	126	.479	78	48	.615	150	300	13.6
52-53	24	....	370	169	.457	180	115	.639	248	453	18.9
53-54	27	....	432	208	.481	137	98	.715	223	514	19.0
56-57	27	....	398	174	.437	202	155	.767	288	503	18.6
Totals	100	....	1463	677	.463	597	416	.697	909	1770	17.7

NOTE: In military service during 1954-55 and 1955-56 seasons.

NBA REGULAR SEASON RECORD

Sea.—Team	G.	Min.	FGA	FGM	Pct.	FTA	FTM	Pct.	Reb.	Ast.	PF	Disq.	Pts.	Avg.
57-58—Boston	56	594	233	100	.429	84	60	.714	160	37	42	0	260	4.6
58-59—Boston	71	1466	703	305	.434	196	151	.770	428	101	102	0	761	10.7
59-60—Boston	74	1512	782	355	.454	220	168	.764	375	125	101	1	878	11.9
60-61—Boston	78	2028	1069	480	.449	268	211	.787	421	217	148	1	1171	15.0
61-62—Boston	78	2388	1284	596	.464	297	243	.818	458	232	149	0	1435	18.4
62-63—Boston	76	2323	1305	621	.476	324	257	.793	396	241	162	1	1499	19.7
63-64—Boston	76	2381	1359	612	.450	318	249	.783	349	202	192	1	1473	19.4
64-65—Boston	80	2885	1818	821	.452	522	428	.820	411	223	176	0	2070	25.9
65-66—Boston	67	2155	1335	626	.469	407	325	.799	347	216	170	0	1577	23.2
66-67—Boston	72	2325	1406	638	.454	371	318	.857	338	217	191	1	1594	22.1
67-68—Boston	73	2408	1348	621	.461	376	311	.827	357	216	181	0	1553	21.3
68-69—Boston	70	1820	1103	496	.450	189	148	.783	265	182	121	0	1140	16.3
Totals	871	24285	13745	6271	.456	3572	2869	.803	4305	2209	1735	5	15411	17.7

NBA PLAYOFF RECORD

Sea.—Team	G.	Min.	FGA	FGM	Pct.	FTA	FTM	Pct.	Reb.	Ast.	PF	Disq.	Pts.	Avg.
57-58—Boston	8	75	22	10	.455	16	11	.688	24	4	7	0	31	3.9
58-59—Boston	11	192	108	40	.370	39	33	.846	63	17	14	0	113	10.3
59-60—Boston	13	197	117	45	.385	21	17	.809	41	18	15	0	107	8.2
60-61—Boston	10	258	112	50	.446	35	31	.886	54	22	22	0	131	13.1
61-62—Boston	14	504	277	123	.444	60	42	.700	99	44	30	0	288	20.6
62-63—Boston	13	450	248	120	.484	83	69	.831	81	32	42	1	309	23.8
63-64—Boston	10	356	180	91	.506	68	50	.735	47	23	24	0	232	23.2
64-65—Boston	12	495	294	135	.459	84	73	.869	55	30	39	1	343	28.6
65-66—Boston	17	602	343	154	.449	136	114	.838	86	53	65	1	422	24.8
66-67—Boston	9	326	207	95	.459	58	50	.862	46	28	30	1	240	26.7
67-68—Boston	19	685	367	162	.441	84	66	.786	64	50	58	0	390	20.5
68-69—Boston	18	514	296	124	.419	69	55	.797	58	37	45	1	303	16.8
Totals	154	4654	2571	1149	.447	753	611	.811	718	358	391	5	2909	18.9

NBA ALL-STAR GAME RECORD

Season—Team	Min.	FGA	FGM	Pct.	FTA	FTM	Pct.	Reb.	Ast.	PF	Disq.	Pts.
1962—Boston	14	8	1	.125	1	0	.000	1	0	1	0	2
1964—Boston	27	20	8	.400	0	0	.000	4	3	2	0	16
1965—Boston	24	12	2	.167	2	2	1.000	5	3	2	0	6
1966—Boston	22	11	5	.455	2	2	1.000	2	5	0	0	12
1968—Boston	15	5	2	.400	1	1	1.000	2	4	1	0	5
Totals	102	56	18	.321	6	5	.833	14	15	6	0	41

Elected to Naismith Memorial Basketball Hall of Fame, 1983. . . . Named to NBA 25th Anniversary All-Time Team, 1970. . . . NBA All-Star Second Team, 1965, 1966, 1967. . . . Member of NBA championship teams, 1959, 1960, 1961, 1962, 1963, 1964, 1965, 1966, 1968, 1969. . . . Elected to NAIA Basketball Hall of Fame, 1962.

JOHN G. KERR
(Red)

Born August 17, 1932 at Chicago, Ill.   Height 6:09.   Weight 230.
High School—Chicago, Ill., Tilden.
College—University of Illinois, Champaign, Ill.
Drafted by Syracuse on first round, 1954 (6th pick).

Syracuse franchise transferred to Philadelphia, 1963.
Traded by Philadelphia to Baltimore for Wally Jones, September 22, 1965; selected from Baltimore by Chicago Bulls in expansion draft, April 30, 1966.

—COLLEGIATE RECORD—

Year	G.	Min.	FGA	FGM	Pct.	FTA	FTM	Pct.	Reb.	Pts.	Avg.
50-51			(Freshman team did not play intercollegiate schedule.)								
51-52	26	....	365	143	.392	124	71	.573	....	357	13.7
52-53	22	....	397	153	.385	123	80	.650	....	386	17.5
53-54	22	....	520	210	.404	214	136	.636	....	556	25.3
Varsity Totals	70	....	1282	506	.395	461	287	.623	....	1299	18.6

NBA REGULAR SEASON RECORD

Sea.—Team	G.	Min.	FGA	FGM	Pct.	FTA	FTM	Pct.	Reb.	Ast.	PF	Disq.	Pts.	Avg.
54-55—Syracuse	72	1529	718	301	.419	223	152	.682	474	80	165	2	754	10.5
55-56—Syracuse	72	2114	935	377	.403	316	207	.655	607	84	168	3	961	13.3
56-57—Syracuse	72	2191	827	333	.403	313	225	.719	807	90	190	3	891	12.4
57-58—Syracuse	72	2384	1020	407	.399	422	280	.664	963	88	197	4	1094	15.2
58-59—Syracuse	72	2671	1139	502	.441	367	281	.766	1008	142	183	1	1285	17.8
59-60—Syracuse	75	2361	1111	436	.392	310	233	.752	913	168	207	4	1105	14.7
60-61—Syracuse	79	2676	1056	419	.397	299	218	.729	951	199	230	4	1056	13.4
61-62—Syracuse	80	2767	1220	541	.443	302	222	.735	1176	243	282	7	1304	16.3
62-63—Syracuse	80	2561	1069	507	.474	320	241	.753	1049	214	208	3	1255	15.7
63-64—Philadelphia	80	2938	1250	536	.429	357	268	.751	1018	275	187	2	1340	16.8
64-65—Philadelphia	80	1810	714	264	.370	181	126	.696	551	197	132	1	654	8.2
65-66—Baltimore	71	1770	692	286	.413	272	209	.768	586	225	148	0	781	11.0
Totals	905	27772	11751	4909	.418	3682	2662	.723	10103	2005	2297	34	12480	13.8

NBA PLAYOFF RECORD

Sea.—Team	G.	Min.	FGA	FGM	Pct.	FTA	FTM	Pct.	Reb.	Ast.	PF	Disq.	Pts.	Avg.
54-55—Syracuse	11	363	151	59	.391	61	34	.557	118	13	27	0	152	13.8
55-56—Syracuse	8	213	77	37	.481	33	15	.455	68	10	23	0	89	11.1
56-57—Syracuse	5	162	65	28	.431	29	20	.690	69	6	7	0	76	15.2
57-58—Syracuse	3	116	55	18	.327	18	14	.778	61	3	5	0	50	16.7
58-59—Syracuse	9	312	142	50	.352	33	30	.909	108	24	20	0	130	14.4
59-60—Syracuse	3	104	51	15	.294	12	11	.917	25	9	9	0	41	13.7
60-61—Syracuse	8	210	88	30	.341	23	16	.696	99	20	18	0	76	9.5
61-62—Syracuse	5	193	109	41	.376	8	6	.750	80	10	15	0	88	17.6
62-63—Syracuse	5	187	60	26	.433	21	16	.762	75	9	12	0	68	13.6
63-64—Philadelphia	5	185	83	40	.482	20	15	.750	69	16	12	0	95	19.0
64-65—Philadelphia	11	181	67	24	.358	21	15	.714	38	28	20	0	63	5.7
65-66—Baltimore	3	49	11	2	.182	2	1	.500	17	4	5	0	5	1.7
Totals	76	2275	959	370	.386	281	193	.687	827	152	173	0	933	12.3

NBA ALL-STAR GAME RECORD

Season—Team	Min.	FGA	FGM	Pct.	FTA	FTM	Pct.	Reb.	Ast.	PF	Disq.	Pts.
1956—Syracuse	16	4	2	.500	1	0	.000	8	0	2	0	4
1959—Syracuse	21	14	3	.214	2	1	.500	9	2	0	0	7
1963—Syracuse	11	4	0	.000	2	2	1.000	2	1	3	0	2
Totals	48	22	5	.227	5	3	.600	19	3	5	0	13

NBA COACHING RECORD

		Regular Season				Playoffs	
Sea.	Club	W.	L.	Pct.	Pos.	W.	L.
1966-67—Chicago		33	48	.407	4†	0	3
1967-68—Chicago		29	53	.354	4†	1	4
1968-69—Phoenix..............		16	66	.195	7†	..	..
1969-70—Phoenix..............		15	23	.395	..†	..	..
Totals (4 years)		93	190	.329		1	7

†Western Division.

Named NBA Coach of the Year, 1967.... Member of NBA championship team, 1955.

ROBERT JERRY LANIER JR.
(Bob)

Born September 10, 1948 at Buffalo, N. Y.   Height 6:11.   Weight 265.
High School—Buffalo, N. Y., Bennett.
College—St. Bonaventure University, St. Bonaventure, N. Y.
Drafted by Detroit on first round, 1970 (1st pick).

Traded by Detroit to Milwaukee for Kent Benson and a 1980 1st round draft choice, February 4, 1980.

—COLLEGIATE RECORD—

Year	G.	Min.	FGA	FGM	Pct.	FTA	FTM	Pct.	Reb.	Pts.	Avg.
66-67†	15	....	....	....	....	....	....	....	....	450	30.0
67-68	25	....	466	272	.584	175	112	.640	390	656	26.2
68-69	24	....	460	270	.587	181	114	.630	374	654	27.3
69-70	26	....	549	308	.561	194	141	.727	416	757	29.1
Varsity Totals	75	....	1475	850	.576	550	367	.667	1180	2067	27.6

— 323 —

NBA REGULAR SEASON RECORD

Sea.—Team	G.	Min.	FGA	FGM	Pct.	FTA	FTM	Pct.	Reb.	Ast.	PF	Disq.	Pts.	Avg.
70-71—Detroit	82	2017	1108	504	.455	376	273	.726	665	146	272	4	1281	15.6
71-72—Detroit	80	3092	1690	834	.493	505	388	.768	1132	248	297	6	2056	25.7
72-73—Detroit	81	3150	1654	810	.490	397	307	.773	1205	260	278	4	1927	23.8

								—Rebounds—						
Sea.—Team	G.	Min.	FGA	FGM	Pct.	FTA	FTM	Pct.	Off.	Def.	Tot.	Ast.	PF	Dq.	Stl.	Blk.	Pts.	Avg.
73-74—Detroit	81	3047	1483	748	.504	409	326	.797	269	805	1074	343	273	7	110	247	1822	22.5
74-75—Detroit	76	2987	1433	731	.510	450	361	.802	225	689	914	350	237	1	75	172	1823	24.0
75-76—Detroit	64	2363	1017	541	.532	370	284	.768	217	529	746	217	203	2	79	86	1366	21.3
76-77—Detroit	64	2446	1269	678	.534	318	260	.818	200	545	745	214	174	0	70	126	1616	25.3
77-78—Detroit	63	2311	1159	622	.537	386	298	.772	197	518	715	216	185	2	82	93	1542	24.5
78-79—Detroit	53	1835	950	489	.515	367	275	.749	164	330	494	140	181	5	50	75	1253	23.6
79-80—Det.-Milw.	63	2131	867	466	.537	354	277	.782	152	400	552	184	200	3	74	89	1210	19.2
80-81—Milwaukee	67	1753	716	376	.525	277	208	.751	128	285	413	179	184	0	73	81	961	14.3
81-82—Milwaukee	74	1986	729	407	.558	242	182	.752	92	296	388	219	211	3	72	56	996	13.5
82-83—Milwaukee	39	978	332	163	.491	133	91	.684	58	142	200	105	125	2	34	24	417	10.7
83-84—Milwaukee	72	2007	685	392	.572	274	194	.708	141	314	455	186	228	8	58	51	978	13.6
Totals	959	32103	15092	7761	.514	4858	3724	.767			9698	3007	3048	47	777	1100	19248	20.1

Three-Point Field Goals: 1979-80, 1-for-6 (.167). 1980-81, 1-for-1. 1981-82, 0-for-2. 1982-83, 0-for-1. 1983-84, 0-for-3. Totals, 2-for-13 (.154).

NBA PLAYOFF RECORD

								—Rebounds—						
Sea.—Team	G.	Min.	FGA	FGM	Pct.	FTA	FTM	Pct.	Off.	Def.	Tot.	Ast.	PF	Dq.	Stl.	Blk.	Pts.	Avg.
73-74—Detroit	7	303	152	77	.507	38	30	.789	26	81	107	21	28	1	4	14	184	26.3
74-75—Detroit	3	128	51	26	.510	12	9	.750	5	27	32	19	10	0	4	12	61	20.3
75-76—Detroit	9	359	172	95	.552	50	45	.900	39	75	114	30	34	1	8	21	235	26.1
76-77—Detroit	3	118	54	34	.630	19	16	.842	13	37	50	6	10	0	3	7	84	28.0
79-80—Milwaukee	7	256	101	52	.515	42	31	.738	17	48	65	31	23	0	7	8	135	19.3
80-81—Milwaukee	7	236	85	50	.588	32	23	.719	12	40	52	28	18	0	12	8	123	17.6
81-82—Milwaukee	6	212	80	41	.513	25	14	.560	18	27	45	22	21	2	8	5	96	16.0
82-83—Milwaukee	9	250	89	51	.573	35	21	.600	17	46	63	23	32	2	5	14	123	13.7
83-84—Milwaukee	16	499	171	82	.480	44	39	.886	32	85	117	55	57	1	11	10	203	12.7
Totals	67	2361	955	508	.532	297	228	.768	179	466	645	235	233	7	62	99	1244	18.6

Three-Point Field Goals: 1981-82, 0-for-1.

NBA ALL-STAR GAME RECORD

Season—Team	Min.	FGA	FGM	Pct.	FTA	FTM	Pct.	Reb.	Ast.	PF	Disq.	Pts.
1972—Detroit	5	2	0	.000	3	2	.667	3	0	0	0	2
1973—Detroit	12	9	5	.556	0	0	.000	6	0	1	0	10

							—Rebounds—						
Season—Team	Min.	FGA	FGM	Pct.	FTA	FTM	Pct.	Off.	Def.	Tot.	Ast.	PF	Dq.	Stl.	Blk.	Pts.
1974—Detroit	26	15	11	.733	2	2	1.000	2	8	10	2	1	0	0	2	24
1975—Detroit	12	4	1	.250	0	0	.000	2	5	7	2	3	0	2	0	2
1977—Detroit	20	8	7	.875	3	3	1.000	5	5	10	4	3	0	1	1	17
1978—Detroit	4	0	0	.000	2	1	.500	2	0	2	0	0	0	0	0	1
1979—Detroit	31	10	5	.500	0	0	.000	1	3	4	4	4	0	1	1	10
1982—Milwaukee....	11	7	3	.429	2	2	1.000	2	1	3	0	3	0	0	0	8
Totals	121	55	32	.582	12	10	.833			45	12	15	0	4	4	74

Named to NBA All-Rookie Team, 1971. . . . NBA All-Star Game MVP, 1974. . . . Named to THE SPORTING NEWS All-America First Team, 1970.

JERRY RAY LUCAS
(Luke)

Born March 30, 1940 at Middletown, O.   Height 6:08.   Weight 235.

High School—Middletown, O.

College—Ohio State University, Columbus, O.

Drafted by Cincinnati on first round (territorial choice), 1962.

Signed by Cleveland ABL, 1962; Cleveland dropped out of ABL prior to 1962-63 season; did not play pro basketball, 1962-63.

Traded by Cincinnati to San Francisco for Jim King and Bill Turner, October 25, 1969.
Traded by San Francisco to New York for Cazzie Russell, May 7, 1971.

—COLLEGIATE RECORD—

Year	G.	Min.	FGA	FGM	Pct.	FTA	FTM	Pct.	Reb.	Pts.	Avg.
58-59†			Freshman team did not play an intercollegiate schedule.								
59-60	27	....	444	283	.637	187	144	.770	442	710	26.3
60-61	27	....	411	256	.623	208	159	.764	470	671	24.9
61-62	28	....	388	237	.611	169	135	.799	499	609	21.8
Varsity Totals	82	....	1243	776	.624	564	438	.777	1411	1990	24.3

JERRY LUCAS

NBA REGULAR SEASON RECORD

Sea.—Team	G.	Min.	FGA	FGM	Pct.	FTA	FTM	Pct.	Reb.	Ast.	PF	Disq.	Pts.	Avg.
63-64—Cincinnati	79	3273	1035	545	.527	398	310	.779	1375	204	300	6	1400	17.7
64-65—Cincinnati	66	2864	1121	558	.498	366	298	.814	1321	157	214	1	1414	21.4
65-66—Cincinnati	79	3517	1523	690	.453	403	317	.787	1668	213	274	5	1697	21.5
66-67—Cincinnati	81	3558	1257	577	.459	359	284	.791	1547	268	280	2	1438	17.8
67-68—Cincinnati	82	3619	1361	707	.519	445	346	.778	1560	251	243	3	1760	21.4
68-69—Cincinnati	74	3075	1007	555	.551	327	247	.755	1360	306	206	0	1357	18.3
69-70—Cinn.-S.F.	67	2420	799	405	.507	255	200	.784	951	173	166	2	1010	15.1
70-71—San Fran.	80	3251	1250	623	.498	367	289	.787	1265	293	197	0	1535	19.2
71-72—New York	77	2926	1060	543	.512	249	197	.791	1011	318	218	1	1283	16.7
72-73—New York	71	2001	608	312	.513	100	80	.800	510	317	157	0	704	9.9

Sea.—Team	G.	Min.	FGA	FGM	Pct.	FTA	FTM	Pct.	Off.	Def.	Tot.	Ast.	PF	Dq.	Stl.	Blk.	Pts.	Avg.
									—Rebounds—									
73-74—New York	73	1627	420	194	.462	96	67	.698	62	312	374	230	134	0	28	24	455	6.2
Totals	829	32131	11441	5709	.499	3365	2635	.783			12942	2730	2389	20			14053	17.0

NBA PLAYOFF RECORD

Sea.—Team	G.	Min.	FGA	FGM	Pct.	FTA	FTM	Pct.	Reb.	Ast.	PF	Disq.	Pts.	Avg.
63-64—Cincinnati	10	370	123	48	.390	37	26	.703	125	34	37	1	122	12.2
64-65—Cincinnati	4	195	75	38	.507	22	17	.773	84	9	12	0	93	23.3
65-66—Cincinnati	5	231	85	40	.471	35	27	.771	101	14	14	0	107	21.4
66-67—Cincinnati	4	183	55	24	.436	2	2	1.000	77	8	15	0	50	12.5
70-71—San Fran.	5	171	77	39	.506	16	11	.688	50	16	14	0	89	17.8
71-72—New York	16	737	238	119	.500	71	59	.831	173	85	49	1	297	18.6
72-73—New York	17	368	112	54	.482	23	20	.870	85	39	47	0	128	7.5

Sea.—Team	G.	Min.	FGA	FGM	Pct.	FTA	FTM	Pct.	Off.	Def.	Tot.	Ast.	PF	Dq.	Stl.	Blk.	Pts.	Avg.
									—Rebounds—									
73-74—New York	11	115	21	5	.238	0	0	.000	6	16	22	9	9	0	4	0	10	0.9
Totals	72	2370	786	367	.467	206	162	.786			717	214	197	2			896	12.4

NBA ALL-STAR GAME RECORD

Season—Team	Min.	FGA	FGM	Pct.	FTA	FTM	Pct.	Reb.	Ast.	PF	Disq.	Pts.
1964—Cincinnati	36	6	3	.500	6	5	.833	8	0	5	0	11
1965—Cincinnati	35	19	12	.632	1	1	1.000	10	1	2	0	25
1966—Cincinnati	23	11	4	.364	2	2	1.000	19	0	2	0	10
1967—Cincinnati	22	5	3	.600	1	1	1.000	7	2	3	0	7
1968—Cincinnati	21	9	6	.667	4	4	1.000	5	4	3	0	16
1969—Cincinnati	17	5	2	.400	5	4	.800	6	1	3	0	8
1971—San Francisco	29	9	5	.556	2	2	1.000	9	4	2	0	12
Totals	183	64	35	.547	21	19	.905	64	12	20	0	89

Elected to Naismith Memorial Basketball Hall of Fame, 1979.... Named to NBA All-Star First Team, 1965, 1966, 1968.... NBA All-Star Second Team, 1964 and 1967.... NBA Rookie of the Year, 1964.... NBA All-Rookie Team, 1964. ... Led NBA in field-goal percentage, 1964.... NBA All-Star Game MVP, 1965.... Member of NBA championship team, 1973.... THE SPORTING NEWS College Player of the Year, 1961 and 1962.... Named to THE SPORTING NEWS All-America First Team, 1960, 1961, 1962.... Member of NCAA championship team, 1960.... Member of U.S. Olympic team, 1960.... Led NCAA in rebounding, 1961 and 1962.... Led NCAA in field-goal percentage, 1960, 1961, 1962.... One of only seven players to average over 20 points and 20 rebounds per game in NCAA career.

CHARLES EDWARD MACAULEY JR.
(Easy Ed)

Born March 22, 1928 at St. Louis, Mo.   Height 6:08.   Weight 190.

High School—St. Louis, Mo., St. Louis University High.

College—St. Louis University, St. Louis, Mo.

Selected by St. Louis as a territorial choice (first round)
in Basketball Association of America draft, 1949.

Drafted by Boston NBA from St. Louis NBA in dispersal draft, April 25, 1950.
Traded with draft rights to Cliff Hagan by Boston NBA to St. Louis NBA for a 1st round draft choice, April 29, 1956.

—COLLEGIATE RECORD—

Year	G.	Min.	FGA	FGM	Pct.	FTA	FTM	Pct.	Reb.	Pts.	Avg.
45-46	23	....	...	94	....	...	71	....	....	259	11.3
46-47	28	....	...	141	....	...	104	....	....	386	13.8
47-48	27	....	324	132	.407	159	104	.654	....	368	13.6
48-49	26	....	275	144	.524	153	116	.758	....	404	15.5
Totals	104	....	...	511	....	...	395	....	....	1417	13.6

NBA REGULAR SEASON RECORD

Sea.—Team	G.	Min.	FGA	FGM	Pct.	FTA	FTM	Pct.	Reb.	Ast.	PF	Disq.	Pts.	Avg.
49-50—St. Louis	67	....	882	351	.398	528	379	.718	....	200	221	....	1081	16.1
50-51—Boston	68	....	985	459	.466	614	466	.759	616	252	205	4	1384	20.4
51-52—Boston	66	2631	888	384	.432	621	496	.799	529	232	174	0	1264	19.2
52-53—Boston	69	2902	997	451	.452	667	500	.750	629	280	188	0	1402	20.3

Sea.—Team	G.	Min.	FGA	FGM	Pct.	FTA	FTM	Pct.	Reb.	Ast.	PF	Disq.	Pts.	Avg.
53-54—Boston	71	2792	950	462	.486	554	420	.758	571	271	168	1	1344	18.9
54-55—Boston	71	2706	951	403	.424	558	442	.792	600	275	171	0	1248	17.6
55-56—Boston	71	2354	995	420	.422	504	400	.794	422	211	158	2	1240	17.5
56-57—St. Louis	72	2582	987	414	.419	479	359	.749	440	202	206	2	1187	16.5
57-58—St. Louis	72	1908	879	376	.428	369	267	.723	478	143	156	2	1019	14.2
58-59—St. Louis	14	196	75	22	.293	35	21	.600	40	13	20	1	65	4.6
Totals	641	....	8589	3742	.436	4929	3750	.761	....	2079	1667	12	11234	17.5

NBA PLAYOFF RECORD

Sea.—Team	G.	Min.	FGA	FGM	Pct.	FTA	FTM	Pct.	Reb.	Ast.	PF	Disq.	Pts.	Avg.
50-51—Boston	2	....	36	17	.472	16	10	.625	18	8	4	0	44	22.0
51-52—Boston	3	129	49	27	.551	19	16	.842	33	11	11	1	70	23.3
52-53—Boston	6	278	71	31	.437	54	39	.722	58	21	23	2	101	16.8
53-54—Boston	5	127	22	8	.364	13	9	.692	21	21	14	0	25	5.0
54-55—Boston	7	283	93	43	.462	54	41	.759	52	32	21	0	127	18.1
55-56—Boston	3	73	30	12	.400	11	7	.636	15	5	6	0	31	10.3
56-57—St. Louis	10	297	109	44	.404	74	54	.730	62	22	39	3	142	14.2
57-58—St. Louis	11	227	89	36	.404	50	36	.720	62	18	23	0	108	9.8
Totals	47	....	499	218	.437	291	212	.729	321	138	141	6	648	13.8

NBA ALL-STAR GAME RECORD

Season—Team	Min.	FGA	FGM	Pct.	FTA	FTM	Pct.	Reb.	Ast.	PF	Disq.	Pts.
1951—Boston	...	12	7	.583	7	6	.857	6	1	3	0	20
1952—Boston	28	7	3	.429	9	9	1.000	7	3	2	0	15
1953—Boston	35	12	5	.417	8	8	1.000	7	3	2	0	18
1954—Boston	25	11	4	.364	6	5	.833	1	3	2	0	13
1955—Boston	27	5	1	.200	5	4	.800	4	2	1	0	6
1956—Boston	20	9	1	.111	4	2	.500	2	3	3	0	4
1957—St. Louis	19	6	3	.500	2	1	.500	5	3	0	0	7
Totals	...	62	24	.387	41	35	.854	32	18	13	0	83

NBA COACHING RECORD

		Regular Season				Playoffs	
Sea.	Club	W.	L.	Pct.	Pos.	W.	L.
1958-59—St. Louis		43	19	.694	1†	2	4
1959-60—St. Louis		46	29	.613	1†	7	7
Totals (2 seasons)		89	48	.650		9	11

†Western Division.

Elected to Naismith Memorial Basketball Hall of Fame, 1960. . . . Named to NBA All-Star First Team, 1951, 1952, 1953. . . . NBA All-Star Second Team, 1954. . . . NBA All-Star Game MVP, 1951. . . . Member of NBA championship team, 1958. . . . Led NBA in field-goal percentage, 1954. . . . Named to THE SPORTING NEWS All-America First Team, 1949. . . . Led NCAA in field-goal percentage, 1949.

PETER PRESS MARAVICH
(Pete)

Born June 22, 1947 at Aliquippa, Pa.   Height 6:05.   Weight 200.

Died January 5, 1988.

High Schools—Clemson, S. C., Daniels (Fr. and Soph.) and
Raleigh, N. C., Needham Broughton (Jr. and Sr.).

Prep School—Salemburg, N. C., Edwards Military Institute.

College—Louisiana State University, Baton Rouge, La.

Drafted by Atlanta on first round, 1970 (3rd pick).

Traded by Atlanta to New Orleans for Dean Meminger, Bob Kauffman and four draft choices (1st round in 1974, 1st and 2nd in 1975, 2nd in 1976), May 3, 1974.
Waived by Utah, January 17, 1980; signed by Boston as a free agent, January 22, 1980.
Franchise moved from New Orleans to Utah, 1979.

—COLLEGIATE RECORD—

Year	G.	Min.	FGA	FGM	Pct.	FTA	FTM	Pct.	Reb.	Pts.	Avg.
66-67†	17	....	604	273	.452	234	195	.833	176	741	43.6
67-68	26	....	1022	432	.423	338	274	.811	195	1138	43.8
68-69	26	....	976	433	.444	378	282	.746	169	1148	44.2
69-70	31	....	1168	522	.447	436	337	.773	164	1381	44.5
Varsity Totals	83	....	3166	1387	.438	1152	893	.775	528	3667	44.2

NBA REGULAR SEASON RECORD

Sea.—Team	G.	Min.	FGA	FGM	Pct.	FTA	FTM	Pct.	Reb.	Ast.	PF	Disq.	Pts.	Avg.
70-71—Atlanta	81	2926	1613	738	.458	505	404	.800	298	355	238	1	1880	23.2
71-72—Atlanta	66	2302	1077	460	.427	438	355	.811	256	393	207	0	1275	19.3
72-73—Atlanta	79	3089	1788	789	.441	606	485	.800	346	546	245	1	2063	26.1

Sea.—Team	G.	Min.	FGA	FGM	Pct.	FTA	FTM	Pct.	Off.	Def.	Tot.	Ast.	PF	Dq.	Stl.	Blk.	Pts.	Avg.
									—Rebounds—									
73-74—Atlanta	76	2903	1791	819	.457	568	469	.826	98	276	374	396	261	4	111	13	2107	27.7
74-75—N. Orleans	79	2853	1562	655	.419	481	390	.811	93	329	422	488	227	4	120	18	1700	21.5
75-76—N. Orleans	62	2373	1316	604	.459	488	396	.811	46	254	300	332	197	3	87	23	1604	25.9
76-77—N. Orleans	73	3041	2047	886	.433	600	501	.835	90	284	374	392	191	1	84	22	2273	31.1
77-78—N. Orleans	50	2041	1253	556	.444	276	240	.870	49	129	178	335	116	1	101	8	1352	27.0
78-79—N. Orleans	49	1824	1035	436	.421	277	233	.841	33	88	121	243	104	2	60	18	1105	22.6
79-80—Utah-Bos.	43	964	543	244	.449	105	91	.867	17	61	78	83	79	1	24	6	589	13.7
Totals	658	24316	14025	6187	.441	4344	3564	.820			2747	3563	1865	18	587	108	15948	24.2

Three-Point Field Goals: 1979-80, 10-for-15 (.667).

NBA PLAYOFF RECORD

Sea.—Team	G.	Min.	FGA	FGM	Pct.	FTA	FTM	Pct.	Reb.	Ast.	PF	Disq.	Pts.	Avg.
70-71—Atlanta	5	199	122	46	.377	26	18	.692	26	24	14	0	110	22.0
71-72—Atlanta	6	219	121	54	.446	71	58	.817	32	28	24	0	166	27.7
72-73—Atlanta	6	234	155	65	.419	34	27	.794	29	40	24	1	157	26.2

Sea.—Team	G.	Min.	FGA	FGM	Pct.	FTA	FTM	Pct.	Off.	Def.	Tot.	Ast.	PF	Dq.	Stl.	Blk.	Pts.	Avg.
									—Rebounds—									
79-80—Boston	9	104	51	25	.490	3	2	.667	0	8	8	6	12	0	3	0	54	6.0
Totals	26	756	449	190	.423	134	105	.784			95	98	74	1	3	0	487	18.7

Three-Point Field Goals: 1979-80, 2-for-6 (.333).

NBA ALL-STAR GAME RECORD

Season—Team	Min.	FGA	FGM	Pct.	FTA	FTM	Pct.	Off.	Def.	Tot.	Ast.	PF	Dq.	Stl.	Blk.	Pts.
								—Rebounds—								
1973—Atlanta	22	8	4	.500	0	0	.000			3	5	4	0			8
1974—Atlanta	22	15	4	.267	9	7	.778	1	2	3	4	2	0	0	0	15
1977—N. Orleans	21	13	5	.385	0	0	.000	0	0	4	1	0	4	0	0	10
1978—N. Orleans						Selected—Injured, Did Not Play										
1979—N. Orleans	14	8	5	.625	0	0	.000	0	2	2	2	1	0	0	0	10
Totals	79	44	18	.409	9	7	.778			8	15	8	0	4	0	43

Elected to Naismith Memorial Basketball Hall of Fame, 1986.... Named to NBA All-Star First Team, 1976 and 1977.... NBA All-Star Second Team, 1973 and 1978.... NBA All-Rookie Team, 1971.... Shares NBA record for most free-throw attempts in one quarter, 16, vs. Chicago, January 2, 1973. ... Led NBA in scoring, 1977. ... THE SPORTING NEWS College Player of the Year, 1970.... Named to THE SPORTING NEWS All-America First Team, 1968, 1969, 1970.... Led NCAA in scoring, 1968, 1969, 1970.... Holds the following NCAA career records: most points, highest scoring average, most games scoring at least 50 points (28), most field goals made, most field goals attempted, most free throws made (3-year career) and most free throws attempted (3-year career).... Holds the following NCAA season records: most points, highest scoring average, most games scoring at least 50 points (10 in 1970), most field goals made and most field goals attempted.... Holds NCAA record for most free throws made in one game, 30, vs. Oregon State in 31 attempts, December 22, 1969.... Son of former NBL and BAA guard and former college coach Press Maravich.

SLATER MARTIN
(Dugie)

Born October 22, 1925 at Houston, Tex.   Height 5:10.   Weight 170.

High School—Houston, Tex., Thomas Jefferson.

College—University of Texas, Austin, Tex.

Drafted by Minneapolis, 1949.

Drafted by Minneapolis in BAA draft, 1949 (BAA merged with NBL to form NBA later in 1949).
Traded by Minneapolis with Jerry Bird and a player to be named later to New York for Walter Dukes and draft rights to Burdette Haldorson, October 26, 1956.
Traded by New York to St. Louis for Willie Naulls, December 10, 1956.

—COLLEGIATE RECORD—

Year	G.	Min.	FGA	FGM	Pct.	FTA	FTM	Pct.	Reb.	Pts.	Avg.
43-44	14	....	...	75		....	...	34	....	....	184	13.2
44-45 and 45-46					Military Service						
46-47	27	....	...	109		....	...	37	....	....	255	9.4
47-48	25	....	...	126		....	85	65	.765	....	317	12.7
48-49	24	....	...	165		....	...	54	....	....	384	16.0
Totals	90	....	...	475		....	...	190	....	....	1140	12.7

NBA REGULAR SEASON RECORD

Sea.—Team	G.	Min.	FGA	FGM	Pct.	FTA	FTM	Pct.	Reb.	Ast.	PF	Disq.	Pts.	Avg.
49-50—Minneapolis	67	....	302	106	.351	93	59	.634	....	148	162	....	271	4.0
50-51—Minneapolis	68	....	627	227	.362	177	121	.684	246	235	199	3	575	8.5
51-52—Minneapolis	66	2480	632	237	.375	190	142	.747	228	249	226	9	616	9.3
52-53—Minneapolis	70	2556	634	260	.410	287	224	.780	186	250	246	4	744	10.6
53-54—Minneapolis	69	2472	654	254	.388	243	176	.724	166	253	198	3	684	9.9
54-55—Minneapolis	72	2784	919	350	.381	359	276	.769	260	427	221	7	976	13.6
55-56—Minneapolis	72	2838	863	309	.358	395	329	.833	260	445	202	2	947	13.2
56-57—N.Y.-St. L.	66	2401	736	244	.332	291	230	.790	288	269	193	1	718	10.9
57-58—St. Louis	60	2098	768	258	.336	276	206	.746	228	218	187	0	722	12.0

Sea.—Team	G.	Min.	FGA	FGM	Pct.	FTA	FTM	Pct.	Reb.	Ast.	PF	Disq.	Pts.	Avg.
58-59—St. Louis	71	2504	706	245	.347	254	197	.776	253	336	230	8	687	9.4
59-60—St. Louis	64	1756	383	142	.371	155	113	.729	187	330	174	2	397	6.2
Totals	745	....	7224	2632	.364	2720	2073	.762	...	3160	2238	..	7337	9.8

NBA PLAYOFF RECORD

Sea.—Team	G.	Min.	FGA	FGM	Pct.	FTA	FTM	Pct.	Reb.	Ast.	PF	Disq.	Pts.	Avg.
49-50—Minneapolis	12	....	50	21	.420	24	14	.583	....	25	35	....	56	4.7
50-51—Minneapolis	7	....	51	18	.353	27	14	.519	42	25	20	....	50	7.1
51-52—Minneapolis	13	523	110	38	.345	56	41	.732	37	56	64	4	117	9.0
52-53—Minneapolis	12	453	103	41	.398	51	39	.765	31	43	49	1	121	10.1
53-54—Minneapolis	13	533	112	37	.330	70	52	.743	29	60	52	1	126	9.7
54-55—Minneapolis	7	315	94	28	.298	49	40	.816	28	31	23	0	96	13.7
55-56—Minneapolis	3	121	37	17	.459	24	20	.833	7	15	9	0	54	18.0
56-57—St. Louis	10	439	155	55	.355	74	56	.757	42	49	39	2	166	16.6
57-58—St. Louis	11	416	137	44	.321	63	39	.619	48	40	40	1	127	11.5
58-59—St. Louis	1	18	5	4	.800	0	0	.000	3	2	2	0	8	8.0
59-60—St. Louis	3	58	13	1	.077	4	1	.250	3	8	9	0	3	1.0
Totals	92	2876	867	304	.351	442	316	.715	270	354	342	9	924	10.0

NBA ALL-STAR GAME RECORD

Season—Team	Min.	FGA	FGM	Pct.	FTA	FTM	Pct.	Reb.	Ast.	PF	Disq.	Pts.
1953—Minneapolis	26	10	2	.200	1	1	1.000	2	1	2	0	5
1954—Minneapolis	23	5	1	.200	0	0	.000	0	3	3	0	2
1955—Minneapolis	23	5	2	.400	2	1	.500	2	5	3	0	5
1956—Minneapolis	29	7	3	.429	3	3	1.000	1	7	5	0	9
1957—St. Louis	31	11	4	.364	0	0	.000	2	3	1	0	8
1958—St. Louis	26	9	2	.222	4	2	.500	2	8	3	0	6
1959—St. Louis	22	6	2	.333	2	1	.500	6	1	2	0	5
Totals	180	53	16	.302	12	8	.667	15	28	19	0	40

NBA COACHING RECORD

		Regular Season			
Sea.	Club	W.	L.	Pct.	Pos.
1956-57—St. Louis		5	3	.625	..†

ABA COACHING RECORD

		Regular Season				Playoffs	
Sea.	Club	W.	L.	Pct.	Pos.	W.	L.
1967-68—Houston		29	49	.372	4†	0	3
1968-69—Houston		3	9	.250	...†	..	..
Totals (2 years)		32	58	.356		..	..

†Western Division.

Named to NBA All-Star Second Team, 1954, 1956, 1957, 1958, 1959.... Member of NBA championship teams, 1950, 1952, 1953, 1954, 1958.... Named to THE SPORTING NEWS All-America Fifth Team, 1949.

ROBERT ALLEN McADOO
(Bob)

Born September 25, 1951 at Greensboro, N. C. Height 6:09. Weight 225.

High School—Greensboro, N. C., Ben Smith.

Colleges—Vincennes University, Vincennes, Ind., and
University of North Carolina, Chapel Hill, N. C.

Drafted by Buffalo on first round as hardship case, 1972 (2nd pick).

Traded by Buffalo with Tom McMillen to New York Knicks for John Gianelli and cash, December 9, 1976.
Traded by New York to Boston for three 1979 1st round draft choices and a player to be named later, February 12, 1979. New York acquired Tom Barker to complete the deal, February 14, 1979.
Acquired from Boston by Detroit for two 1980 1st round draft choices to complete compensation for Boston's earlier signing of Veteran Free Agent M. L. Carr, September 6, 1979.
Waived by Detroit, March 11, 1981; signed by New Jersey as a free agent, March 13, 1981.
Traded by New Jersey to Los Angeles for a 1983 2nd round draft choice and cash, December 24, 1981.
Signed by Philadelphia as a Veteran Free Agent, January 31, 1986; Los Angeles Lakers relinquished their right of first refusal.
Played in Italy during 1986-87 season.

—COLLEGIATE RECORD—
Vincennes

Year	G.	Min.	FGA	FGM	Pct.	FTA	FTM	Pct.	Reb.	Pts.	Avg.
69-70	32	....	...	258	....	134	101	.754	320	617	19.3
70-71	27	....	...	273	....	164	129	.787	297	675	25.0
JC Totals	59	....	...	531	...	298	230	.772	617	1292	21.9

North Carolina

Year	G.	Min.	FGA	FGM	Pct.	FTA	FTM	Pct.	Reb.	Pts.	Avg.
71-72	31	....	471	243	.516	167	118	.707	312	604	19.5

NBA REGULAR SEASON RECORD

Sea.—Team	G.	Min.	FGA	FGM	Pct.	FTA	FTM	Pct.	Off.	Def.	Tot.	Ast.	PF	Dq.	Stl.	Blk.	Pts.	Avg.
72-73—Buffalo	80	2562	1293	585	.452	350	271	.774			728	139	256	6			1441	18.0
73-74—Buffalo	74	3185	1647	901	.547	579	459	.793	281	836	1117	170	252	3	88	246	2261	30.6
74-75—Buffalo	82	3539	2138	1095	.512	796	641	.805	307	848	1155	179	278	3	92	174	2831	34.5
75-76—Buffalo	78	3328	1918	934	.487	734	559	.762	241	724	965	315	298	5	93	160	2427	31.1
76-77—Buf-Knicks	72	2798	1445	740	.512	516	381	.738	199	727	926	205	262	3	77	99	1861	25.8
77-78—New York	79	3182	1564	814	.520	645	469	.727	236	774	1010	298	297	6	105	126	2097	26.5
78-79—N.Y.-Bos.	60	2231	1127	596	.529	450	295	.656	130	390	520	168	189	3	74	67	1487	24.8
79-80—Detroit	58	2097	1025	492	.480	322	235	.730	100	367	467	200	178	3	73	65	1222	21.1
80-81—Det.-N.J.	16	321	157	68	.433	41	29	.707	17	50	67	30	38	0	17	13	165	10.3
81-82—Los Angeles	41	746	330	151	.458	126	90	.714	45	114	159	32	109	1	22	36	392	9.6
82-83—Los Angeles	47	1019	562	292	.520	163	119	.730	76	171	247	39	153	2	40	40	703	15.0
83-84—Los Angeles	70	1456	748	352	.471	264	212	.803	82	207	289	74	182	0	42	50	916	13.1
84-85—L.A. Lakers	66	1254	546	284	.520	162	122	.753	79	216	295	67	170	0	18	53	690	10.5
85-86—Philadelphia	29	609	251	116	.462	81	62	.765	25	78	103	35	64	0	10	18	294	10.1
Totals	852	28327	14751	7420	.503	5229	3944	.754			8048	1951	2726	35	751	1147	18787	22.1

Three-Point Field Goals: 1979-80, 3-for-24 (.125). 1980-81, 0-for-1. 1981-82, 0-for-5. 1982-83, 0-for-1. 1983-84, 0-for-5. 1984-85, 0-for-1. Totals, 3-for-37 (.081).

NBA PLAYOFF RECORD

Sea.—Team	G.	Min.	FGA	FGM	Pct.	FTA	FTM	Pct.	Off.	Def.	Tot.	Ast.	PF	Dq.	Stl.	Blk.	Pts.	Avg.
73-74—Buffalo	6	271	159	76	.478	47	38	.809	14	68	82	9	25	1	6	13	190	31.7
74-75—Buffalo	7	327	216	104	.481	73	54	.740	25	69	94	10	29	1	6	19	262	37.4
75-76—Buffalo	9	406	215	97	.451	82	58	.707	31	97	128	29	37	3	7	18	252	28.0
77-78—New York	6	238	126	61	.484	35	21	.600	11	47	58	23	19	0	7	12	143	23.8
81-82—Los Angeles	14	388	179	101	.564	47	32	.681	21	74	95	22	43	2	10	21	234	16.7
82-83—Los Angeles	8	166	84	37	.440	14	11	.786	15	31	46	5	23	0	11	10	87	10.9
83-84—Los Angeles	20	447	215	111	.516	81	57	.704	30	78	108	12	63	0	12	27	279	14.0
84-85—L.A. Lakers	19	398	193	91	.472	47	35	.745	25	61	86	15	66	2	9	26	217	11.4
85-86—Philadelphia	5	73	36	20	.556	16	14	.875	8	6	14	2	13	0	4	5	54	10.8
Totals	94	2714	1423	698	.491	442	320	.724	180	531	711	127	318	9	72	151	1718	18.3

Three-Point Field Goals: 1982-83, 2-for-6 (.333). 1983-84, 0-for-1. 1984-85, 0-for-1. Totals, 2-for-8 (.250).

NBA ALL-STAR GAME RECORD

Season—Team	Min.	FGA	FGM	Pct.	FTA	FTM	Pct.	Off.	Def.	Tot.	Ast.	PF	Dq.	Stl.	Blk.	Pts.
1974—Buffalo	13	4	3	.750	8	5	.625	1	2	3	1	4	0	0	1	11
1975—Buffalo	26	9	4	.444	3	3	1.000	4	2	6	2	4	0	0	0	11
1976—Buffalo	29	14	10	.714	4	2	.500	2	5	7	1	5	0	0	0	22
1977—Knicks	38	23	13	.565	4	4	1.000	3	7	10	2	3	0	3	1	30
1978—New York	20	14	7	.500	0	0	.000	3	1	4	0	2	0	1	0	14
Totals	126	64	37	.578	19	14	.737	13	17	30	6	18	0	4	2	88

Named NBA Most Valuable Player, 1975.... All-NBA First Team, 1975.... All-NBA Second Team, 1974.... NBA Rookie of the Year, 1973.... NBA All-Rookie Team, 1973.... Led NBA in scoring, 1974, 1975, 1976.... Led NBA in field-goal percentage, 1974.... Member of NBA championship teams, 1982 and 1985.... Named to THE SPORTING NEWS All-America First Team, 1972.

GEORGE McGINNIS

Born August 12, 1950 at Indianapolis, Ind.   Height 6:08.   Weight 235.

High School—Indianapolis, Ind., Washington.

College—Indiana University, Bloomington, Ind.

Drafted by Philadelphia on second round, 1973 (22nd pick).

Signed as an undergraduate free agent by Indiana ABA in lieu of a 1972 1st round draft choice, 1971.

Invoked proviso that he could buy his way out of contract with Indiana ABA; signed by Philadelphia NBA, July 10, 1975, after Commissioner Larry O'Brien revoked a contract McGinnis had signed with New York NBA, May 30, 1975.

Traded by Philadelphia to Denver for Bobby Jones and Ralph Simpson, August 16, 1978.

Traded by Denver to Indiana for Alex English and a 1980 1st round draft choice, February 1, 1980.

Waived by Indiana, October 27, 1982.

—COLLEGIATE RECORD—

Year	G.	Min.	FGA	FGM	Pct.	FTA	FTM	Pct.	Reb.	Pts.	Avg.
69-70†					Did Not Play—Ineligible						
70-71	24	....	615	283	.460	249	153	.614	352	719	30.0

ABA REGULAR SEASON RECORD

			—2-Point—			—3-Point—									
Sea.—Team	G.	Min.	FGM	FGA	Pct.	FGM	FGA	Pct.	FTM	FTA	Pct.	Reb.	Ast.	Pts.	Avg.
71-72—Indiana	78	2179	459	961	.478	6	38	.158	298	462	.645	711	137	1234	16.9
72-73—Indiana	82	3347	860	1723	.499	8	32	.250	517	778	.665	1022	205	2261	27.6
73-74—Indiana	80	3266	784	1652	.475	5	34	.147	488	715	.683	1197	267	2071	25.9
74-75—Indiana	79	3193	811	1759	.461	62	175	.354	545	753	.724	1126	495	2353	29.8
Totals	319	11985	2914	6095	.478	81	279	.290	1848	2708	.682	4056	1194	7919	24.8

ABA PLAYOFF RECORD

			2-Point			3-Point									
Sea.—Team	G.	Min.	FGM	FGA	Pct.	FGM	FGA	Pct.	FTM	FTA	Pct.	Reb.	Ast.	Pts.	Avg.
71-72—Indiana	20	633	102	246	.415	4	15	.267	94	150	.627	277	52	310	15.5
72-73—Indiana	18	732	161	352	.457	0	5	.000	109	149	.732	222	39	431	23.9
73-74—Indiana	14	585	117	254	.461	2	7	.286	96	129	.744	166	47	336	24.0
74-75—Indiana	18	731	190	382	.497	23	73	.315	132	192	.688	286	148	581	32.3
Totals	70	2681	570	1234	.462	29	100	.290	431	620	.695	901	286	1658	23.7

ABA ALL-STAR GAME RECORD

		2-Point			3-Point								
Sea.—Team	Min.	FGM	FGA	Pct.	FGM	FGA	Pct.	FTM	FTA	Pct.	Reb.	Ast.	Pts.	Avg.
72-73—Indiana	34	10	14	.714	0	1	.000	3	6	.500	15	2	23	23.0
73-74—Indiana	30	7	21	.333	0	0	.000	0	0	.000	11	1	4	14.0
74-75—Indiana	32	6	13	.462	0	1	.000	6	11	.545	12	5	18	18.0
Totals	96	23	48	.479	0	2	.000	9	17	.529	38	8	55	18.3

NBA REGULAR SEASON RECORD

									—Rebounds—								
Sea.—Team	G.	Min.	FGA	FGM	Pct.	FTA	FTM	Pct.	Off.	Def.	Tot.	Ast.	PF	Dq.	Stl.	Blk.	Pts.	Avg.
75-76—Philadelphia	77	2946	1552	647	.417	642	475	.740	260	707	967	359	334	13	198	41	1769	23.0
76-77—Philadelphia	79	2769	1439	659	.458	546	372	.681	324	587	911	302	299	4	163	37	1690	21.4
77-78—Philadelphia	78	2533	1270	588	.463	574	411	.716	282	528	810	294	287	6	137	27	1587	20.3
78-79—Denver	76	2552	1273	603	.474	765	509	.665	256	608	864	283	321	16	129	52	1715	22.6
79-80—Den.-Ind.	73	2208	886	400	.451	488	270	.553	222	477	699	333	303	12	101	23	1072	14.7
80-81—Indiana	69	1845	768	348	.453	385	207	.538	164	364	528	210	242	3	99	28	903	13.1
81-82—Indiana	76	1341	378	141	.373	159	72	.453	93	305	398	204	98	4	96	28	354	4.7
Totals	528	16194	7566	3386	.448	3559	2316	.651	1601	3576	5177	1985	1984	58	923	236	9090	17.2

Three-Point Field Goals: 1979-80, 2-for-15 (.133). 1980-81, 0-for-7. 1981-82, 0-for-3. Totals, 2-for-25 (.080).

NBA PLAYOFF RECORD

									—Rebounds—								
Sea.—Team	G.	Min.	FGA	FGM	Pct.	FTA	FTM	Pct.	Off.	Def.	Tot.	Ast.	PF	Dq.	Stl.	Blk.	Pts.	Avg.
75-76—Philadelphia	3	120	61	29	.475	18	11	.611	9	32	41	12	14	1	1	4	69	23.0
76-77—Philadelphia	19	603	273	102	.374	114	65	.570	62	136	198	69	83	2	23	6	269	14.2
77-78—Philadelphia	10	273	125	53	.424	49	41	.837	24	54	78	30	40	1	15	1	147	14.7
80-81—Indiana	2	39	15	3	.200	8	4	.500	2	8	10	7	6	0	2	0	10	5.0
Totals	34	1035	474	187	.395	189	121	.640	97	230	327	118	143	4	41	11	495	14.6

NBA ALL-STAR GAME RECORD

							—Rebounds—							
Season—Team	Min.	FGA	FGM	Pct.	FTA	FTM	Pct.	Off.	Def.	Tot.	Ast.	PF	Dq.	Stl.	Blk.	Pts.
1976—Philadelphia	19	9	4	.444	4	2	.500	1	6	7	2	2	0	0	0	10
1977—Philadelphia	26	9	2	.222	2	0	.000	5	2	7	2	3	0	4	0	4
1979—Denver	25	12	5	.417	11	6	.545	2	4	6	3	4	0	5	0	16
Totals	70	30	11	.367	17	8	.471	8	12	20	7	9	0	9	0	30

Named to NBA All-Star First Team, 1976. . . . NBA All-Star Second Team, 1977. . . . ABA Co-Most Valuable Player, 1975. . . . ABA All-Star First Team, 1974 and 1975. . . . ABA All-Star Second Team, 1973. . . . ABA All-Rookie Team, 1972. . . . ABA Playoff MVP, 1973. . . . Member of ABA championship teams, 1972 and 1973. . . . Led ABA in scoring, 1975.

RICHARD J. McGUIRE
(Dick)

Born January 25, 1926 at Huntington, N. Y.   Height 6:00.   Weight 180.

High School—New York, N. Y., LaSalle Academy.

Colleges—St. John's University, Brooklyn, N. Y., and Dartmouth College, Hanover, N. H.

Drafted by New York on first round, 1949.

Drafted by New York on first round of BAA draft, 1949 (BAA merged with NBL later that year to form the NBA). Traded by New York to Detroit for first-round draft choice, September, 1957.

—COLLEGIATE RECORD—

St. John's

Year	G.	Min.	FGA	FGM	Pct.	FTA	FTM	Pct.	Reb.	Pts.	Avg.
43-44	16	....	...	43	....	...	20	....	....	106	6.6

Dartmouth

Year	G.	Min.	FGA	FGM	Pct.	FTA	FTM	Pct.	Reb.	Pts.	Avg.
43-44	5	....	...	17	....	10	9	.900	....	43	8.6
44-45, 45-46						Military Service					

St. John's

Year	G.	Min.	FGA	FGM	Pct.	FTA	FTM	Pct.	Reb.	Pts.	Avg.
46-47	21	....	...	63	....	...	37	....	....	163	7.8
47-48	22	....	...	75	....	115	72	.626	....	222	10.1
48-49	25	....	...	121	....	125	72	.576	....	314	12.6

NBA REGULAR SEASON RECORD

Sea.—Team	G.	Min.	FGA	FGM	Pct.	FTA	FTM	Pct.	Reb.	Ast.	PF	Disq.	Pts.	Avg.
49-50—New York	68	....	563	190	.337	313	204	.652	....	386	160	....	584	8.6
50-51—New York	64	....	482	179	.371	276	179	.649	334	400	154	2	537	8.4
51-52—New York	64	2018	474	204	.430	290	183	.631	332	388	181	4	591	9.2
52-53—New York	61	1783	373	142	.381	269	153	.569	280	296	172	3	437	7.2
53-54—New York	68	2343	493	201	.408	345	220	.638	310	354	199	3	622	9.1
54-55—New York	71	2310	581	226	.389	303	195	.643	322	542	143	0	647	9.1
55-56—New York	62	1685	438	152	.347	193	121	.627	220	362	146	0	425	6.9
56-57—New York	72	1191	366	140	.383	163	105	.644	146	222	103	0	385	5.3
57-58—Detroit	69	2311	544	203	.373	225	150	.667	291	454	178	0	556	8.1
58-59—Detroit	71	2063	543	232	.427	258	191	.740	285	443	147	1	655	9.2
59-60—Detroit	68	1466	402	179	.445	201	124	.617	264	358	112	0	482	7.1
Totals	738	17170	5259	2048	.382	2836	1825	.644	2784	4205	1695	13	5921	8.0

NBA PLAYOFF RECORD

Sea.—Team	G.	Min.	FGA	FGM	Pct.	FTA	FTM	Pct.	Reb.	Ast.	PF	Disq.	Pts.	Avg.
49-50—New York	5	....	52	22	.423	26	19	.731	....	27	21	....	63	12.6
50-51—New York	14	....	80	25	.313	53	24	.453	83	78	50	1	74	5.3
51-52—New York	14	546	107	48	.449	86	49	.570	71	90	46	1	145	10.4
52-53—New York	11	360	59	24	.407	55	35	.636	63	70	25	0	83	7.5
53-54—New York	4	68	16	4	.250	5	3	.600	4	5	12	0	11	2.8
54-55—New York	3	75	19	6	.316	12	8	.667	9	12	7	0	20	6.7
57-58—Detroit	7	236	60	25	.417	24	17	.708	33	40	13	0	67	9.6
58-59—Detroit	3	109	32	20	.625	11	7	.636	17	19	10	0	47	15.7
59-60—Detroit	2	42	12	5	.417	3	1	.333	4	9	3	0	11	5.5
Totals	63	1436	437	179	.410	275	163	.593	284	350	187	2	521	8.3

NBA ALL-STAR GAME RECORD

Season—Team	Min.	FGA	FGM	Pct.	FTA	FTM	Pct.	Reb.	Ast.	PF	Disq.	Pts.
1951—New York	..	4	3	.750	0	0	.000	5	10	2	0	6
1952—New York	18	0	0	.000	3	1	.333	1	4	0	0	1
1954—New York	24	5	2	.400	0	0	.000	4	2	1	0	4
1955—New York	25	2	1	.500	2	1	.500	3	6	1	0	3
1956—New York	29	9	2	.222	5	2	.400	0	3	1	0	6
1958—Detroit	31	4	2	.500	0	0	.000	7	10	4	0	4
1959—Detroit	24	7	2	.286	2	1	.500	3	3	2	0	5
Totals	..	31	12	.387	12	5	.417	23	38	11	0	29

NBA COACHING RECORD

Sea. Club	Regular Season W.	L.	Pct.	Pos.	Playoffs W.	L.	Sea. Club	Regular Season W.	L.	Pct.	Pos.	Playoffs W.	L.
1959-60—Detroit	17	24	.415	2†	0	2	1965-66—New York	24	35	.407	4‡	..	..
1960-61—Detroit	34	45	.430	3†	2	3	1966-67—New York	36	45	.444	4	‡1	3
1961-62—Detroit	37	43	.463	3†	5	5	1967-68—New York	15	22	.405	..‡	..	..
1962-63—Detroit	34	46	.425	3†	1	3	Totals (7 years)	197	260	.431		9	16

†Western Division.   ‡Eastern Division.

Named to NBA All-Star Second Team, 1951. . . . Led NBA in assists, 1950. . . . Named to THE SPORTING NEWS All-America Second Team, 1944.

GEORGE LAWRENCE MIKAN JR.

Born June 18, 1924 at Joliet, Ill.   Height 6:10.   Weight 245.

High Schools—Joliet, Ill., Catholic (freshman, did not play basketball) and Chicago, Ill., Quigley Prep (sophomore, junior and senior).

College—DePaul University, Chicago, Ill.

Signed by Chicago of National Basketball League, March 16, 1946.

Chicago dropped out of National Basketball League and entered Professional Basketball League of America for 1947-48 season.

PBLA disbanded, November 13, 1947; Chicago was refused a franchise in the NBL and Mikan was awarded to Minneapolis at an NBL meeting, November 17, 1947. (Mikan scored 193 points in the eight PBLA games played by Chicago before the league folded, and led the league in total points and scoring average.)

Signed by Minneapolis NBL, November, 1947.

—COLLEGIATE RECORD—

Year	G.	Min.	FGA	FGM	Pct.	FTA	FTM	Pct.	Reb.	Pts.	Avg.
41-42†	..	....	...	....	....	...	...	....	....	....	....
42-43	24	....	...	97	....	111	77	.694	....	271	11.3
43-44	26	....	...	188	....	169	110	.655	....	486	18.7
44-45	24	....	...	218	....	199	122	.613	....	558	23.3
45-46	24	....	...	206	....	186	143	.769	....	555	23.1
Varsity Totals	98	....	...	709	....	665	454	.680	....	1870	19.1

NOTE: Mikan played five years at DePaul.

NBL AND NBA REGULAR SEASON PLAYING RECORD

Sea.—Team	G.	Min.	FGA	FGM	Pct.	FTA	FTM	Pct.	Reb.	Ast.	PF	Disq.	Pts.	Avg.
46-47—Chicago-NBL	25	....	....	147	....	164	119	.726	....	....	90	..	413	16.5
47-48—Minn.-NBL	56	....	....	406	....	500	383	.752	....	....	210	..	1195	21.3
48-49—Minneapolis	60	....	1403	583	.416	689	532	.772	....	218	260	..	1698	28.3
49-50—Minneapolis	68	....	1595	649	.407	728	567	.779	....	197	297	..	1865	27.4
50-51—Minneapolis	68	....	1584	678	.428	717	576	.803	958	208	308	14	1932	28.4
51-52—Minneapolis	64	2572	1414	545	.385	555	433	.780	866	194	286	14	1523	23.8
52-53—Minneapolis	70	2651	1252	500	.399	567	442	.780	1007	201	290	12	1442	20.6
53-54—Minneapolis	72	2362	1160	441	.380	546	424	.777	1028	174	268	4	1306	18.1
54-55—					Voluntarily Retired									
55-56—Minneapolis	37	765	375	148	.395	122	94	.770	308	53	153	6	390	10.5
Totals	520	....	....	4097	....	4588	3570	.778	....	....	2162	..	11764	22.6

NBL AND NBA PLAYOFF RECORD

Sea.—Team	G.	Min.	FGA	FGM	Pct.	FTA	FTM	Pct.	Reb.	Ast.	PF	Disq.	Pts.	Avg.
46-47—Chicago-NBL	11	....	....	72	....	104	73	.702	....	....	48	..	217	19.6
47-48—Minn.-NBL	10	....	....	88	....	97	68	.701	....	....	37	..	244	24.4
48-49—Minneapolis	10	....	227	103	.454	121	97	.802	....	21	44	..	303	30.3
49-50—Minneapolis	12	....	316	121	.383	170	134	.788	....	36	47	..	376	31.3
50-51—Minneapolis	7	....	152	62	.408	55	44	.800	74	9	25	1	168	24.0
51-52—Minneapolis	13	553	261	99	.379	138	109	.790	207	36	63	3	307	23.6
52-53—Minneapolis	12	463	213	78	.366	112	82	.732	185	23	56	5	238	19.8
53-54—Minneapolis	13	424	190	87	.458	96	78	.813	171	25	56	1	252	19.4
55-56—Minneapolis	3	60	35	13	.371	13	10	.769	28	5	14	0	36	12.0
Totals	91	....	....	723	....	906	695	.767	....	....	390	..	2141	23.5

NBA ALL-STAR GAME RECORD

Season—Team	Min.	FGA	FGM	Pct.	FTA	FTM	Pct.	Reb.	Ast.	PF	Disq.	Pts.
1951—Minneapolis	....	17	4	.235	6	4	.667	11	3	2	0	12
1952—Minneapolis	29	19	9	.474	9	8	.889	15	1	5	0	26
1953—Minneapolis	40	26	9	.346	4	4	1.000	16	2	2	0	22
1954—Minneapolis	31	18	6	.333	8	6	.750	9	1	5	0	18
Totals	....	80	28	.350	27	22	.815	51	7	14	0	78

NBA COACHING RECORD

		Regular Season			
Sea.	Club	W.	L.	Pct.	Pos.
1957-58—Minneapolis		9	30	.231	4†

†Western Division.

Elected to Naismith Memorial Basketball Hall of Fame, 1959. . . . Named to NBA 25th and 35th Anniversary All-Time Teams, 1970 and 1980. . . . NBA All-Star First Team, 1949, 1950, 1951, 1952, 1953, 1954. . . . Led NBA in scoring, 1949, 1950, 1952. . . . Led NBA in rebounding, 1953. . . . NBA All-Star Game MVP, 1953. . . . Member of NBA championship teams, 1949, 1950, 1952, 1953, 1954. . . . Member of NBL championship teams, 1947 and 1948. . . . Named to THE SPORTING NEWS All-America First Team, 1944 and 1945. . . . ABA Commissioner during 1968-69 season. . . . Brother of former NBA forward-center Ed Mikan and father of former NBA forward Larry Mikan.

ARILD VERNER AGERSKOV MIKKELSEN
(Vern)

Born October 21, 1928 at Fresno, Calif. Height 6:07. Weight 230.

High School—Askov, Minn.

College—Hamline University, St. Paul, Minn.

Drafted by Minneapolis on first round, 1949.

—COLLEGIATE RECORD—

Year	G.	Min.	FGA	FGM	Pct.	FTA	FTM	Pct.	Reb.	Pts.	Avg.
45-46					Statistics Unavailable						
46-47	26	....	...	102	....	...	52	....	....	256	9.8
47-48	31	....	...	199	....	...	119	....	....	517	16.7
48-49	30	...	377	203	.538	177	113	.638	....	519	17.3

NBA REGULAR SEASON RECORD

Sea.—Team	G.	Min.	FGA	FGM	Pct.	FTA	FTM	Pct.	Reb.	Ast.	PF	Disq.	Pts.	Avg.
49-50—Minneapolis	68	....	722	288	.399	286	215	.752	....	123	222	...	791	11.6
50-51—Minneapolis	64	....	893	359	.402	275	186	.676	655	181	260	13	904	14.1
51-52—Minneapolis	66	2345	866	363	.419	372	283	.761	681	180	282	16	1009	15.3
52-53—Minneapolis	70	2465	868	378	.435	387	291	.752	654	148	289	14	1047	15.0
53-54—Minneapolis	72	2247	771	288	.374	298	221	.742	615	119	264	7	797	11.1
54-55—Minneapolis	71	2559	1043	440	.422	598	447	.747	722	145	319	14	1327	18.7
55-56—Minneapolis	72	2100	821	317	.386	408	328	.804	608	173	319	17	962	13.4
56-57—Minneapolis	72	2198	854	322	.377	424	342	.807	630	121	312	18	986	13.7
57-58—Minneapolis	72	2390	1070	439	.410	471	370	.786	805	166	299	20	1248	17.3
58-59—Minneapolis	72	2139	904	353	.390	355	286	.806	570	159	246	8	992	13.8
Totals	699	....	8812	3547	.403	3874	2969	.766	....	1515	2812	...	10063	14.4

NBA PLAYOFF RECORD

Sea.—Team	G.	Min.	FGA	FGM	Pct.	FTA	FTM	Pct.	Reb.	Ast.	PF	Disq.	Pts.	Avg.
49-50—Minneapolis	12	....	149	55	.369	60	46	.767	....	18	32	....	156	13.0
50-51—Minneapolis	7	....	96	39	.406	47	31	.660	67	17	35	3	109	15.6
51-52—Minneapolis	13	496	139	60	.432	64	53	.826	110	20	66	4	173	13.3
52-53—Minneapolis	12	400	133	44	.331	66	56	.848	104	24	59	3	144	12.0
53-54—Minneapolis	13	375	111	51	.459	36	31	.861	73	17	52	1	133	10.2
54-55—Minneapolis	7	209	85	30	.353	46	36	.783	78	13	36	4	96	13.7
55-56—Minneapolis	3	90	26	11	.423	20	18	.900	17	2	14	2	40	13.3
56-57—Minneapolis	5	162	83	33	.398	34	22	.647	43	17	29	4	88	17.6
58-59—Minneapolis	13	371	177	73	.412	73	56	.767	93	24	54	3	202	15.5
Totals	85	....	999	396	.396	446	349	.783	....	152	377	...	1141	13.4

NBA ALL-STAR GAME RECORD

Season—Team	Min.	FGA	FGM	Pct.	FTA	FTM	Pct.	Reb.	Ast.	PF	Disq.	Pts.
1951—Minneapolis	..	11	4	.364	4	3	.750	9	1	3	0	11
1952—Minneapolis	23	8	5	.625	2	2	1.000	10	0	2	0	12
1953—Minneapolis	19	13	3	.231	0	0	.000	6	3	3	0	6
1955—Minneapolis	25	15	7	.467	3	2	.667	9	1	5	0	16
1956—Minneapolis	22	13	5	.385	7	6	.857	9	2	4	0	16
1957—Minneapolis	21	10	3	.300	4	0	.000	9	1	3	0	6
Totals (6 games)	..	70	27	.386	20	13	.650	52	8	20	0	67

ABA COACHING RECORD

		Regular Season			
Sea.	Club	W.	L.	Pct.	Pos.
1968-69—Minnesota		6	7	.462	...

Named to NBA All-Star Second Team, 1951, 1952, 1953, 1955. . . . Holds NBA record for most disqualifications. . . . Member of NBA championship team, 1950, 1952, 1953, 1954. . . . Led NCAA Division II in field-goal percentage, 1949. . . . Named to NAIA Basketball Hall of Fame, 1956. . . . THE SPORTING NEWS All-America Fourth Team, 1949.

EARL MONROE
(The Pearl)

Born November 21, 1944 at Philadelphia, Pa.   Height 6:03½.   Weight 190.

High School—Philadelphia, Pa., Bartram.

College—Winston-Salem State University, Winston-Salem, N. C.

Drafted by Baltimore on first round, 1967 (2nd pick).

Traded by Baltimore to New York for Dave Stallworth, Mike Riordan and cash, November 10, 1971.

—COLLEGIATE RECORD—

Year	G.	Min.	FGA	FGM	Pct.	FTA	FTM	Pct.	Reb.	Pts.	Avg.
63-64	23	....	...	71	....	...	21	....	....	163	7.1
64-65	30	....	...	286	....	176	125	.710	211	697	23.2
65-66	25	....	519	292	.563	187	162	.866	167	746	29.8
66-67	32	....	839	509	.607	391	311	.795	218	1329	41.5
Totals	110	....	....	1158	....	....	619	....	.....	2935	26.7

NBA REGULAR SEASON RECORD

Sea.—Team	G.	Min.	FGA	FGM	Pct.	FTA	FTM	Pct.	Reb.	Ast.	PF	Disq.	Pts.	Avg.
67-68—Baltimore	82	3012	1637	742	.453	649	507	.781	465	349	282	3	1991	24.3
68-69—Baltimore	80	3075	1837	809	.440	582	447	.768	280	392	261	1	2065	25.8
69-70—Baltimore	82	3051	1557	695	.446	641	532	.830	257	402	258	3	1922	23.4
70-71—Baltimore	81	2843	1501	663	.442	506	406	.802	213	354	220	1	1732	21.4
71-72—Balt.-N.Y.	63	1337	662	287	.434	224	175	.781	100	142	139	1	749	11.9
72-73—New York	75	2370	1016	496	.488	208	171	.822	245	288	195	1	1163	15.5

Sea.—Team	G.	Min.	FGA	FGM	Pct.	FTA	FTM	Pct.	Off.	Def.	Tot.	Ast.	PF	Dq.	Stl.	Blk.	Pts.	Avg.
									|— Rebounds —|									
73-74—New York	41	1194	513	240	.468	113	93	.823	22	99	121	110	97	0	34	19	573	14.0
74-75—New York	78	2814	1462	668	.457	359	297	.827	56	271	327	270	200	0	108	29	1633	20.9
75-76—New York	76	2889	1354	647	.478	356	280	.787	48	225	273	304	209	1	111	22	1574	20.7
76-77—Knicks	77	2656	1185	613	.517	366	307	.839	45	178	223	366	197	0	91	23	1533	19.9
77-78—New York	76	2369	1123	556	.495	291	242	.832	47	135	182	361	189	0	60	19	1354	17.8
78-79—New York	64	1393	699	329	.471	154	129	.838	26	48	74	189	123	0	48	6	787	12.3
79-80—New York	51	633	352	161	.457	64	56	.875	16	20	36	67	46	0	21	3	378	7.4
Totals	926	29636	14898	6906	.464	4513	3642	.807			2796	3594	2416	13	473	121	17454	18.8

—DID YOU KNOW—

That the Lakers' Magic Johnson holds a three-game edge over the Celtics' Larry Bird in head-to-head duels in both regular-season competition (9-6) and the playoffs (11-8) since they each entered the league in 1979? The Lakers lost two of the three games Johnson missed against the Celtics early in his career.

NBA PLAYOFF RECORD

Sea.—Team	G.	Min.	FGA	FGM	Pct.	FTA	FTM	Pct.	Reb.	Ast.	PF	Disq.	Pts.	Avg.
68-69—Baltimore	4	171	114	44	.386	31	25	.806	21	16	10	0	113	28.3
69-70—Baltimore	7	299	154	74	.481	60	48	.800	23	28	23	0	196	28.0
70-71—Baltimore	18	671	356	145	.407	135	107	.793	64	74	56	0	397	22.1
71-72—New York	16	429	185	76	.411	57	45	.789	45	47	41	0	197	12.3
72-73—New York	16	504	211	111	.526	48	36	.750	51	51	39	0	258	16.1

Sea.—Team	G.	Min.	FGA	FGM	Pct.	FTA	FTM	Pct.	Off.	Def.	Tot.	Ast.	PF	Dq.	Stl.	Blk.	Pts.	Avg.
73-74—New York	12	407	165	81	.491	55	47	.855	8	40	48	25	26	0	8	9	209	17.4
74-75—New York	3	89	45	12	.267	22	18	.818	1	8	9	6	6	0	4	2	42	14.0
77-78—New York	6	145	62	24	.389	18	11	.611	1	4	5	17	15	0	6	0	59	9.8
Totals	82	2715	1292	567	.439	426	337	.791			266	264	216	0	18	11	1471	17.9

NBA ALL-STAR GAME RECORD

Season—Team		Min.	FGA	FGM	Pct.	FTA	FTM	Pct.	Reb.	Ast.	PF	Disq.	Pts.
1969—Baltimore		27	15	6	.400	12	9	.750	4	4	4	0	21
1971—Baltimore		18	9	3	.333	0	0	.000	5	2	3	0	6

Season—Team	Min.	FGA	FGM	Pct.	FTA	FTM	Pct.	Off.	Def.	Tot.	Ast.	PF	Dq.	Stl.	Blk.	Pts.
1975—New York	25	8	3	.375	5	3	.600	0	3	3	2	2	0	1	0	9
1977—Knicks..........	15	7	2	.286	0	0	.000	0	0	0	3	1	0	0	0	4
Totals	85	39	14		359	17	12	.706			12	11	10	0	1		40

Named to NBA All-Star First Team, 1969.... NBA Rookie of the Year, 1968.... NBA All-Rookie Team, 1968.... Member of NBA championship team, 1973.... Holds NCAA Division II record for most points in a season, 1967.... Outstanding player in 1967 NCAA College Division tournament.... Member of NCAA College Division tournament championship team, 1967.... Named to THE SPORTING NEWS All-America First Team, 1966.... Named to NAIA Basketball Hall of Fame, 1975.

CALVIN JEROME MURPHY

Born May 9, 1948 at Norwalk, Conn.   Height 5:09.   Weight 165.

High School—Norwalk, Conn.

College—Niagara University, Niagara University, N. Y.

Drafted by San Diego on second round, 1970 (18th pick).

—COLLEGIATE RECORD—

Year	G.	Min.	FGA	FGM	Pct.	FTA	FTM	Pct.	Reb.	Pts.	Avg.
66-67†	19	....	719	364	.506	239	201	.841	102	929	48.9
67-68	24	....	772	337	.437	288	242	.840	118	916	38.2
68-69	24	....	700	294	.420	230	190	.826	87	778	32.4
69-70	29	....	692	316	.457	252	222	.881	103	854	29.4
Varsity Totals	77	....	2164	947	.438	770	654	.849	308	2548	33.1

NBA REGULAR SEASON RECORD

Sea.—Team	G.	Min.	FGA	FGM	Pct.	FTA	FTM	Pct.	Reb.	Ast.	PF	Disq.	Pts.	Avg.
70-71—San Diego	82	2020	1029	471	.458	434	356	.820	245	329	263	4	1298	15.8
71-72—Houston	82	2538	1255	571	.455	392	349	.890	258	393	298	6	1491	18.2
72-73—Houston	77	1697	820	381	.465	269	239	.888	149	262	211	3	1001	13.0

Sea.—Team	G.	Min.	FGA	FGM	Pct.	FTA	FTM	Pct.	Off.	Def.	Tot.	Ast.	PF	Dq.	Stl.	Blk.	Pts.	Avg.
73-74—Houston	81	2922	1285	671	.522	357	310	.868	51	137	188	603	310	8	157	4	1652	20.4
74-75—Houston	78	2513	1152	557	.484	386	341	.883	52	121	173	381	281	8	128	4	1455	18.7
75-76—Houston	82	2995	1369	675	.493	410	372	.907	52	157	209	596	294	3	151	6	1722	21.0
76-77—Houston	82	2764	1216	596	.490	307	272	.886	54	118	172	386	281	6	144	8	1464	17.9
77-78—Houston	76	2900	1737	852	.491	267	245	.918	57	107	164	259	241	4	112	3	1949	25.6
78-79—Houston	82	2941	1424	707	.496	265	246	.928	78	95	173	351	288	5	117	4	1660	20.2
79-80—Houston	76	2676	1267	624	.493	302	271	.897	68	82	150	299	269	3	143	9	1520	20.0
80-81—Houston	76	2014	1074	528	.492	215	206	.958	33	54	87	222	209	0	111	6	1266	16.7
81-82—Houston	64	1204	648	277	.427	110	100	.909	20	41	61	163	142	0	43	1	655	10.2
82-83—Houston	64	1423	754	337	.447	150	138	.920	34	40	74	158	163	3	59	4	816	12.8
Totals	1002	30607	15030	7247	.482	3864	3445	.892			2103	4402	3250	53	1165	51	17949	17.9

Three-Point Field Goals: 1979-80, 1-for-25 (.040). 1980-81, 4-for-17 (.235). 1981-82, 1-for-16 (.063). 1982-83, 4-for-14 (.286). Totals, 10-for-72 (.139).

NBA PLAYOFF RECORD

Sea.—Team	G.	Min.	FGA	FGM	Pct.	FTA	FTM	Pct.	Off.	Def.	Tot.	Ast.	PF	Dq.	Stl.	Blk.	Pts.	Avg.
74-75—Houston	8	305	156	72	.462	57	51	.895	9	10	19	45	36	2	14	1	195	24.4
76-77—Houston	12	420	213	102	.479	30	28	.933	7	12	19	75	47	1	19	2	232	19.3
78-79—Houston	2	73	31	9	.290	9	8	.889	2	1	3	6	9	0	8	1	26	13.0
79-80—Houston	7	265	108	58	.537	13	13	1.000	4	6	10	26	29	1	11	0	131	18.7
80-81—Houston	19	540	287	142	.495	60	58	.967	7	17	24	57	69	0	26	0	344	18.1
81-82—Houston	3	57	22	5	.227	8	7	.875	2	1	3	4	7	0	1	0	17	5.7
Totals	51	1660	817	388	.475	177	165	.932	31	47	78	213	197	4	79	4	945	18.5

Three-Point Field Goals: 1979-80, 2-for-4 (.500). 1980-81, 2-for-7 (.286). 1981-82, 0-for-3. Totals, 4-for-14 (.286).

Season—Team	Min.	FGA	FGM	Pct.	FTA	FTM	Pct.	Off.	Def.	Tot.	Ast.	PF	Dq.	Stl.	Blk.	Pts.
								—Rebounds—								
1979—Houston	15	5	3	.600	0	0	.000	0	0	1	5	4	0	2	0	6

Three-Point Field Goals: 1979-80, 2-for-4 (.500). 1980-81, 2-for-7 (.286). Totals, 4-for-11 (.364).

Named to NBA All-Rookie Team, 1971. . . . Holds NBA records for highest free-throw percentage in one season, 1981, and most consecutive free throws made, 78, December 27, 1980 through February 28, 1981. . . . Led NBA in free-throw percentage, 1981 and 1983. . . . Named to THE SPORTING NEWS All-America Second Team, 1969 and 1970.

ROBERT LEE PETTIT JR.
(Bob)

Born December 12, 1932 at Baton Rouge, La.   Height 6:09.   Weight 215.

High School—Baton Rouge, La.

College—Louisiana State University, Baton Rouge, La.

Drafted by Milwaukee on first round, 1954.

Milwaukee franchise transferred to St. Louis, 1955.

—COLLEGIATE RECORD—

Year	G.	Min.	FGA	FGM	Pct.	FTA	FTM	Pct.	Reb.	Pts.	Avg.
50-51†	10	....	...	...	....	...	...	....	...	270	27.0
51-52	23	....	549	237	.432	192	115	.599	315	589	25.6
52-53	21	....	394	193	.490	215	133	.619	263	519	24.7
53-54	25	....	573	281	.490	308	223	.724	432	785	31.4
Varsity Totals	69	....	1516	711	.469	715	471	.659	1010	1893	27.4

NBA REGULAR SEASON RECORD

Sea.—Team	G.	Min.	FGA	FGM	Pct.	FTA	FTM	Pct.	Reb.	Ast.	PF	Disq.	Pts.	Avg.
54-55—Milwaukee	72	2659	1279	520	.407	567	426	.751	994	229	258	5	1466	20.4
55-56—St. Louis	72	2794	1507	646	.429	757	557	.736	1164	189	202	1	1849	25.7
56-57—St. Louis	71	2491	1477	613	.415	684	529	.773	1037	133	181	1	1755	24.7
57-58—St. Louis	70	2528	1418	581	.410	744	557	.745	1216	157	222	6	1719	24.6
58-59—St. Louis	72	2873	1640	719	.438	879	667	.758	1182	221	200	3	2105	29.2
59-60—St. Louis	72	2896	1526	669	.438	722	544	.753	1221	257	204	0	1882	26.1
60-61—St. Louis	76	3027	1720	769	.447	804	582	.724	1540	262	217	1	2120	27.9
61-62—St. Louis	78	3282	1928	867	.450	901	695	.771	1459	289	296	4	2429	31.1
62-63—St. Louis	79	3090	1746	778	.446	885	685	.774	1191	245	282	9	2241	28.4
63-64—St. Louis	80	3296	1708	791	.463	771	608	.789	1224	259	300	3	2190	27.4
64-65—St. Louis	50	1754	923	396	.429	405	332	.820	621	128	167	0	1124	22.5
Totals	792	30690	16872	7349	.436	8119	6182	.761	12849	2369	2529	33	20880	26.4

NBA PLAYOFF RECORD

Sea.—Team	G.	Min.	FGA	FGM	Pct.	FTA	FTM	Pct.	Reb.	Ast.	PF	Disq.	Pts.	Avg.
55-56—St. Louis	8	274	128	47	.367	70	59	.843	84	18	20	0	153	19.1
56-57—St. Louis	10	430	237	98	.414	133	102	.767	168	25	33	0	298	29.8
57-58—St. Louis	11	430	230	90	.391	118	86	.729	181	20	31	0	266	24.2
58-59—St. Louis	6	257	137	58	.423	65	51	.785	75	14	20	0	167	27.8
59-60—St. Louis	14	576	292	129	.442	142	107	.753	221	52	43	1	365	26.1
60-61—St. Louis	12	526	284	117	.412	144	109	.757	211	38	42	0	343	28.6
62-63—St. Louis	11	463	259	119	.459	144	112	.778	166	33	34	0	350	31.8
63-64—St. Louis	12	494	226	93	.412	79	66	.835	174	33	44	0	252	21.0
64-65—St. Louis	4	95	41	15	.366	20	16	.800	24	8	10	0	46	11.5
Totals	88	3545	1834	766	.418	915	708	.774	1304	241	277	1	2240	25.5

NBA ALL-STAR GAME RECORD

Season—Team	Min.	FGA	FGM	Pct.	FTA	FTM	Pct.	Reb.	Ast.	PF	Disq.	Pts.
1955—Milwaukee	27	14	3	.214	4	2	.500	9	2	0	0	8
1956—St. Louis	31	17	7	.412	7	6	.857	24	7	4	0	20
1957—St. Louis	31	18	8	.444	6	5	.833	11	2	2	0	21
1958—St. Louis	38	21	10	.476	10	8	.800	26	1	1	0	28
1959—St. Louis	34	21	8	.381	9	9	1.000	16	5	1	0	25
1960—St. Louis	28	15	4	.267	6	3	.500	14	2	2	0	11
1961—St. Louis	32	22	13	.591	7	3	.429	9	0	2	0	29
1962—St. Louis	37	20	10	.500	5	5	1.000	27	2	5	0	25
1963—St. Louis	32	16	7	.438	12	11	.917	13	0	1	0	25
1964—St. Louis	36	15	6	.400	9	7	.778	17	2	3	0	19
1965—St. Louis	34	14	5	.357	5	3	.600	12	0	4	0	13
Totals	360	193	81	.420	80	62	.775	178	23	25	0	224

NBA COACHING RECORD

Sea.	Club		Regular Season			
		W.	L.	Pct.	Pos.	
1961-62—St. Louis		4	2	.667	...†	

†Western Division.

Elected to Naismith Memorial Basketball Hall of Fame, 1970. . . . Named to NBA 25th and 35th Anniversary All-Time Teams, 1970 and 1980. . . . NBA Most Valuable Player, 1956 and 1959. . . . Named to NBA All-Star First Team, 1955, 1956, 1957, 1958, 1959, 1960, 1961, 1962, 1963, 1964. . . . NBA All-Star Second Team, 1965. . . . NBA Rookie of the Year, 1955. . . . Holds NBA championship series game records for most free-throw attempts, 24, and most free throws made, 19, vs. Boston, April 9, 1958. . . . Holds NBA championship series record for most field goals made in one half, 13, vs. Boston, April 9, 1957. . . . Shares NBA championship series record for most field goals made in one quarter, 8, vs. Boston, April 12, 1958. . . . Shares NBA championship series record for most free-throw attempts in one quarter, 11, vs. Boston, April 9, 1958. . . . NBA All-Star Game MVP, 1956, 1958, 1962. . . . NBA All-Star Game co-MVP, 1959. . . . Holds NBA All-Star Game records for most rebounds in one game, 27, in 1962, and most rebounds in one quarter, 10, in 1962. . . . Shares NBA All-Star Game record for most rebounds in one half, 16, in 1962. . . . Member of NBA championship team, 1958. . . . Led NBA in scoring, 1956 and 1959. . . . Led NBA in rebounding, 1956.

ANDREW MICHAEL PHILLIP
(Andy)

Born March 7, 1922 at Granite City, Ill. Height 6:02. Weight 195.

High School—Granite City, Ill.

College—University of Illinois, Champaign, Ill.

Drafted by Chicago BAA, 1947.

Drawn by Philadelphia NBA in dispersal of Chicago NBA team, October 6, 1950.

—COLLEGIATE RECORD—

Year	G.	Min.	FGA	FGM	Pct.	FTA	FTM	Pct.	Reb.	Pts.	Avg.
40-41†					(Freshman team did not play intercollegiate schedule)						
41-42	23	....	....	87	....	....	58		....	232	10.1
42-43	18	....	....	131		57	43	.754		305	16.9
			(In military service, 1943-44, 1944-45 and 1945-46 seasons.)								
46-47	20	....	....	81	....	61	30	.492	....	192	9.6
Varsity Totals	61	....	....	299		....	131		....	729	12.0

BBA AND NBA REGULAR SEASON RECORD

Sea.—Team	G.	Min.	FGA	FGM	Pct.	FTA	FTM	Pct.	Reb.	Ast.	PF	Disq.	Pts.	Avg.
47-48—Chicago	32	....	425	143	.336	103	60	.583	....	74	75	..	346	10.8
48-49—Chicago	60	....	818	285	.348	219	148	.676	....	319	205	..	718	12.0
49-50—Chicago	65	....	814	284	.349	270	190	.704	....	377	210	..	758	11.7
50-51—Philadelphia	66	....	690	275	.399	253	190	.751	446	414	221	8	740	11.2
51-52—Philadelphia	66	2933	762	279	.366	308	232	.753	434	539	218	6	790	12.0
52-53—Ft. Wayne	70	2690	629	250	.397	301	222	.737	364	397	229	9	722	10.3
53-54—Ft. Wayne	71	2705	680	255	.375	330	241	.730	265	449	204	4	751	10.6
54-55—Ft. Wayne	64	2332	545	202	.371	308	213	.692	290	491	166	1	617	9.6
55-56—Ft. Wayne	70	2078	405	148	.365	199	112	.563	257	410	155	2	408	5.8
56-57—Boston	67	1476	277	105	.379	137	88	.642	181	168	121	1	298	4.4
57-58—Boston	70	1164	273	97	.355	71	42	.592	158	121	121	0	236	3.4
Totals	701	15378	6318	2323	.368	2499	1738	.695	2395	3759	1925	31	6384	9.1

BBA AND NBA PLAYOFF RECORD

Sea.—Team	G.	Min.	FGA	FGM	Pct.	FTA	FTM	Pct.	Reb.	Ast.	PF	Disq.	Pts.	Avg.
47-48—Chicago	5	....	46	13	.283	14	10	.714	....	4	11	..	36	7.2
48-49—Chicago	2	....	36	14	.389	11	11	1.000	....	12	9	..	39	19.5
49-50—Chicago	2	....	27	7	.259	13	10	.769	....	12	8	..	24	12.0
50-51—Philadelphia	2	....	15	6	.400	6	3	.500	15	14	9	..	15	7.5
51-52—Philadelphia	3	122	19	8	.421	24	19	.792	14	22	16	1	35	11.7
52-53—Ft. Wayne	8	329	71	24	.338	51	34	.667	32	30	23	1	82	10.3
53-54—Ft. Wayne	4	136	38	13	.342	12	9	.750	12	17	9	0	35	8.8
54-55—Ft. Wayne	11	445	93	30	.323	40	34	.850	60	78	37	0	94	8.5
55-56—Ft. Wayne	10	173	27	9	.333	25	11	.440	26	35	16	0	29	2.9
56-57—Boston	10	128	22	8	.364	15	6	.400	20	17	18	0	22	2.2
57-58—Boston	10	91	21	5	.238	9	7	.778	14	7	20	0	17	1.7
Totals	67	1424	415	137	.330	220	154	.700	193	248	176	2	428	6.4

NBA ALL-STAR GAME RECORD

Season—Team	Min.	FGA	FGM	Pct.	FTA	FTM	Pct.	Reb.	Ast.	PF	Disq.	Pts.
1951—Philadelphia	....	8	3	.375	0	0	.000	10	8	1	0	6
1952—Philadelphia	30	6	4	.667	3	3	1.000	3	6	1	0	11
1953—Ft. Wayne	36	9	4	.444	1	1	1.000	6	8	2	0	9
1954—Ft. Wayne	19	4	1	.250	1	0	.000	3	3	1	0	2
1955—Ft. Wayne	28	4	3	.750	0	0	.000	3	6	3	0	6
Totals	....	31	15	.484	5	4	.800	25	31	8	0	34

NBA COACHING RECORD

		Regular Season			
Sea.	Club	W.	L.	Pct.	Pos.
1958-59—St. Louis		6	4	.600	..

Sea. Club	Regular Season W. L. Pct. Pos.
1961-62—Chicago	39 44 .470 3†

†Eastern Division.

Elected to Naismith Memorial Basketball Hall of Fame, 1961.... Named to NBA All-Star Second Team, 1952 and 1953.... Led NBA in assists, 1951 and 1952.... Member of NBA championship team, 1957.... Named THE SPORTING NEWS College Player of the Year, 1943.... Played minor league baseball in the St. Louis Cardinals' organization.

JAMES C. POLLARD
(Jim)

Born July 9, 1922 at Oakland, Calif.   Height 6:05. Weight 185.

High School—Oakland, Calif., Tech.

College—Stanford University, Stanford, Calif.

Signed by Minneapolis NBL, 1947.

—COLLEGIATE RECORD—

Year	G.	Min.	FGA	FGM	Pct.	FTA	FTM	Pct.	Reb.	Pts.	Avg.
40-41†						Statistics Unavailable					
41-42	23	....	...	103	....	48	35	.729	....	241	10.5
Varsity Totals	23	...	...	103	...	48	35	.729	....	241	10.5

Note: In military service during 1942-43, 1943-44 and 1944-45 seasons. Played with Alameda, Calif., Coast Guard team.

AMERICAN BASKETBALL LEAGUE RECORD
(Amateur Athletic Union League)

Year—Team	G	FG	FT	Pts.	Avg.
45-46—San Diego Dons	15	84	55	223	14.9
46-47—Oakland Bittners	20	..	..	279	14.0

(Led league in scoring both seasons.)

NBL AND NBA REGULAR SEASON RECORD

Sea.—Team	G.	Min.	FGA	FGM	Pct.	FTA	FTM	Pct.	Reb.	Ast.	PF	Disq.	Pts.	Avg.
47-48—Minn-N L	59	....	....	310	....	207	140	.676	....	....	147	....	760	12.9
48-49—Minneapolis	53	....	792	314	.396	227	156	.687	....	142	144	....	784	14.8
49-50—Minneapolis	66	....	1140	394	.346	242	185	.764	....	252	143	....	973	14.7
50-51—Minneapolis	54	....	728	256	.352	156	117	.750	484	184	157	4	629	11.6
51-52—Minneapolis	65	2545	1155	411	.356	260	183	.704	593	234	199	4	1005	15.5
52-53—Minneapolis	66	2403	933	333	.357	251	193	.769	452	231	194	3	859	13.0
53-54—Minneapolis	71	2483	882	326	.370	230	179	.778	500	214	161	0	831	11.7
54-55—Minneapolis	63	1960	749	265	.354	186	151	.812	458	160	147	3	681	10.8
Totals	497	....	....	2609	....	1759	1304	.741	....	....	1292	....	6522	13.1

NBA PLAYOFF RECORD

Sea.—Team	G.	Min.	FGA	FGM	Pct.	FTA	FTM	Pct.	Reb.	Ast.	PF	Disq.	Pts.	Avg.
48-49—Minneapolis	10	....	147	43	.293	62	44	.710	....	39	31	....	130	13.0
49-50—Minneapolis	12	....	175	50	.286	62	44	.710	....	56	36	....	144	12.0
50-51—Minneapolis	7	....	108	35	.324	30	25	.833	62	27	27	1	95	13.6
51-52—Minneapolis	11	469	173	70	.405	50	37	.740	71	33	34	1	177	16.1
52-53—Minneapolis	12	455	167	62	.371	62	48	.774	86	49	37	2	172	14.3
53-54—Minneapolis	13	543	155	56	.361	60	48	.800	110	41	27	0	160	12.3
54-55—Minneapolis	7	257	104	33	.317	46	33	.717†	78	14	13	0	99	14.1
Totals	72	....	1029	349	.339	372	279	.750	....	259	205	....	977	13.6

NBA ALL-STAR GAME RECORD

Season—Team	Min.	FGA	FGM	Pct.	FTA	FTM	Pct.	Reb.	Ast.	PF	Disq.	Pts.
1951—Minneapolis	..	11	2	.182	0	0	.000	4	5	1	0	4
1952—Minneapolis	29	17	2	.118	0	0	.000	11	5	3	0	4
1954—Minneapolis	41	22	10	.455	5	3	.600	3	3	3	0	23
1955—Minneapolis	27	19	7	.368	3	3	1.000	4	0	1	0	17
Totals (4 games)	..	69	21	.304	8	6	.750	22	13	8	0	48

NBA COACHING RECORD

Sea. Club	Regular Season W. L. Pct. Pos.	Playoffs W. L.
1959-60—Minneapolis	14 25 .359 3	5 4
1961-62—Chicago	18 62 .225 5	.. ..
Totals (2 years)	32 87 .269	5 4

ABA COACHING RECORD

Sea. Club	Regular Season				Playoffs	
	W.	L.	Pct.	Pos.	W.	L.
1967-68—Minnesota..........	50	28	.641	2	4	6
1968-69—Miami................	43	35	.551	2	5	7
1969-70—Miami................	5	15	.250	...	..	..
Totals (3 years)	98	78	.557		9	13

COLLEGIATE COACHING RECORD

Sea. Club	Regular Season			
	W.	L.	Pct.	Pos.
1955-56—La Salle	15	10	.600	
1956-57—La Salle	17	9	.653	
1957-58—La Salle	16	9	.640	

Elected to Naismith Memorial Basketball Hall of Fame, 1977. . . . Named to NBA All-Star First Team, 1949 and 1950. . . . NBA All-Star Second Team, 1952 and 1954. . . . Member of NBA championship teams, 1949, 1950, 1952, 1953, 1954. . . . Member of NBL championship team, 1948. . . . Member of NCAA Division I championship team, 1942.

FRANK VERNON RAMSEY JR.

Born July 31, 1931 at Corydon, Ky.   Height 6:03.   Weight 190.
High School—Madisonville, Ky.
College—University of Kentucky, Lexington, Ky.
Drafted by Boston on first round, 1953.

—COLLEGIATE RECORD—

Year	G.	Min.	FGA	FGM	Pct.	FTA	FTM	Pct.	Reb.	Pts.	Avg.
49-50†	16	....	274	109	.398	71	46	.648	..	264	16.5
50-51	34	....	413	135	.327	123	75	.610	434	345	10.1
51-52	32		470	185	.394	214	139	.650	383	509	15.9
52-53			Did Not Play—Kentucky had no team								
53-54	25	....	430	179	.416	181	132	.729	221	490	19.6
Varsity Totals	91	....	1313	499	.380	518	346	.668	1038	1344	14.8

NBA REGULAR SEASON RECORD

Sea.—Team	G.	Min.	FGA	FGM	Pct.	FTA	FTM	Pct.	Reb.	Ast.	PF	Disq.	Pts.	Avg.
54-55—Boston	64	1754	592	236	.399	322	243	.755	402	185	250	11	715	11.2
55-56—Boston			Did Not Play—In Military Service											
56-57—Boston	35	807	349	137	.393	182	144	.791	178	67	113	3	418	11.9
57-58—Boston	69	2047	900	377	.419	472	383	.811	504	167	245	8	1137	16.5
58-59—Boston	72	2013	1013	383	.378	436	341	.782	491	147	266	11	1107	15.4
59-60—Boston	73	2009	1062	422	.397	347	273	.787	506	137	251	10	1117	15.3
60-61—Boston	79	2019	1100	448	.407	354	295	.833	431	148	284	13	1191	15.1
61-62—Boston	79	1913	979	436	.445	405	334	.825	387	109	245	9	1206	15.3
62-63—Boston	77	1541	743	284	.382	332	271	.816	288	95	259	13	839	10.9
63-64—Boston	75	1227	604	226	.374	233	196	.841	233	81	245	7	648	8.6
Totals	623	15330	7342	2949	.402	3083	2480	.804	3410	1136	2158	85	8378	13.4

NBA PLAYOFF RECORD

Sea.—Team	G.	Min.	FGA	FGM	Pct.	FTA	FTM	Pct.	Reb.	Ast.	PF	Disq.	Pts.	Avg.
54-55—Boston	7	154	54	28	.519	26	19	.731	35	16	27	0	75	10.7
56-57—Boston	10	229	82	38	.463	59	46	.780	43	17	36	1	122	12.2
57-58—Boston	11	352	174	74	.425	59	54	.915	90	16	50	3	202	18.4
58-59—Boston	11	303	192	95	.495	81	65	.802	68	20	52	4	255	23.2
59-60—Boston	13	459	196	81	.413	63	55	.873	100	27	51	1	217	16.7
60-61—Boston	10	300	136	55	.407	75	61	.813	64	23	40	0	171	17.1
61-62—Boston	13	210	104	39	.375	45	41	.911	38	10	38	3	119	9.1
62-63—Boston	13	251	104	37	.356	47	34	.723	35	12	43	1	108	8.3
63-64—Boston	10	138	63	22	.349	21	18	.857	21	10	25	0	62	6.2
Totals	98	2396	1105	469	.424	476	393	.826	494	151	362	13	1331	13.6

ABA COACHING RECORD

Sea. Club	Regular Season				Playoffs	
	W.	L.	Pct.	Pos.	W.	L.
1970-71—Kentucky...........	32	35	.478	2†	11	8

†Eastern Division.

Elected to Naismith Memorial Basketball Hall of Fame, 1981. . . . Holds NBA championship series game record for most free throws made in one quarter, 9, vs. Minneapolis, April 4, 1959. . . . Member of NBA championship teams, 1957, 1959, 1960, 1961, 1962, 1963, 1964. . . . Named to THE SPORTING NEWS All-America Second Team, 1951. . . . Member of NCAA championship team, 1951.

OSCAR PALMER ROBERTSON
(Big O)

Born November 24, 1938 at Charlotte, Tenn.   Height 6:05.   Weight 220.
High School—Indianapolis, Ind., Crispus Attucks.
College—University of Cincinnati, Cincinnati, O.
Drafted by Cincinnati on first round (territorial choice), 1960.

Traded by Cincinnati to Milwaukee for Flynn Robinson and Charlie Paulk, April 21, 1970.

—COLLEGIATE RECORD—

Year	G.	Min.	FGA	FGM	Pct.	FTA	FTM	Pct.	Reb.	Pts.	Avg.
56-57†	13	....	...	151	....	178	127	.713	....	429	33.0
57-58	28	1085	617	352	.571	355	280	.789	425	984	35.1
58-59	30	1172	650	331	.509	398	316	.794	489	978	32.6
59-60	30	1155	701	369	.526	361	273	.756	424	1011	33.7
Varsity Totals	88	3412	1968	1052	.535	1114	869	.780	1338	2973	33.8

NBA REGULAR SEASON RECORD

Sea.—Team	G.	Min.	FGA	FGM	Pct.	FTA	FTM	Pct.	Reb.	Ast.	PF	Disq.	Pts.	Avg.
60-61—Cincinnati	71	3012	1600	756	.473	794	653	.822	716	690	219	3	2165	30.5
61-62—Cincinnati	79	3503	1810	866	.478	872	700	.803	985	899	258	1	2432	30.8
62-63—Cincinnati	80	3521	1593	825	.518	758	614	.810	835	758	293	1	2264	28.3
63-64—Cincinnati	79	3559	1740	840	.483	938	800	.853	783	868	280	3	2480	31.4
64-65—Cincinnati	75	3421	1681	807	.480	793	665	.839	674	861	205	2	2279	30.4
65-66—Cincinnati	76	3493	1723	818	.475	881	742	.842	586	847	227	1	2378	31.3
66-67—Cincinnati	79	3468	1699	838	.493	843	736	.873	486	845	226	2	2412	30.5
67-68—Cincinnati	65	2765	1321	660	.500	660	576	.873	391	633	199	2	1896	29.2
68-69—Cincinnati	79	3461	1351	656	.486	767	643	.838	502	772	231	2	1955	24.7
69-70—Cincinnati	69	2865	1267	647	.511	561	454	.809	422	558	175	1	1748	25.3
70-71—Milwaukee	81	3194	1193	592	.496	453	385	.850	462	668	203	0	1569	19.4
71-72—Milwaukee	64	2390	887	419	.472	330	276	.836	323	491	116	0	1114	17.4
72-73—Milwaukee	73	2737	983	446	.454	281	238	.847	360	551	167	0	1130	15.5

Sea.—Team	G.	Min.	FGA	FGM	Pct.	FTA	FTM	Pct.	Off.	Def.	Tot.	Ast.	PF	Dq.	Stl.	Blk.	Pts.	Avg.
									—Rebounds—									
73-74—Milw.	70	2477	772	338	.438	254	212	.835	71	208	279	446	132	0	77	4	888	12.7
Totals	1040	43866	19620	9508	.485	9185	7694	.838			7804	9887	2931	18			26710	25.7

NBA PLAYOFF RECORD

Sea.—Team	G.	Min.	FGA	FGM	Pct.	FTA	FTM	Pct.	Reb.	Ast.	PF	Disq.	Pts.	Avg.
61-62—Cincinnati	4	185	81	42	.519	39	31	.795	44	44	18	1	115	28.8
62-63—Cincinnati	12	570	264	124	.470	154	133	.864	156	108	41	0	381	31.8
63-64—Cincinnati	10	471	202	92	.455	127	109	.858	89	84	30	0	293	29.3
64-65—Cincinnati	4	195	89	38	.427	39	36	.923	19	48	14	0	112	28.0
65-66—Cincinnati	5	224	120	49	.408	68	61	.897	38	39	20	1	159	31.8
66-67—Cincinnati	4	183	64	33	.516	37	33	.892	16	45	9	0	99	24.8
70-71—Milwaukee	14	520	210	102	.486	69	52	.754	70	124	39	0	256	18.3
71-72—Milwaukee	11	380	140	57	.407	36	30	.833	64	83	29	0	144	13.1
72-73—Milwaukee	6	256	96	48	.500	34	31	.912	28	45	21	1	127	21.2

Sea.—Team	G.	Min.	FGA	FGM	Pct.	FTA	FTM	Pct.	Off.	Def.	Tot.	Ast.	PF	Dq.	Stl.	Blk.	Pts.	Avg.
									—Rebounds—									
73-74—Milw.	16	689	200	90	.450	52	44	.846	15	39	54	149	46	0	15	4	224	14.0
Totals	86	3673	1466	675	.460	655	560	.855			578	769	267	3			1910	22.2

NBA ALL-STAR GAME RECORD

Season—Team	Min.	FGA	FGM	Pct.	FTA	FTM	Pct.	Reb.	Ast.	PF	Disq.	Pts.
1961—Cincinnati	34	13	8	.615	9	7	.778	9	14	5	0	23
1962—Cincinnati	37	20	9	.450	14	8	.571	7	13	3	0	26
1963—Cincinnati	37	15	9	.600	4	3	.750	3	6	5	0	21
1964—Cincinnati	42	23	10	.435	10	6	.600	14	8	4	0	26
1965—Cincinnati	40	18	8	.444	13	12	.923	6	8	5	0	28
1966—Cincinnati	25	12	6	.500	6	5	.833	10	8	0	0	17
1967—Cincinnati	34	20	9	.450	10	8	.800	2	5	4	0	26
1968—Cincinnati	22	9	7	.778	7	4	.571	1	5	2	0	18
1969—Cincinnati	32	16	8	.500	8	8	1.000	6	5	3	0	24
1970—Cincinnati	29	11	9	.818	4	3	.750	6	4	3	0	21
1971—Milwaukee	24	6	2	.333	3	1	.333	2	2	3	0	5
1972—Milwaukee	24	9	3	.333	10	5	.500	3	3	4	0	11
Totals	380	172	88	.512	98	70	.714	69	81	41	0	246

Elected to Naismith Memorial Basketball Hall of Fame, 1979. . . . Named to NBA 35th Anniversary All-Time Team, 1980. . . . NBA Most Valuable Player, 1964. . . . Named to NBA All-Star First Team, 1961, 1962, 1963, 1964, 1965, 1966, 1967, 1968, 1969. . . . NBA All-Star Second Team, 1970 and 1971. . . . NBA Rookie of the Year, 1961. . . . Holds NBA record for most free throws attempted, 22, and most free throws made, 19, in one half, vs. Baltimore, December 27, 1964. . . . Shares NBA record for most free throws attempted in one quarter, 16, vs. Baltimore, December 27, 1964. . . . NBA all-time leader in free throws made, assists and rebounds by guard. . . . NBA All-Star Game MVP, 1961, 1964, 1969. . . . Shares NBA All-Star Game records for most career free throws attempted; most free throws made in one game, 12, in 1965. . . . Member of NBA championship team, 1971. . . . Led NBA in assists, 1961, 1962, 1964, 1965, 1966, 1969. . . . Led NBA in free-throw percentage, 1964 and 1968. . . . THE SPORTING NEWS College Player of the Year, 1958, 1959, 1960. . . . Named to THE SPORTING NEWS All-America First Team, 1958, 1959, 1960. . . . Led NCAA in scoring, 1958, 1959, 1960. . . . Member of U.S. Olympic team, 1960.

OSCAR ROBERTSON

GUY WILLIAM RODGERS JR.

Born September 1, 1935 at Philadelphia, Pa.   Height 6:00.   Weight 185.
High School—Philadelphia, Pa., Northeast.
College—Temple University, Philadelphia, Pa.
Drafted by Philadelphia on first round (territorial choice), 1958.

Philadelphia franchise transferred to San Francisco, 1962.
Traded by San Francisco to Chicago for a draft choice, cash and two players to be designated, September 7, 1966.
Jim King and Jeff Mullins sent to San Francisco to complete deal.
Traded by Chicago to Cincinnati for Flynn Robinson, cash and two draft choices, October 20, 1967.
Selected from Cincinnati by Milwaukee in expansion draft, May 6, 1968.

—COLLEGIATE RECORD—

Year	G.	Min.	FGA	FGM	Pct.	FTA	FTM	Pct.	Reb.	Pts.	Avg.
54-55†	15	....	...	...	....	...	...	....	....	278	18.5
55-56	31	....	552	243	.440	155	87	.561	186	573	18.5
56-57	29	....	565	216	.382	224	159	.710	202	591	20.4
57-58	30	....	564	249	.441	171	105	.614	199	603	20.1
Varsity Totals	90	....	1681	708	.421	550	351	.638	587	1767	19.6

NBA REGULAR SEASON RECORD

Sea.—Team	G.	Min.	FGA	FGM	Pct.	FTA	FTM	Pct.	Reb.	Ast.	PF	Disq.	Pts.	Avg.
58-59—Philadelphia	45	1565	535	211	.394	112	61	.545	281	261	132	1	483	10.7
59-60—Philadelphia	68	2483	870	338	.388	181	111	.613	391	482	196	3	787	11.6
60-61—Philadelphia	78	2905	1029	397	.386	300	206	.687	509	677	262	3	1000	12.3
61-62—Philadelphia	80	2650	749	267	.356	182	121	.599	348	643	312	12	655	8.2
62-63—San Francisco	79	3249	1150	445	.387	286	208	.725	394	825	296	7	1098	14.1
63-64—San Francisco	79	2695	923	337	.365	280	198	.707	328	556	245	4	872	11.0
64-65—San Francisco	79	2699	1225	465	.380	325	223	.686	323	565	256	4	1153	14.6
65-66—San Francisco	79	2902	1571	586	.373	407	296	.727	421	846	241	6	1468	18.6
66-67—Chicago	81	3063	1377	538	.391	475	383	.806	346	908	243	1	1459	18.0
67-68—Chi.-Cinn.	79	1546	426	148	.347	133	107	.805	150	380	167	1	403	5.1
68-69—Milwaukee	81	2157	862	325	.377	232	184	.793	226	561	207	2	834	10.3
69-70—Milwaukee	64	749	191	68	.356	90	67	.744	74	213	73	1	203	3.2
Totals	892	28663	10908	4125	.378	3003	2165	.721	3791	6917	2630	45	10415	11.7

NBA PLAYOFF RECORD

Sea.—Team	G.	Min.	FGA	FGM	Pct.	FTA	FTM	Pct.	Reb.	Ast.	PF	Disq.	Pts.	Avg.
59-60—Philadelphia	9	370	136	49	.360	36	20	.555	77	54	39	3	118	13.1
60-61—Philadelphia	3	121	57	21	.368	20	11	.550	21	15	16	2	53	17.7
61-62—Philadelphia	13	482	145	52	.359	55	35	.636	7	88	57	3	139	11.6
63-64—San Francisco	12	419	173	57	.329	47	33	.702	58	90	46	1	147	12.3
66-67—Chicago	3	97	40	15	.375	5	4	.800	6	18	11	0	34	11.3
69-70—Milwaukee	7	68	14	4	.286	12	9	.750	4	21	7	0	17	2.4
Totals	47	1557	565	198	.350	175	112	.640	173	286	176	9	508	10.8

NBA ALL-STAR GAME RECORD

Season—Team	Min.	FGA	FGM	Pct.	FTA	FTM	Pct.	Reb.	Ast.	PF	Disq.	Pts.
1963—San Francisco	17	6	3	.500	2	1	.500	2	4	2	0	7
1964—San Francisco	22	6	3	.500	0	0	.000	2	2	4	0	6
1966—San Francisco	34	11	4	.364	0	0	.000	7	11	4	0	8
1967—Chicago	28	4	0	.000	1	1	1.000	2	8	3	0	1
Totals	101	27	10	.370	3	2	.667	13	25	13	0	22

Led NBA in assists, 1963 and 1967.... Named to THE SPORTING NEWS All-America First Team, 1958.

WILLIAM FELTON RUSSELL
(Bill)

Born February 12, 1934 at Monroe, La.   Height 6:10.   Weight 220.
High School—Oakland, Calif., McClymonds.
College—University of San Francisco, San Francisco, Calif.
Drafted by Boston on first round, 1956. (3rd pick—Boston traded Ed Macauley and Cliff Hagan to St. Louis for its first-round choice, April 29, 1956.)

—COLLEGIATE RECORD—

Year	G.	Min.	FGA	FGM	Pct.	FTA	FTM	Pct.	Reb.	Pts.	Avg.
52-53†	23	....	...	...	....	...	....	....	...	461	20.0
53-54	21	....	309	150	.485	212	117	.552	403	417	19.9
54-55	29	....	423	229	.541	278	164	.590	594	622	21.4
55-56	29	....	480	246	.513	212	105	.495	609	597	20.6
Varsity Totals	79	....	1212	625	.516	702	386	.550	1606	1636	20.7

NBA REGULAR SEASON RECORD

Sea.—Team	G.	Min.	FGA	FGM	Pct.	FTA	FTM	Pct.	Reb.	Ast.	PF	Disq.	Pts.	Avg.
56-57—Boston	48	1695	649	277	.427	309	152	.492	943	88	143	2	706	14.7
57-58—Boston	69	2640	1032	456	.442	443	230	.519	1564	202	181	2	1142	16.6
58-59—Boston	70	2979	997	456	.457	428	256	.598	1612	222	161	3	1168	16.7
59-60—Boston	74	3146	1189	555	.467	392	240	.612	1778	277	210	0	1350	18.2
60-61—Boston	78	3458	1250	532	.426	469	258	.550	1868	268	155	0	1322	16.9
61-62—Boston	76	3433	1258	575	.457	481	286	.594	1790	341	207	3	1436	18.9
62-63—Boston	78	3500	1182	511	.432	517	287	.555	1843	348	189	1	1309	16.8
63-64—Boston	78	3482	1077	466	.433	429	236	.550	1930	370	190	0	1168	15.0
64-65—Boston	78	3466	980	429	.438	426	244	.573	1878	410	204	1	1102	14.1
65-66—Boston	78	3386	943	391	.415	405	223	.551	1779	371	221	4	1005	12.9
66-67—Boston	81	3297	870	395	.454	467	285	.610	1700	472	258	4	1075	13.4
67-68—Boston	78	2953	858	365	.425	460	247	.537	1451	357	242	2	977	12.5
68-69—Boston	77	3291	645	279	.433	388	204	.526	1484	374	231	2	762	9.9
Totals	963	40726	12930	5687	.440	5614	3148	.561	21620	4100	2592	24	14522	15.1

NBA PLAYOFF RECORD

Sea.—Team	G.	Min.	FGA	FGM	Pct.	FTA	FTM	Pct.	Reb.	Ast.	PF	Disq.	Pts.	Avg.
56-57—Boston	10	409	148	54	.365	61	31	.508	244	32	41	1	139	13.9
57-58—Boston	9	355	133	48	.361	66	40	.606	221	24	24	0	136	15.1
58-59—Boston	11	496	159	65	.409	67	41	.612	305	40	28	1	171	15.5
59-60—Boston	13	572	206	94	.456	75	53	.707	336	38	38	1	241	18.5
60-61—Boston	10	462	171	73	.427	86	45	.523	299	48	24	0	191	19.1
61-62—Boston	14	672	253	116	.458	113	82	.726	370	70	49	0	314	22.4
62-63—Boston	13	617	212	96	.453	109	72	.661	326	66	36	0	264	20.3
63-64—Boston	10	451	132	47	.356	67	37	.552	272	44	33	0	131	13.1
64-65—Boston	12	561	150	79	.527	76	40	.526	302	76	43	2	198	16.5
65-66—Boston	17	814	261	124	.475	123	76	.618	428	85	60	0	324	19.1
66-67—Boston	9	390	86	31	.360	52	33	.635	198	50	32	1	95	10.6
67-68—Boston	19	869	242	99	.409	130	76	.585	434	99	73	1	274	14.4
68-69—Boston	18	829	182	77	.423	81	41	.506	369	98	65	1	195	10.8
Totals	165	7497	2335	1003	.430	1106	667	.603	4104	770	546	8	2673	16.2

NBA ALL-STAR GAME RECORD

Season—Team	Min	FGA	FGM	Pct.	FTA	FTM	Pct.	Reb.	Ast.	PF	Disq.	Pts.
1958—Boston	26	12	5	.417	3	1	.333	11	2	5	0	11
1959—Boston	27	10	3	.300	1	1	1.000	9	1	4	0	7
1960—Boston	27	7	3	.429	2	0	.000	8	3	1	0	6
1961—Boston	28	15	9	.600	8	6	.750	11	1	2	0	24
1962—Boston	27	12	5	.417	3	2	.667	12	2	2	0	12
1963—Boston	37	14	8	.571	4	3	.750	24	5	3	0	19
1964—Boston	42	13	6	.462	2	1	.500	21	2	4	0	13
1965—Boston	33	12	7	.583	9	3	.333	13	5	6	1	17
1966—Boston	23	6	1	.167	0	0	.000	10	2	2	0	2
1967—Boston	22	2	1	.500	0	0	.000	5	5	2	0	2
1968—Boston	23	4	2	.500	0	0	.000	9	8	5	0	4
1969—Boston	28	4	1	.250	2	1	.500	6	3	1	0	3
Totals	343	111	51	.459	34	18	.529	139	39	37	1	120

NBA COACHING RECORD

Sea. Club	Regular Season W.	L.	Pct.	Pos.	Playoffs W.	L.	Sea. Club	Regular Season W.	L.	Pct.	Pos.	Playoffs W.	L.
1966-67—Boston	60	21	.741	2†	4	5	1975-76—Seattle	43	39	.524	2‡	2	4
1967-68—Boston*	54	28	.659	2†	12	7	1976-77—Seattle	40	42	.488	4‡	..	..
1968-69—Boston*	48	34	.585	4†	12	6	1987-88—Sacramento	17	41	.293	..‡	..	..
1973-74—Seattle	36	46	.439	3‡	..	..	Totals (8 seasons)	341	290	.540		34	27
1974-75—Seattle	43	39	.524	2‡	4	5							

*Won NBA championship. †Eastern Division. ‡Pacific Division.

Selected as "Greatest Player in the History of the NBA" by Professional Basketball Writers' Association of America, 1980. . . . Elected to Naismith Memorial Basketball Hall of Fame, 1974. . . . Named to NBA 25th and 35th Anniversary All-Time Teams, 1970 and 1980. . . . NBA Most Valuable Player, 1958, 1961, 1962, 1963, 1965. . . . Named to NBA All-Star First Team, 1959, 1963, 1965. . . . NBA All-Star Second Team, 1958, 1960, 1961, 1962, 1964, 1966, 1967, 1968. . . . NBA All-Defensive First Team, 1969. . . . Holds NBA record for most rebounds in one half, 32, vs. Philadelphia, November 16, 1957. . . . NBA all-time playoff leader in rebounds. . . . Holds NBA championship series game record for most rebounds, 40, vs. St. Louis, March 29, 1960, and vs. Los Angeles, April 18, 1962. . . . Holds NBA championship series game record for most free throws attempted in one half, 15, vs. St. Louis, April 11, 1961. . . . Holds NBA championship series game record for most rebounds in one quarter, 19, vs. Los Angeles, April 18, 1962. . . . NBA All-Star Game MVP, 1963. . . . Member of NBA championship teams, 1957, 1959, 1960, 1961, 1962, 1963, 1964, 1965, 1966, 1968 (also coach), 1969 (also coach). . . . Led NBA in rebounding, 1957, 1958, 1964, 1965. . . . NCAA Tournament Most Outstanding Player, 1955. . . . Member of NCAA championship teams, 1955 and 1956. . . . Member of U.S. Olympic team, 1956. . . . One of only seven players to average over 20 points and 20 rebounds per game during NCAA career.

BILL RUSSELL

ADOLPH SCHAYES
(Dolph)

Born May 19, 1928 at New York, N. Y.   Height 6:08.   Weight 220.
High School—Bronx, N. Y., DeWitt Clinton.
College—New York University, New York, N. Y.
Drafted by Tri-Cities NBL, 1948.

NBL draft rights obtained by Syracuse from Tri-Cities, 1948; Syracuse franchise transferred to Philadelphia, 1963.

—COLLEGIATE RECORD—

Year	G.	Min.	FGA	FGM	Pct.	FTA	FTM	Pct.	Reb.	Pts.	Avg.
44-45	11	....	...	46	....	...	23	....	....	115	10.5
45-46	22	....	...	54	....	...	41	....	....	149	6.8
46-47	21	....	...	66	....	...	63	....	....	195	9.3
47-48	26	....	...	124	....	...	108	....	....	356	13.7
Totals	80			290			235	....	....	815	10.2

NBL AND NBA REGULAR SEASON RECORD

Sea.—Team	G.	Min.	FGA	FGM	Pct.	FTA	FTM	Pct.	Reb.	Ast.	PF	Disq.	Pts.	Avg.
48-49—Syr. NBL	63	....	....	272	...	369	267	.724	....	....	232	..	811	12.8
49-50—Syracuse	64	....	903	348	.385	486	376	.774	....	259	225	..	1072	16.8
50-51—Syracuse	66	....	930	332	.357	608	457	.752	1080	251	271	9	1121	17.0
51-52—Syracuse	63	2004	740	263	.355	424	342	.807	773	182	213	5	868	13.8
52-53—Syracuse	71	2668	1002	375	.367	619	512	.827	920	227	271	9	1262	17.8
53-54—Syracuse	72	2655	973	370	.380	590	488	.827	870	214	232	4	1228	17.1
54-55—Syracuse	72	2526	1103	422	.383	587	489	.833	887	213	247	6	1333	18.5
55-56—Syracuse	72	2517	1202	465	.387	632	542	.858	891	200	251	9	1472	20.4
56-57—Syracuse	72	2851	1308	496	.379	691	625	.904	1008	229	219	5	1617	22.5
57-58—Syracuse	72	2918	1458	581	.398	696	629	.904	1022	224	244	6	1791	24.9
58-59—Syracuse	72	2645	1304	504	.387	609	526	.864	962	178	280	9	1534	21.3
59-60—Syracuse	75	2741	1440	578	.401	597	533	.892	959	256	263	10	1689	22.5
60-61—Syracuse	79	3007	1595	594	.372	783	680	.868	960	296	296	9	1868	23.6
61-62—Syracuse	56	1480	751	268	.357	319	286	.896	439	120	167	4	822	14.7
62-63—Syracuse	66	1438	575	223	.388	206	181	.879	375	175	177	2	627	9.5
63-64—Phila.	24	350	143	44	.308	57	46	.807	110	48	76	3	134	5.6
Totals	1059	....	15427	6135	.380	8273	6979	.844	11256	3072	3664	90	19249	18.2

NBA PLAYOFF RECORD

Sea.—Team	G.	Min.	FGA	FGM	Pct.	FTA	FTM	Pct.	Reb.	Ast.	PF	Disq.	Pts.	Avg.
48-49—Syr. NBL	6	....	...	27	...	42	32	.762	....	26	..	86	14.3	
49-50—Syracuse	11	....	148	57	.385	101	74	.733	....	28	43	..	188	17.1
50-51—Syracuse	7	....	105	47	.448	64	49	.766	102	20	28	2	143	20.4
51-52—Syracuse	7	248	91	41	.451	78	60	.769	90	15	34	2	142	20.3
52-53—Syracuse	2	58	16	4	.250	13	10	.769	17	1	7	0	18	9.0
53-54—Syracuse	13	374	140	64	.457	108	80	.741	136	24	40	1	208	16.0
54-55—Syracuse	11	363	167	60	.359	106	89	.840	141	40	48	3	209	19.0
55-56—Syracuse	8	310	142	52	.366	83	73	.880	111	27	27	0	177	22.1
56-57—Syracuse	5	215	95	29	.305	55	49	.891	90	14	18	0	107	21.4
57-58—Syracuse	3	131	64	25	.391	36	30	.833	45	6	10	0	80	26.7
58-59—Syracuse	9	351	195	78	.400	107	98	.916	117	41	36	0	254	28.2
59-60—Syracuse	3	126	66	30	.454	30	28	.933	48	8	10	0	88	29.3
60-61—Syracuse	8	308	152	51	.335	70	63	.900	91	21	32	2	165	20.6
61-62—Syracuse	5	95	66	24	.364	13	9	.692	35	5	21	0	57	11.5
62-63—Syracuse	5	108	44	20	.455	12	11	.917	28	7	17	0	51	10.2
Totals	103	2687	1491	609	.390	918	755	.822	1051	257	397	10	1973	19.2

NBA ALL-STAR GAME RECORD

Season—Team	Min.	FGA	FGM	Pct.	FTA	FTM	Pct.	Reb.	Ast.	PF	Disq.	Pts.
1951—Syracuse	..	10	7	.700	2	1	.500	14	3	1	0	15
1952—Syracuse				Selected—Injured, Did Not Play								
1953—Syracuse	26	7	2	.286	4	4	1.000	13	3	3	0	8
1954—Syracuse	24	3	1	.333	6	4	.667	12	1	1	0	6
1955—Syracuse	29	12	6	.500	3	3	1.000	13	1	4	0	15
1956—Syracuse	25	8	4	.500	10	6	.600	4	2	2	0	14
1957—Syracuse	25	6	4	.667	1	1	1.000	10	1	1	0	9
1958—Syracuse	39	15	6	.400	6	6	1.000	9	2	4	0	18
1959—Syracuse	22	14	3	.214	8	7	.875	13	1	6	1	13
1960—Syracuse	27	19	8	.421	3	3	1.000	10	0	3	0	19
1961—Syracuse	27	15	7	.467	7	7	1.000	6	3	4	0	21
1962—Syracuse	4	0	0	.000	0	0	.000	1	0	3	0	0
Totals	248	109	48	.440	50	42	.840	105	17	32	1	138

NBA COACHING RECORD

Sea. Club	Regular Season W.	L.	Pct.	Pos.	Playoffs W.	L.	Sea. Club	Regular Season W.	L.	Pct.	Pos.	Playoffs W.	L.
1963-64—Philadelphia	34	46	.425	3†	2	3	1970-71—Buffalo	22	60	.268	4‡	..	..
1964-65—Philadelphia	40	40	.500	3†	6	5	1971-72—Buffalo	0	1	.000	..‡	..	..
1965-66—Philadelphia	55	25	.688	1†	1	4	Totals (5 seasons)	151	172	.467		9	12

†Eastern Division.   ‡Atlantic Division.

Elected to Naismith Memorial Basketball Hall of Fame, 1972. . . . Named to NBA 25th Anniversary All-Time Team, 1970. . . . NBA All-Star First Team, 1952, 1953, 1954, 1955, 1957, 1958. . . . NBA All-Star Second Team, 1950, 1951, 1956, 1959, 1960, 1961. . . . Member of NBA championship team, 1955. . . . Led NBA in rebounding, 1951. . . . Led NBA in free-throw percentage, 1958, 1960, 1962. . . . NBA Coach of the Year, 1966. . . . Former NBA Supervisor of Referees. . . . Father of Denver Nuggets center Dan Schayes.

WILLIAM WALTON SHARMAN
(Bill)

Born May 25, 1926 at Abilene, Tex.   Height 6:01.   Weight 190.

High Schools—Lomita, Calif., Narbonne (Soph.) and
Porterville, Calif. (Jr. and Sr.)

College—University of Southern California, Los Angeles, Calif.

Drafted by Washington on second round, 1950.

Selected by Fort Wayne in dispersal draft of Washington franchise, January 8, 1951. (Did not report to Fort Wayne).

Traded by Fort Wayne with Bob Brannum to Boston for NBA rights to Charlie Share, 1951.

Signed as player-coach by Los Angeles of American Basketball League, 1961.

—COLLEGIATE PLAYING RECORD—

Year	G.	Min.	FGA	FGM	Pct.	FTA	FTM	Pct.	Reb.	Pts.	Avg.
46-47	10	....	....	....	....	....	....	....	....	41	4.1
47-48	24	....	....	100	....	44	38	.864	....	238	9.9
48-49	24	....	....	142	....	125	98	.784	....	382	15.9
49-50	24	....	421	171	.406	129	104	.806	....	446	18.6
Totals	82	....	....	....	....	....	...	....	....	1107	13.5

NOTE: In military service during 1944-45 and 1945-46 seasons.

NBA REGULAR SEASON RECORD

Sea.—Team	G.	Min.	FGA	FGM	Pct.	FTA	FTM	Pct.	Reb.	Ast.	PF	Disq.	Pts.	Avg.
50-51—Washington	31	....	361	141	.391	108	96	.889	96	39	86	3	378	12.2
51-52—Boston	63	1389	628	244	.389	213	183	.859	221	151	181	3	671	10.7
52-53—Boston	71	2333	925	403	.436	401	341	.850	288	191	240	7	1147	16.2
53-54—Boston	72	2467	915	412	.450	392	331	.844	255	229	211	4	1155	16.0
54-55—Boston	68	2453	1062	453	.427	387	347	.897	302	280	212	2	1253	18.4
55-56—Boston	72	2698	1229	538	.438	413	358	.867	259	339	197	1	1434	19.9
56-57—Boston	67	2403	1241	516	.416	421	381	.905	286	236	188	1	1413	21.1
57-58—Boston	63	2214	1297	550	.424	338	302	.893	295	167	156	3	1402	22.3
58-59—Boston	72	2382	1377	562	.408	367	342	.932	292	179	173	1	1466	20.4
59-60—Boston	71	1916	1225	559	.456	291	252	.866	262	144	154	2	1370	19.3
60-61—Boston	61	1538	908	383	.422	228	210	.921	223	146	127	0	976	16.0
Totals	711	21793	11168	4761	.426	3559	3143	.883	2779	2101	1925	27	12665	17.8

NBA PLAYOFF RECORD

Sea.—Team	G.	Min.	FGA	FGM	Pct.	FTA	FTM	Pct.	Reb.	Ast.	PF	Disq.	Pts.	Avg.
51-52—Boston	1	27	12	7	.583	1	1	1.000	3	7	4	0	15	15.0
52-53—Boston	6	201	60	20	.333	32	30	.938	15	15	26	1	70	11.7
53-54—Boston	6	206	81	35	.432	50	43	.860	25	10	29	2	113	18.3
54-55—Boston	7	290	110	55	.500	38	35	.921	38	38	24	1	145	20.7
55-56—Boston	3	119	46	18	.391	17	16	.941	7	12	7	0	52	17.3
56-57—Boston	10	377	197	75	.381	64	61	.953	35	29	23	1	211	21.1
57-58—Boston	11	406	221	90	.407	56	52	.929	54	25	28	0	232	21.1
58-59—Boston	11	322	193	82	.425	59	57	.966	36	28	35	0	221	20.1
59-60—Boston	13	364	209	88	.421	53	43	.811	45	20	22	1	219	16.8
60-61—Boston	10	261	133	68	.511	36	32	.889	27	17	22	0	168	16.8
Totals	78	2573	1262	538	.426	406	370	.911	285	201	220	6	1446	18.5

NBA ALL-STAR GAME RECORD

Season—Team	Min.	FGA	FGM	Pct.	FTA	FTM	Pct.	Reb.	Ast.	PF	Disq.	Pts.
1953—Boston	26	8	5	.625	1	1	1.000	4	0	2	0	11
1954—Boston	30	9	6	.667	4	2	.500	2	3	3	0	14
1955—Boston	18	10	5	.500	5	5	.500	4	2	4	0	15
1956—Boston	24	8	2	.250	4	3	.750	7	2	6	1	7
1957—Boston	23	17	5	.294	2	2	1.000	3	2	2	0	10
1958—Boston	25	19	6	.316	3	3	1.000	4	3	2	0	15
1959—Boston	24	12	3	.250	6	5	.833	2	0	1	0	11
1960—Boston	26	21	8	.381	1	1	1.000	6	2	1	0	17
Totals	196	104	40	.385	26	22	.846	32	14	21	1	100

ABL REGULAR SEASON RECORD

			—2-Point—			—3-Point—								
Sea.—Team	G.	Min.	FGM	FGA	Pct.	FGM	FGA	Pct.	FTM	FTA	Pct.	Reb.	Ast.	Pts.	Avg.
61-62—Los Angeles	19	346	80	35	.438	8	1	.125	37	34	.919	43	37	107	5.6

Sea.	Club	Regular Season			
		W.	L.	Pct.	Pos.
1962-63—Cal St.-Los Ang..		10	12	.454	4§
1963-64—Cal St.-Los Ang..		17	8	.680	2§

§California Collegiate Athletic Association.

NBA COACHING RECORD

Sea.	Club	Regular Season				Playoffs	
		W.	L.	Pct.	Pos.	W.	L.
1966-67—San Francisco ...		44	37	.543	1†	9	6
1967-68—San Francisco ...		43	39	.524	3†	4	6
1971-72—Los Angeles*		69	13	.841	1‡	12	3
1972-73—Los Angeles		60	22	.732	1‡	9	8
1973-74—Los Angeles		47	35	.573	1‡	1	4
1974-75—Los Angeles		30	52	.366	5‡	..	..
1975-76—Los Angeles		40	42	.488	4‡	..	..
Totals (7 seasons)		333	240	.581		35	27

*Won NBA Championship.   †Western Division.   ‡Pacific Division.

ABL AND ABA COACHING RECORD

Sea.	Club	Regular Season				Playoffs	
		W.	L.	Pct.	Pos.	W.	L.
1961-62—LA-Clev. ABL......		43	26	.615	..	5	2
1968-69—Los Ang. ABA....		33	45	.423	5†	..	..
1969-70—Los Ang. ABA....		43	41	.512	4†	10	7
1970-71—Utah ABA*		57	27	.679	2†	12	6
Totals (4 seasons)		176	139	.559		27	15

Note: Los Angeles Jets had 24-15 record when they folded after first half of season. Sharman then guided the Cleveland Pipers to ABL championship.

*Won ABA Championship.   †Western Division.

Elected to Naismith Memorial Basketball Hall of Fame, 1974. . . . Named to NBA 25th Anniversary All-Time Team, 1970. . . . NBA All-Star First Team, 1956, 1957, 1958, 1959. . . . NBA All-Star Second Team, 1953, 1955, 1960. . . . NBA All-Star Game MVP, 1955. . . . Holds NBA All-Star Game record for most field goals attempted in one quarter, 12, in 1960. . . . Member of NBA championship teams, 1957, 1959, 1960, 1961. . . . Led NBA in free-throw percentage, 1953, 1954, 1955, 1956, 1957, 1959, 1961. . . . NBA Coach of the Year, 1972. . . . Coach of NBA championship team, 1972. . . . ABA Co-Coach of the Year, 1970. . . . Coach of ABA championship team, 1971. . . . Coach of ABL championship team, 1962. . . . Played minor league baseball as an outfielder in Brooklyn Dodgers' organization, 1950 through 1953. . . . Named to THE SPORTING NEWS All-America First Team, 1950. . . . THE SPORTING NEWS All-America Third Team, 1949.

PAUL THERON SILAS

Born July 12, 1943 at Prescott, Ariz.   Height 6:07.   Weight 230.

High School—Oakland, Calif., McClymonds.

College—Creighton University, Omaha, Neb.

Drafted by St. Louis on second round, 1964 (12th pick).

Traded by Atlanta to Phoenix for Gary Gregor, May 8, 1969.

Traded by Phoenix to Boston, September 19, 1972, to complete deal in which Phoenix acquired draft rights to Charlie Scott, March 14, 1972.

Traded by Boston to Denver in three-team deal, in which Curtis Rowe was traded by Detroit to Boston, and Ralph Simpson was traded by Denver to Detroit, October 20, 1976.

Traded by Denver with Willie Wise and Marvin Webster to Seattle for Tom Burleson, Bob Wilkerson and a 1977 2nd round draft choice, May 24, 1977.

Signed by San Diego as Veteran Free Agent, May 21, 1980; Seattle received a 1985 2nd round draft choice as compensation.

Played in Eastern Basketball League with Wilkes Barre, 1965-66.

—COLLEGIATE RECORD—

Year	G.	Min.	FGA	FGM	Pct.	FTA	FTM	Pct.	Reb.	Pts.	Avg.
60-61†	21	....	...	225	....	119	96	.807	568	546	26.0
61-62	25	....	524	213	.406	215	125	.581	563	551	22.0
62-63	27	....	531	220	.414	228	133	.583	557	573	21.2
63-64	29	....	529	210	.397	194	117	.603	631	537	18.5
Varsity Totals	81	....	1584	643	.406	637	375	.589	1751	1661	20.5

NBA REGULAR SEASON RECORD

Sea.—Team	G.	Min.	FGA	FGM	Pct.	FTA	FTM	Pct.	Reb.	Ast.	PF	Disq.	Pts.	Avg.
64-65—St. Louis	79	1243	375	140	.373	164	83	.506	576	48	161	1	363	4.6
65-66—St. Louis	46	586	173	70	.405	61	35	.574	236	22	72	0	175	3.8
66-67—St. Louis	77	1570	482	207	.429	213	113	.531	669	74	208	4	527	6.9
67-68—St. Louis	82	2652	871	399	.458	424	299	.705	958	162	243	4	1097	13.4
68-69—Atlanta	79	1853	575	241	.419	333	204	.613	745	140	166	0	686	8.7
69-70—Phoenix	78	2836	804	373	.464	412	250	.607	916	214	266	5	996	12.8
70-71—Phoenix	81	2944	789	338	.428	416	285	.685	1015	247	227	3	961	11.9
71-72—Phoenix	80	3082	1031	485	.470	560	433	.773	955	343	201	2	1403	17.5
72-73—Boston	80	2618	851	400	.470	380	266	.700	1039	251	197	1	1066	13.3

Sea.—Team	G.	Min.	FGA	FGM	Pct.	FTA	FTM	Pct.	Off.	Def.	Tot.	Ast.	PF	Dq.	Stl.	Blk.	Pts.	Avg.
73-74—Boston	82	2599	772	340	.440	337	264	.783	334	581	915	186	246	3	63	20	944	11.5
74-75—Boston	82	2661	749	312	.417	344	244	.709	348	677	1025	224	229	3	60	22	868	10.6
75-76—Boston	81	2662	740	315	.426	333	236	.709	365	660	1025	203	227	3	56	33	866	10.7
76-77—Denver	81	1959	572	206	.360	255	170	.667	236	370	606	132	183	0	58	23	582	7.2
77-78—Seattle	82	2172	464	184	.397	186	109	.586	289	377	666	145	182	0	65	16	477	5.8
78-79—Seattle	82	1957	402	170	.423	194	116	.598	259	316	575	115	177	3	31	19	456	5.6
79-80—Seattle	82	1595	299	113	.378	136	89	.654	204	232	436	66	120	0	25	5	315	3.8
Totals	1254	34989	9949	4293	.432	4748	3196	.673			12357	2572	3105	32	358	138	11782	9.4

NBA PLAYOFF RECORD

Sea.—Team	G.	Min.	FGA	FGM	Pct.	FTA	FTM	Pct.	Reb.	Ast.	PF	Disq.	Pts.	Avg.
64-65—St. Louis	4	42	10	4	.400	4	3	.750	18	1	6	0	11	2.8
65-66—St. Louis	7	80	18	5	.278	11	8	.727	34	2	11	0	18	2.6
66-67—St. Louis	8	122	36	9	.250	18	11	.611	52	6	17	0	29	3.6
67-68—St. Louis	6	178	51	22	.431	38	27	.711	57	21	17	0	71	11.8
68-69—Atlanta	11	258	58	21	.362	37	19	.514	92	21	32	0	61	5.5
69-70—Phoenix	7	286	109	46	.422	32	21	.656	111	30	29	1	113	16.1
72-73—Boston	13	512	120	47	.392	50	31	.620	196	39	39	0	125	9.6

—Rebounds—

Sea.—Team	G.	Min.	FGA	FGM	Pct.	FTA	FTM	Pct.	Off.	Def.	Tot.	Ast.	PF	Dq.	Stl.	Blk.	Pts.	Avg.
73-74—Boston	18	574	126	50	.397	53	44	.830	53	138	191	47	51	2	13	9	144	8.0
74-75—Boston	11	405	92	42	.457	25	16	.640	46	84	130	40	45	1	12	2	100	9.1
75-76—Boston	18	741	154	69	.448	69	56	.812	78	168	246	42	67	1	24	6	194	10.8
76-77—Denver	6	141	33	14	.424	24	13	.542	16	24	40	16	23	1	2	4	41	6.8
77-78—Seattle	22	605	94	33	.351	60	41	.683	73	114	187	36	59	0	12	6	107	4.9
78-79—Seattle	17	418	54	21	.389	46	31	.674	40	58	98	19	44	1	9	5	73	4.3
79-80—Seattle	15	257	43	13	.302	13	11	.846	33	42	75	15	29	0	9	2	37	2.5
Totals	163	4619	998	396	.397	480	332	.692			1527	335	469	7	81	34	1124	6.9

NBA ALL-STAR GAME RECORD

—Rebounds—

Season—Team	Min.	FGA	FGM	Pct.	FTA	FTM	Pct.	Off.	Def.	Tot.	Ast.	PF	Dq.	Stl.	Blk.	Pts.
1972—Phoenix	15	6	0	.000	3	2	.667			9	1	1	0			2
1975—Boston	15	4	2	.500	2	2	1.000	0	2	2	2	2	0	4	0	6
Totals	30	10	2	.200	5	4	.800			11	3	3	0			8

EBL REGULAR SEASON RECORD

Sea.—Team	G.	Min.	2-Point FGM	2-Point FGA	Pct.	3-Point FGM	3-Point FGA	Pct.	FTM	FTA	Pct.	Reb.	Ast.	Pts.	Avg.
65-66—Wilkes Barre	5	....	25	....	....	0	0	.000	13	21	.619	85	9	63	12.6

NBA COACHING RECORD

Sea. Club	Regular Season W.	L.	Pct.	Pos.
1980-81—San Diego	36	46	.439	5†
1981-82—San Diego	17	65	.207	6†
1982-83—San Diego	25	57	.305	6†
Totals (3 seasons)	78	168	.317	

†Pacific Division.

Named to NBA All-Defensive First Team, 1975 and 1976. . . . NBA All-Defensive Second Team, 1971, 1972, 1973. . . . Member of NBA championship teams, 1974, 1976, 1979. . . . Holds NCAA record for most rebounds in 3-year career. . . . Led NCAA in rebounding, 1963. . . . One of only seven players to average over 20 points and 20 rebounds per game during NCAA career.

NATHANIEL THURMOND
(Nate)

Born July 25, 1941 at Akron, O. Height 6:11. Weight 235.

High School—Akron, O., Central.

College—Bowling Green State University, Bowling Green, O.

Drafted by San Francisco on first round, 1963.

Franchise named changed to Golden State, 1971.
Traded by Golden State to Chicago for Clifford Ray, cash and a 1975 1st round draft choice, September 3, 1974.
Traded by Chicago with Rowland Garrett to Cleveland for Steve Patterson and Eric Fernsten, November 27, 1975.

—COLLEGIATE RECORD—

Year	G.	Min.	FGA	FGM	Pct.	FTA	FTM	Pct.	Reb.	Pts.	Avg.
59-60†	17	....	....	....	....	....	....	....	208	225	13.2
60-61	24	....	427	170	.398	129	87	.674	449	427	17.8
61-62	25	....	358	163	.455	113	67	.593	394	393	15.7
62-63	27	....	466	206	.442	197	124	.629	452	536	19.9
Varsity Totals	76	....	1251	539	.431	439	278	.633	1295	1356	17.8

NATE THURMOND

NBA REGULAR SEASON RECORD

Sea.—Team	G.	Min.	FGA	FGM	Pct.	FTA	FTM	Pct.	Reb.	Ast.	PF	Disq.	Pts.	Avg.
63-64—San Fran.	76	1966	554	219	.395	173	95	.549	790	86	184	2	533	7.0
64-65—San Fran.	77	3173	1240	519	.419	357	235	.658	1395	157	232	3	1273	16.5
65-66—San Fran.	73	2891	1119	454	.406	428	280	.654	1312	111	223	7	1188	16.3
66-67—San Fran.	65	2755	1068	467	.437	445	280	.629	1382	166	183	3	1214	18.7
67-68—San Fran.	51	2222	929	382	.411	438	282	.644	1121	215	137	1	1046	20.5
68-59—San Fran.	71	3208	1394	571	.410	621	382	.615	1402	253	171	0	1524	21.5
69-70—San Fran.	43	1919	824	341	.414	346	261	.754	762	150	110	1	943	21.9
70-71—San Fran.	82	3351	1401	623	.445	541	395	.730	1128	257	192	1	1641	20.0
71-72—Golden St.	78	3362	1454	628	.432	561	417	.743	1252	230	214	1	1673	21.4
72-73—Golden St.	79	3419	1159	517	.446	439	315	.718	1349	280	240	2	1349	17.1

Sea.—Team	G.	Min.	FGA	FGM	Pct.	FTA	FTM	Pct.	—Rebounds— Off.	Def.	Tot.	Ast.	PF	Dq.	Stl.	Blk.	Pts.	Avg.
73-74—Gld. St.	62	2463	694	308	.444	287	191	.666	249	629	878	165	179	4	41	179	807	13.0
74-75—Chicago	80	2756	686	250	.364	224	132	.589	259	645	904	328	271	6	46	195	632	7.9
75-76—Chi.-Clev.	78	1393	337	142	.421	123	62	.504	115	300	415	94	160	1	22	98	346	4.4
76-77—Cleveland	49	997	246	100	.407	106	68	.642	121	253	374	83	128	2	16	81	268	5.5
Totals	964	35875	13105	5521	.421	5089	3395	.667			14464	2575	2624	34	125	553	14437	15.0

NBA PLAYOFF RECORD

Sea.—Team	G.	Min.	FGA	FGM	Pct.	FTA	FTM	Pct.	Reb.	Ast.	PF	Disq.	Pts.	Avg.
63-64—San Fran.	12	410	98	42	.429	53	36	.679	148	12	46	0	120	10.0
66-67—San Fran.	15	690	215	93	.433	91	52	.571	346	47	52	1	238	15.9
68-69—San Fran.	6	263	102	40	.392	34	20	.588	117	28	18	0	100	16.7
71-71—San Fran.	5	192	97	36	.371	20	16	.800	51	15	20	0	88	17.6
71-72—Golden St.	5	230	122	53	.434	28	21	.750	89	26	12	0	127	25.4
72-73—Golden St.	11	460	161	64	.398	40	32	.800	145	40	30	1	160	14.5

Sea.—Team	G.	Min.	FGA	FGM	Pct.	FTA	FTM	Pct.	—Rebounds— Off.	Def.	Tot.	Ast.	PF	Dq.	Stl.	Blk.	Pts.	Avg.
74-75—Chicago	13	254	38	14	.368	37	18	.486	24	63	87	31	36	0	5	21	46	3.5
75-76—Chi.-Cle.	13	375	79	37	.468	32	13	.406	38	79	117	28	52	2	6	29	87	6.7
76-77—Cleveland	1	1	0	0	.000	0	0	.000	0	1	1	0	0	0	0	1	0	0.0
Totals	81	2875	912	379	.416	335	208	.621			1101	227	266	4	11	51	966	11.9

NBA ALL-STAR GAME RECORD

Season—Team	Min.	FGA	FGM	Pct.	FTA	FTM	Pct.	Reb.	Ast.	PF	Disq.	Pts.
1965—San Francisco	10	2	0	.000	0	0	.000	3	0	1	0	0
1966—San Francisco	33	16	3	.188	3	1	.000	16	1	1	0	7
1967—San Francisco	42	16	7	.438	4	2	.500	18	0	1	0	16
1968—San Francisco	Selected—Injured, Did Not Play											
1970—San Francisco	Selected—Injured, Did Not Play											
1973—Golden State	14	5	2	.400	0	0	.000	4	1	2	0	4

Season—Team	Min.	FGA	FGM	Pct.	FTA	FTM	Pct.	—Rebounds— Off.	Def.	Tot.	Ast.	PF	Dq.	Stl.	Blk.	Pts.
1974—Golden St.	5	4	2	.500	1	0	.000	1	2	3	0	0	0	0	0	4
Totals	104	43	14	.326	8	3	.375			44	2	5	0			31

Elected to Naismith Memorial Basketball Hall of Fame, 1984. . . . Named to NBA All-Defensive First Team, 1969 and 1971. . . . NBA All-Defensive Second Team, 1972, 1973, 1974. . . . NBA All-Rookie Team, 1964. . . . Holds NBA record for most rebounds in one quarter, 18, vs. Baltimore, February 28, 1965. . . . Named to THE SPORTING NEWS All-America First Team, 1963. . . . Holds NCAA Tournament record for most rebounds in one game, 31, vs. Mississippi State, 1963.

JOHN KENNEDY TWYMAN
(Jack)

Born May 11, 1934 at Pittsburgh, Pa.   Height 6:06. Weight 210.
High School—Pittsburgh, Pa., Central Catholic.
College—University of Cincinnati, Cincinnati, O.
Drafted by Rochester on second round, 1955 (10th pick).

Rochester franchise transferred to Cincinnati, 1957.

—COLLEGIATE RECORD—

Year	G.	Min.	FGA	FGM	Pct.	FTA	FTM	Pct.	Reb.	Pts.	Avg.
51-52	16	....	83	27	.325	27	13	.481	55	67	4.2
52-53	24	716	323	136	.421	143	89	.622	362	361	15.0
53-54	21	777	443	174	.393	145	110	.759	347	458	21.8
54-55	29	1097	628	285	.454	192	142	.740	478	712	24.6
Totals	90	....	1477	622	.421	507	354	.698	1242	1598	17.8

NBA REGULAR SEASON RECORD

Sea.—Team	G.	Min.	FGA	FGM	Pct.	FTA	FTM	Pct.	Reb.	Ast.	PF	Disq.	Pts.	Avg.
55-56—Rochester	72	2186	987	417	.422	298	204	.685	466	171	239	4	1038	14.4
56-57—Rochester	72	2338	1023	449	.439	363	276	.760	354	123	251	4	1174	16.3
57-58—Cincinnati	72	2178	1028	465	.452	396	307	.775	464	110	224	3	1237	17.2
58-59—Cincinnati	72	2713	1691	710	.420	558	437	.783	653	209	277	6	1857	25.8

Sea.—Team	G.	Min.	FGA	FGM	Pct.	FTA	FTM	Pct.	Reb.	Ast.	PF	Disq.	Pts.	Avg.
59-60—Cincinnati	75	3023	2063	870	.422	762	598	.785	664	260	275	10	2338	31.2
60-61—Cincinnati	79	2920	1632	796	.488	554	405	.731	669	225	279	5	1997	25.3
61-62—Cincinnati	80	2991	1542	739	.479	435	353	.815	638	323	315	5	1831	22.9
62-63—Cincinnati	80	2523	1335	641	.480	375	304	.811	598	214	286	7	1586	19.8
63-64—Cincinnati	68	2004	993	447	.450	228	189	.829	364	137	267	7	1083	19.9
64-65—Cincinnati	80	2236	1081	479	.443	239	198	.828	383	137	239	4	1156	14.5
65-66—Cincinnati	73	943	498	224	.450	117	95	.812	168	60	122	1	543	7.4
Totals	823	26055	13873	6237	.450	4325	3366	.778	5421	1969	2774	56	15840	19.2

NBA PLAYOFF RECORD

Sea.—Team	G.	Min.	FGA	FGM	Pct.	FTA	FTM	Pct.	Reb.	Ast.	PF	Disq.	Pts.	Avg.
57-58—Cincinnati	2	74	45	15	.333	12	7	.583	22	1	6	0	37	18.5
61-62—Cincinnati	4	149	78	34	.436	8	8	1.000	29	12	18	0	76	19.0
62-63—Cincinnati	12	410	205	92	.449	77	65	.844	98	30	47	1	249	20.8
63-64—Cincinnati	10	354	176	83	.472	49	29	.796	87	16	41	1	205	20.5
64-65—Cincinnati	4	97	48	19	.396	11	11	1.000	17	3	16	0	49	12.3
65-66—Cincinnati	2	11	4	2	.500	2	1	.500	2	0	3	0	5	2.5
Totals	34	1095	556	245	.441	159	131	.824	255	62	131	2	621	18.3

NBA ALL-STAR GAME RECORD

Season—Team	Min.	FGA	FGM	Pct.	FTA	FTM	Pct.	Reb.	Ast.	PF	Disq.	Pts.
1957—Rochester	17	8	1	.125	3	1	.333	0	1	1	0	3
1958—Cincinnati	25	13	8	.615	2	2	1.000	3	0	3	0	18
1959—Cincinnati	23	12	8	.667	4	2	.500	8	3	4	0	18
1960—Cincinnati	28	17	11	.647	8	5	.625	5	1	4	0	27
1962—Cincinnati	8	6	4	.667	3	3	1.000	1	2	0	0	11
1963—Cincinnati	16	12	6	.500	0	0	.000	4	1	2	0	12
Totals	117	68	38	.559	20	13	.650	21	8	14	0	89

Elected to Naismith Memorial Basketball Hall of Fame, 1982. . . . Named to NBA All-Star Second Team, 1960 and 1962. . . . Led NBA in field-goal percentage, 1958.

CHESTER WALKER
(Chet)

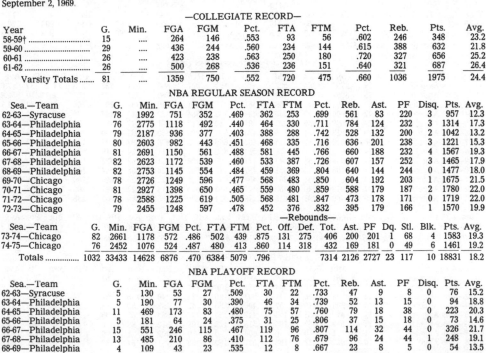

Born February 22, 1940 at Benton Harbor, Mich.   Height 6:07. Weight 220.

High School—Benton Harbor, Mich.

College—Bradley University, Peoria, Ill.

Drafted by Syracuse on second round, 1962 (14th pick).

Franchise transferred from Syracuse to Philadelphia, 1963.
Traded with Shaler Halimon by Philadelphia to Chicago for Jim Washington and a player to be named later, September 2, 1969.

—COLLEGIATE RECORD—

Year	G.	Min.	FGA	FGM	Pct.	FTA	FTM	Pct.	Reb.	Pts.	Avg.
58-59†	15	....	264	146	.553	93	56	.602	246	348	23.2
59-60	29	....	436	244	.560	234	144	.615	388	632	21.8
60-61	26	....	423	238	.563	250	180	.720	327	656	25.2
61-62	26	....	500	268	.536	236	151	.640	321	687	26.4
Varsity Totals	81	....	1359	750	.552	720	475	.660	1036	1975	24.4

NBA REGULAR SEASON RECORD

Sea.—Team	G.	Min.	FGA	FGM	Pct.	FTA	FTM	Pct.	Reb.	Ast.	PF	Disq.	Pts.	Avg.
62-63—Syracuse	78	1992	751	352	.469	362	253	.699	561	83	220	3	957	12.3
63-64—Philadelphia	76	2775	1118	492	.440	464	330	.711	784	124	232	3	1314	17.3
64-65—Philadelphia	79	2187	936	377	.403	388	288	.742	528	132	200	2	1042	13.2
65-66—Philadelphia	80	2603	982	443	.451	468	335	.716	636	201	238	3	1221	15.3
66-67—Philadelphia	81	2691	1150	561	.488	581	445	.766	660	188	232	4	1567	19.3
67-68—Philadelphia	82	2623	1172	539	.460	533	387	.726	607	157	252	3	1465	17.9
68-69—Philadelphia	82	2753	1145	554	.484	459	369	.804	640	144	244	0	1477	18.0
69-70—Chicago	78	2726	1249	596	.477	568	483	.850	604	192	203	1	1675	21.5
70-71—Chicago	81	2927	1398	650	.465	559	480	.859	588	179	187	2	1780	22.0
71-72—Chicago	78	2588	1225	619	.505	568	481	.847	473	178	171	0	1719	22.0
72-73—Chicago	79	2455	1248	597	.478	452	376	.832	395	179	166	1	1570	19.9

								—Rebounds—								
Sea.—Team	G.	Min.	FGA	FGM	Pct.	FTA	FTM	Pct.	Off.	Def.	Tot.	Ast.	PF	Dq.	Stl.	Blk.	Pts.	Avg.
73-74—Chicago	82	2661	1178	572	.486	502	439	.875	131	275	406	200	201	1	68	4	1583	19.3
74-75—Chicago	76	2452	1076	524	.487	480	413	.860	114	318	432	169	181	0	49	6	1461	19.2
Totals	1032	33433	14628	6876	.470	6384	5079	.796			7314	2126	2727	23	117	10	18831	18.2

NBA PLAYOFF RECORD

Sea.—Team	G.	Min.	FGA	FGM	Pct.	FTA	FTM	Pct.	Reb.	Ast.	PF	Disq.	Pts.	Avg.
62-63—Syracuse	5	130	53	27	.509	30	22	.733	47	9	8	0	76	15.2
63-64—Philadelphia	5	190	77	30	.390	46	34	.739	52	13	15	0	94	18.8
64-65—Philadelphia	11	469	173	83	.480	75	57	.760	79	18	38	0	223	20.3
65-66—Philadelphia	5	181	64	24	.375	31	25	.806	37	15	18	0	73	14.6
66-67—Philadelphia	15	551	246	115	.467	119	96	.807	114	32	44	0	326	21.7
67-68—Philadelphia	13	485	210	86	.410	112	76	.679	96	24	44	1	248	19.1
68-69—Philadelphia	4	109	43	23	.535	12	8	.667	23	8	5	0	54	13.5

Sea.—Team	G.	Min.	FGA	FGM	Pct.	FTA	FTM	Pct.	Reb.	Ast.	PF	Disq.	Pts.	Avg.
69-70—Chicago	5	178	83	35	.422	33	27	.818	42	11	14	0	97	19.4
70-71—Chicago	7	234	100	44	.440	24	17	.708	50	22	20	0	105	15.0
71-72—Chicago	4	97	38	16	.421	16	13	.813	14	4	7	0	45	11.3
72-73—Chicago	7	229	121	42	.347	37	33	.892	62	14	15	0	117	16.7

Sea.—Team	G.	Min.	FGA	FGM	Pct.	FTA	FTM	Pct.	—Rebounds— Off.	Def.	Tot.	Ast.	PF	Dq.	Stl.	Blk.	Pts.	Avg.
73-74—Chicago	11	403	159	81	.509	79	68	.861	26	35	61	18	26	0	10	1	230	20.9
74-75—Chicago	13	432	164	81	.494	75	66	.880	10	50	60	24	32	2	13	1	228	17.5
Totals	105	3688	1531	687	.449	689	542	.787			737	212	286	3	23	2	1916	18.2

NBA ALL-STAR GAME RECORD

Season—Team	Min.	FGA	FGM	Pct.	FTA	FTM	Pct.	Reb.	Ast.	PF	Disq.	Pts.
1964—Philadelphia	12	5	2	.400	0	0	.000	0	0	1	0	4
1966—Philadelphia	25	10	3	.300	3	2	.667	6	4	2	0	8
1967—Philadelphia	22	9	6	.667	4	3	.750	4	1	2	0	15
1970—Chicago	17	3	1	.333	2	2	1.000	2	1	2	0	4
1971—Chicago	19	9	3	.333	5	4	.800	3	1	1	0	10
1973—Chicago	16	5	1	.200	2	2	1.000	1	0	2	0	4

Season—Team	Min.	FGA	FGM	Pct.	FTA	FTM	Pct.	—Rebounds— Off.	Def.	Tot.	Ast.	PF	Dq.	Stl.	Blk.	Pts.
1974—Chicago	14	5	4	.800	4	4	1.000	0	2	2	1	1	0	0	0	12
Totals	125	46	20	.435	20	17	.850			18	8	11	0			57

Named to NBA All-Rookie Team, 1963. . . . Led NBA in free-throw percentage, 1971. . . . Member of NBA championship team, 1967. . . . Named to THE SPORTING NEWS All-America First Team, 1962. . . . THE SPORTING NEWS All-America Second Team, 1961.

JEROME ALAN WEST
(Jerry)

Born May 28, 1938 at Cheylan, W. Va.   Height 6:02.   Weight 185.
High School—East Bank, W. Va.
College—West Virginia University, Morgantown, W. Va.
Drafted by Minneapolis on first round, 1960 (2nd pick).

Minneapolis franchise transferred to Los Angeles, 1960.

—COLLEGIATE RECORD—

Year	G.	Min.	FGA	FGM	Pct.	FTA	FTM	Pct.	Reb.	Pts.	Avg.
56-57†	17	...	...	114	...	...	104	....	....	332	19.5
57-58	28	799	359	178	.496	194	142	.732	311	498	17.8
58-59	34	1210	656	340	.518	320	223	.697	419	903	26.6
59-60	31	1129	645	325	.504	337	258	.766	510	908	29.3
Varsity Totals	93	3138	1660	843	.508	851	623	.732	1240	2309	24.8

NBA REGULAR SEASON RECORD

Sea.—Team	G.	Min.	FGA	FGM	Pct.	FTA	FTM	Pct.	Reb.	Ast.	PF	Disq.	Pts.	Avg.
60-61—Los Angeles	79	2797	1264	529	.419	497	331	.666	611	333	213	1	1389	17.6
61-62—Los Angeles	75	3087	1795	799	.445	926	712	.769	591	402	173	4	2310	30.8
62-63—Los Angeles	55	2163	1213	559	.461	477	371	.778	384	307	150	1	1489	27.1
63-64—Los Angeles	72	2906	1529	740	.484	702	584	.832	443	403	200	2	2064	28.7
64-65—Los Angeles	74	3066	1655	822	.497	789	648	.821	447	364	221	2	2292	31.0
65-66—Los Angeles	79	3218	1731	818	.473	977	840	.860	562	480	243	1	2476	31.3
66-67—Los Angeles	66	2670	1389	645	.464	686	602	.878	392	447	160	1	1892	28.7
67-68—Los Angeles	51	1919	926	476	.514	482	391	.811	294	310	152	1	1343	26.3
68-69—Los Angeles	61	2394	1156	545	.471	597	490	.821	262	423	156	1	1580	25.9
69-70—Los Angeles	74	3106	1673	831	.497	785	647	.824	338	554	160	3	2309	31.2
70-71—Los Angeles	69	2845	1351	667	.494	631	525	.832	320	655	180	0	1859	26.9
71-72—Los Angeles	77	2973	1540	735	.477	633	515	.814	327	747	209	0	1985	25.8
72-73—Los Angeles	69	2460	1291	618	.479	421	339	.805	289	607	138	0	1575	22.8

Sea.—Team	G.	Min.	FGA	FGM	Pct.	FTA	FTM	Pct.	—Rebounds— Off.	Def.	Tot.	Ast.	PF	Dq.	Stl.	Blk.	Pts.	Avg.
73-74—L. A.	31	967	519	232	.447	198	165	.833	30	86	116	206	80	0	81	23	629	20.3
Totals	932	36571	19032	9016	.474	8801	7160	.814			5376	6238	2435	17			25192	27.0

NBA PLAYOFF RECORD

Sea.—Team	G.	Min.	FGA	FGM	Pct.	FTA	FTM	Pct.	Reb.	Ast.	PF	Disq.	Pts.	Avg.
60-61—Los Angeles	12	461	202	99	.490	106	77	.726	104	63	39	0	275	22.9
61-62—Los Angeles	13	557	310	144	.465	150	121	.807	88	57	38	0	409	31.5
62-63—Los Angeles	13	538	286	144	.503	100	74	.740	106	61	34	0	362	27.8
63-64—Los Angeles	5	206	115	57	.496	53	42	.792	36	17	20	0	156	31.2
64-65—Los Angeles	11	470	351	155	.442	155	137	.884	63	58	37	0	447	40.6
65-66—Los Angeles	14	619	357	185	.518	125	109	.872	88	79	40	0	479	34.2
66-67—Los Angeles	1	1	0	0	.000	0	0	.000	1	0	0	0	0	0.0
67-68—Los Angeles	15	622	313	165	.527	169	132	.781	81	82	47	0	462	30.8

JERRY WEST

Sea.—Team	G.	Min.	FGA	FGM	Pct.	FTA	FTM	Pct.	Reb.	Ast.	PF	Disq.	Pts.	Avg.
68-69—Los Angeles	18	757	423	196	.463	204	164	.804	71	135	52	1	556	30.9
69-70—Los Angeles	18	830	418	196	.469	212	170	.802	66	151	55	1	562	31.2
71-72—Los Angeles	15	608	340	128	.376	106	88	.830	73	134	39	0	344	22.9
72-73—Los Angeles	17	638	336	151	.449	127	99	.780	76	132	49	1	401	23.6

Sea.—Team	G.	Min.	FGA	FGM	Pct.	FTA	FTM	Pct.	Off.	Def.	Tot.	Ast.	PF	Dq.	Stl.	Blk.	Pts.	Avg.
								—Rebounds—										
73-74—L. A.	1	14	9	2	.222	0	0	.000	0	2	2	1	1	0	0	0	4	4.0
Totals	153	6321	3460	1622	.469	1507	1213	.805			855	970	451	3			4457	29.1

NBA ALL-STAR GAME RECORD

Season—Team	Min.	FGA	FGM	Pct.	FTA	FTM	Pct.	Reb.	Ast.	PF	Disq.	Pts.
1961—Los Angeles	25	8	2	.250	6	5	.833	2	4	3	0	9
1962—Los Angeles	31	14	7	.500	6	4	.667	3	1	2	0	18
1963—Los Angeles	32	15	5	.333	4	3	.750	7	5	1	0	13
1964—Los Angeles	42	20	8	.400	1	1	1.000	4	5	3	0	17
1965—Los Angeles	40	16	8	.500	6	4	.667	5	6	2	0	20
1966—Los Angeles	11	5	1	.200	2	2	1.000	1	0	2	0	4
1967—Los Angeles	30	11	6	.545	4	4	1.000	3	6	3	0	16
1968—Los Angeles	32	17	7	.412	4	3	.750	6	6	4	0	17
1969—Los Angeles	Selected—Injured, Did Not Play											
1970—Los Angeles	31	12	7	.583	12	8	.667	5	5	3	0	22
1971—Los Angeles	20	4	2	.500	3	1	.333	1	9	1	0	5
1972—Los Angeles	27	9	6	.667	2	1	.500	6	5	2	0	13
1973—Los Angeles	20	6	3	.500	0	0	.000	4	3	2	0	6
1974—Los Angeles	Selected—Injured, Did Not Play											
Totals	341	137	62	.453	50	36	.720	47	55	28	0	160

NBA COACHING RECORD

Sea. Club	W.	L.	Pct.	Pos.	Playoffs W.	L.	Sea. Club	W.	L.	Pct.	Pos.	Playoffs W.	L.
1976-77—Los Angeles	53	29	.646	1†	4	7	1978-79—Los Angeles	47	35	.573	3†	3	5
1977-78—Los Angeles	45	37	.549	4†	1	2	Totals (3 seasons)	145	101	.589		8	14

†Pacific Division.

Elected to Naismith Memorial Basketball Hall of Fame, 1979. . . . Named to NBA 35th Anniversary All-Time Team, 1980. . . . NBA All-Star First Team, 1962, 1963, 1964, 1965, 1966, 1967, 1970, 1971, 1972, 1973. . . . NBA All-Star Second Team, 1968 and 1969. . . . NBA All-Defensive First Team, 1970, 1971, 1972, 1973. . . . NBA All-Defensive Second Team, 1969. . . . NBA Playoff MVP, 1969. . . . Holds NBA record for most free throws made in one season, 1966. . . . NBA all-time playoff leader in free throws made and scoring average. . . . Holds NBA playoff game record for most free throws made in one half, 14, vs. Baltimore, April 5, 1965. . . . NBA All-Star Game MVP, 1972. . . . Member of NBA championship team, 1972. . . . Led NBA in assists, 1972. . . . Led NBA in scoring, 1970. . . . Named to THE SPORTING NEWS All-America First Team, 1959 and 1960. . . . NCAA Tournament Most Outstanding Player, 1959. . . . Member of U.S. Olympic team, 1960.

JOSEPH HENRY WHITE
(Jo Jo)

Born November 16, 1946 at St. Louis, Mo. Height 6:03. Weight 190.

High Schools—St. Louis, Mo., Vashon (Soph.) and McKinley (Jr.-Sr.)

College—University of Kansas, Lawrence, Kan.

Drafted by Boston on first round, 1969 (9th pick).

Traded by Boston to Golden State for a 1979 1st round draft choice, January 30, 1979.
Sold by Golden State to Kansas City, September 10, 1980.

—COLLEGIATE RECORD—

Year	G.	Min.	FGA	FGM	Pct.	FTA	FTM	Pct.	Reb.	Pts.	Avg.
64-65†	2	....	34	11	.324	15	11	.733	25	33	16.5
65-66†	6	....	88	35	.398	27	18	.667	32	88	14.7
65-66	9	....	112	44	.393	26	14	.538	68	102	11.3
66-67	27	....	416	170	.409	72	59	.819	150	399	14.8
67-68	30	....	462	188	.407	115	83	.722	107	459	15.3
68-69	18	....	286	134	.469	79	58	.734	84	326	18.1
Varsity Totals	84		1276	536	.420	292	214	.733	409	1286	15.3

NBA REGULAR SEASON RECORD

Sea.—Team	G.	Min.	FGA	FGM	Pct.	FTA	FTM	Pct.	Reb.	Ast.	PF	Disq.	Pts.	Avg.
69-70—Boston	60	1328	684	309	.452	135	111	.822	169	145	132	1	729	12.2
70-71—Boston	75	2787	1494	693	.464	269	215	.799	376	361	255	5	1601	21.3
71-72—Boston	79	3261	1788	770	.431	343	285	.831	446	416	227	1	1825	23.1
72-73—Boston	82	3250	1665	717	.431	228	178	.781	414	498	185	2	1612	19.7

Sea.—Team	G.	Min.	FGA	FGM	Pct.	FTA	FTM	Pct.	Off.	Def.	Tot.	Ast.	PF	Dq.	Stl.	Blk.	Pts.	Avg.
									—Rebounds—									
73-74—Boston	82	3238	1445	649	.449	227	190	.837	100	251	351	448	185	1	105	25	1488	18.1
74-75—Boston	82	3220	1440	658	.457	223	186	.834	84	227	311	458	207	1	128	17	1502	18.3
75-76—Boston	82	3257	1492	670	.449	253	212	.838	61	252	313	445	183	2	107	20	1552	18.9
76-77—Boston	82	3333	1488	638	.429	383	333	.869	87	296	383	492	193	5	118	22	1609	19.6
77-78—Boston	46	1641	690	289	.419	120	103	.858	53	127	180	209	109	2	49	7	681	14.8
78-79—Bos.-G.S.	76	2338	910	404	.444	158	139	.880	42	158	200	347	173	1	80	7	947	12.5

JOJO WHITE

Sea.—Team	G.	Min.	FGA	FGM	Pct.	FTA	FTM	Pct.	Off.	Def.	Tot.	Ast.	PF	Dq.	Stl.	Blk.	Pts.	Avg.
									\-Rebounds-\									
79-80—Golden St.	78	2052	706	336	.476	114	97	.851	42	139	181	239	186	0	88	13	770	9.9
80-81—Kan. City	13	236	82	36	.439	18	11	.611	3	18	21	37	21	0	11	1	83	6.4
Totals	837	29941	13884	6169	.444	2471	2060	.834			3345	4095	2056	21	686	112	14399	17.2

Three-Point Field Goals: 1979-80, 1-for-6 (.167)

NBA PLAYOFF RECORD

Sea.—Team	G.	Min.	FGA	FGM	Pct.	FTA	FTM	Pct.	Reb.	Ast.	PF	Disq.	Pts.	Avg.
71-72—Boston	11	432	220	109	.495	48	40	.833	59	58	31	0	258	23.5
72-73—Boston	13	583	300	135	.450	54	49	.907	54	83	44	2	319	24.5

Sea.—Team	G.	Min.	FGA	FGM	Pct.	FTA	FTM	Pct.	Off.	Def.	Tot.	Ast.	PF	Dq.	Stl.	Blk.	Pts.	Avg.
									\-Rebounds-\									
73-74—Boston	18	765	310	132	.426	46	34	.739	17	58	75	98	56	1	15	2	298	16.6
74-75—Boston	11	462	227	100	.441	33	27	.818	18	32	50	63	32	0	11	4	227	20.6
75-76—Boston	18	791	371	165	.445	95	78	.821	12	59	71	98	51	0	23	1	408	22.7
76-77—Boston	9	395	201	91	.453	33	28	.848	10	29	39	52	27	0	14	0	210	23.3
Totals	80	3428	1629	732	.449	309	256	.828			348	452	241	3	63	7	1720	21.5

NBA ALL-STAR GAME RECORD

Season—Team	Min.	FGA	FGM	Pct.	FTA	FTM	Pct.	Reb.	Ast.	PF	Disq.	Pts.
1971—Boston	22	10	5	.500	0	0	.000	9	2	2	0	10
1972—Boston	18	15	6	.400	2	0	.000	4	3	1	0	12
1973—Boston	18	7	3	.429	0	0	.000	5	5	0	0	6

Season—Team	Min.	FGA	FGM	Pct.	FTA	FTM	Pct.	Off.	Def.	Tot.	Ast.	PF	Dq.	Stl.	Blk.	Pts.
								\-Rebounds-\								
1974—Boston	22	12	6	.500	3	1	.333	2	4	6	4	1	0	2	1	13
1975—Boston	13	2	1	.500	6	5	.833	0	1	1	4	1	0	0	0	7
1976—Boston	16	7	3	.429	0	0	.000	0	1	1	1	1	0	2	0	6
1977—Boston	15	7	5	.714	0	0	.000	0	1	1	2	0	0	0	0	10
Totals	124	60	29	.483	11	6	.545			27	21	6	0	4	1	64

Named to NBA All-Star Second Team, 1975 and 1977.... NBA All-Rookie Team, 1970.... NBA Playoff MVP, 1976. ... Member of NBA championship teams, 1974 and 1976.... Named to THE SPORTING NEWS All-America First Team, 1968 and 1969.... Member of U. S. Olympic team, 1968.

GEORGE HARRY YARDLEY

Born November 23, 1928 at Hollywood, Calif. Height 6:05. Weight 195.

High School—Balboa, Calif.

College—Stanford University, Stanford, Calif.

Drafted by Ft. Wayne on first round, 1950.

Played with the San Francisco Stewart Chevrolets in the National Industrial Basketball League, an Amateur Athletic Union League, during 1950-51 season. (Finished third in the league in scoring with a 13.1-point averge on 104 field goals and 53 field goals for 261 points in 20 games.)

In military service during 1951-52 and 1952-53 seasons. Played with Los Alamitos, Calif., Naval Air Station.

Signed by Ft. Wayne NBA, 1953.

Ft. Wayne franchise transferred to Detroit, 1957.

Traded by Detroit to Syracuse for Ed Conlin, February 13, 1959.

Played in American Basketball League with Los Angeles, 1961-62.

—COLLEGIATE RECORD—

Year	G.	Min.	FGA	FGM	Pct.	FTA	FTM	Pct.	Reb.	Pts.	Avg.
46-47†					Statistics Unavailable						
47-48	18	....	...	22	....	20	8	.400	....	52	2.9
48-49	28	....	377	126	.334	131	93	.710	....	345	12.3
49-50	25	....	452	164	.363	130	95	.731	....	423	16.9
Varsity Totals	71	....	...	312	....	281	196	.698	....	820	11.5

NBA REGULAR SEASON RECORD

Sea.—Team	G.	Min.	FGA	FGM	Pct.	FTA	FTM	Pct.	Reb.	Ast.	PF	Disq.	Pts.	Avg.
53-54—Ft. Wayne	63	1489	492	209	.425	205	146	.712	407	99	166	3	564	9.0
54-55—Ft. Wayne	60	2150	869	363	.418	416	310	.745	594	126	205	7	1036	17.3
55-56—Ft. Wayne	71	2353	1067	434	.407	492	365	.742	686	159	212	2	1233	17.4
56-57—Ft. Wayne	72	2691	1273	522	.410	639	503	.787	755	147	231	2	1547	21.5
57-58—Detroit	72	2843	1624	673	.414	808	655	.811	768	97	226	2	2001	27.8
58-59—Det.-Syr.	61	1839	1042	446	.428	407	317	.779	431	65	159	2	1209	19.8
59-60—Syracuse	73	2390	1214	549	.452	462	377	.816	570	123	227	3	1475	20.2
Totals	472	15755	7581	3196	.422	3429	2673	.780	4211	816	1426	22	9065	19.2

NBA PLAYOFF RECORD

Sea.—Team	G.	Min.	FGA	FGM	Pct.	FTA	FTM	Pct.	Reb.	Ast.	PF	Disq.	Pts.	Avg.
53-54—Ft. Wayne	4	107	33	16	.485	12	10	.833	24	3	10	0	42	10.5
54-55—Ft. Wayne	11	420	143	57	.399	79	60	.759	99	36	37	2	174	15.8
55-56—Ft. Wayne	10	406	183	77	.421	98	76	.776	139	26	25	0	230	23.0
56-57—Ft. Wayne	2	85	53	24	.453	11	9	.818	19	8	7	0	57	28.5
57-58—Detroit	7	254	127	52	.409	67	60	.896	72	17	26	0	164	23.4
58-59—Syracuse	9	333	189	83	.439	70	60	.857	87	21	29	0	226	25.1
59-60—Syracuse	3	88	39	15	.385	12	10	.833	17	1	9	0	40	13.3
Totals	46	1693	767	324	.422	349	285	.817	457	112	143	2	933	20.3

Season—Team	Min.	FGA	FGM	Pct.	FTA	FTM	Pct.	Reb.	Ast.	PF	Disq.	Pts.
1955—Fort Wayne	22	11	4	.364	4	3	.750	4	2	2	0	11
1956—Fort Wayne	19	7	3	.429	3	2	.667	6	1	1	0	8
1957—Fort Wayne	25	10	4	.400	1	1	1.000	9	0	2	0	9
1958—Detroit	32	15	8	.533	5	3	.600	9	1	1	0	19
1959—Detroit	17	8	2	.250	2	2	1.000	4	0	3	0	6
1960—Syracuse	16	9	5	.556	2	1	.500	3	0	4	0	11
Totals	131	60	26	.433	17	12	.706	35	4	13	0	64

ABL REGULAR SEASON RECORD

Sea.—Team	G.	Min.	2-Point FGM	2-Point FGA	Pct.	3-Point FGM	3-Point FGA	Pct.	FTM	FTA	Pct.	Reb.	Ast.	Pts.	Avg.
1961-62—L.A.	25	948	378	159	.421	37	14	.378	148	122	.824	172	65	482	19.2

Named to NBA All-Star First Team, 1958.... NBA All-Star Second Team, 1957.... Led league in scoring in 1958 when he became first NBA player ever to score over 2,000 points in a season.

MAX ZASLOFSKY

Born December 7, 1925 at Brooklyn, N. Y.   Height 6:02.   Weight 170.

Died October 15, 1985.

High School—Brooklyn, N. Y., Thomas Jefferson.

College—St. John's University, Brooklyn, N. Y.

Signed as free agent by Chicago BAA, 1946.

His name drawn out of a hat by New York NBA for $15,000 in dispersal of Chicago franchise, 1950.
Traded by New York to Baltimore for Jim Baechtold, 1953.
Traded by Baltimore to Milwaukee, November, 1953.
Traded by Milwaukee to Fort Wayne, December, 1953.
Coached in ABA with New Jersey Americans and New York Nets, 1967-68 and 1968-69.

—COLLEGIATE PLAYING RECORD—

Year	G.	Min.	FGA	FGM	Pct.	FTA	FTM	Pct.	Reb.	Pts.	Avg.
45-46	18	....	...	59	....	38	22	.579	...	140	7.8

NOTE: Played only one year of college basketball. In Military Service during 1944-45 season.

NBA REGULAR SEASON RECORD

Sea.—Team	G.	Min.	FGA	FGM	Pct.	FTA	FTM	Pct.	Reb.	Ast.	PF	Disq.	Pts.	Avg.
46-47—Chicago	61	....	1020	336	.320	278	205	.737	...	40	121	...	877	14.4
47-48—Chicago	48	....	1156	373	.323	333	261	.784	...	29	125	...	1007	21.0
48-49—Chicago	58	....	1216	425	.350	413	347	.840	...	149	156	...	1197	20.6
49-50—Chicago	68	....	1132	397	.351	381	321	.843	...	155	185	...	1115	16.4
50-51—New York	66	....	853	302	.354	298	231	.775	228	136	150	...	835	12.7
51-52—New York	66	....	958	322	.336	380	287	.755	194	156	183	...	931	14.1
52-53—New York	29	....	320	123	.384	142	98	.690	75	55	81	...	344	11.9
53-54—Balt.-Mil.-F.W.	65	....	756	278	.368	357	255	.714	160	154	142	...	811	12.5
54-55—Fort Wayne	70	....	821	269	.328	352	247	.702	191	203	130	...	785	11.2
55-56—Fort Wayne	9	....	81	29	.358	35	30	.857	16	16	18	...	88	9.8
Totals	540	...	8313	2854	.343	2969	2282	.769	...	1093	1291	...	7990	14.8

NBA PLAYOFF RECORD

Sea.—Team	G.	Min.	FGA	FGM	Pct.	FTA	FTM	Pct.	Reb.	Ast.	PF	Disq.	Pts.	Avg.
46-47—Chicago	11	....	199	60	.302	44	29	.659	...	4	26	..	149	13.5
47-48—Chicago	5	....	88	30	.341	47	37	.787	...	0	17	..	97	19.4
48-49—Chicago	2	....	49	15	.306	18	14	.778	...	6	3	..	44	22.0
49-50—Chicago	2	....	32	15	.469	18	15	.833	...	6	7	..	45	22.5
50-51—New York	14	....	217	88	.406	100	74	.740	58	38	43	..	250	17.9
51-52—New York	14	....	185	69	.373	110	89	.809	44	23	51	..	227	16.2
53-54—Fort Wayne	4	....	36	11	.306	15	13	.867	3	6	7	..	35	8.8
54-55—Fort Wayne	11	....	44	18	.409	20	16	.750	16	18	20	..	52	4.7
Totals	63	....	850	306	.360	372	287	.772	...	101	174	..	899	14.3

NBA ALL-STAR GAME RECORD

Season—Team	Min.	FGA	FGM	Pct.	FTA	FTM	Pct.	Reb.	Ast.	PF	Disq.	Pts.
1952—New York	....	7	3	.429	5	5	1.000	4	2	0	0	11

ABA COACHING RECORD

Sea. Club	Regular Season W.	L.	Pct.	Pos.
1967-68—New Jersey	36	42	.462	4T†
1968-69—New York	17	61	.218	5†
Totals (2 seasons)	53	103	.339	

†Eastern Division.

Named to NBA All-Star First Team, 1947, 1948, 1949, 1950. . . . Led NBA in scoring, 1948. . . . Led NBA in free-throw percentage, 1950.

COACHES

ALVIN A. ATTLES
(Al)

Born November 7, 1936 at Newark, N. J.   Height 6:00.   Weight 185.
High School—Newark, N. J., Weequahic.
College—North Carolina A&T State University, Greensboro, N. C.
Drafted by Philadelphia on fifth round, 1960 (39th pick).

Philadelphia franchise transferred to San Francisco, 1962.

COLLEGIATE PLAYING RECORD

Year	G.	Min.	FGA	FGM	Pct.	FTA	FTM	Pct.	Reb.	Pts.	Avg.
56-57					Statistics Unavailable						
57-58					Statistics Unavailable						
58-59	29	....	225	105	.467	91	56	.615	....	266	9.2
59-60	24	....	301	190	.631	71	47	.662	80	427	17.8

NBA REGULAR SEASON RECORD

Sea.—Team	G.	Min.	FGA	FGM	Pct.	FTA	FTM	Pct.	Reb.	Ast.	PF	Disq.	Pts.	Avg.
60-61—Philadelphia	77	1544	543	222	.409	162	97	.599	214	174	235	5	541	7.0
61-62—Philadelphia	75	2468	724	343	.474	267	158	.592	355	333	279	8	844	11.3
62-63—San Fran.	71	1876	630	301	.478	206	133	.646	205	184	253	7	735	10.4
63-64—San Fran.	70	1883	640	289	.452	275	185	.673	236	197	249	4	763	10.9
64-65—San Fran.	73	1733	662	254	.384	274	171	.624	239	205	242	7	679	9.3
65-66—San Fran.	79	2053	724	364	.503	252	154	.611	322	225	265	7	882	11.2
66-67—San Fran.	70	1764	467	212	.454	151	88	.583	321	269	265	13	512	7.3
67-68—San Fran.	67	1992	540	252	.467	216	150	.694	276	390	284	9	654	9.8
68-69—San Fran.	51	1516	359	162	.451	149	95	.638	181	306	183	3	419	8.2
69-70—San Fran.	45	676	202	78	.386	113	75	.664	74	142	103	0	231	5.1
70-71—San Fran.	34	321	54	22	.407	41	24	.585	40	58	59	2	68	2.0
Totals	712	17826	5545	2499	.451	2106	1330	.632	2463	2483	2417	65	6328	8.9

NBA PLAYOFF RECORD

Sea.—Team	G.	Min.	FGA	FGM	Pct.	FTA	FTM	Pct.	Reb.	Ast.	PF	Disq.	Pts.	Avg.
60-61—Philadelphia	3	110	26	12	.462	14	5	.357	12	9	14	0	29	9.7
61-62—Philadelphia	12	338	76	28	.368	31	17	.548	55	27	54	4	73	6.1
63-64—San Fran.	12	386	144	58	.403	56	30	.536	37	30	54	5	146	12.2
66-67—San Fran.	15	237	46	20	.435	16	6	.375	62	38	45	1	46	3.1
67-68—San Fran.	10	277	62	25	.403	30	23	.767	53	70	49	2	73	7.3
68-69—San Fran.	6	109	21	7	.333	4	1	.250	18	21	17	0	15	2.5
70-71—San Fran.	4	47	7	4	.571	7	4	.571	8	11	13	0	12	3.0
Totals	62	1504	382	154	.403	158	86	.544	245	206	246	12	394	6.4

NBA COACHING RECORD

Sea. Club	Regular Season W.	L.	Pct.	Pos.	Playoffs W.	L.	Sea. Club	Regular Season W.	L.	Pct.	Pos.	Playoffs W.	L.
1969-70—San Francisco ...	8	22	.267	6†	..	..	1976-77—Golden State	46	36	.561	3‡	5	5
1970-71—San Francisco ...	41	41	.500	2‡	1	4	1977-78—Golden State	43	39	.524	5‡	..	..
1971-72—Golden State	51	31	.622	2‡	1	4	1978-79—Golden State	38	44	.463	6‡	..	..
1972-73—Golden State	47	35	.573	2‡	5	6	1979-80—Golden State	18	43	.295	6‡	..	..
1973-74—Golden State	44	38	.537	2‡	..	..	1980-81—Golden State	39	43	.476	4‡	..	..
1974-75—Golden State*	48	34	.585	1‡	12	5	1981-82—Golden State	45	37	.549	4‡	..	..
1975-76—Golden State	59	23	.720	1‡	7	6	1982-83—Golden State	30	52	.366	5‡	..	..
							Totals (14 seasons)	557	518	.518		31	30

†Western Division. ‡Pacific Division.
*Won NBA championship.
Coach of NBA championship team, 1975.

ARNOLD JACOB AUERBACH
(Red)

Born September 20, 1917 at Brooklyn, N. Y.   Height 5:10.   Weight 170.
High School—Brooklyn, N. Y., Eastern District.
Colleges—Seth Low Junior College, New York, N. Y., and
George Washington University, Washington, D. C.

—COLLEGIATE PLAYING RECORD—

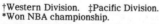

Seth Low JC

Year	G.	Min.	FGA	FGM	Pct.	FTA	FTM	Pct.	Reb.	Pts.	Avg.
					Statistics Unavailable						

Year	G.	Min.	FGA	George Washington FGM	Pct.	FTA	FTM	Pct.	Reb.	Pts.	Avg.
37-38	17	....	...	22	....	12	8	.667	....	52	3.1
38-39	20	....	...	54	....	19	12	.632	....	120	6.0
39-40	19	....	...	69	....	39	24	.727	....	162	8.5
Totals	56	....	...	145	....	64	44	.688	....	334	6.0

COLLEGIATE COACHING RECORD

Assistant, Duke University, 1949-50.

NBA COACHING RECORD

Sea. Club	W.	L.	Pct.	Pos.	W.	L.	Sea. Club	W.	L.	Pct.	Pos.	W.	L.
1946-47—Washington	49	11	.817	1†	2	4	1957-58—Boston	49	23	.681	1†	6	5
1947-48—Washington	28	20	.583	4†	..	..	1958-59—Boston	52	20	.722	*1†	8	3
1948-49—Washington	38	22	.633	1†	6	5	1959-60—Boston	59	16	.787	*1†	8	5
1949-50—Tri-Cities	28	29	.491	3‡	1	2	1960-61—Boston	57	22	.722	*1†	8	2
1950-51—Boston	39	30	.565	2†	0	2	1961-62—Boston	60	20	.750	*1†	8	6
1951-52—Boston	39	27	.591	2†	1	2	1962-63—Boston	58	22	.725	*1†	8	5
1952-53—Boston	46	25	.568	3†	3	3	1963-64—Boston	59	21	.738	*1†	8	2
1953-54—Boston	42	30	.583	2T†	2	4	1964-65—Boston	62	18	.775	*1†	8	4
1954-55—Boston	36	36	.500	3†	3	4	1965-66—Boston	54	26	.675	*2†	11	6
1955-56—Boston	39	33	.542	2†	1	2	Totals (20 seasons)	938	479	.662		99	69
1956-57—Boston	44	28	.611	*1†	7	3							

*Won NBA Championship.   †Eastern Division.   ‡Western Division.

Selected as the "Greatest Coach in the History of the NBA" by the Professional Basketball Writers' Association of America, 1980. . . . Elected to the Naismith Memorial Basketball Hall of Fame, 1968. . . . Named NBA Coach of the Year, 1965. . . . NBA Executive of the Year, 1980. . . . Winningest coach in history of NBA. . . . Coach of NBA championship teams, 1957, 1959, 1960, 1961, 1962, 1963, 1964, 1965, 1966.

LAWRENCE R. COSTELLO
(Larry)

Born July 2, 1931 at Minoa, N. Y.   Height 6:01.   Weight 188.

High School—Minoa, N. Y.

College—Niagara University, Niagara Falls, N. Y.

Drafted by Philadelphia on second round, 1954.

Sold by Philadelphia to Syracuse, October 10, 1957.
Syracuse franchise moved to Philadelphia, 1963.
Drafted by Milwaukee from Philadelphia in expansion draft, May 6, 1968.
Played in Eastern Basketball League with Wilkes-Barre Barons, 1965-66.

—COLLEGIATE PLAYING RECORD—

Year	G.	Min.	FGA	FGM	Pct.	FTA	FTM	Pct.	Reb.	Pts.	Avg.
50-51†					Statistics Unavailable						
51-52	28	....	...	131	....	87	58	.667	....	320	11.4
52-53	28	....	...	185	....	191	140	.733	....	510	18.2
53-54	29	....	...	160	....	152	125	.822	....	445	15.3
Totals	85	....	...	476	....	430	323	.751	....	1275	15.0

NBA REGULAR SEASON RECORD

Sea.—Team	G.	Min.	FGA	FGM	Pct.	FTA	FTM	Pct.	Reb.	Ast.	PF	Disq.	Pts.	Avg.
54-55—Philadelphia	19	463	139	46	.331	32	26	.813	49	78	37	0	118	6.2
55-56—Philadelphia					Did Not Play—Military Service									
56-57—Philadelphia	72	2111	497	186	.374	222	175	.788	323	236	182	2	547	7.6
57-58—Syracuse	72	2746	888	378	.426	378	320	.847	378	317	246	3	1076	14.9
58-59—Syracuse	70	2750	948	414	.437	349	280	.802	365	379	263	7	1108	15.8
59-60—Syracuse	71	2469	822	372	.453	289	249	.862	388	449	234	4	993	14.0
60-61—Syracuse	75	2167	844	407	.482	338	270	.799	292	413	286	9	1084	14.5
61-62—Syracuse	63	1854	726	310	.427	295	247	.837	245	359	220	5	867	13.7
62-63—Syracuse	78	2066	660	285	.432	327	288	.881	237	334	263	4	858	11.0
63-64—Philadelphia	45	1137	408	191	.476	170	147	.865	105	167	150	3	529	11.8
64-65—Philadelphia	64	1967	695	309	.445	277	243	.877	169	275	242	10	861	13.5
66-67—Philadelphia	49	976	293	130	.444	133	120	.902	103	140	141	2	380	7.8
67-68—Philadelphia	28	492	148	67	.453	81	67	.827	51	68	62	0	201	7.2
Totals	706	21198	7068	3095	.438	2891	2432	.841	2705	3215	2326	49	8622	12.2

NBA PLAYOFF RECORD

Sea.—Team	G.	Min.	FGA	FGM	Pct.	FTA	FTM	Pct.	Reb.	Ast.	PF	Disq.	Pts.	Avg.
56-57—Philadelphia	2	16	8	3	.375	1	0	.000	5	2	3	0	6	3.0
57-58—Syracuse	3	134	34	10	.294	14	14	1.000	25	12	6	0	34	11.3
58-59—Syracuse	9	361	121	54	.446	61	51	.836	53	54	40	2	159	17.7
59-60—Syracuse	3	122	47	20	.425	12	10	.833	14	20	15	1	50	16.7

Sea.—Team	G.	Min.	FGA	FGM	Pct.	FTA	FTM	Pct.	Reb.	Ast.	PF	Disq.	Pts.	Avg.
60-61—Syracuse	8	269	103	42	.408	55	47	.854	35	52	39	3	131	16.4
61-62—Syracuse	5	167	51	22	.431	33	29	.879	16	28	21	0	73	14.6
62-63—Syracuse	5	134	37	16	.432	23	19	.826	4	23	27	2	51	10.2
63-64—Philadelphia	5	36	14	3	.214	10	10	1.000	3	4	14	1	16	3.2
64-65—Philadelphia	10	207	53	22	.415	16	11	.688	12	20	43	2	55	5.5
66-67—Philadelphia	2	25	8	6	.750	5	5	1.000	4	3	2	0	17	8.5
Totals	52	1471	476	198	.416	230	196	.852	171	218	210	11	592	11.4

NBA ALL-STAR GAME RECORD

Season—Team	Min.	FGA	FGM	Pct.	FTA	FTM	Pct.	Reb.	Ast.	PF	Disq.	Pts.
1958—Syracuse	17	6	0	.000	1	1	1.000	1	4	2	0	1
1959—Syracuse	18	8	3	.375	1	1	1.000	3	3	1	0	7
1960—Syracuse	20	9	5	.556	0	0	.000	4	2	1	0	10
1961—Syracuse	5	2	1	.500	0	0	.000	0	0	2	0	2
1962—Syracuse				Selected—Injured, Did Not Play								
1965—Philadelphia	11	7	2	.286	0	0	.000	1	2	2	0	4
Totals	71	32	11	.344	2	2	1.000	9	11	8	0	24

EBL REGULAR SEASON RECORD

			—2-Point—			—3-Point—								
Sea.—Team	G.	Min.	FGM	FGA	Pct.	FGM	FGA	Pct.	FTM	FTA	Pct.	Reb.	Ast.	Pts.	Avg.
65-66—Wilkes-Barre	12	....	54	...	...	2	...	....	53	59	.898	22	83	167	13.9

NBA COACHING RECORD

	Regular Season				Playoffs				Regular Season				Playoffs	
Sea. Club	W.	L.	Pct.	Pos.	W.	L.	Sea. Club	W.	L.	Pct.	Pos.	W.	L.
1968-69—Milwaukee	27	55	.329	7†	..	..	1974-75—Milwaukee	38	44	.463	4‡	..	..
1969-70—Milwaukee	56	26	.683	2†	5	5	1975-76—Milwaukee	38	44	.463	1‡	1	2
1970-71—Milwaukee	66	16	.805	*1†	12	2	1976-77—Milwaukee	3	15	.167	6‡	..	..
1971-72—Milwaukee	63	19	.768	1‡	6	5	1978-79—Chicago	20	36	.357	3‡	..	..
1972-73—Milwaukee	60	22	.732	1‡	2	4	Totals (10 seasons)	430	300	.589		37	23
1973-74—Milwaukee	59	23	.720	1‡	11	5							

*Won NBA championship.   †Eastern Division.   ‡Midwest Division.

COLLEGIATE COACHING RECORD

	Regular Season			
Sea. Club	W.	L.	Pct.	Pos.
1980-81—Utica	13	12	.520	..
1981-82—Utica	4	22	.154	..
1982-83—Utica	11	15	.423	..
1983-84—Utica	11	15	.423	..
1984-85—Utica	15	12	.556	..
1985-86—Utica	13	14	.481	..
1986-87—Utica	10	16	.385	..
Totals (7 seasons)	77	106	.421	

NOTE: Costello coached the Milwaukee Does of the Women's Professional Basketball League during 1979-80 season. He also coached at Minoa, N. Y., High School during 1965-66 season.

Named to NBA All-Star Second Team, 1961. . . . Led NBA in free-throw percentage, 1963 and 1965. . . . Member of NBA championship team, 1967. . . . Coach of NBA championship team, 1971.

WILLIAM JOHN CUNNINGHAM
(Billy)

Born June 3, 1943 at Brooklyn, N. Y.   Height 6:07.   Weight 210.

High School—Brooklyn, N. Y., Erasmus.

College—University of North Carolina, Chapel Hill, N. C.

Drafted by Philadelphia on first round, 1965.

Signed by Carolina ABA as a free agent, August, 1969.
Returned to Philadelphia, 1974.

—COLLEGIATE PLAYING RECORD—

Year	G.	Min.	FGA	FGM	Pct.	FTA	FTM	Pct.	Reb.	Pts.	Avg.
61-62†	10	....	162	81	.500	78	45	.577	127	207	20.7
62-63	21	....	380	186	.489	170	105	.618	339	477	22.7
63-64	24	....	526	233	.443	249	157	.631	379	623	26.0
64-65	24	....	481	237	.493	213	135	.634	344	609	25.4
Varsity Totals	69	....	1387	656	.473	632	397	.628	1062	1709	24.8

NBA REGULAR SEASON RECORD

									—Rebounds—							
Sea.—Team	G.	Min.	FGA	FGM	Pct.	FTA	FTM	Pct.	Off.	Def.	Tot.	Ast.	PF	Dq.	Stl.	Blk.	Pts.	Avg.
65-66—Philadelphia	80	2134	1011	431	.426	443	281	.634			599	207	301	12			1143	14.3
66-67—Philadelphia	81	2168	1211	556	.459	558	383	.686			589	205	260	2			1495	18.5
67-68—Philadelphia	74	2076	1178	516	.438	509	368	.723			562	187	260	3			1400	18.9
68-69—Philadelphia	82	3345	1736	739	.426	754	556	.737			1050	287	329	10			2034	24.8
69-70—Philadelphia	81	3194	1710	802	.469	700	510	.729			1101	352	331	15			2114	26.1

Sea.—Team	G.	Min.	FGA	FGM	Pct.	FTA	FTM	Pct.	Off.	Def.	Tot.	Ast.	PF	Dq.	Stl.	Blk.	Pts.	Avg.
70-71—Philadelphia	81	3090	1519	702	.462	620	455	.734			946	395	328	5			1859	23.0
71-72—Philadelphia	75	2900	1428	658	.461	601	428	.712			918	443	295	12			1744	23.3
74-75—Philadelphia	80	2859	1423	609	.428	444	345	.777	130	596	726	442	270	4	91	35	1563	19.5
75-76—Philadelphia	20	640	251	103	.410	88	68	.773	29	118	147	107	57	1	24	10	274	13.7
Totals	654	22406	11467	5116	446	4717	3394	.720			6638	2625	2431	64	115	45	13626	20.8

NBA PLAYOFF RECORD

Sea.—Team	G.	Min.	FGA	FGM	Pct.	FTA	FTM	Pct.	Off.	Def.	Tot.	Ast.	PF	Dq.	Stl.	Blk.	Pts.	Avg.
65-66—Philadelphia	4	69	31	5	.161	13	11	.846			18	10	11	0			21	5.3
66-67—Philadelphia	15	339	221	83	.376	90	59	.656			93	33	53	1			225	15.0
67-68—Philadelphia	3	86	43	24	.558	17	14	.824			22	10	16	1			62	20.7
68-69—Philadelphia	5	217	117	49	.419	38	24	.632			63	12	24	1			122	24.4
69-70—Philadelphia	5	205	123	61	.496	36	24	.667			52	20	19	0			146	29.2
70-71—Philadelphia	7	301	142	67	.472	67	47	.701			108	40	28	0			181	25.9
Totals	39	1217	677	289	.427	261	179	.686			356	125	151	3			757	19.4

NBA ALL-STAR GAME RECORD

Season—Team	Min.	FGA	FGM	Pct.	FTA	FTM	Pct.	Off.	Def.	Tot.	Ast.	PF	Dq.	Stl.	Blk.	Pts.
1969—Philadelphia	22	10	5	.500	0	0	.000			5	1	3	0			10
1970—Philadelphia	28	13	7	.538	5	5	1.000			4	2	3	0			19
1971—Philadelphia	19	8	2	.250	2	1	.500			4	3	1	0			5
1972—Philadelphia	24	13	4	.308	8	6	.750			10	3	4	0			14
Totals	93	44	18	.409	15	12	.800			23	9	11	0			48

ABA REGULAR SEASON RECORD

Sea.—Team	G.	Min.	2-Point FGM	FGA	Pct.	3-Point FGM	FGA	Pct.	FTM	FTA	Pct.	Reb.	Ast.	Pts.	Avg.
72-73—Carolina	84	3248	757	1534	.493	14	49	.286	472	598	.789	1012	530	2028	24.1
73-74—Carolina	32	1190	252	529	.476	1	8	.125	149	187	.797	331	150	656	20.5
Totals	116	4438	1009	2063	.489	15	57	.263	621	785	.791	1343	680	2684	23.1

ABA PLAYOFF RECORD

Sea.—Team	G.	Min.	2-Point FGM	FGA	Pct.	3-Point FGM	FGA	Pct.	FTM	FTA	Pct.	Reb.	Ast.	Pts.	Avg.
72-73—Carolina	12	472	111	219	.507	1	4	.250	57	83	.687	142	61	282	23.5
73-74—Carolina	3	61	9	29	.310	0	2	.000	4	5	.800	16	6	22	7.3
Totals	15	533	120	248	.484	1	6	.167	61	88	.693	158	67	304	20.3

ABA ALL-STAR GAME RECORD

Sea.—Team	Min.	2-Point FGM	FGA	Pct.	3-Point FGM	FGA	Pct.	FTM	FTA	Pct.	Reb.	Ast.	Pts.	Avg.
1973—Carolina.............	20	9	11	.818	0	1	.000	0	0	.000	6	4	18	18.0

NBA COACHING RECORD

Sea.	Club	Regular Season W.	L.	Pct.	Pos.	Playoffs W.	L.	Sea.	Club	Regular Season W.	L.	Pct.	Pos.	Playoffs W.	L.
1977-78	Philadelphia	53	23	.697	1†	6	4	1982-83	Philadelphia*	65	17	.793	1†	12	1
1978-79	Philadelphia	47	35	.573	2†	5	4	1983-84	Philadelphia	52	30	.634	2†	2	3
1979-80	Philadelphia	59	23	.720	2†	12	6	1984-85	Philadelphia	58	24	.707	2†	8	5
1980-81	Philadelphia	62	20	.756	1T†	9	7		Totals (8 seasons)	454	196	.698		66	39
1981-82	Philadelphia	58	24	.707	2†	12	9								

*Won NBA championship. †Atlantic Division.

Elected to Naismith Memorial Basketball Hall of Fame, 1985. . . . Named to All-NBA First Team, 1969, 1970, 1971. . . . All-NBA Second Team, 1972. . . . NBA All-Rookie Team, 1966. . . . Member of NBA championship team, 1967. . . . Coach of NBA championship team, 1983. . . . ABA Most Valuable Player, 1973. . . . ABA All-Star First Team, 1973. . . . Led ABA in steals, 1973. . . . Named to THE SPORTING NEWS All-America Second Team, 1965.

WILLIAM CHARLES FITCH
(Bill)

Born May 19, 1934 at Davenport, Iowa.

High School—Cedar Rapids, Iowa.

College—Coe College, Cedar Rapids, Iowa.

—COLLEGIATE PLAYING RECORD—

Year	G.	Min.	FGA	FGM	Pct.	FTA	FTM	Pct.	Reb.	Pts.	Avg.
50-51					Statistics Unavailable						
51-52	20	....	...	63	....	...	50	....	....	176	8.8
52-53	19	....	...	83	....	...	72	....	....	238	12.5
53-54	22	....	...	123	....	...	92	....	....	338	15.4

Sea. Club	W.	L.	Pct.	Pos.
1958-59—Coe College	11	9	.550	6
1959-60—Coe College	12	9	.571	5T
1960-61—Coe College	10	12	.455	4T
1961-62—Coe College	11	10	.524	6T
1962-63—North Dakota	14	13	.519	
1963-64—North Dakota	10	16	.385	
1964-65—North Dakota	26	5	.839	

Sea. Club	W.	L.	Pct.	Pos.
1965-66—North Dakota	24	5	.828	
1966-67—North Dakota	20	6	.769	
1967-68—Bowl. Green	18	7	.720	
1968-69—Minnesota	12	12	.500	5T
1969-70—Minnesota	13	11	.542	5
Totals (12 seasons)	181	115	.611	

NBA COACHING RECORD

Sea. Club	W.	L.	Pct.	Pos.	Playoffs W.	L.	Sea. Club	W.	L.	Pct.	Pos.	Playoffs W.	L.
1970-71—Cleveland	15	67	.183	4†	..	..	1980-81—Boston*	62	20	.756	1T‡	12	5
1971-72—Cleveland	23	59	.280	4†	..	..	1981-82—Boston	63	19	.768	1‡	7	5
1972-73—Cleveland	32	50	.390	4†	..	..	1982-83—Boston	56	26	.683	2‡	2	5
1973-74—Cleveland	29	53	.354	4†	..	..	1983-84—Houston	29	53	.354	6§	..	..
1974-75—Cleveland	40	42	.488	3†	..	..	1984-85—Houston	48	34	.585	2§	2	3
1975-76—Cleveland	49	33	.598	1†	6	7	1985-86—Houston	51	31	.622	1§	13	7
1976-77—Cleveland	43	39	.524	4†	1	2	1986-87—Houston	42	40	.512	3§	5	5
1977-78—Cleveland	43	39	.524	3†	0	2	1987-88—Houston	46	36	.561	4§	1	3
1978-79—Cleveland	30	52	.366	4T†	..	..	Totals (18 seasons)	762	714	.516		54	48
1979-80—Boston	61	21	.744	1‡	5	4							

*Won NBA championship. †Central Division. ‡Atlantic Division. §Midwest Division.

Named NBA Coach of the Year, 1976 and 1980.... Coach of NBA championship team, 1981.

ALEXANDER MURRAY HANNUM
(Alex)

Born July 19, 1923 at Los Angeles, Calif.   Height 6:07.   Weight 225.

High School—Los Angeles, Calif., Hamilton.

College—University of Southern California, Los Angeles, Calif.

Signed by Oshkosh NBL, 1948.

Sold by Oshkosh NBA to Syracuse NBA, 1949.
Traded with Fred Scolari by Syracuse to Baltimore for Red Rocha, 1951.
Sold by Baltimore to Rochester during 1951-52 season.
Sold by Rochester to Milwaukee, 1954.
Milwaukee franchise moved to St. Louis, 1955.
Released by St. Louis, signed by Ft. Wayne, 1956.
Released by Ft. Wayne, December 12, 1956; signed by St. Louis, December 17, 1956.
Played for Los Angeles Shamrocks, an Amateur Athletic Union team, during 1945-46 season (averaged 9.8 points per game).

—COLLEGIATE PLAYING RECORD—

Year	G.	Min.	FGA	FGM	Pct.	FTA	FTM	Pct.	Reb.	Pts.	Avg.
41-42†					Statistics Unavailable						
42-43	15	....		23	....	20	9	.450	....	55	3.7
43-44-45-46					In Military Service.						
46-47	24	....	...	...	....	...	...	....	....	251	10.5
47-48	23	....	108	...	...	...	...	....	....	263	11.4
Varsity Totals	62	....	....	....	...	...	...	....	....	569	9.2

NBA REGULAR SEASON RECORD

Sea.—Team	G.	Min.	FGA	FGM	Pct.	FTA	FTM	Pct.	Reb.	Ast.	PF	Disq.	Pts.	Avg.
48-49—Oshkosh NBL	62	....		126	...	191	113	.592	...	...	188	...	365	5.9
49-50—Syracuse	64	....	488	177	.363	186	128	.688	...	129	264	...	482	7.5
50-51—Syracuse	63	....	494	182	.368	197	107	.543	301	119	271	...	471	7.5
51-52—Balt.-Roch.	66	....	462	170	.368	138	98	.710	336	133	271	...	438	6.6
52-53—Rochester	68	....	360	129	.358	133	88	.662	279	81	258	...	346	5.1
53-54—Rochester	72	....	503	175	.348	164	102	.622	350	105	279	...	452	6.3
54-55—Milwaukee	53	....	358	126	.352	107	61	.570	245	105	206	...	313	5.9
55-56—St. Louis	71	....	453	146	.322	154	93	.604	344	157	271	...	385	5.4
56-57—Ft. W.-St. Louis	59	....	223	77	.345	56	37	.661	158	28	135	...	191	3.2
Totals	578	....	....	1308	....	1326	827	.624	...	...	2143	...	3443	6.0

NBA PLAYOFF RECORD

Sea.—Team	G.	Min.	FGA	FGM	Pct.	FTA	FTM	Pct.	Reb.	Ast.	PF	Disq.	Pts.	Avg.
49-50—Syracuse	11	....	86	38	.442	34	17	.500	....	10	50	....	93	8.5
50-51—Syracuse	7	....	39	17	.436	10	8	.800	47	17	37	3	42	6.0
51-52—Rochester	6	146	42	16	.381	13	8	.615	26	8	30	3	40	6.7
52-53—Rochester	3	52	10	4	.400	8	3	.375	4	2	16	1	11	3.7
53-54—Rochester	6	107	29	12	.414	24	15	.625	22	5	28	3	39	6.5
55-56—St. Louis	8	159	66	21	.318	35	19	.543	29	10	36	3	61	7.6
56-57—St. Louis	2	6	2	0	.000	0	0	.000	0	0	2	0	0	0.0
Totals	43	....	274	108	.394	124	70	.565	...	52	199	....	286	6.7

NBA COACHING RECORD

Sea.	Club	W.	L.	Pct.	Pos.	W.	L.
1956-57	St. Louis	15	16	.484	1T†	6	4
1957-58	St. Louis	41	31	.569	*1†	8	3
1960-61	Syracuse	38	41	.481	3‡	4	4
1961-62	Syracuse	41	39	.513	3‡	2	3
1962-63	Syracuse	48	32	.600	2‡	2	3
1963-64	San Francisco	48	32	.600	1†	5	7
1964-65	San Francisco	17	63	.213	5†	..	..
1965-66	San Francisco	35	45	.438	4†	..	..
1966-67	Philadelphia	68	13	.840	*1‡	11	4
1967-68	Philadelphia	62	20	.756	1‡	7	6
1969-70	San Diego	18	38	.321	7†	..	..
1970-71	San Diego	40	42	.488	3§	..	..
Totals (12 Seasons)		471	412	.533		45	34

*Won NBA Championship.

ABA COACHING RECORD

Sea.	Club	W.	L.	Pct.	Pos.	W.	L.
1968-69	Oakland*	60	18	.769	1†	12	4
1971-72	Denver	34	50	.405	4†	3	4
1972-73	Denver	47	37	.560	3†	1	4
1973-74	Denver	37	47	.440	4T†	0	0
Totals (4 seasons)		178	152	.539		16	12

*Won ABA Championship.
†Western Division. ‡Eastern Division. §Pacific Division.

NBA Coach of the Year, 1964.... Coach of NBA championship teams, 1958 and 1967.... ABA Coach of the Year, 1969.... Coach of ABA championship team, 1969.

THOMAS W. HEINSOHN
(Tom)

Born August 26, 1934 at Jersey City, N. J. Height 6:07. Weight 218.

High School—Union City, N. J., St. Michael's.

College—Holy Cross College, Worcester, Mass.

Drafted by Boston on first round (territorial choice), 1956.

—COLLEGIATE RECORD—

Year	G.	Min.	FGA	FGM	Pct.	FTA	FTM	Pct.	Reb.	Pts.	Avg.
52-53†	15	....	....	97	....	....	70	....	....	264	17.6
53-54	28	....	364	175	.481	142	94	.662	300	444	15.9
54-55	26	....	499	232	.465	215	141	.656	385	605	23.3
55-56	27	....	630	254	.403	304	232	.763	569	740	27.4
Varsity Totals	81	....	1493	661	.443	661	467	.707	1254	1789	22.1

NBA REGULAR SEASON RECORD

Sea.—Team	G.	Min.	FGA	FGM	Pct.	FTA	FTM	Pct.	Reb.	Ast.	PF	Disq.	Pts.	Avg.
56-57—Boston	72	2150	1123	446	.397	343	271	.790	705	117	304	12	1163	16.2
57-58—Boston	69	2206	1226	468	.382	394	294	.746	705	125	274	6	1230	17.8
58-59—Boston	66	2089	1192	465	.390	391	312	.798	638	164	271	11	1242	18.8
59-60—Boston	75	2420	1590	673	.423	386	283	.734	794	171	275	8	1629	21.7
60-61—Boston	74	2256	1566	627	.400	424	325	.767	732	141	260	7	1579	21.3
61-62—Boston	79	2383	1613	692	.429	437	358	.819	747	165	280	2	1742	22.1
62-63—Boston	76	2004	1300	550	.423	407	340	.835	569	95	270	4	1440	18.9
63-64—Boston	76	2040	1223	487	.398	342	283	.827	460	183	268	3	1257	16.5
64-65—Boston	67	1706	954	365	.383	229	182	.795	399	157	252	5	912	13.6
Totals	654	19254	11787	4773	.405	3353	2648	.790	5749	1318	2454	58	12194	18.6

NBA PLAYOFF RECORD

Sea.—Team	G.	Min.	FGA	FGM	Pct.	FTA	FTM	Pct.	Reb.	Ast.	PF	Disq.	Pts.	Avg.
56-57—Boston	10	370	231	90	.390	69	49	.710	117	20	40	1	229	22.9
57-58—Boston	11	349	194	68	.351	72	56	.778	119	18	52	3	192	17.5
58-59—Boston	11	348	220	91	.414	56	37	.661	98	32	41	0	219	19.9
59-60—Boston	13	423	267	112	.419	80	60	.750	126	27	53	2	284	21.8
60-61—Boston	10	291	201	82	.408	43	33	.767	99	20	36	1	197	19.7
61-62—Boston	14	445	291	116	.399	76	58	.763	115	34	58	4	290	20.7
62-63—Boston	13	413	270	123	.456	98	75	.765	116	15	55	2	321	24.7
63-64—Boston	10	308	180	70	.412	42	34	.810	80	26	36	0	174	17.4
64-65—Boston	12	276	181	66	.365	32	20	.625	84	23	46	1	152	12.7
Totals	104	3223	2035	818	.402	568	422	.743	954	215	417	14	2058	19.8

NBA ALL-STAR GAME RECORD

Season—Team	Min.	FGA	FGM	Pct.	FTA	FTM	Pct.	Reb.	Ast.	PF	Disq.	Pts.
1957—Boston	23	17	5	.294	2	2	1.000	7	0	3	0	12
1961—Boston	19	16	2	.125	0	0	.000	6	1	4	0	4
1962—Boston	13	11	4	.364	2	2	1.000	2	1	4	0	10
1963—Boston	21	11	6	.545	4	3	.750	2	1	4	0	15
1964—Boston	21	12	5	.417	0	0	.000	3	0	5	0	10
1965—Boston					Selected—Injured, Did Not Play							
Totals	97	67	22	.328	8	7	.875	20	3	20	0	51

Sea. Club	W.	L.	Pct.	Pos.	W.	L.	Sea. Club	W.	L.	Pct.	Pos.	W.	L.
1969-70—Boston	34	48	.415	6†	..	..	1974-75—Boston	60	22	.732	1‡	6	5
1970-71—Boston	44	38	.537	3‡	..	..	1975-76—Boston	54	28	.659	*1‡	12	6
1971-72—Boston	56	26	.683	1‡	5	6	1976-77—Boston	44	38	.537	2‡	5	4
1972-73—Boston	68	14	.829	1‡	7	6	1977-78—Boston	11	23	.324	3‡	..	..
1973-74—Boston	56	26	.683	*1‡	12	6	Totals (9 seasons)	427	263	.619		47	33

*Won NBA Championship. †Eastern Division. ‡Atlantic Division.

Elected to Naismith Memorial Basketball Hall of Fame, 1985. . . . Named to NBA All-Star Second Team, 1961, 1962, 1963, 1964. . . . NBA Rookie of the Year, 1957. . . . Member of NBA championship teams, 1957, 1959, 1960, 1961, 1962, 1963, 1964, 1965. . . . NBA Coach of the Year, 1973. . . . Coach of NBA championship teams, 1974 and 1976.

WILLIAM HOLZMAN
(Red)

Born August 10, 1920 at Brooklyn, N. Y.   Height 5:10.   Weight 175.

High School—Brooklyn, N. Y., Franklin Lane.

Colleges—University of Baltimore, Baltimore, Md., and City College of New York, New York, N. Y.

Signed by Rochester NBL, 1945.

Acquired by Milwaukee NBA from Rochester NBA, 1953.
Played in American Basketball League with New York 1945-46.

—COLLEGIATE PLAYING RECORD—

Baltimore

Year	G.	Min.	FGA	FGM	Pct.	FTA	FTM	Pct.	Reb.	Pts.	Avg.
38-39					Statistics Unavailable						

CCNY

Year	G.	Min.	FGA	FGM	Pct.	FTA	FTM	Pct.	Reb.	Pts.	Avg.
39-40					Did Not Play—Transfer Student						
40-41	21	....	...	96	....	...	37	....	...	229	10.9
41-42	18	....	...	87	....	...	51	....	...	225	12.5
Varsity Totals	39	....	...	183	....	...	88	....	...	454	11.6

NOTE: In Military Service during 1942-43, 1943-44 and 1944-45 seasons. Played at Norfolk, Va., Naval Training Station and scored 305 points in 1942-43 and 258 points in 1943-44.

NBL AND NBA REGULAR SEASON RECORD

Sea.—Team	G.	Min.	FGA	FGM	Pct.	FTA	FTM	Pct.	Reb.	Ast.	PF	Disq.	Pts.	Avg.
45-46—Roch. NBL	34	....	....	144	....	115	77	.669	....	....	54	....	365	10.7
46-47—Roch. NBL	44	....	....	227	....	139	74	.532	....	....	68	....	528	12.0
47-48—Roch. NBL	60	....	....	246	....	182	117	.643	....	....	58	....	609	10.2
48-49—Rochester	60	....	691	225	.326	157	96	.611	....	149	93	....	546	9.1
49-50—Rochester	68	....	625	206	.330	210	144	.686	....	200	67	....	556	8.2
50-51—Rochester	68	....	561	183	.326	179	130	.726	152	147	94	0	496	7.3
51-52—Rochester	65	1065	372	104	.280	85	61	.718	106	115	95	1	269	4.1
52-53—Rochester	46	392	149	38	.255	38	27	.711	40	35	56	2	103	2.2
53-54—Milwaukee	51	649	224	74	.330	73	48	.658	46	75	73	1	196	3.8
Totals	496	....	....	1447	....	1178	774	.666	....	....	658	....	3668	7.4

NBL AND NBA PLAYOFF RECORD

Sea.—Team	G.	Min.	FGA	FGM	Pct.	FTA	FTM	Pct.	Reb.	Ast.	PF	Disq.	Pts.	Avg.
45-46—Roch. NBL	7	....	....	30	....	31	21	.677	....	....	10	....	81	11.6
46-47—Roch. NBL	11	....	....	42	....	29	22	.759	....	....	22	....	106	9.6
47-48—Roch. NBL	10	....	....	35	....	15	10	.667	....	....	6	....	80	8.0
48-49—Rochester	4	....	40	18	.450	6	5	.833	....	13	3	....	41	10.3
49-50—Rochester	2	....	9	3	.333	2	1	.500	....	0	3	....	7	3.5
50-51—Rochester	14	....	76	31	.408	34	23	.676	19	20	14	....	85	6.1
51-52—Rochester	6	65	15	3	.200	6	1	.167	6	2	3	0	7	1.2
52-53—Rochester	2	14	5	1	.200	4	1	.250	1	1	4	0	3	1.5
Totals	56	....	....	163	....	127	84	.661	....	....	65	....	410	7.3

NBA COACHING RECORD

Sea. Club	W.	L.	Pct.	Pos.	W.	L.	Sea. Club	W.	L.	Pct.	Pos.	W.	L.
1953-54—Milwaukee	10	16	.385	4†	..	..	1973-74—New York	49	33	.598	2§	5	7
1954-55—Milwaukee	26	46	.361	4†	..	..	1974-75—New York	40	42	.488	3§	1	2
1955-56—St. Louis	33	39	.458	2T†	4	4	1975-76—New York	38	44	.463	4§	..	..
1956-57—St. Louis	14	19	.424	1†	..	..	1976-77—New York	40	42	.488	3§	..	..
1967-68—New York	28	17	.622	3‡	2	4	1978-79—New York	25	43	.368	4§	..	..
1968-69—New York	54	28	.659	3‡	6	4	1979-80—New York	39	43	.476	3T§	..	..
1969-70—New York*	60	22	.732	1‡	12	7	1980-81—New York	50	32	.610	3§	0	2
1970-71—New York	52	30	.634	1§	7	5	1981-82—New York	33	49	.402	5§	..	..
1971-72—New York	48	34	.667	2§	9	7	Totals (18 seasons)	696	604	.535		58	47
1972-73—New York*	57	25	.695	2§	12	5							

*Won NBA championship.
†Western Division. ‡Eastern Division. §Atlantic Division.

Elected to Naismith Memorial Basketball Hall of Fame, 1985.... NBA Coach of the Year, 1970.... Coach of NBA championship teams, 1970 and 1973.... Member of NBL championship team, 1946.... Member of NBA championship team, 1951.... Named to NBL All-Star First Team, 1946 and 1948.... NBL All-Star Second Team, 1947.

K.C. JONES

Born May 25, 1932 at San Francisco, Calif. Height 6:01. Weight 200.

High School—San Francisco, Calif., Commerce.

College—University of San Francisco, San Francisco, Calif.

Drafted by Boston on second round, 1956.

In military service, 1956-57 and 1957-58; played at Fort Leonard Wood, Mo.; named to Amateur Athletic Union All-America team as a member of 1957-58 Fort Leonard Wood team.
Played in Eastern Basketball League with Hartford, 1967-68.

—COLLEGIATE RECORD—

Year	G.	Min.	FGA	FGM	Pct.	FTA	FTM	Pct.	Reb.	Pts.	Avg.
51-52	24	....	128	44	.344	64	46	.719	....	134	5.6
52-53	23	....	159	163	.396	149	81	.544	....	207	9.0
53-54	1	....	12	3	.250	2	2	1.000	....	8	8.0
54-55	29	....	293	105	.358	144	97	.674	148	307	10.6
55-56	25	....	208	76	.365	142	93	.655	130	245	9.8
Totals	102	....	800	291	.364	501	319	.637	....	901	8.8

(Jones underwent an appendectomy after one game of the 1953-54 season and was granted an extra year of eligibility by the University of San Francisco; however, he was ineligible for the 1955-56 NCAA tournament because he was playing his fifth season of college basketball.)

EBL REGULAR SEASON RECORD

Sea.—Team	G.	Min.	FGA	FGM	Pct.	FTA	FTM	Pct.	Reb.	Ast.	PF	Disq.	Pts.	Avg.
67-68—Hartford	6	....	....	15	....	18	9	.500	24	41	..	..	39	6.5

NBA REGULAR SEASON RECORD

Sea.—Team	G.	Min.	FGA	FGM	Pct.	FTA	FTM	Pct.	Reb.	Ast.	PF	Disq.	Pts.	Avg.
58-59—Boston	49	609	192	65	.339	68	41	.603	127	70	58	0	171	3.5
59-60—Boston	74	1274	414	169	.408	170	128	.752	199	189	109	1	466	6.3
60-61—Boston	78	1607	601	203	.337	320	186	.581	279	253	200	3	592	7.6
61-62—Boston	79	2023	707	289	.409	231	145	.628	291	339	204	2	723	9.1
62-63—Boston	79	1945	591	230	.389	177	112	.633	263	317	221	3	572	7.2
63-64—Boston	80	2424	722	283	.392	168	88	.524	372	407	253	0	654	8.2
64-65—Boston	78	2434	639	253	.396	227	143	.630	318	437	263	5	849	8.3
65-66—Boston	80	2710	619	240	.388	303	209	.690	304	503	243	4	689	8.6
66-67—Boston	78	2446	459	182	.397	189	110	.630	239	389	273	7	483	6.2
Totals	675	17472	4944	1914	.387	1853	1171	.632	2392	2904	1824	25	4999	7.4

NBA PLAYOFF RECORD

Sea.—Team	G.	Min.	FGA	FGM	Pct.	FTA	FTM	Pct.	Reb.	Ast.	PF	Disq.	Pts.	Avg.
58-59—Boston	8	75	20	5	.250	5	5	1.000	12	10	8	0	15	1.9
59-60—Boston	13	232	80	27	.337	22	17	.773	45	14	28	0	71	5.522
60-61—Boston	9	103	30	9	.300	14	7	.500	19	15	17	0	25	2.8
61-62—Boston	14	329	102	44	.431	53	38	.717	56	55	50	1	126	9.0
62-63—Boston	13	250	64	19	.297	30	21	.700	36	37	42	1	59	4.5
63-64—Boston	10	312	72	25	.347	25	13	.520	37	68	40	0	63	6.3
64-65—Boston	12	396	104	43	.413	45	35	.778	39	74	49	1	121	10.1
65-66—Boston	17	543	109	45	.413	57	39	.684	52	75	65	0	129	7.6
66-67—Boston	9	254	75	24	.320	18	11	.611	24	48	36	1	59	6.6
Totals	105	2494	656	241	.367	269	186	.691	320	396	335	4	668	6.4

NBA COACHING RECORD

		Regular Season				Playoffs	
Sea.	Club	W.	L.	Pct.	Pos.	W.	L.
1973-74—Capital		47	35	.573	1†	3	4
1974-75—Washington		60	22	.732	1†	8	9
1975-76—Washington		48	34	.585	2†	3	4
1983-84—Boston*		62	20	.756	1‡	15	8
1984-85—Boston		63	19	.768	1‡	13	8
1985-86—Boston*		67	15	.817	1‡	15	3
1986-87—Boston		59	23	.720	1‡	13	10
1987-88—Boston		57	25	.695	1‡	9	8
Totals (8 seasons)		463	193	.706		79	54

*Won NBA championship. †Central Division. ‡Atlantic Division.
Assistant coach, Los Angeles Lakers, 1972; Milwaukee Bucks, 1977; Boston Celtics, 1980-83.

Member of U.S. Olympic team, 1956.... Member of NCAA championship team, 1955.... Member of NBA championship teams, 1959, 1960, 1961, 1962, 1963, 1964, 1965, 1966.... Coach of NBA championship teams, 1984 and 1986.... Drafted by Los Angeles Rams in 30th round of 1955 National Football League draft.

JOHN KUNDLA

Born July 3, 1916 at Star Junction, Pa.

Height 6:02.   Weight 180.

High School—Minneapolis, Minn., Central.

College—University of Minnesota, Minneapolis, Minn.

—COLLEGIATE PLAYING RECORD—

Year	G.	Min.	FGA	FGM	Pct.	FTA	FTM	Pct.	Reb.	Pts.	Avg.
35-36†					Statistics unavailable						
36-37	15	....	...	53	....	53	34	.641	....	140	9.3
37-38	20	....	...	62	....	77	41	.532	....	165	8.3
38-39	17	....	...	71	....	63	40	.635	....	182	10.7
Varsity Totals	52	....	...	186	....	193	115	.596	....	487	9.4

NBA COACHING RECORD

Sea. Club	Regular Season W.	L.	Pct.	Pos.	Playoffs W.	L.	Sea. Club	Regular Season W.	L.	Pct.	Pos.	Playoffs W.	L.
1948-49—Minneapolis	44	16	.733	*2†	8	2	1955-56—Minneapolis	33	39	.458	2T†	1	2
1949-50—Minneapolis	51	17	.750	*1T†	10	2	1956-57—Minneapolis	34	38	.472	1T†	2	3
1950-51—Minneapolis	44	24	.647	1†	3	4	1957-58—Minneapolis	10	23	.303	4†	..	..
1951-52—Minneapolis	40	26	.606	*2†	9	4	1958-59—Minneapolis	33	39	.458	2†	6	7
1952-53—Minneapolis	48	22	.686	*1†	9	3	Totals (11 seasons)	423	302	.583		60	35
1953-54—Minneapolis	46	26	.639	*1†	9	4							
1954-55—Minneapolis	40	32	.556	2†	3	4							

*Won NBA Championship.   †Western Division.

COLLEGIATE COACHING RECORD

Sea. Club	Regular Season W.	L.	Pct.	Pos.	Sea. Club	Regular Season W.	L.	Pct.	Pos.
1946-47—St. Thomas	11	11	.500	....	1964-65—Minnesota	19	5	.792	2
1959-60—Minnesota	12	12	.500	3T	1965-66—Minnesota	14	10	.583	5T
1960-61—Minnesota	10	13	.435	4T	1966-67—Minnesota	9	15	.375	9
1961-62—Minnesota	10	14	.417	7	1967-68—Minnesota	7	17	.292	9T
1962-63—Minnesota	12	12	.500	4T	Totals (10 seasons)	121	116	.511	
1963-64—Minnesota	17	7	.708	3					

NBL COACHING RECORD

Sea. Club	Regular Season W.	L.	Pct.	Pos.	Playoffs W.	L.
1947-48—Minneapolis	43	17	.717	1†	8	2

†Western Division.

Coach of NBA championship teams, 1950, 1952, 1953, 1954.

JOSEPH BOHOMIEL LAPCHICK
(Joe)

Born April 12, 1900 at Yonkers, N. Y.   Height 6:05½.   Weight 185.

Died August 10, 1970.

Did not play high school or college basketball.

Played with independent teams, including the Original Celtics, in 1917-18 through 1919-20; 1923-24 through 1925-26 and 1931-32 through 1935-36 seasons.

PRO RECORD

Year Team	League	G	FG	FT	Pts.	Avg.
1920-21—Holyoke	IL	11	14	40	68	6.2
1921-22—Schenectady-Troy	NYSL	32	12	95	119	3.7
1921-22—Brooklyn	MBL	10	6	20	32	3.2
1922-23—Brooklyn	MBL	33	34	109	177	5.4
1922-23—Troy	NYSL	24	13	59	85	3.5
1926-27—New York	NBL	..	..	..	..	7.3
1926-27—Brooklyn	ABL	32	35	131	201	6.3
1927-28—New York	ABL	47	103	110	316	6.7
1928-29—Cleveland	ABL	39	51	86	188	4.8
1929-30—Cleveland	ABL	52	47	92	186	3.6
1930-31—Cleveland-Toledo	ABL	30	22	49	93	3.1
ABL Pro Totals		200	258	468	984	4.9

COLLEGIATE COACHING RECORD

Sea. Club	Regular Season W.	L.	Pct.	Pos.	Sea. Club	Regular Season W.	L.	Pct.	Pos.
1936-37—St. John's	12	7	.632	....	1946-47—St. John's	16	7	.696	....
1937-38—St. John's	15	4	.789	....	1956-57—St. John's	14	9	.609	....
1938-39—St. John's	18	4	.818	....	1957-58—St. John's	18	8	.692	....
1939-40—St. John's	15	5	.750	....	1958-59—St. John's	20	6	.769	....
1940-41—St. John's	11	6	.647	....	1959-60—St. John's	17	8	.680	....
1941-42—St. John's	16	5	.762	....	1960-61—St. John's	20	5	.800	....
1942-43—St. John's	21	3	.875	....	1961-62—St. John's	21	5	.808	....
1943-44—St. John's	18	5	.783	....	1962-63—St. John's	9	15	.375	....
1944-45—St. John's	21	3	.875	....	1963-64—St. John's	14	11	.560	....
1945-46—St. John's	17	6	.739	....	1964-65—St. John's	21	8	.724	....
					Totals (20 seasons)	334	130	.720	

NBA COACHING RECORD

Sea. Club	Regular Season W.	L.	Pct.	Pos.	Playoffs W.	L.
1947-48—New York	26	22	.542	2†	1	2
1948-49—New York	32	28	.533	2†	3	3
1949-50—New York	40	28	.588	2†	3	2
1950-51—New York	36	30	.545	3†	8	6
1951-52—New York	37	29	.561	3†	8	6
1952-53—New York	47	23	.671	1†	6	5
1953-54—New York	44	28	.611	1†	0	4
1954-55—New York	38	34	.528	2†	1	2
1955-56—New York	26	25	.510		....	....
Totals (9 seasons)	326	247	.569		30	30

†Eastern Division
Elected to Naismith Memorial Basketball Hall of Fame, 1966.

JOHN RICHARD MOTTA
(Dick)

Born September 3, 1931 at Medvale, Utah.   Height 5:10.   Weight 170.
High School— Jordan, Utah (did not play varsity basketball).
College—Utah State University, Logan, Utah (did not play basketball).

—COLLEGIATE COACHING RECORD—

Sea. Club	Regular Season W.	L.	Pct.	Pos.	Sea. Club	Regular Season W.	L.	Pct.	Pos.
1962-63—Weber State	22	4	.846	..	1966-67—Weber State	18	7	.720	1
1963-64—Weber State	17	8	.680	2	1967-68—Weber State	21	6	.778	1
1964-65—Weber State	22	3	.880	1	Totals (6 seasons)	120	33	.784	
1965-66—Weber State	20	5	.800	1T					

NBA COACHING RECORD

Sea. Club	Regular Season W.	L.	Pct.	Pos.	Playoffs W.	L.	Sea. Club	Regular Season W.	L.	Pct.	Pos.	Playoffs W.	L.
1968-69—Chicago	33	49	.402	5†	..	..	1978-79—Washington	54	28	.659	1x	9	10
1969-70—Chicago	39	43	.476	3T†	1	4	1979-80—Washington	39	43	.476	3†	0	2
1970-71—Chicago	51	31	.622	2‡	3	4	1980-81—Dallas	15	67	.183	6‡	..	..
1971-72—Chicago	57	25	.695	2‡	0	4	1981-82—Dallas	28	54	.341	5‡	..	..
1972-73—Chicago	51	31	.622	2‡	3	4	1982-83—Dallas	38	44	.463	4‡	..	..
1973-74—Chicago	54	28	.659	2‡	4	7	1983-84—Dallas	43	39	.524	2‡	4	6
1974-75—Chicago	47	35	.573	1‡	7	6	1984-85—Dallas	44	38	.537	3‡	1	3
1975-76—Chicago	24	58	.293	4‡	..	..	1985-86—Dallas	44	38	.537	3‡	5	5
1976-77—Washington	48	34	.585	2§	4	5	1986-87—Dallas	55	27	.671	1‡	1	3
1977-78—Washington	44	38	.537	2§	14	7	Totals (19 seasons)	808	750	.519		56	70

*Won NBA championship.   †Western Division.   ‡Midwest Division.   §Central Division.   xAtlantic Division.
Named NBA Coach of the Year, 1971. . . . Coach of NBA championship team, 1978.

—DID YOU KNOW—

That Portland Trail Blazers General Manager Jon Spoelstra was the "other considerations" in a 1983 trade between the Trail Blazers and Indiana Pacers? The Blazers, in need of a backcourt replacement for the injured Darnell Valentine in January 1983, gave Don Buse, a free-agent guard formerly with the Pacers, an offer sheet. As an inducement to the Pacers not to exercise their right of first refusal, Portland offered Indiana "cash and other considerations." The "considerations" were for Spoelstra, the Blazers' vice president of marketing at the time, to spend 40 hours in Indianapolis helping to develop the Pacers' marketing program.

NOTES